Robert E. Sche

11·29 13th

Boulder

Fri. – 1 to middle of page 13

THE DESIGN OF STEEL MILL BUILDINGS

AND

THE CALCULATION OF STRESSES IN FRAMED STRUCTURES

BY

MILO S. KETCHUM, C.E., Sc.D.

M.Am.Soc.C.E.

Dean of College of Engineering and Director of Engineering Experiment Station, University of Illinois; Consulting Engineer

FIFTH EDITION

SECOND THOUSAND

TOTAL ISSUE, TWENTY-FIVE THOUSAND

(Printed, 1935)

McGRAW-HILL BOOK COMPANY, Inc.

NEW YORK AND LONDON

1932

PRINTED IN THE UNITED STATES OF AMERICA

PREFACE TO THE FIFTH EDITION.

This edition contains a chapter on the calculation of the stresses in stiff frames by moment distribution as developed by Professor Hardy Cross, and detailed descriptions and designs of several typical steel frame buildings, a hangar and an air dock. The specifications for steel frame mill buildings as given in Appendix I have been revised to bring them in line with the latest practice. Numerous minor changes have been made in the text and all known errors have been corrected.

The aim in this book has been to develop the methods of calculating the stresses in framed structures in such a way that the student or the engineer may be able to calculate the stresses in any structure even though the framework may be of a new or novel type. Both algebraic and graphic methods are developed for both statically determinate and statically indeterminate structures. The details of the design of steel frame buildings are developed for the completed structure.

Credit is due Milo S. Ketchum, Jr. for assistance in writing the chapter on moment distribution and the preparation of the drawings.

M. S. K.

URBANA, ILLINOIS,
Sept, 1, 1932.

PREFACE TO FOURTH EDITION.

This book covers the calculation of the stresses in framed structures, and also the design of buildings having a self-supporting steel frame with a light covering, usually fireproof. In this edition the book has been rewritten and enlarged, the type has been reset and the plates have been recast. The type page is the same size as that used in the author's "Structural Engineers' Handbook." The scope of the book has been enlarged by the addition of a concise discussion of the calculation of the stresses in statically indeterminate trusses and frames, several problems in framed structures and detailed designs of a crane girder, a roof truss, and a steel frame mill building. The book is written to serve as a text book in structural engineering and also as a book of reference for engineers.

The book is divided into three parts and in addition has one appendix.

Part I covers the calculation of the stresses in simple beams, trusses, portals, the transverse bent, and the three-hinged arch. The stresses in pins and the stresses due to bending stress combined with compression and tension, and due to eccentric loading are briefly discussed. This part contains 40 problems which cover the calculation of the stresses in practically all types of simple trusses, bents and portals. Part I covers the ground required for a preliminary course in stresses in framed structures.

Part II covers the calculation of the deflections of structures, the calculation of the stresses in statically indeterminate girders, trusses and frames, and secondary stresses in trusses. The stresses in stiff frames, the two-hinged arch, and the steel head frame are calculated and explained in detail. This part contains the detail solutions of nine problems and the statements of six additional problems. The discussion of statically indeterminate structures in this section covers most problems in building construction and is preliminary to a study of movable bridges, arch, cantilever and suspension bridges.

Part III covers the design and construction of steel frame buildings for mines, mills, smelters and other industrial plants. The detailed design of a crane girder, a roof truss and a steel building are given. The design and construction of floors, roof coverings, foundations, corrugated steel, windows, doors, wall covering and other details of steel frame buildings are fully discussed.

A complete specification for steel frame mill buildings is given in Appendix I.

While this book is a companion volume to the author's "Structural Engineers' Handbook," the two books are independent.

As far as practicable, credit has been given in the body of the book for drawings and data. Credit is due Professor R. S. Wallis, Iowa State College, for assistance in making drawings, to Professor W. C. Huntington, University of Colorado, for assistance in preparing material for Chapters XVII and XXII, and in making drawings, and to C. L. Eckel, Assistant Professor of Civil Engineering, University of Pennsylvania, for assistance in making calculations, making drawings, and reading proof.

The author wishes to acknowledge the appreciation with which the previous editions have been received by engineers and instructors.

UNIVERSITY OF PENNSYLVANIA,
PHILADELPHIA, PA.,
November 1, 1921.

M. S. K.

PREFACE TO FIRST EDITION.

This book is intended to provide a short course in the calculation of stresses in framed structures and to give a brief discussion of mill building construction. The book is intended to supplement the elementary books on stresses on the one hand, and the more elaborate treatises on bridge design on the other. While the book is concerned chiefly with mill buildings it is nevertheless true that much of the matter will apply equally well to all classes of steel frame construction.

In the course in stresses an attempt has been made to give a concise, logical and systematic treatment. Both the algebraic and graphic methods of calculating stresses are fully described and illustrated. Each step in the solution is fully explained and analyzed so that the student will get a definite idea of the underlying principles.

Attention is called to the graphic solutions of the transverse bent, the portal and the two-hinged arch, which are believed to be new, and have proved their worth by actual test in the class room. The diagram for finding the stress in eye-bars due to their own weight is new, and its use will save considerable time in designing bridges.

In the discussion of mill building construction the aim has been to describe the methods of construction and the material used, together with a brief treatment of mill building design, and the making of estimates of weight and cost. The underlying idea has been to give methods, data and details not ordinarily available, and to discuss the matter presented in a way to assist the engineer in making his designs and the detailer in developing the designs in the drafting room. Every engineer should be familiar and be provided with one or more of the standard handbooks, and therefore only such tables as are not ordinarily available are given.

The present book is a result of two years experience as designing engineer and contracting agent for the Gillette-Herzog Mfg. Co., Minneapolis, Minn., and four years experience in teaching the subject at the University of Illinois. This book represents the course given by the author in elementary stresses and in the design of metal structures, preliminary to a course in bridge design. While written primarily for the author's students it is hoped that the book will be of interest to others, especially to the younger engineers.

The author will consider it a favor to have errors brought to his notice.

UNIVERSITY OF ILLINOIS,
CHAMPAIGN, ILL.,
August 17, 1903.

M. S. K.

TABLE OF CONTENTS

PART I. STRESSES IN FRAMED STRUCTURES

Chapter I. Graphic Statics

Chapter II. Stresses in Framed Structures

Chapter III. Stresses in Simple Roof Trusses

Chapter IV. Simple Beams

Chapter V. Moving Loads on Beams

Chapter VI. Stresses in Highway Bridge Trusses

Chapter VII. Influence Diagrams

Chapter VIII. Stresses in Railway Bridge Trusses

Chapter IX. Stresses in Portals

Chapter X. Stresses in a Transverse Bent

CHAPTER XI. STRESSES IN THREE-HINGED ARCH

CHAPTER XII. STRESSES IN PINS, COMBINED AND ECCENTRIC STRESSES

Chapter XIII. Problems in the Calculation of Stresses in Framed tructures

PART II. DEFLECTIONS OF STRUCTURES AND STRESSES IN STATICALLY INDETERMINATE STRUCTURES

Chapter XIV. Area Moments and Curved Influence Lines

Chapter XV. Deflection of Framed Structures

Chapter XVI. Stresses in Statically Indeterminate Structures

Chapter XVII. Stresses in Stiff Frames by Area Moments

Chapter XVIII. Stresses in Stiff Frames by Slope Deflections

Chapter XVIIIA. Stresses in Stiff Frames by Moment Distribution

Chapter XIX. Secondary Stresses

CHAPTER XX. STRESSES IN A TWO-HINGED ARCH

CHAPTER XXI. STRESSES IN A STATICALLY INDETERMINATE HEAD FRAME

CHAPTER XXII. PROBLEMS IN THE CALCULATION OF STRESSES IN STATICALLY INDETERMINATE STRUCTURES, CAMBER, ETC.

PART III. DESIGN OF STEEL MILL BUILDINGS

CHAPTER XXIII. GENERAL DESIGN

Chapter XXIV. Loads

Chapter XXV. Framework

Chapter XXVI. Examples of Industrial Buildings

Chapter XXVII. Data for Design of Framework

CHAPTER XXVIII. CORRUGATED STEEL

CHAPTER XXIX. ROOF COVERINGS

CHAPTER XXX. SIDE WALLS

CHAPTER XXXI. FOUNDATIONS

CHAPTER XXXII. FLOORS

Chapter XXXIII. Windows, Skylights and Ventilators

Chapter XXXIV. Doors

Chapter XXXV. Paints and Painting

Chapter XXXVI. Design of a Steel Roof Truss

CHAPTER XXXVII. DESIGN OF BEAMS AND PLATE GIRDERS

CHAPTER XXXVIII. DESIGN OF A STEEL MILL BUILDING

CHAPTER XXXIX. ERECTION OF STEEL MILL BUILDINGS

CHAPTER XL. ESTIMATE OF WEIGHT AND COST OF STEEL MILL BUILDINGS

Appendix I. General Specifications for Steel Frame Buildings

THE DESIGN OF STEEL MILL BUILDINGS.

INTRODUCTION.

This book covers primarily the design and construction of buildings made by covering a self-supporting steel frame with a light covering, usually fireproof. The design of steel structures of this type requires the solution of many problems not usually met in the design of bridges, as well as the design of girders and trusses for moving loads.

This book is used by the author as a text in three courses given to civil engineering students as follows:

(1) Part I is used as a text in the calculation of stresses in framed structures in the junior year; (2) Part II is used as a text in the calculation of stresses in statically indeterminate structures in the senior year, while (3) Part III is used as a text in the design of steel frame buildings in the senior year. To make the courses in stresses complete, it has been necessary to consider the calculation of the stresses in simple bridge trusses due to equal joint loads and due to concentrated loads as well as a full discussion of influence diagrams. The scope of each section of the book will be briefly discussed.

The discussion in Part I covers the calculation of the stresses in simple beams, trusses, portals, the transverse bent and the three-hinged arch. The stresses in pins, the stresses due to combined compression and tension, and due to eccentric loading are also briefly discussed. The forty problems in Chapter XIII cover the calculation of the stresses in practically all types of simple trusses, bents and portals. In each case a problem is stated and fully solved, and the details of the solution are discussed. A second problem, similar to the first problem, is given without a solution. The student is required to study the solution of the first problem and to make an independent solution of the unsolved problem.

A very satisfactory course in framed structures can be given by requiring the student to solve about three-fourths of the problems in Chapter XIII.

The discussion in Part II covers the calculation of the deflections of structures, the calculation of the stresses in statically indeterminate girders, trusses and frames, and the calculation of secondary stresses in trusses. The most important methods for the calculation of deflections are described in detail. The stresses in stiff frames, the two-hinged arch, and the steel head frame are calculated and explained in detail. The detail solutions of nine problems and the statements of six additional problems are given in Chapter XXII. The discussion of statically indeterminate structures in this section is preliminary to a study of movable bridges, arch, cantilever and suspension bridges.

The discussion in Part III covers the design and construction of steel frame buildings for mines, mills, smelters and other industrial plants. The detailed design of a crane girder, a roof truss, and a steel frame mill building are given. The design and construction of floors, roof coverings, foundations, corrugated steel, windows, doors, ventilators, wall covering, and other details of steel frame buildings are fully discussed. A complete specification for steel frame mill buildings is given in Appendix I. For properties of sections reference is made to the author's "Structural Engineers' Handbook." While this book is a companion volume to the "Structural Engineers' Handbook," the two books are independent.

For a brief course in structural engineering for mechanical or electrical engineering students Chapter VII, Chapter VIII, and all of Part II may be omitted.

PART I.

STRESSES IN FRAMED STRUCTURES.

CHAPTER I.

Graphic Statics.

Introduction.—Structures are acted upon by external forces consisting of the loads and the reactions of the supports. The loads may be due to the weight of the structure, due to the weights carried by the structure, or be due to snow or wind. The external forces acting on a structure are held in equilibrium by internal forces called stresses. If a straight member is acted upon at its ends by two equal external forces in the direction of its length, equilibrium at any right section of the member will be maintained by internal forces called stresses acting on opposite sides of the section, equal in amount, but opposite in direction to the external forces. When the external forces tend to elongate the member, the stress is tension; when the external forces tend to shorten the member the stress is compression; while when the external forces tend to shear the member off, the stress is shear. Strain is the deformation caused by stress, the ratio of stress to strain being equal to a quantity, usually a constant, called the modulus of elasticity. Compressive stresses will be considered positive stresses, while tensile stresses will be considered negative stresses. Forces are concurrent when their lines of action meet in a common point, non-concurrent when their lines of action do not all meet in a common point. Forces acting in a plane are called coplanar; forces acting in different planes are called non-coplanar forces. Coplanar forces only will be considered in this chapter.

The moment of a force about a point is its tendency to produce rotation about that point. Moment is measured by the product of the magnitude of the force and the perpendicular dropped from the point to the line of action of the force. Moments are commonly measured in foot-pounds, inch-pounds, foot-tons or inch-tons.

The resultant of a system of forces is a single force that will replace the system. The force equal and opposite to the resultant will be the equilibrant of the system of forces. Where the system of forces reduces to a couple no one force will replace the system, but the resultant and equilibrant of the system will each be a couple.

Equilibrium.—Statics considers forces as at rest and therefore in equilibrium. To have static equilibrium in any system of forces there must be neither translation nor rotation and the following conditions must be fulfilled for coplanar forces (forces in one plane).

$$\Sigma \text{ horizontal components of forces } = 0 \quad (1)$$

$$\Sigma \text{ vertical components of forces } = 0 \quad (2)$$

$$\Sigma \text{ moments of forces about any point } = 0 \quad (3)$$

Representation of Forces.—A force is determined when its magnitude, line of action, and direction are known, and it may be represented graphically in magnitude by the length of a line, in line of action by the position of the line, and in direction by an arrow placed on the line, pointing in the direction in which the force acts. A force may be considered as applied at any point in its line of action.

Force Triangle.—The resultant, R, of the two forces P_1 and P_2 meeting at the point a in Fig. 1 is represented in magnitude and direction by the diagonal, R, of the parallelogram a–b–c–d. The combining of the two forces P_1 and P_2 into the force R is termed composition of forces. The reverse process is called resolution of forces.

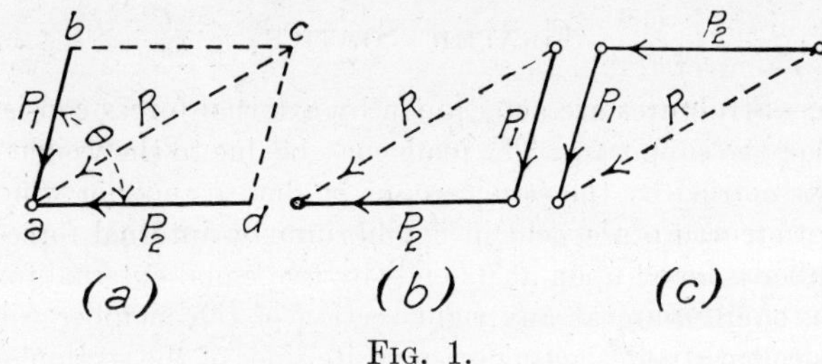

FIG. 1.

The value of R may also be found from the equation

$$R^2 = P_1^2 + P_2^2 + 2P_1 \cdot P_2 \cos \theta$$

It is not necessary to construct the entire force parallelogram as in (a) Fig. 1, the force triangle (b) below or (c) above the resultant R being sufficient.

If only one force together with the line of action of the two others be given in a system containing three forces in equilibrium, the magnitude and direction of the two forces may be found by means of the force triangle.

If the resultant R in Fig. 1 is replaced by a force E equal in amount but opposite in direction, the system of forces will be in equilibrium, (a) or (b) Fig. 2. The force E is the equilibrant of the system of forces P_1 and P_2.

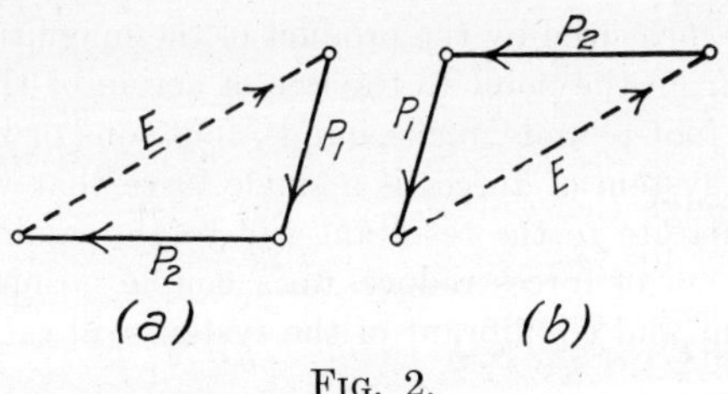

FIG. 2.

It is immaterial in what order the forces are taken in constructing the force triangle, as in Fig. 2, as long as the forces all act in the same direction around the triangle. The force triangle is the foundation of the science of graphic statics.

Force Polygon.—If more than three concurrent forces (forces which meet in a point) are in equilibrium as in (*a*) Fig. 3, R_1 in (*b*) will be the resultant of P_1 and P_2, R_2 will be the resultant of R_1 and P_3, and will also be the equilibrant of P_4 and P_5.

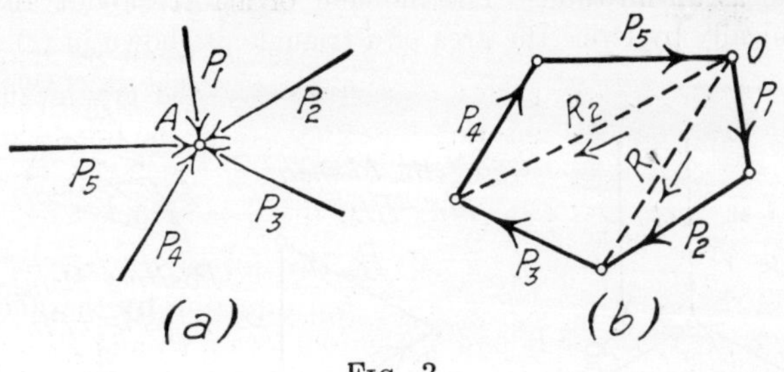

FIG. 3.

The force polygon in (*b*) is therefore only a combination of force triangles. The force polygon for any system of forces may be constructed as follows:—Beginning at any point draw in succession lines representing in magnitude and direction the given forces, each line beginning where the preceding one ends. If the polygon closes the system of forces is in equilibrium, if not the line joining the first and last points represents the resultant in magnitude and direction. As in the case of the force triangle, it is immaterial in what order the forces are applied as long as they all act in the same direction around the polygon. A force polygon is analogous to a traverse of a field in which the bearings and the distances are measured progressively around the field in either direction. The conditions for closure in the two cases are also identical.

It will be seen that any side in the force polygon is the equilibrant of all the other sides, and that any side reversed in direction is the resultant of all the other sides.

Equilibrium of Concurrent Forces.—The necessary condition for equilibrium of concurrent coplanar forces therefore is that the force polygon close. This is equivalent to the algebraic condition that Σ horizontal components of forces $= 0$, and Σ vertical components of forces $= 0$. If the system of concurrent forces is not in equilibrium the resultant can be found in magnitude and direction by completing the force polygon. The resultant of a system of concurrent forces is always a single force acting through their point of intersection.

Equilibrium of Non-concurrent Forces.—If the forces are non-concurrent (do not all meet in a common point), the condition that the force polygon close is a necessary, but not a sufficient condition for equilibrium. For example, take the three equal forces P_1, P_2 and P_3, making an angle of 120° with each other as in (*a*) Fig. 4.

The force polygon (*b*) closes, but the system is not in equilibrium. The resultant, R, of P_2 and P_3 acts through their intersection and is parallel to P_1, but is opposite in direction. The system of forces is in equilibrium for translation, but is not in equilibrium for rotation.

The resultant of this system is a couple with a moment $= - P_1 \cdot h$, moments clockwise being considered negative and counter-clockwise positive, (*c*) Fig. 4. The equilibrant of the system in (*a*) Fig. 4 is a couple with a moment $= + P_1 \cdot h$.

A couple.—A couple consists of two parallel forces equal in amount, but opposite in direction. The arm of the couple is the perpendicular distance between the forces.

The moment of a couple is equal to one of the forces multiplied by the arm. The moment of a couple is constant about any point in the plane and may be represented graphically by twice the area of the triangle having one of the forces as a base and the arm of the couple as an altitude. The moment of a force about any point may be represented graphically by twice the area of a triangle as shown in (*c*) Fig. 4.

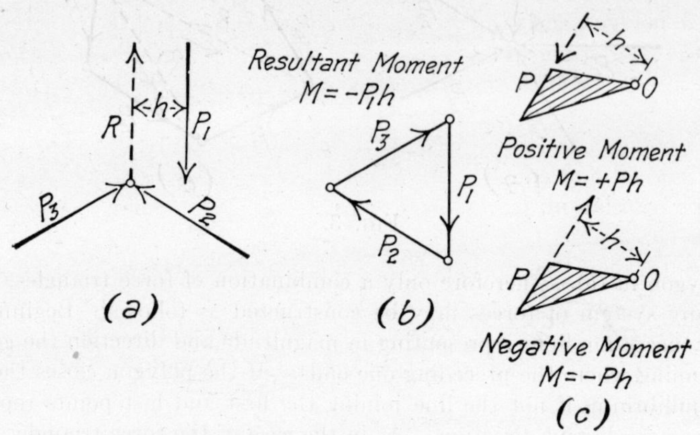

FIG. 4.

It will be seen from the preceding discussion that in order that a system of non-concurrent forces be in equilibrium it is necessary that the resultant of all the forces save one shall coincide with the one and be opposite in direction. Three non-concurrent forces can not be in equilibrium unless they are parallel. The resultant of a system of non-concurrent forces may be a single force or a couple.

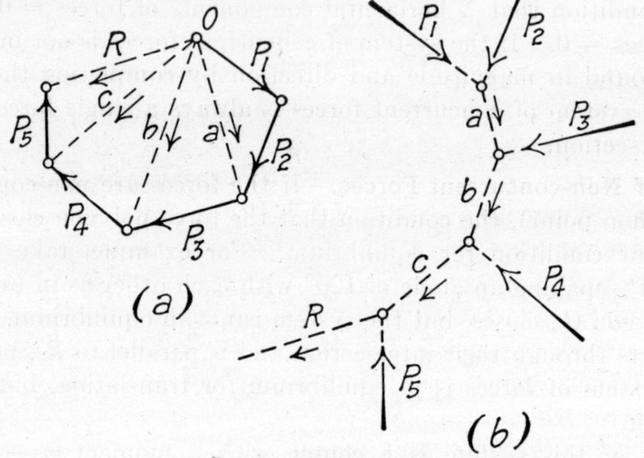

FIG. 5.

Equilibrium Polygon.—*First Method.*—In Fig. 5 the resultant, *a*, of P_1 and P_2 acts through their intersection and is equal and parallel to *a* in the force polygon (*a*); the resultant, b, of a and P_3 acts through their intersection and is equal and parallel to b in the force polygon; the resultant, c, of b and P_4 acts through their intersection and is equal and parallel to c in the force polygon; and finally the resultant, R, of c and P_5 acts through their intersection and is equal and parallel to R in the force polygon. R is therefore the resultant of the entire system of forces. If R is replaced by an equal and opposite force, E, the system of forces will be in equilibrium. Polygon (a) in Fig. 5 is called a force polygon and (b) is called a funicular or an equilibrium polygon. It will be seen that the magnitude and direction of the resultant of a system of forces is given by the closing line of the force polygon, and the line of action is given by the equilibrium polygon.

The force polygon in (a) Fig. 6 closes and the resultant, R, of the forces P_1, P_2, P_3, P_4, P_5 is parallel and equal to P_6, and is opposite in direction. The system is in equilibrium for translation, but is not in equilibrium for rotation. The resultant is a

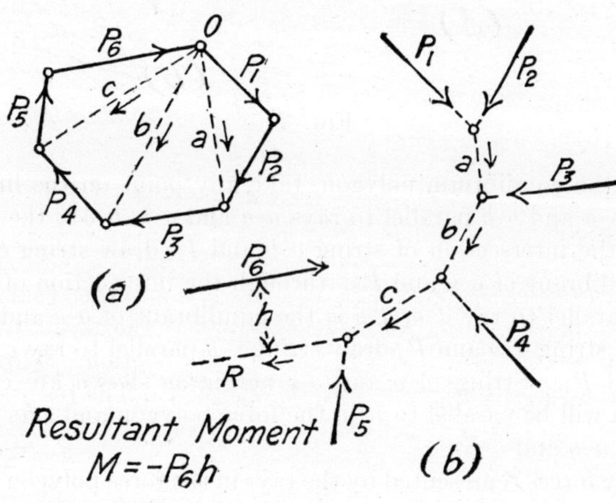

FIG. 6.

couple with a moment $= - P_6 \cdot h$. The equilibrant of the system of forces will be a couple with a moment $= + P_6 \cdot h$. From the preceding discussion it will be seen that if the force polygon for any system of non-concurrent forces closes the resultant will be a couple. If there is perfect equilibrium the arm of the couple will be zero.

Second Method.—Where the forces do not intersect within the limits of the drawing board, or where the forces are parallel, it is not possible to draw the equilibrium polygon as shown in Fig. 5 and Fig. 6, and the following method is used.

The point O, (a) Fig. 7, which is called the pole of the force polygon, is selected so that the strings a–o, b–o, c–o, d–o and e–o in the equilibrium polygon (b), which are drawn parallel to the corresponding rays in the force polygon (a), will make good intersections with the forces which they replace or equilibrate.

In the force polygon (a), P_1 is equilibrated by the imaginary forces represented by the rays o–a and b–o acting as indicated by the arrows within the triangle; P_2 is equilibrated by the imaginary forces represented by the rays o–b and c–o acting as indicated by the arrows within the triangle; P_3 is equilibrated by the imaginary forces represented by the rays o–c and d–o acting as indicated by the arrows within the triangle;

and P_4 is equilibrated by the imaginary forces *o–d* and *e–o* acting as indicated by the arrows within the triangle. The imaginary forces are all neutralized except *a–o* and *o–e*, which are seen to be components of the resultant *R*.

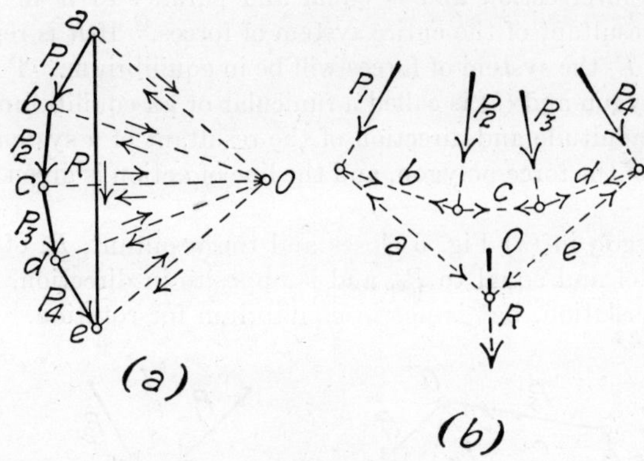

FIG. 7.

To construct the equilibrium polygon, take any point on the line of action of P_1 and draw strings *o–a* and *o–b* parallel to rays *o–a* and *o–b*, *b–o* is the equilibrant of *o–a* and P_1; through the intersection of string *o–b* and P_2 draw string *c–o* parallel to ray *c–o*, *c–o* is the equilibrant of *o–b* and P_2; through the intersection of string *c–o* and P_3 draw string *d–o* parallel to ray *d–o*, *d–o* is the equilibrant of *o–c* and P_3; and through the intersection of string *d–o* and P_4 draw string *e–o* parallel to ray *e–o*, *e–o* is the equilibrant of *o–d* and P_4. Strings *a–o* and *o–e* acting as shown are components of the resultant *R*, which will be parallel to *R* in the force polygon and acts through the intersections of strings *a–o* and *o–e*.

The imaginary forces represented by the rays in the force polygon may be considered as components of the forces and the analysis made on that assumption with equal ease.

It is immaterial in what order the forces are taken in drawing the force polygon, as long as the forces all act in the same direction around the force polygon, and the strings meeting on the lines of the forces in the equilibrium polygon are parallel to the rays drawn to the ends of the same forces in the force polygon.

The imaginary forces *a–o*, *b–o*, *c–o*, *d–o*, *e–o* are represented in magnitude and in direction by the rays of the force polygon to the same scale as the forces P_1, P_2, P_3, P_4. The strings of the equilibrium polygon represent the imaginary forces in line of action and direction, but not in magnitude.

Reactions of a Simple Beam.—The equilibrium polygon may be used to obtain the reactions of a beam loaded with a load *P* as in Fig. 8.

The force polygon (*b*) is drawn with a pole *O* at any convenient point and rays *o–a* and *o–c* are drawn. Now from the fundamental conditions for equilibrium for translation we have $P = R_1 + R_2$. At any convenient point in the line of action of *P* draw the strings *o–a* and *o–c* parallel to the rays *o–a* and *o–c*, respectively, in the force polygon. The imaginary forces *o–a* and *c–o* acting as shown equilibrate the force *P*. The imaginary force *a–o* acting in a reverse direction as shown is an equilibrant of R_1, and the imaginary force *o–c* acting in a reverse direction is an equilibrant of R_2. The remaining equilibrant of R_1 and of R_2 must coincide and be equal in amount, but opposite in direction. The string b–o is the remaining equilibrant of R_1 and of R_2 and is called the closing line of the equilibrium polygon. The ray b–o drawn parallel to the string b–o divides P in two parts which are equal to the reactions R_1 and R_2 (for reactions of overhanging beam see Chapter IV).

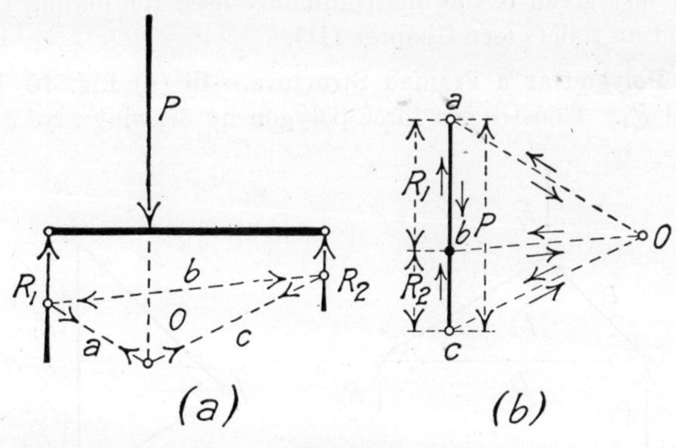

FIG. 8.

Reactions of a Cantilever Truss.—In the cantilever truss shown in Fig. 9, the direction and point of application B of the reaction R_1 are known, while the point of application A of the reaction R_2 only is known. The direction of reaction R_2 may be found by applying the principle that if a body is in equilibrium under the action of three external forces which are not parallel, they must all meet in a common point,

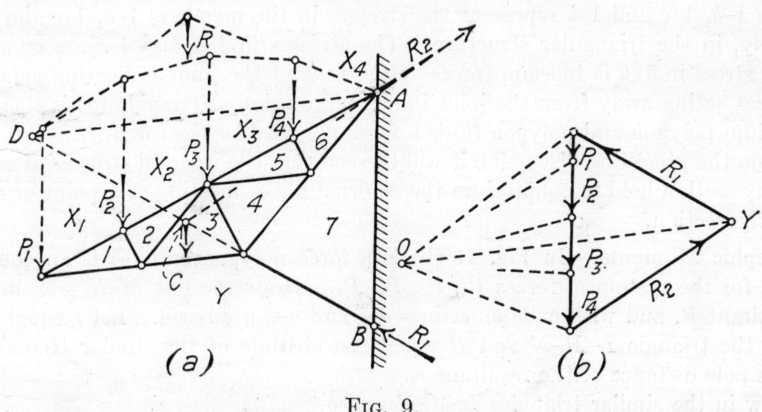

FIG. 9.

i. e., the forces must be concurrent. The resultant of all the loads acts through the point c, which is also the point of intersection of the reactions R_1 and R_2. Having the direction of the reaction R_2, the values of the reactions may be found by means of a force polygon.

The direction of reaction R_2 may be found by means of a force and equilibrium polygon as follows: Construct the force polygon (b) with pole O and draw equilibrium polygon (a) starting with point A, the only known point on the reaction R_2, and draw the polygon as previously described. A line drawn through point O in the force polygon parallel to the closing line of the equilibrium polygon will meet R_1, drawn parallel to reaction R_1, in the point y, which is also a point on R_2. The reactions R_1 and R_2 are therefore completely determined in direction and amount.

The method just given is the one commonly used for finding the reactions in a truss with one end on rollers (see Chapter III).

Equilibrium Polygon as a Framed Structure.—In (a) Fig. 10, the rigid triangle supports the load P_1. Construct a force polygon by drawing rays a–1 and c–1 in (b)

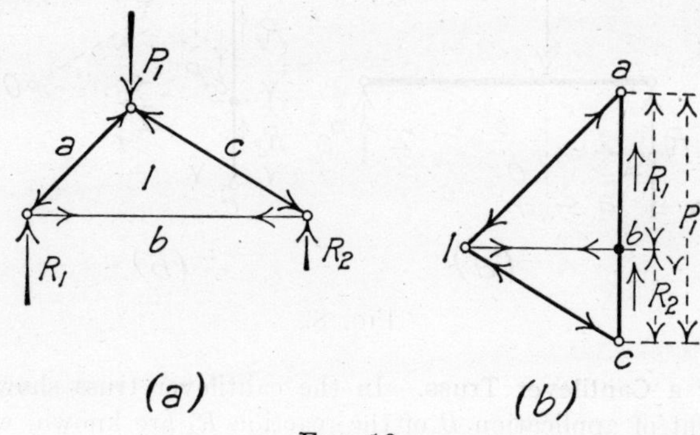

FIG. 10.

parallel to sides a–1 and c–1, respectively, in (a), and through pole 1 draw 1–b parallel to side 1–b in (a). The reactions R_1 and R_2 will be given by the force polygon (b), and the rays 1–a, 1–c and 1–b represent the stresses in the members 1–a, 1–c and 1–b, respectively, in the triangular structure. The stresses in 1–a and 1–c are compression and the stress in 1–b is tension, forces acting toward the joint indicating compression and forces acting away from the joint indicating tension. Triangle (a) is therefore an equilibrium polygon and polygon (b) is a force polygon for the force P_1.

From the preceding discussion it will be seen that the internal stresses at any point or on any section hold in equilibrium the external forces meeting at a point or on either side of the section.

Graphic Moments.—In Fig. 11 (b) is a force polygon and (a) is an equilibrium polygon for the system of forces P_1, P_2, P_3, P_4. Draw the line M–N = Y parallel to the resultant R, and with ends on strings o–e and o–a produced. Let r equal the altitude of the triangle L–M–N and H equal the altitude of the similar triangle o–e–a. H is the pole distance of the resultant R.

Now in the similar triangles L–M–N and o–e–a

$$R : Y :: H : r$$

and

$$R \cdot r = H \cdot Y$$

But $R \cdot r = M$ = moment of resultant R about any point in the line M–N and therefore

$$M = H \cdot Y$$

The statement of the principle just demonstrated is as follows: The moment of any system of coplanar forces about any point in the plane is equal to the intercept on a line drawn through the center of moments and parallel to the resultant of all the forces, cut off by the strings which meet on the resultant, multiplied by the pole distance of the resultant. *It should be noted that in all cases the intercept is a distance and the pole distance is a force.*

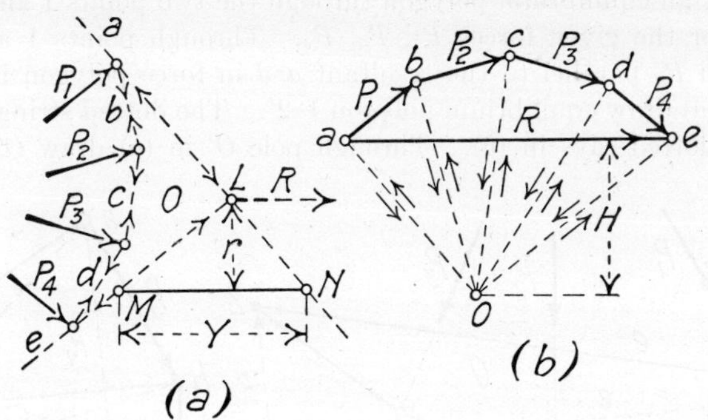

FIG. 11.

This property of the equilibrium polygon is frequently used in finding the bending moments in beams and trusses which are loaded with vertical loads.

Bending Moments in a Beam.—It is required to find the moment at the point M in the simple beam loaded as in (*b*) Fig. 12. The moment at M will be the algebraic

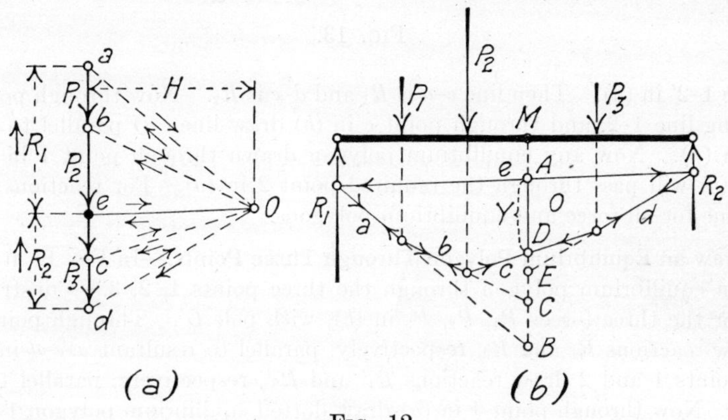

FIG. 12.

sum of the moments of the forces to the left of M. The moment of $P_1 = H \times B\text{–}C$, the moment of $P_2 = H \times C\text{–}D$ and the moment of $R_1 = - H \times B\text{–}A$. The moment at M will therefore be

$$M_1 = H \times B\text{–}C + H \times C\text{–}D - H \times B\text{–}A = H \times A\text{–}D = - H \cdot y$$

The moment of the forces to the right of M may in like manner be shown to be

$$M_1 = + H \cdot y$$

In like manner the bending moment at any point in the beam may be shown to be the ordinate of the equilibrium polygon multiplied by the pole distance. The ordinate is a distance and is measured by the same scale as the beam, while the pole distance is a force and is measured by the same scale as the loads.

To Draw an Equilibrium Polygon Through Two Points.—In Fig. 13 it is required to draw an equilibrium polygon through the two points 1 and 2. Construct a force polygon for the given forces P_1, P_2, P_3. Through points 1 and 2 in (*a*) draw reactions R_1 and R_2 parallel to the resultant *a–d* in force polygon in (*b*). Beginning with point 1 in (*a*) draw equilibrium polygon 1–2′. The dotted strings in (*a*) are drawn parallel to the dotted rays in (*b*). Through pole *O*′ in (*b*) draw *O*′–*e* parallel to the

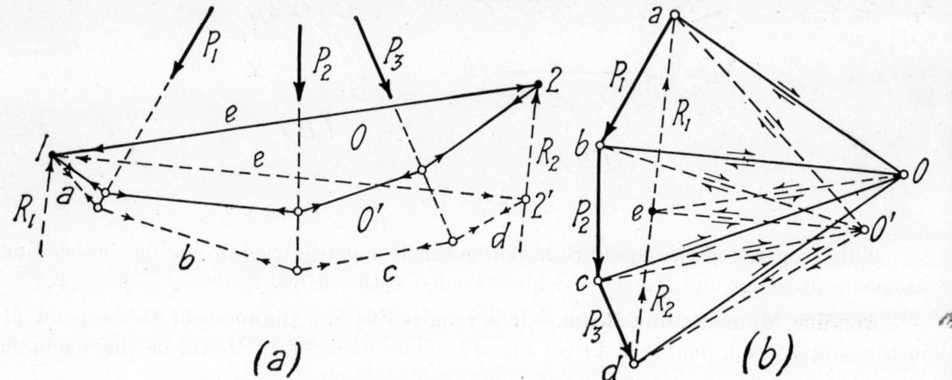

FIG. 13.

closing line 1–2′ in (*a*). Then line *e–a* is R_1 and *d–e* is R_2. Now through point 1 in (*a*) draw closing line 1–2, and through point *e* in (*b*) draw line *e–O* parallel to the closing line 1–2 in (*a*). Now any equilibrium polygon drawn through point 1 in (*a*) with a pole *O* in (*b*) will pass through the required point 2 in (*a*). For reactions R_1 and R_2 are the same for all force and equilibrium polygons.

To Draw an Equilibrium Polygon Through Three Points.—In Fig. 14, it is required to draw an equilibrium polygon through the three points 1, 2, 3. Construct a force polygon for the three forces P_1, P_2, P_3 in (*b*), with pole *O*′. Through points 1 and 3 in (*a*) draw reactions R_1 and R_2, respectively, parallel to resultant *a–e–d* in (*b*). Also through points 1 and 2 draw reactions R_1' and R_2', respectively, parallel to resultant *a–c* in (*b*). Now through point 1 in (*a*) draw dotted equilibrium polygon 1–2′–3′, with strings parallel to the dotted rays in (*b*). In force polygon (*b*) draw line *O*′–*e* parallel to closing line 1–3′ in (*a*). Then in (*b*), $e\text{–}a = R_1$, and $d\text{–}e = R_2$. Also draw line *O*′–*f* in (*b*) parallel to closing line 1–2′ in (*a*). Then $f\text{–}a = R_1'$ and $c\text{–}f = R_2'$. In (*a*) draw closing lines 1–2, and 1–3, respectively. Through points *e* and *f* in (*b*) draw lines parallel to closing lines 1–3, and 1–2 in (*a*), respectively. Now every equilibrium polygon having its pole on the line *e–O* will pass through points 1 and 3, and every equilibrium polygon having its pole on the line *f–O* will pass through points 1 and 2. Point *O* is common to both force polygons, and therefore an equilibrium polygon with a pole at *O*, may be drawn through the given points 1, 2, 3.

It will be seen that while an infinite number of equilibrium polygons may be drawn through two points, only one equilibrium polygon can be drawn through three points.

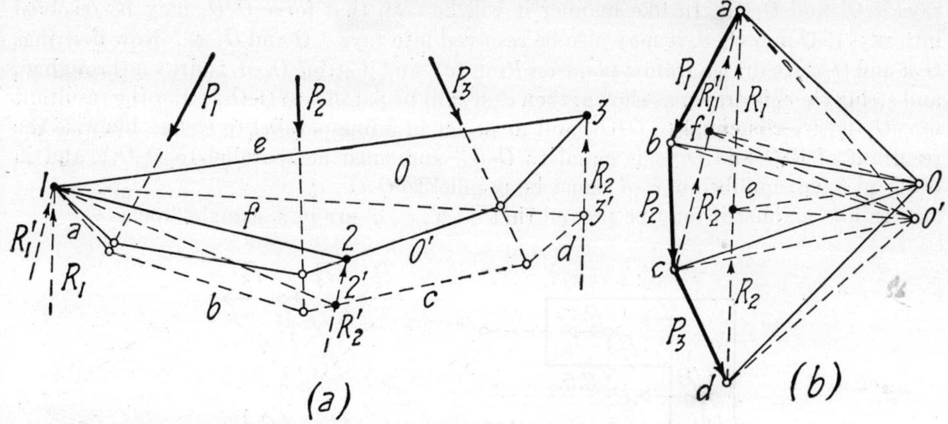

FIG. 14.

Properties of Equilibrium Polygons.—Given the forces P_1, P_2, P_3 in (*a*) Fig. 15. Construct the force polygon in (*b*) and draw resultant a–d = R. Now with pole O in force polygon (*b*) draw equilibrium polygon a–b–c–d in (*a*). Also with pole O_1 in force

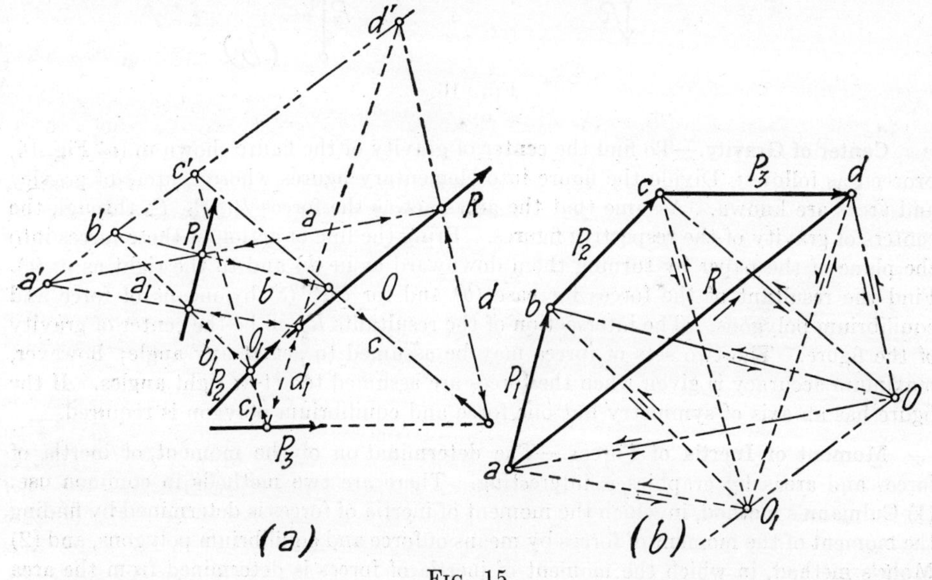

FIG. 15.

polygon (*b*) draw equilibrium polygon a_1, b_1, c_1, d_1 in (*a*). Now the intersections of strings a–O and a_1–O_1; b–O and b_1–O_1; c–O and c_1–O_1; d–O and d_1 O_1 will meet at the points a', b', c', d', respectively, which will be on a straight line parallel to the line O–O_1 which passes through the poles O and O_1 in (b). This relation is due to the reciprocal relation of the force and equilibrium polygons, and may be proved as follows: In force polygon (b) force P_3 may be resolved into rays d–O and O–c, it may also be resolved into rays d–O_1 and O_1–c. In like manner it will be seen that force O–O_1 may be resolved into rays d–O and O_1–d, it may also be resolved into rays c–O and O_1–c. Now if strings O–d and O–c are drawn from a point on P_3 in (a), and if string O_1–d_1 is drawn through d^1, and string O_1–c_1 is drawn as shown, then c'–d' will be parallel to O–O_1. For the resultant of c–O and O_1–c is equal to O–O_1, and must act in a line parallel to O–O_1; likewise the resultant of d–O and O_1–d is equal to O–O_1, and must act parallel to O–O_1; and in order to have equilibrium c'–d' must be parallel to O–O_1.

In like manner it may be proved that a', b', c', d' are in a straight line.

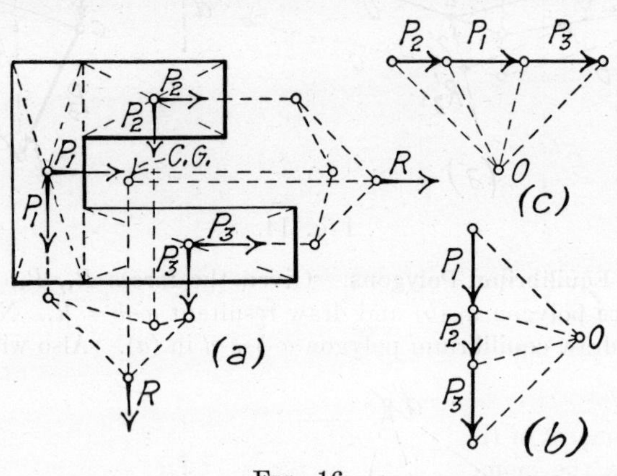

FIG. 16.

Center of Gravity.—To find the center of gravity of the figure shown in (a) Fig. 16, proceed as follows: Divide the figure into elementary figures whose centers of gravity and areas are known. Assume that the areas act as the forces P_1, P_2, P_3 through the centers of gravity of the respective figures. Bring the line of action of these forces into the plane of the paper by turning them downward as in (b) and to the right as in (c). Find the resultant of the forces for case (b) and for case (c) by means of force and equilibrium polygons. The intersection of the resultants R will be the center of gravity of the figure. The two sets of forces may be assumed to act at any angle; however, maximum accuracy is given when the forces are assumed to act at right angles. If the figure has an axis of symmetry but one force and equilibrium polygon is required.

Moment of Inertia of Forces.—The determinat on of the moment of inertia of forces and areas by graphics is interesting. There are two methods in common use: (1) Culmann's method, in which the moment of inertia of forces is determined by finding the moment of the moment of forces by means of force and equilibrium polygons, and (2) Mohr's method, in which the moment of inertia of forces is determined from the area of the equilibrium polygon. The moment of inertia of a force about a parallel axis is equal to the force multiplied by the square of the distance between the force and the axis.

Culmann's Method.—It is required to find the moment of inertia, I, of the system of forces P_1, P_2, P_3, P_4, Fig. 17, about the axis M–N. Construct the force polygon (a)

with a pole distance H, draw the equilibrium polygon a–b–c–d–e, and produce the strings until they intersect the axis M–N. Now the moment of P_1 about axis M–N equals $E–D \times H$; moment of P_2 equals $D–C \times H$; moment of P_3 equals $C–B \times H$; moment of P_4 equals $B–A \times H$; and moment of resultant R equals $E–A \times H$. With intercepts E–D, D–C, C–B, B–A, as forces acting in place of P_1, P_2, P_3, P_4, respectively, construct force polygon (*b*) with pole distance H', and draw equilibrium polygon (*c*).

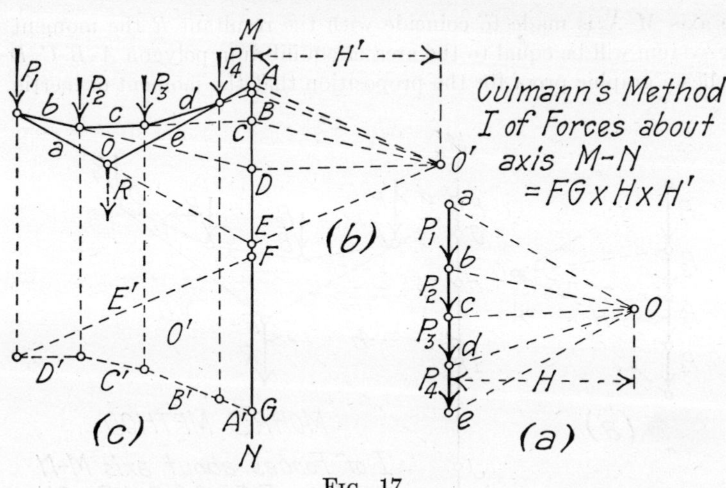

FIG. 17.

As before the moments of the forces will be equal to the products of the intercepts and pole distance and the moment of the system of forces represented by the intercepts will be equal to the intercept G–F multiplied by pole distance H'. But the intercepts E–D, D–C, C–B, B–A, multiplied by the pole distance H equal moments of the forces P_1, P_2, P_3, P_4, respectively, about the axis M–N, and the moment of inertia of the system of forces P_1, P_2, P_3, P_4, about the axis M–N will be equal to the intercept G–F multiplied by the product of the two pole distances H and H', and

$$I = F–G \times H \times H'$$

Mohr's Method.—It is required to find the moment of inertia, I, of the system of forces P_1, P_2, P_3, P_4, Fig. 18, about the axis M–N. Construct the force polygon (*a*) with a pole distance H, and draw the equilibrium polygon (*b*). Now the moment of P_1 about the axis M–N equals intercept F–G multiplied by the pole distance H, and the moment of inertia of P_1 about the axis M–N equals the moment of the moment of P_1 about the axis, $= F–G \times H \times d$. But $F–G \times d$ equals twice the area of the triangle F–G–A, and we have the moment of inertia of P_1 equal to the area of the triangle $F–G–A \times 2H$. In like manner the moment of inertia of P_2 may be shown equal to area of the triangle $G–H–B \times 2H$; moment of inertia of P_3 equal to area of the triangle $H–I–C \times 2H$; and moment of inertia of P_4 equal to area of the triangle $I–J–D \times 2H$. Summing up these values we have the moment of inertia of the system of forces equal to the area of the equilibrium polygon multiplied by twice the pole distance, H, and

$$I = \text{area } F–A–B–C–D–E–J–F \times 2H$$

To find the radius of gyration, r, we use the formula

$$I = R \cdot r^2$$

In Fig. 18 the moment of inertia, I_r, of the resultant of the system of forces about the axis M–N, can in like manner be shown to be equal to area of the triangle F–E–J $\times$ $2H$.

If the axis M–N is made to coincide with the resultant R the moment of inertia $I_{c.g.}$ of the system will be equal to the area of equilibrium polygon A–B–C–D–E $\times$ $2H$. This furnishes a graphic proof for the proposition that the moment of inertia, I, of any

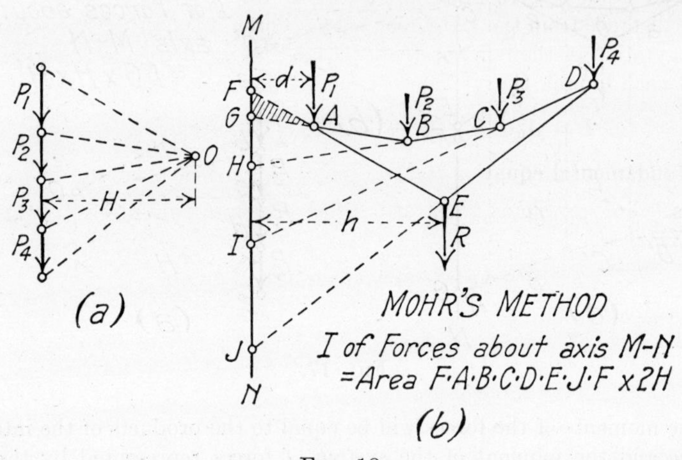

FIG. 18.

system of parallel forces about an axis parallel to the resultant of the system is equal to the moment of inertia, $I_{c.g.}$, of the forces about an axis through their centroid plus the moment of inertia, I_r, of their resultant about the given axis.

$$I = I_{c.g.} + R \cdot h^2$$

$$= I_{c.g.} + I_r$$

It will be seen from the foregoing discussion that the moment of inertia of a system of forces about an axis through the centroid of the system is a minimum.

Moment of Inertia of Areas.—The moment of inertia of an area about an axis in the same plane is equal to the summation of the products of the differential areas which compose the area and the squares of the distances of the differential areas from the axis.

The moment of inertia of an area about a neutral axis (axis through center of gravity of the area) is less than that about any parallel axis, and is the moment of inertia used in the fundamental formula for flexure in beams

$$M = \frac{f \cdot I}{c}$$

where

M = bending moment at section in inch-pounds;
f = extreme fibre stress in pounds;
I = moment of inertia of section in inches to the fourth power;
c = distance from neutral axis to extreme fibre in inches.

An approximate value of the moment of inertia of an area may be obtained by either of the preceding methods by dividing the area into laminae and assuming each area to be a force acting through the center of gravity of the lamina, the smaller the laminae the greater the accuracy. The true value may be obtained by either of the above methods if each one of the forces is assumed to act at a distance from the given axis equal to the radius of gyration of the area with reference to the axis, $d = \sqrt{a^2 + r^2}$, where a is the distance from the given axis to the center of gravity of the lamina and r is the radius of gyration of the lamina about an axis through its center of gravity. If A_0 is the area of each lamina the moment of inertia of the lamina will be

$$I = A_0 \cdot d^2 = A_0 \cdot a^2 + A_0 \cdot r^2 = A_0 \cdot a^2 + I_{c.g.}$$

which is the fundamental equation for transferring moments of inertia to parallel axes.

Problems.—For problems illustrating the principles discussed in this chapter, see Chapter XIII.

CHAPTER II.

Stresses in Framed Structures.

Methods of Calculation.—The determination of the reactions of simple framed structures usually requires the use of the three fundamental equations of equilibrium,

$$\Sigma \text{ horizontal components of forces } = 0 \qquad (1)$$

$$\Sigma \text{ vertical components of forces } = 0 \qquad (2)$$

$$\Sigma \text{ moments of forces about any point } = 0 \qquad (3)$$

Having completely determined the external forces, the internal stresses may be obtained by either equations (1) and (2) (resolution), or equation (3) (moments). These equations may be solved by graphics or by algebra. There are, therefore, four methods of calculating stresses:

Resolution of Forces { Algebraic Method, Graphic Method }

Moments of Forces { Algebraic Method, Graphic Method }

The stresses in any simple framed structure can be calculated by using any one of the four methods. However, all the methods are not equally well suited to all problems, and there is in general one method that is best suited to each particular problem.

The common practice of dividing methods of calculation of stresses into analytic and graphic methods is meaningless and misleading for the reason that both algebraic and graphic methods are analytical, *i. e.* capable of analysis.

The loads on trusses are usually considered as concentrated at the joints in the plane of the loaded chord.

Algebraic Resolution.—In calculating the stresses in a truss by algebraic resolution, the fundamental equations for equilibrium for translation,

$$\Sigma \text{ horizontal components of forces } = 0 \qquad (1)$$

$$\Sigma \text{ vertical components of forces } = 0 \qquad (2)$$

are applied (1) to each joint, or (2) to the members and forces on one side of a section cut through the truss.

(*a*) *Forces at a Joint.*—The reactions having been found, the stresses in the members of the truss shown in Fig. 1 are calculated as follows: Beginning at the left reaction, R_1, we have by applying equations (1) and (2)

$$1\text{-}x \cdot \sin\theta - 1\text{-}y \cdot \sin\alpha = 0 \qquad (4)$$

$$1\text{-}x \cdot \cos\theta - 1\text{-}y \cdot \cos\alpha - R_1 = 0 \qquad (5)$$

The stresses in members 1–x and 1–y may be obtained by solving equations (4) and (5). The direction of the forces which represent the stresses in amount will be

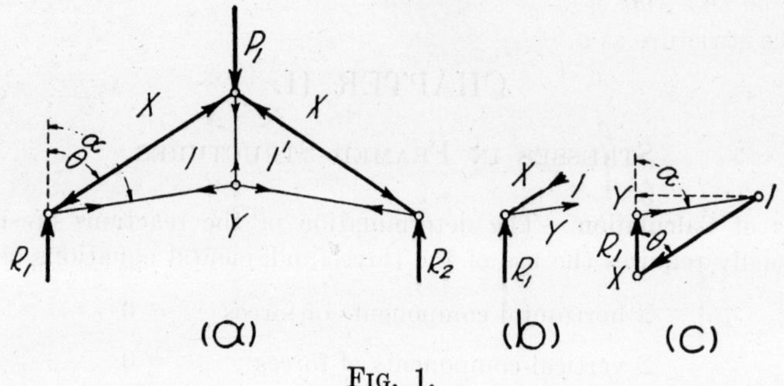

FIG. 1.

determined by the signs of the results, plus signs indicating compression and minus signs indicating tension. Arrows pointing toward the joint indicate that the member is in compression; arrows pointing away from the joint indicate that the member is in tension. The stresses in the members of the truss at the remaining joints in the truss are calculated in the same way.

The direction of the forces and the kind of stress can always be determined by sketching in the force polygon for the forces meeting at the joint as in (c) Fig. 1.

It will be seen from the foregoing that the method of algebraic resolution consists in applying the principle of the force polygon to the external forces and internal stresses at each joint.

Since we have only two fundamental equations for translation (resolution) we can not solve a joint if there are more than two forces or stresses unknown.

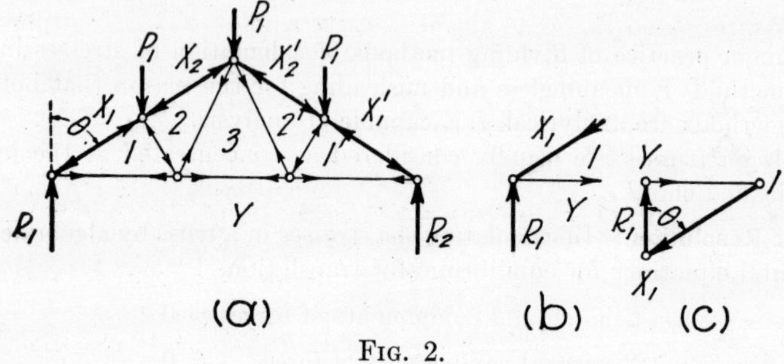

FIG. 2.

Where the lower chord of the truss is horizontal as in Fig. 2, we have by applying fundamental equations (1) and (2) to the joint at the left reaction,

$$1\text{–}x = +\,R_1 \cdot \sec\,\theta \tag{6}$$

$$1\text{–}y = -\,R_1 \cdot \tan\,\theta \tag{7}$$

the plus sign indicating compression and the minus sign tension. Equations (6) and (7) may be obtained directly from force triangle (c). Equations (6) and (7) are used in calculating the stresses in trusses with parallel chords and lead to the method of coefficients (Chapter VI).

(b) *Forces on One Side of a Section.*—The principle of resolution of forces may be applied to the structure as a whole or to a portion of the structure.

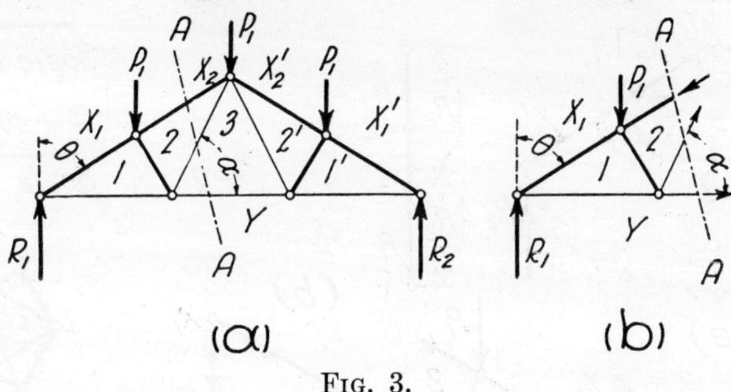

Fig. 3.

If the truss shown in Fig. 3 is cut by the plane A–A, the internal stresses and external forces acting on either segment, as in (b) will be in equilibrium. The external forces acting on the cut members as shown in (b) are equal to the internal stresses in the cut members and are opposite in direction.

Applying equations (1) and (2) to the cut section

$$3\text{–}y + 2\text{–}3\cdot\cos\alpha - 2\text{–}x\cdot\sin\theta = 0 \tag{8}$$

$$2\text{–}3\cdot\sin\alpha - 2\text{–}x\cdot\cos\theta + R_1 - P_1 = 0 \tag{9}$$

Now, if all but two of the external forces are known, the unknowns may be found by solving equations (8) and (9). If more than two external forces are unknown the problem is indeterminate as far as equations (8) and (9) are concerned.

In the Warren truss in Fig. 4 the stresses at a joint may be calculated by com-

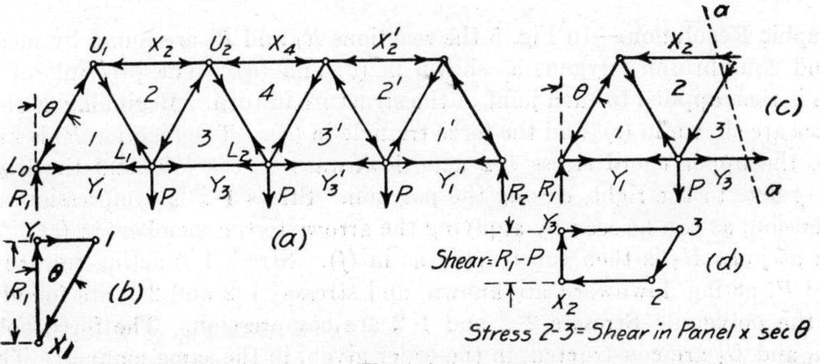

Fig. 4.

pleting the force polygon as at the left reaction in (b) Fig. 4. Applying equations (1) and (2) to a section as in (c)

$$2\text{–}x + 2\text{–}3\cdot\sin\theta - 3\text{–}y = 0 \tag{10}$$

$$-\ 2\text{–}3\cdot\cos\theta - P + R_1 = 0 \tag{11}$$

Now, $R_1 - P$ = shear in the panel. Therefore the stress in 2–3 = $-(R_1 - P) \sec \theta$ = shear in panel $\times \sec \theta$. This analysis leads directly to the method of coefficients as explained in detail in Chapter VI.

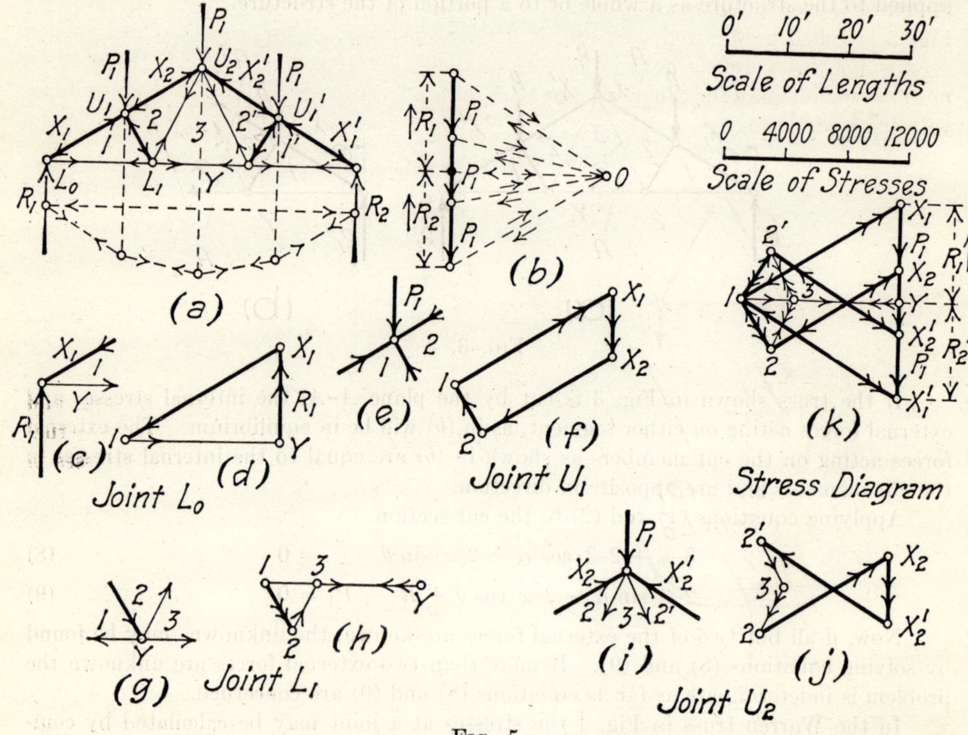

FIG. 5.

Graphic Resolution.—In Fig. 5 the reactions R_1 and R_2 are found by means of the force and equilibrium polygons as shown in (*b*) and (*a*). The principle of the force polygon is then applied to each joint of the structure in turn. Beginning at the joint L_0 the forces are shown in (*c*), and the force triangle in (*d*). The reaction R_1 is known and acts up, the upper chord stress 1–x acts downward to the left, and the lower chord stress 1–y acts to the right, closing the polygon. Stress 1–x is compression and stress 1–y is tension, as can be seen by applying the arrows to the members in (*c*). The force polygon at joint U_1 is then constructed as in (*f*). Stress 1–x acting toward joint U_1 and load P_1 acting downward are known, and stresses 1–2 and 2–x are found by completing the polygon. Stresses 2–x and 1–2 are compression. The force polygons at joints L_1 and U_2 are constructed, in the order given, in the same manner. The known forces at any joint are indicated in direction in the force polygon by double arrows, and the unknown forces are indicated in direction by single arrows.

The stresses in the members of the right segment of the truss are the same as in the left, and the force polygons are, therefore, not constructed for the right segment. The force polygons for all the joints of the truss are grouped into the stress diagram shown in (*k*). Compression in the stress diagram and truss is indicated by arrows acting toward the ends of the stress lines and toward the joints, respectively, and tension is indicated by arrows acting away from the ends of the stress lines and away from the joints, respectively. The first time a stress is used a single arrow, and the second time the stress is used a double arrow is used to indicate direction. The stress diagram in (*k*) Fig. 5 is called a Maxwell diagram or a reciprocal polygon diagram. The notation used is known as Bow's notation. The method of graphic resolution is the method most commonly used for calculating stresses in roof trusses and simple framed structures with inclined chords.

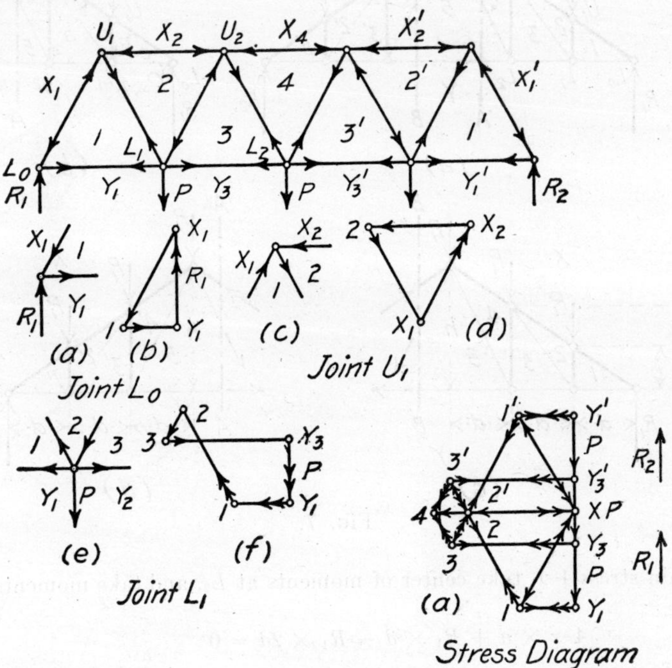

FIG. 6.

Warren Bridge Truss.—In Fig. 6 the dead load stresses in a Warren bridge truss loaded on the lower chord, are calculated by the method of graphic resolution. In the stress diagram the loads are laid off from the bottom upwards. The details of the solution can easily be followed by reference to Fig. 6 and Fig. 5. It will be seen that the upper chord of the truss is in compression, while the lower chord is in tension.

Algebraic Moments.—The reactions may be found by applying the fundamental equations of equilibrium to the structure as a whole. In the truss in (*a*) Fig. 7, by taking moments about the right reaction we have

$$R_1 \times 6d = 5P_1 \times 3d$$

$$R_1 = \tfrac{5}{2}P_1 = R_2$$

To find the stresses in the members of the truss in (*a*) Fig. 7, proceed as follows: Cut the truss by means of plane *AA*, as in (*b*), and replace the stresses in the members cut away with external forces. These forces are equal to the stresses in the members in amount, but opposite in direction, and produce equilibrium.

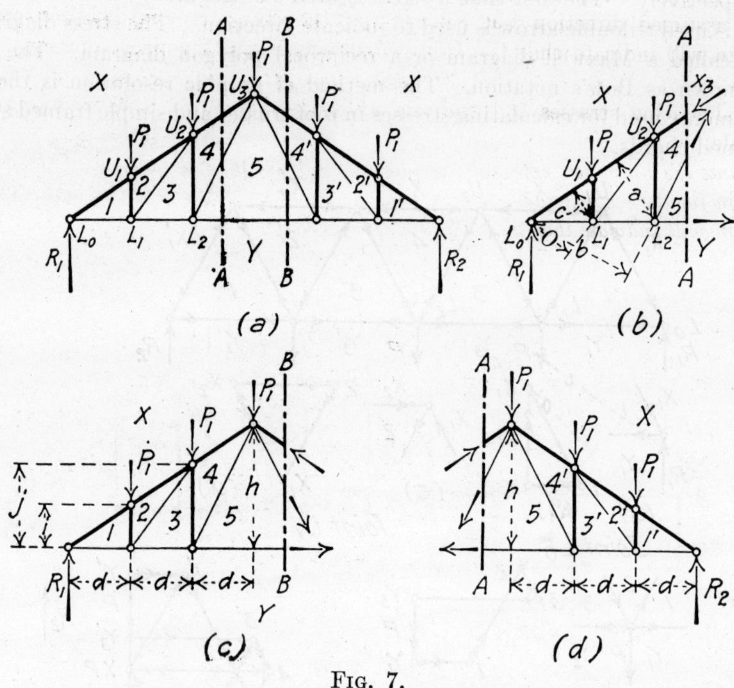

FIG. 7.

To obtain stress $4\text{–}x$, take center of moments at L_2, and take moments of external forces

$$4\text{–}x \times a + P_1 \times d - R_1 \times 2d = 0$$

$$4\text{–}x = \frac{R_1 \times 2d - P_1 \cdot d}{a} = \frac{4P \cdot d}{a} \text{ (compression)}$$

To obtain stress in 4–5 take center of moments at L_0, and take moments of external forces

$$4\text{–}5 \times b - 2P_1 \times \tfrac{3}{2}d = 0$$

$$4\text{–}5 = \frac{3P \cdot d}{b} \text{ (tension)}$$

To obtain the stress in $5\text{–}y$ take center of moments at joint U_3 in (*c*), and take moments of external forces

$$5\text{–}y \times h - R_1 \times 3d + 3P_1 \cdot d = 0$$

$$5\text{–}y = \frac{3R_1 \cdot d - 3P_1 \cdot d}{h} = \frac{9P_1 \cdot d}{2h} \text{ (tension)}$$

To Determine Kind of Stress.—If the unknown external force is always taken as acting from the outside toward the cut section, *i. e.*, is always assumed to cause compression, the sign of the result will indicate the kind of stress. A plus sign will indicate that the assumed direction was correct and that the stress is compression, while a minus sign will indicate that the assumed direction was incorrect and that the stress is tension.

In calculating stresses by algebraic moments, therefore, always observe the following rule:

Assume the unknown external force as acting from the outside toward the cut section; a plus sign for the result will then show that the stress in the member is compression, and a minus sign will indicate that the stress in the member is tension.

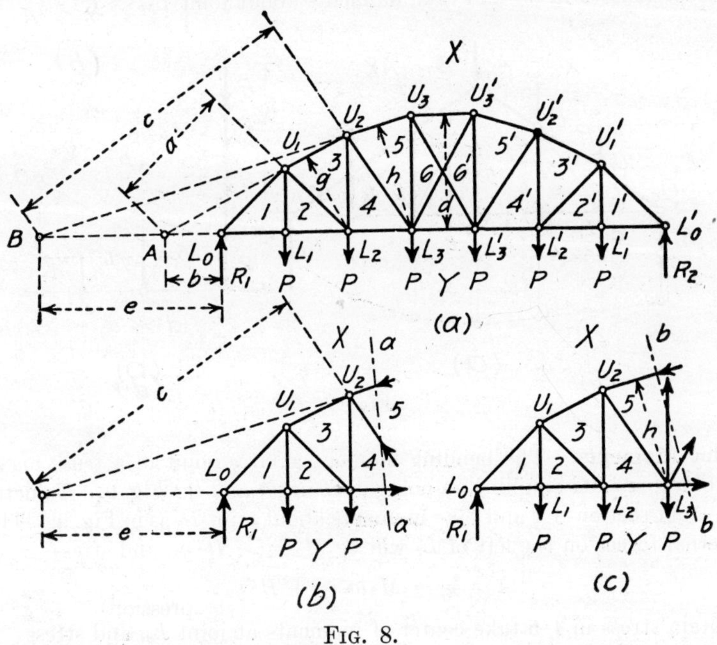

FIG. 8.

The stresses in the web members 3–4, 2–3, 1–2, are found by taking moments about joint L_0 as a center. The stresses in y–3 and y–1 are found by taking moments about joints U_2 and U_1, respectively; and the stresses in x–2 and x–1 are found by taking moments about joint L_1.

The method of algebraic moments is the most common method used for calculating the stresses in bridge trusses with inclined chords and similar frameworks which carry moving loads.

Stresses in a Bridge Truss.—Calculate reaction R_1, Fig. 8, by taking moments of the vertical forces about joint L_0'. Then $R_1 \times L = 6P \cdot L/2$, and $R_1 = 3P = R_2$. To calculate the stress in any member in the truss, pass a section cutting the member in which the stress is required, and cutting away the truss on one side of the section.

The stresses in the members cut away are assumed as replaced by external forces acting in the line of the member and equal to the stresses in amount.

To calculate the stresses take the center of moments so that there will be but one unknown stress The solution of the equation of moments about this center of moments will give the required stress. To calculate the stress in 4–5 in (*b*) Fig. 8, pass the section *a–a*, cutting away the right side of the truss, and take the center of moments at the intersection of the top and bottom chords. Now 5–*x* and 4–*y* act through the center of moments and produce no moment. The moment of the stress in 4–5 acting from the outside toward the cut section with an arm *c*, holds in equilibrium the reaction R_1, and the two loads, *P*. The sign of the result will determine the kind of stress, minus for tension and plus for compression. To calculate the stress in the top chord U_2U_3, pass section *b–b* in (*c*) and take moments about joint L_3.

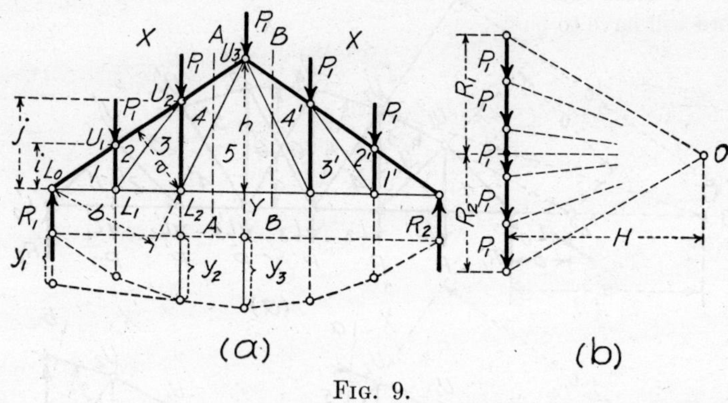

FIG. 9.

Graphic Moments.—The bending moment at any point in a truss may be found by means of a force and equilibrium polygon as in (*b*) and (*a*) Fig. 9. To determine the stress in 4–*x* cut section *AA* and take moments about joint L_2 as in Fig. 9. The moment of the external forces on the left of L_2 will be $M_2 = -H \cdot y_2$, and stress

$$4\text{–}x = -M_2/a = +H \cdot y_2/a$$

To obtain stress in 4–5 take center of moments at joint L_0, and stress

$$4\text{–}5 = M_1/b = = H \cdot y_1/b$$

To obtain stress in 5–*y* take center of moments at joint U_3, and stress

$$5\text{–}y = M_3/h = -H \cdot y_3/h$$

The method of graphic moments is principally used to explain other methods and is little used as a direct method of calculation.

Problems.—For problems illustrating the principles discussed in this chapter, see Chapter XIII.

CHAPTER III.

Stresses in Simple Roof Trusses.

Loads.—The stresses in roof trusses are due (1) to the dead load, (2) the snow load, (3) the wind load, and (4) concentrated and moving loads. The stresses due to dead, snow, wind and concentrated loads will be discussed in this chapter in the order given.

Dead Load Stresses.—The dead load is made up of the weight of the truss and roof covering and is usually considered as applied at the panel points of the upper chord in computing stresses in roof trusses. If the purlins do not come at the panel points, the upper chord will have to be designed for both direct stress and stress due to flexure.

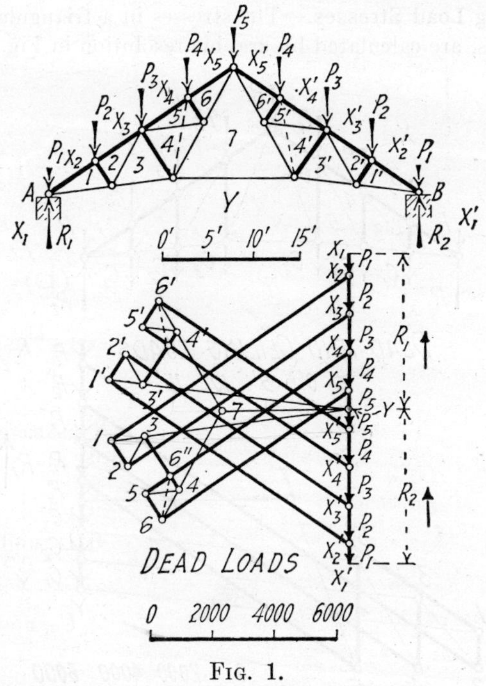

Fig. 1.

The dead load is usually specified as a certain number of pounds per sq. ft. of horizontal projection of roof supported.

The stresses in a Fink truss due to dead load are calculated by graphic resolution in Fig. 1.

The loads are laid off, the reactions found, and the stresses calculated beginning at joint L_0, as explained in Fig. 5, Chapter II. The stress diagram for the right half of the truss need not be drawn where the truss and loads are symmetrical as in Fig. 1; however it gives a check on the accuracy of the work and is well worth the extra time required. The loads P_1 on the abutments have no effect on the stresses in the truss and may be omitted in this solution.

In calculating the stresses at joint P_3, the stresses in the members 3–4, 4–5 and x–5 are unknown, and the solution appears to be indeterminate. The solution is easily made by cutting out members 4–5 and 5–6, and replacing them with the dotted member shown. The stresses in the members in the modified truss are now obtained up to and including stresses 6–x and 6–7. Since the stresses 6–x and 6–7 are independent of the form of the framework to the left, as can easily be seen by cutting a section through the members 6–x, 6–7 and 7–y, the solution can be carried back and the apparent ambiguity removed. The ambiguity can also be removed by calculating the stress in 7–y by algebraic moments and substituting it in the stress diagram. It will be noted that all top chord members are in compression and all bottom chord members are in tension.

The dead load stresses can also be calculated by any of the three remaining methods, as previously described.

Dead and Ceiling Load Stresses.—The stresses in a triangular Pratt truss due to dead and ceiling loads, are calculated by graphic resolution in Fig. 2.

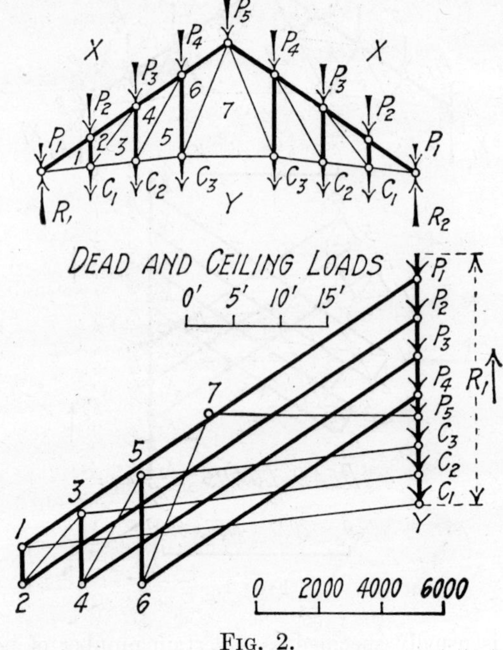

FIG. 2.

For simplicity the stresses are shown for one side only. The reaction R_1 is equal to one-half of the entire load on the truss. The solution will appear more clear when it is noted that the stress diagram shown consists of two diagrams, one due to loads on the upper chord and the other due to loads on the lower chord, combined in one, the loads in each case coming between the stresses in the members on each side of the load. The top chord loads are laid off in order downward, while the bottom chord loads are laid off in order upward.

Snow Load Stresses.—Large snow storms nearly always occur in still weather, and the maximum snow load will therefore be a uniformly distributed load. A heavy wind may follow a sleet storm and a snow load equal to the minimum given in Fig. 2, Chapter XXIV should be considered as acting at the same time as the wind load. The stresses due to snow load are found in the same manner as the dead load stresses.

Wind Load Stresses.—The stresses in trusses due to wind load will depend upon the direction and intensity of the wind, and the condition of the end supports. The wind is commonly considered as acting horizontally, and the normal component, as determined by one of the formulas in Fig. 4, Chapter XXIV, is taken.

The ends of the truss may (1) be rigidly fixed to the abutment walls, (2) be equally free to move, or (3) have one end fixed and the other end on rollers. When both ends of the truss are rigidly fixed to the abutment walls (1) the reactions are parallel to each other and to the resultant of the external loads; where both ends of the truss are equally free to move (2) the horizontal components of the reactions are equal; and where one end is fixed and the other end is on frictionless rollers (3) the reaction at the roller end will always be vertical. Either case (1) or case (3) is commonly assumed in calculating wind load stresses in trusses. Case (2) is the condition in a portal or framed bent. The vertical components of the reactions are independent of the condition of the ends.

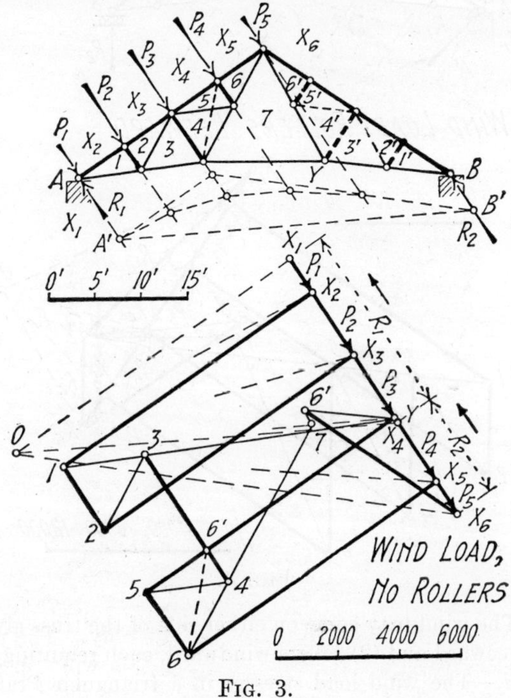

Fig. 3.

Wind Load Stresses: No Rollers.—The stresses due to a normal wind load, in a Fink truss with both ends fixed to rigid walls, are calculated by graphic resolution in Fig. 3. The reactions are parallel and their sum equals sum of the external loads;

they are found by means of force and equilibrium polygons as in Fig. 8, Chapter I, and Fig. 5, Chapter II. The stress diagram is constructed in the same manner as that for dead loads. Heavy lines in truss and stress diagram indicate compression, and light lines indicate tension.

The ambiguity at joint P_3 is removed by means of the dotted member as in the case of the dead load stress diagram. It will be seen that there are no stresses in the dotted web members in the right segment of the truss. It is necessary to carry the solution entirely through the truss, beginning at the left reaction and checking up at the right reaction. It will be seen that the load P_1 has no effect on the stresses in the truss in this case.

Wind Load Stresses: Rollers.—Trusses longer than 70 feet are usually fixed at one end, and are supported on rollers at the other end. The reaction at the roller end is then vertical—the horizontal component of the external wind force being all taken

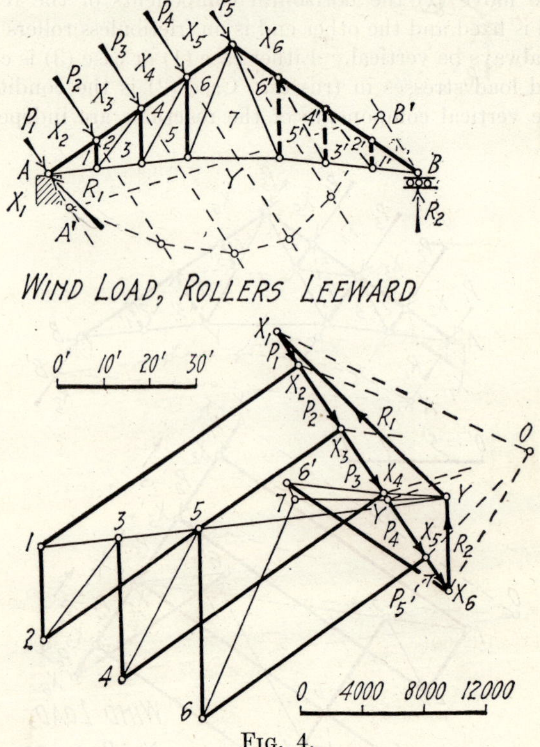

FIG. 4.

by the fixed end. The wind may come on either side of the truss giving rise to two conditions; (1) rollers leeward and (2) rollers windward, each requiring a separate solution.

Rollers Leeward.—The wind load stresses in a triangular Pratt truss with rollers under the leeward side are calculated by graphic resolution in Fig. 4.

The reactions in Fig. 4 were first determined by means of force and equilibrium polygons, on the assumption that they were parallel to each other and to the resultant of the external loads. Then since the reaction at the roller end is vertical and the horizontal component at the fixed end is equal to the horizontal component of the external wind forces, the true reactions were obtained by closing the force polygon.

In order that the truss be in equilibrium under the action of the three external forces R_1, R_2 and the *resultant of the wind loads*, the three external forces must meet in a point if produced. This furnishes a method for determining the reactions, where the direction and line of action of one and a point in the line of action of the other are known, providing the point of intersection of the three forces comes within the limits of the drawing board.

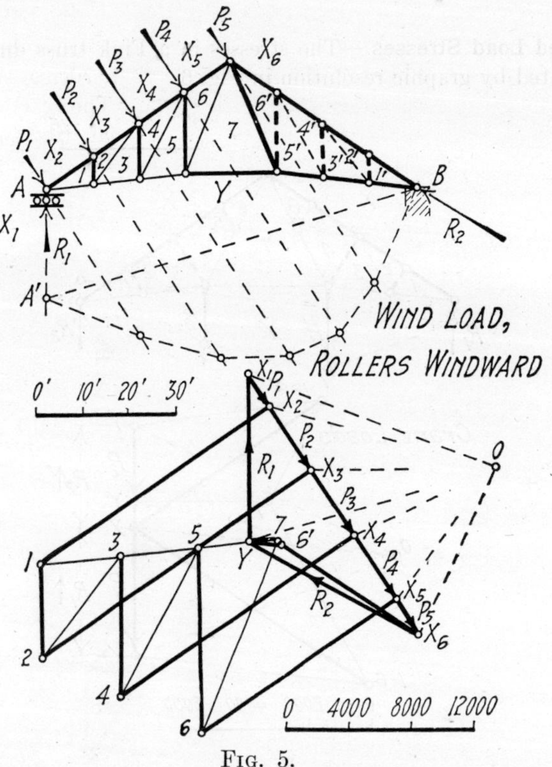

FIG. 5.

The stress diagram is constructed in the same way as the stress diagram for dead loads. It will be seen that the load P_1 has no effect on the stresses in the truss in this case. Heavy lines in truss and stress diagram indicate compression and light lines indicate tension.

Rollers Windward.—The wind load stresses in the same triangular Pratt truss as shown in Fig. 4, with rollers under the windward side of the truss are calculated by graphic resolution in Fig. 5.

The true reactions were determined directly by means of force and equilibrium polygons as in Fig. 9, Chapter I. The direction of the reaction R_1 is known to be vertical, but the direction of the reaction R_2 is unknown, the only known point in its line of action being the right abutment. The equilibrium polygon is drawn to pass through the right abutment and the direction of the right reaction is determined by connecting the point of intersection of the vertical reaction R_1 and the line drawn through O parallel to the closing line of the equilibrium polygon, with the lower end of the load line.

Since the vertical components of the reactions are independent of the conditions of the ends of the truss, the vertical components of the reactions in Fig. 4 and Fig. 5 are the same. It will be seen that the load P_1 produces stress in the members of the truss with rollers windward. If the line of action of R_2 drops below the point P_5 the lower chord of the truss will be in compression, as will be seen by taking moments about P_5.

Concentrated Load Stresses.—The stresses in a Fink truss due to unequal crane loads are calculated by graphic resolution in Fig. 6.

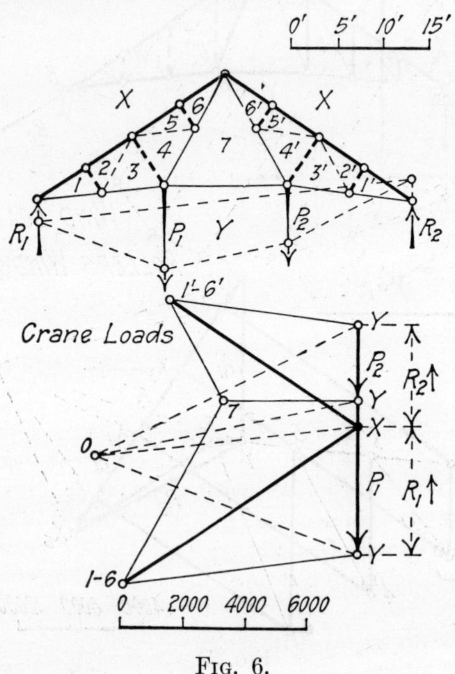

FIG. 6.

The reactions were found by means of force and equilibrium polygons. The truss is reduced to three triangles for the loading shown. The solution of this problem is similar to that for ceiling loads in Fig. 2. The moving crane trolley will produce maximum moment when it is at the center of the truss, and this case should be investigated in solving the problem.

The method of graphic resolution is commonly used for calculating the stresses in roof trusses and similar structures. For examples of the calculation of stresses in trusses by algebraic resolution, algebraic and graphic moments, see Chapter VI and Chapter XIII.

Problems.—For problems illustrating the principles discussed in this chapter, see Chapter XIII.

CHAPTER IV.

SIMPLE BEAMS.

Reactions of a Simple Beam.—A force and an equilibrium polygon may be used to obtain the reactions of a beam loaded with a load *P*, as in Fig. 1.

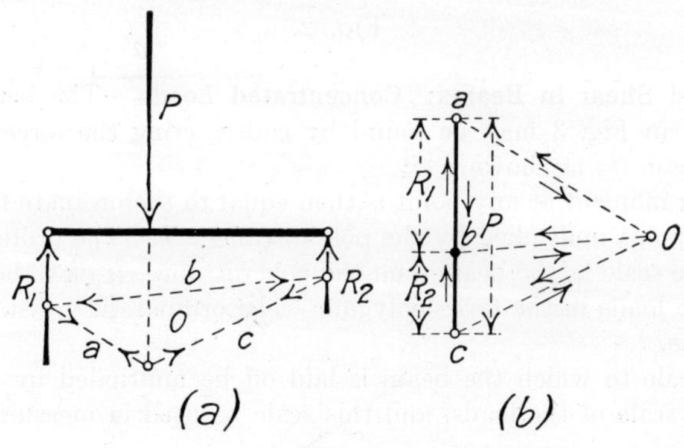

FIG. 1.

The force polygon (*b*) is drawn with a pole *O* at any convenient point, and rays *O–a* and *O–c* are drawn. Now from the fundamental conditions for equilibrium for translation we have $P = R_1 + R_2$. At any convenient point in the line of action of *P*, draw the strings *O–a* and *O–c* parallel to the rays *a–O* and *O–c*, respectively, in the force polygon. The imaginary forces *O–a* and *O–c* acting as shown, equilibrate the force *P*. The imaginary force *a–O* acting in a reverse direction, as shown, is an equilibrant of R_1, and the imaginary force *c–O*, acting in a reverse direction, is an equilibrant of R_2. The remaining equilibrant of R_1 and of R_2 must coincide and be equal in amount, but opposite in direction. The string *b–O* is the remaining equilibrant of R_1 and also of R_2, and is called the closing line of the equilibrium polygon. The ray *b–O* drawn parallel to the string *b–O* divides *P* in two parts, which are equal to the reactions R_1 and R_2.

Reactions of a Cantilever Beam.—As a second example let it be required to find the reactions of the overhanging beam shown in Fig. 2.

Construct a force polygon with pole *O*, as in (*b*), and draw an equilibrium polygon, as in (*a*). The ray *O–d*, drawn parallel to the closing line *O–d* in (*a*), determines the reactions. In this case reaction R_1 is negative. It should be noted that the closing line in an equilibrium polygon must have its ends on the two reactions.

The ordinate to the equilibrium polygon at any point, multiplied by the pole distance, *H*, will give the bending moment in the beam at a point immediately above it.

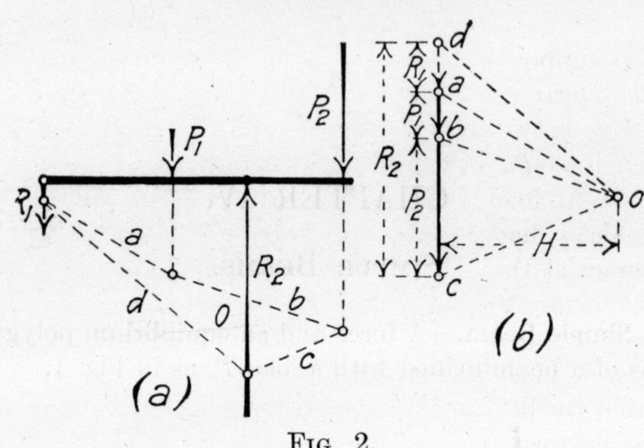

FIG. 2.

Moment and Shear in Beams: Concentrated Loads.—The bending moment in the beam shown in Fig. 3 may be found by constructing the force polygon (*a*) and equilibrium polygon (*b*) as shown.

The bending moment at any point is then equal to the ordinate to the equilibrium polygon at that point multiplied by the pole distance, *H*. The ordinate is to be measured to the same scale as the beam, and the pole distance, *H*, is to be measured to the same scale as the loads in the force polygon. The ordinate is a distance and the pole distance is a force.

Or, if the scale to which the beam is laid off be multiplied by the pole distance measured to the scale of the loads, and this scale be used in measuring the ordinates,

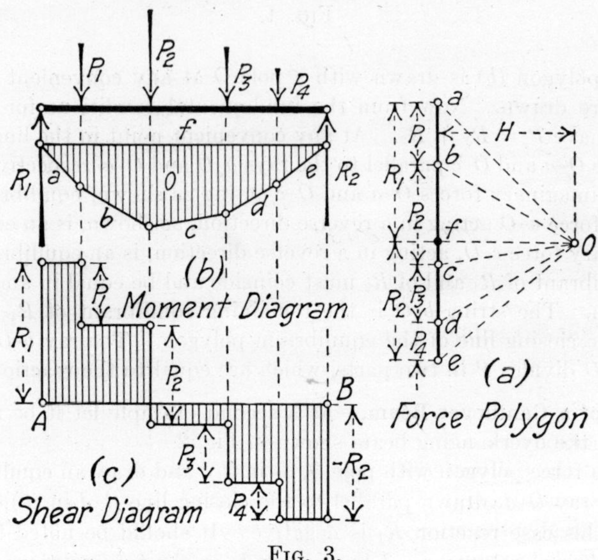

FIG. 3.

the ordinates will be equal to the bending moments at the corresponding points. This is the same as making the pole distance equal to unity. Diagram (*b*) is called a moment diagram.

Between the left support and the first load the shear is equal to R_1; between the loads P_1 and P_2 the shear equals $R_1 - P_1$; between the loads P_2 and P_3 the shear equals $R_1 - P_1 - P_2$; between the loads P_3 and P_4 the shear equals $R_1 - P_1 - P_2 - P_3$; and between load P_4 and the right reaction the shear equals $R_1 - P_1 - P_2 - P_3 - P_4 = - R_2$. At load P_2 the shear changes from positive to negative. Diagram (*c*) is called a shear diagram. It will be seen that the maximum ordinate in the moment diagram comes at the point of zero shear.

The bending moment at any point in the beam is equal to the algebraic sum of the shear areas on either side of the point in question. From this we see that the shear areas on each side of P_2 must be equal. This property of the shear diagram depends upon the principle that the bending moment at any point in a simple beam is the definite integral of the shear between either point of support and the point in question. This will be taken up again in the discussion of beams uniformly loaded which will now be considered.

Moment and Shear in Beams: Uniform Loads.—In the beam loaded with a uniform load of w lb. per lineal foot shown in Fig. 4, the reaction $R_1 = R_2 = \frac{1}{2}w \cdot L$. At a

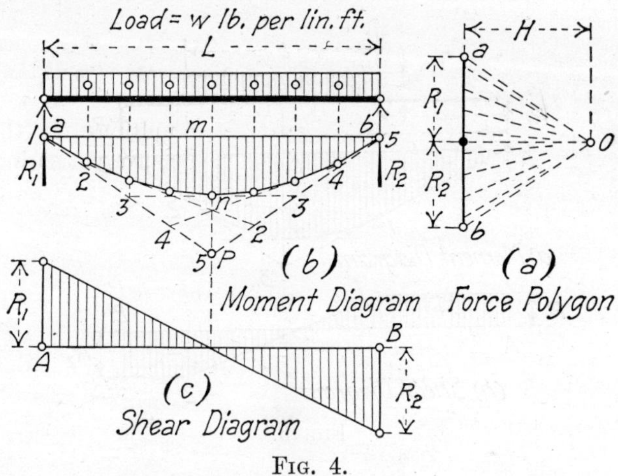

FIG. 4.

distance x from the left support, the bending moment is

$$M = R_1 \cdot x - \tfrac{1}{2}w \cdot x^2 = \tfrac{1}{2}w\,(L \cdot x - x^2) \tag{1}$$

which is the equation of a parabola.

The parabola may be constructed by means of the force and equilibrium polygons by assuming that the uniform load is concentrated at points in the beam, as is assumed in a bridge truss, and drawing the force and equilibrium polygons in the usual way, as in Fig. 4. The greater the number of segments into which the uniform load is divided the more nearly will the equilibrium polygon approach the bending moment parabola.

The parabola may be constructed without drawing the force and equilibrium polygons as follows: Lay off ordinate m–n = n–p = bending moment at center of beam = $\frac{1}{8}w \cdot L^2$. Divide a–p and b–p into the same number of equal parts and number them as shown in (*b*). Join the points with like numbers by lines, which will be tangents to the required parabola. It will be seen in Fig. 4 that points on the parabola are also obtained.

The shear at any point x, will be

$$S = R_1 - w \cdot x = \tfrac{1}{2} w \cdot L - w \cdot x = w(\tfrac{1}{2}L - x) \qquad (2)$$

which is the equation of the inclined line shown in (c) Fig. 4. The shear at any point is therefore represented by the ordinate to the shear diagram at the given point.

Proper y of the Shear Diagram.—Integrating the equation for shear between the limits, $x = o$ and $x = x$ we have

$$\int_0^x S \cdot dx = \int_0^x w(\tfrac{1}{2}L - x)dx = \tfrac{1}{2}w(L \cdot x - x^2) \qquad (3)$$

which is the equation for the bending moment at any point, x, in the beam, and is also the area of the shear diagram between the limits given. From this we see that the bending moment at any point in a simple beam uniformly loaded is equal to the area of the shear diagram to the left of the point in question. The bending moment is also equal to the algebraic sum of the shear areas on either side of the point.

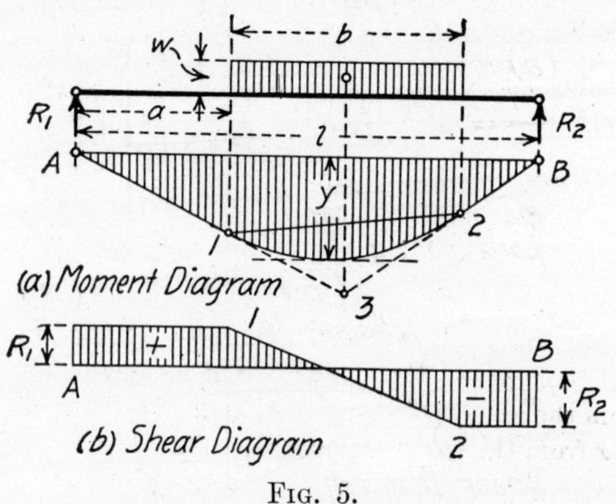

FIG. 5.

Beam with Partial Uniform Load.—The beam in Fig. 5 is loaded with a load w extending over a length b. The bending moments between the left end of the uniform load and the left reaction is $R_1 \cdot x$, represented by the ordinates to the straight line A–1 in (a); the bending moments in that part of the beam covered by the uniform load is represented by ordinates to the curved line 1–2; while the bend'ng moments to the right of the uniform load are represented by ordinates to the straight line 2–B. The ordinates from the straight line 1–2 to the curve 1–2 are the same as for a simple beam with a span b loaded with a uniform load w. The shear diagram is shown in (b). It will be seen that the maximum bending moment comes at the point of zero shear.

Problems.—For problems illustrating the principles discussed in this chapter, see Chapter XIII.

CHAPTER V.

MOVING LOADS ON BEAMS.

Uniform Moving Loads.—Let the beam in Fig. 1 be loaded with a uniform load of p lb. per lineal foot, which can be moved on or off the beam.

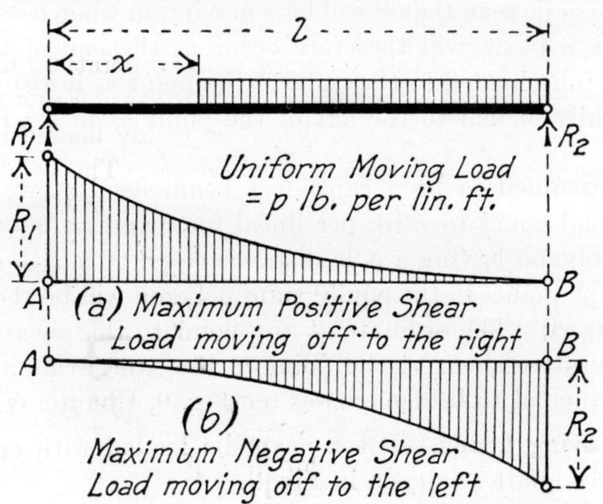

FIG. 1.

To find the position of the moving load that will produce a maximum moment at a point a distance a from the left support, proceed as follows: Let the end of the uniform load be at a distance x from the left reaction. Then taking moments about R_2 we have

$$R_1 = \frac{(l - x)^2}{2l} p \tag{1}$$

and the moment at the point whose abscissa is a will be

$$M = R_1 \cdot a - \frac{(a - x)^2}{2} p = \frac{(l - x)^2}{2l} a \cdot p - \frac{(a - x)^2}{2} p \tag{2}$$

Differentiating (2) and placing derivative of M with respect to x equal to zero, we have after solving

$$x = 0 \tag{3}$$

Therefore the maximum moment at any point in a beam will occur when the beam is fully loaded.

The bending moment diagram for a beam loaded with a uniform moving load is constructed as in Fig. 4, Chapter IV.

To find the position of the moving load for maximum shear at any point in a beam loaded with a moving uniform load, proceed as follows: The left reaction when the end of the moving load is at a distance x from the left reaction, will be

$$R_1 = \frac{(l - x)^2}{2l} p \tag{1}$$

and the shear at a point at a distance a from the left reaction will be

$$S = R_1 - (a - x)p = \frac{(l - x)^2}{2l} p - (a - x)p \tag{4}$$

which is the equation of a parabola.

By inspection it can be seen that S will be a maximum when $a = x$. The maximum shear at any point in a beam will therefore occur at the end of the uniform moving load, the beam being fully loaded to the right of the point as in (*a*) Fig. 1 for maximum positive shear, and fully loaded to the left of the point as in (*b*) Fig. 1 for maximum negative shear.

If the beam is assumed to be a cantilever beam fixed at A, and loaded with a stationary uniform load equal to p lb. per lineal foot, and an equilibrium polygon be drawn with a force polygon having a pole distance equal to length of span, l, the parabola drawn through the points in the equilibrium polygon will be the maximum positive shear diagram, (*a*) Fig. 1. The ordinate at any point to this shear diagram will represent the maximum positive shear at the point to the same scale as the loads (for the application of this principal to bridge trusses see Fig. 9, Chapter VI).

Concentrated Moving Loads.—Let a beam be loaded with concentrated moving loads at fixed distances apart as shown in Fig. 2.

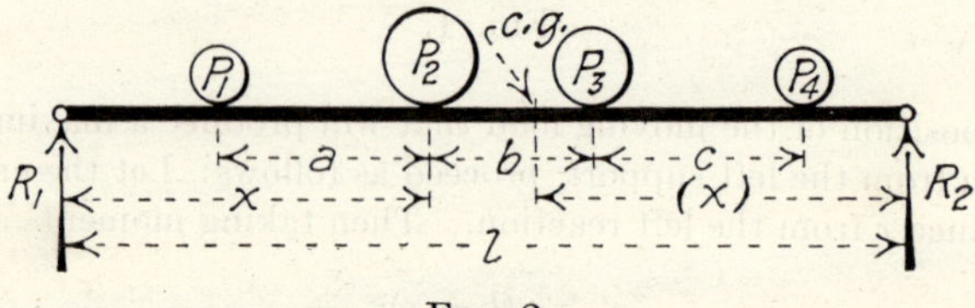

FIG. 2.

First Proof.—To find the position of the loads for maximum moment and the amount of the maximum moment, proceed as follows: The load P_2 will be considered first. Let x be the distance of the load P_2 from the left support when the loads produce a maximum moment under load P_2.

Taking moments about R_2 we have

$$\begin{aligned} R_1 \cdot l &= P_1(l - x + a) + P_2(l - x) + P_3(l - x - b) + P_4(l - x - b - c) \\ &= (l - x)(P_1 + P_2 + P_3 + P_4) + P_1 \cdot a - P_3 \cdot b - P_4(b + c) \end{aligned} \tag{5}$$

and the bending moment under load P_2 will be

$$\begin{aligned} M &= R_1 \cdot x - P_1 \cdot a \\ &= \frac{x(l - x)(P_1 + P_2 + P_3 + P_4) + x(P_1 \cdot a - P_3 \cdot b - P_4(b + c))}{l} - P_1 \cdot a \end{aligned} \tag{6}$$

Differentiating (6) we have

$$\frac{dM}{dx} = \frac{(l - 2x)(P_1 + P_2 + P_3 + P_4) + P_1 \cdot a - P_3 \cdot b - P_4(b + c)}{l} = 0 \qquad (7)$$

and solving (7) for x we have

$$x = \frac{l}{2} + \frac{P_1 \cdot a - P_3 \cdot b - P_4(b + c)}{2(P_1 + P_2 + P_3 + P_4)} \qquad (8)$$

Now $P_1 \cdot a - P_3 \cdot b - P_4(b + c)$, is the static moment of the loads about P_2 and $\frac{P_1 \cdot a - P_3 \cdot b - P_4(b + c)}{P_1 + P_2 + P_3 + P_4}$ = distance from P_2 to center of the gravity of all the loads.

Therefore, for a maximum moment under load P_2, it must be as far from one end as the center of gravity of all the loads is from the other end of the beam, Fig. 2

The above criterion holds for all the loads on the beam. The only way to find which load produces the greatest maximum is to try each one, however, it is usually possible to determine by inspection which load will produce a maximum bending moment. For example the maximum moment in the beam in Fig. 2 will certainly come under the heavy load P_2. The above proof may be generalized without difficulty and the criterion above shown to be of general application.

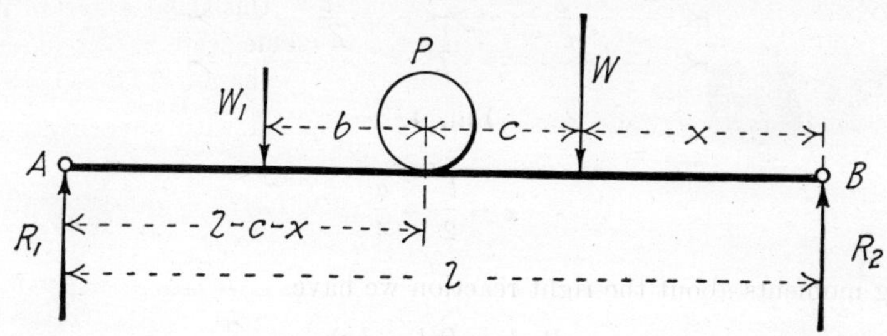

FIG. 3.

Second Proof.—Let several moving loads at fixed distances apart pass over the girder with span l in Fig. 3. It is required to calculate the point in the beam where some intermediate load P will produce a maximum moment. Let the sum of the loads to the left of the load P be equal to W_1 acting through the center of gravity of the loads, and let the sum of all the loads on the span be equal to W acting through the center of gravity of all the loads. It is assumed that all loads remain on the span during this discussion. In general the point of maximum moment will come under a heavy load.

Let load P be at a distance b to the right of W_1, and at a distance c to the left of W; and let W be at a distance x from the right end of the span. Then the left reaction will be found by taking moments about the right reaction, and

$$R_1 \cdot l = W \cdot x \qquad (9)$$

and the bending moment under the load P will be equal to the moment of the left reaction about the load P minus the moment of the load W_1 about load P, and

$$M = R_1 \cdot (l - c - x) - W_1 \cdot b \qquad (10)$$

$$M = \frac{W \cdot x}{l}(l - c - x) - W_1 \cdot b \tag{11}$$

Differentiating M with respect to x, and solving for a maximum

$$\frac{dM}{dx} = \frac{W}{l}(l - c - 2x) = 0$$

and

$$x + \tfrac{1}{2}c = \tfrac{1}{2}l \tag{12}$$

which shows that maximum moment under any load will occur when the load is as far from one end of the span as the center of gravity of all the loads on the span is from the other end of the span.

For two equal loads $P = P$ at a fixed distance, a, apart as in the case of a traveling crane, Fig. 4, the maximum moment will occur under one of the loads when

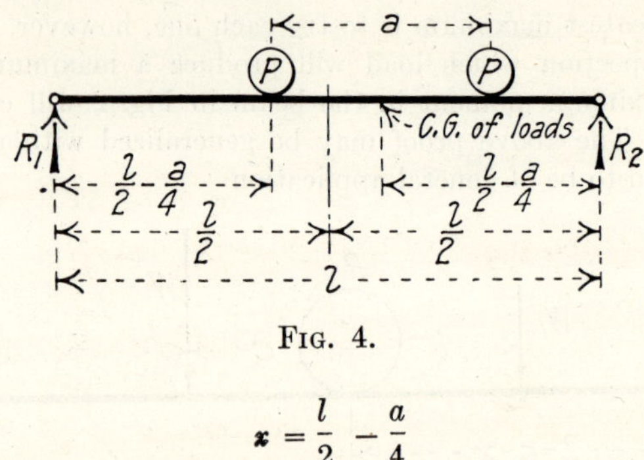

FIG. 4.

$$x = \frac{l}{2} - \frac{a}{4}$$

Taking moments about the right reaction we have

$$R_1 \cdot l = P(l - \tfrac{1}{2}a) \tag{13}$$

and the maximum bending moment is

$$M = R_1(\tfrac{1}{2}l - \tfrac{1}{4}a)$$

$$= \frac{P(l - \frac{1}{2}a)^2}{2l} \tag{14}$$

There will be a maximum moment when either of the loads satisfies the above criterion, the bending moments being equal.

By equating the maximum moment above to the moment due to a single load at the center of the beam, it will be found that the above criterion holds only when

$$a < 0.586\, l \tag{15}$$

Where two unequal moving loads are at a fixed distance apart the greater maximum bending moment will always come under the heavier load.

The maximum end shear at the left support for a system of concentrated loads on a simple beam, as in Fig. 2, will occur when the left reaction, R_1, is a maximum. This will occur when one of the wheels is infinitely near the left abutment (usually said to be over the left abutment). The load which produces maximum end shear can be easily found by trial.

The maximum shear at any point in the beam will occur when one of the loads is over the point. The criterion for determining which load will cause a maximum shear at any point, x, in a beam will now be determined.

In Fig. 2, let the total load on the beam, $P_1 + P_2 + P_3 + P_4 = W$, and let x be the distance from the left support to the point at which we wish to determine the maximum shear.

When load P_1 is at the point, the shear will be equal to the left reaction, which is found by substituting $x + a$ for x in (5) to be

$$S_1 = R_1 = \frac{(l - x - a)W + P_1 \cdot a - P_3 \cdot b - P_4(b + c)}{l} \tag{16}$$

and when P_2 is at the point the shear will be

$$S_2 = \frac{(l - x)W + P_1 \cdot a - P_3 \cdot b - P_4(b + c)}{l} - P_1 \tag{17}$$

Subtracting S_2 from S_1 we have

$$S_1 - S_2 = \frac{P_1 \cdot l - W \cdot a}{l} \tag{18}$$

Now S_1 will be greater than S_2 if $P_1 \cdot l$ is greater than $W \cdot a$, or if

$$P_1 \cdot l > W \cdot a \tag{19}$$

The criterion for maximum shear at any point therefore is as follows:

The maximum positive shear in any section of a beam occurs when the foremost load is at the section, provided $W \cdot a$ is not greater than $P_1 \cdot l$. If $W \cdot a$ is greater than $P_1 \cdot l$, the greatest shear will occur when some succeeding load is at the point.

Having determined the position of the moving loads for maximum moment and maximum shear, the amount of the moment and shear can be obtained as in the case of beams loaded with stationary loads.

Problems.—A simple girder with a span l carries moving concentrated loads coming on the girder from the right end. Show that the point of maximum moment and the amount of the moment are as follows:—

1. Two unequal loads P_1 and P_2, at a fixed distance apart $= a$. Load $P_1 > P_2$. Load P_1 will be at a distance from the left end of the girder

$$x = \tfrac{1}{2}\,[l - P_2 \cdot a/(P_1 + P_2)] \tag{20}$$

and

$$M = (P_1 + P_2)\, x^2/l \tag{21}$$

2. Three equal loads P, at fixed distances apart $= a$. Middle load will be at center of span, and

$$M = P\,(3\,l/4 - a) \tag{22}$$

If a is greater than 0.450 l, two loads will give a maximum moment as in Fig. 4.

3. Four equal loads P, at fixed distances apart $= a$. The second load from the left will be at a point

$$x = \tfrac{1}{2}\,(l - \tfrac{1}{2}a) \tag{23}$$

and

$$M = P\,(l - 2a + a^2/4l) \tag{24}$$

If a is greater than 0.268 l, three loads give a maximum moment as above.

CHAPTER VI.

Stresses in Highway Bridge Trusses.

LOADS.—The loads on highway bridges are commonly specified as a certain number of pounds per square foot of floor surface, or per lineal foot of truss or bridge. The live load is assumed as applied at the panel points of the loaded chord, while the dead load may be assumed as all applied on the loaded chord, or assumed as partly applied on the loaded chord and partly on the unloaded chord (usually two-thirds on the loaded chord and one-third on the unloaded chord). In this discussion the dead load will be assumed as applied at the panel points in the loaded chord. Equal panel lengths and joint loads will also be assumed.

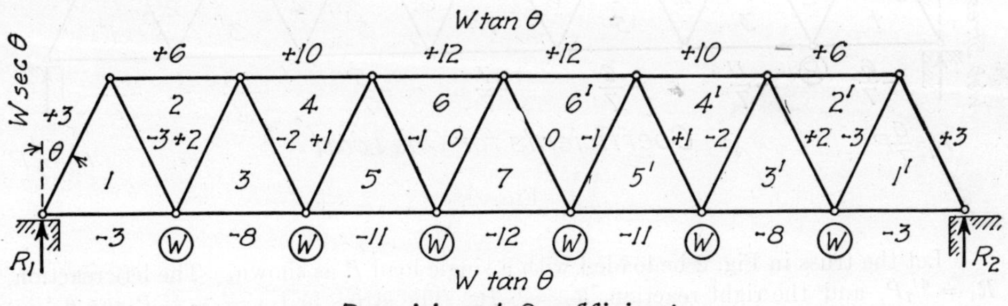

Fig. 1.

Algebraic Resolution.*—Let the Warren truss in Fig. 1 have dead loads applied at the joints as shown. From the fundamental equations for equilibrium for translation, reaction $R_1 = R_2 = 3W$.

The stresses in the members are calculated as follows: Resolving at the left reaction, stress in $1\text{–}x = +\ 3W \cdot \sec\theta$, and stress in $1\text{–}y = -\ 3W \cdot \tan\theta$. Resolving at first joint in upper chord, stress in $1\text{–}2 = -\ 3W \cdot \sec\theta$, and stress in $2\text{–}x = +\ 6W \cdot \tan\theta$. Resolving at second joint in lower chord, stress $2\text{–}3 = +\ 2W \cdot \sec\theta$, and stress $3\text{–}y = -\ 8W \cdot \tan\theta$. And in like manner the stresses in the remaining members are found as shown. The coefficients shown in Fig. 1 for the chords are to be multiplied by $W \cdot \tan\theta$; while those for the webs are to be multiplied by $W \cdot \sec\theta$.

It will be seen that the coefficients for the web stresses are equal to the shear in the respective panels. Having found the shears in the different panels of the truss, the remaining coefficients may be found by resolution. Pass a section through any panel and the algebraic sum of the coefficients will be equal to zero. Therefore, if two coefficients are known, the third may be found by addition.

* Also called "Method of Sections."

Beginning with member 1–y, which is known and equals -3;

$$\text{coefficient of } 2\text{–}x = -(-\ 3-3) = +\ 6;$$
$$\text{coefficient of } 3\text{–}y = -(+\ 6+2) = -\ 8;$$
$$\text{coefficient of } 4\text{–}x = -(-\ 8-2) = +10;$$
$$\text{coefficient of } 5\text{–}y = -(+10+1) = -11;$$
$$\text{coefficient of } 6\text{–}x = -(-11-1) = +12;$$
$$\text{coefficient of } 7\text{–}y = -(+12+0) = -12.$$

Loading for Maximum Stresses.—The effect of different positions of the loads on a Warren truss will now be investigated.

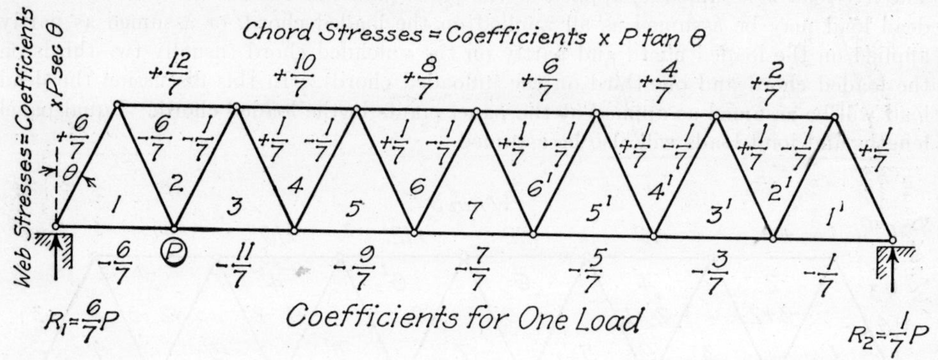

FIG. 2.

Let the truss in Fig. 2 be loaded with a single load P as shown. The left reaction, $R_1 = {}^6/_7P$, and the right reaction, $R_2 = {}^1/_7P$. The stress in 1–y = $-{}^6/_7P\cdot\tan\theta$, and stress in 1–x = $+{}^6/_7P\cdot\sec\theta$. The stress in 1–2 = $-{}^6/_7P\cdot\sec\theta$ and stress in 2–3 = $-{}^1/_7P\cdot\sec\theta$, etc. The remaining coefficients are found as in the case of dead loads by adding coefficients algebraically and changing the sign of the result.

In Fig. 3 the coefficients for a load applied at each joint in turn are shown for the different members; the coefficients for the load on left being given in the top line.

The following conclusions may be drawn from Fig. 3.

(1) All loads produce a compressive stress in the top chord and a tensile stress in the bottom chord.

(2) All the loads on one side of a panel produce the same kind of stress in the web members that are inclined in the same direction on that side.

For maximum stresses in the chords, therefore, the truss should be fully loaded. For maximum stresses in the web members, the longer segment into which the panel divides the truss should be fully loaded; while for minimum stresses in the web members, the shorter segment of the truss should be fully loaded.

The conditions for maximum loading of a truss with equal joint loads are therefore seen to be essentially the same as the maximum loading of a beam with a uniform live load.

Stresses in Warren Truss.—The coefficients for maximum and minimum stresses in a Warren truss due to live load are shown in Fig. 4.

These coefficients are seen to be the algebraic sum of the coefficients for the individual loads given in Fig. 3. The live load chord coefficients are the same as for dead load, and if found directly are found in the same manner.

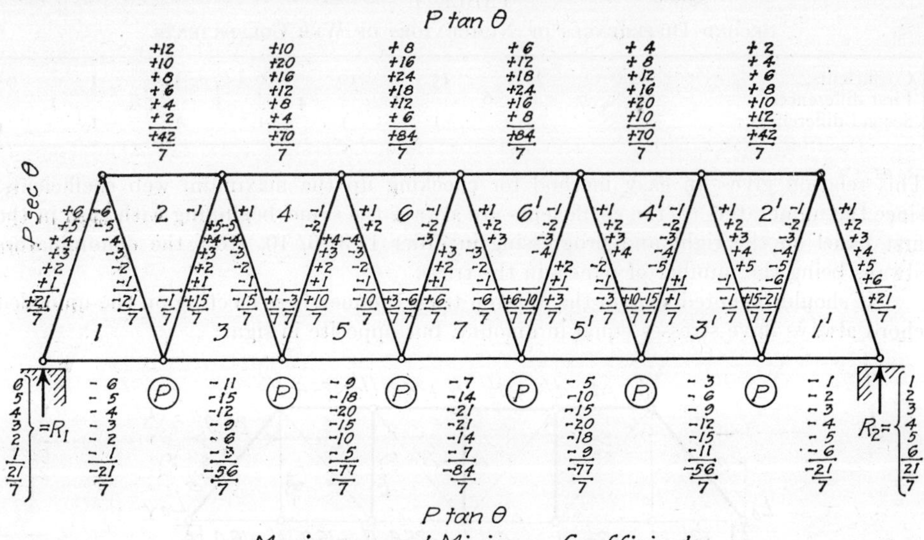

FIG. 3.

The maximum web coefficients may be found directly by taking off one load at a time beginning at the left. The left reaction, which may be found by algebraic moments, will in each case be the coefficient of the maximum stress in the panel to the left

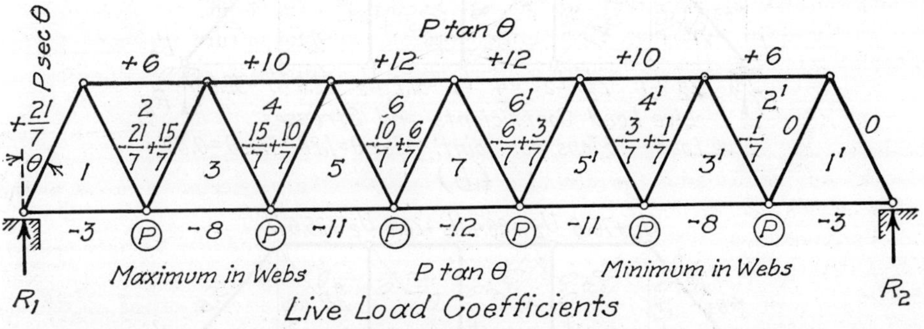

FIG. 4.

of the first load. A rule for finding the coefficient of left reaction for any loading is as follows: Multiply the number of loads on the truss by the number of loads plus unity, and divide the product by twice the number of panels in the truss and the result will be the coefficient of the left reaction.

If the second differences of the maximum coefficients in the web members are calculated, they will be found to be constant, which shows that the coefficients are equal to the ordinates of a parabola.

TABLE I.

SECOND DIFFERENCES OF NUMERATORS OF WEB COEFFICIENTS.

Coefficients,	28		21		15		10		6		3		1		0
First differences,		7		6		5		4		3		2		1	
Second differences,			1		1		1		1		1		1		

This relation gives an easy method for checking up the maximum web coefficients, since the numerators of the coefficients are always the same beginning with zero in the first panel on the right and progressing in order 1, 3, 6, 10, etc.; the denominators always being the number of panels in the truss.

It should be noted that in the Warren truss the members meeting on the unloaded chord always have stresses equal in amount, but opposite in sign.

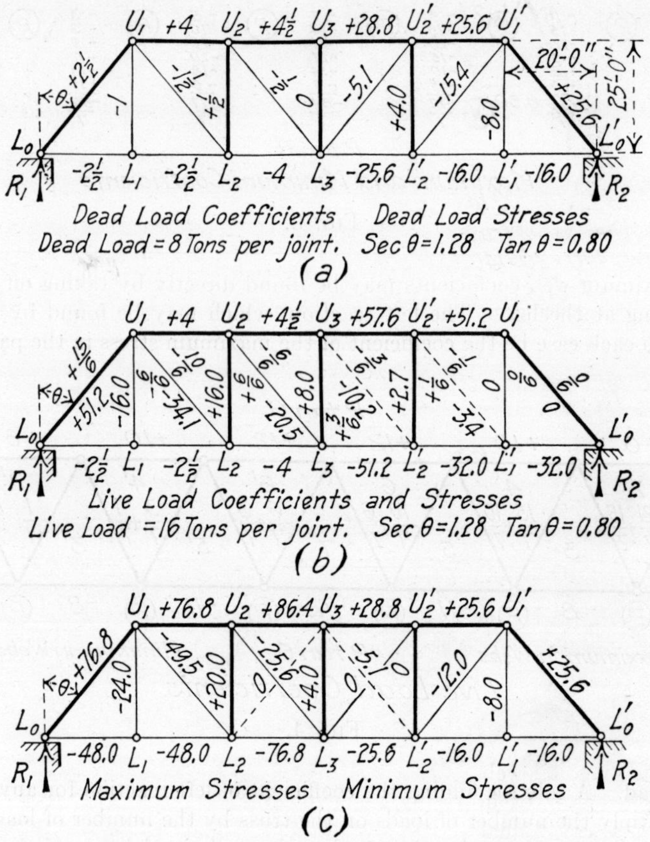

Dead Load Coefficients Dead Load Stresses
Dead Load = 8 Tons per joint. Sec θ = 1.28 Tan θ = 0.80
(a)
Live Load Coefficients and Stresses
Live Load = 16 Tons per joint. Sec θ = 1.28 Tan θ = 0.80
(b)
Maximum Stresses Minimum Stresses
(c)

FIG. 5.

Stresses in Pratt Truss.—In the Pratt truss the diagonal members are tension members and counters (see dotted members in (*c*) Fig. 5) must be supplied where there is a reversal of stress. The coefficients for the dead and live load stresses in the Pratt truss shown in (*a*) and (*b*) Fig. 5, are found in the same manner as for a Warren truss. The member U_1L_1 acts as a hanger and carries only the load at its lower end. The stresses in the chords are found by multiplying the coefficients by $W \cdot \tan \theta$, and in the inclined webs by multiplying the coefficients by $W \cdot \sec \theta$. The stresses in the posts are equal to the vertical components of the stresses in the inclined web members meeting them on the unloaded chord.

The maximum chord stresses shown on the left of (*c*) are equal to the sum of the live and dead load chord stresses. The minimum chord stresses shown on the right of (*c*) are equal to the dead load chord stresses.

The maximum and minimum web stresses are found by adding algebraically the stresses in the members due to dead and live loads.

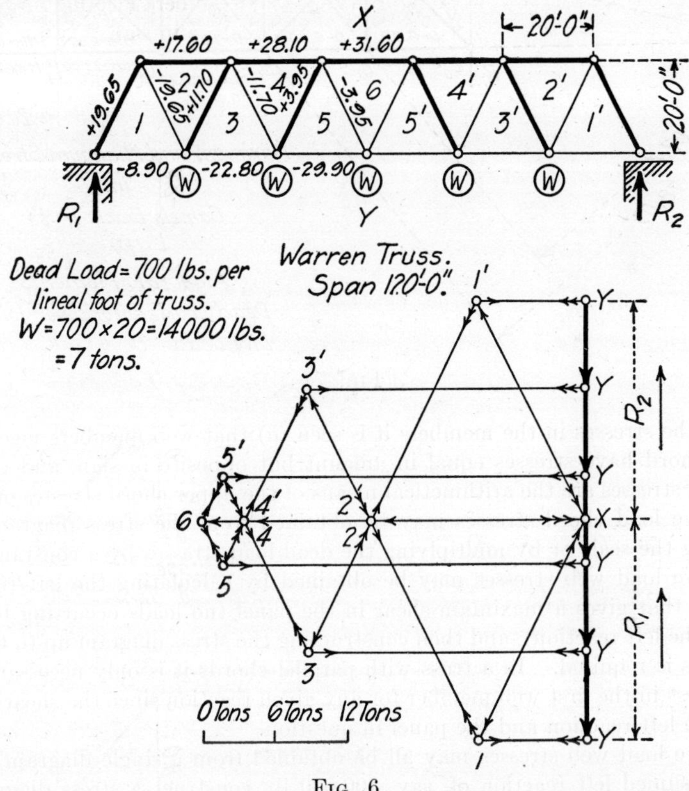

FIG. 6.

Since the diagonal web members in a Pratt truss can take tension only, counters must be supplied as U_3L_2' in panel $L_2'L_3$. The tensile stress in a counter in a panel of a Pratt truss is always equal to the compressive stress that would occur in the main diagonal web member in the panel if it were possible for it to take compression. Care must always be used to calculate the corresponding stresses in the vertical posts.

Graphic Resolution.—The stresses in a Warren truss due to dead loads are calculated by graphic resolution in Fig. 6. The solution is the same as for ceiling loads in a roof truss. The loads beginning with the first load on the left are laid off from the bottom upwards; or if the loads beginning with the first load are laid off from the top downwards, the stress diagram will be on the right hand side of the load line. The analysis of the solution is shown on the stress diagram and truss and needs no explanation.

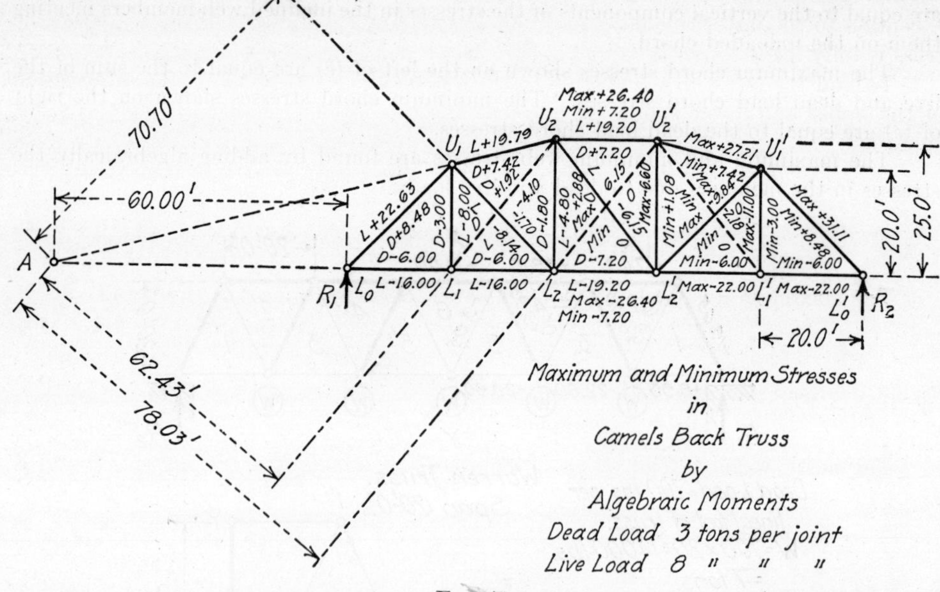

FIG. 7.

From the stresses in the members it is seen (*a*) that web members meeting on the unloaded chord have stresses equal in amount but opposite in sign, and (*b*) that the lower chord stresses are the arithmetical means of the upper chord stresses on each side.

The live load chord stresses may be obtained from the stress diagram in Fig. 6 by changing the scale or by multiplying the dead load stresses by a constant.

The live load web stresses may be obtained by calculating the left reactions for the loading that gives a maximum shear in the panel (no loads occurring between the panel and the left reaction), and then constructing the stress diagram up to the member whose stress is required. In a truss with parallel chords it is only necessary to calculate the stress in the first web member for any given reaction since the shear is constant between the left reaction and the panel in question.

The live load web stresses may all be obtained from a single diagram as follows: With an assumed left reaction of, say, 100,000 lb. construct a stress diagram on the assumption that the truss is a cantilever fixed at the right abutment and that there are no loads on the truss. Then the maximum stress in any web member will be equal to the stress scaled from the diagram, divided by 100,000, multiplied by the left reaction that produces the maximum stress. This method is a very convenient one for finding the stresses in a truss with inclined chords. See Problem 36, Chapter XIII.

Algebraic Moments.—The dead and live load stresses in a truss with inclined chords are calculated by algebraic moments in Fig. 7. The conditions for maximum loading are the same in this truss as in a truss with parallel chords, and are as follows: Maximum chord stresses occur when all loads are on; minimum chord stresses occur when no live load is on; maximum web stresses in main members occur when the longer segment of the truss is loaded; and minimum stresses in main members and maximum stresses in counters occur when the shorter segment of the truss is loaded. An apparent exception to the latter rule occurs in post U_2L_2 which has a maximum stress when the truss is fully loaded with dead and live loads.

To find the stress in member U_1L_2 take moments about point A, the intersection of the upper and lower chords produced. The dead load stress is then given by the equation

$$U_1L_2 \times 70.7 + R_1 \times 60 - W \times 80 = 0$$

$$U_1L_2 \times 70.7 = -6 \times 60 + 3 \times 80 = -120 \text{ foot-tons}$$

$$U_1L_2 = -1.70 \text{ tons}$$

The maximum live load stress occurs when all loads are on except L_1, and

$$U_1L_2 \times 70.7 + R_1 \times 60 = 0$$

$$U_1L_2 \times 70.7 = -\tfrac{6}{5}P \times 60 = -576 \text{ foot-tons}$$

$$U_1L_2 = -8.14 \text{ tons}$$

The maximum live load stress in counter U_2L_1 occurs with a load at L_1, and is given by the equation

$$-U_2L_1 \times 62.43 + R_1 \times 60 - P \times 80 = 0$$

$$U_2L_1 \times 62.43 = \tfrac{4}{5}P \times 60 - 8 \times 80 = -256 \text{ foot-tons}$$

$$U_2L_1 = -4.10 \text{ tons}$$

The dead load stress in counter U_2L_1 when main member U_1L_2 is not acting will be

$$U_2L_1 \times 62.43 = +120 \text{ foot-tons}$$

$$U_2L_1 = +1.92 \text{ tons}$$

The maximum stress in U_1L_2 is therefore $-1.70 - 8.14 = -9.84$ tons, and the minimum stress is zero. The maximum stress in counter U_2L_1 is $+1.92 - 4.10 = -2.18$ tons, and the minimum stress is zero.

The stresses in the remaining members may be found in the same manner. To obtain stresses in upper chords U_1U_2 and U_2U_2, take moments about L_2 as a center; to obtain stress in lower chord L_0L_1 take moments about U_1 as a center. The dead load and maximum live load stress in post U_2L_2 is equal to the vertical component of the dead and live loads, respectively, in upper chord U_1U_2. The stresses in L_0U_1, L_0L_2, L_2L_2', U_2U_2' and U_2L_2' are most easily found by algebraic resolution.

Graphic Moments.—The dead load stresses in the chords of a Warren truss are calculated by graphic moments in Fig. 8.

Bending Moment Polygon.—The upper chord stresses are given by the ordinates to the bending moment parabola direct, while the lower chord stresses are arithmetical means of the upper chord stresses on each side, and are given by the ordinates to the chords of the parabola as shown in Fig. 8.

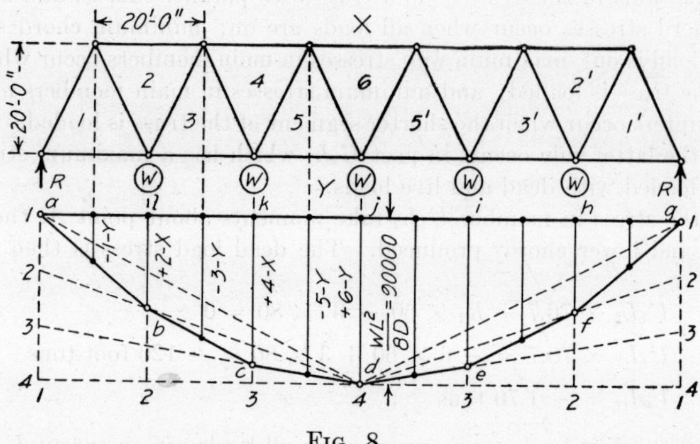

FIG. 8.

The parabola is constructed as follows: The mid-ordinate, 4–j, is made equal to the bending moment at the center of the truss divided by the depth; in this case the mid-ordinate is the stress in 6–x; if the number of panels in the truss were odd the mid-ordinate would not be equal to any chord stress. The parabola is then constructed as shown in Fig. 8. The live load chord stresses may be found from Fig. 8 by changing the scale or by multiplying the dead load chord stresses by a constant.

Shear Polygon.—In Chapter V it was shown that the maximum shear in a beam at any point could be represented by the ordinate to a parabola at any point. The same principle holds for a bridge truss loaded with equal joint loads, as will now be proved.

In Fig. 9 assume that the simple Warren truss is fixed at the left end as shown, and that right reaction R_2 is not acting. Then with all joints fully loaded with a live load P, construct a force polygon as shown, with pole o and pole distance H = span L, and beginning at point a in the load line of the force polygon construct the equilibrium polygon a–g–h for the cantilever truss.

Now the bending moment at the left support will be equal to ordinate Y_1 multiplied by the pole distance H. But the truss is a simple truss and the moment of the right reaction will be equal to the moment at the left abutment and.

$$Y_1 \cdot H = R_1 \cdot L$$

and since $H = L$

$$Y_1 \cdot L = R_1 \cdot L$$

and

$$Y_1 = R_1$$

Now, with the loads remaining stationary, move the truss one panel to the right as shown by the dotted truss. With the same force polygon draw a new equilibrium polygon as above. This equilibrium polygon will be identical with a part of the first equilibrium polygon as shown. As above, the bending moment at left reaction is

$Y_3 \cdot H = Y_3 \cdot L = R_3 \cdot L$, and $Y_3 = R_3$. In like manner Y_5 can be shown to be the right reaction with three loads on, etc. Since the bridge is symmetrical with reference to the center line, the ordinates to the shear polygon in Fig. 9, are equal to the maximum shears in the panel to the right of the ordinate as the load moves off the bridge to the right.

The shear parabola may be drawn without the use of the force and equilibrium polygons as shown in Problem 35, Chapter XIII: At a distance of a panel length to the left of the left abutment lay off to scale a load line equal to one-half the total load

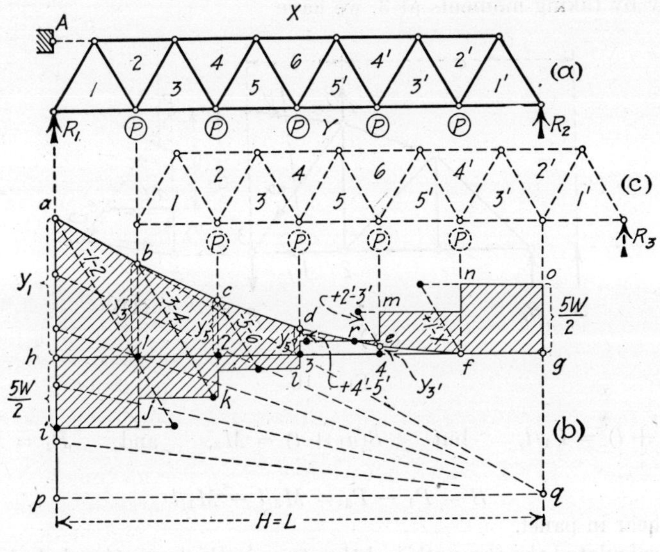

FIG. 9.

on the truss, divide this load line into as many parts as there are panels in the truss, and beginning at the top, which call 1, number the points of division of the load line 1, 2, 3, etc. Drop vertical lines from the panel points and number them 1, 2, 3, etc. Now connect the numbered points in the load line with the point 7, which is under the first panel to the left of the right abutment; and the intersection of like numbered lines will give points on the shear parabola. It should be noted that the line 8–8 is a secant to the parabola and not a tangent as might be expected.

The dead load shear is laid off positive downward in Fig. 9 to the same scale as the live load shears, and the maximum and minimum shears due to dead and live loads are added graphically. The stresses in the web members are calculated graphically in Fig. 9. For the solution of the stresses in a Warren truss by graphic moments, see Problem 35, Chapter XIII.

Resolution of the Shear.—In Fig. 10 the stresses U, D and L hold in equilibrium the external forces on the left of the section cutting these members. These external forces consist of a left reaction, R, at the left abutment and a force at 2, equal to the reaction of the stringer 2–3. The resultant, S, of these two forces acts at a point a little to the left of the left reaction. Its position may be determined by moments. Referring to Fig. 10, let the resultant, S, be replaced by the two forces P_1 and P_3, P_1 acting upwards at 1 and P_3 acting downward at 3 as shown. Now taking moments about point 1, and

$$S \cdot a = P_3 \cdot l \tag{1}$$

Now the bending moment at 1 equals M_1, and

$$P_3 = S \cdot a/l = M_1/l \tag{2}$$

Similarly by taking moments at 3, we have

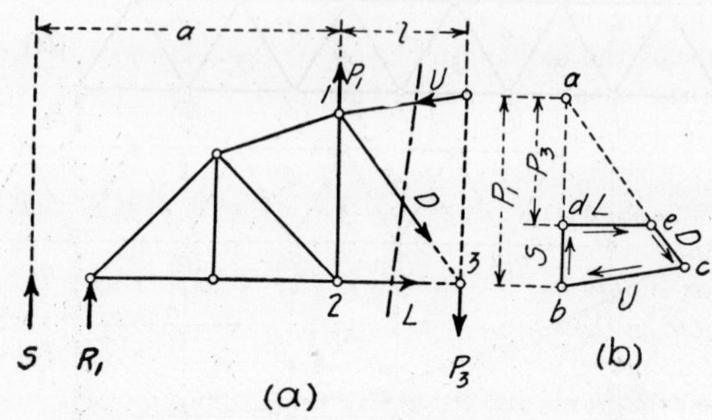

FIG. 10.

$$S(a + l) = P_1 \cdot l, \quad \text{but} \quad S(a_1 + l) = M_3, \quad \text{and} \quad P_1 = M_3/l$$

Now

$$S = P_1 - P_3 = M_3/l - M_1/l \tag{3}$$

where S = shear in panel.

Having calculated the shear, S, and the stress in the lower chord, L, for the loading that will give a maximum stress, the stress in D may be calculated by completing the force polygon as in (*b*), Fig. 10.

Method of Shear Increments.—The loads on a beam or truss first produce shears, which in turn produce bending stresses in the chords. In (a) Fig. 5 it will be seen that member U_2L_3 carries the shear in the panel of $\frac{1}{2}W$, which produces a stress of $-\frac{1}{2}W \cdot \sec\theta$ in the member. The difference in the stresses in U_1U_2 and U_2U_3 is seen to be the horizontal component of the stress in U_2L_3, or the shear increment in the panel. The shear increment may be calculated as follows: The shear in the panel L_2L_3 is $\frac{1}{2}W$ and may be assumed to act a differential to the right of joint L_2. Now take moments about L_3, and pass a section cutting U_2U_3, U_2L_3 and L_2L_3 just to the right of L_2, and cutting away the truss to the left. Now the shear, S, represents the resultant of the vertical forces to the left of the panel. Then for equilibrium the stress in U_2U_3 will be equal to the stress in U_1U_2 found by taking moments about joint L_2, plus the shear increment $I = (S \times l)/d$, $= \frac{1}{2}W \cdot \tan\theta$, where l = panel length and d = depth of truss.

Problems.—For problems illustrating the principles discussed in this chapter, see Chapter XIII.

CHAPTER VII.

INFLUENCE DIAGRAMS.

Definition.—An influence diagram shows the variation at a given point of the effect of a single moving load occupying different positions on the structure. The effect may be the shear, the bending moment, or the deflection at a point of the structure; or it may be the shear in a panel, the reaction at a support, or the stress in a member. A shear or a moment influence diagram represents the shear or moment at a certain point or in a certain member for any position of a moving load; while a shear or a moment diagram gives the shear or the moment at all points of the structure for a single position of the loads. Influence diagrams constructed for unit loads are called unit influence diagrams. A unit influence diagram will be referred to in the discussion which follows. An influence diagram is also a diagram which gives the rate of change of shear, moment, stress, etc., at a point or in a member for a change in an external load. Shear diagrams and bending moment diagrams are summation diagrams, while influence diagrams are derivative diagrams.

Influence Diagrams for a Simple Beam.—Influence diagrams for reaction, shear, bending moment and deflection will be constructed for a simple beam.

Reaction Influence Diagram.—In the simple beam in (*a*), Fig. 1, the influence diagram for the right reaction, (*b*), Fig. 1, will have a unit height under the right reac-

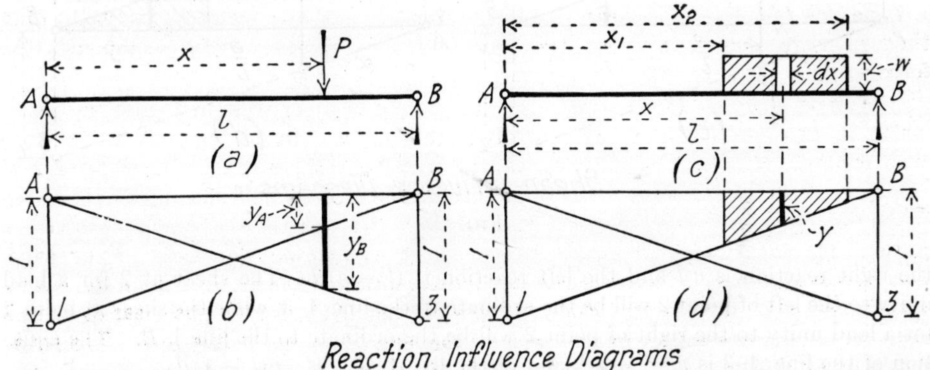

FIG. 1.

tion and will be the straight line A–3, with ordinates varying from unity at B to zero at A. For a unit load at a distance x from the left support the right reaction will be y_B, and for a load P the right reaction will be $P \cdot y_B$. The influence diagram for the left reaction will have a unit height under the left reaction and will be the straight line 1–B, with ordinates varying from unity at A to zero at B.

The equation of the line A–3 is $R_2 = P \cdot y_B = P \cdot x/l$ and the equation of the line 1–B is $R_1 = P \cdot y_A = P(l - x)/l$. It will be seen that $y_A + y_B = 1$ (unity) for every point of the span.

The reaction for several loads is the sum of the reactions for the separate loads.

For a uniform load, (*c*), Fig. 1, the influence diagram, (*d*), Fig. 1, is the same as for concentrated loads, (*b*), Fig. 1. The left reaction for a differential length of the load will be $dR_A = w \cdot dx \cdot y = w \cdot y \cdot dx = w$ times the area of the influence diagram covered by the uniform load; and the left reaction for a uniform load, w, extending from x_1 to x_2 will be $R_A = w \int_{x_1}^{x_2} y \cdot dx = w$ times the area of the influence diagram covered by the uniform load.

Shear Influence Diagram.—The shear influence diagram in (*b*), Fig. 2, gives the shear at the point 2 at a distance a from the left support for a load unity at a distance x from the left support. The shear at any point is the left reaction minus the load to the left of the point. The influence diagram for shear at the point 2 consists of the influence diagram for the right reaction on the left of the point 2, and the influence diagram for the left reaction on the right of the point. With a load unity at the point 2,

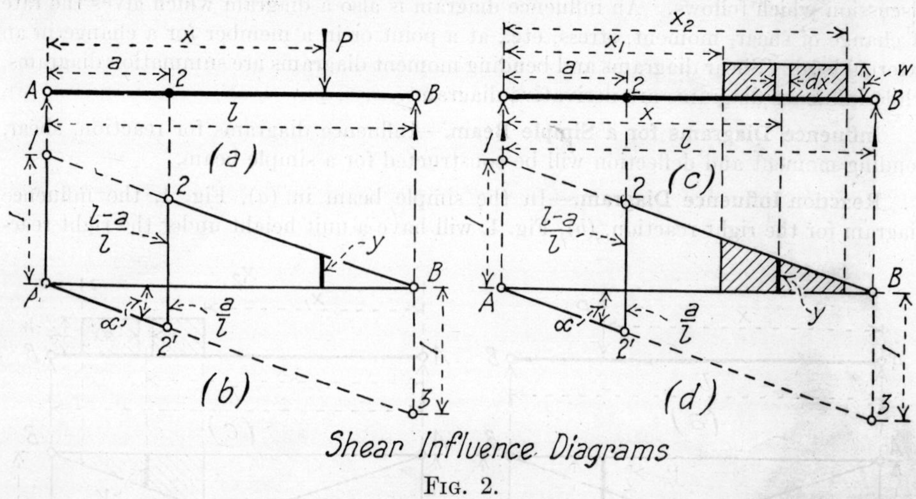

FIG. 2.

the right reaction is a/l and the left reaction is $(l - a)/l$. The shear at 2 for a load unity to the left of point 2 will be the ordinate to the line A–3, while the shear at point 2 for a load unity to the right of point 2 will be the ordinate to the line 1–B. The equation of the line A–3 is $y = -x/l$, and of the line 1–B is $y' = (l - x)/l$.

The shear at 2 for several loads is the sum of the shears for the separate loads. For a uniform load, (*d*), Fig. 2, the influence diagram is the same as for concentrated loads, (*b*), Fig. 2. The shear at point 2 for a differential length of load will be $dV = w \cdot dx \cdot y = w \cdot y \cdot dx = w$ times the area of the influence diagram covered by the uniform load; and the shear for a uniform load, w, extending from x_1 to x_2 will be $V = w \int_{x_1}^{x_2} y \cdot dx = w$ times the area of the influence diagram covered by the uniform load. From, (d), Fig. 2 it will be seen that to obtain maximum shear at any point the uniform load should cover the longer segment of the beam.

Moment Influence Diagram.—The moment influence diagram in (b), Fig. 3, gives the moment at the point 2 at a distance a from the left support, for a load unity at a distance x from the left support. For a load to the left of point 2, the bending moment at point 2 will be the right reaction multiplied by the distance $l - a$. For a load at a distance x from the left support, where x is less than a, the equation of the influence line A–3 will be $y = x(l - a)/l$, with a maximum value under the point 2 of $y = a(l-a)/l$. For a load to the right of the point 2 the bending moment at point 2 will be the left

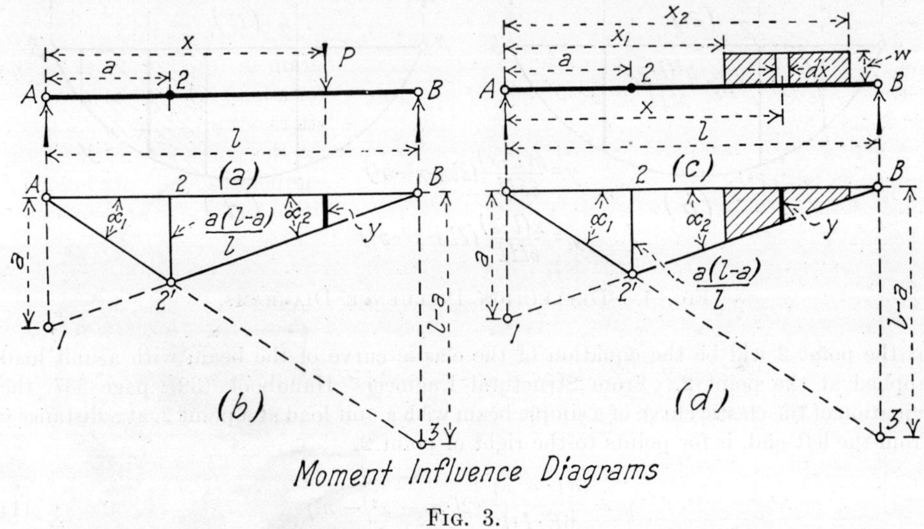

Moment Influence Diagrams

FIG. 3.

reaction multiplied by the distance a. For a load at a distance x from the left support, where x is greater than a, the equation of the influence line $2'$–B will be $y = a(l - x)/l$, with a maximum value under the point 2 of $y = a(l - a)/l$. The influence diagram for any point, 2, may be calculated by placing a unit load at point 2, and calculating the bending moment due to the load unity. The influence diagram may also be constructed by laying off the vertical line A–1 $= a$, and the vertical line B–3 $= l - a$ and the influence diagram is the figure A–$2'$–B. The moment at point 2 for any number of loads will be equal to the sum of the products of each load by the intercept y under the load.

For a uniform load, (d), Fig. 3, the influence diagram is the same as for concentrated loads, (b), Fig. 3. The moment at the point 2 for a differential length of load will be $dM = w \cdot dx \cdot y = w \cdot y \cdot dx = w$ times the area of the influence diagram covered by the uniform load; and the moment for a uniform load extending from x_1 to x_2 will be $M = w \int_{x_1}^{x_2} y \cdot dx = w$ times the area of the influence diagram covered by the uniform load. The moment at point 2 will be a maximum when the uniform load covers the entire span. For the span fully loaded with the uniform load w, the moment at point 2 will be $M = w$ times the area of the influence diagram $A–2'–B = \frac{1}{2}w \cdot a(l - a)$. Where $a = \frac{1}{2}l$, the moment will be $M = \frac{1}{8}w \cdot l^2$.

Deflection Influence Diagram.—The deflection influence diagram in (*b*), Fig. 4, gives the deflection at point 2 at a distance *a* from the left support for a load unity at a distance *x* from the left support. The equation of the influence diagram for deflection

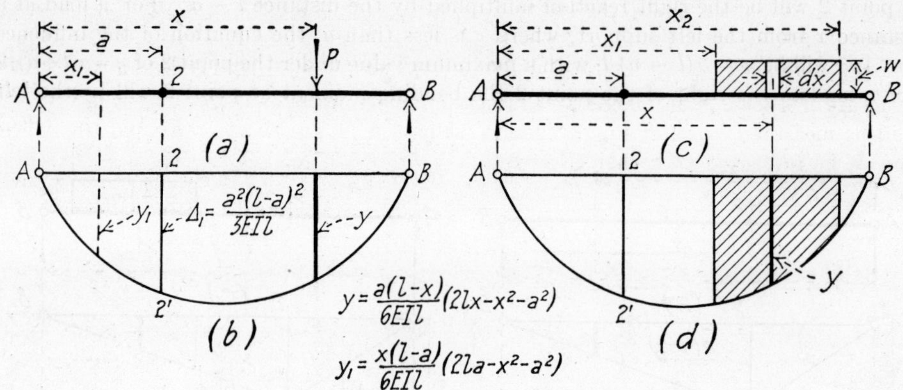

FIG. 4. DEFLECTION INFLUENCE DIAGRAMS.

at the point 2 will be the equation of the elastic curve of the beam with a unit load applied at the point 2. From Structural Engineers' Handbook (39), page 537, the equation of the elastic curve of a simple beam with a unit load at a point 2, at a distance *a* from the left end, is for points to the right of point 2.

$$y = \frac{a(l - x)}{6E \cdot I \cdot l}\,(2l \cdot x - x^2 - a^2) \tag{1}$$

and for point to the left of point 2,

$$y_1 = \frac{x(l - a)}{6E \cdot I \cdot l}\,(2l \cdot a - x^2 - a^2) \tag{2}$$

In both equations (1) and (2) the deflection at point 2 for a unit load at the point 2 will be found by substituting $x = a$, and

$$\Delta_1 = \frac{a(l - a)}{6E \cdot I \cdot l}\,(2l \cdot a - 2a^2)$$

$$= \frac{a^2(l - a)^2}{3E \cdot I \cdot l}$$

If $a = \frac{1}{2}l$, then $\Delta_1 = l^3/48E \cdot I$.

If *x* and *a* are interchanged in equations (1) and (2), *x* being a constant and *a* being a variable, the resulting equations will be a deflection influence diagram for the point 3, at a distance *x* from the left support.

For any two points, 2 and 3, in a beam therefore it follows that the deflection at point 2 for a unit load at point 3, will be equal to the deflection at point 3 for a unit load at point 2. This is known as Maxwell's Theorem, which will presently be proved to hold for all structures in equilibrium.

For a uniform load the deflection at point 2 in (*c*), Fig. 4, for a load $w \cdot dx$ will be $\Delta y = w \cdot dx \cdot y = w \cdot y \cdot dx$; and the deflection at point 2 for a uniform load extending from x_1 to x_2 will be $\Delta = \int_{x_1}^{x_2} w \cdot y \cdot dx = w$ times the area of the deflection influence diagram covered by the load.

Maxwell's Theorem.—The general statement of Maxwell's Theorem is "In a structure if a load P be placed at 1, and the deflection Δ_2 of the structure due to the load be measured at 2, (*a*) Fig. 5, then if the load P be placed at 2, (*b*), and the deflection Δ_1 be measured at 1, then $\Delta_1 = \Delta_2$."

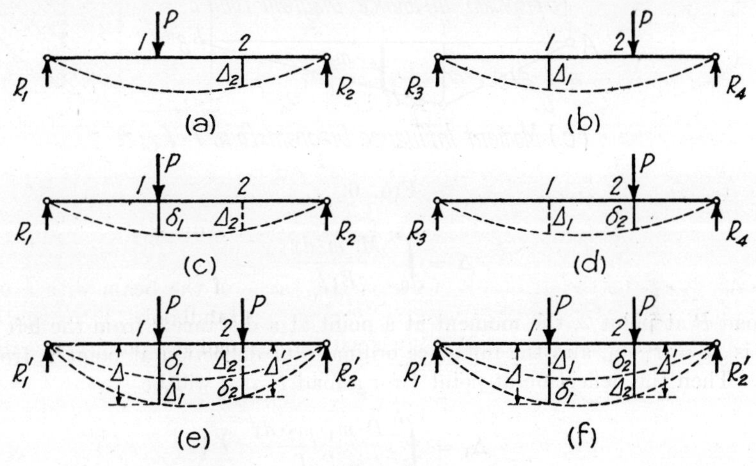

Fig. 5.

First Proof.—Let the load P be gradually applied at point (1) (*c*), Fig. 5 and the work on the structure will be $W_1 = \frac{1}{2}P \cdot \delta_1$, and the deflection at 2 will be Δ_2. Then if a load P be applied gradually at point 2, the deflection at 1 will be Δ_1, (*e*) Fig. 5, and the work due to both loads will be

$$W = \tfrac{1}{2}P \cdot \delta_1 + P \cdot \Delta_1 + \tfrac{1}{2}P \cdot \delta_2 \tag{3}$$

Now in (*d*), Fig. 5, let P be gradually applied at 2, producing a deflection Δ_1 at 1, and the work on the beam will be $W_2 = \frac{1}{2}P \cdot \delta_2$. Then if load P be applied at point 1 in (*f*), Fig. 5, the deflection at point 2 will be Δ_2, and the work due to both loads will be

$$W = \tfrac{1}{2}P \cdot \delta_1 + \tfrac{1}{2}P \cdot \delta_2 + P \cdot \Delta_2 \tag{4}$$

Now the work due to both loads will be independent of the order of the application of the loads, and equating (3) and (4) and solving gives $\Delta_1 = \Delta_2$, which proves the theorem.

Second Proof for Maxwell's Theorem as Applied to a Beam.—In (*a*), Fig. 6 it is required to prove that the deflection at point 1 with a load P at point 2, will be equal to the deflection at point 2 with a load P at point 1. An influence diagram for moment for point 2 is given in (*b*) and an influence diagram for moment for point 1 is given in (*c*) Fig. 6. Now the deflection of a point in a beam is given by the general formula

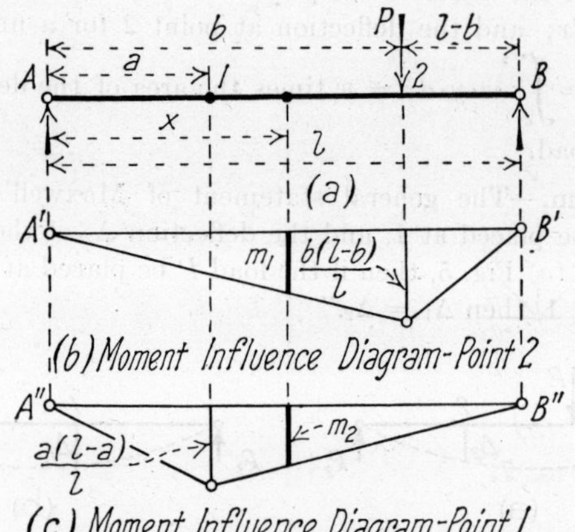

FIG. 6.

$$\Delta = \int_0^l \frac{M \cdot m \cdot dx}{E \cdot I} \tag{5}$$

With a load P at point 2, the moment at a point at a distance x from the left support from (*b*) is $M = P \cdot m_1$, and the influence ordinate for deflection at point 1, from (*c*) is $m = m_2$. Then the deflection at point 1 for a load P at 2 will be

$$\Delta_1 = \int_0^l \frac{P \cdot m_1 \cdot m_2 \cdot dx}{E \cdot I} \tag{6}$$

In a similar manner the deflection at point 2 for a load P at 1 will be

$$\Delta_2 = \int_0^l \frac{P \cdot m_2 \cdot m_1 \cdot dx}{E \cdot I} \tag{7}$$

But the right-hand members of both equations are equal, and $\Delta_1 = \Delta_2$.

Stress Influence Diagram.—A stress influence diagram for stresses in a beam with a constant moment of inertia due to bending moment may be constructed by using the stress $f = M \cdot c/I$ at any point in place of the bending moment. The stress influence diagram for a beam is then of the same form as for bending moments as given in Fig. 3, except that the scale is changed to give stresses in place of bending moments. The stress influence diagram for stresses due to shear in a beam with a constant cross section may be constructed as in Fig. 2, by using a scale that gives stresses in place of shears.

A stress influence diagram for a truss may be constructed by applying a load unity at the point, acting in the required direction. The stresses in each member due to the unit load will then be the influence values, called the U stresses. An algebraic stress influence diagram for point B in the Pratt truss is given in (a), and a graphic diagram in (b), Fig. 7; and a graphic diagram for a horizontal force at the point B in a roof truss is given in Fig. 8. If P is the force at B and S is the stress in any member due to P, then $U = \frac{dS}{dP}$, and diagrams in Fig. 7 and Fig. 8 are derivative diagrams.

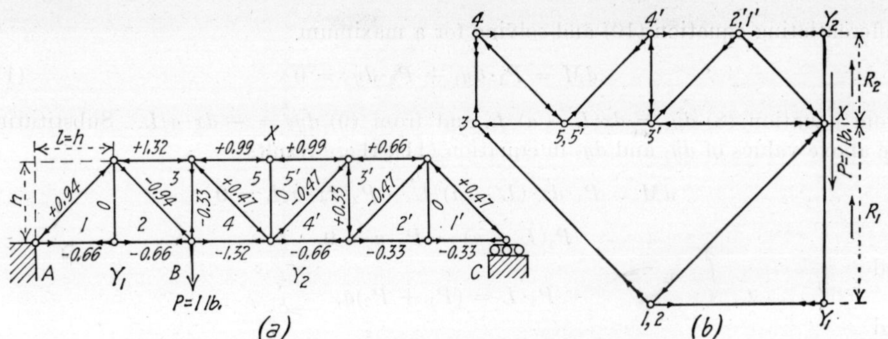

FIG. 7. STRESS INFLUENCE DIAGRAM.

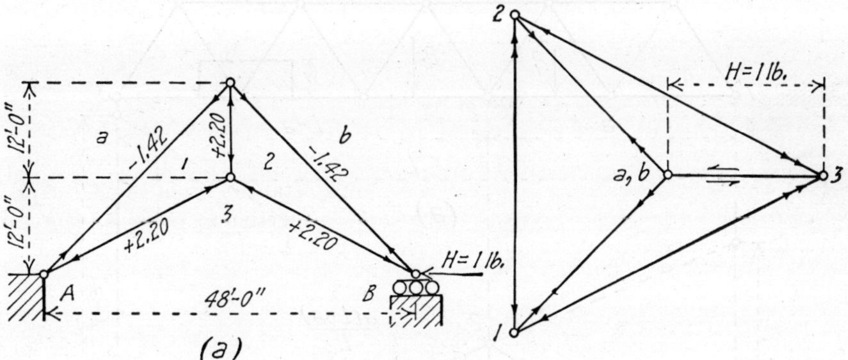

FIG. 8. STRESS INFLUENCE DIAGRAM.

Maximum Moment in the Loaded Chord of a Truss or in a Beam.—Let P_1 in Fig. 9 represent the summation of the moving loads to the left of the panel point 2′, and P_2 represent the summation of the loads to the right of the point 2′.

The influence diagram for the point 2′ is constructed by calculating the bending moment at 2′ due to a unit load $= m = a(L - a)/L =$ ordinate 2–4, and drawing lines 1–2 and 2–3. The equation of the line 1–2 is,

$$y_1 = x(L - a)/L \tag{8}$$

and the equation of the line 2–3 is,

$$y_2 = a(L - x)/L \tag{9}$$

when $x = a$, the two lines have a common ordinate which is equal to $y = a(L - a)/L$. When $x = L$, the ordinate to 1–2 $= L - a$, while when $x = 0$, the ordinate to 2–3 $= a$, as is seen in Fig. 9. This relation gives an easy method for constructing an influence diagram for moments at any point in a beam or truss.

It is required to determine the criterion for maximum moment at the joint 2′.

First Proof.—Now in Fig. 9, the bending moment at point 2′ due to the loads P_1 and P_2, is

$$M = P_1 \cdot y_1 + P_2 \cdot y_2 \tag{10}$$

Differentiating equation (10) and solving for a maximum

$$dM = P_1 \cdot dy_1 + P_2 \cdot dy_2 = 0 \tag{11}$$

From equation (8) $dy_1 = dx(L - a)/L$, and from (9) $dy_2 = - dx \cdot a/L$. Substituting the above values of dy_1 and dy_2 in equation (11), there results

$$dM = P_1 \cdot dx \cdot (L - a)/L - P_2 \cdot dx \cdot a/L = 0$$

$$P_1(L - a) - P_2 \cdot a = 0,$$

and

$$P_1 \cdot L = (P_1 + P_2)a,$$

and

$$P_1/a = (P_1 + P_2)/L \tag{12}$$

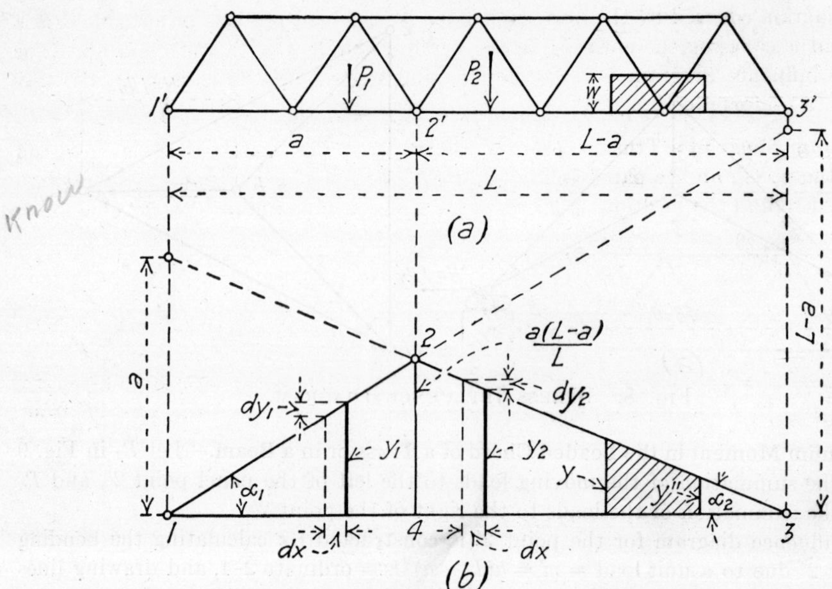

FIG. 9. MOMENT INFLUENCE DIAGRAM.

Second Proof.—In Fig. 9 the bending moment at 2′ due to the loads P_1 and P_2 is

$$M = P_1 \cdot y_1 + P_2 \cdot y_2 \tag{13}$$

Now move the loads P_1 and P_2 a short distance to the left, the distance being assumed so small that the distribution of the loads will not be changed, and

$$M + dM = P_1(y_1 - dy_1) + P_2(y_2 + dy_2) \tag{14}$$

Subtracting (13) from (14), and placing $dM = 0$, we have

$$dM = -P_1 \cdot dy_1 + P_2 \cdot dy_2 = 0 \tag{15}$$

But $dy_1 = dx \cdot \tan \alpha_1 = dx \dfrac{L-a}{L}$, and $dy_2 = dx \cdot \tan \alpha_2 = dx \dfrac{a}{L}$, and

$$dM = -P_1 \frac{L-a}{L} dx + P_2 \frac{a}{L} dx = 0 \tag{16}$$

from which $P_1 \cdot a - P_1 \cdot L + P_2 \cdot a = 0$, and $(P_1 + P_2)a = P_1 \cdot L$.

and

$$P_1/a = (P_1 + P_2)/L \tag{12}$$

From equation (12) it follows "That the maximum bending moment at point 2′ occurs when the average load on the left of the section is equal to the average load on the entire span." The criterion will be satisfied for a bridge loaded with equal joint loads when the bridge is fully loaded.

Uniform Loads.—In Fig. 9 the bending moment at 2′ due to a uniform load of $w \cdot dx$ will be $w \cdot y \cdot dx$. But $y \cdot dx$ is the area of the influence diagram under the uniform load, and the bending moment at 2′ due to a uniform load w will be equal to the area of the influence diagram covered by the load, multiplied by the load per unit of length. For a uniform load w covering the entire span the bending moment at 2′ will be w times the area of the influence diagram 1–2–3. For maximum moment the span must be fully loaded with a uniform load.

Maximum Shear in a Truss.—Let P_1, P_2 and P_3, in Fig. 10 represent the loads on the left of the panel, on the panel and to the right of the $(m+1)$st panel, respectively. It is required to find the position of the moving loads for a maximum shear in the panel.

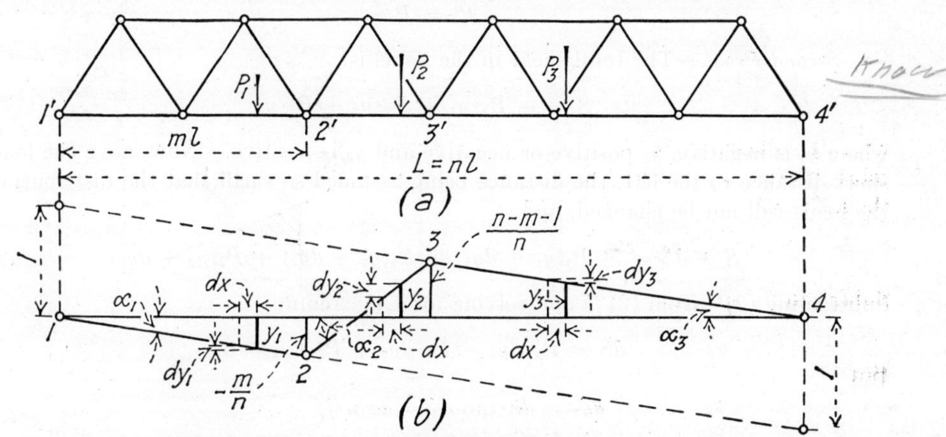

FIG. 10. SHEAR INFLUENCE DIAGRAM.

The influence diagram for loads to the left of the panel and to the right of the panel are constructed as in Fig. 2, while the influence line for the panel is the line 2–3 as shown. With a load unity at 2′ the right reaction is $R_2 = m \cdot l/n \cdot l = m/n$, and the shear in the panel 2′–3′, is $-m/n$. With a load unity at 3′ the left reaction is $R_1 = (n-m-1)l/n \cdot l = (n-m-1)/n$ = the shear in the panel 2′–3′. For a load unity on the panel the shear will vary from $-m/n$ at 2′ to $(n-m-1)/n$ at 3′, as given by the influence line 2–3.

The equation of the influence line 1–2 is

$$y_1 = -x/n \cdot l \tag{18}$$

The equation of line 2–3 is

$$y_2 = x(n-1)/n \cdot l - m \tag{19}$$

The equation of line 3–4 is

$$y_3 = (n \cdot l - x)/n \cdot l \tag{20}$$

It is required to determine the criterion for maximum shear in the panel 2′–3′.

First Proof.—Now the total shear in the panel is

$$S = P_1 \cdot y_1 + P_2 \cdot y_2 + P_3 \cdot y_3 \tag{21}$$

Differentiating (21) and solving for a maximum

$$dS = P_1 \cdot dy_1 + P_2 \cdot dy_2 + P_3 \cdot dy_3 = 0 \tag{22}$$

Now $dy_1 = -dx/n \cdot l$, $dy_2 = dx(n-1)/n \cdot l$, and $dy_3 = -dx/n \cdot l$. Substituting values of dy_1, dy_2, and dy_3 in equation (22), and solving

$$-P_1/n \cdot l + P_2(n-1)/n \cdot l - P_3/n \cdot l = 0$$

and

$$-P_1 + P_2(n-1) - P_3 = 0 \tag{22′}$$

Solving and substituting

$$P = P_1 + P_2 + P_3$$

the criterion is

$$P_2 = P/n \tag{23}$$

Second Proof.—The total shear in the panel is

$$S = -P_1 \cdot y_1 + P_2 \cdot y_2 + P_3 \cdot y_3 \tag{21′}$$

where y_1 is negative, y_2 positive or negative and y_3 is positive. Now move the loads a short distance to the left, the distance being assumed so small that the distribution of the loads will not be changed, and

$$S + dS = -P_1(y_1 - dy_1) + P_2(y_2 - dy_2) + P_3(y_3 + dy_3) \tag{21″}$$

Subtracting (21′) from (21″) and solving for a maximum

$$dS = P_1 \cdot dy_1 - P_2 \cdot dy_2 + P_3 \cdot dy_3 = 0$$

But

$$dy_1 = dx \cdot \tan \alpha_1 = dx/n \cdot l$$

$$dy_2 = dx \cdot \tan \alpha_2 = dx(n-1)/n \cdot l$$

$$dy_3 = dx \cdot \tan \alpha_3 = dx/n \cdot l$$

and substituting we have

$$dS = P_1 \cdot dx/n \cdot l - P_2 \cdot dx(n-1)/n \cdot l + P_3 \cdot dx/n \cdot l = 0$$

$$P_1 - P_2(n-1) + P_3 = 0$$

and

$$P_1 + P_2 + P_3 = P_2 \cdot n$$

and

$$P_2 = P/n \tag{23}$$

From equation (23) it follows that the maximum shear in the panel will occur when the average load on the panel is equal to the average load on the span.

Uniform Loads.—As proved for Fig. 2 the shear in the panel due to a uniform load is equal to the area of the influence diagram covered by the load, multiplied by the intensity of the uniform load per linear unit. From Fig. 10 it will be seen that maximum shear in the panel will occur when the uniform load covers the longer segment of the truss and extends to the point in the panel where the shear changes sign (the load divide), while for minimum shear (maximum negative shear) the shorter segment of the truss should be loaded. For equal joint loads, load the longer segment of the truss for maximum shear, and load the shorter segment for minimum shear.

Maximum Floorbeam Reaction.—The loads on the panels 1′–2′ and 2′–3′ in (*a*) Fig. 11, are carried to the floorbeam at 2′ by stringers acting as simple beams. The influence diagram for floorbeam reaction at 2′ will then consist of reaction influence diagrams for panels 1′–2′ and 2′–3′, respectively, drawn as in Fig. 1. The influence

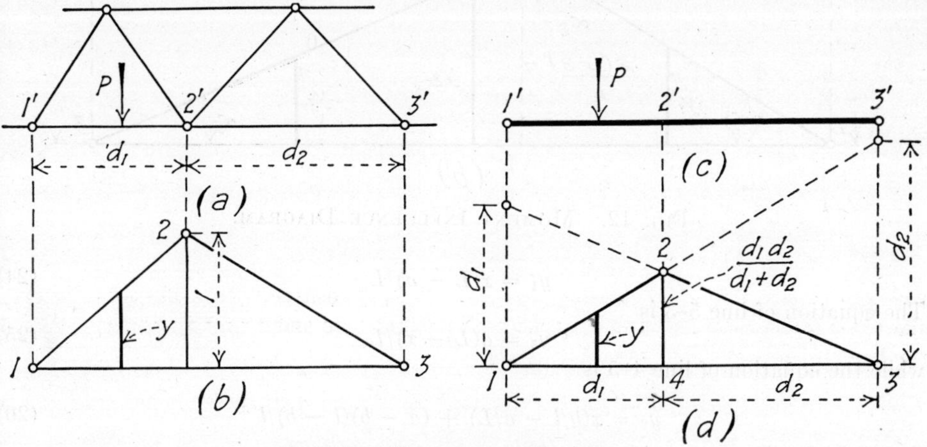

FIG. 11. FLOORBEAM REACTION.

diagram for moment at the point 2′ in a simple beam 1′–3′ with a span equal to $d_1 + d_2$ is shown in (*d*) Fig. 11. Now diagram (*d*) differs from diagram (*b*) only in the value of the mid ordinate 2–4. Ordinates to the influence diagram in (*b*) are equal to ordinates at the same point in diagram (*d*) multiplied by $(d_1 + d_2)/d_1 \cdot d_2$. *Therefore to calculate the maximum floorbeam reaction, calculate the maximum bending moment in a simple span equal to the sum of the two adjacent panel lengths, at a point in the simple beam corresponding to the panel point. The maximum moment multiplied by* $(d_1 + d_2)/d_1 \cdot d_2$ *will be the maximum floorbeam reaction.* If the two panels are equal, the maximum moment at the center of a beam equal to two panel lengths multiplied by two divided by the panel length $(2/d)$ will give the maximum floorbeam reaction.

Maximum Moment in the Unloaded Chord of a Through Warren Truss.—In Fig. 12, let P_1 represent the summation of the moving loads to the left of the panel 4′–5′, P_2 represent the summation of the moving loads on the panel, and P_3 represent the summation of the moving loads to the right of the panel 4′–5′. The influence diagram for the point 2 is the figure 1–4–5–3, the lines 1–4 and 5–3 being the same as the lines 1–2 and 2–3, respectively, in Fig. 9, while 4–5 is the influence line for the panel 4′–5′. The equation of line 1–4 is

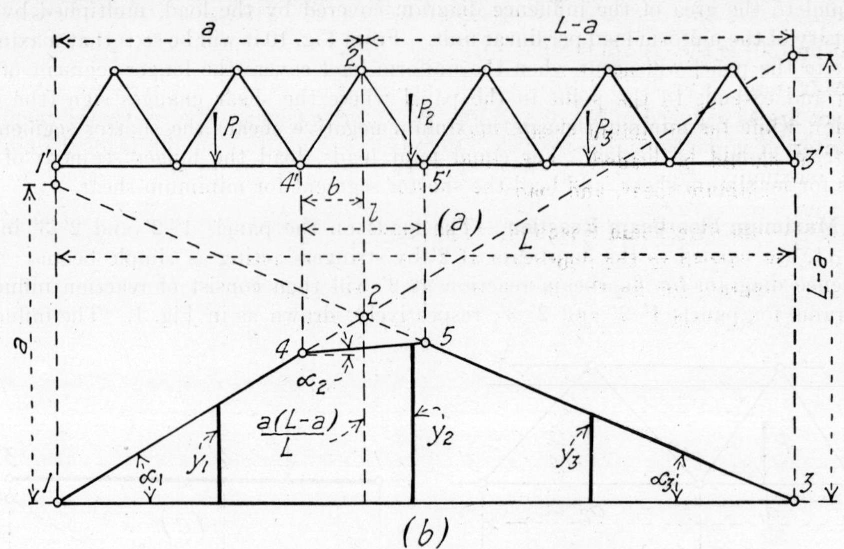

FIG. 12. MOMENT INFLUENCE DIAGRAM.

$$y_1 = x(L - a)/L \tag{24}$$

The equation of line 5–3 is

$$y_3 = a(L - x)/L \tag{25}$$

while the equation of line 4–5 is

$$y_2 = x(b/l - a/L) + (a - b)(l - b)/l \tag{26}$$

Now the bending moment at 2 due to the three loads is

$$M = P_1 \cdot y_1 + P_2 \cdot y_2 + P_3 \cdot y_3 \tag{27}$$

Differentiating (27) and solving for a maximum

$$dM = P_1 \cdot dy_1 + P_2 \cdot dy_2 + P_3 \cdot dy_3 = 0 \tag{28}$$

Now from (24)

$$dy_1 = dx(L - a)/L,$$

from (26)

$$dy_2 = dx(b/l - a/L),$$

and from (25)

$$dy_3 = - dx \cdot a/L$$

Substituting values of dy_1, dy_2, and dy_3 in equation (28), and solving

$$P_1(L - a)/L + P_2(b/l - a/L) - P_3 \cdot a/L = 0 \qquad (29)$$

$$P_1 \cdot l \cdot L - P_1 \cdot a \cdot l + P_2 \cdot b \cdot L - P_2 \cdot a \cdot l - P_3 \cdot a \cdot l = 0$$

$$(P_1 + P_2 + P_3)a \cdot l = P_1 \cdot l \cdot L + P_2 \cdot b \cdot L$$

Solving and placing $P = P_1 + P_2 + P_3$

$$P/L = (P_1 \cdot l + P_2 \cdot b)/a \cdot l \qquad (30)$$

Equation (30) is the criterion required.

Maximum Stresses in a Bridge with Inclined Chords.—The criteria for maximum moment are as deduced in Fig. 9 and Fig. 12. For maximum stresses in web members the criterion is developed as follows. Required the position of the loads P_2 and P_3 for a maximum stress in web U_24', Fig. 13. The stress in U_24' is equal to the

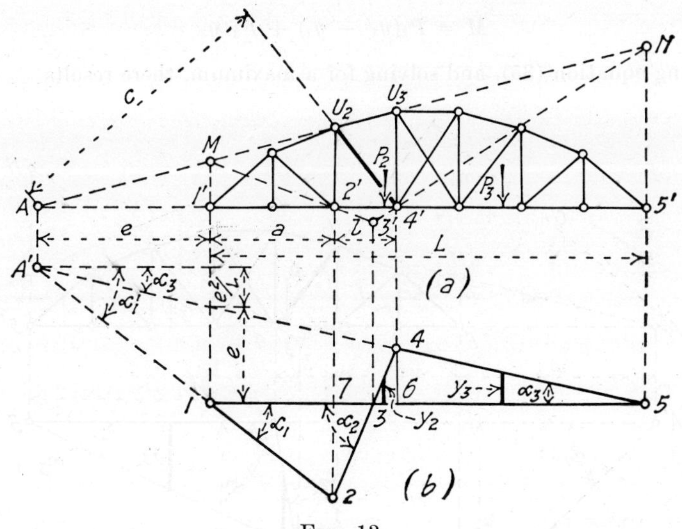

FIG. 13.

moment about point A, of the reaction and the loads to the left of the cut section in the panel, divided by the arm c. The stress in web U_24' will then be a maximum when the moment at A is a maximum. To draw the influence diagram for moment at the point A, calculate the bending moments about A for a unit load at 2′ and a unit load at 4′, respectively. With a unit load at 4′ the moment about point A is line 4–6 = $(L - a - l)e/L$, and with a load unity at 2′ the moment about point A is line 7–2 $= (L - a)e/L - (a + e) = -a(e + L)/L$, a minus quantity, and the influence diagram is the diagram 1–2–4–5 as given in Fig. 13. From Fig. 13 it will be seen that the maximum stress will occur in general when load P_2 is to the right of the load divide in the panel. The maximum moment at A will be

$$M = P_2 \cdot y_2 + P_3 \cdot y_3 \qquad (31)$$

From Fig. 13 it will be seen that $\tan \alpha_3 = e/L$, and $\tan \alpha_1 = -(e + L)/L$.

The influence diagram in Fig. 13 may be constructed as follows.

Draw the horizontal line 1–5. At point 1 erect a vertical line = e. Draw line 5–4 to A'. Then draw A'–1–2. Also draw influence line 2–4.

The equations of the influence diagrams are in simpler form if the influence diagram is drawn as in Fig. 14. Referring to Fig. 14, with origin of coördinates at point A', the equation of line 1–2′ is

$$y_1 = -x \tag{32}$$

The equation of line 2–4′ is

$$y_2 = x(e+a)/l - (e+a+l)(a+e)/l \tag{33}$$

The equation of line 1–5 is

$$y_3 = x \cdot e/L - (e+L)e/L \tag{34}$$

Now in Fig. 14 the moment at point A for loads P_2 and P_3, will be

$$M = P_2(y_3' - y_2) + P_3 \cdot y_3 \tag{35}$$

Differentiating equation (35), and solving for a maximum, there results

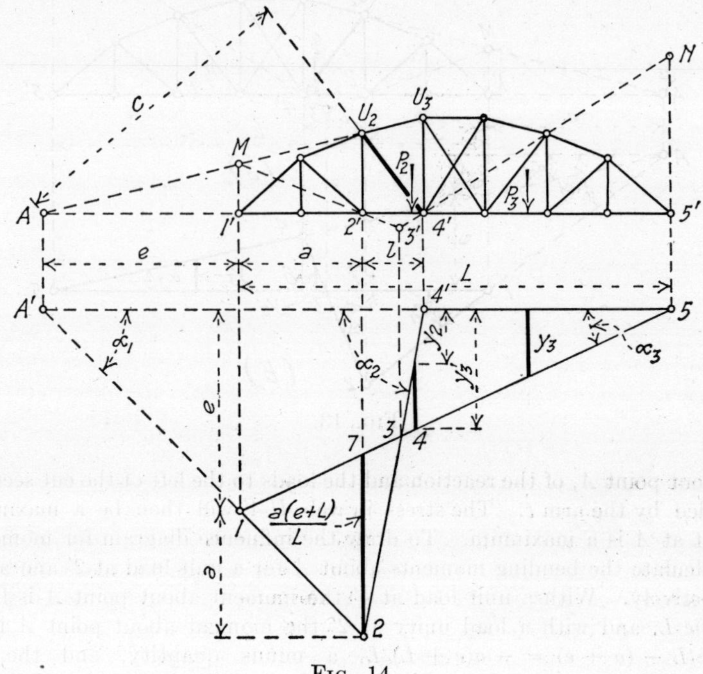

FIG. 14.

$$P_2 \cdot dy_3 - P_2 \cdot dy_2 + P_3 \cdot dy_3 = 0 \tag{36}$$

Now from equation (33), $dy_2 = dx(e+a)/l$, and from equation (34) $dy_3 = dx \cdot e/L$. Substituting in equation (36), there results

$$P_2 \cdot e/L - P_2(e + a)/l + P_3 \cdot e/L = 0$$
$$(P_2 + P_3)/L = P_2(1 + a/e)/l$$
$$P/L = P_2(1 + a/e)/l \tag{37}$$

which is the criterion required.

For a bridge with parallel chords $e = \infty$, and the criterion is the familiar criterion for maximum shear in a panel. For a uniform load the longer segment should be loaded up to point 3′, the load divide, for a maximum stress, while the shorter segment should be loaded for a minimum stress in $U_2 4'$.

By comparing Fig. 13 and Fig. 14 with Fig. 9 it will be seen that the moment influence diagram may be constructed by laying off at the left abutment the distance from the left abutment to the center of moments = a in Fig. 9, and e in Fig. 13 and Fig. 14.

The influence diagram for the maximum stress in the upper chord U_2U_3 may be constructed as in Fig. 15, without calculating the moment due to a unit load at the center of moments 4′. It will be noted that the criterion is the same as for moment at a joint in the loaded chord of a truss with parallel chords.

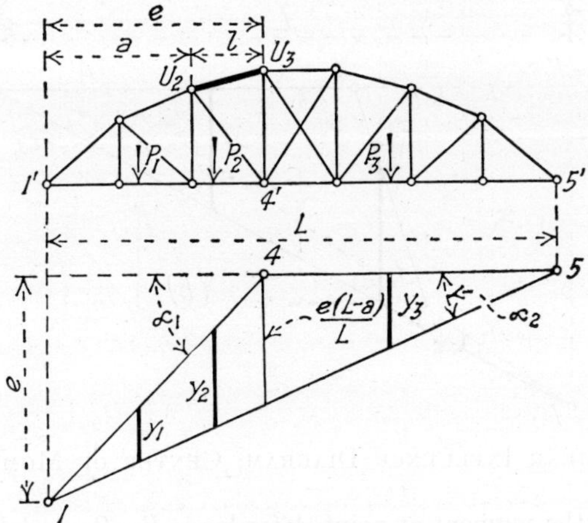

FIG. 15.

Minimum Stresses in Vertical Posts.—The minimum stress in the vertical post $U_2 2'$ in Fig. 13 will be tension and will occur for the loading that gives no stress in the main tie $U_2 4'$ and the counter $U_3 2'$. The dead load stress in $U_2 2'$ having been calculated, the position of the wheels that will make the live load compression in $U_2 2'$ equal the dead load tension is calculated by trial, using the influence diagram in Fig. 13.

Maximum Stress in Web of a Truss of Arch Type.—In Fig. 16 it is required to find the position of the loads P_1, P_2, P_3 that will give a maximum stress in the member U_1–4′. The center of moments used in calculating the stress in U_1–4′ is at A, a distance e to the right of the left abutment. The influence diagram is constructed as in Fig. 16, by laying off a distance e at the left abutment, and by drawing 1–A' and 1–5. Also draw line 3–4. Then the figure 1–3–4–5 is the influence diagram for moment at the point A. It will be noted that there is no load divide in the panel as in Fig. 14, and that all segments of the span should be loaded to give a maximum moment at point A.

The equation of influence line 1–A', with the origin at point A' is

$$y_1 = x \tag{38}$$

The equation of line 3–4 is

$$y_2 = x(e - a)/l - (-e + a + l)(a - e)/l \tag{39}$$

The equation of line 1–5 is

$$y_3 = x \cdot e/L - (L - e)e/L \tag{40}$$

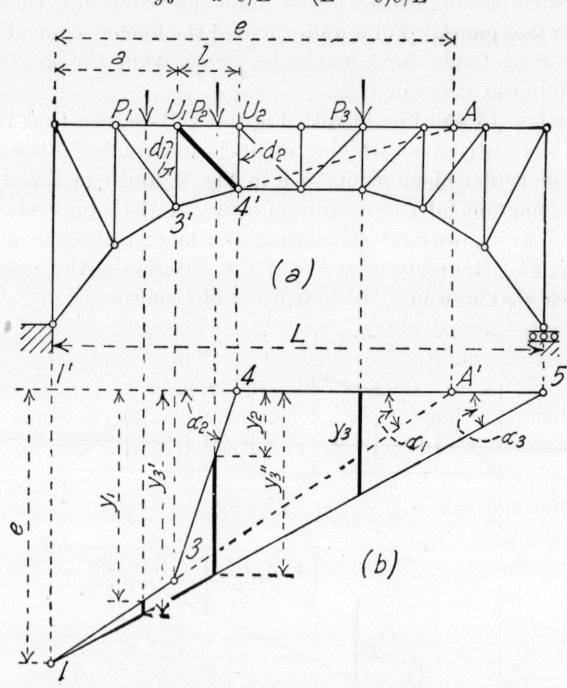

FIG. 16. SHEAR INFLUENCE DIAGRAM, CENTER OF MOMENTS AT A.

Now in Fig. 16 the moment at point A for loads P_1, P_2, and P_3, will be

$$M = P_1(y_3' - y_1) + P_2(y_3'' - y_2) + P_3 \cdot y_3 \tag{41}$$

Differentiating equation (41), and solving for a maximum

$$dM = P_1 \cdot dy_3 - P_1 \cdot dy_1 + P_2 \cdot dy_3 - P_2 \cdot dy_2 + P_3 \cdot dy_3 = 0 \tag{42}$$

Now $dy_1 = dx$, $dy_2 = dx(e - a)/l$, and $dy_3 = dx \cdot e/L$, which substituted in equation (42) gives after solving

$$P_1 \cdot e/L - P_1 + P_2 \cdot e/L - P_2(e - a)/l + P_3 \cdot e/L = 0 \tag{43}$$

and

$$P_1 \cdot e \cdot l - P_1 \cdot l \cdot L + P_2 \cdot e \cdot l + P_2 \cdot a \cdot L - P_2 \cdot e \cdot L + P_3 \cdot e \cdot l = 0$$

$$(P_1 + P_2 + P_3)e \cdot l = (P_1 \cdot l + P_2 \cdot e - P_2 \cdot a)L \tag{44}$$

and

$$P/L = P_1/e + P_2(e - a)/e \cdot l \tag{45}$$

which is the criterion required.

By comparing Fig. 14 with Fig. 16 it will be seen that the criteria are the same except that all segments are loaded and that e is negative.

CHAPTER VIII.

Stresses in Railway Bridge Trusses.

LOADS.—The dead load of a railway bridge is assumed to act at the joints the same as in a highway bridge. The dead joint loads are commonly assumed to act on the loaded chord, but may be assumed as divided between the panel points of the two chords, one-third and two-thirds of the dead loads usually being assumed as acting at the panel points of the unloaded and the loaded chords, respectively.

The live load on a railway bridge consists of wheel loads, the weights and spacing of the wheels depending upon the type of the rolling stock used. The locomotives and cars differ so much that it would be difficult if not impossible to design bridges on a railway system for the actual conditions, and conventional systems of loading, which approximate the actual conditions are assumed. The conventional systems for calculating the live load stresses in railway bridges that have been most favorably received are: (1) Cooper's Conventional System of Wheel Concentrations; (2) the use of an Equivalent Uniform Load; and (3) the use of a uniform load and one or two wheel concentrations. In addition to these some railroads specify special engine loadings. The first and second methods will be discussed in this chapter.

Cooper's Conventional System of Wheel Concentrations.—In Cooper's loadings two consolidation locomotives are followed by a uniformly distributed train load. The typical loading for Cooper's Class E loadings are shown in Fig. 1. The loads on the drivers in thousands of pounds and the uniform train load in hundreds of pounds are the same as the class number. The wheel spacings are the same for all classes. The stresses for Cooper's loadings calculated for one class may be used to obtain the stresses due to any other class loading. For example, the stresses in any truss due to Cooper's Class E 50 are equal to $\frac{5}{4}$ of the stresses in the same truss due to Class E 40 loading. The E 55 and the E 60 loadings are those most used for steam railways in the United States. In bridges designed for Class E 40 loading and under the floor system must in addition be designed for two moving loads of 50,000 lb. each, spaced 6′ 0″ apart on each track. The corresponding loads for Class E 50 are 60,000 lb. with the same spacing. The American Railway Engineering Association has adopted Cooper's loadings, except that the special loads are spaced 7′ 0″. The values for moment, M, shear, S, and floorbeam reaction, R, for Class E 60 are given in Table I.

Equivalent Uniform Load System.—The equivalent uniform load for calculating the stresses in trusses and the bending moments in beams, is the uniform load that will produce the same bending moment at the quarter points of the truss or beam as the maximum bending moment produced by the wheel concentrations. The equivalent uniform loads for different spans for Cooper's E 40 loading are given in Fig. 2. The uniform loadings for any class are proportional. In calculating the stresses in the truss members select the equivalent load for the given span, and calculate the chord and web stresses by the use of equal joint loads, as for highway bridges. In designing the stringers for bending moment take a loading for a span equal to one panel length, and for the maximum floorbeam reaction take a loading for a span equal to two panel lengths. It is necessary to calculate the maximum end shears and the shears at intermediate points by wheel concentrations, or to use equivalent uniform loads calculated for wheel concentrations.

Live load stresses calculated by the method of equivalent uniform loads are too small for the chords and webs between the ends of the truss and the quarter points, and are too large between the quarter points. The stresses obtained for the counters are

Class	8′	5′	5′	5′	9′	5′	6′	5′	8′	8′	5′	5′	5′	9′	5′	6′	5′	5′	Uniform Load
E-40	20 000	40 000	40 000	40 000	40 000	26 000	26 000	26 000	26 000	20 000	40 000	40 000	40 000	40 000	26 000	26 000	26 000	26 000	4 000 lb. per lin. Ft.
E-45	22 500	45 000	45 000	45 000	45 000	29 250	29 250	29 250	29 250	22 500	45 000	45 000	45 000	45 000	29 250	29 250	29 250	29 250	4500 lb. per lin. Ft.
E-50	25 000	50 000	50 000	50 000	50 000	32 500	32 500	32 500	32 500	25 000	50 000	50 000	50 000	50 000	32 500	32 500	32 500	32 500	5 000 lb. per lin. Ft.
E-55	27 500	55 000	55 000	55 000	55 000	35 750	35 750	35 750	35 750	27 500	55 000	55 000	55 000	55 000	35 750	35 750	35 750	35 750	5 500 lb. per lin. Ft.
E-60	30 000	60 000	60 000	60 000	60 000	39 000	39 000	39 000	39 000	30 000	60 000	60 000	60 000	60 000	39 000	39 000	39 000	39 000	6 000 lb. per lin. Ft.

FIG. 1. COOPER'S CONVENTIONAL ENGINE LOADINGS. (LOADS FOR ONE TRACK.)

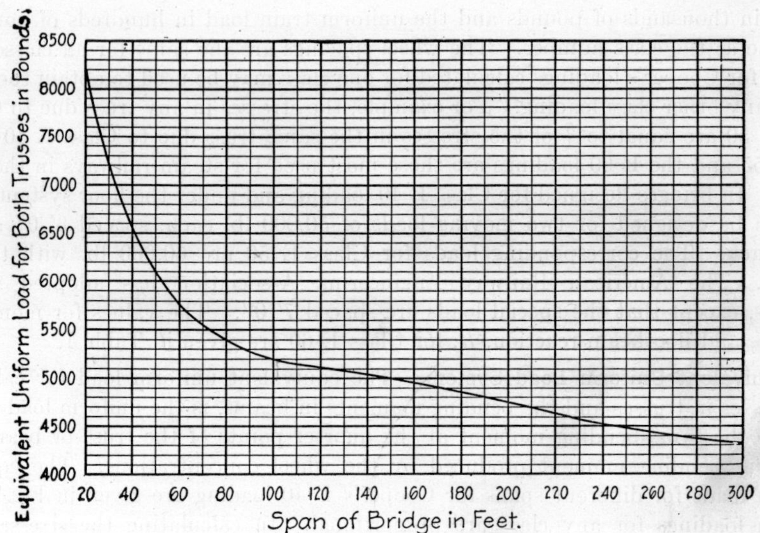

FIG. 2. EQUIVALENT UNIFORM LIVE LOAD FOR COOPER'S E 40 LOADING FOR RAILWAY BRIDGES.

TABLE I.

Maximum Moments, M; End Shears, S; and Floorbeam Reactions, R; Per Rail, for Girders.

Cooper's E 60 Loading (A. R. E. A.).

Loading Two E 60 Engines and Train Load of 6,000 Pounds per Foot or Special Loading Two 75,000 Pound Axle Loads 7 Ft. C. to C.

Moments in Thousands of Foot-Pounds. Shears and Floorbeam Reactions in Thousands of Pounds.

Results for One Rail. Results from Special Loading marked*. A.R.E.A. Impact Formula, (1).

Span L, Ft.	Maximum Moments M.	Moment Impact M′.	End Shear S.	End Shear Impact S′.	Floorbeam Reaction R.	Floorbeam Impact R′.	Span L, Ft.	Maximum Moments M.	Moment Impact M′.	End Shear S.	End Shear Impact S′.
5	* 46.9	* 46.1	*37.5	*36.9	*37.5	*36.3	50	1426.3	1222.6	130.8	112.1
6	* 56.2	* 55.1	*37.5	*36.8	40.0	38.5	51	1474.7	1260.4	132.5	113.2
7	* 65.6	* 64.2	38.6	37.7	47.1	45.0	52	1522.8	1297.8	134.1	114.3
8	* 75.0	* 73.0	*42.2	*41.2	52.5	49.8	53	1571.0	1335.1	135.7	115.3
9	* 84.4	* 82.0	*45.8	*44.5	56.7	53.5	54	1621.5	1374.2	137.4	116.4
10	* 93.7	* 90.7	*48.8	*47.2	60.0	56.3	55	1675.2	1415.7	139.0	117.5
11	*103.0	* 99.5	*51.1	*49.3	65.5	61.0	56	1728.0	1456.7	140.6	118.5
12	120.0	115.4	*53.2	*51.1	70.0	64.8	57	1781.9	1497.4	142.2	119.5
13	142.5	136.6	55.4	53.1	73.9	68.0	58	1834.5	1537.4	143.8	120.5
14	165.0	157.6	57.8	55.2	78.2	71.5	59	1891.4	1580.6	145.4	121.5
15	187.5	178.6	60.0	57.2	82.0	74.5	60	1949.4	1624.5	147.0	122.5
16	210.0	199.3	63.8	60.6	85.3	77.1	61	2007.5	1668.3	148.6	123.5
17	232.5	220.0	67.1	63.5	88.2	79.2	62	2064.3	1710.8	150.2	124.5
18	255.0	240.5	70.0	66.0	91.0	81.3	63	2123.4	1754.9	152.0	125.6
19	280.0	263.2	72.6	68.3	94.3	83.7	64	2183.3	1799.4	153.8	126.8
20	309.5	290.5	75.0	70.3	98.3	86.7	65	2246.3	1846.3	155.7	128.0
21	339.0	316.8	77.1	72.1	101.9	89.4	66	2309.3	1893.0	157.5	129.1
22	368.5	343.3	79.1	73.7	105.2	91.7	67	2378.3	1943.2	159.6	130.5
23	398.2	369.8	80.9	75.1	108.2	93.8	68	2435.4	1985.3	161.7	131.8
24	427.8	396.1	83.1	76.9	110.9	95.6	69	2498.4	2031.2	163.8	133.2
25	457.5	422.3	85.2	78.6	113.5	97.3	70	2561.3	2076.8	165.8	134.4
26	487.2	448.3	87.1	80.2	116.6	99.4	71	2624.5	2122.2	167.7	135.6
27	516.9	474.2	88.9	81.6	120.1	101.8	72	2688.0	2168.0	170.0	137.1
28	548.3	501.5	90.6	82.9	123.4	104.0	73	2750.9	2212.5	172.2	138.5
29	582.0	530.7	92.3	84.2	126.5	106.0	74	2818.5	2260.7	174.4	139.9
30	615.8	559.8	94.6	86.0	129.4	107.8	75	2888.6	2310.9	176.5	141.2
31	649.3	588.5	96.6	87.5	132.7	110.0	76	2958.0	2360.1	178.6	142.5
32	683.2	617.3	98.6	89.1	136.5	112.5	77	3028.6	2410.0	180.6	143.7
33	716.9	645.8	100.4	90.5	140.0	114.8	78	3096.6	2457.6	182.5	144.8
34	750.6	674.2	102.1	91.7	143.2	116.7	79	3168.2	2507.8	184.4	146.0
35	784.5	702.5	103.8	93.0	146.4	118.7	80	3240.7	2558.5	186.3	147.1
36	823.0	734.9	105.9	94.6	149.3	120.4	81	3311.4	2607.4	188.4	148.4
37	861.6	767.0	107.8	96.0	152.2	122.1	82	3385.1	2658.4	190.4	149.5
38	900.0	798.8	109.7	97.4	155.6	124.2	83	3459.6	2709.8	192.3	150.6
39	940.0	831.8	111.4	98.6	158.8	126.0	84	3534.6	2761.4	194.2	151.7
40	983.4	867.7	113.1	99.8	162.0	127.9	85	3610.4	2813.3	196.1	152.8
41	1027.0	903.5	115.2	101.3	....	....	86	3689.4	2867.4	198.1	154.0
42	1070.4	938.9	117.2	102.8	....	....	87	3766.5	2919.8	200.1	155.1
43	1113.9	974.2	119.0	104.1	....	....	88	3846.0	2973.7	202.1	156.3
44	1157.4	1009.4	120.8	105.3	....	....	89	3924.3	3026.5	204.0	157.3
45	1201.1	1044.4	122.5	106.5	Viaduct	....	90	4005.8	3081.4	205.8	158.3
46	1244.4	1078.9	124.2	107.7	Span	....	91	4084.4	3133.8	207.7	159.4
47	1287.9	1113.4	125.9	108.8	30′–60′	....	92	4164.0	3186.7	209.7	160.5
48	1331.4	1147.8	127.5	109.9	179.2	....	93	4246.6	3241.6	211.6	161.5
49	1378.3	1184.8	129.2	111.1	....	....	94	4328.0	3295.4	213.5	162.6

TABLE I.—*Continued.*

MAXIMUM MOMENTS, M; END SHEARS, S; AND FLOORBEAM REACTIONS, R; PER RAIL, FOR GIRDERS.

Cooper's E 60 Loading (A. R. E. A.).

Span L, Ft.	Maximum Moments M.	Moment Impact, M′.	End Shear S.	End Shear Impact S′.	Floorbeam Reaction R.	Floorbeam Impact R′.	Span L, Ft.	Maximum Moments M.	Moment Impact M′.	End Shear S.	End Shear Impact S′.
95	4408.4	3348.2	215.4	163.6	Viaduct	....	110	5829.6	4265.5	243.0	177.8
96	4490.7	3402.0	217.2	164.5	Span	....	111	5937.4	4333.9	244.8	178.7
97	4573.5	3456.0	219.2	165.6	40′–60′	....	112	6040.0	4398.1	246.6	179.5
98	4659.8	3512.4	221.2	166.7	197.2	....	113	6148.2	4466.0	248.3	180.3
99	4743.8	3566.7	223.1	167.7	....	....	114	6258.0	4534.8	250.0	181.2
100	4830.0	3622.5	225.0	168.8	Viaduct	....	115	6366.8	4602.5	251.8	182.0
101	4916.9	3678.5	226.8	169.7	Span	....	116	6478.0	4671.6	253.6	182.9
102	5004.0	3734.4	228.6	170.6	40′–80′	....	117	6586.1	4738.2	255.3	183.6
103	5115.5	3808.1	230.4	171.5	236.5	....	118	6696.6	4806.1	257.0	184.4
104	5212.8	3870.9	232.3	172.5	....	....	119	6808.3	4874.7	258.8	185.3
105	5306.5	3930.7	234.1	173.4	....	....	120	6921.6	4944.0	260.5	186.1
106	5401.3	3991.1	235.9	174.3	....	....	121	7030.5	5009.9	262.2	186.9
107	5499.2	4053.4	237.7	175.2	....	....	122	7143.8	5078.5	264.0	187.7
108	5617.0	4130.1	239.4	176.0	....	....	123	7260.1	5148.9	265.7	188.4
109	5727.6	4201.1	241.2	176.9	....	....	124	7376.4	5219.1	267.4	189.2
							125	7495.2	5290.7	269.1	190.0

too large. The live load stresses calculated by the method of equivalent uniform loads are sufficiently accurate for all practical purposes. Even though the equivalent uniform load method is simple to apply and gives sufficiently accurate results, it is now seldom used.

KINDS OF STRESS.—The live loads on a railway bridge produce stresses as follows:

(1) Static stresses due to the live load in any position;

(2) Vibratory stresses due to the moving of the live load, generally included in the term "Impact";

(3) Horizontal static stresses due to centrifugal forces, if the bridge is on a curve;

(4) Longitudinal static stresses due to the momentum of the train, and the friction on the rails when the brakes are applied.

Vibratory stresses cannot be calculated with our present knowledge, but are provided for by taking a percentage of the static live load as "Impact Stress," or by using smaller working stresses. Horizontal and static stresses can be calculated.

IMPACT STRESSES.—As a load moves over the bridge it causes shocks and vibrations whereby the actual stresses are increased over those due to static loads alone. It is shown in mechanics of materials that a load suddenly applied to a bar or a beam will produce stresses equal to twice the stresses produced by the same load gradually applied. A bridge is a complex structure and it is not possible to determine the exact effect of the moving loads. It has been found by experiment that the ultimate strength for repeated loads is much less than the ordinary ultimate strength. In a bridge it will be seen that the dead load is a fixed load and that the live load is a varying load.

Impact Formulas.—The formula in most common use is given in the form

$$I = S\left(\frac{a}{L + b}\right) \tag{1}$$

where I = impact stress to be added to the static live load stress, S = the static live load stress, L = the length in feet of the portion of the bridge that is loaded to produce the maximum stress in the member, and a and b are constants expressed in feet. The American Railway Engineering Association prior to 1920 specified for railway bridges, $a = b = 300$ ft.

After an extensive series of tests the committee on Iron and Steel Structures of the American Railway Engineering Association has recommended the following formula for impact in railway bridges.

$$I = S \cdot \frac{30{,}000}{30{,}000 + L^2} \tag{2}$$

where L is the length of the span. This formula was included in the revised specifications for railway bridges adopted by the Association in 1920, but the new formula has been adopted by very few roads as yet.

For additional data on impact see the author's "Structural Engineers' Handbook," and "Design of Highway Bridges of Steel, Timber and Concrete."

CALCULATION OF STRESSES DUE TO WHEEL CONCENTRATIONS.—The maximum stresses in any member of a truss may be found by trail, that is, by assuming a number of positions of the live load, calculating the stress for each position, and then comparing the results. This method is long and tiresome and considerable time may be saved by the application of certain simple criteria, which are developed in Chapter VII by means of influence diagrams. These criteria may also be developed by algebraic methods.

MAXIMUM STRESSES.—The conditions of live loading for maximum stresses in beams and trusses are as follows.

Uniform Live Load on Beam or Girder.—For bending moment the span should be fully loaded. For shear the longer segment of the span should be loaded.

Equal Joint Loads.—For bending moment (chord stresses) the bridge should be fully loaded. For shear (web stresses in trusses with parallel chords) the longer segment of the truss should be loaded for maximum stress, and the shorter segment of the truss should be loaded for maximum counter stress (minimum stress).

Point of Maximum Bending Moment in a Beam.—The maximum bending moment in a beam loaded with moving loads will come under a heavy load when this load is as far from one end of the beam as the center of gravity of all the moving loads then on the beam is from the other end of the beam.

Wheel Loads, Bridge with Parallel Chords.—The max mum bending moment at any joint in the loaded chord will occur when the average load on the left of the section is equal to the average load on the entire span.

The maximum bending moment at any joint in the unloaded chord of a symmetrical Warren truss will occur when the average load on the entire span is equal to the average

Position of Wheels for Maximum Moment; Table III.

The wheel loads that will produce maximum moment at a point a given distance from the left end of a beam, or at any loaded panel point in a bridge, are given in Table III. For example in an 8-panel Pratt truss of 200 ft. span, maximum moment at panel point L_1, 25 ft. from the left end, occurs with wheel No. 4, at the point; a maximum moment at L_2 occurs with wheel No. 7 at the point; etc.

Instructions for Use of Moment Table; Table II.

Line (1) is summation of loads from head of uniform load.
Line (2) is summation of loads from wheel No. 1.
Line (3) is the number of each wheel from wheel No. 1.
Line (4) is amount of each wh e' load in thousand pounds.
Line (5) is distance c. to c. of the wheels, in feet.
Line (6) is distance of any wheel, or the head of uniform load, from wheel No. 1.
Line (7) is distance of any wheel from head of uniform load.
Line (8) is summation of moments of all wheels to right of any wheel, including the wheel in question, about head of uniform load.

Lines (9) to (25) are summations of moments of all wheels to left of the stepped line, including wheel on left of value, about the wheel just above the heavy vertical stepped line on each line.

The values to the right of the stepped lines are moments about the stepped line, including wheel to right of moment value given.

EXAMPLES.—Problem 1.—Calculate moment of wheels Nos. 1 to 15, inclusive, about wheel No. 15.

Follow vertical line passing through wheel No. 15 down to stepped line, and follow over to the left on line (12), and find 16,220 thousand ft.-lb. to right of vertical line through wheel No. 1.

Problem 2.—Calculate the moment of wheels Nos. 17, 16, 15, 14, about wheel No. 13.

Follow vertical line passing through wheel No. 13 down to the stepped line, and follow line (14), to right, and to left of the vertical line through wheel No. 17, find 1,281 thousand ft.-lb.

Problem 3.—Given a 200-ft. span, 8 panel Pratt railway bridge The moments and shears are calculated as follows:

Moments.—Panel point L_1. From Table III, there will be a maximum moment at L_1 with wheel No. 4 at the joint; and from Table II, line (7) it is 91 ft. from wheel No. 4 to the end of the uniform load, and it is also 175 ft. from joint L_1 to the end of the bridge, and there will be $175 - 91 = 84$ ft. of uniform load on the bridge. Then, $R_1 \times 200 = 24{,}550 + 426 \times 84 + 3 \times 84^2/2 = 70{,}918$ thousand ft.-lb.; and $R_1 = 354.6$ thousand lb. The moment at L_1 is $M_1 = 354.6 \times 25 - 720 = 8{,}145$ thousand ft.-lb.

Shear in Panel L_0L_1 is $S_1 = R_1 - 720/25 = 354.6 - 28.8 = 325.8$ thousand lb. (720 is the moment of wheels Nos. 1, 2, 3, about wheel

TABLE III.

Loading for Maximum Moment in Bridges for Cooper's Loadings.

Spans	10'	15'	20'	25'	30'	35'	40'	45'	50'	55'	60'	65'	70'	80'	90'	100'	110'	120'	130'	140'
300' to 260'	2	3	3	4	4	5	5	6	7	7	8	9	10	11	12	13	14	15	17	18
250' to 200'	2	3	3	4	4	5	5	6	7	8	8	9	10	11	12	13	14	15	17	18
190' to 150'	2	3	3	4	4	5	5	6	7	8	9	9	11	12	12	13	14	15	17	18
140'	3	3	3	4	4	5	5	6	7	8	9	10	11	12	12	13	14	15	17	18
130'	3	3	3	4	4	5	5	6	7	8	9	10	11	12	12	13	14	15	17	
120'	3	3	3	4	4	5	5	6	7	8	9	10	11	12	13	13	14	15		
110'	3	3	3	4	4	5	6	7	7	8	9	10	11	12	13	13	14			
100'	3	3	3	4	5	5	6	$\overline{14}$	$\overline{14}$	$\overline{14}$	$\overline{13}$	$\overline{13}$	11	12	13	13				
90'	3	3	4	4	5	$\overline{13}$	$\overline{13}$	$\overline{13}$	$\overline{13}$	$\overline{13}$	$\overline{13}$	$\overline{13}$	$\overline{13}$	12	13					
80'	3	3	4	4	$\overline{13}$	$\overline{13}$	$\overline{13}$	$\overline{12}$	$\overline{12}$	$\overline{12}$	$\overline{12}$	$\overline{12}$	$\overline{12}$	12						
70'	3	3	4	4	$\overline{13}$	$\overline{13}$	$\overline{12}$	$\overline{12}$	$\overline{12}$	$\overline{12}$	$\overline{11}$	$\overline{11}$	11							
65'	3	3	4	4	$\overline{12}$	$\overline{12}$	$\overline{12}$	$\overline{12}$	$\overline{12}$	$\overline{11}$	$\overline{11}$	11								
60'	3	3	4	4	5	$\overline{13}$	$\overline{12}$	$\overline{11}$	$\overline{11}$	$\overline{11}$	11									
55'	12	12	12	4	12	$\overline{13}$	$\overline{12}$	$\overline{12}$	$\overline{13}$	11										
50'	12	12	12	12	12	$\overline{13}$	$\overline{13}$	$\overline{13}$	12											
45'	12	12	12	12	12	$\overline{13}$	$\overline{13}$	13												
40'	3	3	3	12	12	$\overline{13}$	13													
35'	3	3	4	4	13	13														
30'	3	3	4	4	13															
25'	3	3	4	4																
20'	$\overline{4}$	3	4																	
15'	3	3																		
10'	3																			

WHEEL DETERMINING MAXIMUM MOMENT
COOPER'S LOADINGS
C·M·& ST·P·RY.

The shorter span is ahead followed by the longer one except wheel is over-lined.

TABLE II.

Moment Table for Cooper's E 60 Loading.

1	426	411	381	351	321	291	271.5	252	232.5	213	198	168	138	108	78	58.5	39	19.5
2	15	45	75	105	135	154.5	174	193.5	213	228	258	288	318	348	367.5	387	406.5	426
3	1	2	3	4	5	6	7	8	9	10	11	12	13	14	15	16	17	18
4	15	30	30	30	30	19.5	19.5	19.5	19.5	15	30	30	30	30	19.5	19.5	19.5	19.5
5	8'	5'	5'	5'	9'	5'	6'	5'	8'	8'	5'	5'	5'	9'	5'	6'	5'	5'
6	8'	13'	18'	23'	32'	37'	43'	48'	56'	64'	69'	74'	79'	88'	93'	99'	104'	109'
7	109'	101'	96'	91'	86'	77'	72'	66'	61'	53'	45'	40'	35'	30'	21'	16'	10'	5'
8	24550	22910	19880	17000	14270	11690	10190	8790	7500	6310	5514	4164	2965	1914	1014	605	292.5	97.5
9	22420	20860	17980	15250	12670	10240	8830	7530	6340	5240	4524	3325	2275	1374	624	312	97.5	
10	20380	18900	16170	13590	11160	8880	7570	6360	5270	4280	3632	2580	1682	932	331.5	117	97.5	
11	18060	16670	14120	11720	9470	7370	6180	5090	4110	3230	2678	1808	1088	518	97.5	117	331.5	
12	16220	14900	12500	10250	8155	6200	5110	4120	3240	2460	1980	1260	690	270	97.5	312	624	
13	13090	11910	9780	7800	5970	4290	3370	2550	1850	1245	900	450	150	175.5	448.5	838.5	1326	
14	11500	10400	8410	6580	4900	3370	2555	1830	1227	720	450	150	150	423	793.5	1281	1866	
15	10060	9030	7200	5520	3990	2605	1885	1262	755	345	150	150	450	820.5	1288.5	1873	2556	
16	8770	7810	6130	4600	3220	1992	1368	842	432	120	150	450	900	1368	1933.5	2620	3396	
17	6950	6110	4670	3380	2240	1248	780	409.5	156	240	630	1170	1860	2484	3205.5	4044	4980	
18	5240	4524	3325	2275	1374	624	312	97.5										
19	4280	3632	2580	1682	932	331.5	117											
20	3230	2678	1808	1088	518	97.5												
21	2460	1980	1260	690	270													
22	1245	900	450	150														
23	720	450	150															
24	345	150																
25	120																	

Uniform Load 3000# per lin. Ft.

MOMENT TABLE
COOPER'S E-60 LOADING
TWO 213 TON ENGINES + 6000 LBS. PER FOOT.
MOMENT IN THOUSAND FOOT POUNDS FOR ONE RAIL.
LOADS IN THOUSANDS OF POUNDS FOR ONE RAIL.

load on the left of the section, one-half of the load on the panel under the joint being considered as part of the load on the left of the section.

The maximum shear in any panel of a truss will occur when the average load on the panel is equal to the average load on the entire bridge.

Wheel Loads, Bridge with Inclined Chords.—The criterion for maximum bending moment in a bridge with vertical posts is the same as for bridges with parallel chords.

For web members the criterion is that

$$P/L = P_2(1 + a/e)/l \qquad (3)$$

where P = total load on the bridge;
P_2 = load on the panel in question;
L = span of bridge;
l = panel length;
a = distance from left abutment to left end of panel in question;
e = distance from left abutment to intersection of top chord section of the panel produced and the lower chord. (The intersection is to the left and outside of the span.)

For the proof of the above criteria see Chapter VII.

For the calculation of the stresses in truss bridges due to wheel loads, see problem in Chapter XIII.

Moment Table.—A moment table for Cooper's E 60 loading is given in Table II. The use of the moment table is explained in detail on page 74.

CHAPTER IX.

Stresses in Portals.

Introduction.—Portal bracing is frequently used for bracing the sides of mill buildings and open sheds. Portal bracing is placed at the ends of through bridges in the planes of the end-posts to transfer the wind loads from the upper lateral system to the abutments, and also as sway bracing at intermediate posts. There are many forms of portal bracing in use, a few of the most common of which are shown in Fig. 1.

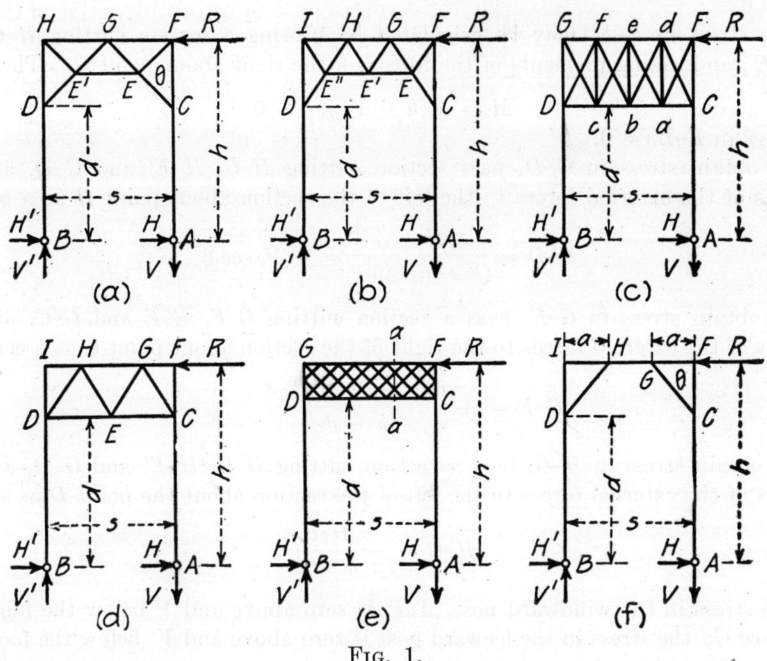

Fig. 1.

Portal bracing may be in separate panels of mill buildings or may be continuous. The columns may be hinged or fixed at the base in either case.

CASE I. STRESSES IN SIMPLE PORTALS: Columns Hinged.—The deflections of the columns in the portals shown in Fig. 1 are assumed to be equal and

$$H = H' = \tfrac{1}{2}R$$

Taking moments about the foot of the windward column

$$V' = -V = R \cdot h/s$$

Having found the external forces, the stresses in the members may be found by either algebraic or graphic methods.

Algebraic Solution.—*Portal* (*a*).—To obtain the stress in member *G–C*, (*a*) Fig. 1, pass a section cutting *G–F*, *E–F* and *G–C*, and take moments of the external forces to the right of the section about point *F* as a center.

$$G\text{–}C = -\frac{H\cdot h}{(h-d)\sin\theta} \tag{1}$$

But $H = \frac{1}{2}R$, and $(h-d)\sin\theta = \frac{1}{2}s\cdot\cos\theta$. Substituting these values in (1) we have

$$G\text{–}C = -\frac{R\cdot h,}{s\cdot\cos\theta} = -V\cdot\sec\theta \tag{2}$$

Resolving at *E* and *F* we have, stress in $E\text{–}F = 0$, and also stresses *E–E′* and $H\text{–}E' = 0$.

The stress in *E–E′* may be calculated by passing a section cutting *H–G*, *E′–G* and *E–E′*, and taking moments of the forces on the right about point *G*. Then

$$M = H\cdot h - V\cdot\tfrac{1}{2}s\cdot = 0 \tag{3}$$

and stress in $E\text{–}E' = 0$.

To obtain stress in *G–D*, pass section cutting *H–G*, *H–E′* and *G–D*, and take moments of the external forces to the left of the section about point *H* as a center.

$$G\text{–}D = \frac{H\cdot h}{(h-d)\sin\theta} = +V\cdot\sec\theta \tag{4}$$

To obtain stress in *G–F*, pass a section cutting *G–F*, *E–F* and *G–C*, and take moments of the external forces to the right of the section about point *C* as a center.

$$G\text{–}F = +\frac{R(h-d) + H\cdot d}{h-d} \tag{5}$$

To obtain stress in *H–G*, pass a section cutting *H–G*, *H–E′* and *G–D*, and take moments of the external forces to the left of the section about the point *D* as a center.

$$H\text{–}G = -\frac{H\cdot d}{h-d} \tag{6}$$

The stress in the windward post, *A–F*, is zero above and *V* below the foot of the knee brace *C*; the stress in the leeward post is zero above and *V′* below the foot of the knee brace *D*.

The shear in the posts is *H* below the foot of the knee brace, and above the foot of the knee brace is given by the formula

$$S = \frac{H\cdot d}{h-d} = \text{stress in } H\text{–}G \tag{7}$$

The maximum moment in the posts occurs at the foot of the knee braces *C* and *D*, and is

$$M = H\cdot d \tag{8}$$

For the actual stresses, moments and shears in a portal of this type, see Fig. 2.

Portal (*b*).—The stresses in portal (*b*) Fig. 1, are found in the same manner as in portal (*a*). The graphic solution of a similar portal with one more panel is given in Fig. 3, which see. It should be noted that all members are stressed in portals (*b*) and (*d*).

Portal (*c*).—The stresses in portal (*c*) Fig. 1, may be obtained (1) by separating the portal into two separate portals with simple bracing, the stresses found by calculating the separate simple portals with a load $= \frac{1}{2}R$ being combined algebraically, to give the stresses in the portal; or (2) by assuming that the stresses are all taken by the system of bracing in which the diagonal ties are in tension. The latter method is the one usually employed and is the simpler.

Maximum moment, shear, and stresses in the columns are given by the same formulas as in (*a*) Fig. 1.

Portal (*e*).—In portal (*e*) Fig. 1, the flanges G–F and D–C are assumed to take all the bending moment, and the lattice web bracing is assumed to take all the shear. The maximum compression in the upper flange G–F occurs at F, and is

$$G\text{–}F = + \frac{R(h - d) + H \cdot d}{h - d} \tag{9}$$

The maximum tension in the upper flange G–F is

$$G\text{–}F = - \frac{H \cdot d}{h - d} \tag{10}$$

The maximum stress in the lower flange D–C is

$$D\text{–}C = \pm \frac{H \cdot h}{h - d} \tag{11}$$

maximum tension occurring at C, and maximum compression occurring at D.

The maximum shear in the portal strut is V, which is assumed as taken equally by the lattice members cut by a section, as a–a.

Maximum moment, shear, and stresses in the columns are given by the same formulas as in (*a*) Fig. 1.

Portal (*f*).—The maximum moment in the portal strut I–F in (*f*) Fig. 1, occurs at H and G, and is

$$M = + H \cdot h - V \cdot a \tag{12}$$

The maximum direct stress in H–G is $+ H$, and in I–H is

$$I\text{–}H = - \frac{H \cdot d}{h - d} \tag{13}$$

The maximum stress in G–F is given by formula (5).

The maximum shear in girder I–F is equal to V. To calculate direct stress in I–D, take moments about H, and stress $I\text{–}D = (H \cdot h - V \cdot a) \div a = H \cdot h/a - V$. The stress in H–D is $(H \cdot h/a - V + V) \sec \theta = (H \cdot h/a) \sec. \theta$.

Portal strut I–F is designed as a girder to take the maximum moment, shear and direct stress.

Maximum moment, shear and stress in the columns below the knee brace are given by the same formulas as in (*a*) Fig. 1.

Graphic Solution.—To make the solution of the stresses statically determinate, replace the columns in the portal with trussed framework as in Fig. 2. The stresses in the interior members are not affected by the change and will be correctly given by graphic resolution.

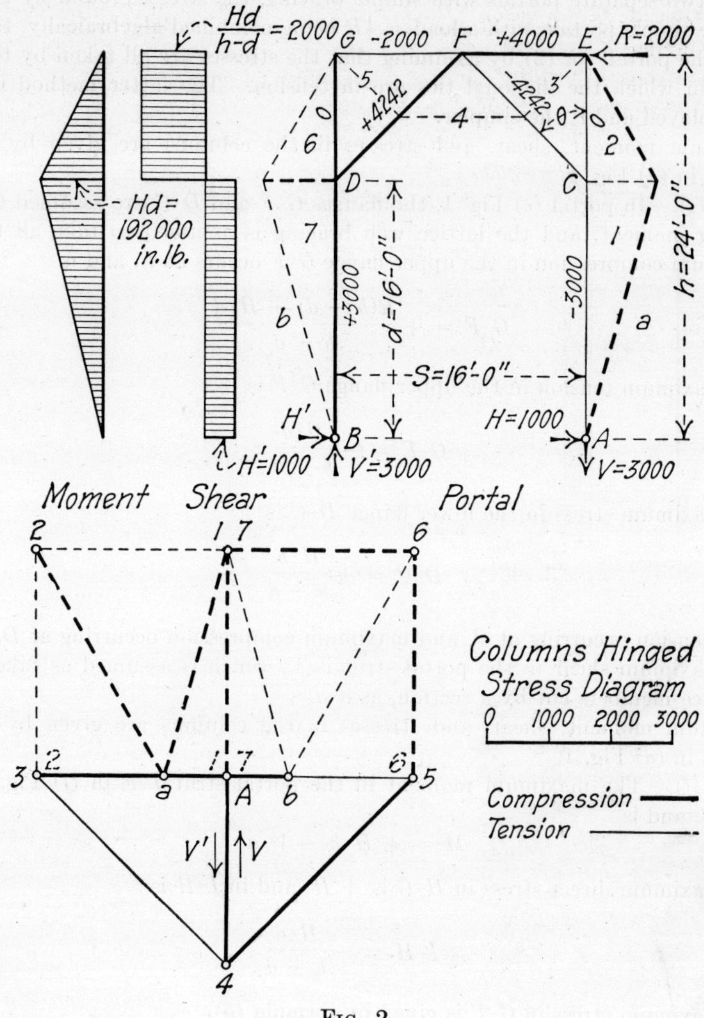

FIG. 2.

As before

$$H = H' = \tfrac{1}{2}R \qquad \text{and} \qquad V = -V' = \frac{R \cdot h}{s}$$

Having the calculated H, H', V, and V', the stresses are calculated by graphic resolution as follows: Beginning at the base of the column A, lay off A–a = H = 1,000 lb. acting to the right, and A–4 = V = 3,000 lb. acting downward. Then a–1 and 4–1 are the stresses in members a–1 and 4–1, respectively, heavy lines indicating compression and light lines tension. At joint in auxiliary truss to right of C the stress in 1–a is known and stresses in 1–2 and 2–a are found by closing the polygon. The stresses in the remaining members are found in like manner, taking joints C, E, F, etc., in order, and finally checking up at the base of the column B. The full lines in the stress diagram represent stresses in the portal; the dotted lines represent stresses in the auxiliary members or stresses in members due to auxiliary members, and are of no consequence. The shears and moments are shown in the diagram.

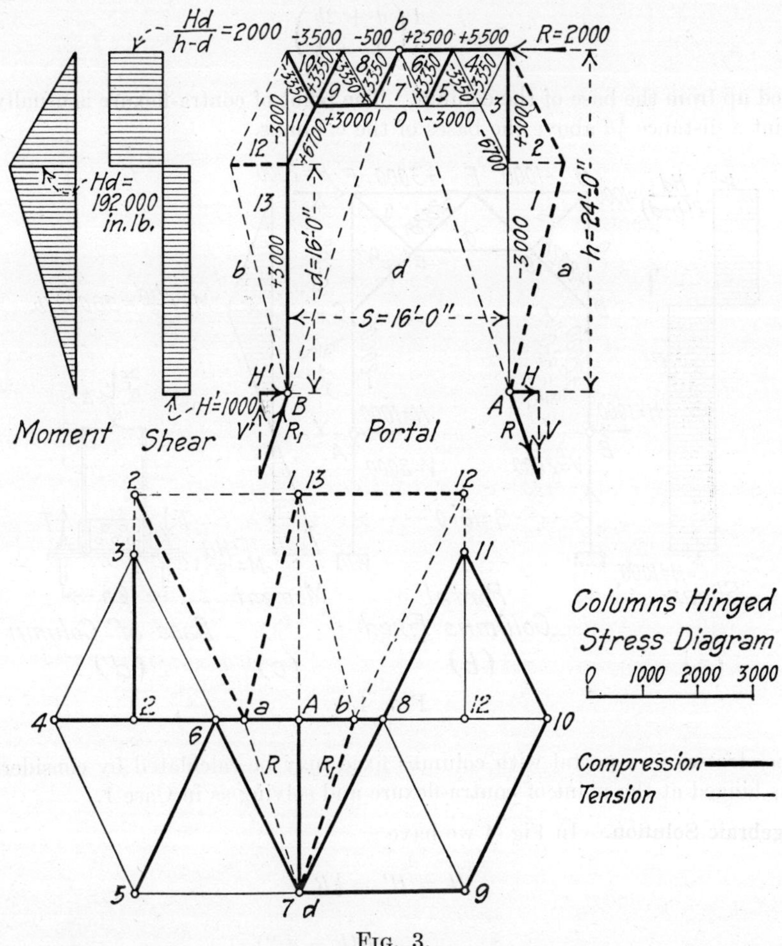

FIG. 3.

Simple Portal as a Three-Hinged Arch.—In a simple portal the resultant reactions and the external load R meet in a point at the middle of the top strut, and the portal then becomes a three-hinged arch (see Chapter XI), provided there is a joint at that point (point b, Fig. 3).

In Fig. 3 the reactions were calculated graphically and the stresses in the portal were calculated by graphic resolution. Full lines in the stress diagram represent required stresses in the members. Stresses 3–2 and 11–12 were determined by dropping verticals from points 3 and 11 to the load line 4–10.

CASE II. STRESSES IN SIMPLE PORTALS: Columns Fixed.—The calculation of the stresses in a portal with columns fixed at the base is similar to the calculation of stresses in a transverse bent with columns fixed at the base, for which see Chapter X. The point of contra-flexure is at the point

$$y_0 = \frac{d}{2}\left(\frac{d + 2h}{2d + h}\right) \tag{14}$$

measured up from the base of the column. The point of contra-flexure is usually taken at a point a distance $\frac{1}{2}d$ above the bases of the columns.

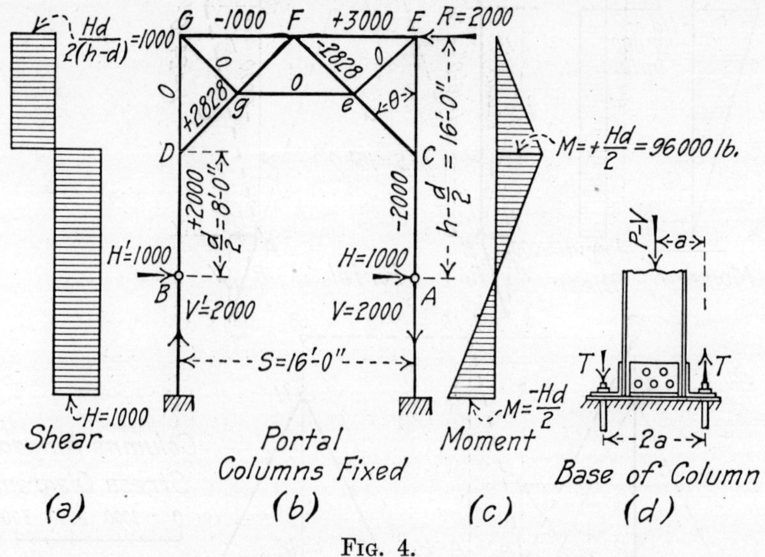

FIG. 4.

The stresses in a portal with columns fixed may be calculated by considering the columns hinged at the point of contra-flexure and solving as in Case 1.

Algebraic Solution.—In Fig. 4 we have

$$H = H' = \tfrac{1}{2}R$$

and

$$V = -V' = \frac{R(h - d/2)}{s}$$

Having found the reactions H and H', V and V', the stresses in the members are found by taking moments as in (*a*) Fig. 1, considering the columns as hinged at the point of contra-flexure.

The shear diagram for the columns is as shown in (*a*) and the moment diagram as in (*c*) Fig. 4.

Anchorage of Columns.—In order that the columns be fixed, the anchorage of each column must be capable of developing a resisting moment greater than the overturning moment $M = -\frac{1}{2}H \cdot d$, shown in (*c*) Fig. 4. The anchorage required on the wind-

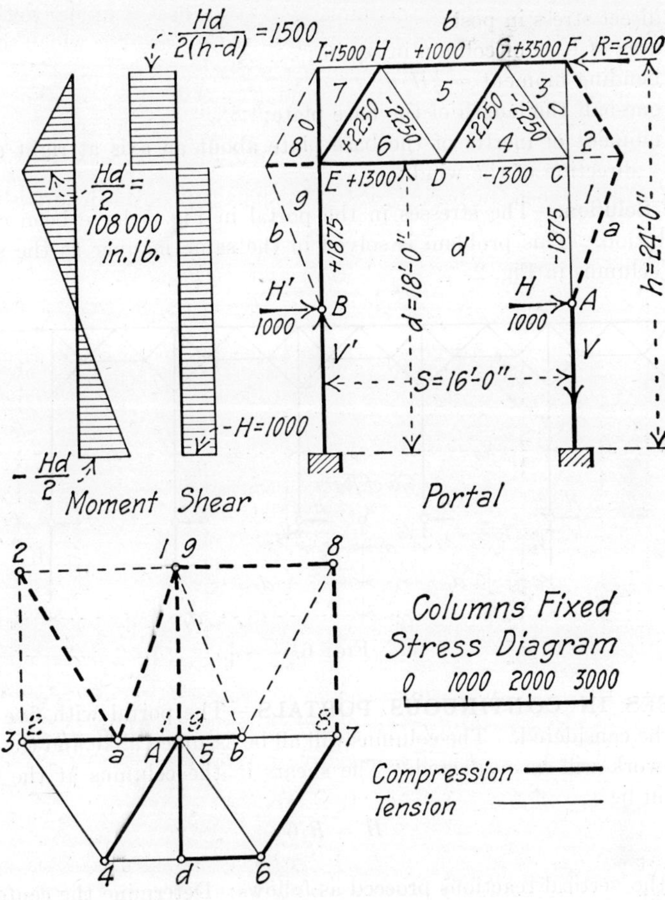

FIG. 5.

ward side is a maximum and may be calculated as follows: Let T be the tension in the windward anchor bolt, $2a$ be the distance center to center of anchor bolts, and P be the direct load on the column. Taking moments about the leeward anchor bolt we have

$$2T \cdot a - (P - V)a + \tfrac{1}{2}H \cdot d = 0$$

$$T = -H \cdot d/4a + \tfrac{1}{2}(P - V) \tag{15}$$

If the nuts on the anchor bolts are not screwed down tight, there will be a tendency for the column to rotate about the leeward edge of the base plate, and both anchor bolts will resist overturning.

The maximum pressure on the masonry will occur under the leeward edge of the base plate and will be

$$f = W/A + M \cdot c/I$$

where W = direct stress in post;
A = area of base of column in sq. in.;
M = bending moment = $\frac{1}{2}H \cdot d$;
c = one-half the length of the base plate;
I = moment of inertia of the base plate about an axis at right angles to the direction of the wind.

Graphic Solution.—The stresses in the portal in Fig. 5 have been calculated by graphic resolution. This problem is solved in the same manner as the simple portal with hinged columns in Fig. 2.

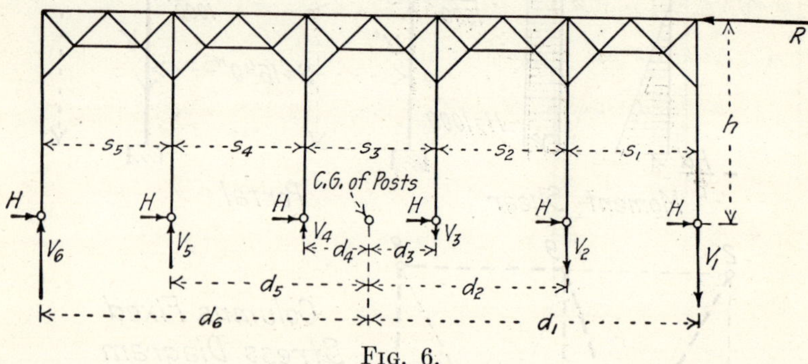

FIG. 6.

STRESSES IN CONTINUOUS PORTALS.—The portal with five bays shown in Fig. 6 will be considered. The columns will all be assumed alike and the deformation of the framework will be neglected. The shears in the columns at the base will be equal, and will be

$$H = R/6$$

To find the vertical reactions proceed as follows: Determine the center of gravity of the columns by taking moments about the base of one of the columns. Now there will be tension in each one of the columns on the windward side and compression in each one of the columns on the leeward side of the center of gravity of the columns. The sum of the moments of the reactions must be equal to the moment of the external wind load, R. The reactions at the bases of the columns will vary as the distance from the center of gravity and their moments will vary as the square of the distance from the center of gravity. Now if a equals the reaction of a column at a unit distance from the center of gravity, we will have $V_1 = -a \cdot d_1$, $V_2 = -a \cdot d_2$, $V_3 = -a \cdot d_3$, $V_4 = +a \cdot d_4$, $V_5 = +a \cdot d_5$, and $V_6 = +a \cdot d_6$ and the moment

$$M = a(d_1^2 + d_2^2 + d_3^2 + d_4^2 + d_5^2 + d_6^2) = R \cdot h$$

$$a\Sigma d^2 = R \cdot h$$

$$a = R \cdot h / \Sigma d^2 \qquad (16)$$

Having found a, the vertical reactions may be found.

Now having found the external forces H and V, the stresses can be calculated by either algebraic or graphic methods.

Stresses in a Double Portal.—To illustrate the general problem the stresses in a double portal are calculated by graphic resolution in Fig. 7. In this case

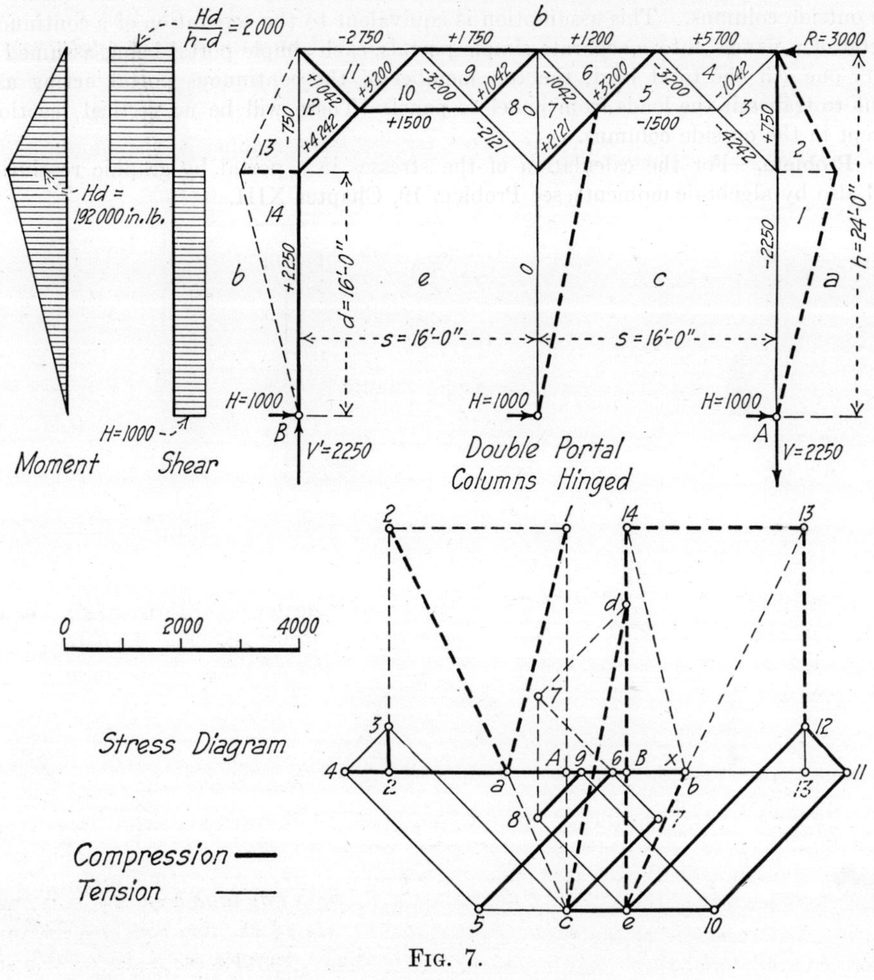

FIG. 7.

$$H = H = H = R/3 = 1{,}000 \text{ lb.}$$

and

$$V = -V' = R \cdot h/2s = 2{,}250 \text{ lb.}$$

The vertical reaction of the middle column is zero. By substituting the dotted members as shown, the stresses can be calculated as in the case of the simple portal. The full lines represent stresses in the portal members. The shear in the columns is equal and is H below, and $(H \cdot d)/(h - d)$ above the foot of the knee brace.

The maximum bending moment occurs at the foot of the knee brace and is

$$M = H \cdot d = 192{,}000 \text{ in-lb.}$$

Note.—In calculating the stresses in a building frame in Problem 7, Chapter XXII, the horizontal shears on the interior columns are taken equal to twice the shears on the outside columns. This assumption is equivalent to the separation of a continuous portal of n panels, into n separate simple portals, each simple portal being assumed to carry one nth the total load; the top member of the continuous portal acting as a strut to transmit the loads from panel to panel. There will be no vertical reactions except in the outside columns.

Problem.—For the calculation of the stresses in a portal by graphic resolution and also by algebraic moments, see Problem 19, Chapter XIII.

CHAPTER X.

Stresses in a Transverse Bent.

Introduction.—A transverse bent as used in shop or mill buildings consists of a roof truss supported on two columns and braced by diagonal knee braces joining the truss to the columns. The transverse bent is not statically determinate but is (1) a two-hinged arch if the columns are free to turn at the bases, or is (2) a fixed arch if the columns are fixed at the bases. The combination of columns that take bending with a framed truss makes the calculation of the true stresses a matter of considerable difficulty. In addition, in order to calculate the true stresses it is necessary to have the actual sizes of the members of a transverse bent. In view of the above it has been the custom for designers to use approximate methods for obtaining the stresses in a transverse bent. The methods given in this chapter were proposed by the author in the first edition of this book published in 1903. These methods have been checked by the author and others* by calculating the true stresses, assuming that the transverse bent is a statically indeterminate structure.

The results obtained by the approximate methods given in this chapter have been shown to be more accurate than for any other method proposed, and to give a safe and satisfactory design. The errors tend to compensate, and the combined stresses used in design are more accurate than are the stresses obtained for dead and wind loads, when considered separately.

If a flag pole carries a horizontal load at its top as in (*a*), Fig. 1; the load, P, will be transferred to the base of the pole by means of a shear P at every section of the pole, and a bending moment $M_1 = P \cdot h$ at the base of the flag pole. There will be no vertical reaction at the base of the flag pole.

If a rigid truss is supported on two flag poles with identical sections as in (*b*), Fig. 1; the load, P, will be carried to the base of the flag poles by means of a shear $\frac{1}{2}P$ at every point in each flag pole, and a bending moment at the base of each flag pole of $M_1 = M_2 = \frac{1}{2}P \cdot h$. If the truss is not rigid but decreases in length the shear in the windward flag pole will be greater than in the leeward flag pole, and the shears will vary as the deflections of the tops of the flag poles. There will be no vertical reactions at the bases of the flag poles.

If the load P is carried to the bases of the columns by means of a transverse bent as in (*c*), Fig. 1; with columns free to turn at the base, there will be shears $H_1 = H_2 = \frac{1}{2}P$ in each column if the truss is rigid. The vertical reactions will be equal but opposite in direction, and will be $V_1 = -V_2 = P \cdot h/s$.

If the load P is carried to the bases of the columns by means of a transverse bent as in (*d*) Fig. 1, with columns fixed at the base, there will be shears H_1 and H_2 in the columns, moments M_1 and M_2 at the bases, and vertical reactions V_1 and V_2 at the

* "An investigation of the Stresses in the Transverse Bent for Steel Mill Buildings," by C. S. Sperry; Proceedings of the Colorado Scientific Society, Vol. XI, pp. 253–268.

bases in the windward and leeward columns, respectively. The moments in each column will vary from $+H_2(d - y_0)$ at the foot of the knee brace to $H_2 \cdot y_0$ at the base of the column, with a point of contraflexure at a distance y_0 above the base of the column. The transverse bent in (*d*) is a combination as shown in (*e*), of a transverse bent with columns free to turn as in (*c*) and two flag poles as in (*b*). The moment at the base of the leeward column is equal to the shear in the column multiplied by y_0. The vertical reaction is equal to, $V_1 = P(h - y_0)/s$.

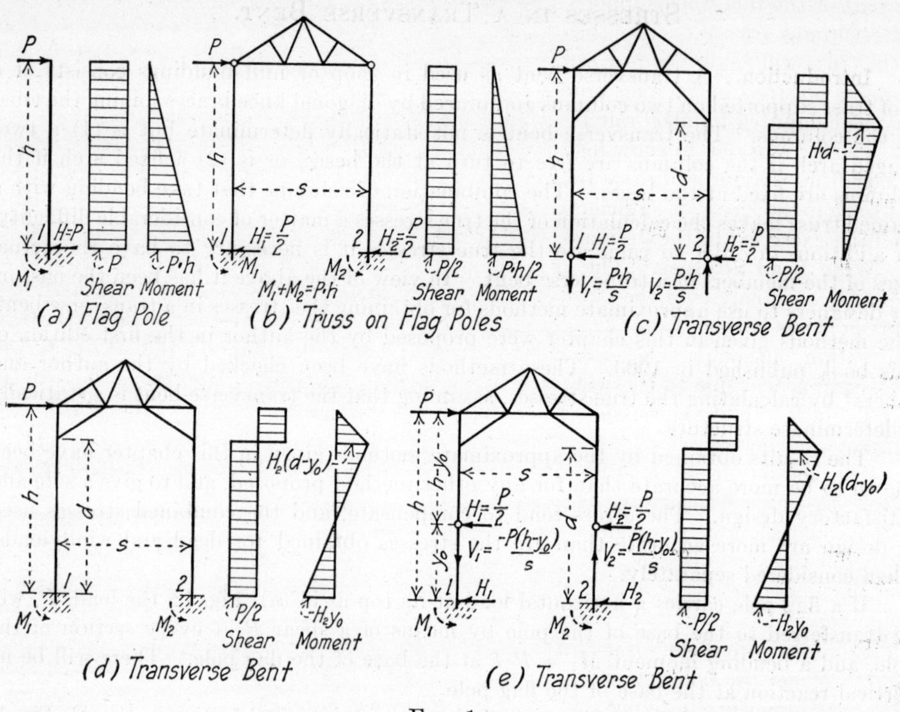

FIG. 1.

If the truss is not rigid, or the columns are not of identical section the shears will not be equal.

The transverse bent with columns free to turn as in (*c*), Fig. 1, is a two-hinged arch and the true stresses can only be calculated by taking the deformations of the members into account as in Chapter XX. When the true shears in the columns are calculated as in Chapter XX, the problem becomes statically determinate.

The transverse bent with columns fixed at the base as in (*d*) Fig. 1 is a fixed arch. This structure has three redundant members, or three more members than are necessary for static equilibrium. If the two knee braces and the middle panel in the lower chord of the truss be removed the structure becomes a three-hinged arch, and is statically determinate. The bending moments M_1 and M_2 and the shear in one column may also be taken as the three redundant or extra stresses. If the shears in the columns are known and the point of contra-flexure in each column is known, the moments M_1 and M_2 can be calculated and the structure in (*d*) becomes statically determinate.

KETCHUM'S APPROXIMATE SOLUTION. The following approximate solution for the calculation of the stresses in transverse bents have been generally used since first published in 1903.

Dead and Snow Load Stresses.—The stresses due to the dead load in the trusses of a transverse bent are assumed to be the same as if the trusses were supported on solid walls. The stresses in the supporting columns are due to the dead load of the roof and the part of the side walls supported by the columns, and are direct compressive stresses if the columns are not fixed at the top. If the columns are fixed at the top the deflection of the truss will cause bending stress in the columns. It is assumed that the dead load produces no stress in the knee braces of a bent of the type shown in Fig. 2. The stresses may be computed by algebraic or graphic methods.

The stresses due to snow load are found in the same way as the dead load stresses. In localities having a heavy fall of snow freezing and thawing often causes icicles to form on the eaves of sufficient weight to tear off the cornice, unless particular care has been exercised in the design of this detail.

Wind Load Stresses.—The analysis of the stresses in a bent due to wind loads is similar to the analysis of the stresses in the portal of a bridge. The external wind force is taken (1) as horizontal or (2) as normal to all surfaces. The first is the more common assumption, although the second is more nearly correct. For a comparison of the stresses in a bent due to the wind acting horizontal and normal, see Figs. 5, 6, 7 and 8 and Table I. In the discussion which immediately follows, the wind force will be assumed to act horizontally.

The magnitude of the wind stresses in the trusses, knee braces and columns will depend (*a*) upon whether the bases of the columns are fixed or free to turn, (*b*) upon whether the columns are rigidly fixed to the truss at the top, and (*c*) upon the knee brace and truss connections. Of the numerous assumptions that might be made, only two, the most probable, will be considered, viz.: (I) columns pin-connected (free to turn) at the base and top, and (II) columns fixed at the base and pin-connected at the top.

Columns in mill buildings are usually fixed by means of heavy bases and anchor bolts. Where the columns support heavy loads the dead load stress in the columns will assist somewhat in fixing them. Where the dead load stress plus algebraically the vertical component of the wind stress in the column, multiplied by one-half the width of the base of the column parallel to the direction of the wind, is greater than the bending moment developed at the base of the leeward column when the columns are considered as fixed, the columns will be fixed without anchor bolts (see Chapter IX, Fig. 4). In any case the resultant moment is all that will be taken by the anchor bolts. The dead load stresses in mill buildings are seldom sufficient to give material assistance in fixing the columns. Unless care is used in anchoring columns it is best to design mill buildings for columns hinged at the base.

The general problem of stresses in a transverse bent for Case I and Case II, in which the stresses and forces are determined by algebraic methods, will now be considered. The application of the general problem will be further explained by the graphic solution of a particular problem.

ALGEBRAIC CALCULATION OF STRESSES. Case I. Columns Free to Turn at Base and Top.—In Fig. 2, $H = H' = \frac{1}{2}W$ = horizontal reaction at the base of the column due to external wind force, W.

$V = -V' = W \cdot l/2s$ = vertical reaction at base of column due to the wind force, W.

The wind produces bending in the columns, and also the direct stresses V and V'. Maximum bending occurs at the foot of the knee brace and is equal to $(H - W_7)d$ on the windward side, and $H' \cdot d$ on the leeward side. These bending moments are the same as the bending moments in a simple beam supported at both ends and loaded with

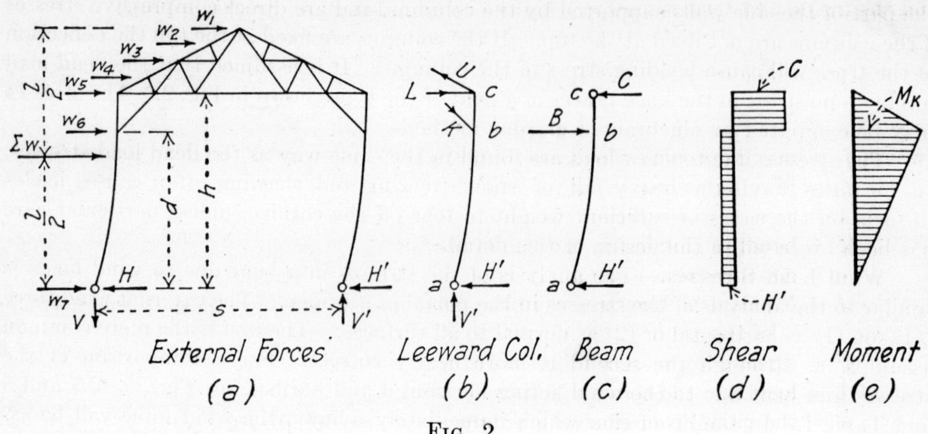

FIG. 2.

a concentrated load at the point of maximum moment. Since the maximum moment occurs at the foot of the knee brace in the leeward column, we will consider only that side. We will assume that the leeward column (*b*), Fig. 2, acts as a simple beam with reactions H' and C and a concentrated load B, as in (*c*). The reaction C and load B will now be calculated.

From the fundamental equation of equilibrium, summation horizontal forces equal zero, we have

$$B = H' + C \tag{1}$$

Taking moments about b, we have

$$C(h - d) = H' \cdot d$$

$$C = \frac{H' \cdot d}{h - d} \tag{2}$$

The stresses K, U and L can be computed by means of the following formulas:

$$K = B \cdot \text{cosecant } m \tag{3}$$

where m = angle knee brace makes with column;

$$U = (V' - K \cdot \cos m) \text{ cosecant } n \tag{4}$$

where n = angle of pitch of roof; and

$$L = C + U \cdot \cos n \tag{5}$$

In calculating the corresponding stresses on the windward side, the wind components acting at the points (*a*), (*b*) and (*c*) must be subtracted from H, B and C.

The shear in the leeward column is equal to H' below and C above the foot of the knee brace, (*d*) Fig. 2.

The moment in the column is shown in (*e*), Fig. 2, and is a maximum at the foot of the knee brace and is, $M = H' \cdot d$.

The maximum fibre stress due to wind moment and direct loading in the columns will occur at the foot of the knee brace in the leeward column, and will be compression on the inside and tension on the outside fibres, and is given by the formula*

$$f_2 + f_1 = \frac{P}{A} + \frac{M \cdot c}{I \pm \dfrac{P \cdot h^2}{10E}} \tag{6}$$

where f_1 = maximum fibre stress due to flexure;
f_2 = fibre stress due to direct load P;
A = area of cross-section of column in square inches;
M = bending moment in inch-pounds = $H' \cdot d$;
c = distance from neutral axis to extreme fibre of column in inches;
I = Moment of Inertia of column about an axis at right angles to the direction of the wind;
P = direct compression in the column in pounds;
h = length of the column in inches;
E = the modulus of elasticity of steel = 30,000,000 lb. per sq. in.;
$\dfrac{P \cdot h^2}{10E}$ is minus when P is compression and plus when P is tension.

The maximum compressive wind stress is added to the direct dead and minimum snow load compression and governs the design of the column.

Having the stresses K, U, and L, the remaining stresses in the truss can be obtained by ordinary algebraic or graphic methods.

For a simple graphic solution of the stresses in a bent for Case I, in which these stresses are computed graphically, see Fig. 5 for wind horizontal, and Fig. 7 for wind normal to all surfaces.

Case II. Columns Fixed at the Base.—With columns fixed at the base the columns may be (1) hinged at the top, or (2) rigidly fixed to the truss.

(1) *Columns fixed at the base and hinged at the top.*—It will be further assumed that the deflections at the foot of the knee brace and the top of the column, Fig. 3, are equal. In Fig. 3 we have as in Case I

$$H = H' = \tfrac{1}{2}W \tag{7}$$

V and V' are not as easily found as in Case I, but will be calculated presently.

The leeward column will be considered and will have horizontal external forces acting on it as shown in (*c*) Fig. 3. For convenience we will consider the leeward column as a beam fixed at a and acted upon by the horizontal forces B and C as shown in (*c*) Fig. 3, the deflection of the points b and c being equal by hypothesis.

From the fundamental condition of equilibrium, summation horizontal forces equal zero, we have

* This formula was first deduced by Prof. J. B. Johnson. For deduction of the formula see Chapter XII.

$$B = H' + C \tag{8}$$

To obtain B and C a second equation is necessary.

From the theory of flexure we have for the bending moment in the column at any point y, where the origin is taken at the base of the column, when $y \leqq d$

$$M = E \cdot I \frac{d^2x}{dy^2} = B(d - y) - C(h - y) \tag{9}$$

Integrating (9) between the limits $y = 0$ and $y = d$, we have

$$E \cdot I \frac{dx}{dy} = \left(B \cdot d \cdot y - \frac{B \cdot y^2}{2} - C \cdot h \cdot y + \frac{C \cdot y^2}{2} + F \right)_{y = o}^{y = d}$$

$$= - C(h \cdot d - \tfrac{1}{2}d^2) + \tfrac{1}{2}B \cdot d^2 \tag{10}$$

Now (10) equals $E \cdot I$ times the angular change in the direction of the neutral axis of the column from $y = o$ to $y = d$.

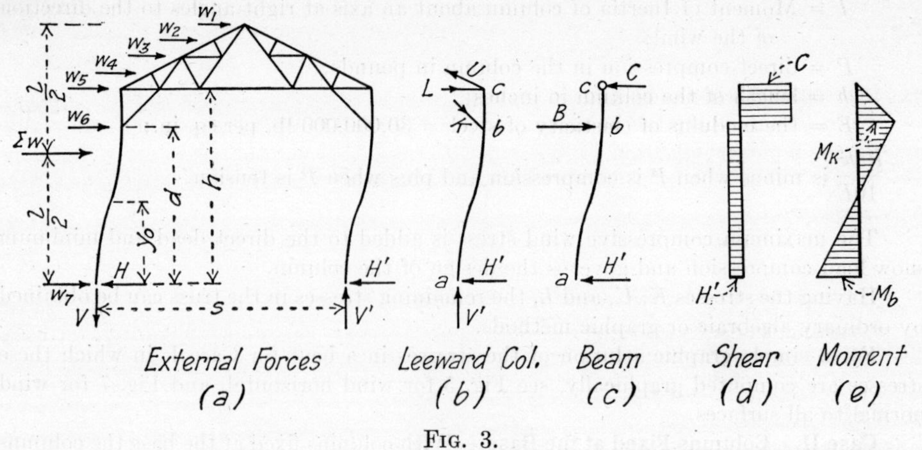

FIG. 3.

When $y \geqq d$, we have

$$M = E \cdot I \frac{d^2x}{dy^2} = - C(h - y) \tag{11}$$

Integrating (11) we have

$$E \cdot I \frac{dx}{dy} = - C \cdot h \cdot y + \tfrac{1}{2}C \cdot y^2 + F_2 \tag{12}$$

Now (12) equals $E \cdot I$ times the change in direction of the neutral axis of the column at any point from $y = d$ to $y = h$.

To determine constant F_2 in (12) we have the condition that the angle of slope at $y = d$ must be the same whether determined from equation (10) or equation (12). Equating (10) and (12) and making $y = d$, we have

$$F_2 = \tfrac{1}{2}B \cdot d^2$$

Substituting this value of F_2 in (12) we have

$$E \cdot I \frac{dx}{dy} = - C \cdot h \cdot y + \tfrac{1}{2} C \cdot y^2 + \tfrac{1}{2} B \cdot d^2 \qquad (13)$$

Integrating (13) between the limits $y = d$ and $y = h$, we have

$$E \cdot I \cdot x = \left(- \frac{C \cdot h \cdot y^2}{2} + \frac{C \cdot y^3}{6} + \frac{B \cdot d^2 \cdot y}{2} \right)_{y = d}^{y = h}$$

$$= C \left(\frac{h \cdot d^2}{2} - \frac{d^3}{6} - \frac{h^3}{3} \right) + B \left(\frac{d^2 \cdot h}{2} - \frac{d^3}{2} \right) \qquad (14)$$

Now (14) equals $E \cdot I$ times the deflection of the column from $y = d$ to $y = h$, which equals zero by hypothesis.

Solving (14) we have

$$\frac{C}{B} = \frac{3d^2 \cdot h - 3d^3}{- 3h \cdot d^2 + d^3 + 2h^3}$$

$$= \frac{3d^2}{2h^2 + 2d \cdot h - d^2} \qquad (15)$$

In a beam fixed at one end there is a point of inflection at some point, between $y = o$ and $y = d$, where the bending moment equals zero. Now if y_0 equals the value of y for the point of inflection, we have from (9)

$$B(d - y_0) = C(h - y_0)$$

and

$$\frac{C}{B} = \frac{d - y_0}{h - y_0} \qquad (16)$$

Equating the second members of equations (15) and (16) and solving for y_0, we have

$$y_0 = \frac{d}{2} \left(\frac{d + 2h}{2d + h} \right) \qquad (17)$$

For the derivation of this formula by Area Moments, see Chapter XIV.

To find the relations between y_0 and d, substitute h in terms of d in (17) and solve for y_0.

For

$$d = \tfrac{1}{2} h, \qquad y_0 = 5d/8$$

$$d = 2h/3, \qquad y_0 = 4d/7$$

$$d = h, \qquad y_0 = \tfrac{1}{2} d \, *$$

Solving (8) and (15) for C, we have

$$C = \frac{H'}{2} \times \frac{3d^2}{(h - d)(h + 2d)} \qquad (18)$$

To find the moment M_b' at the base of the leeward column, we have from (9)

$$M_b' = B \cdot d - C \cdot h$$

* For column fixed at top. If column is pin-connected at top, $y_0 = h$.

8

Substituting the value of B given in (8) we have

$$M_b' = H'\cdot d + C\cdot d - C\cdot h \tag{19}$$

Eliminating h and d by means of (17) and (18) we have finally

$$M_b' = H'\cdot y_0 \tag{20}$$

In like manner it can be shown that the moment at the base of the windward column is

$$M_b = H\cdot y_0 - \frac{w\cdot d^2}{8} \tag{21}$$

where w equals the wind load per foot of height.

To find V, we will take moments about the leeward column. The moments M_b' and M_b at the bases of the columns respectively, resist overturning and we have

$$V = -V' = \left(\frac{w\cdot l^2}{2} - M_b' - M_b\right)\Big/ s$$

and since

$$H = \frac{w\cdot l}{2}$$

$$V = \left(H\cdot l - 2H\cdot y_0 + \frac{w\cdot d^2}{8}\right)\Big/ s \tag{22}$$

Now if $\frac{1}{2}d$ is taken equal to y_0, we have after transposing

$$V = -V' = (2H - w\cdot y_0)\left(\frac{l - y_0}{2}\right)\Big/ s \tag{23}$$

It will be seen that (23) is the same value of V and V' that we would obtain if the bent were hinged at the point of contra-flexure.

From (20) and (23) it will be seen that we may consider the columns as hinged at the point of contra-flexure and solve the problem as in Case I, taking into account the wind above the point of contra-flexure only. The maximum shear in the column is shown in (d) Fig. 3.

The maximum positive moment occurs at the foot of the leeward knee brace and is $M_k = H(d - y_0)$; the maximum negative moment occurs at the base of the leeward column and is equal to $M_b' = H\cdot y_0$.

The maximum fibre stress occurs at the foot of the knee brace, and is given by the formula

$$f_2 + f_1 = \frac{P}{A} + \frac{M\cdot c}{I \pm \dfrac{P\cdot h^2}{10E}} \tag{24}$$

The nomenclature being the same as for (6) except h, which is the distance in inches from the point of contra-flexure to the top of the column.

(2) *Columns fixed at the base and top.*—In this case it can be seen by inspection that the point of inflection is at a point $y_0 = \frac{1}{2}d$, and we have for this case

$$B = H' + C \tag{25}$$

$$M_b' = \frac{H' \cdot d}{2} = M_k \tag{26}$$

$$C = \frac{H' \cdot d}{2(h - d)} \tag{27}$$

It is difficult to realize the exact conditions in either (1) or (2), in Case II, and it is probable that when an attempt is made to fix columns at the base, the actual conditions lie some place between (1) and (2). It would therefore seem reasonable to assume the minimum value, $y_0 = \frac{1}{2}d$ as the best value to use in practice. This assumption is commonly made and will be made in the problems which follow.

Having the external forces H', B, C and V', the stresses K, U and L are computed by formulas (3), (4) and (5). The remaining stresses in the truss can then be computed by the ordinary algebraic or graphic methods.

For a simple graphic solution of this problem, where the external forces B and C are not computed, see Fig. 6 and Fig. 8.

Maximum Stresses.—It is not probable that the maximum snow and wind loads will ever come on the building at the same time, and it is therefore not necessary to design the structure for the sum of the maximum stresses due to dead load, snow load and wind load. A common method is to combine the dead load stresses with the snow or the wind load stresses that will produce maximum stresses in the members. It is, however, the practice of the author to consider that a heavy sleet may be on the roof at the time of a heavy wind, and to design the structure for the maximum stresses caused by dead and snow load; dead load, minimum snow load and wind load; or dead load and wind load. It should be noted that the maximum reversals occur when the dead and wind load are acting. For a comparison of the stresses due to the different combinations see Table II.

A common method of computing the stresses in a truss of the Fink type for small steel frame mill buildings is to use an equivalent uniform vertical dead load; the knee braces and the members affected directly by the knee braces being designed according to the judgment of the engineer. This method is satisfactory and expeditious when used by an experienced man, but like other short cuts is dangerous when used by the inexperienced. For a comparison of the stresses in a 60-foot Fink truss by the exact and the approximate method above, see Table II.

Stresses in End Framing.—The external wind force on an end bent will be one-half what it would be on an intermediate transverse bent, and the shear in the columns may be taken as equal to the total external wind force divided by the number of columns in the braced panels. The stresses in the diagonal rods in the end framing will then be equal to the external wind force H, divided by the number of braced panels, multiplied by the secant of the angle the diagonal rod makes with a vertical line. (For analysis of portal bracing see Chapter IX.)

Bracing in the Upper Chord and Sides.—The intensity of the wind pressure is taken the same on the ends as on the sides, and the wind loads are applied at the bracing connection points along the end rafters and the corner columns. The shear transferred by each braced panel is equal to the total shear divided by the number of braced panels. The stresses in the diagonals in each braced panel are computed by applying wind loads at the points above referred to, the wind loads being equal to the total wind loads divided by the number of panels. The stresses are computed as in a cantilever truss. The bracing in the plane of the lower chord is designed to prevent undue deflection of the end columns and to brace the lower chords of the trusses. All wind braces should be designed for, say, 5,000 pounds initial stress in each member, and the struts and connections should be proportioned to take the resulting stresses.

It should be noted that a mill building can be braced so as to be rigid without knee braces if the bracing be made sufficiently strong.

GRAPHIC CALCULATION OF STRESSES.—Data.—To illustrate the method of calculating the stresses in a transverse bent by graphic methods, the following data for a transformer building similar to one designed by the author will be taken.

The building will consist of a rigid steel frame covered with corrugated steel and will have the following dimensions: Length of building, 80′ 0″; width of building, 60′ 0″; height of columns, 20′ 0″; pitch of truss, $\frac{1}{4}$ (6″ in 12″); total height of building, 35′ 0″; the trusses will be spaced 16′ 0″ center to center. See Fig. 4. The trusses will be riveted Fink trusses. Purlins will be placed at the panel points of the trusses and will be spaced for a normal roof load of 30 lb. per square foot. The roof covering will consist of No. 20 corrugated steel with $2\frac{1}{2}$-inch corrugations, laid with 6-inch end laps and two corrugations side lap, with anti-condensation lining (see Chapter XXVII). The side covering will consist of an outside covering of No. 22 corrugated steel with $2\frac{1}{2}$-inch corrugations, laid with 4-inch end laps and one corrugation side lap; and an inside lining of No. 24 corrugated steel with $1\frac{1}{4}$-inch corrugations, laid with 4-inch end laps and one corrugation side lap. For additional warmth two layers of tar paper will be put inside of the lining. Three 36-inch Star ventilators placed on the ridge of the roof will be used for ventilation. The general arrangement of the framing and bracing will be as in Fig. 1, Chapter XXV.

The approximate weight of the roof per square foot of horizontal projection will be as follows:

Trusses	3.6 lb. per sq. ft.
Purlins and Bracing	3.0 " " " "
Corrugated Steel	2.4 " " " "
Roof Lining	1.0 " " " "
Total	10.0 " " " "

The maximum snow load will be taken at 20 pounds, and the minimum snow load at 10 pounds per square foot of horizontal projection of roof.

The wind load will be taken at 20 pounds per square foot on a vertical projection for the sides and ends of the building, 20 pounds per square foot on a vertical surface when the wind is considered as acting horizontally on the vertical projection of the roof, and 30 pounds per square foot on a vertical surface when the wind is considered as acting normal to the roof.

The stresses in an intermediate transverse bent will be calculated for the following:

CASE 1. Permanent dead and snow loads.

CASE 2. A horizontal wind load of 20 pounds per square foot on the sides and vertical projections of the roof, with the columns hinged at the base.

CASE 3. Same wind load as in Case 2, with columns fixed at the base.

CASE 4. A horizontal wind load of 20 pounds per square foot on the sides, and the normal component of a horizontal wind load of 30 pounds per square foot on the roof, with columns hinged at the base.

CASE 5. Same wind load as in Case 4, with columns fixed at the base.

Case 1. Permanent Dead and Snow Load Stresses.—On account of the limited size of the stress diagram the secondary members have been omitted and the loads

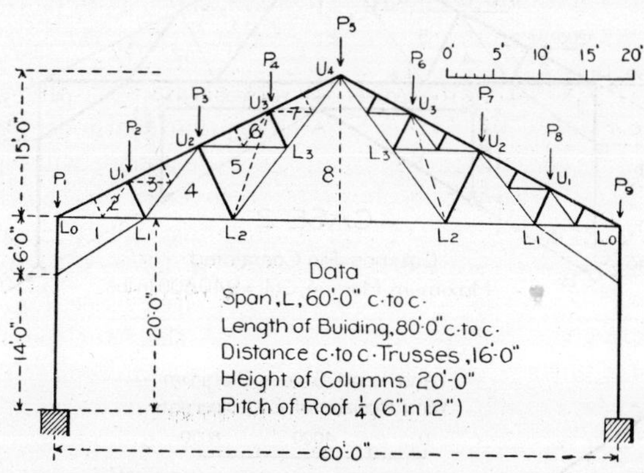

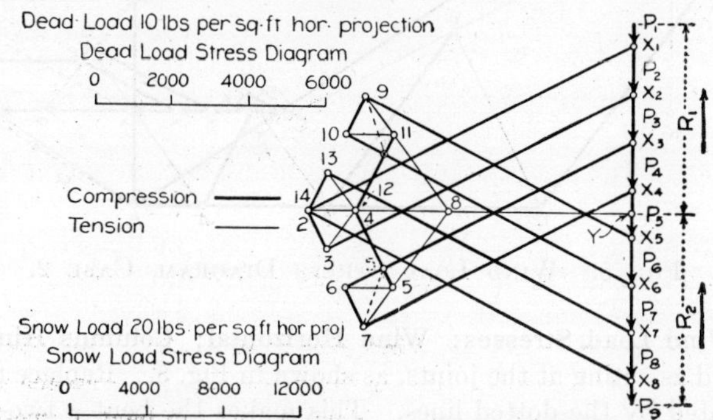

FIG. 4. DEAD AND SNOW LOAD STRESS DIAGRAM.

applied as shown in Fig. 4. The loads producing stresses in the truss are laid off to the prescribed scale, x_1–y being the left, and y–x_8 the right reaction. The stresses are calculated as follows: Beginning with the left reaction, x_1–y, draw lines through x_1 and y, parallel to the upper and lower chords of the truss, respectively, and the line x_1–2 will represent the compressive stress in the member x_1–2 and y–2 will represent the tensile stress in the member y–2 to the scale of the stress diagram.

Calculate the stresses in the remaining members in like manner, being careful to take the members in order around a joint in completing any polygon. The indeterminate case at the joint U_2, can be solved by calculating the stress in 5–6 and substituting it in the diagram, or by substituting an auxiliary member as shown. Compression and tension in the truss and stress diagram in Fig. 4 are indicated by heavy and light lines respectively.

The stress in each column is equal to one-half the sum of the vertical loads, plus the load carried directly by the column.

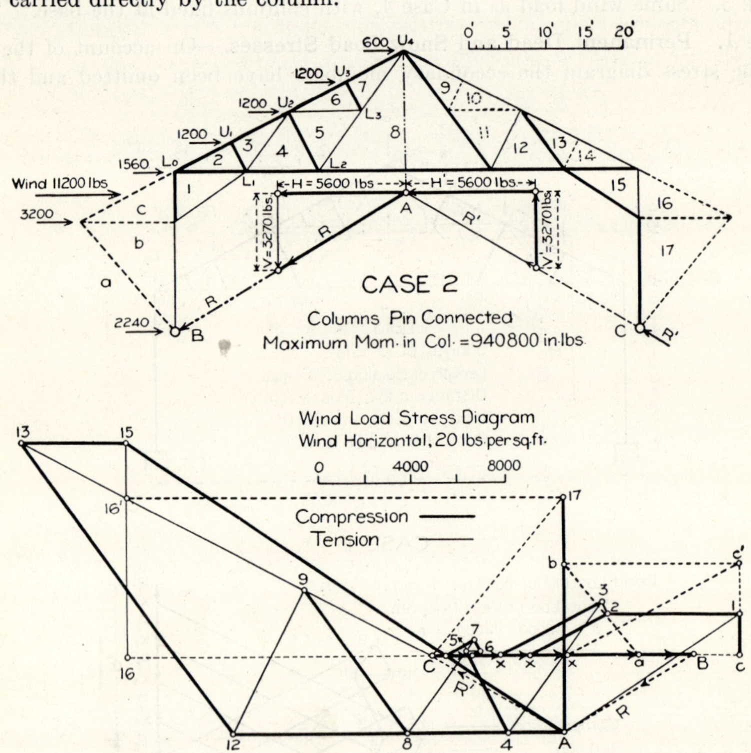

FIG. 5. WIND LOAD STRESS DIAGRAM, CASE 2.

Case 2. Wind Load Stresses: Wind Horizontal; Columns Hinged.—The wind will be considered as acting at the joints, as shown in Fig. 5. Replace the columns with trusses as indicated by the dotted lines. This makes the bent a two-hinged arch (see Chapter XX), and the stresses will be statically determinate as soon as the horizontal reactions H and H' at the bases of the columns, have been determined. The usual assumption in mill buildings and portals of bridges is that $H = H' = \frac{1}{2}W$ where W = the horizontal component of the external wind force. To calculate V and V' graphically, produce the line of resultant wind until it intersects a vertical line through the center of the truss, and connect the intersection A with the bases of the columns B and C. From A lay off $H = H' = \frac{1}{2}W$, as shown in Fig. 5, and complete the triangles by drawing vertical lines through the ends of these lines. The vertical closing lines will be $V = -V'$, as shown in Fig. 5.

The stresses are calculated as follows: Beginning with the foot of the column B, lay off the dotted line A–B = R. At B, lay off the load a–B = 2,240 lb.; through a

draw a line parallel to auxiliary truss member a–b, and through A draw a line parallel to the column b–A, completing the polygon A–B–a–b.

The line a–b in the stress diagram will be the compression in the auxiliary member a–b, and A–b will be the tension in the column A–b. It should be noted that V is equal to the algebraic sum of the vertical components of the stresses in a–b and A–b. Next lay off x–a = 3,200 lb. and complete the polygon x–c'–b–a by drawing lines through

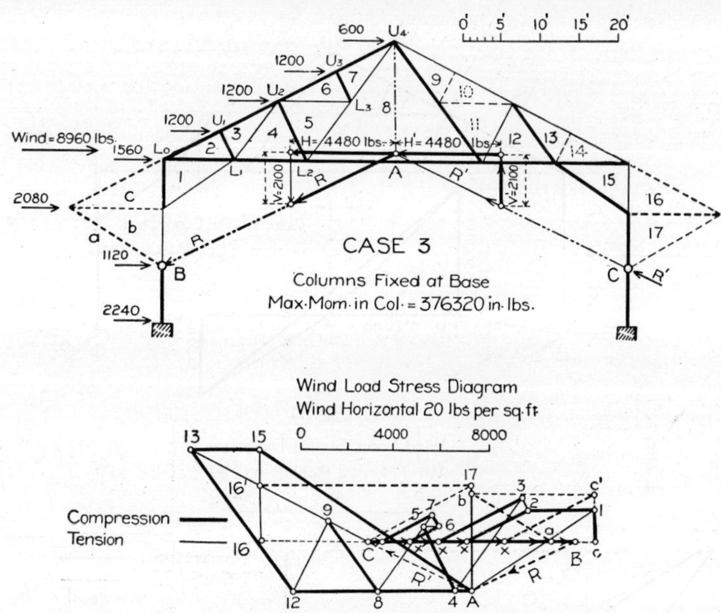

FIG. 6. WIND LOAD STRESS DIAGRAM, CASE 3.

x and b parallel to the auxiliary truss members x–c and b–c respectively. In like manner determine the stresses at the foot of the knee brace by constructing the polygon c'–b–A–1; and at the top of the column by constructing the polygon x–x–c'–1–2, etc., until the diagram is checked up at C with C–A = R'. The indeterminate case at the joint U_2, can be solved by computing the stress in 5–6 (component due to stress in 6–7), and substituting it in the diagram, or by substituting an auxiliary member.

The stresses in the auxiliary members are represented by dotted lines and are of no value in designing the bent. It should be noted that the auxiliary members do not affect the stresses in the trusses and knee braces, which are correctly given in the stress diagram.

The maximum stress in the knee brace A–15 is compression, and occurs on the leeward side.

The maximum shear in the leeward column below the knee brace is H' = 5,600 lb.; the maximum shear above the knee brace is 13,100 lb. The maximum moment occurs at the foot of the knee brace and is $H' \times 14 \times 12$ = 940,800 in.-lb.

Case 3. Wind Load Stresses: Wind Horizontal; Columns Fixed at Base.—This is Case 2 with the base of the column hinged at the point of contra-flexure. In calculating H and V, Fig. 6, the wind above the point of contra-flexure only (see formula (23)) produces stresses in the bent. The value of fixing the columns at the base is seen by comparing the stresses in Case 2 with those in Case 3, both being drawn to the same scale. Maximum shear in the leeward column below the knee brace is $H' = 4{,}480$ lb.;

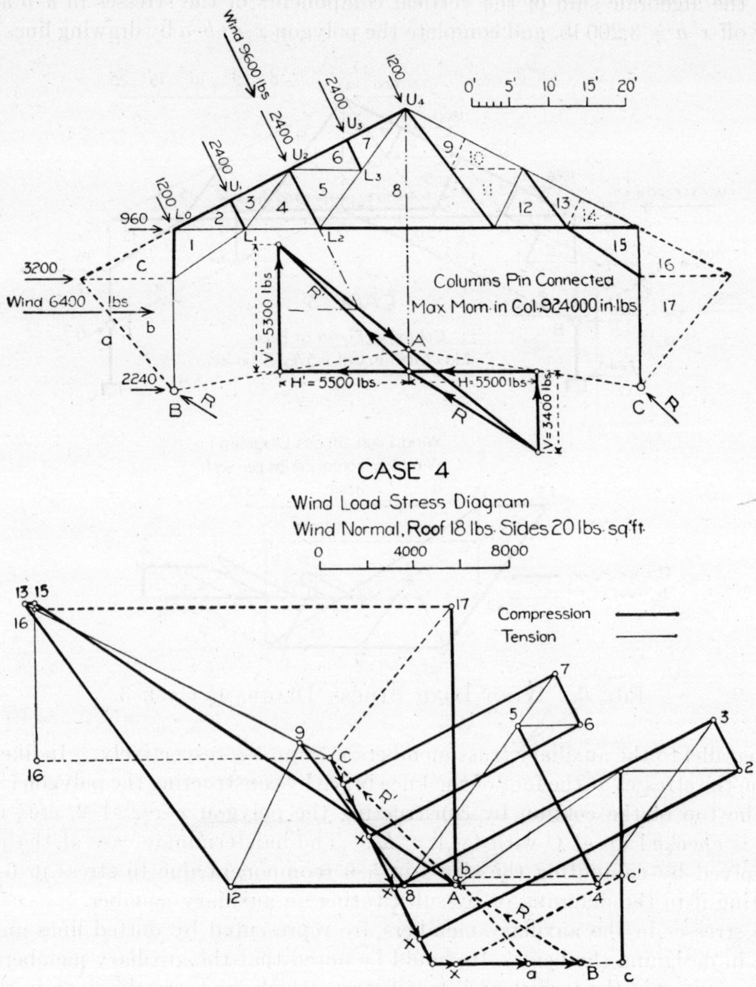

FIG. 7. WIND LOAD STRESS DIAGRAM, CASE 4.

above the knee brace is 5,230 lb. The maximum positive moment occurs at the foot of the knee brace and the maximum negative moment occurs at the foot of the column, and is $H' \times 7 \times 12 = 376{,}320$ in.-lb.

Case 4. Wind Load Stresses: Wind Normal; Columns Hinged.—In Fig. 7 the resultant of the external wind forces on the sides and the roof acts through their intersection, and is parallel to $C\text{–}B$ in the stress diagram (line $C\text{–}B$ is not drawn). To calculate V and V' connect the point of intersection, A, of the resultant wind and the vertical line through the center of truss, with the bases of the columns B and C. From A lay off one-half of resultant wind on each side, and from the extreme ends drop vertical lines V and V' to the dotted lines A–B and A–C. The vertical lines V and V' will be the vertical reactions, the horizontal lines will be H and H', and R and R' will be the

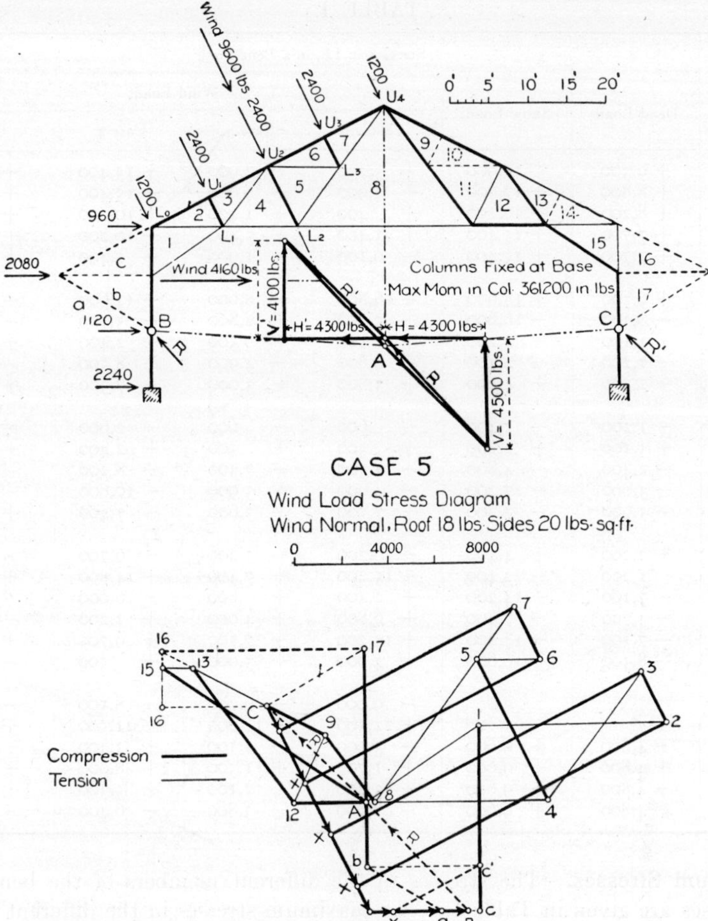

FIG. 8. WIND LOAD STRESS DIAGRAM, CASE 5.

resultants of the horizontal and vertical reactions at B and C respectively. The stresses are calculated by beginning at the base of the column B as in Case 2. In the polygon a–B–A–b at B, A–B = R, a–B = 2,240 lb., and a–b and A–b are the stresses in a–b and A–b respectively.

The maximum shear in the leeward column below the knee brace is $H' = 5{,}500$ lb., above the knee brace is 12,800 lb.; the maximum moment occurs at the foot of the knee brace and is $H' \times 14 \times 12 = 924{,}000$ in.-lb.

Case 5. Wind Load Stresses: Wind Normal; Columns Fixed at Base.—This is Case 4 with the base of the column moved up to the point of contra-flexure. The maximum shear in the leeward column below the knee brace is 4,300 lb., above the knee brace is 5,000 lb.; the maximum positive moment occurs at the foot of the knee brace and the maximum negative moment occurs at the foot of the column, and is $H' \times 7 \times 12 = 361{,}200$ in.-lb. For analysis see Fig. 8.

TABLE I.

Name of Piece.	Stresses in Lb. in a Bent For					
	Dead Load	Snow Load.	Wind Load.			
			Case 2.	Case 3.	Case 4.	Case 5.
x–2	+ 9,300	+ 18,900	+ 3,700	+ 2,900	+ 15,400	+ 14,900
x–3	+ 8,800	+ 17,600	+ 4,900	+ 4,000	+ 15,400	+ 14,900
x–6	+ 8,200	+ 16,400	+ 400	+ 1,400	+ 10,200	+ 11,200
x–7	+ 7,700	+ 15,400	+ 1,400	+ 3,400	+ 10,200	+ 11,200
x–9	+ 7,700	+ 15,400	− 6,100	− 1,900	− 1,400	+ 2,800
x–13	+ 9,300	+ 18,600	− 19,800	− 8,600	− 14,600	− 3,600
1–2	− 8,300	− 16,600	+ 5,700	+ 2,800	− 5,100	− 8,000
2–3	+ 1,100	+ 2,200	+ 500	+ 500	+ 2,400	+ 2,400
3–4	− 1,200	− 2,400	− 6,800	− 4,900	− 8,500	− 6,700
4–5	+ 2,200	+ 4,400	+ 3,800	+ 3,000	+ 7,300	+ 6,600
5–6	− 1,200	− 2,400	− 600	− 600	− 2,600	− 2,600
6–7	+ 1,100	+ 2,200	+ 500	+ 500	+ 2,400	+ 2,400
5–8	− 2,400	− 4,800	− 4,300	− 3,300	− 8,200	− 7,400
7–8	− 3,600	− 7,200	− 4,900	− 3,900	− 10,800	− 10,000
8–9	− 3,600	− 7,200	+ 7,500	+ 3,600	+ 7,400	+ 3,500
9–12	+ 2,200	+ 4,400	− 6,700	− 3,200	− 6,700	− 3,200
12–13	− 1,200	− 2,400	+ 15,200	+ 7,400	+ 14,800	+ 7,000
y–4	− 7,100	− 14,200	+ 2,400	+ 800	− 6,000	− 7,700
y–8	− 4,700	− 7,400	+ 6,800	+ 4,000	+ 2,200	− 400
y–12	− 7,100	− 14,200	+ 14,200	+ 7,700	+ 9,700	+ 2,100
13–15	− 8,300	− 16,600	+ 4,600	+ 3,000	+ 500	− 1,300
A–1	......	......	− 9,000	− 6,200	− 8,500	− 6,700
A–15	......	......	+ 22,300	+ 11,000	+ 21,500	+ 10,400
A–*b*	+ 4,800	+ 9,600	− 3,200	− 2,100	+ 3,400	+ 4,500
C–1	+ 4,800	+ 9,600	+ 1,700	+ 1,300	+ 8,000	+ 7,600
A–17	+ 4,800	+ 9,600	+ 3,200	+ 2,100	+ 5,300	+ 4,100
15–16	+ 4,800	+ 9,600	− 8,600	− 3,800	− 6,400	− 2,400

Maximum Stresses.—The stresses in the different members of the bent for the different cases are given in Table I. The maximum stresses in the different members of the bent for (1) dead load plus maximum snow load; (2) dead load plus wind load, Case 4; (3) dead load plus minimum snow load plus wind load, Case 4; and (4) a vertical dead load of 40 lb. per sq. ft. horizontal projection of the roof are given in Table II. The stresses which control the design of the members may be seen in Table II. By comparing these values with the stresses given in the last column the accuracy of the equivalent load method can be seen.

Graphic Calculation of Reactions.—The graphic method for calculating the reactions given in Fig. 7 and Fig. 8 may be proved as follows: In Fig. 9 the intersection of ΣW and the center line of the bent is at A. Draw A–B and A–C, lay off ΣW so

TABLE II.

Name of Piece.	Maximum Stresses in Lb. in a Bent For			
	Dead Load + Max. Snow Load	Dead Load + Wind Load, Case 4.	Dead Load + Min. Snow Load + Wind Load, Case 4.	Vert. Dead Load of 40 lb. per Sq. Ft. of Horizontal Projection.
x–2	+ 28,200	+ 24,700	+ 34,300	+ 37,200
x–3	+ 26,400	+ 24,200	+ 33,000	+ 35,200
x–6	+ 26,400	+ 18,400	+ 26,600	+ 32,800
x–7	+ 23,100	+ 17,900	+ 25,600	+ 30,800
x–9	+ 23,100	+ 6,300	+ 14,000	+ 30,800
x–13	+ 28,200	− 5,300	+ 4,000	+ 37,200
1–2	− 24,900	− 13,400	− 21,700	− 33,200
2–3	+ 3,300	+ 3,500	+ 4,600	+ 4,400
3–4	− 3,600	− 9,700	− 10,900	− 4,800
4–5	+ 6,600	+ 9,500	+ 11,700	+ 8,800
5–6	− 3,600	− 3,800	− 5,000	− 4,800
6–7	+ 3,300	+ 3,500	+ 4,600	+ 4,400
5–8	− 7,200	− 10,600	− 13,000	− 9,600
7–8	− 10,800	− 14,400	− 18,000	− 14,400
8–9	− 10,800	+ 3,800	+ 200	− 14,400
9–12	+ 6,600	− 4,500	− 2,300	+ 8,800
12–13	− 3,600	+ 13,600	+ 12,400	− 4,800
y–4	− 21,300	− 13,100	− 20,200	− 28,400
y–8	− 14,100	− 2,500	− 5,200	− 14,800
y–12	− 23,100	+ 2,600	− 4,500	− 28,400
13–15	− 24,900	− 7,800	− 16,100	− 32,400
A–1	......	− 8,500	− 8,500	......
A–15	......	+ 21,500	− 21,500	......
A–*b*	+ 14,400	+ 8,200	+ 13,000	+ 19,200
C–1	+ 14,400	+ 12,800	+ 17,600	+ 19,200
A–17	+ 14,400	+ 10,100	+ 14,900	+ 19,200
15–16	+ 14,400	− 1,600	+ 3,200	+ 19,200

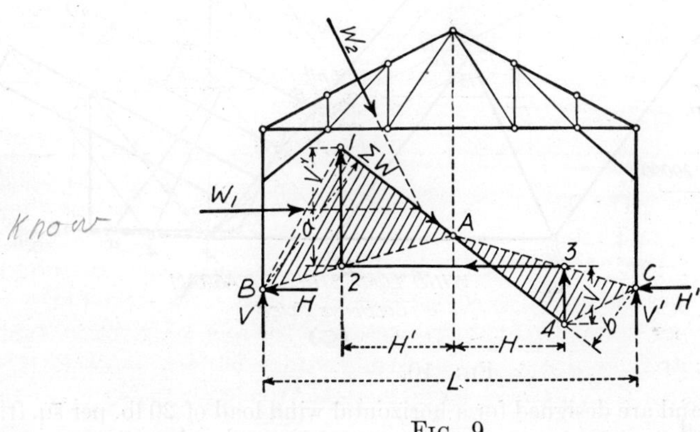

FIG. 9.

that it is bisected by the point *A*, and draw 1–2 and 3–4. Then 1–2 equals *V′* and 3–4 equals *V* as shown in the following proof:

Proof.—To calculate V take moments of external forces about C, and

$$V = \frac{\Sigma W \times b}{L} = \frac{4 \text{ times area triangle } A\text{–}4\text{–}C}{L}$$

But area triangle A–4–C is also equal to $\frac{3\text{–}4 \times L}{4}$, and $V = \frac{3\text{–}4 \times L}{L} = 3\text{–}4$ which proves the construction. It may be proved in like manner that $1\text{–}2 = V'$.

TRANSVERSE BENT WITH VENTILATOR.—The calculation of the wind stresses in a transverse bent with a monitor ventilator is shown in Fig. 10. The bents are

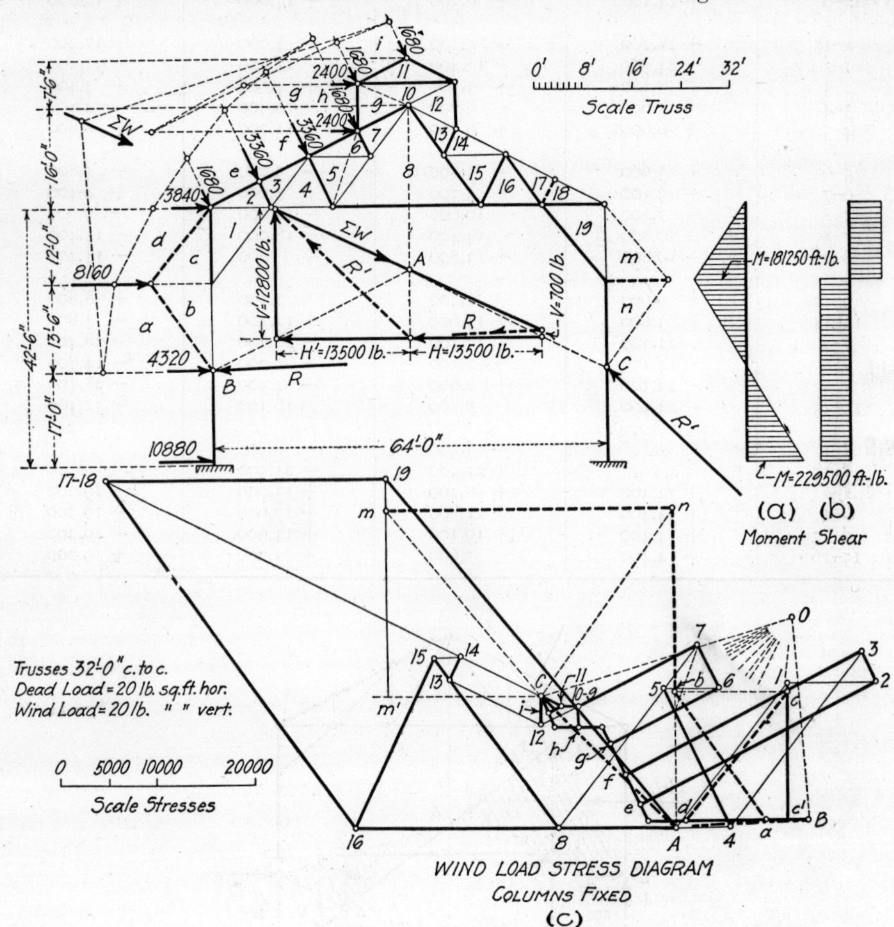

FIG. 10.

spaced 32′ 0″ centers and are designed for a horizontal wind load of 20 lb. per sq. ft., the normal wind roof load being obtained by Hutton's formula as shown in Chapter XXIV.

The point of contra-flexure is found by substituting in formula (17) to be at a point $y_0 = 17.0$ ft. The external forces are calculated for the bent above the point of contra-flexure by multiplying the area supported at the point by the intensity of the wind pressure. For example, the load at B is $32' \times 6.75' \times 20$ lb. $= 4{,}320$ lb.

The line of application and the amount of the external wind load, ΣW, are found by means of a force and an equilibrium polygon. ΣW acts through the intersection of the strings parallel to the rays O–B and O–C, and is equal to C–B (line C–B is not drawn in force polygon) in amount. The reactions R and R' are calculated by the graphic method as previously described.

The calculation of stresses is begun at point B in the windward column, and in the stress diagram the stresses at B are found by drawing the force polygon a–B–A–b–a. The remaining stresses are calculated as for a simple truss. In calculating the stresses in the ventilator it was assumed that diagonals 9–10 and 10–12 are tension members, so that 9–10 will not be in action when the wind is acting as shown. Before solving the stresses at the joint 6–7–9 it was necessary to calculate the stresses in members i–11, 10–11, and 9–h. The remainder of the solution offers no difficulty to one familiar with the principles of graphic statics.

The stress in post b–A is equal to V, while the stress in 1–c is found by extending 1–c to c' in the stress diagram, c' being a point on the load line. The stress in post n–A is equal to V', while the stress in 19–m is found by extending 19–m to m' in the stress diagram, m' being a point on the horizontal line drawn through C. The kind of stress in the different members is shown by the weight of lines in the bent diagram and in the stress diagram, light lines indicating tension and heavy lines indicating compression.

TRANSVERSE BENT WITH SIDE SHEDS.—Transverse bents with side sheds are quite often used in the design of shops and mills. The calculation of the stresses due to wind load in a bent of this type is an interesting application of the author's graphic solution of stresses in transverse bents.

It is required to calculate the stresses due to a horizontal wind load of 30 lb. per square foot on the sides and the normal component of 30 lb. (Hutton's formula) on the roof, the bents being spaced 20′ 0″ centers, as in Fig. 11. The loads are calculated, and by means of a force polygon in (d) and an equilibrium polygon in (a) the resultant wind ΣW is found to pass through point E, and to be equal to 30,800 lb.

Calculation of Reactions.—The horizontal shear of 25,400 lb. will be taken by the columns in proportion to their rigidities—in this case the rigidities of the columns are assumed equal and the shear at the foot of each column will be 6,350 lb. The vertical reactions will be due to two forces: (1) a vertical load of 17,200 lb., which will be taken equally by the four columns, making a load of 4,300 lb. on each; and (2) to a bending moment of 25,400 lb. × 9.2 ft. = 233,680 ft.-lb. (the bending moment about C. G. is also equal to 30,800 lb. × 7.6 ft.), which will be resisted by the columns and will cause reactions varying as the distance from the center of gravity of the columns, (E), as in the case of the continuous portal, Chapter IX.

Let v_1', v_2', v_3', and v_4' represent the reactions due to moment in the columns, respectively; then if a is the reaction on a column at a units distance from the center of gravity we will have $v_1' = -a\,40$, $v_2' = -a\,20$, $v_3' = +a\,20$, and $v_4' = +a\,40$. The resisting moment of each column will be equal to the reaction multiplied by the distance from the center of gravity, and $a\,40^2 + a\,20^2 + a\,20^2 + a\,40^2 = 233{,}680$ ft.-lb. from which $a = 58.42$ lb. and $v_1' = -2{,}340$ lb.; $v_2' = -1{,}170$ lb.; $v_3' = +1{,}170$ lb.; $v_4' = +2{,}340$ lb.

Now adding the reactions due to (1) and (2) we have

$$V_1 = 4{,}300 - 2{,}340 = +\ 1{,}960 \text{ lb.},$$
$$V_2 = 4{,}300 - 1{,}170 = +\ 3{,}130 \text{ lb.},$$
$$V_3 = 4{,}300 + 1{,}170 = +\ 5{,}470 \text{ lb.},$$
$$V_4 = 4{,}300 + 2{,}340 = +\ 6{,}640 \text{ lb.}$$

Combining the horizontal and vertical reactions we have $R_1 = a_1\text{–}A = 6{,}600$ lb.; $R_2 = A\text{–}B = 7{,}200$ lb.; $R_3 = B\text{–}C = 8{,}400$ lb.; $R_4 = C\text{–}D = 9{,}100$ lb. These reactions close the force polygon in (*d*).

Calculation of Stresses.—Auxiliary members are substituted as shown by the broken lines. It will be seen that these members are arranged so that all bending is removed from the columns and that the stresses in the truss members are correctly given in the stress diagram. The calculation is started at point A at the foot of the left-hand column as in the case of the simple transverse bent, and reactions R_2 and R_3 are substituted as the calculation progresses, the stress diagram finally closing at the base of the leeward column, point D. The stresses are given on the members in (*a*). The direct stresses in the columns are easily found by algebraic resolution beginning at the foot of the columns where the direct stress is equal to V_1, V_2, V_3 and V_4, respectively. The stresses in the leeward side of the main truss are very large due to the small depth of truss in line of the member 29–30.

Moment and Shear in Columns.—The bending moment in the main leeward column is shown in (*b*), the maximum moment is at the foot of the knee brace and is $M_1 = 274{,}500$ ft.-lb. The shear diagram is shown in (*c*), the maximum shear is between the foot of the knee brace and the top of the column and is $S_0 = 45{,}750$ lb.

Note.—The stresses in a bent with side sheds obtained by the preceding method are approximate for the reason that the assumed conditions are probably never entirely realized. In the exact calculation of the stresses, of which the above solution is the first approximation, the deformation of the framework is considered in a manner similar to that of the two-hinged arch in Chapter XX. The approximate solution is entirely adequate for all practical purposes. In designing a transverse bent with side sheds it would be better to omit the knee braces in the side sheds; in which case the shear will all be taken by the main columns.

STRESSES IN MILL BUILDING COLUMNS CARRYING CRANE LOADS.—The stresses produced in columns of mill buildings by crane loads eccentrically applied depend upon the method used in bracing the structure against lateral forces. If the knee braces are omitted or only very small knee braces are used, the columns are practically hinged at the top and the lateral thrust due to the eccentric crane loads must be carried to the ends of the building by the lateral bracing in the planes of the chords of the trusses. Proper bracing must then be provided in the end bents.

If rigid knee braces are provided the columns may be considered as fixed at the top and a transverse bent may be considered as carrying its load directly to the foundations. The lateral load will in reality be distributed between the direct path down the columns and the indirect path along the lateral bracing in the planes of the chords to the end bents. The portion carried by each route will depend upon the relative rigidity of the routes. Since the transverse bent is much more rigid than the lateral bracing, all of the load may be considered as carried by the transverse bent.

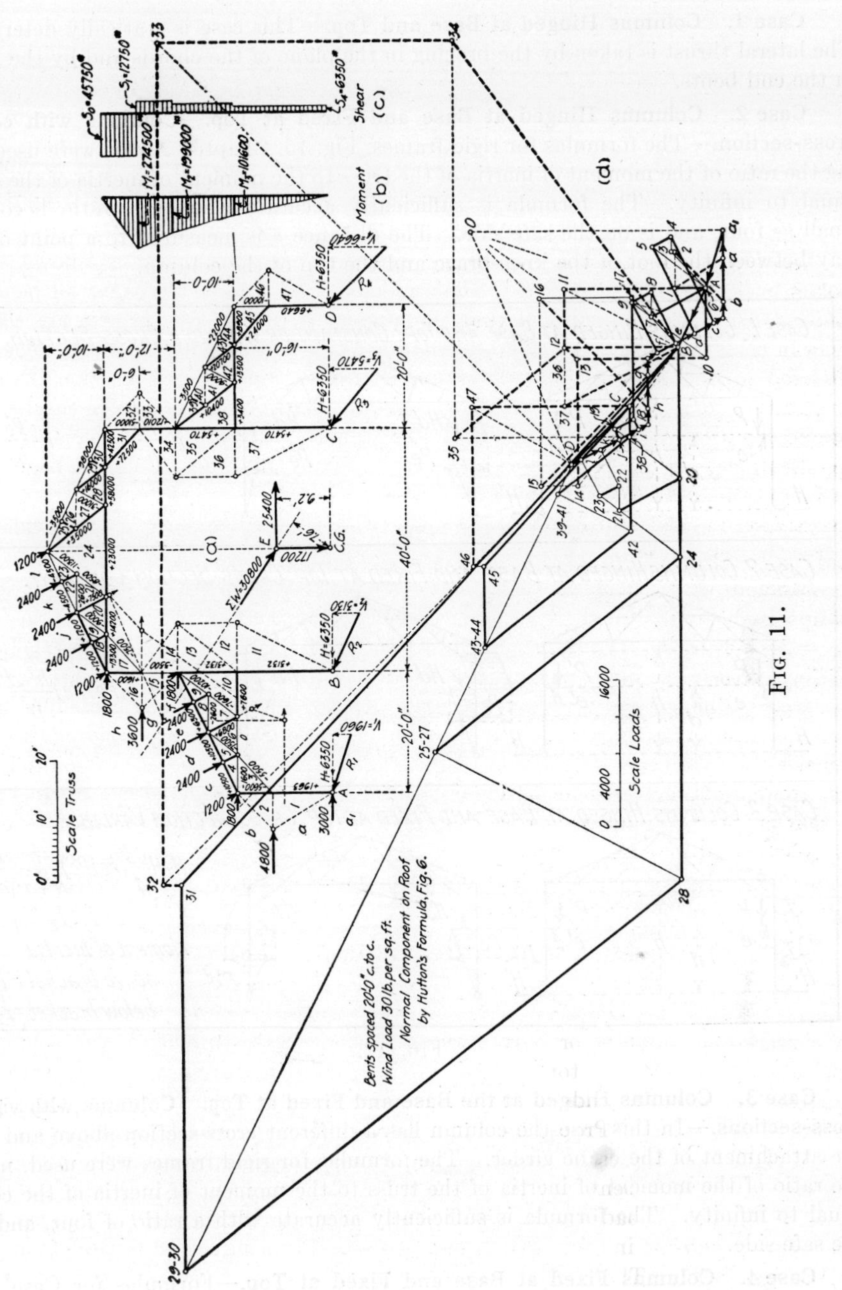
Bents spaced 20'-0" c. to c.
Wind Load 30 lb. per sq. ft.
Normal Component on Roof
by Hutton's Formula, Fig. 6.
Scale Truss
Scale Loads
Moment (b)
Shear (c)
(a)
(d)

FIG. 11.

In Fig. 12 three cases are considered.

Case 1. Columns Hinged at Base and Top.—This case is statically determinate. The lateral thrust is taken by the bracing in the plane of the chords and by the bracing in the end bents.

Case 2. Columns Hinged at Base and Fixed at Top.—Columns with constant cross-section.—The formulas for rigid frames, Fig. 15, Chapter XVII, were used, making the ratio of the moment of inertia of the truss to the moment of inertia of the column equal to infinity. The formula is sufficiently accurate when this ratio becomes as small as four, and is on the safe side. The distance h is measured to a point one-half way between the foot of the knee-brace and the top of the column.

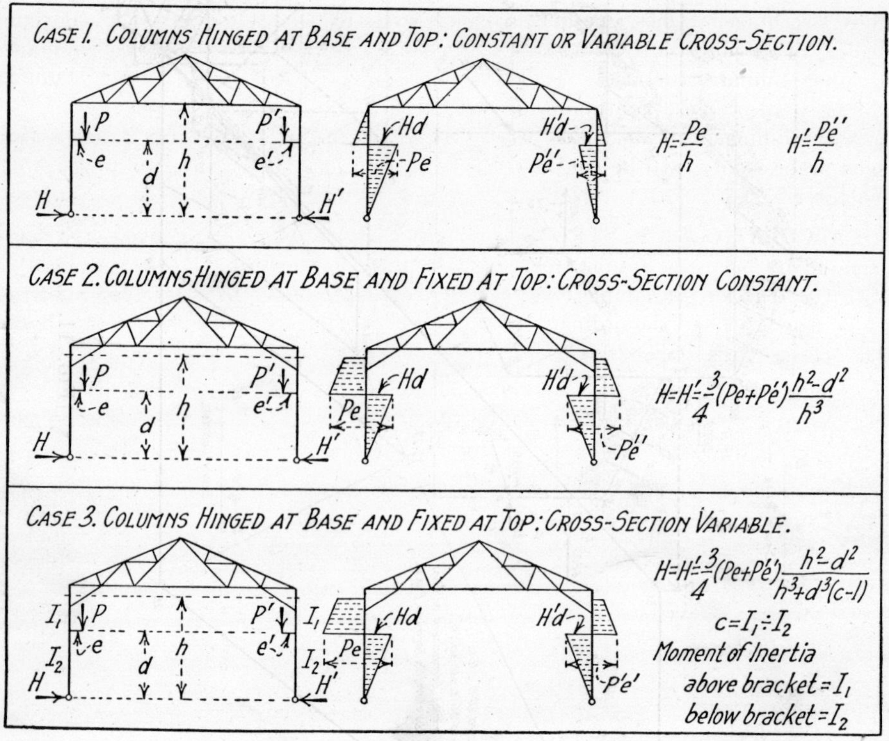

FIG. 12.

Case 3. Columns Hinged at the Base and Fixed at Top. Columns with variable cross-sections.—In this case the column has a different cross-section above and below the attachment of the crane girder. The formulas for rigid frames were used, making the ratio of the moment of inertia of the truss to the moment of inertia of the column equal to infinity. The formula is sufficiently accurate with a ratio of four, and is on the safe side.

Case 4. Columns Fixed at Base and Fixed at Top.—Formulas for Case 2 and Case 3 may be used, the value of h being taken as the distance from the point of contra-flexure to a point midway between the foot of the knee brace and the top of the column. The point of contra-flexure may be calculated by formula (17).

CHAPTER XI.

Stresses in Three-hinged Arch.

Introduction.—An arch is a structure in which the reactions are inclined for vertical loads. Arches are divided, according to the number of hinges, into three-hinged arches, two-hinged arches, one-hinged arches, and arches without hinges or continuous arches. Three-hinged arches are in common use for exposition buildings, train sheds and other similar structures. Two-hinged arches are used for steel frame buildings and long span bridges; continuous arches are used only in dome construction.

A three-hinged arch is made up of two simple beams or trusses. Trussed three-hinged arches, only, will be considered in this chapter, and trussed two-hinged arches in Chapter XX.

CALCULATION OF STRESSES.—The reactions for a three-hinged arch can be calculated by means of simple statics with slightly more work than that necessary to obtain the reactions in simple trusses. Having determined the reactions the stresses may be calculated by the ordinary algebraic and graphic methods used in the solution of the stresses in simple roof trusses.

Calculation of Reactions. Algebraic Method.—Let H and V, H' and V' be the horizontal and vertical reactions at the left and right supports for a concentrated load P, placed at a distance x from the center hinge C in the three-hinged arch in Fig. 1.

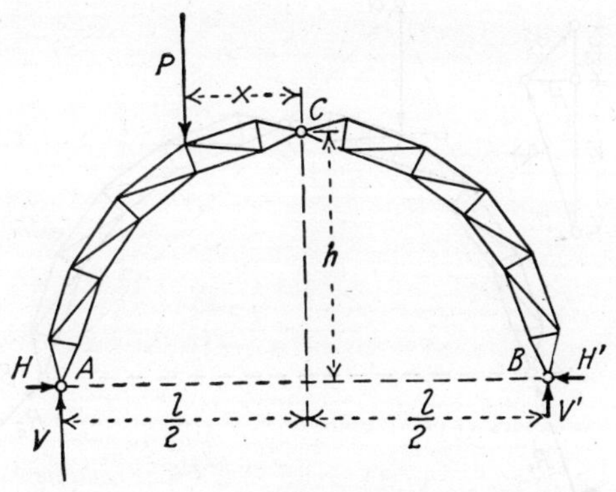

Fig. 1.

From the three fundamental equations of equilibrium

$$\Sigma \text{ horizontal components of forces} = 0 \quad (1)$$

$$\Sigma \text{ vertical components of forces} = 0 \quad (2)$$

$$\Sigma \text{ moments of forces about any point} = 0 \quad (3)$$

we have

$$H = H' \tag{4}$$

and

$$V + V' = P \tag{5}$$

Taking moments about B, we have

$$V \cdot l - P(\tfrac{1}{2}l + x) = 0 \tag{6}$$

and taking moments about center hinge C, we have

$$\tfrac{1}{2}V \cdot l - H \cdot h - P \cdot x = 0 \tag{7}$$

Solving (6) we have

$$V = \frac{P}{l}(\tfrac{1}{2}l + x) \tag{8}$$

and

$$V' = P - V = \frac{P}{l}(\tfrac{1}{2}l - x) \tag{9}$$

Substituting (7) in (8), we have

$$H = H' = \frac{P}{2h}(\tfrac{1}{2}l - x) \tag{10}$$

The horizontal reactions at the crown are the same as at the supports. Reactions for an inclined load may be found by substituting the proper moment arms.

Calculation of Reactions. Graphic Method.—Let P, Fig. 2, be the resultant of all the loads on the left segment. Since there is no bending moment at hinge C, the line

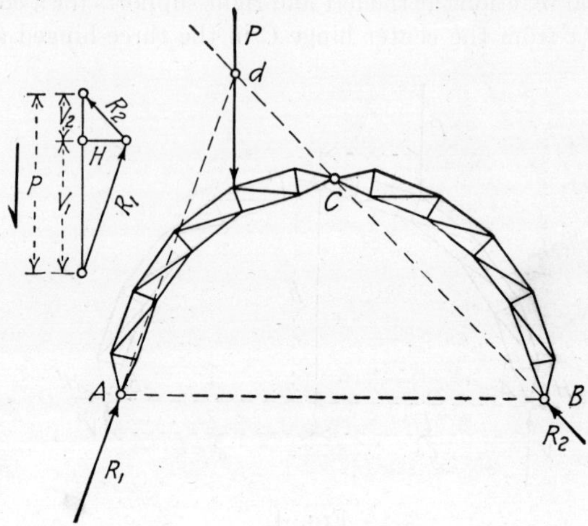

FIG. 2.

of action of the reaction R_2 must pass through the hinge at the crown. This determines the direction of reaction R_2, and since the three external forces R_1, R_2, and P produce equilibrium in the structure they must meet in a point. Therefore to find the direction of R_1 produce B–C to d and join d and A.

The values of R_1 and R_2 may then be obtained from the force polygon.

The reactions due to loads on the right segment may be found in the same manner. The two operations may be combined in one as illustrated in the solution of the dead load stresses in a three-hinged arch, Fig. 3.

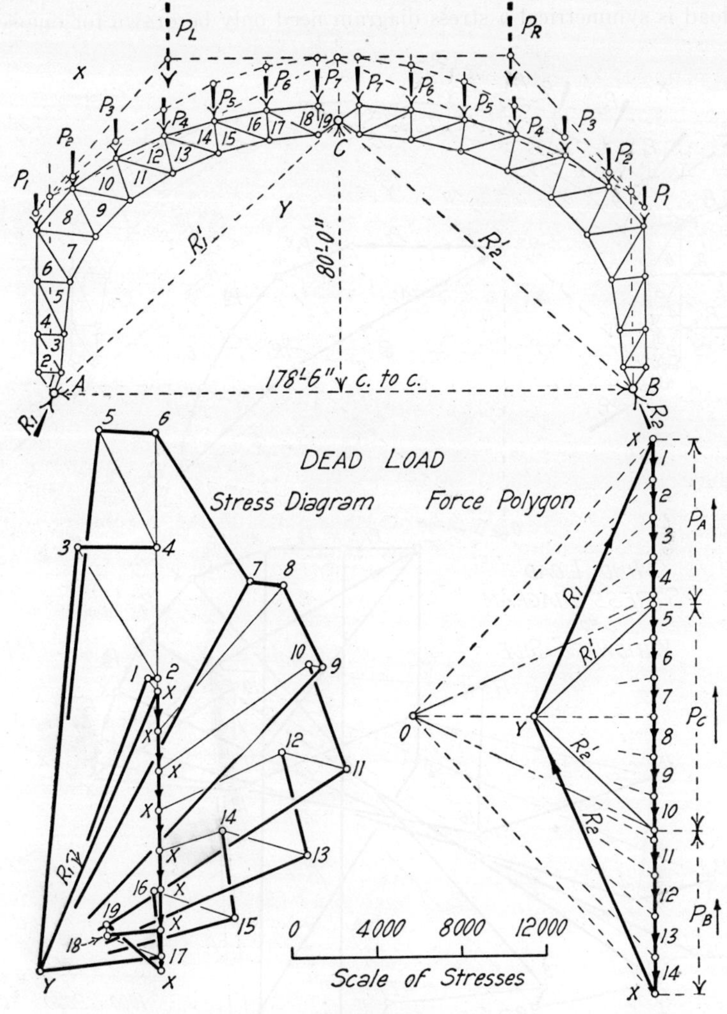

FIG. 3.

Calculation of Dead Load Stresses.—To find the reactions for the dead loads in Fig. 3, the loads are laid off on the load line of the force polygon in order, beginning at the left reaction A, and two equilibrium polygons, one for each segment, are drawn using the same force polygon. The vertical reactions at the crown, P_C, and at abutments, P_A and P_B, are found by drawing a line through pole O of the force polygon parallel to the closing lines of the equilibrium polygons. The load P_C at the crown causes reactions R_1' and R_2', and combining reactions R_1' and P_A at A, and R_2' and P_B at B, we have the true reactions R_1 and R_2.

Having obtained the reactions, the stresses in the members are found in the same manner as in simple trusses. In Fig. 3 the stresses in the left segment are calculated by graphic resolution. The diagram is begun with the left reaction x–y = R_1. Where the dead load is symmetrical a stress diagram need only be drawn for one segment.

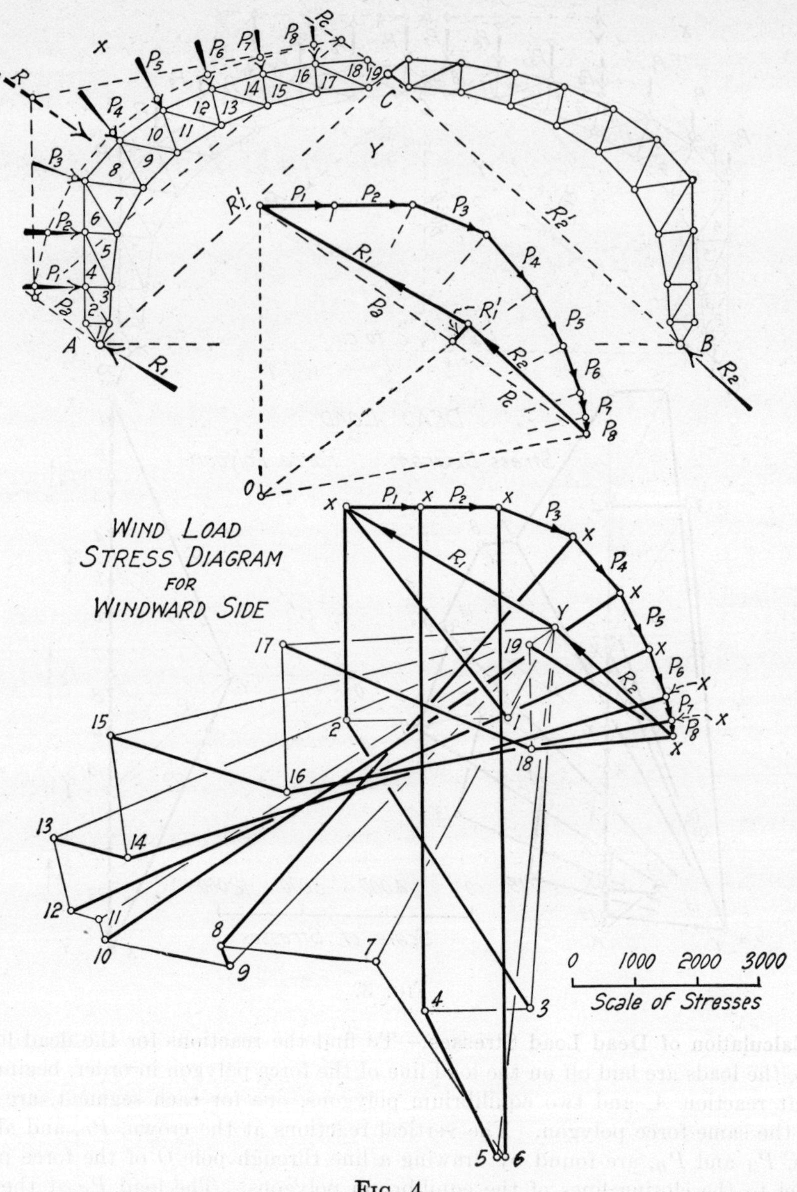

FIG. 4.

Calculation of Wind Load Stresses.—The reactions for wind load in Fig. 4 are found as follows:

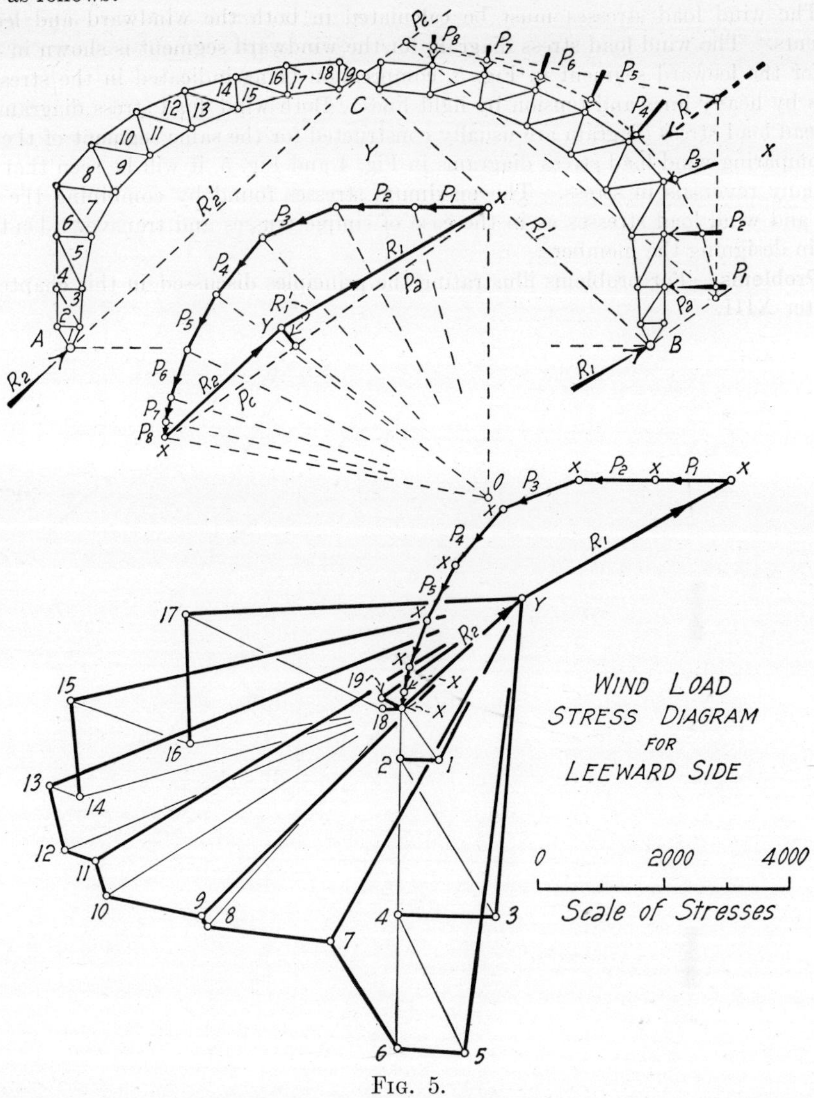

FIG. 5.

The reactions P_a and P_c for the windward segment, considering it a simple truss supported at the hinges, are found by means of force and equilibrium polygons. The lines of action of P_a and P_c are parallel to each other and to the resultant R. The line of action of the right reaction, R_2, must pass through the center hinge C, and the reaction P_c will be replaced by two reactions R_2 and R_1' parallel to R_2' and R_1' in the arch respectively, and the force triangle will be closed by drawing R_1 in the force polygon. The intersection of force R and reactions R_1 and R_2 falls outside the limit of the diagram.

Having obtained the reactions, the stresses in the members are calculated in the same manner as in a simple truss.

The wind load stresses must be calculated in both the windward and leeward segments. The wind load stress diagram for the windward segment is shown in Fig. 4 and for the leeward segment in Fig. 5, compression being indicated in the stress diagrams by heavy lines and tension by light lines. Both wind load stress diagrams and the dead load stress diagram are usually constructed for the same segment of the arch. By comparing wind load stress diagrams in Fig. 4 and Fig. 5, it will be seen that there are many reversals in stress. The maximum stresses found by combining the dead, snow and wind load stresses as in the case of simple trusses and transverse bents, are used in designing the members.

Problems.—For problems illustrating the principles discussed in this chapter, see Chapter XIII.

CHAPTER XII.

Stresses in Pins, Combined and Eccentric Stresses.

STRESSES IN PINS.—A pin under ordinary conditions is a short beam and must be designed (1) for bending, (2) for shear, and (3) for bearing. If a pin becomes bent the distribution of the loads and the calculation of the stresses are very uncertain.

The cross-bending stress, f, is found by means of the fundamental formula for flexure, $f = M \cdot c/I$, where the maximum bending moment, M, is found as explained later; I is the moment of inertia; and c is one-half the diameter of a solid or hollow pin.

The safe shearing stresses given in standard specifications are for a uniform distribution of the shear over the entire cross-section, and the actual unit shearing stress to be used in designing will be equal to the maximum shear divided by the area of the cross-section of the pin.

The bearing stress is found by dividing the stress in the member by the bearing area of the pin, found by multiplying the thickness of the bearing plates by the diameter of the pin.

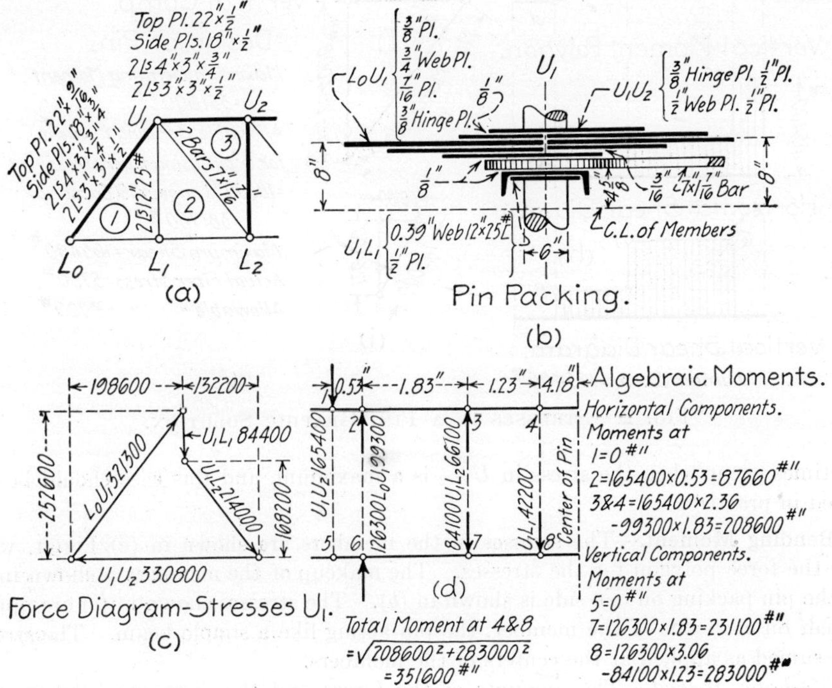

Fig. 1. Stresses in a Pin; Algebraic Solution.

Calculation of Stresses.—The method of calculation will be illustrated by calculating the stresses in the pin at U_1 in (*a*) Fig. 1. In the complete investigation of the pin U_1, it would be necessary to calculate the stresses when the stress in U_1U_2 was a maximum, and when the stress in U_1L_2 was a maximum. Only the case where the stress in U_1U_2 is a maximum will be considered. However, maximum stresses in pins

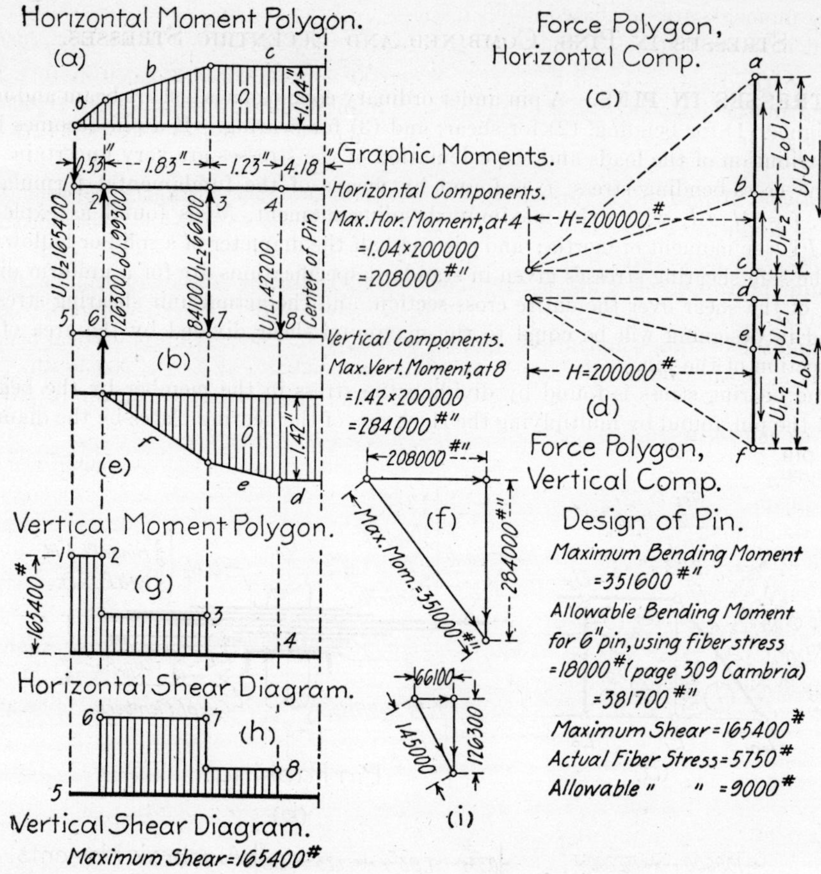

FIG. 2. STRESSES IN A PIN; GRAPHIC SOLUTION.

sometimes occur when the stress in U_1L_2 is a maximum, and this case should be considered in practice.

Bending Moment.—The stresses in the members are shown in (c) Fig. 1, which gives the force polygon for the stresses. The makeup of the members is shown in (*a*), and the pin packing on one side is shown in (*b*). The stresses shown in (*c*) are applied one-half on each side of the member, the pin acting like a simple beam. The stresses are assumed as applied at the centers of the members.

Algebraic Method.—The amounts of the forces and the distances between their points of application as calculated from (*b*) are shown in (*d*) Fig. 1. The horizontal and vertical components of the forces are considered separately, the maximum horizontal bending moment and the maximum vertical bending moment are calculated for the same point, and the resultant moment is then found by means of the force triangle.

In (*d*) the horizontal bending moments are calculated about the points 1, 2, 3, 4; the maxim ım horizontal moment is to the right of 3, and is 208,600 in.-lb. The vertical bending moments are calculated about points 5, 6, 7, 8; the maximum vertical bending moment is to the right of 8, and is 283,000 in.-lb. The maximum bending moment is at and to the right of 4 and 8, and is $\sqrt{208{,}600^2 + 283{,}000^2} = 351{,}600$ in.-lb. Substituting in the formula $f = M \cdot c/I$, the maximum bending stress is $f = 16{,}600$ lb. The allowable bending stress for which this bridge was designed was 18,000 lb. per sq. in.

Graphic Method.—The amounts of the forces and the distances between their points of application are shown in (*b*) Fig. 2. The force polygon for the horizontal components i; given in (*c*), and the bending moment polygon is given in (*a*). The maximum horizontal bending moment will be to the right of 3, and will be $H \times y = 200{,}000 \times 1.04 = 208{,}000$ in.-lb. The force polygon for the vertical forces is given in (*d*), and the bending moment polygon is given in (*e*). The maximum vertical bending moment is to the right of 8, and is $H \times y = 200{,}000 \times 1.42 = 284{,}000$ in.-lb. The maximum bending moment will occur at and to the right of 4 and 8, and will be 351,000 in.-lb., as shown in (*f*).

Shear.—The shear is found for both the horizontal and vertical components as in a simple beam, and is equal to the summation of all the forces to the left of the section. The horizontal shear diagram is shown in (*g*), and the vertical shear diagram is shown in (*h*) Fig. 2. The maximum horizontal shear is between 1 and 2, and is 165,400 lb. The shear between 2 and 3 is $165{,}400 - 99{,}300 = 66{,}100$ lb. The maximum vertical shear is between 6 and 7, and is 126,300 lb. The resultant shear between 2 and 3, and 6 and 7, is $\sqrt{126{,}300^2 + 66{,}100^2} = 145{,}000$ lb. as in (*i*), which is less than the horizontal shear between 1 and 2. The maximum shear, therefore, comes between 1 and 2, and is 165,400 lb. The maximum shearing unit stress is 5,750 lb. The allowable shearing stress was 9,000 lb.

Bearing.—The bearing stress in L_0U_1 is $160{,}650 \div (6 \times 1.94) = 13{,}800$ lb. Bearing stress in U_1U_2 is $165{,}400 \div (6 \times 1.88) = 14{,}600$ lb. Bearing stress in U_1L_1 is $42{,}200 \div (6 \times 0.89) = 7{,}900$ lb. Bearing stress in U_1L_2 is $107{,}000 \div (6 \times 1\tfrac{7}{16}) = 12{,}400$ lb. The allowable bearing stress was 15,000 lb. per sq. in.

COMBINED AND ECCENTRIC STRESSES.—The combined stress due to direct and cross-bending in a tie or strut is given by the formula

$$f = f_2 \pm f_1 = \frac{P}{A} \pm \frac{M_1 \cdot c}{I \pm \dfrac{P \cdot l^2}{k \cdot E}} \qquad (1)$$

where P = total direct stress in the member in lb.;
l = length of the member in in.;
I = moment of inertia of the member in in. to the fourth power;
c = distance in in. from the neutral axis to the most remote fiber on the side for which the stress is desired;

E = modulus of elasticity of the material in lb. per sq. in.;
A = area of the member in sq. in.;
f_1 = fiber stress due to cross-bending;
$f_2 = P/A$ = direct unit stress;
M_1 = bending moment on the section in in.-lb.
k = a coefficient depending upon the method of loading and the condition of the ends, and is usually taken as 10 for struts with hinged ends, 24 for struts with one end hinged and the other end fixed, and 32 for both ends fixed.

Derivation of Formula.—The total bending moment in a strut or a tie which carries a direct total stress P, and a cross-bending M_1 will $M = M_1 \pm P \cdot v$, where v = maximum deflection of strut or tie, and

$$M = M_1 \pm P \cdot v = \frac{f_1 \cdot I}{c} \tag{2}$$

But from Applied Mechanics

$$v = \frac{f_1 \cdot l^2}{k \cdot E \cdot c} \tag{3}$$

in which k is a constant depending upon the condition of the ends, and the manner in which the beam is loaded.

Substituting this value of v in (2) and reducing

$$f_1 = \frac{M_1 \cdot c}{I \pm \dfrac{P \cdot l^2}{k \cdot E}} \tag{1}$$

The plus sign in the denominator of (1) is to be used when P is a tensile stress, and the minus sign is to be used when P is a compressive stress. If the member is inclined at an angle θ to the vertical, the stress f_1 should be multiplied by $\sin\theta$. For an eccentric stress, the bending moment is $M_1 = P \cdot e$, where P is the total direct stress in the member and e is the eccentricity of the load in in. (distance from the line of action of the force to the neutral axis of the member).

Combined Compression and Cross-bending.—The method of calculating direct and cross-bending stresses will be illustrated by calculating the stresses in the end-post of a bridge, Fig. 3, due to direct compression, weight, eccentricity of loading, and wind moment.

End-Post.—Design the end-post, Fig. 3, for a 160 ft. span through highway bridge. Panel length, 20′ 0″; depth of truss c. to c. of pins, 24′ 0″; length of end-post, 31′ 3″. The direct stresses are as follows: dead load stress = 30,000 lb.; live load stress = 60,000 lb.; impact = 100/(160 + 300) × 60,000 = 13,000 lb.; total direct stress due to dead load, live load and impact = 103,000 lb. The bridge is to be a class C bridge designed according to the "General Specifications for Highway Bridges," in Ketchum's "Structural Engineers' Handbook." From § 38 of the specifications the allowable unit stress is $f_c = 16{,}000 - 70\,l/r$. The section will be made of two channels and one cover plate. Try a section made of two 10 in. channels @ 15 lb., and one 14 in. by $\frac{5}{16}$ in. plate, (*b*), Fig. 3. From Table 82, "Structural Engineers' Handbook," the radius of gyration about horizontal axis A–A, is $r_A = 3.99$ in., and about the vertical axis $B-B$ is, $r_B = 4.67$ in., and the eccentricity is, $e = 1.70$ in. The allowable stress is then $f_c = 16{,}000 - \dfrac{70 \times 375}{3.99} = 9{,}400$ lb. per sq. in. The required area will be $= 103{,}000 \div 9{,}400 = 10.96$ sq. in. The actual area is 13.30 sq. in. While the section appears to be excessive, it will be investigated for stress due to weight, eccentric loading and wind before rejecting it.

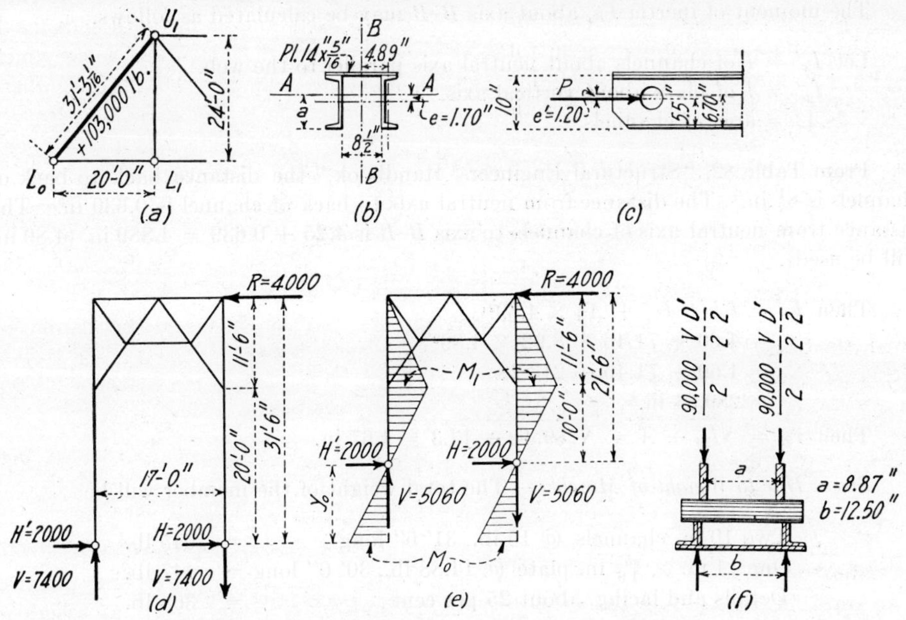

FIG. 3. END-POST OF A HIGHWAY BRIDGE.

The area, radii of gyration and the eccentricity may be calculated as follows. To calculate the area. From the "Structural Engineers' Handbook."

area of two 10 in. channels	=	8.92 sq. in.
area of one 14 in. by $\frac{5}{16}$ in. plate	=	4.38 sq. in.
Total area	=	13.30 sq. in.

To locate the neutral axis $A-A$, take moments about the lower edge of the channels

$$d = \frac{8.92 \times 5 + 4.38 \times 10.156}{13.30} = 6.70 \text{ in.}$$

The eccentricity is $e = 6.70 - 5.00 = 1.70$ in.

The moment of inertia I_A, about axis $A-A$ may be calculated as follows:

Let $I_c = I$ of channels about center of channels.

$I_p = I$ of plate about center of plate.

$A_c =$ area of channels.

$A_p =$ area of plate.

Then

$$\begin{aligned} I_A &= I_c + I_p + A_c \times 1.70^2 + A_p \times 3.456^2. \\ &= 2 \times 66.9 + 0.04 + 8.92 \times 1.70^2 + 4.38 \times 3.456^2 \\ &= 133.8 + 0.04 + 25.76 + 52.20 \\ &= 211.80 \text{ in.}^4 \end{aligned}$$

Then $r_A = \sqrt{I_A \div A} = \sqrt{211.80 \div 13.3} = 3.99$ in.

The moment of inertia I_B, about axis B–B may be calculated as follows.

Let I_c' = I of channels about neutral axis parallel to the web.
I_p' = I of plate about vertical axis.
A_c = area of channels.

From Table 82, "Structural Engineers' Handbook," the distance back to back of channels is $8\frac{1}{2}$ in. The distance from neutral axis to back of channel is 0.639 in. The distance from neutral axis of channels to axis B–B is $4.25 + 0.639 = 4.889$ in. (4.89 in. will be used).

Then

$$\begin{aligned} I_B &= I_c' + I_p' + A_c \times 4.89^2 \\ &= 4.60 + 71.46 + 8.92 \times 4.89^2 \\ &= 4.60 + 71.46 + 213.28 \\ &= 289.34 \text{ in.}^4 \end{aligned}$$

Then $r_B = \sqrt{I_B \div A} = \sqrt{289.34 \div 13.3} = 4.67$ in.

Stress Due to Weight of Member.—The total weight of the member will be

Two 10 in. channels @ 15 lb., 31′ 6″ long	=	945 lb.
One 14 in. × $\frac{5}{16}$ in. plate @ 14.88 lb., 30′ 0″ long	=	447 lb.
Details and lacing, about 25 per cent	=	308 lb.
Total Weight, W	=	1,700 lb.

The bending moment due to weight of member is $M = \frac{1}{8} W \cdot l \cdot \sin\theta$.
Stress due to weight

$$f_w = \frac{M \cdot c}{I_A - \dfrac{P \cdot l^2}{10E}} = \frac{\frac{1}{8} W \cdot l \cdot \sin\theta \cdot c}{I_A - \dfrac{P \cdot l^2}{10E}} \tag{4}$$

The stress due to weight in the upper fiber will be

$$f_w = \frac{\frac{1}{8} \times 1{,}700 \times 375 \times 0.645 \times 3.6125}{211.8 - \dfrac{103{,}000 \times 375^2}{10 \times 30{,}000{,}000}}$$

$$= 940 \text{ lb. per sq. in.}$$

The stress due to weight in the lower fiber is

$$\begin{aligned} f_w' &= -\,6.70 \times 940 \div 3.6125 \\ &= -\,1{,}745 \text{ lb. per sq. in.} \end{aligned}$$

Stress Due to Eccentric Loading.—The pins were placed ½ inch above the center of the channels, and the stress due to eccentric loading will be

$$f_e = \frac{M_1 \cdot c}{I - \dfrac{P \cdot l^2}{10E}} = \frac{P \times (1.70 - 0.5) \times c}{I - \dfrac{P \cdot l^2}{10E}} \tag{5}$$

The eccentric stress in the upper fiber will be

$$f_e = \frac{103{,}000 \times 1.20 \times 3.6125}{211.8 - \dfrac{103{,}000 \times 375^2}{10 \times 30{,}000{,}000}}$$

$$= - 2{,}280 \text{ lb. per sq. in.}$$

The eccentric stress in the lower fiber is

$$f_e = + 6.70 \times 2{,}280 \div 3.6125$$

$$= + 4{,}230 \text{ lb. per sq. in.}$$

The resultant stress due to weight and eccentric loading is $f_1 = f_w + f_e = + 940 - 2{,}280 = - 1{,}340$ lb. in the upper fiber, and $- 1{,}745 + 4{,}230 = 2{,}485$ lb. per sq. in. in the lower fiber.

The allowable stress due to weight and eccentric loading is greater than 10 per cent of the allowable stress and must be considered, with the allowable unit stress increased by 10 per cent.

The total unit stress in the member will be, $f = 103{,}000 \div 13.30 + 2{,}485 = 7{,}752 + 2{,}485 = 10{,}237$ lb. per sq. in. The allowable unit stress when weight and eccentric loading are considered is $9{,}400 \times 1.10 = 10{,}340$ lb. per sq. in., which is sufficient.

Stress Due to Wind Moment.—The load on the portal and the direct wind stresses in the end-post when the end-post is assumed as pin-connected at the base are shown in (*d*) and (*e*) Fig. 3. The end-posts may both be assumed as fixed if the windward end-post is fixed. To fix the windward end-post the bending moment must not be greater than the resisting moment which will be

$$M_0 = H \cdot y_0 = \tfrac{1}{2}a(90{,}000 - V - D')$$

where $V = 5{,}060$ lb. and $D' = 7{,}000$ lb. the direct stress due to wind, and a = distance center to center of metal in the sides of the end-post = 8.87 in., (*f*), Fig. 3. (The impact stress is omitted.) If y_0 is taken equal to $\frac{1}{2}d = 10' \ 0'' = 120$ in., we will have

$$2{,}000 \times 120 \leqq (90{,}000 - 5{,}060 - 7{,}000)8.87/2$$

which makes $240{,}000 < 345{,}600$, and the end-post may be assumed as fixed at the base. The stress due to bending moment due to wind loads in the leeward end-post will be,

$$f_w = \frac{M \cdot c}{I - \dfrac{P \cdot l^2}{10E}} \tag{6}$$

$$= \frac{240{,}000 \times 7}{289.4 - \dfrac{(90{,}000 + 5{,}060 + 7{,}000)258^2}{10 \times 30{,}000{,}000}} = 6{,}730 \text{ lb. per sq. in.}$$

The total stress due to direct wind load will be $f_w = (5{,}060 + 7{,}000)/13.30 = +\ 910$ lb. per sq. in. The total maximum wind load stress will come on the windward fiber of the leeward end-post, and will be $f_w'' = +\ 6{,}370 + 910 = +\ 7{,}280$ lb. per sq. in.

The maximum stress due to direct dead and live loads (not including impact) and wind load stresses will be

$$\begin{aligned} f &= 90{,}000 \div 13.30 + 7{,}280 \\ &= 6{,}770 + 7{,}280 = 14{,}050 \text{ lb. per sq. in.} \end{aligned}$$

From the specifications the allowable stress may be increased 50 per cent when direct and flexural wind stresses are considered.

The allowable stress when both direct and flexural wind stress are considered is then

$$f_c = 9{,}400 \times 1.50 = 14{,}100 \text{ lb. per sq. in.}$$

The stresses in the windward post will be less than in the leeward end-post calculated above.

While the section assumed appeared to be excessive, the additional area and the width of plate are required to take the flexure due to wind loads.

Combined Tension and Cross-bending.—The stress due to cross-bending when the member is also subjected to direct tension is given by the formula

$$f_1 = \frac{M_1 \cdot c}{I + \dfrac{P \cdot l^2}{k \cdot E}} \tag{7}$$

the nomenclature being the same as in (1). The constant k is taken equal to 10 where the ends are hinged.

Stress in a Bar Due to its Own Weight.—Let b = breadth of bar in inches; h = depth of bar in inches; w = weight of bar per lineal inch = $0.28\, b \cdot h$ lb.; $f_2 = P/b \cdot h$ = direct unit stress in lb. per sq. in.

We will also have $c = \frac{1}{2}h$; $M_1 = \frac{1}{8}w \cdot l^2$; $P = f_2 \cdot b \cdot h$.

Substituting in (7), we have

$$f_1 = \frac{\frac{1}{8}w \cdot l^2 \cdot \frac{1}{2}h}{\dfrac{b \cdot h^3}{12} + \dfrac{f_2 \cdot b \cdot h \cdot l^2}{10 \times 28{,}000{,}000}} = \frac{4{,}900{,}000h}{f_2 + 23{,}000{,}000\left(\dfrac{h}{l}\right)^2} \tag{8}$$

where f_1 is the extreme fiber stress in the bar due to weight, and is tension in lower fiber and compression in upper fiber.

If the bar is inclined, the stress obtained by formula (8) must be multiplied by the sine of the angle that the bar makes with a vertical line. Formula (8) is much more convenient for actual use than formula (7).

Diagram for Stress in Bars Due to Their Own Weight.—Taking the reciprocal of (8), we have

$$\frac{1}{f_1} = \frac{f_2}{4{,}900{,}000h} + \frac{23{,}000{,}000\left(\dfrac{h}{l}\right)^2}{4{,}900{,}000h} = y_1 + y_2$$

and

$$f_1 = 1/(y_1 + y_2) \tag{9}$$

Fig. 4 gives values of y_1 for different values of f_2, and values of y_2 for different values of the length in feet, L. The values of y_1 and y_2 can be read off the diagram directly for any value of h, f_2 and L. And then, if the sum of y_1 and y_2 be taken on the lower part of the diagram, the reciprocal, which is the fiber stress f_1, may be read off the right hand side.

The use of the diagram will be illustrated by two problems:

PROBLEM 1.—Required the stress in a 4 in. × 1 in. eye-bar, 20 ft. 0 in. long, which has a direct tension of 56,000 lb.

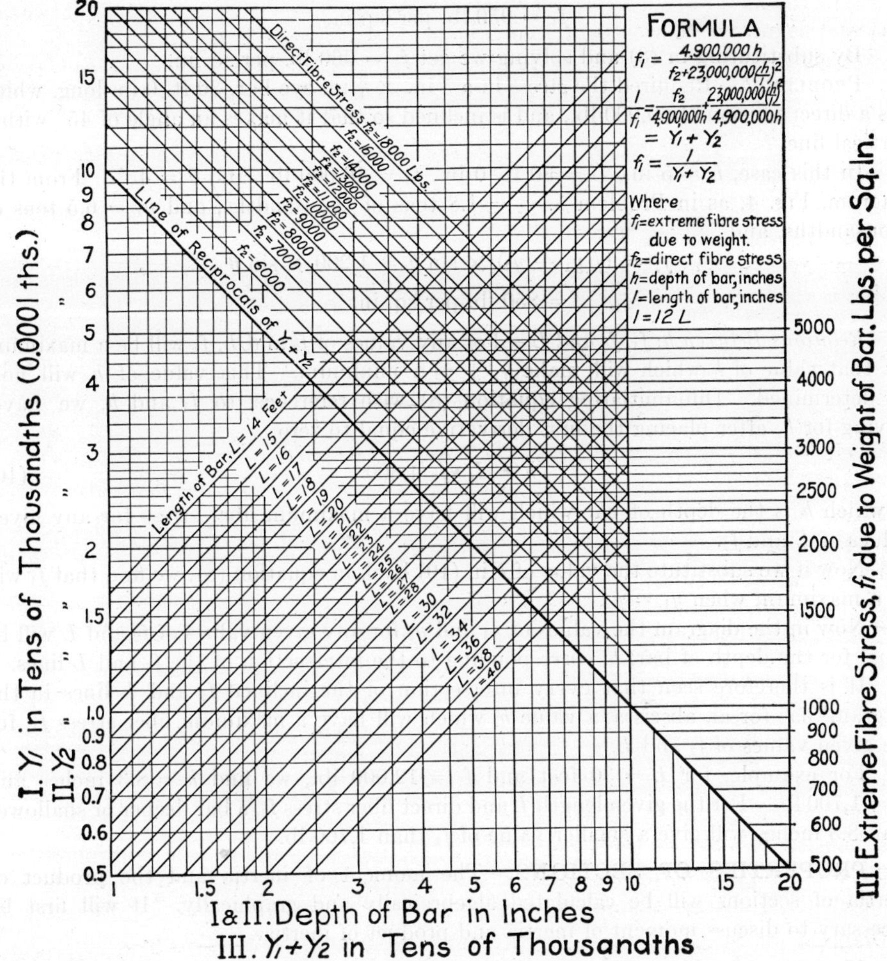

FIG. 4. DIAGRAM FOR FINDING STRESS IN BARS DUE TO THEIR OWN WEIGHT.

In this case, h = 4 in., L = 20 ft. 0 in., and f_2 = 14,000 lb. per sq. in. The stress due to weight, f_1, is found as follows: On the bottom of the diagram, Fig. 4, find h = 4 inches, follow up the vertical line to its intersection with inclined line marked, L = 20 feet, and then follow the horizontal line passing through the point of intersection out to the left margin and find, $y_2 = 3.3$ tens of thousandths; then follow the vertical line, $h = 4$ inches, up to its intersecçion with inclined line marked, $f_2 = 14{,}000$, and then follow the horizontal line passing through the point of intersection out to the left margin and find, $y_1 = 7.2$ tens of thousandths.

Now to find the reciprocal of $y_1 + y_2 = 7.2 + 3.3 = 10.5$, find value of $y_1 + y_2 = 10.5$ on lower edge of diagram, follow vertical line to its intersection with inclined line marked " Line of Reciprocals " and find stress f_1 by following horizontal line to right hand margin to be

$$f_1 = 950 \text{ lb. per sq. in.}$$

By substituting in (8) and solving we get $f_1 = 960$ lb. per sq. in.

PROBLEM 2.—Required the stress in a 5 in. $\times \frac{3}{4}$ in. eye-bar, 30 ft. 0 in. long, which has a direct tension of 60,000 lb., and is inclined so that it makes an angle of 45° with a vertical line.

In this case, $h = 5$ in., $L = 30$ ft. 0 in., $f_2 = 16{,}000$ lb., and $\theta = 45°$. From the diagram, Fig. 4, as in Problem 1, $y_2 = 1.8$ tens of thousandths, and $y_1 = 6.5$ tens of thousandths, and

$$f_1 = 1/(y_1 + y_2) \times \sin\theta = 1{,}200 \times \sin\theta$$
$$= 850 \text{ lb. per sq. in.}$$

Relations Between h, f_1, f_2 and L.—For any values of f_2 and L, f_1 will be a maximum for that value of h which will make $y_1 + y_2$ a minimum. This value of h will now be determined. Differentiating equation (8) with reference to f_1 and h, we have, solving for h, after placing the first derivative equal to zero

$$h = L\sqrt{f_2}/4{,}800 \tag{10}$$

in which h is the depth of bar which will have a maximum fiber stress for any given values of L and f_2.

Now if we substitute the value of h in (10) back in equation (8), we find that f_1 will be a maximum when $y_1 = y_2$.

Now in the diagram the values of y_1 and y_2 for any given values of f_2 and L will be equal for the depth of bar, h, corresponding to the intersection of the f_2 and L lines.

It is therefore seen that every intersection of the inclined f_2 and L lines in the diagram, has for an abscissa, a value h, which will have a maximum fiber stress f_1, for the given values of f_2 and L.

For example, for $L = 30$ feet and $f_2 = 12{,}000$ lb., we find $h = 8.3$ inches and $f_1 = 1{,}700$ lb. For the given length L and direct fiber stress f_2, a bar deeper or shallower than 8.3 inches will give a smaller value of f_1 than 1,700 lb.

PROPERTIES OF SECTIONS.—The moment of inertia and the product of inertia of sections will be calculated algebraically and graphically. It will first be necessary to discuss moment of inertia and product of inertia.

Moment of Inertia.—The moment of inertia, I, of a plane area about an axis is the summation of the product of each differential area, dA, multiplied by the square of the distance, y, of the differential area from the axis, and

$$I = \Sigma y^2 \cdot dA \tag{11}$$

For an axis through the centroid of the section (the neutral axis)

$$I = A \cdot r^2 \qquad (12)$$

where A = area of the section, and r = radius of gyration = distance from the neutral axis to a point at which the entire area A may be considered as concentrated. If A is in sq. in. and r is in inches, I will be in.[4] For an axis parallel to the neutral axis and at a distance d, from the neutral axis

$$I_d = I + A \cdot d^2 \qquad (13)$$

Product of Inertia.—The product of inertia, Z, of a plane area about a pair of rectangular axis is the summation of the product of each differential area, dA, multiplied by y, the distance of the differential area from the X-axis and x, the distance of the differential area from the Y-axis.

$$Z_{xy} = \Sigma x \cdot y \cdot dA \qquad (14)$$

The product of inertia, Z, may be written

$$Z_{xy} = A \cdot c_x \cdot r_x = A \cdot c_y \cdot r_y \qquad (15)$$

where r_x and r_y are the radii of gyration of the area referred to the YY-axis and the XX-axis, respectively, and c_x and c_y are lengths known as product abscissas.

The product of inertia of a rectangle with height a and breadth b, about rectangular axes coinciding with the left side and lower edge will be

$$Z = (a \cdot b)\tfrac{1}{2}b \cdot \tfrac{1}{2}a = \tfrac{1}{4}a^2 \cdot b^2$$

The product of inertia, Z, of a section may be positive, negative or zero, depending upon the location of the axes. For an axis of symmetry, the product of inertia, Z, will be zero. If the figure is measured in inches the product of inertia will be given in in[4].

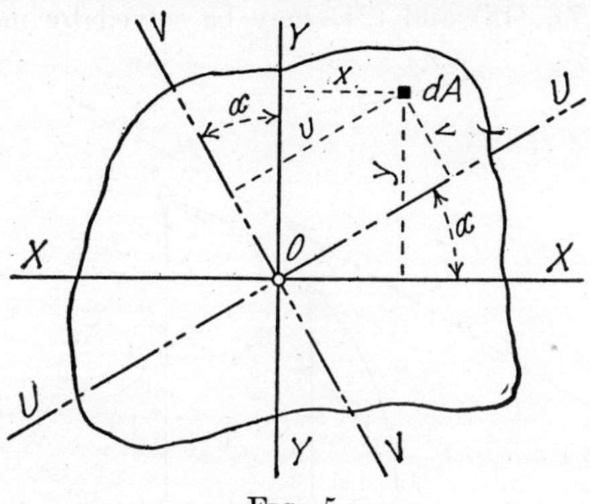

FIG. 5.

Moment of Inertia, Rotation of Axes.—Let the rectangular axes OX and OY in Fig. 5, be revolved through an angle α to the position OU and OV, respectively.

Then,
$$u = y \cdot \sin \alpha + x \cdot \cos \alpha$$
$$v = y \cdot \cos \alpha - x \cdot \sin \alpha$$

Substituting these values of u and v in equations for I_u, I_v and Z_{uv}

$$\begin{aligned} I_u &= \Sigma v^2 \cdot dA \\ &= \Sigma(y \cdot \cos \alpha - x \cdot \sin \alpha)^2 dA \\ &= \Sigma y^2 \cdot \cos^2 \alpha \cdot dA + \Sigma x^2 \cdot \sin^2 \alpha \cdot dA - 2\Sigma x \cdot y \cdot \sin \alpha \cdot \cos \alpha \cdot dA \\ &= I_x \cdot \cos^2 \alpha + I_y \cdot \sin^2 \alpha - Z_{xy} \cdot \sin 2\alpha \qquad (16) \end{aligned}$$

Also, in a similar manner

$$I_v = I_x \cdot \sin^2 \alpha + I_y \cdot \cos^2 \alpha + Z_{xy} \sin 2\alpha \tag{17}$$

and

$$\begin{aligned} Z_{uv} &= \Sigma u \cdot v \cdot dA \\ &= \Sigma(y \cdot \sin \alpha + x \cdot \cos \alpha)(y \cdot \cos \alpha - x \cdot \sin \alpha) dA \\ &= \Sigma y^2 \cdot \sin \alpha \cdot \cos \alpha \cdot dA + \Sigma x \cdot y \cdot \cos^2 \alpha \cdot dA - \Sigma x \cdot y \cdot \sin^2 \alpha \cdot dA - \Sigma x^2 \cdot \sin \alpha \cdot \cos \alpha \cdot dA \\ &= \tfrac{1}{2}(I_x - I_y) \sin 2\alpha + Z_{xy} \cdot \cos 2a \end{aligned} \tag{18}$$

Adding equations (16) and (17),

$$I_u + I_v = I_x + I_y \tag{19}$$

and

$$r_u^2 + r_v^2 = r_x^2 + r_y^2 \tag{20}$$

Principal Axes.—To obtain the value of $\alpha = \beta$ for the principal axes (axes for which $Z = 0$), place Z_{uv} in (18) equal to zero, and

$$\tan 2\beta = -\frac{2Z_{xy}}{I_x - I_y} \tag{21}$$

If I_1 and I_2 are the moments of inertia for the principal axes, by substituting (21) in (16) and (17), we have

$$I_1 = I_y - Z_{xy} \cdot \tan \beta \tag{22}$$

$$I_2 = I_x + Z_{xy} \cdot \tan \beta \tag{23}$$

Equations (16), (17), (18) and (21) may be solved by means of the "Circle of Inertia."

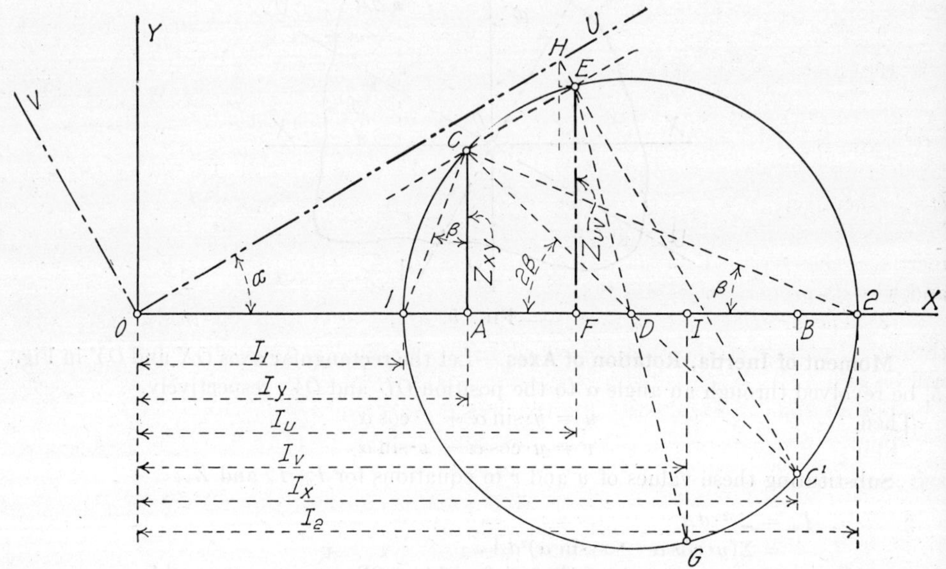

FIG. 6. CIRCLE OF INERTIA.

Circle of Inertia.—From any point O, Fig. 6, along the axis OX, lay off $OA = I_y$ and $OB = I_x$. At point A lay off $AC = Z_{xy}$ upward if plus, and downward if minus. Bisect the line AB at point D. With radius CD and center D, describe the circle 1–C–2. Circle 1–C–2 is the "Circle of Inertia" for the given section.

To calculate I_u, I_v and Z_{uv}, for the axes OU and OV, making an angle α with axes OX and OY, respectively, proceed as follows:

Through C draw CE parallel to OU. Drop a perpendicular EF on axis OX. Draw EG through center of circle. Drop perpendicular from G to axis OX at I. Then

$$OF = I_u$$

$$OI = I_v$$

$$EF = Z_{uv}$$

Proof:—

$$OF = OH \cdot \cos\alpha + HE \cdot \sin\alpha \tag{24}$$

$$EF = OH \cdot \sin\alpha - HE \cdot \cos\alpha \tag{25}$$

But

$$OH = I_x \cdot \cos\alpha - Z_{xy} \cdot \sin\alpha \tag{26}$$

$$HE = I_y \cdot \sin\alpha - Z_{xy} \cdot \cos\alpha \tag{27}$$

Substituting in (24) and (25)

$$OF = I_x \cdot \cos^2\alpha + I_y \cdot \sin^2\alpha - Z_{xy} \cdot \sin 2\alpha \tag{29}$$

$$EF = \tfrac{1}{2}(I_x - I_y)\sin 2\alpha + Z_{xy} \cdot \cos 2\alpha \tag{30}$$

By comparing (29) and (30) with (16) and (18), it will be seen that,

$$OF = I_u \tag{31}$$

$$EF = Z_{uv} \tag{32}$$

Also

$$OI = I_v \tag{33}$$

By construction angle $CDA = 2\beta$, and (21) follows from inspection.

From Fig. 6 it will be seen.

(1) The maximum and minimum values of the moment of inertia will be O-2 and O-1, respectively;

(2) For maximum and minimum values of the moment of inertia, the product of inertia equals zero. This shows why the term product of inertia is not often used, and why its properties are not familiar;

(3) The principal axes will be parallel to the lines C-1 and C-2; for a line drawn through C parallel to the axis OU will pass through point 1, and the product of inertia will be zero.

For an application of the "Inertia circle," see Problem 7, Chapter XIII.

Ellipse of Inertia.—For the principal axes, angle $\alpha = \beta$, the product of inertia is zero, and equation (16) becomes

$$I_u = I_x \cdot \cos^2\beta + I_y \cdot \sin^2\beta$$

$$A \cdot r_u^2 = A \cdot r_x^2 \cdot \cos^2\beta + A \cdot r_y^2 \cdot \sin^2\beta$$

$$r_u^2 = r_x^2 \cdot \cos^2\beta + r_y^2 \cdot \sin^2\beta \tag{34}$$

Now let $x = r_x \cdot r_y \cdot \cos \beta / r_u$, and $y = r_x \cdot r_y \cdot \sin \beta / r_u$, then

$$\frac{x^2}{r_y^2} + \frac{y^2}{r_x^2} = 1 \tag{35}$$

Equation (35) is the equation of an ellipse in which r_x and r_y are the major and minor semi-axes.

It is required to calculate a tangent to the point B in Fig. 7 which shall be normal to the axis A-O.

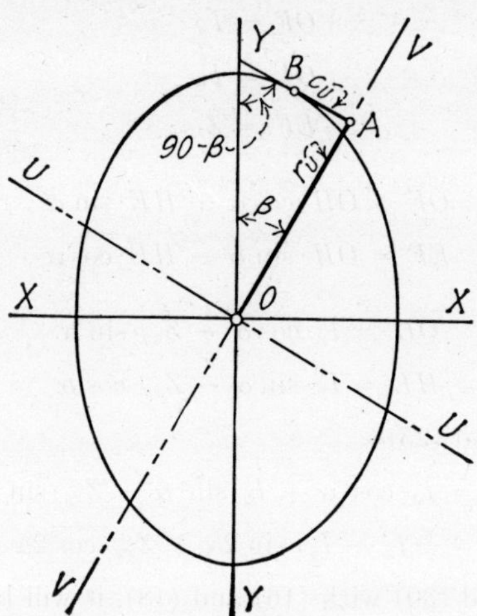

FIG. 7. ELLIPSE OF INERTIA.

Differentiate equation (35) with reference to x, and the equation of the tangent to the ellipse at B, coordinates x, y, will be

$$\frac{x_1 \cdot dx}{r_y^2} + \frac{y_1 \cdot dy}{r_x^2} = 0 \tag{36}$$

and

$$\frac{dy}{dx} = - \frac{x_1 \cdot r_x^2}{y_1 \cdot r_y^2} = \tan \beta$$

from which

$$x_1 = - \frac{y_1 \cdot r_y^2 \cdot \sin \beta}{r_x^2 \cdot \cos \beta} \tag{37}$$

Substitute x_1 in (37) in (35), and

$$\frac{y_1^2 \cdot r_y^2 \cdot \sin^2 \beta}{r_x^4 \cdot \cos^2 \beta} + \frac{y_1^2}{r_x^2} = 1 \tag{38}$$

Solving (38),

$$y_1^2 = \frac{r_x^4 \cdot \cos^2 \beta}{r_y^2 \cdot \sin^2 \beta + r_x^2 \cdot \cos^2 \beta} \tag{39}$$

But the denominator in (39) is equal to r_u^2 in (34), and

$$y_1^2 = \frac{r_x^4 \cdot \cos^2 \beta}{r_u^2}$$

and

$$y_1 = \frac{r_x^2 \cdot \cos \beta}{r_u} \tag{40}$$

also

$$x_1 = \frac{r_y^2 \cdot \sin \beta}{r_u} \tag{41}$$

Now

$$OA = x_1 \cdot \sin \beta + y_1 \cdot \cos \beta = \frac{r_y^2 \cdot \sin^2 \beta + r_x^2 \cdot \cos^2 \beta}{r_u} = r_u \tag{42}$$

Also, $BA = y \cdot \sin \beta - x \cdot \cos \beta = c_u$

$$= \frac{r_x^2 \cdot \cos \beta \cdot \sin \beta}{r_u} - \frac{r_y^2 \cdot \sin \beta \cdot \cos \beta}{r_u}$$

$$= \frac{(I_x - I_y) \sin 2\beta}{2 r_u \cdot A}$$

From (18) $Z_{xy} = 0$, and $Z_{uv} = (I_x - I_y) \sin 2\beta$, then

$$c_u = \frac{Z_{uv}}{r_u \cdot A} \tag{43}$$

and

$$Z_{uv} = c_u \cdot r_u \cdot A \tag{44}$$

Therefore, if a tangent be drawn parallel to any axis the radius of gyration about this axis will be the perpendicular distance between this axis and the tangent; and the product of inertia will be equal to the product of this radius of gyration and the distance from the point of tangency of this tangent to the intersection of this tangent with the major axis.

For the principal axes, $c_x = 0$, and $Z_{xy} = 0$.

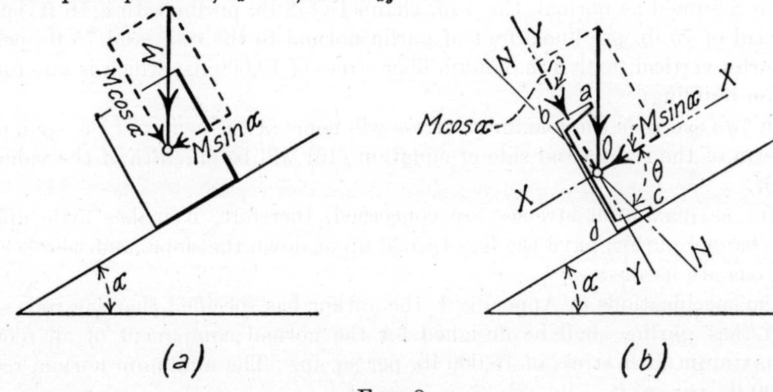

FIG. 8.

OBLIQUE LOADING ON BEAMS.—Steel purlins on roofs are made of channels or I-beams with the web normal to the roof. The wind loads are usually assumed as normal to the roof while dead and snow loads are vertical. The bending moment due to the vertical loading = M, may be resolved into a component, $M \cdot \sin \alpha$, parallel to the roof, and a component, $M \cdot \cos \alpha$, normal to the roof. The total fiber stress due to the vertical loading will be

$$f = f_x + f_y = \frac{M \cdot y \cdot \cos \alpha}{I_x} + \frac{M \cdot x \cdot \sin \alpha}{I_y} \tag{45}$$

The stress f_x will be compression on the top and tension on the bottom edges. For simple spans the stress f_y will be compression on the upper and tension on the lower flanges. For a simple span the maximum compression will be at the point a in Fig. 8.

For a 6 in channel @ 8 lb. on a roof with $\frac{1}{4}$ pitch ($\alpha = 26° 34'$), $I_x = 13.0$ in.^{4}, $I_y = 0.70$ in.^{4}, $y = 3$ in., $x = 1.403$ in. to point a with the flanges turned up the slope as in Fig. 8, and $x_1 = 0.517$ in. to the upper right hand fiber with the flanges turned down the slope. Then the total fiber stress in the upper right hand fiber with the flanges of the channel turned up the slope will be

$$f = f_x + f_y = 0.206M + 0.896M = 1.102M \tag{46}$$

If the flanges of the channel are turned down the slope the maximum fiber stress will be tension and will be on the top of the lower flange and will have the same value as the maximum compression given in equation (46).

With a purlin made of a 6 in. channel @ 8 lb., 16 ft. long, a vertical load of 40 lb. per lineal foot of purlin will give a maximum fiber stress by inserting in (46) of 17,000 lb. per sq. in. In practice 6 in. channels @ 8 lb. with about a 5 ft. spacing are used up to spans of 16 ft., the center of the purlin being supported by a sag rod placed in the plane of the roof. If the sag rod is drawn up so that there is no deflection of the center of the purlin in the plane of the roof, the bending moment in the plane of the roof will be one-fourth of that given in (46), and the maximum fiber stress will be

$$f = f_x + f_y = 0.206M + 0.224M = 0.430M \tag{47}$$

With a sag rod at the middle of the 16-ft span a vertical load of 100 lb. per lineal foot of purlin will produce a maximum fiber stress of 16,500 lb. per sq. in. If one-half the load is assumed as normal, the 6 in. channel @ 8 lb. purlin with a 16 ft. span will carry a load of 75 lb. per lineal foot of purlin normal to the roof, and 75 lb. per lineal foot of purlin vertical, with a maximum fiber stress of 19,000 lb., which is safe for rolled sections on buildings.

With two sag rods the maximum stress will come at the center of the span and the second term of the right hand side of equation (46) will be one-fifth of the value given or $0.195M$.

As far as maximum stresses are concerned, therefore, it makes little difference whether channel purlins have the legs turned up or down the slope, and whether one or two sag rods are used.

In the specifications in Appendix I, the author has specified that sag rods shall be used and that purlins shall be designed for the normal component of all roof loads with a maximum fiber stress of 16,000 lb. per sq. in. The minimum normal roof load is to be 30 lb. per sq. ft.

ECCENTRIC RIVETED CONNECTIONS.—The actual shearing stresses in riveted connections are often very much in excess of the stresses due to direct shear. This will be illustrated by the calculation of the shearing stresses in the rivets of the standard connection in Fig. 9.

The eccentric force, P, may be replaced by a direct force P, acting through the center of gravity of the rivets and parallel to its original direction, and a couple with a moment, $M = P \times 3'' = 60{,}000$ in.-lb. Each rivet will then take a direct shear equal to P divided by n, where n = total number of rivets in the connection, and a shear due to bending moment M.

The shear on any rivet due to twisting moment will vary as the distance, and the resisting moment exerted by each rivet will vary as the square of the distance from the center of gravity of all the rivets.

Now if a is taken as the resultant shear due to twisting moment on a rivet at a unit distance from the center of gravity of all the rivets, we will have the relation

$$M = a(d_1^2 + d_2^2 + d_3^2 + d_4^2 + d_5^2)$$
$$= a\Sigma d^2$$

and

$$a = \frac{M}{\Sigma d^2} = \frac{60{,}000}{23.10} \tag{48}$$
$$= 2{,}600 \text{ lb.}$$

The remainder of the calculations are shown in Table I. The resultant shears on the rivets are given in the last column of Table I, and are much larger than would be expected.

TABLE I.

Direct shear, $S = 20{,}000 \div 5 = 4{,}000$ lb

Moment = $20{,}000 \times 3 = 60{,}000$ in.-lb. = $a(d_1^2+d_2^2+d_3^2+d_4^2+d_5^2)$ where a = moment shear on rivet 3 = 2,600 lb.

Rivet.	d, In.	d^2, In.².	Moment, In.-Lb.	M, Lb.	S, Lb.	R, Lb.
1	2.70	7.25	18,850	6,820	4,000	9,260
2	1.95	3.80	9,875	5,070	4,000	3,250
3	1.00	1.00	2,600	2,600	4,000	6,600
4	1.95	3.80	9,875	5,070	4,000	3,250
5	2.70	7.25	18,850	6,820	4,000	9,260
		23.10	60,000		20,000	

$a\Sigma d^2 = 23.10\, a = 60{,}000$ in.-lb.
$a = 2{,}600$ lb. = moment shear on rivet 3
M = shear due to moment
S = shear due to direct load, P.
R = resultant shear

The force and equilibrium polygons for the resultant shears and the load P, drawn in Fig. 9, close, which shows that the connection is in equilibrium.

Center of Motion.—The total shear on rivet 3 is $4{,}000 + 2{,}600 = 6{,}600$ lb., and is parallel to the resultant force P. There will be some point to the right of rivet 3 where the total shear on a rivet will be zero. This point will be at a distance to the right of rivet 3 equal to $6{,}600 \div 2{,}600 = 2.54$ in. The center of motion of all of the rivets of the group will then be at a distance to the right of the center of gravity of the rivets equal to $2.54 - 1.00 = 1.54$ in. The total shear on each rivet will be equal to a (2,600 lb.) multiplied by the distance of the rivet from the center of motion. The direction of the shear on each rivet will be normal to the rotation arm.

Let the distance from the center of motion to any rivet be represented by the distance z, and the distances of the rivets will be
$z_3 = 2.54$ in., $z_2 = z_4 = \sqrt{1.25^2 + 0.04^2} = 1.25$ in., $z_1 = z_5 = \sqrt{2.54^2 + 2.5^2} = 3.56$ in.
The total shears on the rivets will then be

$$R_3 = 2.54 \times 2{,}600 = 6{,}600 \text{ lb.}$$
$$R_2 = R_4 = 1.25 \times 2{,}600 = 3{,}250 \text{ lb.}$$
$$R_1 = R_5 = 3.56 \times 2{,}600 = 9{,}260 \text{ lb.}$$

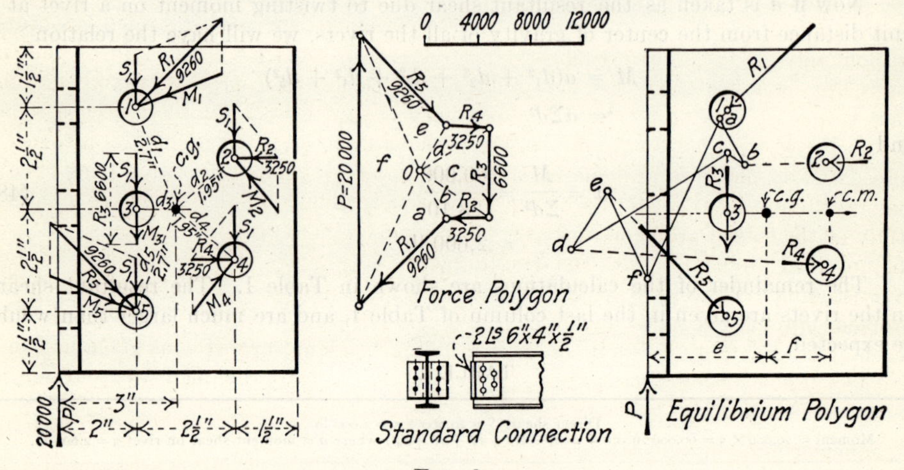

FIG. 9.

The value of Σd^2 about the center of gravity of the rivets may be calculated as follows. If the coordinates of the rivets are represented by x and y, then

$$\Sigma d^2 = \Sigma(x^2 + y^2) = 23.10 \text{ in.}^2$$

and $a = M/\Sigma d^2 = 2{,}600$ lb. as above. Let e be the distance from the line of action of P to the center of gravity of the rivets and f be the distance from the center of gravity to the center of motion, Fig. 9. Now the moment of the direct shears on the rivets about the line of action of force P will be equal to the twisting moment of the rivets about the center of gravity, and since the direct shears on the rivets parallel to line of action of force P is $f.n.a.$,

$$f \times n \times a \times e = a\Sigma d^2$$

and

$$f = \frac{\Sigma d^2}{n \cdot e}$$

and since number of rivets is $n = 5$

$$f = \frac{\Sigma d^2}{5e} = 23.10/15 = 1.54 \text{ in.}$$

which gives a method for calculating f for any connection. The center of motion will be on a line drawn normal to the line of action of P and passing through the center of gravity.

See Ketchum's "Structural Engineers' Handbook," page 729 for the calculation of the stresses in four types of eccentric rivet connections.

CHAPTER XIII.

Problems in the Calculation of Stresses in Framed Structures.

Introduction.—It is impossible for the student to gain a working knowledge of algebraic and graphic statics and of the calculation of stresses in framed structures without solving numerous problems. In order to save the time of the student and the instructor, it is necessary that the problems be selected with great care and that the data be put in working form. The problems given in this chapter have been used by the author in his classes and have proved their usefulness. The student is assigned a solved and an unsolved problem involving the same principles, but with different data. Before attempting the solution of the unsolved problem, the student makes a careful study of the solved problem, and uses the principles there explained in the solution of the unsolved problem. With the definite instructions given, the student loses no time in proceeding to the solution of the problem, and not only gains a knowledge of the given problem but also acquires facility in solving additional problems. This method of teaching is essentially the same as the method of teaching surveying as given in Pence and Ketchum's "Surveying Manual." By slightly changing the quantities and dimensions, the data for new problems may be easily obtained.

Instructions.—(1) Plate.—The standard plate is to be $9'' \times 10\frac{1}{2}''$, with a $1''$ border on the left-hand side, and a $\frac{1}{2}''$ border on the top, bottom, and right-hand side of the plate. The plate inside the border is to be $7\frac{1}{2}'' \times 9\frac{1}{2}''$. (2) Co-ordinates.—Unless stated to the contrary, co-ordinates given in the data will refer to the lower left-hand corner of border as the origin of co-ordinates. In defining the force, $P \dfrac{1500}{150^\circ}$ (5.0″, 3.0″), the force is 1500 lb., makes 150° with the X-axis (lies in the second quadrant), and passes through a point 5.0″ to the right, and 3.0″ above the lower left-hand corner of border. (3) Data.—Complete data shall be placed on each problem so that the solution will be self explanatory. (4) Scales.—The scales of forces, and of frames or trusses shall be given as 1″ = (   ) lb., or ft.; and by a graphic scale as well. (5) Name.—The name of the student is to be placed outside the border in the lower right-hand corner. (6) Equations.—All equations shall be given, but details of the solution may be indicated. (7) Lettering.—Engineering News lettering is to be used on all drawings. Titles may be vertical, all other figures and lettering shall be inclined. Height of letters and figures shall be as follows: Main titles—capitals ¼ in., small capitals 1/5 in., other lettering—capitals, full height lower case letters and numerals. 5/30 in., lower case letters 3/30 in. All lettering and drawings are to be executed in pencil. (8) References.—References are to "The Design of Steel Mill Buildings," and to the author's "Structural Engineer's Handbook."

Note.—It should be noted that all the problems have been reduced so that all dimensions are about five-eighths of the original dimensions given in the statements of the problems.

PROBLEM 1. RESULTANT OF CONCURRENT FORCES.

(a) **Problem.**—Given the following concurrent forces:

$$P_1\frac{1900}{120°};\quad P_2\frac{950}{30°};\quad P_3\frac{1700}{315°};\quad P_4\frac{750}{240°};\quad P_5\frac{2200}{150°}.$$

Forces are given in pounds. Required to find the resultant, R, by means of a force diagram. Check by calculating R by the algebraic method. Give all equations. Also construct check force polygon. Give amount and direction of the resultant. Scale for force polygon, 1″ = 400 lb.

(b) **Methods.**—Start P_1 at point 4″, 3½″ (x, y, using lower left-hand corner of the border as the origin of co-ordinates) and take the forces in the order, P_1, P_2, P_3, P_4, P_5. Draw check polygon starting at the same point and drawing the forces in the order P_2, P_4, P_5, P_3, P_1, as described in Chapter I.

Calculate the value of R in amount, line of action and direction as described in Chapter I.

(c) **Results.**—The resultant is a force R acting through the point of intersection of the given forces, and is parallel to the closing line in the force polygon. It will be seen that it is immaterial in what order the forces are taken in calculating the resultant, R. In the algebraic solution the summation of the horizontal components of the forces, including the resultant, R, are placed equal to zero, and the summation of the vertical components of the forces, including the resultant, R, are placed equal to zero. Solving these equations we have the value of R, and the angle θ, which R makes with the X-axis.

This problem is essentially the same as the closure of a survey in which the sum of the departures east and west of the point of closure must equal zero, and the sum of the latitudes north and south of the point of closure must equal zero. If the survey does not close, the length of the closing course will equal the square root of the sum of the square of the sum of the departures and the square of the sum of the latitudes. The tangent of the angle of the closing course will be equal to the sum of the departures divided by the sum of the latitudes.

PROBLEM 1a. RESULTANT OF CONCURRENT FORCES.

(a) **Problem.**—Given the following concurrent forces:

$$P_1\frac{1800}{120°};\quad P_2\frac{1000}{30°};\quad P_3\frac{1700}{315°};\quad P_4\frac{750}{240°};\quad P_5\frac{2100}{150°}.$$

Forces are given in pounds. Required to find the resultant, R, by means of a force diagram. Check by calculating R by the algebraic method. Give all equations. Also construct check force polygon. Give amount and direction of the resultant. Scale for force polygon, 1″ = 400 lb.

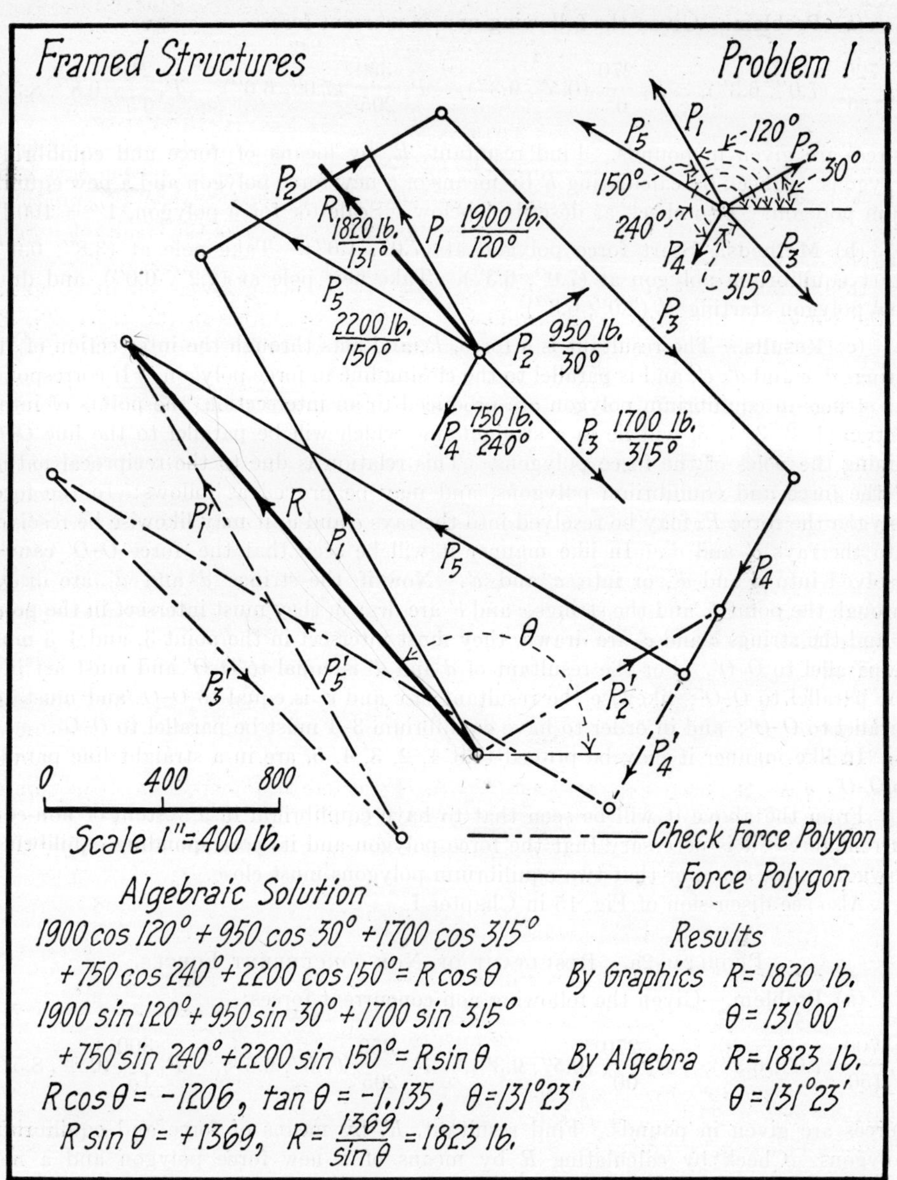

Framed Structures
Problem 1
P1
P2
P3
P4
P5
R
-120°
30°
150°
240°
315°
1820 lb.
131°
1900 lb.
120°
2200 lb.
150°
950 lb.
30°
750 lb.
240°
1700 lb.
315°
P'1
P'2
P'3
P'4
P'5
θ
0
400
800
Scale 1"=400 lb.
Check Force Polygon
Force Polygon
Algebraic Solution
1900 cos 120° + 950 cos 30° + 1700 cos 315°
+ 750 cos 240° + 2200 cos 150° = R cos θ
1900 sin 120° + 950 sin 30° + 1700 sin 315°
+ 750 sin 240° + 2200 sin 150° = R sin θ
R cos θ = -1206, tan θ = -1.135, θ = 131°23'
R sin θ = +1369, R = 1369/sin θ = 1823 lb.
Results
By Graphics R = 1820 lb.
θ = 131°00'
By Algebra R = 1823 lb.
θ = 131°23'

PROBLEM 2. RESULTANT OF NON-CONCURRENT FORCES.

(a) **Problem.**—Given the following non-concurrent forces:

$P_1 \frac{720}{150°}$ (7.0″, 6.3″), $P_2 \frac{270}{0°}$ (0.5″, 9.3″), $P_3 \frac{350}{205°}$ (7.0″, 6.6″), $P_4 \frac{210}{15°}$ (0.8″, 8.5′.)

Forces are given in pounds. Find resultant, R, by means of force and equilibrium polygons. Check by calculating R by means of a new force polygon and a new equilibrium polygon. Also check as described below. Scale for force polygon, 1″ = 100 lb.

(b) **Methods.**—Start force polygon at (7.0″, 1.0″). Take pole at (3.8″, 0.0″). Start equilibrium polygon at (7.0″, 6.3″). Take new pole at (2.2″, 0.0″), and draw new polygon starting at (7.0″, 6.3″).

(c) **Results.**—The resultant is a force, R, and acts through the intersection of the strings d, e and d', e', and is parallel to the closing line in force polygon. If corresponding strings in equilibrium polygon are produced to an intersection the points of intersection, 1, 2 3, 4, 5, will lie in a straight line which will be parallel to the line O–O' joining the poles of the force polygons. This relation is due to the reciprocal nature of the force and equilibrium polygons, and may be proved as follows: In the force polygon the force P_4 may be resolved into the rays c and d, it may likewise be resolved into the rays c' and d'. In like manner it will be seen that the force O–O' can be resolved into d and d', or into c and c'. Now if the strings d and d' are drawn through the point 4, and the strings c and c' are drawn, they must intersect in the point 4, and the strings c and c' are drawn, they must intersect in the point 3, and 4–3 must be parallel to O–O'. For the resultant of d and d' is equal to O–O' and must act in a line parallel to O–O'; likewise the resultant of c and c' is equal to O–O' and must act parallel to O–O'; and in order to have equilibrium 3–4 must be parallel to O–O'.

In like manner it may be proved that 1, 2, 3, 4, 5, are in a straight line parallel to O–O'.

From the above it will be seen that to have equilibrium in a system of non-concurrent forces it is necessary that the force polygon and its corresponding equilibrium polygons must close, or that two equilibrium polygons must close.

Also see discussion of Fig. 15 in Chapter I.

PROBLEM 2a. RESULTANT OF NON-CONCURRENT FORCES.

(a) **Problem.**—Given the following non-concurrent forces:

$P_1 \frac{700}{150°}$ (7.0″, 6.3″), $P_2 \frac{270}{00°}$ (0.5″, 9.3″), $P_3 \frac{350}{205°}$ (7.0″, 6.6″), $P_4 \frac{300}{15°}$ (0.8″, 8.5″).

Forces are given in pounds. Find resultant, R, by means of force and equilibrium polygons. Check by calculating R by means of a new force polygon and a new equilibrium polygon. Also check as described in Problem 2. Scale for force polygon, 1″ = 100 lb.

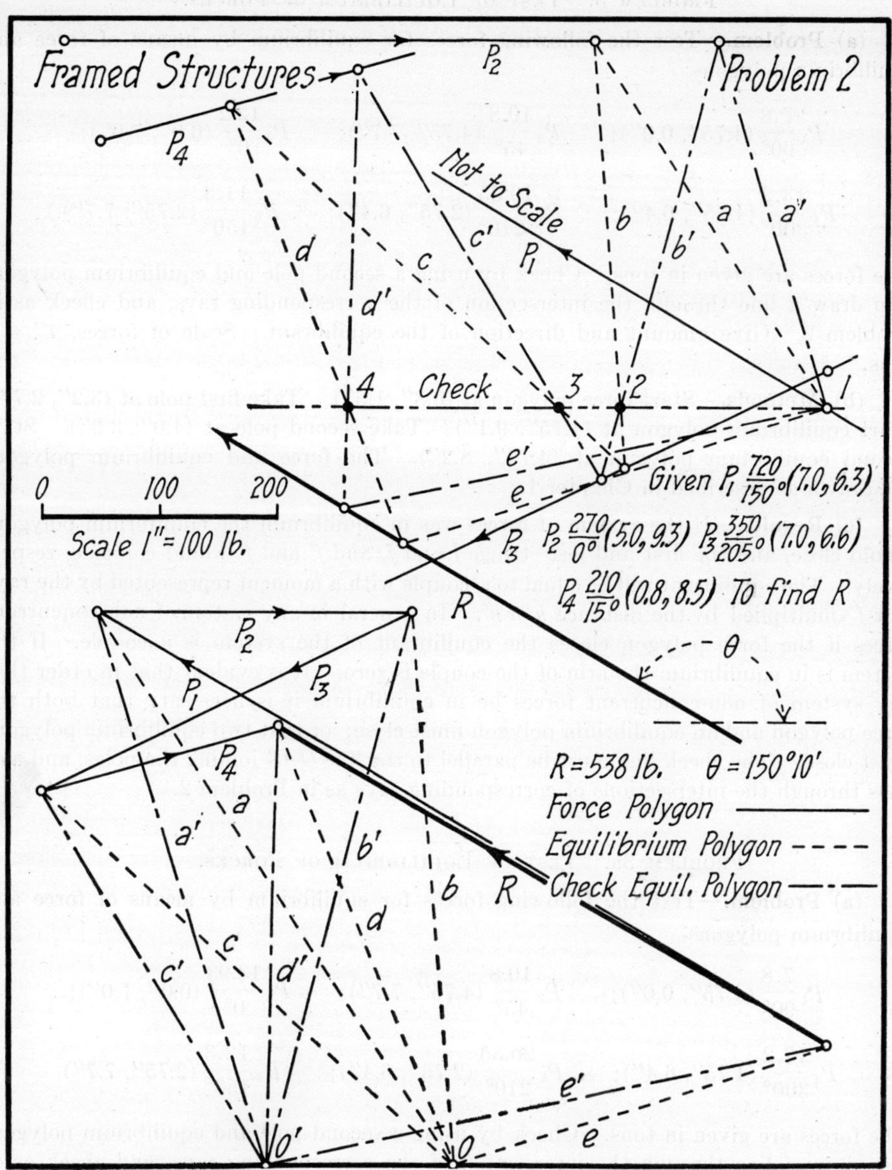

Framed Structures
Problem 2
Not to Scale
Check
Given P_1 $\frac{720}{150^\circ}$ (7.0, 6.3)
P_2 $\frac{270}{0^\circ}$ (5.0, 9.3) P_3 $\frac{350}{205^\circ}$ (7.0, 6.6)
P_4 $\frac{210}{15^\circ}$ (0.8, 8.5)   To find R
0   100   200
Scale 1" = 100 lb.
R = 538 lb.   θ = 150° 10'
Force Polygon
Equilibrium Polygon
Check Equil. Polygon

PROBLEM 3. TEST OF EQUILIBRIUM OF FORCES.

(a) **Problem.**—Test the following forces for equilibrium by means of force and equilibrium polygons:

$P_1 \frac{7.8}{90°}$ (4.75″, 0.0″); $P_2 \frac{10.8}{45°}$ (4.75″, 7.7″); $P_3 \frac{12.2}{0°}$ (0.0″, 7.0″);

$P_4 \frac{13.2}{300°}$ (4.75″, 6.4″); $P_5 \frac{19.35}{210°}$ (2.75″, 6.4″); $P_6 \frac{11.3}{150°}$ (2.75″, 7.7″).

The forces are given in tons. Check by using a second pole and equilibrium polygon; also draw a line through the intersection of the corresponding rays, and check as in Problem 2. Give amount and direction of the equilibrant. Scale of forces, 1″ = 5 tons.

(b) **Methods.**—Start force polygon at (0.8″, 1.5″). Take first pole at (3.2″, 2.7″). Start equilibrium polygon at (4.75″, 9.1″). Take second pole at (4.0″, 3.2″). Start second equilibrium polygon at (4.75″, 8.2″). The force and equilibrium polygons are drawn as described in Chapter I.

(c) **Results.**—If the system of forces was in equilibrium the equilibrium polygons would close, and the first and last strings f and f, and f' and f' would coincide, respectively. The equilibrant will be equal to a couple with a moment represented by the rays f or f' multiplied by the distance h or h'. In general in any system of non-concurrent forces if the force polygon closes the equilibrant of the system is a couple. If the system is in equilibrium the arm of the couple is zero. It is evident that in order that any system of non-concurrent forces be in equilibrium it is necessary that both the force polygon and an equilibrium polygon must close; or that two equilibrium polygons must close. The check line must be parallel to the line O–O' joining the poles, and also pass through the intersections of corresponding rays as in Problem 2.

PROBLEM 3a. TEST OF EQUILIBRIUM OF FORCES.

(a) **Problem.**—Test the following forces for equilibrium by means of force and equilibrium polygons:

$P_1 \frac{7.8}{90°}$ (4.75″, 0.0″); $P_2 \frac{10.8}{45°}$ (4.75″, 7.7″); $P_3 \frac{13.93}{0°}$ (0.0″, 7.0″);

$P_4 \frac{13.2}{300°}$ (4.75″, 6.4″); $P_5 \frac{20.35}{210°}$ (2.75″, 6.4″); $P_6 \frac{12.3}{150°}$ (2.75″, 7.7″).

The forces are given in tons. Check by using a second pole and equilibrium polygon; also draw a line through the intersection of the corresponding rays, and check as in Problem 2. Give amount and direction of the equilibrant. Scale of forces, 1″ = 5 tons.

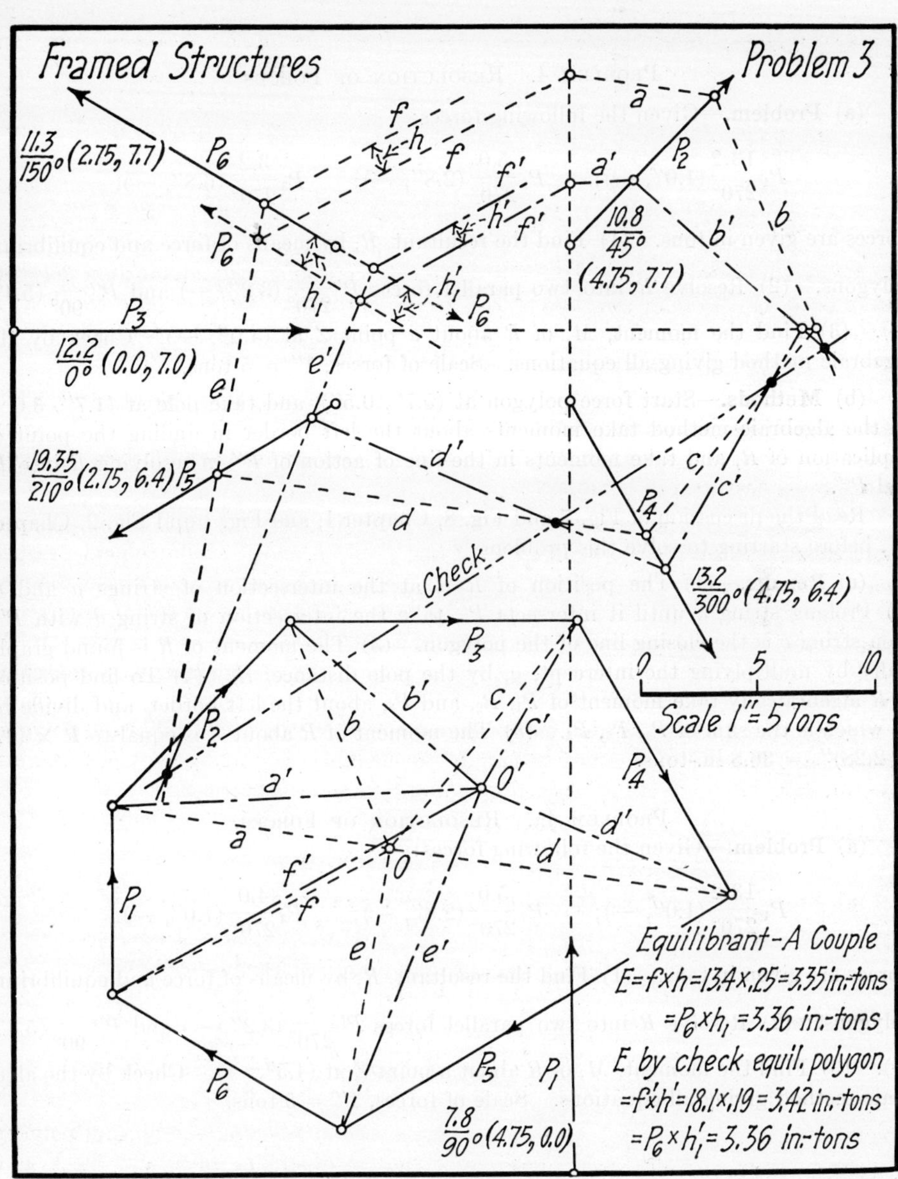
Framed Structures
Problem 3
11.3 / 150° (2.75, 7.7)
P6
10.8 / 45°
(4.75, 7.7)
P2
P3
12.2 / 0° (0.0, 7.0)
19.35 / 210° (2.75, 6.4) P5
13.2 / 300° (4.75, 6.4)
P4
Check
0 5 10
Scale 1" = 5 Tons
P1
Equilibrant-A Couple
E = f×h = 13.4×.25 = 3.35 in.-tons
= P6×h1 = 3.36 in.-tons
E by check equil. polygon
= f'×h' = 18.1×.19 = 3.42 in.-tons
= P6×h'1 = 3.36 in.-tons
7.8 / 90° (4.75, 0.0)

PROBLEM 4. RESOLUTION OF FORCES

(a) **Problem.**—Given the following forces:

$$P_1 \frac{13.2}{270°} (1.0'', —); \quad P_2 \frac{5.0}{270°} (2.8'', —); \quad P_3 \frac{3.2}{270°} (6.8'', —).$$

Forces are given in tons. (1) Find the resultant, R, by means of force and equilibrium polygons. (2) Resolve R into two parallel forces $P' \frac{?}{270°} (3.2'', —)$ and $P'' \frac{?}{90°} (5.4'', —)$. (3) Find the moment, M, of R about a point Z at $(4.0'', —)$. Check by the algebraic method giving all equations. Scale of forces, $1'' = 5$ tons.

(b) **Methods.**—Start force polygon at $(5.7'', 0.5'')$, and take pole at $(1.7'', 3.0'')$. In the algebraic method take moments about the left border in finding the point of application of R, and take moments in the line of action of P'' in resolving R into P' and P''.

Read the discussion of Fig. 7 and Fig. 8, Chapter I, and Fig. 1 and Fig. 2, Chapter IV, before starting to solve this problem.

(c) **Results.**—(1) The position of R is at the intersection of strings a and d. (2) Prolong string a until it intersects P', take the intersection of string d with P''; then string e is the closing line of the polygon. (3) The moment of R is found graphically by multiplying the intercept, y, by the pole distance, H. (4) To find position of R algebraically take moment of P_1, P_2, and P_3, about the left border, and divide by R, which is the sum of P_1, P_2, P_3. (5) The moment of R about Z is equal to $R \times (4.0 - 2.28)'' = 36.8$ in.-tons.

PROBLEM 4a. RESOLUTION OF FORCES.

(a) **Problem.**—Given the following forces:

$$P_1 \frac{13.2}{270°} (1.0'', —); \quad P_2 \frac{5.0}{270°} (2.8'', —); \quad P_3 \frac{4.0}{270°} (7.0'', —).$$

Forces are given in tons. (1) Find the resultant, R, by means of force and equilibrium polygons. (2) Resolve R into two parallel forces $P' \frac{?}{270°} (3.2'', —)$ and $P'' \frac{?}{90°} (5.4'', —)$. (3) Find the moment, M, of R about a point Z at $(4.5'', —)$. Check by the algebraic method giving all equations. Scale of forces, $1'' = 5$ tons.

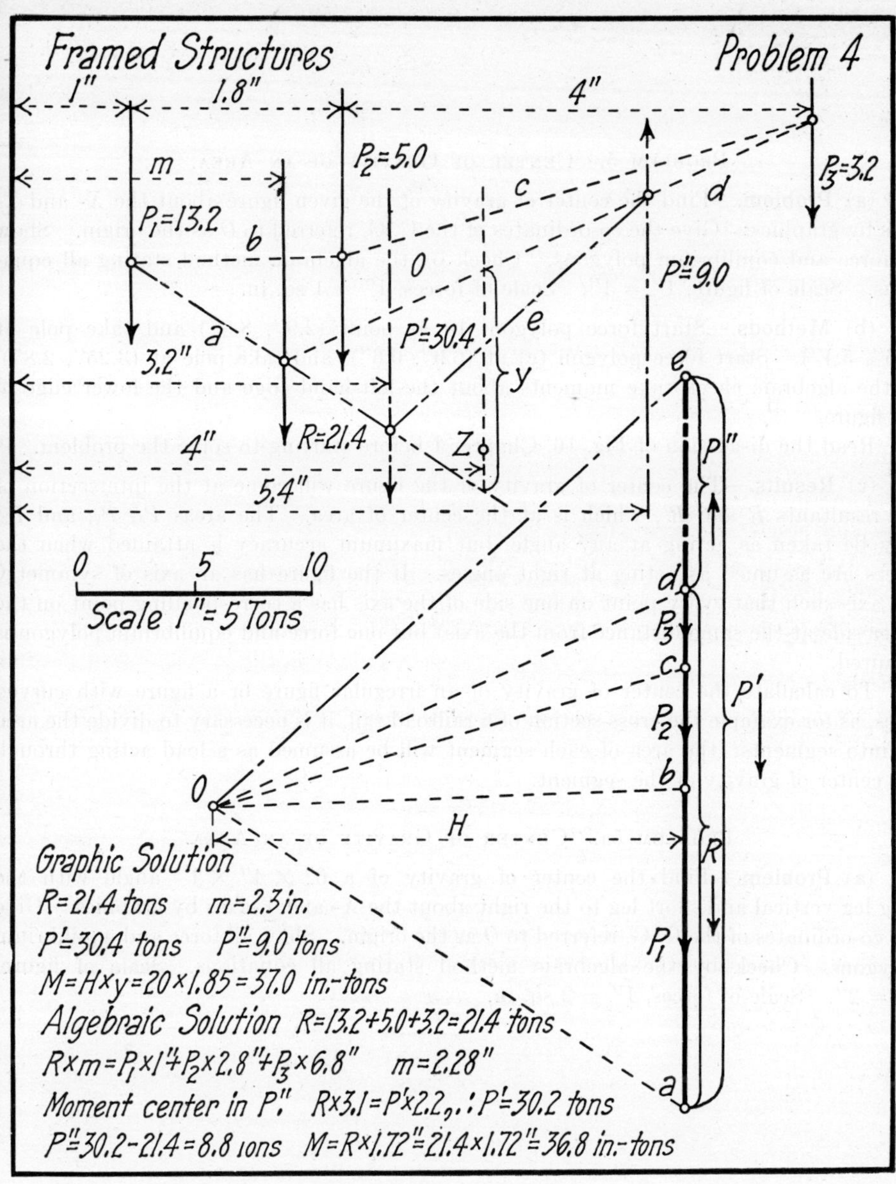
Framed Structures
Problem 4
1"
1.8"
4"
m
$P_2=5.0$
$P_3=3.2$
$P_1=13.2$
c
d
b
0
P"=9.0
a
e
P'=30.4
3.2"
e
y
4"
R=21.4
Z
P"
5.4"
0 5 10
Scale 1"=5 Tons
d
P_3
c
P'
P_2
b
0
H
R
P_1
Graphic Solution
R=21.4 tons m=2.3 in.
P'=30.4 tons P"=9.0 tons
M=H×y=20×1.85=37.0 in.-tons
Algebraic Solution R=13.2+5.0+3.2=21.4 tons
$R\times m=P_1\times 1"+P_2\times 2.8"+P_3\times 6.8"$ m=2.28"
Moment center in P". R×3.1=P'×2.2,.: P'=30.2 tons
P"=30.2-21.4=8.8 tons M=R×1.72"=21.4×1.72"=36.8 in.-tons
a

PROBLEM 5. CENTER OF GRAVITY OF AN AREA.

(a) **Problem.**—Find the center of gravity of the given figure about the *X*- and *Y*-axes by graphics. Give the co-ordinates of the C. G. referred to *O* as the origin. Show all force and equilibrium polygons. Check by the algebraic method stating all equations. Scale of figure, 1″ = 1″. Scale of forces, 1″ = 1 sq. in.

(b) **Methods.**—Start force polygon (b) at point (2.9″, 8.8″) and take pole at (5.6″, 5.4″). Start force polygon (c) at (6.9″, 0.6″), and take pole at (3.25″, 2.8″). In the algebraic check take moments about the left-hand edge and the lower edge of the figure.

Read the discussion of Fig. 16, Chapter I before starting to solve the problem.

(c) **Results.**—The center of gravity of the figure will come at the intersection of the resultants *R* and *R′*, which is at the center of area. The areas P_1, P_2, and P_3, may be taken as acting at any angle, but maximum accuracy is attained when the forces are assumed as acting at right angles. If the figure has an axis of symmetry (an axis such that every point on one side of the axis has a corresponding point on the other side at the same distance from the axis) but one force and equilibrium polygon is required.

To calculate the center of gravity of an irregular figure or a figure with curved sides, as for example the cross-section of a railroad rail, it is necessary to divide the area up into segments; the area of each segment will be assumed as a load acting through the center of gravity of the segment.

PROBLEM 5a. CENTER OF GRAVITY OF AN AREA.

(a) **Problem.**—Find the center of gravity of a 6″ × 4″ × 1″ angle with the long leg vertical and short leg to the right about the *X*- and *Y*-axes by graphics. Give the co-ordinates of the C. G. referred to *O* as the origin. Show all force and equilibrium polygons. Check by the algebraic method stating all equations. Scale of figure, 1″ = 2″. Scale of forces, 1″ = 2 sq. in.

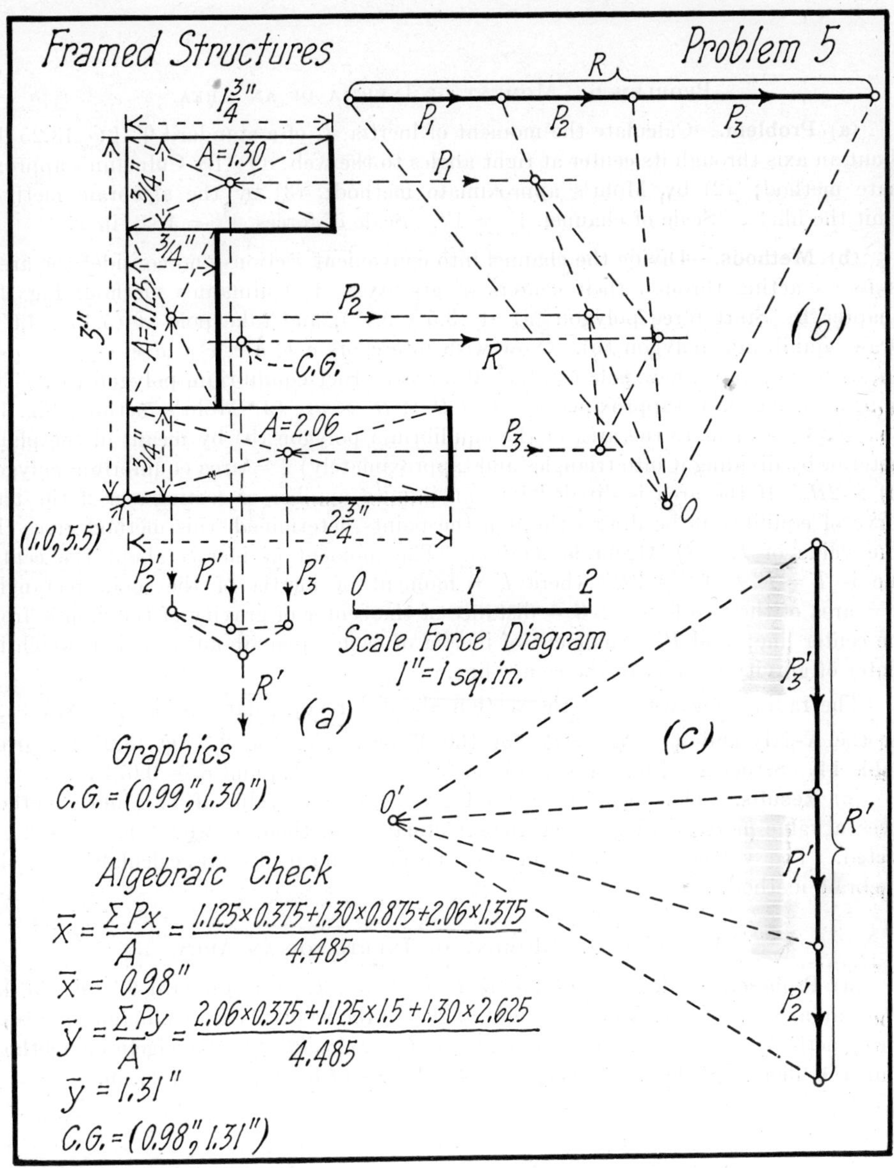

Framed Structures
Problem 5
R
P1
P2
P3
1 3/4"
A=1.30
3/4"
3"
3/4"
A=1.125
C.G.
R
(b)
A=2.06
3/4"
O
(1.0, 5.5)
2 3/4"
P2'
P1'
P3'
0
1
2
Scale Force Diagram
1" = 1 sq. in.
R'
(a)
(c)
Graphics
C.G. = (0.99", 1.30")
O'
R'
Algebraic Check
x̄ = ΣPx / A = (1.125×0.375+1.30×0.875+2.06×1.375) / 4.485
x̄ = 0.98"
ȳ = ΣPy / A = (2.06×0.375+1.125×1.5+1.30×2.625) / 4.485
ȳ = 1.31"
C.G. = (0.98", 1.31")

Problem 6. Moment of Inertia of an Area.

(a) **Problem.**—Calculate the moment of inertia, I, of a standard 9″ [@ 13.25 lb., about an axis through its center at right angles to the web: (1) By Culmann's approximate method; (2) by Mohr's approximate method; (3) by the algebraic method. Omit the fillets. Scale of channel, 1″ = 1″. Scale of forces, 1″ = 1 sq. in.

(b) **Methods.**—Divide the channel into convenient sections and consider the areas as forces acting through their centers of gravity. (1) Culmann's method, Fig. 17, Chapter I. Start force polygon (a) at (3.5″, 9.1″), and take pole at (5.45″, 4.6″). Draw equilibrium polygon (b). Now with intercepts a–b, b–c, c–d, d–e, e–f, f–g, g–h, h–i, as forces, and a new pole at (4.5″, 0.1″) construct equilibrium polygon (d). The moment of inertia is (approximately) $I = H \times H' \times y$. (2) Mohr's method, Fig. 18, Chapter I. Calculate the area of the equilibrium polygon (b) by means of the planimeter or by dividing it into triangles and (approximately) I = area equilibrium polygon (b) $\times\ 2H$. If the area is divided into an infinite number of sections, or if the true curve of equilibrium be drawn through the points determined, this method gives the true value of I. (3) Algebraic method. The moment of inertia about the center line is $I = I' + Ad^2 + 2I''$ where I' = moment of inertia of the main rectangle; A = area of the two flanges; d = distance of the center of gravity of the flanges from the center line; and I'' = moment of inertia of each flange about an axis through its center of gravity parallel to the center line.

The radius of gyration of the section about a rectangular axis is $r_x = \sqrt{I_x \div A}$, for the X-axis and $r_y = \sqrt{I_y \div A}$, for the Y-axis. For the 9″ [@ 13.25 lb., from Table 14, "Structural Engineers' Handbook," r_x = 3.49 in., and r_y = 0.674 in.

(c) **Results.**—The algebraic method gives the true value of I; Mohr's method gives a value more nearly correct than Culmann's method, as would have been expected. The values of I given in the various hand-books are calculated by the algebraic method.

Problem 6a. Moment of Inertia of an Area.

(a) **Problem.**—Calculate the moment of inertia, I, of a standard 9″ [@ 15 lb., about an axis through its center at right angles to the web: (1) By Culmann's approximate method; (2) by Mohr's approximate method; (3) by the algebraic method. Omit the fillets. Scale of channel, 1″ = 1″. Scale of forces, 1″ = 1 sq. in.

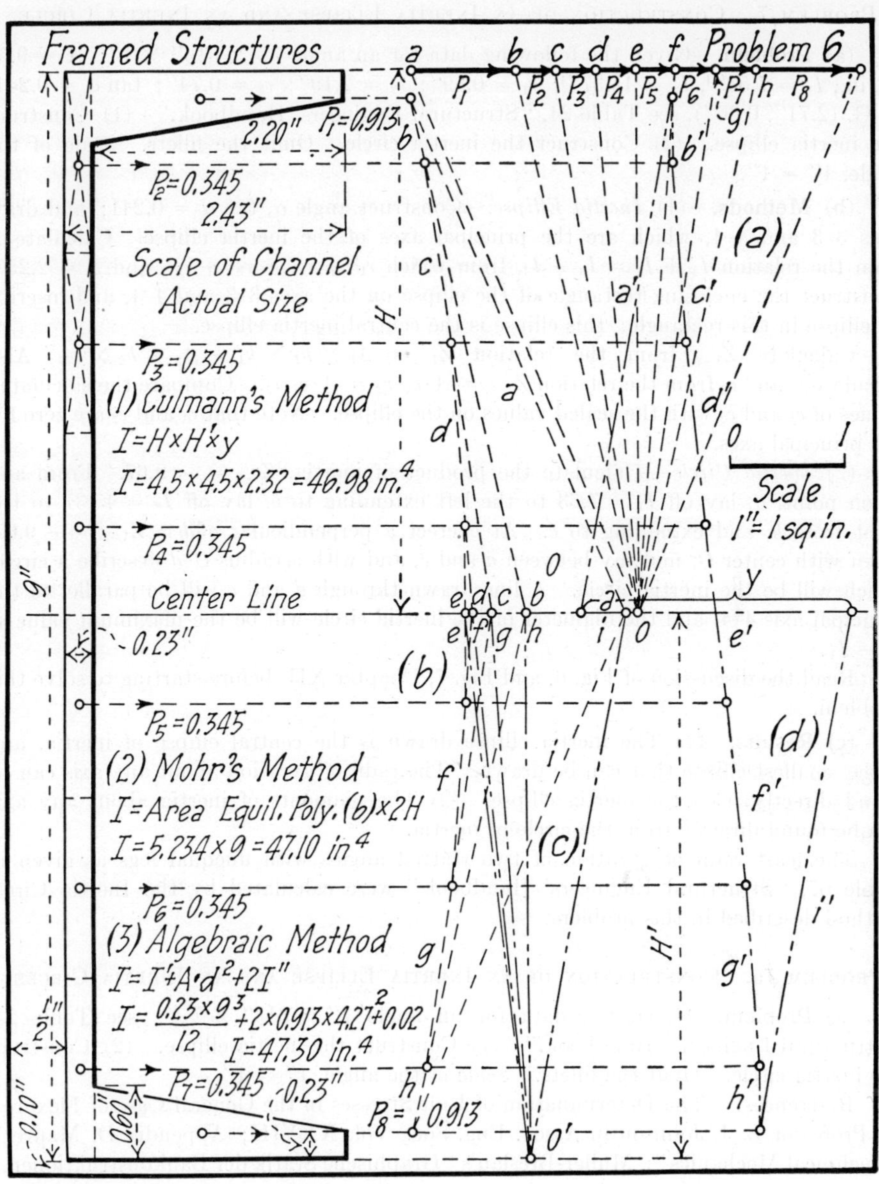
Framed Structures
Problem 6
Scale of Channel
Actual Size
2.20"
2.43"
$P_1 = 0.913$
$P_2 = 0.345$
$P_3 = 0.345$
$P_4 = 0.345$
$P_5 = 0.345$
$P_6 = 0.345$
$P_7 = 0.345$
$P_8 = 0.913$
(1) Culmann's Method
$I = H \times H' \times y$
$I = 4.5 \times 4.5 \times 2.32 = 46.98$ in.^{4}
(2) Mohr's Method
I = Area Equil. Poly. (b) × 2H
$I = 5.234 \times 9 = 47.10$ in^4
(3) Algebraic Method
$I = I' + A \cdot d^2 + 2I''$
$I = \frac{0.23 \times 9^3}{12} + 2 \times 0.913 \times 4.27^2 + 0.02$
$I = 47.30$ in.^{4}
Center Line
Scale
1" = 1 sq. in.
9"
0.23"
0.10"
0.60"
1/2"
(a)
(b)
(c)
(d)

PROBLEM 7. CONSTRUCTION OF AN INERTIA ELLIPSE AND AN INERTIA CIRCLE.

(a) **Problem.**—Given the following data for an angle 7″ × 3½″ × 1″; $A = 9.50$ sq. in., $I_1 = 7.53''^4$, $I_2 = 45.37''^4$; $r_1 = 0.89''$; $r_2 = 2.19''$; $r_3 = 0.74''$; $\tan \alpha = 0.241$; C. G. (2.71″, 0.96″), see Table 24, "Structural Engineers' Handbook." (1) Construct the inertia ellipse. (2) Construct the inertia circle. Omit the fillets. Scale of the angle, 1″ = 1″.

(b) **Methods.**—(1) *Inertia Ellipse.*—Construct angle α, $\tan \alpha = 0.241$; and draw axes 3–3 and 4–4, which are the principal axes of the inertia ellipse. Calculate r_4 from the relation $I_1 + I_2 = I_3 + I_4$, from which $r_1^2 + r_2^2 = r_3^2 + r_4^2$, and $r_4 = 2.25''$. Construct the enclosing rectangle of the ellipse on the axes 3–3 and 4–4, and inscribe an ellipse in this rectangle; this ellipse is the central inertia ellipse.

Calculate Z_{1-2} from the relation $Z_{1-2} = A_1 \times h_1 \times k_1 + A_2 \times h_2 \times k_2$. Also calculate c_1 and c_2 from the relation $Z_{1-2} = A \cdot c_1 \cdot r_2 = A \cdot c_2 \cdot r_1$. Compare the calculated values of c_1 and c_2 with the scaled values on the ellipse. Note that c_1 and c_2 are zero for the principal axes.

(2) *Inertia Circle.*—Calculate the product of inertia, $Z_{1-2} = -9.67$. From any given point, a, lay off $I_1 = 7.53$ to the left extending to b, lay off $I_2 = 45.37$ to the right from b, and extending to c. At a erect a perpendicular a–d = $Z_{1-2} = -9.67$. Then with center O, midway between a and c, and with a radius O–d describe a circle, which will be the inertia circle. A line drawn through d and e will be parallel to the principal axis 4–4, and the diameter of the inertia circle will be the maximum value of $I_2 - I_1$.

Read the discussion of Fig. 6, and Fig. 7, Chapter XII, before starting to solve this problem.

(c) **Results.**—(1) The inertia ellipse drawn is the central ellipse of inertia, and is the smallest ellipse that can be drawn. The radii of gyration about any axis can be found directly from the inertia ellipse. (2) The moments of inertia about any axis can be found directly from the circle of inertia.

The least radii of gyration of two starred angles with unequal legs as given in Table 67, "Structural Engineers' Handbook" were calculated by the Inertia Circle method described in this problem.

PROBLEM 7a. CONSTRUCTION OF AN INERTIA ELLIPSE AND AN INERTIA CIRCLE.

(a) **Problem.**—Given the data for an angle 7″ × 3½″ × ⅞″; see Table 24, "Structural Engineers' Handbook." (1) Construct the inertia ellipse. (2) Construct the inertia circle. Omit the fillets. Scale of the angle, 1″ = 1″.

References: "The Determination of Unit Stresses in the General Case of Flexure" by Professor L. J. Johnson in Assoc. Eng. Soc., Vol. XXVIII; Appendix D. Maurer's "Technical Mechanics"; Muller-Breslau's "Graphische Statik der Baukonstruktionen," Band I.

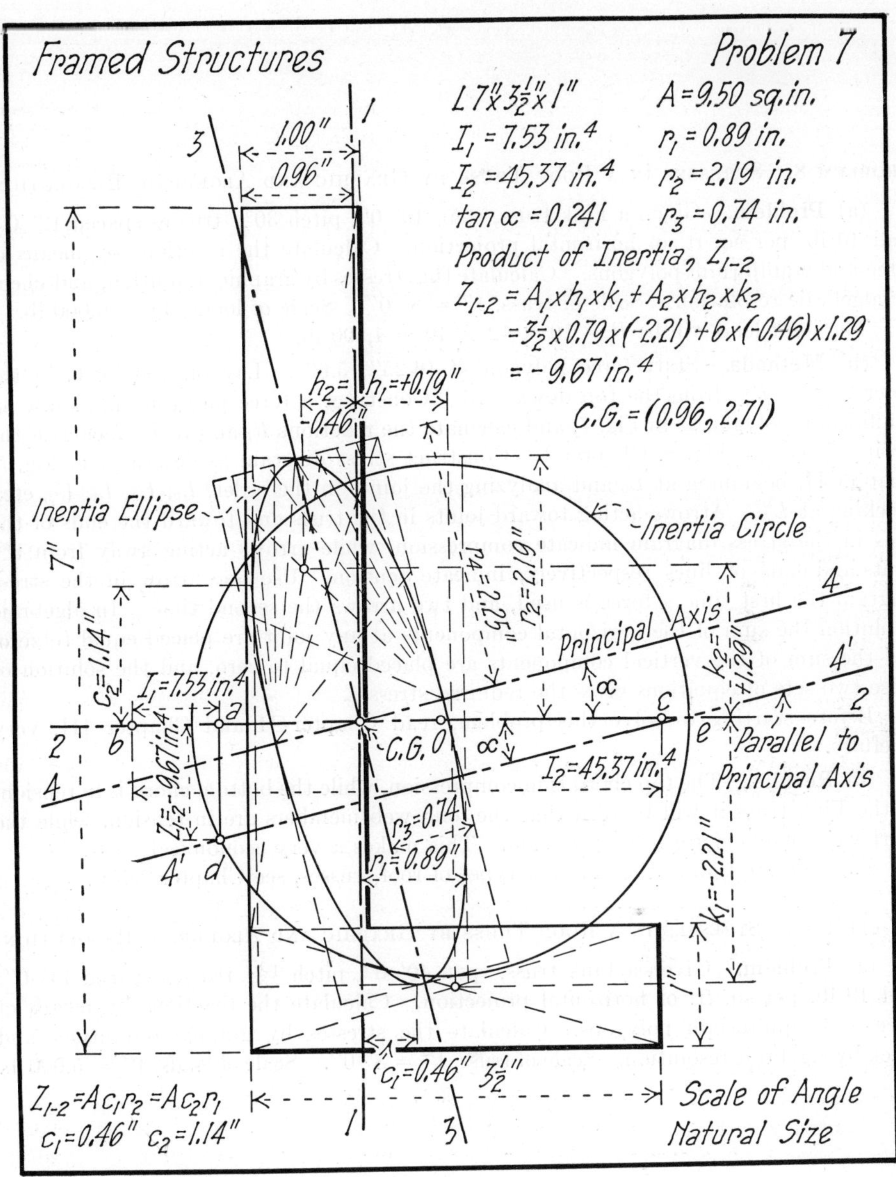

Framed Structures
Problem 7
L 7" x 3½" x 1"
A = 9.50 sq.in.
I1 = 7.53 in.4
r1 = 0.89 in.
I2 = 45.37 in.4
r2 = 2.19 in.
tan ∝ = 0.241
r3 = 0.74 in.
Product of Inertia, Z1-2
Z1-2 = A1 x h1 x k1 + A2 x h2 x k2
= 3½ x 0.79 x (-2.21) + 6 x (-0.46) x 1.29
= -9.67 in.4
C.G. = (0.96, 2.71)
1.00"
0.96"
h2 = -0.46"
h1 = +0.79"
Inertia Ellipse
Inertia Circle
Principal Axis
Parallel to Principal Axis
I1 = 7.53 in.4
I2 = 45.37 in.4
Z1-2 = 9.67 in.4
c2 = 1.14"
r4 = 2.25"
r2 = 2.19"
k2 = +1.29"
k1 = -2.21"
r3 = 0.74"
r1 = 0.89"
C.G.
c1 = 0.46"
3½"
Z1-2 = Ac1r2 = Ac2r1
c1 = 0.46" c2 = 1.14"
Scale of Angle
Natural Size

PROBLEM 8. STRESSES IN A ROOF TRUSS BY GRAPHIC AND ALGEBRAIC RESOLUTION.

(a) **Problem.**—Given a Fink truss, span 40′–0″, pitch 30°; trusses spaced 12′–0″; load 40 lb. per sq. ft. of horizontal projection. Calculate the reactions by means of force and equilibrium polygons. Calculate the stresses by graphic resolution, and check by algebraic resolution. Scale of truss, 1″ = 8′–0″. Scale of loads, 1″ = 6,000 lb.

The joint load will be $P = 10 \times 12 \times 40 = 4{,}800$ lb.

(b) **Methods.**—Start force polygon at (6.25″, 5.6″). Lay off the loads in the order P_1, P_2, P'_1, from the top downward. Construct a force polygon, and draw an equilibrium polygon as in Fig. 7, and calculate the reactions R_1 and R_2 by means of the closing line as in Fig. 8, Chapter I. Construct stress diagram as described in Fig. 5, Chapter II, beginning at L_0 and analyzing the joints in the order, L_0, U_1, L_1, U_2, etc., checking at L'_0. Arrows acting toward joints in the truss and toward the ends of the lines in the stress diagram indicate compression, while arrows acting away from the joints and ends of lines respectively, indicate tension. Use one arrow in the stress diagram the first time a force is used, and two arrows the second time. In algebraic resolution the sum of the horizontal components at any joint are placed equal to zero, and the sum of the vertical components are placed equal to zero, and the solution of these two sets of equations gives the required stresses.

Before starting to solve this problem, read Chapter II and Chapter III, very carefully.

(c) **Results.**—The top chord is in compression, while the bottom chord is in tension. In the Fink truss it will be seen that the long web members are in tension, while the short web members are in compression. This makes a very economical truss.

For a description of the different types of roof trusses, see Chapter XXV.

PROBLEM 8a. STRESSES IN A ROOF TRUSS BY GRAPHIC AND ALGEBRAIC RESOLUTION.

(a) **Problem.**—Given a Fink truss, span 40′–0″, pitch ⅓; trusses spaced 14′–0″; load 40 lb. per sq. ft. of horizontal projection. Calculate the reactions by means of force and equilibrium polygons. Calculate the stresses by graphic resolution, and check by algebraic resolution. Scale of truss, 1″ = 8′–0″. Scale of loads, 1″ = 5,000 lb.

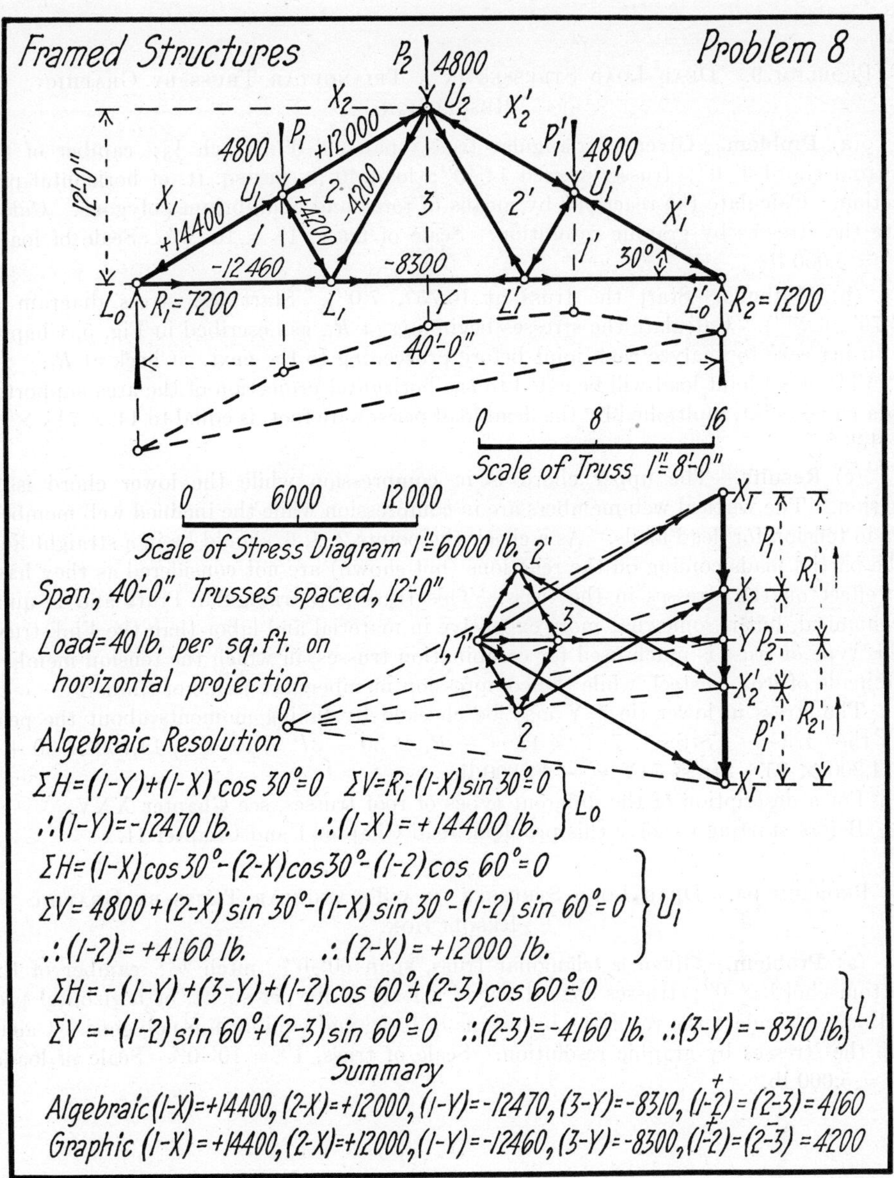
Framed Structures
Problem 8
P2 4800
X2 U2 X'2
4800 P1 +12000
P'1 4800
X1 U1 2 -4200 3 2' U'1 X'1
+14400 +4200
1 1' 30°
12'-0"
-12460 -8300
L0 R1=7200 L1 Y L'1 L'0 R2=7200
40'-0"
0 8 16
Scale of Truss 1"=8'-0"
0 6000 12000
Scale of Stress Diagram 1"=6000 lb.
Span, 40'-0". Trusses spaced, 12'-0"
Load=40 lb. per sq. ft. on horizontal projection
X1 P1 R1 X2 P2 Y X'2 R2 P'1 X'1
2' 3 1,1' 0 2
Algebraic Resolution
ΣH=(1-Y)+(1-X) cos 30°=0 ΣV=R1-(1-X)sin 30°=0
∴(1-Y)=-12470 lb. ∴(1-X)=+14400 lb. L0
ΣH=(1-X)cos 30°-(2-X)cos30°-(1-2)cos 60°=0
ΣV=4800+(2-X)sin 30°-(1-X)sin 30°-(1-2) sin 60°=0 U1
∴(1-2)=+4160 lb. ∴(2-X)=+12000 lb.
ΣH=-(1-Y)+(3-Y)+(1-2)cos 60°+(2-3)cos 60°=0
ΣV=-(1-2)sin 60°+(2-3)sin 60°=0 ∴(2-3)=-4160 lb. ∴(3-Y)=-8310 lb. L1
Summary
Algebraic (1-X)=+14400, (2-X)=+12000, (1-Y)=-12470, (3-Y)=-8310, (1-2)=(2-3)=4160
Graphic (1-X)=+14400, (2-X)=+12000, (1-Y)=-12460, (3-Y)=-8300, (1-2)=(2-3)=4200

PROBLEM 9. DEAD LOAD STRESSES IN A TRIANGULAR TRUSS BY GRAPHIC RESOLUTION.

(a) **Problem.**—Given a triangular truss, span 60′–0″; pitch ⅓; camber of the bottom chord 3′–0″; trusses spaced 14′–0″; load 40 lb. per sq. ft. of horizontal projection. Calculate the reactions by means of force and equilibrium polygons. Calculate the stresses by graphic resolution. Scale of truss, 1″ = 10′–0″. Scale of loads, 1″ = 5,000 lb.

(b) **Methods.**—Start the truss at (0.75″, 7.0″). Start the stress diagram at (6.75″, 6.25″). Calculate the stresses beginning at R_1, as described in Fig. 5, Chapter II, using care to analyze each joint before proceeding to the next. Check at R_2.

The dead joint load will be equal to the horizontal projection of the area supported by a panel point, multiplied by the dead load per square foot, is equal to $14 \times 7\frac{1}{2} \times 40 = 4,200$ lb.

(c) **Results.**—The upper chord is in compression while the lower chord is in tension. The vertical web members are in compression while the inclined web members are in tension for dead loads. As a check the points 2, 4, 6, should be in a straight line. The partial loads coming on the reactions (not shown) are not considered as they have no effect on the stresses in the truss. This truss is a triangular Pratt and is quite economical, but is somewhat more expensive in material and labor than the Fink truss. This type of truss is much used for combination trusses, in which the tension members are made of iron or steel, while the compression members are made of timber.

The stress in lower tie 7–Y may be checked by taking moments about the peak of the truss. Stress $7\text{–}Y \times 17 = -R_1 \times 30 + 3P \times 15 = -14,700 \times 30 + 3 \times 4,200 \times 15$. Stress 7–Y = − 14,800 lb.

For a description of the different types of roof trusses, see Chapter XXV.

Before starting to solve this problem, read Chapter I and Chapter II.

PROBLEM 9a. DEAD LOAD STRESSES IN A TRIANGULAR TRUSS BY GRAPHIC RESOLUTION.

(a) **Problem.**—Given a triangular truss, span 60′–0″; pitch ⅓; camber of the bottom chord 2′–0″; trusses spaced 16′–0″; load 40 lb. per sq. ft. of horizontal projection. Calculate the reactions by means of force and equilibrium polygons. Calculate the stresses by graphic resolution. Scale of truss, 1″ = 10′–0″. Scale of loads, 1″ = 5,000 lb.

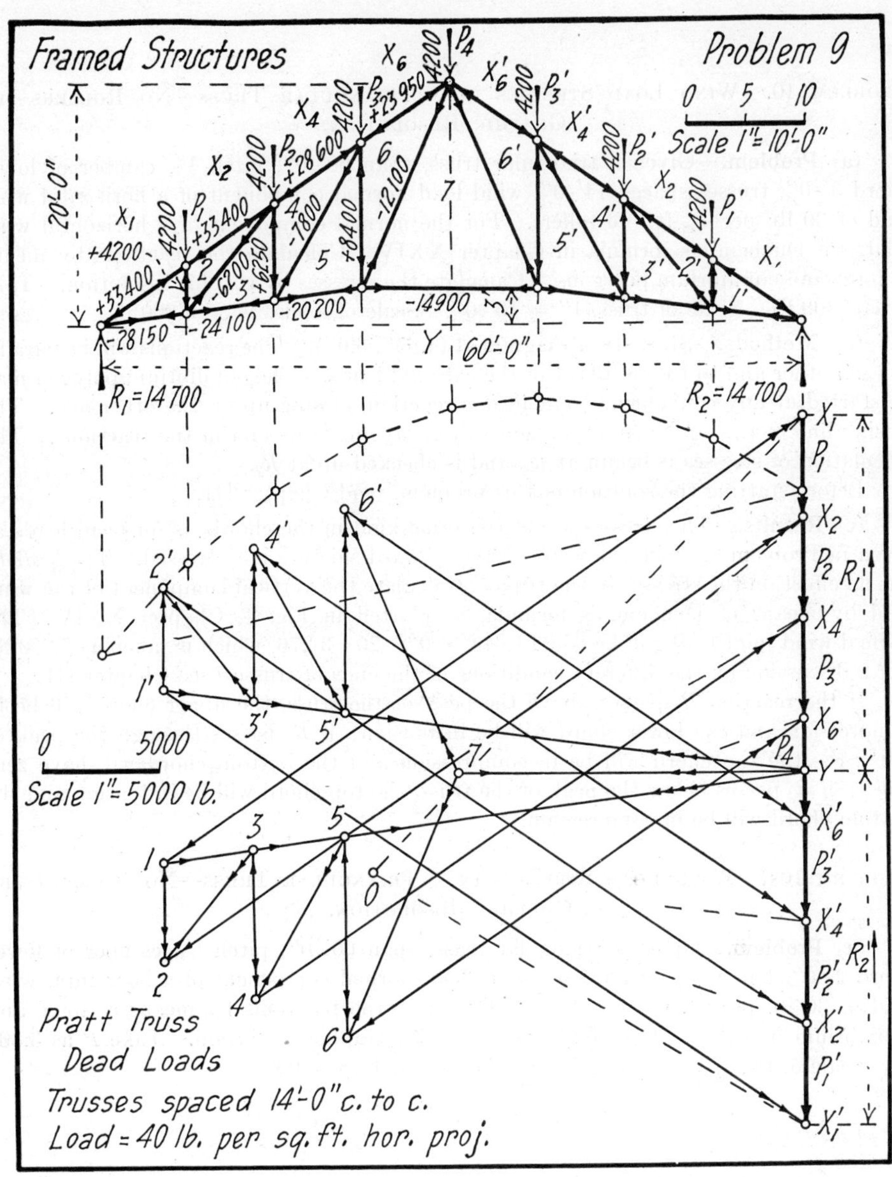
Framed Structures
Problem 9
0 5 10
Scale 1" = 10'-0"
20'-0"
60'-0"
R₁ = 14700
R₂ = 14700
+4200
+33400
+33400
+28600
+23950
-28150
-24100
-20200
-14900
-6200
+6250
-7800
+8400
-12100
4200
0 5000
Scale 1" = 5000 lb.
Pratt Truss
Dead Loads
Trusses spaced 14'-0" c. to c.
Load = 40 lb. per sq. ft. hor. proj.

PROBLEM 10. WIND LOAD STRESSES IN A TRIANGULAR TRUSS—NO ROLLERS—BY GRAPHIC RESOLUTION.

(a) **Problem.**—Given a triangular truss, span 60′–0″, pitch ⅓, camber of lower chord 3′–0″, trusses spaced 14′–0″, wind load normal component of a horizontal wind load of 30 lb. per sq. ft., no rollers. For the normal component of a horizontal wind load, see Duchemin's formula in Chapter XXIV. Calculate the reactions by means of force and equilibrium polygons. Calculate the stresses by graphic resolution. Take P as 3,300 lb. Scale of truss, 1″ = 10′–0″. Scale of loads, 1″ = 3,000 lb.

(b) **Methods.**—Start stress diagram at (4.65″, 6.6″). The reactions will be parallel to each other and to the resultant of the external loads. The equilibrium polygon may be started at any convenient point in one reaction, closing up on the other one. The closing line of the equilibrium polygon will always have its end in the reactions. The calculation of stresses is begun at R_1, and is checked up at R_2.

Before starting the solution of this problem, read Chapter III.

(c) **Results.**—The stresses are of the same kind in the chords as for dead loads as given in Problem 9, while the webs on the leeward side are not stressed. The load P_0 has no effect on the stresses in the truss. Calculate the vertical component of the wind load by means of Duchemin's formula, as plotted in Fig. 4, Chapter XXIV. The normal wind joint load will be equal to 14 × 9 × 26 = 3,276, which is taken as 3,300 lb. For a discussion on the different conditions of the ends of trusses, see Chapter III.

If the reaction R_2 passes above the peak of the truss, the upper chord will be in compression and the lower chord will be in tension; if R_2 passes through the peak of the truss, the top chord will be in compression and the bottom chord wil' have zero stress; if R_2 passes below the peak of the truss, the top chord will be in tension and the bottom chord will be in compression.

PROBLEM 10a. WIND LOAD STRESSES IN A TRIANGULAR TRUSS—NO ROLLERS—BY GRAPHIC RESOLUTION.

(a) **Problem.**—Given a triangular truss, span 60′–0″, pitch 1/3, camber of lower chord 2′–0″, trusses spaced 16′–0″, wind load normal component of a horizontal wind load of 30 lb. per sq. ft., no rollers. Calculate the reactions by means o force and equilibrium polygons. Calculate the stresses by graphic resolution. Take P as 3,800 lb. Scale of truss, 1″ = 10′–0″. Scale of loads, 1 = 3,000 lb.

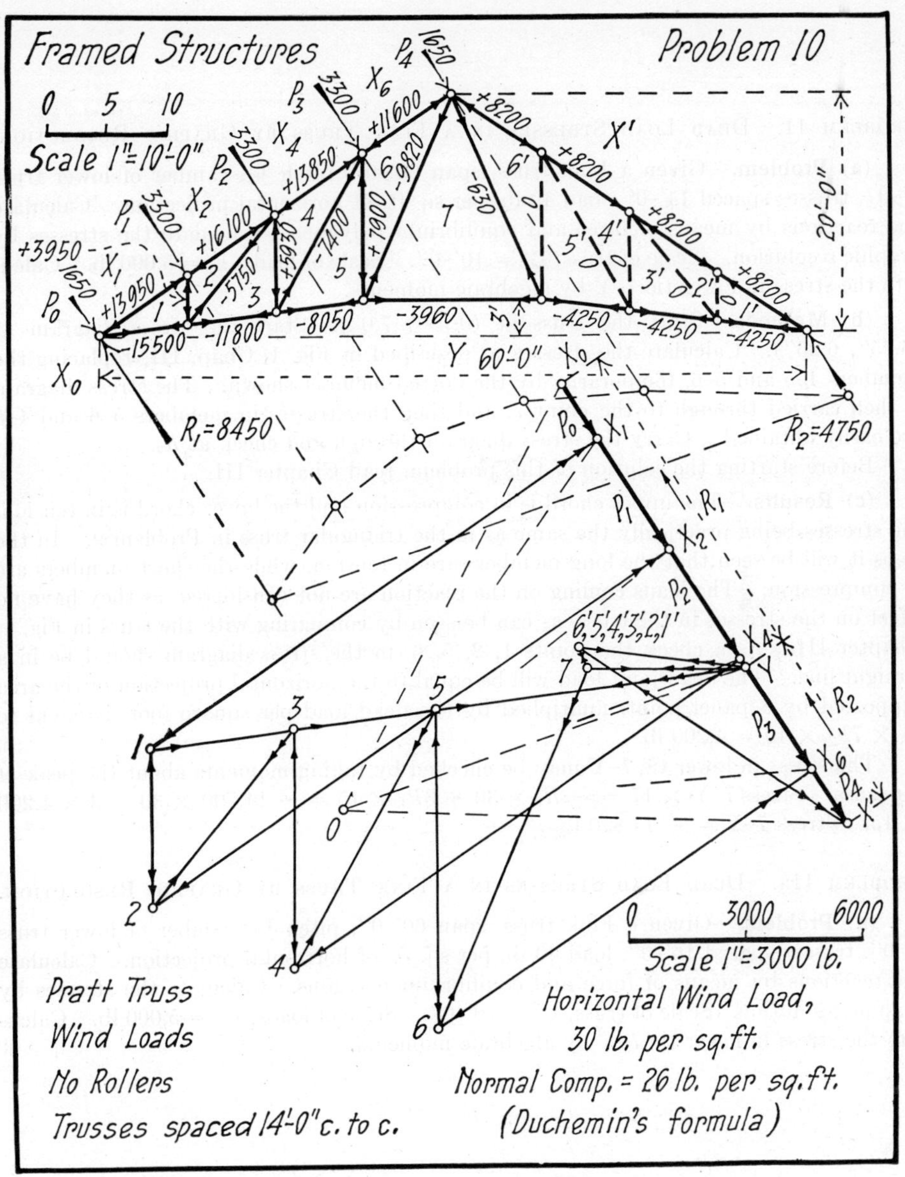
Framed Structures
Problem 10
0 5 10
Scale 1"=10'-0"
+3950
+13950
+16100
+13850
+11600
+8200
+8200
+8200
+8200
-15500
-11800
-8050
-3960
-4250
-4250
-4250
-5750
+5930
-7400
+7900
-9820
-630
20'-0"
60'-0"
R1=8450
R2=4750
0 3000 6000
Scale 1"=3000 lb.
Pratt Truss
Wind Loads
No Rollers
Trusses spaced 14'-0" c. to c.
Horizontal Wind Load,
30 lb. per sq.ft.
Normal Comp. = 26 lb. per sq.ft.
(Duchemin's formula)

PROBLEM 11. DEAD LOAD STRESSES IN A FINK TRUSS BY GRAPHIC RESOLUTION.

(a) **Problem.**—Given a Fink truss, span 60′–0″, pitch ⅓, camber of lower truss 3′–0″, trusses spaced 14′–0″, load 40 lb. per sq. ft. of horizontal projection. Calculate the reactions by means of force and equilibrium polygons. Calculate the stresses by graphic resolution. Scale of truss, 1″ = 10′–0″. Scale of loads, 1″ = 5,000 lb. Calculate the stress in lower tie 7–Y by algebraic moments.

(b) **Methods.**—Start the truss at (0.75″, 7.0″). Start the stress diagram at (6.75″, 6.25″). Calculate the stresses as described in Fig. 1, Chap. III, replacing the members 4–5 and 5–6, temporarily by the dotted member shown. The stress diagram is then carried through to the point 7, and then the stresses in members 5–6 and 4–5 are easily obtained. Carry the stress diagram through and check at R_2.

Before starting the solution of this problem, read Chapter III.

(c) **Results.**—The upper chord is in compression and the lower chord is in tension, the stresses being practically the same as in the triangular truss in Problem 9. In the webs it will be seen that the long members are in tension, while the short members are in compression. The loads coming on the reaction are not considered, as they have no effect on the stresses in the truss, as can be seen by comparing with the truss in Fig. 1, Chapter III. As a check the points 1, 2, 5, 6, in the stress diagram shou'd be in a straight line. The dead joint load will be equal to the horizontal projection of the area supported by a panel point, multiplied by the dead load per square foot, is equal to $14 \times 7\frac{1}{2} \times 40 = 4{,}200$ lb.

The stress in lower tie 7–Y may be checked by taking moments about the peak of the truss. Stress 7–Y $\times 17 = - R_1 \times 30 + 3P_1 \times 15 = - 14{,}700 \times 30 - 3 \times 4{,}200 \times 15$. Stress 7–Y $= - 14{,}820$ lb.

PROBLEM 11a. DEAD LOAD STRESSES IN A FINK TRUSS BY GRAPHIC RESOLUTION.

(a) **Problem.**—Given a Fink truss, span 60′–0″, pitch ⅓, camber of lower truss 2′–0″, trusses spaced 16′–0″, load 40 lb. per sq. ft. of horizontal projection. Calculate the reactions by means of force and equilibrium polygons. Calculate the stresses by graphic resolution. Scale of truss, 1″ = 10′–0″. Scale of loads, 1″ = 5,000 lb. Calculate the stress in lower tie 7–Y by algebraic moments.

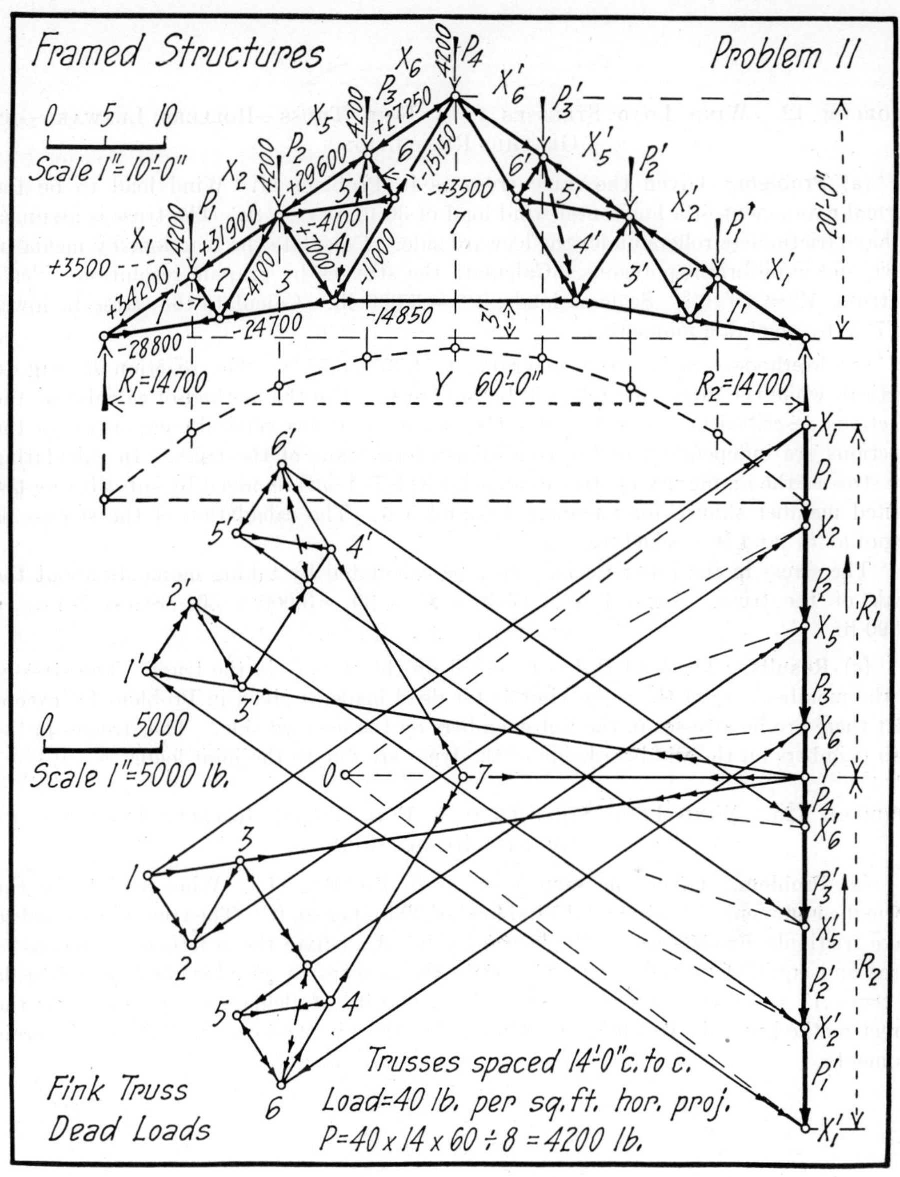

Framed Structures
Problem 11
Scale 1"=10'-0"
Scale 1"=5000 lb.
+3500
+34200
+31900
+29600
+27250
-28800
-24700
-14850
-4100
-4100
+7000
-11000
-15150
+3500
R₁=14700
R₂=14700
60'-0"
20'-0"
Fink Truss
Dead Loads
Trusses spaced 14'-0" c. to c.
Load=40 lb. per sq. ft. hor. proj.
P=40 x 14 x 60 ÷ 8 = 4200 lb.

PROBLEM 12. WIND LOAD STRESSES IN A FINK TRUSS—ROLLERS LEEWARD—BY GRAPHIC RESOLUTION.

(a) **Problem.**—Given the same truss as in Problem 11. Wind load to be the normal component of a horizontal wind load of 30 lb. per sq. ft. The truss is assumed to have frictionless rollers under the leeward side. Calculate the reactions by means of force and equilibrium polygons. Calculate the stresses by graphic resolution. Scale of truss, 1″ = 10′-0″. Scale of loads, 1″ = 3,000 lb. Calculate the stress in lower tie 7–Y by algebraic moments.

(b) **Methods.**—Start stress diagram at (4.75″, 6.55″). The reaction R_2 will be vertical, while the direction of R_1 will be unknown. Use the method of calculating the reactions described in Fig. 4, Chapter III; noting that the vertical components of the reactions are independent of the conditions of the ends of the truss. In calculating the stresses the ambiguity of stresses at point 3–4–7–4–y is removed by substituting the dotted member shown, for members 4–5 and 5–6. The calculation of the stresses is begun at R_1 ,and is checked up at R_2.

The stress in the lower tie 7–Y may be calculated by taking moments about the peak of the truss. Stress 7–Y × 17 = − R_2 × 30 = 3,900 × 30. Stress 7-Y= − 6,890 lb.

(c) **Results.**—The load P_1 has no effect on the stresses in the truss. The stresses in the members are of the same kind as for dead loads as given in Problem 11, except that there are no stresses in the web members on the leeward side. The stresses in the web members on the windward side of the truss are due to the joint loads.

PROBLEM 12a. WIND LOAD STRESSES IN A FINK TRUSS—ROLLERS LEEWARD—BY GRAPHIC RESOLUTION.

(a) **Problem.**—Given the same truss as in Problem 11a. Wind load to be the normal component of a horizontal wind load of 30 lb. per sq. ft. The truss is assumed to have frictionless rollers under the leeward side. Calculate the reactions by means of force and equilibrium polygons. Calculate the stresses by graphic resolution. Scale of truss ,1″ = 10′-0″. Scale of loads, 1″ = 3,000 lb. Calculate the reactions by the direct method used in Problem 13. Check the stress in the lower tie 7–Y by algebraic moments.

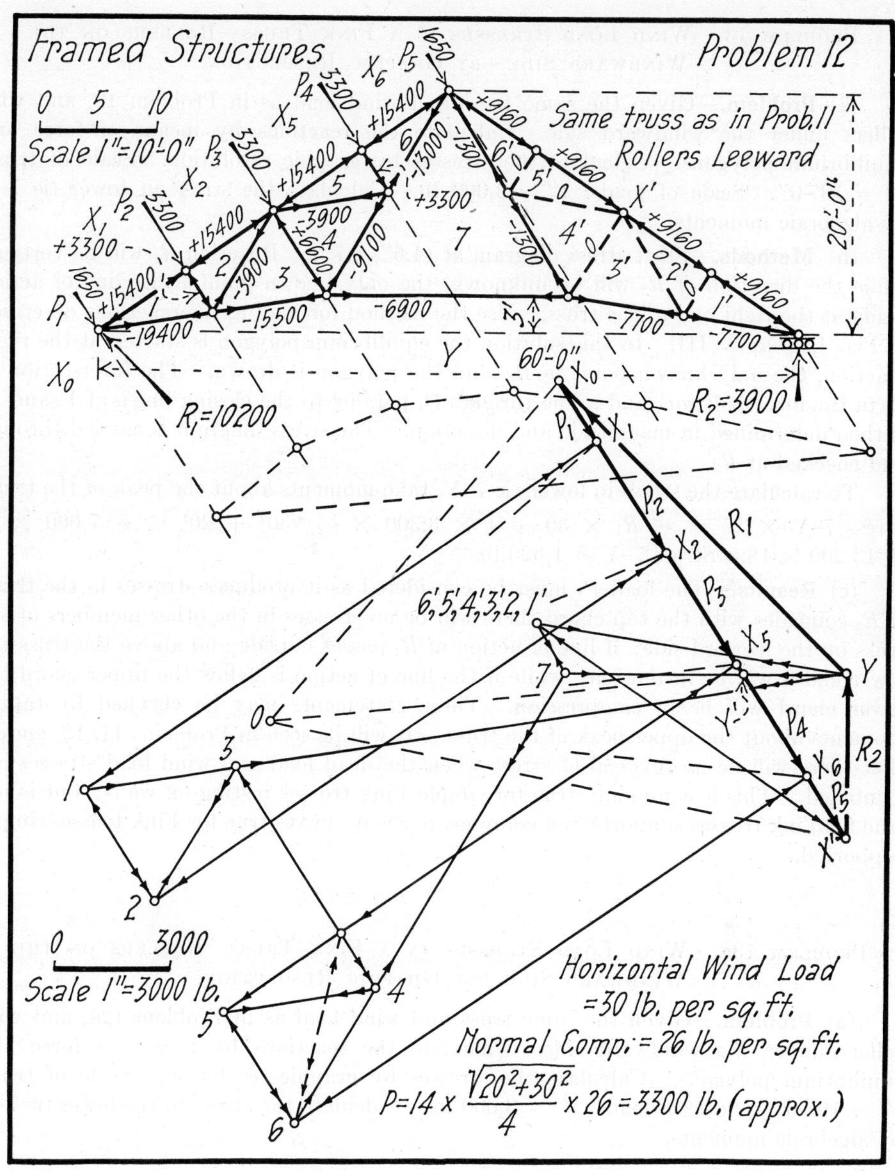
Framed Structures
Problem 12
0 5 10
Scale 1"=10'-0"
Same truss as in Prob. 11
Rollers Leeward
20'-0"
60'-0"
+3300
+15400
+15400
+15400
+15400
+9160
+9160
+9160
+9160
-19400
-15500
-6900
-7700
-7700
-3900
-3900
-13000
-1300
-1300
+6600
-9100
+3300
R_1=10200
R_2=3900
0 3000
Scale 1"=3000 lb.
Horizontal Wind Load
=30 lb. per sq. ft.
Normal Comp. = 26 lb. per sq. ft.
$P=14\times\frac{\sqrt{20^2+30^2}}{4}\times 26=3300$ lb. (approx.)

PROBLEM 13. WIND LOAD STRESSES IN A FINK TRUSS—ROLLERS ON THE WINDWARD SIDE—BY GRAPHIC RESOLUTION.

(a) **Problem.**—Given the same truss and wind load as in Problem 12, and with rollers under the windward side. Calculate the reactions by means of force and equilibrium polygons. Calculate the stresses by graphic resolution. Scale of truss, 1″ = 10′-0″. Scale of loads, 1″ = 3,000 lb. Calculate the stress in lower tie 7–Y by algebraic moments.

(b) **Methods.**—Start stress diagram at (4.6″, 6.7″). Reaction R_1 will be vertical, while the direction of R_2 will be unknown, the only known point in its line of action being at the right end of the truss. Use the method for finding the reactions described in Fig. 4, Chapter III. In this solution the equilibrium polygon is started at the right reaction, the only known point in R_2, and the polygon is drawn. The intersection of R_1 in the force polygon, and a line through O, parallel to the closing line is at Y, and R_2 is then determined in magnitude and direction. The stress diagram is carried through and checked at R_2.

To calculate the stress in lower tie 7–Y, take moments about the peak of the truss. Stress 7–Y $\times$ 17 $= - R_1 \times 30 + 4 \times 3{,}300 \times \frac{1}{2}\sqrt{30^2 + 20^2} = -7{,}000 \times 30 + 13{,}200 \times 18$. Stress 7–Y = 1,620 lb.

(c) **Results.**—The load P_1 must be considered as it produces stresses in the truss. If R_2 coincides with the top chord there will be no stresses in the other members of the truss on the leeward side; if line of action of R_2 passes outside and above the truss the lower chord will be in tension; while if the line of action is below the upper chord the lower chord will be in compression. These statements may be checked by taking moments about the upper peak of the truss. It will be seen in Problems 11, 12, and 13 that there will be no reversal of stress when the dead load and wind load stresses are combined. This is commonly true for simple Fink trusses resting on walls; but is not true for Fink trusses supported on columns. nor is it always true for Fink trusses simply supported.

PROBLEM 13a. WIND LOAD STRESSES IN A FINK TRUSS—ROLLERS ON THE WINDWARD SIDE—BY GRAPHIC RESOLUTION.

(a) **Problem.**—Given the same truss and wind load as in Problem 12a, and with rollers under the windward side. Calculate the reactions by means of force and equilibrium polygons. Calculate the stresses by graphic resolution. Scale of truss, 1″ = 10′-0′. Scale of loads, 1″ = 3,000 lb. Calculate the stress in the lower tie 7–Y by algebraic moments.

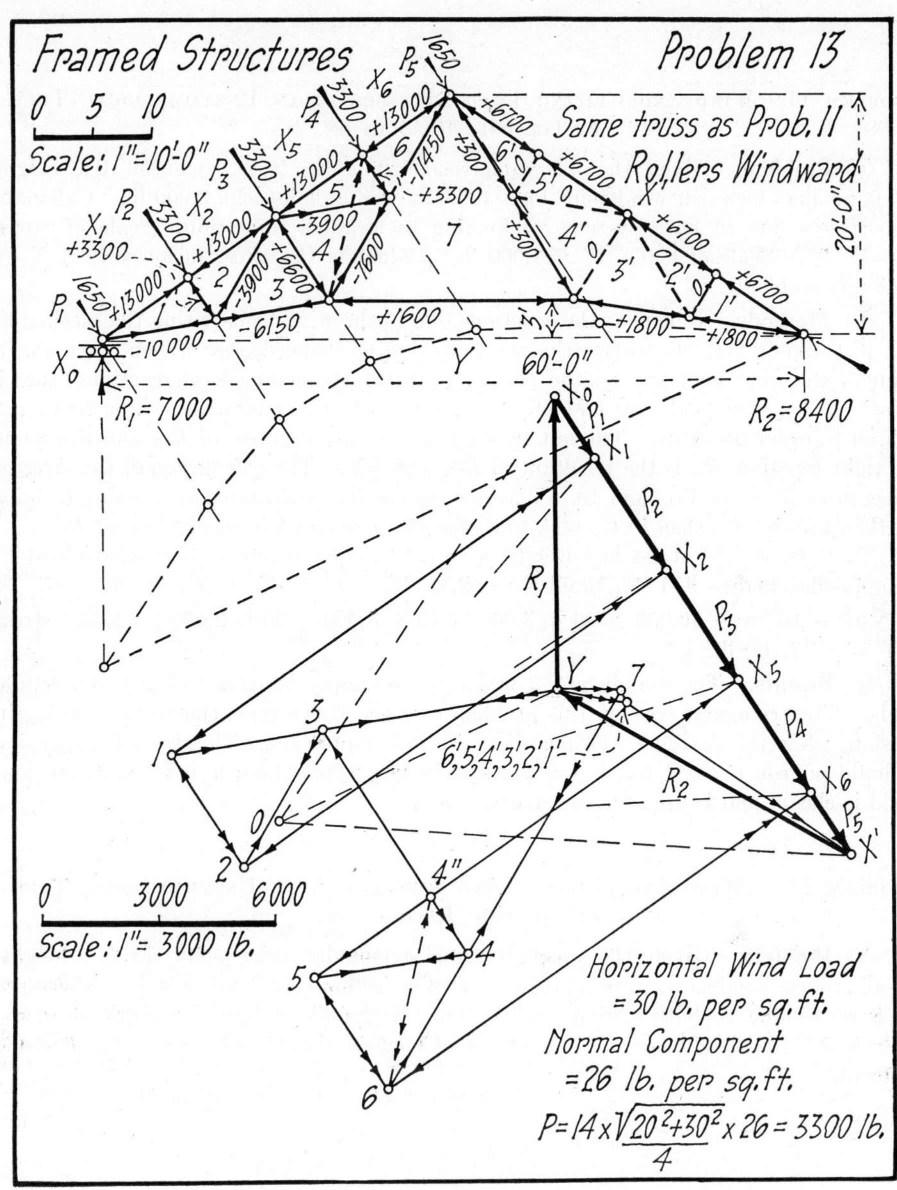
Framed Structures
Problem 13
Scale: 1"=10'-0"
Same truss as Prob. 11
Rollers Windward
20'-0"
60'-0"
R1 = 7000
R2 = 8400
Scale: 1"= 3000 lb.
Horizontal Wind Load
= 30 lb. per sq. ft.
Normal Component
= 26 lb. per sq. ft.
P = 14 x √(20² + 30²)/4 x 26 = 3300 lb.

PROBLEM 14. WIND AND CEILING LOAD STRESSES IN AN UNSYMMETRICAL TRUSS, BY GRAPHIC RESOLUTION.

(a) **Problem.**—Given the unsymmetrical triangular truss, span 50′–0″, height 16′–0″, rollers leeward, wind joint load 4,000 lb., ceiling joint load 3,000 lb. Calculate the stresses due to both systems of loading by graphic resolution. Scale of truss, 1″ = 8′–0″. Scale of loads, 1″ = 4,000 lb. Calculate the stress in lower tie 4–Y by algebraic moments.

(b) **Methods.**—Calculate the reactions due to the wind loads, using the method of Fig. 3, Chapter III. Calculate the reactions due to ceiling loads. Then place the Y point of the wind load line on the point separating the ceiling load reactions (the X point). The wind loads are laid off in order downwards, while the ceiling loads are laid off in order upwards. The left reaction, R_1, is the resultant of R_{1W} and R_{1D} whlie the right reaction, R_2, is the resultant of R_{2W} and R_{2D}. The calculation of the stresses is begun at R_1, as in Problem 10. The stresses are then calculated by passing to joint C_1, then to joint P_2, then to C_2, etc., until the stress diagram is checked up at R_2.

To calculate the stress in lower tie 4–Y take moments about joint where load P_3 is applied. Stress $4\text{-}Y \times 10.67 = -R_2 \times 30 + C_3 \times 10 + C_4 \times 20 + P_4 \times \frac{1}{3}\sqrt{30^2 + 16^2} = -10{,}050 \times 30 + 3{,}000 \times 10 + 3{,}000 \times 20 + 2{,}000 \times 11.33$. Stress 4–Y = − 17,700 lb.

(c) **Results.**—The members 1–2 and 7–8 are simply hangers to carry the ceiling loads. The triangular truss in this problem is of the Howe type, the verticals being in tension, while the diagonal web members are in compression. This truss is expensive to build of iron or steel but is quite a satisfactory type where iron is expensive and wood is cheap, and is used for the struts.

PROBLEM 14a. WIND AND CEILING LOAD STRESSES IN AN UNSYMMETRICAL TRUSS, BY GRAPHIC RESOLUTION.

(a) **Problem.**—Given the unsymmetrical triangular truss span 50′–0″, height, 16′–0″, rollers windward, wind joint load 4,000 lb., ceiling joint load 3,000 lb. Calculate the stresses due to both systems of loading by graphic resolution. Scale of truss, 1″ = 8′–0″. Scale of loads, 1″ = 4,000 lb. Calculate the stress in tie 4–Y by algebraic moments.

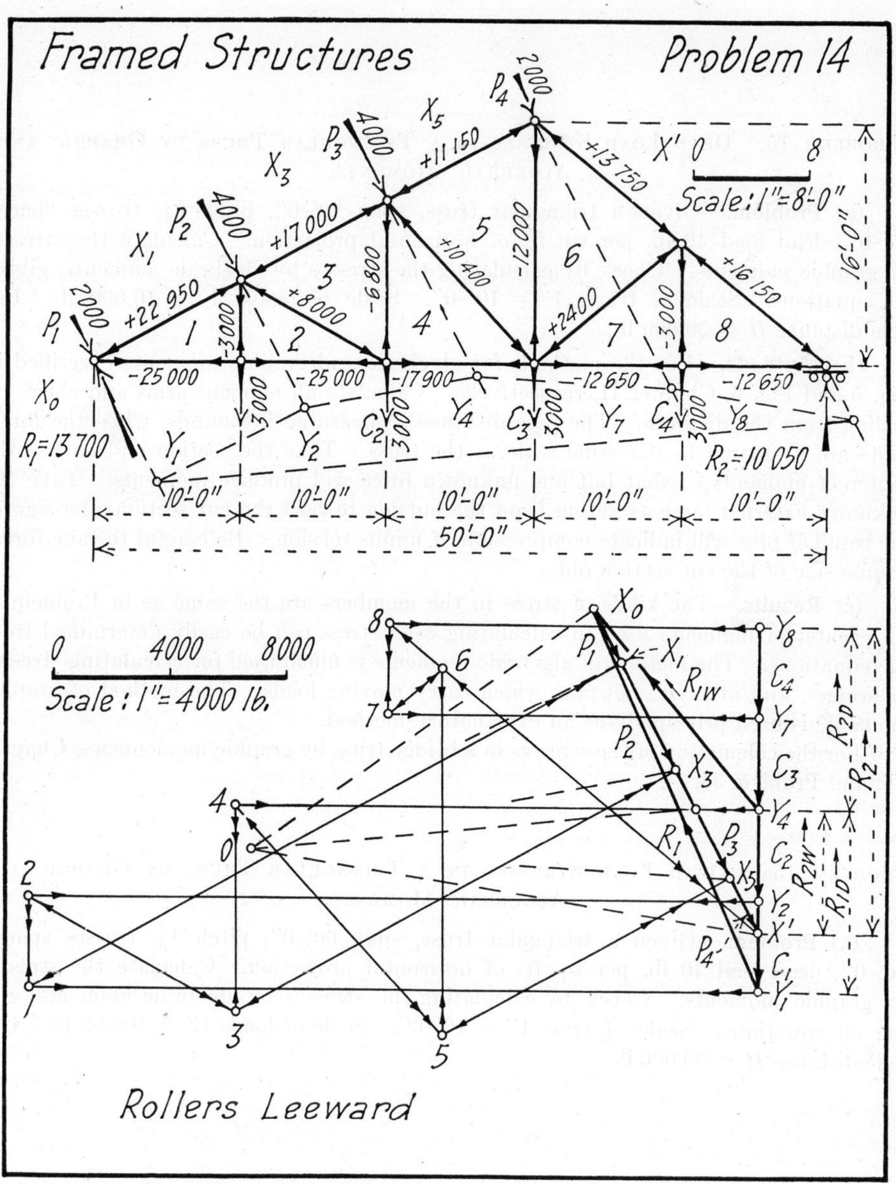
Framed Structures
Problem 14
Scale: 1"=8'-0"
16'-0"
+22 950
+17 000
+11 150
+13 750
+16 150
+8000
+10 400
+2400
-6 800
-3000
-3000
12 000
-25 000
-25 000
-17 900
-12 650
-12 650
3000
3000
3000
3000
R₁=13 700
R₂=10 050
10'-0"
10'-0"
10'-0"
10'-0"
10'-0"
50'-0"
0 4000 8000
Scale: 1"=4000 lb.
Rollers Leeward

PROBLEM 15. DEAD LOAD STRESSES IN A TRIANGULAR TRUSS BY GRAPHIC AND ALGEBRAIC MOMENTS.

(a) **Problem.**—Given a triangular truss, span 60′–0″, pitch ¼, trusses spaced 15′–0″, dead load 40 lb. per sq. ft. of horizontal projection. Calculate the stresses by graphic moments. Check by calculating the stresses by algebraic moments, giving all equations. Scale of truss, 1″ = 10′–0″. Scale of loads, 1″ = 10,000 lb. Use pole distance H = 30,000 lb.

(b) **Methods.**—Use the methods for algebraic and graphic moments described in Fig. 5 and Fig. 6, Chapter II, respectively. Calculate all moment arms and check by scaling from the diagram. The pole distance is measured in pounds, while the intercepts are measured to the same scale as the truss. Take the section and choose the center of moments so that but one unknown force will produce moments. Take the unknown external force as acting from the outside toward the cut section, the sign of the result if plus will indicate compression, if minus tension. Be careful to take forces on one side of the cut section only.

(c) **Results.**—The kinds of stress in the members are the same as in Problem 9. The center of moments used in calculating each stress can be easily determined from the equations. The method of algebraic moments is much used for calculating stresses in bridges, and other frameworks which carry moving loads. The method of graphic moments is used principally as an explanatory method.

For the calculation of the stresses in a bridge truss by graphic moments see Chapter VI, and Problem 35.

PROBLEM 15a. DEAD LOAD STRESSES IN A TRIANGULAR TRUSS BY GRAPHIC AND ALGEBRAIC MOMENTS.

(a) **Problem.**—Given a triangular truss, span 60′–0″, pitch ⅓, trusses spaced 16′–0″, dead lead 40 lb. per sq. ft. of horizontal projection. Calculate the stresses by graphic moments. Check by calculating the stresses by algebraic moments, giving all equations. Scale of truss 1″ = 10′–0″. Scale of loads 1″ = 10,000 lb. Use pole distance H = 30,000 lb.

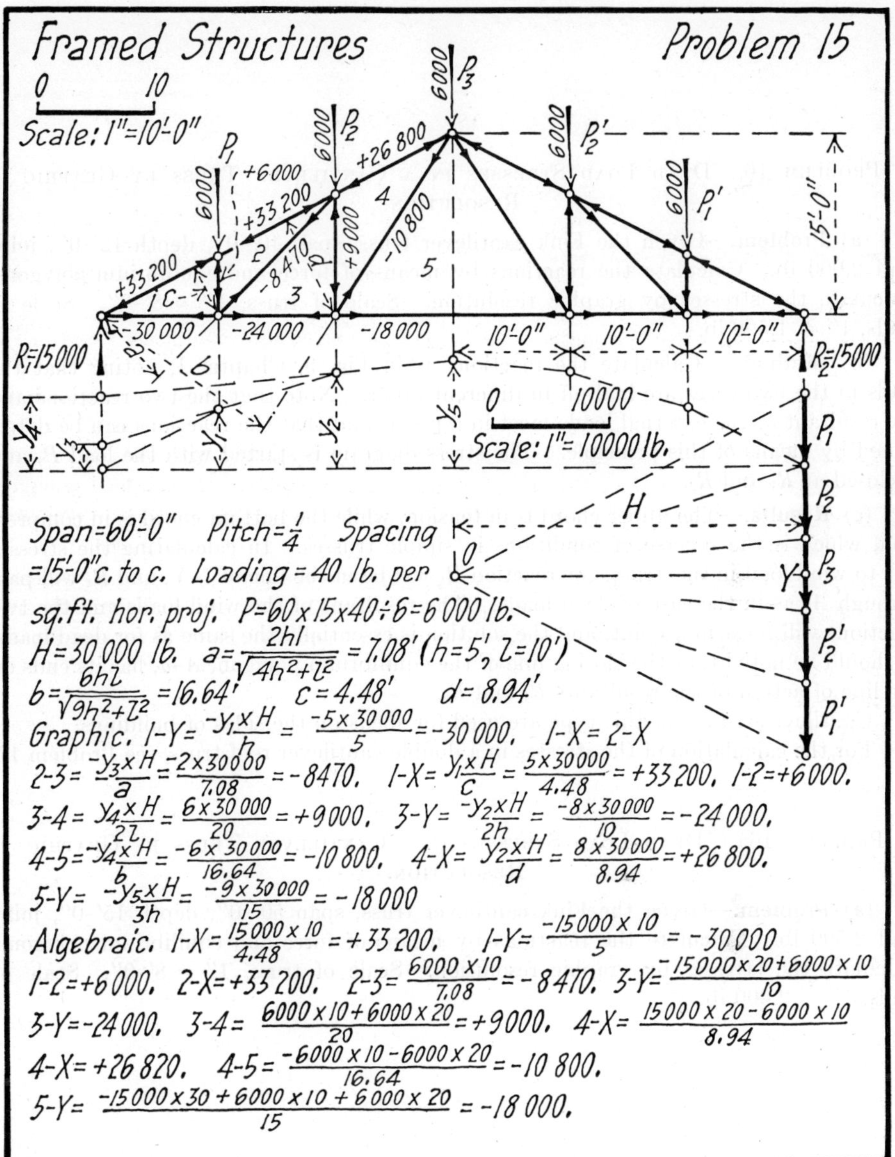
Framed Structures
Problem 15
0 10
Scale: 1"=10'-0"
6000 P1
6000 P2
6000 P3
6000 P2'
6000 P1'
+6000
+33 200
+33 200
+26 800
-8 470
+9000
-10 800
-30 000
-24 000
-18 000
1 C 2 3 4 5 6
10'-0" 10'-0" 10'-0"
15'-0"
R1=15000
R2=15000
y4 y3 y1 y2 y5
0 10000
Scale: 1"=10000 lb.
H
0
Y
Span=60'-0" Pitch=1/4 Spacing
=15'-0" c. to c. Loading = 40 lb. per
sq. ft. hor. proj. P=60x15x40÷6=6 000 lb.
H=30 000 lb. a = 2hl / √(4h²+l²) = 7.08' (h=5', l=10')
b = 6hl / √(9h²+l²) = 16.64' c = 4.48' d = 8.94'
Graphic. 1-Y = -y1 x H / h = -5 x 30 000 / 5 = -30 000. 1-X = 2-X
2-3 = -y3 x H / a = -2 x 30000 / 7.08 = -8470. 1-X = y1 x H / c = 5 x 30000 / 4.48 = +33 200. 1-2 = +6000.
3-4 = y4 x H / 2l = 6 x 30 000 / 20 = +9000. 3-Y = -y2 x H / 2h = -8 x 30000 / 10 = -24 000.
4-5 = -y4 x H / b = -6 x 30 000 / 16.64 = -10 800. 4-X = y2 x H / d = 8 x 30000 / 8.94 = +26 800.
5-Y = -y5 x H / 3h = -9 x 30 000 / 15 = -18 000
Algebraic. 1-X = 15 000 x 10 / 4.48 = +33 200. 1-Y = -15 000 x 10 / 5 = -30 000
1-2 = +6000. 2-X = +33 200. 2-3 = 6000 x 10 / 7.08 = -8470. 3-Y = -15 000 x 20 + 6000 x 10 / 10
3-Y = -24 000. 3-4 = 6000 x 10 + 6000 x 20 / 20 = +9000. 4-X = 15 000 x 20 - 6000 x 10 / 8.94
4-X = +26 820. 4-5 = -6000 x 10 - 6000 x 20 / 16.64 = -10 800.
5-Y = -15 000 x 30 + 6000 x 10 + 6000 x 20 / 15 = -18 000.

PROBLEM 16. DEAD LOAD STRESSES IN A CANTILEVER TRUSS BY GRAPHIC RESOLUTION.

(a) **Problem.**—Given the Fink cantilever truss, span 40′–0″, depth 12′–0″, joint load 2,000 lb. Calculate the reactions by means of force and equilibrium polygons. Calculate the stresses by graphic resolution. Scale of truss, 1″ = 8′–0″. Scale of loads, 1″ = 1,500 lb.

(b) **Methods.**—Calculate the reactions as in Fig. 9, Chapter I, noting that the loads in the two cases are laid off in different order. Note that the two reactions and the resultant of the external loads meet in a point, and that the reactions can be determined by means of this principle. The stress diagram is started with the load P_1 and is closed at R_1 and R_2.

(c) **Results.**—The upper chord is in tension, while the bottom chord is in compression, which is the reverse of conditions in simple trusses. In calculating the stresses due to wind load in this truss, the reaction R_1 will be in the line of 7–Y, and R_2 will pass through A, as in the case of dead loads. The resultant of the wind loads and the two reactions will meet in a point, and the solution is essentially the same as for dead loads. It should be noted that the closing line of the equilibrium polygon, A–a, has its ends on the line of action of the resultants R_1 and R_2.

Cantilever trusses of this type are used for sheds on the sides of buildings.

For the calculation of the stresses in a double cantilever roof truss, see Problem 17.

PROBLEM 16a. DEAD LOAD STRESSES IN A CANTILEVER TRUSS BY GRAPHIC RESOLUTION.

(a) **Problem.**—Given the Fink cantilever truss, span 50′–0″, depth 15′–0″, joint load 2,500 lb. Calculate the reactions by means of force and equilibrium polygons. Calculate the stresses by graphic resolution. Scale of truss, 1″ = 8′–0″. Scale of loads, 1″ = 2,000 lb.

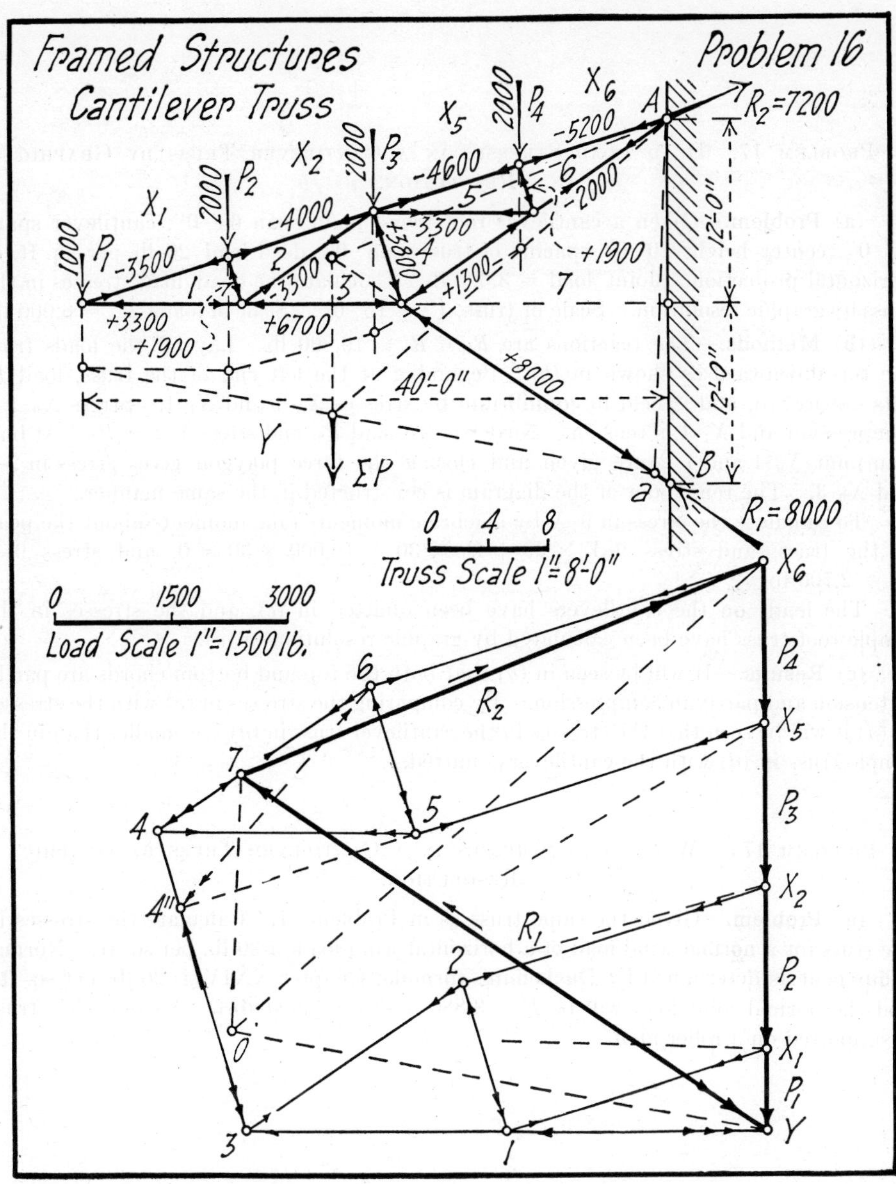
Framed Structures
Cantilever Truss
Problem 16
R₂=7200
R₁=8000
Truss Scale 1"=8'-0"
Load Scale 1"=1500 lb.
40'-0"
12'-0"
12'-0"
+8000
-5200
-4600
-4000
-3500
+3300
+6700
+1900
-2000
+1900
+1300
-3300
-3300
+3800

PROBLEM 17. DEAD LOAD STRESSES IN A CANTILEVER TRUSS BY GRAPHIC RESOLUTION.

(a) **Problem.**—Given a cantilever roof truss, main span 60′–0″, cantilever spans 20′–0″, center height 20′–0″, spacing of trusses 18′–0″, dead load 20 lb. per sq. ft. of horizontal projection. Joint load = 3,600 lb. Calculate the dead load stresses in the truss by graphic resolution. Scale of truss, 1″ = 15′–0″. Scale of loads, 1″ = 6,000 lb.

(b) **Methods.**—The reactions are $R_1 = R_2 = 19,800$ lb. Lay off the loads from the top downward as shown in (*b*). Beginning at the left end of the truss, load P_1 acts downward, and is held in equilibrium by stresses X_0–1 and X_1–1. Stress X_0–1 is compression and X_1–1 is tension. Next pass to load P_2, and stress 1–2 = P_2. At bottom joint X_0–1 and 1–2 are given and closing the force polygon gives stress in 2–3 and X_0–3. The remainder of the diagram is constructed in the same manner.

To calculate the stress in 9–X by algebraic moments take moments about the peak of the truss, and stress 9–$Y \times 20 + R_1 \times 30 - 18,000 \times 30 = 0$, and stress 9–$Y = -2,700$ lb.

The loads on the cantilevers have been omitted in (*c*), and the stresses in the simple roof truss have been calculated by graphic resolution in (*d*).

(c) **Results.**—It will be seen in (*a*) that both the top and bottom chords are partly in tension and partly in compression. By comparing the stresses in (*a*) with the stresses in (*d*) it will be seen that the stresses in the cantilever truss in (*a*) are smaller than in the simple truss in (*d*) with the cantilevers omitted.

PROBLEM 17a. WIND LOAD STRESSES IN A CANTILEVER TRUSS BY GRAPHIC RESOLUTION.

(a) **Problem.**—Given the same truss as in Problem 17. Calculate the stresses in the truss for a normal wind load of a horizontal wind load of 30 lb. per sq. ft. Normal component as determined by Duchemin's formula, Chapter XXIV, is 20 lb. per sq. ft., and the normal joint load will be $P = 3,880$ lb. (use 3,900 lb.). Assume that truss is supported on a roller at R_2.

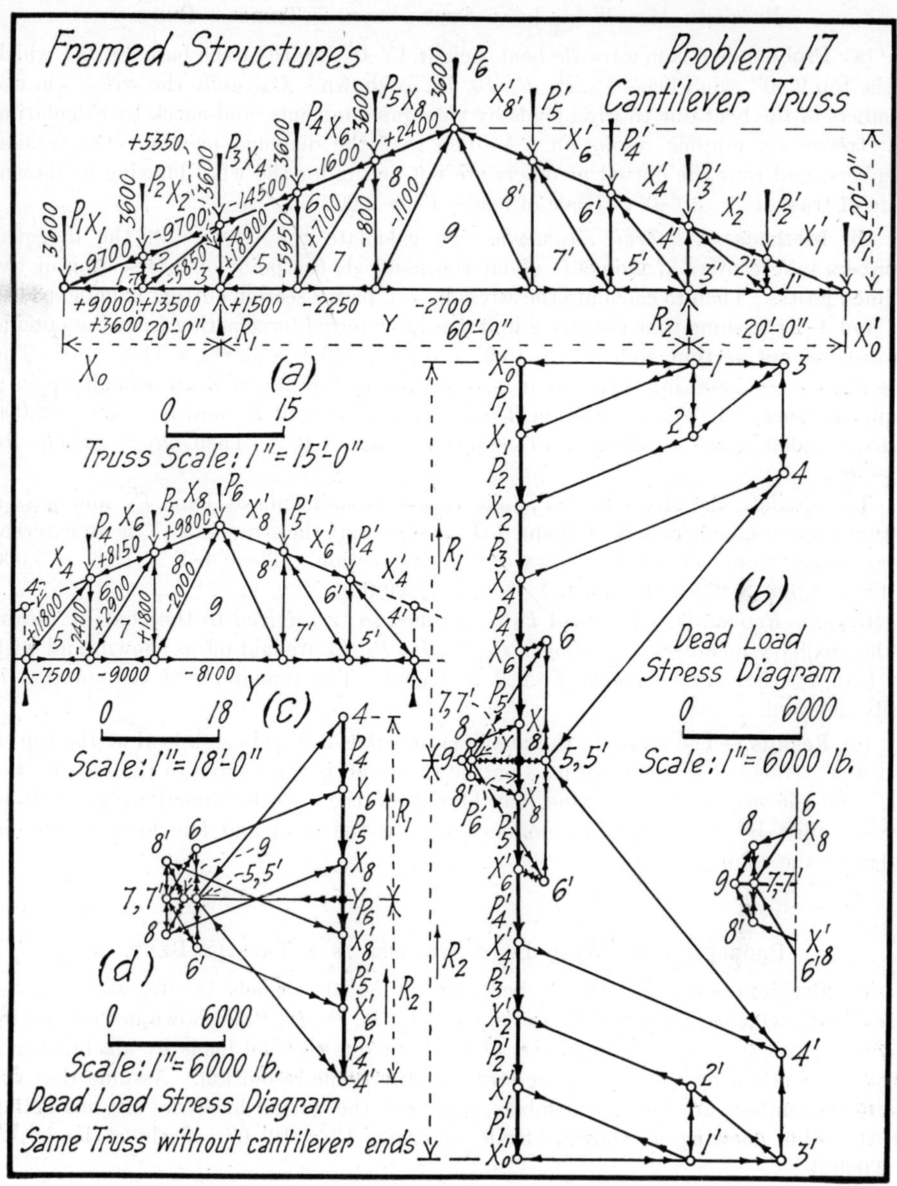
Framed Structures
Problem 17
Cantilever Truss
(a)
Truss Scale: 1" = 15'-0"
(b)
Dead Load
Stress Diagram
Scale: 1" = 6000 lb.
(c)
Scale: 1" = 18'-0"
(d)
Scale: 1" = 6000 lb.
Dead Load Stress Diagram
Same Truss without cantilever ends

PROBLEM 18. WIND LOAD STRESSES IN A TRESTLE BENT.

(a) **Problem.**—Given a trestle bent, height 45′–0″, width at the base 30′–0″, width at the top 9′–0″, wind loads P_0, P_1, P_2, P_3, P_4, as shown. Calculate the stresses in the members of the bent due to wind loads by algebraic moments, and check by calculating the stresses by graphic resolution. Assume that the diagonal members are tension members, and that the dotted members are not acting for the wind blowing as shown. Scale of truss, 1″ = 10′–0″. Scale of loads, 1″ = 2,000 lb.

(b) **Methods.**—*Algebraic Moments.*—To calculate the stresses in the diagonal members take centers of moments about the point A, the point of intersection of the inclined posts. Then to calculate the stress in 3–4, pass a section cutting members 3–X, 3–4 and 4–Y; assume that the stress in 3–4 is an external force acting from the outside toward the cut section, and 3–4 × 15.9′ + 3,000 × 19.3′ + 3,000 × 11.3′ = 0. The stress 3–4 = – 5,800 lb. Stresses in 4–5, 5–6, 6–7, 7–8 and 8–Z are calculated in a similar manner. To obtain reaction R_1 take moments about R_2, and R_1 × 30′ – 2,000 × 15′ – 2,000 × 30′ – 3,000 × 45′ – 3,000 × 53′ = 0. Then R_1 = 12,800 lb. = – R_2.

To calculate the stress in 4–Y, take center of moments at joint P_2, and pass a section cutting members 5–X, 4–5 and 4–Y, and assume the stress in 4–Y as an external force acting from the outside toward the cut section. Then 4–Y × 15.6′ – 3,000 × 15′ – 3,000 × 23′ = 0. Then 4–Y = + 7,300 lb.

Graphic Resolution.—The load P_0 is assumed as transferred to the bent by means of the auxiliary members. The loads P_0, P_1, P_2, P_3, P_4 are laid off as shown, and with the load P_0 the stress triangle Y–X–2 is drawn. The remainder of the solution is easily followed.

(c) **Results.**—The stress in the auxiliary member 2–Y acts as a load at the top of post 4–Y. Load P_0 is the wind load on the train and is transferred to the rails by the car. For the reason that the wind may blow from the opposite direction, both sets of stresses must be considered in combination with the dead and live load stresses in designing the columns.

PROBLEM 18a. WIND LOAD STRESSES IN A TRESTLE BENT.

(a) **Problem.**—Given a trestle bent, height 54′–0″, panels 18′–0″, width at the base 30′–0″, width at the top 8′–0″, wind loads P_0, P_1, P_2, P_3, P_4 as shown in Problem 18. Calculate the stresses in the members of the bent due to wind loads by algebraic moments, and check by calculating the stresses by graphic resolution. Assume that the diagonal members are tension members, and that the dotted members are not acting for the wind blowing as shown. Scale of truss, 1″ = 10′–0″. Scale of loads, 1″ = 2,000 lb.

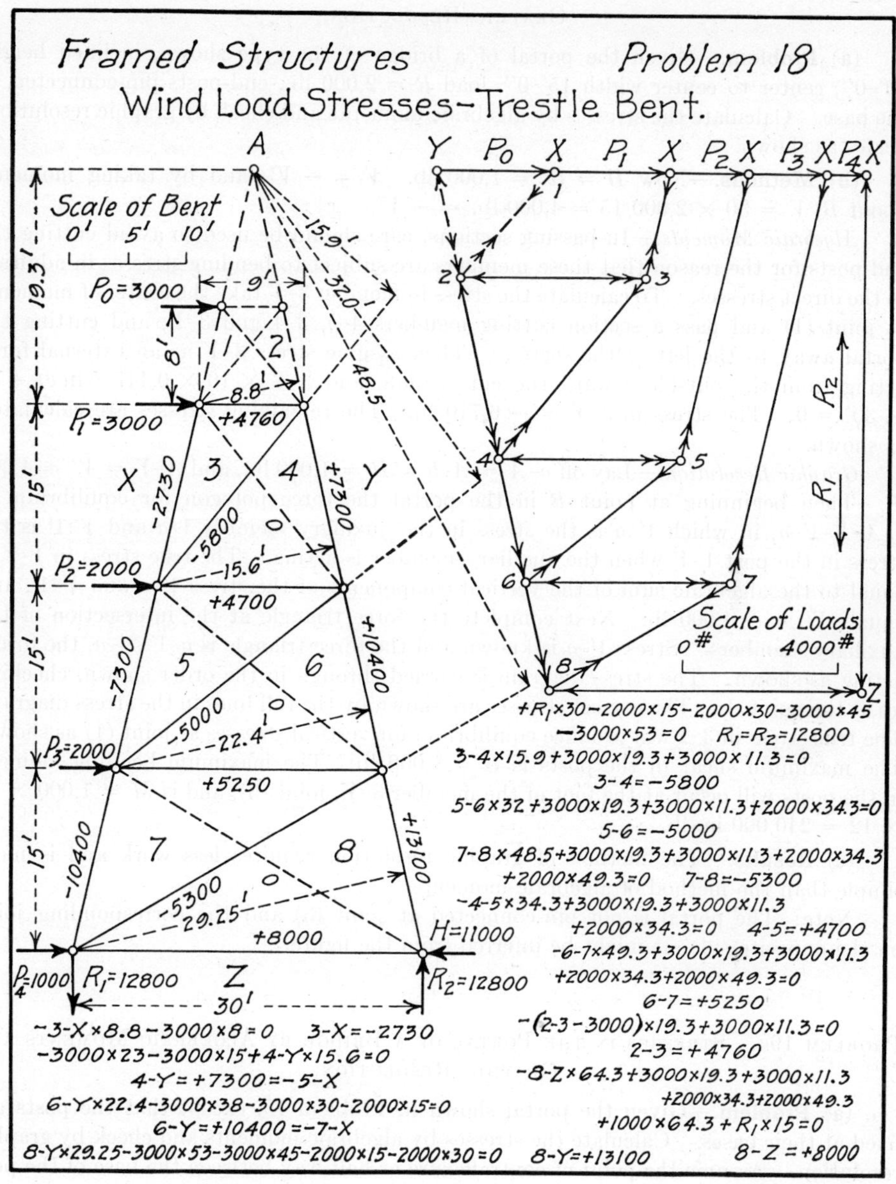
Framed Structures
Problem 18
Wind Load Stresses-Trestle Bent.
Scale of Bent
0' 5' 10'
A
P0=3000
P1=3000
P2=2000
P3=2000
P4=1000
R1=12800
R2=12800
H=11000
19.3'
8'
9'
15.9'
32.0'
48.5
8.8'
15.6'
22.4'
29.25'
15'
30'
X
Y
Z
+4760
+4700
+5250
+8000
-2730
-5800
-7300
-5000
-10400
-5300
+7300
+10400
+13100
Y P0 X P1 X P2 X P3 X P4 X
R2
R1
Scale of Loads
0# 4000#
+R1×30-2000×15-2000×30-3000×45
-3000×53=0 R1=R2=12800
3-4×15.9+3000×19.3+3000×11.3=0
3-4=-5800
5-6×32+3000×19.3+3000×11.3+2000×34.3=0
5-6=-5000
7-8×48.5+3000×19.3+3000×11.3+2000×34.3
+2000×49.3=0 7-8=-5300
-4-5×34.3+3000×19.3+3000×11.3
+2000×34.3=0 4-5=+4700
-6-7×49.3+3000×19.3+3000×11.3
+2000×34.3+2000×49.3=0
6-7=+5250
-(2-3-3000)×19.3+3000×11.3=0
2-3=+4760
-8-Z×64.3+3000×19.3+3000×11.3
+2000×34.3+2000×49.3
+1000×64.3+R1×15=0
8-Z=+8000
-3-X×8.8-3000×8=0 3-X=-2730
-3000×23-3000×15+4-Y×15.6=0
4-Y=+7300=-5-X
6-Y×22.4-3000×38-3000×30-2000×15=0
6-Y=+10400=-7-X
8-Y×29.25-3000×53-3000×45-2000×15-2000×30=0 8-Y=+13100

PROBLEM 19. STRESSES IN THE PORTAL OF A BRIDGE BY ALGEBRAIC MOMENTS AND GRAPHIC RESOLUTION.

(a) **Problem.**—Given the portal of a bridge of the type shown, inclined height 30′-0″, center to center width 15′-0″, load $R = 2{,}000$ lb., end-posts pin-connected at the base. Calculate the stresses by algebraic moments and check by graphic resolution. Scales as shown.

(b) **Methods.**—Now $H = H' = 1{,}000$ lb. $V = -V'$, and by taking moments about B, $V = 30 \times 2{,}000/15 = 4{,}000$ lb. $= -V'$.

Algebraic Moments.—In passing sections, care should be used to avoid cutting the end-posts for the reason that these members are subject to bending stresses in addition to the direct stresses. To calculate the stress in member 3–Y take the center of moments at joint (1) and pass a section cutting members 4–b, 3–4 and 3–Y, and cutting the portal away to the left of the section. Then assume stress 3–Y as an external force acting from the outside toward the cut section, and 3–$Y \times 10 \times 0.447$ $(\sin \theta) + H \times 30' = 0$. The stress in 3–$Y = -6{,}710$ lb. The remaining stresses are calculated as shown.

Graphic Resolution.—Lay off a–A = A–b = $H = 1{,}000$ lb., and A–Y = $V' = 4{,}000$ lb. Then beginning at point B in the portal the force polygon for equilibrium is a–A–Y–1′–a, in which 1′–a is the stress in the auxiliary member 1–a and Y–1′ is the stress in the post 1–Y when the auxiliary member is acting. The true stress in 1–Y is equal to the algebraic sum of the vertical components of the stress 1′–a and Y–1′, and equals $V' = -4{,}000$ lb. Next complete the force triangle at the intersection of the auxiliary members. Stress 1′–a is known and the force triangle is a–1′–2′–a, the forces acting as shown. The stress diagram is carried through in the order shown, checking up at the point A. The correct stresses are shown by the full lines in the stress diagram. The true stress in 3–2 will produce equilibrium for vertical stresses at joint (1) as shown. The maximum shear in the posts is $H = 1{,}000$ lb. The maximum bending moment in the posts will occur at the foot of the member 3–Y, joint (3), and is $M = 1{,}000 \times 20 \times 12 = 240{,}000$ in.-lb.

(c) **Results.**—The method of graphic resolution requires less work and is more simple than the method of algebraic moments.

Note: The portal is not pin-connected at joint (3) and the corresponding joint on the opposite side, as might be inferred from the figure.

PROBLEM 19a. STRESSES IN THE PORTAL OF A BRIDGE BY ALGEBRAIC MOMENTS AND GRAPHIC RESOLUTION.

(a) **Problem.**—Given the portal shown in Problem 19, except that the posts are fixed at their bases. Calculate the stresses by algebraic moments and check by graphic resolution. Assume the point of contraflexure as half way between the base of the post and the foot of the knee brace. Scales as in Problem 19.

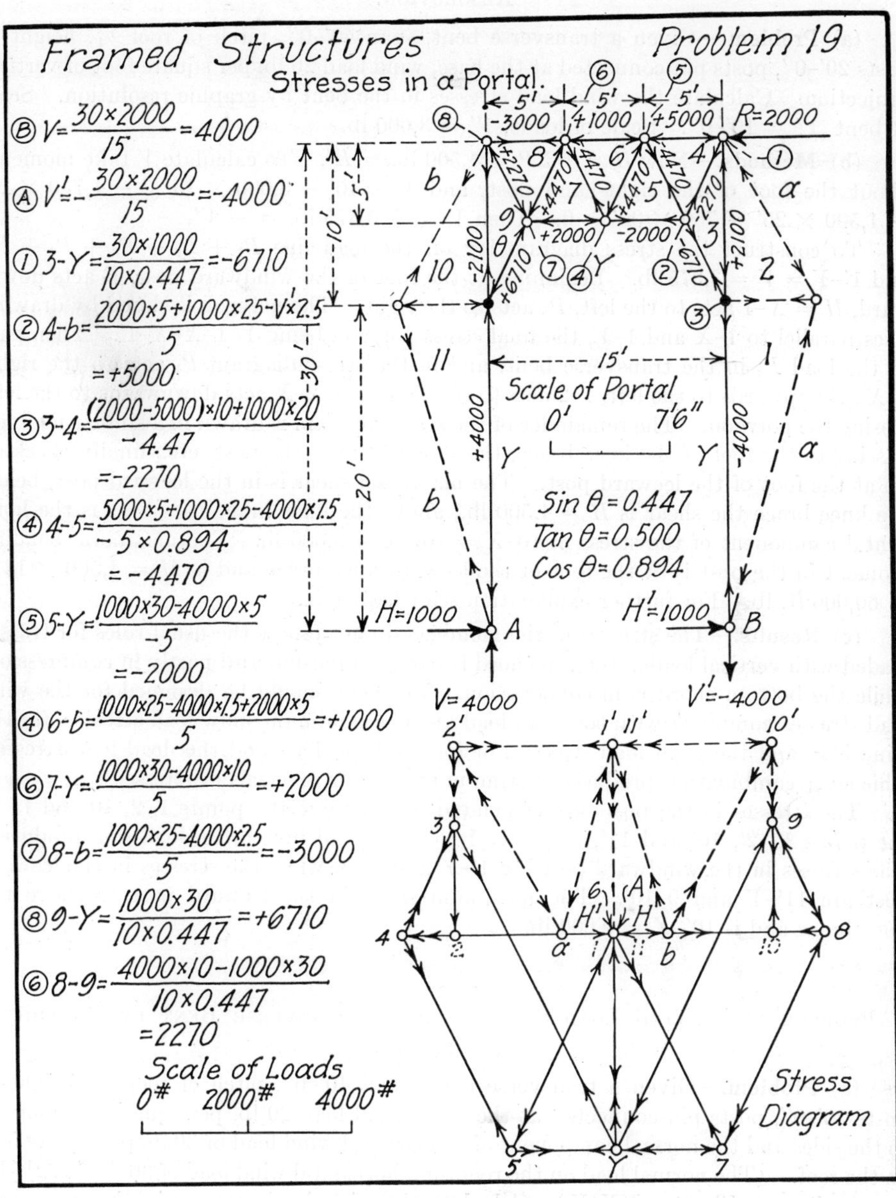
Framed Structures
Problem 19
Stresses in a Portal.
(B) V = 30×2000 / 15 = 4000
(A) V' = - 30×2000 / 15 = -4000
(1) 3-Y = -30×1000 / 10×0.447 = -6710
(2) 4-b = 2000×5+1000×25-V'×2.5 / 5 = +5000
(3) 3-4 = (2000-5000)×10+1000×20 / -4.47 = -2270
(4) 4-5 = 5000×5+1000×25-4000×7.5 / -5×0.894 = -4470
(5) 5-Y = 1000×30-4000×5 / -5 = -2000
(4) 6-b = 1000×25-4000×7.5+2000×5 / 5 = +1000
(6) 7-Y = 1000×30-4000×10 / 5 = +2000
(7) 8-b = 1000×25-4000×2.5 / 5 = -3000
(8) 9-Y = 1000×30 / 10×0.447 = +6710
(6) 8-9 = 4000×10-1000×30 / 10×0.447 = 2270
Scale of Loads
0# 2000# 4000#
5'
5'
5'
-3000
+1000
+5000
R=2000
+2270
+4470
+4470
+4470
-4470
-2270
+2000
-2000
-6710
+6710
-2100
+2100
10'
5'
30'
20'
15'
Scale of Portal
0' 7'6"
Sin θ=0.447
Tan θ=0.500
Cos θ=0.894
+4000
-4000
H=1000
H'=1000
A
B
V=4000
V'=-4000
Stress Diagram

PROBLEM 20. WIND LOAD STRESSES IN A TRANSVERSE BENT BY GRAPHIC RESOLUTION.

(a) **Problem.**—Given a transverse bent, span 40′-0″, pitch of roof ¼, height of posts 20′-0″, posts pin-connected at the base, wind load 20 lb. per square foot of vertical projection. Calculate the wind load stresses in the bent by graphic resolution. Scale of bent ,1″ = 10′-0″. Scale of loads, 1″ = 3,000 lb.

(b) **Methods.**—Now $H = \frac{1}{2}\Sigma P = 4{,}500$ lb. $= H'$. To calculate V take moments about the foot of the right-hand post, and $V \times 40' - 3{,}000 \times 13\frac{1}{3}' - 1{,}750 \times 20' - 1{,}500 \times 25' - 750 \times 30' = 0$. Then $V = +3{,}375$ lb. $= -V'$.

To construct the stress diagram lay off the load line $P_1 + P_2 + P_3 + P_4 + P_5$, and $1'-Y = V = 3{,}375$ lb. Beginning at the foot of the windward post, V acts downward, $H = X-1$ acts to the left, P_5 acts to the right. The polygon is closed by drawing lines parallel to $1-X$ and $1-Y$, the final stress polygon being $Y-1-X-X-1'$. Then pass to the load P_4 in the transverse bent, and in the stress diagram P_4 acts to the right, $1-X$ acts upwards to the left, 1–2 acts to the right, and $2-X$ acts downwards to the left, closing the polygon. The remainder of the stress diagram is drawn in a similar manner, passing to the foot of the knee brace, then to the top of the post, etc., finally checking up at the foot of the leeward post. The maximum shear is in the leeward post, below the knee brace the shear is $H = 4{,}500$ lb., above the knee brace the shear is the horizontal component of the stress in $10-X = 10'-X = 9{,}000$ lb. The maximum bending moment in the post is at the foot of the leeward knee brace and is $M = 4{,}500 \times 13\frac{1}{3} = 60{,}000$ ft.-lb. For further explanation see Chapter X.

(c) **Results.**—The stresses in the members do not follow the usual rules for trusses loaded with vertical loads; the top chord is partly in tension and partly in compression, while the bottom chord is in compression. The bent should be designed for the wind load stresses combined with the dead load and the minimum snow load stresses, for the wind load and the dead load stresses, or for the wind load and the dead load stresses, whichever combination produces maximum stresses or reversals of stresses.

The stresses in the posts are calculated by dropping the points 1, 2, 10 and 11 to the points 1′, 2′, 10′ and 11′, respectively, on the load line, or on load line produced. The stresses in the windward post are $1'-Y$ and $2'-3$, while the stresses in the leeward post are $11'-Y$ and $9-10'$. The maximum shear in the leeward post is above the knee brace and is $10'-X = 9{,}000$ lb.

PROBLEM 20a. WIND LOAD STRESSES IN A TRANSVERSE BENT BY GRAPHIC RESOLUTION.

(a) **Problem.**—Given a transverse bent, span 40′-0″, pitch of roof ¼, height of posts 20′-0″, posts pin-connected at the base, wind load 20 lb. per square foot normal to the sides and the normal component of a horizontal wind load of 30 lb. per square foot on the roof. (The normal load on the roof for a horizontal wind load of 30 lb., is 22½ lb. per sq. ft., see Chapter XXIV.) Calculate the wind load stresses in the transverse bent by graphic resolution. Scale of bent, 1″ = 10′-0″. Scale of loads, 1″ = 3,000 lb.

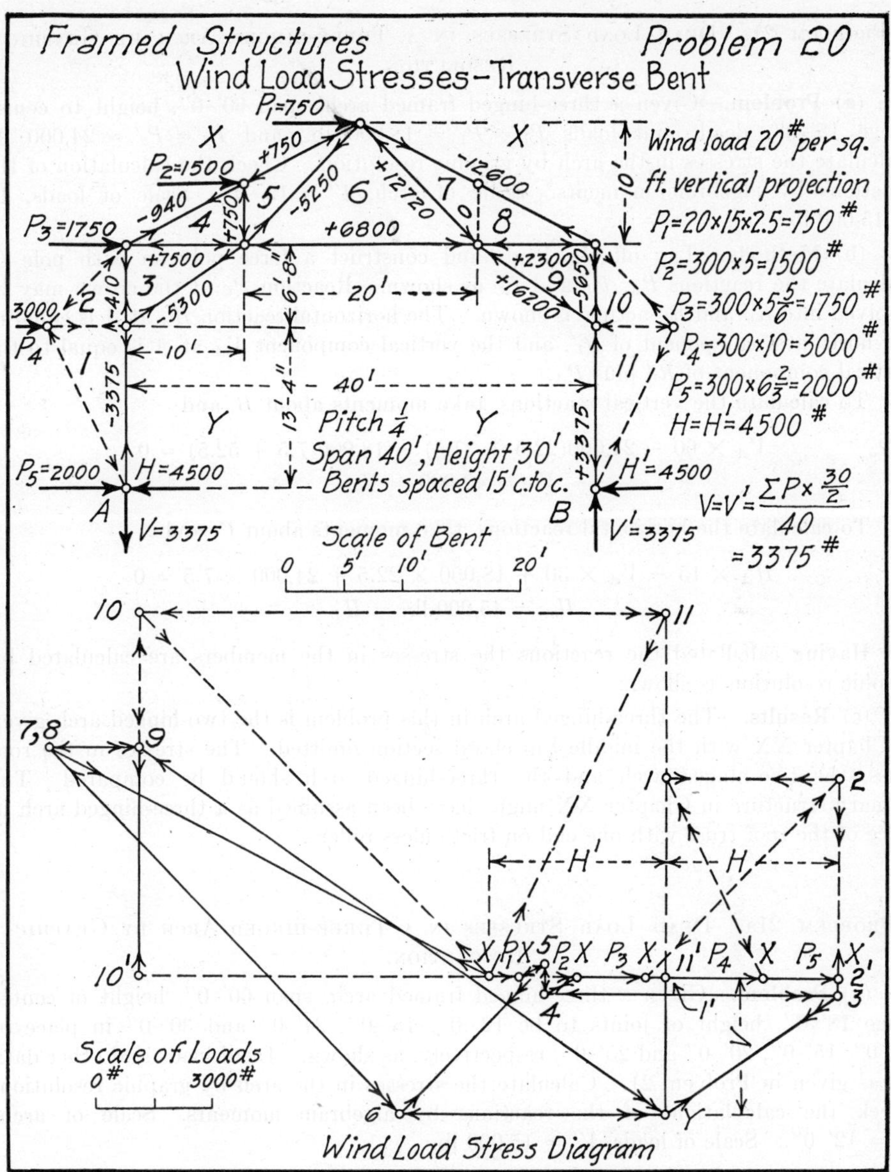
Framed Structures
Problem 20
Wind Load Stresses-Transverse Bent
Wind load 20# per sq. ft. vertical projection
P1=20×15×2.5=750#
P2=300×5=1500#
P3=300×5 5/6=1750#
P4=300×10=3000#
P5=300×6 2/3=2000#
H=H'=4500#
V=V'=ΣP× 30/2 / 40 =3375#
Pitch 1/4
Span 40', Height 30'
Bents spaced 15' c. to c.
Scale of Bent
Scale of Loads
Wind Load Stress Diagram

PROBLEM 21. DEAD LOAD STRESSES IN A THREE-HINGED ARCH BY GRAPHIC RESOLUTION.

(a) **Problem.**—Given a three-hinged framed arch, span 60′–0″, height to center hinge 15′–0″, dead joint loads $P_1 = P_1' = 18{,}000$ lb., and $P_2 = P_2' = 24{,}000$ lb. Calculate the stresses in the arch by graphic resolution. Check the calculation of the reactions by algebraic moments. Scale of arch, 1″ = 12′–0″. Scale of loads, 1″ = 15,000 lb.

(b) **Methods.**—Lay off the loads and construct a force polygon with pole O. Calculate the reactions P_A, P_B and P_C as shown. Reaction P_C at the crown may be resolved into R_1' and R_2' acting as shown. The horizontal reaction H_A at A is equal to the horizontal component of R_1', and the vertical component V_A at A is equal to the vertical component of R_1' plus P_A.

To calculate the vertical reactions, take moments about B, and

$$V_A \times 60 - 24{,}000(22.5 + 37.5) - 18{,}000(7.5 + 52.5) = 0$$
$$V_A = 42{,}000 = V_B$$

To calculate the horizontal reactions, take moments about C, and

$$H_A \times 15 - V_A \times 30 + 18{,}000 \times 22.5 + 24{,}000 \times 7.5 = 0$$
$$H_A = 45{,}000 \text{ lb.} = H_B$$

Having calculated the reactions the stresses in the members are calculated by graphic resolution as shown.

(c) **Results.**—The three-hinged arch in this problem is the two-hinged arch given in Chapter XX with the middle top chord section omitted. The stresses in the roof truss, the two-hinged arch and the three-hinged arch shou'd be compared. The primary structure in Chapter XX migh have been assumed as a three-hinged arch in place of the roof truss with one end on frict'onless rollers.

PROBLEM 21a. DEAD LOAD STRESSES IN A THREE-HINGED ARCH BY GRAPHIC RESOLUTION.

(a) **Problem.**—Given a three-hinged framed arch, span 60′–0″, height of center h'nge 18′–0″, height of joints to be 12–0″, 18′–0″, 24′–0″ and 30′–0″ in place of 10′–0″, 15′–0″, 20′–0″ and 25′–0 , respectively, as shown. Dead loads and other data are as given in Prob'em 21. Calculate the stresses in the arch by graphic resolution. Check the calculations of the reactions by algebraic moments. Scale of arch, 1″ = 12′–0″. Scale of loads, 1″ = 15,000 lb.

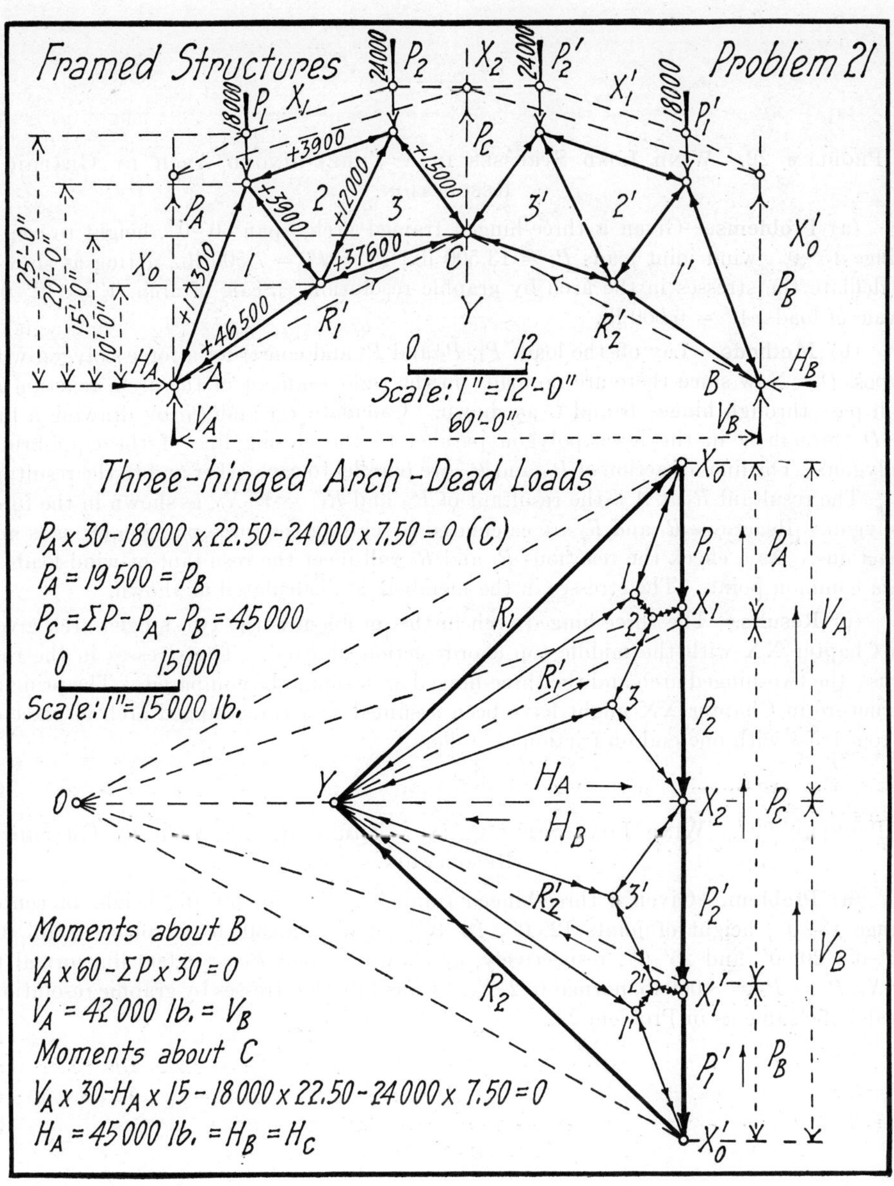
Framed Structures
Problem 21
Three-hinged Arch - Dead Loads
$P_A \times 30 - 18000 \times 22.50 - 24000 \times 7.50 = 0$ (C)
$P_A = 19500 = P_B$
$P_C = \Sigma P - P_A - P_B = 45000$
0 15000
Scale: 1" = 15000 lb.
Scale: 1" = 12'-0"
60'-0"
Moments about B
$V_A \times 60 - \Sigma P \times 30 = 0$
$V_A = 42000$ lb. $= V_B$
Moments about C
$V_A \times 30 - H_A \times 15 - 18000 \times 22.50 - 24000 \times 7.50 = 0$
$H_A = 45000$ lb. $= H_B = H_C$

PROBLEM 22. WIND LOAD STRESSES IN A THREE-HINGED ARCH BY GRAPHIC RESOLUTION.

(a) **Problems.**—Given a three-hinged framed arch, span 60′–0″, height to center hinge 15′–0″, wind joint loads P_1 = 13,500 lb., $P_2 = P_3$ = 7,500 lb., acting as shown. Calculate the stresses in the arch by graphic resolution. Scale of arch, 1″ = 12′–0′. Scale of loads, 1″ = 6,000 lb.

(b) **Methods.**—Lay off the loads P_1, P_2 and P_3 and construct a force polygon with a pole O. Now since there are no loads on the right segment of the arch, reaction R_2 will pass through hinges B and C as shown. Calculate P_A and P_C by drawing a line O–D through O in the force polygon parallel to the closing line of the equilibrium polygon. The lines of action of P_A and P_C are parallel to each other and to the resultant R. The resultant R_1 at A is the resultant of P_A and $R_1' = Y - X_0$, as shown in the force polygon. Reactions R_1 and R_2 are calculated by closing the force polygon of loads and react ons. As a check the reactions R_1 and R_2 will meet the resu tant of wind loads R in a common point. The stresses in the members are calculated as shown.

(c) **Results.**—The three-hinged arch in this problem is the two-hinged arch given in Chapter XX with the middle top chord section omitted. The stresses in the roof truss, the two-hinged arch and the three-hinged arch should be compared. The primary structure in Chapter XX might have been assumed as a three-hinged arch in place of a roof truss with one end on frictionless rollers.

PROBLEM 22a. WIND LOAD STRESSES IN A THREE-HINGED ARCH BY GRAPHIC RESOLUTION.

(a) **Problem.**—Given a three-hinged framed arch, span 60′–0″, height of center hinge 18′–0″, height of joints 12′–0″, 18′–0″, 24′–0″ and 30′–0″ in place of 10′–0″, 15′–0′, 20′–0″ and 25′–0″, respectively, as shown. Load P_1 = 16,000 lb. normal to 1–X_0, $P = P_3$ = 8,000 lb. normal to 2–X_2. Calculate the stresses by graphic resolution. Scales the same as in Problem 22.

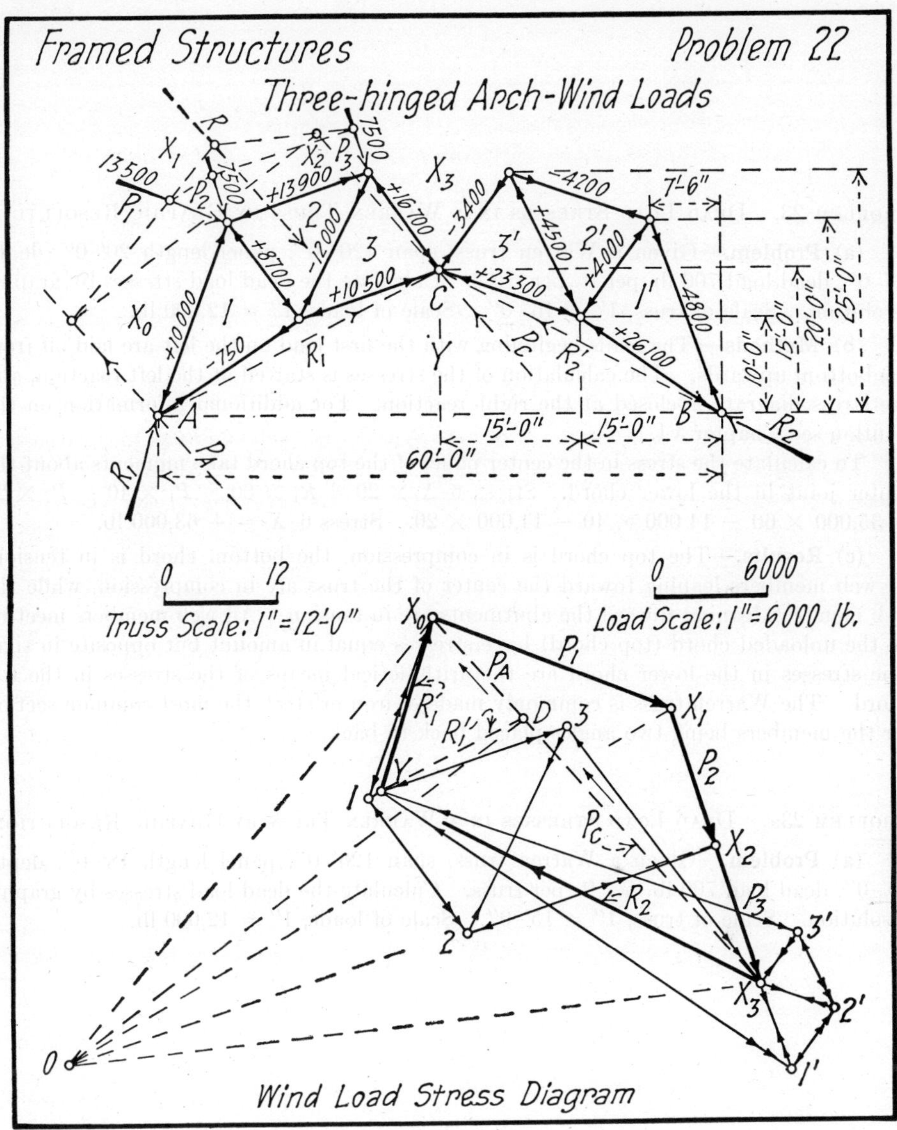
Framed Structures
Problem 22
Three-hinged Arch-Wind Loads
13 500
7500
7500
+13900
+16700
-3400
-4200
+4500
+4000
-4800
7'-6"
-12000
+8700
+10 500
+23 300
+26100
+10000
-750
15'-0"
20'-0"
25'-0"
10'-0"
60'-0"
15'-0"
15'-0"
Truss Scale: 1" = 12'-0"
Load Scale: 1" = 6000 lb.
Wind Load Stress Diagram

PROBLEM 23. DEAD LOAD STRESSES IN A WARREN TRUSS BY GRAPHIC RESOLUTION.

(a) **Problem.**—Given a Warren truss, span 120′–0″, panel length 20′–0″, depth 20′–0″, dead load 700 lb. per ft. per truss. Calculate the dead load stresses by graphic resolution. Scale of truss, 1″ = 16′–0″. Scale of loads, 1″ = 12,000 lb.

(b) **Methods.**—The loads beginning with the first load on the left are laid off from the bottom upwards. The calculation of the stresses is started at the left reaction, and the stress diagram is closed at the right reaction. For additional information on the solution see Chapter VI.

To calculate the stress in the center panel of the top chord take moments about the center joint in the lower chord. Stress $6–X \times 20 = R_1 \times 60 - P_1 \times 40 - P_2 \times 20 = 35{,}000 \times 60 - 14\ 000 \times 40 - 14{,}000 \times 20$. Stress $6–X = +\ 63{,}000$ lb.

(c) **Results.**—The top chord is in compression, the bottom chord is in tension; all web members leaning toward the center of the truss are in compression, while the web members leaning toward the abutments are in tension. All web members meeting on the unloaded chord (top chord) have stresses equal in amount but opposite in sign. The stresses in the lower chord are the arithmetical means of the stresses in the top chord. The Warren truss is commonly made of iron or steel, the most common section for the members being two angles placed back to back.

PROBLEM 23a. DEAD LOAD STRESSES IN A WARREN TRUSS BY GRAPHIC RESOLUTION.

(a) **Problem.**—Given a Warren truss, span 126′–0″, panel length 18′–0″, depth 20′–0″, dead load 700 lb. per ft. per truss. Calculate the dead load stresses by graphic resolution. Scale of truss, 1″ = 15′–0″. Scale of loads, 1″ = 12,000 lb.

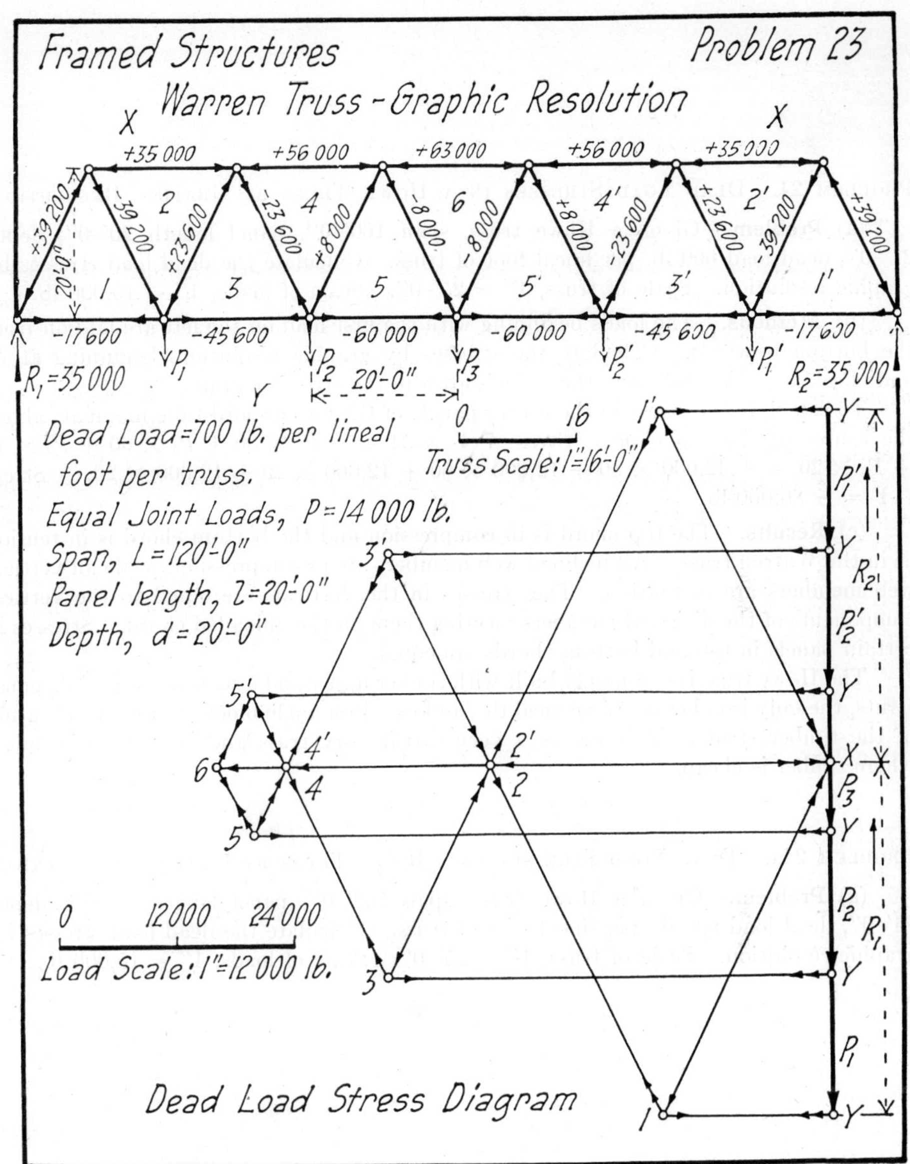
Framed Structures
Problem 23
Warren Truss - Graphic Resolution
X
+35 000
+56 000
+63 000
+56 000
+35 000
+39 200
-39 200
+23 600
-23 600
+8 000
-8 000
-8 000
+8 000
-23 600
+23 600
-39 200
+39 200
20'-0"
-17 600
-45 600
-60 000
-60 000
-45 600
-17 600
R1=35 000
R2=35 000
20'-0"
Y
Dead Load=700 lb. per lineal foot per truss.
Equal Joint Loads, P=14 000 lb.
Span, L=120'-0"
Panel length, l=20'-0"
Depth, d=20'-0"
0 16
Truss Scale: 1"=16'-0"
0 12000 24 000
Load Scale: 1"=12 000 lb.
Dead Load Stress Diagram

Problem 24. Dead Load Stresses in a Howe Truss by Graphic Resolution.

(a) **Problem.**—Given a Howe truss, span 160′–0″, panel length 20′–0″, depth 24′–0″, dead load 600 lb. per lineal foot of truss. Calculate the dead load stresses by graphic resolution. Scale of truss, 1″ = 25′–0″. Scale of loads, 1″ = 15,000 lb.

(b) **Methods.**—The loads beginning with the first load on the left are laid off from the bottom upwards. Calculate the stresses by graphic resolution, beginning at R_1 and checking at R_2, following the order shown in the stress diagram.

To calculate the stress in the center panels of the lower chord take moments about the center of the top chord. Stress $7\text{–}Y \times 24 = -R_1 \times 80 + P_1 \times 60 + P_2 \times 40 + P_3 \times 20 = -42{,}000 \times 80 + 12{,}000 \times 60 + 12{,}000 \times 40 + 12{,}000 \times 20$. Stress $7\text{–}Y = -80{,}000$ lb.

(c) **Results.**—The top chord is in compression and the bottom chord is in tension as in the Warren truss. All inclined web members are in compression, while all vertical web members are in tension. The stresses in the verticals are equal to the vertical components of the diagonal members meeting them on the unloaded chord. Stresses in certain panels in top and bottom chords are equal.

The Howe truss is commonly built with timber upper and lower chords and diagonal struts, the only iron being the vertical ties and cast iron angle blocks to take the bearing of the timber struts. This makes a very satisfactory truss and is quite economical where timber is cheap.

Problem 24a. Dead Load Stresses in a Howe Truss by Graphic Resolution.

(a) **Problem.**—Given a Howe truss, span 162′–0″, panel length 18′–0″, depth 24′–0″, dead load 600 lb. per lineal foot of truss. Calculate the dead load stresses by graphic resolution. Scale of truss, 1″ = 25′–0″. Scale of loads, 1″ = 15,000 lb.

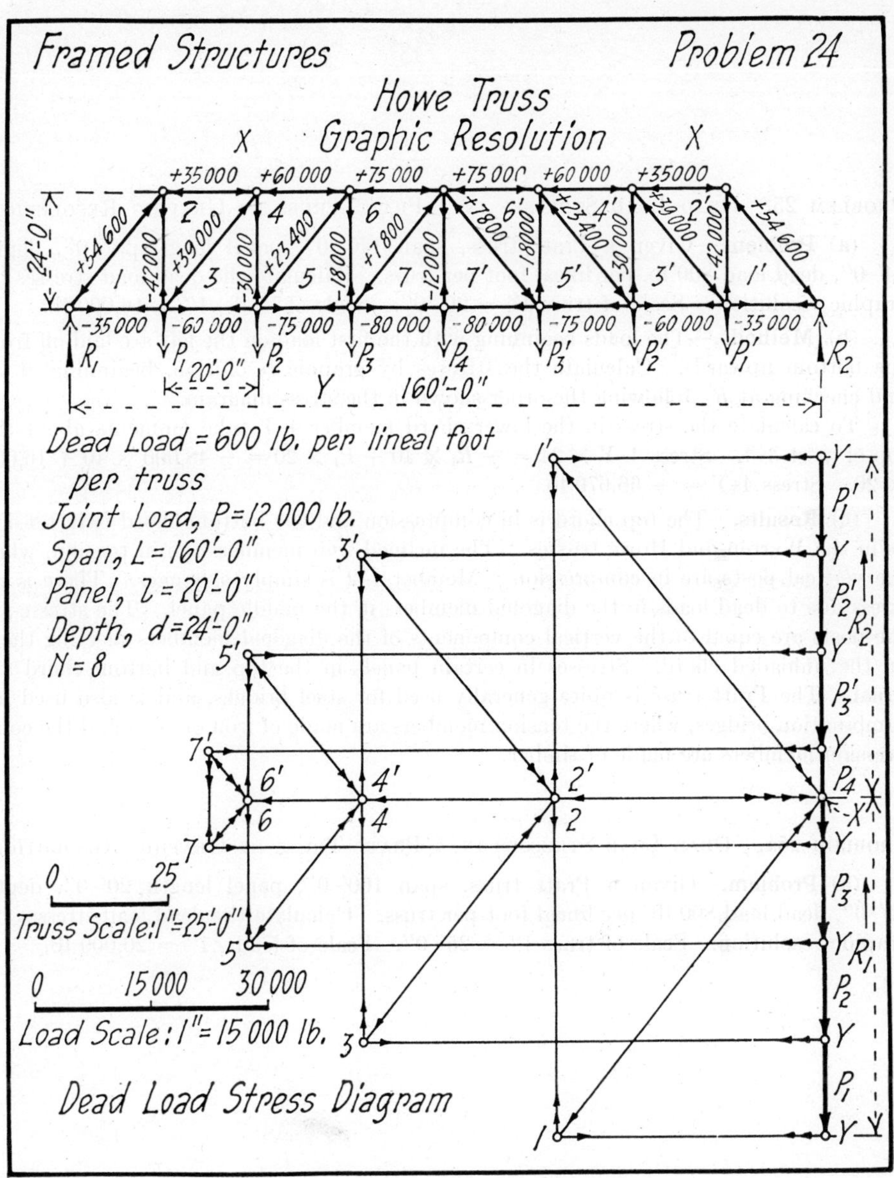
Framed Structures
Problem 24
Howe Truss
Graphic Resolution
X
X
+35 000
+60 000
+75 000
+75 000
+60 000
+35000
24'-0"
+54 600
-42000
+39 000
-30 000
+23 400
-18000
+7800
-12000
+7800
-18000
+23 400
-30 000
+39 000
-42 000
+54 600
-35 000
-60 000
-75 000
-80 000
-80 000
-75 000
-60 000
-35 000
R1
P1
P2
P3
P4
P'3
P'2
P'1
R2
20'-0"
Y
160'-0"
Dead Load = 600 lb. per lineal foot per truss
Joint Load, P=12 000 lb.
Span, L=160'-0"
Panel, l=20'-0"
Depth, d=24'-0"
N=8
0
25
Truss Scale: 1"=25'-0"
0
15 000
30 000
Load Scale: 1"=15 000 lb.
Dead Load Stress Diagram

PROBLEM 25. DEAD LOAD STRESSES IN A PRATT TRUSS BY GRAPHIC RESOLUTION.

(a) **Problem.**—Given a Pratt truss, span 140′-0″, panel length 20′-0″, depth 24′-0″, dead load 800 lb. per lineal foot per truss. Calculate the dead load stresses by graphic resolution. Scale of truss 1″ = 20′-0″. Scale of loads, 1″ = 16,000 lb.

(b) **Methods.**—The loads beginning with the first load on the left are laid off from the bottom upwards. Calculate the stresses by graphic resolution, beginning at R_1 and checking at R_2, following the order shown in the stress diagram.

To calculate the stress in the lower chord member 4–Y take moments about the top of post 3–4. Stress 4–$Y \times 24 = -R_1 \times 40 + P_1 \times 20 = -48{,}000 \times 40 + 16{,}000 \times 20$. Stress 4–$Y = -66{,}670$ lb.

(c) **Results.**—The top chord is in compression and the bottom chord is in tension as in the Warren and Howe trusses. The inclined web members are in tension, while the vertical posts are in compression. Member 1–2 is simply a hanger. There is no stress due to dead loads in the diagonal members in the middle panel. The stresses in the posts are equal to the vertical components of the diagonal members meeting them on the unloaded chord. Stresses in certain panels in the top and bottom chord are equal. The Pratt truss is quite generally used for steel bridges, and is also used for combination bridges, where the tension members are made of iron or steel and the compression members are made of timber.

PROBLEM 25a. DEAD LOAD STRESSES IN A PRATT TRUSS BY GRAPHIC RESOLUTION.

(a) **Problem.**—Given a Pratt truss, span 160′-0″, panel length 20′-0″, depth 24′-0″, dead load 800 lb. per lineal foot per truss. Calculate the dead load stresses by graphic resolution. Scale of truss 1″ = 25′-0″. Scale of loads, 1″ = 20,000 lb.

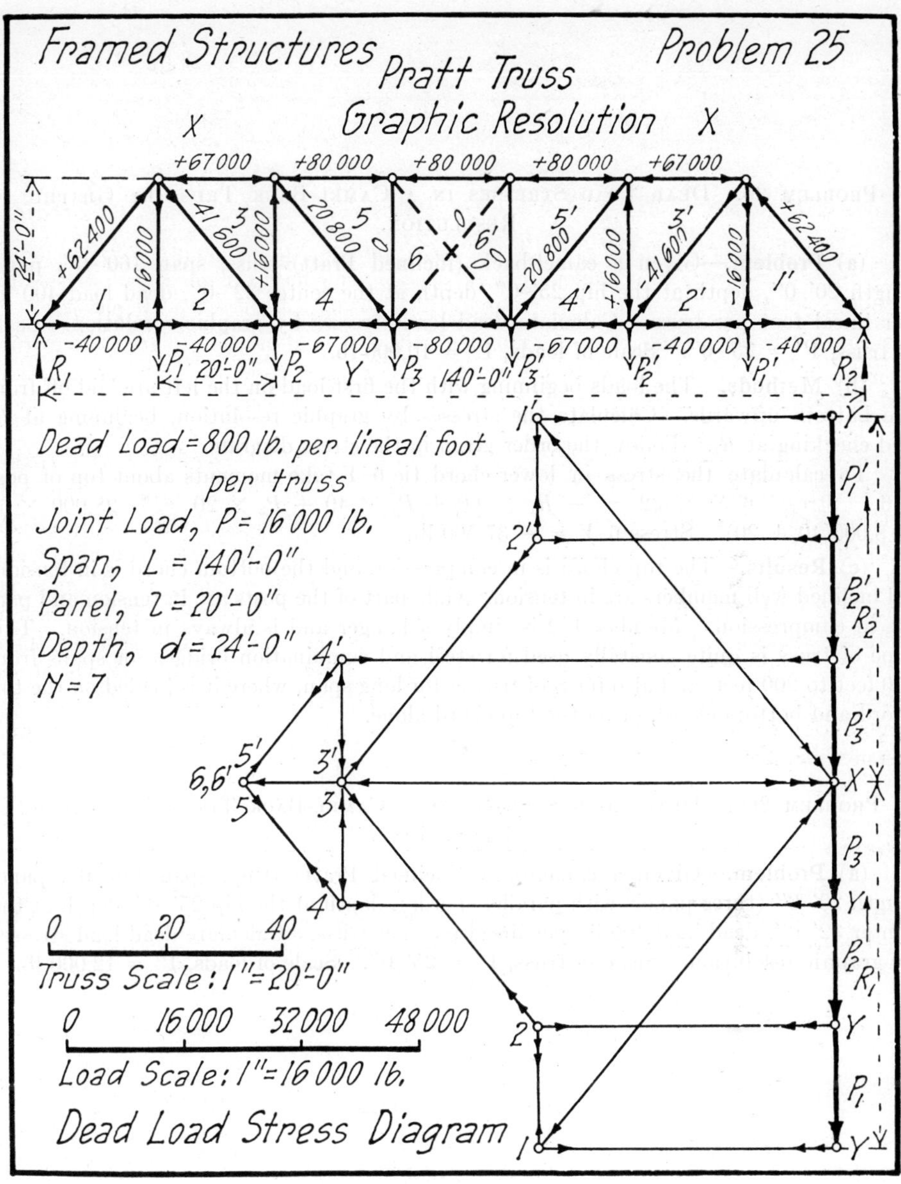
Framed Structures
Problem 25
Pratt Truss
Graphic Resolution
X
X
+67 000
+80 000
+80 000
+80 000
+67 000
24'-0"
+62 400
-16 000
41 600
+16 000
20 800
0
0
20 800
+16 000
41 600
16 000
+62 400
1
2
3
4
5
6
6'
5'
4'
3'
2'
1'
-40 000
-40 000
-67 000
-80 000
-67 000
-40 000
-40 000
R_1
P_1
P_2
P_3
P_3'
P_2'
P_1'
R_2
20'-0"
Y
140'-0"
Dead Load = 800 lb. per lineal foot per truss
Joint Load, P = 16 000 lb.
Span, L = 140'-0"
Panel, l = 20'-0"
Depth, d = 24'-0"
N = 7
0 20 40
Truss Scale: 1" = 20'-0"
0 16 000 32 000 48 000
Load Scale: 1" = 16 000 lb.
Dead Load Stress Diagram
6,6'
X

PROBLEM 26. DEAD LOAD STRESSES IN A CAMEL-BACK TRUSS BY GRAPHIC RESOLUTION.

(a) **Problem.**—Given a camel-back (inclined Pratt) truss, span 160′–0″, panel length 20′–0″, depth at the hip 25′–0″, depth at the center 32′–0″, dead load 400 lb. per lineal foot per truss. Calculate dead load stresses by graphic resolution. Scale of truss, 1″ = 25′–0″. Scale of loads, 1″ = 10,000 lb.

(b) **Methods.**—The loads beginning with the first load on the left are laid off from the bottom upwards. Calculate the stresses by graphic resolution, beginning at R_1 and checking at R_2. Follow the order given in the stress diagram.

To calculate the stress in lower chord tie 6–*Y* take moments about top of post 5–6. Stress 6–Y $\times$ 32 $= - R_1 \times 60 + P_1 \times 40 + P_2 \times 20 = - 28{,}000 \times 60 + 8{,}000(40 + 20)$. Stress 6–*Y* $= - 37{,}500$ lb.

(c) **Results.**—The top chord is in compression and the bottom chord is in tension. All inclined web members are in tension; while part of the posts are in tension and part are in compression. Member 1–2 is simply a hanger and is always in tension. This type of truss is quite generally used for steel and combination bridges for spans from 150 feet to 200 feet, and also for roof trusses for long span, where it is loaded on the top chord and bottom chord, or on the top chord alone.

PROBLEM 26a. DEAD LOAD STRESSES IN A CAMEL-BACK TRUSS BY GRAPHIC RESOLUTION.

(a) **Problem.**—Given a camel-back (inclined Pratt) truss, span 180′–0″, panel length 20′- 0″ (three panels with parallel chords), depth at the hip 25′–0″, depth at the center 32′–0″, dead load 400 lb. per lineal foot per truss. Calculate dead load stresses by graphic resolution. Scale of truss, 1″ = 25′–0″. Scale of loads, 1″ = 12,000 lb.

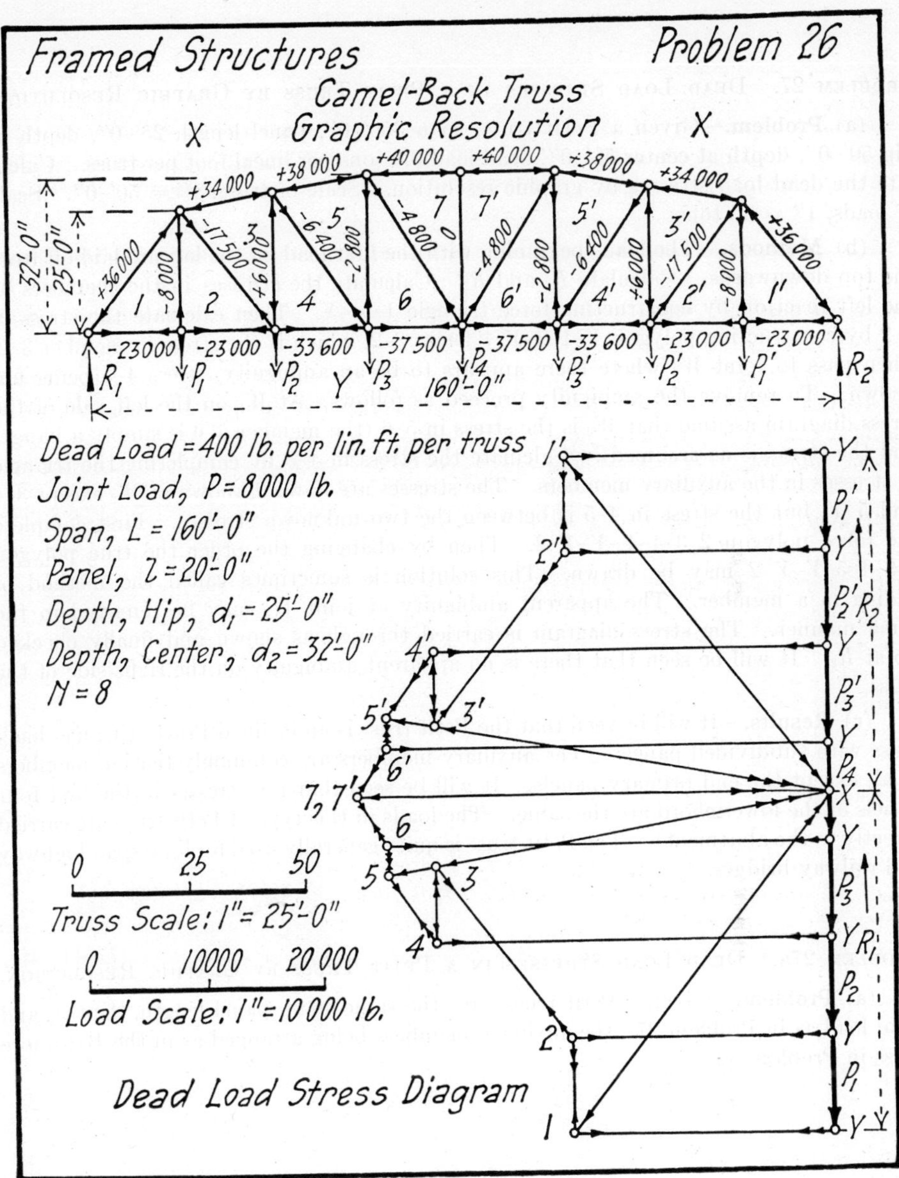

Framed Structures
Problem 26
Camel-Back Truss
Graphic Resolution
X
X
Y
32'-0"
25'-0"
+34 000
+38 000
+40 000
+40 000
+38 000
+34 000
+36 000
+36 000
-17 500
-17 500
-8 000
-8 000
+6000
+6000
-6 400
-6 400
-2 800
-2 800
-4 800
-4 800
0
-23000
-23 000
-33 600
-37 500
-37 500
-33 600
-23 000
-23 000
R1
R2
P1
P2
P3
P4
P3'
P2'
P1'
160'-0"
Dead Load = 400 lb. per lin. ft. per truss
Joint Load, P = 8 000 lb.
Span, L = 160'-0"
Panel, l = 20'-0"
Depth, Hip, d1 = 25'-0"
Depth, Center, d2 = 32'-0"
N = 8
0 25 50
Truss Scale: 1" = 25'-0"
0 10000 20 000
Load Scale: 1" = 10 000 lb.
Dead Load Stress Diagram

PROBLEM 27. DEAD LOAD STRESSES IN A PETIT TRUSS BY GRAPHIC RESOLUTION.

(a) **Problem.**—Given a Petit truss, span 350′–0″, panel length 25′–0″, depth at hip 50′–0″, depth at center 58′–0″, dead load 0.9 tons per lineal foot per truss. Calculate the dead load stresses by graphic resolution. Scale of truss, 1″ = 50′–0″. Scale of loads, 1″ = 45 tons.

(b) **Methods.**—The loads beginning with the first load on the left are laid off from the top downwards. Calculate R_1 and R_2. Calculate the stresses in the members at the left reaction by constructing force triangle 1–Y–X. Then calculate the stress in 1–2 by constructing polygon Y–1–2–Y. Draw 3–2, which is the stress in member 3–2. Then pass to joint W_2 where there appears to be an ambiguity, stress 4–5 being unknown. To remove the ambiguity proceed as follows: At W_3 on the left side of the stress diagram assume that W_3 is the stress in 5–6 (the member 5–6 is simply a hanger and the stress is as assumed). Calculate the stress in 4–5 by completing the triangle of stresses in the auxiliary members. The stresses are now all known at W_2 except 3–4 and 5–Y, but the stress in 4–5 is between the two unknown stresses. First complete the force polygon 2–3–4–4′–Y–Y–2. Then by changing the order the true polygon 2–3–4–5–Y–Y–2 may be drawn. This solution is sometimes called the method of sliding in a member. The apparent ambiguity at joint W_4 may be removed in the same manner. The stress diagram is carried through as shown and finally checked up at R_2. It will be seen that there is no apparent ambiguity on the right side of the truss.

(c) **Results.**—It will be seen that the Petit truss is an inclined Pratt or Camel-back truss with subdivided panels. The auxiliary members are commonly tension members in all except the end primary panels. It will be seen that the stresses in the first four panels of the lower chord are the same. The loads in this type of Petit truss are carried directly to the abutments. The Petit truss is quite generally used for long span highway and railway bridges.

PROBLEM 27a. DEAD LOAD STRESSES IN A PETIT TRUSS BY GRAPHIC RESOLUTION.

(a) **Problem.**—Given a Petit truss with the same span, panel length, depths, and dead load as in Problem 27; the auxiliary members being arranged as in the Baltimore truss in Problem 32.

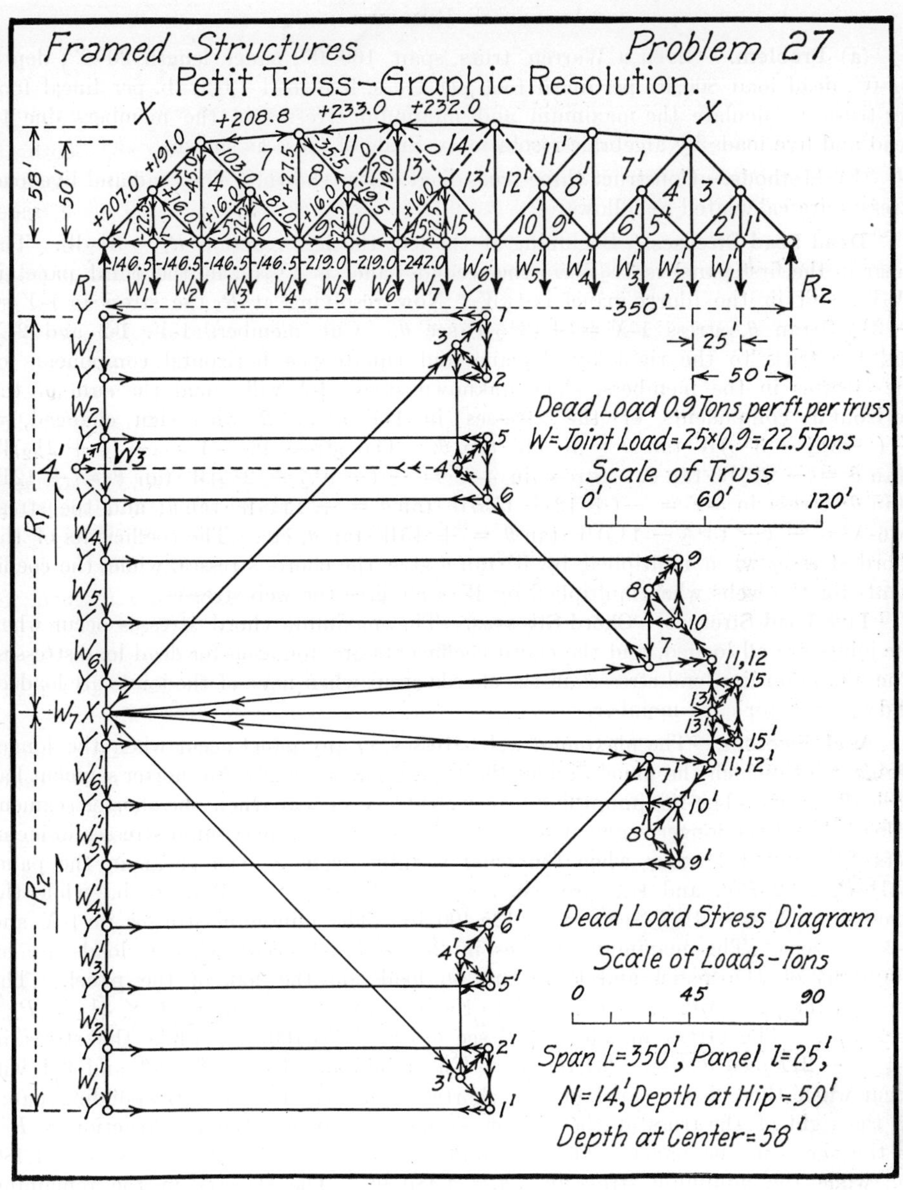
Framed Structures
Problem 27
Petit Truss–Graphic Resolution.
Dead Load 0.9 Tons per ft. per truss
W=Joint Load=25×0.9=22.5 Tons
Scale of Truss
0' 60' 120'
Dead Load Stress Diagram
Scale of Loads–Tons
0 45 90
Span L=350', Panel l=25',
N=14', Depth at Hip=50'
Depth at Center=58'

PROBLEM 28. MAXIMUM AND MINIMUM STRESSES IN A WARREN TRUSS BY ALGEBRAIC RESOLUTION.

(a) **Problem.**—Given a Warren truss, span 160′-0″, panel length 20′-0″, depth 20′-0″, dead load 800 lb. per lineal foot per truss, live load 1,600 lb. per lineal foot per truss. Calculate the maximum and minimum stresses in the members due to dead and live loads by algebraic resolution. Scale of truss as shown.

(b) **Methods.**—Construct three truss diagrams as shown. The dead and live load stresses are calculated as follows:—

Dead Load Stresses.—Beginning at the left the left reaction $R_1 = 3\frac{1}{2}W$. The shear in the first panel is $3\frac{1}{2}W$, in the second panel is $2\frac{1}{2}W$, in the third panel is $1\frac{1}{2}W$, and in the fourth panel is $\frac{1}{2}W$. Now resolving at R_1 the stress in 1-Y = $-3\frac{1}{2}W\cdot\tan\theta$, stress 1-$X$ = $+3\frac{1}{2}W\cdot\sec\theta$. Cut members 1-$Y$, 1-2 and 2-$X$ and the truss to the right by a plane and equate the horizontal components of the stresses in the members. The unknown stress 2-X will equal the sum of the horizontal components of the stresses in 1-Y and 1-2 with sign changed, $= -(-3\frac{1}{2} - 3\frac{1}{2})W\cdot\tan\theta = +7W\cdot\tan\theta$. The stress in 3-$Y = -(7 + 2\frac{1}{2})W\cdot\tan\theta = -9\frac{1}{2}W\cdot\tan\theta$. Stress in 4-$X = -(-9\frac{1}{2} - 2\frac{1}{2})W\cdot\tan\theta = +12W\cdot\tan\theta$; stress in 5-$Y = -(+12 + 1\frac{1}{2})W\cdot\tan\theta = +13\frac{1}{2}W\cdot\tan\theta$; and the stress in 6-$X = -(-13\frac{1}{2} - 1\frac{1}{2})W\cdot\tan\theta = +15W\cdot\tan\theta$, etc. The coefficients of the chord stresses when multiplied by $W\cdot\tan\theta$ give the chord stresses, while the coefficients for the webs when multiplied by $W\cdot\sec\theta$ give the web stresses.

Live Load Stresses.—Chord Stresses.—The maximum chord stresses occur when the joints are all loaded, and the chord coefficients are found as for dead load stresses. The minimum live load stresses in the chords occur when none of the joints are loaded, and are zero for each member.

Web Stresses.—The maximum web stresses in any panel occur when the longer segment into which the panel divides the truss is loaded, while the shorter segment has no loads on it. The minimum live load web stresses occur when the shorter segment is loaded and the longer segment has no loads on it. The maximum stresses in members 1-X and 1-2 occur when the truss is fully loaded. The shear in the panel is $3\frac{1}{2}P$, or $28P/8$, and the stress in 1-$X = 3\frac{1}{2}P\cdot\sec\theta = +125{,}400$ lb., while the stress in 1-2 $= -3\frac{1}{2}P\cdot\sec\theta = -125{,}400$ lb. The minimum stresses in 1-X and 1-2 are zero. The maximum stresses in 2-3 and 3-4 occur when 6 loads are on the right of the panel and there are no loads on the left of the panel. The shear in the panel will then be equal to the left reaction, $= R_1 = (6 \times 3\frac{1}{2} \times P)/8 = 21P/8$. The stress in 2-3 $= 21P\cdot\sec\theta/8 = +94{,}100$ lb., while the stress in 3-4 $= -21P\cdot\sec\theta/8 = -94{,}100$ lb. The minimum stresses in 2-3 and 3-4 will occur when there is one load on the shorter segment. In the corresponding panel on the right of the truss, if the shorter segment is loaded, the left reaction $= P/8$ = the shear in the panel. The minimum stress in 2-3 $= -P\cdot\sec\theta/8 = -4{,}480$ lb., while the minimum stress in 3-4 = 4,480 lb. The stresses in the remaining panels are calculated in the same manner.

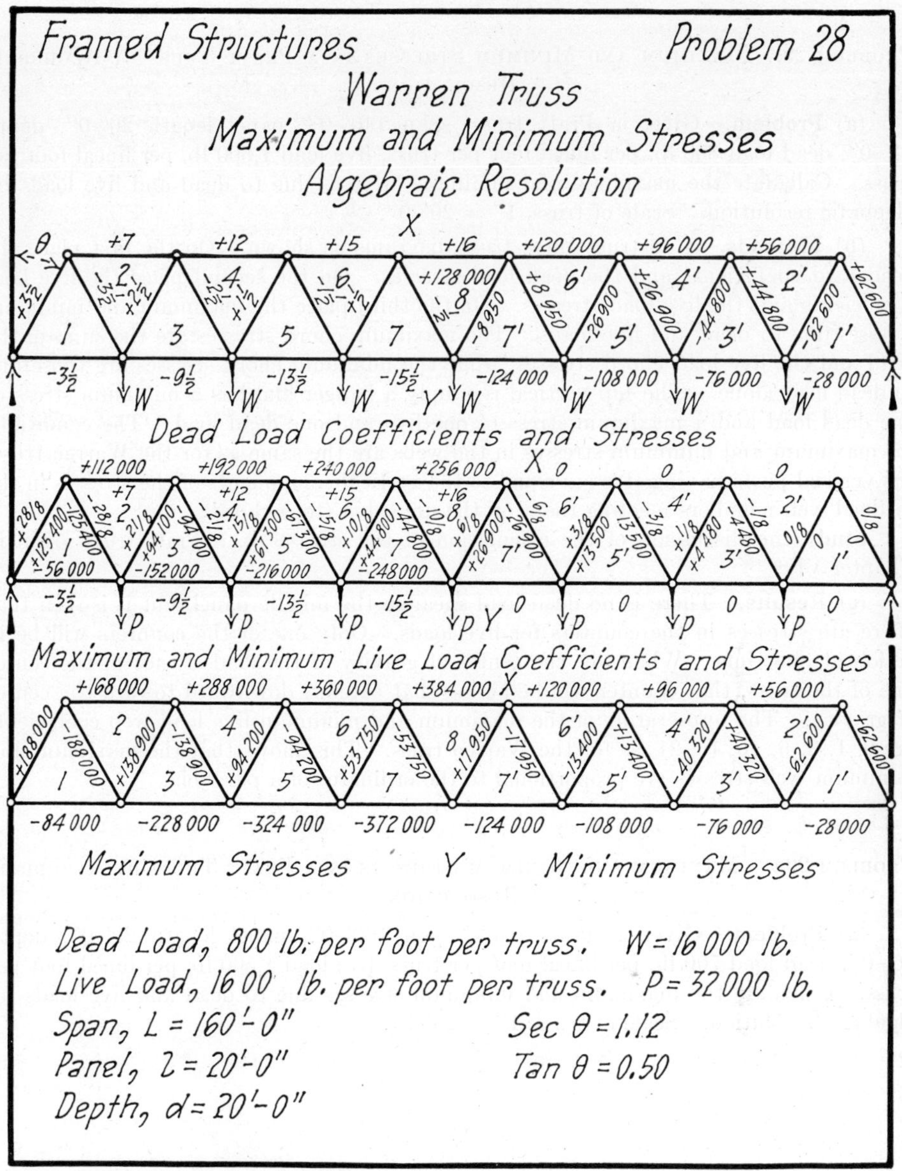

PROBLEM 28a. MAXIMUM AND MINIMUM STRESSES IN A WARREN TRUSS BY ALGEBRAIC RESOLUTION.

(a) Problem.—Given a Warren truss, span 180′-0″, panel length 20′-0″, depth 24-0″, dead load 900 lb. per lineal foot per truss, live load 1,800 lb. per lineal foot per truss. Calculate the maximum and minimum stresses in the members due to dead and live loads by algebraic resolution.

PROBLEM 29. MAXIMUM AND MINIMUM STRESSES IN A PRATT TRUSS BY ALGEBRAIC RESOLUTION.

(a) **Problem.**—Given a Pratt truss, span 140′-0″, panel length 20′-0″, depth 24′-0″, dead load 800 lb. per lineal foot per truss, live load 1,600 lb. per lineal foot per truss. Calculate the maximum and minimum stresses due to dead and live loads by algebraic resolution. Scale of truss, 1″ = 20′-0″.

(b) **Methods.**—Construct three truss diagrams as shown. On the first place the dead load coefficients and the dead load stresses. On the second place the live load coefficients and the live load stresses. On the third place the maximum and minimum stresses due to dead and live loads. The maximum chord stresses are the sums of the dead and the live load chord stresses, while the minimum chord stresses are those due to dead load alone. The hip vertical is simply a hanger and has a minimum stress of one dead load and a maximum stress of one live and one dead load. The conditions for maximum and minimum stresses in the webs are the same as for the Warren truss, the vertical posts having stresses equal to the vertical components of the stresses in the inclined web members meeting them on the unloaded (top) chord.

Study the discussion of the calculation of the stresses in a Pratt truss given in Chapter VI.

(c) **Results.**—There is no dead load shear in the middle panel, but it is seen that there are stresses in the counters for live loads. Only one of the counters will be in action at one time. Whenever the center of gravity of the loads is not in the center line of the truss, that counter will be acting that extends downward toward the center of gravity. The numerators of the maximum and minimum live load web coefficients are 0, 1, 3, 6, 10, 15, 21, as for the Warren truss. This shows that the maximum and minimum web stresses are proportional to the ordinates of a parabola.

PROBLEM 29a. MAXIMUM AND MINIMUM STRESSES IN A PRATT TRUSS BY ALGEBRAIC RESOLUTION.

(a) **Problem.**—Given a Pratt truss, span 160′-0″, panel length 20′-0″, depth 26′-0″, dead load 700 lb. per lineal foot per truss, live load 1,500 lb. per lineal foot per truss. Calculate the maximum and minimum stresses due to dead and live loads by algebraic resolution. Scale of truss, 1″ = 25′-0″.

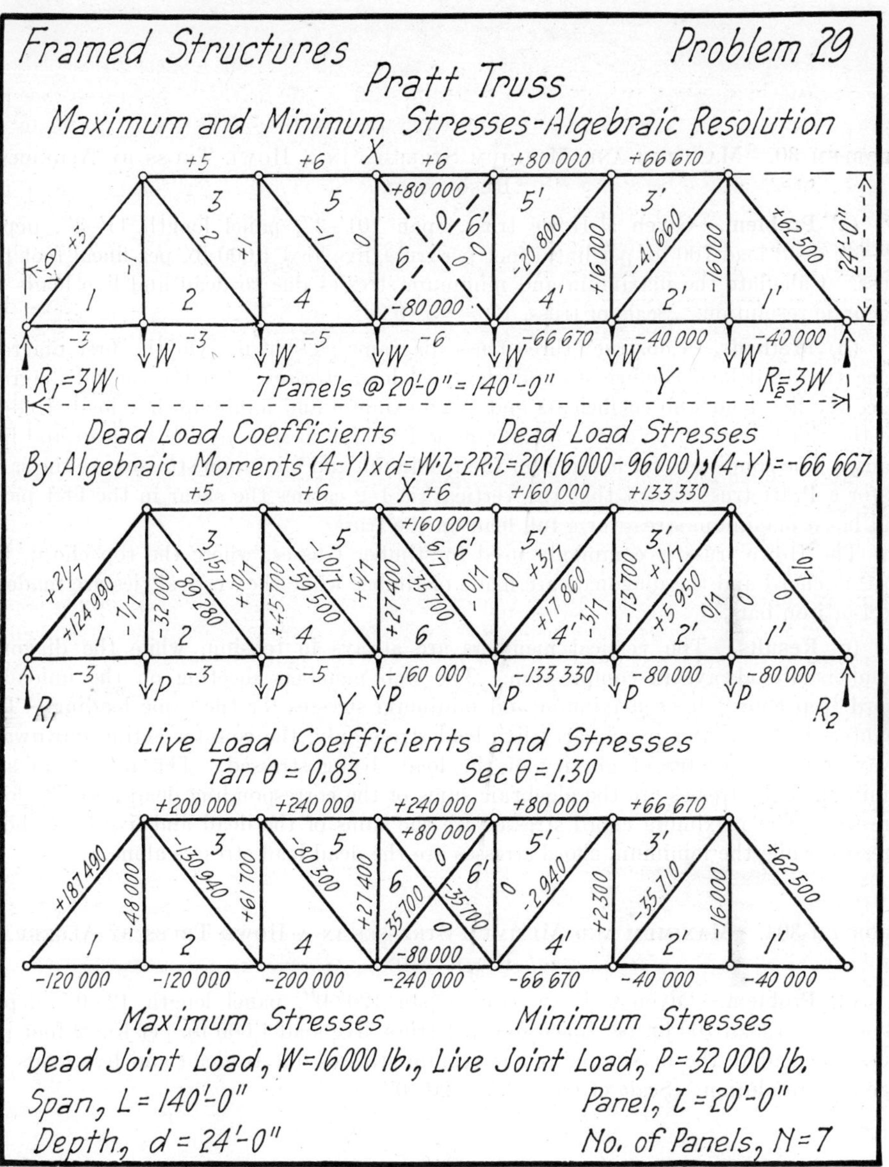
Framed Structures
Problem 29
Pratt Truss
Maximum and Minimum Stresses-Algebraic Resolution
R1=3W
7 Panels @ 20'-0" = 140'-0"
R2=3W
24'-0"
Dead Load Coefficients
Dead Load Stresses
By Algebraic Moments (4-Y)×d=W·l-2R·l=20(16000-96000); (4-Y)=-66 667
Live Load Coefficients and Stresses
Tan θ = 0.83
Sec θ = 1.30
Maximum Stresses
Minimum Stresses
Dead Joint Load, W=16000 lb., Live Joint Load, P=32 000 lb.
Span, L = 140'-0"
Panel, l = 20'-0"
Depth, d = 24'-0"
No. of Panels, N=7

PROBLEM 30. MAXIMUM AND MINIMUM STRESSES IN A HOWE TRUSS BY ALGEBRAIC RESOLUTION.

(a) **Problem.**—Given a Howe truss, span 101′–3″, panel length 11′–3″, depth 22′–6″, dead load 700 lb. per lineal foot per truss, live load 1,000 lb. per lineal foot per truss. Calculate the maximum and minimum stresses due to dead and live loads by algebraic resolution. Scale of truss, 1″ = 15′–0″.

(b) **Methods.**—Construct three truss diagrams as shown. On the first diagram place the dead load coefficients and the dead load stresses. On the second diagram place the live load web coefficients and the maximum and minimum live load stresses. On the third diagram place the maximum and minimum stresses due to dead and live loads. The conditions for loading for the maximum and minimum stresses are the same as for a Pratt truss except that the vertical tie 1–2 carries the shear in the first panel and has a maximum stress for a full load on the truss.

The Howe truss is commonly used for timber trusses, where the top chord, the bottom chord and the diagonals are made of timber while the vertical ties are made of steel or iron bars.

(c) **Results.**—The vertical members are always in tension, while the diagonal members are always in compression. The web members meeting on the unloaded chord (top chord) have maximum and minimum stresses for the same loading. The counters in the center panel carry live load stress only, the counter acting downward away from the center of gravity of the loads being stressed. The maximum and minimum web stresses are the algebraic sums of the corresponding dead and live load stresses. The maximum chord stresses are the sums of the dead and live load chord stresses, while the minimum chord stresses are the dead load stresses alone.

PROBLEM 30a. MAXIMUM AND MINIMUM STRESSES IN A HOWE TRUSS BY ALGEBRAIC RESOLUTION.

(a) **Problem.**—Given a Howe truss, span 120′–0″, panel length 12′–0″, depth 24′–0″, dead load 700 lb. per lineal foot per truss, live load 1,000 lb. per lineal foot per truss. Calculate the maximum and minimum stresses due to dead and live loads by algebraic resolution. Scale of truss, 1″ = 20′–0″.

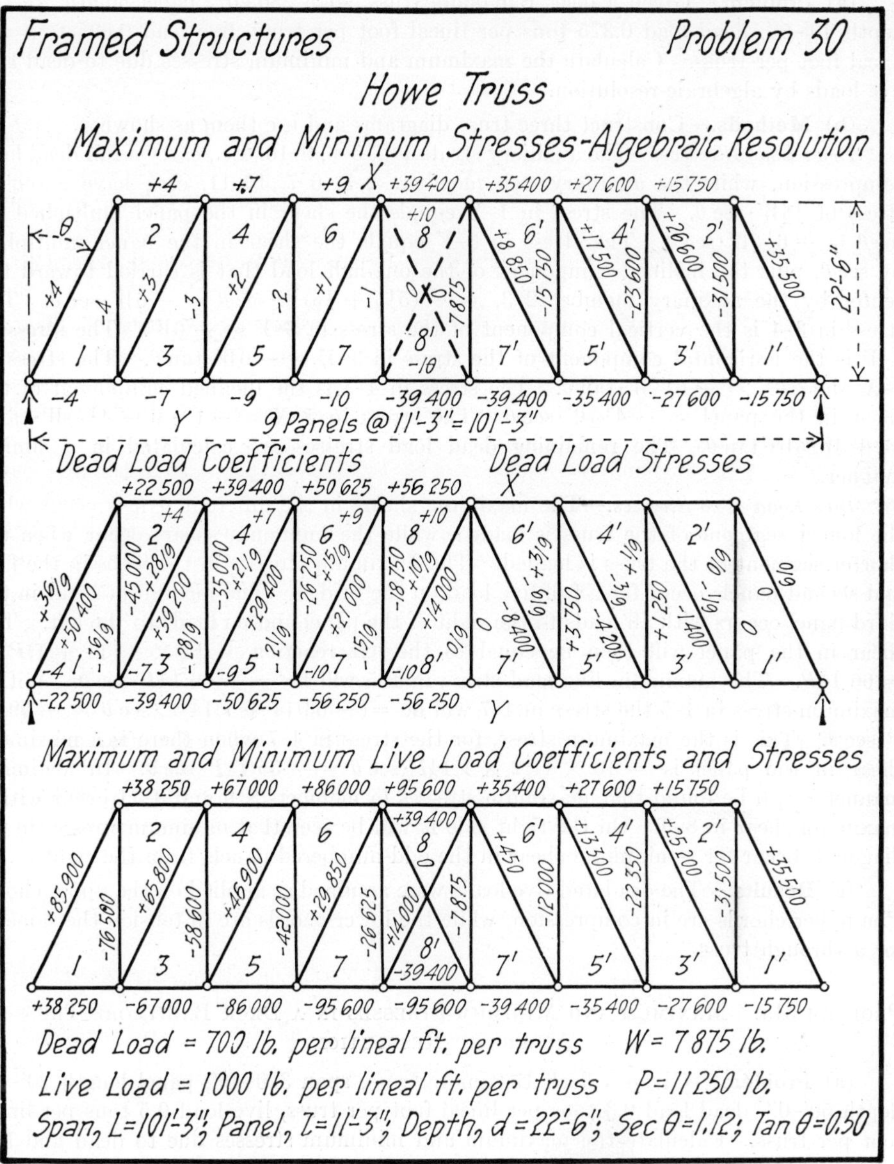
Framed Structures
Problem 30
Howe Truss
Maximum and Minimum Stresses-Algebraic Resolution
+4 +7 +9 X +39 400 +35 400 +27 600 +15 750
+10
θ
2 4 6 8 6' 4' 2'
+4 -4 +3 -3 +2 -2 +1 -1 0 -7 875 +8 850 -15 750 +17 500 -23 600 +26 600 -31 500 +35 500
22'-6"
1 3 5 7 8' 7' 5' 3' 1'
-10
-4 -7 -9 -10 -39 400 -39 400 -35 400 -27 600 -15 750
Y
9 Panels @ 11'-3" = 101'-3"
Dead Load Coefficients
Dead Load Stresses
+22 500 +39 400 +50 625 +56 250 X
+4 +7 +9 +10
2 4 6 8 6' 4' 2'
+36/9 +50 400 -36/9 -45 000 +28/9 +39 200 -28/9 -35 000 +21/9 +29 400 -21/9 -26 250 +15/9 +21 000 -15/9 -18 750 +10/9 +14 000 0/9 0 -8 400 -6/9 +3/9 +3 750 -3/9 +1/9 -4 200 +1 250 -1/9 -1 400 0/9 0 0 0/9
-4 1 -7 3 -9 5 -10 7 -10 8' 7' 5' 3' 1'
-22 500 -39 400 -50 625 -56 250 -56 250
Y
Maximum and Minimum Live Load Coefficients and Stresses
+38 250 +67 000 +86 000 +95 600 +35 400 +27 600 +15 750
+39 400
2 4 6 8 6' 4' 2'
+85 900 -76 500 +65 800 -58 600 +46 900 -42 000 +29 850 -26 625 +14 000 0 -7 875 +450 -12 000 +13 300 -22 350 +25 200 -31 500 +35 500
1 3 5 7 8' 7' 5' 3' 1'
-39 400
+38 250 -67 000 -86 000 -95 600 -95 600 -39 400 -35 400 -27 600 -15 750
Dead Load = 700 lb. per lineal ft. per truss
W = 7 875 lb.
Live Load = 1000 lb. per lineal ft. per truss
P = 11 250 lb.
Span, L = 101'-3"; Panel, l = 11'-3"; Depth, d = 22'-6"; Sec θ = 1.12; Tan θ = 0.50

PROBLEM 31. MAXIMUM AND MINIMUM STRESSES IN A DECK BALTIMORE TRUSS BY ALGEBRAIC RESOLUTION.

(a) **Problem.**—Given a deck Baltimore truss, span 280′–0″, panel length 20′–0″, depth 40′–0″, dead load 0.375 tons per lineal foot per truss, live load 0.625 tons per lineal foot per truss. Calculate the maximum and minimum stresses due to dead and live loads by algebraic resolution.

(b) **Methods.**—Construct three truss diagrams and use them as shown.

Dead Load Stresses.—The auxiliary struts 1–2, 5–6, 9–10, etc., carry a full dead load compression, while the auxiliary web members 2–3, 6–7, 10–11, etc., have a tensile stress of $\frac{1}{2}W \cdot \sec\theta$. The stress in 1–$Y$ equals the shear in the panel multiplied by $\sec\theta = -6\frac{1}{2}W \cdot \sec\theta$. The stress in 3–$Y$ equals the shear in the panel multiplied by $\sec\theta$, plus the inclined component of the one-half load that is carried toward the center by the auxiliary member 2–3, $= -(5\frac{1}{2} + \frac{1}{2})W \cdot \sec\theta = -6W \cdot \sec\theta$. The stress in 3–4 is the vertical component of the stress in 3–$Y = +6W$. The stress in 4–Y is the horizontal component of the stress in 3–$Y = -6W \cdot \tan\theta$. The stress in 1–X and 2–$X = +6\frac{1}{2}W \cdot \tan\theta$. The stress in 4–5 is the inclined component of the shear in the panel $= -4\frac{1}{2}W \cdot \sec\theta$. The stress in 5–$X = -(-6 - 4\frac{1}{2})W \cdot \tan\theta = +10\frac{1}{2}W \cdot \tan\theta$. The remaining dead load stresses are calculated in a similar manner.

Live Load Web Stresses.—The maximum shears in the different panels occur when the longer segment of the truss is loaded, while the minimum shears occur when the shorter segment of the truss is loaded. The maximum stresses in the webs in the first and second panels occur for a full live load on the bridge. The maximum shear in the third panel occurs with all loads to the right of the panel and no loads to the left. The shear in the panel will then be equal to the left reaction $= 11 \times \frac{1}{2}(11 + 1)P/14 = 66/14P$. The maximum live load stress in 4–5 will be $= -66/14P \cdot \sec\theta$. With a maximum stress in 4–5 the stress in 4–7 will be $= (-66/14 + 7/14)P \cdot \sec\theta = -59/14 P \cdot \sec\theta$. This is the maximum stress, for the stress in 4–7 when there is a maximum shear in the panel is $= 10 \times 11/2 \times 1/14P \cdot \sec\theta = -55/14P \cdot \sec\theta$. In a similar manner it will be found that maximum stresses in members 8–9 and 8–11 occur with a maximum shear in 8–9. On the right side it will be seen that minimum stresses in the diagonals occur for a minimum shear in the odd-numbered panels from the right.

(c) **Results.**—The dead and live loads were assumed as applied on the upper chord. The upper chords are in compression, while the lower chords are in tension the same as for a through truss.

PROBLEM 31a. MAXIMUM AND MINIMUM STRESSES IN A DECK BALTIMORE TRUSS BY ALGEBRAIC RESOLUTION.

(a) **Problem.**—Given a deck Baltimore truss, span 320′–0″, panel length 20′–0″, depth 50′–0″, dead load 0.3 tons per lineal foot per truss, live load 0.5 tons per lineal foot per truss. Calculate the maximum and minimum stresses due to dead and live loads by algebraic resolution. Scale of truss, 1″ = 40′–0″.

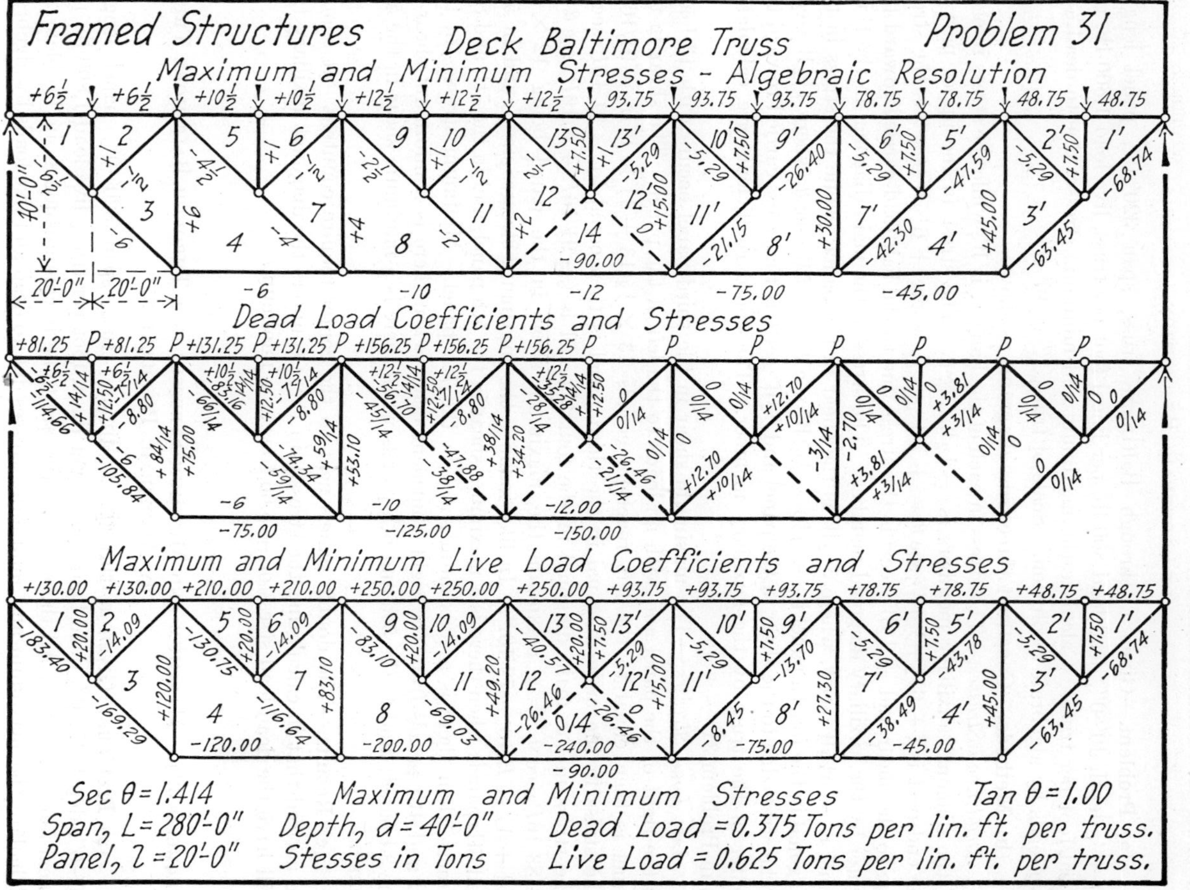
Framed Structures
Deck Baltimore Truss
Problem 31
Maximum and Minimum Stresses - Algebraic Resolution
Dead Load Coefficients and Stresses
Maximum and Minimum Live Load Coefficients and Stresses
Sec θ=1.414
Maximum and Minimum Stresses
Tan θ=1.00
Span, L=280'-0"
Depth, d=40'-0"
Dead Load=0.375 Tons per lin. ft. per truss.
Panel, l=20'-0"
Stesses in Tons
Live Load=0.625 Tons per lin. ft. per truss.

PROBLEM 32. MAXIMUM AND MINIMUM STRESSES IN A THROUGH BALTIMORE TRUSS BY ALGEBRAIC RESOLUTION.

(a) **Problem.**—Given a through Baltimore truss, span 320′–0″, panel length 20′–0″, depth 40′–0″, dead load 800 lb. per lineal foot per truss, live load 1,800 lb. per lineal foot per truss. Calculate the maximum and minimum stresses due to dead and live loads by algebraic resolution. Scale of truss, 1″ = 40′–0″.

(b) **Methods.**—Construct three truss diagrams as shown.

Dead Load Stresses.—The stress in each of the hangers is W, while the stress in each of the diagonal auxiliary members is $-\frac{1}{2}W\cdot\sec\theta$. The stress in the upper part of the end-post is $(+6\frac{1}{2}+\frac{1}{2})W\cdot\sec\theta = +7W\cdot\sec\theta$, where $+6\frac{1}{2}W\cdot\sec\theta$ is the stress due to the shear and $+\frac{1}{2}W\cdot\sec\theta$ is the stress due to the half load carried toward the center by the auxiliary diagonal member. The stress in the main diagonal in the third panel is $-5\frac{1}{2}W\cdot\sec\theta$, where $5\frac{1}{2}W$ is the shear in the panel; while the stress in the diagonal in the fourth panel is $(-4\frac{1}{2}-\frac{1}{2})W\cdot\sec\theta = -5W\cdot\sec\theta$, where $4\frac{1}{2}W\cdot\sec\theta$ is the stress due to the shear in the panel and $\frac{1}{2}W\cdot\sec\theta$ is the stress carried toward the center of the truss by the auxiliary member. The chord coefficients are calculated as in Problem 31.

Live Load Stresses.—The maximum shear in the third panel occurs with 13 loads to the right of the panel and with no loads to the left of the panel. The shear in the panel is then equal to the left reaction, equals $13 \times \frac{1}{2}(13+1) \times P/16 = 91/16P$. The stress in the main diagonal in the third panel is then equal to $-91/16P\cdot\sec\theta$. The stress in the main diagonal in the fourth panel is $(-91/16P + 8/16P)\sec\theta = -83/16P\cdot\sec\theta$, = a maximum, the maximum shear in the panel being $12 \times \frac{1}{2}(12+1) \times P/16 = 78/16P$. In like manner the maximum stresses are found in 5th and 6th panels when there is a maximum shear in the 5th panel, and in the 7th and 8th panels when there is a maximum shear in the 7th panel. Minimum stresses in the 3d and 4th panels from the right abutment occur when there is a minimum shear in the 3d panel; and in the 5th and 6th panels when there is a minimum shear in the 5th panel.

(c) **Results.**—The double panels next to the center require counters. It should be noticed that in calculating the stresses in these counters the diagonal auxiliary ties will have the dead load stress of + 5.66 tons as a minimum.

PROBLEM 32a. MAXIMUM AND MINIMUM STRESSES IN A THROUGH BALTIMORE TRUSS BY ALGEBRAIC RESOLUTION.

(a) **Problem.**—Given a through Baltimore truss, span 320′–0″, panel length 20′–0″, depth 45′–0″, dead load 800 lb. per lineal foot per truss, live load 1,800 lb. per lineal foot per truss. All the auxiliary ties are to be in compression as in Problem 27. Calculate the maximum and minimum stresses due to dead and live loads by algebraic resolution. Scale of truss, 1″ = 40′–0″.

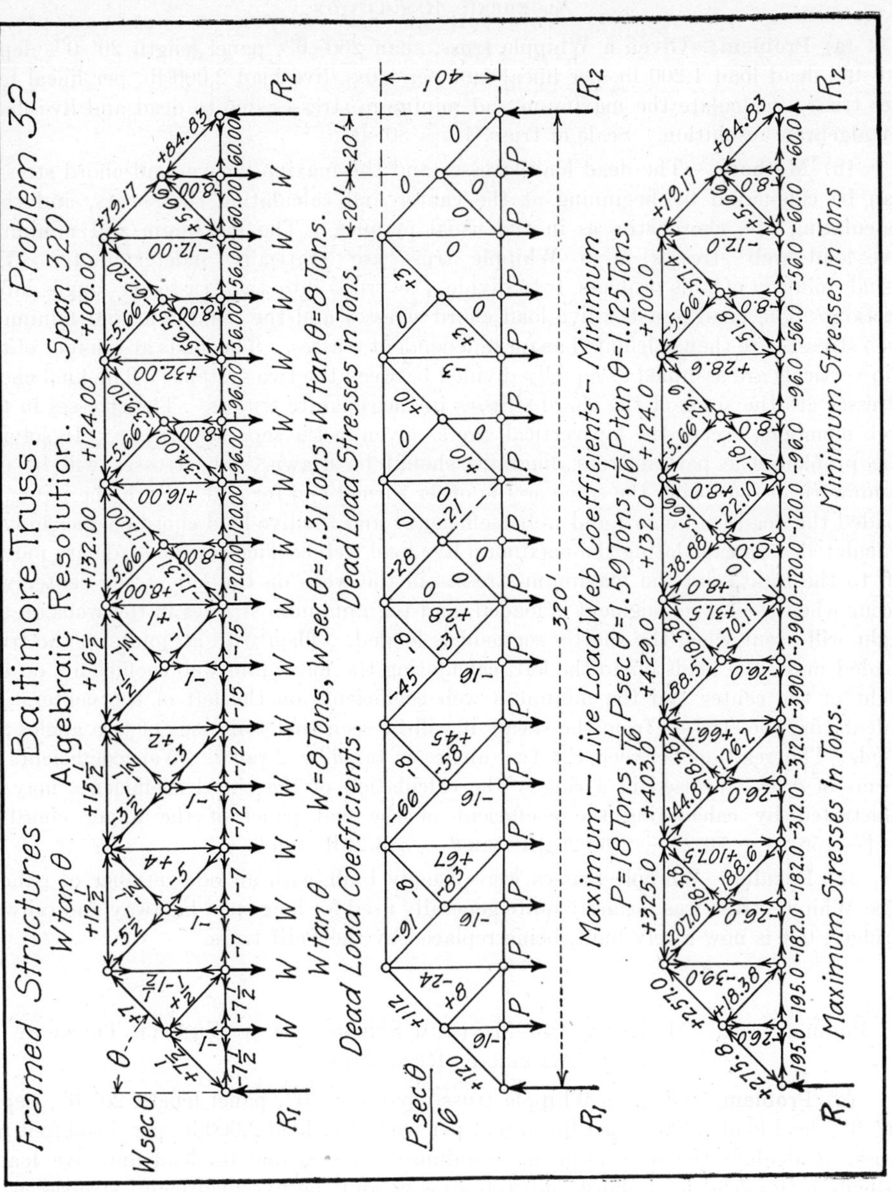
Framed Structures
Baltimore Truss.
Problem 32
Algebraic Resolution.
Span 320'
W tan θ
W sec θ
W=8 Tons, W sec θ=11.31 Tons, W tan θ=8 Tons.
Dead Load Coefficients.
Dead Load Stresses in Tons.
P sec θ / 16
Maximum — Live Load Web Coefficients — Minimum
P=18 Tons, 1/16 P sec θ=1.59 Tons, 1/16 P tan θ=1.125 Tons.
Maximum Stresses in Tons.
Minimum Stresses in Tons
R1
R2

PROBLEM 33. MAXIMUM AND MINIMUM STRESSES IN A WHIPPLE TRUSS BY ALGEBRAIC RESOLUTION.

(a) **Problem.**—Given a Whipple truss, span 260′–0″, panel length 20′–0″, depth 40′–0″, dead load 1,200 lb. per lineal foot per truss, live load 2,000 lb. per lineal foot per truss. Calculate the maximum and minimum stresses due to dead and live loads by algebraic resolution. Scale of truss, 1″ = 30′–0″.

(b) **Methods.**—The dead load stresses and the maximum live load chord stresses can be calculated by beginning at the center and calculating the shears, and then calculating the chord stresses in the usual manner. The maximum and minimum live load web stresses in a Whipple truss are statically indeterminate. The usual solution of this problem is to divide the truss into two trusses of single intersection. The dead and the live load chord stresses and the maximum and minimum web stresses are then calculated as for independent trusses. The loads at the foot of the hip verticals are assumed as equally divided between the two systems. The final chord stresses are the sums of the chord stresses in the separate trusses. The stresses in the web members, except the hip vertical, are as given in the separate trusses. In solving the problem the partial truss diagrams should be drawn. The trusses will be unsymmetrical, one being the same as the other turned end for end. With the joints all loaded the dead load chord and web coefficients, and the live load chord coefficients are calculated. In calculating the maximum live load web coefficients the loads are moved off to the right, and the maximum stresses in the webs on the left of the center will occur when the longer segment is loaded, and the minimum stresses in the webs on the right will occur when the shorter segment is loaded. Then with all joints in the truss loaded move the loads off to the left, calculating the maximum web coefficients on the right of the center and the minimum web coefficients on the left of the center. In calculating the stresses from the shears it will be seen that functions of two angles are used. The relation between the two angles is $\tan\theta' = 2\tan\theta$. Web coefficients in terms of θ are enclosed in a ring. The calculation of the chord coefficients may be illustrated by calculating the coefficient of the end panel of the upper chord = $-[-156/26 - 70/26 - 2(60/26)]W\cdot\tan\theta = 346/26W\cdot\tan\theta$.

(c) **Results.**—Whipple trusses were usually built with an odd number of panels. The Whipple truss was formerly quite generally used for long span highway and railway bridges, but is now rarely built, being replaced by the Petit truss.

PROBLEM 33a. MAXIMUM AND MINIMUM STRESSES IN A WHIPPLE TRUSS BY ALGEBRAIC RESOLUTION.

(a) **Problem.**—Given a Whipple truss, span 300′–0″, panel length 20′–0″, depth 40′–0″, dead load 1,200 lb. per lineal foot per truss, live load 2,000 lb. per lineal foot per truss. Calculate the maximum and minimum stresses due to dead and live loads. Calculate the dead load chord and web stresses and the live load chord stresses as in Problem 33. Scale of truss, 1″ = 30′–0″.

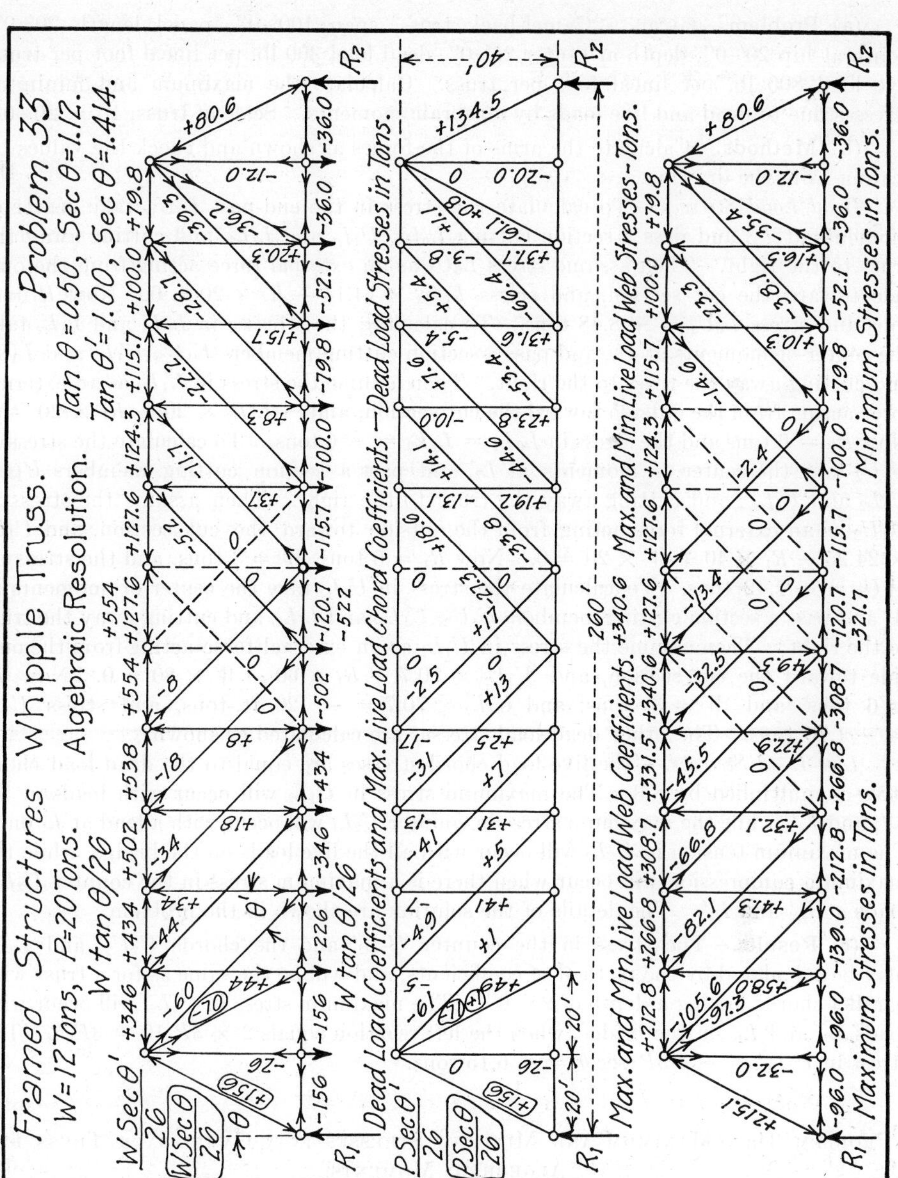
Framed Structures Whipple Truss. Problem 33
W=12 Tons, P=20 Tons. Algebraic Resolution. Tan θ=0.50, Sec θ=1.12.
Tan θ'=1.00, Sec θ'=1.414.
Dead Load Coefficients and Max. Live Load Chord Coefficients — Dead Load Stresses in Tons
Max. and Min. Live Load Web Coefficients. Max. and Min. Live Load Web Stresses – Tons.
Maximum Stresses in Tons. Minimum Stresses in Tons.

PROBLEM 34. MAXIMUM AND MINIMUM STRESSES IN A CAMEL-BACK TRUSS BY ALGEBRAIC MOMENTS.

(a) **Problem.**—Given a Camel-back truss, span 100′-0″, panel length 20′-0″, depth at hip 20′-0″, depth at center 25′-0″, dead load 300 lb. per lineal foot per truss, live load 800 lb. per lineal foot per truss. Calculate the maximum and minimum stresses due to dead and live loads by algebraic moments. Scale of truss, 1″ = 20′-0″.

(b) **Methods.**—Calculate the arms of the forces as shown and check the values by scaling from the drawing.

Dead Load Stresses.—To calculate the stress in the end-post L_0U_1, take center of moments at L_1, and pass a section cutting L_0U_1, U_1L_1 and L_1L_2, and cutting away the truss to the right. Then assume stress L_0U_1 as an external force acting from the outside toward the cut section, and stress $L_0U_1 \times 14.14 - R_1 \times 20 = 0$. Now $R_1 = 6$ tons and stress $L_0U_1 = +\ 8.48$ tons. To calculate the stresses in L_0L_1 and L_1L_2 take the center of moments at U_1, and pass a section cutting members U_1U_2, U_1L_2 and L_1L_2, and cutting away the truss to the right. Then assume the stress in L_1L_2 as an external force acting from the outside toward the cut section, and $-\ L_1L_2 \times 20 - R_1 \times 20 = 0$. Now $R_1 = 6$ tons and the stress in $L_0L_1 = L_1L_2 = -\ 6$ tons. To calculate the stress in U_1U_2 take the center of moments at L_2, and pass a section cutting members U_1U_2, U_2L_2 and L_2L_2', and cutting away the truss to the right. Then assume the stress in U_1U_2 as an external force acting from the outside toward the cut section, and $U_1U_2 \times 24.25 - R_1 \times 40 + W \times 20 = 0$. Now $R_1 = 6$ tons, $W = 3$ tons, and the stress in $U_1U_2 = +\ 7.42$ tons. To calculate the stress in U_1L_2 take the center of moments at A, and pass a section cutting members U_1U_2, U_1L_2, and L_1L_2, and cutting away the truss to the right. Then assume the stress in U_1L_2 as an external force acting from the outside toward the cut section, and $U_1L_2 \times 70.7 + R_1 \times 60 - W \times 80 = 0$. Now $R_1 = 6$ tons and $W = 3$ tons, and $U_1L_2 \times 70.7 = -\ 120$ ft.-tons, and stress $U_1L_2 = -\ 1.70$ tons. The other dead load stresses are calculated as shown.

Live Load Stresses.—The live load chord stresses are equal to the dead load chord stresses multiplied by 8/3. The maximum stress in U_1L_2 will occur with loads at L_2, L_2', and L_1', while the maximum stress in counter U_2L_1 will occur with a load at L_1 only. The maximum tension in U_2L_2 will occur with all the live loads on the bridge, while the maximum compression will occur when there is a maximum stress in the counter U_2L_2', loads at L_2' and L_1'. The details of the solution are shown in the problem.

(c) **Results.**—The stress in the counter U_2L_2' and the chords U_2U_2' and L_2L_2' may be calculated by the method of coefficients, and will be the same as for a truss with parallel chords having a depth of 25′-0″. The maximum stress in U_2L_2' will occur with loads L_2' and L_1' on the bridge, when the left reaction equals $2 \times 3P/10 = 3P/5$. The stress in $U_2L_2' = -\ 3/5P \cdot \sec\theta = -\ 6.15$ tons.

PROBLEM 34a. MAXIMUM AND MINIMUM STRESSES IN A CAMEL-BACK TRUSS BY ALGEBRAIC MOMENTS.

(a) **Problem.**—Given a Camel-back truss, span 120′-0″, panel length 20′-0″, depth at hip 25′-0″, depth at U_2 30′-0″, depth at U_3 30′-0″, dead load 300 lb. per lineal foot per truss, live load 800 lb. per lineal foot per truss. Calculate the maximum and minimum stresses due to dead and live loads.

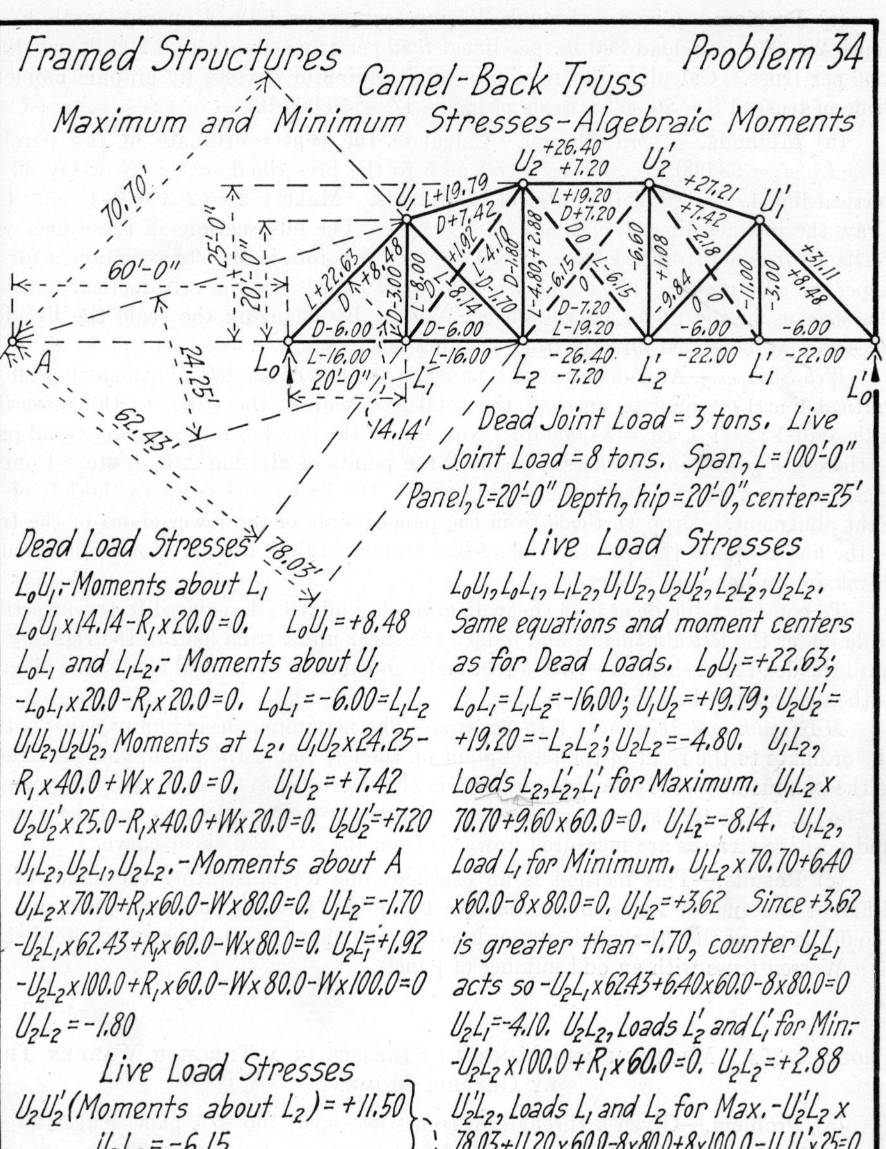

Framed Structures
Problem 34
Camel-Back Truss
Maximum and Minimum Stresses-Algebraic Moments
70.70'
60'-0"
25'-0"
20'-0"
24.25'
62.43'
78.03'
14.14'
20'-0"
A
L_0
L_1
L_2
L_2'
L_1'
L_0'
U_1
U_2
U_2'
U_1'
+26.40
+7.20
L+19.79
D+7.42
L+19.20
D+7.20
+27.21
+7.42
+31.11
+8.48
L+22.63
D+8.48
D-3.00
L-8.00
D+1.92
L-8.14
L-4.10
D-1.70
D-1.80
L-4.80, +2.88
L-6.15
D-0
L-6.15
D-7.20
L-19.20
-6.60
+1.08
-9.84
-2.18
0
-11.00
-3.00
D-6.00
D-6.00
-6.00
-6.00
L-16.00
L-16.00
-26.40
-7.20
-22.00
-22.00
Dead Joint Load = 3 tons. Live
Joint Load = 8 tons. Span, L = 100'-0"
Panel, l = 20'-0" Depth, hip = 20'-0", center = 25'
Dead Load Stresses
L_0U_1. - Moments about L_1
$L_0U_1 \times 14.14 - R_1 \times 20.0 = 0.$ $L_0U_1 = +8.48$
L_0L_1 and L_1L_2. - Moments about U_1
$-L_0L_1 \times 20.0 - R_1 \times 20.0 = 0.$ $L_0L_1 = -6.00 = L_1L_2$
U_1U_2, U_2U_2', Moments at L_2. $U_1U_2 \times 24.25 -$
$R_1 \times 40.0 + W \times 20.0 = 0.$ $U_1U_2 = +7.42$
$U_2U_2' \times 25.0 - R_1 \times 40.0 + W \times 20.0 = 0.$ $U_2U_2' = +7.20$
U_1L_2, U_2L_1, U_2L_2. - Moments about A
$U_1L_2 \times 70.70 + R_1 \times 60.0 - W \times 80.0 = 0.$ $U_1L_2 = -1.70$
$-U_2L_1 \times 62.43 + R_1 \times 60.0 - W \times 80.0 = 0.$ $U_2L_1 = +1.92$
$-U_2L_2 \times 100.0 + R_1 \times 60.0 - W \times 80.0 - W \times 100.0 = 0$
$U_2L_2 = -1.80$
Live Load Stresses
U_2U_2' (Moments about L_2) = +11.50
$U_2L_2 = -6.15$
Live Load Stresses
L_0U_1, L_0L_1, L_1L_2, U_1U_2, U_2U_2', L_2L_2', U_2L_2.
Same equations and moment centers
as for Dead Loads. $L_0U_1 = +22.63$;
$L_0L_1 = L_1L_2 = -16.00$; $U_1U_2 = +19.79$; $U_2U_2' =$
$+19.20 = -L_2L_2'$; $U_2L_2 = -4.80$. U_1L_2,
Loads L_2, L_2', L_1' for Maximum. $U_1L_2 \times$
$70.70 + 9.60 \times 60.0 = 0.$ $U_1L_2 = -8.14.$ U_1L_2,
Load L_1 for Minimum. $U_1L_2 \times 70.70 + 6.40$
$\times 60.0 - 8 \times 80.0 = 0.$ $U_1L_2 = +3.62$ Since +3.62
is greater than -1.70, counter U_2L_1
acts so $-U_2L_1 \times 62.43 + 6.40 \times 60.0 - 8 \times 80.0 = 0$
$U_2L_1 = -4.10.$ U_2L_2, Loads L_2' and L_1' for Min:-
$-U_2L_2 \times 100.0 + R_1 \times 60.0 = 0.$ $U_2L_2 = +2.88$
$U_2'L_2$, Loads L_1 and L_2 for Max. $-U_2'L_2 \times$
$78.03 + 11.20 \times 60.0 - 8 \times 80.0 + 8 \times 100.0 - U_2U_2' \times 25 = 0$

PROBLEM 35. MAXIMUM AND MINIMUM STRESSES IN A THROUGH WARREN TRUS BY GRAPHIC MOMENTS.

(a) **Problem.**—Given a through Warren truss, span 140′–0″, panel length 20′–0″ depth 20′–0″, dead load 800 lb. per lineal foot per truss, live load 1,200 lb. per linea foot per truss. Calculate the maximum and minimum stresses by graphic moments Scale of truss, 1″ = 20′–0″. Scale of loads, 1″ = 50,000 lb.

(b) **Methods.**—*Chord Stresses.*—Calculate the center ordinate of the parabol $= w \cdot L^2/8d$ = 98,000 lb., and lay it off at 5 to the prescribed scale. Now lay off the vertical line 1–5 at the left and right abutments. Make 1–2 = 2–3 = 3–4 = 2 (4–5) Draw the inclined lines 1–5, 2–5, 3–5, 4–5, 5–5. The intersections of these lines with verticals dropped from the lower chord points are points in the stress parabola for the upper chord stresses. The stresses in the lower chords are the arithmetical means of the stresses in the upper chords on each side. By changing the scale the live load stresses may be scaled directly from the diagram.

Web Stresses.—At a distance of a panel to the left of the left abutment lay off the vertical line 1–8 equal to one-half the total live load on the truss, to the prescribed scale, equal 1,200 × 70 = 84,000 lb. Now divide the line 1–8 into as many equal parts as there are panels in the truss, and mark the points of division 2, 3, 4, etc. Connect these points of division with the panel point 7, the first panel point to the left of the right abutment. Drop verticals from the panel points of the lower chord of the truss to the line 1–8, and the intersections of like numbered lines will give points on the curve of maximum live load shears.

To construct the dead load shear diagram, lay off $3W$, downward to the prescribed scale under the left abutment, and reduce the shear under each load to the right by W, until the dead load shear is $-3W$ at the right abutment. The dead load shear diagram is then constructed as shown.

Maximum and Minimum Web Stresses.—The maximum shear in any panel is then the ordinate to the right of the panel point on the left end of the panel, and the stresses in the web members are calculated by drawing lines parallel to the corresponding member as shown. Negative stresses are measured downwards from the live load shear curve, and positive stresses are measured upwards from the live load shear curve.

(c) **Results.**—This method is an excellent one for illustrating the effect of the different systems of loads, but consumes too much time to be of practical use. It should be noted that the maximum ordinate to the chord parabola is not a chord stress in a Warren truss with an odd number of panels.

PROBLEM 35a. MAXIMUM AND MINIMUM STRESSES IN A THROUGH WARREN TRUSS BY GRAPHIC MOMENTS.

(a) **Problem.**—Given a through Warren truss, span 160′–0″, panel length 20′–0″, depth 24′–0″, dead load 900 lb. per lineal foot per truss, live load 1,200 lb. per lineal foot per truss. Calculate the maximum and minimum stresses due to dead and live loads by graphic moments. Scale of truss, 1″ = 25′–0″. Scale of loads, 1″ = 50,000 lb.

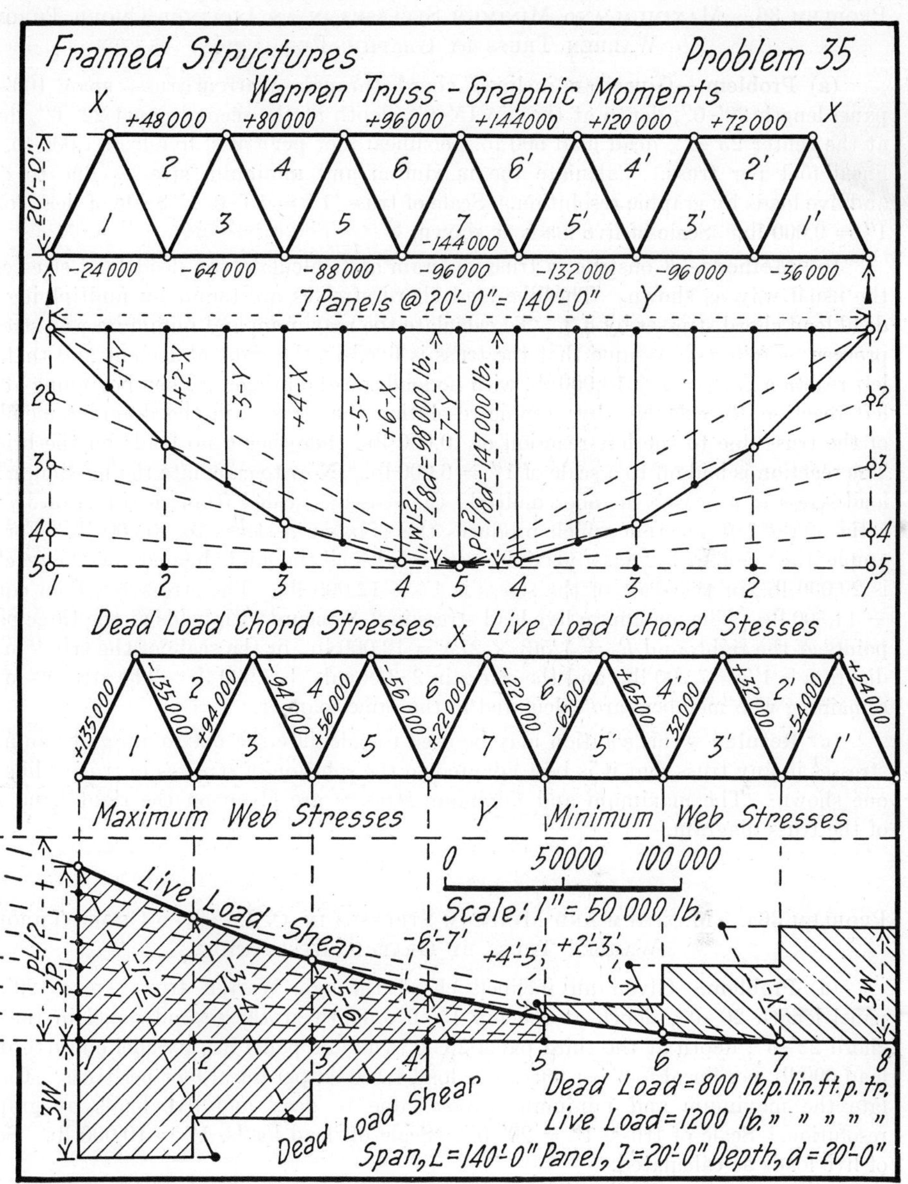

Framed Structures
Problem 35
Warren Truss - Graphic Moments
X
+48000
+80000
+96000
+144000
+120 000
+72000
X
20'-0"
2
4
6
6'
4'
2'
1
3
5
7
5'
3'
1'
-144000
-24000
-64000
-88000
-96000
-132 000
-96000
-36000
7 Panels @ 20'-0" = 140'-0"
Y
-1'-Y
+2-X
-3-Y
+4-X
-5-Y
+6-X
wL²/8d = 98000 lb.
7-Y
pL²/8d = 147000 lb.
Dead Load Chord Stresses
X
Live Load Chord Stesses
+135000
-135000
+94000
-94000
+56000
-56000
+22000
-22000
-6500
+6500
-32000
+32000
-54000
+54000
Maximum Web Stresses
Y
Minimum Web Stresses
0
50000
100 000
Scale: 1" = 50 000 lb.
Live Load Shear
PL/2
3P
-6'-7'
+4'-5'
+2'-3'
3W
Dead Load Shear
Dead Load = 800 lb.p.lin.ft.p.tr.
Live Load = 1200 lb. " " " " "
Span, L=140'-0" Panel, l=20'-0" Depth, d=20'-0"

PROBLEM 36. MAXIMUM AND MINIMUM STRESSES IN AN INCLINED CHORD THROUGH WARREN TRUSS BY GRAPHIC RESOLUTION.

(a) **Problem.**—Given an inclined chord through Warren truss, span 100′–0″, panel length 20′–0″, depth at the hip 15′–0″, depth at the second panel 22′–6″, depth at the center 25′–0″, dead load 600 lb. per lineal foot per truss, live load 1,000 lb. per lineal foot per truss. Calculate the maximum and minimum stresses due to dead and live loads by graphic resolution. Scale of truss, 1″ = 15′–0″. Scale of dead loads, 1″ = 9,000 lb. Scale of live loads as shown.

(b) **Methods.**—Construct a truss diagram and calculate the dead load stresses in the usual way as shown. The live load chord stresses are found by multiplying the dead load chord stresses by 5/3. To calculate the maximum and minimum web stresses proceed as follows: Assume that the truss is fixed at the right abutment and that the left reaction is R_1 = say 10,000 lb. with no loads on the bridge. Then beginning at the left reaction R_1, calculate by graphic resolution the stresses in the different members of the truss due to the left reaction of 10,000 lb., there being no loads on the bridge. The reaction is laid off to a scale of 1″ = 6,000 lb. Now to calculate the maximum live load stress in any web member multiply the stress as scaled from the diagram by the ratio of the left reaction which produces the maximum stress to 10,000 lb. For example, the member 1–2 has a maximum stress with all the joints loaded and the reaction is 20,000 lb., or the scale of the stress is 1″ = 12,000 lb. The stress 1–2 then equals − 14,500 lb. The maximum live load stress in 2–3 occurs with loads at the three panel points at the right, and $R_3 = 1/5(3 \times 2P)$ = 12,000 lb., or the scale of the stress in the diagram is 1″ = 7,200 lb., and the stress in 2–3 equals + 7,900 lb. The stresses in the remaining web members are calculated in the same manner.

(c) **Results.**—This solution may be used to calculate the maximum and minimum stresses in any truss, but it is best adapted to the solution of stresses in trusses like the one shown. The maximum and minimum stresses are given on the right hand side of the truss diagram.

PROBLEM 36a. MAXIMUM AND MINIMUM STRESSES IN AN INCLINED CHORD THROUGH WARREN TRUSS BY GRAPHIC RESOLUTION.

(a) **Problem.**—Given an inclined chord through Warren truss, span 120′–0″, panel length 20′–0″, depth at the hip 15′–0″, depth at the second panel in the top chord 22′–6″, depth at the third panel 25′–0″ (middle panel has parallel chords), dead load 600 lb. per lineal foot per truss, live load 1,100 lb. per lineal foot per truss. Calculate the maximum and minimum stresses due to dead and live loads by graphic resolution. Scale of truss, 1″ = 20′–0″. Scale of dead loads, 1″ = 10,000 lb. Scale of live loads as calculated.

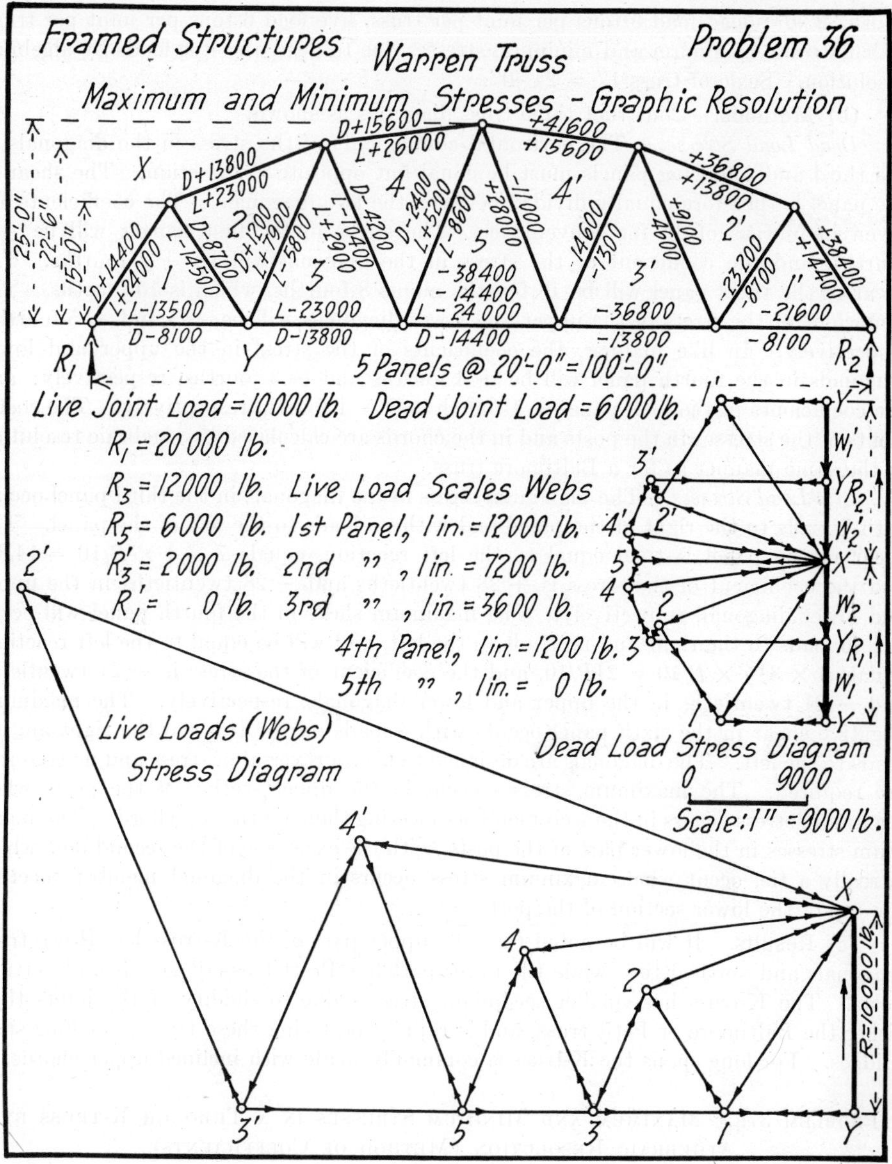
Framed Structures
Problem 36
Warren Truss
Maximum and Minimum Stresses - Graphic Resolution
25'-0"
22'-6"
15'-0"
X
D+15600
L+26000
+41600
+15600
D+13800
L+23000
+36800
+13800
D+14400
L+24000
D-1450
D-8700
D+1200
L+7900
L-5800
L+2900
L-10400
D-4200
D-2400
L+5200
L-8600
+2800
-11000
14600
-1300
+9100
-4600
-23200
-8700
+14400
+38400
1
2
3
4
5
4'
3'
2'
1'
-38400
-14400
L-24000
D-14400
-36800
-13800
L-13500
D-8100
L-23000
D-13800
-21600
-8100
R1
Y
R2
5 Panels @ 20'-0" = 100'-0"
Live Joint Load = 10000 lb.
Dead Joint Load = 6000 lb.
R1 = 20 000 lb.
R3 = 12000 lb.
R5 = 6000 lb.
R'3 = 2000 lb.
R'1 = 0 lb.
Live Load Scales Webs
1st Panel, 1 in. = 12000 lb.
2nd " , 1 in. = 7200 lb.
3rd " , 1 in. = 3600 lb.
4th Panel, 1 in. = 1200 lb.
5th " , 1 in. = 0 lb.
W1'
W2'
W2
W1
Dead Load Stress Diagram
0
9000
Scale: 1" = 9000 lb.
Live Loads (Webs)
Stress Diagram
R = 10000 lb.

PROBLEM 37. MAXIMUM AND MINIMUM STRESSES IN A THROUGH K-TRUSS BY ALGEBRAIC RESOLUTION (METHOD OF COEFFICIENTS).

(a) **Problem.**—Given a through K-truss, span 160′–0″, panel length 16′–0″, depth 32′–0″, dead load 5 tons per joint per truss, live load 6 tons per joint per truss. Calculate the maximum and minimum stresses due to dead and live loads by algebraic resolution. Scale of truss 1″ = 24′–0″.

(b) **Methods.**—Construct three truss diagrams as shown.

Dead Load Stresses.—The horizontal components of the stress in the diagonals in the third and following panels must be equal but opposite in direction. The shear in the panel is therefore equally divided between the two diagonals. The coefficients are given in fourths of W for convenience. The stress in the first hanger will be − 4 fourths, and the coefficient of the stress in the diagonal will be + 2 fourths. The shear in the third panel will be 18 fourths minus 8 fourths, which is 10 fourths. The coefficient of the stress in the upper and lower diagonals will be + 5 and − 5 fourths, respectively. In like manner, the coefficients of the stress in the upper and lower diagonals in the fourth panel will be + 3 fourths and − 3 fourths, respectively; and the coefficients in the fifth panel + 1 fourth and − 1 fourth, respectively. The coefficients of the stresses in the posts and in the chords are calculated by algebraic resolution in the same manner as for a Baltimore truss.

Live Load Stresses.—The maximum stress in the diagonals in the third panel occurs with 7 loads to the right of the panel and with no loads to the left of the panel. The shear in the panel is then equal to the left reaction, equals $7 \times 4 \times P/10 = 14P/5$ and the coefficient of the stress is + 28 twentieths and − 28 twentieths in the upper and lower diagonal, respectively. The maximum shear in the fourth panel will occur with 6 loads to the right and no loads to the left, and will be equal to the left reaction, equals $6 \times 3\frac{1}{2} \times P/10 = 21P/10$, and the coefficient of the stress is + 21 twentieths and − 21 twentieths in the upper and lower diagonals, respectively. The maximum negative shear in the sixth panel occurs with 4 loads on the truss to the right and no loads to the left. The diagonals are designed to take a reversal of stress and no counters are required. The maximum stresses occur in the upper section of the posts when maximum stress occurs in the web members meeting them on the top chord. The maximum stresses in the lower part of the posts, with the exception of the second post which is really a tie, occur when maximum stress occurs in the diagonal member meeting the top of the lower section of the post.

(c) **Results.**—It will be noted that the upper part of the K-truss has Howe truss diagonals and vertical ties, while the lower part has Pratt truss diagonals and vertical posts. The K-truss has smaller secondary stresses due to rigidity of the joints than either the Baltimore or Petit truss, and is rapidly replacing these trusses for long span bridges. For long spans the K-truss is commonly made with inclined upper chords.

PROBLEM 37a. MAXIMUM AND MINIMUM STRESSES IN A THROUGH K-TRUSS BY ALGEBRAIC RESOLUTION (METHOD OF COEFFICIENTS).

(a) **Problem.**—Given a through K-truss, span 216′–0″, panel length 18′–0″, depth 36′–0″, dead load 5 tons per joint per truss, live load 6 tons per joint per truss. Calculate the maximum and minimum stresses due to dead and live loads by algebraic resolution. Scale of truss 1″ = 30′–0″.

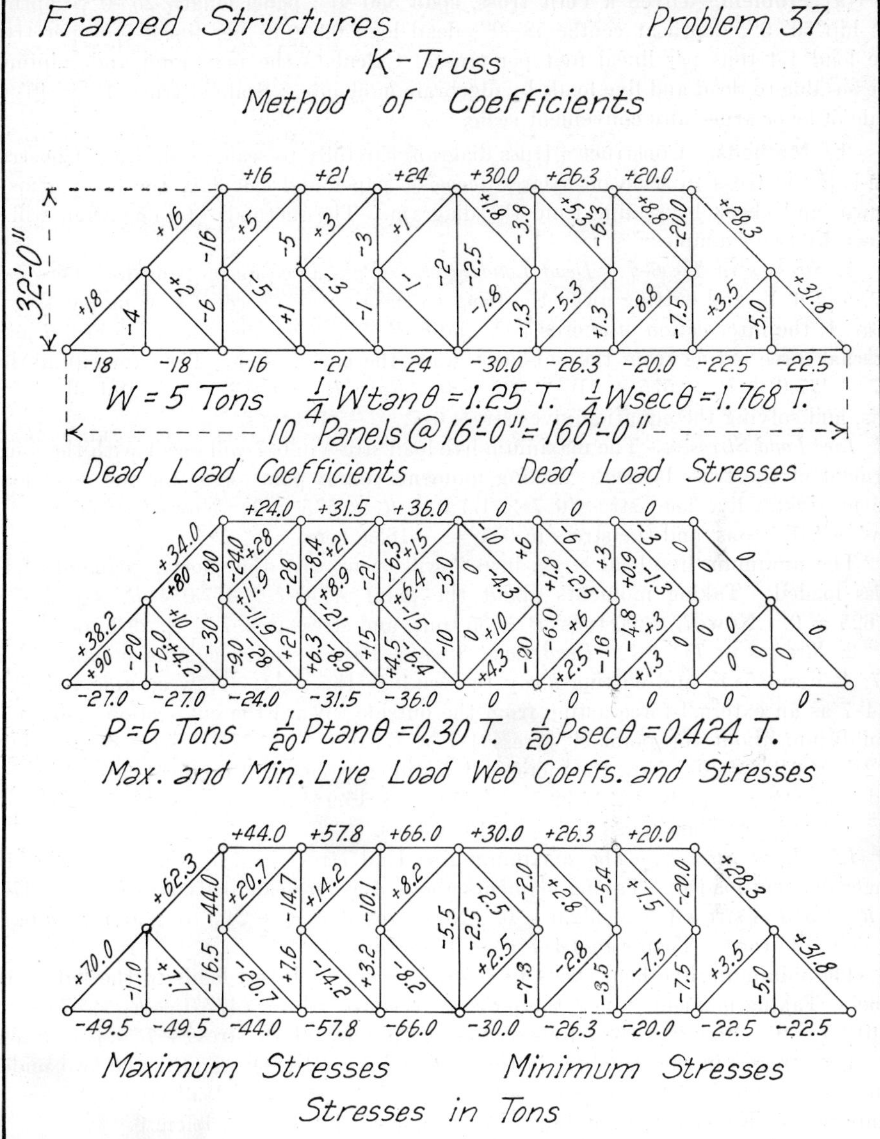
Framed Structures
Problem 37
K-Truss
Method of Coefficients
32'-0"
+16 +21 +24 +30.0 +26.3 +20.0
-18 -18 -16 -21 -24 -30.0 -26.3 -20.0 -22.5 -22.5
W = 5 Tons 1/4 W tan θ = 1.25 T. 1/4 W sec θ = 1.768 T.
10 Panels @ 16'-0" = 160'-0"
Dead Load Coefficients
Dead Load Stresses
+24.0 +31.5 +36.0 0 0 0
-27.0 -27.0 -24.0 -31.5 -36.0 0 0 0 0 0
P = 6 Tons 1/20 P tan θ = 0.30 T. 1/20 P sec θ = 0.424 T.
Max. and Min. Live Load Web Coeffs. and Stresses
+44.0 +57.8 +66.0 +30.0 +26.3 +20.0
-49.5 -49.5 -44.0 -57.8 -66.0 -30.0 -26.3 -20.0 -22.5 -22.5
Maximum Stresses
Minimum Stresses
Stresses in Tons

PROBLEM 38. MAXIMUM AND MINIMUM STRESSES IN A PETIT TRUSS BY ALGEBRAIC MOMENTS.

(a) **Problem.**—Given a Petit truss, span 350′–0″, panel length 25′–0″, depth at the hip 50′–0″, depth at center 58′–0″, dead load 0.9 tons per lineal foot per truss, live load 1.4 tons per lineal foot per truss. Calculate the maximum and minimum stresses due to dead and live loads by algebraic moments. Scale of truss, 1″ = 40′–0″. Scale of lever arms, any convenient scale.

(b) **Methods.**—Construct a truss diagram carefully to scale as shown. Construct one-half the truss to scale on a large piece of paper and calculate the lever arms as shown, and check by scaling from the diagram. The methods of calculation will be shown by two examples:

1. *Stresses in Tie 6–7. Dead Load Stress.*—Pass a section cutting members 7–X, 6–7, and 6–Y, and cutting away the truss to the right. The center of moments will be at A, the intersection of chords 7–X and 6–Y. Now assume the stress in 6–7 as an external force acting from the outside toward the cut section. Then for equilibrium 6–7 $\times$ 477.0 + $R_1 \times 575 - 3W \times 625 = 0$. Now $R_1 = 146.25$ tons and $W = 22.5$ tons, and solving the equation gives stress 6–7 = − 87.8 tons.

Live Load Stresses. The maximum live load stress in 6–7 will occur with the longer segment of the truss loaded. Taking moments about point A as for the dead loads the maximum live load stress 6–7 $\times$ 477.0 + $R_1 \times 575 = 0$. Now $R_1 = 55/14 \times 35$ tons = 137.5 tons, and the stress in 6–7 = − 165.8 tons.

The minimum live load stress in 6–7 will occur with the shorter segment of the truss loaded. Taking moments about the point A, 6–7 $\times$ 477.0 + $R_1 \times 575 - 3P \times 625 = 0$. Now $R_1 = 90$ tons, $P = 35$ tons, and stress in 6–7 = + 29.1 tons.

2. *Stresses in Tie 4–7. Dead Load Stress.*—Pass a section cutting members 7–X, 4–7, 4–5 and 5–Y, and cutting away the truss to the right. Now assume the stress in 4–7 as an external force acting from the outside toward the cut section. Then for equilibrium about the point A, stress 4–7 $\times$ 477.0 + $R_1 \times 575$ − stress 4–5 $\times$ 442.0 − $2W \times 612.5 = 0$. Now the member 4–5 will carry one-half the load carried by 5–6, and the stress equals $1/2 \times 22.5 \times 1.414 = + 15.9$ tons. $R_1 = 146.25$ tons, and $2W = 45$ tons. Then stress 4–7 = − 103.6 tons.

Live Load Stresses.—The maximum live load stress in 4–7 will occur with the longer segment loaded. Taking moments about A as for dead loads, stress 4–7 $\times$ 477.0 + $R_1 \times 575$ − stress 4–5 $\times$ 442.0 = 0. Now stress 4–5 = + 24.8 tons, and $R_1 = 66/14 \times 35 = 165$ tons. Then stress 4–7 = − 175.7 tons.

The minimum live load stress in 4–7 will occur with two loads to the left of the panel. Taking moments about the point A, the stress 4–7 $\times$ 477.0 + $R_1 \times 575 - 2P \times 612.5 = 0$. Now $R_1 = 62.5$ tons and $2P = 70$ tons. Then stress 4–7 = + 14.5 tons.

The stresses in the members in the first and second panels and in the two middle panels may be calculated by coefficients. Check up the dead load chord stresses by comparing with the stresses obtained by graphic resolution in Problem 6.

(c) **Results.**—The auxiliary members carry the stresses directly toward the abutments and there is no ambiguity of loading as in the case of a truss subdivided as in Problem 32. The Petit truss is quite generally used for long span pin-connected highway and railway bridges.

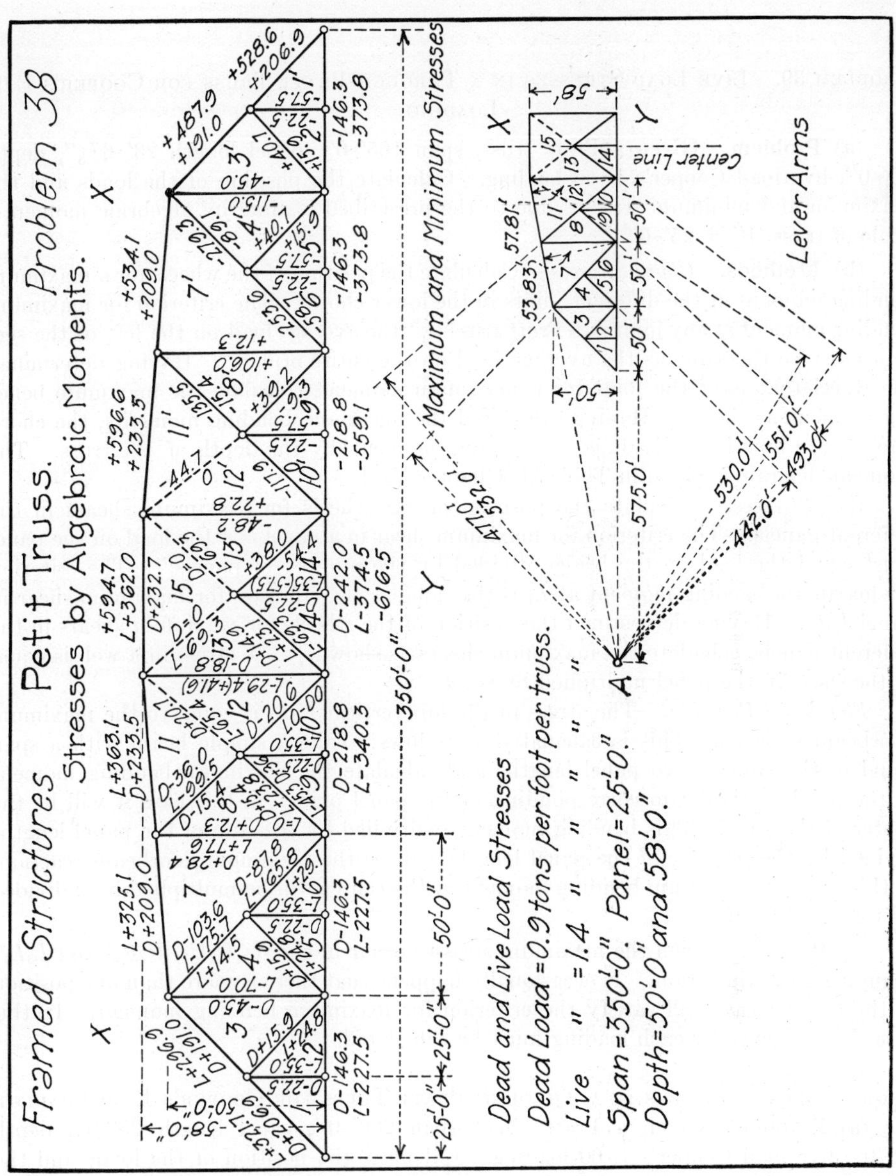

PROBLEM 38a. MAXIMUM AND MINIMUM STRESSES IN A PETIT TRUSS BY ALGEBRAIC MOMENTS.

(a) **Problem.**—Given a Petit truss with the same span and loads as in Problem 38, the auxiliary bracing to be the same as in Problem 32. Calculate the maximum and minimum stresses due to dead and live loads by algebraic moments.

PROBLEM 39. LIVE LOAD STRESSES IN A THROUGH PRATT TRUSS FOR COOPER'S E 60 LOADING.

(a) **Problem.**—Given a Pratt truss, span 165′–0″, panel length 23′–6⅞″, depth 30′–0″, live load Cooper's E 60 loading. Calculate the position of the loads and the maximum and minimum stresses due to the prescribed loading by algebraic moments. Scale of truss, 1″ = 25′–0″.

(b) **Methods.** *Chord Stresses.*—Calculate the position of the wheels for a maximum bending moment at the different joints in the lower chord. The criterion for maximum bending moment at any joint in a Pratt truss is, "the average load on the left of the section must be the same as the average load on the entire bridge." Having determined the wheel that is at the joint for a maximum moment, calculate the maximum bending moment as shown. Having calculated the maximum bending moments, the chord stresses are found by dividing the bending moment by the depth of the truss. The moment diagram is given in Table II, Chapter VIII.

Web Stresses.—Calculate the position of the wheels for maximum shears in the different panels. The criterion for maximum shear in a panel is, "the load on the panel must equal the load on the bridge divided by the number of panels." The criterion for maximum bending moment at L_1 is the same as the criterion for maximum shear in panel L_0L_1. Having determined the position of the wheels for maximum shears in the different panels, calculate the maximum shears as shown. The stress in a web is equal to the shear in the panel multiplied by sec θ.

Floorbeam Reaction.—The stress in the hip vertical U_1L_1 is equal to the maximum floorbeam reaction. This is calculated as follows: Take a simple beam with a span equal to the sum of two panel lengths and calculate the maximum bending moment at the point in the beam corresponding to the panel point; in this case it will be the center of the span. This bending moment multiplied by the sum of the panel lengths divided by the product of the panel lengths will be the maximum floorbeam reaction; in this case the maximum bending moment at the center will be multiplied by 2 divided by the panel length.

(c) **Results.**—When the maximum stresses occur in chords U_2U_3, U_3U_3' and L_3L_3', counter $U_3'L_3$ is in action. It occasionally happens that there is more than one position of the loading that will satisfy the criterion for maximum bending moment. In this case the moments for each loading must be calculated.

PROBLEM 39a. STRESSES IN A THROUGH PRATT TRUSS FOR COOPER'S E 60 LOADING.

(a) **Problem.**—Given a Pratt truss, span 200′–0″, panel length 25′–0″, depth 32′–0″, live load Cooper's E 60 loading. Calculate the position of the loads and the maximum and minimum stresses due to the prescribed loading by algebraic moments. Check the concentrated live load stresses by calculating the maximum and minimum stresses for the equivalent uniform live load as given in Fig. 2, Chapter VIII. Scale of truss, 1″ = 30′–0″.

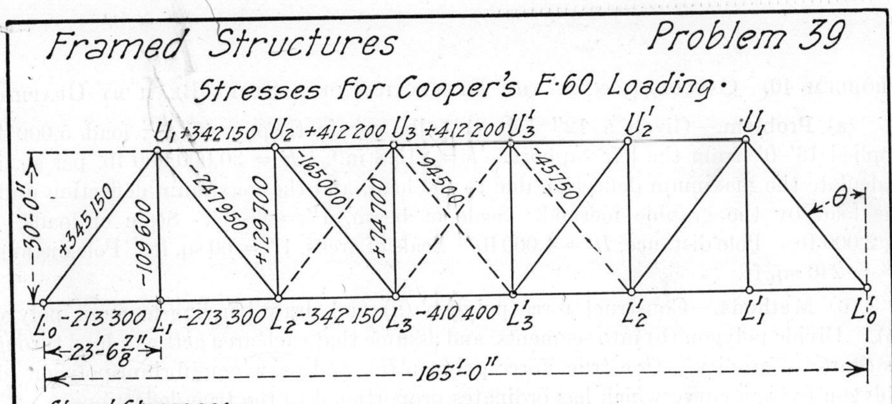

Chord Stresses:–

L_1, Maximum Moment at.–Try wheel 4 at L_1. Total Load on Bridge = 426 + 50·43 × 3 = 577·29. Average panel load = 577·29 ÷ 7 = 82·47. Load on left of L_1 = 75 or 105. Wheel 4 gives maximum moment at L_1.
L_2, Maximum Moment at.–Try wheel 7 at L_2. Total Load on Bridge = 426 + 45·86 × 3 = 563·58. Average panel load = 563·58 ÷ 7 = 80·51. Average panel load on left of L_2 = 154·5/2 or 174/2 = 77·25 or 87. Wheel 7 gives maximum moment at L_2. The other loadings are found in like manner.

Maximum Moments and Chord Stresses.

Center of Moments	Wheel giving Max. Mom.	Maximum Moment, Thousand Foot-Pounds	Stresses in Chords Max. Mom. ÷ 30	
			Member	Stress, Lb.
L_1	4	$[24550+426\times 50{\cdot}43+\frac{3}{2}(50{\cdot}43)^2]\,1/7-720=6400$.	L_0L_1 & L_1L_2	213 300
L_2	7	$[24550+426\times 45{\cdot}86+3/2(45{\cdot}86)^2]\,2/7-3230=10215$.	U_1U_2 & L_2L_3	342 150
L_3	11	$[24550+426\times 49{\cdot}29+3/2(49{\cdot}29)^2]\,3/7-8770=12366$.	U_2U_3 & U_3U_3'	412 200
L_3'	13	$[24550+426\times 35{\cdot}71+3/2(35{\cdot}71)^2]\,4/7-11500=12310$.	L_3L_3'.	410 400

Web Stresses:–

Panel L_0L_1. Maximum Shear. Wheel 4 at L_1 gives maximum shear
Panel L_1L_2. Maximum Shear. Try wheel 3 at L_2. Average load on bridge = [426 + (117·86 − 96) × 3] 1/7 = 70·23. Load on panel = 45 or 75. Wheel 3 at L_2 gives maximum shear in panel L_1L_2. The other loadings are found in like manner.

Maximum Shears and Web Stresses.

Panel	Wheel giving Max. Shear	Maximum Shear, Thousand Pounds.	Stresses in Webs. Shear × Sec θ (1·272)	
			Member	Stress, Lb.
L_0L_1	4 at L_1	$[24550+426\times 50{\cdot}43+3/2(50{\cdot}43)^2\div 165-720\div 23{\cdot}57=271{\cdot}40$	L_0U_1	345 150
L_1L_2	3 at L_2	$[24550+426\times 21{\cdot}86+3/2(21{\cdot}86)^2]\div 165-345\div 23{\cdot}57=194{\cdot}91$	U_1L_2	247 950
L_2L_3	3 at L_3	$[24550+426\times 1{\cdot}72]\div 165-345\div 23{\cdot}57=129{\cdot}69$	U_2L_3	165 000
L_3L_3'	3 at L_3'	$[13090+348\times 4{\cdot}71]\div 165-345\div 23{\cdot}57=74{\cdot}64$	U_3L_3'	94 500
$L_3'L_2'$	2 at L_2'	$[5240+213\times 7{\cdot}14]\div 165-120\div 23{\cdot}57=35{\cdot}91$	$U_3'L_2'$	45 750

Stress U_2L_2 = Shear in panel L_2L_3 = 129,700; Stress U_3L_3 = Shear in panel L_3L_3' = 74 700
Stress in U_1L_1 = Maximum Floorbeam Reaction = 109 650 lb.

Problem 40. Calculation of the Deflection of a Steel Beam by Graphics.

(a) **Problem.**—Given a 12″ I @ 31½ lb. per foot, span 40′–0″, load 5,000 lb. applied 16′–0″ from the left support. $I = 215.8$ in.[4]. $E = 30{,}000{,}000$ lb. per sq. in. Calculate the maximum deflection due to the load, and the maximum deflection under the load by the graphic method. Scale of beam, 1″ = 6′–0″. Scale of loads, 1″ = 2,000 lb. Pole distance, $H = 4{,}000$ lb. Scale of areas, 1″ = 60 sq. ft. Pole distance, $H' = 240$ sq. ft.

(b) **Methods.**—Construct force polygon (a) and draw bending-moment polygon (b). Divide polygon (b) into segments, and assume that each area acts as a load through its center of gravity. Construct force polygon (c), and draw equilibrium polygon (d). Polygon (d) is a curve which has ordinates proportional to the true deflections.

(c) **Results.**—The maximum deflection comes between the load and the center of the beam. If the area of the polygon (b) is measured in square inches and the ordinates in (d) measured in inches the deflection will be $\Delta = y \times H \times H' \div E \cdot I$. In the problem this result must be multiplied by 1,728. The closing lines of polygons (b) and (d) need not be horizontal. The solution given above may be very simply stated as follows: Construct the bending-moment polygon for the given loading on the beam. Load the beam with this bending-moment polygon, and with a force polygon having a pole distance equal to $E \cdot I$, construct an equilibrium polygon; this polygon will be the elastic curve of the beam. It is not commonly convenient to use a pole distance equal to $E \cdot I$, and a pole distance H is used, where $n \cdot H$ equals $E \cdot I$. For a discussion of this subject see Chapter XIV. Compare this problem with Fig. 6, Chapter XIV.

It will be seen that the maximum deflection of the beam will not come under the load but will occur at a point between the load and the center of the beam. For the equation of the elastic curve of the beam and the point of maximum deflection in the beam, see "Structural Engineers' Handbook," page 537.

Problem 40a. Calculation of the Deflection of a Steel Beam by Graphics.

(a) **Problem.**—Given a 12″ I @ 31½ lb .per foot, span 40′–0″, load 3,000 lb. applied 16′–0″ from the left support, and 3,000 lb. applied 12′–0″ from the right support. $I = 215.8$ in.[4]. $E = 30{,}000{,}000$. Calculate the maximum deflection due to the load, and the maximum deflection under the load by the graphic method. Scale of beam, 1″ = 6′–0″. Scale of loads, 1″ = 2,000 lb. Pole distance, $H = 4{,}000$ lb. Scale of areas, 1″ = 60 sq. ft. Pole distance, $H' = 240$ sq. ft.

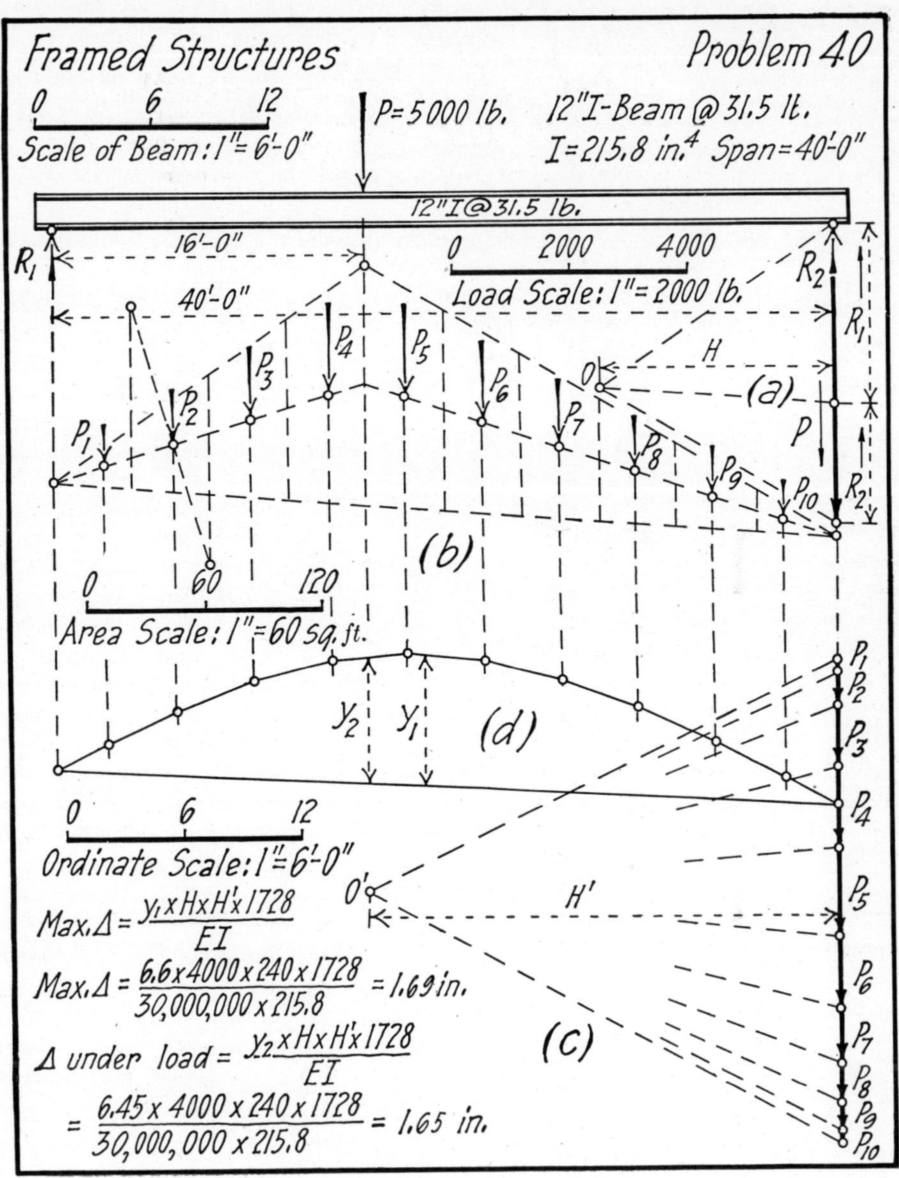
Framed Structures
Problem 40
0 6 12
Scale of Beam: 1" = 6'-0"
P = 5000 lb.
12" I-Beam @ 31.5 lb.
I = 215.8 in.4 Span = 40'-0"
12" I @ 31.5 lb.
16'-0"
40'-0"
0 2000 4000
Load Scale: 1" = 2000 lb.
R1
R2
H
O
(a)
P
P1
P2
P3
P4
P5
P6
P7
P8
P9
P10
(b)
0 60 120
Area Scale: 1" = 60 sq. ft.
y2
y1
(d)
0 6 12
Ordinate Scale: 1" = 6'-0"
O'
H'
(c)
Max. Δ = y1 x H x H' x 1728 / EI
Max. Δ = 6.6 x 4000 x 240 x 1728 / 30,000,000 x 215.8 = 1.69 in.
Δ under load = y2 x H x H' x 1728 / EI
= 6.45 x 4000 x 240 x 1728 / 30,000,000 x 215.8 = 1.65 in.

to end of Quarter

PART II.

DEFLECTIONS OF STRUCTURES AND STRESSES IN STATICALLY INDETERMINATE STRUCTURES.

CHAPTER XIV.

Area Moments and Curved Influence Lines.

Introduction.—With a simple beam carrying vertical loads, if a force polygon be constructed for the given loads with a pole distance unity, and an equilibrium polygon be constructed with this force polygon, the resulting equilibrium polygon will be the bending moment polygon for the beam with the given loading. In a similar manner if the same beam be loaded with the bending moment polygon due to the given loading, if a force polygon be constructed for the new loads with a pole distance equal to $E \cdot I$, and an equilibrium polygon be constructed with this force polygon, the resulting polygon will be the elastic curve for the beam when carrying the given loading.

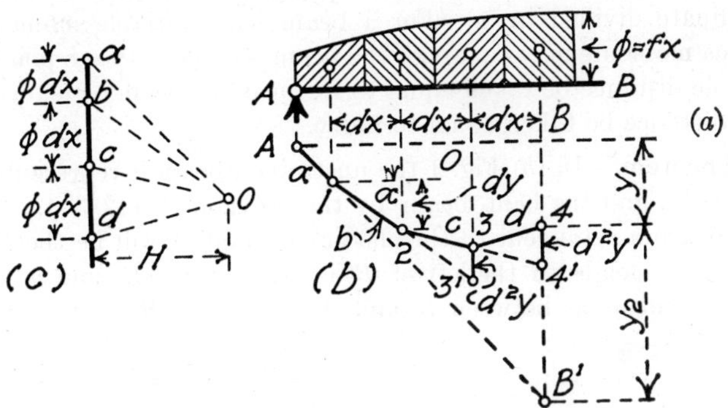

Fig. 1.

AREA MOMENTS.—First Theorem.—Load a simple beam with a continuous load represented by the equation $\phi = fx$, as in (*a*) Fig. 1. Assume that each differential load, $\phi \cdot dx$, acts through its center of gravity. Now construct a force polygon as in (*c*) and an equilibrium polygon as in (*b*) Fig. 1. Now in (*b*) the tangent of the angle between any side of the equilibrium polygon and the X-axis is $\tan \alpha = dy/dx$. If string b–O in (*b*) be produced until it cuts the vertical line through 3, it will cut off the intercept 3–3′, which is the difference between two consecutive values of dy, and therefore equals d^2y.

Now it has been proved in Chapter I, that the moment of the force acting through point 2 in (*b*) about point 3, is equal to the intercept 3–3′ multiplied by the pole distance H, is equal to $d^2y \cdot H$. But the moment of the differential load $fx \cdot dx$ which acts through point 2 about point 3, is $fx \cdot dx^2$, and

$$fx \cdot dx^2 = d^2y \cdot H$$

and

$$\frac{d^2y}{dx^2} = \frac{fx}{H} \tag{1}$$

which is the differential equation of the equilibrium polygon in (*b*).

Now if the loading be taken so that $\phi = fx = M$, where M is the bending moment at any point due to a given loading, and if the pole distance H be taken equal $E \cdot I$, where E is the modulus of elasticity and I is the moment of inertia of the beam, equation (1) becomes

$$\frac{d^2y}{dx^2} = \frac{M}{E \cdot I} \tag{2}$$

which has been proved in Applied Mechanics to be the differential equation of the elastic curve of the given beam. If fx in (*a*) be made equal to M, and in (*c*) the pole distance H be made equal to $E \cdot I$, the resulting equilibrium polygon in (*b*) will be the elastic curve of the beam.

The first or beam area moment theorem then is as follows:—"*Construct the bending moment polygon for the given loading on the beam. Load the beam with this bending moment polygon, and with a force polygon having a pole distance $E \cdot I$, construct an equilibrium polygon; this polygon will be the elastic curve of the given beam.*" If a pole distance H is used where $n \cdot H = E \cdot I$, the deflection at any point will be equal to the measured ordinate divided by n. For a beam with variable moment of inertia the theorem of area moments may be used if the beam is loaded at each point with M divided by I, and a pole distance be taken equal to E; or if the beam be loaded with $M \div E \cdot I$, and the pole distance be taken equal to unity.

Second Theorem.—In (*b*) Fig. 1 the unstrained beam is represented by the dotted straight line A–B', and the bent beam by the polygon A–1–2–3–4. The deflection of the beam at B' from a tangent to the elastic curve at A will be the distance y_2. But the moment of the loads to the left of B' is equal to $y_2 \cdot H$, and y_2 = static moment about B' of moment areas between B' and A divided by H.

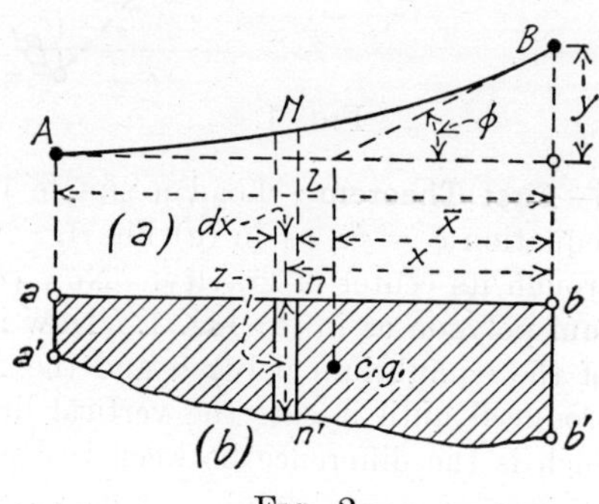

FIG. 2.

Now if a beam is loaded with the bending moment polygon due to the given loading, and the pole distance H be taken equal to $E \cdot I$, the following theorem will follow.—"*In a beam with a constant cross-section the deflection of the point B from a tangent* *to the beam at the point A, will be equal to the static moment of the moment area between A and B about B, divided by $E \cdot I$.*"

This theorem may also be proved as follows:—In Fig. 2 the polygon a–a'–b–b' is the moment polygon of the beam A–B. Now from Applied Mechanics the deflection of B from a tangent at A, is

$$y = \int_A^B M \cdot m \cdot dx / E \cdot I \tag{3}$$

Now if a unit load be placed at B, the moment at a point a distance x from B will be $m = x$. Now if H is the pole distance of the force polygon used in drawing the moment polygon, then $M = H \cdot z$, and substituting in (3)

$$y = H \int_A^B z \cdot x \cdot dx / E \cdot I \tag{4}$$

But $H \cdot z \cdot dx$ is the differential moment area, and $H \cdot z \cdot x \cdot dx$ is the static moment of the differential moment area about B, and the second theorem is proved.

The change in curvature at any point may be calculated as follows:—The angular change at any point in a beam may be found by integrating equation (2), and

$$\phi' = dy/dx = \int M \cdot dx / E \cdot I$$

and the total angular change between A and B will be

$$\phi = \int_A^B M \cdot dx / E \cdot I = H \int_A^B z \cdot dx / E \cdot I \tag{5}$$

which proves that "*The angular change between any two points A and B, is equal to the moment area between A and B divided by $E \cdot I$.*"

Simple Beam.—*Concentrated Load at Center of Beam.*—The simple beam in (a), Fig. 3, is loaded with a load, P, at the center. The bending moment diagram is shown in (b), and the beam is loaded with the bending moment diagram in (c), Fig. 3.

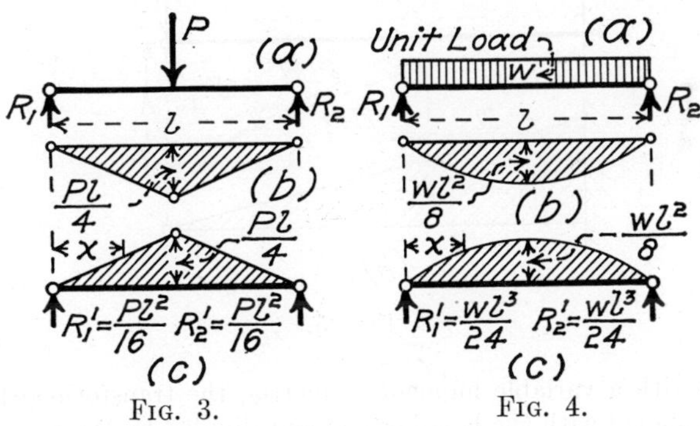

FIG. 3. FIG. 4.

To find the equation of the elastic curve, take moments of the forces to the left of a point at a distance x, from the left support, and the deflection of the beam at any point in the beam (a), Fig. 3, will be equal to the bending moment at the corresponding point in the beam, (b), Fig. 3, divided by $E \cdot I$, and

$$-E \cdot I \cdot y = P \cdot l^2 \cdot x/16 - Px^3/12 \tag{6}$$

and

$$48E \cdot I \cdot y = P(4x^3 - 3l^2 \cdot x) \tag{7}$$

The maximum deflection will occur when $x = l/2$ in equation (7), or it may be found by taking moments of forces to the left of $x = l/2$, to be

$$\Delta = P \cdot l^3/48E \cdot I \tag{8}$$

The slope of the tangent to the elastic curve at the supports will be equal to the left reactions of beam in (*c*), divided by $E \cdot I$; and $\tan \phi = P \cdot l^2/16E \cdot I$.

Beam Uniformly Loaded.—The simple beam in (*a*), Fig. 4, is loaded with a uniform load of w per linear foot. The bending moment parabola is shown in (*b*), and the beam is loaded with the bending moment parabola in (*c*). To find the equation of the elastic curve, take moments of forces to the left of a point at a distance, x, from the left support.

The equation of the bending moment parabola with the origin of the co-ordinates at the left support is $y = \frac{1}{2}w \cdot l \cdot x - \frac{1}{2}w \cdot x^2$; the area of a segment of the parabola is

$$A = \tfrac{1}{4}w \cdot l \cdot x^2 - \tfrac{1}{6}w \cdot x^3 \tag{9}$$

and the center of gravity measured back from x is

$$-\bar{x} = x(2l - x)/(6l - 4x) \tag{10}$$

Taking moments of forces to the left of a point x, and reducing, we have

$$24E \cdot I \cdot y = w(-x^4 + 2l \cdot x^3 - l^3 \cdot x) \tag{11}$$

The deflection is a maximum when $x = l/2$, and may be found directly by taking moments, or may be found from equation (11), and is

$$\Delta = 5w \cdot l^4 \cdot /384E \cdot I \tag{12}$$

(See Fig. 12 for areas and centroids of moment diagrams.)

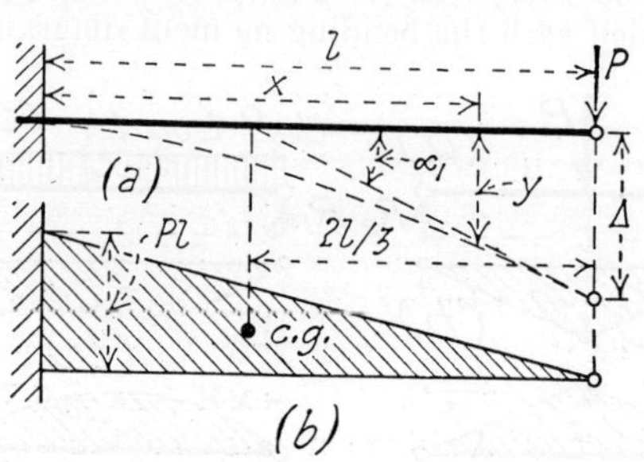

FIG. 5.

For a beam with a variable moment of inertia, the transformed beams, (*b*), Figs. 3 or 4, should be loaded with the bending moment divided by the moment of inertia, I, at each point, or with the bending moment divided by $E \cdot I$ at each point, if both the modulus of elasticity and the moment of inertia are variable.

The slope of the tangents to the elastic curve at the supports will be equal to the reactions of the beam (*c*), Fig. 4, divided by $E \cdot I$, and $\tan \phi = w \cdot l^3/24E \cdot I$.

Cantilever Beam.—*Concentrated Load.*—The cantilever beam in Fig. 5 carries a load P at its free end. Load the beam with the bending moment polygon due to the load P as shown in (*b*) Fig. 5. Then from the second moment area theorem, the deflection y at a distance x from the left end will be given by the equation

$$6E \cdot I \cdot y = 3P \cdot l \cdot x^2 - P \cdot x^3 \tag{13}$$

The maximum value of y will occur when $x = l$, and

$$\Delta = P \cdot l^3 / 3E \cdot I \tag{14}$$

The slope of the beam at the end is

$$a_1 = \tan \phi = \int_0^l M \cdot dx / E \cdot I = P \cdot l^2 / 2E \cdot I \tag{15}$$

From (*c*) Fig. 6 it will be seen that the tangents to the elastic curve of the beam intersect on a vertical line through the center of gravity of the moment area. The deflection at the end of the beam in Fig. 5, will be $\tan \phi \times 2l/3$ and

$$\Delta = (P \cdot l^2 / 2E \cdot I)(2l/3) = P \cdot l^3 / 3E \cdot I \tag{16}$$

Deflection of a Simple Beam.—*Graphic Method.*—In Fig. 6 a simple beam of constant cross-section is loaded with a load P as shown. With force polygon (*b*) draw moment polygon (*c*). Divide the area of the moment polygon in (*c*) into segments as shown. Assume that these segments are loads acting through their centers of gravity. Construct force polygon (*d*) and draw equilibrium polygon (*e*).

Now the deflection at any point will be

$$\Delta = y \cdot H \cdot H' / E \cdot I \tag{17}$$

If P is in pounds, the area of the moment polygon and pole distance H' are measured in square-foot-pounds, the pole distance H in pounds, and y in feet, the deflection in inches will be

$$\Delta = 1728 y \cdot H \cdot H' / E \cdot I \tag{18}$$

Tangents to Elastic Curve.—If the strings at 1 and 3 be produced until they meet they will intersect at point 2, which is on a vertical line through the center of gravity of the moment-area polygon, and the strings 1–2 and 2–3 will be tangents to the elastic curve at the supports R_1 and R_2, respectively. This gives a simple method for constructing the tangents to the elastic curve at the supports without constructing the elastic curve. It will also be seen that the tangents to the elastic curve at the supports depend only upon the amount of the moment area and the position of its center of gravity, and are independent of the arrangement of the moment areas.

Deflection of Beams Fixed at Ends.—From Fig. 6 it will be seen that the tangents to the elastic curve at the supports depend upon the amount of the bending moment area and upon the position of the center of gravity of the bending moment area. To bring the tangents in (*e*) Fig. 6, back to a horizontal position it will be necessary to load the beam with a negative bending moment area, equal to the positive bending moment area and having its center of gravity in the same vertical line. For a beam fixed at the ends the conditions for fixidity are, (1) that the sum of the moment areas equal zero, $\Sigma M = 0$, and (2) that the static moment of the moment areas about any point equal zero, $\Sigma M \cdot x = 0$. For a beam with a variable moment of inertia the conditions for fixidity are $\Sigma(M \cdot dx/E \cdot I) = 0$, and $\Sigma(M \cdot x \cdot dx/E \cdot I) = 0$.

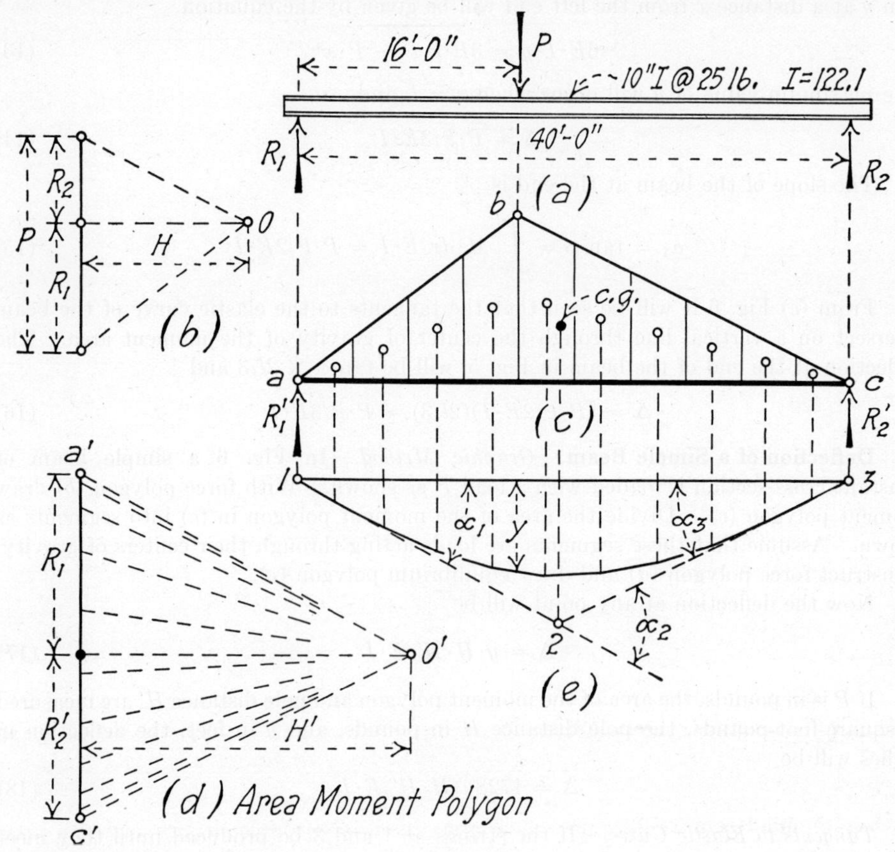

FIG. 6.

In Fig. 7 the beam with span l is fixed at the ends, and carries a load P at a distance a from the left end. The bending moment at the left and right ends is M_1 and M_2, respectively, M_1 and M_2 being negative. The moment under the load is $M_p = P \cdot a(l - a)/l$. To calculate the end reactions we have from the first condition

$$\Sigma M = \tfrac{1}{2}P \cdot a(l - a) + \tfrac{1}{2}(M_1 + M_2)l = 0 \tag{19}$$

Also from the second condition, taking moments about the left reaction

$$\Sigma M \cdot x = \frac{P \cdot a^2(l - a)}{2l} \times \frac{2a}{3} + \frac{P \cdot a(l - a)^2}{2l} \times \left(a + \frac{l - a}{3}\right) + \frac{M_1 \cdot l}{2} \times \frac{l}{3} + \frac{M_2 \cdot l}{2} \times \frac{2l}{3} = 0 \tag{20}$$

The values of M_1 and M_2 can be calculated from equations (19) and (20) for any value of a.

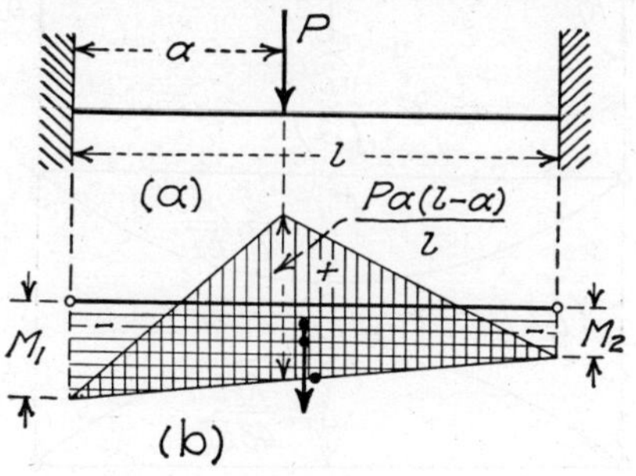

FIG. 7.

In Fig. 7, if $a = l/2$, there results after reduction, from (19)

$$P \cdot l + 4M_1 + 4M_2 = 0 \tag{21}$$

and from (20)

$$3P \cdot l + 8M_1 + 16M_2 = 0 \tag{22}$$

Multiply (21) by 2, and

$$2P \cdot l + 8M_1 + 8M_2 = 0 \tag{23}$$

and subtracting (23) from (22), and

$$P \cdot l + 8M_2 = 0$$

and

$$M_2 = - P \cdot l/8 = M_1 \tag{24}$$

The maximum positive moment will be $M = P \cdot l/8$, and the points of contraflecture will be at the quarter points of the beam. For a load at the center, a beam fixed at the ends is the equivalent of two cantilever beams with spans equal $\frac{1}{4}l$, and a simple beam with a span $\frac{1}{2}l$.

Continuous Beams.—A beam which in an unstrained condition rests on more than two supports is a continuous beam. For a straight beam the supports must be on a level or be in a straight line. Beams of one span with one end fixed and the other end supported, or with both ends fixed, may also be considered as continuous beams.

In a beam with more than two supports with freely supported ends, all reactions in excess of two are redundant (unnecessary for static equilibrium), and the reactions depend upon the elastic properties of the beam. In a continuous beam of two spans continuous over the middle support the middle reaction may be considered redundant as in Fig. 8. The deflection of the beam in line with the reaction, when the middle reaction is taken out, will be equal to the deflection of the unloaded beam due to the middle reaction. In Fig. 8 the deflection at the middle of a span equal to $l' = 2l$ due to the uniform load w will be

$$\Delta_1 = 5w \cdot l'^4/384E \cdot I \tag{25}$$

While the deflection due to the reaction R_2 will be

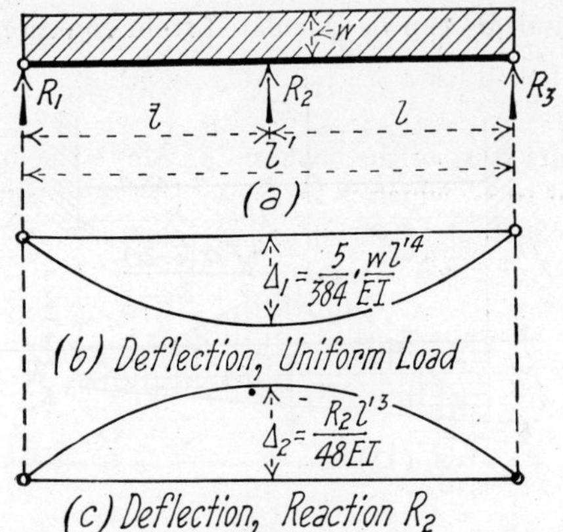

FIG. 8.

$$\Delta_2 = R_2 \cdot l'^3/48E \cdot I \tag{26}$$

Equating Δ_1 and Δ_2 and solving for R_2, there results

$$R_2 = 5w \cdot l'/8 = 5w \cdot l/4 \tag{27}$$

General Theorem.—In Fig. 9 the continuous beam in (a) with spans l_1 and l_2 carries a uniform load w per lineal foot. It is required to calculate the reactions R_1, R_2, and R_3.

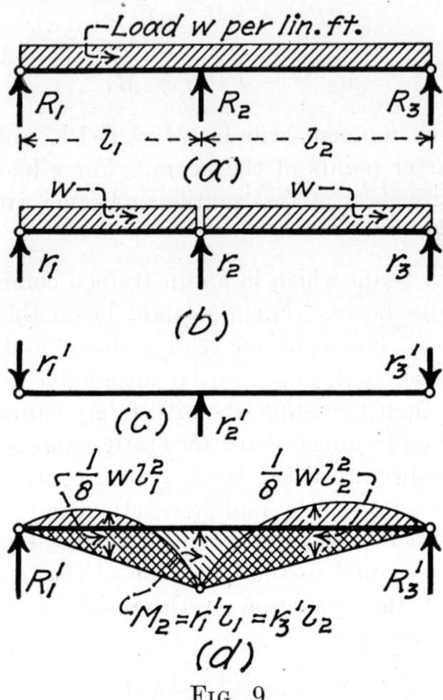

FIG. 9.

The reactions of the continuous beam in (a) may be replaced by the reactions of the two simple beams loaded with the uniform load w in (b), and the reactions and the load of the simple beam with the span $l_1 + l_2$ and carrying a negative load r_2' in (c). The reactions in (a) will then have the following values; $R_1 = r_1 - r_1'$; $R_2 = r_2 + r_2'$; $R_3 = r_3 - r_3'$

Now the upward curvature of the beam in (a) due to the load r_2' will be neutralized by the load above equal to r_2' which is transferred to the reaction R_2 by flexure in the beam. The upward deflection of the beam in (c) at any point will be the bending moment divided by $E \cdot I$ at the same point in (d) due to a bending moment polygon with a maximum moment $M_2 = r_1' \times l_1 = r_3' \times l_2$; and the downward deflection of

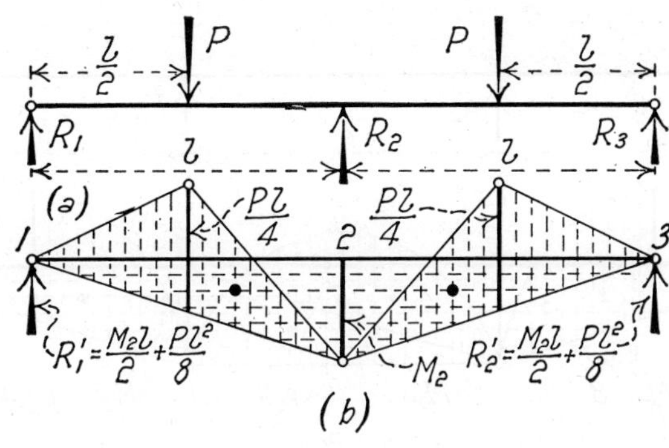

FIG. 10.

the beam in (b) at any point will be the bending moment divided by $E \cdot I$ at the same point in (d) due to the bending moment polygons for a uniform load w covering the simple spans in (b). But the deflection of the beam in (a) is zero at the reaction R_2, and therefore the bending moment at the corresponding point in (d) is zero.

From the above discussion it follows that to calculate the reactions of the continuous beam in (a) by moment areas, take a simple beam with a span equal to $l_1 + l_2$ and load it with the bending moment polygons for beams (b) and (c) as in (d); the bending moment in beam (d) at the points corresponding to the reactions will be equal to zero, and the reactions of the beam (a) can be calculated by statics when the value M_2 is obtained.

Continuous Beam.—*Concentrated Loads.*—In (a) Fig. 10, a continuous beam of two equal spans of length l is loaded with two equal loads P at the centers of the spans. Calculate the bending moments and load a simple beam with a span equal to $2l$, with the positive bending-moment diagram due to a load of P, in each span and also the negative bending moment diagram due to the reaction R_2. Then to find M_2, the bending moment at 2, take moments of forces to the left of 2, and

$$M_2 \cdot l^2/2 + P \cdot l^3/8 - M_2 \cdot l^2/6 - P \cdot l^3/16 = 0$$

and

$$M_2 = -3P \cdot l/16 \tag{28}$$

To calculate R_1 take moments in (a) about R_2, and

$$R_1 \cdot l - P \cdot l/2 + M_2 = 0$$

and

$$R_1 = 5P/16 = R_3 \tag{29}$$

Also

$$R_2 = 11P/8 \tag{30}$$

Beam Uniformly Loaded.—In (*a*) Fig. 11, a continuous beam of three equal spans of length l, is loaded with a uniform load equal to w per foot. Calculate the bending moments due to a uniform load of w on each span, and load a simple beam of span $3l$ with the positive bending-moment diagrams due to load w, and with the negative bending-moment diagrams due to the reactions R_2 and R_3. The bending moment M_2 is equal to M_3. Now the deflection of the beam is zero at 2 and 3, and the bending moments of the moment areas must, therefore, be zero at these points. Taking moments of forces to the left of 2, we have

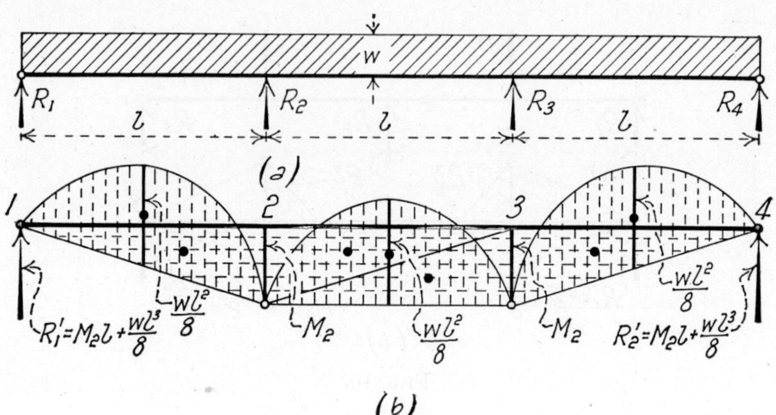

FIG. 11.

$$M_2 \cdot l^2 + w \cdot l^4/8 - w \cdot l^4/24 - M_2 \cdot l^2/6 = 0$$

and

$$M_2 = - w \cdot l^2/10 = M_3$$

To calculate R_1 take moments about 2 in (*a*), and

$$R_1 \cdot l - w \cdot l^2/2 + M_2 = 0$$

$$R_1 = 4w \cdot l/10 = R_4$$

and

$$R_2 = R_3 = 3w \cdot l/2 - 4w \cdot l/10 = 11w \cdot l/10$$

Continuous Beam of n Spans.—To calculate the reactions for a continuous beam of n spans, equal or unequal, loaded with any system or systems of loads proceed as follows:

Calculate the bending moment due to the external load, or loads, or system of loads in each span considered as a simple beam, (*a*) Fig. 13. Take a simple beam having a total length equal to the length of the continuous beam, and load it with the bending moment polygons found as above. Also load the beam with the bending moment polygons due to the reactions, (*b*), Fig. 13. The reactions being unknown, the bending moments at the reactions will be unknown. Now calculate the bending moment in the simple beam at points corresponding to each reaction and place the result equal to zero.

For a continuous beam of n spans there will be $n + 1$ equations which is equal to the number of unknown reactions. Solving these equations, the unknown bending moments will be found, and the reactions may be calculated algebraically.

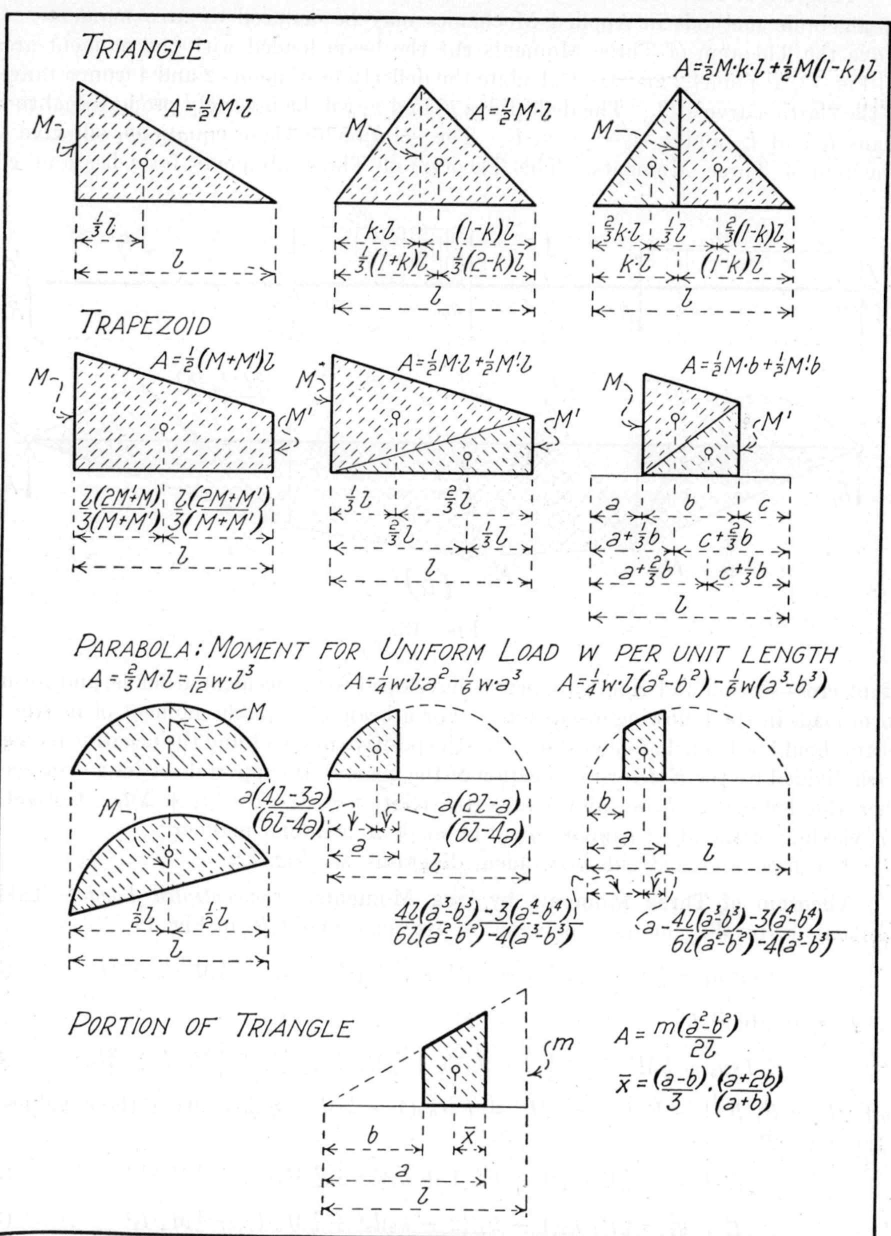

FIG. 12. Areas and Centroids of Moment Diagrams.

Theorem of Three Moments.—The Theorem of Three Moments which was deduced by algebraic methods in Applied Mechanics may be deduced by area moments. To prove the Theorem of Three Moments cut the beam loaded with the moment areas, (*b*) Fig. 13, at points 2 and 4. Calculate the deflections of points 2 and 4 from a tangent to the elastic curve at 3. The deflections y_2 and y_4 will be inversely proportional to the spans l_2 and l_3, and $y_2 \cdot l_3 = - y_4 \cdot l_2$. The solution of these equations will give the Theorem of Three Moments. The Theorem of Three Moments for a beam of con-

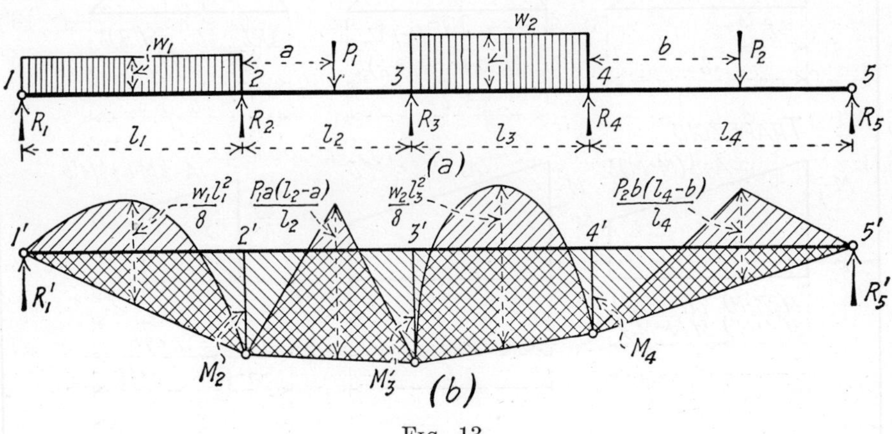

FIG. 13.

stant cross-section and rigid supports is developed for concentrated loads, and for uniform loads in the following discussions. For a beam of variable moment of inertia the beam should be loaded at each point with the positive moment and the negative moment, each divided by the $E \cdot I$ for that section of the beam. If support 4 settles a distance Δ, then the deflections y_2, y_4, and Δ have the relation $y_2 \cdot l_3 = -(y_4 + \Delta)l_2$. Correction for yielding of the other supports may be made in a similar manner.

For areas and centroids of moment diagrams, see Fig. 12,

Theorem of Three Moments by Area Moments.—*Concentrated Loads.*—Taking moments of bending moment polygon for 1st span, about R_1 in Fig. 14.

$$E \cdot I \cdot y_1 = \tfrac{1}{2}M' \cdot l_1 \times \tfrac{1}{3}(1 + k_1)l_1 + \tfrac{1}{2}M_1 \cdot l_1 \times \tfrac{1}{3}l_1 + \tfrac{1}{2}M_2 \cdot l_1 \times \tfrac{2}{3}l_1 \tag{31}$$

for 2d span about R_3.

$$E \cdot I \cdot y_3 = \tfrac{1}{2}M'' \cdot l_2 \times \tfrac{1}{3}(2 - k_2)l_2 + \tfrac{1}{2}M_3 \cdot l_2 \times \tfrac{1}{3}l_2 + \tfrac{1}{2}M_2 \cdot l_2 \times \tfrac{2}{3}l_2, \tag{32}$$

but $M' = P_1 \cdot k_1(1 - k_1)l_1$ and $M'' = P_2 \cdot k_2(1 - k_2)l_2$. Substituting these values in (31) and (32)

$$E \cdot I \cdot y_1 = \tfrac{1}{6}P_1 \cdot k_1(1 - k_1)(1 + k_1)l_1^3 + \tfrac{1}{6}M_1 \cdot l_1^2 + \tfrac{1}{3}M_2 \cdot l_1^2 \tag{33}$$

$$E \cdot I \cdot y_3 = \tfrac{1}{6}P_2 \cdot k_2(1 - k_2)(2 - k_2)l_2^3 + \tfrac{1}{6}M_3 \cdot l_2^2 + \tfrac{1}{3}M_2 \cdot l_2^2 \tag{34}$$

by similar triangles

$$y_1/l_1 = - y_3/l_2 \tag{35}$$

from (33), (34) and (35)

$$\tfrac{1}{6}P_1\cdot k_1(1 - k_1)(1 + k_1)l_1^2 + \tfrac{1}{6}M_1\cdot l_1 + \tfrac{1}{3}M_2\cdot l_1 = -\tfrac{1}{6}P_2\cdot k_2(1 - k_2)(2 - k_2)l_2^2 - \tfrac{1}{6}M_3\cdot l_2 - \tfrac{1}{3}M_2\cdot l_2$$

and

$$\tfrac{1}{6}M_1\cdot l_1 + \tfrac{1}{3}M_2(l_1 + l_2) + \tfrac{1}{6}M_3\cdot l_2 = -\tfrac{1}{6}P_1\cdot k_1(1 - k_1^2)l_1^2 - \tfrac{1}{6}P_2\cdot k_2(2 - 3k_2 + k_2^2)$$

and

$$M_1\cdot l_1 + 2M_2(l_1 + l_2) + M_3\cdot l_2 = -P_1(k_1 - k_1^3)l_1^2 - P_2(2k_2 - 3k_2^2 + k_2^3)l_2^2 \quad (36)$$

If there are several loads on each span

$$M_1\cdot l_1 + 2M_2(l_1 + l_2) + M_3\cdot l_2 = -\Sigma P_1(k_1 - k_1^3)l_1^2 - \Sigma P_2(2k_2 - 3k_2^2 + k_2^3)l_2^2 \quad (37)$$

which is the Equation of Three Moments for concentrated loads.

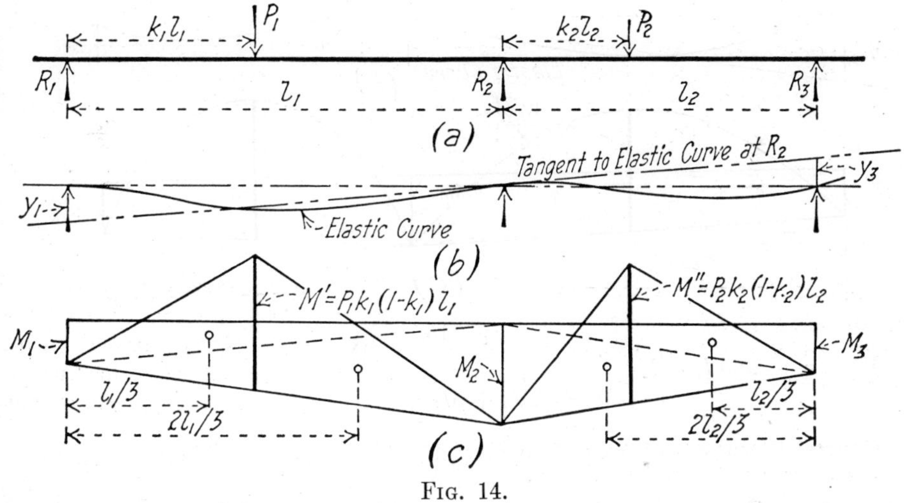

FIG. 14.

If the spans are loaded with uniformly distributed loads of w_1 and w_2 per unit length, P may be replaced by $w\cdot dx$ and k by x/l. Then integrating each of the terms on the right hand side of the preceeding equation, between 0 and l, the equation for uniform loads is obtained; or the theorem may be calculated directly as follows:—

Theorem of Three Moments by Area Moments.—*Uniform Loads.*—Let Fig. 15 represent any two consecutive spans of a continuous girder of any number of spans.

Taking moments of bending moment polygon for 1st span, about R_1 in Fig. 15.

$$E\cdot I\cdot y_1 = \tfrac{1}{12}w_1\cdot l_1^3 \times \tfrac{1}{2}l_1 + \tfrac{1}{2}M_1\cdot l_1 \times \tfrac{1}{3}l_1 + \tfrac{1}{2}M_2\cdot l_1 \times \tfrac{2}{3}l_1 \quad (38)$$

for 2d span, about R_3

$$E\cdot I\cdot y_3 = \tfrac{1}{12}w_2\cdot l_2^3 \times \tfrac{1}{2}l_2 + \tfrac{1}{2}M_3\cdot l_2 \times \tfrac{1}{3}l_2 + \tfrac{1}{2}M_2\cdot l_2 \times \tfrac{2}{3}l_2 \quad (39)$$

but

$$y_1/l_1 = -y_3/l_2 \quad (40)$$

from (38), (39) and (40)

$$\tfrac{1}{24}w_1 \cdot l_1^3 + \tfrac{1}{6}M_1 \cdot l_1 + \tfrac{1}{3}M_2 \cdot l_1 = -\tfrac{1}{24}w_2 \cdot l_2^3 - \tfrac{1}{6}M_3 \cdot l_2 - \tfrac{1}{3}M_2 \cdot l_2$$

and

$$\tfrac{1}{6}M_1 \cdot l_1 + \tfrac{1}{3}M_2(l_1 + l_2) + \tfrac{1}{6}M_3 \cdot l_2 = -\tfrac{1}{24}w_1 \cdot l_1^3 - \tfrac{1}{24}w_2 \cdot l_2^3$$

and

$$M_1 \cdot l_1 + 2M_2(l_1 + l_2) + M_3 \cdot l_2 = -\tfrac{1}{4}w_1 \cdot l_1^3 - \tfrac{1}{4}w_2 \cdot l_2^3 \tag{41}$$

which is the Equation of Three Moments for uniform loads.

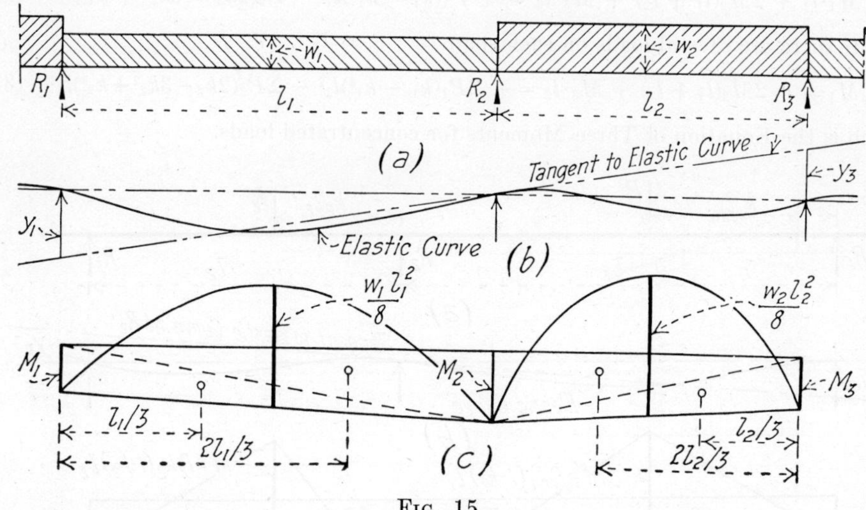

FIG. 15.

If $w_1 = w_2$ and $l_1 = l_2$

$$M_1 + 4M_2 + M_3 = -\tfrac{1}{2}w \cdot l^2 \tag{42}$$

General Discussion of Area Moments.—If a beam be loaded as in (*a*) Fig. 16 the shear at a point in the beam at a distance x from the left support will be equal to the algebraic sum of the forces on the left of the section, and the ordinate at the point in (*b*) will be $V_x = R_A - \int_0^x w \cdot dx$ = definite integral of the loads on the left of the section.

The bending moment at the point a distance x from the left support in (*c*) will be $M_x = \int_0^x V \cdot dx$ = definite integral of the shear area to the left of the section.

The slope at the point a distance x from the left support in (*d*) will be $S_x = S_A - \int_0^x \frac{M \cdot dx}{E \cdot I}$ = definite integral of the moment area to the left of the section divided by $E \cdot I$.

The deflection at the point a distance x from the left support in (*e*) will be $y_x = \int_0^x S \cdot dx$ = definite integral of the slope area to the left of the section.

From the preceding discussion of area moments it will be seen that if the load area in (*a*) Fig. 16 be divided into segments, and each segment be assumed as acting through the center of gravity of the segment, and if a force polygon for these loads be constructed as in (*f*), with a pole distance H = unity, and an equilibrium polygon be drawn as in (*c*); then the equilibrium polygon in (*c*) will be the bending moment polygon for the given loads. Also, if the moment area in (*c*) be divided into segments acting through their centers of gravity, and if a force polygon for these loads be constructed as in (*h*) with a pole distance $H_2 = E \cdot I$, and an equilibrium polygon be drawn as in (*e*); then the equilibrium polygon in (*e*) is the elastic curve of the beam.

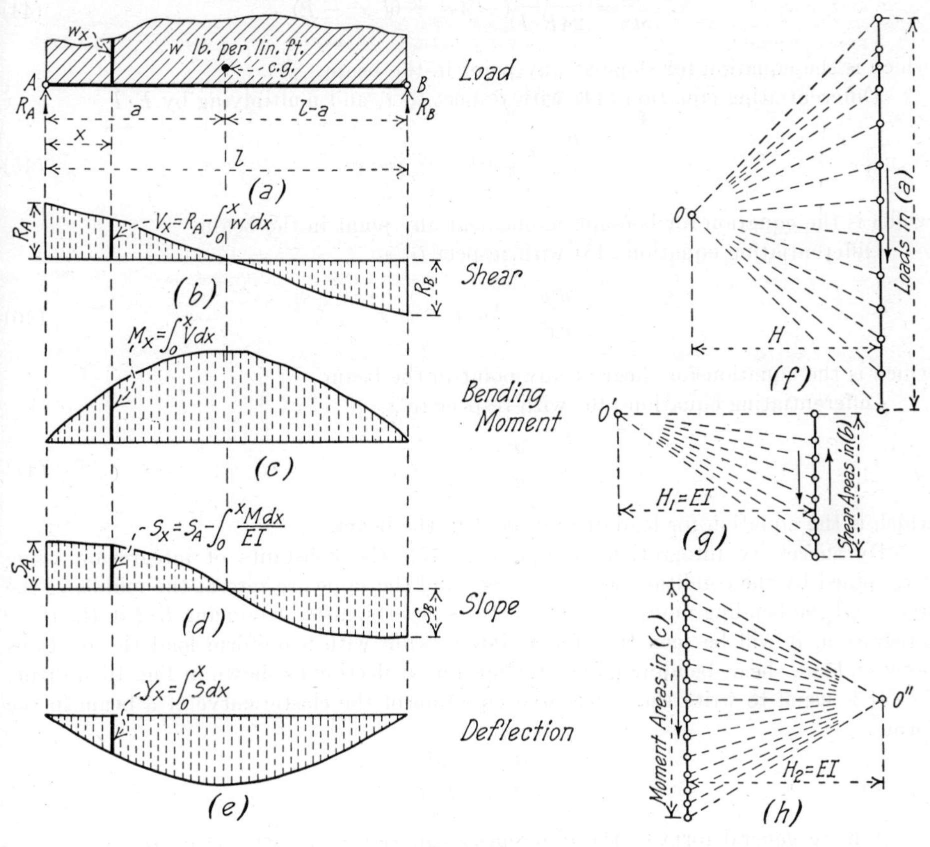

Fig. 16.

It can also be seen that if the shear area in (*b*) be divided into segments acting through the centers of gravity of the segments, and if a force polygon for these loads be drawn as in (*g*) with a pole distance $H_1 = E \cdot I$, and an equilibrium polygon be drawn as in (*d*); then the equilibrium polygon in (*d*) is the slope curve of the beam.

Since a combination of a force polygon with its equilibrium polygon is equivalent to two integrations the relations between load, shear, moment, slope, and deflection as above stated are proved to be true. As an example the relations between load, shear, moment, slope and deflection will be calculated for a simple beam with a span l, loaded with a uniform load w per linear unit. The equation of the elastic curve for a simple beam with a uniform load is

$$y = \frac{w}{24E\cdot I}(-x^4 + 2l\cdot x^3 - l^3\cdot x) \tag{43}$$

Differentiating equation (43) with respect to x,

$$\frac{dy}{dx} = \frac{w}{24E\cdot I}(-4x^3 + 6l\cdot x^2 - l^3) \tag{44}$$

which is the equation for slope at any point in the beam.

Differentiating equation (44) with respect to x, and multiplying by $E\cdot I$,

$$\frac{d^2y}{dx^2} = \tfrac{1}{2}w\cdot l\cdot x - \tfrac{1}{2}w\cdot x^2 \tag{45}$$

which is the equation for bending moment at any point in the beam.

Differentiating equation (45) with respect to x,

$$\frac{d^3y}{dx^3} = \tfrac{1}{2}w\cdot l - w\cdot x \tag{46}$$

which is the equation for shear at any point in the beam.

Differentiating equation (46) with respect to x,

$$\frac{d^4y}{dx^4} = -w \tag{47}$$

which is the equation for load at any point in the beam.

By successive integration of equation (47), the constants of integration being determined by the conditions that the shear and the slope are zero at the middle of the span, and the bending moment is zero at the supports, also introducing $E\cdot I$ in the third integration, it will be seen that for a simple beam with a uniform load the relations between load, shear, bending moment, slope and deflection as shown in Fig. 16 are true.

It is usual to write the differential equation of the elastic curve of a beam in the form

$$\frac{d^2y}{dx^2} = \frac{M}{E\cdot I} \tag{48}$$

A more general form of the differential equation of the elastic curve for a beam with a uniform load is

$$\frac{d^4y}{dx^4} = \frac{-w}{E\cdot I} \tag{49}$$

The differential equation in equation (48) saves two integrations in the solution, and the bending moment, M, is easy to determine, and is to be preferred.

Stresses in Stiff Frames.—For the calculation of the stresses in quadrangular frames with rigid joints, see Chapter XVII.

Method of Elastic Weights.—A method known as the method of elastic weights is used in Chapter XV for calculating the deflections of framed structures. The method of elastic weights as applied to beams is the same as the method of area moments, as will now be shown.

In Fig. 17, a simple beam A–B is loaded with vertical loads in any manner. The deformation of an extreme fiber for a length dx is Δc. Now by definition $\Delta c/c = \Delta\phi = w$, the elastic weight, where c = distance from the neutral axis to the extreme fiber = distance from center of moments used in calculating the stress in the extreme fiber.

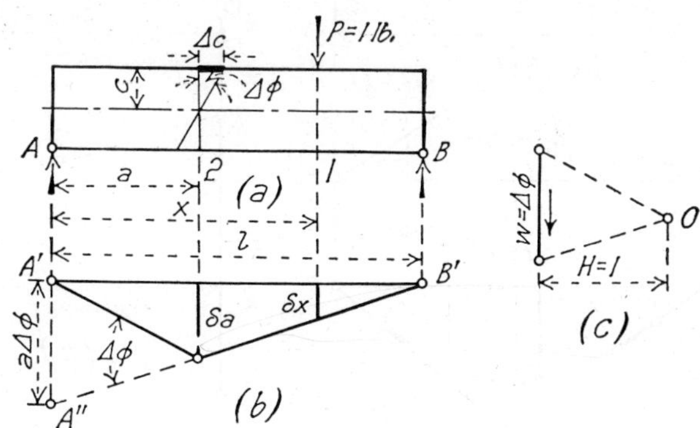

Fig. 17.

Now load the beam at point 2 with the elastic weight $w = \Delta\phi$, construct a force polygon with a pole distance H = unity, as in (c), and draw a moment polygon as in (b), Fig. 17. Now it will be seen that if w is taken equal to unity the moment polygon in (b) will be an influence diagram for the point 2. From (b) $\delta x : a\cdot\Delta\phi : : (l - x) : l$, and

$$\delta x = \frac{a\cdot\Delta\phi(l - x)}{l} \tag{50}$$

where δx = deflection at 1 for a load $\Delta\phi$ at 2. Now if the load at 2 be taken equal to w, then the bending moment at 1 will be

$$M = \frac{w\cdot a(l - x)}{l} \tag{51}$$

from which it may be seen that deflections are given by the moment diagram (b).

Also from the common theory of elasticity of beams

$$\Delta c = S\cdot dx/E,$$

and

$$\Delta\phi = \Delta c/c = S\cdot dx/E\cdot c$$

Now

$$S/c = M/I,$$

and

$$\Delta\phi = w = M\cdot dx/E\cdot I$$

But

$$M\cdot dx/E\cdot I = \text{area moment},$$

which proves that the method of elastic weights is the same as the method of area moments.

In Fig. 18 the elastic curve in (*d*) is calculated by the method of elastic weights. Load the beam $A'B'$ with the bending moment polygon due to the load P. Divide the moment area into segments, and assume that each segment acts through its center

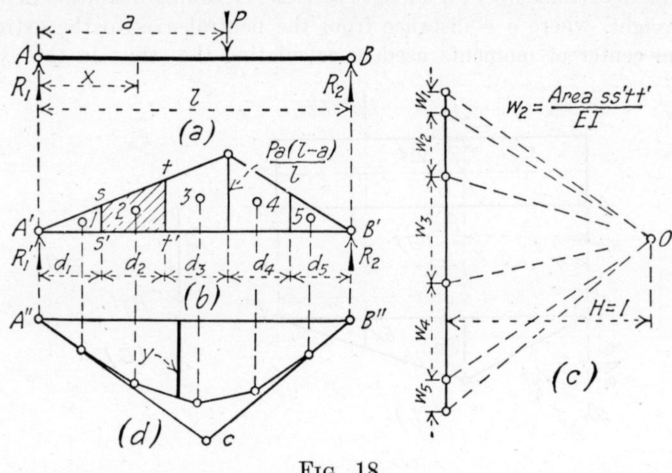

FIG. 18.

of gravity. Each elastic weight is equal to the moment area divided by the value of $E \cdot I$ for the section of the beam covered by the segment. The elastic weight w_2 = area $s\text{-}s'\text{-}t\text{-}t'/E \cdot I$. With the force polygon with a load line w_1 to w_5 inclusive, and a pole

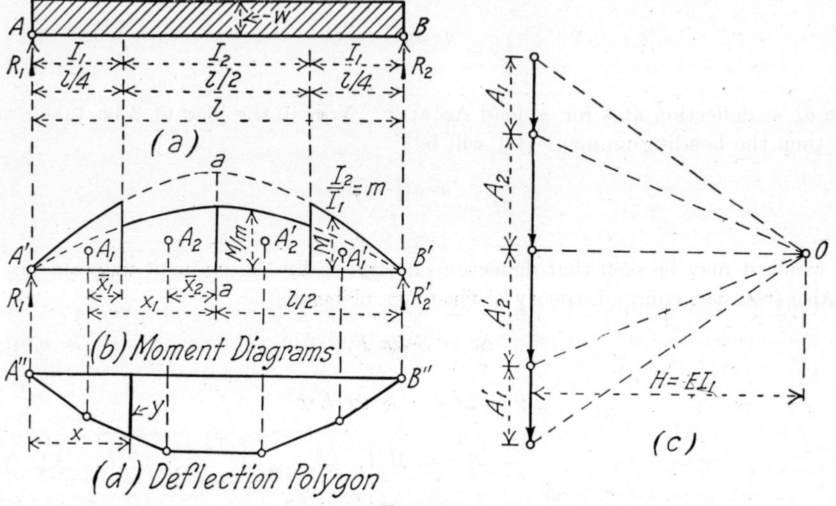

FIG. 19.

distance H = unity, draw equilibrium polygon (*d*). Polygon (*d*) will be the elastic curve of the beam. It will be seen that the method of elastic weights is the same as the method of area moments.

Beams with Variable Moment of Inertia.—For a beam with a variable moment of inertia the beam may be loaded with the moment at each point divided by $E \cdot I$, or if $I_2/I_1 = m$, the ratio of the moment of inertia at each point to the moment of inertia of the end section, the beam may be loaded at each point with M/m, and the deflection diagram can be drawn with a force polygon having a pole distance $H = E \cdot I_1$.

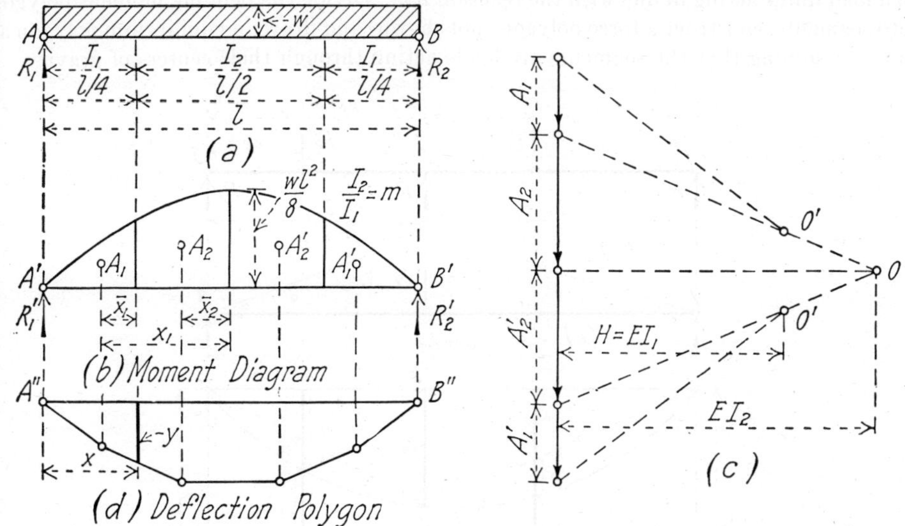

FIG. 20.

If the beam is loaded with the bending moment polygon as in (*b*) Fig. 20, the force polygon may be drawn with a pole distance equal to the $E \cdot I$ for each section of the beam, and the resulting polygon will be the true deflection polygon as shown in (*d*).

Problem 1.—In (*a*) Fig. 19, if the moment of inertia of the middle half of the beam is I_2, and the moment of inertia of the end quarters is I_1, prove by algebraic calculation that the deflection at the center of the beam is

$$\Delta = \frac{w \cdot l^4}{I_1 \cdot I_2 \cdot E}\left(\frac{13}{6{,}144} I_2 + \frac{67}{6{,}144} I_1\right) \qquad (52)$$

Problem 2.—A beam 32 feet long carries a load of 2,000 lb. per lineal foot. Calculate the deflection at the center of the beam, which consists of a 24″ @ 80 lb. *I* beam, with a 10 in. by ½ in. plate 16 ft. long riveted on top of top flange and below bottom flange. Calculate the deflection of the beam at the center with the plates extending the full length of the beam.

CURVED INFLUENCE LINES.—The discussion of influence diagrams in Chapter VII was confined to statically determinate structures, in which the influence diagrams for reaction, shear, moment, and stress had straight lines. In statically indeterminate structures, in which the deformations of the structures must be considered in addition to the usual statical conditions in calculating stresses, the influence diagrams in general have curved lines. Influence lines for continuous beams will be discussed in this chapter, while influence lines for statically indeterminate framed structures will be discussed in Chapter XV.

Continuous Girder of Two Spans.—In Fig. 21 a continuous girder with a constant moment of inertia, and with spans l_1 and l_2 is loaded with loads P_1 and P_2 as in (*a*). In (*b*), load a simple beam having a span $l_1 + l_2$ with the bending moment polygon due to a load unity acting in line with the reaction R_2. Divide the bending moment polygon into segments, construct a force polygon (not shown) and draw an equilibrium polygon as in (*c*), assuming that the segments are loads acting through their centers of gravity.

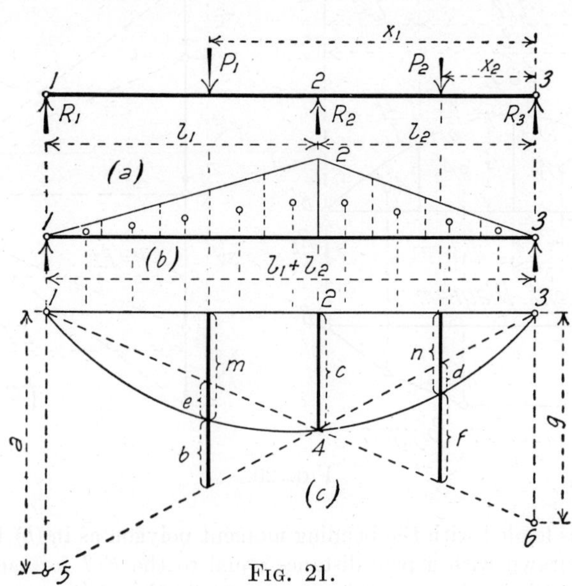

FIG. 21.

The pole distance H may be taken as any convenient length, and the pole O may be taken at any point, in (*c*) the pole O was taken so as to make the closing line 1–2–3 horizontal. Now in (*c*) the reaction may be calculated as follows:

$$R_1 = \frac{P_1 \cdot b - P_2 \cdot d}{a} \tag{53}$$

$$R_2 = \frac{P_1 \cdot m + P_2 \cdot n}{c} \tag{54}$$

$$R_3 = \frac{-P_1 \cdot e + P_2 \cdot f}{g} \tag{55}$$

Proof.—The formula for R_2 will be proved, and the equations for R_1 and R_3 will follow by statics.

In (*c*) the curved line 1–4–3 has ordinates proportional to the ordinates to the elastic curve of the beam when it is loaded with a load at 2. For simplicity it will be assumed that the ordinates are all measured with a scale such that the true deflections for a load unity are given by the diagram. Then if a unit load at 2 will give a deflection m at P_1, by Maxwell's Theorem (see Fig. 5, Chapter VII) a unit load acting in line with P_1 will produce a deflection m at 2, and a load P_1 will produce a deflection $P_1 \cdot m$ at 2. In like manner if a unit load at 2 produces a deflection n at P_2, then a unit load acting in line with P_2 will produce a deflection n at 2, and a load P_2 will produce a deflection $P_2 \cdot n$ at 2.

If a unit load at 2 produces a deflection c, a load R_2 will produce a deflection $R_2 \cdot c$.

Now the final deflection at point 2 is zero, and we have the deflection at point 2 due to the loads P_1 and P_2 equal to the deflection of R_2 at point 2, and

$$R_2 \cdot c = P_1 \cdot m + P_2 \cdot n$$

and

$$R_2 = \frac{P_1 \cdot m + P_2 \cdot n}{c} \tag{54}$$

which proves the theorem.

To calculate R_1 take moments about (3) in (*c*), and

$$R_1(l_1 + l_2) + R_2 \cdot l_2 - P_1 \cdot x_1 - P_2 \cdot x_2 = 0$$

and from reaction influence diagrams

$$R_1 \cdot a + R_2 \cdot c - P_1(m + b) - P_2(n - d) = 0$$

Substituting the values of R_2 from (54), there results

$$R_1 \cdot a = P_1 \cdot b - P_2 \cdot d$$

$$R_1 = \frac{P_1 \cdot b - P_2 \cdot d}{a} \tag{53}$$

Also, since $R_1 + R_2 + R_3 = P_1 + P_2$,

$$R_3 = \frac{- P_1 \cdot e + P_2 \cdot f}{g} \tag{55}$$

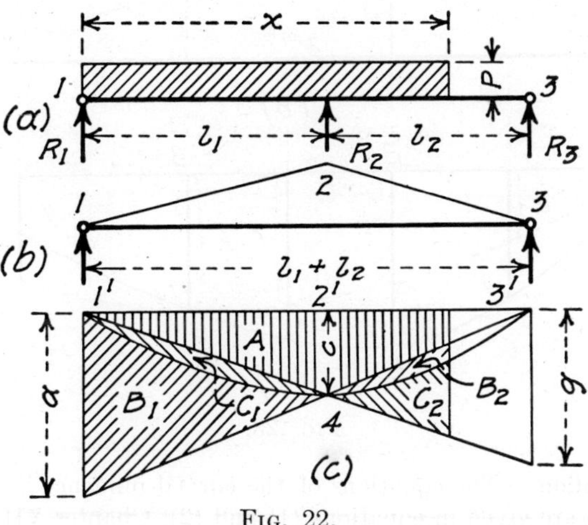

FIG. 22.

The influence diagrams for the reactions R_1, R_2 and R_3 in a continuous beam of two spans are given in Fig. 24*a* and Fig. 24*b*. In Fig. 24*a* the influence diagrams for the reactions in Fig. 21, have been drawn separately. In Fig. 24*b* the influence diagrams for the reactions are shown as calculated separately by applying a unit load in line with each reaction. It will be noted that the curves in (*d*) and (*e*) may be obtained from the curve in (*b*) by taking proportional ordinates. The influence diagrams in Fig. 24*a* and Fig. 24*b* are identical. The influence diagrams are more commonly drawn as in Fig. 24*b*.

Uniform Load.—For a uniform load on a beam the areas of the diagram under the load are to be used in the place of the ordinates, as in the case of influence diagrams with straight lines. For example, in Fig. 22, the reactions are given by the following formulas.

$$R_1 = \frac{p(\text{area } B_1 - \text{area } B_2)}{a} \tag{56}$$

$$R_2 = \frac{p(\text{area } A + \text{area } B_2 + \text{area } C_1)}{c} \tag{57}$$

$$R_3 = \frac{p(\text{area } C_2 - \text{area } C_1)}{g} \tag{58}$$

If the spans are equal, $l_1 = l_2 = l$, the area between the axis and the elastic curve, area A + area B + area $C = 5c \cdot l/4$, and for a full load, $R_2 = 5p \cdot l/4$, a familiar value.

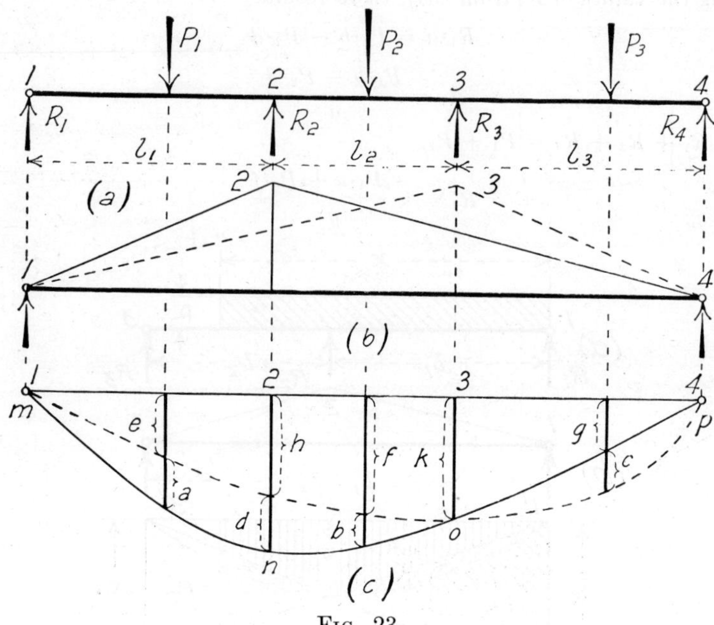

FIG. 23.

Algebraic Solution.—The equations of the curved influence lines for a continuous beam of two spans are given in equations (1) and (2), Chapter VII.

Problem.—For the calculation by influence diagrams of the stresses in a continuous girder of two spans and with a variable moment of inertia, see Problem 2, Chapter XXII.

Continuous Girder of Three Spans.—To calculate the reaction R_2 in Fig. 23 proceed as follows:—With a load represented by the triangle 1–2–4, construct a force polygon (not shown) and draw an equilibrium polygon m–n–o–p. Now, with a load represented by the triangle 1–3–4 construct a force polygon (not shown), and draw an equilibrium polygon through m–o–p. (The method of drawing an equilibrium polygon through three points is given in Chapter I.)

Then in (c) Fig. 23,

$$R_2 \cdot d = P_1 \cdot a + P_2 \cdot b - P_3 \cdot c$$

$$R_2 = \frac{P_1 \cdot a + P_2 \cdot b - P_3 \cdot c}{d} \tag{59}$$

R_3 may be found in a similar manner by drawing an equilibrium polygon through point n.

When the values of R_2 and R_3 have been obtained, the reactions R_1 and R_4 can easily be calculated by algebraic moments.

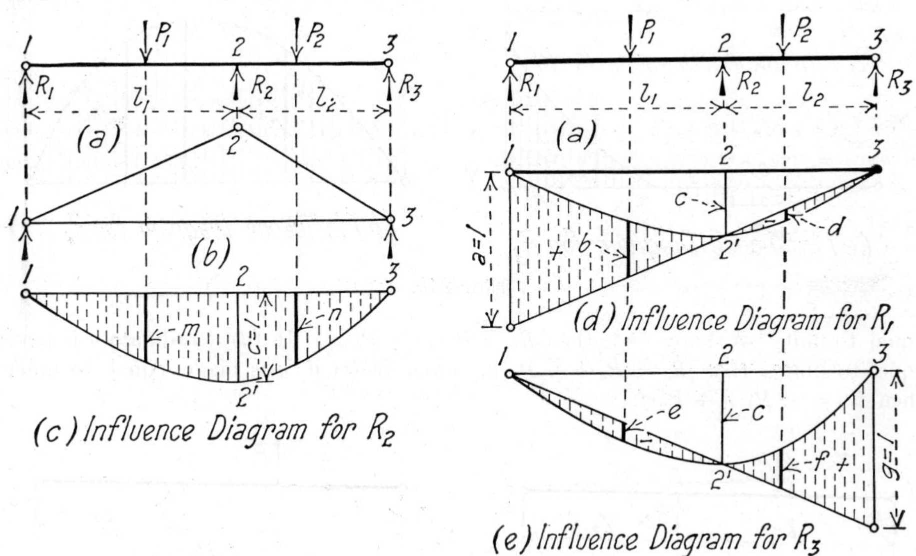

Fig. 24a.

Proof.—With the load 1–2–4 and the full line deflection curve, as in the case of a girder of two spans

$$R_2(d + h) = - R_3 \cdot k + P_1(a + e) + P_2(b + f) + P_3 \cdot g \tag{60}$$

and with the load 1–3–4 and the dotted line deflection curve in like manner

$$R_3 \cdot k = - R_2 \cdot h + P_1 \cdot e + P_2 \cdot f + P_3(c + g) \tag{61}$$

Subtracting (61) from (60) there results

$$R_2 \cdot d = P_1 \cdot a + P_2 \cdot b - P_3 \cdot c$$

$$R_2 = \frac{P_1 \cdot a + P_2 \cdot b - P_3 \cdot c}{d} \tag{59}$$

Problem.—For the calculation by influence diagrams of the stresses in a continuous girder of three spans and with a variable moment of inertia, see Problem 3, Chapter XXII.

17

Influence Diagram for a Continuous Girder of Two Spans.—In Fig. 24*a* and Fig. 24*b* an influence diagram for reaction R_2 is given in (*b*). If the deflection at R_2 is made

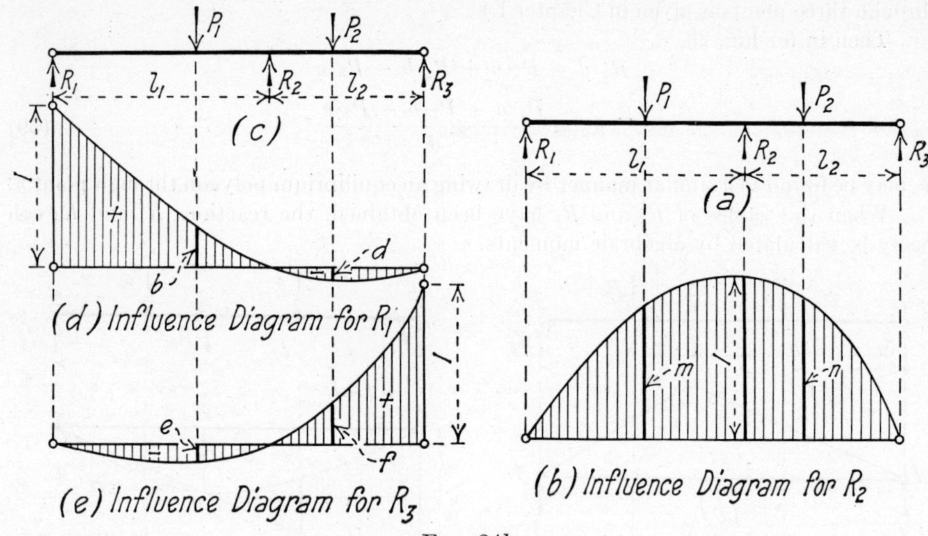

FIG. 24*b*.

equal to unity so that $c = 1$, then $R_2 = P_1 \cdot m + P_2 \cdot n$. In (*d*) if ordinate *a* is made equal to unity, then $R_1 = P_1 \cdot b - P_2 \cdot d$. And in (*e*) if *g* is made equal to unity, then $R_3 = - P_1 \cdot e + P_2 \cdot f$.

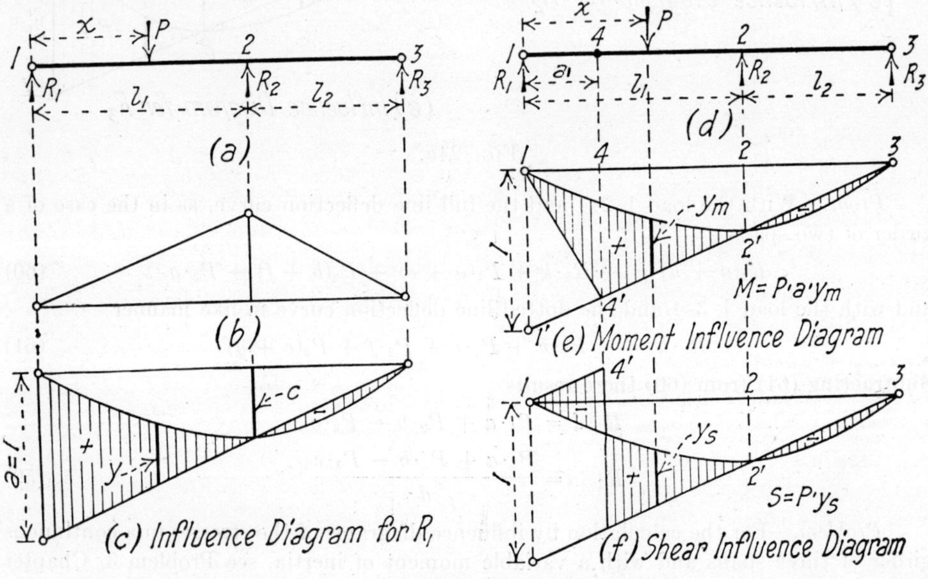

FIG. 25.

An influence diagram for moment at point 4 in the first span is shown in (*e*) Fig. 25. The deflection under the reaction R_1 is taken equal to unity. The moment at point 4 for a load to the right of the point will be equal to the left reaction multiplied by a_1. For points to the left of point 4 the moment will equal the moment of the reaction minus the moment of the load; moment ordinates will be measured from the curved line to the straight line 1–4′. The diagram 1–1′–4′ is the influence diagram for left reaction for a load on a simple beam with a span a_1, with supports at 1 and 4. From which it follows that the shaded area is the true influence diagram. The equation for moment at the point 4 for a load P at x is $M = P \cdot a_1 \cdot y_m$.

An influence diagram for shear at any point 4 in the first span is shown in (*f*) Fig. 25. For points on the right of the point 4, the shear at 4 will be equal to the left reaction. For points to the left the shear at the point is equal to the left reaction minus the load to the left of the point. The shear at 4 for a load P at any point x is $S = P \cdot y_s$.

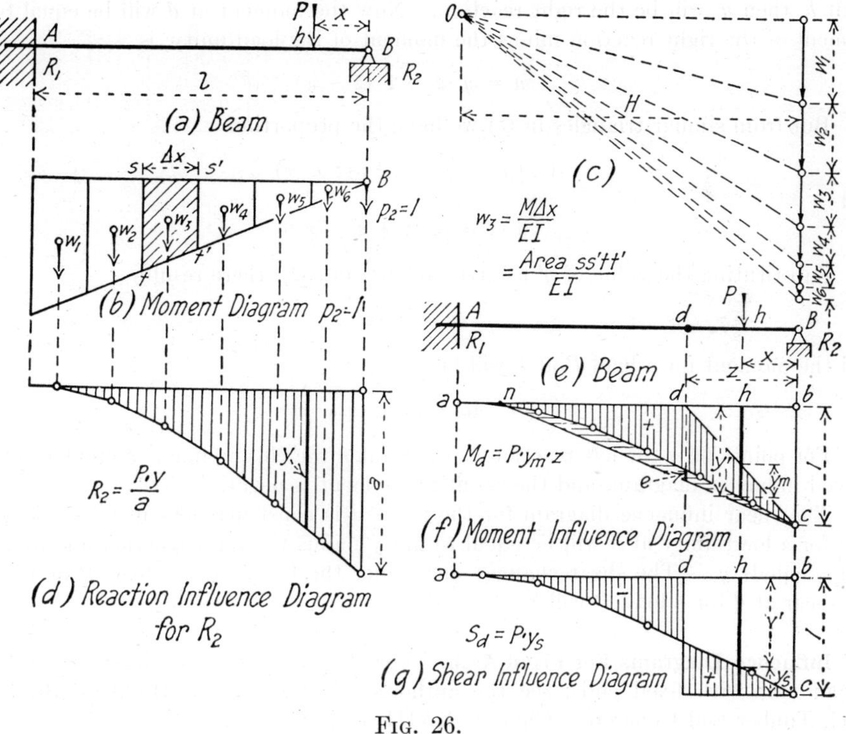

FIG. 26.

Beam Fixed at One End. Supported at Other End.—In (*a*) Fig. 26, the beam has a constant moment of inertia, is fixed at A and is supported at B. The influence diagram for the right reaction is constructed as follows: Remove the right support, B, and load the cantilever beam with a load unity acting in the line of R_2. Load the cantilever beam with a bending moment polygon due to the load unity. Divide the moment diagram into a convenient number of segments, construct a force polygon as in (*c*), with the area of the segments divided by $E \cdot I$ (since both E and I cancel out in the calculation, they may each be taken equal to unity), and with a convenient pole distance construct an equilibrium polygon as in (*d*), assuming that the area of each segment, or elastic weight, acts through the center of gravity of the segment. Now equilibrium polygon (*d*) has ordinates proportional to the elastic curve of a beam fixed at A and loaded with a load unity at B, and is the reaction influence diagram for R_2. For a unit load at B will produce a deflection $k \cdot a$ at B, and a deflection $k \cdot y$ at h; and by Maxwell's Theorem a unit load at h will produce a deflection $k \cdot y$ at B. A unit load at h will then produce a reaction at B equal to $k \cdot y / k \cdot a = y/a$, and a load P at h will produce a reaction $R_2 = P \cdot y/a$ at B.

The moment influence diagram is constructed by dividing each ordinate in the reaction locus (*d*) by the ordinate a, so that the line b–c will be equal to unity as in (*e*). To construct the moment influence diagram for the point d, draw line d–c, and the figure a–c–d is the required influence diagram. For if you take a unit load at the point h, then y' will be the right reaction. Now the moment at d will be equal to the moment of the right reaction minus the moment of the load unity, is

$$m = y' \cdot z - 1 \cdot (z - x) \tag{62}$$

But from similar triangles in (*e*) we have the proportion

$$1 : (y' - y_m) : : z : (z - x)$$

and

$$y' \cdot z = y_m \cdot z + z - x \tag{63}$$

Substituting the value of y' as given in (63) in (62), there results

$$m = y_m \cdot z \tag{64}$$

and the moment for a load P at h will be

$$M = P \cdot y_m \cdot z \tag{65}$$

For points near the left reaction as for point n the closing line n-c drops below the curved influence diagram, and the resulting moment is negative.

The shear influence diagram for the point d is constructed as in (*e*). The shear at d for a load unity at h will be equal to unity minus the right reaction due to a load unity, equals y_s. The shear changes sign under the load. For a load P at point h, the shear at d for a load P will be

$$S = P \cdot y_s \tag{66}$$

Influence Diagrams For Fixed Arch. For the construction of influence diagrams for an arch with fixed ends, see the author's "The Design of Highway Bridges of Steel, Timber and Concrete," Chapter XXIII.

TRANSVERSE BENT.—The problem of the calculation of the point of contraflexure in the columns of a transverse bent will now be solved by the use of moment areas. The nomenclature in Fig. 27 is the same as in Chapter X. It is assumed that the deflections at points b and c are equal.

In (*b*) Fig. 27, the deflection at b from the tangent at a is found by taking moments of the moment areas below b to be

$$E \cdot I \cdot \Delta = \frac{M_0 \cdot d}{2} \times \frac{2d}{3} - \frac{M_1 \cdot d}{2} \times \frac{d}{3}$$

$$\Delta = \frac{2M_0 \cdot d^2 - M_1 \cdot d^2}{6E \cdot I} \tag{67}$$

The deflection at c from the tangent at a is found by taking moments of moment areas below c to be

$$E \cdot I \cdot \Delta' = \frac{M_0 \cdot d}{2}(h - d/3) - \frac{2M_1(h - d)^2}{6} - \frac{M_1 \cdot d}{2}(h - 2/3d)$$

$$\Delta' = \frac{M_0(3d \cdot h - d^2) - M_1(2h^2 - h \cdot d)}{6E \cdot I} \tag{68}$$

But Δ is equal to Δ' by hypothesis, and equating (67) and (68) we have

$$2M_0 \cdot d^2 - M_1 \cdot d^2 = M_0(3d \cdot h - d^2) - M_1(2h^2 - h \cdot d)$$

transposing

$$M_0(3h \cdot d - 3d^2) = M_1(2h^2 - h \cdot d - d^2) \tag{69}$$

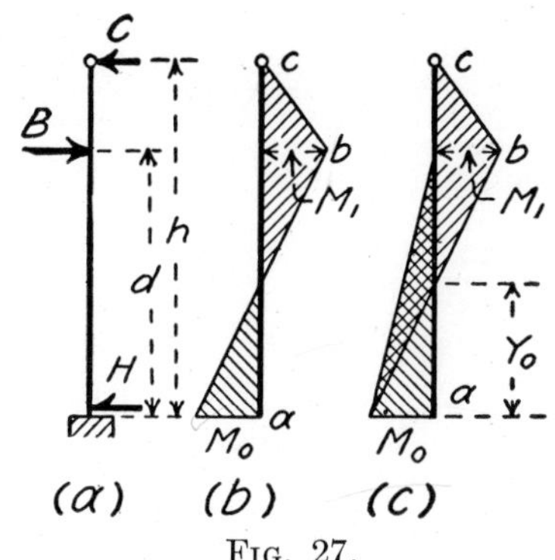

FIG. 27.

Now in (c) Fig. 27, it will be seen that

$$M_0 : M_1 : : y_0 : d - y_0,$$

and

$$M_0(d - y_0) = M_1 \cdot y_0 \tag{70}$$

Solving (69) and (70) for y_0, we have

$$y_0 = \frac{d}{2}\,\frac{(2h + d)}{(h + 2d)} \tag{71}$$

which is the same value as was found by algebraic methods in Chapter X.

For additional problems, see Chapter XXII.

For the calculation of the stresses in framed bents with rigid joints, see Chapter XVII.

References.—The method of area moments was first developed about 1870 by Mohr in Germany and by Green in America. The method has been developed and extended by Mohr, "Technischen Mechanik;" Morley, "Strength of Materials;" Bjorstad, "Die Berechnung von Steifrahmen," and others. The writers above have used the "tangent" or second area moment theorem. The "beam "or first area moment theorem was proposed by the author in an article published in the University of Colorado Journal of Engineering, No. 1, 1905.

CHAPTER XV.

Deflection of Framed Structures.

Introduction.—If a structure is acted upon by external forces which produce stresses in the members, the structure will deflect under the loads. The compression members will be shortened and the tension members will be lengthened, and the total deformation of any joint in the structure will be the sum of the deformations of the particular joint due to the deformation of each member. In addition to changes in length due to stress, there are changes in length due to changes in temperature, to the play in pin joints or in the bolted joints of a bridge when the falsework is removed, or due to errors in workmanship, or due to the substitution of manufactured lengths for the theoretical lengths. Deflections due to stress and to temperature, only, will be considered in this chapter, while both the elastic and the inelastic distortions of structures will be considered in calculating the camber of a bridge. An exact knowledge of the deflections of structures is important in design and erection of all structures, and is necessary for the calculations of the stresses in statically indeterminate structures. In this chapter it is assumed that the structure is perfectly elastic, and that the deformations of the members are small as compared with the lengths of the members themselves, so that the change in the stresses due to the change in form of the truss may be neglected. It is also assumed, as is usual in mechanics, that the deflection of any joint in the structure is the sum of the deflections at the joint due to the individual members, acting consecutively in any order.

The deflection of a framed structure may be calculated algebraically or graphically, or by a combination of algebraic and graphic methods. The algebraic methods are (1) the Method of Algebraic Summation, (2) the Method of Work, commonly called the " Method of Least Work," and (3) the Method of Elastic Weights. The graphic methods are (4) the Williot Diagram in combination with the Mohr Rotation Diagram, and (5) the Method of Elastic Weights solved by graphics. The Williot-Mohr graphical method (4) has the advantage that the changes in positions of all joints of the structure are shown in a single diagram, while the Method of Algebraic Summation (1), and the Method of Work (2), give the deformation of a single joint in one direction only. The Method of Elastic Weights gives the deflections of all joints of a structure in one direction, so that the changes in position of all joints of a structure can be determined by the calculation of the vertical and horizontal displacements, or by two calculations by the Method of Elastic Weights. The Williot-Mohr method is therefore the most satisfactory method to employ for spans of medium length where the deflections of all joints are desired; while the Method of Elastic Weights is the most satisfactory method for long spans or complicated structures where great precision is desired.

METHOD OF ALGEBRAIC SUMMATION.—The method will be illustrated by calculating the deformation of the right end of the truss in Fig. 1.

In Fig. 1 the truss is fixed at L_0, and is free to move at L_0', and is loaded with a load W. Under the action of the load, L_0' will move a distance Δ. Now assume that all the members are rigid with the exception of $1-y$, which is increased in length the distance δ, under the action of the external load W. The movement of the joint L_0' will be Δ', and will be due to the change in length δ, of the member $1-y$. Let H be

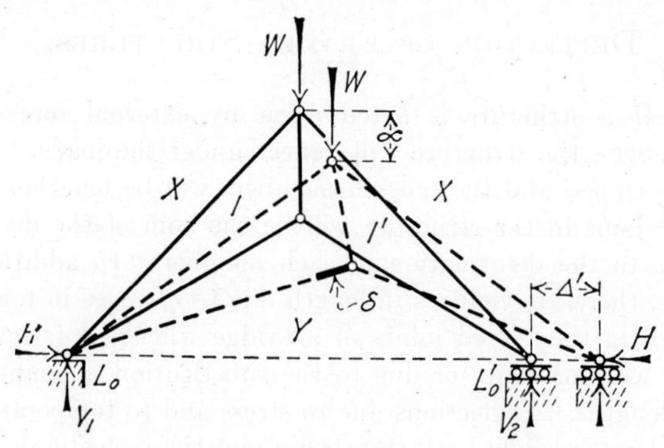

FIG. 1.

the horizontal reaction necessary to bring L_0' back to its original position, and let $U \cdot H$ be the stress in the member $1-y$ due to the horizontal thrust H. Now the internal work $\frac{1}{2}\delta \cdot H \cdot U$ in shortening the member $1-y$ to its original length will be equal to the external work $\frac{1}{2}H \cdot \Delta'$, required to bring the hinge L_0' back to its original position, and

$$\tfrac{1}{2}H \cdot \Delta' = \tfrac{1}{2}\delta \cdot H \cdot U$$

and

$$\Delta' = \delta \cdot U \tag{1}$$

but $\delta = S_1 \cdot L/A \cdot E$, where S_1 is the stress in the member $1-y$ due to the load W; L is the length of the member $1-y$ in the same units as Δ'; A is the area of the member in square inches; and E is the modulus of elasticity of the material of the member in lb. per sq. in. Substituting this value of δ in (1) we have

$$\Delta' = S_1 \cdot U \cdot L/A \cdot E \tag{2}$$

where U is the stress in the member due to a load unity at L_0' acting in the line in which Δ' is measured.

Now if each one of the remaining members of the truss is assumed as distorted in turn, the other members, meanwhile remaining rigid, the deformation at L_0' will be represented by the general equation (2), and the total deformation, Δ, at L_0' will be

$$\Delta = \Sigma \frac{S \cdot U \cdot L}{A \cdot E} \tag{3}$$

Problems.—For detail calculations of the deflections of framed structures by the Method of Algebraic Summation, see Chapters XVI, XX, XXI, and XXII.

METHOD OF WORK.—The deformation of a member under a stress S is equal to $S \cdot L/A \cdot E$, where L is the length of the member, A is the area of the member, and E

is the modulus of elasticity. The work of deformation of the member will be the deformation multiplied by one-half the stress, S, or if W = the work in any member we have

$$W = S^2 \cdot L/2A \cdot E$$

Differentiating the work with reference to a load S, applied in the line of the member,

$$\frac{dW}{dS} = \frac{S \cdot L}{A \cdot E} = \Delta \tag{4}$$

This shows that for direct stress in a straight member the derivative of the work due to any load with reference to the load will be the deformation in line with the load.

This is Castigliano's first theorem for work which will be proved for structures.

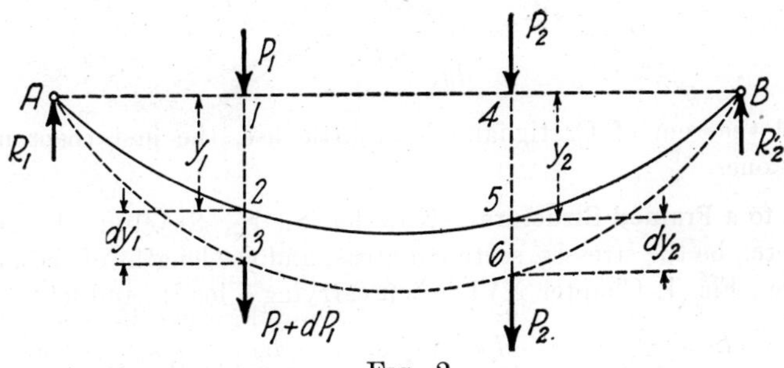

FIG. 2.

THEORY OF WORK.—In Fig. 2 a beam or truss is loaded with two loads, P_1 and P_2, which produce deflections y_1 and y_2. The external work, W, done by the two loads, if both P_1 and P_2 are increased gradually from zero to full load, will be equal to the internal work, and will be

$$W = \tfrac{1}{2}P_1 \cdot y_1 + \tfrac{1}{2}P_2 \cdot y_2 \tag{5}$$

Now let P_1 be increased by a differential load dP_1, producing a further deflection of dy_1 under P_1, and dy_2 under P_2. The external work will then be

$$W + dW = \tfrac{1}{2}P_1 \cdot y_1 + P_1 \cdot dy_1 + \tfrac{1}{2}dP_1 \cdot dy_1 + \tfrac{1}{2}P_2 \cdot y_2 + P_2 \cdot dy_2 \tag{6}$$

since P_1 and P_2 act through the entire distances dy_1 and dy_2, respectively. Subtracting (5) from (6), and dropping the product of differentials

$$dW = P_1 \cdot dy_1 + P_2 \cdot dy_2 \tag{7}$$

Now if $P_1 + dP_1$ and P_2 are increased gradually from zero to full values,

$$W + dW = \tfrac{1}{2}(P_1 + dP_1)(y_1 + dy_1) + \tfrac{1}{2}P_2(y_2 + dy_2)$$

$$= \tfrac{1}{2}P_1 \cdot y_1 + \tfrac{1}{2}P_1 \cdot dy_1 + \tfrac{1}{2}dP_1 \cdot y_1 + \tfrac{1}{2}dP_1 \cdot dy_1 + \tfrac{1}{2}P_2 \cdot y_2 + \tfrac{1}{2}P_2 \cdot dy_2 \tag{8}$$

Subtracting (5) from (8), and dropping products of differentials,

$$dW = \tfrac{1}{2}P_1 \cdot dy_1 + \tfrac{1}{2}dP_1 \cdot y_1 + \tfrac{1}{2}P_2 \cdot dy_2 \tag{9}$$

Now multiply (9) by 2, and subtract from (7), and

$$dW = dP_1 \cdot y_1,$$

and

$$\frac{dW}{dP_1} = y_1 \tag{10}$$

which is Castigliano's first theorem.

Castigliano's first theorem then is, "*The derivative of the total internal work, W, with respect to any one load, or external force, P_1, is equal to the displacement, y_1, in the direction of this load, P_1.*"

Castigliano's second theorem is "*The derivative of the work, W, due to any load, P_1, with respect to the displacement, y_1, in the direction of P_1, is equal to the load, P_1.*"

This can be proved from equation (7) by making P_2 equal zero, then

$$\frac{dW}{dy_1} = P_1 \tag{11}$$

The second theorem of Castigliano is of little use, the first theorem being the more important one.

Application to a Framed Structure.—Now let S_1, S_2, S_3, etc.; A_1, A_2, A_3, etc., and L_1, L_2, L_3, etc., be the stresses, sectional areas, and the lengths of the members of a framed structure , Fig. 1, Chapter XVI, when carrying a load; and let

$$\frac{L_1}{A_1 \cdot E} = B_1; \qquad \frac{L_2}{A_2 \cdot E} = B_2; \qquad \frac{L_3}{A_3 \cdot E} = B_3, \text{ etc.}$$

Then the work of deformation omitting member L_1, will be

$$W = \tfrac{1}{2}S_2^2 \cdot B_2 + \tfrac{1}{2}S_3^2 \cdot B_3 + \text{etc.} \tag{12}$$

Differentiating (12) with reference to S_1, and

$$\frac{dW}{dS_1} = B_2 \cdot S_2 \left(\frac{dS_2}{dS_1}\right) + B_3 \cdot S_3 \left(\frac{dS_3}{dS_1}\right) + \text{etc.}$$

$$= \Sigma B \cdot S \left(\frac{dS}{dS_1}\right) = y_1 \tag{13}$$

where y_1 = deformation of the structure in line with member L_1(3-c).

Now $dS/dS_1 = U$ = the ratio of the change in S as S_1 changes, and equation (13) is identical with equation (3).

Work in Beams.*—The work or resilence in a beam is given in Applied Mechanics as

$$W = \int_0^s \frac{M^2 \cdot ds}{2E \cdot I} \tag{14a}$$

where the integration is over the entire length of the beam. To calculate the deformation at any point in the beam differentiate the work in (14a) with reference to a load acting at the given point in the beam and in the direction in which the deflection is to be measured, and

*For the derivation of formula (14a), see page 264 .

$$\frac{dW}{dP} = \Delta_1 = \int_0^s \frac{M \cdot \frac{dM}{dP} \cdot ds}{E \cdot I} \tag{14b}$$

But $dM/dP = m$, the moment due to a load unity acting in place of P, and we have the familiar formula for deflection at any point in a beam

$$\Delta_1 = \int_0^s \frac{M \cdot m \cdot ds}{E \cdot I} \tag{14c}$$

Least Work.—If the horizontal tie of the two-hinged arch in Fig. I, Chapter XVI, is cut just to the right of the left hinge, and the parts of the cut tie be held in place by applying two stresses equal to S_1 acting away from the cut section, and the deflection of the structure be calculated by equation (13), the condition that the cut ends shall remain in contact, or that the deformation of the cut ends shall be zero, is that the derivative of the total work of deformation of the structure, including the redundant member, with reference to the stress, S_1, in the redundant member shall be zero, or that

$$\frac{dW}{dS_1} = 0 \tag{15}$$

Equation (15) is equivalent to the assumption that the deformation of any structure in line with the redundant member is equal to the deformation of the redundant member. Equation (15) shows that in any framework in static equilibrium and having a redundant member the stresses will be so distributed as to make the work of deformation a minimum, and is the Theorem of Least Work.

In calculating the stresses in statically indeterminate members by the Work Equation (13), the work of deformation of the primary structure, not including the redundant member, is differentiated with reference to the stress in the redundant member and the resulting deformation is placed equal to the deformation of the redundant member. With the Work Equation (15), the total work of deformation, including the redundant member, is differentiated with reference to the stress in the redundant member and the result is placed equal to zero.

Problems.—For the calculation of the stresses in statically indeterminate framed structures by the Method of Work, see Chapters XVI, XXI and XXII.

WILLIOT DEFORMATION DIAGRAM.—When the deformation of the members have been calculated the relative movements of all the joints of the structure may be calculated by a graphic diagram. In (*a*) Fig. 3, the point c is connected with points a and b by lines 1 and 2, respectively, which undergo changes $-\Delta_1$ and $+\Delta_2$, respectively, while the points a and b move to new positions a' and b', respectively. It is required to find the new position of the point c. Now if point a moves to point a', point c will move to point c_1; while if point b moves to point b', point c will move to c_2. Now line 1 will be increased in length by Δ_1, and line 2 will be decreased in length by Δ_2. The final location of point c will be at c' which will be at the intersection of arcs drawn with centers a' and b', and radii equal to the new lengths of the lines 1 and 2, respectively. Since the deformations are very small as compared with the lengths of the members, the new location of point c at the point c' may be found by erecting perpendiculars at the ends of Δ_1 and Δ_2. The construction may be accomplished without drawing members 1 and 2, as in (*b*) Fig. 3. At point *c* in (*b*) lay off *c–a′* equal and parallel to *a–a′* in (*a*), and also *c–b′* equal and parallel to *b–b′* in (*a*). From *a′* in (*b*) lay

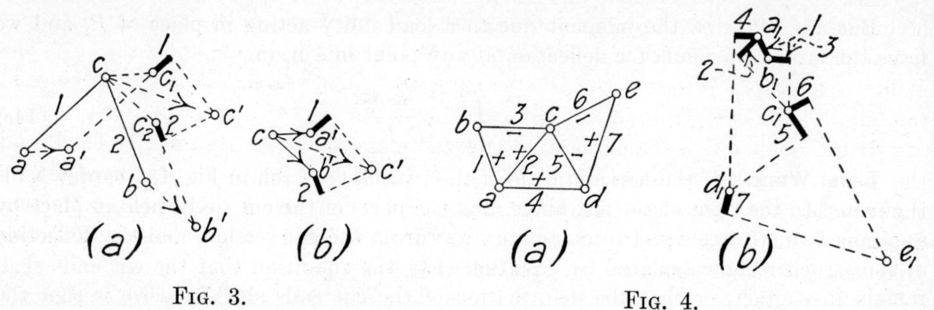

FIG. 3. FIG. 4.

off Δ_1 away from *a′*, in (*a*) and from *b′* lay off Δ_2, toward *b′* in (*a*). The new location of *c* at the point *c′* will then be found by erecting perpendiculars at the ends of the deformations Δ_1 and Δ_2.

With reference to signs, in Fig. 3, $-\Delta_1$ is a lengthening, and is therefore due to tension, and is called minus, while Δ_2 is a shortening, and is therefore due to compression and is called plus. In laying off the deformations in the diagram if *c* remains fixed, a tensile stress, and therefore a minus deformation requires that point *a′* will move away from *a*, and a minus deformation should therefore be laid off on the side of the point on which the member occurs, while a plus deformation should be laid off on the side of the point opposite the side on which the member occurs. The diagram will be properly drawn if the following rule is observed in laying off the deformations: "Lay off minus deformations, tension deformations, so as to cause apparent shortening of the member, and lay off plus deformations so as to cause apparent lengthening of the member."

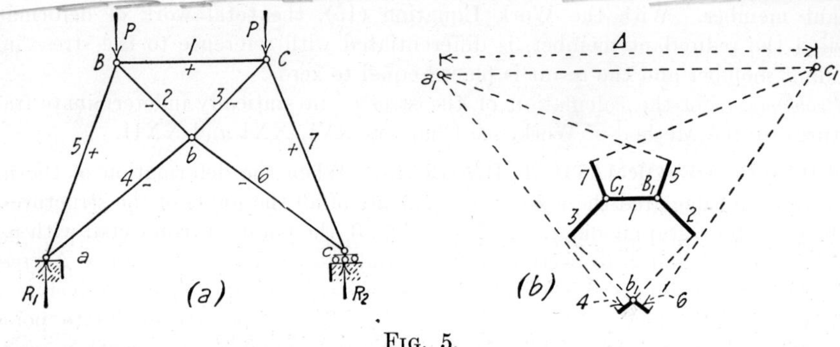

FIG. 5.

The assumption of minus for tensile stresses and plus for compressive stresses is therefore more consistent than the opposite assumption, which is made by some writers.

A Williot diagram is constructed in (*b*), for the truss shown in (*a*) Fig. 5. The member *B–C* is assumed as fixed in direction and its deformation, Δ_1 is laid off to the left of *B* and to the right of *C*, so that points B_1 and C_1 come at the right and left, respectively, of Δ_1. Deformation in member *B–b* is $-\Delta_2$, and is laid off downward from B_1, while deformation in member C–b is $-\Delta_3$, and is laid off downward from C_1. The new position of point b at b_1, will be found by erecting perpendiculars at the outer ends of Δ_2 and Δ_3. The new position of point a at a_1 is found by laying off $-\Delta_4$ at b_1 to cause apparent shortening of the member, because the deformation is minus, and by laying off Δ_5 at B_1 to cause apparent lengthening of the member, because the deformation is plus, and then erecting perpendiculars at the ends of Δ_4 and Δ_5 as shown. The Williot diagram in (*b*) gives the true relative distortions of the joints of the truss in (*a*), Fig. 5.

If the point a is assumed as fixed and the member a–b be assumed as fixed, and the Williot diagram be drawn as in (*b*), Fig. 6, the Williot diagram is distorted due to the fact that both members at point a rotate, and it is necessary to draw a correction diagram. The diagram to correct for rotation, which is called Mohr's Rotation Diagram, will now be constructed and explained.

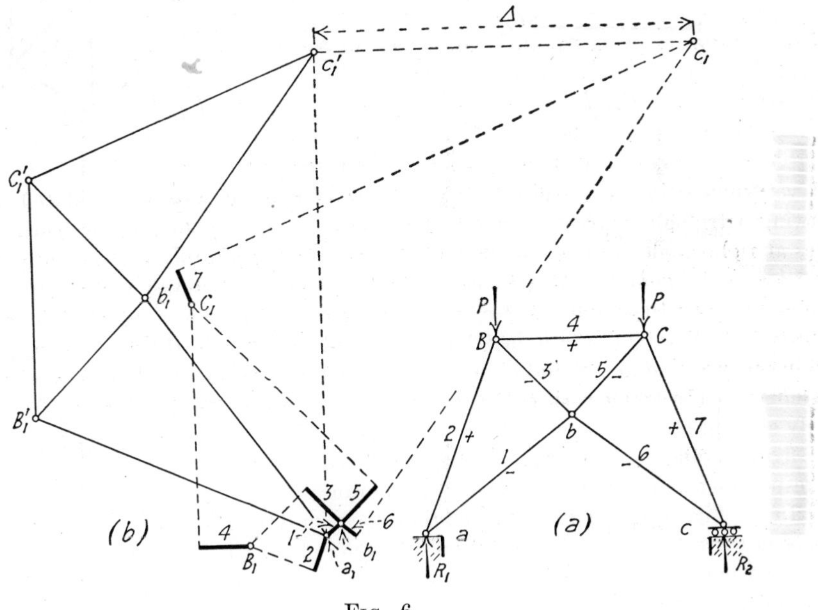

FIG. 6.

Mohr's Rotation Diagram.—In Fig. 4 the framework in (*a*) has deformations as shown and a fixed axis $a-d$. With point a assumed as a fixed point and member a–b marked 1, assumed as a fixed axis the Williot diagram is constructed as in (*b*) Fig. 4. Deformation Δ_1 is plus, and is laid off to cause apparent lengthening in member a–b, so that point b_1 will come at the lower end and point a_1 will come at the upper end of Δ_1 in (*b*). The diagram is completed in the same manner as in Fig. 5. The Williot diagram in (*b*) does not show the true changes of the different joints on account of rotation, and is necessary to construct a correction diagram.

In Fig. 7, assume that the framework in (*a*) is connected by rays with a center O. Now movement about the center O will be indicated in direction by the arrows, and the amount of the rotation will vary as the distance from the center of rotation, O. Through pole O', in (b) draw rays parallel to the arrows indicating rotation in (a). Now lay off the distance of the rotation of point e, equals $o'-e'$ (calculated in a manner

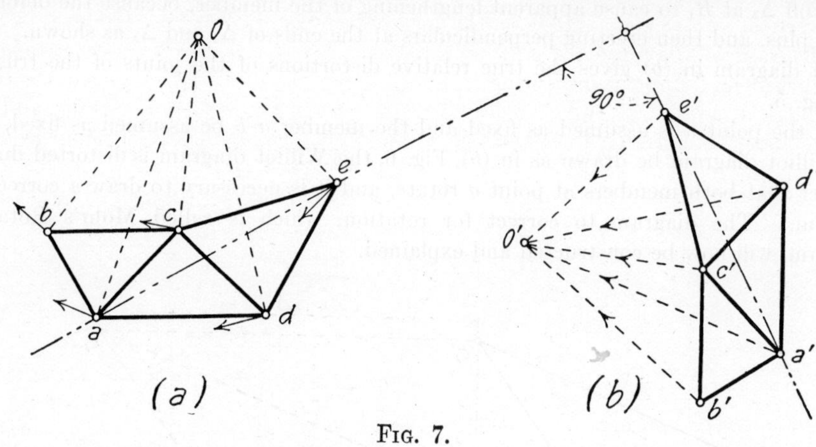

FIG. 7.

not yet known) in (b). The rotation distance of point d may be calculated in (b) by drawing a triangle $o'-e'-d'$ similar to triangle $o-e-d$ in (a), but having corresponding sides at right angles to each other, and ray $o'-d'$ is the rotation distance of point d' in direction and amount. Also to calculate the rotation distance for c, draw triangle $o'-d'-c'$, similar to triangle $o-d-c$, and having corresponding sides at right angles to each other. Points a' and b' in (b) Fig. 7 may be located in the same manner. Connecting points e', d', c', a' and b' in (b) will result in the framework $a'-b'-c'-d'-e'$ which is similar to the framework $a-b-c-d-e$ in (a), and which has similar members respectively at right angles to each other. The rotation diagram for any framework therefore is a figure similar to the original framework with its members at right angles to the corresponding members in the original framework.

In (b) Fig. 8, the Williot deformation diagram drawn for the framework in Fig. 4, has been corrected by Mohr's rotation diagram. In (a) Fig. 8, the point a is assumed as a fixed point and the line $a-d$ is assumed as the axis of rotation. The rotation diagram in (b), Fig. 8 is constructed as follows:

Through the fixed point a_1' in the Williot diagram in (b) draw a line at right angles to the axis of rotation $a-d$ in (a) Fig. 8. The true position of d' in (b) will be found by dropping a perpendicular from d_1 to d_1', on the axis of reference. Point c_1' is determined by the intersection of lines $a_1'-c_1'$ and $d_1'-c_1'$ drawn perpendicular to lines $a-c$ and $d-c$ respectively in (a). The points b_1' and e_1' in the rotation diagram are located in the same manner. The true distortions are a combination of the distortions given by the Williot diagram and the corrections given by the rotation diagram, and can be obtained by measuring the distance from a point on the rotation diagram to the corresponding point on the Williot diagram. For example in (b) Fig. 8, point d_1' moves to d_1, point c_1' moves to c_1, etc.

The Williot deformation diagram drawn in Fig. 6, may now be corrected by means of Mohr's rotation diagram. The Williot diagram in Fig. 6, was drawn, assuming that a is a fixed point. The abutments of the truss are fixed and the axis of rotation will be a line a–c through the hinges of the truss. The Williot diagram is drawn by taking the deformations of the members 1, 2, 3, etc., drawing perpendiculars as shown. The rotation diagram is drawn as follows: Through point a_1 in the Williot diagram draw a vertical line at right angles to the horizontal axis of rotation. Point c_1 of the Williot diagram will be projected on the line of reference at c_1', and the true movement of point c will be found by measuring from c_1' to c_1. To locate b_1' draw intersecting lines through a_1 and c_1' at right angles to members a–b and c–b, respectively, and to locate B_1' draw intersecting lines through a_1 and b_1' at right angles to members a–B

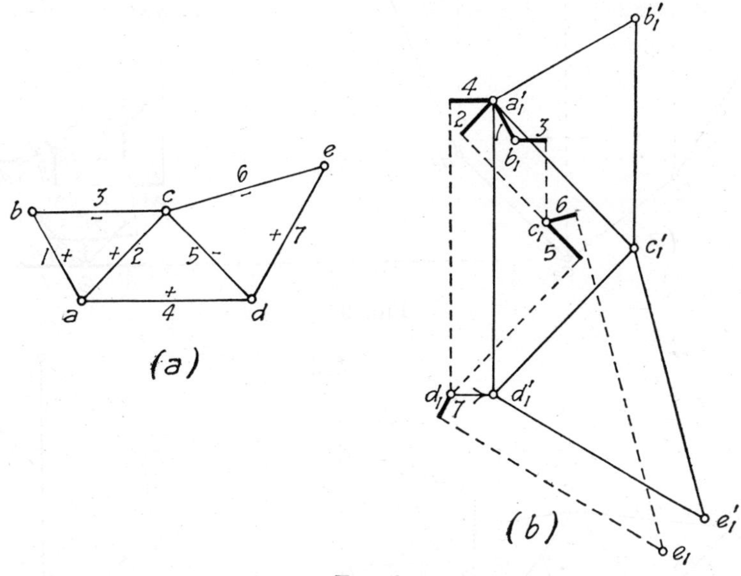

FIG. 8.

and b–B, respectively. The total distortion of point b_1 will be found by measuring from the point b_1' on the rotation diagram to b_1 on the Williot diagram, and the total distortion of point B will be found by measuring from point B_1' on the rotation diagram to point B_1 on the Williot diagram. The deformation diagram for the lower chord points may be constructed by projecting the points on the rotation and Williot diagrams on verticals dropped from the corresponding chord points of the truss The vertical deflection of joint b will be the vertical projection of the line b_1–b_1'.

In Fig. 9 the truss was loaded with an unsymmetrical loading, so that the middle post c–c did not remain fixed during the deformation of the truss. In this case a is the fixed point, and the axis of rotation is horizontal. The rotation diagram was constructed on the axis a'–e' as shown. A deflection polygon for the lower chord was constructed by projecting the points on the rotation diagram and on the Williot diagram on vertical lines drawn through corresponding points. The deflection of the lower chord point b, will be the intercept b_1–b_2 on the deflection diagram in (a).

In Fig. 10, the point a was assumed as fixed and member a–B was assumed as fixed in direction. The axis of rotation is the line a–d in (a), and the line of reference is

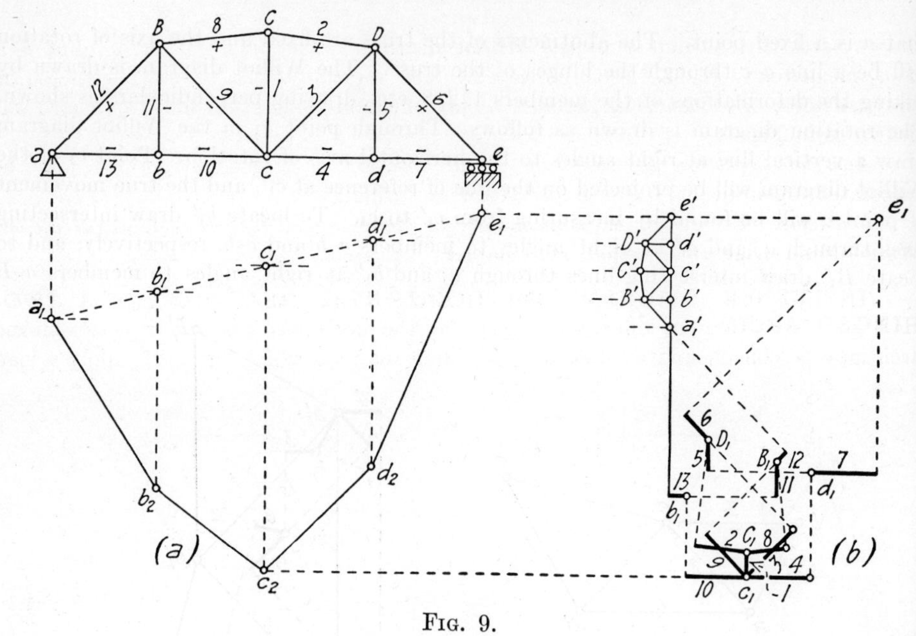

FIG. 9.

FIG. 10.

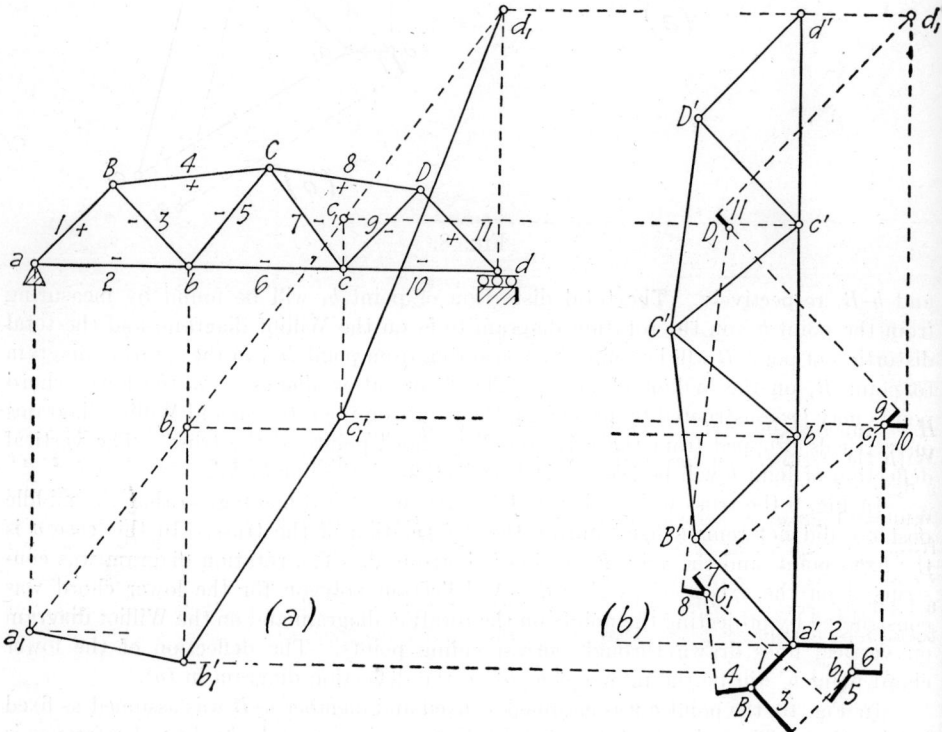

drawn vertically through a' in the Williot diagram. The deformation of joint d is $d'-d_1$ measured in the direction indicated. The rotation diagram was constructed on the base line $a'-d'$ in the usual manner. The deflection polygon for the lower chord was drawn as in Fig. 9.

Algebraic Solution for Rotation.—The rotation of framed structures may be calculated algebraically by formula (34) or by formula (42).

Problems.—For detail calculations of the deflection of framed structures by the Williot-Mohr Diagram Method, see Chapters XX and XXII.

INFLUENCE DIAGRAM FOR HORIZONTAL REACTION OF A TWO-HINGED ARCH.—An influence diagram for the horizontal reaction of a two-hinged arch may be constructed by means of a Williot diagram as in Fig. 11. Apply a load

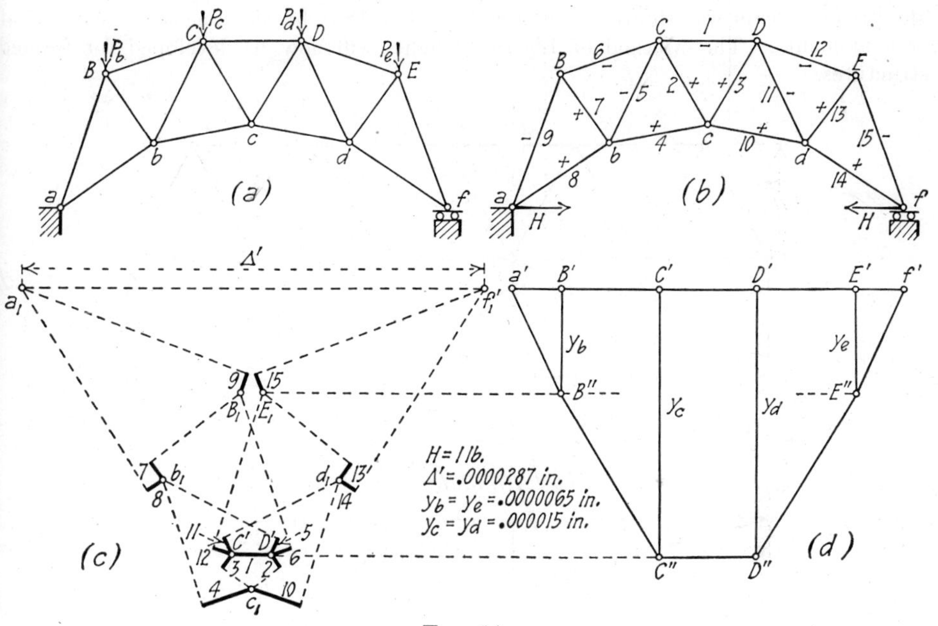

FIG. 11.

H = unity at the right reaction in (b), and calculate the U stresses in the members. With the resulting deformations construct the Williot diagram in (c). Then construct a deflection diagram for the loaded, upper, chord by projecting the points from the Williot diagram to vertical lines through corresponding points of the arch in (d). Now from Maxwell's Theorem if a load unity at f gives a deflection y_b at point B, a load P_b at B will give a deflection $P_b \cdot y_b$ at f. In like manner if the deflection at C due to a load unity at f is y_c, a load P_c will give a deflection $P_c \cdot y_c$ at f, etc. And finally the total deformation at f due to all the loads on the arch will be

$$\Delta = P_b \cdot y_b + P_c \cdot y_c + P_d \cdot y_d + P_e \cdot y_e \tag{16}$$

and the true value of the horizontal reaction will be

$$H = \frac{\Delta}{\Delta'} \tag{17}$$

The arch shown in Fig. 11 is the arch given in Chapter XX. From this problem $\Delta' = 0.0000287$ in.; $P_b = P_e = 18{,}000$ lb.; $P_c = P_d = 24{,}000$ lb.; $y_b = y_e = 0.000065$ in.; $y_c = y_d = 0.00015$ in.

Substituting in equation (16) the values of the loads and deflections, gives the deformation in line with H due to the loads, P_b, P_c, P_d and P_e, and

$$\Delta = 2(18{,}000 \times 0.000065) + 2(24{,}000 \times 0.00015) = 0.954 \text{ in.} \tag{18}$$

Solving for H by substituting values of Δ' and Δ in (17), gives

$$H = 0.954/0.0000287 = 33{,}300 \text{ lb.}$$

METHOD OF ELASTIC WEIGHTS.—The method of elastic weights when applied to a beam was shown in Chapter XIV, Fig. 18 to be the same as the method of area moments. The Method of Elastic Weights will now be developed for framed structures.

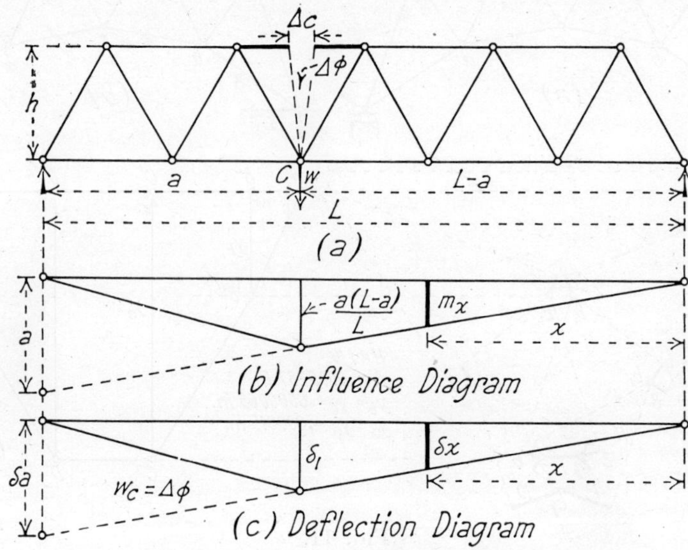

FIG. 12.

Deflections Due to Chord Members.—In the Warren truss with parallel chords in Fig. 12, it is assumed that all members of the truss are rigid except one panel of the top chord, which has a deformation Δc. Now if point c in the lower chord remains fixed in position, the left end of the truss will rise an amount δ_a which may be calculated by the proportion

$$\Delta c : h : : \delta_a : a$$

and

$$\delta_a = a \cdot \frac{\Delta c}{h} = a \cdot \Delta\phi$$
$$= a \cdot w$$

where w = the elastic weight for the point c. Now by comparing the deflection diagram in (c) with the influence diagram for moment at the point c, in (b) it will be seen that the deflection diagram is an influence diagram drawn for the elastic weight w, in place of unity. This leads to the statement of the theory of elastic weights as applied to framed structures, "The deflection of any joint in a framed structure due to the deformation of any member Δc, due to any loading is equal to the bending moment at the joint due to a load unity applied at the joint, multiplied by a quantity w = the elastic weight of the member."

This theorem may be proved as follows:

To calculate the deformation at joint c, Fig. 12, due to a deformation Δc in the upper chord member c, apply a load unity at joint c acting in line with δ_1, and the deflection of the structure at c due to the deformation of the member Δc will be from formula (2)

$$\delta_1 = \frac{U_c : S_c \cdot L_c}{A_c \cdot E}$$

But

$$\frac{S_c \cdot L_c}{A_c \cdot E} = \Delta c,$$

and

$$\delta_1 = U_c \cdot \Delta c$$

Now the stress U_c is equal to m_c/h, where m_c = bending moment at c due to a load unity,

$$m_c = \frac{a(L-a)}{L}$$

in the unit influence diagram in (b) Fig. 12, and h = depth of truss, and

$$\delta_1 = \frac{m_c \cdot \Delta c}{h}$$

$$= m_c \cdot w \tag{19}$$

The deflection δ_x at a distance x from the right end of the truss due to the deformation Δc will be

$$\delta_x = m_x \cdot w \tag{20}$$

Therefore the deformation at any joint of a framed structure due to the deformation of any member will be w times the bending moment at the joint due to a load unity applied at the center of moments used in calculating the stress in the member, and acting parallel to the line in which it is desired to measure the deformation.

The elastic weight for any chord member in a simple truss will be

$$w_c = \Delta_c / r \tag{21}$$

where Δ_c is the deformation due to external loads, temperature, or inelastic changes, and r is the moment arm that is used in calculating the stress in the member by moments. Deformations that shorten the member are plus, and deformations that lengthen the member are minus. Arms measured upward are plus and arms measured downwards are minus. The elastic weights are all positive for both the top chords and bottom chords of simple trusses.

The total deformation at any joint due to the deformations of all members in the framework will be found as follows. Load the framework with the elastic weights for all the members; construct a force polygon for the elastic weights, with a pole distance H = unity, and draw an equilibrium polygon. The equilibrium polygon will be the deflection polygon for the truss. The elastic weights are positive for both top and bottom chords in a simple truss.

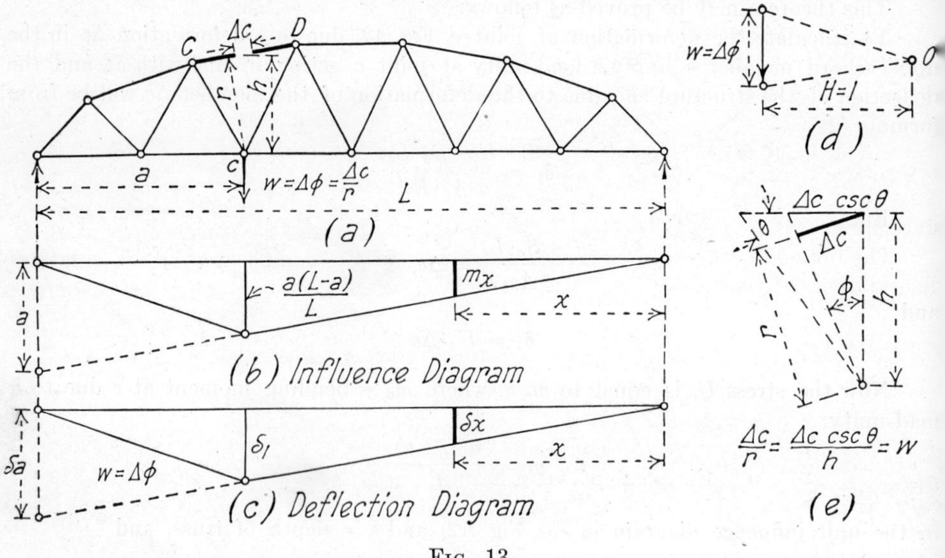

FIG. 13.

In a Warren truss with inclined chords as in Fig. 13, the elastic weight for the upper chord member will be $w_c = \Delta c/r$ and will be applied at the joint c. The deflection at any joint a distance x from the right abutment will then be $\delta_x = m_x \cdot w_c$, as for a bridge with parallel chords.

Deflections Due to Web Members.—In the Warren truss in Fig. 14, it is required to calculate the deflection at any joint due to a deformation Δd_1 in the web member c–D. Now from the definition of an elastic weight the deflection of any joint in the framework due to the deformation in any member may be calculated from the influence diagram drawn for a load $w = \Delta d_1/r$, acting through the center of moments for the member. But point O is outside the truss and the problem may be much simplified by substituting two elastic weights, w_1 acting at joint c, and w_2 acting at joint d, for the elastic weight w at O. The elastic weights w_1 and w_2 may be calculated by the condition (1) that $w = w_1 + w_2$, and (2) that the sum of the moments of w_1 and w_2 about any joint equals moment of w.

Taking moments about joint c, we have

$$w_2 \cdot l = \pm \frac{\Delta d_1 \cdot a}{r} \tag{22}$$

and

$$w_2 = \pm \frac{\Delta d_1 \cdot a}{r \cdot l}$$

$$= \pm \frac{\Delta d_1}{r_2} \qquad (23)$$

since $a/l = r/r_2$.

Taking moments about joint d, we have

$$w_1 \cdot l = \mp \frac{\Delta d_1 \cdot b}{r}$$

$$w_1 = \mp \frac{\Delta d_1 \cdot b}{r \cdot l}$$

$$= \mp \frac{\Delta d_1}{r_1} \qquad (24)$$

since $b/l = r/r_1$.

The influence diagram for maximum moment at the point O will be the influence diagram constructed as in Fig. 14, Chapter VII, and as shown in Fig. 14. The de-

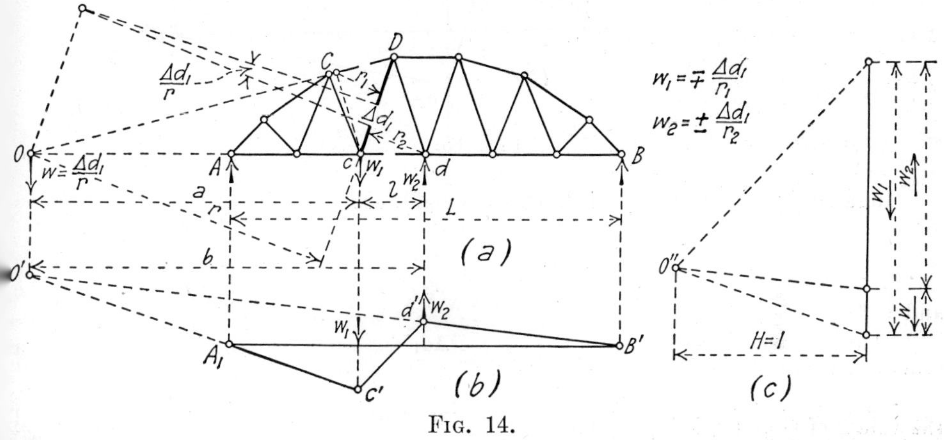

FIG. 14.

flection at any joint in the loaded chord of the truss in Fig. 14, due to the deformation Δd_1 of the web member c–D will then be the algebraic sum of the deformations due to w_1 acting at joint c, and w_2 acting at joint d, calculated as for chord deflections in Fig. 13.

The elastic weights w_1 and w_2 will have opposite signs. *The positive elastic weight will come on that side of the section or panel where the sign of* Δd_1 *is the same as the sign of the stress in the adjacent chord.* If Δd_1 in Fig. 14 is plus, w_2 will be plus and w_1 will be minus.

It has been assumed in this discussion that the lower chord is the loaded chord. If the upper chord is the loaded chord, elastic weights w_1 and w_2 should be calculated in a similar manner for the upper chord joints.

The elastic weights for both web members and chord members at any joint will be the algebraic sum of the elastic weights due to chord members and web members. The elastic weights for web members are all applied on the loaded chord. The deflection diagram for the loaded chord may then be calculated by means of a force polygon with the loads all acting paralle' to the lines of the deflections of the joints, and a pole distance H = unity, and the resulting equilibrium polygon will be the deflection polygon.

Second Solution.—The elastic weights w_1 and w_2 may be applied at the ends of the web members as shown in Fig. 15.

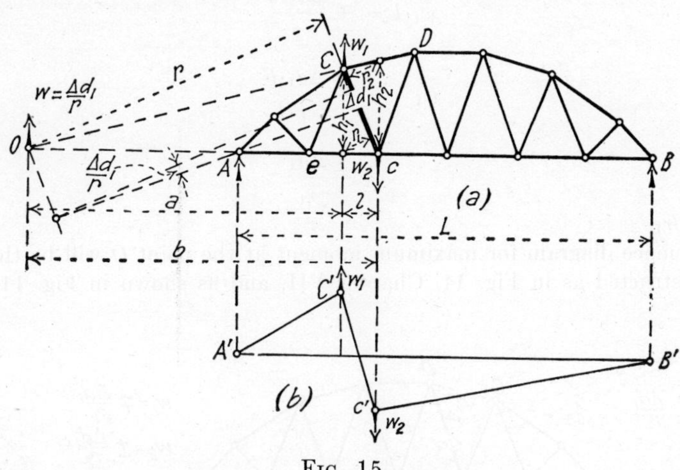

FIG. 15.

In same manner as for Fig. 14 the elastic weights are

$$w_2 = \pm \frac{\Delta d_1}{r_2} \tag{25}$$

and

$$w_1 = \pm \frac{\Delta d_1}{r_1} \tag{26}$$

the values of r_1 and r_2 being as shown in Fig. 15.

For a bridge with vertical posts formulas (23) and (25), and (24) and (26) are identical, respectively.

Deflections for Vertical Posts.—In the Pratt truss with inclined chords in Fig. 16 it is required to calculate the deflection at any joint due to a deformation Δv in the post c–C.

Now the center of moments for calculating the stress in c–C is at O, and the elastic weight $w = \Delta v/r$ will be applied at O. In order that the elastic weights for the vertical posts may be combined with the elastic weights for the chord members it will be necessary to replace elastic weight w with two elastic weights w_1 and w_2 acting at joints C in the unloaded chord and d in the loaded chord. In the same manner as for the elastic weights for web members, we have

$$w_2 \cdot l = \pm \frac{\Delta v \cdot r}{r}$$

and

$$w_2 = \pm \frac{\Delta v}{l} \tag{27}$$

also

$$w_1 \cdot l = \mp \frac{\Delta v \cdot b}{r}$$

and

$$w_1 = \mp \frac{\Delta v}{r} \cdot \frac{b}{l}$$

But

$$\frac{b}{r} = \frac{h_2}{h_1}$$

and

$$w_1 = \mp \frac{\Delta v}{l} \cdot \frac{h_2}{h_1} \tag{28}$$

For a bridge with parallel chords it will be seen that

$$w_1 = -w_2 = -\frac{\Delta v}{l} \tag{29}$$

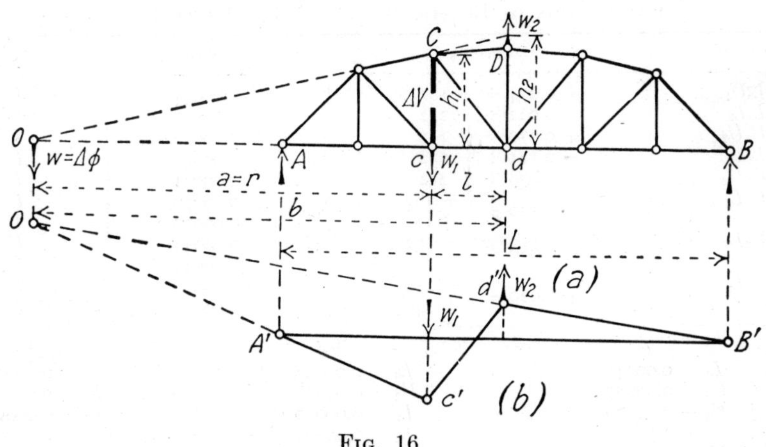

FIG. 16.

The signs of w_1 and w_2 may be obtained by the rule stated for web members. "*The positive elastic weight will come on that side of the section or panel where the sign of Δv is the same as the sign of the stress in the adjacent chord.*" In Fig. 16, Δv is plus and w_1 is minus and w_2 is plus.

Deflection of a Pratt Truss.—A Pratt truss highway bridge of 120 ft. span, for a full load has the deformations of members as shown in Fig. 17. The elastic weights are calculated as shown in Table I. The elastic weights are $w_1' = 0.00058$; $w_2' = 0.00094$; and $\frac{1}{2}w_3' = 0.00083$.

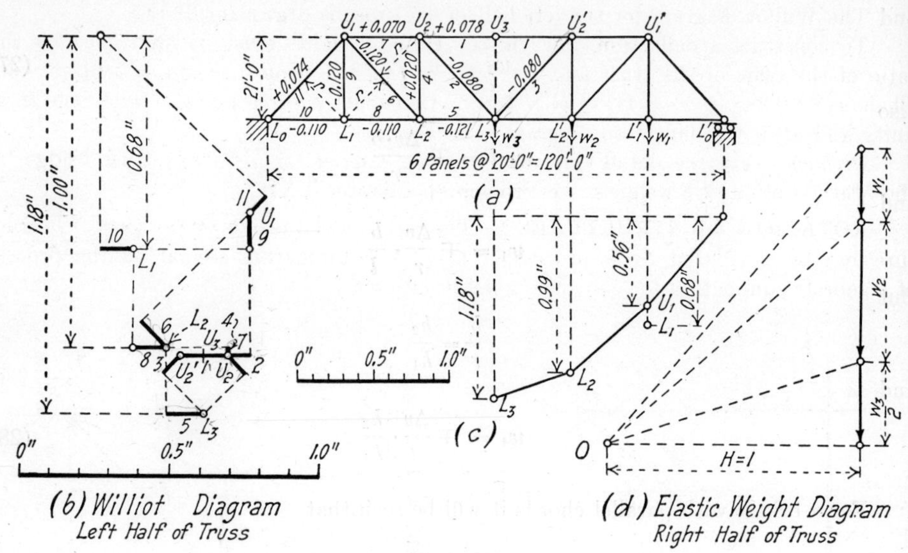

FIG. 17.

TABLE I.

CALCULATION OF ELASTIC WEIGHTS FOR A PRATT TRUSS.

Member.	Calculation.	Elastic Weight.	Point.
L_0U_1	$+0.074 \div +182$	0.00041	L_1
L_0L_2	$-0.022 \div -252$	0.00087	U_1
U_1U_2	$+0.070 \div +252$	0.00028	L_2
L_2L_3	$-0.121 \div -252$	0.00048	U_2
U_2U_3	$+0.078 \div +252$	0.00031	L_3
U_1L_2	$-0.120 \div \{+182$	-0.00070	U_1
	-182	$+0.00070$	L_2
U_2L_3	$-0.080 \div \{+182$	-0.00044	U_2
	-182	$+0.00044$	L_3
U_2L_2	$+0.020 \div \{-240$	-0.00008	L_2
	$+240$	$+0.00008$	L_3

w_1'	w_2'	$\frac{1}{2}w_3'$
L_1 0.00041	L_2 0.00028	L_3 0.00031
U_1 0.00087	U_2 0.00048	L_3 0.00044
$U_1 -$ 0.00070	L_2 0.00070	L_3 0.00008
	$L_2 -$ 0.00008	
$L_1 + U_1 = 0.00058$	$U_2 -$ 0.00044	$L_3 = 0.00083$
	$L_2 + U_2 = 0.00094$	

Scale of Truss 240" = 1" Scale of Polygon 2" = 1"

$$w_1 = w_1' \times 480 = 0.00058 \times 480 = 0.28$$
$$w_2 = w_2' \times 480 = 0.00094 \times 480 = 0.44$$
$$\tfrac{1}{2}w_3 = \tfrac{1}{2}w_3' \times 480 = 0.00083 \times 480 = 0.40$$

The deflections may be calculated as follows.—The left reaction is $R_1 = 0.00058 + 0.00094 + 0.00083 = 0.00235$. Deflection at $L_1 = 0.00235 \times 240 + 0.12 = 0.68$ in.

Deflection at $L_2 = 0.00235 \times 2 \times 240 - 0.00058 \times 240 = 0.99$ in. Deflection at $L_3 = 0.00235 \times 3 \times 240 - 0.00058 \times 2 \times 240 - 0.00094 \times 240 = 1.18$ in.

The Williot diagram for the left half of the truss is drawn in (*b*) Fig. 17.

To construct a deflection diagram the elastic weights must be multiplied by the ratio of the scale of the truss and the scale of the deflection diagram $= 240/\frac{1}{2} = 480$. Then $w_1 = 0.28$; $w_2 = 0.44$; $\frac{1}{2}w_3 = 0.40$. Construct a force polygon with pole $H =$ unity and draw the deflection diagram as in Fig. 17.

Problem.—For the detail calculation of the camber for a railway truss bridge by the Method of Elastic weights, see Problem 9, Chapter XXII.

ROTATION OF STRUCTURES.*—The rotation of the axis of any part of a structure may be calculated by a process of algebraic summation similar to the process of algebraic summation for calculating deformations.

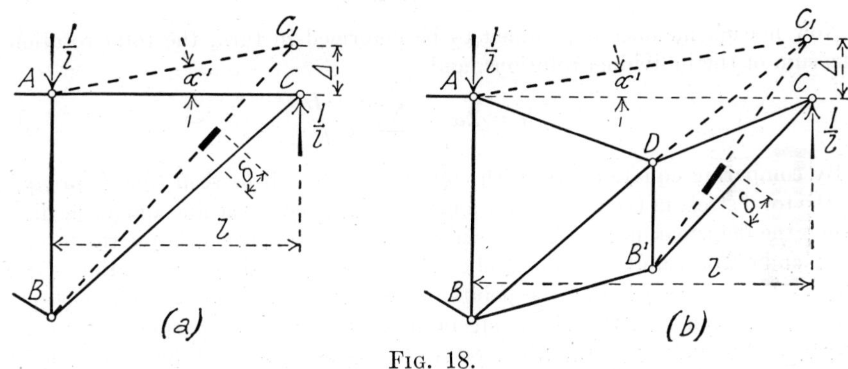

FIG. 18.

Framed Structures.—In Fig. 18 it is required to calculate the rotation about the point A of the member AC in (*a*) or the line joining the points A and C in (*b*). Apply a unit moment at A. This unit moment is applied by means of a couple with forces $1/l$ acting at A and C, and in the direction that the rotation is to be measured. The arm of the couple will then be l, and the moment will be unity.

Now assume that all members of the framework are rigid except member BC in (*a*) or $B'C$ in (*b*), which is deformed an amount δ. Assume that the deformation of the framework at C due to the change in length of BC or $B'C$ is Δ.

Now let P be the external moment due to forces P/l acting in place of $1/l$ that will remove deformations Δ and δ. Then the external work, if P/l is gradually applied, will be

$$W = \tfrac{1}{2}P \cdot \Delta/l$$

But $\Delta = l \cdot \alpha'$, and

$$W = \tfrac{1}{2}P \cdot \alpha' \tag{30}$$

The internal work in removing the deformation δ, will be

*This principle as applied to framed structures was first used by Mohr in his solution of secondary stresses in 1892, see Grimm's "Secondary Stresses," 1908. The use of this principle has been elaborated and extended by Professor George F. Swain in a paper in Proceedings, Am. Soc. C. E. Vol. XLV, March, 1919. This discussion follows Professor Swain's article, which should be consulted for further applications.

$$W = \tfrac{1}{2}P \cdot r \cdot \delta \tag{31}$$

where r = stress in member BC or $B'C$ due to a unit moment acting on the framework (the forces $1/l$ are applied at A and C).

Now the external work is equal to the internal work, and equating equations (30) and (31), there results

$$\alpha' = r \cdot \delta \tag{32}$$

Now the deformation of the member BC or $B'C$ due to any external loading will be $\delta = (S \cdot L)/(A \cdot E)$, where S = total stress in the member, A = area of the cross-section of the member, L = length of the member, and E = modulus of elasticity of the material in lb. per sq. in., and

$$\alpha' = \frac{S \cdot r \cdot L}{A \cdot E} \tag{33}$$

Now if each member is assumed to be deformed in turn, the total rotation will be the sum of the individual rotations, and

$$\alpha = \Sigma\alpha' = \sum \frac{S \cdot r \cdot L}{A \cdot E} \tag{34}$$

By comparing equation (34) with equation (3) it will be seen that U in equation (3) is the total stress in the member for a unit load applied in the line and in the direction in which the deformation is to be measured; while r in equation (34) is the total stress in the member for a unit moment applied at the point about which rotation is desired, the forces $1/l$ being applied at the points between which rotation is to be measured.

It will be seen that this is the algebraic solution of the rotation problem that is solved by a combination of the Mohr rotation diagram and the Williot diagram.

Beams.—The formula for calculating the change in slope of a member stressed in flexure may be calculated by substituting da for A, and dl for L in formula (33). The differential change in slope at the point A in a beam AB will be

$$d\alpha = \frac{S \cdot r \cdot dl}{da \cdot E} \tag{35}$$

The stress S due to an external loading will be

$$S = \frac{M_s \cdot y \cdot da}{I} \tag{36}$$

since the stress S is on a differential area. While the stress due to the unit moment will be

$$r = \frac{M_r \cdot y \cdot da}{I} \tag{37}$$

Substituting the value of S in (36) and r in (37) in (35), we have

$$d\alpha = \frac{M_s \cdot M_r \cdot y^2 \cdot dl \cdot da}{E \cdot I^2} \tag{38}$$

The differential slope in (38) must be integrated over the cross-section and over he length l. If the member is of constant cross-section, the integration over the area will be $\Sigma(y^2 \cdot da) = I$. Integrating from 0 to l equation (38) becomes

$$\alpha = \int_0^l \frac{M_s \cdot M_r \cdot dl}{E \cdot I} \tag{39}$$

Formula (39) differs from the formula for deflection in a beam

$$\Delta = \int_0^l \frac{M_s \cdot m \cdot dl}{E \cdot I} \tag{40}$$

n that M_r is the moment at any point due to unit moment applied at the points in the beam between which the rotation is to be measured, and m is the moment at any point due to a unit load applied at the point at which the deflection of the beam is to be calculated, and acting in the direction that the deflection is to be measured. It should be noted that rotation in (39) is about a point at one end of the integration. In a rigid frame, a structure consisting of several beams, the rotation about a point will be

$$\alpha = \sum \int_0^l \frac{M_s \cdot M_r \cdot dl}{E \cdot I} \tag{41}$$

Framework with Bending and Direct Stress.—In a structure in which the members have direct stress, or flexure, or both, the change in slope about a fixed point will be found by combining the values of the slope calculated by equation (34) and equation (39), and

$$\alpha = \sum \frac{S \cdot r \cdot L}{A \cdot E} + \sum \int_0^l \frac{M_s \cdot M_r \cdot dl}{E \cdot I} \tag{42}$$

From equation (42) it will be seen that:

(1) If in any member, either the external load, or the applied moment, $M_r = 1$, cause a direct stress only, and the other a flexural stress only, the value of α for that member will be zero.

(2) The flexure in any member may be neglected unless both the external loads and the applied moment, $M_r = 1$, cause flexural stress in it.

(3) The direct stress in any member may be neglected unless both the external loads and the applied moment, $M_r = 1$, cause a direct stress in it.

Problem.—Required the slope at the loaded end of a cantilever beam with a span l, carrying a load P at the end. The load P produces a moment at any section a distance x from the end, $M_s = P \cdot x$. The applied couple $M_r = 1$, at the free end, produces a negative moment, $M_r = -1$, at any point. Substituting in equation (39)

$$\alpha = -\int_0^l \frac{M_s \cdot M_r \cdot dl}{E \cdot I} = -\int_0^l \frac{P \cdot x \cdot dl}{E \cdot I} = -\frac{P \cdot l^2}{2E \cdot I} \tag{43}$$

WORK OF FLEXURE.—Let Fig. 19 be a portion of a beam which is in flexure under the action of an external load or loads, and has a bending moment M at the

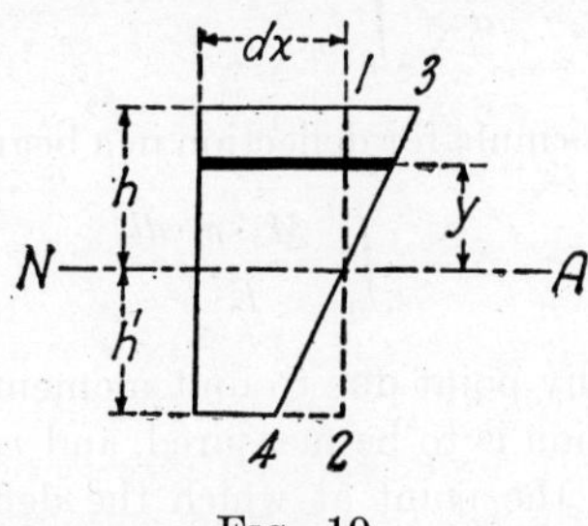

FIG. 19

section *1–2*. Then the stress in any fiber at a distance y from the neutral axis NA is $S' = \frac{M \cdot y}{I}$; and the deformation of any differential length dx at a distance y from the neutral axis NA will be

$$d\Delta = \frac{S'}{E} dx = \frac{M}{E \cdot I} y \cdot dx \tag{44}$$

where E is the modulus of elasticity of the material composing the beam, and I is the moment of inertia of the section *1–2* about the neutral axis NA. Then the deformation of a fiber of length dx at the outer fiber will be

$$d\Delta' = \frac{M}{E \cdot I} h \cdot dx \tag{45}$$

If z is the breadth of the beam at a distance y from NA, then the stress on a differential area dA of the fiber at a distance y from NA will be

$$S = \frac{M}{I} z \cdot y \cdot dy \tag{46}$$

and the work of resistance of the differential fiber will be $\frac{1}{2} S \cdot d\Delta$, and

$$dw = \frac{1}{2} \frac{M}{E \cdot I} y \cdot dx \times \frac{M}{I} z \cdot y \cdot dy \tag{47}$$

Integrating (47) between the limits $+h$ and $-h'$, the work of resistance on the length of beam dx, is

$$dW = \frac{1}{2} \frac{M^2}{E \cdot I^2} dx \int_{-h'}^{+h} z \cdot y^2 \cdot dy \tag{48}$$

Now

$$\int_{-h'}^{+h} z \cdot y^2 \cdot dy = I, \text{ and } dW = \frac{1}{2} \frac{M^2}{E \cdot I} dx \tag{49}$$

The total work of resistance in a beam with a length l will be

$$W = \int_0^l \frac{M^2}{2E \cdot I} dx \tag{50}$$

CHAPTER XVI.

Stresses in Statically Indeterminate Structures.

Introduction.—In simple structures the reactions and the internal stresses may be calculated by the static condition equations for translation, Σ horizontal components of forces equal zero, Σ vertical components of forces equal zero, and Σ lateral forces equal zero; and the equation for rotation, Σ moments of forces about any point equal zero. By projecting the forces on a vertical and a horizontal plane, the condition equations for coplanar forces may be applied to the components in each plane. The problem is commonly simplified by having all internal and external forces in one plane, usually a vertical plane.

A statically indeterminate structure is one in which the above conditions for static equilibrium do not give sufficient equations to determine the unknown external forces, or the unknown internal stresses, or both. Structures may be statically indeterminate externally, or internally, or both externally and internally. A continuous beam is statically indeterminate externally; a two-hinged arch with a horizontal tie is statically indeterminate internally; while a two-hinged arch with fixed abutments may be considered to have a statically indeterminate horizontal reaction, or a member may be considered as a tie and the primary structure is a statically determinate three-hinged arch, and the two-hinged arch is statically indeterminate internally. The stresses in statically indeterminate structures depend upon the rigidity of the members, or the reactions, or of both the members and the reactions; and it is therefore necessary to know the exact sizes and dimensions of the members before the stresses can be calculated.

If a structure is acted upon by an external force which produces stresses in the structure, the structure will deflect under the load, and the stresses in the members will cause the compression members to shorten and the tension members to lengthen. The external work will be equal to one-half the product of the load and the deflection of the structure under the load—it is assumed that the external load has been gradually applied, if the load were suddenly applied the work would be equal to the product of the force and the deflection, which would double the stresses due to a load gradually applied and would cause the structure to vibrate until it came to rest under the conditions first assumed, providing the stresses in the structure have not exceeded the elastic limit of the material. The internal work in the structure will be equal to the sum of one-half the stress in each member multiplied by the deformation of the member due to the stress. Now, since the structure simply stores up the energy due to the application of the external loads, the work of the external loads must be equal to the work of the internal stresses. A fourth condition for equilibrium of a structure then is, that the work of the external forces is equal to the work of the internal stresses.

The additional conditions required to calculate the stresses in statically indeterminate structures may be derived either from the condition (1) that the external work done by the external forces on any structure in elastic equilibrium must be equal to the internal work done by the internal stresses acting on the internal members, or (2) that the deformation of any structure in line with a redundant member is equal to the deformation of the redundant member. The work equation and the deformation equation both depend upon the law of conservation of energy. They are not independent, for each method will follow from the other. In the calculation of the stresses in statically indeterminate structures of any type, the first step is to remove all the redundant members or redundant reactions, leaving a statically determinate structure, called the primary structure. Second, calculate the stresses, S' in each member due to the external loads acting on the primary structure. Third, by applying the conditions of equal work or of equal deformations to each redundant member or each redundant reaction, in turn, there will be formed as many equations as there are redundant conditions; the simultaneous solutions of these equations will give the values of all redundant stresses and reactions. The final stress in any member will then be the stress in the member due to the external loads acting on the primary structure, plus the stress in the member due to each redundant member or reaction acting as a load, considered in turn. If U_1 is the stress in the member due to a unit load acting in line with the redundant member having a final stress S_1; if U_2 is the stress in the member due to a unit load acting in line with the redundant member having a final stress S_2; etc.; then the final stress in the member will be

$$S = S' + S_1 \cdot U_1 + S_2 \cdot U_2 + \text{etc.}$$

In all cases it is assumed (1) that the structure is perfectly elastic, or if not, its condition will be known, and (2) that the deformations are relatively small so that the form of the structure is not materially changed by the elastic changes.

In a statically indeterminate structure the stresses for any loading will be such that the internal work of deformation will be a minimum, as was proved in Chapter XV. There are therefore three general methods for the calculation of stresses in statically indeterminate structures, (1) the Method of Equal Work, (2) the Method of Least Work, and (3) the Method of Equal Deformations.

Method of Equal Deformations.—The principle of the method of equal deformations is; *The deformation of any structure in line with any redundant member is equal to the deformation of the redundant member.* The Method of Equal Deformations is the most easily understood, and it has the added advantage that the deformations may be calculated by work equations, by area moments, by elastic weights, by the Williot diagram, by algebraic summation, or by a combination of these methods.

STRESSES IN A FRAMEWORK WITH ONE REDUNDANT MEMBER.

Method of Algebraic Summation.—The framework in (*a*), Fig. 1 is a two-hinged arch with a horizontal tie, one end being fixed and the other end resting on frictionless rollers. The stress in the tie 3–*c* will depend upon the rigidity of the triangular truss and of the tie, the deformation of the tie 3–*c* being equal to the horizontal deformation of the arch. The arch carries a load W, which produces vertical reactions R_1 and R_2, which are statically determinate.

In (*b*), Fig. 1, assume that the tie 3–*c* is replaced by the horizontal stress, S_1, acting in place of the tie. Assume that all members of the framework are rigid except member 1–3, which is increased in length, δ, under the action of the load, W, and that the right end of the arch moves a distance Δ to the right. Let s be the horizontal force necessary to bring the right reaction back to its original position. Now, the internal work in the member 1–3 will be $\frac{1}{2}s \cdot U \cdot \delta$, where U is the stress in 1–3 due to a stress S_1 = unity, and the external work in bringing the right abutment back to its original position is $\frac{1}{2}s \cdot \Delta$. Now, since the internal work is equal to the external work

$$\Delta = U \cdot \delta \tag{1}$$

But $\delta = \dfrac{S_{1-3} \cdot L}{A \cdot E}$, where L = length of the member in inches, A = area of the cross-section of the member in square inches, E = modulus of elasticity of member in pounds

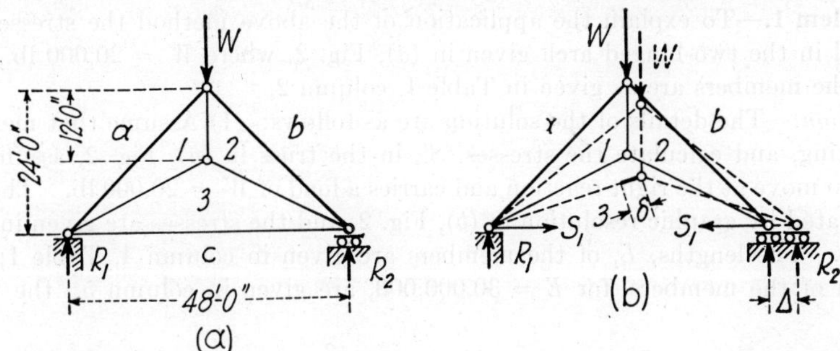

FIG. 1.

per square inch, and S_{1-3} = stress in member 1–3 due to load W, and substituting in (1)

$$\Delta = \frac{S_{1-3} \cdot U \cdot L}{A \cdot E} \tag{2}$$

Now, if all the members in turn are assumed to carry stress, the deformation of the right end of the truss will be

$$\Delta_1 = \sum \frac{S \cdot U \cdot L}{A \cdot E} \tag{3}$$

Now, if $s \cdot U$ is the stress in member 1–3 due to the stress s acting in line with S_1 at the right hinge, then in the same manner as above

$$\Delta = U \cdot \delta \tag{1}$$

and since

$$\delta = \frac{s \cdot U \cdot L}{A \cdot E}$$

$$\Delta = \frac{s \cdot U^2 \cdot L}{A \cdot E} \tag{4}$$

Now, if all the members in turn are assumed to carry stress, the right end of the truss will be brought back a distance

$$\Delta' = \sum \frac{s \cdot U^2 \cdot L}{A \cdot E} \tag{5}$$

Now $\Sigma s = S_1$, and

$$\Delta' = S_1 \sum \frac{U^2 \cdot L}{A \cdot E} \tag{6}$$

Now the deformation of the tie 3–c is $\Delta'' = (S_1 \cdot l)/(A_1 \cdot E)$, where l = length of 3–c. Then since the deformation of the tie = deformation of right end of truss, $\Delta_1 = \Delta' + \Delta''$, and

$$S_1 = \frac{\sum \frac{S \cdot U \cdot L}{A \cdot E}}{\sum \frac{U^2 \cdot L}{A \cdot E} + \frac{l}{A_1 \cdot E}} \tag{7}$$

Problem 1.—To explain the application of the above method the stresses will be calculated in the two-hinged arch given in (a), Fig. 2, where W = 20,000 lb., and the areas of the members are as given in Table I, column 2.

Solution.—The details of the solution are as follows: (1) Assume that member 3–c is not acting, and calculate the stresses, S', in the truss in (a), Fig. 2, assuming that it is free to move at the right reaction and carries a load of W = 20,000 lb. The stresses are calculated by graphic resolution in (b), Fig. 2, and the stresses are given in Table I, column 3. The lengths, L, of the members are given in column 4, Table I; the deformation of the members, for E = 30,000,000, are given in column 5; the values of

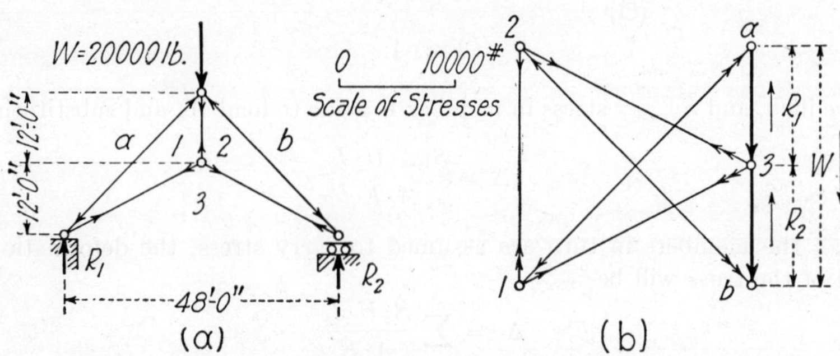

FIG. 2.

U—calculated as will be explained presently—are given in column 6; and the values of $(S' \cdot U \cdot L)/(A \cdot E)$ are given in column 7. The total horizontal deformation of the truss under the load W, is 1.142 in.

TABLE I.

DEFORMATION OF SIMPLE TRUSS FOR W = 20,000 LB.

1	2	3	4	5	6	7
Member.	Area, A, Sq. In.	Stress, S', Lb.	Length, L, In.	$\frac{S' \cdot L}{A \cdot E}$.	U	$\frac{S' \cdot U \cdot L}{A \cdot E}$.
a–1	2.00	+ 28,000	400	+ 0.187	− 1.42	− 0.266
1–3	2.00	− 22,000	320	− 0.117	+ 2.20	− 0.257
1–2	2.00	− 20,000	144	− 0.048	+ 2.00	− 0.096
2–b	2.00	+ 28,000	400	+ 0.187	− 1.42	− 0.266
2–3	2.00	− 22,000	320	− 0.117	+ 2.20	− 0.257
						$\Sigma \frac{S' \cdot U \cdot L}{A \cdot E}$ = − 1.142 in.

(2) The stresses in the framework due to stress S_1 = unity, are then calculated. It was not convenient to use a unit load and a stress of $S_1 = 10{,}000$ lb. was taken, and the stresses U in each member were then equal to the calculated stresses divided by 10,000. The stresses in the members due to $S_1 = 10{,}000$ lb. are called S''. The stresses

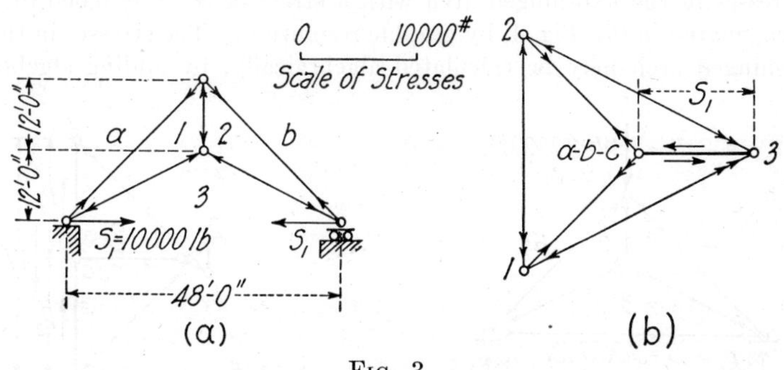

Fig. 3.

S'' for each member are calculated in (*b*), Fig. 3, by graphic resolution, and are given in column 3, Table II. The stress (U) in each member due to a stress of unity in the horizontal tie are equal to stress S'' divided by 10,000 and are given in column 6. The deformation of the framework for $S_1 = 10{,}000$ lb. is 0.880 in. The deformation of the tie 3–*c* for a stress of 10,000 lb. will be 0.384 in.

TABLE II.

Deformation of Simple Truss for $S_1 = 10{,}000$ Lb.

1	2	3	4	5	6	7
Member.	Area, A, Sq. In.	Stress, S'', Lb.	Length, L, In.	$\frac{U \cdot L}{A \cdot E} \times 10{,}000$.	U	$\frac{U^2 \cdot L}{A \cdot E} \times 10{,}000$.
a–1	2.00	− 14,200	400	− 0.095	− 1.42	0.135
1–3	2.00	+ 22,000	320	+ 0.117	+ 2.20	0.257
1–2	2.00	+ 20,000	144	+ 0.048	+ 2.00	0.096
2–*b*	2.00	− 14,200	400	− 0.095	− 1.42	0.135
2–3	2.00	+ 22,000	320	+ 0.117	+ 2.20	0.257
				$\Sigma \frac{U^2 \cdot L}{A \cdot E} \times 10{,}000 = 0.880$ in.		
3–*c*	0.50	− 10,000	576	− 0.384	− 1.00	0.384

$$S_1 = \frac{-1.142}{\frac{0.880}{10{,}000} + \frac{0.384}{10{,}000}}. \qquad S_1 = -9{,}060 \text{ lb.}$$

(3) Now the deformation of the framework will be equal to the deformation of the tie. The total deformation will be equal to deformation of the tie for a stress of one lb., plus the deformation of the framework for a stress of one lb., both multiplied by the true stress in the tie; and from equation (7) the true stress will be equal to the deformation of the framework divided by the sum of the deformation of the framework and tie for a force of one lb., and

$$S_1 = \frac{-1.142}{\frac{0.880}{10,000} + \frac{0.384}{10,000}} = -9,060 \text{ lb.} \tag{8}$$

The stresses in the two-hinged arch with a stress of $S_1 = -9,060$ lb. in the tie, have been calculated in (*b*), Fig. 4, by graphic resolution. The stresses in the members of the two-hinged arch may be calculated algebraically, by adding algebraically the

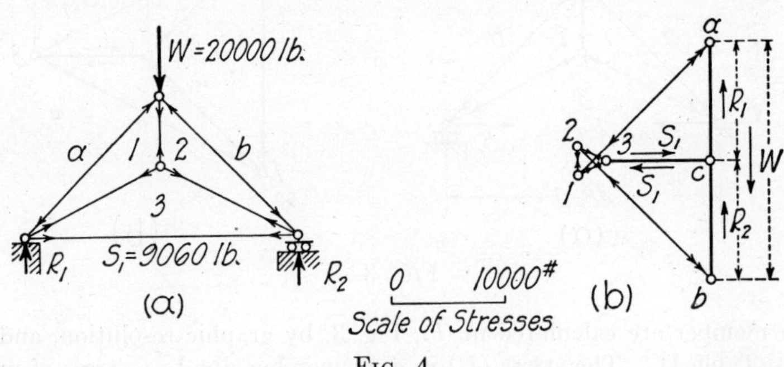

FIG. 4.

stress S' in Table I to the stress $U \times 9,060$ for the corresponding member in Table I. For example the stress in member a–1 in the two-hinged arch $= +28,000 - 1.42 \times 9,060 = +15,150$ lb.

TABLE III.

DEFORMATION OF FRAMEWORK.

1	2	3	4	5	6	7
Member.	Area, A, Sq. In.	Stress, S, Lbs.	Length, L, In.	$\frac{S \cdot L}{A \cdot E}$.	U	$\frac{S \cdot U \cdot L}{A \cdot E}$.
a–1	2.00	+ 15,150	400	+ 0.101	− 1.42	− 0.144
1–3	2.00	− 2,100	320	− 0.011	+ 2.20	− 0.026
1–2	2.00	− 1,900	144	− 0.004	+ 2.00	− 0.008
2–b	2.00	− 15,150	400	+ 0.101	− 1.42	− 0.144
2–3	2.00	− 2,100	320	− 0.011	+ 2.20	− 0.026
					$\Sigma \frac{S \cdot U \cdot L}{A \cdot E}$ =	− 0.348
Deformation of tie 1–3.						
3–c	0.50	− 9,060	576	− 0.348	− 1.00	+ 0.348

The deformation of the framework has been calculated in Table III. It will be seen that the deformation of the framework is equal to the deformation of the tie, which checks the solution.

Problems.—For additional problems showing detail calculations for the calculation of the stresses in statically indeterminate framed structures by the Method of Algebraic Summation, see Chapters XX, XXI and XXII.

STRESSES IN A FRAMEWORK WITH ONE REDUNDANT MEMBER. Method of Work.—The framework in (*a*), Fig. 5, carries a load, $P = 20,000$ lb. The

TABLE IV.

CALCULATION OF WORK EQUATIONS FOR $P = 20{,}000$ LB.

1	2	3	4	5	6	7
Member.	Area A, Sq. In.	Length, L, In.	Stress S, in Terms of S_5.	$\frac{dS}{dS_5} = U.$	$\frac{L}{A \cdot E} = B.$	$B \cdot S\left(\frac{dS}{dS_5}\right)$
S_1	2.00	120	$-P - 0.707S_5$	-0.707	$\frac{1}{500{,}000}$	$\frac{0.707}{500{,}000}(P + 0.707S_5)$
S_2	2.00	120	$-0.707S_5$	-0.707	$\frac{1}{500{,}000}$	$\frac{0.500}{500{,}000}S_5$
S_3	2.00	120	$-0.707S_5$	-0.707	$\frac{1}{500{,}000}$	$\frac{0.500}{500{,}000}S_5$
S_4	2.00	170	$1.414P + S_5$	$+1.000$	$\frac{1.414}{500{,}000}$	$\frac{2.00}{500{,}000}(P + 0.707S_5)$
				$\frac{dW}{dS_5} = \Sigma B \cdot S\left(\frac{dS}{dS_5}\right) = y_1 =$		$\frac{2.707}{500{,}000}P + \frac{2.914}{500{,}000}S_5$
S_5	2.00	170	S_5	$+1.00$	$\frac{1.414}{500{,}000}$	$-y_1 = \frac{1.414}{500{,}000}S_5$

$$\frac{2.707}{500{,}000}P + \frac{2.914}{500{,}000}S_5 + \frac{1.414}{500{,}000}S_5 = 0; \quad S_5 = -0.625P = -12{,}500 \text{ lb.}$$

If member S_2 is rigid the second value in column 7 is zero, and

$$\frac{2.707}{500{,}000}P + \frac{2.414}{500{,}000}S_5 + \frac{1.414}{500{,}000}S_5 = 0; \qquad S_5 = -0.707P = -14{,}140 \text{ lb.} = -S_4$$

area of each member is $A = 2$ sq. in. The framework would be stable with either member AD (S_5) or member CB (S_4), and has therefore one redundant member.

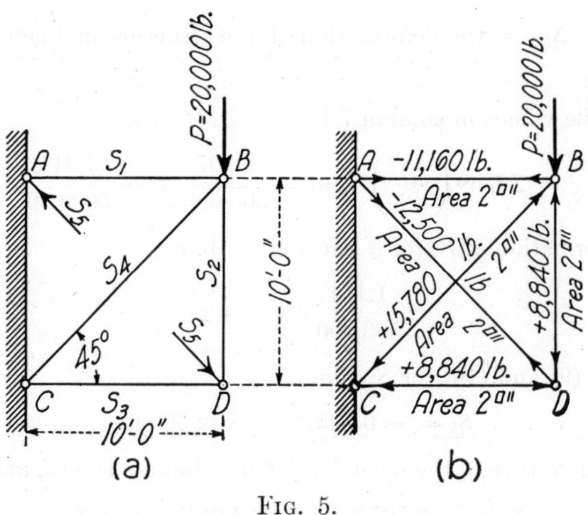

FIG. 5.

Solution.—Replace the member AD by the stress in the member S_5, which will be calculated later. Then calculate the stresses in the remaining members in terms of the stress in S_5. The stresses in the members are given in Table IV, column 4. The derivative of the stress in each member with reference to S_5 is given in column 5. The deformation in each member for a stress unity, is $B = L/A \cdot E$, where L = length of the member in in., A = area of cross-section of member in sq. in., and E = 30,000,000 = modulus of elasticity of steel. Now if S_5 is assumed as unity, then $\frac{dS}{dS_5} = U$, and the stresses in column 5 are the stresses in the members due to a stress of unity acting

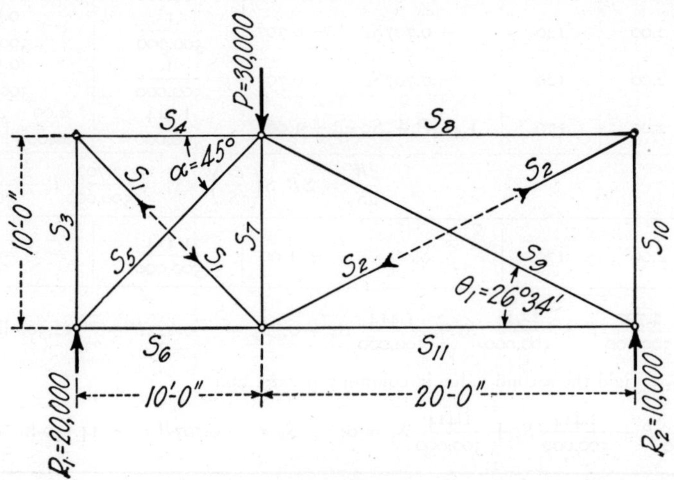

FIG. 6.

in place of S_5. The derivative of the work of each member with reference to S_5, will be $= B \cdot S \cdot \left(\frac{dS}{dS_5}\right) = \Delta y_1$ = the deformation of the structure in line of member S_5, due to stress of S.

The sum of the values in column 7 is

$$\frac{dW}{dS_5} = \Sigma B \cdot S \left(\frac{dS}{dS_5}\right) = y_1 = \frac{2.707}{500,000} P + \frac{2.914}{500,000} S_5 \tag{9}$$

Now the deformation of S_5 for a stress of S_5 lb. is

$$\frac{1.414}{500,000} S_5 = -y_1 \tag{10}$$

Solving equations (9) and (10) for S_5 gives

$$S_5 = -0.625P = -12,500 \text{ lb.}$$

If the member S_2 is rigid the second value in column 7 is zero, and solving as above

$$S_5 = -0.707P = -14,140 \text{ lb.} = -S_4,$$

stresses S_4 and S_5 being equal, as they should be.

Since the modulus of elasticity, E, cancels out in the calculations, a value of E = unity may be used and the work shortened.

TABLE V.

CALCULATION OF WORK EQUATIONS FOR $P = 30,000$ LB.

1	2	3	4	5	6	7	8	9
Member.	Area, A Sq. In.	Length, L, In.	Stress S in Terms of S_1 and S_2.	$\frac{d\cdot S}{dS_1} = U.$	$\frac{dS}{dS_2} = U'.$	$\frac{L}{A\cdot E} = B.$	$B\cdot S\left(\frac{dS}{dS_1}\right).$	$B\cdot S\left(\frac{dS}{dS_2}\right).$
S_3	2.00	120	$-0.707S_1$	-0.707		$\frac{1}{500,000}$	$+\frac{0.500}{500,000}S_1$	
S_4	2.00	120	$-0.707S_1$	-0.707		$\frac{1}{500,000}$	$+\frac{0.500}{500,000}S_1$	
S_5	1.00	170	$+28,280 + S_1$	$+1.00$		$\frac{2.83}{500,000}$	$+\frac{80,000}{500,000}+\frac{2.83}{500,000}S_1$	
S_6	1.00	120	$-20,000 - 0.707S_1$	-0.707		$\frac{2}{500,000}$	$+\frac{28,280}{500,000}+\frac{1.00}{500,000}S_1$	
S_7	2.00	120	$-0.707S_1 - 0.448S_2$	-0.707	-0.448	$\frac{1}{500,000}$	$+\frac{0.500}{500,000}S_1+\frac{0.317}{500,000}S_2$	$+\frac{0.317}{500,000}S_1+\frac{0.200}{500,000}S_2$
S_8	2.00	240	$-0.895S_2$		-0.895	$\frac{2}{500,000}$		$+\frac{1.600}{500,000}S_2$
S_9	1.00	268	$+22,333 + S_2$		$+1.00$	$\frac{4.47}{500,000}$		$+\frac{99,800}{500,000}+\frac{4.47}{500,000}S_2$
S_{10}	2.00	120	$-0.448S_2$		-0.448	$\frac{1}{500,000}$		$+\frac{0.200}{500,000}S_2$
S_{11}	1.00	240	$-20,000 - 0.895S_2$		-0.895	$\frac{4}{500,000}$		$+\frac{71,600}{500,000}+\frac{3.20}{500,000}S_2$
							$y_1 = +\frac{108,280}{500,000}+\frac{5.33}{500,000}S_1 + \frac{0.317}{500,000}S_2$	$y_2 = +\frac{171,400}{500,000}+\frac{0.317}{500,000}S_1 + \frac{9.67}{500,000}S_2$
S_1	1.00	170	S_1	$+1.00$		$\frac{2.83}{500,000}$	$+\frac{2.83}{500,000}S_1 = -y_1$	
S_2	1.00	268	S_2		$+1.00$	$\frac{4.47}{500,000}$		$+\frac{4.47}{500,000}S_2 = -y_2$

$$(1)\quad 8.160S_1 + 0.317S_2 = -108,280$$
$$(2)\quad 0.317S_1 + 14.140S_2 = -171,400$$
$$(3)\quad 363.982S_1 + 14.140S_2 = -4,829,905$$
$$(4)\quad 363.665S_1 = -4,658,500$$
$$S_1 = -12,810$$
$$S_2 = -11,840$$

STRESSES IN A FRAMEWORK WITH TWO REDUNDANT MEMBERS.— The framework in Fig. 6 would be stable with either of the diagonal members in each panel, and therefore has two redundant members. The framework is statically determinate for external forces; $R_1 = 20{,}000$ lb., and $R_2 = 10{,}000$ lb.

To calculate the stresses in the redundant member , replace the truss members by stresses S_1 and S_2, respectively, and solve for the unknown stresses. In Table V the stresses in the membe:s of the framework in terms of S_1 and S_2 are given in column 4; $dS/dS_1 = U$, and $dS/dS_2 = U'$ are given in columns 5 and 6, respectively; values of $L/A \cdot E = B$ are given in column 7; values of $B \cdot S(dS/dS_1)$ in column 8 and $B \cdot S(dS/dS_2)$ in column 9. Now the sum of column 8 is equal to the displacement in line of member $S_1 = y_1$; also $y_1 = -\dfrac{2.83}{500{,}000} S_1$. The sum of column 9 is equal to the displacement in line of member $S_2 = y_2$; also $y_2 = -\dfrac{4.47}{500{,}000} S_2$. Equating the values of y_1 and y_2, and solving we have

$$8.160 S_1 + 0.317 S_2 = -108{,}280 \tag{11}$$
$$0.317 S_1 + 14.140 S_2 = -171{,}400 \tag{12}$$

Multiply (11) by 14.14/0.317, and

$$363.982 S_1 + 14.140 S_2 = -4{,}829{,}905 \tag{13}$$

and subtracting (12) from (13) we have

$$363.665 S_1 = -4{,}658{,}500 \text{ lb.}$$
$$S_1 = -12{,}810 \text{ lb.}$$

also

$$S_2 = -11{,}840 \text{ lb.}$$

Substituting in column 4, Table V, gives $S_5 = +15{,}470$ lb., and $S_9 = +10{,}490$ lb.

The detail calculations may be simplified by taking $E =$ unity.

STRESSES IN A FRAMEWORK WITH THREE REDUNDANT MEMBERS. —For the calculation of the stresses in a trestle bent with three redundant members, see Problem 6, Chapter XXII.

STRESSES IN STIFF FRAMES.—The stresses in stiff frames are calculated by the Method of Area Moments in Chapter XVII, and by the Method of Slope Deflections in Chapter XVIII. The stresses in the portal with pin-connected columns in Fig. 12, Chapter XVII may be calculated by the Method of Work as follows:

The total work of deformation will be

$$W = \int_A^D \frac{M^2 \cdot ds}{2E \cdot I} \tag{14}$$

If the frame is free to move horizontally at D, the movement will be

$$\frac{dW}{dH} = \Delta = \int_A^D \frac{M \cdot \dfrac{dM}{dH} \cdot ds}{E \cdot I} = \int_A^D \frac{M \cdot m \cdot ds}{E \cdot I} \tag{15}$$

(For temperature, $\Delta = e \cdot t \cdot l$, where $e = 0.0000067$ for steel, $t =$ variation temperature degrees Fah., $l =$ span.)

Now apply one lb. horizontally at D, and the distance that the frame will be brought back will be

$$\delta' = \int_A^D \frac{m \cdot m \cdot ds}{E \cdot I} \tag{16}$$

A horizontal thrust H will bring the point D back to its original position. and

$$\Delta = H \int_A^D \frac{m^2 \cdot ds}{E \cdot I} \tag{17}$$

Equating equations (15) and (17), and solving

$$H = \frac{\displaystyle\int_A^D \frac{M \cdot m \cdot ds}{E \cdot I}}{\displaystyle\int_A^D \frac{m^2 \cdot ds}{E \cdot I}} \tag{18}$$

This solution is the same as the Area Moment Solution in equation (53), Chapter XVII.

STRESSES IN CONTINUOUS GIRDERS OF TWO SPANS.—The stresses in continuous girders may be calculated by algebraic or by graphic methods.

Constant Moment of Inertia.—*Algebraic Method.*—Applying the theorem of three moments given in equation (36), Chapter XIV, the following values are derived for the reactions for a single load P on the first span of a girder with spans l_1 and l_2.

$$R_1 = -\frac{P \cdot l_1}{2(l_1 + l_2)}(k - k^3) + P\left(1 - k\right) \tag{19}$$

$$R_3 = -\frac{P \cdot l_1^2}{2l_2(l_1 + l_2)}(k - k^3) \tag{20}$$

$$R_2 = P - R_1 - R_3 \tag{21}$$

For equal spans

$$l_1 = l_2 = l$$

$$R_1 = \tfrac{1}{4}P(4 - 5k + k^3) \tag{23}$$

$$R_2 = \tfrac{1}{2}P(3k - k^3) \tag{24}$$

$$R_3 = -\tfrac{1}{4}P(k - k^3) \tag{25}$$

Applying the theorem of three moments given in equation (41), Chapter XIV, the following values for the reactions are derived for a uniform load w covering the entire first span of a girder with spans l_1 and l_2.

$$R_1 = \tfrac{1}{8}w \cdot l_1\left(\frac{3l_1 + 4l_2}{l_1 + l_2}\right) \tag{26}$$

$$R_3 = -\tfrac{1}{8}w \cdot l_1^3/(l_1 + l_2)l_2 \tag{27}$$

$$R_2 = w \cdot l_1 - R_1 - R_3 \tag{28}$$

For equal spans $l_1 = l_2 = l$

$$R_1 = 7w \cdot l/16 \tag{29}$$

$$R_2 = 5w \cdot l/8 \tag{30}$$

$$R_3 = -w \cdot l/16 \tag{31}$$

For a girder with both spans loaded $R_1 = R_3 = 3w \cdot l/8$, and $R_2 = 5w \cdot l/4$.

Having calculated the reactions the shear and the moment at any point may be calculated in the same manner as for simple beams.

Graphic Method.—For a method by means of influence diagrams, see Chapter XIV.

Variable Moment of Inertia.—The stresses in a continuous girder of two spans with variable moment of inertiaare calculated by area moments in Problem 2, Chapter XXII.

STRESSES IN A CONTINUOUS GIRDER OF THREE SPANS.—Continuous girders of three spans when used for draw spans usually have the end spans equal, $l = l$, and the middle span $= nl\cdot$.

Constant Moment of Inertia.—*Algebraic Method.*—Applying the theorem of three moments in equation (36), Chapter XIV, the following values for the reactions are obtained for a single load P in the first span.

$$R_1 = P(1 - k) - \frac{2 + 2n}{N} P(k - k^3) \tag{32}$$

$$R_2 = P\cdot k + \frac{2 + 5n + 2n^2}{n\cdot N} P(k - k^3) \tag{33}$$

$$R_3 = -\frac{2 + 3n + n^2}{n\cdot N} P(k - k^3) \tag{34}$$

$$R_4 = \frac{n}{N} P(k - k^3) \tag{35}$$

where $N = 4 + 8n + 3n^2$.

For a uniform load w extending over the entire girder, from (41), Chapter XIV,

$$R_1 = R_4 = \frac{w\cdot l}{4}\left[\frac{3 + 6n - n^3}{2 + 3n}\right] \tag{36}$$

$$R_2 = R_3 = \frac{w\cdot l}{4}\left[\frac{5 + 10n + 6n^2 + n^3}{2 + 3n}\right] \tag{37}$$

Having calculated the reactions the shear and the moment at any point may be calculated in the same manner as for simple beams.

Graphic Method.—For a method by means of influence diagrams, see Chapter XIV.

Variable Moment of Inertia.—The stresses in a continuous girder of three spans with a variable moment of inertia are calculated by area moments in Problem 3, Chapter XXII.

STRESSES IN CONTINUOUS TRUSSES.—Continuous trusses of two or three spans are the most common and these two cases only will be discussed.

Approximate Solution.—By assuming that the trusses have a constant moment of inertia, the reactions may be calculated in the same manner as for girders. The stresses calculated on the assumption of a constant moment of inertia are sufficiently exact for the preliminary design. Having made the preliminary design, the reactions should be calculated by calculating the deformations of the members of the truss, all but two of the reactions being considered as redundant.

Calculation of True Reactions.—For the dead load and for a full live load, the redundant reactions may be calculated by the methods explained above for structures with one redundant member and with two redundant members. For maximum live load stresses, influence diagrams similar to those constructed for a continuous girder in Chapter XIV should be used.

CONTINUOUS TRUSS OF TWO SPANS.—Having made a preliminary design based on approximate values of the reactions calculated for a continuous girder with a constant moment of inertia, the true reactions for maximum and minimum stresses due to dead and live loads may be calculated by the influence diagram method.

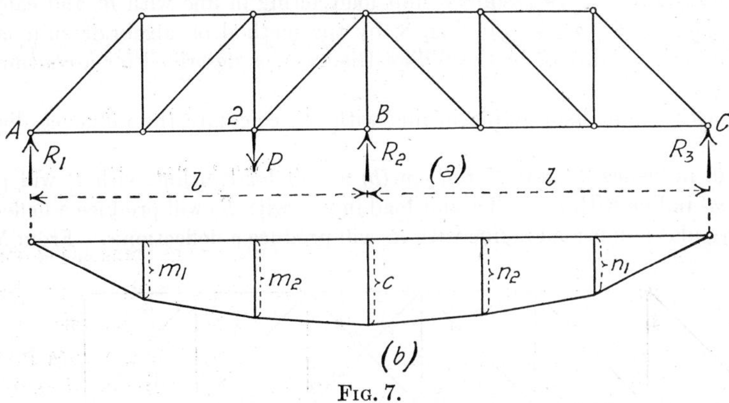

Fig. 7.

The influence diagram in (*b*), Fig. 7, may be calculated by several different methods.

(*a*) *Method of Algebraic Summation.*—To calculate deflection c, apply a unit load in line with R_2 (R_2 = unity) and calculate the deflection c by means of equation (6). To calculate deflection m_2, assume a unit load acting in line with P, and calculate the stresses, U_2, in all members. Also assume a unit load acting in line with R_2 and calculate stresses, U, in all members. Then from equation (3), $m_2 = \Sigma(U_2 \cdot U \cdot L/A \cdot E)$. Also calculate m_1 by placing a unit load in line with m_1, and also a unit load in line with R_2 and substitute in equation (3). Now by applying Maxwell's theorem it will be seen that with a unit load at the first joint, m_1 = deflection in line with R_2; with a unit load at the second joint, m_2 = deflection in line with R_2, etc.

(*b*) *Method of the Williot Diagram.*—Apply a unit load in line with R_2, calculate the stresses in the members due to the unit load, and construct a Williot diagram and an influence diagram as in Fig. 11, Chapter XV.

(*c*) *Method of Elastic Weights.*—Apply a unit load in line with R_2, calculate the stresses in the members due to the unit load, and calculate the deflections of the loaded chord as shown in Table I and Fig. 17, Chapter XV, and in Problem 9, Chapter XXII. The method of the Williot Diagram is the shortest method, while the method of Elastic Weights is capable of the greatest precision and should be used for large structures. For a symmetrical truss $m_1 = n_1$ and $m_2 = n_2$.

Having constructed the influence diagram by one of the above methods, the center reaction for a unit load at a joint, by Maxwell's Theorem will be

$$R_2 = m_2/c \tag{38}$$

and for a load P the center reaction will be

$$R_2 = P \cdot m_2/c \tag{39}$$

The influence diagrams for moment and for shear may be calculated in the same manner as for a girder with two spans as given in Fig. 25, Chapter XIV.

CONTINUOUS TRUSS OF THREE SPANS.—Having made a preliminary design based on approximate values of the reactions calculated as for a continuous girder with a constant moment of inertia, the true reactions may be calculated by the influence diagram method.

Assume that the reactions R_2 and R_3 are not acting and that the truss is supported at R_1 and R_4. Now assume a unit load acting in line with R_2 and calculate the influence diagram for R_2 in (*b*), Fig. 8, by the method of algebraic summation, the method of elastic weights or by the Williot Diagram, as described for a continuous truss of two spans.

Also, with a unit load acting in line with R_3, calculate the influence diagram for R_3 in (*c*), Fig. 8.

Now in influence diagram for R_2 in (*b*) a unit load in line with P will produce a deflection m_2 in line with R_2, and a unit load in line with R_2 will produce a deflection k in line with R_3, also a unit load in line with R_2 will produce a deflection c. From Maxwell's Theorem

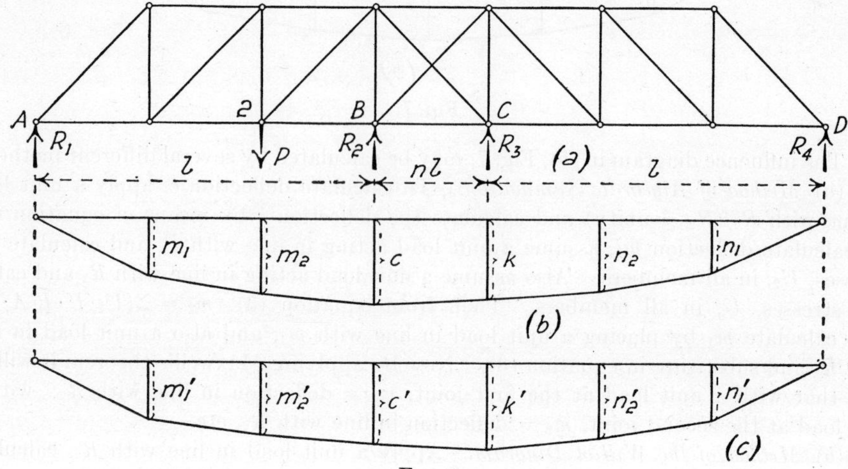

FIG. 8.

$$R_2 \cdot c + R_3 \cdot k - P \cdot m_2 = 0 \tag{40}$$

Also in like manner in (*c*),

$$R_2 \cdot c' + R_3 \cdot k' - P \cdot m_2' = 0 \tag{41}$$

Now let $k/k' = g$.

Multiply equation (41) by g, and

$$R_2 \cdot c'g + R_3 \cdot k' \cdot g - P \cdot m_2' \cdot g = 0 \tag{42}$$

Subtract (42) from (40) and

$$R_2 = \frac{P(m_2 - m_2' \cdot g)}{c - c' \cdot g} \tag{43}$$

In like manner let $c/c' = h$ and

$$R_3 = \frac{P(m_2 - m_2' \cdot h)}{k - k' \cdot h} \tag{44}$$

Having calculated the reactions moments and shears may be calculated by statics.

CHAPTER XVII.

Stresses in Stiff Frames by Area Moments.

Introduction.—In this chapter the stresses in stiff frames due to rigidity of the joints will be calculated. It will be assumed (1) that the members have large sections and that the distortions due to direct stresses are small and may be neglected; (2) that the joints are perfectly rigid, and (3) that deformations due to shear are zero.

GENERAL SOLUTION.—A general solution using the principles of area moments will first be developed. Formulas for several particular cases will then be calculated.

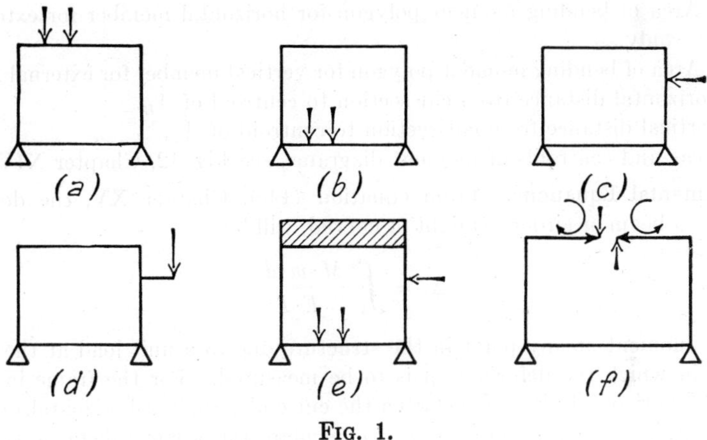

Fig. 1.

Let it be required to find the stresses in a quadrangular frame carrying some loading such as shown in Fig. 1.

Consider an unloaded member, such as the upper member in (*f*), Fig. 1, as cut at the center and equilibriate the stresses which are at this section by a direct stress, a shearing stress, and a bending moment.

Calculate the horizontal distance between the cut ends, the vertical distance, and the difference in slope of the tangents at the cut ends, first for the internal stresses and then for the loads only. Since the cut ends must stay together and have a common tangent, the total horizontal distance, the total vertical distance, and the total difference in slope, must each equal zero.

There are then three equations with which to determine the three unknown quantities at the cut section. After these quantities have been determined the stresses at any other section can be found by simple statics.

NOMENCLATURE:

l = width of frame at the neutral axis.

h = height of frame at the neutral axis.

V_0, H_0, and M_0 = shear, direct stress and moment at cut section, respectively.

I_0, I_1 and I_2 = moments of inertia of members as designated on diagrams, I_0 always being for the cut member.

x_H, x_V, x_M = horizontal distances between cut ends due to H_0, V_0, and M_0, respectively.

y_H, y_V, y_M = vertical distances between cut ends due to H_0, V_0, and M_0, respectively.

ϕ_H, ϕ_V, ϕ_M = angles between tangents at cut ends due to H_0, V_0, and M_0, respectively.

x_L, y_L, ϕ_L = corresponding quantities due to external loads.

M_H, M_V, M_M = moments in structure due to H_0, V_0 and M_0, respectively.

M_L = moments in structure due to external loads.

C_1, C_2, C_3, C_4, C_5 = constants depending on dimensions of frame and are independent of the loading.

A_H = Area of bending moment polygon for horizontal member for external loads only.

A_V = Area of bending moment polygon for vertical member for external loads only.

$\bar{x}$ = horizontal distance from cut section to centroid of A_H.

$\bar{y}$ = vertical distance from cut section to centroid of A_V.

For areas and centroids of moment diagrams, see Fig. 12, Chapter XIV.

Fundamental Equations.—From equation (14*c*), Chapter XV, the deflection at any point in a beam or girder, straight or curved, will be

$$\Delta_1 = \int_0^s \frac{M \cdot m \cdot ds}{E \cdot I}$$

where m = moment at any point in the structure due to a unit load at the point and in the line in which the deformation is to be measured. For the frame in Fig. 1, to calculate the horizontal distance between the cut ends, apply a horizontal unit load on each cut end at the point, and $m = y$; to calculate the vertical distance between the cut ends, apply a vertical unit load on each cut end, and $m = x$; for the rotation of the cut ends, apply a unit moment at the cut ends (see equation (39), Chapter XV), and m = unity. (For another proof of these equations see the author's "Design of Highway Bridges of Steel, Timber and Concrete," Chapter XXIII.)

The horizontal distance between the cut ends, the vertical distance between the cut ends, and the angle between the tangents at the cut ends are as follows:

The horizontal distance between the cut ends due to a given loading is

$$x_1 = \Sigma \frac{M \cdot y}{E \cdot I} ds \tag{1}$$

where M = the moment at any point due to the given loading.

The vertical distance is

$$y_1 = \Sigma \frac{M \cdot x}{E \cdot I} ds \tag{2}$$

The angle between the tangents at the cut ends is

$$\phi = \Sigma \frac{M}{E \cdot I} ds \tag{3}$$

These equations may be written as follows; and may be equated to zero since the cut ends must stay in contact and the member must be continuous:

$$x_1 = x_H + x_V + x_M + x_L = \Sigma \frac{M_H \cdot y}{E \cdot I} ds + \Sigma \frac{M_V \cdot y}{E \cdot I} ds + \Sigma \frac{M_M \cdot y}{E \cdot I} ds + \Sigma \frac{M_L \cdot y}{E \cdot I} ds = 0 \tag{4}$$

$$y_1 = y_H + y_V + y_M + y_L = \Sigma \frac{M_H \cdot x}{E \cdot I} ds + \Sigma \frac{M_V \cdot x}{E \cdot I} ds + \Sigma \frac{M_M \cdot x}{E \cdot I} ds + \Sigma \frac{M_L \cdot x}{E \cdot I} ds = 0 \tag{5}$$

$$\phi = \phi_H + \phi_V + \phi_M + \phi_L = \Sigma \frac{M_H}{E \cdot I} ds + \Sigma \frac{M_V}{E \cdot I} ds + \Sigma \frac{M_M}{E \cdot I} ds + \Sigma \frac{M_L}{E \cdot I} ds = 0 \tag{6}$$

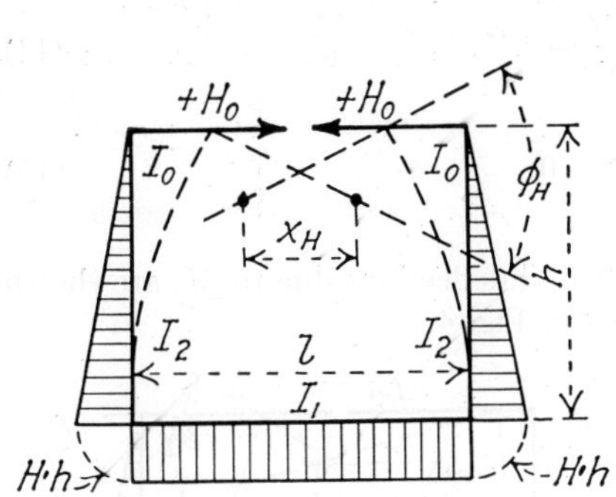

FIG. 2.

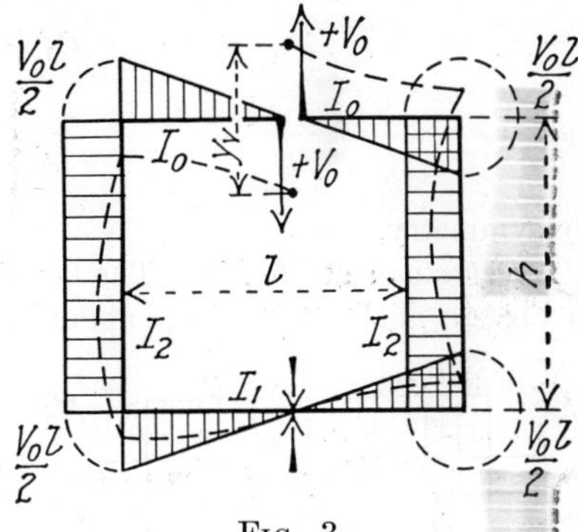

FIG. 3.

Deflections.—*Deflections due to H_0.*—The bending moments and deflections due to H_0 are shown in Fig. 2.

Taking moments about the cut section in Fig. 2.

$$x_H = \Sigma \frac{M_H \cdot y}{E \cdot I} ds = \frac{H_0 \cdot h \cdot h}{E \cdot I_2} \times \frac{2}{3} h + \frac{H_0 \cdot h \cdot l}{E \cdot I_1} \times h = \frac{H_0 \cdot h^2}{E \cdot I_1}\left(\frac{2}{3} h \frac{I_1}{I_2} + l\right) = \frac{H_0 \cdot h^2}{E \cdot I_1} \times C_1 \tag{7}$$

where

$$C_1 = \frac{2}{3} h \frac{I_1}{I_2} + l \tag{8}$$

$$y_H = \Sigma \frac{M_H \cdot x}{E \cdot I} ds = 0 \tag{9}$$

by symmetry.

$$\phi_H = \Sigma \frac{M_H}{E \cdot I} ds = \frac{H_0 \cdot h \cdot h}{E \cdot I_2} + \frac{H_0 \cdot h \cdot l}{E \cdot I_1} = \frac{H_0 \cdot h}{E \cdot I_1}\left(h \frac{I_1}{I_2} + l\right) = \frac{H_0 \cdot h}{E \cdot I_1} \times C_2 \tag{10}$$

where

$$C_2 = h \frac{I_1}{I_2} + l \tag{11}$$

Deflections due to V_0.—The bending moments and deflections due to V_0 are shown in Fig. 3. Taking moments about the cut section in Fig. 3.

$$x_V = \Sigma \frac{M_V \cdot y}{E \cdot I} ds = 0 \tag{12}$$

by symmetry.

$$y_V = \Sigma \frac{M_V \cdot x}{E \cdot I} ds = 2 \frac{V_0 \cdot \frac{1}{2}l \cdot \frac{1}{2}l}{2E \cdot I_0} \times \frac{l}{3} + 2 \frac{V_0 \cdot \frac{1}{2}l \cdot h}{E \cdot I_2} \times \frac{l}{2} + 2 \frac{V_0 \cdot \frac{1}{2}l \cdot \frac{1}{2}l}{2E \cdot I_1} \times \frac{l}{3}$$

$$= \frac{V_0 \cdot l^2}{12E \cdot I_1} \left(l \frac{I_1}{I_0} + 6h \frac{I_1}{I_2} + l \right)$$

$$y_V = \frac{V_0 \cdot l^2}{12E \cdot I_1} \cdot C_3 \tag{13}$$

where

$$C_3 = l \frac{I_1}{I_0} + 6h \frac{I_1}{I_2} + l \tag{14}$$

$$\phi_V = \Sigma \frac{M_V}{E \cdot I} ds = 0 \tag{15}$$

by symmetry.

Deflections due to M_0.—The bending moments and deflections due to M_0 are shown in Fig. 4. Taking moments about the cut section in Fig. 4.

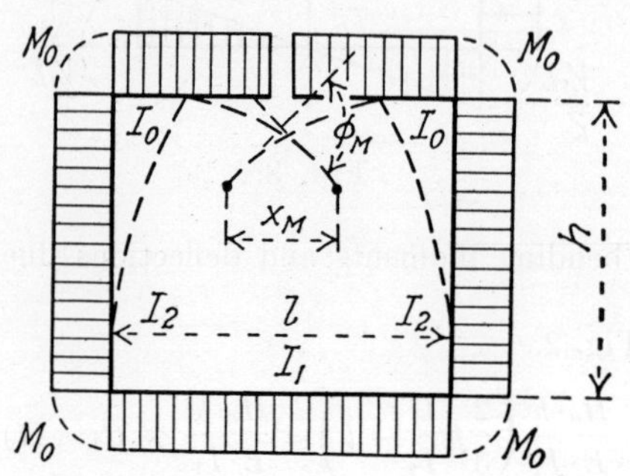

FIG. 4.

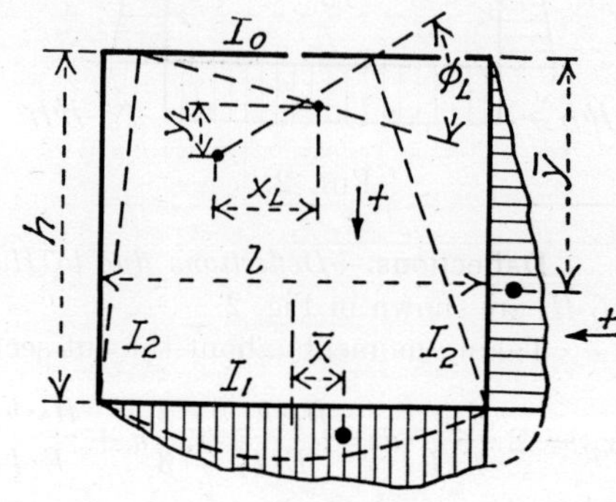

FIG. 5.

$$x_M = \Sigma \frac{M_M \cdot y}{E \cdot I} ds = \frac{2M_0 \cdot h}{E \cdot I_2} \times \frac{h}{2} + \frac{M_0 \cdot l}{E \cdot I_1} \times h = \frac{M_0 \cdot h}{E \cdot I_1} \left(h \frac{I_1}{I_2} + l \right) = \frac{M_0 \cdot h}{E \cdot I_1} \times C_2 \tag{16}$$

where in (11)

$$C_2 = h \frac{I_1}{I_2} + l \tag{17}$$

$$y_M = \Sigma \frac{M_M \cdot x}{E \cdot I} ds = 0 \tag{18}$$

by symmetry.

$$\phi_M = \Sigma \frac{M_M}{E \cdot I} ds = \frac{M_0 \cdot l}{E \cdot I_0} + \frac{2M_0 \cdot h}{E \cdot I_2} + \frac{M_0 \cdot l}{E \cdot I_1} = \frac{M_0}{E \cdot I_1}\left(l \frac{I_1}{I_0} + 2h \frac{I_1}{I_2} + l \right) = \frac{M_0}{E \cdot I_1} \times C_4 \quad (19)$$

where

$$C_4 = l \frac{I_1}{I_0} + 2h \frac{I_1}{I_2} + l \quad (20)$$

* *Deflections due to any external loading.*—The deflections and bending moments due to any loading on the bottom member and on the right side are shown in Fig. 5. Taking moments about the cut section in Fig. 5.

$$x_L = \Sigma \frac{M_L \cdot y}{E \cdot I} ds = \frac{A_H}{E \cdot I_1} \times h + \frac{A_V}{E \cdot I_2} \times \bar{y} = \frac{A_H}{E \cdot I_1} \times h + \frac{A_V}{E \cdot I_1} \times \bar{y} \times \frac{I_1}{I_2}$$

$$= \frac{1}{E \cdot I_1} (A_H \cdot h + A_V \cdot \bar{y} \cdot C_5) \quad (21)$$

where

$$C_5 = \frac{I_1}{I_2} \quad (22)$$

$$y_L = \Sigma \frac{M_L \cdot x}{E \cdot I} ds = \frac{A_H}{E \cdot I_1} \bar{x} + \frac{A_V}{E \cdot I_2} \times \frac{l}{2} = \frac{A_H}{E \cdot I_1} \bar{x} + \frac{A_V}{E \cdot I_1} \times \frac{l}{2} \times \frac{I_1}{I_2}$$

$$= \frac{1}{E \cdot I_1}\left(A_H \cdot \bar{x} + A_V \cdot \frac{l}{2} \cdot C_5 \right) \quad (23)$$

$$\phi_L = \Sigma \frac{M_L}{E \cdot I} ds = \frac{A_H}{E \cdot I_1} + \frac{A_V}{E \cdot I_2} = \frac{A_H}{E \cdot I_1} + \frac{A_V}{E \cdot I_1} \times \frac{I_1}{I_2} = \frac{1}{E \cdot I_1} (A_H + A_V \cdot C_5) \quad (24)$$

Solution for Internal Stresses H_0, V_0 and M_0.—From (4), (7), (12), (16), and (21)

$$\frac{H_0 \cdot h^2}{E \cdot I_1} \times C_1 + 0 + \frac{M_0 \cdot h}{E \cdot I_1} \times C_2 + \frac{A_H}{E \cdot I_1} \times h + \frac{A_V}{E \cdot I_1} \times \bar{y} \cdot C_5 = 0$$

$$H_0 = -\frac{1}{C_1 \cdot h^2} \cdot (M_0 \cdot h \cdot C_2 + A_H \cdot h + A_V \cdot \bar{y} \cdot C_5) \quad (25)$$

From (6), (10), (15), (19), and (24)

$$\frac{H_0 \cdot h}{E \cdot I_1} \times C_2 + 0 + \frac{M_0}{E \cdot I_1} \times C_4 + \frac{A_H}{E \cdot I_1} + \frac{A_V}{E \cdot I_1} \times C_5 = 0$$

$$H_0 = -\frac{1}{C_2 \cdot h} \cdot (M_0 \cdot C_4 + A_H + A_V \cdot C_5) \quad (26)$$

From (25) and (26)

$$\frac{1}{C_1 \cdot h^2} (M_0 \cdot h \cdot C_2 + A_H \cdot h + A_V \cdot \bar{y} \cdot C_5) = \frac{1}{C_2 \cdot h} (M_0 \cdot C_4 + A_H + A_V \cdot C_5)$$

$$M_0 = \frac{A_H(C_1 - C_2) + A_V \cdot C_5 \left(C_1 - C_2 \cdot \frac{\bar{y}}{h} \right)}{C_2^2 - C_1 \cdot C_4} \quad (27)$$

* For temperature, in (21), $x_L = e \cdot t \cdot l$, y_L in (23) $= 0$, ϕ_L in (24) $= 0$, $e = 0.0000067$, t = variation degrees Fah.

From (26) and (27)

$$H_0 = -\frac{1}{C_2 \cdot h}\left(\frac{A_H(C_1 - C_2)C_4 + A_V \cdot C_5\left(C_1 - C_2 \cdot \frac{\bar{y}}{h}\right)C_4}{C_2^2 - C_1 \cdot C_4} + A_H + A_V \cdot C_5\right)$$

$$= -\frac{1}{h} \cdot \frac{A_H(C_2 - C_4) + A_V \cdot C_5\left(C_2 - C_4 \cdot \frac{\bar{y}}{h}\right)}{C_2^2 - C_1 \cdot C_4} \tag{28}$$

From (5), (9), (13), (18) and (23)

$$0 + \frac{V_0 \cdot l^2}{12E \cdot I_1} \times C_3 + 0 + \frac{A_H}{E \cdot I_1} \times \bar{x} + \frac{A_V}{E \cdot I_1} \times \frac{l}{2} \cdot C_5 = 0$$

$$V_0 = -\frac{6}{C_3 \cdot l^2}(2A_H \cdot \bar{x} + A_V \cdot l \cdot C_5) \tag{29}$$

Stresses at any Section.—After the values of V_0, H_0 and M_0 have been determined the stresses at any section can be found by simple statics.

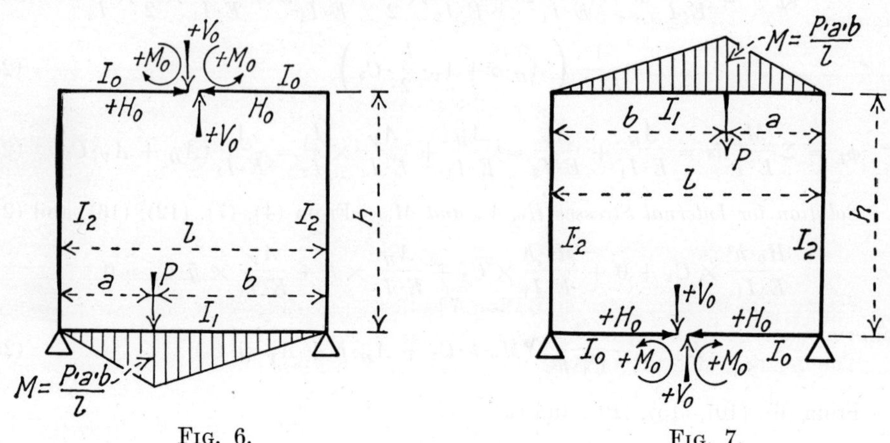

FIG. 6. FIG. 7.

Frame with Concentrated Loads on Bottom Member.—A rigid frame with a single concentrated load on the lower member is shown in Fig. 6.

The bending moment under the load is

$$M = \frac{P \cdot a \cdot b}{l}$$

$$A_H = \frac{P \cdot a \cdot b}{l} \times \frac{l}{2} = \frac{P \cdot a \cdot b}{2}; \qquad A_V = 0; \qquad \bar{x} = \frac{a - b}{6}$$

From (27)

$$M_0 = \frac{P \cdot a \cdot b}{2} \times \frac{C_1 - C_2}{C_2^2 - C_1 \cdot C_4} \tag{30}$$

From (28)

$$H_0 = -\frac{P\cdot a\cdot b}{2h}\times\frac{C_2 - C_4}{C_2^2 - C_1\cdot C_4} \tag{31}$$

From (29)

$$V_0 = -\frac{P\cdot a\cdot b}{l^2}\times\frac{a - b}{C_3} \tag{33}$$

For several loads

$$M_0 = \frac{\Sigma P\cdot a\cdot b}{2}\times\frac{C_1 - C_2}{C_2^2 - C_1\cdot C_4} \tag{34}$$

$$H_0 = -\frac{\Sigma P\cdot a\cdot b}{2h}\times\frac{C_2 - C_4}{C_2^2 - C_1\cdot C_4} \tag{35}$$

$$V_0 = -\frac{\Sigma P\cdot a\cdot b(a - b)}{l^2\cdot C_3} \tag{36}$$

Frame with Concentrated Loads on Top Member.—A rigid frame with a single concentrated load on the top member is shown in Fig. 7.

If the load in Fig. 6 be reversed in direction, the deformations and stresses will be reversed, and if the whole system be rotated 180° the case shown in Fig. 7 will result. Equations (34) (35) and (36) may then be written

$$M_0 = -\frac{\Sigma P\cdot a\cdot b}{2}\times\frac{C_1 - C_2}{C_2^2 - C_1\cdot C_4} \tag{37}$$

$$H_0 = +\frac{\Sigma P\cdot a\cdot b}{2h}\times\frac{C_2 - C_4}{C_2^2 - C_1\cdot C_4} \tag{38}$$

$$V_0 = -\frac{\Sigma P\cdot a\cdot b(a - b)}{l^2\cdot C_3} \tag{39}$$

Frame with Uniform Load on Bottom Member.—A frame with the bottom member uniformly loaded is shown in Fig. 8.

The bending moment at the center, A_H, A_V, and $\bar{x}$ are

$$M = \frac{1}{8}w\cdot l^2; \qquad A_H = \frac{1}{12}w\cdot l^3; \qquad A_V = 0; \qquad \bar{x} = 0$$

From (27)

$$M_0 = \frac{1}{12}w\cdot l^3\times\frac{C_1 - C_2}{C_2^2 - C_1\cdot C_4} \tag{40}$$

From (28)

$$H_0 = -\frac{w\cdot l^3}{12h}\times\frac{C_2 - C_4}{C_2^2 - C_1\cdot C_4} \tag{41}$$

From (29)

$$V_0 = 0 \tag{42}$$

Frame with Uniform Load on Top Member.—A rigid frame with top member uniformly loaded, is shown in Fig. 9. For reasons given in solving Fig. 7, the signs of formulas (40), (41), and (42) are changed for this case.

$$M_0 = -\frac{w \cdot l^3}{12} \times \frac{C_1 - C_2}{C_2^2 - C_1 \cdot C_4} \qquad (43)$$

$$H_0 = \frac{w \cdot l^3}{12h} \times \frac{C_2 - C_4}{C_2^2 - C_1 \cdot C_4} \qquad (44)$$

$$V_0 = 0 \qquad (45)$$

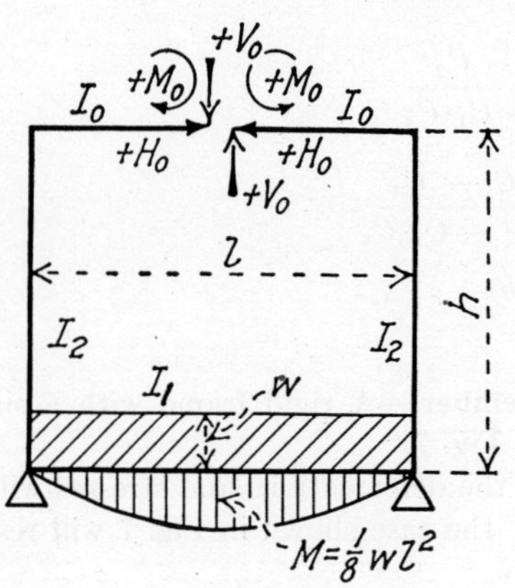

FIG. 8.

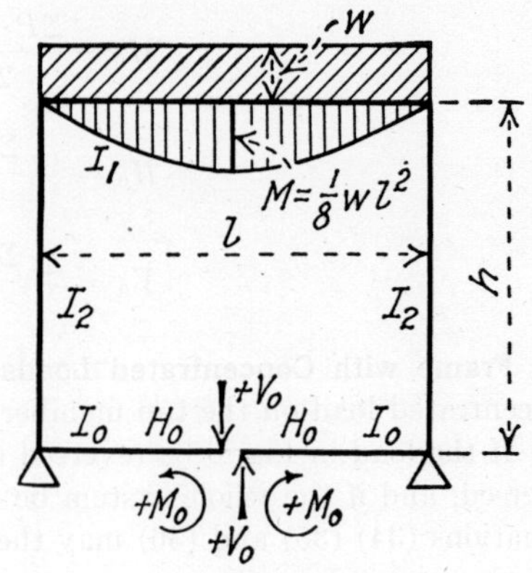

FIG. 9.

Frame with Concentrated Loads on Side Member.—A rigid frame with a single load on one side is shown in Fig. 10.

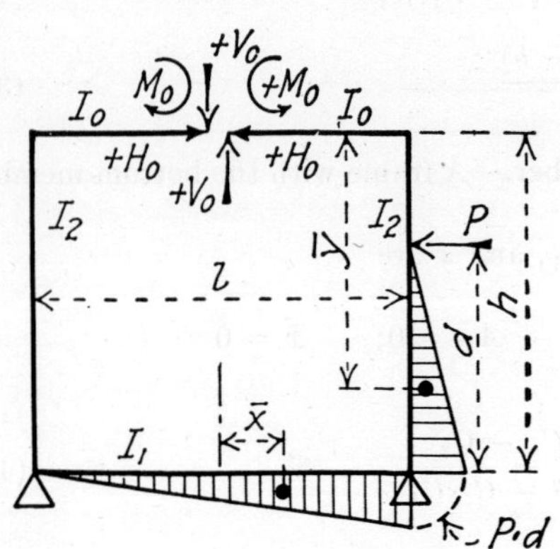

FIG. 10.

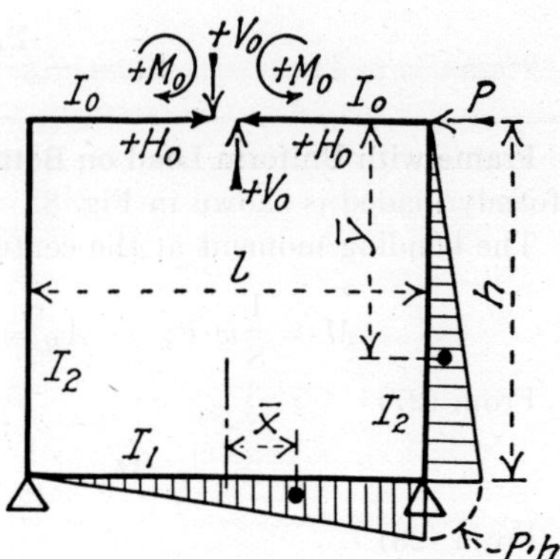

FIG. 11.

$$A_H = \frac{P \cdot d \cdot l}{2}; \qquad A_V = \frac{P \cdot d^2}{2}; \qquad \bar{x} = \frac{l}{6}; \qquad \bar{y} = h - \frac{d}{3}$$

From (27)

$$M_0 = \frac{P \cdot d}{2(C_2^2 - C_1 \cdot C_4)} \cdot \left[l(C_1 - C_2) + d\left(C_1 - C_2\left(1 - \frac{d}{3h}\right)\right) C_5 \right] \qquad (46)$$

From (28)

$$H_0 = \frac{P \cdot d}{2h(C_2^2 - C_1 \cdot C_4)} \cdot \left[l(C_2 - C_4) + d\left(C_2 - C_4\left(1 - \frac{d}{3h}\right)\right) C_5 \right] \tag{47}$$

From (29)

$$V_0 = -\frac{P \cdot d}{C_3 \cdot l}(l + 3d \cdot C_5) \tag{48}$$

For $d = h$

$$M_0 = \frac{P \cdot h}{2(C_2^2 - C_1 \cdot C_4)} \cdot [l(C_1 - C_2) + h(C_1 - \tfrac{2}{3}C_2)C_5] \tag{49}$$

$$H_0 = \frac{P}{2(C_2^2 - C_1 \cdot C_4)} \cdot [l(C_2 - C_4) + h(C_2 - \tfrac{2}{3}C_4)C_5] \tag{50}$$

$$V_0 = -\frac{P \cdot h}{C_3 \cdot l}(l + 3h \cdot C_5) \tag{51}$$

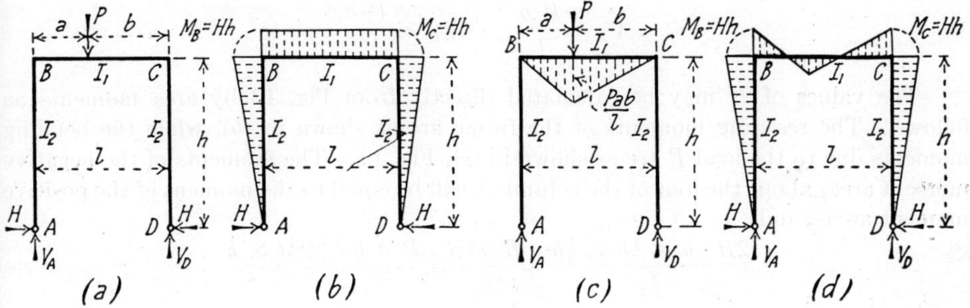

FIG. 12.

Frame with Pin-connected Ends.—*Concentrated Load.*—The stresses in the frame in (*a*) Fig. 12 may be calculated by means of formulas (37), (38) and (39) as deduced from Fig. 7, by assuming that I_0 is zero.

Now

$$C_1 = \frac{2}{3} h \frac{I_1}{I_2} + l \tag{8}$$

$$C_2 = h \frac{I_1}{I_2} + l \tag{11}$$

$$C_3 = l \frac{I_1}{I_0} + 6h \frac{I_1}{I_2} + l \tag{14}$$

$$C_4 = l \frac{I_1}{I_0} + 2h \frac{I_1}{I_2} + l \tag{20}$$

$$C_5 = \frac{I_1}{I_2} \tag{22}$$

Substituting values of C_1, C_2, and C_4 in formula (37) and making $I_0 = 0$, we have

$$M_0 = 0 \tag{52}$$

Substituting values of C_1, C_2 and C_4 in formula (38)

$$H = \frac{3P\cdot a\cdot b}{2h\cdot l\left(2\frac{h}{l}\cdot\frac{I_1}{I_2}+3\right)} \tag{53}$$

If

$$\frac{h}{l}\cdot\frac{I_1}{I_2} = k$$

$$H = \frac{3P\cdot a\cdot b}{2h\cdot l(2k+3)} \tag{54}$$

Substituting C_3 in equation (39)

$$V_0 = 0 \tag{55}$$

The vertical reactions can be calculated by moments, and are

$$V_A = \frac{P\cdot b}{l}, \quad V_D = \frac{P\cdot a}{l}$$

The values of H may be calculated directly from Fig. 12 by area moments as follows. The resisting moments of the frame are as shown in (*b*), while the bending moments due to the load P are as shown in (*c*), Fig. 12. The moments of the negative moment areas about the foot of the column A will be equal to the moment of the positive moment areas, and

$$\frac{2H\cdot h\times\frac{1}{2}h\times\frac{2}{3}h}{I_2}+\frac{H\cdot h^2\cdot l}{I_1}=\frac{P\cdot a\cdot b/l\times\frac{1}{2}l\times h}{I_1}$$

$$H = \frac{3P\cdot a\cdot b}{2h\cdot l\left(2\frac{h}{l}\cdot\frac{I_1}{I_2}+3\right)} = \frac{3P\cdot a\cdot b}{2h\cdot l(2k+3)} \tag{54}$$

For temperature, horizontal movement $= e\cdot t\cdot l$, and $H = (3E\cdot I_1\cdot e\cdot t)/h^2(2k+3)$.

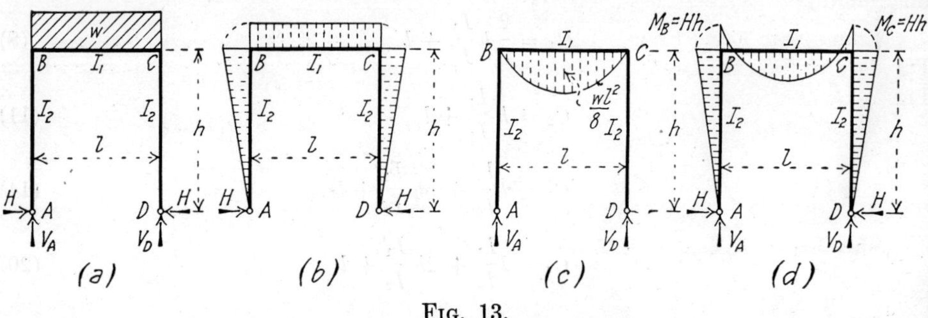

FIG. 13.

Frame with Pin-connected Ends.—*Uniform Loads.*—The stresses in the frame in (*a*) Fig. 13 may be calculated by means of formulas (43), (44) and (45) as deduced from Fig. 9, by assuming that I_0 is zero.

Substituting values of C_1, C_2, and C_4 in formula (43), and making $I_0 = 0$, we have

$$M_0 = 0$$

Substituting values of C_1, C_2, and C_4 in formula (44)

$$H = \frac{w \cdot l^2}{4h(2k+3)} \tag{56}$$

where

$$k = \frac{h}{l} \cdot \frac{I_1}{I_2}$$

also by symmetry

$$V_0 = 0$$

The vertical reactions are

$$V_A = V_D = \tfrac{1}{2} w \cdot l$$

The value of H may be calculated directly from Fig. 13 by area moments as follows. The resisting moments of the frame are as shown in (b), while the bending moments due to the external loading are as shown in (c) Fig. 13. The moments of the negative moment areas about the foot of the column A will be equal to the moment of the positive moment areas, and

$$\frac{2H \cdot h \times \frac{1}{2}h \times \frac{2}{3}h}{I_2} + \frac{H \cdot h \times l \times h}{I_1} = \frac{\frac{1}{8}w \cdot l^2 \times \frac{2}{3}l \times h}{I_1}$$

$$H = \frac{w \cdot l^2}{4h\left(2\frac{h}{l} \cdot \frac{I_1}{I_2} + 3\right)}$$

$$= \frac{w \cdot l^2}{4h(2k+3)} \tag{56}$$

Formula (56) may be obtained from formula (54) by substituting the area of the moment diagram due to the external load, $\frac{1}{12} w \cdot l^3$ in Fig. 13, for the area of the moment diagram due to the external load, $\frac{1}{2} P \cdot a \cdot b$.

Frame with Fixed Ends.—*Concentrated Load.*—The stresses in the frame in (a) Fig. 14 may be calculated by means of formulas (37), (38) and (39) as deduced from Fig. 7, by assuming that I_0 is infinity.

Substituting values of C_1, C_2 and C_4 in formula (38) and making $I_0 = \infty$, we have

$$H_0 = H_A = H_D = \frac{3P \cdot a \cdot b}{2h \cdot l(k+2)} \tag{57}$$

Substituting value of C_3 in (39), and making $I_0 = \infty$

$$V_0 = -\frac{P \cdot a \cdot b(a-b)}{l^3(6k+1)} \tag{58}$$

Substituting values of C_1, C_2 and C_4 in formula (37), and making $I_0 = \infty$

$$M_0 = \frac{P \cdot a \cdot b}{2l(k+2)} \tag{59}$$

The shear V_0 is the difference between the vertical reaction for a pin-connected and a fixed column at A, and

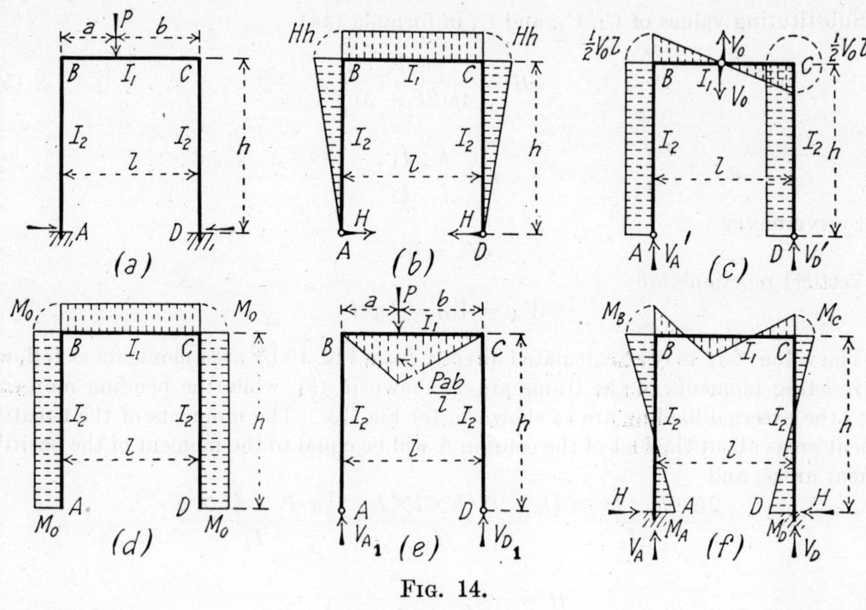

FIG. 14.

$$V_A = \frac{P \cdot b}{l} + V_0$$

$$= \frac{P \cdot b}{l}\left(\frac{6k + 1 + s - 2s^2}{6k + 1}\right) \tag{60}$$

where $a/l = s$, and

$$V_D = \frac{P \cdot a}{l}\left(\frac{6k + 3s - 2s^2}{6k + 1}\right) \tag{61}$$

The bending moment at A is found by taking moments about the center of the base, and

$$M_A = M_0 + \tfrac{1}{2} V_0 \cdot l$$

$$= \frac{P \cdot a \cdot b}{2l}\left(\frac{5k - 1 + 2s(k + 2)}{(k + 2)(6k + 1)}\right) \tag{62}$$

and

$$M_D = \frac{P \cdot a \cdot b}{2l}\left(\frac{3 + 7k - 2s(k + 2)}{(k + 2)(6k + 1)}\right) \tag{63}$$

$$M_B = -M_A + H \cdot h \tag{64}$$

$$M_C = -M_D + H \cdot h \tag{65}$$

Frame with Fixed Ends.—*Uniform Load.*—The stresses in a frame with columns fixed at the base and carrying a uniform load of w lb. per lineal foot on the top member may be obtained from formulas (57), (58) and (59). The value of the horizontal reac-

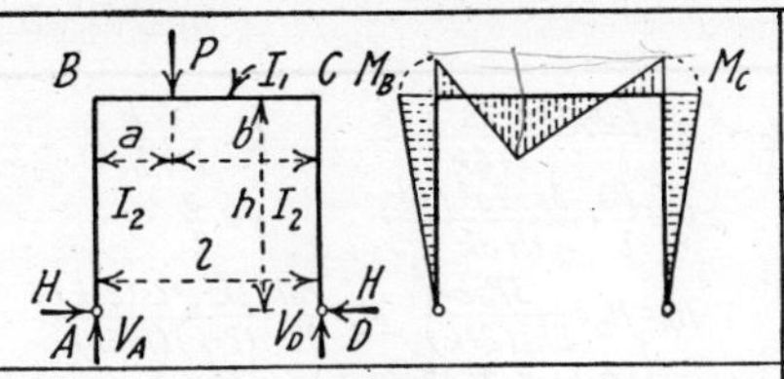	GENERAL CASE $H=\frac{3Pab}{2hl(2k+3)}$; $k=\frac{I_1}{I_2}\cdot\frac{h}{l}$ $V_A=\frac{Pb}{l}$; $V_D=\frac{Pa}{l}$ $M_B=M_C=-Hh$	LOAD IN CENTER; $a=b$ $H=\frac{3Pl}{8h(2k+3)}$; $k=\frac{I_1}{I_2}\cdot\frac{h}{l}$ $V_A=\frac{P}{2}$ $V_D=\frac{P}{2}$ $M_B=M_C=-Hh$
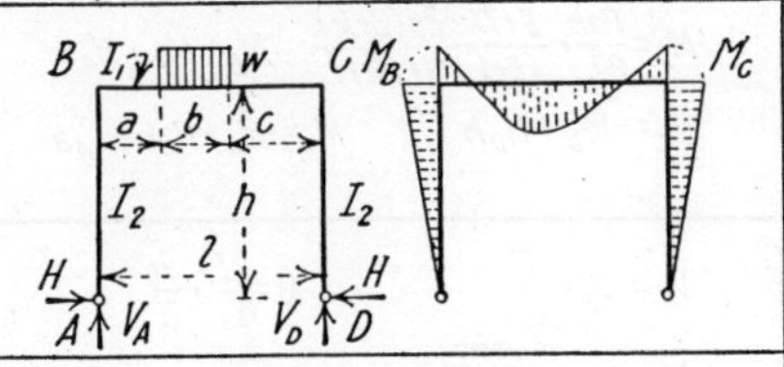	GENERAL CASE $H=\frac{wb}{4}\cdot\frac{[6ac+b(3l-2b)]}{hl(2k+3)}$; $k=\frac{I_1}{I_2}\cdot\frac{h}{l}$ $V_A=\frac{wb}{2l}(2c+b)$; $V_D=\frac{wb}{2l}(2a+b)$ $M_B=M_C=-Hh$	TOP FULLY LOADED; $b=l$ $H=\frac{wl^2}{4h(2k+3)}$; $k=\frac{I_1}{I_2}\cdot\frac{h}{l}$ $V_A=V_D=\frac{wl}{2}$ $M_B=M_C=-Hh$
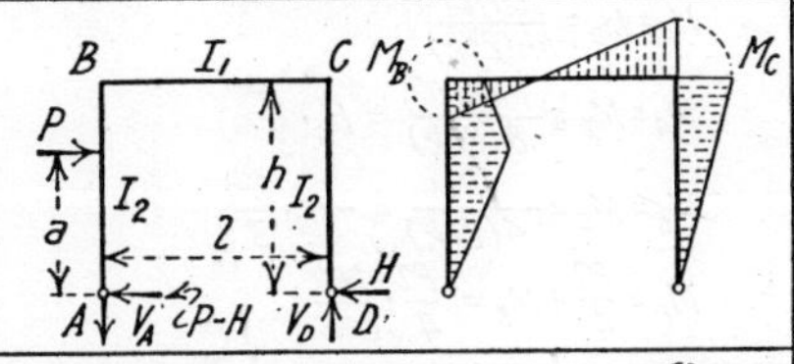	GENERAL CASE $H=\frac{Pa}{2}\cdot\frac{3h^2+k(3h^2-a^2)}{h^3(2k+3)}$; $k=\frac{I_1}{I_2}\cdot\frac{h}{l}$ $V_A=V_D=\frac{Pa}{l}$ $M_B=Pa-Hh$; $M_C=-Hh$	LOAD AT B; $a=h$ $H=\frac{P}{2}$ $V_A=V_D=\frac{Ph}{l}$ $M_B=+\frac{1}{2}Ph$; $M_C=-\frac{1}{2}Ph$
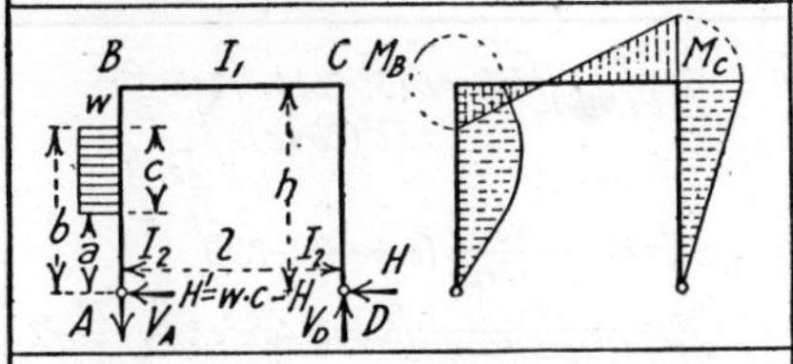	GENERAL CASE $H=\frac{w[6h^2(1+k)(b^2-a^2)-k(b^4-a^4)]}{8h^3(2k+3)}$ $V_A=V_D=\frac{w(b^2-a^2)}{2l}$ $k=\frac{I_1}{I_2}\cdot\frac{h}{l}$ $M_B=V_Dl-Hh$; $M_C=-Hh$	SIDE FULLY LOADED; $c=h$ $H=\frac{wh}{8}\cdot\frac{6+5k}{2k+3}$ $V_A=V_D=\frac{wh^2}{2l}$; $k=\frac{I_1}{I_2}\cdot\frac{h}{l}$ $M_B=V_Dl-Hh$; $M_C=-Hh$
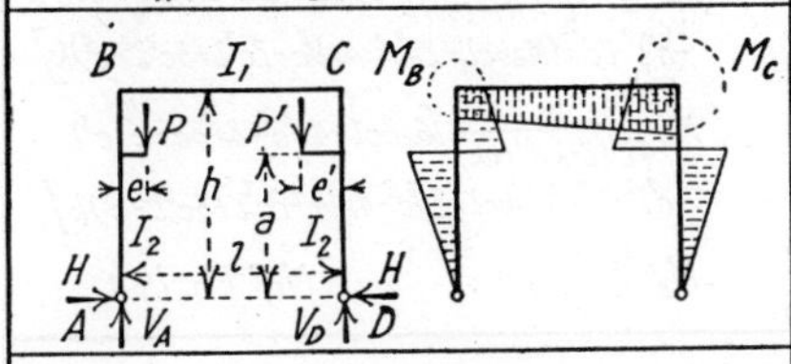	GENERAL CASE $H=3(Pe+P'e')\frac{k(h^2-a^2)+h^2}{2h^3(2k+3)}$; $k=\frac{I_1}{I_2}\cdot\frac{h}{l}$ $V_A=\frac{P'e'+P(l-e)}{l}$; $V_D=\frac{Pe+P'(l-e')}{l}$ $M_B=Pe-Hh$; $M_C=P'e'-Hh$	LOAD ON ONE SIDE; $P'=0$ $H=3Pe\frac{k(h^2-a^2)+h^2}{2h^3(2k+3)}$ $V_A=\frac{P(l-e)}{l}$; $V_D=\frac{Pe}{l}$; $k=\frac{I_1}{I_2}\cdot\frac{h}{l}$ $M_B=Pe-Hh$; $M_C=-Hh$
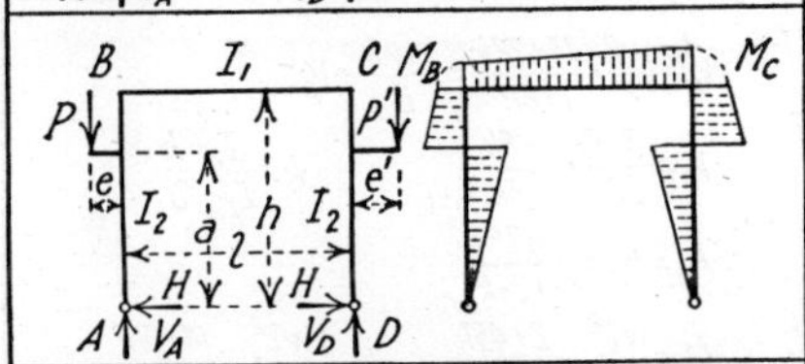	GENERAL CASE $H=3(Pe+P'e')\frac{k(h^2-a^2)+h^2}{2h^3(2k+3)}$; $k=\frac{I_1}{I_2}\cdot\frac{h}{l}$ $V_A=\frac{P(l+e)-P'e'}{l}$; $V_D=\frac{P'(l+e')-Pe}{l}$ $M_B=Hh-Pe$; $M_C=Hh-P'e'$	LOADS AT TOP; $a=h$ $H=\frac{3(Pe+P'e')}{2h(2k+3)}$; $k=\frac{I_1}{I_2}\cdot\frac{h}{l}$ V_A and V_D are the same as in general case. For sides, $M_B=M_C=Hh$
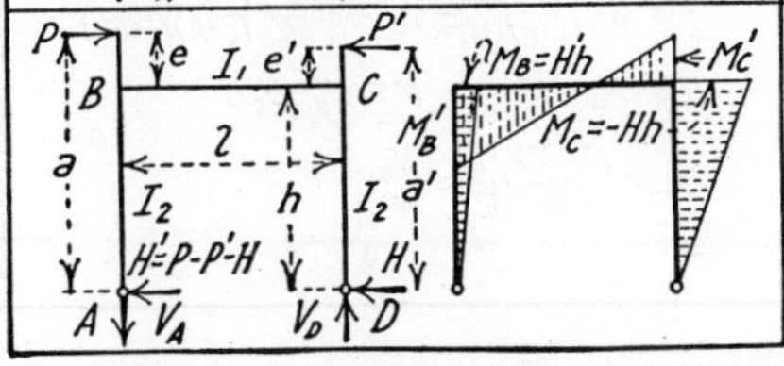	GENERAL CASE $H=\frac{(P-P')2kh+3(Pa+P'a')-6P'h}{2h(2k+3)}$ $V_A=V_D=\frac{Pa-P'a'}{l}$; $k=\frac{I_1}{I_2}\cdot\frac{h}{l}$ $M_B=H'h$; $M_B'=M_B+Pe$; $M_C'=M_C+P'e'$.	LOAD ON ONE SIDE; $P'=0$. $H=\frac{P(2kh+3a)}{2h(2k+3)}$ $V_A=V_D=\frac{Pa}{l}$; $k=\frac{I_1}{I_2}\cdot\frac{h}{l}$ $M_B'=M_B+Pe$; $M_C'=M_C$

FIG. 15. STRESSES IN STIFF FRAMES WITH PIN-CONNECTED COLUMNS.

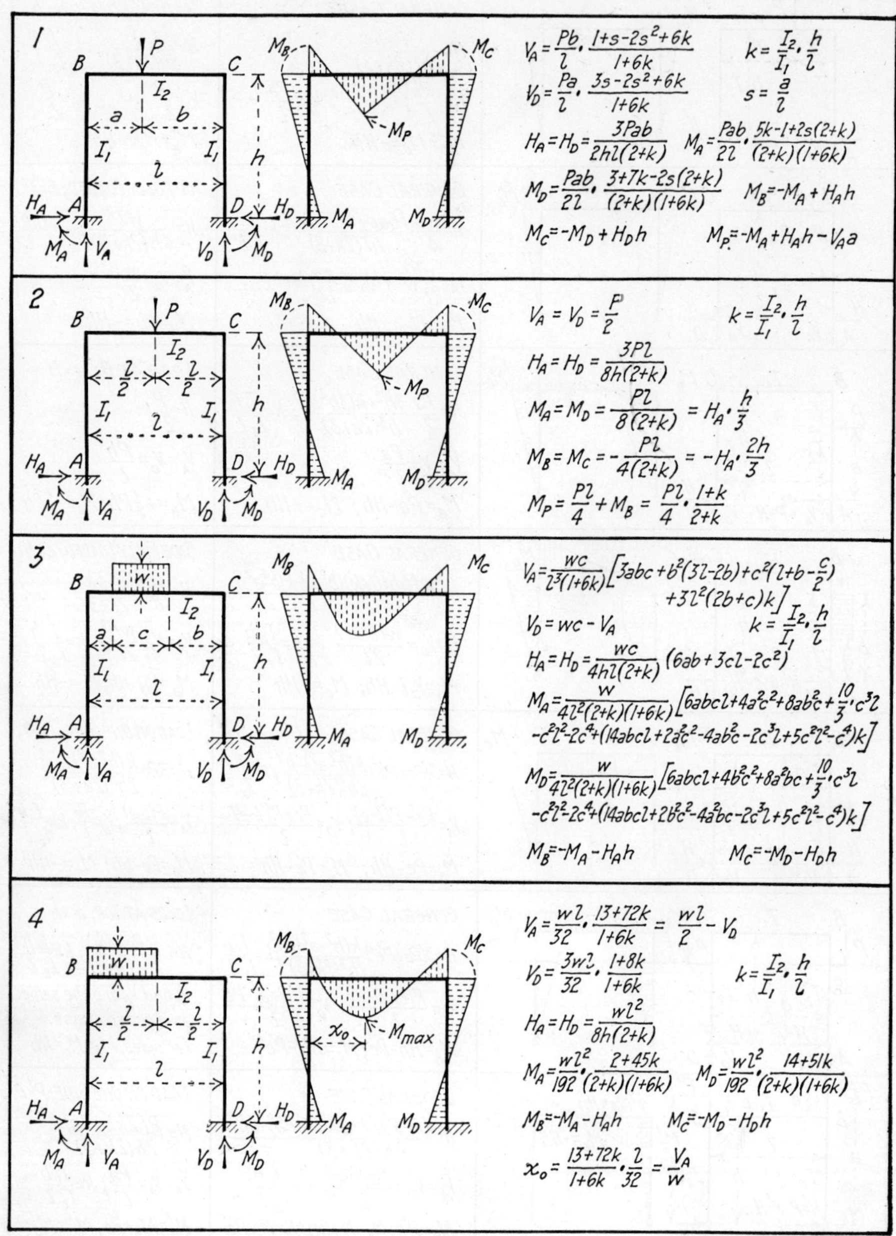

FIG. 16. STRESSES IN STIFF FRAMES WITH FIXED COLUMNS.

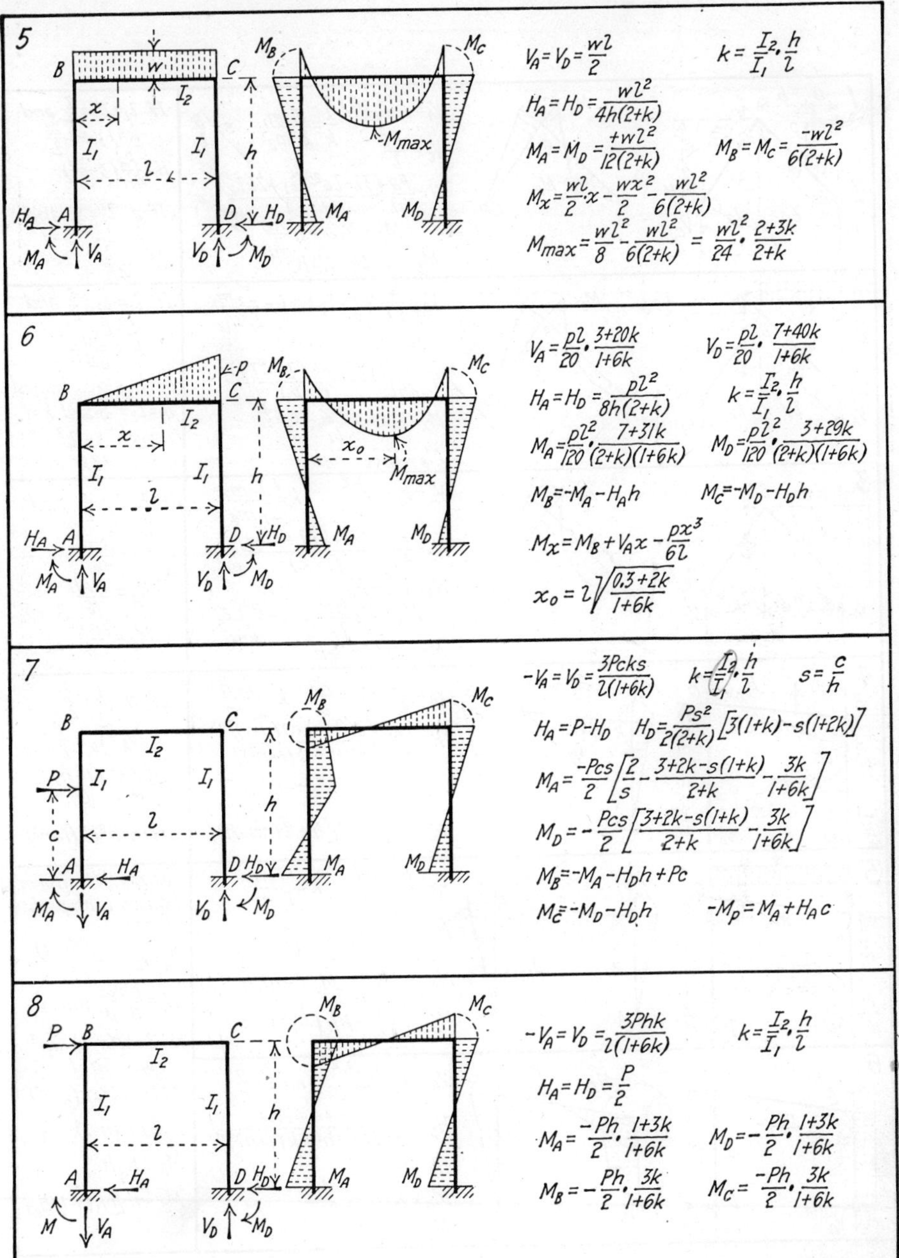

5
$V_A = V_D = \frac{wl}{2}$
$k = \frac{I_2}{I_1} \cdot \frac{h}{l}$
$H_A = H_D = \frac{wl^2}{4h(2+k)}$
$M_A = M_D = \frac{+wl^2}{12(2+k)}$
$M_B = M_C = \frac{-wl^2}{6(2+k)}$
$M_x = \frac{wl}{2} x - \frac{wx^2}{2} - \frac{wl^2}{6(2+k)}$
$M_{max} = \frac{wl^2}{8} - \frac{wl^2}{6(2+k)} = \frac{wl^2}{24} \cdot \frac{2+3k}{2+k}$
6
$V_A = \frac{pl}{20} \cdot \frac{3+20k}{1+6k}$
$V_D = \frac{pl}{20} \cdot \frac{7+40k}{1+6k}$
$H_A = H_D = \frac{pl^2}{8h(2+k)}$
$k = \frac{I_2}{I_1} \cdot \frac{h}{l}$
$M_A = \frac{pl^2}{120} \cdot \frac{7+31k}{(2+k)(1+6k)}$
$M_D = \frac{pl^2}{120} \cdot \frac{3+29k}{(2+k)(1+6k)}$
$M_B = -M_A - H_A h$
$M_C = -M_D - H_D h$
$M_x = M_B + V_A x - \frac{px^3}{6l}$
$x_0 = l\sqrt{\frac{0.3+2k}{1+6k}}$
7
$-V_A = V_D = \frac{3Pcks}{l(1+6k)}$
$k = \frac{I_2}{I_1} \cdot \frac{h}{l}$
$s = \frac{c}{h}$
$H_A = P - H_D$
$H_D = \frac{Ps^2}{2(2+k)}[3(1+k) - s(1+2k)]$
$M_A = \frac{-Pcs}{2}\left[\frac{2}{s} - \frac{3+2k-s(1+k)}{2+k} - \frac{3k}{1+6k}\right]$
$M_D = -\frac{Pcs}{2}\left[\frac{3+2k-s(1+k)}{2+k} - \frac{3k}{1+6k}\right]$
$M_B = -M_A - H_D h + Pc$
$M_C = -M_D - H_D h$
$-M_P = M_A + H_A c$
8
$-V_A = V_D = \frac{3Phk}{l(1+6k)}$
$k = \frac{I_2}{I_1} \cdot \frac{h}{l}$
$H_A = H_D = \frac{P}{2}$
$M_A = \frac{-Ph}{2} \cdot \frac{1+3k}{1+6k}$
$M_D = -\frac{Ph}{2} \cdot \frac{1+3k}{1+6k}$
$M_B = -\frac{Ph}{2} \cdot \frac{3k}{1+6k}$
$M_C = \frac{-Ph}{2} \cdot \frac{3k}{1+6k}$

FIG. 17. STRESSES IN STIFF FRAMES WITH FIXED COLUMNS.

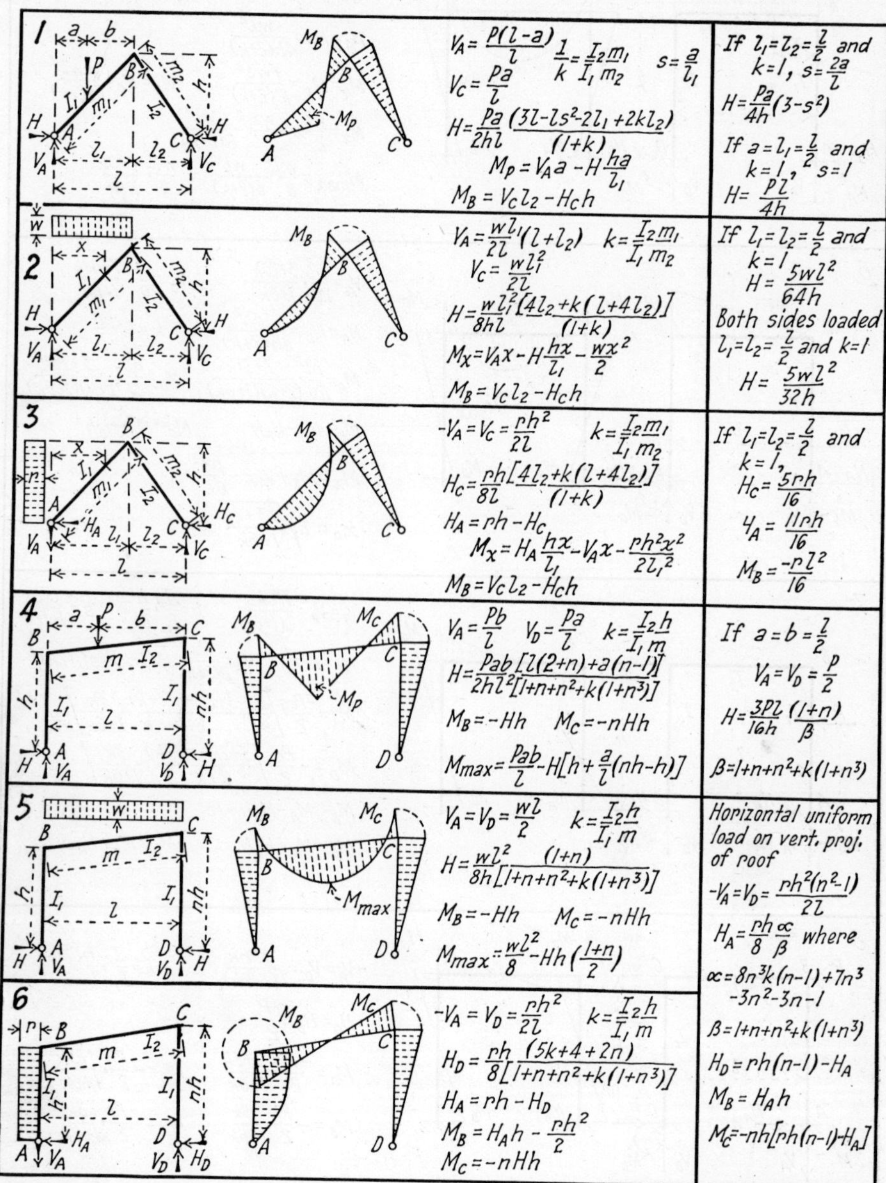

FIG. 18. STRESSES IN STIFF BUILDING FRAMES.

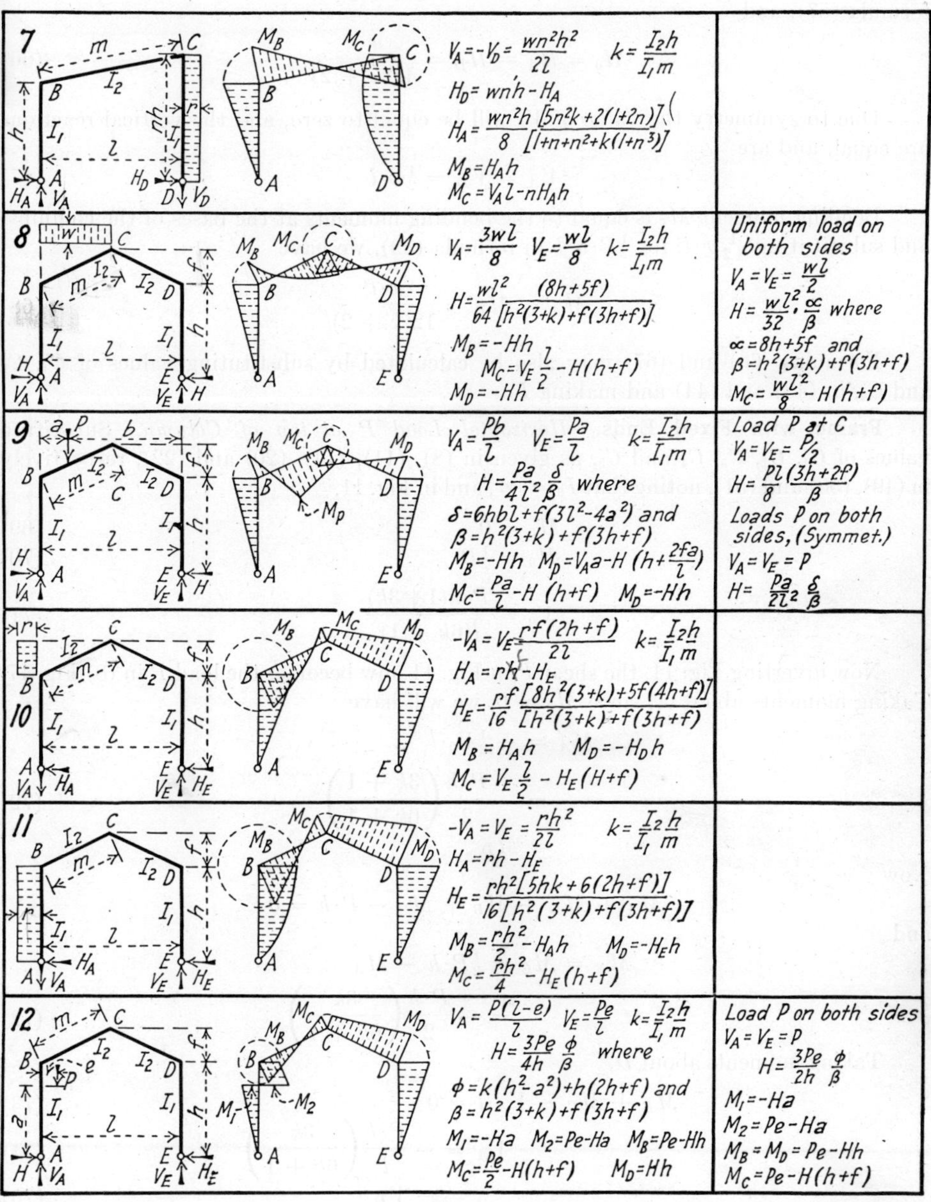

7
$V_A = -V_D = \frac{wn^2h^2}{2l}$ $k = \frac{I_2h}{I_1m}$
$H_D = wnh - H_A$
$H_A = \frac{wn^2h}{8} \frac{[5n^2k + 2(1+2n)]}{[1+n+n^2+k(1+n^3)]}$
$M_B = H_Ah$
$M_C = V_Al - nH_Ah$
8
$V_A = \frac{3wl}{8}$ $V_E = \frac{wl}{8}$ $k = \frac{I_2h}{I_1m}$
$H = \frac{wl^2}{64} \frac{(8h+5f)}{[h^2(3+k)+f(3h+f)]}$
$M_B = -Hh$
$M_C = V_E\frac{l}{2} - H(h+f)$
$M_D = -Hh$
Uniform load on both sides
$V_A = V_E = \frac{wl}{2}$
$H = \frac{wl^2}{32} \cdot \frac{\alpha}{\beta}$ where
$\alpha = 8h+5f$ and
$\beta = h^2(3+k)+f(3h+f)$
$M_C = \frac{wl^2}{8} - H(h+f)$
9
$V_A = \frac{Pb}{l}$ $V_E = \frac{Pa}{l}$ $k = \frac{I_2h}{I_1m}$
$H = \frac{Pa}{4l^2} \frac{\delta}{\beta}$ where
$\delta = 6hbl + f(3l^2 - 4a^2)$ and
$\beta = h^2(3+k) + f(3h+f)$
$M_B = -Hh$ $M_P = V_Aa - H(h + \frac{2fa}{l})$
$M_C = \frac{Pa}{l} - H(h+f)$ $M_D = -Hh$
Load P at C
$V_A = V_E = P/2$
$H = \frac{Pl}{8} \frac{(3h+2f)}{\beta}$
Loads P on both sides, (Symmet.)
$V_A = V_E = P$
$H = \frac{Pa}{2l^2} \frac{\delta}{\beta}$
10
$-V_A = V_E = \frac{rf(2h+f)}{2l}$ $k = \frac{I_2h}{I_1m}$
$H_A = rh - H_E$
$H_E = \frac{rf}{16} \frac{[8h^2(3+k)+5f(4h+f)]}{[h^2(3+k)+f(3h+f)]}$
$M_B = H_Ah$ $M_D = -H_Dh$
$M_C = V_E\frac{l}{2} - H_E(H+f)$
11
$-V_A = V_E = \frac{rh^2}{2l}$ $k = \frac{I_2h}{I_1m}$
$H_A = rh - H_E$
$H_E = \frac{rh^2[5hk + 6(2h+f)]}{16[h^2(3+k)+f(3h+f)]}$
$M_B = \frac{rh^2}{2} - H_Ah$ $M_D = -H_Eh$
$M_C = \frac{rh^2}{4} - H_E(h+f)$
12
$V_A = \frac{P(l-e)}{l}$ $V_E = \frac{Pe}{l}$ $k = \frac{I_2h}{I_1m}$
$H = \frac{3Pe}{4h} \frac{\phi}{\beta}$ where
$\phi = k(h^2 - a^2) + h(2h+f)$ and
$\beta = h^2(3+k) + f(3h+f)$
$M_1 = -Ha$ $M_2 = Pe - Ha$ $M_B = Pe - Hh$
$M_C = \frac{Pe}{2} - H(h+f)$ $M_D = Hh$
Load P on both sides
$V_A = V_E = P$
$H = \frac{3Pe}{2h} \frac{\phi}{\beta}$
$M_1 = -Ha$
$M_2 = Pe - Ha$
$M_B = M_D = Pe - Hh$
$M_C = Pe - H(h+f)$

FIG. 19. STRESSES IN STIFF BUILDING FRAMES.

tion H_0, may be obtained by substituting the area of the moment diagram due to uniform load, $= \frac{1}{12}w \cdot l^3$ for the area of the moment area due to the load P, $= \frac{1}{2}P \cdot a \cdot b$ in formula (57), and

$$H_0 = H_A = H_D = \frac{w \cdot l^2}{4h(k+2)} \tag{66}$$

Due to symmetry the value of V_0 will be equal to zero, and the vertical reactions are equal, and are

$$V_A = V_D = \tfrac{1}{2}w \cdot l \tag{67}$$

Bending moment M_0 is equal to the bending moments at the bases of the columns; and substituting $\frac{1}{12}w \cdot l^3$ for $\frac{1}{2}P \cdot a \cdot b$ in formula (59), we have

$$M_A = M_D = \frac{w \cdot l^2}{12(k+2)} \tag{68}$$

Formulas (66) and (67) may also be calculated by substituting values of C_1, C_2 and C_4, in (43) and (44) and making $I_0 = \infty$.

Frame with Fixed Ends.—*Horizontal Load P at top of Column.*—Substitute values of C_1, C_2, C_3, C_4 and C_5, as given in (8), (11), (14), (20) and (22), respectively in (49), (50) and (51), noting that $I_0 = \infty$, and in Fig. 11,

$$M_0 = 0 \tag{69}$$

$$H_0 = \tfrac{1}{2}P \tag{70}$$

$$V_0 = \frac{P \cdot h(1+3k)}{l(6k+1)} \tag{71}$$

Now inverting Fig. 11, the shear P in Fig. 11 now becomes the load P in (8) Fig. 17. Taking moments about A, since $M_0 = 0$, we will have

$$\begin{aligned} M_A &= -\tfrac{1}{2}V_0 \cdot l \\ &= -\frac{P \cdot h}{2}\left(\frac{3k+1}{6k+1}\right) \\ &= M_D \end{aligned} \tag{72}$$

Now

$$M_A + M_D + M_B + M_C - P \cdot h = 0$$

and

$$\begin{aligned} M_B = M_C &= \tfrac{1}{2}P \cdot h - M_A \\ &= -\frac{P \cdot h}{2}\left(\frac{3k}{6k+1}\right) \end{aligned} \tag{72}$$

Taking moments about D,

$$M_B + M_C - V_A \cdot l = 0 \tag{73}$$

$$V_A = -\frac{P \cdot h}{l}\left(\frac{3k}{6k+1}\right) \tag{74}$$

$$= -V_D \tag{75}$$

Stresses in Stiff Frames.—Stresses in stiff frames with pin-connected columns are given for different loadings in Fig. 15. Stresses in stiff frames with fixed columns are given for different loadings in Fig. 16 and Fig. 17. Stresses in several types of stiff building frames are given in Fig. 18 and Fig. 19.

CHAPTER XVIII.

Stresses in Stiff Frames by Slope Deflections

Slope Deflections.—The moments in stiff frames may be calculated by area moments using the slopes of the members and also the slope deflections. The analysis is based on the theorem proved in Chapter XIV, "*that the change in slope between two points A and B in a beam is equal to the moment area between A and B divided by $E \cdot I$.*

In making the calculations of the stresses in stiff frames it will be assumed, (1) that the connections are perfectly rigid; (2) that the lengths of the members are not changed by axial stress, and (3) that the shear deformation is zero.

Signs of Moments and Deflections.—The moment at the end of any member will be positive if the external moment at the end acts in a clockwise direction. In the member AB the moment at the end A will be M_{AB}, and at the end B will be M_{BA}.

The change in slope of the tangent to a member will be considered positive when the tangent has turned in a clockwise direction.

The deflection of any point in a member will be measured normal to and away from base line or line of original position. The sign of deflection will be considered positive when measured in the same direction from the base line as are positive slopes.

The bending moment diagrams will be plotted on the tension side of the member.

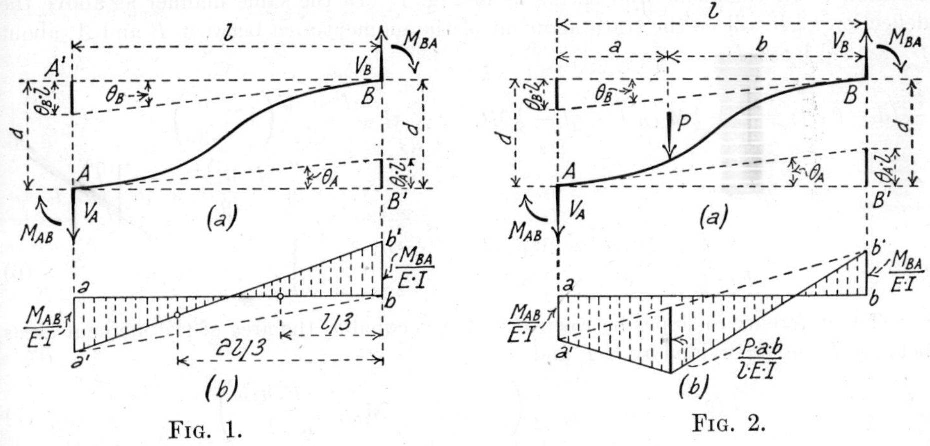

Fig. 1. Fig. 2.

No Transverse Loads.—The member AB in Fig. 1 is acted upon by moments and shears at the ends. Let AB' be the original position of the member AB, and BA' be the original position of the member BA. The angles θ_A and θ_B, and the distance d are negative.

The total deflection d at B is partly due to the change in slope at A, and partly due to flexure of the member. The distance $d - \theta_A \cdot l$ is equal to the deflection due to flexure, and is the static moment of the moment area between B and A, about B, divided by $E \cdot I$, and

$$-(d - \theta_A \cdot l) = (+\tfrac{1}{2}M_{AB} \cdot l \times \tfrac{2}{3}l - \tfrac{1}{2}M_{BA} \cdot l \times \tfrac{1}{3}l)/E \cdot I$$

$$= \frac{l^2}{E \cdot I}\left(+\frac{M_{AB}}{3} - \frac{M_{BA}}{6}\right) \tag{1}$$

The change in slope of the member from B to A is $\theta_A - \theta_B$, and is equal to the area of the moment diagram between B and A, divided by $E \cdot I$, and

$$\theta_A - \theta_B = (+\tfrac{1}{2}M_{AB} \cdot l - \tfrac{1}{2}M_{BA} \cdot l)/E \cdot I$$

$$= \frac{l}{2E \cdot I}(+M_{AB} - M_{BA}) \tag{2}$$

Solving equations (1) and (2) for M_{AB}, there results

$$M_{AB} = \frac{2E \cdot I}{l}\left(2\theta_A + \theta_B - \frac{3d}{l}\right) \tag{3}$$

Substituting $K = I/l$ and $R = d/l$, and

$$M_{AB} = 2E \cdot K(2\theta_A + \theta_B - 3R) \tag{4}$$

also

$$M_{BA} = 2E \cdot K(2\theta_B + \theta_A - 3R) \tag{5}$$

These are the general equations for moment at the ends of a member carrying no transverse loads.

Transverse Loads.—In (*a*) Fig. 2, the member AB carries a transverse load P in addition to the moments and shears as in Fig. 1. In the same manner as above the deflection at B will be the static moment of the moment area between B and A, about B, divided by $E \cdot I$.

$$-(d - \theta_A \cdot l) = \left[+\tfrac{1}{2}M_{AB} \cdot l \times \tfrac{2}{3}l - \tfrac{1}{2}M_{BA} \cdot l \times \tfrac{1}{3}l + \frac{P \cdot a^2 \cdot b}{2l}\left(b + \frac{a}{3}\right) + \frac{P \cdot a \cdot b^2}{2l} \times \tfrac{2}{3}b\right] \Big/ E \cdot I$$

$$= \frac{l}{E \cdot I}\left[+\frac{M_{AB} \cdot l}{3} - \frac{M_{BA} \cdot l}{6} + \frac{P \cdot a \cdot b}{6l}(l + b)\right] \tag{6}$$

The difference in slopes between B and A is equal to the area of the moment areas between B and A, divided by $E \cdot I$, and

$$(\theta_A - \theta_B) = \frac{l}{2E \cdot I}\left(+\mathrm{M}_{AB} - \mathrm{M}_{BA} + \frac{P \cdot a \cdot b}{l}\right) \tag{7}$$

Solving equations (6) and (7) for M_{AB}, there results

$$M_{AB} = 2E \cdot K(2\theta_A + \theta_B - 3R) - \frac{P \cdot a \cdot b^2}{l^2} \tag{8}$$

and also

$$M_{BA} = 2E \cdot K(2\theta_B + \theta_A - 3R) + \frac{P \cdot a^2 \cdot b}{l^2} \tag{9}$$

If the transverse load on the member is symmetrical the last term in equations (8) and (9) are equal to F/l, where F is the area of the moment diagram, and

$$M_{AB} = 2E \cdot K(2\theta_A + \theta_B - 3R) - \frac{F}{l} \tag{10}$$

$$M_{BA} = 2E \cdot K(2\theta_B + \theta_A - 3R) + \frac{F}{l} \tag{11}$$

For a load P at the center of the beam, $F/l = \frac{1}{8}P \cdot l$; for two loads P at a distance a from each end, $F/l = P \cdot a(l - a)/l$; for two loads P equally spaced, $F/l = 2P \cdot l/9$; for three loads P equally spaced, $F/l = 5P \cdot l/16$; for a uniform load w, $F/l = \frac{1}{12}w \cdot l^2$; for a triangular load varying from zero at the ends to a maximum at the center, total load $= W$, $F/l = 5W \cdot l/48$; for triangular load varying from a maximum at the ends to zero at center, total load $= W$, $F/l = W \cdot l/16$; for a parabolic loading, total load $= W$, $F/l = W \cdot l/10$. These are the general equations for moments at the ends of members carrying transverse loads.

Several problems will be solved.

For several transverse loads on a member the last term in (8) and (9) will be the sum of the values for the individual loads, and

$$M_{AB} = 2E \cdot K(2\theta_A + \theta_B - 3R) - \Sigma(P \cdot a \cdot b^2)/l^2 \tag{8'}$$

$$M_{BA} = 2E \cdot K(2\theta_B + \theta_A - 3R) + \Sigma(P \cdot a^2 \cdot b)/l^2 \tag{9'}$$

Beam Fixed at Ends.—Load at distance a from left end. In this case $\theta_A = 0$, $\theta_B = 0$, and $R = 0$, and

$$M_{AB} = -\frac{P \cdot a \cdot b^2}{l^2} \tag{12}$$

$$M_{BA} = +\frac{P \cdot a^2 \cdot b}{l^2} \tag{13}$$

For a load at the middle of the beam, $a = b = \frac{1}{2}l$

$$M_{AB} = -M_{BA} = -\tfrac{1}{8}P \cdot l \tag{14}$$

(Moments M_{AB} and M_{BA} are restraining moments and both are usually assumed as negative, although acting in opposite directions.)

Beam Free to Turn at Support, Bending at other end, carrying Load P.—Let the beam AB with span l in Fig. 2, be hinged at support A, have a bending moment M_{BA} at B, and carry a load P at a distance a from the left end and b from the right end.

Substituting $M_{AB} = 0$ in equation (8),

$$0 = 2E \cdot K(2\theta_A + \theta_B - 3R) - \frac{P \cdot a \cdot b^2}{l^2} \tag{15}$$

also

$$M_{BA} = 2E \cdot K(2\theta_B + \theta_A - 3R) + \frac{P \cdot a^2 \cdot b}{l^2} \tag{16}$$

Eliminating θ_A between (15) and (16), and

$$M_{BA} = E \cdot K(3\theta_B - 3R) + \frac{P \cdot a \cdot b}{l^2}(a + \tfrac{1}{2}b) \tag{17}$$

Stresses in a Portal.—The portal in Fig. 3 with columns free to turn at the base carries a load P at a distance a from the left support.

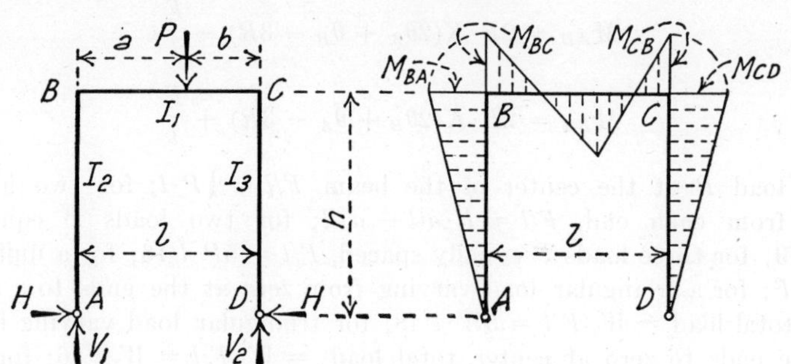

FIG. 3.

Let $K = I_1/l = k \cdot I_2/h = s \cdot I_3/h$.
Now from Fig. 3, it will be seen that

$$M_{BA} + M_{CD} = 0 \tag{18}$$

From equation (17), since the load is on the top strut.

$$M_{BA} = \frac{E \cdot K}{k}(3\theta_B - 3R) \tag{19}$$

Also

$$M_{CD} = \frac{E \cdot K}{s}(3\theta_C - 3R) \tag{20}$$

From equations (8) and (9), noting that there is no vertical deflection,

$$M_{BC} = 2E \cdot K(2\theta_B + \theta_C) - \frac{P \cdot a \cdot b^2}{l^2} \tag{21}$$

$$M_{CB} = 2E \cdot K(2\theta_C + \theta_B) + \frac{P \cdot a^2 \cdot b}{l^2} \tag{22}$$

Subtract (20) from (19), and substitute $M_{CD} = -M_{CB}$

$$k \cdot M_{BA} + s \cdot M_{CB} = E \cdot K(3\theta_B - 3\theta_C) \tag{23}$$

Subtract (22) from (21) and substitute $M_{BC} = -M_{BA}$, and

$$-M_{BA} - M_{CB} = 2E \cdot K(\theta_B - \theta_C) - \frac{P \cdot a \cdot b}{l} \tag{24}$$

Eliminate $(\theta_B - \theta_C)$ between (23) and (24), and

$$M_{BA}(3 + 2k) + M_{CB}(3 + 2s) = \frac{3P \cdot a \cdot b}{l} \tag{25}$$

Now from (18), since $M_{CD} = -M_{CB}$,

$$M_{BA} - M_{CB} = 0 \tag{26}$$

Substitute M_{CB} from (26) in (25), and

$$M_{BA} = \frac{3P \cdot a \cdot b}{2l(k + s + 3)} \tag{27}$$

$$= + M_{CB}$$

Now if H = horizontal reaction at A and D, then

$$H \cdot h = M_{BA}$$

and

$$H = \frac{3P \cdot a \cdot b}{2h \cdot l(k + s + 3)} \tag{28}$$

If $k = s$, then

$$M_{BA} = \frac{3P \cdot a \cdot b}{2l(2k + 3)} \tag{29}$$

and

$$H = \frac{3P \cdot a \cdot b}{2h \cdot l(2k + 3)} \tag{30}$$

Equation (30) is the same as equation (54), Chapter XVII, which was calculated by Area Moments.

STRESSES IN A QUADRANGULAR BRIDGE TRUSS.—The quadrangular truss with a span $2l$ and depth h carries a load P at the center of the truss. The moments of inertia of the members are as shown in Fig. 4. The joints of the truss are assumed as

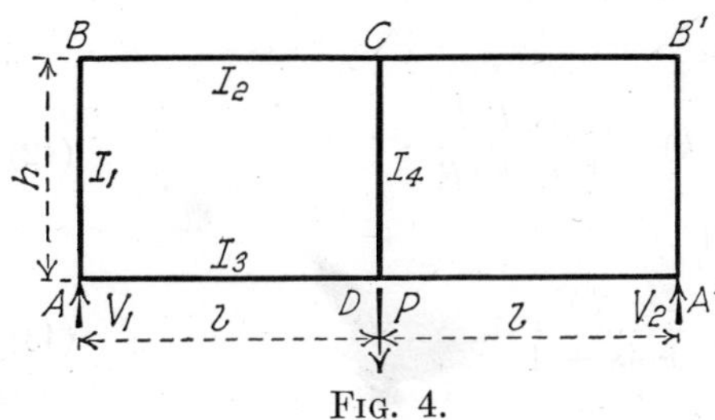

FIG. 4.

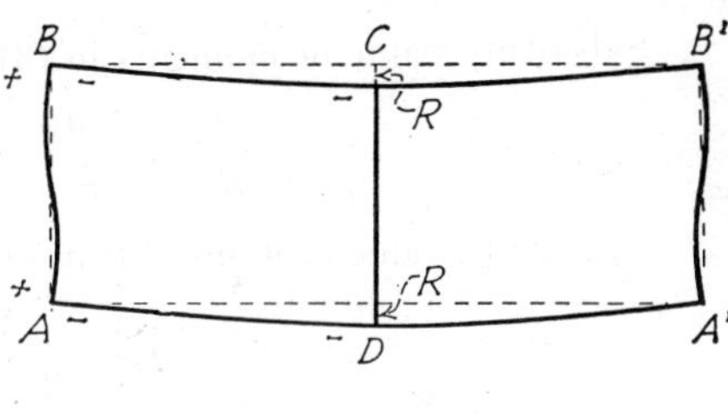

FIG. 5.

rigid. Assume that

$$K = I_1/h, \quad = s \cdot I_2/l = k \cdot I_3/l = r \cdot I_4/h$$

From the deformed truss diagram in Fig. 5, it will be seen that if the longitudinal deformations of the truss members be neglected, the deflection of point B will be zero and that the deflections of points C and D will be equal to R. From symmetry, it will be seen that $\theta_C = \theta_D = 0$.

Solution.—Take moments of forces to the left of a vertical section through C–D, and

$$M_{AD} + M_{DA} + M_{BC} + M_{CB} + \tfrac{1}{2}P \cdot l = 0 \tag{31}$$

Applying equations (4) and (5) to the members of the truss, noting from symmetry $M_{CD} = M_{DC} = 0$, there results

$$M_{AB} = 2E\cdot K(2\theta_A + \theta_B) \tag{32}$$

$$M_{AD} = \frac{2E\cdot K}{k}(2\theta_A - 3R) \tag{33}$$

$$M_{DA} = \frac{2E\cdot K}{k}(\theta_A - 3R) \tag{34}$$

$$M_{BA} = 2E\cdot K(2\theta_B + \theta_A) \tag{35}$$

$$M_{BC} = \frac{2E\cdot K}{s}(2\theta_B - 3R) \tag{36}$$

$$M_{CB} = \frac{2E\cdot K}{s}(\theta_B - 3R) \tag{37}$$

Also, since the joints A and B are in equilibrium,

$$M_{AB} + M_{AD} = 0 \tag{38}$$

$$M_{BA} + M_{BC} = 0 \tag{39}$$

Substitute (32) and (33) in (38), and

$$\frac{\theta_B}{R} = \frac{3}{k} - \frac{2\theta_A}{R}\left(\frac{1+k}{k}\right) \tag{40}$$

Substitute (35) and (36) in (39), and

$$\frac{2\theta_B}{R}(1+s) + \frac{s\cdot\theta_A}{R} = 3 \tag{41}$$

Substitute value of moments in (31), and

$$\frac{s\cdot\theta_A}{R} + \frac{k\cdot\theta_B}{R} = 2(s+k) - \frac{k\cdot s\cdot P\cdot l}{12E\cdot K\cdot R} \tag{42}$$

Substitute value of θ_B in (40) in (41), and

$$\theta_A = \frac{3R(2s+2-k)}{3k\cdot s + 4k + 4s + 4} \tag{43}$$

Substitute value of θ_A in (43) in (40), and

$$\theta_B = \frac{3R(2k+2-s)}{3k\cdot s + 4k + 4s + 4} \tag{44}$$

Substitute θ_A from (43) and θ_B from (44) in (42), and

$$R = \frac{k\cdot s\cdot P\cdot l}{12E\cdot K}\cdot\frac{3k\cdot s + 4k + 4s + 4}{2(3k\cdot s^2 + 11k\cdot s + s^2 + s + 3k^2\cdot s + k^2 + k)} \tag{45}$$

Let

$$\frac{1}{N} = (3k\cdot s^2 + 11k\cdot s + s^2 + s + 3k^2\cdot s + k^2 + k)$$

and

$$R = \frac{k\cdot s\cdot P\cdot l\cdot N}{24E\cdot K}(3k\cdot s + 4k + 4s + 4) \tag{46}$$

Substitute R in (46) in (43), and

$$\theta_A = \frac{P \cdot l \cdot N \cdot k \cdot s}{8E \cdot K}(2s + 2 - k) \tag{47}$$

Substitute R in (46) in (44), and

$$\theta_B = \frac{P \cdot l \cdot N \cdot k \cdot s}{8E \cdot K}(2k + 2 - s) \tag{48}$$

Substitute values of θ_A and θ_B in (32), and

$$M_{AB} = \tfrac{3}{4}P \cdot l \cdot N \cdot k \cdot s(s + 2) \tag{49}$$

From (38)

$$M_{AD} = - M_{AB} = - \tfrac{3}{4}P \cdot l \cdot N \cdot k \cdot s(s + 2) \tag{50}$$

Substitute θ_A and θ_B in equation (35), and

$$M_{BA} = \tfrac{3}{4}P \cdot l \cdot N \cdot k \cdot s(k + 2) \tag{51}$$

From equation (39)

$$M_{BC} = - M_{BA} = - \tfrac{3}{4}P \cdot l \cdot N \cdot k \cdot s(s + 2) \tag{52}$$

Substitute R from equation (46) and θ_A from equation (43) in equation (34), and

$$M_{DA} = - \tfrac{1}{4}P \cdot l \cdot N \cdot s(2s + 2 + 5k + 3k \cdot s) \tag{53}$$

Substitute R from equation (46) and θ_B from equation (44), in equation (37), and

$$M_{CB} = - \tfrac{1}{4}P \cdot l \cdot N \cdot k(2k + 2 + 5s + 3k \cdot s) \tag{54}$$

The longitudinal stress at the center of the lower chord AD, will be

$$H_D = - \frac{P \cdot l}{2h} - \left(\frac{M_{CB} + M_{DA}}{h}\right) \tag{55}$$

$$= - H_C$$

Now if members AD and BC have the same moment of inertia, $I_3 = I_2$, and $s = k$

$$k = \frac{I_1}{I_2}\frac{l}{h}$$

and

$$M_{AD} = M_{BC} = - \frac{P \cdot l}{4} \cdot \frac{3k}{6k + 1} \tag{56}$$

$$M_{CB} = M_{DA} = - \frac{P \cdot l}{4} \cdot \frac{3k + 1}{6k + 1} \tag{57}$$

The longitudinal stress at the center of the lower chord AD, will be

$$H_D = - \frac{P \cdot l}{2h} + \frac{P \cdot l}{2h} \cdot \frac{3k + 1}{6k + 1}$$

$$= - \frac{3P \cdot l \cdot k}{2h(6k + 1)} \tag{58}$$

$$= - H_C$$

If $I_1/h = I_2/l = I_3/l$ ($k = s = 1$)

$$M_{AD} = M_{BC} = -\tfrac{3}{28}P\cdot l \tag{59}$$

$$M_{CB} = M_{DA} = -\tfrac{4}{28}P\cdot l \tag{60}$$

$$M_{AB} = M_{BA} = +\tfrac{3}{28}P\cdot l \tag{61}$$

$$H_D = -\frac{3}{14}\frac{P\cdot l}{h} \tag{62}$$

$$= -H_C$$

When $k = s = 1$, the direct stress in $AB = \tfrac{1}{4}P$, and the direct stress in $CD = -\tfrac{1}{2}P$.

For any quadrangular truss with stiff joints, the equations may be written as above. There will always be as many equations as there are unknowns. If the truss is symmetrical about a center line as was the above truss, the problem is much simplified.

By passing a vertical plane through the center of the truss CD in Fig. 4, it will be seen that the left half of the truss is a portal with stiff joints, with columns fixed at C and D ($\theta_C = \theta_D = 0$), and carrying a load of $\tfrac{1}{2}P$. For the solution of a portal with fixed columns by Area Moments, see Chapter XVII.

Problems.—The stresses in the stiff frames given in Fig. 15 to Fig. 19, inclusive, Chapter XVII, may be calculated by the method of "Slope Deflections."

For the solutions of additional problems by the "Method of Slope Deflections," see "Analysis of Statically Indeterminate Structures by the Slope Deflection Method," by Wilson, Richart and Weiss, University of Illinois, Eng. Sta. Bul. No. 108.

References.—The method of slope deflections was first deduced by Manderla in 1878, and was used in the solution of secondary stresses. The method of slope deflections has been developed by several writers, among whom are: Mohr, Otto, "Abhandlungen aud dem Gebiete der technischen Mechanik, 1906." Kunz, F. C., "Engineering News," Oct. 5, 1911. Wilson and Maney, "Wind Stresses in Steel Frames of Office Buildings," University of Ill. Eng. Exp. Sta., Bul. 80, 1915. Wilson, Richart and Weiss, "Analysis of Statically Indeterminate Structures by the Slope Deflection Method," Univ. of Ill. Eng. Exp. Sta. Bul. 108, 1918.

CHAPTER XVIIIA.

STRESSES IN STIFF FRAMES BY MOMENT DISTRIBUTION.

Introduction.—The method of moment distribution is due to Professor Hardy Cross of the University of Illinois.* This method may be explained as the solution of the theorem of three moments by a series of successive approximations. It is essentially a method involving numerical computation for a specific structure rather than an algebraic computation for a series of similar structures as illustrated by the method of area moments. The method of moment distribution is readily understood and easily remembered because each step has a definite physical significance.

Constants.—Three constants for every member must be defined for the moment distribution method. These constants are (1) "stiffness," (2) "carry-over factor," and (3) "fixed-end moment."

(1) **Stiffness.**—Stiffness is defined as the moment at the end of a member necessary to produce a unit rotation of that end when the other end is fixed. The stiffness factor at A in Fig. 1 is $K = M_A/\theta_A$. The significance of the stiffness factor in this discussion is

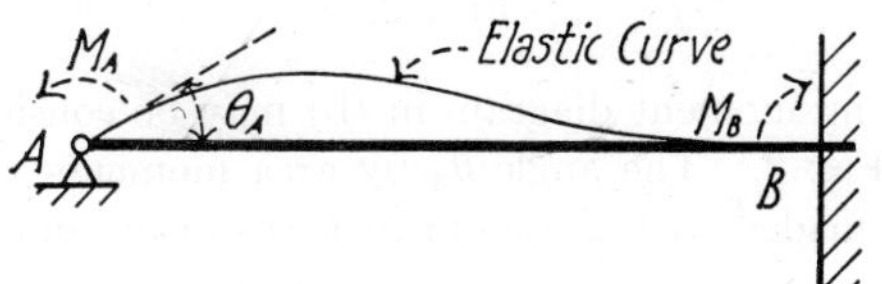

FIG. 1.

that at any joint the moment will be distributed in proportion to the stiffness of the members meeting at that point. For members with a constant moment of inertia the stiffness is proportional to I/l where I is the moment of inertia and l is the span.

(2) **Carry-over Factor.**—The carry-over factor is defined as the ratio of the moment at the point A, Fig. 1, to the moment at point B. For members with a constant moment of inertia the carry-over factor is $\frac{1}{2}$.

(3) **Fixed-end Moment.**—By fixed-end moment is meant the moment at the end of a member if its ends are fixed against rotation. For a member having a constant moment of inertia the fixed-end moment is equal to $\mp \frac{1}{12} w \cdot l^2$ for a uniform load of w lb. per lineal foot. For a concentrated load P at a distance a from the left end and b from the right end the fixed-end moment at the left end is $\frac{P \cdot a^2 \cdot b}{l^2}$, and at the right end is $\frac{P \cdot a \cdot b^2}{l^2}$.

Derivation of Constants for Members of Uniform Section.—The "stiffness" and "carry-over factor" in this discussion are derived by area moments although they may be derived by work, slope deflection or other standard methods.

* See Transactions of the American Society of Civil Engineers, vol. 96, 1932.

Stiffness.—The "stiffness factor" has been defined as the moment at the end of a member necessary to produce a unit rotation of that end when the other end is fixed. Such a condition is represented by (a), Fig. 2.

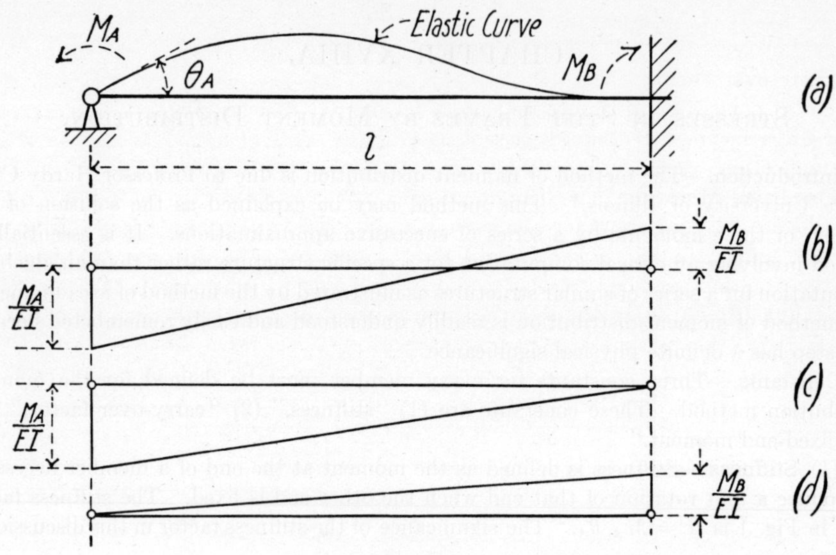

FIG. 2.

The resulting bending moment diagram in (b) may be considered as the sum of two diagrams (c) and (d), Fig. 2. The angle θ_A by area moments will be the reaction of a simple beam of length l loaded with the moment areas in (c) and (d), and

$$\theta_A = \frac{M_A}{E \cdot I} \cdot \frac{l}{2} \cdot \frac{2l}{3} \div l + \frac{M_B}{E \cdot I} \cdot \frac{l}{2} \cdot \frac{l}{3} \div l$$

and

$$\theta_A = \frac{M_A \cdot l}{3E \cdot I} + \frac{M_B \cdot l}{6E \cdot I} \tag{1}$$

Also the deflection of point A must be zero and the moments of the area moments about A must be zero, and

$$\frac{M_A}{E \cdot I} \cdot \frac{l}{2} \cdot \frac{l}{3} + \frac{M_B}{E \cdot I} \cdot \frac{l}{2} \cdot \frac{2l}{3} = 0$$

and

$$M_A = -2M_B \tag{2}$$

Substituting M_B as given in (2) in (1) we have

$$\theta_A = \frac{M_A \cdot l}{3E \cdot I} - \frac{1}{12} \cdot \frac{M_A \cdot l}{E \cdot I}$$

and

$$E \cdot \theta_A = \frac{M_A \cdot l}{4I} \tag{3}$$

The stiffness is defined as

$$K = \frac{M_A}{\theta_A}$$

and from (3) we have

$$K = \frac{4E \cdot I}{l} \qquad (4)$$

Carry-over Factor.—The "carry-over factor" has been defined as the ratio of the moment at point A to the moment at point B, Fig. 1. From equation (2) the carry-over factor for a member of uniform section is $\frac{1}{2}$, if the signs of moments are taken as in slope deflection.

Fixed-end Moment.—The "fixed-end moment" is derived here for a single concentrated load. The procedure for a uniform load or a series of concentrated loads is essentially the same. In Fig. 3, (a) and (b) show a concentrated load on a fixed-end beam with the resulting bending moment diagram which may be considered as the sum of the areas of (c), (d) and (e). M_P is the bending moment on a simple beam and in this case

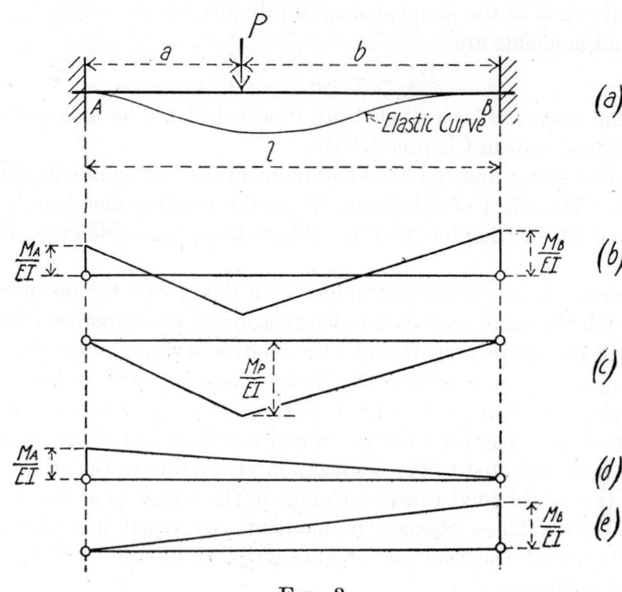

FIG. 3.

is equal to $\frac{P \cdot a \cdot b}{l}$.

The slope of the elastic curve of the beam at the point A is zero. By area moments the sum of the areas from B to A must be zero, and

$$\frac{M_P \cdot l}{2E \cdot I} - \frac{M_A \cdot l}{2E \cdot I} - \frac{M_B \cdot l}{2E \cdot I} = 0 \qquad (5)$$

Also the moment of the area moments about A must be zero, and

$$\frac{M_P}{E \cdot I}\frac{a}{2}\frac{2a}{3} + \frac{M_P}{E \cdot I}\frac{b}{2}\left(a + \frac{b}{3}\right) - \frac{M_A}{E \cdot I}\frac{l^2}{6} - \frac{M_B}{E \cdot I}\frac{l^2}{3} = 0 \qquad (6)$$

Solving (5) and (6) and changing signs to conform to slope deflection sign conventions, we have

$$M_A = \frac{M_P \cdot b}{l} = -\frac{P \cdot a \cdot b^2}{l^2} \tag{7}$$

and

$$M_B = \frac{M_P \cdot a}{l} = \frac{P \cdot a^2 \cdot b}{l^2} \tag{8}$$

For several transverse loads on a member the fixed-end moments are

$$M_A = -\frac{\Sigma(P \cdot a \cdot b^2)}{l^2} \tag{9}$$

and

$$M_B = \frac{\Sigma(P \cdot a^2 \cdot b)}{l^2} \tag{10}$$

If the transverse load on the member is symmetrical the fixed-end moment at each end is equal to the area of the moment diagram divided by the length l. For a uniform load the fixed-end moments are

$$M_A = -M_B = -\tfrac{1}{12} w \cdot l^2 \tag{11}$$

The fixed-end moments for a single load, P, as calculated by area moments are given in equations (12) and (13) in Chapter XVIII.

The carry-over factor and the fixed-end moments are given in equations (8) and (9) Chapter XVIII. The effect of side sway, R, on the bending moments is also shown in equations (8) and (9) in Chapter XVIII. Where there is no side sway, R, will be equal to zero.

Joint Rotation.—In any framed structure with rigid joints the members at any joint will rotate through the same angle when deformation of the structure takes place. The end moments will change in proportion to the relative stiffness of the members. Before rotation takes place the sum of the "fixed-end moments" will not be zero, after the rotation takes place and the joint is released the sum of the end moments at the joint must be equal to zero. The total change in end moments or the "unbalanced fixed-end moment" must be distributed to the members in proportion to the stiffness of the members. The rotation of the joint causes a change in the moments at the other ends of the connecting members. These changes in moments are equal in each member to the moments distributed at the rotating point multiplied by the "carry-over factor" at the rotating end of the member.

Moment Distribution.—The method of moment distribution is applied as follows to a structure without side sway.

(1) Assume that all joints in the structure are fixed against rotation and compute the moments for this condition. The moments will not be in equilibrium and must be balanced.

(2) Distribute the unbalanced fixed-end moments to the connecting members at each joint in proportion to their stiffness.

(3) Add to the moment at the opposite end of every member the proportion of the moment just distributed as defined by the carry-over factor for that member.

(4) The moments at all joints will again be unbalanced so perform step (2) again.

(5) Carry over the balanced moments as in step (3).

Repeat the process until the moments carried over are small enough to be neglected. Add up the fixed-end moments, the distributed moments, and the carry-over moments and the result will be the moments in the frame.

For a framework where there is no side sway or settlement of the reactions the method of moment distribution as given above leads to exact results if the distribution is carried to a conclusion. For a framework in which side sway or other movements of the joints occur the above method of moment distribution must be modified to take care of the moments due to side sway—see calculation of moments in a transverse bent with an unsymmetrical load, Problem 6.

Examples.—Several examples with a detailed explanation of each step will now be given. The sign conventions are the same as for slope deflections, see Chapter XVIII.

Problem 1.—The beam in Fig. 4 is a beam fixed at D and continuous over supports B and C. The moment of inertia of the beams with the corresponding ratios of the stiffness factor K are as shown in Fig. 4. The beam carries a concentrated load of 20,000 lb. at a point 14 ft. from A and a uniform load of 1,000 lb. per lineal foot on the center span. The computation of the fixed-end moments is indicated in Fig. 4. These quantities are written in a line across the page below the figure as shown. The steps necessary to solve the problem are explained in detail. The moments are given in thousands of foot-pounds.

Problem 2.—The beam in Fig. 5 is fixed at the left end, is continuous over the middle support, carries a continuous load of 150 lb. per lineal foot in the left hand span and a concentrated load of 5,000 lb. at a distance of 15 ft. from the end of the center span. The moment of inertia and the stiffness factor K is given for each span in Fig. 5. The details of balancing the moments and the calculation of the carry-over factor are given in the solution of the problem. The moments in the beam at the supports are found by adding algebraically the columns of moments.

Problem 3.—The framework in Fig. 6 consists of a three span bent fixed at the left end and supported at the right end. The column at B is fixed at the base, while the column at C is hinged at the base. The bent carries a concentrated load of 5,000 lb. in the first span, and a uniform load of 150 lb. per lineal foot on the third span. The moments of inertia for the members and the values of stiffness factor K are given in the diagram. The percentages of K values for each member are written at the end of each member. The moments at the left end of each span are written below the member while the moments at the right end of each span are written above the span. The moments at the top of the column are written on the left at the top of the column while the moments at the bottom are written on the left at the bottom of the column. The fixed-end moments in each span are calculated as shown in Fig. 6. The moments are distributed and carried-over in the manner previously described.

Problem 4.—This problem involves a section in a building frame as shown in Fig. 7. The columns and the girders are assumed as fixed at the ends. The middle span is loaded in such a manner that the fixed-end moments are 25,000 ft.-lb. at each end of the girder. The value of K is given for each member. For the reason that there is no carry over from the fixed-ends of the columns and girders it is not necessary to write the carry-over moments at the fixed ends. The moment at each fixed-end is one-half the moment at the other end of the column or girder.

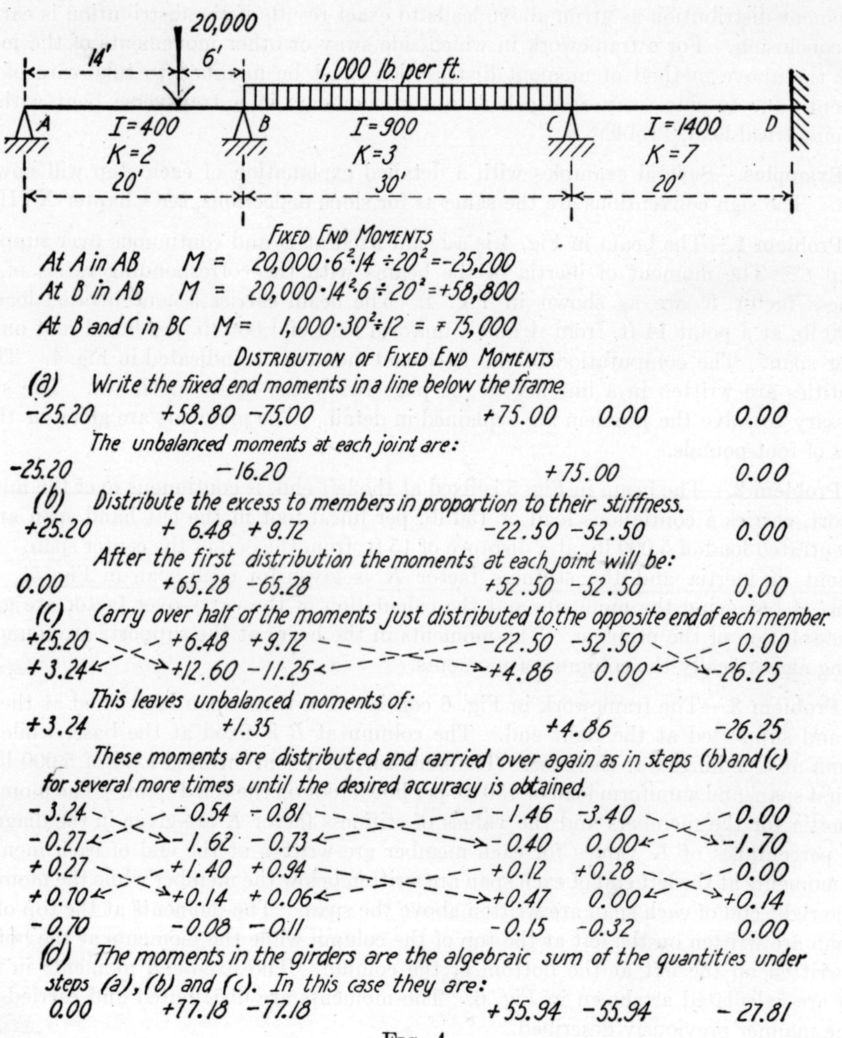
20,000
14'
6'
1,000 lb. per ft.
A
I=400
K=2
20'
B
I=900
K=3
30'
C
I=1400
K=7
20'
D
FIXED END MOMENTS
At A in AB M = 20,000·6²·14 ÷ 20² = -25,200
At B in AB M = 20,000·14²·6 ÷ 20² = +58,800
At B and C in BC M = 1,000·30² ÷ 12 = ∓75,000
DISTRIBUTION OF FIXED END MOMENTS
(a) Write the fixed end moments in a line below the frame.
-25.20 +58.80 -75.00 +75.00 0.00 0.00
The unbalanced moments at each joint are:
-25.20 -16.20 +75.00 0.00
(b) Distribute the excess to members in proportion to their stiffness.
+25.20 + 6.48 + 9.72 -22.50 -52.50 0.00
After the first distribution the moments at each joint will be:
0.00 +65.28 -65.28 +52.50 -52.50 0.00
(c) Carry over half of the moments just distributed to the opposite end of each member.
+25.20 + 6.48 + 9.72 -22.50 -52.50 0.00
+3.24 +12.60 -11.25 +4.86 0.00 -26.25
This leaves unbalanced moments of:
+3.24 +1.35 +4.86 -26.25
These moments are distributed and carried over again as in steps (b) and (c) for several more times until the desired accuracy is obtained.
- 3.24 - 0.54 - 0.81 - 1.46 -3.40 - 0.00
- 0.27 - 1.62 - 0.73 - 0.40 0.00 -1.70
+ 0.27 +1.40 + 0.94 + 0.12 +0.28 - 0.00
+ 0.10 +0.14 + 0.06 +0.47 0.00 +0.14
- 0.70 -0.08 - 0.11 - 0.15 -0.32 0.00
(d) The moments in the girders are the algebraic sum of the quantities under steps (a), (b) and (c). In this case they are:
0.00 +77.18 -77.18 +55.94 -55.94 - 27.81

FIG. 4.

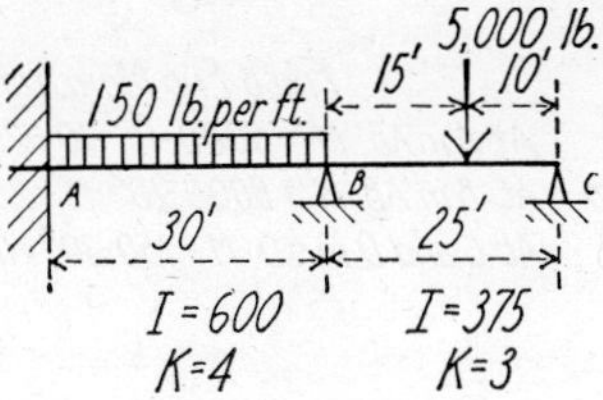

5,000 lb.; 150 lb. per ft.; 15′; 10′; A; B; C; 30′; 25′; $I = 600$, $K = 4$; $I = 375$, $K = 3$

FIXED END MOMENTS

At A and B in AB $M = \frac{150 \cdot 30^2}{12} = \mp 11,250$

At B in BC $M = \frac{5,000 \cdot 10^2 \cdot 15}{25^2} = +12,000$

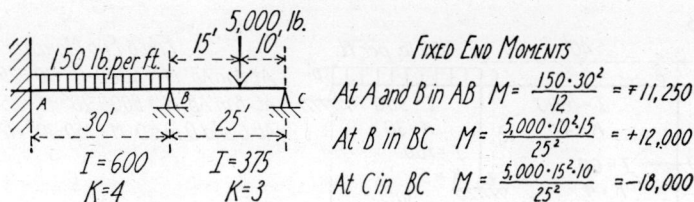

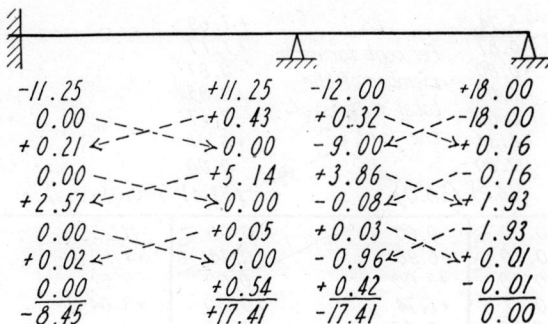

At C in BC $M = \frac{5,000 \cdot 15^2 \cdot 10}{25^2} = -18,000$

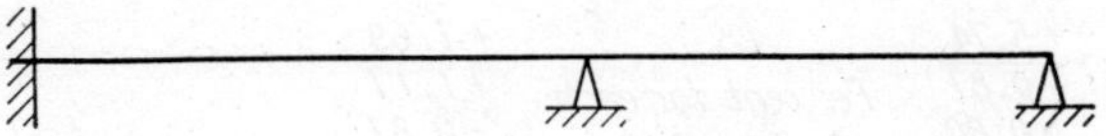

A	B (AB)	B (BC)	C
−11.25	+11.25	−12.00	+18.00
0.00	+0.43	+0.32	−18.00
+0.21	0.00	−9.00	+0.16
0.00	+5.14	+3.86	−0.16
+2.57	0.00	−0.08	+1.93
0.00	+0.05	+0.03	−1.93
+0.02	0.00	−0.96	+0.01
0.00	+0.54	+0.42	−0.01
−8.45	+17.41	−17.41	0.00

FIG. 5.

Stresses in Frames Subject to Side Sway.—If the joints in a frame move due to the application of a load or loads, the distribution of the moments as outlined above will not give the correct results without a correction for the change in moment due to the movement of the joint. In the method of slope deflections the side sway is represented by the factor R as in equations (4) and (5) in Chapter XVIII. An example of a frame in which side sway occurs is a simple bent loaded with a concentrated load as in Fig. 8. A special case for this frame is where the load is symmetrical about the center line.

The following solution for finding the stresses in frames subject to side sway has been developed by Professor C. T. Morris in Bulletin No. 66, Engineering Experiment Station, Ohio State University. This solution includes the moments in the columns due to side sway and consists of the following steps:

(1) Compute the "fixed-end moments."

(2) Distribute these moments to the members in proportion to their "stiffness."

(3) "Carry-over" these moments to the other ends of the members.

(4) To satisfy the conditions of static equilibrium the sum of the moments in the columns must equal the horizontal shear times the story height. If there is no side sway there will be no horizontal shear and the sums of the moments at the tops and bottoms of the columns will equal zero. In Fig. 8 the sums of the moments at the tops and bottoms of the columns after (2) and (3) will be $5.4 + 2.7 - 3.6 - 1.8 = +2.7$. This "shear

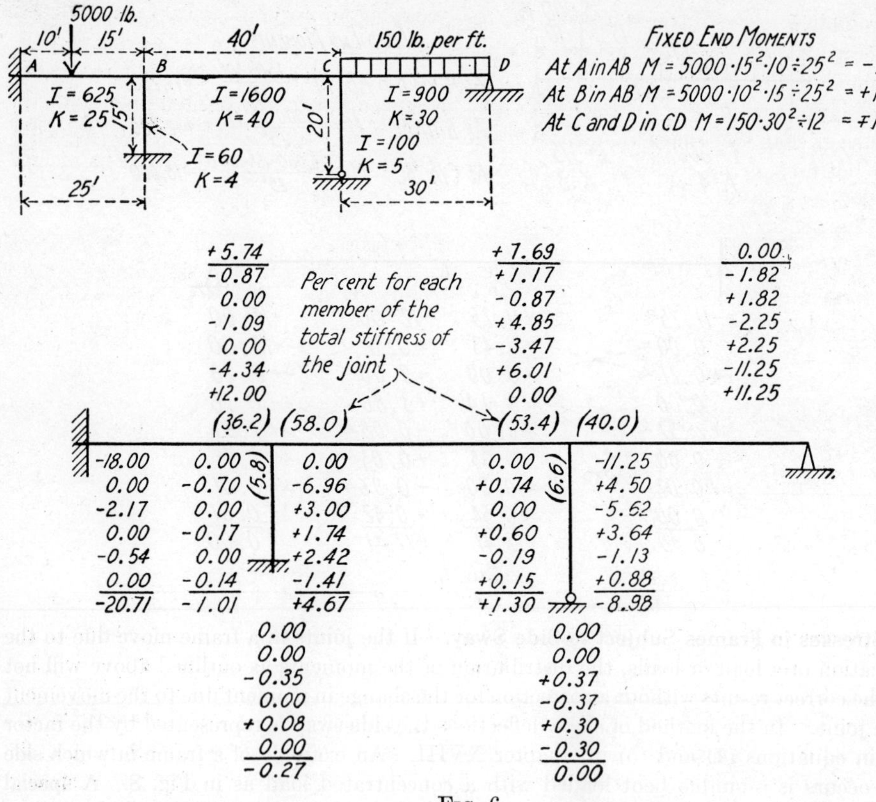

FIG. 6.

moment" will be distributed between the columns in proportion to I/l^2 for each column. In this case the columns having the same K, the unbalanced "shear moment" at the top and bottom of each column will be $+2.7/4 = +0.68$. The shear moment to balance will be -0.68 at the top and bottom of each column.

(5) Distribute the moments found under steps (3) and (4).

(6) Repeat the steps (3), (4) and (5) until the desired accuracy is obtained.

Problem 5.—A stiff frame fixed at the base carrying an unsymmetrical load of 15,000 lb. is shown in Fig. 8. The fixed-end moments in the top member are −32.4 and +21.6. The moments are distributed in (2), the moments carried over in (3), and the shear moments are given in (4). The solution may be carried out to any desired precision. It will be seen that two shear-moments (4) give quite satisfactory results. The moments at the bottoms of the columns were calculated using the area moment equations in Fig. 16, p. 292, as a check.

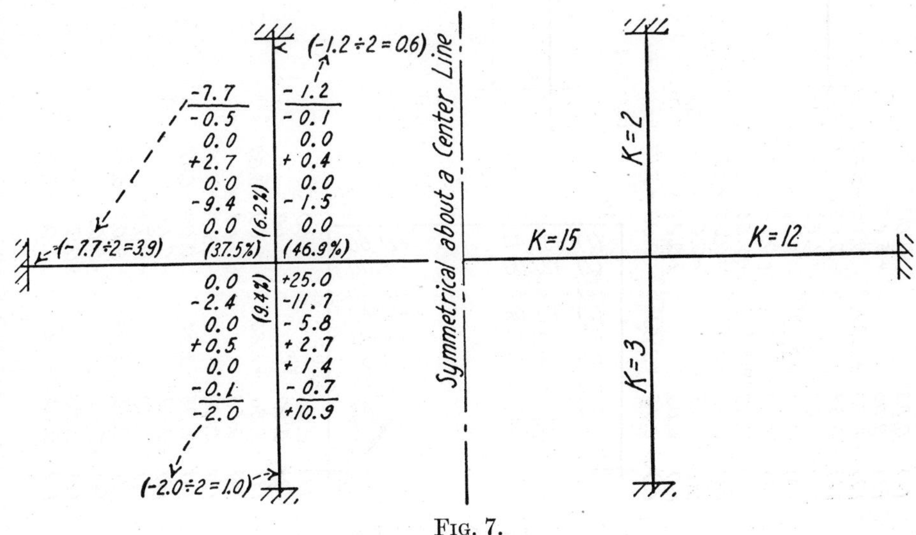

Fig. 7.

Stresses in a Building Frame.—The bending moments in the steel building frame given in Problem 7, Chapter XXII will now be calculated by moment distribution, and the moments will be compared with the moments obtained by means of the author's modified portal system.

Problem 6.—The column and girder sections and the stiffness factors were obtained from calculated areas using the stresses given in Problem 7, Chapter XXII and dead and live load stresses. The fixed-end moments are calculated, the moments are distributed to the members in proportion to their stiffness, and the moments are carried over to the other ends of the members as in Fig. 9. The "shear-moments" are then calculated by multiplying the shear in any story by the story height. The "shear-moments" are distributed to the columns in proportion to I/l^2 where I is the moment of inertia of the column, and l is the story height. By comparing the resulting bending moments in Fig. 9 with the bending moments calculated in Problem 7, Chapter XXII, it will be seen that the approximate method gives results that are quite satisfactory for design.

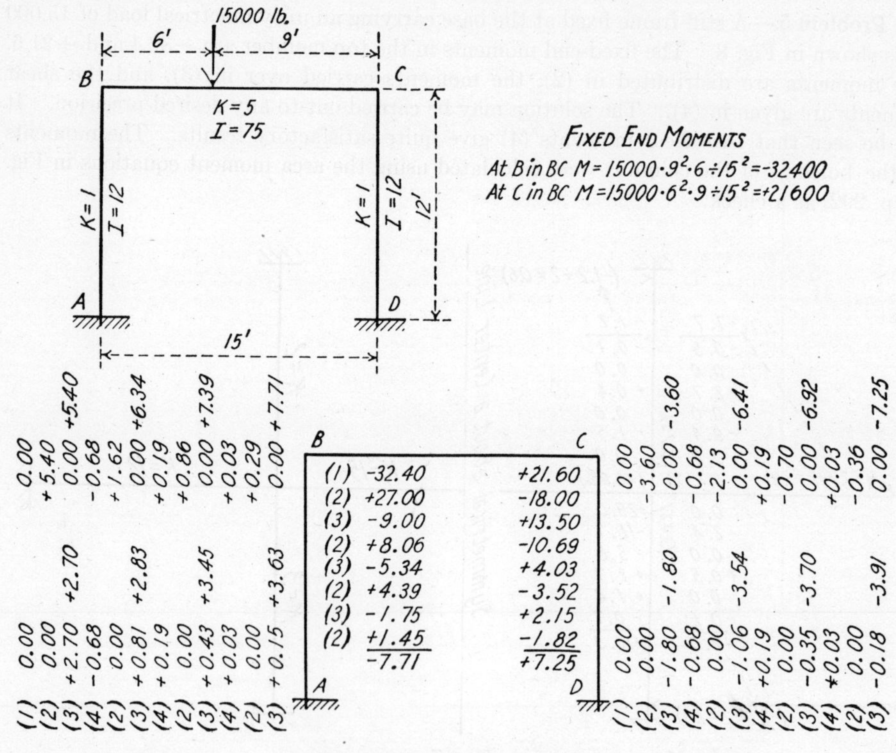

FIG. 8.

Calculation of Stiffness, Carry-over Factor and Fixed-end Moments for Members of Variable Section.—For members with variable moment of inertia it is necessary to calculate the stiffness, carry-over factor and fixed-end moments in a manner similar to that for members with a constant cross-section but including the effect of the variation of the moment of inertia. It is possible to develop algebraic equations for the simple types of sections, but in general these equations are long and complicated. An example of the calculations for specific sections will be given.

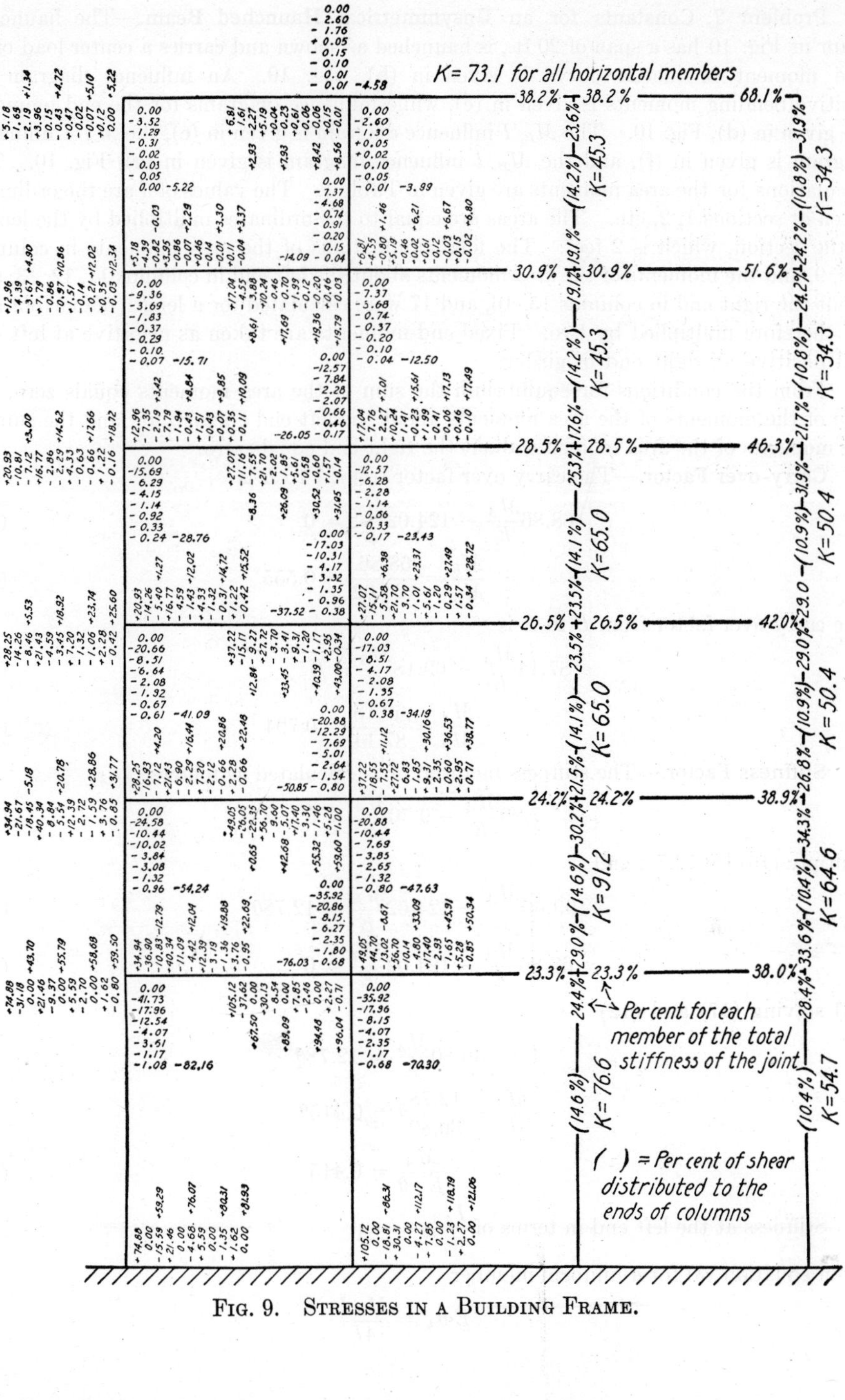

K = 73.1 for all horizontal members

38.2% — 38.2% — 68.1%

30.9% — 30.9% — 51.6%

28.5% — 28.5% — 46.3%

26.5% — 26.5% — 42.0%

24.2% — 24.2% — 38.9%

23.3% — 23.3% — 38.0%

K = 45.3 K = 34.3

K = 45.3 K = 34.3

K = 65.0 K = 50.4

K = 65.0 K = 50.4

K = 91.2 K = 64.6

K = 76.6 K = 54.7

Per cent for each member of the total stiffness of the joint

( ) = Per cent of shear distributed to the ends of columns

FIG. 9. STRESSES IN A BUILDING FRAME.

Problem 7. Constants for an Unsymmetrical Haunched Beam.—The haunched beam in Fig. 10 has a span of 20 ft., is haunched as shown and carries a center load of P. The moment of inertia curve is given in (b), Fig. 10. An influence diagram for positive bending moments is given in (c), while influence diagrams for the end moments are given in (d), Fig. 10. The M_P/I influence diagram is given in (e), the M_A/I influence diagram is given in (f), and the M_B/I influence diagram is given in (g), Fig. 10. The calculations for the area moments are given in Table I. The values of d are the ordinates taken at sections 1, 2, etc. The areas are equal to the ordinates multiplied by the length of the section, which is 2 feet. The final summations of the area moments in columns 7, 8, 9, and the moments of the area moments about the left end in columns 11, 12, 13, and about the right end in columns 15, 16, and 17 were calculated for a length of one foot and are therefore multiplied by two. Fixed end-moments are taken as negative at left end and positive at right end of girder.

From the conditions for equilibrium the sum of the area moments equals zero, the sum of the moments of the area moments about the left end equals zero, and the sum of the moments of the area moments about the right end equals zero.

Carry-over Factor.—The carry over factor from A to B is

$$68.86\frac{M_A}{E} - 124.02\frac{M_B}{E} = 0 \tag{12}$$

$$\frac{M_B}{M_A} = \frac{68.86}{124.02} = 0.555 \tag{13}$$

The carry-over factor from B to A is

$$87.14\frac{M_A}{E} - 69.18\frac{M_B}{E} = 0 \tag{14}$$

$$\frac{M_A}{M_B} = \frac{69.18}{87.14} = 0.794 \tag{15}$$

Stiffness Factor.—The stiffness factor at A is calculated as follows:

$$7.80\frac{M_A}{E} - 9.70\frac{M_B}{E} = \theta \tag{16}$$

multiply (16) by 12.78, and

$$99.66\frac{M_A}{E} - 124.02\frac{M_B}{E} = 12.78\theta \tag{17}$$

$$68.86\frac{M_A}{E} - 124.02\frac{M_B}{E} = 0 \tag{12}$$

and solving (17) and (12)

$$30.80\frac{M_A}{E} = 12.78\theta$$

$$\frac{M_A}{E} = \frac{12.78}{30.80}\theta = 0.415\theta$$

$$\frac{M_A}{E \cdot \theta} = 0.415 \tag{18}$$

Stiffness at the left end in terms of $\frac{I_A}{l}$ is

From equation (3) for a uniform member

$$E \cdot \theta_A = \frac{M_A \cdot l}{4I} \tag{3}$$

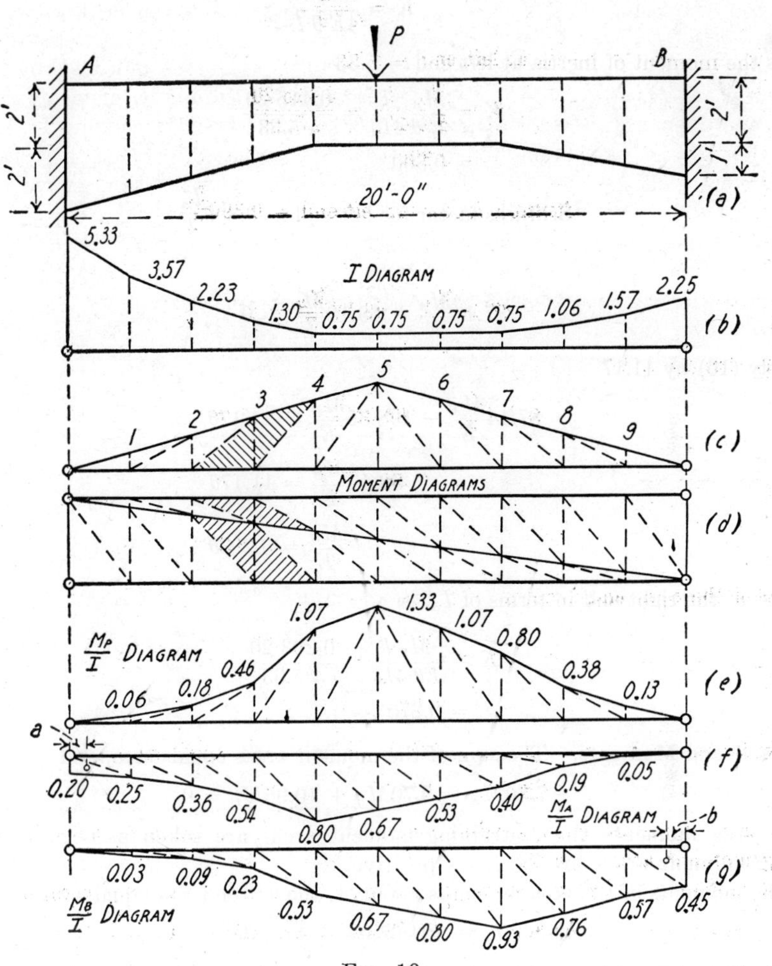
P
A
B
2'
2'
2'
1'
20'-0"
(a)
5.33
3.57
2.23
1.30
0.75
0.75
0.75
0.75
1.06
1.57
2.25
I DIAGRAM
(b)
1
2
3
4
5
6
7
8
9
(c)
MOMENT DIAGRAMS
(d)
$\frac{M_P}{I}$ DIAGRAM
0.06
0.18
0.46
1.07
1.33
1.07
0.80
0.38
0.13
(e)
a
0.20
0.25
0.36
0.54
0.80
0.67
0.53
0.40
0.19
0.05
(f)
$\frac{M_A}{I}$ DIAGRAM
b
0.03
0.09
0.23
0.53
0.67
0.80
0.93
0.76
0.57
0.45
(g)
$\frac{M_B}{I}$ DIAGRAM

FIG. 10.

and for a non-uniform member

$$E \cdot \theta_A = \frac{M_A \cdot l}{4K \cdot I} \tag{19}$$

and

$$K = \frac{M_A \cdot l}{4E \cdot \theta \cdot I} \tag{20}$$

If I_A is the moment of inertia at left end = 5.33

$$K = \frac{M_A}{E \cdot \theta} \frac{l}{4I_A} = \frac{0.415 \cdot 20}{4 \cdot 5.33}$$

$$= 0.390$$

$$\text{Stiffness factor for left end} = 0.390 \frac{I_A}{l} \tag{21}$$

At B

$$87.14 \frac{M_A}{E} - 69.18 \frac{M_B}{E} = 0 \tag{14}$$

Multiply (16) by 11.17

$$87.14 \frac{M_A}{E} - 108.35 \frac{M_B}{E} = 11.17\theta$$

$$38.17 \frac{M_B}{E} = 11.17\theta$$

$$\frac{M_B}{E} = 0.293\theta \tag{22}$$

Stiffness of the right end in terms of I_A, is

$$K = \frac{M_B \cdot l}{E\theta \cdot 4I_B} = \frac{0.293 \cdot 20}{4 \cdot 5.33}$$

$$= 0.275 \tag{23}$$

Fixed-end Moments.—The sum of the moment areas equals zero, and

$$-7.80M_A - 9.70M_B + 10.96M_P = 0 \tag{24}$$

In area moments the restraining moment areas are taken as negative and the bending moment areas are taken as positive.

The moments of the area moments about A, the left end will equal zero, and

$$-68.86M_A - 124.02M_B + 115.84M_P = 0 \tag{25}$$

And the moments of the area moments about B, the right end will equal zero, and

$$-87.14M_A - 69.18M_B + 103.36M_P = 0 \tag{26}$$

Solving equations (24) and (25) or (24) and (26) for M_A and M_B in terms of the simple beam bending moment, $M_P = \frac{P \cdot l}{4}$.

$$M_A = -0.787M_P = -0.197P \cdot l \tag{27}$$

$$M_B = 0.498M_P = 0.125P \cdot l \tag{28}$$

TABLE I.

Calculations of Area Moments.

Section	d	$I=\frac{1}{12}b\cdot d^3$	M_A	M_B	M_P	$\frac{M_A}{I}$	$\frac{M_B}{I}$	$\frac{M_P}{I}$	Moment Arm from $A=R_A$	$\frac{M_A}{I}\times R_A$	$\frac{M_B}{I}\times R_A$	$\frac{M_P}{I}\times R_A$	Moment Arm from $B=R_B$	$\frac{M_A}{I}\times R_B$	$\frac{M_B}{I}\times R_B$	$\frac{M_P}{I}\times R_B$
1	2	3	4	5	6	7	8	9	10	11	12	13	14	15	16	17
a	3.8	4.72	0.48*	.....	....	0.10	....	.....	0.7	0.07	......	......	19.3	1.93		
1	3.5	3.57	0.90	0.10	0.20	0.25	0.03	0.06	2.0	0.50	0.06	0.12	18.0	4.50	0.54	1.08
2	3.0	2.23	0.80	0.20	0.40	0.36	0.09	0.18	4.0	1.44	0.36	0.72	16.0	5.76	1.44	2.88
3	2.5	1.30	0.70	0.30	0.60	0.54	0.23	0.46	6.0	3.24	1.38	2.76	14.0	7.56	3.22	6.44
4	2.0	0.75	0.60	0.40	0.80	0.80	0.53	1.07	8.0	6.40	4.24	8.56	12.0	9.60	6.36	12.84
5	2.0	0.75	0.50	0.50	1.00	0.67	0.67	1.33	10.0	6.70	6.70	13.30	10.0	6.70	6.70	13.30
6	2.0	0.75	0.40	0.60	0.80	0.53	0.80	1.07	12.0	6.36	9.60	12.84	8.0	4.24	6.40	8.56
7	2.0	0.75	0.30	0.70	0.60	0.40	0.93	0.80	14.0	5.60	13.02	11.20	6.0	2.40	5.58	4.80
8	2.3	1.06	0.20	0.80	0.40	0.19	0.76	0.38	16.0	3.04	12.16	6.08	4.0	0.76	3.04	1.52
9	2.7	1.57	0.10	0.90	0.20	0.06	0.57	0.13	18.0	1.08	10.26	2.34	2.0	0.12	1.14	0.26
b	2.8	2.00	.....	0.48*	....	.....	0.24	.....	19.3	.....	4.23	......	0.7	.....	0.17	
						3.90	4.85	5.48	......	34.43	62.01	57.92	......	43.57	34.59	51.68
			Multiply by 2 =			7.80	9.70	10.96	......	68.86	124.02	115.84	......	87.14	69.18	103.36

* Area of triangle.

CHAPTER XIX

SECONDARY STRESSES.

Introduction.—In calculating the stresses in structures it is usual to assume (1) that the joints are free to turn, (2) that the neutral axes of the members meet in a point at the joints, (3) that all loads, including the weights of the members themselves, are applied at the joints. The stresses so calculated are direct or axial stresses and are commonly called primary stresses. The above assumed conditions are not realized in practice. The stresses due to stiffness of joints, to eccentric joints, to members not being straight, to weight of members, etc., are called secondary stresses. The secondary stresses due to rigidity of joints only will be considered in this chapter. The primary stresses must first be calculated, and the secondary stresses due to shear and bending moment are then calculated. The secondary stresses due to shear are commonly very small and may be neglected.

For the calculation of combined and eccentric stresses, see Chapter XII.

Secondary Stresses Due to Rigidity of Joints.—The rigid triangle *a-b-c*, in Fig. 1, is subject to direct unit stresses, S_{ab}, S_{bc}, S_{ca}, and the lengths of the corresponding members are l_{ab}, l_{bc}, l_{ca}. Then the change in length of each member will be

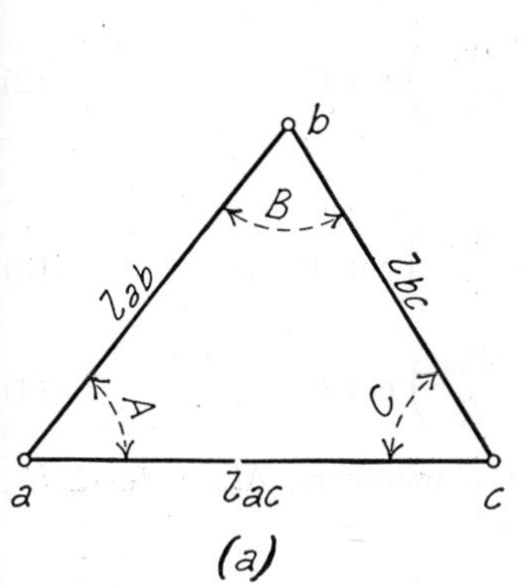

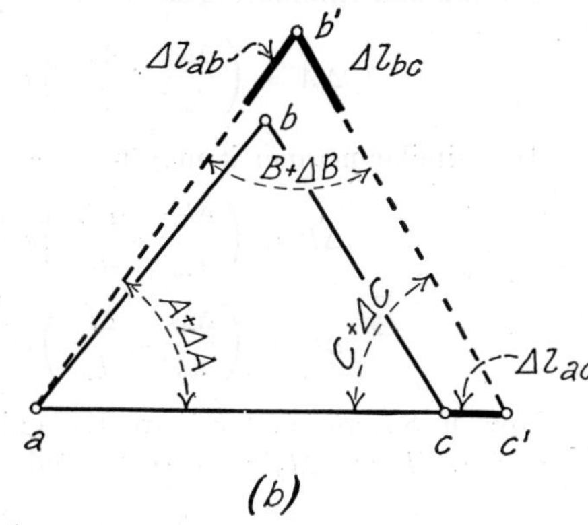

FIG. 1.

$$\Delta_{ab} = (S_{ab} \cdot l_{ab})/E \tag{1}$$

$$\Delta_{bc} = (S_{bc} \cdot l_{bc})/E \tag{2}$$

$$\Delta_{ca} = (S_{ca} \cdot l_{ca})/E \tag{3}$$

If the joints do not offer any resistance, the angles in the new triangle due to the changed sides may be calculated as follows. By the law of sines

$$(l_{bc} + \Delta l_{bc}) : (l_{ca} + \Delta l_{ca}) :: \sin (A + \Delta A) : \sin (B + \Delta B) \tag{4}$$

and

$$(l_{ca} + \Delta l_{ca}) \sin (A + \Delta A) = (l_{bc} + \Delta l_{bc}) \sin (B + \Delta B) \tag{5}$$

Expanding and placing $\cos \Delta A = \cos \Delta B = 1$, and $\sin \Delta A = \Delta A$, and $\sin \Delta B = \Delta B$; also dropping products of differentials

$$l_{ac} \cdot \sin A + l_{ac} \cdot \cos A \cdot \Delta A + \sin A \cdot \Delta l_{ac} = l_{bc} \cdot \sin B + l_{bc} \cdot \cos B \cdot \Delta B + \sin B \cdot \Delta l_{bc} \tag{6}$$

and

$$\Delta A = -\frac{\sin A(l_{ca} + \Delta l_{ca})}{l_{ca} \cdot \cos A} + \frac{\sin B(l_{bc} + \Delta l_{bc})}{l_{ca} \cdot \cos A} + \frac{\Delta B \cdot \cos B \cdot l_{bc}}{l_{ca} \cdot \cos A} \tag{7}$$

From law of sines

$$\sin B : \sin A :: l_{ca} : l_{bc}$$

and

$$\sin B = \sin A \cdot l_{ca}/l_{bc} \tag{8}$$

Substituting the value of $\sin B$ from (8) in (7)

$$\Delta A = \left(\frac{\Delta l_{bc}}{l_{bc}} - \frac{\Delta l_{ca}}{l_{ca}}\right) \tan A + \Delta B \frac{\tan A}{\tan B} \tag{9}$$

In a similar manner

$$\Delta C = \left(\frac{\Delta l_{ab}}{l_{ab}} - \frac{\Delta l_{ca}}{l_{ca}}\right) \tan C + \Delta B \frac{\tan C}{\tan B} \tag{10}$$

Also

$$\Delta A + \Delta B + \Delta C = 0 \tag{11}$$

Solving and eliminating ΔB from (9) and (10)

$$\Delta A = \left(\frac{\Delta l_{bc}}{l_{bc}} - \frac{\Delta l_{ab}}{l_{ab}}\right) \cot B - \left(\frac{\Delta l_{ca}}{l_{ca}} - \frac{\Delta l_{bc}}{l_{bc}}\right) \cot C \tag{12}$$

In a similar manner it may be shown that

$$\Delta B = \left(\frac{\Delta l_{ca}}{l_{ca}} - \frac{\Delta l_{bc}}{l_{bc}}\right) \cot C - \left(\frac{\Delta l_{ab}}{l_{ab}} - \frac{\Delta l_{ca}}{l_{ca}}\right) \cot A \tag{13}$$

$$\Delta C = \left(\frac{\Delta l_{ab}}{l_{ab}} - \frac{\Delta l_{ca}}{l_{ca}}\right) \cot A - \left(\frac{\Delta l_{bc}}{l_{bc}} - \frac{\Delta l_{ab}}{l_{ab}}\right) \cot B \tag{14}$$

Now if S_{ab}, S_{bc} and S_{ca} are the unit stresses in the members, $\Delta l_{ab} = S_{ab} \cdot l_{ab}/E$, $\Delta l_{bc} = S_{bc} \cdot l_{bc}/E$, and $\Delta l_{ca} = S_{ca} \cdot l_{ca}/E$, and

$$\Delta A = \frac{S_{bc} - S_{ab}}{E} \cdot \cot B - \frac{S_{ca} - S_{bc}}{E} \cdot \cot C \tag{15}$$

$$\Delta B = \frac{S_{ca} - S_{bc}}{E} \cdot \cot C - \frac{S_{ab} - S_{ca}}{E} \cdot \cot A \tag{16}$$

$$\Delta C = \frac{S_{ab} - S_{ca}}{E} \cdot \cot A - \frac{S_{bc} - S_{ab}}{E} \cdot \cot B \tag{17}$$

Equations (15), (16) and (17) will give the angular changes if the joints of the triangle are free to turn.

Deflection Angles of a Beam Due to Bending at Ends.—The beam AB in (*a*), Fig. 2, has bending moments M_{ab} and M_{ba}, and shears V_a and V_b at the ends and has no intermediate loads. The bending moment diagram is shown in (*b*), Fig. 2. To calculate the deflection at B from a tangent at A, take the static moment of the moment area between A and B about B and divide the result by $E \cdot I.$, and

$$E \cdot I \cdot y_b = -\frac{M_{ba} \cdot l}{2} \times \frac{l}{3} + \frac{M_{ab} \cdot l}{2} \times \tfrac{2}{3}l$$

$$y_b = \frac{l^2}{6E \cdot I}(2M_{ab} - M_{ba}) \tag{18}$$

and the deflection angle is,

$$\theta_a = y_b/l = \frac{l}{6E \cdot I}(2M_{ab} - M_{ba}) \tag{19}$$

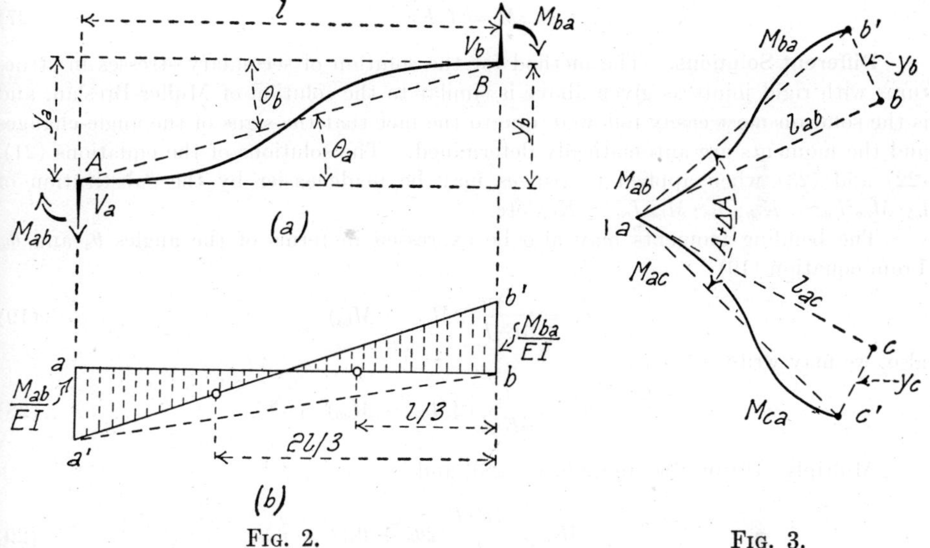

FIG. 2. FIG. 3.

Moments clockwise are taken as positive the same as in Chapter XVIII. The opposite assumption may be made, in which case the signs of all moments are changed.

In Fig. 3, it will be seen that the change in angle A will be

$$\Delta A = \angle\, bac - \angle\, b'ac'$$

and

$$\Delta A = y_c/l_{ca} - y_b/l_{ab} \tag{20}$$

and from (19) and applying (19) to Fig. 3,

$$\Delta A = \frac{l_{ac}}{6E \cdot I_{ac}}(2M_{ac} - M_{ca}) - \frac{l_{ab}}{6E \cdot I_{ab}}(2M_{ab} - M_{ba}) \tag{21}$$

also

$$\Delta B = \frac{l_{ab}}{6E \cdot I_{ab}}(2M_{ba} - M_{ab}) - \frac{l_{bc}}{6E \cdot I_{bc}}(2M_{bc} - M_{cb}) \tag{22}$$

$$\Delta C = \frac{l_{bc}}{6E \cdot I_{bc}}(2M_{cb} - M_{bc}) - \frac{l_{ca}}{6E \cdot I_{ca}}(2M_{ca} - M_{ac}) \tag{23}$$

Now since at each joint $\Sigma M = 0$, in the triangle in Fig. 1,

$$M_{ab} + M_{ac} = 0 \tag{24}$$

$$M_{ba} + M_{bc} = 0 \tag{25}$$

$$M_{cb} + M_{ca} = 0 \tag{26}$$

The values of ΔA, ΔB and ΔC are calculated by solving equations (15), (16) and (17), respectively. The values of ΔA, ΔB and ΔC will then be substituted in equations (21), (22) and (23), respectively. Equations (21) to (26) inclusive give six equations containing six unknown moments. By solving these simultaneous equations the unknown bending moments may be calculated.

Having calculated the bending moments, the secondary stresses may be calculated by means of the usual formula for flexure

$$M = f \cdot I/c \tag{27}$$

Different Solutions.—The method for the solution of secondary stresses in structures with rigid joints as given above is similar to the solution of Muller-Breslau, and is the solution most easily followed, due to the fact that the signs of the angle-changes and the moments are automatically determined. The solutions of the equations (21), (22) and (23) when applied to trusses may be made easier by the substitution of $l_{ab} \cdot M_{ab}/I_{ab} = K_{ab}$; $l_{ba} \cdot M_{ba}/I_{ba} = K_{ba}$, etc.

The bending moments may also be expressed in terms of the angles θ_a and θ_b. From equation (19)

$$\theta_a = \frac{l}{6E \cdot I}(2M_{ab} - M_{ba}) \tag{19}$$

also, we may write

$$\theta_b = \frac{l}{6E \cdot I}(2M_{ba} - M_{ab}) \tag{28}$$

Multiply (19) by two and add to (28), and

$$M_{ab} = \frac{2E \cdot I}{l}(2\theta_a + \theta_b) \tag{29}$$

In like manner

$$M_{ba} = \frac{2E \cdot I}{l}(2\theta_b + \theta_a) \tag{30}$$

The bending moments at the joints may be expressed in terms of the deflection angles. There will be as many equations as there are unknown moments. This method, which is a slope deflection method, is a simplification of Manderla's method. This is the method given in Johnson, Bryan and Turneaure's "Framed Structures," Part II.

Mohr's method for calculating secondary stresses is also a slope deflection method. For a full discussion of Mohr's method see, article entitled "Secondary Stresses," by F. C. Kunz, "Engineering News," Oct. 5, 1911.

For a discussion of the methods of Manderla, Muller-Breslau, Ritter, Mohr, and the Method of Least Work, see Grimm's "Secondary Stresses in Bridge Trusses."

Problem.—It is required to calculate the secondary stresses in the riveted triangular truss in (*a*), Fig. 4. The joints of the truss are assumed as rigid.

The lengths of members are, $l_{ab} = l_{bc} = 25$ ft. $l_{bd} = l_{ac} = 30$ ft.

The moments of inertia of the members are, $I_{ab} = I_{bd} = 360$ in.^{4}, $I_{bc} = 60$ in.^{4}, $I_{ac} = 40$ in.^{4} The unit stresses in the members due to the external loads, are

$$S_{ab} = S_{de} = \quad 7{,}000 \text{ lb. per sq. in.}$$
$$S_{ac} = S_{ce} = -\,7{,}300 \text{ lb. per sq. in.}$$
$$S_{bd} = \quad 7{,}330 \text{ lb. per sq. in.}$$
$$S_{bc} = S_{cd} = -\,8{,}000 \text{ lb. per sq. in.}$$

$$\cot BAC = \cot BCA = \cot CBD = 0.7500$$
$$\cot BDC = \cot DCE = \cot DEC = 0.7500$$
$$\cot ABC = \cot BCD = \cot CDE = 0.2915$$

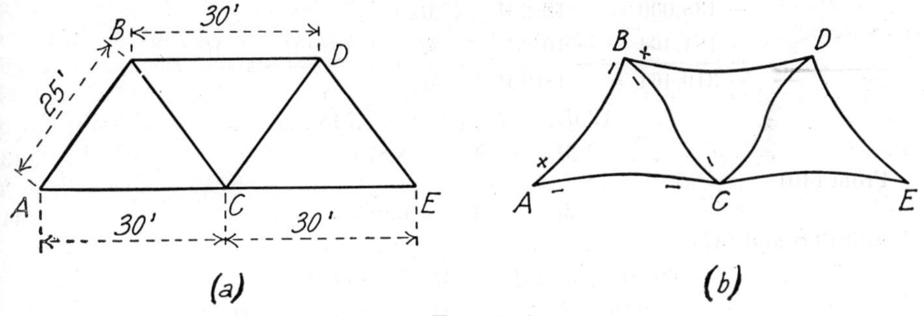

FIG. 4.

Substituting in equations (15), (16) and (17), and reducing

$$E \cdot \Delta BAC = (-\,8{,}000 - 7{,}000)0.2915 - (-\,7{,}330 + 8{,}000)0.75 = -\;\;4{,}875 \quad (31)$$
$$E \cdot \Delta ABC = (-\,7{,}300 + 8{,}000)0.75 - (7{,}000 + 7{,}300)0.75 = -\,10{,}245 \quad (32)$$
$$E \cdot \Delta BCA = (7{,}000 + 7{,}330)0.75 - (-\,8{,}000 - 7{,}000)0.2915 = 15{,}122 \quad (33)$$
$$E \cdot \Delta DBC = (-\,8{,}000 + 8{,}000)0.2915 - (7{,}330 + 8{,}000)0.75 = -\,11{,}500 \quad (34)$$
$$E \cdot \Delta BCD = (7{,}330 + 8{,}000)0.75 - (-\,8{,}000 - 7{,}330)0.75 = 23{,}000 \quad (35)$$

Writing the equations for moments (21), (22) and (23), for all angles, and substituting the values of ΔBAC, etc., there results

$$-\,6 \times 4{,}875 = \tfrac{360}{40}(2M_{ac} - M_{ca}) - \tfrac{300}{360}(2M_{ab} - M_{ba}) \quad (36)$$
$$-\,6 \times 10{,}245 = \tfrac{300}{360}(2M_{ba} - M_{ab}) - \tfrac{300}{60}(2M_{bc} - M_{cb}) \quad (37)$$
$$6 \times 15{,}122 = \tfrac{300}{60}(2M_{cb} - M_{bc}) - \tfrac{360}{40}(2M_{ca} - M_{ac}) \quad (38)$$
$$-\,6 \times 11{,}500 = \tfrac{300}{60}(2M_{bc} - M_{cb}) - \tfrac{360}{360}(2M_{bd} - M_{db}) \quad (39)$$
$$6 \times 23{,}000 = \tfrac{300}{60}(2M_{cd} - M_{dc}) - \tfrac{300}{60}(2M_{cb} - M_{bc}) \quad (40)$$

Also, since $\Sigma M = 0$ for each joint

$$M_{ab} + M_{ac} = 0 \quad (41)$$

$$M_{ba} + M_{bc} + M_{bd} = 0 \quad (42)$$

From symmetry, $M_{cd} = -M_{cb}$, $M_{dc} = -M_{bc}$, and $M_{db} = -M_{bd}$. Substituting these values in equations (39) and (40) and reducing, the equations are as follows:

$$-\ 29{,}250 = 9(2M_{ac} - M_{ca}) - \tfrac{5}{6}(2M_{ab} - M_{ba}) \quad (36)$$

$$-\ 61{,}470 = \tfrac{5}{6}(2M_{ba} - M_{ab}) - 5(2M_{bc} - M_{cb}) \quad (37)$$

$$90{,}732 = 5(2M_{cb} - M_{bc}) - 9(2M_{ca} - M_{ac}) \quad (38)$$

$$-\ 69{,}000 = 5(2M_{bc} - M_{cb}) - 3M_{bd}. \quad (39)$$

$$-\ 138{,}000 = 10(2M_{cb} - M_{bc}) \quad (40)$$

$$M_{ab} + M_{ac} = 0 \quad (41)$$

$$M_{ba} + M_{bc} + M_{bd} = 0 \quad (42)$$

Solution of Equations.—Multiply (38) by two, and subtract from (40)

$$\begin{aligned} -\ 138{,}000 &= 10(2M_{cb} - M_{bc}) \\ -\ 181{,}464 &= -10(2M_{cb} - M_{bc}) + 18(2M_{ca} - M_{ac}) \\ \hline -\ 319{,}464 &= 18(2M_{ca} - M_{ac}) \end{aligned}$$

$$(2M_{ca} - M_{ac}) = -\ 17{,}748$$

$$M_{ca} = \tfrac{1}{2}M_{ac} - 8{,}874 \quad (43)$$

From (40)

$$M_{cb} = \tfrac{1}{2}M_{bc} - 6{,}900 \quad (44)$$

Add (39) and (37)

$$\begin{aligned} -\ 69{,}000 &= 5(2M_{bc} - M_{cb}) - 3M_{bd} \\ -\ 61{,}470 &= \tfrac{5}{6}(2M_{ba} - M_{ab}) - 5(2M_{bc} - M_{cb}) \\ \hline -\ 130{,}470 &= \tfrac{5}{6}(2M_{ba} - M_{ab}) - 3M_{bd} \end{aligned} \quad (45)$$

Subtract (36) from twice (37)

$$\begin{aligned} -\ 122{,}940 &= \tfrac{5}{6}(4M_{ba} - 2M_{ab}) - 10(2M_{bc} - M_{cb}) \\ +\ 29{,}250 &= -\ 9(2M_{ac} - M_{ca}) + \tfrac{5}{6}(2M_{ab} - M_{ba}) \\ \hline -\ 93{,}690 &= -\ 9(2M_{ac} - M_{ca}) + \tfrac{15}{6}M_{ba} - 10(2M_{bc} - M_{cb}) \end{aligned} \quad (46)$$

Substitute M_{cb} in (44) in (39)

$$-\ 69{,}000 = 5(\tfrac{3}{2}M_{bc} + 6{,}900) - 3M_{bd}$$

$$-\ 103{,}500 = \tfrac{15}{2}M_{bc} - 3M_{bd} \quad (47)$$

In (45) substitute $M_{ca} = \frac{1}{2}M_{ca} - 8{,}874$ from (43), $M_{cb} = \frac{1}{2}M_{bc} - 6{,}900$ from (44), and $M_{ac} = -M_{ab}$ from (41).

$$-\ 93{,}690 = 9(\tfrac{3}{2}M_{ab} - 8{,}874) + \tfrac{15}{6}M_{ba} - 10(\tfrac{3}{2}M_{bc} + 6{,}900)$$

Reducing

$$110{,}350 = 27M_{ab} + 5M_{ba} - 30M_{bc} \quad (48)$$

Substitute $M_{bd} = -M_{ba} - M_{bc}$, from (42) in (45),

$$-\ 130{,}470 = \tfrac{5}{6}(2M_{ba} - M_{ab}) + 3M_{ba} + 3M_{bc}$$

$$= \tfrac{28}{6}M_{ba} - \tfrac{5}{6}M_{ab} + 3M_{bc} \quad (49)$$

Multiply (49) by ten and add to (48)

$$-1{,}304{,}700 = \tfrac{280}{6}M_{ba} - \tfrac{50}{6}M_{ab} + 30M_{bc}$$

$$110{,}350 = 5M_{ba} + 27M_{ab} - 30M_{bc}$$

$$-1{,}194{,}350 = \tfrac{310}{6}M_{ba} + \tfrac{112}{6}M_{ab}$$

$$-7{,}166{,}100 = 310M_{ba} + 112M_{ab} \qquad (50)$$

Substitute from (42), $M_{bc} = -M_{ba} - M_{bd}$, in (47)

$$-103{,}500 = -\tfrac{15}{2}M_{ba} - \tfrac{15}{2}M_{bd} - 3M_{bd}$$

$$-207{,}000 = -15M_{ba} - 21M_{bd}$$

Solving:

$$M_{bd} = -\tfrac{5}{7}M_{ba} + 9{,}857 \qquad (51)$$

Substitute (51) in (45)

$$-130{,}470 = \tfrac{5}{6}(2M_{ba} - M_{ab}) + \tfrac{15}{7}M_{ba} - 29{,}570$$

Reducing

$$-100{,}900 = \tfrac{160}{42}M_{ba} - \tfrac{5}{6}M_{ab} \qquad (52)$$

Multiply (52) by 672/5 and add to (50)

$$-13{,}560{,}960 = 512M_{ba} - 112M_{ab} \qquad (53)$$

$$-7{,}166{,}100 = 310M_{ba} + 112M_{ab} \qquad (50)$$

$$-20{,}727{,}060 = 822M_{ba}$$

$$M_{ba} = -25{,}220 \text{ in.-lb.} \qquad (54)$$

Substitute M_{ba} in (51)

$$M_{bd} = \tfrac{5}{7} \times 25{,}220 + 9{,}857$$

$$= 27{,}870 \text{ in.-lb.} \qquad (55)$$

Substitute M_{ba} and M_{bd} in (42)

$$-25{,}220 + 27{,}870 + M_{bc} = 0$$

$$M_{bc} = -2{,}650 \text{ in.-lb.} \qquad (56)$$

Substitute M_{ba} in (53)

$$112M_{ab} = 512(-25{,}220) + 13{,}560{,}960$$

$$M_{ab} = +5{,}790 \text{ in.-lb.} \qquad (57)$$

Substitute M_{bc} in (44)

$$M_{cb} = -1{,}325 - 6{,}900$$

$$= -8{,}225 \text{ in.-lb.} \qquad (58)$$

From (41)

$$M_{ac} = -M_{ab} = -5{,}790 \text{ in.-lb.} \qquad (59)$$

Substitute $M_{ac} = -5{,}790$ in (43)

$$M_{ca} = -2{,}895 - 8{,}874$$

$$= -11{,}769 \text{ in.-lb.} \qquad (60)$$

Collecting the values of M,

$$M_{ab} = + \ 5{,}790 \text{ in.-lb.}$$
$$M_{ac} = - \ 5{,}790 \text{ in.-lb.}$$
$$M_{ba} = - \ 25{,}220 \text{ in.-lb.}$$
$$M_{bc} = - \ 2{,}650 \text{ in.-lb.}$$
$$M_{bd} = + \ 27{,}870 \text{ in.-lb.}$$
$$M_{ca} = - \ 11{,}769 \text{ in.-lb.}$$
$$M_{cb} = - \ 8{,}225 \text{ in.-lb.}$$

The signs of the moments are shown in the distorted truss in (*b*), Fig. 4. There are points of contra-flexure in members BC, DC, AC and CE.

Secondary Stresses.—The values of c, the distance from the neutral axis to the extreme fiber on the side of the member in which the secondary stress is of the same kind as the primary stress are as follows:

AB = 9 in. to compression side
BD = 9 in. to compression side
BC = 6 in. to tension side
AC = 6 in. to tension side

Substituting in the formula $f = M \cdot c/I$, there results for the secondary stresses

Stress in AB =	$25{,}220 \times 9/360$ =	630 lb. per sq. in.	(compression)
Stress in BD =	$27{,}870 \times 9/360$ =	690 " " " "	"
Stress in BC =	$-\ 8{,}225 \times 6/60$ =	$-$ 822 " " " "	(tension)
Stress in AC =	$-\ 11{,}769 \times 6/40$ =	$-$ 1,766 " " " "	"

Discussion of Secondary Stresses.—The preceding analysis has omitted (1) the bending moments due to the direct or primary stress, acting with an arm equal to the deflection of the member, and (2) the effect of the secondary stresses in reducing the primary stresses. Both of these were included in Manderla's solution published in 1880, which is much longer and more laborious than the approximate method given above. The effects of (1) and (2) tend to neutralize each other and the approximate results are generally sufficiently exact. It should be noted that (2) is very large in stiff frames, see Chapter XVII and Chapter XVIII. The secondary stresses in simple riveted railway bridge trusses of the Pratt or Warren type may vary from 20 to 40 per cent of the primary or direct stresses, depending upon the design. For a truss with subdivided panels the secondary stresses are commonly larger than for a truss with simple bracing. The secondary stresses in a truss with K-bracing are less than for any other type of subdivided truss.

The secondary stresses in a member vary directly as the moment of inertia in the plane of bending and inversely as the length of member. Sections with a large moment of inertia and small area, such as T-sections, have large secondary stresses.

In designing railway bridges with riveted trusses, the secondary stresses should be calculated in any member where the width of the member in the plane of the truss is greater than one-tenth of its length.

CHAPTER XX.

Stresses in a Two-hinged Arch.

Introduction.—A two-hinged arch is a frame-work or beam with hinged ends which has inclined reactions for vertical loads. The bottom chords of two-hinged arches are usually cambered, however, a simple truss becomes a two-hinged arch if the ends are fixed to the abutments so that deformation in the direction of the length of the truss is prevented.

The horizontal components of the reactions may be supplied either by the abutments or by a tie connecting the hinges. In the latter case the deformation of the tie must be considered in determining the horizontal reactions. Two-hinged arches are statically indeterminate structures and their design is subject to the same uncertainties as continuous and swing bridges.

Two-hinged roof arches are rigid and economical, but have been used to a very limited extent on account of the difficulties experienced in their design. The methods outlined in this chapter are quite simple in principle, although they necessarily require quite extended calculations. Two-hinged roof arches with open framework, only, will be considered in this chapter.

For the calculation of the stresses in a fixed arch, see the author's "The Design of Highway Bridges of Steel, Timber and Concrete."

CALCULATION OF STRESSES.—The vertical reactions in a two-hinged arch are the same as in a simple truss or a three-hinged arch having the same loads and span. The horizontal reactions, however, depend upon the deformation of the framework and cannot be determined by simple statics alone. Before the deformations can be calculated, the sizes of the members must be known, and conversely, before the sizes of the members can be calculated, the stresses which depend upon the deformations must be known. Any method for the calculation of the stresses in a two-hinged arch is, therefore, necessarily a method of successive approximations. With a skilled computer, however, it is rarely necessary to make more than two or three trials before obtaining satisfactory results in designing roof arches. Two-hinged bridge arches require somewhat more work to design than roof arches on account of the greater number of conditions for maximum stresses in the members.

Having determined the correct value of the horizontal thrust, H, the stresses in a two-hinged arch may be calculated by the ordinary algebraic or graphic methods used in the solution of the stresses in simple trusses.

The stresses in a two-hinged roof arch will be calculated by the Method of Algebraic Summation and also by the Williott-Mohr Diagram Method, as already explained in Chapter XV.

Calculation of the Reactions.—In Fig. 1 the vertical reactions, R_1 and R_2, are the same as for a simple truss. The horizontal reactions, H, will be equal and will be the forces which would prevent change in length of span if the ends of the arch were free to move. The horizontal thrust, H, will therefore be the force which, applied at the roller end of a simple truss, will prevent deformation and make the truss a two-hinged arch.

The deformation of the right end of the truss due to the external loads from equation (3), Chapter XVI, will be

$$\Delta' = \Sigma \frac{S \cdot U \cdot L}{A \cdot E} \tag{1}$$

where S is the stress in the member in lb. per sq. in.; U is the stress in the member due to a load of 1 lb. acting in line with the deformation Δ'; L = length of the member in inches; A = area of the member in sq. in.; and E = modulus of elasticity of the member in lb. per sq. in.

The deformation of the right end of the truss due to the horizontal reaction H, from equation (6), Chapter XVI, will be

$$\Delta' = H\Sigma \frac{U^2 \cdot L}{A \cdot E} \tag{2}$$

By equating the values of Δ' in equations (1) and (2), we have

$$H = \frac{\Sigma \frac{S \cdot U \cdot L}{A \cdot E}}{\Sigma \frac{U^2 \cdot L}{A \cdot E}} \tag{3}$$

For a two-hinged arch with a horizontal tie, the deformation of the right end of the arch will be equal to the deformation of the horizontal tie. The deformation of the horizontal tie for a stress H, will be

$$\Delta'' = (H \cdot l)/(A_1 \cdot E) \tag{4}$$

where l = length of tie in inches, and A_1 = area of tie in sq. in.

Then the deformation of the truss will be equal to the sum of the distance that the horizontal tie will bring the right end back and the deformation of the horizontal tie. Placing equation (1) equal to the sum of equations (2) and (4) and solving

$$H = \frac{\Sigma \frac{S \cdot U \cdot L}{A \cdot E}}{\Sigma \frac{U^2 \cdot L}{A \cdot E} + \frac{l}{A_1 \cdot E}} \tag{5}$$

The method of finding the correct value of the horizontal reaction, H, is as follows: (1) calculate the stresses in the arch for the given loading on the assumption that it is a simple truss with one end supported on frictionless rollers (*b*) Fig. 1; (2) calculate the stresses in the arch for an assumed horizontal reaction, H' = 1 lb. on the assumption that it is a simple truss on frictionless rollers (*d*) Fig. 1; (3) calculate the deformation, Δ, of the free end of the truss for the given loads by means of formula (1); (4) calculate the deformation, Δ' of the free end of the truss for the assumed horizontal reaction H' = 1 lb. by means of formula (2). The true value of H is then given by formula (3).

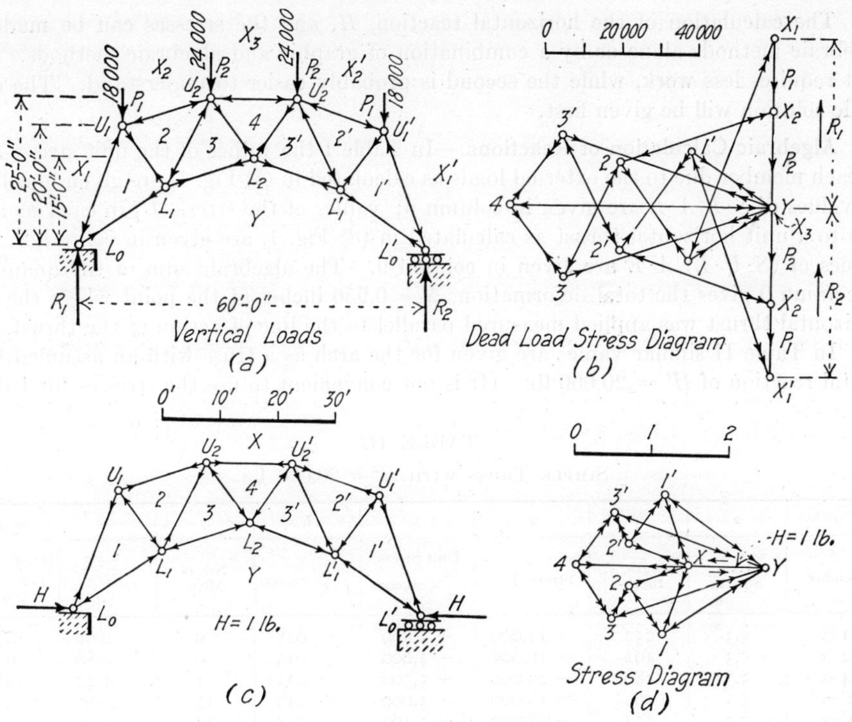

FIG. 1. STRESS DIAGRAMS FOR THE TRUSS.

TABLE I.

SIMPLE TRUSS WITH VERTICAL LOADS

1	2	3	4	5	6	7	8	9
Member.	Area, Sq. In.	Length, L, In.	Stress, Lb.	Unit Stress, $\frac{S}{A}$, Lb.	$\frac{S \cdot L}{A \cdot E}$.	No. of Mem	U	$\frac{S \cdot U \cdot L}{A \cdot E}$.
1–x	5.3	252	+ 60,000	+ 11,320	+ .095	9	− 0.90	− .086
2–x	5.3	192	+ 41,000	+ 7,740	+ .050	6	− 0.80	− .040
4–x	5.3	180	+ 67,000	+ 12,650	+ .076	1	− 1.45	− .110
2′–x	5.3	192	+ 41,000	+ 7,740	+ .050	12	− 0.80	− .040
1′–x	5.3	252	+ 60,000	+ 11,320	+ .095	15	− 0.90	− .086
1–y	5.3	216	− 25,000	− 4,720	− .034	8	+ 1.60	− .054
3–y	5.3	192	− 57,000	− 10,760	− .069	4	+ 2.05	− .141
3′–y	5.3	192	− 57,000	− 10,760	− .069	10	+ 2.05	− .141
1′–y	5.3	216	− 25,000	− 4,720	− .034	14	+ 1.60	− .054
1–2	2.0	150	− 30,000	− 15,000	− .075	7	+ 0.75	− .056
2–3	4.0	204	+ 32,000	+ 8,000	+ .054	5	− 0.45	− .024
3–4	4.0	150	− 22,000	− 5,500	− .028	2	+ 0.80	− .022
3′–4	4.0	150	− 22,000	− 5,500	− .028	3	+ 0.80	− .022
2′–3′	4.0	204	+ 32,000	+ 8,000	+ .054	11	− 0.45	− .024
1′–2′	2.0	150	− 30,000	− 15,000	− .075	13	+ 0.75	− .056

$$\text{Total Deformation} = \Sigma \frac{S \cdot U \cdot L}{A \cdot E} = - .956$$

The calculation of the horizontal reaction, H, and the stresses can be made by algebraic methods alone or by a combination of graphic and algebraic methods. The first requires less work, while the second is probably easier to understand. The algebraic solution will be given first.

Algebraic Calculation of Reactions.—In Table I the values of the unit stress, S/A, in each member due to the external loads as calculated in (b) Fig. 1, are given in column 5; values of $S \cdot L/A \cdot E$ are given in column 6; values of the stress, U, in each member due to a unit horizontal thrust as calculated in (d) Fig. 1, are given in column 8; and values of $(S \cdot U \cdot L)/A \cdot E$ are given in column 9. The algebraic sum of the quantities in column 9 gives the total deformation, $\Delta = 0.956$ inches at the point where the unit horizontal thrust was applied measured parallel to the line of action of the thrust.

In Table II similar values are given for the arch as a truss with an assumed horizontal reaction of $H' = 20{,}000$ lb. (It is not convenient to use the stresses for 1 lb. in

TABLE II.

SIMPLE TRUSS WITH $H' = 20{,}000$ LB.

1	2	3	4	5	6	7	8	9
Member	Area, Sq. In.	Length, L, Inches.	Stress, Lb.	Unit Stress, $\frac{U}{A} \times 20{,}000$.	$\frac{U \cdot L}{A \cdot E} \times 20{,}000$.	No. of Mem.	U	$\frac{U^2 \cdot L}{A \cdot E} \times 20{,}000$
1–x	5.3	252	− 18,000	− 3,400	− .028	9	− 0.90	.025
2–x	5.3	192	− 16,000	− 3,000	− .019	6	− 0.80	.015
4–x	5.3	180	− 29,000	− 5,500	− .033	1	− 1.45	.048
2′–x	5.3	192	− 16,000	− 3,000	− .019	12	− 0.80	.015
1′–x	5.3	252	− 18,000	− 3,400	− .028	15	− 0.90	.025
1–y	5.3	216	+ 32,000	+ 6,000	+ .043	8	+ 1.60	.069
3–y	5.3	192	+ 41,000	+ 7,800	+ .050	4	+ 2.05	.102
3′–y	5.3	192	+ 41,000	+ 7,800	+ .050	10	+ 2.05	.102
1′–y	5.3	216	+ 32,000	+ 6,000	+ .043	14	+ 1.60	.069
1–2	2.0	150	+ 15,000	+ 7,500	+ .038	7	+ 0.75	.029
2–3	4.0	204	− 9,000	− 2,250	− .015	5	− 0.45	.007
3–4	4.0	150	+ 16,000	+ 4,000	+ .020	2	+ 0.80	.016
3′–4	4.0	150	+ 16,000	+ 4,000	+ .020	3	+ 0.80	.016
2′–3′	4.0	204	− 9,000	− 2,250	− .015	11	− 0.45	.007
1′–2′	2.0	150	+ 15,000	+ 7,500	+ .038	13	+ 0.75	.029
Total Deformation $= \Sigma \frac{U^2 \cdot L}{A \cdot E} \times 20{,}000 = .574$								

tabulation or in drawing the deformation diagram for H as in (c) Fig. 2.) The algebraic sum of the quantities in column 9 gives the total deformation, $\Delta' = 0.574$ inches at the point where the horizontal thrust was applied.

The correct value of H is given by the proportion

$$H : H' : : \Delta' : \Delta'$$

$$H = \frac{20{,}000 \times 0.956}{0.574} = 33{,}400 \text{ lb.}$$

In Table III the deformation, Δ, for the same arch considered as a simple truss and acted upon by dead and wind loads is 1.357 in., and

$$H = \frac{20,000 \times 1.357}{0.574} = 47,300 \text{ lb.}$$

Graphic Calculation of Reactions.—In the graphic solution of the horizontal reactions the total amount of the deformations, Δ and Δ' are found by means of Williot deformation diagrams as given in Fig. 2. Before constructing the deformation diagrams the quantities in the first seven columns in Tables I and II or II and III must be calculated. The stresses given in column 4 are calculated as shown in Fig. 1. Column 6, giving deformations of each member, and column 7, giving the order in which these deformations are used, are, however, the only values used in constructing the deformation diagrams.

TABLE III.

SIMPLE TRUSS WITH DEAD AND WIND LOADS.

1	2	3	4	5	6	7	8	9
Member	Area, Sq. In	Length, L, Inches.	Stress, Lb.	Unit Stress, $\frac{S}{A}$, Lb.	$\frac{S \cdot L}{A \cdot E}$	No. of Mem.	U	$\frac{S \cdot U \cdot L}{A \cdot E}$.
1–x	5.3	252	+ 87,000	+ 16,400	+ .138	9	− 0.90	− .124
2–x	5.3	192	+ 72,000	+ 13,600	+ .087	6	− 0.80	− .069
4–x	5.3	180	+ 95,000	+ 17,800	+ .107	1	− 1.45	− .155
2′–x	5.3	192	+ 52,000	+ 9,800	+ .063	12	− 0.80	− .050
1′–x	5.3	252	+ 72,000	+ 13,600	+ .114	15	− 0.90	− .103
1–y	5.3	216	− 58,000	− 10,900	− .078	8	+ 1.60	− .125
3–y	5.3	192	− 87,000	− 16,400	− .105	4	+ 2.05	− .215
3′–y	5.3	192	− 74,000	− 14,000	− .090	10	+ 2.05	− .185
1′–y	5.3	216	− 30,000	− 5,650	− .041	14	+ 1.60	− .064
1–2	2.0	150	− 36,000	− 18,000	− .090	7	+ 0.75	− .067
2–3	4.0	204	+ 28,000	+ 7,000	+ .048	5	− 0.45	− .022
3–4	4.0	150	− 22,000	− 5,500	− .028	2	+ 0.80	− .022
3′–4	4.0	150	− 42,000	− 10,500	− .053	3	+ 0.80	− .042
2′–3′	4.0	204	+ 46,000	+ 11,500	+ .078	11	− 0.45	− .035
1′–2′	2.0	150	− 42,000	− 21,000	− .105	13	+ 0.75	− .079

$$\text{Total Deformation} = \Sigma \frac{S \cdot U \cdot L}{A \cdot E} = -1.357$$

The Williot Deformation Diagram.—The principle upon which the construction of the Williot deformation diagram is based is as follows: Take the two members a–c and c–b in (d) Fig. 2, meeting at the point c. Assume that a–c is shortened and b–c is lengthened the amounts indicated. It is required to find the new position, c', of the point c. With center at a' and a radius equal to the new length of a –c', describe an arc. The new position of c must be some place on this arc. Then with a center at b' and a radius equal to the new length of b'–c', describe an arc cutting the first arc in c'. The new position of c must be some place on this arc and will therefore be at the intersection of the two arcs, c'. Since the deformations of the members are always very small as compared with the lengths of the members, the arcs may be replaced by perpendiculars, and the members themselves need not be drawn, (e) Fig. 2.

For a further discussion of the Williot deformation diagram, see Chapter XV.

To draw the deformation diagram, (b) Fig. 2, for the arch as a truss with one end on frictionless rollers and loaded with vertical loads, proceed as follows: Begin with the member marked 1, lay off its deformation = + .076 in. (Table I, column 6) to scale and parallel to member 1. Now lay off the deformation of 2 = − .028 in. away, from the joint U_2 and parallel to the member 2, and lay off deformation of 3 = − .028 in., away from the joint U_2' and parallel to the member 3. Perpendiculars erected at the ends of deformations 2 and 3 will meet in the new position of L_2. The vertical distance between the deformation 1 and point L_2 represents to scale the change in position of L_2

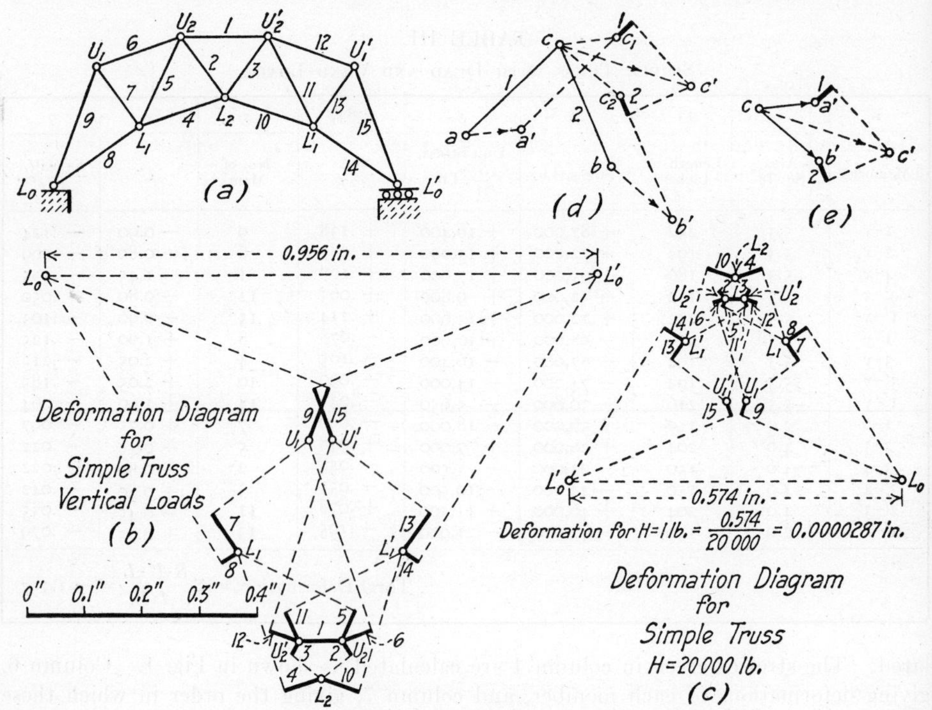

FIG. 2. WILLIOT DEFORMATION DIAGRAMS.

relative to the member U_2U_2'. At L_2 in the deformation diagram lay off deformation of 4 = − .069 in., away from the joint and parallel to the member 4, and at U_2 lay off deformation of 5 = + .054 in., toward the joint and parallel to the member 5. The perpendiculars erected at the ends of the deformations 4 and 5 determine the new position of joint L_1 relative to the other points. In like manner perpendiculars erected at the ends of deformations 6 and 7 determine U_1, and finally perpendiculars erected at the ends of deformations 8 and 9 determine L_0. The deformation diagram for the right half of the truss is constructed in the same manner. The horizontal line joining L_0 and L_0' represents to scale the movement of the joint L_0'.

The Williot deformation diagram for the truss with a horizontal thrust of H = 20,000 lb. is drawn in (*c*), Fig. 2, in the same manner using the values in Table II.

Calculation of Dead Load Stresses in Arch.—In Fig. 1, (*b*) is the stress diagram for the arch as a simple truss with vertical loads as shown in (*a*); and (*d*) is the stress diagram for the arch as a simple truss with a horizontal thrust, H', of 1 lb. as shown in (c). The quantities for calculating the deformations of the simple truss with vertical loads are given in Table I, and the deformation diagram is shown in (b) Fig. 2. The quantities for calculating the deformations of the simple truss with a horizontal thrust of 20,000 lb. are given in Table II, and the deformation diagram is shown in (c) Fig. 2. The true value of H is found by the proportion

$$H : 20{,}000 :: 0.956 : 0.574$$
$$H = 33{,}400 \text{ lb.}$$

The stress diagram for the two-hinged arch with $V = V' = 42{,}000$ lb., and $H = H = 33{,}400$ lb. is shown in (b) Fig. 3.

The difference in the stresses in the members of a simple truss and a two-hinged arch may be seen by comparing stress diagram (b) Fig. 1, and stress diagram (b) Fig. 3,

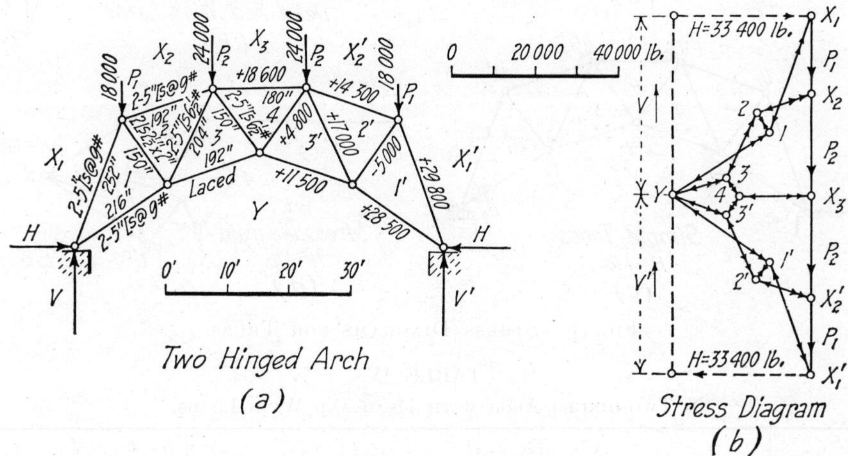

FIG. 3. STRESS DIAGRAM FOR ARCH.

both diagrams being drawn to the same scale. The stresses in the arch may be found from the stresses given in Tables I and II by adding the stresses in column 4, Table I, to the corresponding stresses in column 4, Table II, multiplied by 1.67, the ratio between the actual and assumed horizontal reactions. For example, the stress in 1–x in the arch equals $+ 60{,}000 - 18{,}000 \times 1.67 = + 29{,}800$ lb. Stress in 1–y equals $- 25{,}000 + 32{,}000 \times 1.67 = + 28{,}440$ lb.

Dead and Wind Load Stresses in Arch.—In Fig. 4, (b) is the stress diagram for the arch as a simple truss loaded with dead and wind loads as shown in (a). Table III gives the same data for this case as are given in Table I for the simple truss with vertical loads. The deformation diagram for the deformations given in column 6, Table III, is shown in (b) Fig. 5. In drawing the deformation diagram for this case the member marked 1 was assumed to be fixed in position and the other members were assumed free to move. The horizontal distance between L_0 and L_0' will be the total deformation required.

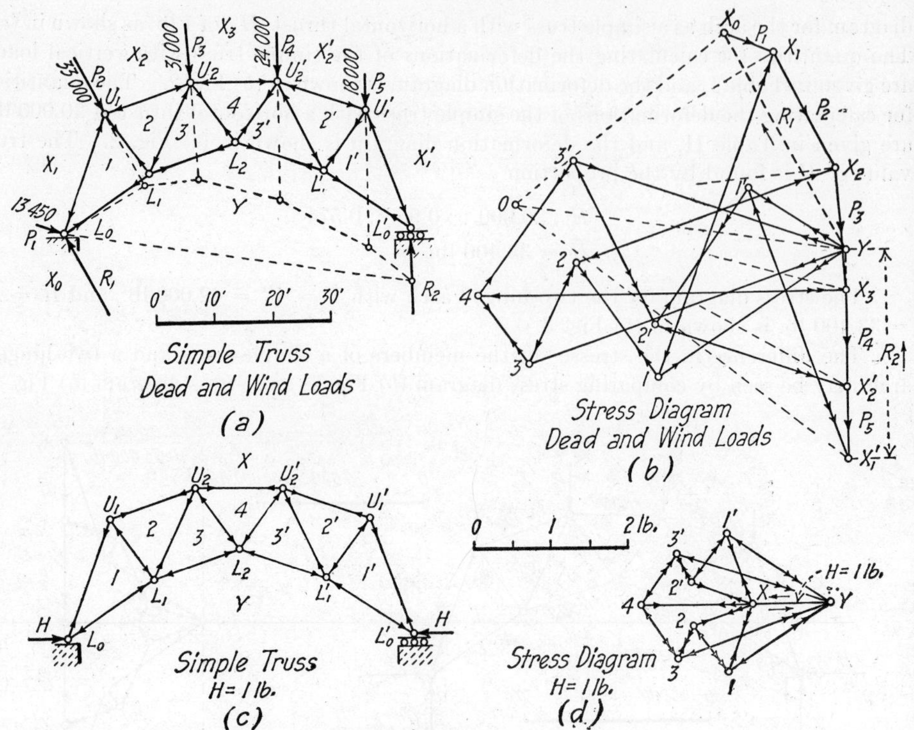

FIG. 4. STRESS DIAGRAMS FOR TRUSS.

TABLE IV.

TWO-HINGED ARCH WITH DEAD AND WIND LOADS.

1	2	3	4	5	6	8	9
Member.	Area, Sq. In.	Length. L, Inches.	Stress, S. Lb.	Unit Stress, $\frac{S}{A}$ Lb.	$\frac{S \cdot L}{A \cdot E}$	U	$\frac{S \cdot U \cdot L}{A \cdot E}$.
1–x	5.3	252	+ 43,500	+ 8,220	+ .069	− 0.90	− .063
2–x	5.3	192	+ 34,200	+ 6,450	+ .041	− 0.80	− .033
4–x	5.3	180	+ 26,500	+ 5,000	+ .030	− 1.45	− .045
2′–x	5.3	192	+ 14,200	+ 2,660	+ .017	− 0.80	− .014
1′–x	5.3	252	+ 29,500	+ 5,550	+ .047	− 0.90	− .042
1–y	5.3	216	+ 18,000	+ 3,400	+ .024	+ 1.60	+ .038
3–y	5.3	192	+ 10,000	+ 1,890	+ .012	+ 2.05	+ .025
3′–y	5.3	192	+ 23,000	+ 4,350	+ .028	+ 2.05	+ .057
1′–y	5.3	216	+ 46,000	+ 8,700	+ .062	+ 1.60	+ .099
1–2	2.0	150	− 500	− 250	− .001	+ 0.75	− .001
2–3	4.0	204	+ 6,500	+ 1,625	+ .011	− 0.45	− .005
3–4	4.0	150	+ 15,800	+ 3,950	+ .020	+ 0.80	+ .016
3′–4	4.0	150	− 4,200	− 1,050	− .005	+ 0.80	− .004
2′–3′	4.0	204	+ 22,800	+ 5,700	+ .039	− 0.45	− .018
1′–2′	2.0	150	− 5,000	− 2,500	− .013	+ 0.75	− .010
Total Deformation $= \Sigma \frac{S \cdot U \cdot L}{A \cdot E} = .000$							

The member marked 1 was assumed as moving parallel to its original position which was incorrect as is shown by the twist in the deformation diagram in (*b*), Fig. 5. The Mohr rotation diagram, assuming that L_0' holds fast, and L_0 moves is drawn in (*b*), Fig. 5. The movement of a joint will be the distance measured from the point on the

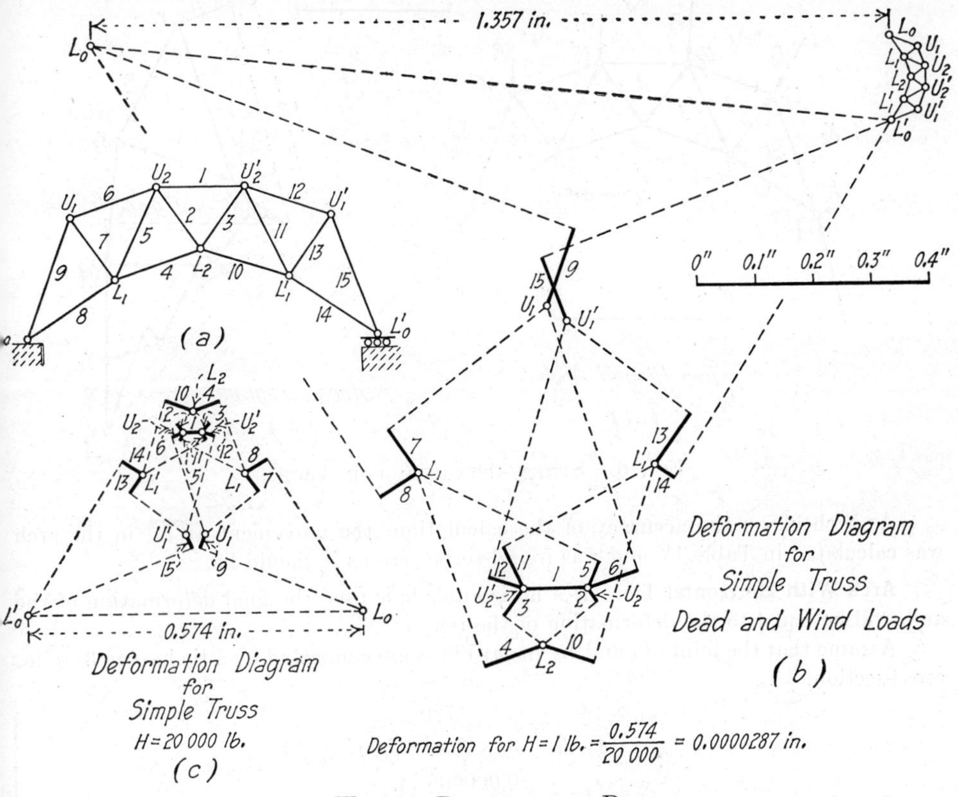

FIG. 5. WILLIOT DEFORMATION DIAGRAMS.

rotation diagram to the corresponding point on the Williot deformation diagram. For example joint L_1 moves from L_1 on the rotation diagram to L_1 on the Williot deformation diagram; L_0, moves from L_0 on the rotation diagram to L_0 on the Williot deformation diagram. (The rotation diagram should preferably be drawn at the left end, L_0.)

For a further discussion of the Mohr rotation diagram, see Chapter XV.

The deformation diagram for the simple truss with a horizontal thrust, H', of 20,000 lb. is given in (*c*) Fig. 5 and is the same as that given in (*c*) Fig. 2.

The true value of H is found by the proportion

$$H : 20{,}000 :: 1.357 : 0.574$$

$$H = 47{,}300 \text{ lb.}$$

The stress diagram for the two-hinged arch with dead and wind loads and a horizontal thrust, H, of 47,300 lb. is given in (*b*) Fig. 6. The stresses in the arch for this case may be found from the stresses in Tables III and II by adding the stresses in column 4, Table III, to the corresponding stresses in column 4, Table II, multiplied by 2.865, the ratio between the actual and assumed horizontal reactions.

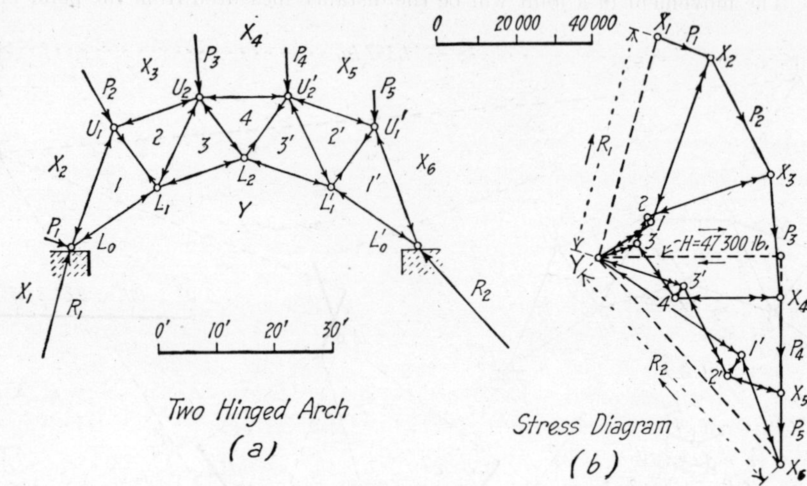

FIG. 6. STRESS DIAGRAM FOR ARCH.

As a check on the accuracy of the calculations the movement at L_0' in the arch was calculated in Table IV and was found to be zero as it should be.

Arch With Horizontal Tie.—If a horizontal tie is used the final deformation of the arch will be equal to the deformation of the tie.

Assume that the joints L_0 and L_0' in (*a*) Fig. 3 are connected by a tie having 3 sq. in. cross-section.

$$\frac{l}{A_1 \cdot E} = \frac{720}{3 \times 30{,}000{,}000}$$
$$= 0.000008 \text{ in.}$$

From equation (5)

$$H = \frac{0.956}{\dfrac{0.574}{20{,}000} + 0.000008}$$
$$= 26{,}050 \text{ lb.}$$

Temperature Stresses.—Where a horizontal tie is used and all parts of the structure are exposed to the same conditions and range of temperature, the entire arch will contract and expand freely and temperature stresses will not enter into the calculations. Where the tie is protected and where rigid abutments are used the temperature stresses must receive careful attention.

The deformation Δ' due to a uniform change of temperature of t degrees Fahr. when the arch is assumed to be a truss supported on frictionless rollers, will be $e \cdot t \cdot L$, where e is the coefficient of expansion of steel per degree Fahr. = .00000665; t equals change in temperature in degrees Fahr.; and L equals the length of the span.

For a change of 75 degrees Fahr. from the mean, the deformation will be

$$\Delta' = \pm .00000665 \times 75L$$
$$= \pm \frac{L}{2,000} \qquad (6)$$

For the arch in Fig. 3

$$\Delta' = \pm \frac{720''}{2,000} = \pm 0.36 \text{ in.}$$

This will be equivalent to a change in H of $\pm \frac{0.36}{0.0000287} = \pm 12,540$ lb. The stresses due to temperature in the two-hinged arch will be equal to the stresses in column 4, Table II, multiplied by ± 0.627. The maximum stresses due to external loads and temperature will be found by adding algebraically the temperature stresses to the stresses due to the external loads. If the arch is not erected at a mean temperature this fact must be taken into account in setting the pedestals.

Design of Two-hinged Arch.—In designing a two-hinged roof arch proceed as follows: (1) With one end free to move, calculate the stresses in the arch as a simple truss; (2) with an assumed horizontal reaction, H', of, say, 1 lb., calculate the stresses in the arch as a simple truss; (3) as a first approximation assume that all members have a unit area and that E is a constant. Then

$$H = \frac{\Sigma S \cdot U \cdot L}{\Sigma U^2 \cdot L} \qquad (7)$$

where S = total stress in each member due to external loads;
U = stress in each member due to a load of 1 lb. acting in line with the horizontal reaction H.

For the two-hinged arch carrying dead loads from Table I and Table II, the approximate value of H as found by substituting in (7) is, H = 33,000 lb., which checks the true value very closely; (4) design the members for approximate stresses in the arch; (5) calculate the deformation of the arch as a truss for the approximate sections and stresses; (6) determine a more accurate value of H from the deformations as previously described; (7) recalculate the stresses in the arch, redesign the members, recalculate the deformations, recalculate a new value of H, etc., until satisfactory sections are obtained. The second approximation is usually sufficient. Corrections for horizontal tie and temperature should be applied in making the approximations The gross area of the sections of all members should be used in determining the deformation of the members. If riveted tension members are much weakened, a somewhat smaller value of E, say, 26,000,000, may be used than the 30,000,000 commonly used for the compression members.

Problem.—For the details of the calculation of the stresses in a two-hinged arch with a horizontal tie, see Problem 5, Chapter XXII.

CHAPTER XXI.

STRESSES IN A STATICALLY INDETERMINATE HEAD FRAME.

Introduction.—Head frames of the 4-post type are statically indeterminate to a greater or less degree depending upon the details of the design. The 4-post head frame in Fig. 1 is statically indeterminate both internally and externally. It is statically indeterminate externally because the reactions cannot be calculated by statics, the

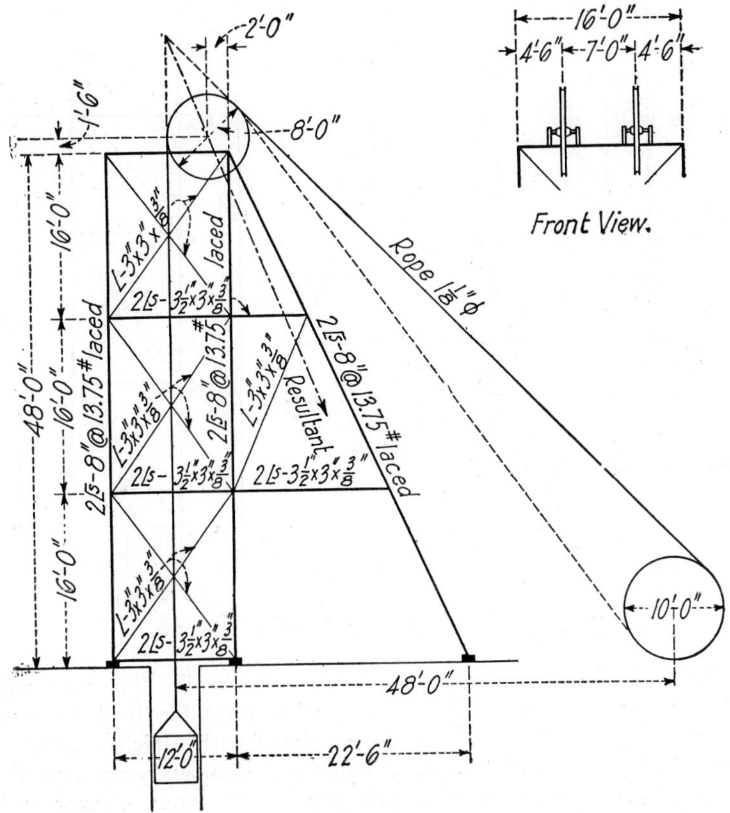

FIG. 1. 4-POST HEAD FRAME.

distribution of the load between the tower and back brace not being known; and is statically indeterminate internally because there are redundant members in the 4-post tower and in the bracing between the tower and the back brace.

The dimensions of the head frame and the make-up of the members are given in Fig. 1. The head sheaves are 8 ft. in diameter, the hoisting drum is placed 48 ft. from the center of the shaft. The hoisting rope is $1\frac{1}{8}$ in. round with an ultimate strength of 84,000 lb. The calculations will be made for the right hand or near frame for the full breaking load of one hoisting rope, it being assumed that both ropes break at the same time. Stresses for other conditions may be calculated from the stresses due to

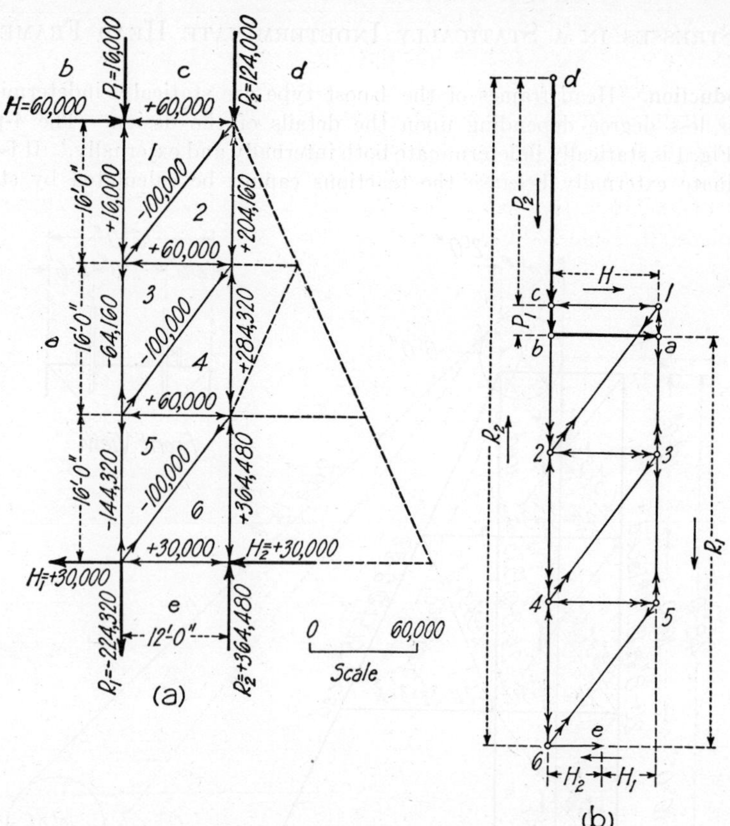

FIG. 2. STRESSES DUE DIRECT LOADING.

84,000 lb., the live load stresses being proportional to the loads. The dead load stresses may be calculated in a manner similar to the method given for live loads, or since the dead load stresses are small, they may be calculated with sufficient accuracy by an approximate solution by assuming that the redundant members carry none of the dead load. The wind load stresses may be calculated in the same manner as live load stresses, or as in the general custom the 4-post tower may be assumed to carry all the wind loads, and the bracing calculated upon that assumption.

CALCULATION OF THE STRESSES.—The diagonal bracing in the tower will be assumed as ties not having initial tension, and the redundant diagonals may then be omitted. The back brace and the bracing between the tower and back brace are redundant. There will be two cases, depending upon whether (1) the back brace alone is considered redundant and the bracing is omitted, or (2) where the back brace and the upper horizontal strut are both considered redundant. The solution will cover Case 1, One Redundant Member, and Case 2, Two Redundant Members. With high frames it is often necessary to solve for 3 or even 4 redundant members.

Case 1. One Redundant Member.—The stresses may be calculated by the "Theory of Work," described in Chapter XVI, or the method used in the calculation of the stresses in a two-hinged arch in Chapter XX may be used.

Method of Work.—The breaking stress of 84,000 lb. in the hoisting rope produces a resultant which falls inside of the back brace. The resultant of the stress in the rope is replaced by its components, a horizontal force H = 60,000 lb. acting in line with the top strut, a vertical force P_1 = 16,000 lb. acting in line with the left post, and P_2 = 124,000 lb. acting in line with the right vertical post. These external forces were calculated by moments in the usual manner.

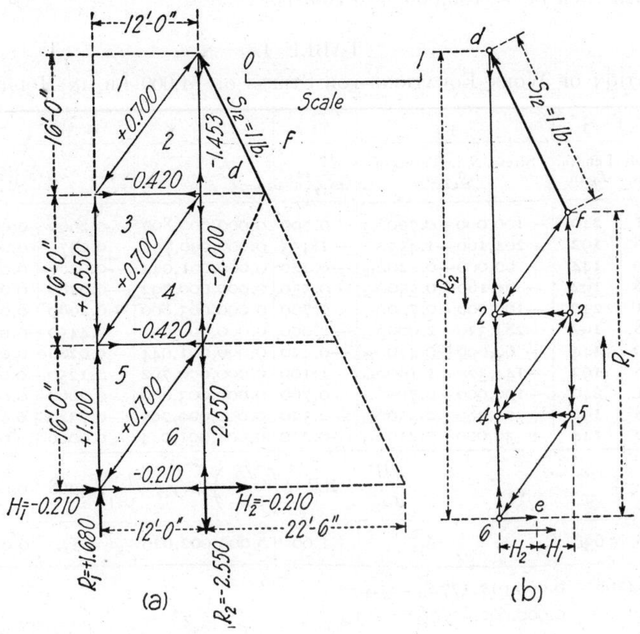

FIG. 3. VALUES OF U.

The stresses in the tower—the back brace being redundant is omitted—for the external loads H, P_1 and P_2 were calculated in (b) by graphic resolution, and the stresses in the members are given in (a), Fig. 2.

The values of $\dfrac{dS}{dS_{12}} = U$ are calculated in (b), Fig. 3, for a load of 1 lb. acting in line of the back brace S_{12}. The values of $\dfrac{dS}{dS_{12}} = U$ are given in (a), Fig. 3.

Work Equations.—The work equations are given in Table I. The members as marked in Fig. 5, are given in column 1; the cross-sectional areas of the members are given in column 2; the lengths, L, of the members are given in column 3; the stresses in the members in terms of S_{12}—the stress in the back brace—the method of calculating which will be given presently are given in column 4; the values of $\frac{dS}{dS_{12}} = U$ are given in column 5; values of $B = \frac{L}{A \cdot E}$, for $E = 30,000,000$, are given in column 6; while values of $B \cdot S \left(\frac{dS}{dS_{12}}\right)$ are given in column 7. The stresses in column 4 may be calculated directly by algebraic resolution, or the stress in each member is equal to the stress due to the direct loads, as given in (a), Fig. 2, plus S_{12} times the stress U, in the member due to a unit load. For example the direct stress in S_1 from (a), Fig. 2, is $-$ 100,000 lb., while the stress U from (a), Fig. 3, is $+$ 0.700. The true stress in the member S_1 will then be $-$ 100,000 $+$ 0.700S_{12}.

TABLE I.

CALCULATION OF WORK EQUATIONS FOR STRESS OF 84,000 LB. IN HOISTING ROPE.

1	2	3	4	5	6	7
Member.	Area, A, Sq In.	Length, L, In.	Stress, S, in Terms of S_{12}.	$\frac{dS}{dS_{12}} = U$	$\frac{L}{A \cdot E} = B$	$B \cdot S\left(\frac{dS}{dS_{12}}\right)$
S_1	2.11	240	$-100,000+0.700S_{12}$	$+0.700$	0.000,003,800	$-0.2660+0.000,001,862S_{12}$
S_2	8.08	192	$+204,160-1.453S_{12}$	-1.453	0.000,000,792	$-0.2370+0.000,001,670S_{12}$
S_3	4.60	144	$+60,000-0.420S_{12}$	-0.420	0.000,001,044	$-0.0266+0.000,000,188S_{12}$
S_4	8.08	192	$-64,160+0.550S_{12}$	$+0.550$	0.000,000,792	$-0.0280+0.000,000,238S_{12}$
S_5	2.11	240	$-100,000+0.700S_{12}$	$+0.700$	0.000,003,800	$-0.2660+0.000,001,862S_{12}$
S_6	8.08	192	$+284,320-2.000S_{12}$	-2.000	0.000,000,792	$-0.4450+0.000,003,160S_{12}$
S_7	4.60	144	$+60,000-0.420S_{12}$	-0.420	0.000,001,044	$-0.0266+0.000,000,188S_{12}$
S_8	8.08	192	$-144,320+1.100S_{12}$	$+1.100$	0.000,000,792	$-0.1250+0.000,000,950S_{12}$
S_9	2.11	240	$-100,000+0.700S_{12}$	$+0.700$	0.000,003,800	$-0.2660+0.000,001,862S_{12}$
S_{10}	8.08	192	$+364,480-2.550S_{12}$	-2.550	0.000,000,792	$-0.7340+0.000,005,150S_{12}$
S_{11}	4.60	144	$+30,000-0.210S_{12}$	-0.210	0.000,001,044	$-0.0066+0.000,000,047S_{12}$
			$\frac{dW}{dS_{12}} = \Sigma B \cdot S\left(\frac{dS}{dS_{12}}\right) = y_{12} =$			$-2.4268+0.000,017,177S_{12}$
S_{12}	8.08	636	S_{12}	$+1.00$	0.000,002,620	$-y_{12}=0.000,002,620S_{12}$

(1) $-2.4268 + 0.000,017,177S_{12} = y_{12}$
(2) $0.000,002,620S_{12} = -y_{12}$
(3) $0.000,019,797S_{12} = 2.4268$
$S_{12} = +123,000$ lb.

The sum of the values of $B \cdot S\left(\frac{dS}{dS_{12}}\right)$ in column 7 for members S_1 to S_{11} is $\frac{dW}{dS_{12}} = \Sigma B \cdot S\left(\frac{dS}{dS_{12}}\right) = -2.4268 + 0.000,017,177S_{12} = y_{12}$. The deformation of the member S_{12} due to a stress of S_{12} will be $0.000,002,620S_{12} = -y_{12}$. Equating the two values of y_{12} and solving, we have $S_{12} = +123,000$ lb.

Having the stress $S_{12} = +123{,}000$ lb. the stresses in the head frame are calculated by graphic resolution as in Fig. 4. The stresses may also be calculated by substituting $S_{12} = 123{,}000$ lb. in the stresses in the members as given in column 4, Table I. For

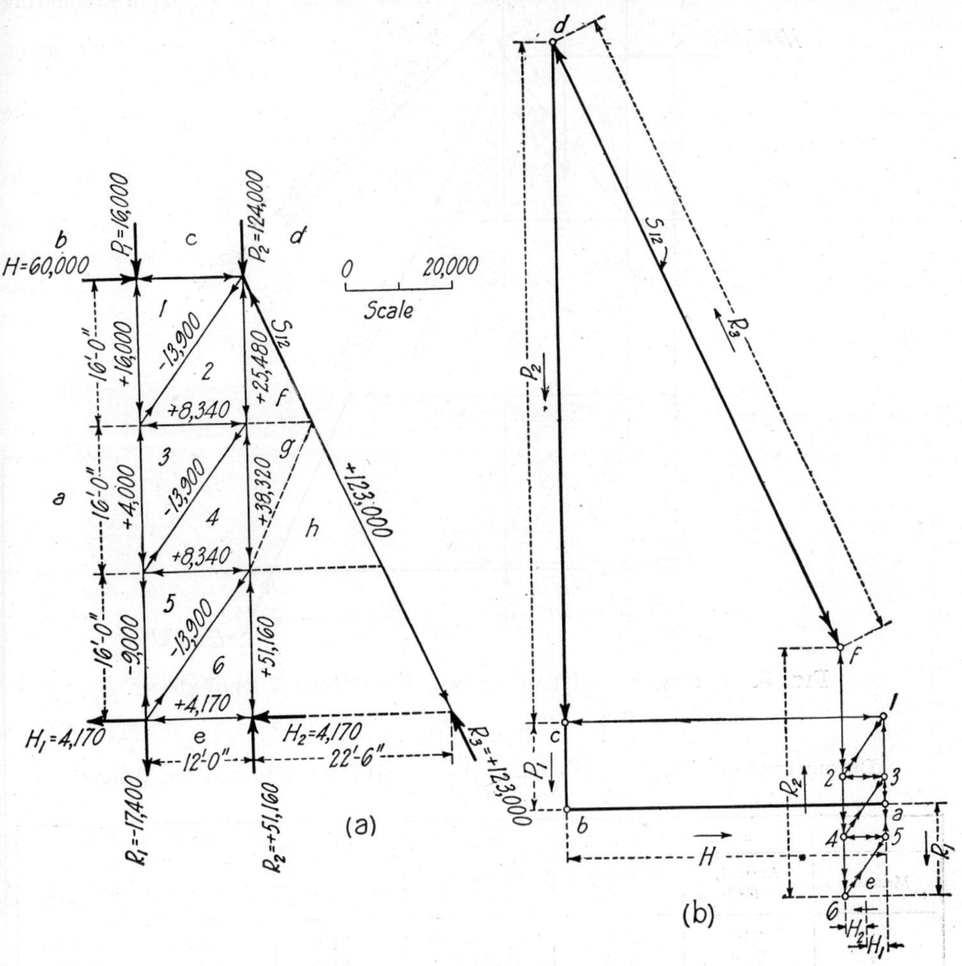

FIG. 4. STRESSES IN HEAD FRAME, BACK BRACE REDUNDANT.

example the stress in (1-3) $= S_1 = -100{,}000 + 0.700 S_{12} = -100{,}000 + 0.700 \times 123{,}000 = -100{,}000 + 86{,}100 = -13{,}900$ lb. The remaining stresses may be calculated in the same manner.

The final stresses in the head frame for live load are given in Fig. 5.

Method of Two-Hinged Arch.—The stresses, S, in the tower due to the external loads, the back brace not acting are calculated as in Fig. 2. The values of U for a load of 1 lb. acting in line with the back brace, are calculated as in Fig. 3. The deformation

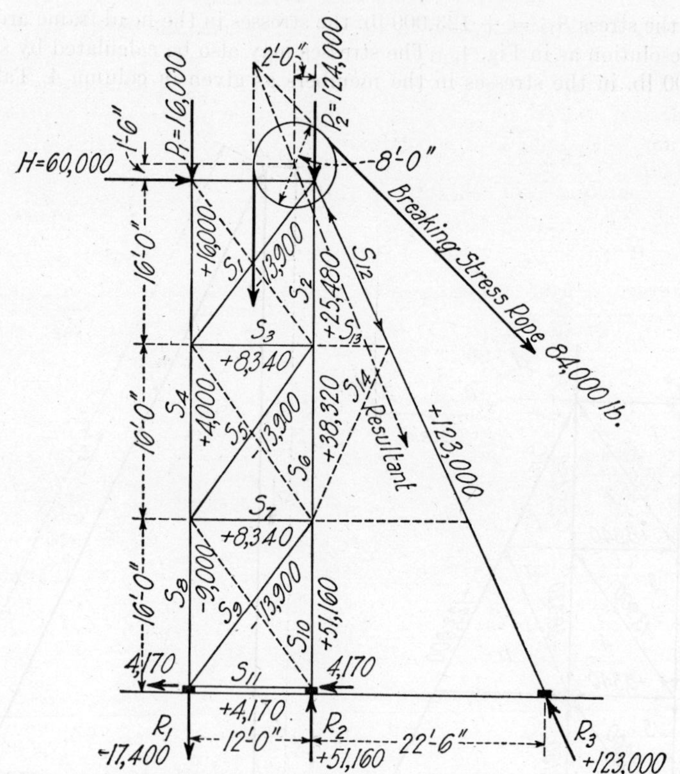

FIG. 5. STRESSES IN HEAD FRAME, BACK BRACE REDUNDANT.

TABLE II.

DEFORMATION AT TOP OF HEAD FRAME DUE TO HOISTING ROPE, BACK BRACE, S_{12} NOT ACTING.

1	2	3	4	5	6	7
Member.	Area, A, Sq. In.	Length, L, In.	Stress, S, Lb.	$\frac{S \cdot L}{A \cdot E}$.	U	$\frac{S \cdot U \cdot L}{A \cdot E}$.
S_1	2.11	240	− 100,000	− 0.380	+ 0.700	− 0.2660
S_2	8.08	192	+ 204,160	+ 0.163	− 1.453	− 0.2370
S_3	4.60	144	+ 60,000	+ 0.0625	− 0.420	− 0.0266
S_4	8.08	192	− 64,160	− 0.0510	+ 0.550	− 0.0280
S_5	2.11	240	− 100,000	− 0.380	+ 0.700	− 0.2660
S_6	8.08	192	+ 284,320	+ 0.225	− 2.000	− 0.4450
S_7	4.60	144	+ 60,000	+ 0.0625	− 0.420	− 0.0266
S_8	8.08	192	− 144,320	− 0.114	+ 1.100	− 0.1250
S_9	2.11	240	− 100,000	− 0.380	+ 0.700	− 0.2660
S_{10}	8.08	192	+ 364,480	+ 0.287	− 2.550	− 0.7340
S_{11}	4.60	144	+ 30,000	+ 0.0312	− 0.210	− 0.0066
					$\Sigma \frac{S \cdot U \cdot L}{A \cdot E}$ =	− 2.4268

of the upper right hand point of the head frame in line with the back brace is then calculated in Table II. Columns 1, 2 and 3 in Table II are the same as the respective columns in Table I. The stresses S in column 4 are the stresses in the tower when the back brace is not acting, and are obtained from Fig. 2. The deformation of each member is given in column 5; the values of U, obtained from Fig. 3, are given in column 6, while values of $\frac{S \cdot U \cdot L}{A \cdot E}$ are given in column 7.

TABLE III.

DEFORMATION AT TOP OF HEAD FRAME DUE TO A VALUE OF S_{12} = 100,000 LB.

1	2	3	4	5	6	7
Member.	Area, A, Sq. In.	Length, L, In.	Stress, S', Lb.	$\frac{U \cdot L}{A \cdot E} \times 100{,}000$.	U	$\frac{U^2 \cdot L}{A \cdot E} \times 100{,}000$
S_1	2.11	240	+ 70,000	+ 0.2600	+ 0.700	0.1862
S_2	8.08	192	− 145,300	− 0.1150	− 1.453	0.1670
S_3	4.60	144	− 42,000	− 0.0430	− 0.420	0.0188
S_4	8.08	192	+ 54,800	+ 0.0434	+ 0.550	0.0238
S_5	2.11	240	+ 70,000	− 0.2600	+ 0.700	0.1862
S_6	8.08	192	− 200,000	− 0.1580	− 2.000	0.3160
S_7	4.60	144	− 42,000	− 0.0430	− 0.420	0.0188
S_8	8.08	192	+ 110,000	+ 0.0864	+ 1.100	0.0950
S_9	2.11	240	+ 70,000	+ 0.2600	+ 0.700	0.1862
S_{10}	8.08	192	− 254,800	− 0.2030	− 2.550	0.5150
S_{11}	4.60	144	− 21,000	− 0.0215	− 0.210	0.0047
						$\Sigma \frac{U^2 \cdot L}{A \cdot E} \times 100{,}000 = 1.7177$
S_{12}	8.08	636	100,000	0.2622	+ 1.00	0.2620

$$S_{12} = \frac{2.4268}{\frac{1.7177}{100{,}000} + \frac{0.262}{100{,}000}} = 123{,}000 \text{ lb.}$$

The deformation of the upper right hand point of the tower in line with the back brace is $y_{12} = -2.4268$ in. The deformation of the upper right hand point of the tower for a value of S_{12} = 100,000 lb. is calculated in Table III, and is $y_{12} = +1.7177$ in. The deformation of S_{12} for a stress of 100,000 lb. = 0.262 in. The total deformation will then be

$$S_{12} = \frac{2.4268}{\frac{1.7177}{100{,}000} + \frac{0.262}{100{,}000}} = 123{,}000 \text{ lb.}$$

This is the value of the stress in S_{12} that was calculated by work equations.

Case 2. Two Redundant Members.—If it is assumed that the two upper diagonal braces between the tower and the back brace carry stress the structure has two redundant members. This problem can only be solved by the "Theory of Least Work," the method of the two-hinged arch, "Algebraic Summation," not being applicable to this problem.

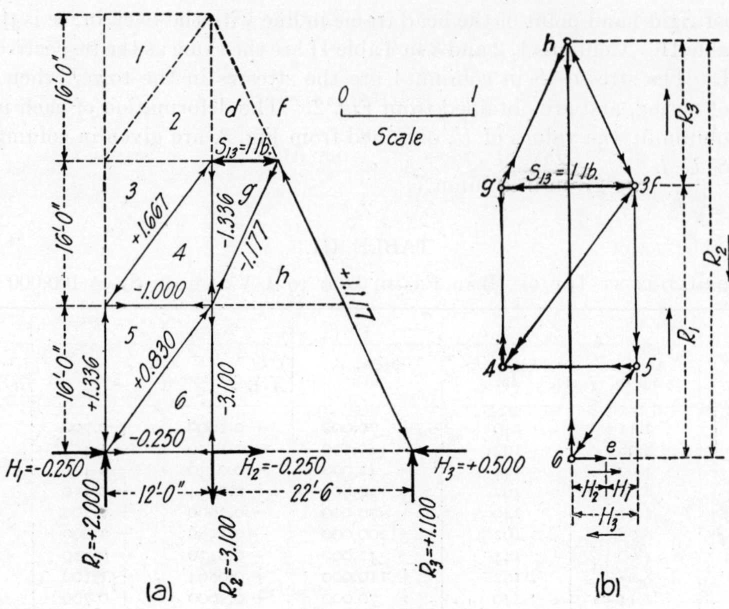

FIG. 6. VALUES OF U'.

Solution.—The stresses in the tower due to the external loads are calculated in Fig. 2, and are the same as in Case 1. The stresses, U, in the members due to a stress of 1 lb. in the back brace are calculated in Fig. 3. The values of U are the values of $\frac{dS}{dS_{12}}$ for the corresponding members. The stresses, U', in the members due to a stress of 1 lb. in the top horizontal strut are calculated in Fig. 6. The values of U' are the values of $\frac{dS}{dS_{13}}$ for the corresponding members.

Work Equations.—The work equations are given in Table IV. The values in columns 1, 2 and 3 are the same as in Table I. The stresses in the members in terms of the unknown stresses S_{12} and S_{13} are given in column 4—these stresses may be calculated directly by algebraic resolution, or may be found by adding to the stresses in the tower due to direct loads the unknown stress S_{12} multiplied by the values of $\frac{dS}{dS_{12}}$ (U), and the unknown stress S_{13} multiplied by $\frac{dS}{dS_{13}}$ (U'). The values of $\frac{dS}{dS_{13}} = U$ were calculated in Fig. 3; while the values of $\frac{dS}{dS_{13}} = U'$ were calculated in Fig. 6. The values of B in column 7 were calculated for E = 30,000,000. The values of $B \cdot S\left(\frac{dS}{dS_{12}}\right)$ are given in column 8, and of $B \cdot S\left(\frac{dS}{dS_{13}}\right)$ are given in column 9. Now the deformation of the back brace will be equal to the deformation of the tower in line of the back brace, and from column 8 the deformations are

$$- y_{12} = 0.000,000,874 S_{12} \tag{1}$$

and

$$y_{12} = 0.000,018,925 S_{12} + 0.000,018,646 S_{13} - 2.4268 \tag{2}$$

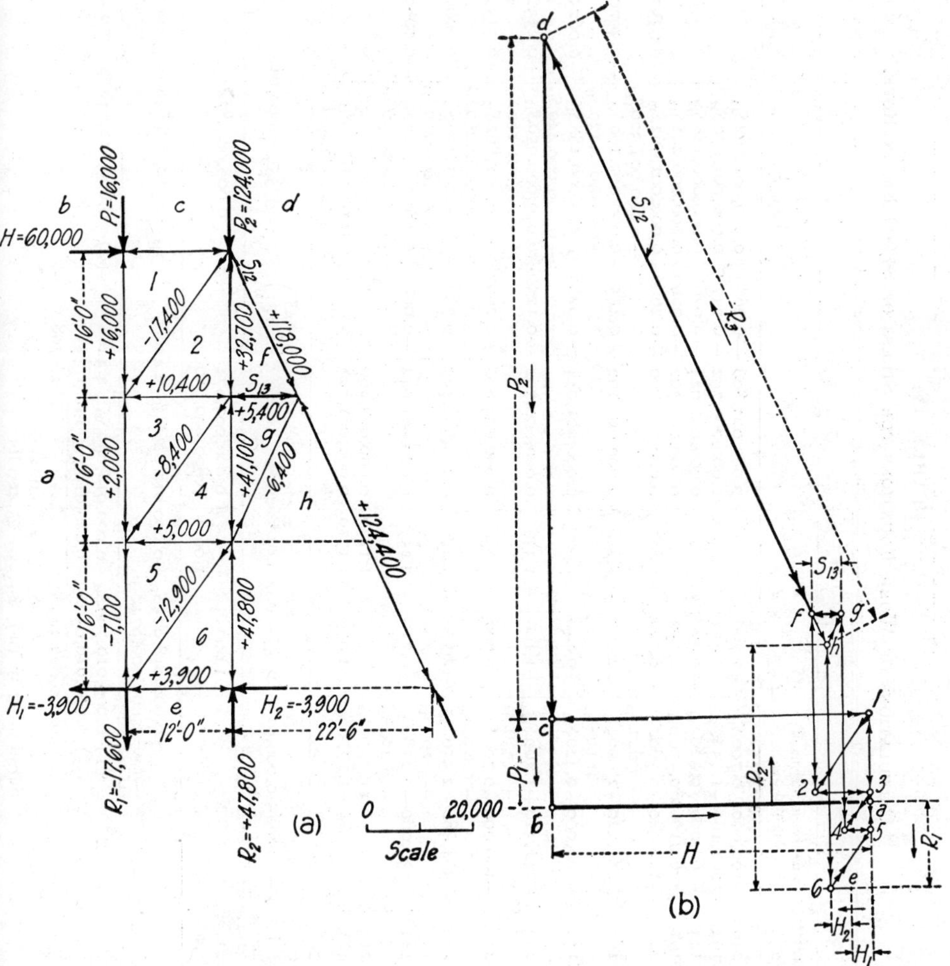

FIG. 7. STRESSES IN HEAD FRAME, TWO MEMBERS REDUNDANT.

Adding equations (1) and (2) gives

$$0.000,019,799 S_{12} + 0.000,018,646 S_{13} = 2.4268 \tag{3}$$

From column 9 the deformation of the strut, and the tower in line with the strut are

$$- y_{13} = + 0.000,000,650 S_{13} \tag{4}$$

TABLE IV.

CALCULATIONS OF WORK EQUATIONS FOR STRESS OF 84,000 LB. IN ROPE.

1	2	3	4	5	6	7	8	9
Member.	Area, A, Sq. In.	Length, L, In.	Stresses in Terms of S_{12} and S_{13}.	$\frac{dS}{dS_{12}} = U$	$\frac{dS}{dS_{13}} = U'$	$\frac{L}{A \cdot E} = B$	$B \cdot S\left(\frac{dS}{dS_{12}}\right)$	$B \cdot S\left(\frac{dS}{dS_{13}}\right)$
S_1	2.11	240	$-100,000+0.700S_{12}$	$+0.700$		0.000,003,800	$-0.2660+0.000,001,862S_{12}$	
S_2	8.08	192	$+204,160-1.453S_{12}$	-1.453		0.000,000,792	$-0.2370+0.000,001,670S_{12}$	
S_3	4.60	144	$+60,000-0.420S_{12}$	-0.420		0.000,001,044	$-0.0266+0.000,000,188S_{12}$	
S_4	8.08	192	$-64,160+0.550S_{12}$	$+0.550$		0.000,000,792	$-0.0280+0.000,000,238S_{12}$	
S_5	2.11	240	$-100,000+0.700S_{12}$ $+1.667S_{13}$	$+0.700$	$+1.667$	0.000,003,800	$-0.2660+0.000,001,862S_{12}$ $+0.000,004,320S_{13}$	$-0.6350+0.000,004,320S_{12}$ $+0.000,010,600S_{13}$
S_6	8.08	192	$+284,320-2.000S_{12}$ $-1.336S_{13}$	-2.000	-1.336	0.000,000,792	$-0.4450+0.000,003,160S_{12}$ $+0.000,002,120S_{13}$	$-0.3020+0.000,002,120S_{12}$ $+0.000,001,420S_{13}$
S_7	4.60	144	$+60,000-0.420S_{12}$ $-S_{13}$	-0.420	-1.000	0.000,001,044	$-0.0266+0.000,000,188S_{12}$ $+0.000,000,440S_{13}$	$-0.0625+0.000,000,440S_{12}$ $+0.000,001,044S_{13}$
S_8	8.08	192	$-144,320+1.100S_{12}$ $+1.336S_{13}$	$+1.100$	$+1.336$	0.000,000,792	$-0.1250+0.000,000,950S_{12}$ $+0.000,001,160S_{13}$	$-0.1530+0.000,001,160S_{12}$ $+0.000,001,420S_{13}$
S_9	2.11	240	$-100,000+0.700S_{12}$ $+0.830S_{13}$	$+0.700$	$+0.830$	0.000,003,800	$-0.2660+0.000,001,862S_{12}$ $+0.000,002,260S_{13}$	$-0.3150+0.000,002,260S_{12}$ $+0.000,002,620S_{13}$
S_{10}	8.08	192	$+364,480-2.550S_{12}$ $-3.100S_{13}$	-2.550	-3.100	0.000,000,792	$-0.7340+0.000,005,150S_{12}$ $+0.000,006,250S_{13}$	$-0.9000+0.000,006,250S_{12}$ $+0.000,007,600S_{13}$
S_{11}	4.60	144	$+30,000-0.210S_{12}$ $-0.250S_{13}$	-0.210	-0.250	0.000,001,044	$-0.0066+0.000,000,047S_{12}$ $+0.000,000,056S_{13}$	$-0.0080+0.000,000,056S_{12}$ $+0.000,000,065S_{13}$
S_{14}	2.11	212	$-1.1770S_{13}$		-1.1770	0.000,003,460		$+0.000,004,800S_{13}$
S_{15}	8.08	424	$S_{12}+1.1770S_{13}$	1.000	$+1.1770$	0.000,001,748	$0.000,001,748S_{12}$ $+0.000,002,040S_{13}$	$+0.000,002,040S_{12}$ $+0.000,002,420S_{13}$

$$\Sigma B \cdot S\left(\frac{dS}{dS_{12}}\right) = -2.4268+0.000,018,925S_{12}+0.000,018,646S_{13} \qquad \Sigma B \cdot S\left(\frac{dS}{dS_{13}}\right) = -2.3755+0.000,018,646S_{12}+0.000,031,999S_{13}$$

S_{12}	8.08	212	S_{12}	1.000		0.000,000,874	$0.000,000,874S_{12}$	
S_{13}	4.60	90	S_{13}		1.000	0.000,000,650		$0.000,000,650S_{13}$

$$y_{12}=0.000,018,925S_{12}+0.000,018,646S_{13}-2.4268 \qquad y_{13}=0.000,018,646S_{12}+0.000,031,999S_{13}-2.3755$$

$$-y_{12}=0.000,000,874S_{12} \qquad -y_{13}= \quad +0.000,000,650S_{13}$$

$$(1) \quad 0.000,019,799S_{12}+0.000,018,646S_{13}=2.4268 \qquad (2) \quad 0.000,018,646S_{12}+0.000,032,649S_{13}=2.3755$$

$$(3) \quad 0.000,010,650S_{12}+0.000,018,646S_{13}=1.3550$$

$$0.000,009,149S_{12} = 1.0708$$

$$S_{12}=+118,000 \text{ lb.}$$

Substituting in (1), $S_{13}=+\ 5,400$ lb.

and $$y_{13} = 0.000,018,646S_{12} + 0.000,031,999S_{13} - 2.3755 \tag{5}$$

Adding equations (4) and (5) gives

$$0.000,018,646S_{12} + 0.000,032,649S_{13} = 2.3755 \tag{6}$$

Solving equations (3) and (6) for S_{12} and S_{13} gives

$$S_{12} = +\ 118,000 \text{ lb.}$$
$$S_{13} = +\quad 5,400 \text{ lb.}$$

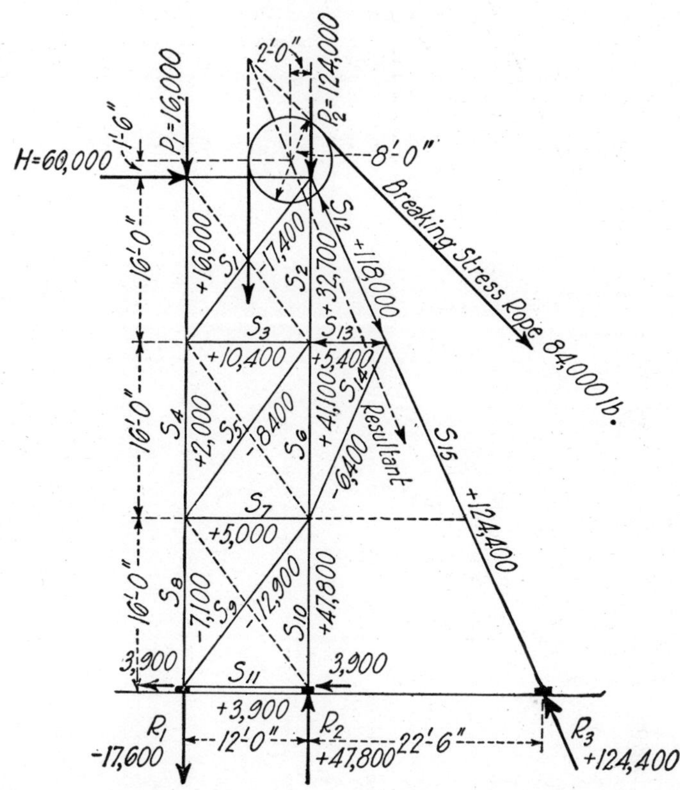

FIG. 8. STRESSES IN HEAD FRAME, TWO MEMBERS REDUNDANT.

The stresses in the members of the head frame were calculated by graphic resolution in Fig. 7. The stresses in members may be calculated by substituting the true values of S_{12} and S_{13} in column 4, Table IV. For example the stress in

$$S_5 = -\ 100,000 + 0.700S_{12} + 1.667S_{13}$$
$$S_5 = -\ 100,000 + 82,600 + 9,000$$
$$= -\ 8,400 \text{ lb.}$$

The stresses in the different members of the head frame are given in Fig. 8.

The work may be shortened and simplified if E is taken as equal to unity. For the reason that E cancels out in solving the equations, relative values of E may be used.

CHAPTER XXII.

Problems in the Calculation of Stresses in Statically Indeterminate Structures, Camber, etc.

Introduction.—The problems given in this chapter illustrate the application of the principles given in the preceding chapters. In addition to the subjects already discussed in Part II, the calculation of the stresses in the frames of steel office buildings and the camber of truss bridges are discussed in detail. The actual details for the solution of the first nine problems are shown, while the details of the solution of the remaining problems are left to the student. The problems in this chapter are those solved in advanced structures by the civil engineering students in the University of Pennsylvania. This course is given as a preliminary to a study of cantilever, arch and suspension bridges.

Instructions.—The problems are to be solved on paper 18″ × 24″ with a 1″ border on the left and a ½″ border on the three remaining sides of the sheet. The drawings are to be neatly finished in pencil. The specifications for executing the drawings are the same as for the problems given in Chapter XIII.

Problem 1. Deflections of Simple and Constrained Beams.

(a) **Problems.**—(1) Calculate by area moments the deflection at the center of a simple girder, span 16′–0″; uniform load, w = 4,000 lb. per lineal ft.; girder consists of one 15″ I @ 42 lb., and two plates 6″ × ½″ × 16′–0″. (2) Calculate by area moments the deflection at the center of a simple girder, span 16′–0″; uniform load, w = 4,000 lb. per lineal ft.; girder consists of one 15″ I @ 42 lb., and two plates 6″ × ½″ × 12″–0″. (3) Calculate by the calculus method the horizontal deflection of the upper right hand corner of a girder consisting of one 24″ I @ 80 lb.; span 30′–0″; load at center, P = 30,000 lb. (4) Calculate by the calculus method the horizontal deflection of the upper right-hand corner of the girder given in (3) for a uniform load, w = 2,000 lb. per lineal ft. (5) Calculate the stress in an elastic steel prop with a length of 10 ft., and an area of 4 sq. in., that supports the center of a beam, made of one 24″ I @ 80 lb.; span 24 ft.; uniform load w = 6,000 lb. per lineal ft. (6) Calculate the stresses in elastic ties P_1 and P_2 which support a 24″ I @ 80 lb., 30 ft. long, resting on end supports; uniform load w = 4,000 lb. per lineal ft.

(b) **Methods.**—The details of the calculations are shown in the problem. The beams in (3) and (4) are supported on the neutral axis of the beam. The foundation of the prop in (5) has settled 3/8 in.

(c) **Results.**—If the prop in (5) is rigid and the base does not settle the stress in the prop will be $P = 5/8w \cdot l = 5/8W$ = 90,000 lb.; and the moment in the beam at a point x from the left end will be $M = \frac{1}{2}(144{,}000 - 90{,}000)x - \frac{1}{2}w \cdot x^2$. If the deflection of the base is equal to the deflection of the beam under full load = 0.715 in., there will be no stress in the prop. It will be noted that the stresses in elastic ties or elastic props will vary directly as the area, and inversely as the length of the tie or prop.

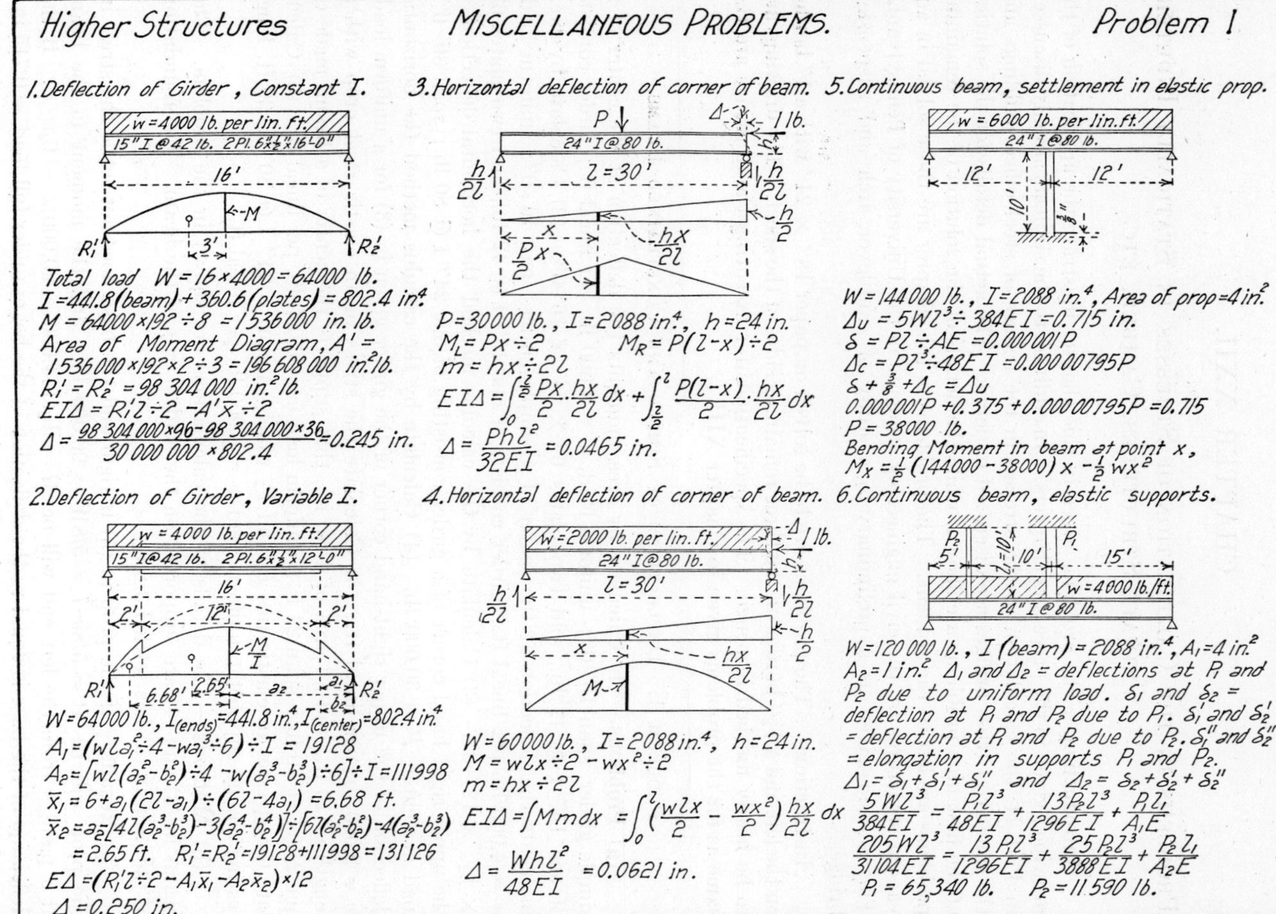
Higher Structures
MISCELLANEOUS PROBLEMS.
Problem I
1. Deflection of Girder, Constant I.
w = 4000 lb. per lin. ft.
15" I @ 42 lb. 2 Pl. 6" x 1/2" x 16'-0"
16'
M
3'
R'1
R'2
Total load W = 16 x 4000 = 64000 lb.
I = 441.8 (beam) + 360.6 (plates) = 802.4 in.⁴
M = 64000 x 192 ÷ 8 = 1536000 in. lb.
Area of Moment Diagram, A' =
1536000 x 192 x 2 ÷ 3 = 196608000 in.² lb.
R'1 = R'2 = 98304000 in.² lb.
EIΔ = R'1 l ÷ 2 − A' x̄ ÷ 2
Δ = (98304000 x 96 − 98304000 x 36) / (30000000 x 802.4) = 0.245 in.
2. Deflection of Girder, Variable I.
w = 4000 lb. per lin. ft.
15" I @ 42 lb. 2 Pl. 6" x 1/2" x 12'-0"
16'
2'
12'
2'
M/I
R'1
6.68'
2.65'
a2
a1
b2
R'2
W = 64000 lb., I(ends) = 441.8 in.⁴, I(center) = 802.4 in.⁴
A1 = (w l a1² ÷ 4 − w a1³ ÷ 6) ÷ I = 19128
A2 = [w l (a2² − b2²) ÷ 4 − w (a2³ − b2³) ÷ 6] ÷ I = 111998
x̄1 = 6 + a1 (2l − a1) ÷ (6l − 4a1) = 6.68 ft.
x̄2 = a2 − [4l (a2³ − b2³) − 3 (a2⁴ − b2⁴)] ÷ [6l (a2² − b2²) − 4 (a2³ − b2³)]
= 2.65 ft. R'1 = R'2 = 19128 + 111998 = 131126
EΔ = (R'1 l ÷ 2 − A1 x̄1 − A2 x̄2) x 12
Δ = 0.250 in.
3. Horizontal deflection of corner of beam.
P
Δ
1 lb.
24" I @ 80 lb.
h/2l
l = 30'
h/2l
h/2
x
hx/2l
Px/2
P = 30000 lb., I = 2088 in.⁴, h = 24 in.
M_L = Px ÷ 2   M_R = P(l − x) ÷ 2
m = hx ÷ 2l
EIΔ = ∫₀^{l/2} (Px/2)·(hx/2l) dx + ∫_{l/2}^{l} (P(l − x)/2)·(hx/2l) dx
Δ = Phl²/32EI = 0.0465 in.
4. Horizontal deflection of corner of beam.
w = 2000 lb. per lin. ft.
Δ
1 lb.
24" I @ 80 lb.
h/2l
l = 30'
h/2l
h/2
x
hx/2l
M
W = 60000 lb., I = 2088 in.⁴, h = 24 in.
M = w l x ÷ 2 − w x² ÷ 2
m = hx ÷ 2l
EIΔ = ∫ M m dx = ∫₀^l (wlx/2 − wx²/2) (hx/2l) dx
Δ = Whl²/48EI = 0.0621 in.
5. Continuous beam, settlement in elastic prop.
w = 6000 lb. per lin. ft.
24" I @ 80 lb.
12'
12'
10'
3/8"
W = 144000 lb., I = 2088 in.⁴, Area of prop = 4 in.²
Δu = 5Wl³ ÷ 384EI = 0.715 in.
δ = Pl ÷ AE = 0.000001P
Δc = Pl³ ÷ 48EI = 0.00000795P
δ + 3/8 + Δc = Δu
0.000001P + 0.375 + 0.00000795P = 0.715
P = 38000 lb.
Bending Moment in beam at point x,
Mx = 1/2 (144000 − 38000) x − 1/2 wx²
6. Continuous beam, elastic supports.
P2
P1
5'
l1 = 10'
10'
15'
w = 4000 lb./ft.
24" I @ 80 lb.
W = 120000 lb., I (beam) = 2088 in.⁴, A1 = 4 in.²
A2 = 1 in.² Δ1 and Δ2 = deflections at P1 and
P2 due to uniform load. δ1 and δ2 =
deflection at P1 and P2 due to P1. δ'1 and δ'2
= deflection at P1 and P2 due to P2. δ"1 and δ"2
= elongation in supports P1 and P2.
Δ1 = δ1 + δ'1 + δ"1 and Δ2 = δ2 + δ'2 + δ"2
5Wl³/384EI = P1l³/48EI + 13P2l³/1296EI + P1l1/A1E
205Wl³/31104EI = 13P1l³/1296EI + 25P2l³/3888EI + P2l1/A2E
P1 = 65,340 lb. P2 = 11590 lb.

PROBLEM 2. STRESSES IN A CONTINUOUS GIRDER OF TWO EQUAL SPANS, WITH VARIABLE MOMENT OF INERTIA. METHOD OF AREA MOMENTS

(a) **Problem.**—Given a girder with two spans of 60 ft. each, the total length being 120 ft. The girder is symmetrical about its center line. The relative values of the moments of inertia, I, at the following distances from the outside ends are:

$$0 \text{ to } 12 \text{ ft.}, I = 1.00$$
$$12 \text{ to } 36 \text{ ft.}, I = 1.38$$
$$36 \text{ to } 48 \text{ ft.}, I = 1.15$$
$$48 \text{ to } 60 \text{ ft.}, I = 1.92.$$

Required (1) to calculate the reactions for a uniform load of w lb. per lineal foot by area moments, and (2) to calculate the bending moments and shears at any point in the girder by means of curved influence diagrams.

(b) **Methods.**—The method of area moments will be used in both solutions.

(1) *Reactions by Area Moments.*—Take a simple beam with a span of l = 120 ft., having the same cross-section as the girder, and loaded with a uniform load of w pounds per lineal foot, as in (*a*). The bending moment diagram will be a parabola with a maximum ordinate at the center, $M = \frac{1}{8}w \cdot l^2 = 1{,}800w$. To calculate the deflection in the beam due to the load, w, load the transformed beam in (*b*) with a load $= M/I$.

The equation of the bending moment parabola with the origin of co-ordinates at the left support is $y = \frac{1}{2}w \cdot l \cdot x - \frac{1}{2}w \cdot x^2$; the area of a segment of the parabola is

$$A = w \cdot l \cdot x^2/4 - w \cdot x^3/6. \tag{1}$$

The areas of the segments divided by I, are as follows:

$$A_1 = 4{,}032w \text{ (sq.-ft.-lb.)}$$
$$A_2 = 19{,}618w \quad \text{"}$$
$$A_3 = 17{,}030w \quad \text{"}$$
$$A_4 = 11{,}100w \quad \text{"}$$

The center of gravity measured back from x is

$$-\bar{x}_1 = \frac{x(2l - x)}{6l - 4x}. \tag{2}$$

(For formulas giving the areas and centroids of moment areas, see Fig. 12, Chapter XIV.)

The centers of gravity of the segments of the parabola were calculated by equation (2) as follows:

$$\bar{x}_1 = \frac{x(240 - x)}{720 - 4x} = \frac{12(240 - 12)}{720 - 48} = 4.07 \text{ ft.},$$

and the distance of the center of gravity of A_1 from the center of the beam, d, is 48 ft. + 4.07 ft. = 52.07 ft.

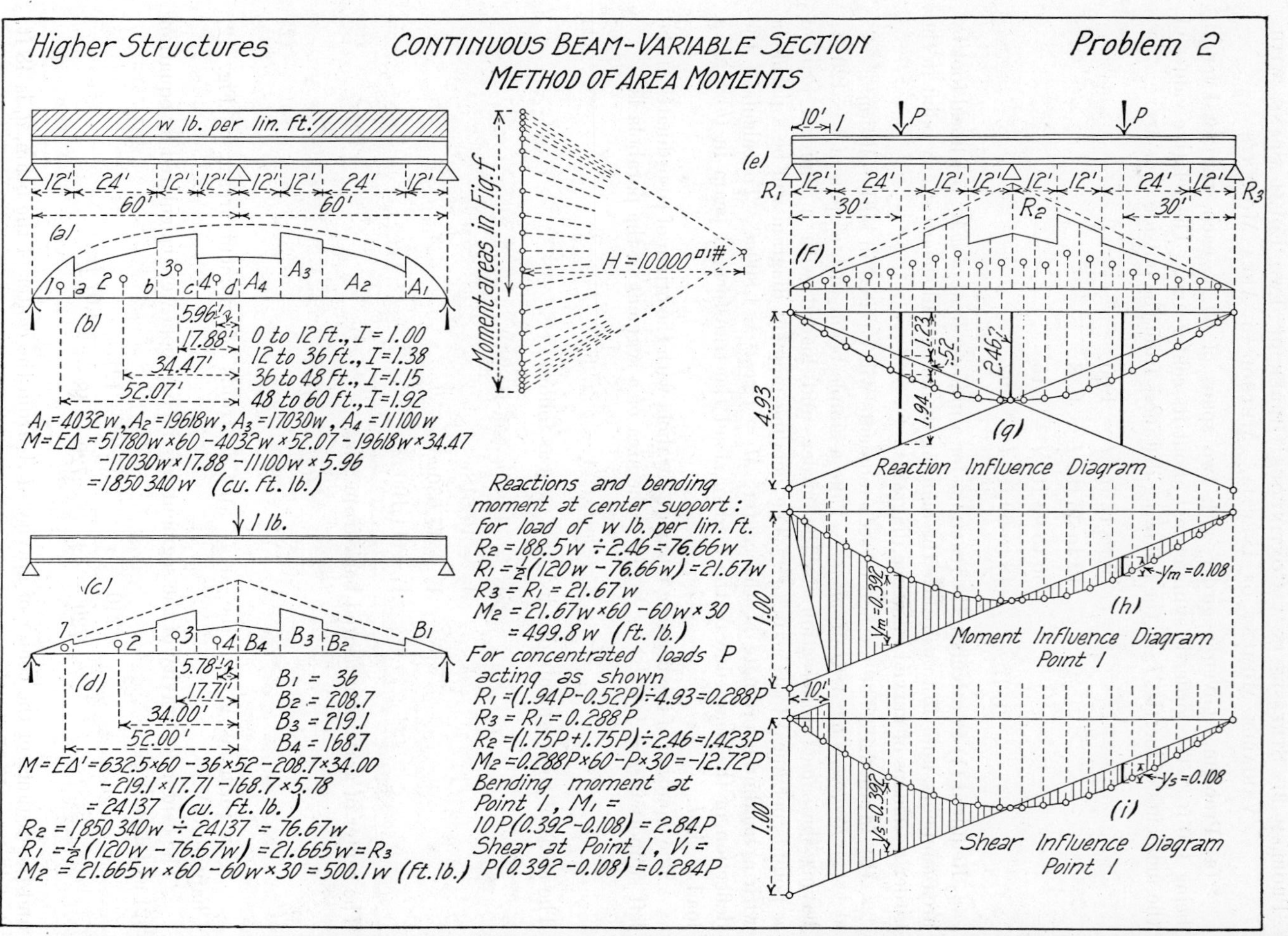

Higher Structures
CONTINUOUS BEAM-VARIABLE SECTION
METHOD OF AREA MOMENTS
Problem 2
w lb. per lin. ft.
12' 24' 12' 12' 12' 12' 24' 12'
60' 60'
(a)
(b)
1 a 2 b 3 c 4 d A4 A3 A2 A1
5.96' 17.88' 34.47' 52.07'
0 to 12 Ft., I = 1.00
12 to 36 Ft., I = 1.38
36 to 48 Ft., I = 1.15
48 to 60 Ft., I = 1.92
A1 = 4032 w, A2 = 19618 w, A3 = 17030 w, A4 = 11100 w
M = EΔ = 51780 w × 60 − 4032 w × 52.07 − 19618 w × 34.47
−17030 w × 17.88 − 11100 w × 5.96
= 1850 340 w (cu. ft. lb.)
1 lb.
(c)
(d)
1 2 3 4 B4 B3 B2 B1
5.78' 17.71' 34.00' 52.00'
B1 = 36
B2 = 208.7
B3 = 219.1
B4 = 168.7
M = EΔ' = 632.5 × 60 − 36 × 52 − 208.7 × 34.00
− 219.1 × 17.71 − 168.7 × 5.78
= 24137 (cu. ft. lb.)
R2 = 1850 340 w ÷ 24137 = 76.67 w
R1 = ½ (120 w − 76.67 w) = 21.665 w = R3
M2 = 21.665 w × 60 − 60 w × 30 = 500.1 w (ft. lb.)
Moment areas in Fig. f
H = 10000 □"#
Reactions and bending
moment at center support:
For load of w lb. per lin. ft.
R2 = 188.5 w ÷ 2.46 = 76.66 w
R1 = ½ (120 w − 76.66 w) = 21.67 w
R3 = R1 = 21.67 w
M2 = 21.67 w × 60 − 60 w × 30
= 499.8 w (ft. lb.)
For concentrated loads P
acting as shown
R1 = (1.94 P − 0.52 P) ÷ 4.93 = 0.288 P
R3 = R1 = 0.288 P
R2 = (1.75 P + 1.75 P) ÷ 2.46 = 1.423 P
M2 = 0.288 P × 60 − P × 30 = −12.72 P
Bending moment at
Point 1, M1 =
10 P (0.392 − 0.108) = 2.84 P
Shear at Point 1, V1 =
P (0.392 − 0.108) = 0.284 P
10' 1 P P
(e)
R1 12' 24' 12' 12' 12' 12' 24' 12' R3
30' R2 30'
(F)
4.93
1.23 .52 2.46 1.94
(g)
Reaction Influence Diagram
1.00
ym = 0.392
ym = 0.108
(h)
Moment Influence Diagram
Point 1
10'
1.00
ys = 0.392
ys = 0.108
(i)
Shear Influence Diagram
Point 1

The center of gravity of the part of the dotted parabola about the point, b, is

$$\bar{x} = \frac{x(240 - x)}{720 - 4x} = \frac{36(240 - 36)}{720 - 144} = 12.75 \text{ ft.}$$

The center of gravity of the dotted A_2 about the point b will be

$$\bar{x}_2 = \frac{(\text{Area } A_1 + \text{Area } A_2)12.75 \text{ ft.} - \text{Area } A_1 \times 28.07 \text{ ft.}}{\text{Area } A_2}$$

$$= \frac{31{,}104w \times 12.75 - 4{,}032w \times 28.07 \text{ ft.}}{27{,}072w}$$

$$= 10.47 \text{ ft.}$$

and the distance of the center of gravity of A_2 from the center of the beam, d, is 24 ft. + 10.47 ft. = 34.47 ft.

The centers of gravity of A_3 and A_4 are calculated in the same manner.

The bending moment at the center of the beam, (b), will be E times the deflection at the center of the beam, (a).

$$M = E \cdot \Delta = R_1 \times 60 \text{ ft.} - A_1 \times 52.07 \text{ ft.} - A_2 \times 34.47 \text{ ft.} - A_3 \times 17.88 \text{ ft.} - A_4 \times 5.96 \text{ ft.}$$

$$= 51{,}780w \times 60 \text{ ft.} - 4{,}032w \times 52.07 \text{ ft.} - 19{,}618w \times 34.47 \text{ ft.} - 17{,}030w \times 17.88 \text{ ft.} - 11{,}100w \times 5.96 \text{ ft.}$$

$$= 1{,}850{,}340w \text{ (cu.-ft.-lb.)} \tag{3}$$

Now load the same beam with a load of 1 lb., as in (c). The bending moment diagram is a triangle with a center height of $M = \frac{1}{4}P \cdot l = 30$ ft.-lb. The beam is loaded with the bending moment divided by the moment of inertia at each point.

The areas of the different sections of the moment diagram are:

$$B_1 = 36 \text{ (sq.-ft.-lb.).}$$
$$B_2 = 208.7 \quad \text{"}$$
$$B_3 = 219.1 \quad \text{"}$$
$$B_4 = 168.7 \quad \text{"}$$

The centers of gravity are as shown in (c). Then the bending moment at the center of the beam (b), will be E times the deflection of the beam (c) due to a center load of 1 lb.

$$M_1 = E \cdot \Delta' = R_1 \times 60 \text{ ft.} - B_1 \times 52 \text{ ft.} - B_2 \times 34 \text{ ft.} - B_3 \times 17.71 \text{ ft.} - B_4 \times 5.78 \text{ ft.}$$

$$= 632.5 \times 60 \text{ ft.} - 36 \times 52 \text{ ft.} - 208.7 \times 34 \text{ ft.} - 219.1 \times 17.71 \text{ ft.} - 168.7 \times 5.78 \text{ ft.}$$

$$= 24{,}137 \text{ (cu.-ft.-lb.).} \tag{4}$$

Now the center reaction of the draw span will be equal to equation (3) divided by equation (4), and

$$R_2 = 1{,}850{,}340w \div 24{,}137$$
$$= 76.67w.$$

The left reaction is

$$R_1 = \tfrac{1}{2}(120w - 76.67w)$$
$$= 21.665w.$$

The bending moment at the center support of the girder is

$$M_2 = 21.665w \times 60 \text{ ft.} - 60w \times 30 \text{ ft.}$$
$$= 500.1w \text{ (ft.-lb.)}.$$

(2) *Reactions and Stresses by Influence Diagrams.*—The girder in (*e*) Problem 2 has the same spans and the same cross-section as the girder in (*a*). Construct a moment area diagram in (*f*) in which the ordinate at each point is equal to the M/I for the point due to a reaction $R_2 = 1$. (The scale in (*f*) is not the same as the scale in (*d*).) Divide the moment area diagram in (*f*) into segments and assume that the area of each segment is a load acting through the center of gravity of the segment. With the segments as loads construct a force polygon with a convenient pole distance as shown; and draw the equilibrium polygon in (*g*). The equilibrium polygon in (*g*) is the influence diagram for the reaction R_2; see Fig. 21 and Fig. 22, Chapter XIV.

For a uniform load w, the middle reaction is, R_2 = (area influence diagram) ÷ (ordinate $c = 2.46$). The area of the curved influence diagram for $H = 10{,}000$ sq.-ft.-lb. as measured by a planimeter is $188.5w$, and

$$R_2 = 188.5w \div 2.46 = 76.66w.$$

For concentrated loads P_1 and P_2 at the mid-spans from equation (54), Chapter XIV,

$$R_2 = (P_1 \times 1.75 + P_2 \times 1.75) \div 2.46 = 0.7115(P_1 + P_2).$$

If $P_1 = P_2 = P$.

$$R_2 = 1.423P.$$

Reactions R_1 and R_3 are calculated as shown.

The moment influence diagram for a point 10 ft. from the left reaction is drawn in (*h*). The shear influence diagram for a point 10 ft. from left reaction is drawn in (*i*). For a discussion of moment and shear influence diagrams, see Chapter XIV.

(c) **Results.**—The area moment solution may be solved algebraically or graphically. The influence diagram solution for a girder with variable moment of inertia is very easy to solve by graphics but very tedious to solve by algebra. The influence diagram has the decided advantage that it gives the reactions, moments, etc. for fixed and moving uniform loads and for fixed and moving concentrated loads.

PROBLEM 3. STRESSES IN CONTINUOUS GIRDER OF THREE SPANS, WITH VARIABLE MOMENT OF INERTIA.

(a) **Problem.**—Given a continuous girder of three spans, 15′–0″, 12′–0″ and 16′–0″, respectively. The moments of inertia of the girder have relative moments of inertia for distances from the left support as follows: 0 to 6 ft., $I' = I$; 6 ft. to 12 ft., $I' = 4/3\ I$; 12 ft. to 18 ft., $I' = 3/2\ I$; 18 ft. to 24 ft., $I' = I$; 24 ft. to 29′–2″, $I' = 3/2\ I$; 29′–8″ to 37′–8″, $I' = 4/3\ I$; 37′–8″ to 43′, $I' = I$. Calculate the reactions R_B and R_C for Cooper's E 60 loading by the influence diagram method.

(b) **Methods.**—The influence diagrams for a continuous girder of three spans may be calculated (1) by the graphic method or (2) by the algebraic method. The graphic method is the simpler and will be given first. The algebraic method will give the greater precision and should ordinarily be used.

(1) *Graphic Solution.*—The method of constructing the influence diagrams for a continuous beam of three spans is explained in Chapter XIV. Apply a unit load in line with R_B and load a simple beam in (*b*) with the bending moment polygon due to a unit load applied at R_B. The diagram in (*b*) is constructed to give $M \div I$ at any point in the beam. The segments of the moment area are assumed to act through the center of gravity of the segment. The areas of the segments, divided by I are given in (*a*). The areas of the segments divided by I are laid off as loads in (*d*) and with a pole H, the equilibrium polygon with full lines in (*c*) is drawn. In the same manner the equilibrium polygon with a unit load in line with R_C is drawn in (*c*′), with force polygon (*d*′) and pole H', and is the polygon with dotted lines. Now redraw the equilibrium polygon given in (*c*′) in (*c*), multiplying each ordinate by $y_c'/y_c = 28.0/22.7$, so that the dotted equilibrium polygon in (*c*) will pass through the point 10. The dotted equilibrium polygon in (*c*) may be drawn by using the force polygon in (*d*′) with a pole distance $H_1' = y_c' \cdot H/y_c = 28.0 \times 8.00 \div 22.7 = 9.86$. The closing line of the force polygon is parallel to the closing line of the equilibrium polygon.

The influence diagram for R_C is drawn in the same manner and is given in (*c*′). With force polygon (*d*) and pole $H_1 = y_B \cdot H \div y'_B = 8.8$ the full equilibrium polygon is drawn in (*c*′) through point 9′.

The influence ordinates in (*c*) are laid off in (*e*) to a scale such that the ordinate at R_B is unity. The influence ordinates in (*c*′) are laid off in (*e*) to a scale such that the ordinate at R_C is unity.

The reaction at R_B for any load P on either span will be equal to the ordinate to curve R_B under the load in (*e*), multiplied by P.

To calculate the reactions for a Cooper's E 60 loading construct diagram in (*f*) on tracing linen. The wheels 1, 2, 3, etc., are spaced to scale as shown. The loads are laid off so that each load represents a unit on the influence diagram.

Now to calculate the reaction R_C for any position of the wheels, place the engine diagram over the influence diagram and record the height of the ordinate in line with each load. The algebraic sum of the ordinates to the influence diagram will be the reaction R_C. With wheel 4 over R_C the reaction at R_C will be, $-3.3 + 5.0 + 20.5 + 30.0 + 30 + 4.5 = 86.7$ thousands of pounds $= 86{,}700$ lb.

Reaction R_B may be calculated in the same manner.

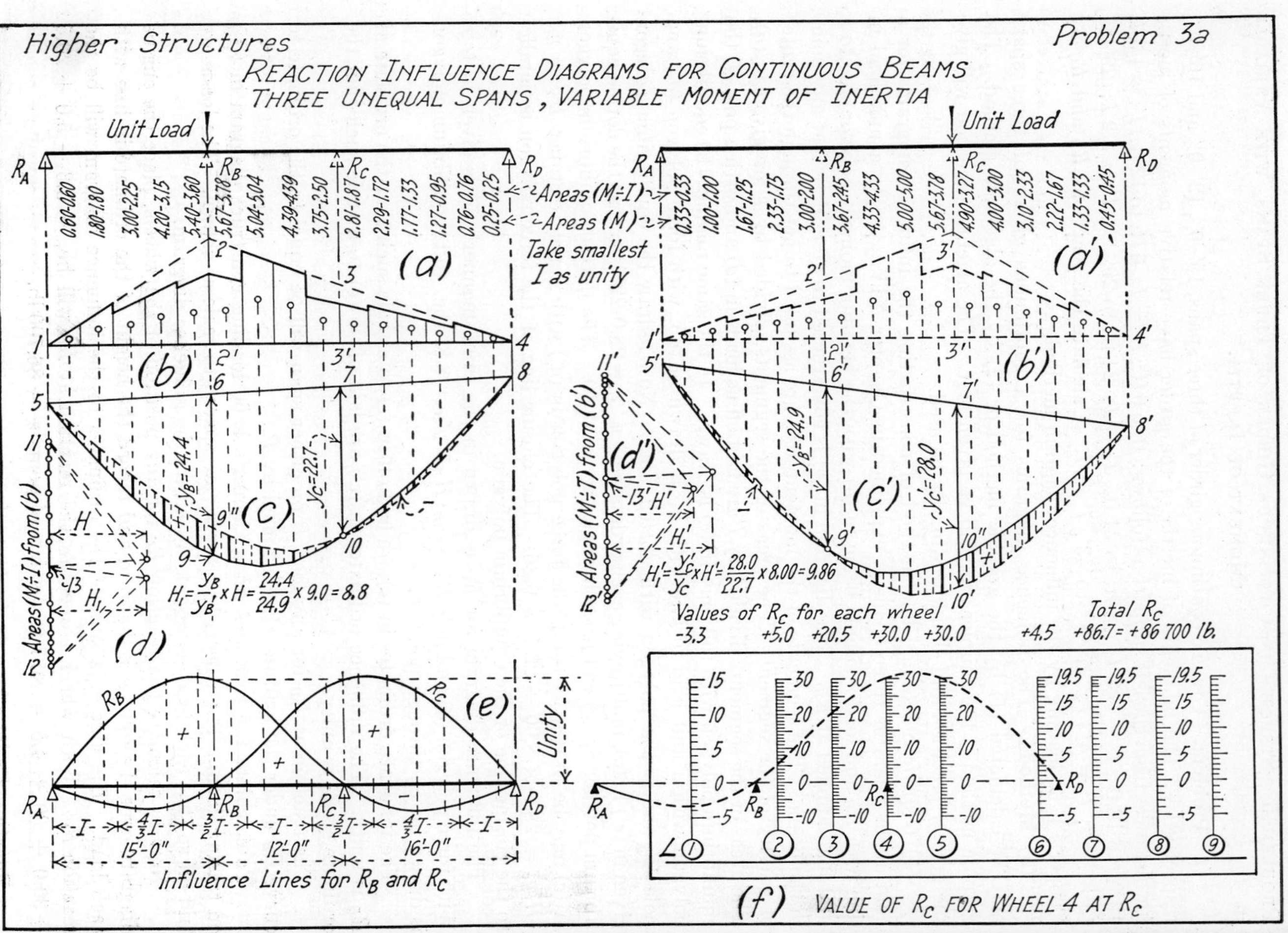
Higher Structures
Problem 3a
REACTION INFLUENCE DIAGRAMS FOR CONTINUOUS BEAMS
THREE UNEQUAL SPANS, VARIABLE MOMENT OF INERTIA
Unit Load
Unit Load
0.60-0.60
1.80-1.80
3.00-2.25
4.20-3.15
5.40-3.60
5.67-3.78
5.04-5.04
4.39-4.39
3.75-2.50
2.81-1.87
2.29-1.72
1.77-1.33
1.27-0.95
0.76-0.76
0.25-0.25
Areas (M÷I)
Areas (M)
Take smallest I as unity
0.33-0.33
1.00-1.00
1.67-1.25
2.33-1.75
3.00-2.00
3.67-2.45
4.33-4.33
5.00-5.00
5.67-3.78
4.90-3.27
4.00-3.00
3.10-2.33
2.22-1.67
1.33-1.33
0.45-0.45
(a)
(a')
(b)
(b')
(c)
(c')
(d)
(d')
(e)
$y_B=24.4$
$y_C=22.7$
$y'_B=24.9$
$y'_C=28.0$
$H_1=\frac{y_B}{y'_B}\times H=\frac{24.4}{24.9}\times 9.0=8.8$
$H'_1=\frac{y'_C}{y_C}\times H'=\frac{28.0}{22.7}\times 8.00=9.86$
Areas (M÷I) from (b)
Areas (M÷I) from (b')
Values of R_C for each wheel
-3.3 +5.0 +20.5 +30.0 +30.0 +4.5
Total R_C
+86.7 = +86 700 lb.
Unity
15'-0"
12'-0"
16'-0"
Influence Lines for R_B and R_C
(f) VALUE OF R_C FOR WHEEL 4 AT R_C

(2) *Algebraic Solution.*—The beam with a span $l_1 + l_2 + l_3 = 43'\text{-}0''$ is loaded in (*b*), Problem 3b with a loading such that the load at any section multiplied by the I of that section will be equal to the bending moment at the given section for a unit load applied in line with R_B. (The ordinate $B\text{-}B'$ in (*b*) was taken equal to 2.00 in place of the correct value for a unit load, which is 0.977. The loading at any section is therefore proportional to the proper loading.) The segments of the beam are taken 3 ft. long in the first span, 3 ft. long in the middle span and 2 ft. 8 in. long in the third span, and the area of each segment is assumed to act through the centroid of the segment. The beam is also loaded in (*b'*) with a similar loading for a unit load applied in line with R_C. (The ordinate $C\text{-}C'$ in (*b'*) was taken equal to 2.00 in place of the correct value for a unit load, which is 1.005. The loading for any section is therefore proportional to the proper loading.)

The bending moments for the beam loaded as in (*b*) are calculated by applying the following theorem. "The bending moment at the right edge of any segment is equal to the bending moment at the right edge of the preceding segment, plus the shear at the left edge of the segment multiplied by the length of the segment, minus the static moment of the segment about the right edge of the segment."

The quantities in Table I are as follows:—The number of the segment is given in column 1. The area of each segment, A, is given in column 2. The distance from the median of each segment to a line through the center of gravity of each segment, e, is given in column 3. The distance from the right edge of each segment to a line through the center of gravity of the segment, e', is given in column 4. Values of $A \div I$ are given in column 5. The distance from the right end of the beam to the center of gravity of each segment is given in column 6. The moment of any segment about the right reaction, $M_1 = A \cdot a/I$, is given in column 7. The value of the left reaction is $R_1 = \Sigma M_1 \div l = 805.53 \div 43.00 = 18.72$. The value of $R_1 - \Sigma A/I$ at the left edge of each segment is given in column 8. The length of each segment is given in column 9. The shear to the left of each segment is multiplied by the length of each segment and the value $= (R_1 - \Sigma A/I)\Delta X$ is given in column 10. The moment increment for each segment is $M' = (R_1 - \Sigma A/I)\Delta X - A \cdot e'/I$, and is given in column 12. The bending moment about the right edge of any segment $M = \Sigma M'$ is given in column 13. From Fig. 23, Chapter XIV, and from Problem 3, it will be seen that the influence ordinates for R_B will be equal to (the ordinates in column 13, Table I) minus (the ordinates in column 13, Table II, multiplied by a factor (K_2) that will make the value of M for segment 5 in Table I equal the value of segment 5 in Table II). $K_2 = 199.29 \div 218.61 = 0.912$. Values of $K_2 \cdot C_2$ are given in column 14. The values of the intercepts between the influence diagrams are given in column 15. The values of the intercepts divided by the intercept at 5 in column 15, are given in column 16. The values in column 16 are the ordinates to the influence diagram at the right of each segment for reaction R_B.

The values in Table II are calculated in the same manner. Due to symmetry, the values of K_1 and K_2 are equal. In general the values of K_1 and K_2 are not equal.

The influence diagrams for R_B and R_C are drawn in (*c*). The ordinate for curve for R_B is unity at section 5, while the ordinate for curve for R_C is unity at section 9.

The influence diagrams when calculated by algebraic methods are more accurate than when calculated by graphic methods, due to the fact that the influence ordinates are equal to the differences of ordinates to bending moment polygons.

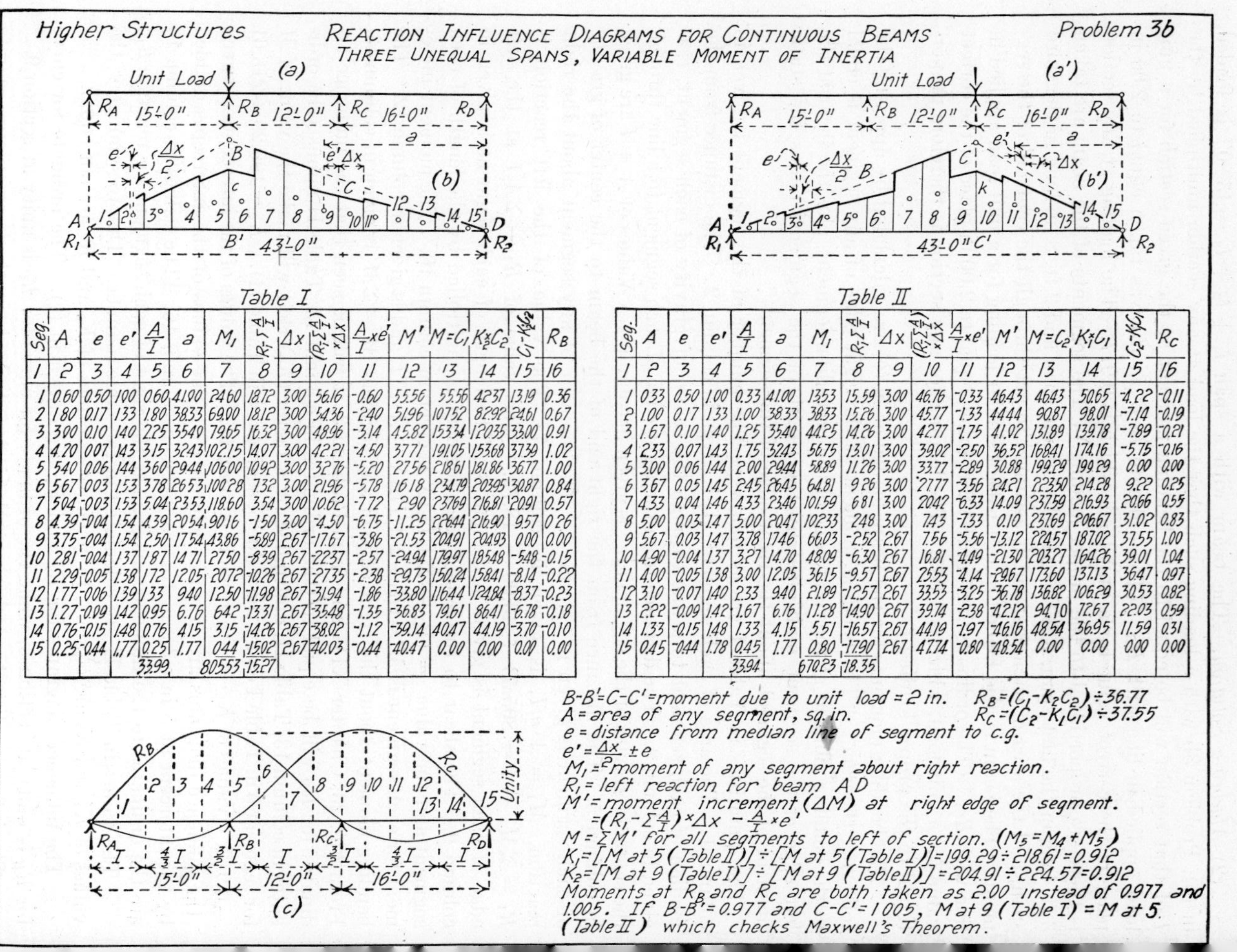

Table I

Seg.	A	e	e'	$\frac{A}{I}$	a	M_1	$R_1-\Sigma\frac{A}{I}$	Δx	$(R_1-\Sigma\frac{A}{I})\times\Delta x$	$\frac{A}{I}\times e'$	M'	$M=C_1$	$K_2\times C_2$	$C_1-K_2C_2$	R_B
1	2	3	4	5	6	7	8	9	10	11	12	13	14	15	16
1	0.60	0.50	1.00	0.60	41.00	24.60	18.72	3.00	56.16	-0.60	55.56	55.56	42.37	13.19	0.36
2	1.80	0.17	1.33	1.80	38.33	69.00	18.12	3.00	54.36	-2.40	51.96	107.52	82.92	24.61	0.67
3	3.00	0.10	1.40	2.25	35.40	79.65	16.32	3.00	48.96	-3.14	45.82	153.34	120.35	33.00	0.91
4	4.20	0.07	1.43	3.15	32.43	102.15	14.07	3.00	42.21	-4.50	37.71	191.05	153.68	37.39	1.02
5	5.40	0.06	1.44	3.60	29.44	106.00	10.92	3.00	32.76	-5.20	27.56	218.61	181.86	36.77	1.00
6	5.67	0.03	1.53	3.78	26.53	100.28	7.32	3.00	21.96	-5.78	16.18	234.79	203.95	30.87	0.84
7	5.04	-0.03	1.53	5.04	23.53	118.60	3.54	3.00	10.62	-7.72	2.90	237.69	216.81	20.91	0.57
8	4.39	-0.04	1.54	4.39	20.54	90.16	-1.50	3.00	-4.50	-6.75	-11.25	226.44	216.90	9.57	0.26
9	3.75	-0.04	1.54	2.50	17.54	43.86	-5.89	2.67	-17.67	-3.86	-21.53	204.91	204.93	0.00	0.00
10	2.81	-0.04	1.37	1.87	14.71	27.50	-8.39	2.67	-22.37	-2.57	-24.94	179.97	185.48	-5.48	-0.15
11	2.29	-0.05	1.38	1.72	12.05	20.72	-10.26	2.67	-27.35	-2.38	-29.73	150.24	158.41	-8.14	-0.22
12	1.77	-0.06	1.39	1.33	9.40	12.50	-11.98	2.67	-31.94	-1.86	-33.80	116.44	124.84	-8.37	-0.23
13	1.27	-0.09	1.42	0.95	6.76	6.42	-13.31	2.67	-35.48	-1.35	-36.83	79.61	86.41	-6.78	-0.18
14	0.76	-0.15	1.48	0.76	4.15	3.15	-14.26	2.67	-38.02	-1.12	-39.14	40.47	44.19	-3.70	-0.10
15	0.25	-0.44	1.77	0.25	1.77	0.44	-15.02	2.67	-40.03	-0.44	-40.47	0.00	0.00	0.00	0.00
				33.99		805.53	-15.27								

Table II

Seg.	A	e	e'	$\frac{A}{I}$	a	M_1	$R_1-\Sigma\frac{A}{I}$	Δx	$(R_1-\Sigma\frac{A}{I})\times\Delta x$	$\frac{A}{I}\times e'$	M'	$M=C_2$	$K_1\times C_1$	$C_2-K_1C_1$	R_C
1	2	3	4	5	6	7	8	9	10	11	12	13	14	15	16
1	0.33	0.50	1.00	0.33	41.00	13.53	15.59	3.00	46.76	-0.33	46.43	46.43	50.65	-4.22	-0.11
2	1.00	0.17	1.33	1.00	38.33	38.33	15.26	3.00	45.77	-1.33	44.44	90.87	98.01	-7.14	-0.19
3	1.67	0.10	1.40	1.25	35.40	44.25	14.26	3.00	42.77	-1.75	41.02	131.89	139.78	-7.89	-0.21
4	2.33	0.07	1.43	1.75	32.43	56.75	13.01	3.00	39.02	-2.50	36.52	168.41	174.16	-5.75	-0.16
5	3.00	0.06	1.44	2.00	29.44	58.89	11.26	3.00	33.77	-2.89	30.88	199.29	199.29	0.00	0.00
6	3.67	0.05	1.45	2.45	26.45	64.81	9.26	3.00	27.77	-3.56	24.21	223.50	214.28	9.22	0.25
7	4.33	0.04	1.46	4.33	23.46	101.59	6.81	3.00	20.42	-6.33	14.09	237.59	216.93	20.66	0.55
8	5.00	0.03	1.47	5.00	20.47	102.33	2.48	3.00	7.43	-7.33	0.10	237.69	206.67	31.02	0.83
9	5.67	0.03	1.47	3.78	17.46	66.03	-2.52	2.67	7.56	-5.56	-13.12	224.57	187.02	37.55	1.00
10	4.90	-0.04	1.37	3.27	14.70	48.09	-6.30	2.67	16.81	-4.49	-21.30	203.27	164.26	39.01	1.04
11	4.00	-0.05	1.38	3.00	12.05	36.15	-9.57	2.67	25.53	-4.14	-29.67	173.60	137.13	36.47	0.97
12	3.10	-0.07	1.40	2.33	9.40	21.89	-12.57	2.67	33.53	-3.25	-36.78	136.82	106.29	30.53	0.82
13	2.22	-0.09	1.42	1.67	6.76	11.28	-14.90	2.67	39.74	-2.38	-42.12	94.70	72.67	22.03	0.59
14	1.33	-0.15	1.48	1.33	4.15	5.51	-16.57	2.67	44.19	-1.97	-46.16	48.54	36.95	11.59	0.31
15	0.45	-0.44	1.78	0.45	1.77	0.80	-17.90	2.67	47.74	-0.80	-48.54	0.00	0.00	0.00	0.00
				33.94		670.23	-18.35								

B-B' = C-C' = moment due to unit load = 2 in. $R_B = (C_1 - K_2C_2) \div 36.77$

A = area of any segment, sq. in. $R_C = (C_2 - K_1C_1) \div 37.55$

e = distance from median line of segment to c.g.

$e' = \frac{\Delta x}{2} \pm e$

M_1 = moment of any segment about right reaction.

R_1 = left reaction for beam AD

M' = moment increment (ΔM) at right edge of segment.
$= (R_1 - \Sigma\frac{A}{I}) \times \Delta x - \frac{A}{I} \times e'$

$M = \Sigma M'$ for all segments to left of section. ($M_5 = M_4 + M'_5$)

K_1 = [M at 5 (Table II)] ÷ [M at 5 (Table I)] = 199.29 ÷ 218.61 = 0.912

K_2 = [M at 9 (Table I)] ÷ [M at 9 (Table II)] = 204.91 ÷ 224.57 = 0.912

Moments at R_B and R_C are both taken as 2.00 instead of 0.977 and 1.005. If B-B' = 0.977 and C-C' = 1.005, M at 9 (Table I) = M at 5 (Table II) which checks Maxwell's Theorem.

Problem 4. Calculation of Stresses in a Trussed Beam.

(c) **Problem.**—Given a timber beam 12 in. wide and 14 in. deep, span 28 ft. center to center of supports. The beam is trussed with a center post 8 in. by 10 in. in cross-section and 5 ft. long, and two rods 1 in. round. Load, including weight of beam, is w = 1,500 lb. per lineal foot. Calculate the stresses in the beam and in the steel rods. Modulus of elasticity for timber is E_t = 1,500,000 lb. per sq. in., for steel is E_s = 30,000,000 lb. per sq. in.

(b) **Methods.**—Take the vertical post, member 1, as the redundant member. Then the vertical deflection of the beam plus the vertical deflection of the steel rods will equal the deformation of the post, member 1. Apply a load of 1 lb. in line with member 1, and calculate the values of U in the members. The stresses in the members due to the load S_1 are calculated as shown. The vertical deflection of the beam in line with the post, due to direct stress will be, $B.S.U. = \Delta_2' = 0.00000261 S_1$, while the vertical deflection of the beam due to a load of w per lineal foot acting downward and a load S_1 acting upward will be $\Delta_2'' = 5W \cdot l^3 \div 384E \cdot I + S_1 \cdot l^3 \div 48E \cdot I = -5.040 + 0.0001920 S_1$. The vertical deformation in the rods due to a load of S_1 will be $\Delta_3 = 2(0.00000838 S_1)$.

The total vertical deformation from the center of the beam to the rods will be $\Delta = \Delta_2' + \Delta_2'' + \Delta_3 = -5.040 + 0.00021137 S_1$, which will equal the deformation of the vertical post, $\Delta_1 = 0.0000005 S_1$. Equating the deformations and solving gives

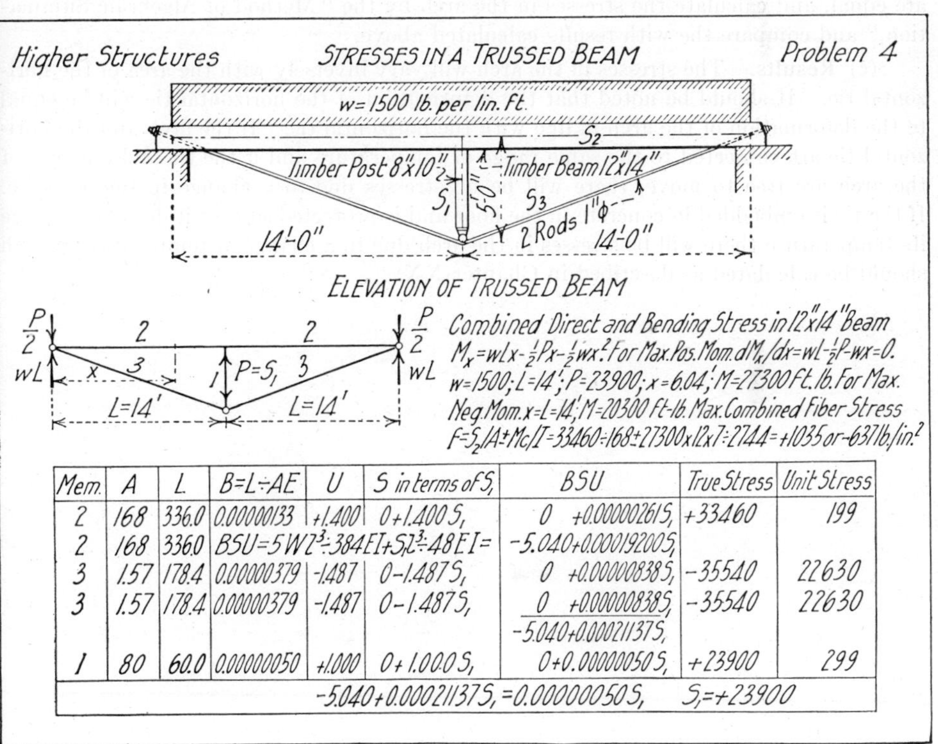

Mem.	A	L	B=L÷AE	U	S in terms of S_1	BSU	True Stress	Unit Stress
2	168	336.0	0.00000133	+1.400	0+1.400 S_1	0 +0.00000261 S_1	+33460	199
2	168	336.0	BSU=5Wl³÷384EI+S₁l³÷48EI=			−5.040+0.00019200 S_1		
3	1.57	178.4	0.00000379	−1.487	0−1.487 S_1	0 +0.00000838 S_1	−35540	22630
3	1.57	178.4	0.00000379	−1.487	0−1.487 S_1	0 +0.00000838 S_1	−35540	22630
						−5.040+0.00021137 S_1		
1	80	60.0	0.00000050	+1.000	0+1.000 S_1	0+0.00000050 S_1	+23900	299
					−5.040+0.00021137 S_1 = 0.00000050 S_1,		S_1=+23900	

$S_1 = +23,900$ lb. The stresses in the beam will be $f_c = +1,035$ or -637 lb. per sq. in. The stresses in the post and rods are as shown in the problem.

(c) **Results.**—The deflection of the beam without the trussed post will be 5.04 in. at the center The deflection at the center of the beam with the truss post acting will be $5.04 - 0.000192 \times 23,900 = 0.45$ in. If the center of the beam did not deflect the load in the center support would be $R_2 = 5w \cdot L/4 = 26,250$ lb.

Approximate Solution.—For an approximate solution assume that the stress in the post is $S_1 = R_2 = 5w \cdot L/4 = 26,250$ lb. The results will be on the safe side.

PROBLEM 5. CALCULATION OF THE STRESSES IN A TWO-HINGED ROOF ARCH.

(a) **Problem.**—Given a two-hinged roof arch with a span of 60′–0″, a rise of 15′–0″, and other dimensions and loads and sections as given in Problem 5. The horizontal tie has a cross-sectional area of 3.00 sq. in. Required to calculate the stresses in the arch by the "Method of Algebraic Summations." Also check the deformations of the arch by the "Williot Diagram Method."

(b) **Methods.**—The stresses are calculated by the "Method of Algebraic Summation" as described in Chapter XV. Draw the Williot deformation diagrams as described in Chapter XV and Chapter XX.

Assume that the areas of all the members of the arch including the horizontal tie are equal, and calculate the stresses in the arch by the "Method of Algebraic Summation," and compare the with results calculated above.

(c) **Results.**—The stresses in the arch will vary inversely with the area of the horizontal tie. It should be noted that the deformation of the horizontal tie will be equal to the deformation of the arch in line with the horizontal tie. If the arch and the horizontal tie are subjected to the same range of temperature and if the tie and one end of the arch are free to move, there will be no stresses due to a change in temperature. If the tie is embedded in concrete in the floor and is protected so that it does not change its temperature there will be stresses in the arch due to a change of temperature, which should be calculated as described in Chapter XX.

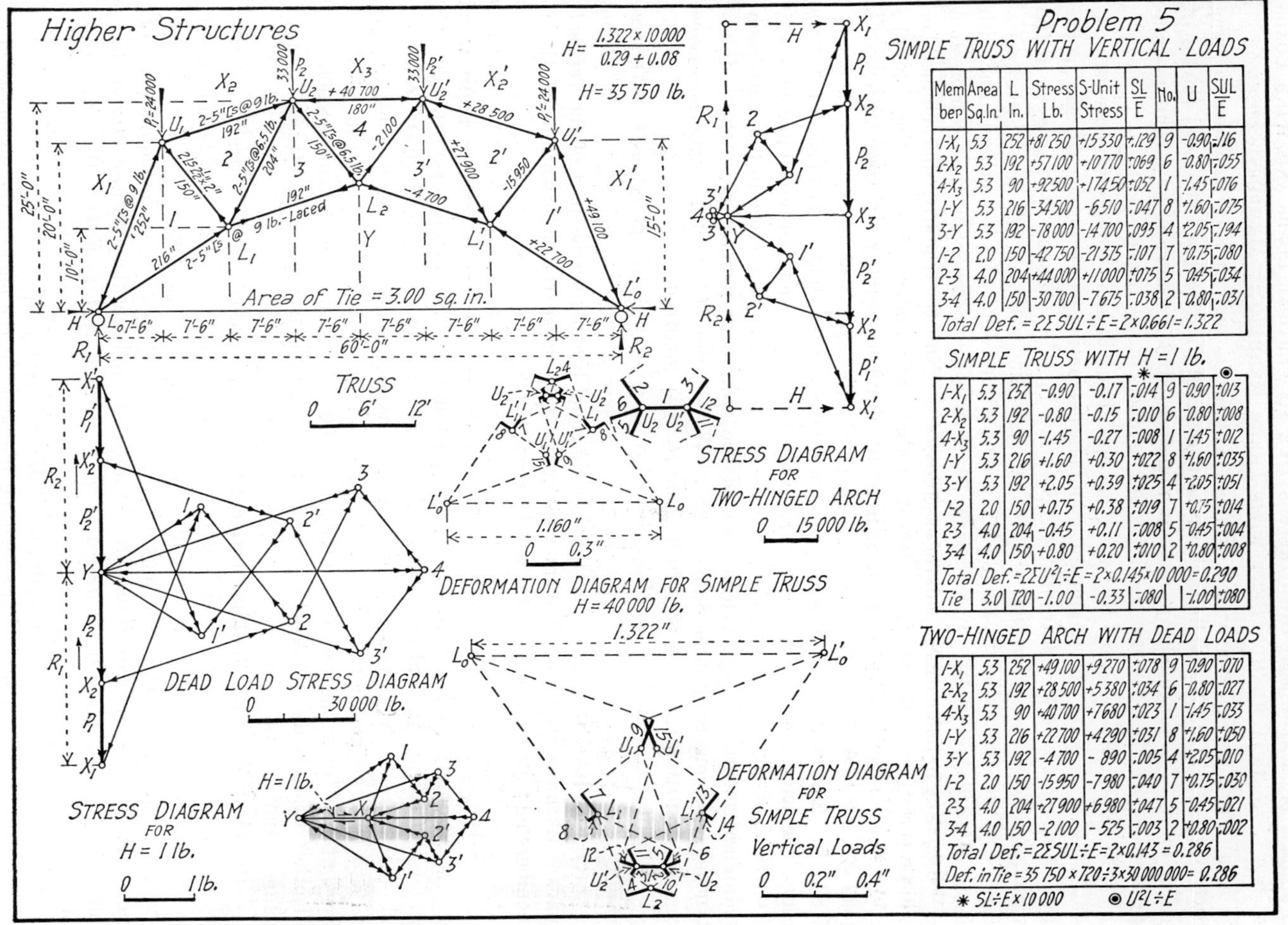

Problem 5

SIMPLE TRUSS WITH VERTICAL LOADS

Member	Area Sq.In.	L In.	Stress Lb.	S-Unit Stress	SL/E	No.	U	SUL/E
1-X1	5.3	252	+81 250	+15 330	+.129	9	-0.90	-.116
2-X2	5.3	192	+57 100	+10 770	+.069	6	-0.80	-.055
4-X3	5.3	90	+92 500	+17 450	+.052	1	-1.45	-.076
1-Y	5.3	216	-34 500	-6 510	-.047	8	+1.60	-.075
3-Y	5.3	192	-78 000	-14 700	-.095	4	+2.05	-.194
1-2	2.0	150	-42 750	-21 375	-.107	7	+0.75	-.080
2-3	4.0	204	+44 000	+11 000	+.075	5	-0.45	-.034
3-4	4.0	150	-30 700	-7 675	-.038	2	-0.80	-.031
Total Def. = 2Σ SUL ÷ E = 2 × 0.661 = 1.322								

SIMPLE TRUSS WITH H = 1 lb.

Member	Area Sq.In.	L In.	Stress Lb.	S-Unit Stress	SL/E *	No.	U	U²L/E ⊙
1-X1	5.3	252	-0.90	-0.17	-.014	9	-0.90	+.013
2-X2	5.3	192	-0.80	-0.15	-.010	6	-0.80	+.008
4-X3	5.3	90	-1.45	-0.27	-.008	1	-1.45	+.012
1-Y	5.3	216	+1.60	+0.30	+.022	8	+1.60	+.035
3-Y	5.3	192	+2.05	+0.39	+.025	4	+2.05	+.051
1-2	2.0	150	+0.75	+0.38	+.019	7	+0.75	+.014
2-3	4.0	204	-0.45	+0.11	-.008	5	-0.45	+.004
3-4	4.0	150	+0.80	+0.20	+.010	2	+0.80	+.008
Total Def. = 2ΣU²L ÷ E = 2 × 0.145 × 10 000 = 0.290								
Tie	3.0	720	-1.00	-0.33	-.080		-1.00	+.080

TWO-HINGED ARCH WITH DEAD LOADS

Member	Area Sq.In.	L In.	Stress Lb.	S-Unit Stress	SL/E	No.	U	SUL/E
1-X1	5.3	252	+49 100	+9 270	+.078	9	-0.90	-.070
2-X2	5.3	192	+28 500	+5 380	+.034	6	-0.80	-.027
4-X3	5.3	90	+40 700	+7 680	+.023	1	-1.45	-.033
1-Y	5.3	216	+22 700	+4 290	+.031	8	+1.60	+.050
3-Y	5.3	192	-4 700	- 890	-.005	4	+2.05	-.010
1-2	2.0	150	-15 950	-7 980	-.040	7	+0.75	-.030
2-3	4.0	204	+27 900	+6 980	+.047	5	-0.45	-.021
3-4	4.0	150	-2 100	- 525	-.003	2	+0.80	-.002
Total Def. = 2Σ SUL ÷ E = 2 × 0.143 = 0.286								
Def. in Tie = 35 750 × 720 ÷ 3 × 30 000 000 = 0.286								

* SL ÷ E × 10 000 ⊙ U²L ÷ E

PROBLEM 6. CALCULATE THE STRESSES DUE TO VERTICAL LOADS AND WIND LOADS IN A FRAMED BENT WITH THREE REDUNDANT MEMBERS.

(a) **Problem.**—Given a steel framed bent 54 ft. high and 12 ft. wide, carrying two vertical loads of 50,000 lb. each, and a horizontal wind load of 4,000 lb. at the top of each story. The diagonals are made of angles capable of taking either tension or compression. Calculate the stresses in all the members of the framed bent.

(b) **Methods.**—Assume that the diagonals that will be in compression are redundant as in (*c*). With the redundant members not acting calculate the stresses in the remaining members of the framework as shown in (*b*). Calculate the stresses in the members due to a compression of 1 lb. acting in line with S_1; call these stresses U_1. Calculate the stresses in the members due to a compression of 1 lb. acting in line with S_2; call these stresses U_2. Calculate the stresses in the members due to a compression of 1 lb. acting in line with S_3; call these stresses U_3. Now the true stress in each member will be the stress in the member when the redundant members are not acting, plus the stress in the member due to the stress in each redundant member acting separately as a load on the structure. The true stress in member 2–*a* will be $S_{2a} = +\ 56{,}000 - 0.833\ S_1$. The true stress in member 2–3 will be $S_{23} = +\ 8{,}000 - 0.555\ S_1 - 0.555\ S_2$, etc. The deformation of the framework in line with S_1, S_2, and S_3, is given in columns 9, 10 and 11, respectively. Equating the deformation of the structure in line with each redundant member to the deformation of the redundant member gives three simultaneous equations containing S_1, S_2 and S_3. The solution of these three equations gives $S_1 = +\ 18{,}670$ lb.; $S_2 = +\ 21{,}570$ lb., and $S_3 = +\ 26{,}070$ lb.

Substituting these values of S_1, S_2 and S_3 in column 8, will give the true stresses as in (*d*).

(c) **Results.**—It will be seen that the diagonal bracing carries part of the vertical loads. If the horizontal members were made very large the deformations of these members may be neglected and it will be seen that $S_1 = S_2 = S_3$.

PROBLEM 7. CALCULATION OF THE STRESSES IN A STEEL BUILDING FRAME.

(a) **Problem.**—Given a 6 story steel frame building. Steel transverse bents 20′–0″ centers. Columns in bent spaced 16′–′0′ centers. Lower story height 20′–0″ centers, all other stories 12′–0″ centers. The bent has six stories and three bays, consisting of vertical columns and horizontal girders, with rigid joints. Wind load 30 lb. per foot horizontal. Upper horizontal wind load = 4,000 lb.; lower wind load = 8,000 lb.; all other wind loads = 6,000 lb. Calculate the moments and direct stresses in the columns and girders.

(b) **Methods.**—The building frame given in this problem is a statically indeterminate structure and the true bending moments and direct stresses can only be calculated by taking the deformations into account. The longitudinal deformations of the columns and girders are very small and may be neglected. The equations for equilibrium of the statically indeterminate frame are obtained by applying the conditions for equilibrium, $\Sigma(M\cdot x\cdot ds/E\cdot I) = 0$, $\Sigma(M\cdot y\cdot ds/E\cdot I) = 0$, and $\Sigma(M\cdot ds/E\cdot I) = 0$, and are as follows:

From the condition for equilibrium $\Sigma(M\cdot x\cdot ds/E\cdot I) = 0$.

(1) The algebraic sum of the bending moments in the ends of the girders in any bay will be equal to the total vertical shear in the bay multiplied by the length of girders center to center of columns.

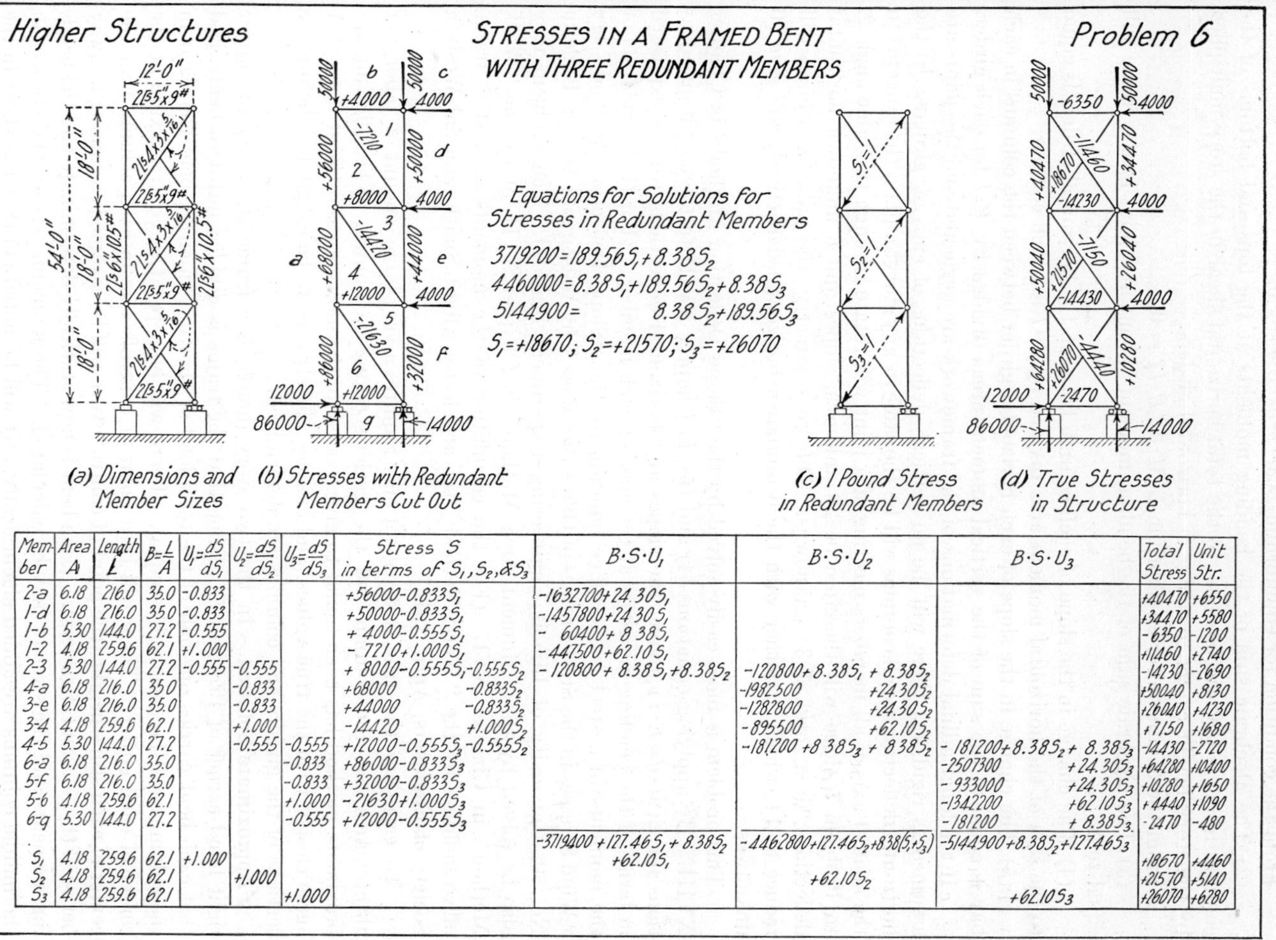

(a) Dimensions and Member Sizes (b) Stresses with Redundant Members Cut Out (c) 1 Pound Stress in Redundant Members (d) True Stresses in Structure

Member	Area A	Length L	$B=\frac{L}{A}$	$U_1=\frac{dS}{dS_1}$	$U_2=\frac{dS}{dS_2}$	$U_3=\frac{dS}{dS_3}$	Stress S in terms of $S_1, S_2, \& S_3$	$B \cdot S \cdot U_1$	$B \cdot S \cdot U_2$	$B \cdot S \cdot U_3$	Total Stress	Unit Str.
2-a	6.18	216.0	35.0	-0.833			$+56000-0.833S_1$	$-1632700+24.30S_1$			+40470	+6550
1-d	6.18	216.0	35.0	-0.833			$+50000-0.833S_1$	$-1457800+24.30S_1$			+34470	+5580
1-b	5.30	144.0	27.2	-0.555			$+4000-0.555S_1$	$-60400+8.38S_1$			-6350	-1200
1-2	4.18	259.6	62.1	+1.000			$-7210+1.000S_1$	$-447500+62.10S_1$			+11460	+2740
2-3	5.30	144.0	27.2	-0.555	-0.555		$+8000-0.555S_1-0.555S_2$	$-120800+8.38S_1+8.38S_2$	$-120800+8.38S_1+8.38S_2$		-14230	-2690
4-a	6.18	216.0	35.0		-0.833		$+68000-0.833S_2$		$-1982500+24.30S_2$		+50040	+8130
3-e	6.18	216.0	35.0		-0.833		$+44000-0.833S_2$		$-1282800+24.30S_2$		+26040	+4230
3-4	4.18	259.6	62.1		+1.000		$-14420+1.000S_2$		$-895500+62.10S_2$		+7150	+1680
4-5	5.30	144.0	27.2		-0.555	-0.555	$+12000-0.555S_3-0.555S_2$		$-181200+8.38S_3+8.38S_2$	$-181200+8.38S_2+8.38S_3$	-14430	-2720
6-a	6.18	216.0	35.0			-0.833	$+86000-0.833S_3$			$-2507300+24.30S_3$	+64280	+10400
5-f	6.18	216.0	35.0			-0.833	$+32000-0.833S_3$			$-933000+24.30S_3$	+10280	+1650
5-6	4.18	259.6	62.1			+1.000	$-21630+1.000S_3$			$-1342200+62.10S_3$	+4440	+1090
6-g	5.30	144.0	27.2			-0.555	$+12000-0.555S_3$			$-181200+8.38S_3$	-2470	-480
								$-3719400+127.46S_1+8.38S_2$	$-4462800+127.46S_2+8.38(S_1+S_3)$	$-5144900+8.38S_2+127.46S_3$		
S_1	4.18	259.6	62.1	+1.000				$+62.10S_1$			+18670	+4460
S_2	4.18	259.6	62.1		+1.000				$+62.10S_2$		+21570	+5140
S_3	4.18	259.6	62.1			+1.000				$+62.10S_3$	+26070	+6280

From the condition for equilibrium $\Sigma(M \cdot y \cdot ds/E \cdot I) = 0$.

(2) The algebraic sum of the bending moments at the tops and bottoms of the columns in any story will be equal to the total horizontal shear in the story multiplied by the story height center to center of horizontal girders.

From the condition for equilibrium $\Sigma(M \cdot ds/E \cdot I) = 0$.

(3) The algebraic sum of the bending moments about any joint in the frame will equal zero.

(4) The change in the slope of each column between the horizontal girders is equal to the sum of the horizontal moment area divided by $E \cdot I$ for each column.

(5) The change in the slope of each horizontal girder between the columns in each bay is equal to the sum of the vertical moment areas divided by $E \cdot I$ for each girder.

If the longitudinal deformations of the framework are neglected and the joints are assumed as rigid, (a) there will be no vertical deflections of ends of girders, (b) the horizontal deflections of all columns will be the same in any story, and (c) the tangents to the neutral axis of all members meeting at a joint will rotate through the same angle θ. In Problem 7 there will therefore be 28 unknown slopes and 6 unknown horizontal deflections, or a total of 34 unknowns. Due to symmetry, the unknown slopes will reduce to 14, which, together with the 6 unknown horizontal deflections, will give 20 unknowns.

This problem is most easily solved by the "Slope Deflection Method" in Chapter XVIII. By applying equations (4) and (5), in Chapter XVIII to the condition equations for $\Sigma(M \cdot ds/E \cdot I)$ above, the slopes and horizontal deflections will be expressed in terms of the bending moments at the ends of each member. (For the calculation of the moments in a steel frame office building by the "Slope Deflection Method," see "Wind Stresses in the Steel Frames of Office Buildings," by Wilson and Maney, Bulletin No. 80, University of Illinois Engineering Experiment Station). The problem may also be solved by the "Moment Area Method" in Chapter XVII, or by the "Work Method" in Chapter XVI. (For the calculation of the moments in a steel frame office building by the "Work Method," see article by Albert Smith, Journal Western Society of Engineers, April, 1915).

To calculate the true stresses not only requires a very large amount of labor but also requires that the column and the girder sections be known. The following approximate method has been found to give values for the moments and the stresses that agree closely with the true values, and enables the stresses to be calculated before the sections of the girders and columns are determined.

Approximate Solution.—In the two story double bay frame shown in the upper right hand corner of Problem 7, assume that the frame is divided into two bents, and that each bent carries one-half of the total load as shown. In either bent the shear in the columns will be assumed as equal. There will be a point of contra-flexure at the center of each girder. There will be a point of contraflexure in each column near the center of each story height (the point of contraflexure will be assumed as coming midway between the horizontal girders). Each bent is now statically determinate and the bending moments and the stresses may be calculated. The moments, shears and stresses in the middle columns are added algebraically. It will be noted (1) that the shear in the center column is twice the shear in the outside columns, and (2) that there will be no vertical stresses in the middle column.

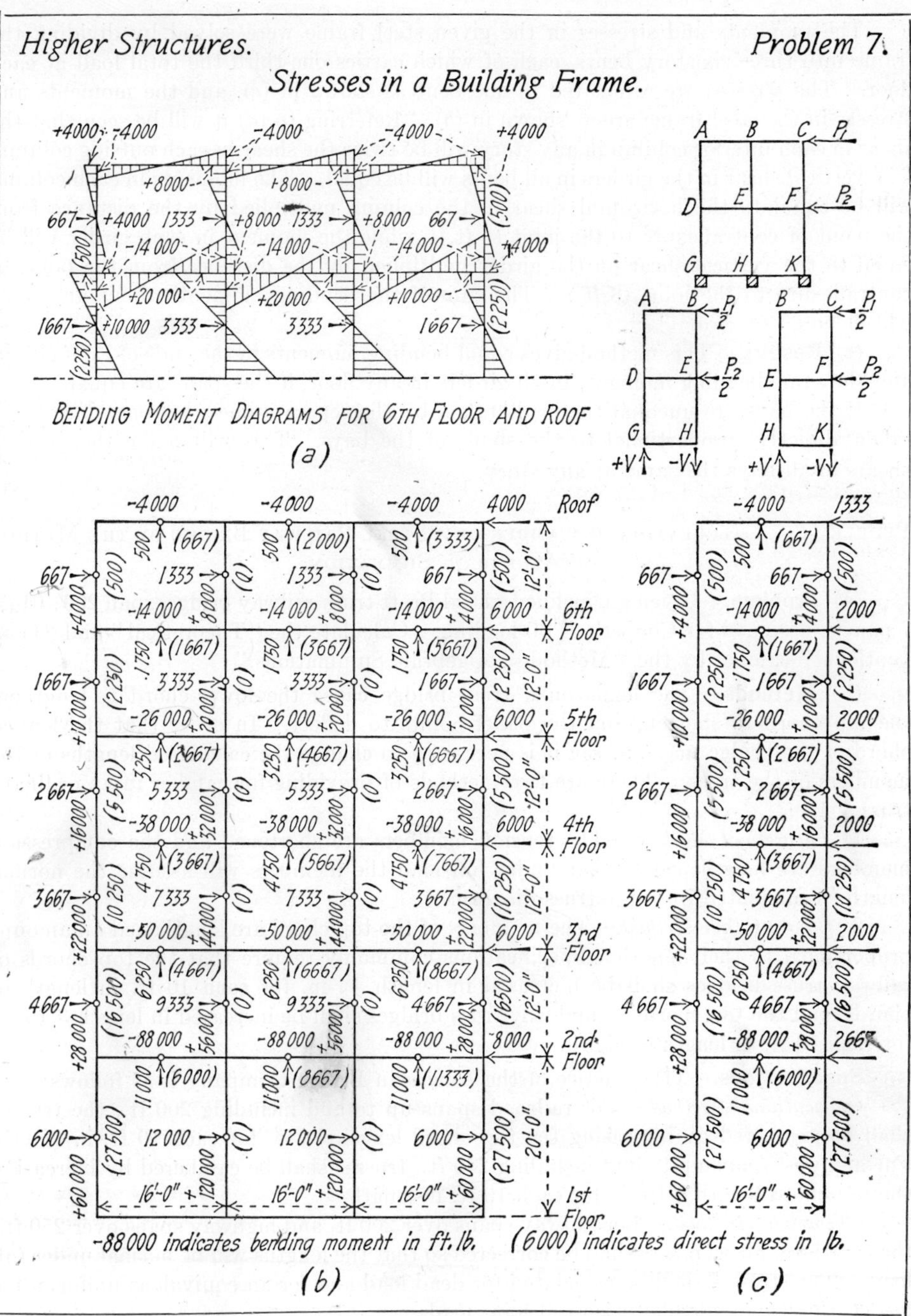

Note.—The moments in this building frame have been calculated by the method of moment distribution in Chapter XVIIIA.

The moments and stresses in the given steel frame were solved by dividing the frame into three six-story bents, each of which carries one-third the total load at each floor. The stresses are calculated in one bent as shown in (*c*), and the moments and stresses in the steel frame are as shown in (*b*). Referring to (*a*) it will be seen that the shear in each interior column in any story will be twice the shear in each outside column. The vertical shear in the girders in all bents will be equal. The moments in each column will be equal to the horizontal shear in the column multiplied by the distance from the point of contraflexure to the joint (6 ft.); while the moment in each girder will be equal to the vertical shear on the girder multiplied by the distance from the point of contraflexure to the joint (8 ft.). The sum of the bending moments about any joint will be equal to zero.

(c) **Results.**—This method gives equal bending moments in the ends of each girder, and the same bending moments in all girders in any floor, if the spans are equal.

If the bays are unequal the loads taken by the separate one-span bents are to be taken directly proportional to the spans of the bays. This will make the vertical shears in all bays the same at any story.

PROBLEM 8. CALCULATION OF CAMBER OF A STEEL RAILWAY BRIDGE BY THE METHOD OF ALGEBRAIC SUMMATION.

(a) **Problem.**—Given an inclined chord Pratt truss railway bridge, span 200′-0⅛″, 7 panels, designed for Cooper's E 60 loading. Calculate the "Theoretical" and "Conventional" camber by the "Method of Algebraic Summations."

(b) **Methods.**—The loads on a truss bridge cause the lower chord to lengthen, the top chord to shorten, and the panel points to deflect. In order that the loaded chord of the bridge may not sag it is necessary to change the calculated lengths of the members of the truss. There are two methods of providing for camber in an ordinary truss span.

1. *Theoretical Method.*—The tension members are shortened and the compression members are lengthened so that under full load the members will assume the normal length as calculated from the truss diagram.

2. *Conventional Method.*—The members of the top chord are lengthened an amount proportional to their length. Specifications commonly require that the top chords of railway truss bridges shall be increased in length ⅛ in. for each 10 ft. in length of chord; and the top chords of highway truss bridges shall be increased in length 3/16 in. for each 10 ft. in length of chord.

Specifications.—The practice of the American Bridge Company is as follows:

Conventional Method.—For railroad spans up to and including 200 ft., the trusses shall be cambered by increasing the top chord length ⅛ in. for each 10 ft. in length. For highway spans up to and including 250 ft., trusses shall be cambered by increasing the top chord length 3/16 in. for each 10 ft. in length.

Theoretical Method.—For railway spans over 200 ft. and highway spans over 250 ft., the lengths of all members shall be corrected so that the lengths will be normal under full load. The stresses shall be calculated for dead load and for an equivalent uniform live load with all joints loaded with full joint loads.

Impact stresses shall be neglected in calculating distortions. The length of members shall be corrected for pin play.

Higher Structures

Problem 8

CAMBER BLOCKING FOR RAILWAY BRIDGE CAMEL-BACK PRATT TRUSSES BY ALGEBRAIC SUMMATIONS THEORETICAL AND CONVENTIONAL METHODS

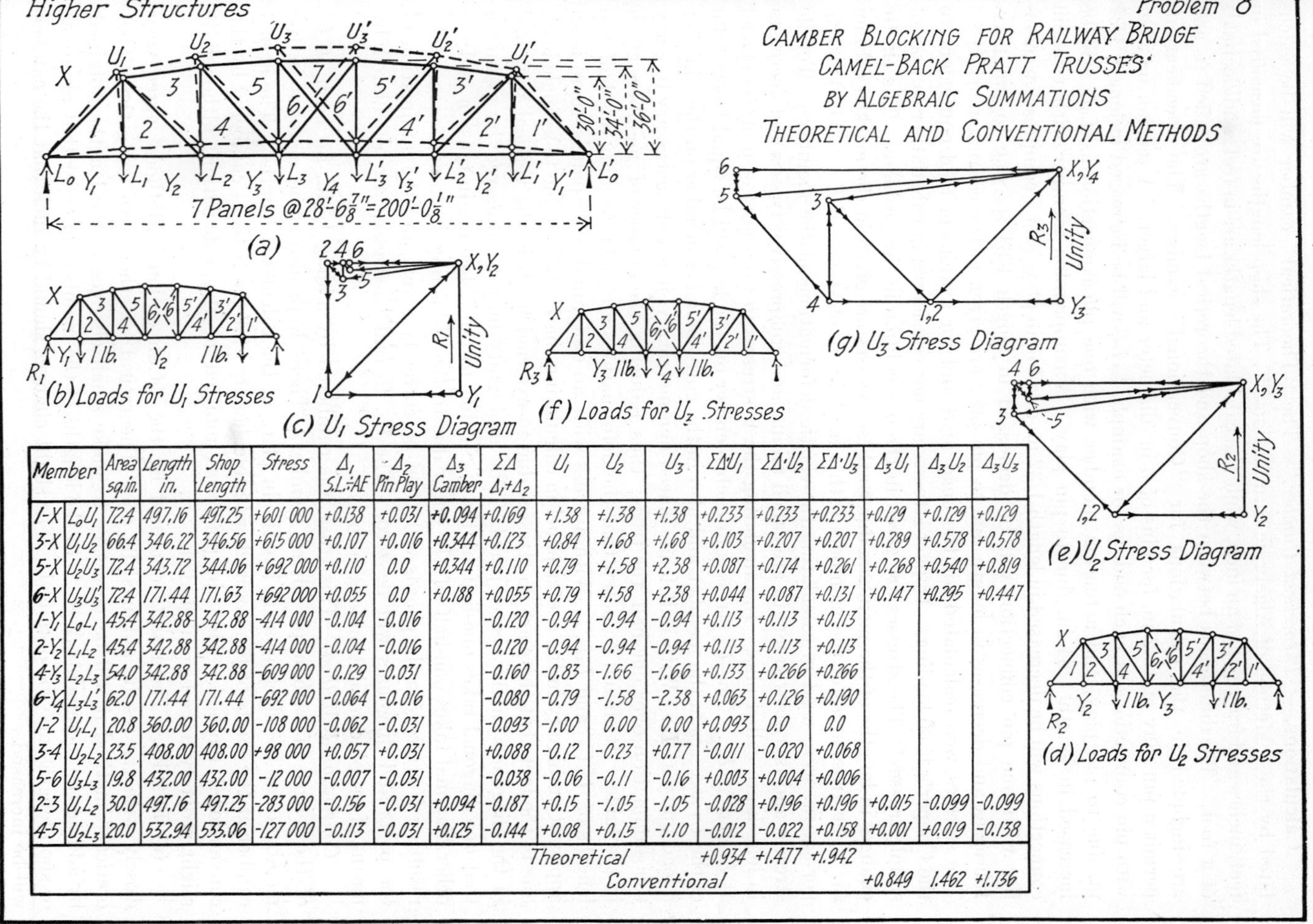

(a)

(b) Loads for U_1 Stresses

(c) U_1 Stress Diagram

(f) Loads for U_3 Stresses

(g) U_3 Stress Diagram

(e) U_2 Stress Diagram

(d) Loads for U_2 Stresses

Member		Area sq.in.	Length in.	Shop Length	Stress	Δ_1 S.L.÷AE	Δ_2 Pin Play	Δ_3 Camber	$\Sigma\Delta$ $\Delta_1+\Delta_2$	U_1	U_2	U_3	$\Sigma\Delta \cdot U_1$	$\Sigma\Delta \cdot U_2$	$\Sigma\Delta \cdot U_3$	$\Delta_3 U_1$	$\Delta_3 U_2$	$\Delta_3 U_3$
1-X	L_0U_1	72.4	497.16	497.25	+601 000	+0.138	+0.031	+0.094	+0.169	+1.38	+1.38	+1.38	+0.233	+0.233	+0.233	+0.129	+0.129	+0.129
3-X	U_1U_2	66.4	346.22	346.56	+615 000	+0.107	+0.016	+0.344	+0.123	+0.84	+1.68	+1.68	+0.103	+0.207	+0.207	+0.289	+0.578	+0.578
5-X	U_2U_3	72.4	343.72	344.06	+692 000	+0.110	0.0	+0.344	+0.110	+0.79	+1.58	+2.38	+0.087	+0.174	+0.261	+0.268	+0.540	+0.819
6-X	U_3U_3'	72.4	171.44	171.63	+692 000	+0.055	0.0	+0.188	+0.055	+0.79	+1.58	+2.38	+0.044	+0.087	+0.131	+0.147	+0.295	+0.447
1-Y_1	L_0L_1	45.4	342.88	342.88	-414 000	-0.104	-0.016		-0.120	-0.94	-0.94	-0.94	+0.113	+0.113	+0.113			
2-Y_2	L_1L_2	45.4	342.88	342.88	-414 000	-0.104	-0.016		-0.120	-0.94	-0.94	-0.94	+0.113	+0.113	+0.113			
4-Y_3	L_2L_3	54.0	342.88	342.88	-609 000	-0.129	-0.031		-0.160	-0.83	-1.66	-1.66	+0.133	+0.266	+0.266			
6-Y_4	L_3L_3'	62.0	171.44	171.44	-692 000	-0.064	-0.016		-0.080	-0.79	-1.58	-2.38	+0.063	+0.126	+0.190			
1-2	U_1L_1	20.8	360.00	360.00	-108 000	-0.062	-0.031		-0.093	-1.00	0.00	0.00	+0.093	0.0	0.0			
3-4	U_2L_2	23.5	408.00	408.00	+98 000	+0.057	+0.031		+0.088	-0.12	-0.23	+0.77	-0.011	-0.020	+0.068			
5-6	U_3L_3	19.8	432.00	432.00	-12 000	-0.007	-0.031		-0.038	-0.06	-0.11	-0.16	+0.003	+0.004	+0.006			
2-3	U_1L_2	30.0	497.16	497.25	-283 000	-0.156	-0.031	+0.094	-0.187	+0.15	-1.05	-1.05	-0.028	+0.196	+0.196	+0.015	-0.099	-0.099
4-5	U_2L_3	20.0	532.94	533.06	-127 000	-0.113	-0.031	+0.125	-0.144	+0.08	+0.15	-1.10	-0.012	-0.022	+0.158	+0.001	+0.019	-0.138
										Theoretical			+0.934	+1.477	+1.942			
											Conventional					+0.849	1.462	+1.736

Calculations.—"*Theoretical Camber.*"—The "Theoretical" camber will be calculated by the "Method of Algebraic Summations." The shop lengths are measured in feet, inches and fractions of an inch, while the calculated lengths are in feet, and decimals of a foot. The differences between the shop and theoretical lengths are called Δ_3 and are included in the calculations for "Conventional" camber. The specifications permit a pin play of 1/32 in. for pins of 5 in. diameter and larger. A tension member with pin connections at each end, as for example U_1L_2, will be increased in length 1/32 in. due to pin play, and a tension member with one pin connection as L_0L_1 will be increased in length 1/64 in. due to pin play. A compression member with two pin connections will be decreased in length 1/32 in. due to pin play, and a compression member with one pin connection will be decreased in length 1/64 in. due to pin play. Increases and decreases in length due to pin play are given in the column marked Δ_2. The stresses were calculated for the dead load and for a uniform load equivalent to the Cooper's E 60 loading. Impact stresses are not considered in calculating camber of simple trusses. The stresses are given in the 6th column in the problem. The elastic changes in lengths of the members due to these stresses are given in the marked column Δ_1. The gross areas of the members with a modulus of elasticity of E = 30,000,000 lb. per sq. in. were used in calculating the elastic deformations of the members. Tensile stresses and increases in length are called minus, and compressive stresses and decreases in length are called plus. In calculating the U stresses in (*b*) a load of unity is placed at L_1 and at L_1'. The U_1 stresses in each member on the left will be equal to the sum of the U_1 stresses in the member and also in the corresponding member on the right for a load unity at L_1. With unit loads placed symmetrically, it is only necessary to carry the summation over one-half the truss; thus reducing the number of members given in the table. It should be noted that the deformations are given for only one-half the lengths of U_3U_3' and L_3L_3'. With a truss with an odd number of panels there is an apparent ambiguity in the center panel in calculating the U stresses due to a single load, due to the fact that there are no stresses due to external loads in the vertical post and in the diagonals in the center panel. The ambiguity may be removed by assuming that one diagonal takes one-half of the shear due to the U-loading in tension and the other diagonal takes one-half of the shear due to the U-loading in compression. The resulting U stresses in the chords will then be correctly given, and the summation of the posts and diagonals will be zero. The U_1, U_2 and U_3 stresses are calculated by means of graphic resolution as shown.

Conventional Method.—This truss was cambered by adding ⅛ in. for each 10 ft. of the length of each upper chord member. There were also some changes in the members due to selecting shop lengths in place of the calculated lengths. The actual camber at the joints of the lower chord are calculated for the truss as cambered by the conventional method. The pin play was omitted in this calculation, although it might properly have been included.

(c) **Results.**—The results obtained by the "Conventional Method" agree very closely with the results obtained by the "Theoretical" method. In using the "Theoretical" method it will be necessary to make small changes in the lengths obtained by adding the increments $\Delta_1 + \Delta_2$ to the lengths of the members in order that practical or shop lengths may be obtained. The slight changes should be such that the camber will be increased.

PROBLEM 9. CALCULATION OF CAMBER OF A STEEL RAILWAY BRIDGE BY THE METHOD OF ELASTIC WEIGHTS, AND BY THE WILLIOT DIAGRAM.

(a) **Problem.**—Given an inclined chord Pratt truss railway bridge, span 200′–0⅛″, 7 panels, designed for Cooper's E 60 loading. Calculate the camber (1) by the "Method of Elastic Weights," and (2) by means of the "Williot diagram method."

(b) **Methods.**—The "Theoretical" camber of the truss will be calculated by the "Method of Elastic Weights" and by the "Williot Diagram Method." The dead load stresses and the live load stresses due to a uniform load equivalent to Cooper's E 60 loading were calculated, and are as given in Problem 8. The elastic and inelastic deformations, $\Sigma\Delta = \Delta_1 + \Delta_2$ as calculated in Problem 8, are given in column 3, Problem 9.

(1) *Method of Elastic Weights.*—The deformations as given in column 3 and the lengths of the members are written on the members of the truss diagram. The moment arms for calculating the chord stresses and the web stresses are written on the truss diagram. The elastic weights of the end-post and of the upper and lower chords given in column 5, are equal to deformations in column 3, divided by arms in column 4.

The elastic weights for the chords are calculated as shown in Fig. 13, Chapter XV. The elastic weights for the chords are all plus, and are each applied at the center of moments that was used in calculating the direct stresses due to dead and live loads. The elastic weights for the post U_2L_2 are from equation (27), Chapter XV, $w_2 = 0.088 \div 28.6 = 0.0031$, applied at L_3; and from equation (28), Chapter XV, $w_1 = 0.088 \div (-28.6 \times 34 \div 38) = -0.0035$, applied at L_2. In calculating the elastic weights for U_3L_3 the elastic weight at L_3' due to U_3L_3 is balanced by the elastic weight at L_3 due to $U_3'L_3'$. The elastic weights for U_1L_2 are from equation (24), Chapter XV, $w_1 = -0.188 \div 20.7 = -0.0091$ applied at L_1, and from equation (23), $w_2 = -0.188 \div (-23.4) = 0.0080$ applied at L_2.

The signs of the elastic weights for webs and posts are determined by the following rule: "The positive elastic weight will come on that side of the section or panel where the sign of the deformation in the given member is the same as the sign of the stress in the adjacent chord." In a Pratt truss the elastic weight for the post will be minus at the panel under the post, and plus on the other side of the panel.

The total elastic weights at the lower chord joints are equal to the algebraic sum of the elastic weights due to the individual members. The bending moments due to the elastic weights are calculated as shown. The deflection at L_1 must be increased by the deformation of U_1L_1, which was omitted in the calculations.

(2) *Williot Diagram Method.*—The deformations are given in column 3. Pass a vertical plane through the center of the truss, lay off deformation of left half of member marked 2 to the right, since the deformation is plus, and at a distance below 2 equal to deformation of 3 lay off one-half of deformation of member marked 1, to the left, since the deformation is minus. At U_3 lay off deformation 4 to the right, since deformation 4 is plus, and at L_3 lay off deformation 6 to the left, since deformation 6 is minus, and perpendiculars erected at ends of deformations 4 and 6 will intersect at joint U_2. The remainder of the diagram is constructed in the same manner. Since the loading is symmetrical the Williot diagram is symmetrical.

(c) **Results.**—The results obtained by the "Method of Elastic Weights" and the "Williot Diagram Method" check the results obtained by the "Method of Algebraic Summation" given in Problem 8.

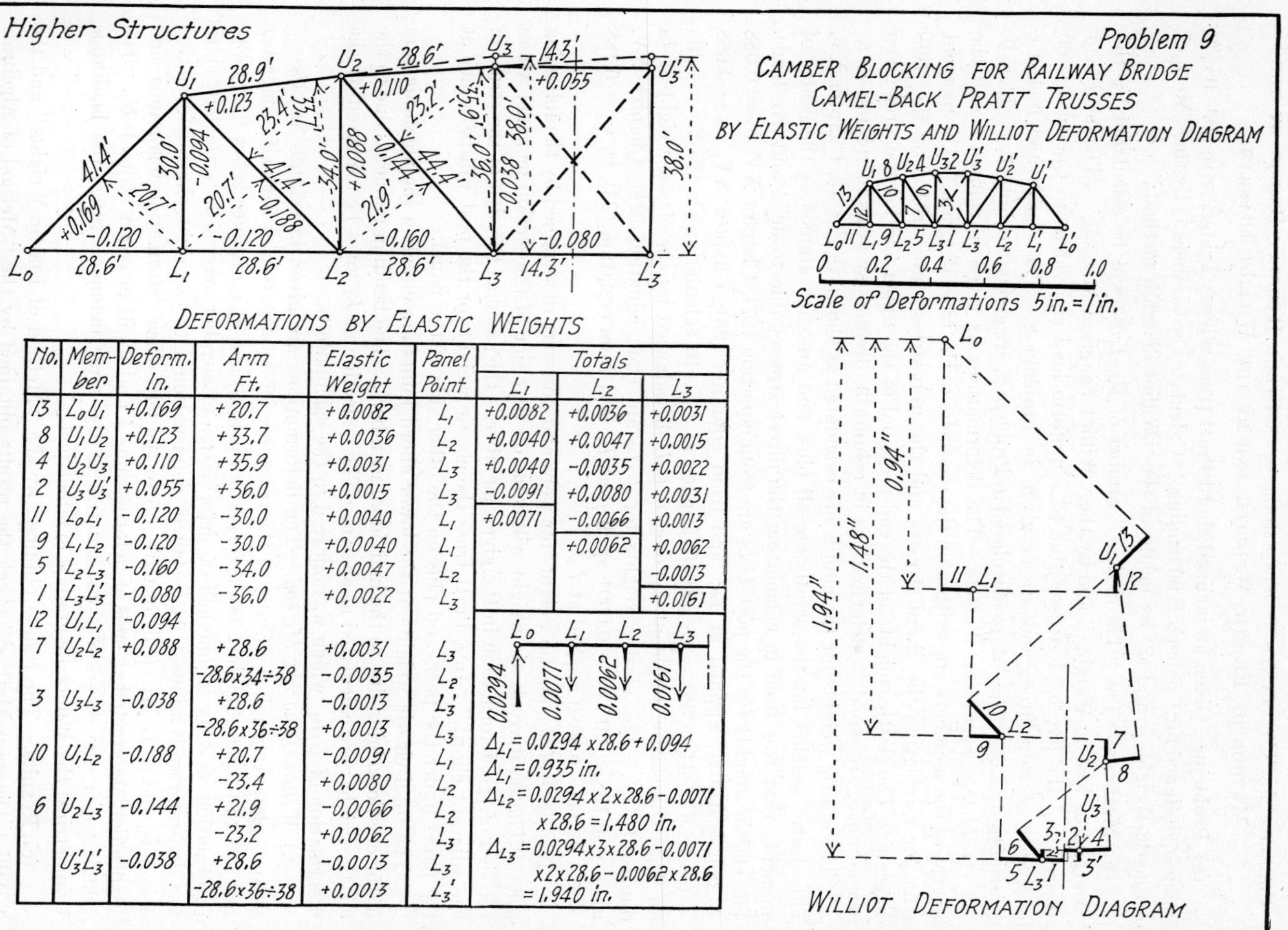

DEFORMATIONS BY ELASTIC WEIGHTS

No.	Member	Deform. In.	Arm Ft.	Elastic Weight	Panel Point	Totals L_1	Totals L_2	Totals L_3
13	L_0U_1	+0.169	+20.7	+0.0082	L_1	+0.0082	+0.0036	+0.0031
8	U_1U_2	+0.123	+33.7	+0.0036	L_2	+0.0040	+0.0047	+0.0015
4	U_2U_3	+0.110	+35.9	+0.0031	L_3	+0.0040	-0.0035	+0.0022
2	U_3U_3'	+0.055	+36.0	+0.0015	L_3	-0.0091	+0.0080	+0.0031
11	L_0L_1	-0.120	-30.0	+0.0040	L_1	+0.0071	-0.0066	+0.0013
9	L_1L_2	-0.120	-30.0	+0.0040	L_1		+0.0062	+0.0062
5	L_2L_3	-0.160	-34.0	+0.0047	L_2			-0.0013
1	L_3L_3'	-0.080	-36.0	+0.0022	L_3			+0.0161
12	U_1L_1	-0.094						
7	U_2L_2	+0.088	+28.6	+0.0031	L_3			
			-28.6×34÷38	-0.0035	L_2			
3	U_3L_3	-0.038	+28.6	-0.0013	L_3'			
			-28.6×36÷38	+0.0013	L_3			
10	U_1L_2	-0.188	+20.7	-0.0091	L_1			
			-23.4	+0.0080	L_2			
6	U_2L_3	-0.144	+21.9	-0.0066	L_2			
			-23.2	+0.0062	L_3			
	$U_3'L_3'$	-0.038	+28.6	-0.0013	L_3			
			-28.6×36÷38	+0.0013	L_3'			

L_0 L_1 L_2 L_3

0.0294 0.0071 0.0062 0.0161

$\Delta_{L_1} = 0.0294 \times 28.6 + 0.094$

$\Delta_{L_1} = 0.935$ in.

$\Delta_{L_2} = 0.0294 \times 2 \times 28.6 - 0.0071 \times 28.6 = 1.480$ in.

$\Delta_{L_3} = 0.0294 \times 3 \times 28.6 - 0.0071 \times 2 \times 28.6 - 0.0062 \times 28.6 = 1.940$ in.

Problem 10. Stresses in a Statically Indeterminate Head Frame.

(a) **Problem.**—Given a 4-post head frame with the same dimensions and sections as for the 4-post head frame in Chapter XXI, except that the distance center to center of vertical columns is reduced to 10 ft. and the center of the sheave is placed 1 ft. from the back column. Calculate the stresses in the head frame, assuming that the back brace and the horizontal brace between the tower and the back brace are statically indeterminate.

(b) **Methods.**—Follow the solution as given in Chapter XXI.

Problem 11. Stresses in a Transverse Bent.

(a) **Problem.**—Calculate the stresses in the transverse bent designed in Chapter XXXVIII, on the assumption that it is a two-hinged arch, with the middle lower chord member a redundant member.

(b) **Method.**—Calculate the deformation of the structure in line with the horizontal tie and place this deformation equal to the deformation of the horizontal tie. Calculate the deformation of the framed structure due to direct stresses by means of the "Method of Algebraic Summation," and the deformation of the structure due to flexure in the columns by area moments. The deformation of the structure in line with the lower tie due to flexure may be obtained from the deflection at the foot of the knee brace by applying Maxwell's theorem.

Problem 12. Stresses in a Quadrangular Bridge Truss Without Diagonals and With Rigid Joints.

(a) **Problem.** Given a bridge with parallel chords, vertical posts, no diagonals and rigid joints. Span, 75′-0″, panel length, 25′-0″, depth 10′-0″. Members have relative moments of inertia as follows: vertical end-posts, $I_1 = 2.00$; top chord, $I_2 = 4.00$; bottom chord, $I_3 = 1.00$; vertical intermediate posts, $I_4 = 2.00$. Truss carries a dead joint load of 5 tons and a live joint load of 10 tons. Calculate the moments at the joints and the direct stresses in the members, for full live and dead loads.

(b) **Methods.**—Use the method of slope deflections and follow methods outlined in the solution of the truss with two panels as given in Chapter XVIII. The deflection R of the top and bottom chords may be assumed as equal at the center of the truss, and the longitudinal deflections of the members may be neglected.

Problem 13. Stresses in a Stiff Frame.

(a) **Problem.**—Given a stiff frame with columns free to turn at base, with loads carried by brackets on inside of columns, as shown in case 5, Fig. 15, Chapter XVII. Deduce the equations given in Fig. 15, Chapter XVII for the general case and for a load on one side. Also assume that $I_1 = \infty$, and $P = P'$ and $e = e'$, and compare with case 2, Fig. 15, Chapter X.

(b) **Methods.**—(1) Use the "Method of Area Moments" as given in Chapter XVII. (2) Also, deduce the equations by using the "Method of Slope Deflections" as given in Chapter XVIII.

PROBLEM 14. STRESSES IN A STIFF FRAME.

(a) **Problem.**—Given a stiff frame consisting of a continuous girder of three equal spans, l, with two intermediate columns of height h, fixed at the base and making rigid joints with the girder at the top. Moment of inertia of girder $= I_1$, and of columns $= I_2$. The frame carries a uniform load w lb. per lineal foot over the middle span. Omit longitudinal deformation of column. Prove that the horizontal reaction at base of each column is

$$H = \frac{w \cdot l^2}{2h(4 + 5k)}$$

and the vertical reaction of each column is

$$V_c = \frac{w \cdot l(8 + 11k)}{4(4 + 5k)}$$

and the vertical reactions at the end of each end girder is

$$V_b = -\frac{w \cdot l \cdot k}{4(4 + 5k)}$$

where

$$k = \frac{I_1}{I_2} \cdot \frac{h}{l}.$$

Also calculate moments at intersections of girders and columns, and the point of contraflexure in each column.

(b) **Methods.**—Use the "Method of Slope Deflections" as given in Chapter XVIII.

(c) **Results.**—For the solution of this problem by the "Method of Work," and for formulas for different cases, see "Analysis and Tests of Rigidly Connected Reinforced Concrete Frames," by Mikishi Abe, University of Illinois Engineering Experiment Station Bulletin, No. 107.

PROBLEM 15. SECONDARY STRESSES IN A TRUSS.

(a) **Problem.**—Calculate the secondary stresses in a triangular truss of two panels with inclined end-posts and vertical tie. Span = 20′–0″; panel length, l = 10′–0″, height, h = 12′–0″. Direct unit stresses in end-posts is f_c = 8,000 lb. per sq. in., in vertical tie is f_t = 15,000 lb. per sq. in., and in lower chord is f_t = 12,000 lb. per sq. in. Moment of inertia of end-post about an axis perpendicular to the plane of the trusses is $I_1 = 400$ in.^{4}, of vertical tie is $I_2 = 400$ in.^{4}, and of lower chord is $I_3 = 300$ in.^{4}. The distance from neutral axis to extreme fiber is, for end-post, c = 8 in., for vertical tie, c = 5 in., for lower chord, c = 5 in. Calculate the secondary stresses in the members.

(b) **Methods.**—Follow the solution given in Chapter XIX.

(c) **Results.**—The maximum bending moment due to rigidity of joints is at the center of the bottom chord and is $M = \pm$ 427,000 in.-lb., and the unit stress will be $\pm$ 7,116 lb. per sq. in. The secondary stresses in the lower chord are very large due to the high unit stress in the vertical tie. From this problem it will be seen that the unit stress in the hip vertical of a Pratt truss railway bridge should be kept low.

PART III.

DESIGN OF STEEL MILL BUILDINGS.

CHAPTER XXIII.

General Design.

Definitions.—A steel mill building may be defined as a structure with a self-supporting steel frame with a light-weight covering, usually fire resistant. The structure may be of a simple one-story type with a framework of trusses and columns; a building with several stories, the multiple-story type; a building with two-hinge or three-hinge arches, or a building with a steel framed dome. Steel mill buildings are used for trainsheds, smelters, rock houses, shaft houses, coal tipples, coal breakers, shaker structures, air docks, hangars, and other industrial structures. A steel office or tier building will be a steel mill building if the multiple-story structure has light-weight walls and roof covering as was used in the engineering and research building built by the A. O. Smith Corporation as described in Chapter XXVI.

General Principles.—The general dimensions and outline of a mill building will be governed by local conditions and requirements. The questions of light, heat, ventilation, foundations for machinery, handling of materials, future extensions, first cost and cost of maintenance should receive proper attention in designing the different classes of structures. One or two of the above items often determines the type and general design of the structure. Where real estate is high, the first cost, including the cost of both land and structure, causes the adoption in many cases of the multiple story building; while on the other hand where the site is not too expensive the single story shop or mill is usually preferred. In coal tipples and shaft houses the handling of materials is the prime object, in railway shops and factories turning out heavy machinery or a similar product, foundations for the machinery required, and convenience in handling materials are most important, while in many other classes of structures such as weaving sheds, textile mills, and factories which turn out a less bulky product with light machinery, and which employ a large number of men, the principal items to be considered in designing are light, heat, ventilation and ease of superintendence.

Shops and factories are preferably located where transportation facilities are good, land is cheap and labor plentiful. Too much care cannot be used in the design of shops and factories, for the reason that defects in design that cause inconvenience in handling materials and workmen, increased cost of operation and maintenance, are permanent and cannot be removed.

The best modern practice inclines toward single floor shops with as few dividing walls and partitions as possible. The advantages of this type over multiple story buildings are (1) the light is better, (2) ventilation is better, (3) buildings are more easily heated, (4) foundations for machinery are cheaper, (5) machinery being set directly on the ground causes no vibrations in the building, (6) floors are cheaper, (7) workmen are more directly under the eye of the superintendent, (8) materials are more easily and cheaply handled, (9) buildings admit of indefinite extension in any direction, (10) the cost of construction is less, and (11) there is less danger from damage due to fire.

The walls of shops and factories are made (1) of brick, stone, or concrete; (2) of brick, hollow tile or concrete curtain walls between steel columns; (3) of curtain walls made of plaster on expanded metal or other reinforcing, and glass; (4) of concrete slabs fastened to the steel frame; and (5) of corrugated steel fastened to the steel frame.

The roof is commonly supported by steel trusses and framework. The roofing may be slate, tile, tar and gravel or other composition, tin or sheet steel, laid on board sheathing or on concrete or gypsum slabs, tile or slate supported directly on the purlins, or corrugated steel supported on board sheathing or directly on the purlins. Where the slope of the roof is flat a first grade tar and gravel roof, or some one of the patent composition roofs is used in preference to tin, and on a steep slope slate or tile is commonly used in preference to tin. Corrugated steel roofing is much used on boiler houses, smelters, forge shops, coal tipples, and similar structures. For buildings that are to be heated the roof sheathing should be a non-conductor of heat, or an anti-condensation lining should be used.

Floors in boiler houses, forge shops and in similar structures are generally made of brick on a gravel or concrete foundation; while in buildings where men have to work at machines the favorite floor is a wooden floor on a foundation of cinders, gravel, or tar concrete. Where concrete is used for the foundation of a wooden floor it should be either a tar or an asphalt concrete, or a layer of tar should be put on top of the cement concrete to prevent decay. Concrete or cement floors are used in many cases with good results, but they are not satisfactory where men have to stand at benches or machines. Wooden racks on cement floors remove the above objection somewhat. Where rough work is done, the upper or wearing surface of wooden floors is often made of yellow pine or oak plank, while in the better classes of structures, the top layer is commonly made of maple. For upper floors some one of the common types of fireproof floors, or as is more common a heavy plank floor or a laminated timber floor supported on beams may be used.

Steel plate floors carried on closely spaced I-beams are now being used for floors in multiple-story buildings. The plates are commonly spot welded to the beams through slots in the plates. A special reinforced concrete floor one inch thick reinforced with two inch diameter steel rings is commonly used. These rings are pressed from thin plate steel and are tack welded to the plates. After the concrete has set the surface is finished by grinding. For office floors the wearing surface may be made of 12 in. square blocks one inch thick fastened to the steel plates with an asphalt mastic.

Care should be used to obtain an ample amount of light in buildings in which men are to work. It is now the common practice to make as much of the roof and side walls of a transparent or translucent material as practicable; in many cases fifty per cent of the total exterior surface is made of glass, while skylights equal to twenty-five to thirty per cent of the roof surface are very common. Direct sunlight causes a glare, and is also objectionable in the summer on account of the heat. Where windows and skylights are directly exposed to the sunlight they may best be curtained with white muslin cloth which admits much of the light and shades perfectly. The "saw tooth" type of roof with the shorter and glazed tooth facing the north, gives the best light and is now coming into quite general use.

Plane glass, wire glass, factory ribbed glass, and translucent fabric are used for glazing windows and skylights. Factory ribbed glass should be placed with the ribs vertical for the reason that with the ribs horizontal, the glass emits a glare which is very trying on the eyes of the workmen. Wire netting should always be stretched under skylights to prevent the broken glass from falling down, where wire glass is not used. Steel sash can now be obtained for practically the same cost as for wooden sash in wooden frames, and are in common use.

Heating in large buildings is generally done by the hot blast system in which fans draw the air across heated coils, which are heated by exhaust steam, and the heated air is conveyed by ducts suspended from the roof or placed under the ground. In smaller buildings, direct radiation from steam or hot water pipes is commonly used. In buildings with light machinery or for research laboratories the air may be conditioned, being cooled in summer and heated in winter.

The proper unit stresses, minimum size of sections and thickness of metal will depend upon whether the building is to be permanent or temporary, and upon whether or not the metal is liable to be subjected to the action of corrosive gases. For permanent buildings the author would recommend 18,000 lb. per square inch for allowable tensile, and $18,000 - 60(l/r)$ lb. per square inch for allowable compressive stress for direct dead, snow and wind stresses and columns; l being the center to center length and r the radius of gyration of the member, both in inches. For wind bracing and flexural stresses in columns due to wind, add 25 per cent to the allowable stresses for dead, snow and wind loads. For temporary structures the above allowable stresses may be increased 20 to 25 per cent.

The minimum size of angles should be 2 in. $\times$ 2 in. $\times$ $\frac{1}{4}$ in., and the minimum thickness of plates $\frac{1}{4}$ in., for both permanent and temporary structures. Where the metal will be subjected to corrosive gases as in smelters and train sheds, the allowable stress should be decreased 20 to 25 per cent, and the minimum thickness of metal increased 25 per cent, unless the metal is fully protected by an acid-proof coating (at present the best paints do little more in any case than delay and retard the corrosion).

While welding has been used for secondary members and details and to a limited extent for the main framework, most steel frame buildings have riveted connections. Small buildings and simple structures not subject to impact of moving machinery or vibration may have bolted connections.

The minimum thickness of corrugated steel should be No. 20 gage for the roof and No. 22 for the sides, where there is certain to be no corrosion Nos. 22 and 24 may be used for the roof and sides respectively.

The different parts of steel mill buildings will be taken up and discussed at some length in the following chapters.

CHAPTER XXIV.

LOADS.

Introduction.—The loads to be provided for in designing a mill building will depend to a large extent upon the use to which the finished structure is to be put. The loads may be classed under (1) dead loads; (2) snow loads; (3) wind loads, and (4) miscellaneous loads. Concentrated floor and roof loads, girder and jib crane, and miscellaneous loads should receive special attention, and proper provision should be made in each case. No general solution can be given for providing for miscellaneous loads, but each problem must be worked out to suit local conditions.

Dead Loads.—Dead loads may be divided into (a) weight of structure; (b) concentrated loads.

The weight of the structure may be divided into (1) the weight of the roof trusses; (2) the weight of the roof sheathing and the roof covering; (3) the weight of the purlins and bracing; (4) the weight of the side and end walls. The first three items, together with the concentrated roof loads, constitute the dead loads used in designing the trusses.

The weights of mill buildings vary so much that it is not possible to give anything more than approximate values for the different items which go to make up the dead load. The following data will, however, materially assist the designer in arriving at approximately the proper dead load to assume for computing stresses, and the approximate weight of steel to use as a basis for preliminary estimates.

Weight of Roof Trusses.—The weight of roof trusses varies with the span, the distance between trusses, the load carried or capacity of the truss, and the pitch.

The empirical formula

$$W = \frac{P}{45} A \cdot L \left(1 + \frac{L}{5 \sqrt{A}} \right) \qquad (1)$$

where

W = weight of steel roof truss in lb.;

P = capacity of truss in lb. per sq. ft. of horizontal projection of roof (30 to 80 lb.);

A = distance center to center of trusses in ft. (8 to 30 ft.);

L = span of truss in ft.;

was deduced by the author from the computed and shipping weights of mill building trusses. The trusses were riveted Fink trusses with purlins placed at panel points, and were made up of angles with connecting plates; minimum size of angles 2 in. × 2 in. × ¼ in., minimum thickness of plates ¼ in. These weights include the weights of monitors and kneebraces. The weights of steel trusses without monitors and resting on walls will be somewhat less.

The trusses whose weights were used in deducing this formula had a pitch of $\frac{1}{4}$ (6 in. in 12 in.), but the formula gives quite accurate results for trusses having a pitch of $\frac{1}{6}$ to $\frac{1}{3}$. The trusses were designed for a tensile stress of 15,000 lb. per sq. in. and a compressive stress of 15,000 − 55 (l/r) lb. per sq. in., where l = length and r = the radius of gyration of the member, both in inches.

The weight of steel roof trusses for a capacity, P, of 40 lb. per sq. ft. for different spacings is given in Fig. 1. The weights of trusses for other capacities can be obtained by multiplying the tabular values by the ratio of the capacities.

Dividing (1) by $A \cdot L$ we have the weight of roof truss, w, per square foot of horizontal projection of the roof

$$w = \frac{P}{45}\left(1 + \frac{L}{5\sqrt{A}}\right) \tag{2}$$

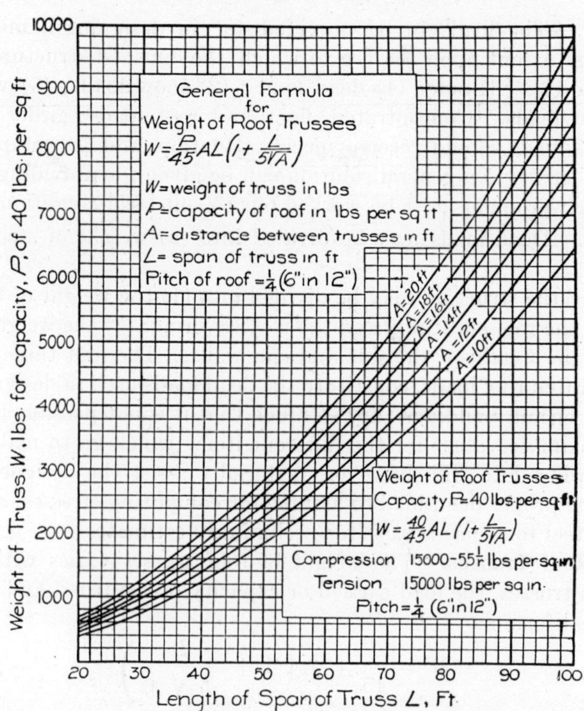

FIG. 1. WEIGHT OF ROOF TRUSSES FOR A CAPACITY OF 40 LB. PER SQUARE FOOT.

It should be noted that w is the dead load per square foot carried by an interior truss. The actual weight of trusses per square foot of horizontal projection for a building with n panels will be $w\,((n-1)/n)$ where end post bent is used, and $w\,((n+1)/n)$ where end truss bent is used, assuming that all trusses are made alike.

Formula (1) gives the weights of mill building trusses and includes the weight of the kneebraces and the ventilator framing. By reducing the details and by skimping the sections the actual weights may be reduced below those given by formula (1). For a comparison of the results as given by several formulas for the weight of roof trusses, see an article by Mr. R. Fleming, in Engineering News-Record, March 20, 1919.

Weight of Purlins, Girts, Bracing, and Columns.—Steel purlins will weigh from 1½ to 4 lb. per sq. ft. of area covered, depending upon the spacing and the capacity of the trusses and the snow load. If possible the actual weight of the purlins should be calculated. Girts and window framing will weigh from 1¼ to 3 lb. per sq. ft. of net surface. Bracing is quite a variable quantity. The bracing in the planes of the upper and lower chords will vary from $\frac{1}{2}$ to 1 lb. per sq. ft. of area. The side and end bracing, eave struts and columns will weigh about the same per sq. ft. of surface as the trusses.

Weight of Covering.—The weight of corrugated steel covering varies from $1\frac{1}{2}$ to 3 lb. per sq. ft. of area. In estimating the weight of corrugated steel allow about 25 per cent for laps where two corrugations side lap and 6 inches end lap are required, and about 15 per cent for laps where one corrugation side lap and 4 inches end lap are required. Nos. 20 and 22 corrugated steel are commonly used on the roof and Nos. 22 and 24 on the sides. For the weight of corrugated steel see Chapter XXVIII.

Weight of Roof Covering.—The approximate weight per square foot of various roof coverings is given in the following table:

Corrugated steel, without sheathing	1 to 3	lb.
Felt and asphalt, without sheathing	2	"
Tar and gravel roofing, without sheathing	8 to 10	"
Slate, 3/16 in. to $\frac{1}{4}$ in., without sheathing	7 to 9	"
Tin, without sheathing	1 to $1\frac{1}{2}$	"
Skylight glass, 3/16 in. to $\frac{1}{2}$ in., including frames	4 to 10	"
White pine sheathing 1 in. thick	3	"
Yellow pine sheathing 1 in. thick	4	"
Tiles, flat	15 to 20	"
Tiles, corrugated	8 to 10	"
Tiles, on concrete slabs	30 to 35	"
Plastered ceiling	10	"

For additional data on weight of roof coverings, see Chapter XXVIII and Chapter XXIX. The actual weight of roof coverings should be calculated if possible.

Weight of the Structure.—The weight of the roof can now be found. The weight of the steel in the sides and ends is approximately the same per square foot as the steel work in the roof.

A very close approximation to the weight of the steel in the entire structure where no sheathing is used and the same weight of corrugated steel is used on sides as on roof may be found as follows: Take the sum of the horizontal projection of the roof and the net surface of the sides and ends, after subtracting one-half of the area of the windows, wooden doors and clear openings; multiply the sum of these areas by the weight per square foot of the horizontal projection of the roof, and the product will be the approximate weight of the steel in the structure.

For the actual weights of steel frame buildings, see Chapter XL.

SNOW LOADS.—The annual snowfall in different localities is a function of the humidity and the latitude, and is quite a variable quantity. The amount of snow on the ground at one time is still more variable. In the Lake Superior region very little of the snow melts as it falls, and almost the entire annual snowfall is frequently on the ground at one time; while on the other hand in the same latitude in the Rocky Mountains the dry winds evaporate the snow in even the coldest weather and a less proportion accumulates. In latitudes of 35 to 45 degrees the heavy snowfalls are often followed by a sleeting rain, and the snow and ice load on roofs sometimes nearly equals the weight of the annual snowfall.

From the records of the snowfall for ten years (previous to 1903), as given in the reports of the U. S. Weather Bureau and data obtained by personal experience, in British Columbia, Montana, the Lake Superior region and central Illinois, the author, in the first edition of this book, proposed the values given in Fig. 2, for snow loads for roofs of different inclinations in different latitudes. For the Pacific coast and localities with low humidity, take one-half of the values given. The weight of newly fallen snow was taken at 5 lb. and packed snow at 12 lb. per cubic foot.

A high wind may follow a heavy sleet, and in designing the trusses the author would recommend the use of a minimum snow and ice load as given in Fig. 2 for all slopes of roofs. The maximum stresses due to the sum of this snow load, the dead and wind loads; the dead and the wind loads; or of the maximum snow load and the dead load is to be used in designing the members.

The snow loads given in Fig. 2 have now been quite generally adopted in specifications.

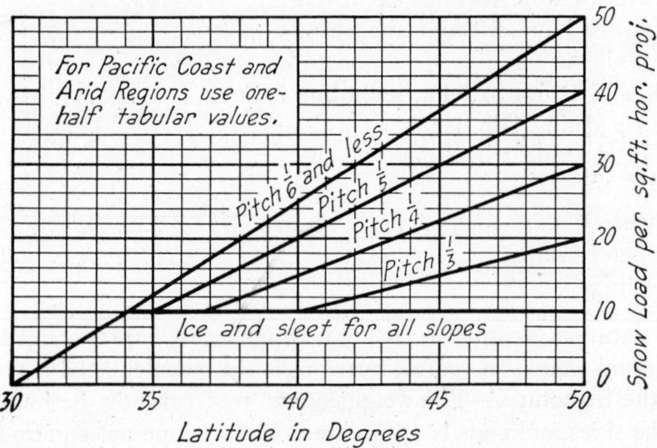

FIG. 2. SNOW LOAD ON ROOFS FOR DIFFERENT LATITUDES, IN LB. PER SQ. FT.

Snow loads per square foot of horizontal projection of roof are specified in various localities as follows: Chicago and New York, 20 lb.; Cincinnati and St. Louis, 10 lb.; New England, 30 lb. The Baltimore and Ohio Railroad specifies 20 lb. per square foot of horizontal projection of roof. For additional data, see Table I.

Schneider's "General Specifications for Structural Work for Buildings," require "A snow load of 25 lb. per sq. ft. of horizontal projection of the roof for all slopes up to 20 degrees; this load to be decreased 1 lb. for every degree of increase of slope up to 45 degrees, above which no snow load is to be considered. The above snow loads are minimum values for localities, where snow is likely to occur. In severe climates these snow loads should be increased in accordance with the actual conditions existing in these localities."

One of the heaviest falls of snow on record occurred at Boulder and Denver, Colorado, on Dec. 5 and 6, 1913, when 36 inches of snow weighing 9 lb. per cu. ft. fell during two days. Many flat roofs were loaded with a snow load of more than 30 lb. per sq. ft., and roofs with a pitch of one-half carried the full snow load of 27 lb. per sq. ft. of horizontal projection.

WIND LOADS.—Wind Pressure.—The wind pressure (P) in lb. per sq. ft. on a flat surface normal to the direction of the wind for any given velocity (V) in miles per hour, is given quite accurately by the formula

$$P = 0.004\ V^2 \tag{3}$$

The following table gives the pressure per sq. ft. on a flat surface normal to the direction of the wind for different velocities, as calculated by formula (3).

Velocity, miles per hour.	Pressure, lb. per sq. ft.	
10	0.4	Fresh breeze.
20	1.6	
30	3.6	Strong wind.
40	6.4	High wind.
50	10.0	Storm.
60	14.4	Violent storm.
80	25.6	Hurricane.
100	40.0	Violent hurricane.

The pressure on other than flat surfaces may be taken in per cents of that given by formula (3) as follows: 80 per cent on a rectangular building; 67 per cent on the convex side of cylinders; 115 to 130 per cent on the concave side of cylinders, channels and flat cups; and 130 to 170 per cent on the concave sides of spheres and deep cups.

The pressure on the vertical sides of buildings is usually taken at 30 lb. per sq. ft., equivalent to P equals $37\frac{1}{2}$ lb. in formula (3). This would give a velocity of 96 miles per hour, which would seem to be sufficient for all except the most exposed positions. The velocity of the wind in the St. Louis tornado was about 120 miles per hour. The records of the U. S. Weather Bureau for ten years show only one instance where the velocity of the wind as recorded by the anemometer was more than 90 miles per hour. The actual pressure of wind gusts has been found to be about 60 per cent and the actual steady wind pressure only about 36 per cent of that registered by ordinary small anemometers, which further reduces the intensity of the observed pressures. The wind pressure has been found to increase as the distance above the ground increases.

Wind Pressure and Wind Suction.—The effect of wind on a building is partly due to an increase in the pressure on the windward side and partly due to a suction on the leeward side. Tests have been made on small models by several observers. Professor Albert Smith in 1912 made tests of the wind pressure on a model building 6 ft. wide by 15 ft. long, and with walls 4, 5 and 6 ft. high. In a paper in Journal Western Society of Engineers, December, 1912, Professor Smith recommends that for roof trusses on masonry walls, or on steel bents with long diagonals, a suction effect of 0.4 of the unit wind pressure be placed on the leeward roof of all closed buildings; the remainder of the wind load to be applied on the windward side. The results obtained by taking one-half the wind load as a suction applied on the leeward side will not differ materially in amount from the results obtained by taking all the wind loads on the windward side, but may give some reverses in stress.

It is the uniform practice to omit the effect of suction in designing closed buildings. The uplifting effect of the wind on open sheds should always be investigated.

Increase of Wind Pressure with Height.—Experiments have shown that the wind pressure increases with the height of the structure. Professor Henry Adams in " Mechanics of Building Construction" gives the following formula for the wind pressure on a surface

$$\log P = 1.125 + 0.32 \log h - 0.12 \log w \qquad (4)$$

where P = wind pressure in lb. per sq. ft.; h = height of center of gravity of surface above ground level in ft.; w = width of surface in. ft.

For a rectangular building 100 ft. in length, from formula (4) the wind pressure per sq. ft. for various heights of building will be as follows:—Height = 20 ft., P = 16 lb.; height = 40 ft., P = 20 lb.; height = 100 ft., P = 26.8 lb.; height = 200 ft., P = 33.5 lb. For a rectangular structure 20 ft. in length, the wind pressure will be as follows:—Height = 20 ft., P = 19.5 lb.; height = 40 ft., P = 24.3 lb.; height = 100 ft., P = 32.5 lb.; height = 200 ft., P = 40.7 lb. The height of the building will be twice the value of h used in formula (4).

Specifications for Wind Loads.—A horizontal wind load of 30 lb. per sq. ft. is required by the building laws of Boston, New York, Baltimore, Cleveland, St. Louis; a horizontal wind load of 20 lb. per sq. ft. by Chicago and San Francisco. For additional data, see Table I.

The practice in England as given by Albert S. Spencer in "The Practical Design of Steel-Framed Sheds" is as follows:—The normal component of a wind pressure of 30 to 40 lb. per sq. ft. on roofs; and a wind load of 20 to 25 lb. per sq. ft. acting on the sides and ends of buildings.

German specifications for design of tall chimneys specify wind loads per sq. ft. as follows:—26 lb. on rectangular chimneys; 67 per cent of 26 lb. on circular chimneys; and 71 per cent of 26 lb. on octagonal chimneys.

The official specifications for the design of steel framework in Prussia have recently been amplified in the matter of wind pressures. For the wind-bracing, as a whole, the wind pressure on the whole building is to be taken as 17 lb. per sq. ft. For proportioning individual frame members, girts, studs, trusses, etc., a higher value of wind pressure must be assumed, viz., 28 to 34 lb. per sq. ft.

Mr. R. Fleming in his book entitled "Wind Stresses," recommends a wind load of 15 lb. per sq. ft. on the sides and ends and the normal component of 15 lb. as determined by Duchemin's formula on the roof. For buildings over 25 ft. to the eaves, he recommends that a wind pressure of 20 lb. per sq. ft. be used in the place of 15 lb. per sq. ft. as given above.

Schneider's "General Specifications for Structural Work for Buildings" requires that:—

"The wind pressure shall be assumed as acting in any direction horizontally: First.—At 20 lb. per sq. ft. on the sides and ends of buildings and on the actually exposed surface, or the vertical projection of roofs; Second.—At 30 lb. per sq. ft. on the total exposed surfaces of all parts composing the metal framework. The framework shall be considered an independent structure, without walls, partitions or floors."

The author's specifications for wind loads on office buildings as given in the "Structural Engineers' Handbook" requires that:—

Wind Loads.—All structures shall be designed to resist the horizontal wind pressure on the surface exposed above surrounding buildings as follows.

a. The wind pressure on roofs shall be taken as the normal component, calculated by Duchemin's formula (formula (6)), of 30 lb. per square foot on the vertical projection of the roof.

b. The wind pressure on the sides and ends of buildings except as otherwise provided in the following paragraph shall be assumed as 20 lb. per square foot acting in any direction horizontally.

c. In designing the steel or reinforced concrete framework of fireproof buildings the framework shall be designed to resist a wind pressure of 30 lb. per square foot acting on the total exposed surface of all parts composing the framework or a horizontal wind pressure of 20 lb. per square foot acting in any direction horizontally on the sides and ends of the completed building. The strength of reinforced concrete floors may be considered in calculating the strength of the framework in the completed structure. The framework before the structure has been completed shall be self-supporting without walls, partitions or floors. In no case shall the overturning moment due to wind pressure exceed 75 per cent of the resisting moment of the structure. In the calculations for wind bracing the working stresses for dead and live loads may be increased 25 per cent providing the sections are not less than required for dead and live loads. Chimneys shall be designed to resist a wind pressure of 20 lb. ($\frac{2}{3}$ of 30 lb.) per square foot acting on the vertical projection of the chimney. Curtain walls carried on the framework of steel or reinforced concrete buildings shall be designed to resist a horizontal pressure of 30 lb. per square foot acting horizontally on the outside of the entire surface of the wall.

From the above discussion it would seem that 30 lb. per square foot on the side and the normal component of a horizontal pressure of 30 lb. on the roof would be sufficient for all except exposed locations. If the building is somewhat protected a horizontal pressure of 20 lb. per square foot on the sides is certainly ample for heights less than, say, 30 feet. For the author's specifications for wind loads on steel frame buildings, see Appendix I.

Wind Pressure on Inclined Surfaces.—The wind is usually taken as acting horizontally and the normal component on inclined surfaces is calculated.

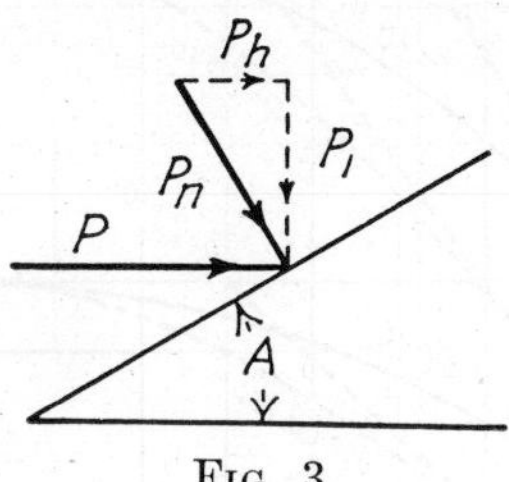

FIG. 3.

The normal component of the wind pressure on inclined surfaces has usually been computed by Hutton's empirical formula

$$P_n = P \cdot \sin A^{1.842 \cos A - 1} \tag{5}$$

where P_n equals the normal component of the wind pressure, P equals the pressure per square foot on a vertical surface, and A equals the angle of inclination of the surface with the horizontal, Fig. 3

The formula due to Duchemin

$$P_n = P \frac{2 \sin A}{1 + \sin^2 A} \tag{6}$$

where P_n, P and A are the same as in (5), gives results considerably larger for ordinary roofs than Hutton's formula, and is coming into quite general use.

The formula

$$P_n = P \cdot A/45 \tag{7}$$

where P_n and P are the same as in (5) and (6), and A is the angle of inclination of the surface in degrees (A being equal to or less than 45°), gives results which agree very closely with Hutton's formula, and is much more simple.

Hutton's formula (5) is based on experiments which were very crude and probably erroneous. Duchemin's formula (6) is based on very careful experiments and is now considered the most reliable formula in use. The Straight Line formula (7) agrees with experiments quite closely and is preferred by many engineers on account of its simplicity.

The values of P_n as determined by Hutton's, Duchemin's and the Straight Line formulas are given in Fig. 4, for P equals 20, 30 and 40 lb. per sq. ft.

It is interesting to note that Duchemin's formula with P equals 30 lb. gives practically the same values for roofs of ordinary inclination as is given by Hutton's and the Straight Line formulas with P equals 40 lb.

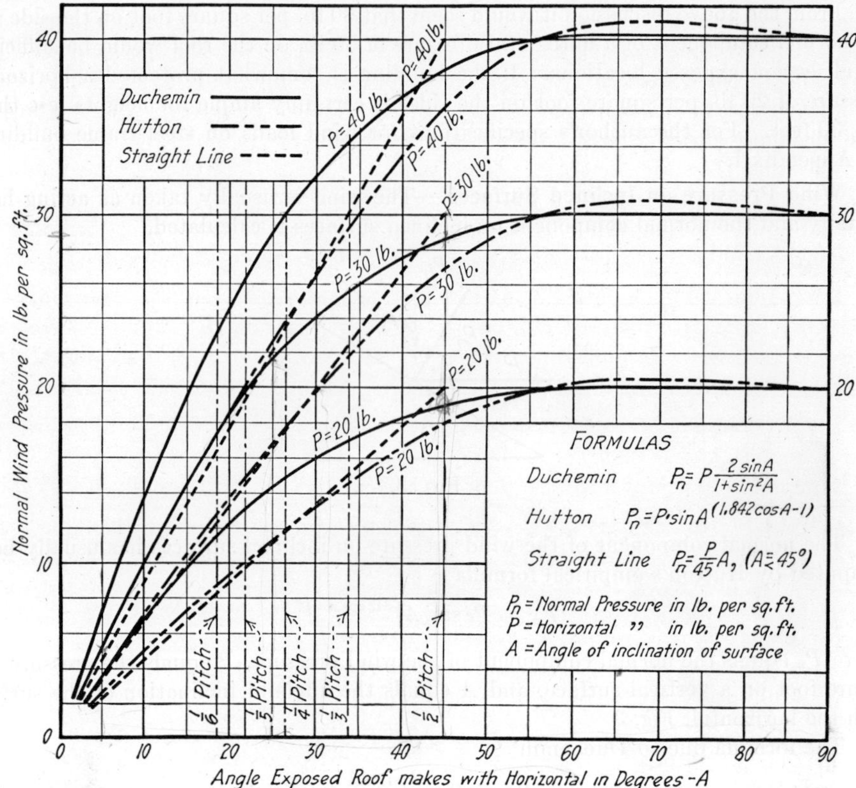

FIG. 4. NORMAL WIND LOAD ON ROOF ACCORDING TO DIFFERENT FORMULAS.

Duchemin has also deduced the formula

$$P_h = P\,\frac{2\sin^2 A}{1+\sin^2 A} \tag{8}$$

where P_h in (8) equals the pressure parallel to the direction of the wind, Fig. 3; and

$$P_l = P \frac{2 \sin A \cdot \cos A}{1 + \sin^2 A} \tag{9}$$

where P_h in (9) equals the pressure at right angles to the direction of the wind, Fig. 3. P_l may be an uplifting, a depressing or a side pressure. With an open shed in exposed positions the uplifting effect of the wind often requires attention. In that case the wind should be taken normal to the inner surface of the building on the leeward side, and the uplifting force determined by using formula (9). If the gables are closed a deep cup is formed, and the normal pressure should be increased 30 to 70 per cent.

That the uplifting force of the wind is often considerable in exposed localities is made evident by the fact that highway bridges are occasionally wrecked by the wind. The most interesting example known to the author is that of a 100-foot span combination bridge in Northwestern Montana which was picked up bodily by the wind, turned about 90 degrees in azimuth and dropped into the middle of the river. The end bolsters were torn loose although drift-bolted to the abutments.*

The wind pressure is not a steady pressure, but varies in intensity, thus producing excessive vibrations which cause the structure to rock if the bracing is not rigid. The bracing in mill buildings should be designed for initial tension, so that the building will be rigid. Rigidity is of more importance than strength in mill buildings.

References.—For additional data on wind pressures, see the following:—(1) "Wind Pressures in Engineering Construction," by Capt. W. H. Bixby, M. Am. Soc. C. E., published in Engineering News, Vol. XXXIII., pp. 175–184, March, 1895. (2) "Wind Stresses in Buildings," by R. Fleming, published by John Wiley & Son's, 1930.

LIVE LOADS ON FLOORS.—Live loads on floors for mill buildings are very hard to classify and should be calculated for each case.

Floor loads as specified in the building laws of various cities are given in Table I.

CONCENTRATED LIVE LOADS.—The loads given in Table II have been proposed for different classes of buildings and are from "Specifications for Structural Steel for Buildings" by Mr. C. C. Schneider. These loads consist of:

(*a*) A uniform load per sq. ft. of floor area;
(*b*) A concentrated load which shall be applied to all points of the floor;
(*c*) A uniform load per linear foot for girders.

The maximum result is to be used in calculations.

The specified concentrated loads shall also apply to the floor construction between the beams for a length of five feet.

If heavy concentrations, like safes, armatures, or special machinery are likely to occur on floors, provision should be made for them.

The weight of floors above ground in mill buildings varies so much that it is useless to give weights.

* For a description of the wreck by the wind of the High Bridge over the Mississippi River at St. Paul, Minn., see article by C. A. P. Turner in Trans. Am. Soc. C. E., Vol. 54, p. 31.

TABLE I.

FLOORS AND ROOFS.

MINIMUM LIVE LOADS, POUNDS PER SQUARE FOOT.

By Building Laws of Various Cities.

American Bridge Company.

Kind of Building.	Boston, 1912.	New York, 1906.	Philadelphia, 1913.	Baltimore, 1908.	Pittsburgh, 1913. (Proposed.)	Cleveland, 1911.	Chicago, 1911.	St. Louis, 1910.	San Francisco, 1910.
Apartments	50	60	70	60	50	50	40	60	60
Public Rooms* and Halls	100	....	....	....	....	80	....	....	....
Assembly Halls	125	90	120	....	125	100	....	100	125
Fixed Seat Auditoriums	....	....	....	75	125	80	100	....	75
Movable Seat Auditoriums	....	....	....	125	....	100	100	....	125
Churches	....	90	....	75	125	....	100	....	125
Dance Halls	200	....	....	....	150	150	100	....	....
Drill Rooms	200	....	....	....	150	....	....	....	....
Riding Schools	200	....	....	....	150	....	....	....	....
Theaters	....	90	....	75	125	....	100	....	125
Dwellings	50	60	70	60	50	40	40	60	60
Public Rooms*	100	....	....	....	....	....	....	....	....
Hotels	50	60	70	60	70	50	50	60	60
First Floors	....	....	....	....	....	....	....	100	....
Corridors	....	....	....	....	....	80	....	....	....
Office Floors	100	....	....	....	....	80	....	....	....
Public Rooms*	100	....	....	....	....	....	....	....	....
Manufacturing	125	120	120	125	125	....	100	....	125
Light Factories	....	120	150	....	125	....	....	150	....
Mercantile	....	....	....	....	....	....	....	....	....
Heavy Storehouses	....	150	150	250	200	200	....	....	250
Retail Stores	125	....	120	125	125	125	100	150	125
Warehouses	250	150	150	....	200	....	100	150	250
Offices	100	75	100	75	70	60	50	70	60
First Floor	100	150	....	150	....	....	....	150	150
Corridors	....	....	....	....	....	100	....	....	....
Schools (Class Rooms)	60	75	....	75	70	60	40	100	75
Assembly Rooms—Halls	125	90	....	....	70	80	75	....	125
Sidewalks	....	300	....	200	....	200	....	....	150
Stables—Carriage Houses	....	75	....	100	....	80	100	....	75
Area less than 500 sq. ft.	....	....	....	....	....	....	40	....	....
Stairways and Landings	70	....	....	....	....	80	100	....	....
Fire Escapes	70	....	....	....	....	80	....	....	....
Roofs—Flat‡	40	50	....	40	50§	40	25	40	30
Horizontal Projection Steep Roofs	....	30	....	20	50§	....	25	....	20
Superficial Surface	....	....	30	....	50§	40	....	....	....
Wind Pressure	....	30	30‖	30	25	30‖	20	30	20

* Area greater than 500 square feet.

† First Floors 200.

‡ Slopes less than 20 degrees.

§ Dead and live, except for one story steel frame buildings, corrugated iron roofs, 35 pounds.

‖ High Buildings, built up districts, 35 pounds; 14 stories or over, 25 pounds at tenth story, $2\frac{1}{2}$ pounds less each story below.

Figures for manufacturing establishments do not include machinery.

TABLE II.

TABLE OF LIVE LOADS, SCHNEIDER'S SPECIFICATIONS.

Classes of Buildings.	Live Loads in Pounds. Distributed Load.	Concentrated Load.	Load per Linear Ft. of Girder.
Dwellings, hotels, apartment-houses, dormitories, hospitals	40	2 000	500
Office buildings, upper stories	50	5 000	1 000
Schoolrooms, theater galleries, churches	60	5 000	1 000
Ground floors of office buildings, corridors and stairs in public buildings	80	5 000	1 000
Assembly rooms, main floors of theaters, ballrooms, gymnasia, or any room likely to be used for drilling or dancing	Floor 100 Columns 50	5 000	1 000
Ordinary stores and light manufacturing, stables and carriage-houses	80	8 000	1 000
Sidewalks in front of buildings	300	10 000	1 000
Warehouses and factories	from 120 up	Special	Special
Charging floors for foundries	" 300 "	"	"
Power houses, for uncovered floors	" 200 "	The actual weights of engines, boilers, stacks, etc., shall be used, but in no case less than 200 lb. per sq. ft.	

TABLE III.

TYPICAL HAND CRANES.*

Capacity in Tons.	Span.	Wheel Base.	Maximum wheel Load in Pounds.	Side Clearance.	Vertical Clearance.	Weight of Rail for: Plate Girders.	Beams.
2	30	4 ft. 0 in.	3 100	7 in.	4 ft. 0 in.	30 lb. per yd.	30
	50	5 " 0 "	4 000	7 "	4 " 0 "	30 "	30
4	30	4 " 0 "	5 400	8 "	4 " 6 "	30 "	30
	50	5 " 0 "	6 500	8 "	4 " 0 "	30 "	30
6	30	6 " 0 "	8 000	9 "	5 " 0 "	35 "	30
	50	7 " 0 "	9 200	9 "	5 " 0 "	35 "	30
8	30	6 " 0 "	10 500	10 "	5 " 0 "	40 "	30
	50	7 " 0 "	11 800	10 "	5 " 0 "	40 "	35
10	30	7 " 0 "	13 000	10 "	5 " 0 "	40 "	35
	50	8 " 0 "	14 400	10 "	5 " 6 "	40 "	40
16	30	7 " 0 "	20 700	10 "	5 " 6 "	45 "	40
	50	8 " 0 "	22 300	10 "	5 " 6 "	45 "	45
20	30	7 " 0 "	26 000	10 "	5 " 6 "	50 "	45
	50	8 " 0 "	28 000	10 "	5 " 6 "	50 "	50
25	30	7 " 0 "	32 300	12 "	6 " 0 "	55 "	50
	50	8 " 0 "	35 000	12 "	6 " 0 "	55 "	50

*Mr. C. C. Schneider in Trans. Am. Soc. C. E., Vol. 54, 1905.

TABLE IV.

Typical Electric Traveling Cranes.*

Capacity in Tons.	Span.	Wheel Base.	Maximum Wheel Load, in Pounds.	s.	v.	Weight of Rail for:	
						Plate Girders.	Beams.
5	40	8 ft. 6 in.	12 000	10 in.	7 ft.	40 lb. per yd.	40
	60	9 " 0 "	13 000	10 "	7 "	40 "	40
10	40	9 " 0 "	19 000	10 "	7 "	45 "	40
	60	9 " 6 "	21 000	10 "	7 "	45 "	40
15	40	9 " 6 "	26 000	10 "	7 "	50 "	50
	60	10 " 0 "	29 000	10 "	7 "	50 "	50
20	40	10 " 0 "	33 000	12 "	8 "	55 "	50
	60	10 " 6 "	36 000	12 "	8 "	55 "	50
25	40	10 " 0 "	40 000	12 "	8 "	60 "	50
	60	10 " 6 "	44 000	12 "	8 "	60 "	50
30	40	10 " 6 "	48 000	12 "	8 "	70 "	60
	60	11 " 0 "	52 000	12 "	8 "	70 "	60
40	40	11 " 0 "	64 000	14 "	9 "	80 "	60
	60	12 " 0 "	70 000	14 "	9 "	80 "	60
50	40	11 " 0 "	72 000	14 "	9 "	100 "	60
	60	12 " 0 "	80 000	14 "	9 "	100 "	60

s = Side clearance from center of rail.

v = Vertical clearance from top of rail.

* Mr. C. C. Schneider in Trans. Am. Soc. C. E., Vol. 54, 1905.

TABLE V.

Weights of Building Materials, Etc. Pounds per Cubic Foot.

Material.	Weight.	Material.	Weight.
Brick, pressed and paving	150	Hemlock	25
" common building	120	White pine	25
" soft building	100	Douglas fir	30
Granite	170	Yellow pine	40
Marble	170	White oak	50
Limestone	160	Mortar	100
Sandstone	150	Stone concrete	150
Cinders	40	Cinder "	110
Slag	160–180	Common brick work	100–120
Granulated furnace slag	53	Rubble masonry, sandstone	130–140
Gravel	120	" " limestone	140
Slate	175	" " granite	150
Sand, clay and earth (dry)	100	Ashlar " sandstone	140–150
" " " " (moist)	120	" " limestone	150
Coal ashes	45	" " granite	165
Paving asphaltum	100	Cast iron	450
Plaster of Paris	140	Wrought iron	480
Glass	160	Steel	490
Water	$62\frac{1}{2}$	Lead	711
Snow, freshly fallen	5	Copper, rolled	490
" packed	12	Brass	523
" wet	50	Plaster, ceiling 10 to 15 lb. per sq. ft.	
Spruce	25		

TABLE VI.

FLOOR LOADS.

CONTENTS OF STORAGE WAREHOUSES.

American Bridge Company.

Material.	Weights per Cubic Foot of Space, Pounds.	Height of Pile, Feet.	Weights per Square Foot of Floor, Pounds.	Recommended Live Loads, Pounds per Square Foot.
Groceries, Wines, Liquors, Etc.				
Beans, in bags	40	8	320	
Canned Goods, in cases	58	6	348	
Coffee, Roasted, in bags	33	8	264	
Coffee, Green, in bags	39	8	312	
Dates, in cases	55	6	330	
Figs, in cases	74	5	370	
Flour, in barrels	40	5	200	
Molasses, in barrels	48	5	240	
Rice, in bags	58	6	348	250 to 300
Sal Soda, in barrels	46	5	230	
Salt, in bags	70	5	350	
Soap Powder, in cases	38	8	304	
Starch, in barrels	25	6	150	
Sugar, in barrels	43	5	215	
Sugar, in cases	51	6	306	
Tea, in chests	25	8	200	
Wines and Liquors, in barrels	38	6	228	
Dry Goods, Cotton, Wool, Etc.				
Burlap, in bales	43	6	258	
Coir Yarn, in bales	33	8	264	
Cotton, in bales, compressed	18	8	144	
Cotton Bleached Goods, in cases	28	8	224	
Cotton Flannel, in cases	12	8	96	
Cotton Sheeting, in cases	23	8	184	
Cotton Yarn, in cases	25	8	200	
Excelsior, compressed	19	8	152	
Hemp, Italian, compressed	22	8	176	200 to 250
Hemp, Manila, compressed	30	8	240	
Jute, compressed	41	8	328	
Linen Damask, in cases	50	5	250	
Linen Goods, in cases	30	8	240	
Linen Towels, in cases	40	6	240	
Sisal, compressed	21	8	168	
Tow, compressed	29	8	232	
Wool, in bales, compressed	48	.	...	
Wool, in bales, not compressed	13	8	104	
Wool, Worsteds, in cases	27	8	216	

Material.	Weights per Cubic Foot of Space, Pounds.	Height of Pile, Feet.	Weights per Square Foot of Floor, Pounds.	Recommended Live Loads, Pounds per Square Foot.
Building Materials				
Cement, Natural	59	6	354	
Cement, Portland	73	6	438	300 to 400
Lime and Plaster	53	5	265	
Hardware, Etc.				
Door Checks	45	.	...	
Hinges	64	.	...	
Locks, in cases, packed	31	.	...	
Sash Fasteners	48	.	...	
Screws	101	.	...	
Sheet Tin, in boxes	278	2	556	300 to 400
Wire Cables, on reels	...	.	425	
Wire, Insulated Copper, in coils	63	5	315	
Wire, Galvanized Iron, in coils	74	$4\frac{1}{2}$	333	
Wire, Magnet, on spools	75	6	450	
Drugs, Paints, Oil, Etc.				
Alum, Pearl, in barrels	33	6	198	
Bleaching Powder, in hogsheads	31	$3\frac{1}{2}$	102	
Blue Vitriol, in barrels	45	5	226	
Glycerine, in cases	52	6	312	
Linseed Oil, in barrels	36	6	216	
Linseed Oil, in iron drums	45	4	180	
Logwood Extract, in boxes	70	5	350	
Rosin, in barrels	48	6	288	200 to 300
Shellac, Gum	38	6	228	
Soda Ash, in hogsheads	62	$2\frac{3}{4}$	167	
Soda, Caustic, in iron drums	88	$3\frac{1}{3}$	294	
Soda, Silicate, in barrels	53	6	318	
Sulphuric Acid	60	$1\frac{2}{3}$	100	
White Lead Paste, in cans	174	$3\frac{1}{2}$	610	
White Lead, dry	86	$4\frac{3}{4}$	408	
Red Lead and Litharge, dry	132	$3\frac{3}{4}$	495	
Miscellaneous				
Glass and Chinaware, in crates	40	8	320	
Hides and Leather, in bales	20	8	160	
Hides, Buffalo, in bundles	37	8	296	
Paper, Newspaper, and Strawboards	35	6	210	300
Paper, Writing and Calendared	60	6	360	
Rope, in coils	32	6	192	

WEIGHT OF CRANES.—The approximate weight of a few of the common sizes of hand cranes are given in Table III.

The weights and dimensions of typical traveling cranes as given in Table IV have been proposed for adoption as a standard.

Specifications for the Design of Crane Girders.—In designing crane girders the following specifications should be complied with.

1. Wheel-load can be assumed as distributed in top flange, over a distance equal to depth of girder, with a maximum limit of 30 in.

2. In addition to the vertical load, the top flanges of the girder shall withstand a lateral loading of two-tenths of the lifting capacity of the crane, equally divided between the four wheels of the crane.

3. The top flanges of the crane girders shall not be of smaller width than one-twentieth of their unsupported length.

WEIGHTS OF MISCELLANEOUS MATERIAL.—The weights of various kinds of merchandise are given in Table V and Table VI.

MINIMUM LOADS ON ROOFS.—Schneider's "General Specifications for Structural Work for Buildings" contains the following specification for loads on ordinary roofs:

"In climates corresponding to that of New York, ordinary roofs, up to 80 ft. span, shall be proportioned to carry the minimum loads in Table VII, per square foot of exposed surface, applied vertically, to provide for dead, wind and snow loads combined:

TABLE VII.

MINIMUM LOADS ON ROOFS.

Gravel or Composition Roofing	On boards, flat slope, 1 to 6, or less	50 lb.
	On boards, steep slope, more than 1 to 6	45 "
	On 3-in. flat tile or cinder concrete	60 "
Corrugated sheeting, on boards or purlins		40 "
Slate	On boards or purlins	50 "
	On 3-in. flat tile or cinder concrete	65 "
Tile, on steel purlins		55 "
Glass		45 "

"For roofs in climates where no snow is likely to occur, reduce the foregoing loads by 10 lb. per sq. ft., but no roof or any part thereof shall be designed for less than 40 lb. per sq. ft.

References.—For additional data on loads, see the author's "Structural Engineers' Handbook."

CHAPTER XXV.

FRAMEWORK.

Definitions.—The following definitions will assist the reader in a study of roof trusses and steel frame buildings.

Steel Mill Building.—A steel mill building is a structure with a self-supporting steel frame with a light-weight covering, usually fire resistant.

Truss.—A truss is a framed structure in which the members are so arranged and fastened at their ends that external loads applied at the joints of the truss will cause only direct stresses in the members. In its simplest form a truss is a triangle or a combination of triangles. In this chapter it will be assumed (1) that the structure is not constrained by the reactions, (2) that the axes of the members meet in a common point at the joints, and (3) that the joints have frictionless hinges.

Transverse Bent.—A transverse bent consists of a truss supported at the ends on columns and braced against longitudinal movement by knee braces attached to the lower chord of the truss and to the columns.

Purlin.—A beam that rests on the top chords of roof trusses and supports the sheathing that carries the roof covering, or supports the roof covering directly, or supports rafters.

Rafter.—A beam that rests on the purlins and supports the sheathing, or may support sub-purlins. Rafters are not commonly used in mill buildings.

Sub-purlin.—A secondary system of purlins that rest on the rafters and are spaced so as to support the tile or slate covering directly without the use of sheathing.

Sheathing.—A covering of boards or reinforced concrete that is carried on the purlins or rafters to furnish a support for the roof covering.

Girt.—A beam that is fastened to the columns to support the side covering either directly or to support the side sheathing.

Monitor Ventilator.—A framework at the top of the roof that carries fixed or movable louvres, or sash in the clerestory.

Clerestory.—The clear opening in the side framework of a monitor ventilator of a building, also the clear opening on the side of a building.

Louvres.—Slats made of metal or wood which are placed in the clerestory of a monitor ventilator to keep out the storm. Louvres may be fixed or movable. The opening of a monitor ventilator is also called a louvre.

Panel.—The distance between two joints in a roof truss or the distance between purlins.

Bay.—The distance between two trusses or transverse bents.

Pitch.—The pitch of a truss is the center height of the truss divided by the span where the truss is symmetrical about the center line.

Other terms are defined when they are first used.

STEEL FRAME MILL BUILDINGS.—The framework of a steel frame mill building consists of a series of transverse bents, which carry the purlins on the tops of the trusses, and girts on the sides of the columns to carry the covering, Fig. 1. The framework is braced by diagonal bracing in the planes of the roof and the sides of the building, and in the plane of the lower chords. A transverse bent consists of a roof truss supported at the ends on columns and is braced against endwise movement by means of knee braces. The framing plan for a steel frame mill building is shown in Fig. 1. Steel mill buildings are also made with end trusses in place of the end framing shown in Fig. 1.

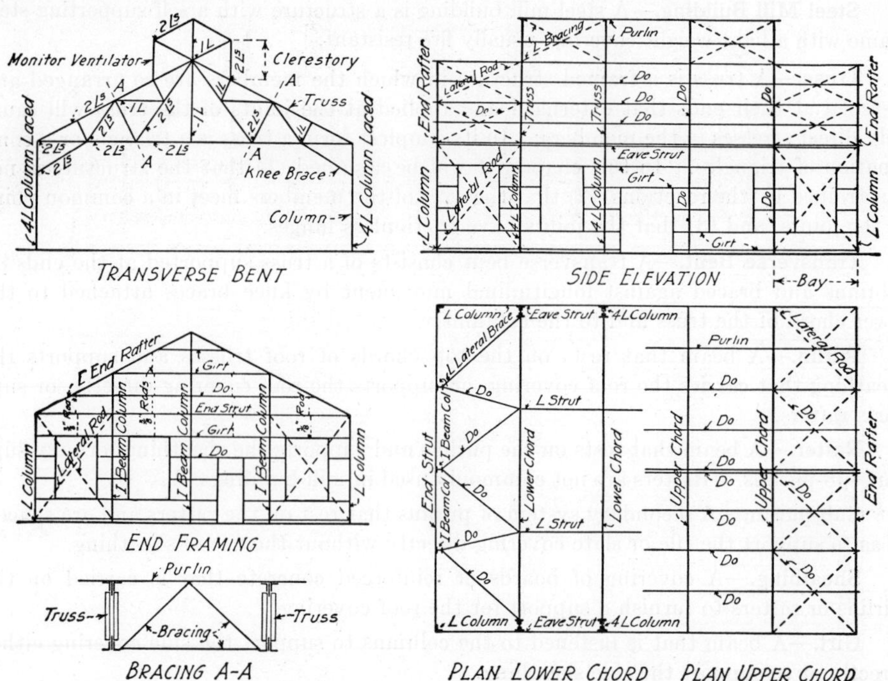

FIG. 1. FRAMEWORK FOR A STEEL MILL BUILDING.

The end post bent, shown in Fig. 1, usually requires less material than the end trussed bent shown in Fig. 2, and is commonly used for simple mill buildings. Extensions can be made with about equal ease in either case, and the choice of methods will usually be determined by the local conditions of the problem and the fancy of the designer. In train sheds and similar structures the end trussed bent, Fig. 2, is used. Where the truss span is quite long, as in train sheds, the end trusses are often designed for lighter loads than are the intermediate trusses, thus saving considerable material. In the case of simple mill buildings of moderate size all trusses are, however, commonly made alike, the extra cost of detailing being usually more than the amount saved in material.

In train sheds, coliseums, and similar structures requiring a large floor space, the two-hinged or the three-hinged arch may be used in place of the typical transverse bent system.

The framework of a steel frame building may be made rigid without the use of knee braced bents. The steel frame warehouse shown in Fig. 3 is 236 ft. 8 in. wide by 378 ft. 6 in. long. The interior columns are spaced 94 ft. $7\frac{1}{2}$ in. centers and support

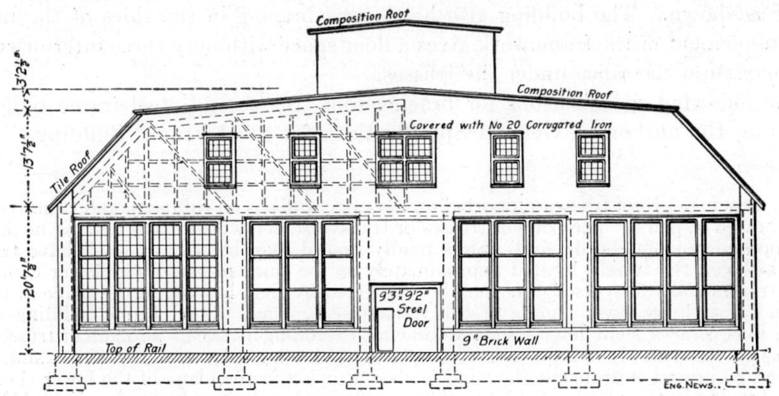

Fig. 2. A. T. & S. F. R. R. Blacksmith Shop, Topeka, Kas.

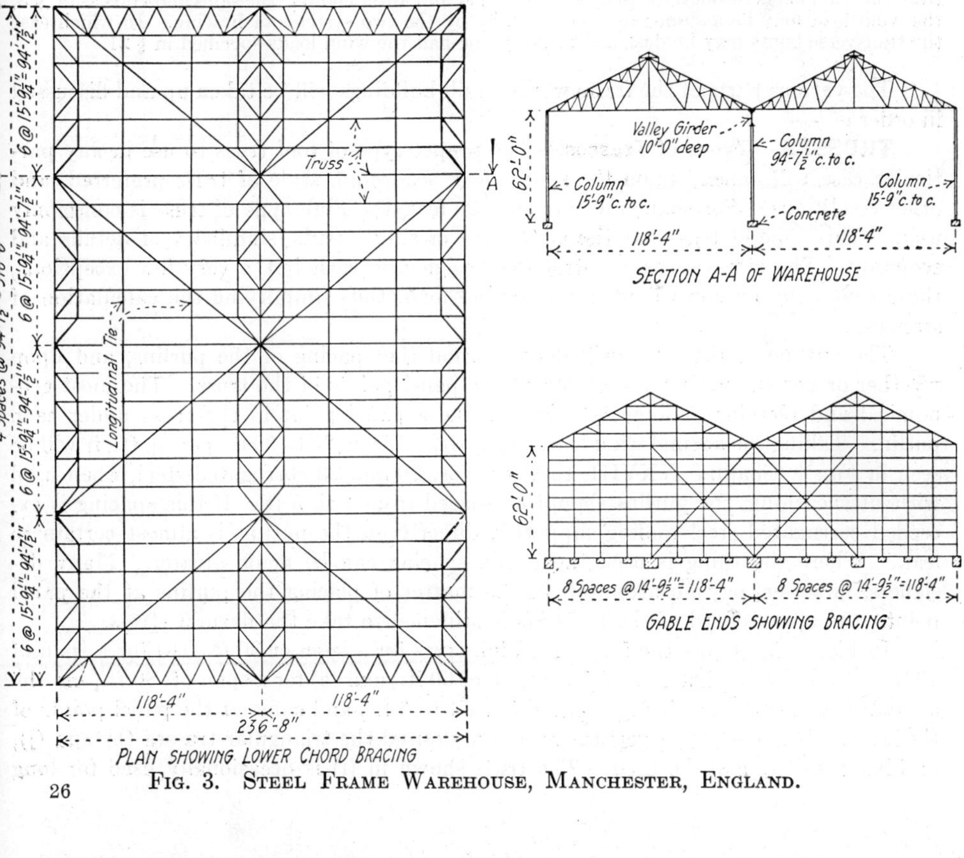

Fig. 3. Steel Frame Warehouse, Manchester, England.

valley girders 10 ft. 0 in. deep. The main trusses are spaced 15 ft. $9\frac{1}{4}$ in. and are supported by outside columns and by the valley girders. The columns are pin-connected at top and bottom. The wind loads coming on the sides of the building are transferred to the ends of the building by stiff bracing in the plane of the lower chords of the trusses; and are transferred to the foundations on the leeward side of the end bents by means of bracing as shown. The building also has lateral bracing in the sides of the building. This arrangement of the framework gives a floor space with only three interior columns, and a maximum clearance under the trusses.

The following specifications for bracing roof trusses and steel frame buildings is taken from the author's "General Specifications for Steel Frame Buildings" in Appendix I.

§ 8. Bracing.—Roof trusses supported on masonry walls or on columns, and transvese bents shall be braced in pairs. The pairs of trusses or transverse bents shall have bracing in the planes of the top and bottom chords, and, unless rigidly braced by other means, shall have transverse bracing between the trusses located approximately at the third points of the lower chord. The pairs of trusses and transverse bents shall be connected by rigid bracing in the plane of the lower chords in line with the lower chords of the transverse bracing. Steel frame buildings without effective knee braces shall have diagonal bracing extending between all pairs of trusses so arranged as to transmit the wind loads to the ends of the building, and the sides and the end bents shall be braced to transmit the wind loads. Bracing in the plane of the lower chords shall be stiff; bracing in the planes of the top chords, sides and ends may be made adjustable.

§ 22. In steel frame buildings having efficient knee-braced bents and also so braced as to transmit wind loads through the planes of the upper and lower chords, the sides and ends as in § 8, the wind load may be assumed as taken equally by the two systems of bracing. In which case the transverse bents may be designed to carry one-half the wind loads specified in § 21.

The various parts of the framework of mill buildings will be taken up and discussed in order.

TRUSSES.—Types of Trusses.—The proper type of roof truss to use in any particular case will depend upon the span, clear headroom, style of truss preferred, and other conditions. For spans up to about 100 feet, the Fink type of truss is commonly used. This type of truss has the advantage of short struts, simplicity of details and economy. The stresses that control the design are, with but a very few exceptions, those caused by an equivalent uniform dead load, thus simplifying the calculation of stresses.

The outline of the truss will depend upon the spacing of the purlins, and upon whether or not the purlins are placed at the panel points of the truss. The most economical and pleasing arrangement is to make a panel point in the truss under each purlin. Taking the normal wind load on the roof at from 25 to 30 lb. per sq. ft., it will be seen in Fig. 4, Chapter XXVIII, that for Nos. 20 and 22 corrugated steel, when used without sheathing, the purlins should be spaced from 4 to 5 ft. If this spacing is exceeded corrugated steel roofing supported directly on the purlins is almost certain to leak. Where sheathing is used the purlin spacing can be made greater. Many designers, however, pay no attention to the matter of placing the purlins at the panel points, the upper chord of the truss being stiffened to take the flexural stress.

In Fig. 4, (a) shows the form of a Fink truss for a span of 30 ft.; (b) for a span of 40 ft.; (c) for a span of 50 ft.; (d) for a span of 60 ft.; and (e) for a span of 80 ft., on the assumption that the purlins are spaced from 4 to 5 ft., and come at the panel points of the truss. If trusses with vertical posts are desired the triangular trusses (h) and (j), or Fink truss (f) may be used. The truss shown in (i) is occasionally used for long

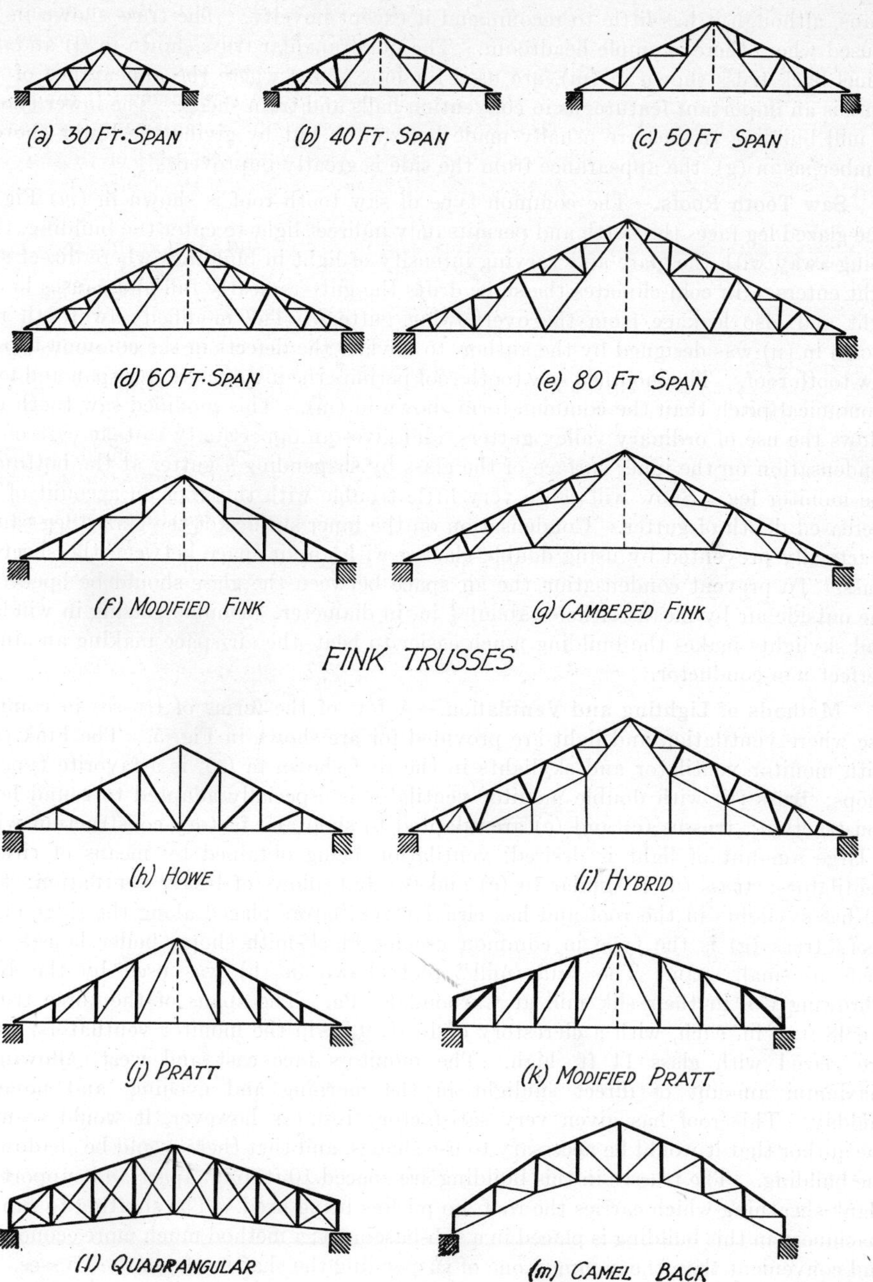

FIG. 4. TYPES OF ROOF TRUSSES.

spans, although it has little to recommend it except novelty. The truss shown in (k) is used where there is ample headroom. The quadrangular truss shown in (l) and the camel-back truss shown in (m), are used for long spans where the appearance of the truss is an important feature, as in convention halls and train sheds. The lower chords of mill building trusses are usually made horizontal, but by giving the lower chord a camber, as in (g), the appearance from the side is greatly improved.

Saw Tooth Roofs.—The common type of saw tooth roof is shown in (*m*) Fig. 5. The glazed leg faces the north and permits only indirect light to enter the building, thus doing away with the glare and varying intensity of light in buildings where direct sunlight enters. In cold climates the snow drifts the gutters nearly full and causes loss of light and also leakage from the overflowing gutters. The modified saw tooth roof shown in (n) was designed by the author, to obviate the defects in the common type of saw tooth roof. The modified saw tooth roof permits the use of a greater span and more economical pitch than the common form shown in (m). This modified saw tooth roof allows the use of ordinary valley gutters, and gives an opportunity to take care of the condensation on the inner surface of the glass by suspending a gutter at the bottom of the monitor leg. Snow will cause very little trouble with this roof on account of the increased depth of gutter. Condensation on the inner surface of the glazed leg can be practically prevented by using double glazing with an air space between the sheets of glass. To prevent condensation the air space between the glass should be opened to the outside air by means of holes about $\frac{1}{8}$ in. in diameter. Double glazing in windows and skylights makes the building much easier to heat, the air space making an almost perfect non-conductor.

Methods of Lighting and Ventilation.—A few of the forms of trusses in common use where ventilation and light are provided for are shown in Fig. 5. The Fink truss with monitor ventilator and skylights in the roof shown in (a), is a favorite type for shops; truss (b) with double monitor ventilator is especially adapted to round house construction; trusses (c) and (e) are adapted to shop and factory construction where a large amount of light is desired, ventilation being obtained by means of circular ventilators; truss (d) is similar to (c) and (e), but allows of better ventilation; truss (f) has skylights in the roof and has circular ventilators placed along the ridge of the roof; truss (g) is the type in common use for blacksmith shops, boiler houses, and roofs of small span. The "silk mill" roof shown in (h) was used by the Klots Throwing Co. in their silk mill at Carbondale, Pa. The spans of the three trusses are 48 ft. 8 in. each, with a clerestory of 13 ft. 9 in. in the monitor ventilators, which are glazed with glass 11 ft. high. The monitors face east and west, allowing a maximum amount of direct sunlight in the morning and evening, and none at midday. This roof has given very satisfactory results; however, it would seem to the author that it would be necessary to use shades, and that there would be shadows in the building. The trusses in this building are spaced 10 ft. 6 in. apart and support the plank sheathing which carries the roof, no purlins being used. The shafting to run the machinery in this building is placed in a sub-basement; a method much more economical and convenient than the common one of suspending the shafting from the trusses.

A roof truss with saw tooth skylights is shown in (l). The common type of saw tooth roof is shown in (m). The modified saw tooth roof proposed by the author in 1903 is shown in (n). The advantages of the modified saw tooth roof have already been

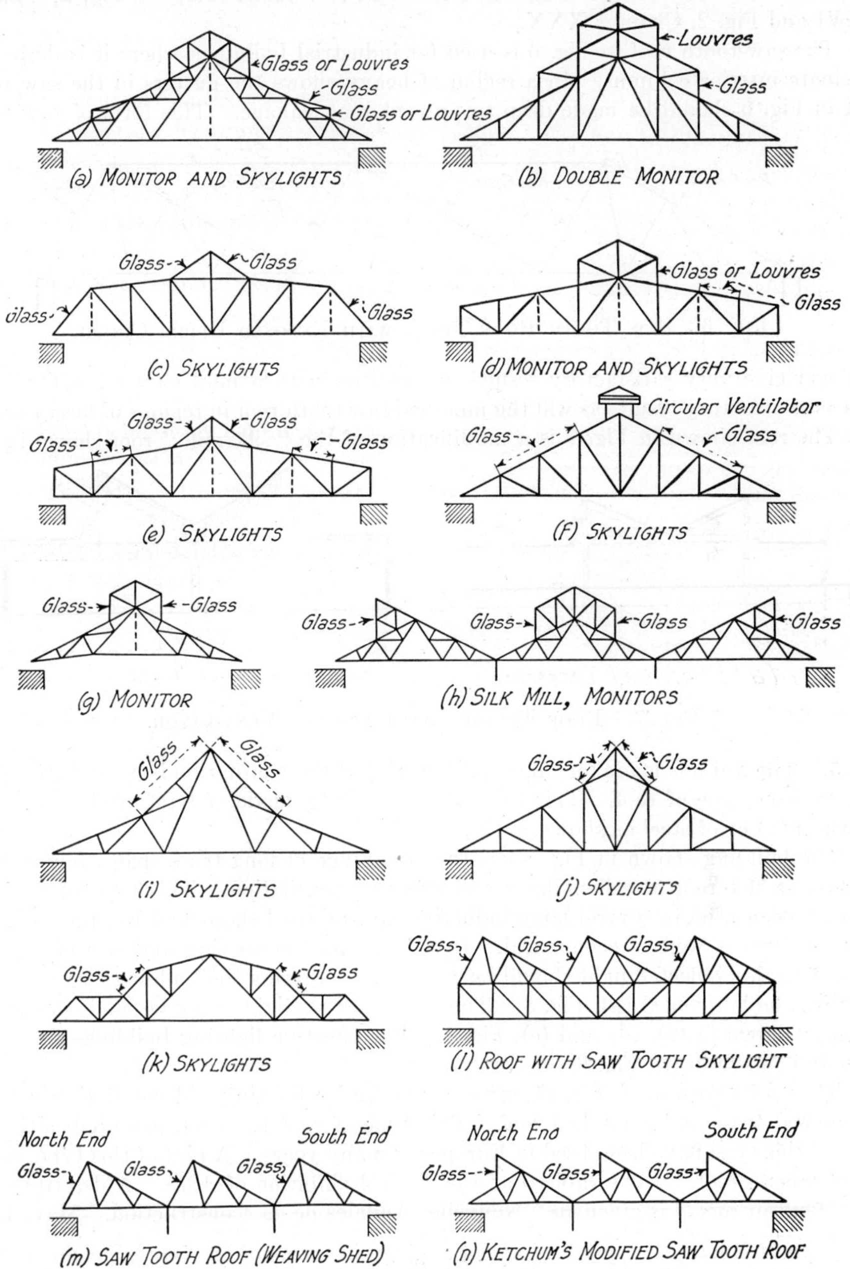

Fig. 5. Roof Trusses Showing Methods of Lighting and Ventilating.

pointed out. For a detail design of a modified saw tooth roof, see Fig. 2, Chapter XXVI and Fig. 2, Chapter XXX.

The saw tooth roof in Fig. 6 is used for industrial buildings where it is desired to eliminate interior columns. In a region of heavy snows the gutters in the saw tooth roof in Fig. 6 should be made deep to prevent roof leakage. This form of saw tooth

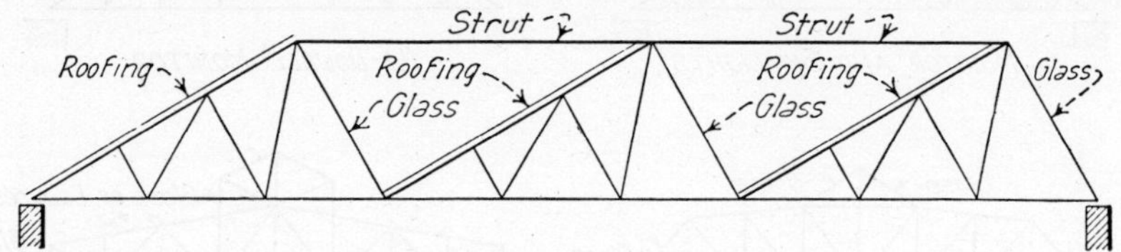

FIG. 6. SAW TOOTH ROOF TRUSS WITH EXPOSED UPPER CHORD.

roof will give very satisfactory results in localities with a mild climate, but will not give as satisfactory results as will the modified saw tooth roof in regions of heavy snows.

The roof shown in Fig. 7 is a modification of the "silk mill" roof shown in (h),

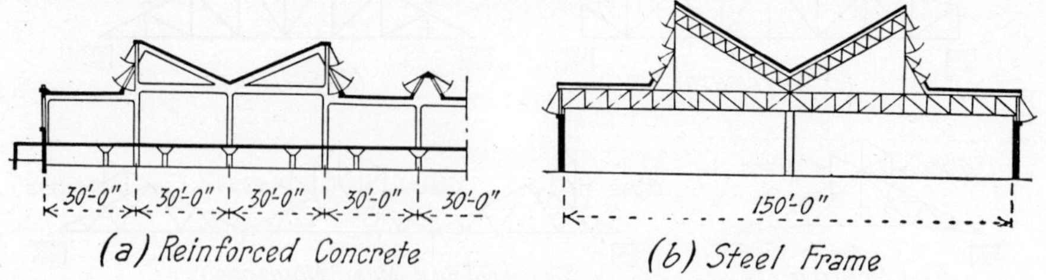

FIG. 7. ROOF TRUSSES WITH DOUBLE VENTILATOR.

Fig. 5. The claim is made for this type of roof that the ventilation is much better than in any other type of roof. This type of roof may be made of reinforced concrete as shown in (a) or of steel as shown in (b), Fig. 7.

The building shown in Fig. 8 has the advantage of long truss spans, few interior columns, a flat roof, excellent light and effective ventilation. This type of roof has recently been used in several large industrial and railroad shops and has proved to be very efficient as well as economical. In calculating the spacing and size of the saw tooth skylights reflected light should be assumed as entering the building at an angle of 45° with the horizontal (h), Fig. 8. The saw tooth skylights may be made of several types as shown in (c), (d) and (e), Fig. 8. For effective lighting buildings should be spaced as shown in (i), Fig. 8.

The roof shown in (i) Fig. 11, gives very effective lighting and ventilation with an economical truss and a pitched roof. This type of roof has been patented, although roofs of this type have been used in Europe for many years. A roof of this type, called the "Boileau roof" was exhibited at the Paris Exhibition of 1878. A description of the "Boileau roof" is given in "Nouvelles Annales de la Construction," May, 1877.

Pitch of Roof.—The pitch of a roof is given in terms of the center height divided by the span; for example a 60-ft. span truss with $\frac{1}{4}$ pitch will have a center height of 15 ft. The minimum pitch allowable in a roof will depend upon the character of the roof covering, and upon the kind of sheathing used. For corrugated steel laid directly on purlins, the pitch should preferably be not less than $\frac{1}{4}$ (6 in. in 12 in.), and the minimum pitch, unless the joints are cemented, not less than $\frac{1}{5}$. Slate and tile should not be used on a less slope than $\frac{1}{4}$ and preferably not less than $\frac{1}{3}$. The lap of the slate and tile should be greater for the less pitch. Tar and gravel should not be used on a roof with a greater pitch than 3 in. in 12 in. Asphalt is inclined to run and should not be used on a roof with a pitch of more than, say, 2 inches to the foot. If the laps are carefully made and cemented a gravel and tar or asphalt roof may be practically flat; a pitch of $\frac{3}{4}$ to 1 inch to the foot is, however, usually preferred. Tin may be used on a roof of any slope if the joints are properly soldered. Most of the patent composition roofings give better

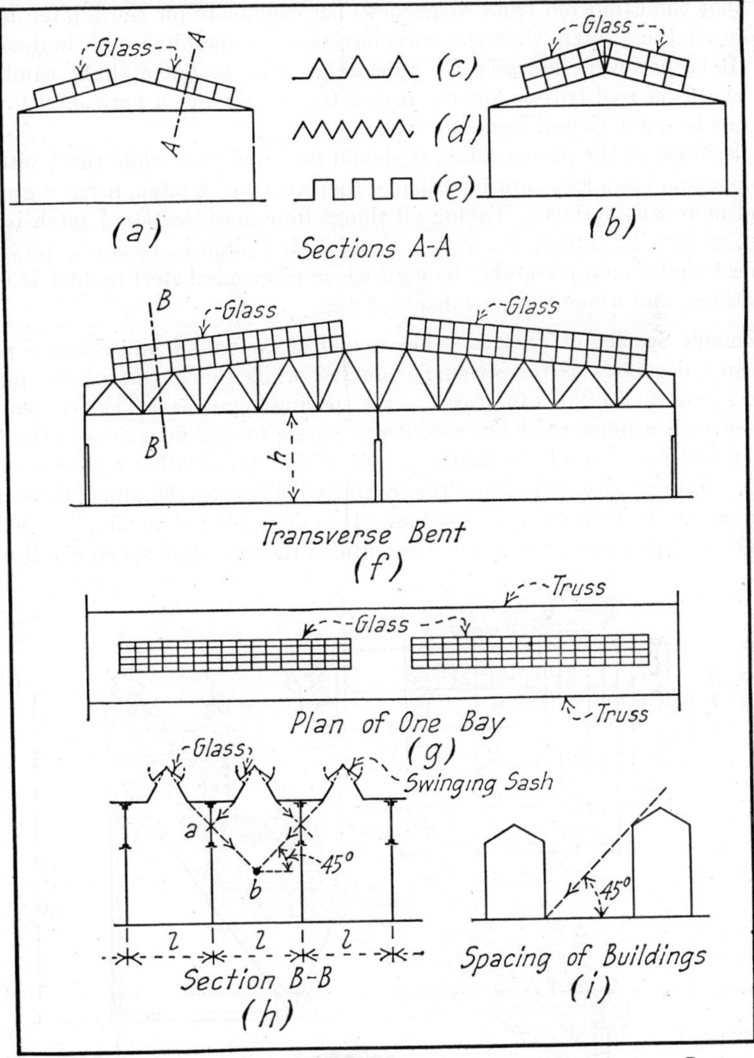

FIG. 8. DETAILS OF SAW TOOTH SKYLIGHTS AND METHODS OF LIGHTING.

satisfaction if laid on a roof with a pitch of $\frac{1}{5}$ to $\frac{1}{4}$. Shingles should not be used on a roof with a pitch less than $\frac{1}{4}$, and preferably the pitch should be $\frac{1}{3}$ to $\frac{1}{2}$.

Pitch of Truss.—There is very little difference in the weight of Fink trusses with horizontal bottom chords, in which the top chord has a pitch of $\frac{1}{5}$, $\frac{1}{4}$, or $\frac{1}{3}$. The difference in weight is quite noticeable, however, when the lower chord is cambered; the truss with the $\frac{1}{3}$ pitch being then more economical than either the $\frac{1}{5}$ or the $\frac{1}{4}$ pitch. Cambering the lower chord of a truss more than, say, 1/40 of the span adds considerable to the weight. For example the computed weights of a 60-ft. Fink truss with a horizontal lower chord, and a 60-ft. Fink truss with a camber of 3 ft. in the lower chord, showed that the cambered truss weighed 40 per cent more for the $\frac{1}{4}$ pitch and 15 per cent more for the $\frac{1}{3}$ pitch, than the truss having the same pitch with horizontal lower chord. It is, however, desirable for appearance sake to put a slight camber in the bottom chords of roof trusses, for the reason that to the eye a horizontal lower chord will appear to sag if viewed from one side.

In deciding on the proper pitch, it should be noted that while the $\frac{1}{3}$ pitch gives a better slope and has a less snow load than a roof with $\frac{1}{4}$ or $\frac{1}{5}$ pitch, it has a greater wind load and more roof surface. Taking all things into consideration $\frac{1}{4}$ pitch is probably the most economical pitch for a roof. A roof with $\frac{1}{3}$ pitch is, however, very nearly as economical, and should preferably be used where corrugated steel roofing is used without sheathing, and where the snow load is large.

Economic Spacing of Trusses.—The weight of the trusses and columns per square foot of area decreases as the spacing increases, while the weight of the purlins and girts per square foot of area increases as the spacing increases. The economic spacing of the trusses is a function of the weight per square foot of floor area of the truss, the purlins, the side girts and the columns, and also of the relative cost of each kind of material. For any given conditions the spacing which makes the sum of these quantities a minimum will be the economic spacing. It is desirable to use simple rolled sections for purlins and girts, and under these conditions the economic spacing will usually be

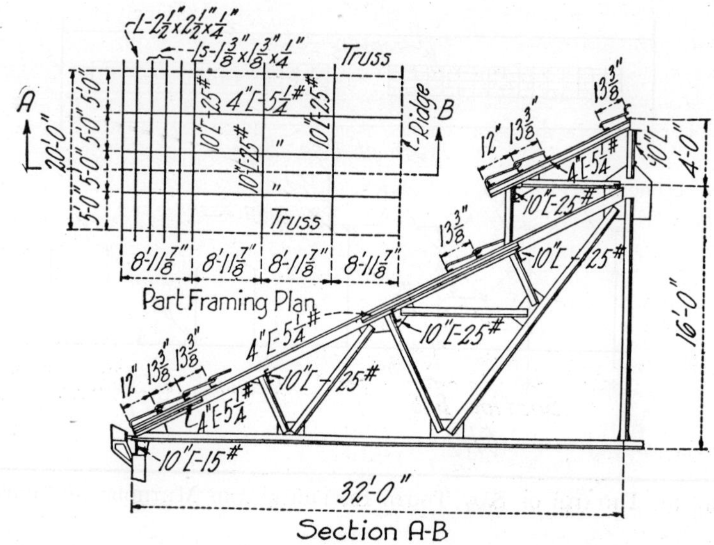

FIG. 9. STEEL ROOF COVERED WITH LUDOWICI TILE.

between 16 and 25 feet. The smaller value being about right for spans up to, say, 60 feet, designed for moderate loads, while the greater value is about right for long spans, designed for heavy loads.

Calculations of a series of simple Fink trusses resting on walls and having a uniform span of 60 feet, and different spacings gave the least weight per square foot of horizontal projection of the roof for a spacing of 18 feet, and the least weight of trusses and purlins combined for a spacing of 10 feet. The weight of trusses per square foot was, however, more for the 10-ft. spacing than for the 18-ft. spacing, so that the actual cost of the steel in the roof was a minimum for a spacing of about 16 feet; the shop cost of the trusses per pound being several times that of the purlins. Local conditions and requirements usually control the spacing of the trusses so that it is not necessary that we know the economic spacing very definitely.

The present (1921) practice is to space trusses 16-ft. centers up to a 50-ft. span, and 20-ft. centers for spans of 60 ft. to 100 ft.

For long spans the economic spacing can be increased by using rafters supported on heavy purlins, placed at greater distances than would be required if the roof were carried directly by the purlins. This method is frequently used in the design of train sheds and roofs of buildings where plank sheathing is used to support slate or tile coverings, or where the tiles are supported by angle sub-purlins spaced close together as shown in Fig. 9.

TRANSVERSE BENTS.—The proper cross-section for a mill building will depend upon the use to which the finished structure is to be put. A number of the common types of transverse bents are shown in Fig. 10. Transverse bents (a), (b), (d) and (h) are commonly used for boiler houses, shops and small train sheds. Where a traveling crane is desired, the crane girders are commonly suspended from the trusses in the bents referred to, although the crane may be made to span the entire building as in (h). Transverse bent (d) was used for a round house with excellent results. Transverse bents (f) and (g) are quite commonly used where it is desired that the main part of the building be open and be provided with a traveling crane that will sweep the building, while the side rooms are used for lighter tools and miscellaneous work. Transverse bent (c) may be used in the same way as (g), by supplying a traveling crane. Transverse bent (e) is very often used for shops.

Several types of transverse bents as used in industrial buildings in Germany are shown in Fig. 11. These designs make use of trussed columns, cantilever trusses and three-hinged arches. The types of structures shown in Fig. 11 may be adopted in designing industrial buildings with profit. The roof with transverse ventilators and skylights shown in (i) has been extensively used in the United States, and has many points of merit. The roof in (i) is known in Europe as the "Boileau roof," a model of which was exhibited at the Paris Exposition of 1878.

In the shops of the American Bridge Co. at Gary, Ind., shown in Fig. 12, the main section has roof trusses of 100-ft. span with a pitched roof; while the remainder of the building has saw tooth skylights carried on trusses with parallel chords. The interior columns are spaced 66 ft. 8 in. in one direction and 100 ft. in the other. This building has very effective lighting and efficient ventilation.

In the Railway Shops of the Central Ry. of Georgia, shown in Fig. 12, saw tooth skylights are carried on longitudinal trusses.

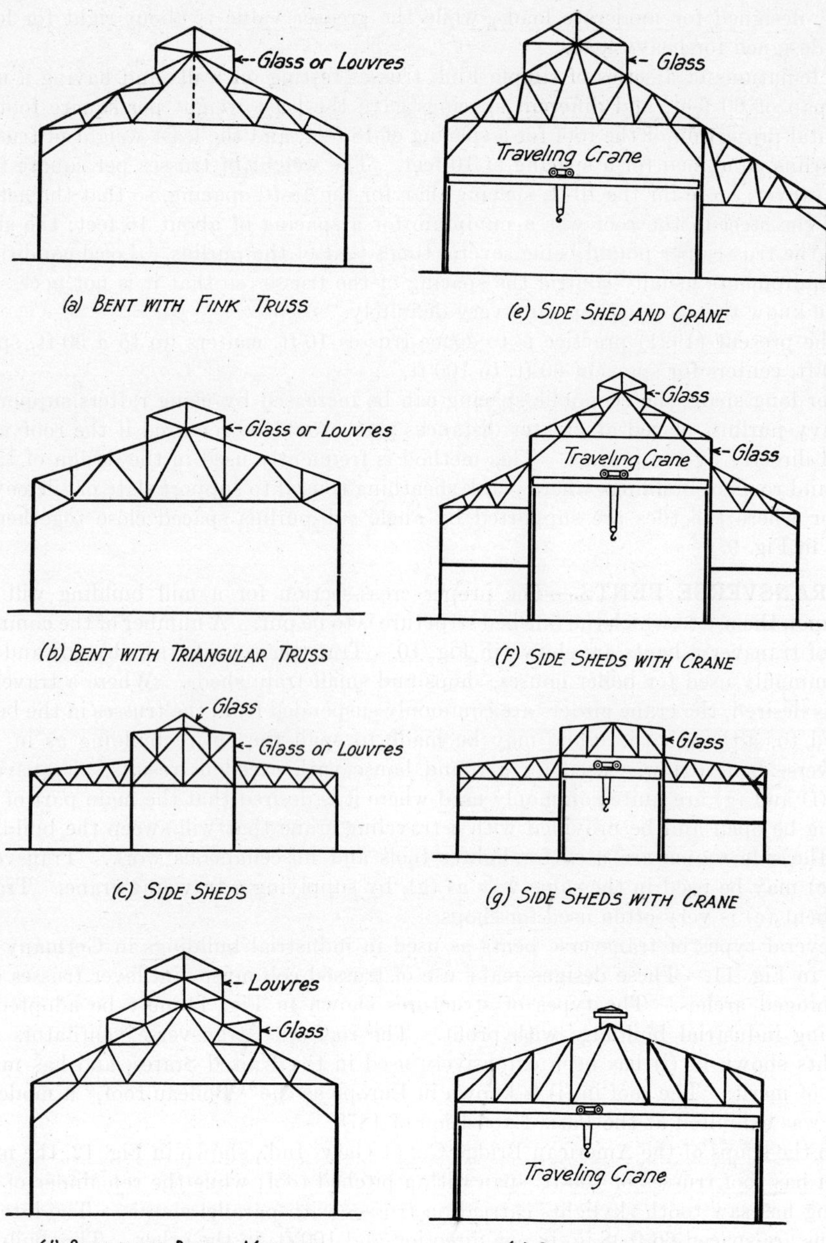

Fig. 10. Types of Transverse Bents.

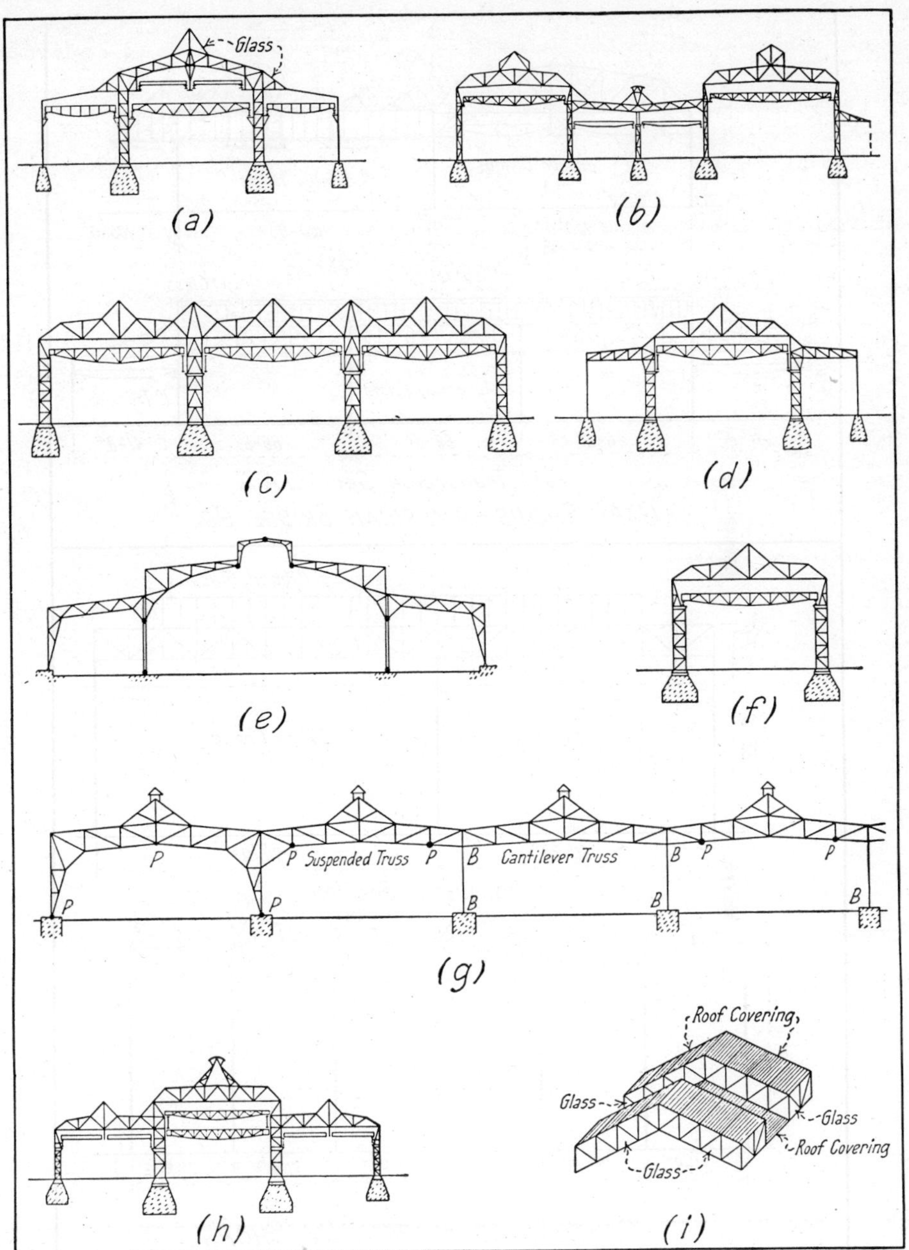

FIG. 11. DETAILS OF TYPES OF TRANSVERSE BENTS USED IN GERMANY.

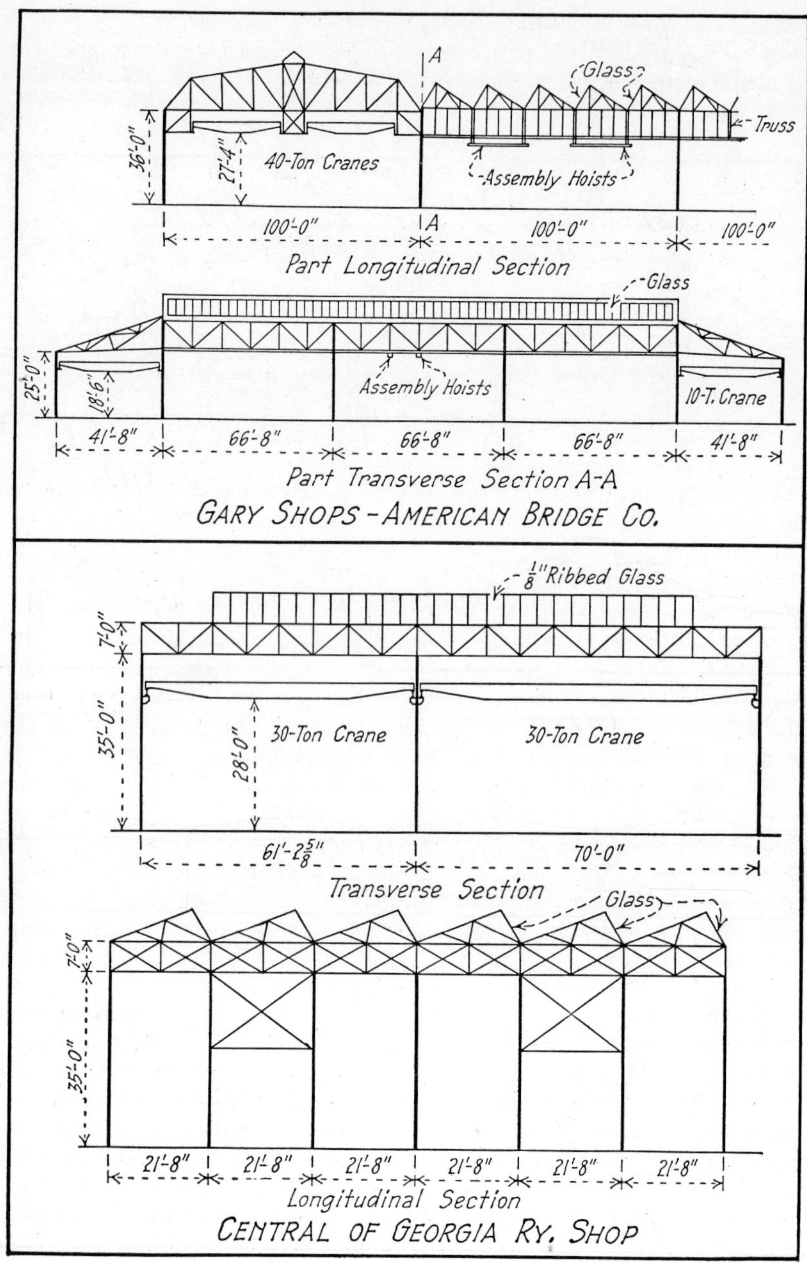

FIG. 12. PLANS OF SHOP BUILDINGS.

The cross-section of a locomotive shop for the Eastern Railway of France is shown in Fig. 13. The entire building is made of fireproof materials, the framework is of iron and the roof of sheet metal and glass. The building extends from east to west and has a saw tooth roof, with the shorter leg facing north, and glazed with crinkled

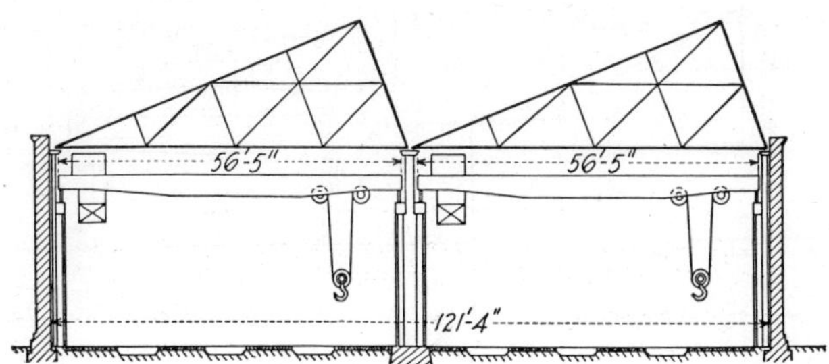

FIG. 13. LOCOMOTIVE SHOP, EASTERN RAILWAY OF FRANCE.

glass. The floor is made of treated oak cubes measuring 3.94 in. on the edge, set with the grain vertical, on a bed of river sand about 8 in. thick. The saw tooth roof is well suited to structures of this class.

The detail design of a transverse bent is given in Chapter XXXVIII.

Cross-sections of the locomotive shops of several of the leading railways are shown in Fig. 14, and the locomotive shops of the A. T. & S. F. R. R. are described in detail in Chapter XXVI. These buildings are built with self-supporting frames, and have brick walls built outside the framing or brick curtain walls built between the columns. The arrangement of the cranes, provisions for lighting and ventilating, and the main dimensions are shown in the cuts and need no explanation.

Riveted trusses are quite generally used in train sheds; a notable exception to this statement, however, being the trusses for the train shed of the C. R. I. & P., and L. S. & M. S. Railways in Chicago. The trusses in this structure have a length of span of 207 ft., a rise of the bottom chord of 40 ft. and a depth of truss at the center of 25 ft. The trusses are pin connected, the compression members being built-up channels and the tension members eye-bars. The building is described in detail in Engineering News, August 6, 1903.

ROOF ARCHES.—Roof arches are used where a large clear floor space is required as in coliseums, exposition buildings and train sheds, Fig. 15. The arches are braced in pairs and carry the roof covering. Arches may have one, two or three hinges, or may be made without hinges. Three-hinged arches are statically determinate structures, while the stresses in all other arches are statically indeterminate. Arches without hinges are used for domes. Three-hinged roof arches have been commonly used in America, although the two-hinged roof arch is more economical and has many advantages. Arches may have a horizontal tie as in the Chicago Stock Pavilion and the Government Building, or the horizontal reactions may be carried by the foundations as in the St. Louis Coliseum, Fig. 15. For the calculation of the stresses in three-hinged arches, see Chapter XI, and in two-hinged roof arches, see Chapter XX. The Government building is described in Chapter XXVI.

TRUSS DETAILS.—Riveted trusses are commonly used for mill buildings and similar structures. For ordinary loads, the upper and lower chords, and the main struts and ties are commonly made of two angles placed back to back, forming a T-section, the connections being made by means of plates. The upper chord should prefer-

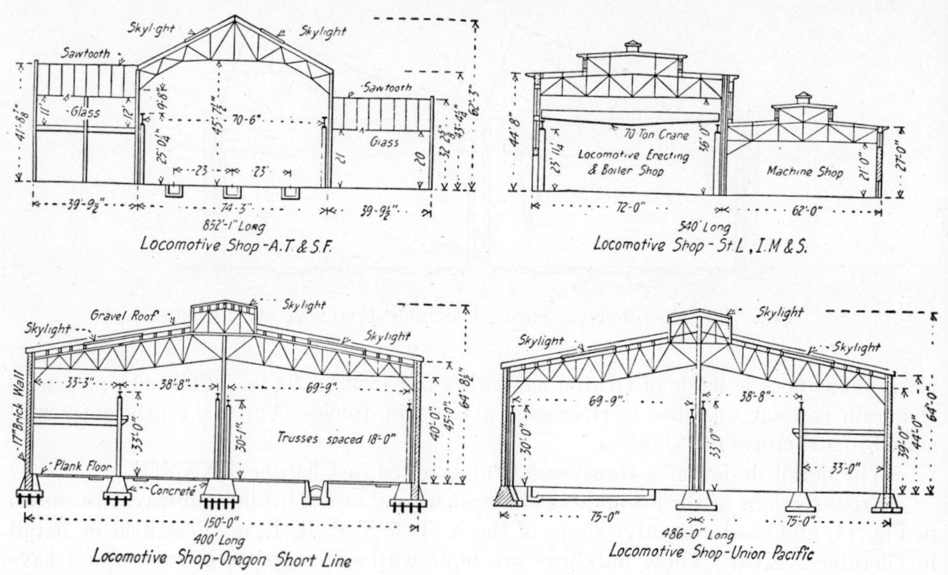

FIG. 14. CROSS-SECTIONS OF RAILWAY SHOPS.

ably be made of unequal legged angles with the long legs turned out. Sub-struts and ties are usually made of one angle. Flats should not be used. Where a truss member is made of two angles placed back to back, the angles should always be riveted together at intervals of 2 to 4 ft.

Trusses that carry heavy loads or that support a traveling crane or hoist, are very often made with a lower chord composed of two channels placed back to back and laced or battened, and are sometimes made with channel chord sections throughout, see Fig. 14, Chapter XXVI.

When the purlins are not placed at the panel points of the truss the upper chord must be designed for flexure as well as for direct stress. The section in most common use for the upper chord, where the purlins are not placed at the panel points, is one composed of two angles and a plate as shown in (d), Fig. 3, Chapter XXVII.

Details of end connections of trusses are shown in Fig. 16. The neutral axes of the members meeting at any joint should intersect. With angle truss members the ideal condition is nearly met when the rivet gage lines meet as shown in (a), (b), (c), (j), (k), and (l), Fig. 16. The types of end connections shown in (a), (b) and (c) should preferably be used for column connections in place of the end truss connections shown in (g), (h) and (i). Column connections may be made as shown. The connection shown in (g) is the most effective and should preferably be used. Expansion ends of trusses may be carried on a steel sliding plate, or on rollers, or on a cast rocker. The

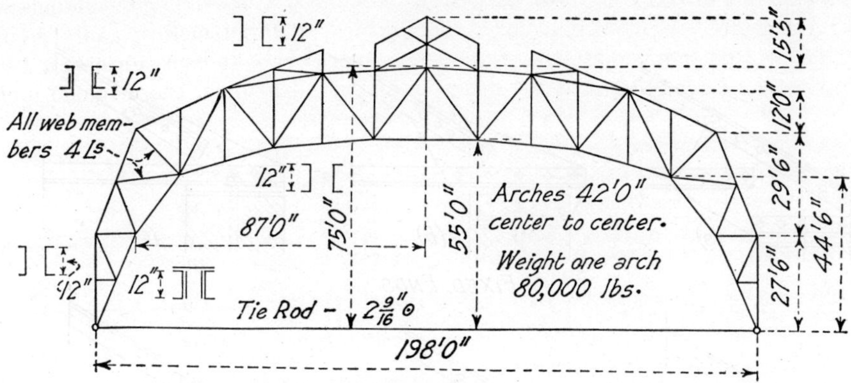

TWO HINGED ARCH, CHICAGO LIVE STOCK PAVILION

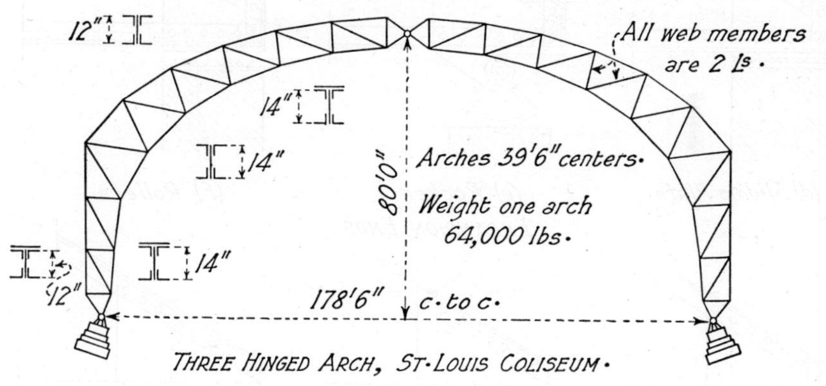

THREE HINGED ARCH, ST. LOUIS COLISEUM.

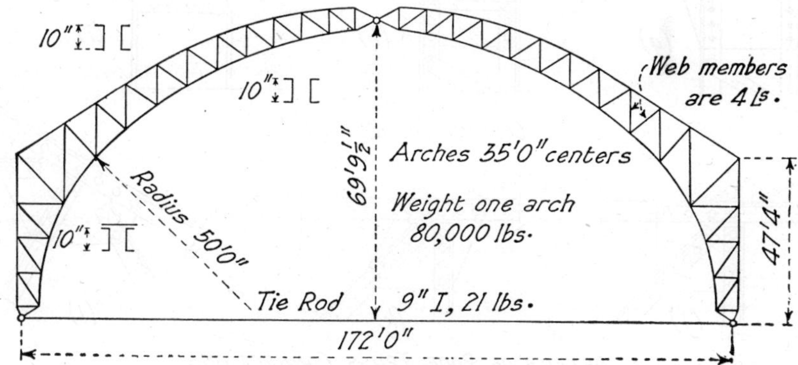

THREE HINGED ARCH, GOVERNMENT BUILDING ST. LOUIS, MO.

FIG. 15. ROOF ARCHES.

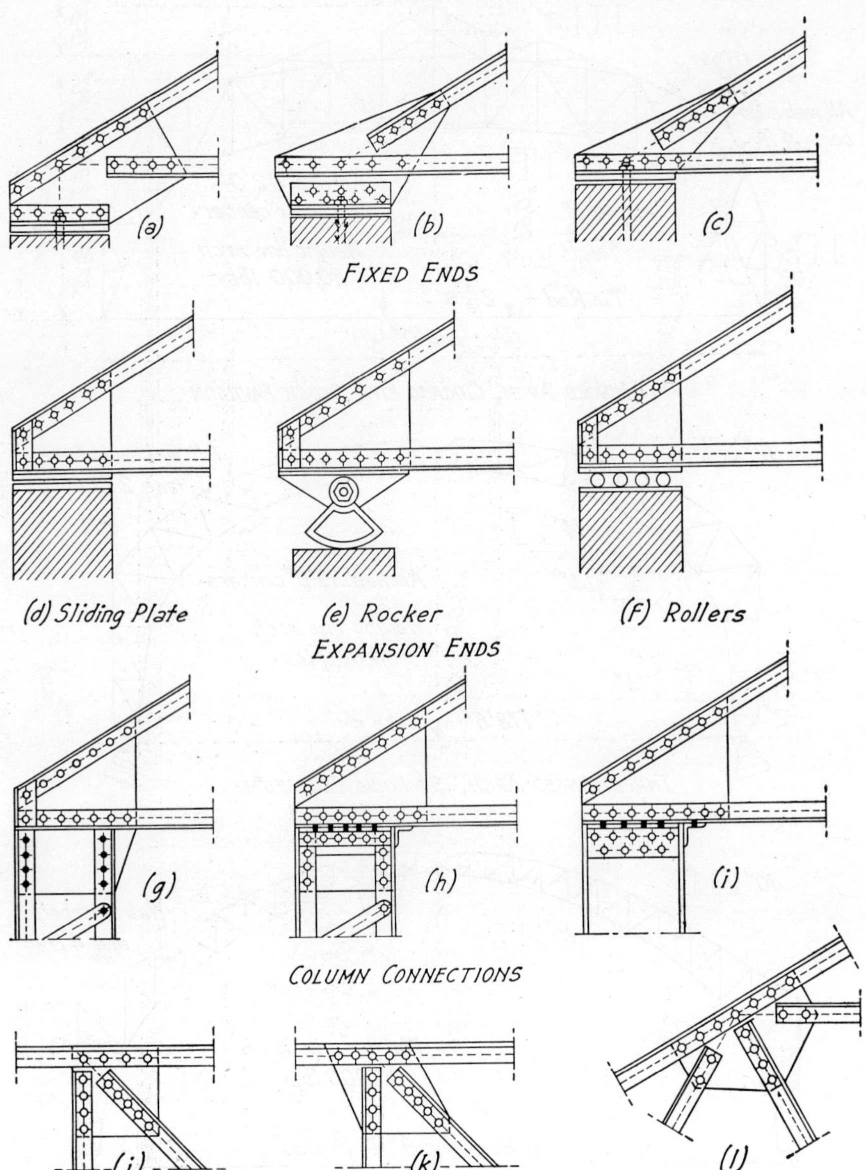

FIG. 16. DETAILS OF TRUSS CONNECTIONS AND JOINTS.

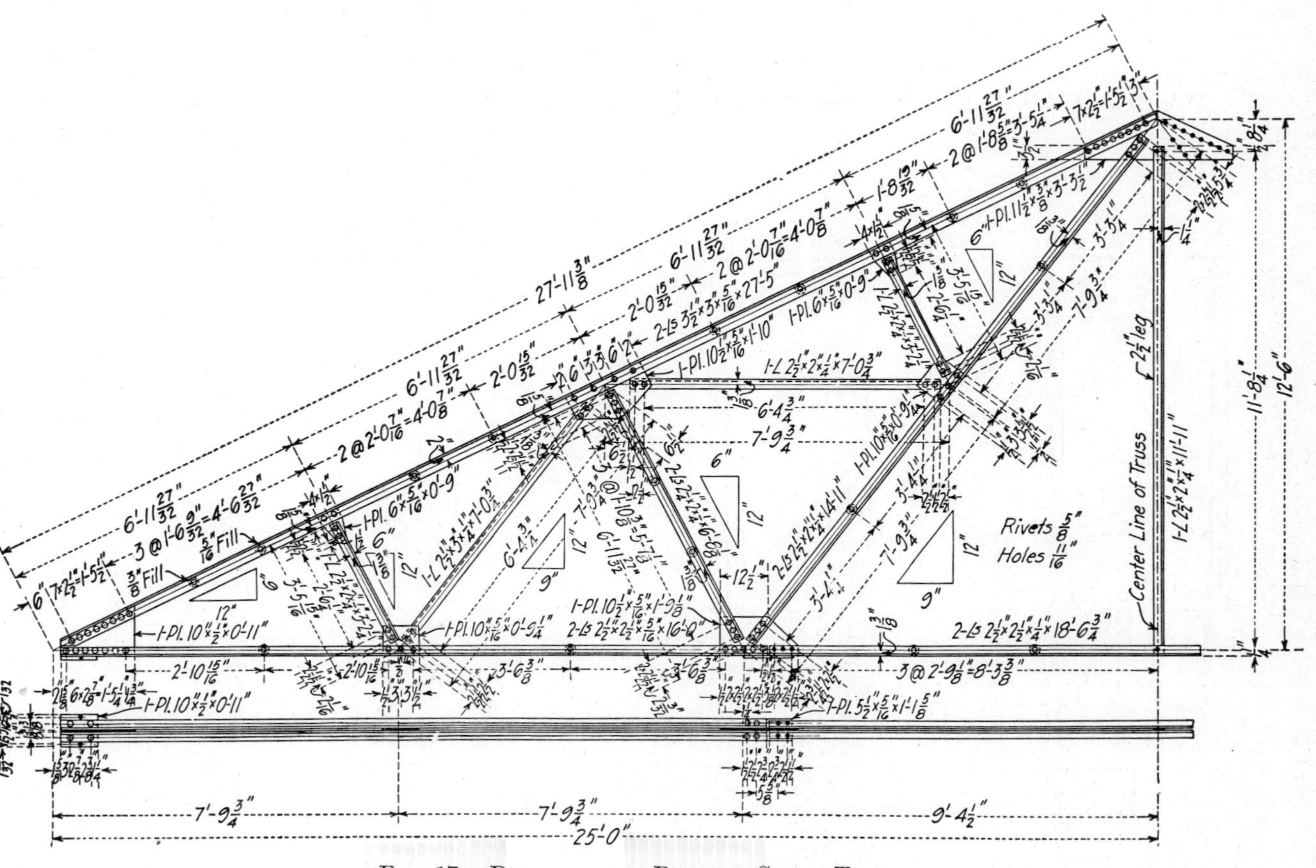

Fig. 17 Details of a Riveted Steel Truss.

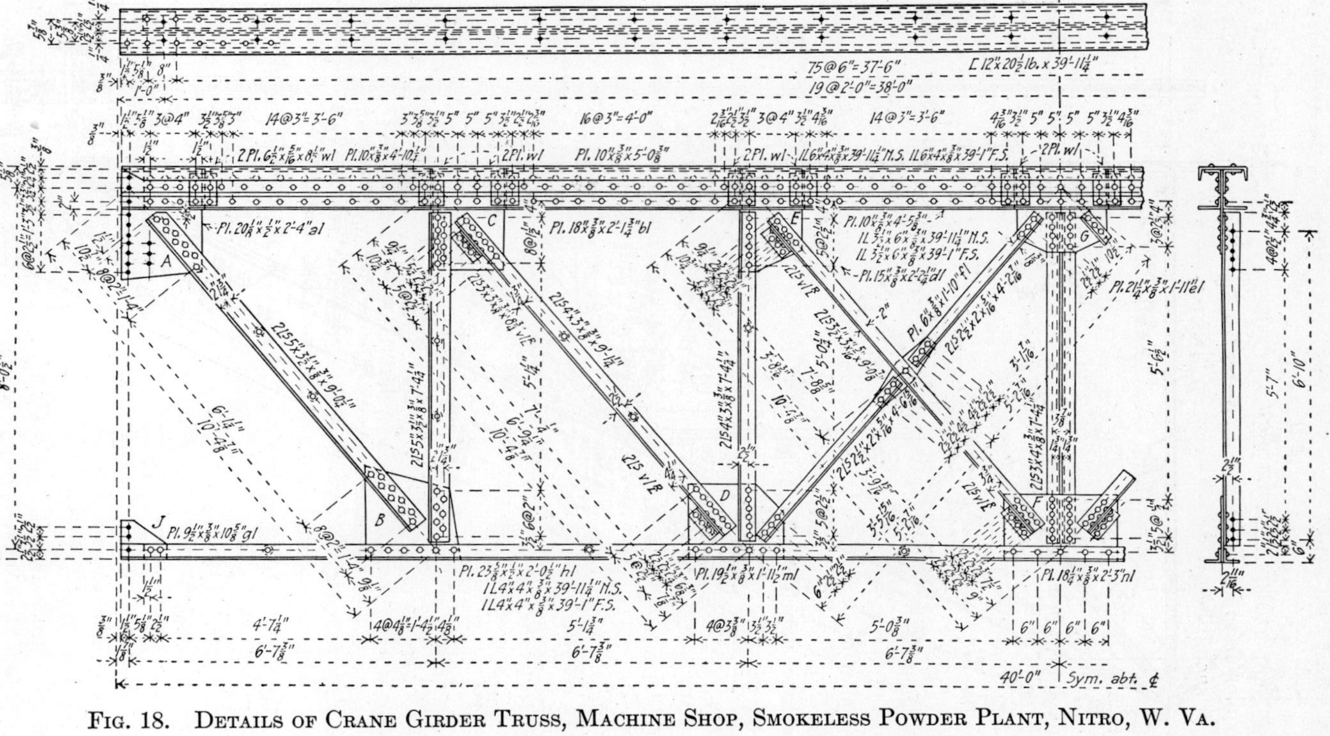

FIG. 18. DETAILS OF CRANE GIRDER TRUSS, MACHINE SHOP, SMOKELESS POWDER PLANT, NITRO, W. VA.

cast rocker is the most satisfactory and effective solution for the expansion end of a roof truss.

Trusses supported directly on masonry walls have one end supported on sliding plates for spans up to about 70 ft.; for greater lengths of span one end should be placed on rollers, or should be carried on a rocker. Trusses for mill buildings should be made with riveted rather than with pin connections, on account of the greater rigidity of the riveted structure. The complete shop drawings of a truss for the machine shop at the University of Illinois are shown in Fig. 17. This truss is more completely detailed than is customary in most bridge shops. The practice in many shops is to sketch the truss, giving main dimensions, number of rivets and lengths of members, and depending on the templet maker for the rest. In Fig. 17 the rivet gage lines are taken as the center lines. This is the most common practice, although many use one leg of the angle as the center line in secondary members. The latter method has the advantage of reducing the length of connection plates without introducing secondary stresses that are liable to be troublesome.

The detail design of a roof truss is given in Chapter XXXVI.

The detail shop drawings of the crane girder truss used in the machine shop built at the U. S. Smokeless Powder Plant, Nitro, W. Va., is shown in Fig. 18. The plans for this machine shop are shown in Fig. 10, Chapter XXVI.

COLUMNS.—The common forms of columns used in mill buildings are shown in Fig. 19. For side columns where the loads are not excessive, column (g) composed of four angles and a web plate is probably the best. In this column a large radius of gyration about an axis at right angles to the direction of the wind is obtained with a small amount of metal. The web plate should be designed to take the shear. The I beam column (i) makes a good side column where proper connections are made, and is commonly used for end columns (see Fig. 1). The best corner column is made of an equal legged angle with 5-, 6- or 8-in. legs, (j) Fig. 19. The column made of 4 angles laced as shown in (h), was formerly much used for side columns, but its use is no longer good practice.

Columns made of two channels laced, or two channels and two plates, are used where moderately heavy loads are to be carried. Channel column (a), with channels turned back to back and laced, is the form most commonly used; column (b), with the backs of the channels turned out and laced, gives a better chance to make connections and can be made to enter an opening without chipping the legs of the channel; column (c) is a closed section and is seldom used on that account. The cost of the shop work on column (b) was formerly considerably more than for column (a), for the reason that it was impossible to use a power riveter for driving all the rivets. A pneumatic riveter is now made, however, that will drive all the rivets in column (b), and the shop cost for columns (a) and (b) are practically the same.

Where very heavy loads are to be carried, columns (d), (e) or (f) are often used. Column (d), composed of two channels and one I beam, is a very economical column and is quite often used as a substitute for the Z-bar column shown in (e), for the reason that it can be built-up out of the material that is in stock or that can be easily obtained. Connections for beams are easily and effectively made with either columns (d) or (e). The H-column in (k) or the built-up H-column in (l) make excellent columns for heavy loads. The Larimer column (m) is a patented column manufactured by Jones &

Laughlins. The Gray column (n) is a patented column and is but little used. Columns made of four angles box-laced, are used where extremely light loads are carried by very long columns. The shop cost of column (o) is somewhat less than that of column (p), although with small angles there is no difficulty in riveting (p) with a machine riveter. Column (q) is a very poorly designed colum , for the reason that the radius of gyration is very small for the area of a cross-section of the column. Columns made of two angles "starred" and fastened at intervals of two or three feet by means of batten plates, are quite frequently used for light loads.

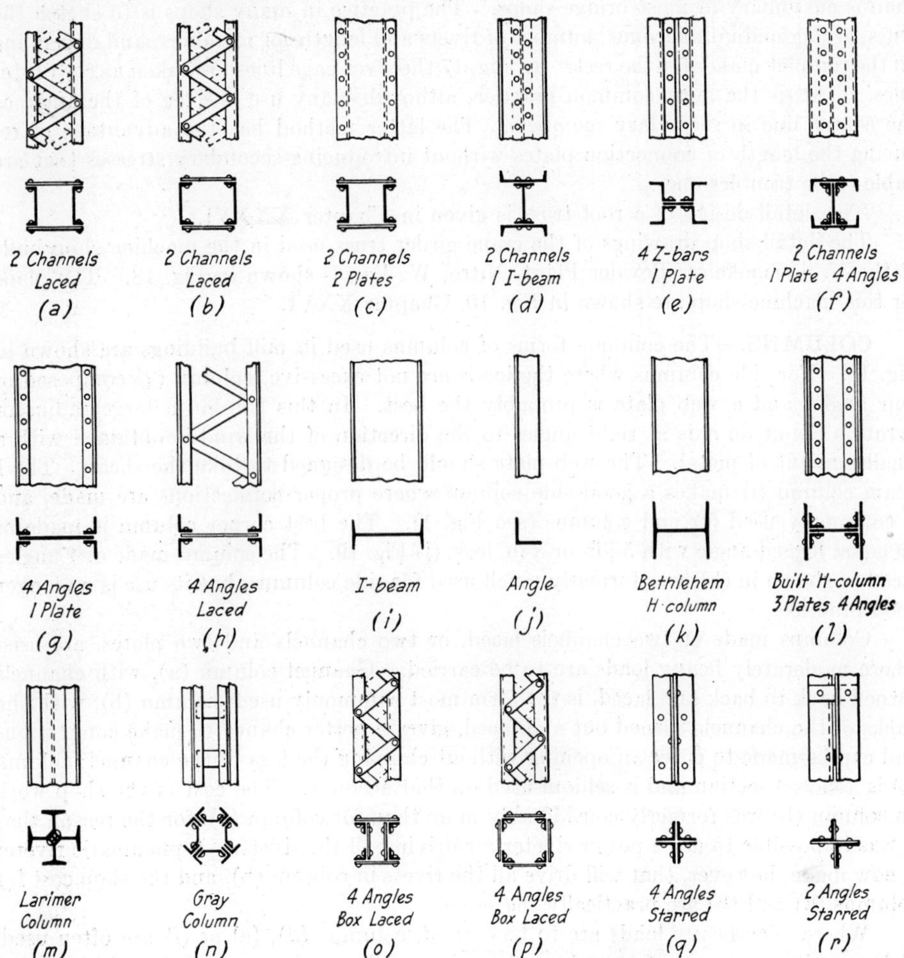

FIG. 19. TYPES OF STEEL MILL BUILDING COLUMNS.

For additional details of column sections, see Fig. 2, Fig. 4, and Fig. 5, Chapter XXVII.

Column Details.—Shop details of a 4-angle column are shown in (a), Fig. 20. This

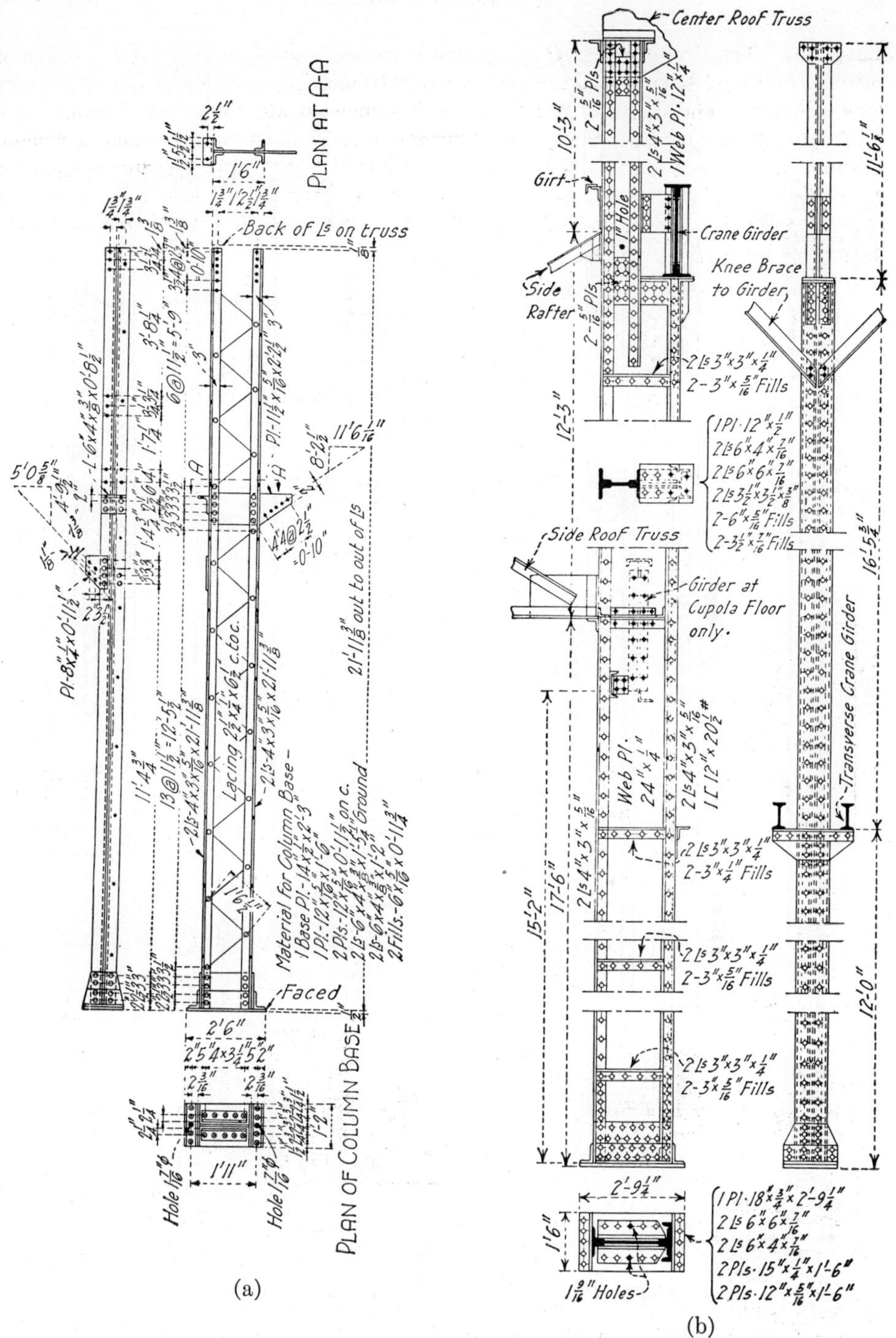

(a)

(b)

Fig. 20. Details of Mill Building Columns.

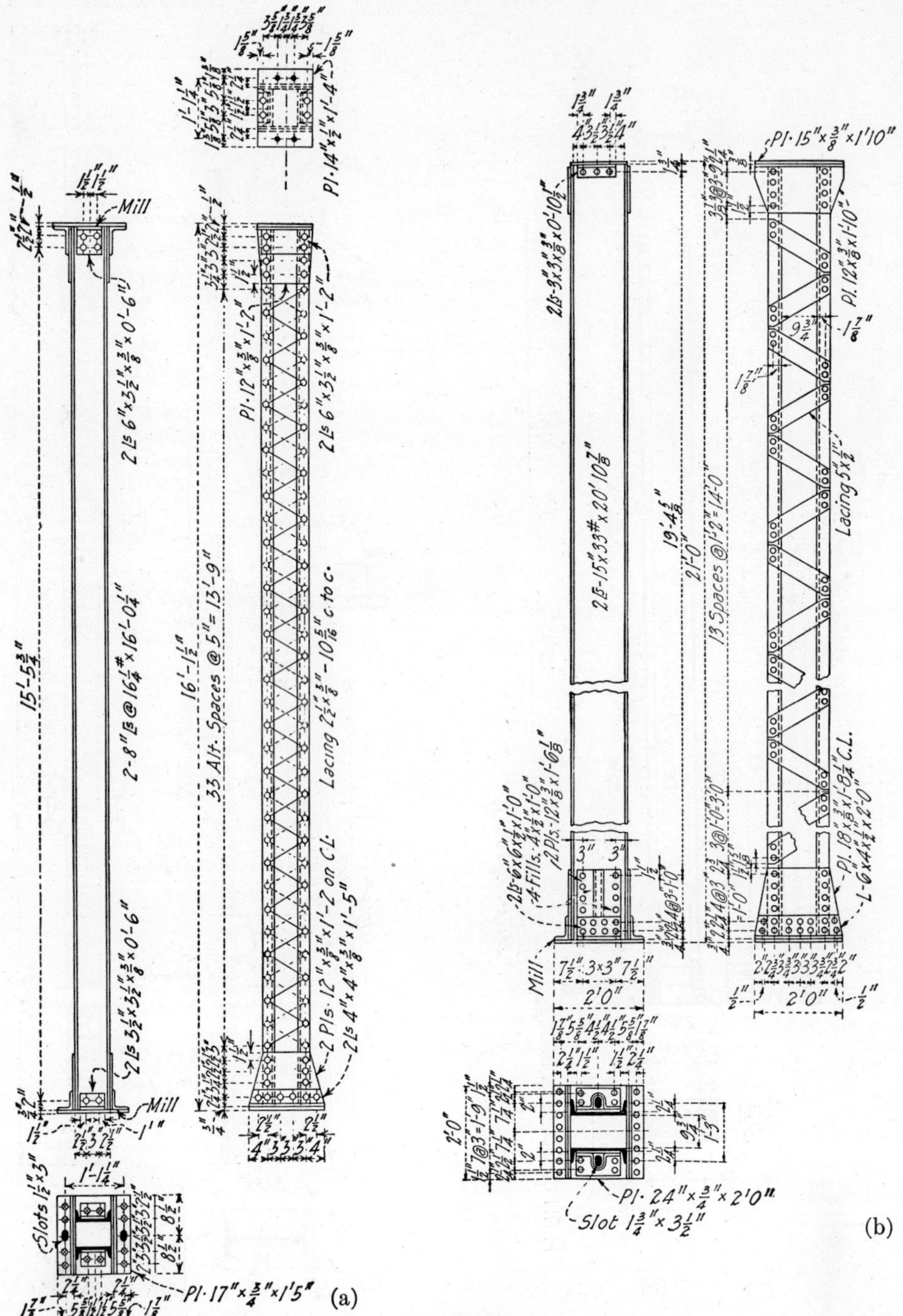

FIG. 21. DETAILS OF MILL BUILDING COLUMNS.

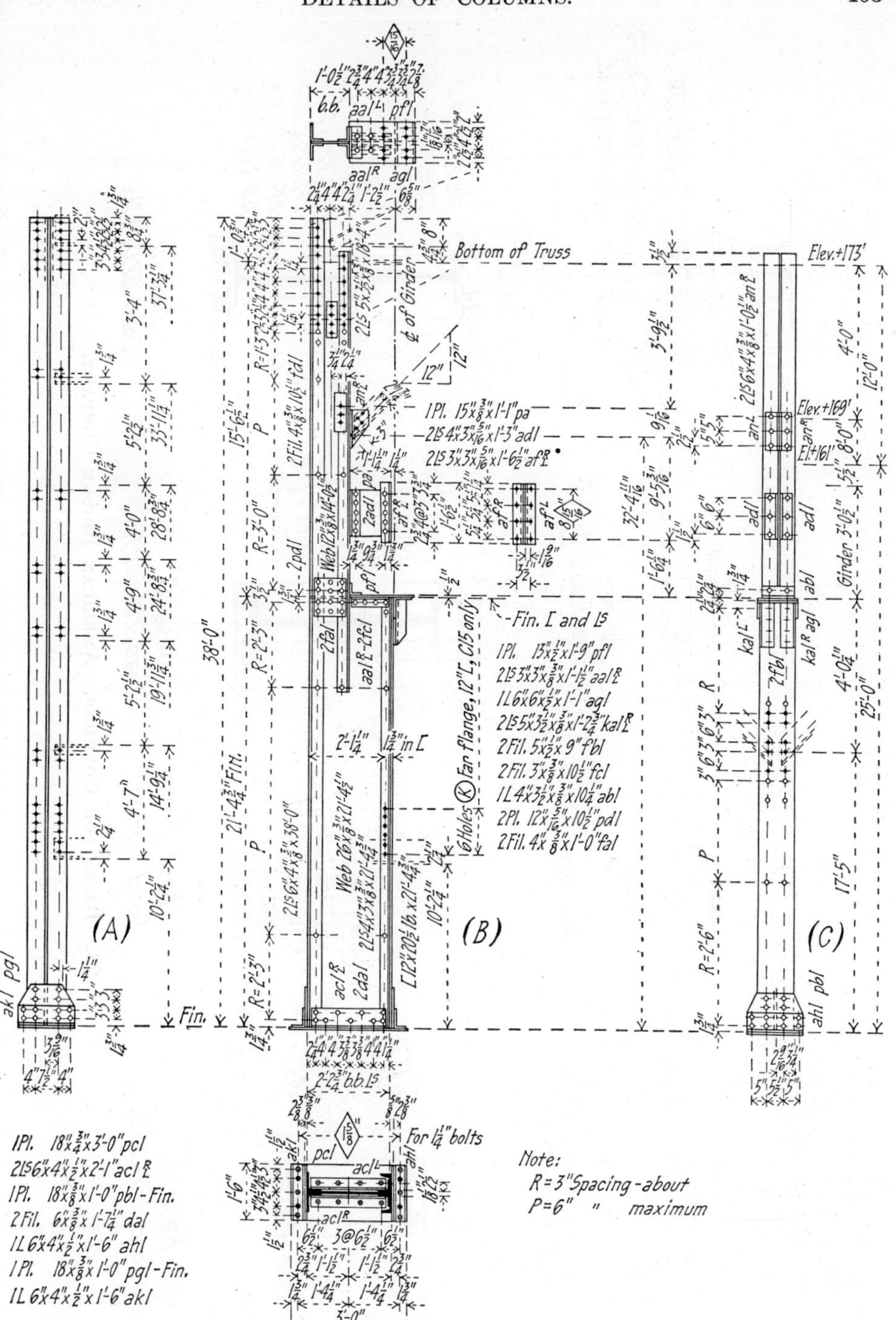

FIG. 22. DETAILS OF COLUMN. AMERICAN BRIDGE COMPANY.

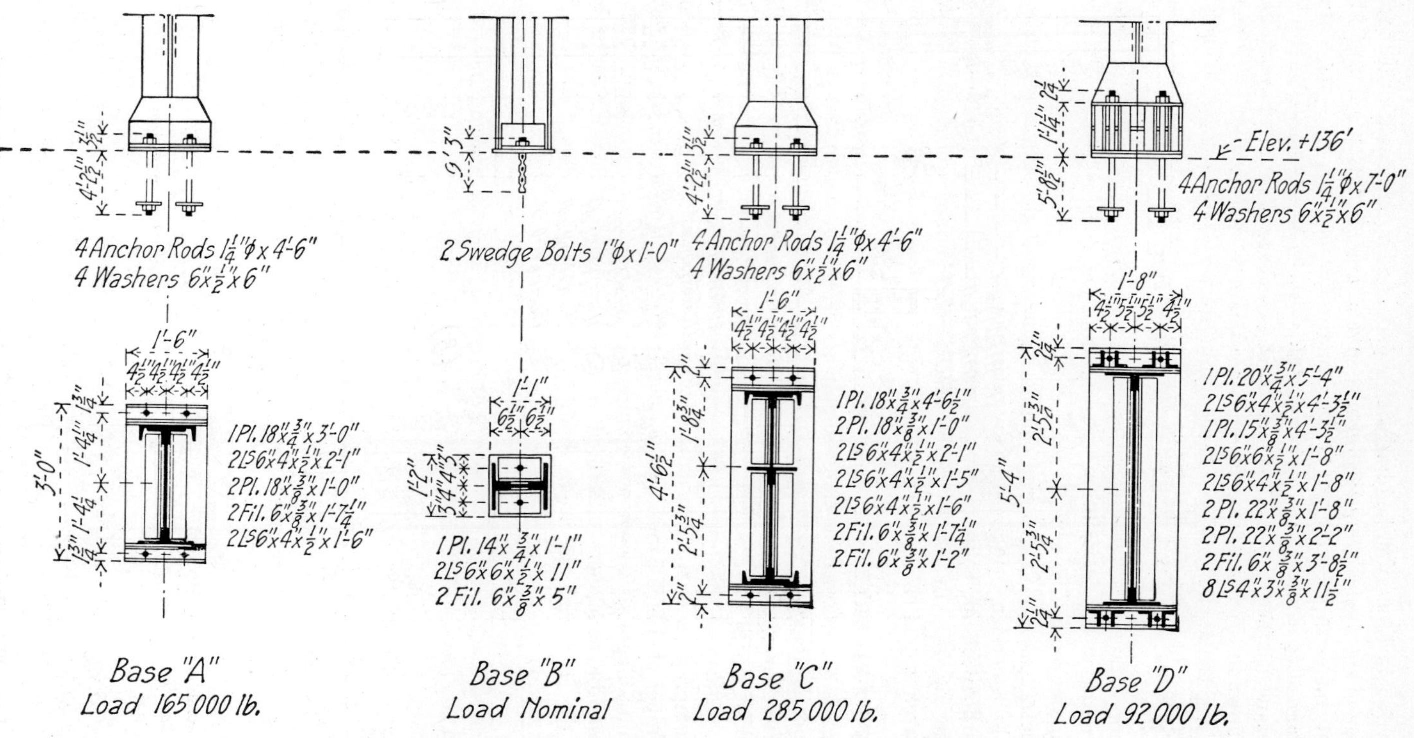

FIG. 23. BASES FOR COLUMNS. AMERICAN BRIDGE COMPANY.

column was designed for a mill building with a span of 60 ft., trusses spaced 16 ft. apart. The long legs of the angles are placed out, to give a larger radius of gyration about an axis at right angles to the direction of the wind. The details of a 4-angle and plate column, designed to carry a crane girder as well as the roof, are shown in (b), Fig. 20.

The details of a heavy column composed of two channels placed back to back and laced, are shown in (b) Fig. 21; the lacing is heavy and is well riveted. The bent plate connections for the anchor bolts on this column are very satisfactory. This is one of the columns used in the A. T. & S. F. R. R. shops at Topeka, Kas., to carry the crane girders.

The shop details of a light channel column are shown in (a), Fig. 21. The single lacing alternates on the two sides of the column. The various details of the columns can be seen, and require no explanation.

Shop details of a crane and roof column made of 4 angles and a web plate, as designed by the American Bridge Company, are shown in Fig. 22.

Standard details for column bases as designed by the American Bridge Company are shown in Fig. 23. Base " A " is the base for the column in Fig. 22. Bases " C " and " D " are for long columns carrying heavy crane loads as well as a roof load.

STRUTS AND BRACING.—Eave struts are very commonly made of four angles laced, made in the same way as the 4-angle posts, Fig. 20. Eave struts made of single channels and an angle, Fig. 7, Chapter XXVII, are more economical, and are equally as good as the laced struts for most cases. End rafters are commonly made of channels. The sides, ends, upper and lower chords are commonly braced as shown in Fig. 1. The bracing in the plane of the lower chords should preferably be made of members capable of taking compression as well as tension. The diagonal bracing in the plane of sides, ends, and upper chords is commonly composed of rods. Initial tension should always be thrown into diagonal rods by screwing up the turnbuckles or adjustable ends. Stiff bracing should be made short, and should be brought into position for riveting by using drift pins; to accomplish this there should be not less than three rivet holes in each lateral connection.

Where rod bracing in the ends and sides of buildings interferes with windows and doors, or where the building is to be left open, portal bracing is used as shown in Fig. 9 and Fig. 10, Chapter XXVI, or in Fig. 4, Chapter XXXVIII. The bents may be braced in pairs, or the portal bracing may be made continuous. Stiff bracing is often placed between the trusses in the plane of the center of the building and materially stiffens the structure, see Fig. 1, and Fig. 14, Chapter XXVI.

PURLINS AND GIRTS.—Purlins are made of channels, angles, Z-bars and I beams, where simple shapes are used. Channel and angle purlins should be fastened by means of angle lugs as shown in Fig. 24. I-beam purlins are very often fastened as shown in Fig. 24, or in the A. T. & S. F. R. R. shops, Fig. 14, Chapter XXVI. Z-bar purlins are bolted directly to the upper chords of the trusses. The channel purlin is the most economical, and the I-beam purlin is the most rigid. Girts are made of channels, angles, and Z-bars, and are fastened in the same manner as purlins.

Where the columns and trusses are placed so far apart that the use of simple rolled shapes is no longer economical, purlins and girts are trussed.

Details of the different types of steel purlin connections are shown in Fig. 24.

The connections of purlins and girts may be bolted to the lug angles. The lug angles are usually riveted in the shop to the truss or to the column.

The minimum sizes of channel purlins for different spans and purlin spaces, designed for a normal load of 30 lb., 40 lb., and 50 lb. per sq. ft. of roof surface and for 16,000 lb. per sq. in. are given in Table I, Table II and Table III, respectively. These purlins will carry 15 lb., 20 lb., and 25 lb., respectively, as a normal load, and 15 lb., 20 lb., and 25 lb. per sq. ft. of horizontal projection, respectively, with a maximum allowable fiber stress of 20,000 lb. per sq. in. when the stresses are calculated as described in Chapter XII, see § 44 and § 57, Specifications in Appendix I.

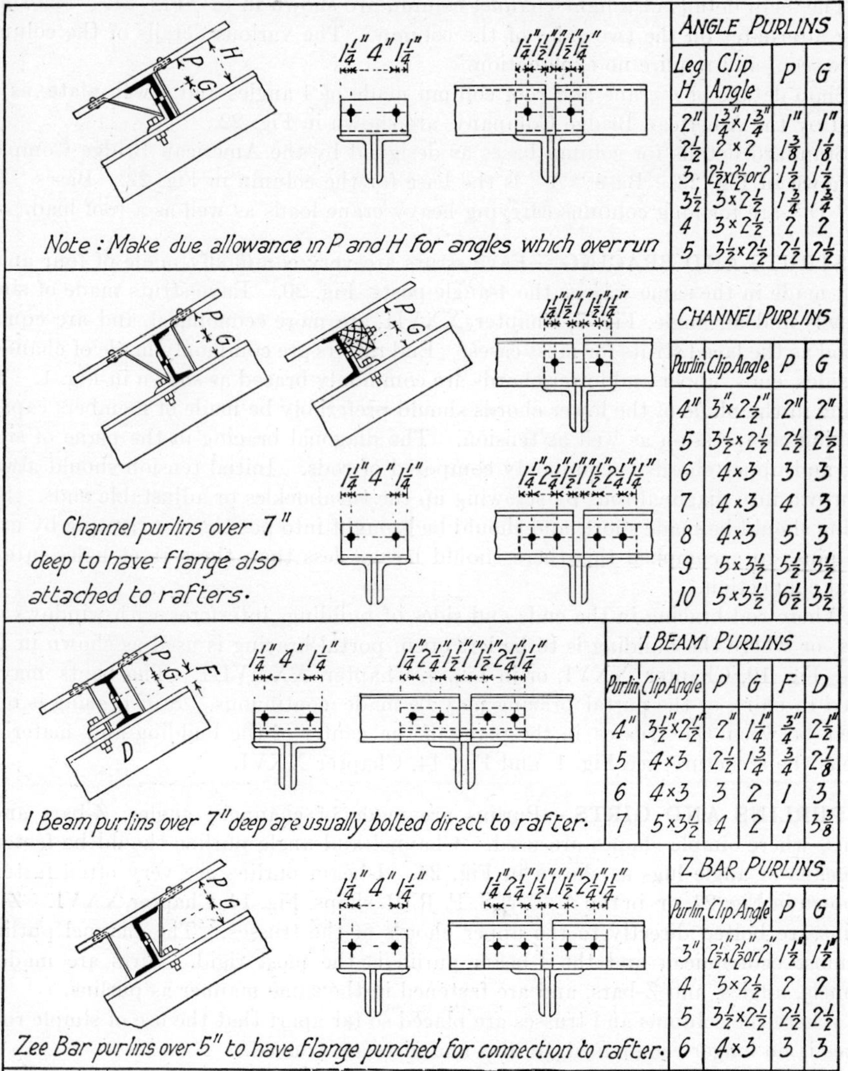

ANGLE PURLINS
Leg H | Clip Angle | P | G
2" | 1¾x1¾" | 1" | 1"
2½ | 2x2 | 1⅜ | 1⅛
3 | 2½x2½ or 2 | 1½ | 1½
3½ | 3x2½ | 1¾ | 1¾
4 | 3x2½ | 2 | 2
5 | 3½x2½ | 2½ | 2½
Note: Make due allowance in P and H for angles which overrun
CHANNEL PURLINS
Purlin | Clip Angle | P | G
4" | 3"x2½" | 2" | 2"
5 | 3½x2½ | 2½ | 2½
6 | 4x3 | 3 | 3
7 | 4x3 | 4 | 3
8 | 4x3 | 5 | 3
9 | 5x3½ | 5½ | 3½
10 | 5x3½ | 6½ | 3½
Channel purlins over 7" deep to have flange also attached to rafters.
I BEAM PURLINS
Purlin | Clip Angle | P | G | F | D
4" | 3½"x2½" | 2" | 1¼" | ¾" | 2½"
5 | 4x3 | 2½ | 1¾ | ¾ | 2⅞
6 | 4x3 | 3 | 2 | 1 | 3
7 | 5x3½ | 4 | 2 | 1 | 3⅜
I Beam purlins over 7" deep are usually bolted direct to rafter.
Z BAR PURLINS
Purlin | Clip Angle | P | G
3" | 2½"x2½" or 2" | 1½" | 1½"
4 | 3x2½ | 2 | 2
5 | 3½x2½ | 2½ | 2½
6 | 4x3 | 3 | 3
Zee Bar purlins over 5" to have flange punched for connection to rafter.

FIG. 24. DETAILS OF STEEL PURLINS.

Sag Rods.—The purlins in Table I were supported by one sag rod for spans of 20 ft. and under, and by two sag rods for spans of over 20 ft. The purlins in Table II and Table III are supported by one sag rod for spans of 14 ft. or under, and by two sag rods placed at the third points of the span for spans of more than 14 ft. Details of roof framing are given in Fig. 25.

The specifications for sag rods in Appendix I are as follows:—

Sag Rods.—With a steel corrugated roof one sag rod, at the center, shall be used for purlin spans of 20 ft. or less, and two sag rods, spaced at the third points, for purlin spans of more than 20 ft. With clay tile, cement tile, slate, gypsum or similar roofs, one sag rod shall be used for purlin spans of 14 ft. or less, and two sag rods spaced at the third points for spans of more than 14 ft. Where one sag rod is used, the sag rod on each side of the roof in any panel shall be rigidly connected through the ridge purlins. Where two sag rods are used in any panel, each sag rod shall be rigidly connected with the peak of the nearest truss by means of a diagonal sag rod in the upper purlin space. Sag rods need not be used in roofs with a pitch of 3 in. in 12 in., or less. With corrugated steel siding, one sag rod shall be used for all girt spacings of 20 ft. or less, and two sag rods spaced at third points for girt spacings of more than 20 ft.

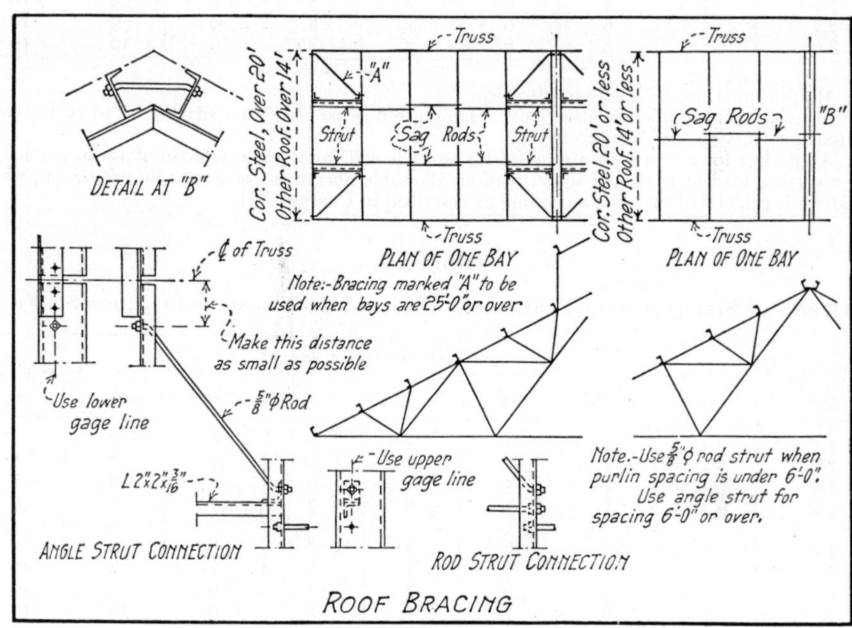

FIG. 25. DETAILS OF ROOF FRAMING.

Sag rods shall be designed to carry the component of the dead load of the purlins and roof covering and the maximum snow load parallel to the roof surface, with a unit stress of 16,000 lb. per sq. in. on net section. Sag rods for the sides shall be designed to carry the weight of the side framing and covering with the same allowable unit stresses as for sag rods for purlins. If sag rods are not upset, the net section shall be taken as the section having a diameter 1/16 in. less than the diameter of the root of the thread. The minimum size of sag rods shall have a diameter of ½ in. if the ends are upset, or ⅝ in. if the ends are not upset.

TABLE I.

Depths of Steel Channel Purlins for a Normal Roof Load of 30 lb. per Sq. Ft. Corrugated Steel Roof.

Purlin Spacing Ft.	Truss Spacing, or Bay, Ft.							
	10	12	14	16	18	20	22	24
2.5	4	4	5*	5*	6*	6*	7*	8*
3.0	4	4	5*	5	6*	6	7*	8*
3.5	4	4	5	5	6	6	7	8*
4.0	4	4	5	5	6	7	7	8
4.5	4	4	5	6	6	7	8	8
5.0	4	5	5	6	7	7	8	8
5.5	4	5	6	6	7	8	8	9
6.0	4	5	6	7	7	8	9	9
6.5	4	5	6	7	7	8	9	9
7.0	5	5	6	7	8	8	9	10
7.5	5	6	6	7	8	9	9	10
8.0	5	6	7	7	8	9	10	10

*Depth must not be less than 1/40 span.

All channels are minimum sections. One sag rod is used for truss spacing up to 20 ft., two sag rods for truss spacing over 20 ft.

All purlins for a roof with a pitch of 1/3 and less will carry a normal load of 15 lb. per sq. ft. and a vertical load of 15 lb. per sq. ft. with an allowable fiber stress of 20,000 lb. per sq. in., when the stress is calculated for oblique loading as described in Chapter XII.

TABLE II.

Depths of Steel Channel Purlins for a Normal Roof Load of 40 lb. per Sq. Ft.

Purlin Spacing Ft.	Truss Spacing, or Bay, Ft.							
	10	12	14	16	18	20	22	24
2.5	4	4	5*	5	6	6	7	8*
3.0	4	4	5	5	6	7	7	8
3.5	4	4	5	6	6	7	8	8
4.0	4	5	5	6	7	7	8	9
4.5	4	5	6	7	7	8	9	9
5.0	4	5	6	7	8	8	9	10
5.5	5	5	6	7	8	9	9	10
6.0	5	6	7	7	8	9	10	10
6.5	5	6	7	8	8	9	10	12
7.0	5	6	7	8	9	9	10	12
7.5	5	6	7	8	9	10	12	12
8.0	5	7	7	8	9	10	12	12

*Depth must not be less than 1/40 span.

All channels are minimum sections. One sag rod is used for truss spacing up to 14 ft., two sag rods for truss spacing over 14 ft.

All purlins for a roof with a pitch of 1/3 or less will carry a normal load of 20 lb. per sq. ft., and a vertical load of 20 lb. per sq. ft., with an allowable stress of 20,000 lb. per sq. in., when the stress is calculated for oblique loading as described in Chapter XII.

TABLE III.

DEPTHS OF STEEL CHANNEL PURLINS FOR A NORMAL ROOF LOAD OF 50 LB. PER SQ. FT.

Purlin Spacing Ft.	Truss Spacing, or Bay, Ft.							
	10	12	14	16	18	20	22	24
2.5	4	4	5	6	6	7	7	8
3.0	4	5	5	6	7	7	8	8
3.5	4	5	6	6	7	8	8	9
4.0	4	5	6	7	8	8	9	10
4.5	5	6	6	7	8	9	9	10
5.0	5	6	7	7	8	9	10	12
5.5	5	6	7	8	9	9	10	12
6.0	5	6	7	8	9	10	12	12
6.5	6	7	7	8	9	10	12	12
7.0	6	7	8	9	10	10	12	12
7.5	6	7	8	9	10	12	12	12
8.0	6	7	8	9	10	12	12	15

All channels are minimum sections. One sag rod is used for truss spacing up to 14 ft., two sag rods for truss spacing over 14 ft.

All purlins for a roof with a pitch of 1/3 or less, will carry a normal load of 25 lb. per sq. ft. and a vertical load of 25 lb. per sq. ft., with an allowable stress of 20,000 lb. per sq. in., when calculated for oblique loading as described in Chapter XII.

Structural Drafting.—For a discussion of structural drafting, see the author's "Structural Engineers' Handbook."

References.—For data on the framework for steel office buildings, see the author's "Structural Engineers' Handbook." For data on the framework for steel bins and steel grain elevators, see the author's "Design of Walls, Bins and Grain Elevators." For data on the framework for head frames, coal tipples and other mine structures, see the author's "Design of Mine Structures."

CHAPTER XXVI.

Examples of Steel Industrial Buildings.

Introduction.—The different types of steel frame industrial buildings will be illustrated by the description of several typical structures. As far as possible, the data used in the design are given.

Saw Tooth Roof Shop.—The detailed drawings of a saw tooth roof bent constructed by the Mathiessen and Hegeler Zinc Works, La Salle, Ill., are shown in Fig. 1. This

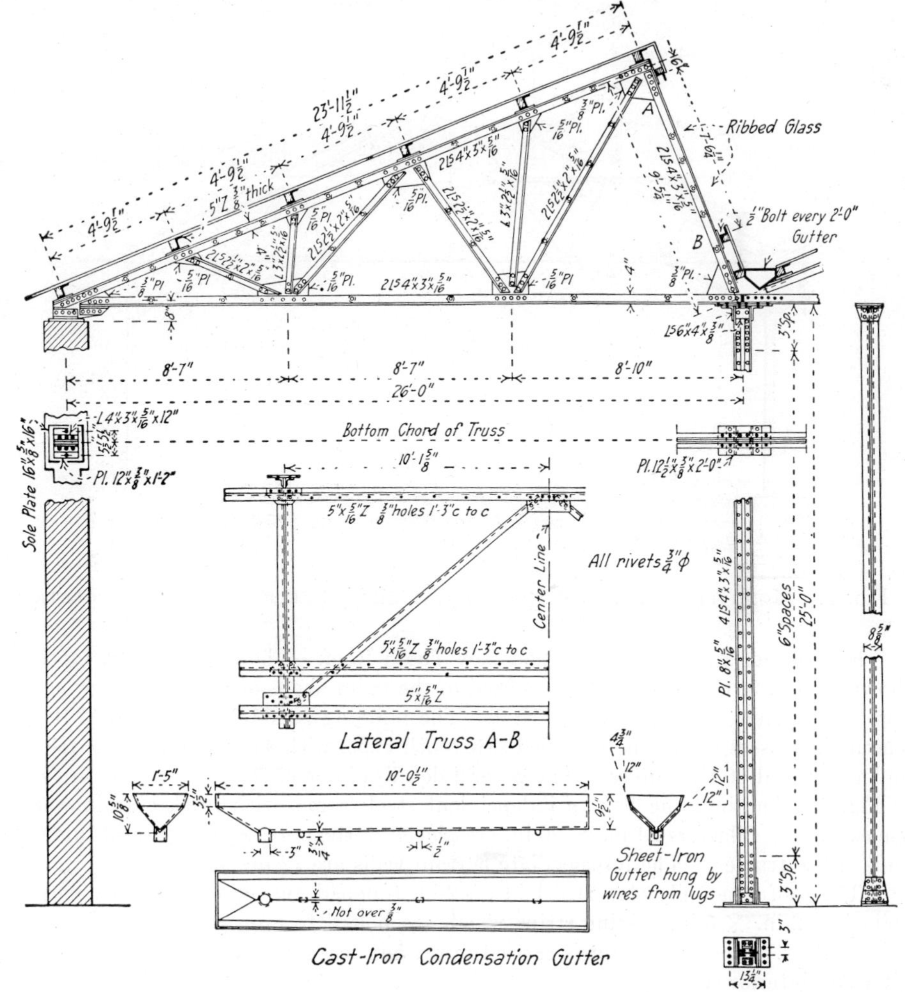

Fig. 1. Cross-section of the Shops of the Mathiessen & Hegeler Zinc Works, La Salle, Ill.

building was erected in 1899 along the lines suggested by an experience with a similar saw tooth roof building erected in 1874. The roof is a composition roof laid on plank sheathing, which is spiked to nailing strips that are bolted to Z-bar purlins. The water from the roof and the condensation from the glass surface in the saw tooth are carried by cast iron gutters to galvanized iron down spouts. These gutters are so placed that the galvanized iron down spouts are next to the post, there being two down spouts at each post. The condensation gutters are fastened to the cast iron gutters. The saw tooth is glazed with ribbed glass. Snow and ice have never caused any trouble by forming in the gutters. The original saw tooth roof shop built by this firm is still in use, and is one of the first, if not the first, saw tooth roof built in America.

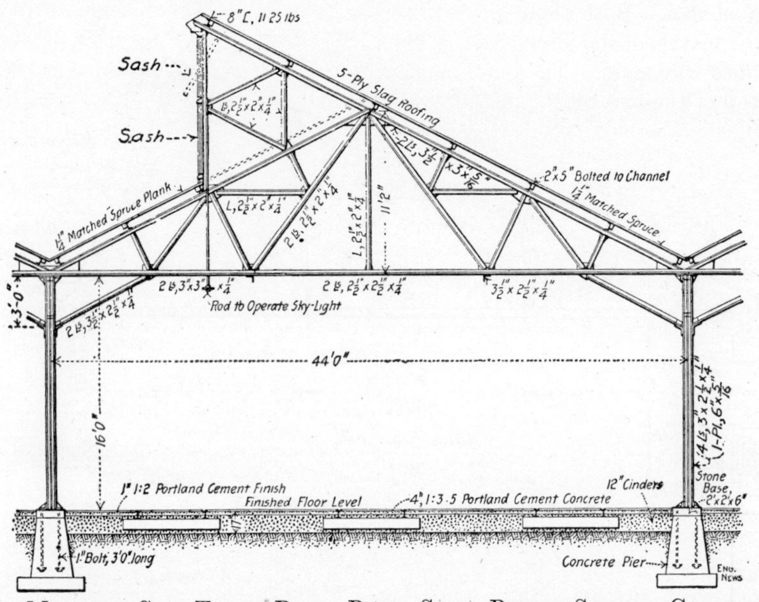

FIG. 2. MODIFIED SAW TOOTH ROOF, PAINT SHOP, PUBLIC SERVICE CORPORATION.

Example of Ketchum's Modified Saw Tooth Roof.—The modified saw tooth roof shown in Fig. 5, Chapter XXV, was used in the paint shops of the Public Service Corporation of New Jersey, Newark, N. J. The building is 135 ft. wide by 354 ft. long. The main trusses are of the modified saw tooth type, with 44-ft. spans and a rise of $\frac{1}{4}$, and are spaced 16 ft. centers. The general details of one of the main trusses are shown in Fig. 2. The building has an independent steel frame, with brick curtain walls on the exterior. Pilasters 24 in. × 20 in. are placed in the outside curtain walls under the ends of the trusses. The intermediate curtain walls are 12 in. thick.

The roof is a 5-ply slag roof laid on 2-in. tongued and grooved spruce sheathing spiked to 2-in. × 5-in. spiking strips which are bolted to 8-in. channel purlins spaced 6 ft. centers. The roof water is carried down 5-in. cast iron down spouts attached to alternate interior columns.

The sash in the vertical leg of the saw tooth are in two rows, the upper row being hinged at the center, thus providing ample ventilation. Condensation gutters are placed below the vertical leg to take the drip. The skylight area is about 20 per cent of the roof area, the window area is about 45 per cent of the outside walls, while about 28 per cent of the entire outside surface of the building is of glass. All windows and skylights are glazed with 1/8-in. ribbed wire glass, with ribs placed vertical. The skylight frames and moldings are made of No. 24 galvanized steel, while the entire roof is flashed with 16-oz. copper sheets, 4 ft. wide, and are counterflashed with sheet lead.

Louisville and Nashville R. R. Shops.—The saw tooth roof shown in Fig. 3 was used in the South Louisville Shops of the Louisville and Nashville R. R. The pitched roof is covered with a composition roof, while the flat roof is covered with an asphalt and gravel roof. Both the composition roof and the asphalt and gravel roof are laid on $1\frac{3}{4}$-in. matched and dressed sheathing. The short leg of the saw tooth is glazed with ribbed wire glass. The building is ventilated by means of 12-in. ventilators placed at the top of the saw tooth, spaced 30 ft. 2 in.

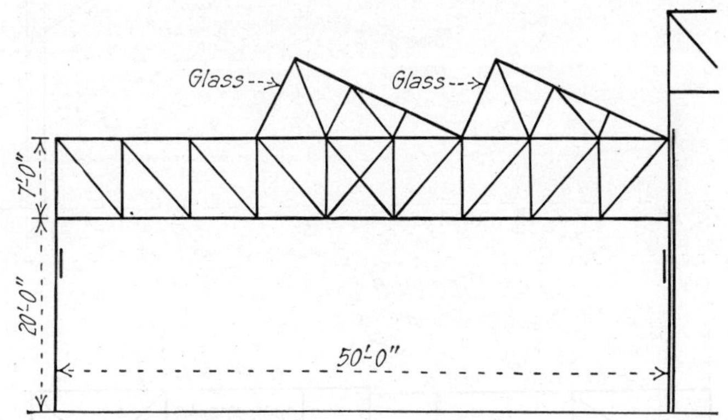

FIG. 3. SAW TOOTH ROOF, LOUISVILLE AND NASHVILLE R. R. SHOPS.

Rock Drill Building, Ingersoll-Sargent Drill Company.—The design of the saw tooth roof is shown in Fig. 4. The building is covered with a composition roof laid on

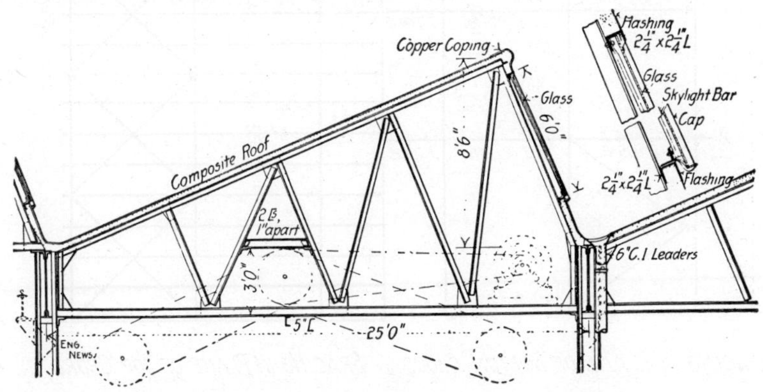

FIG. 4. SAW TOOTH FOR ROCK DRILL BUILDING.

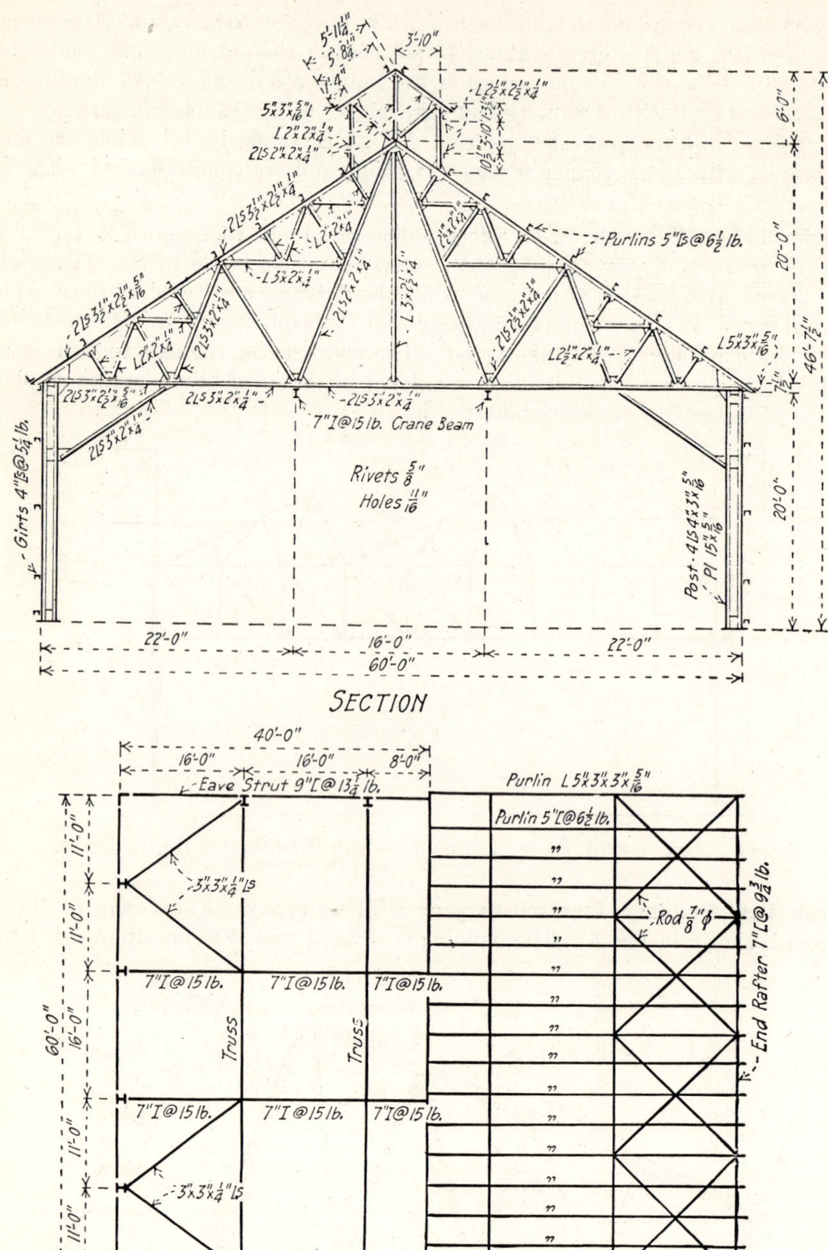

Fig. 5. Plans of a Steel Transformer Building.

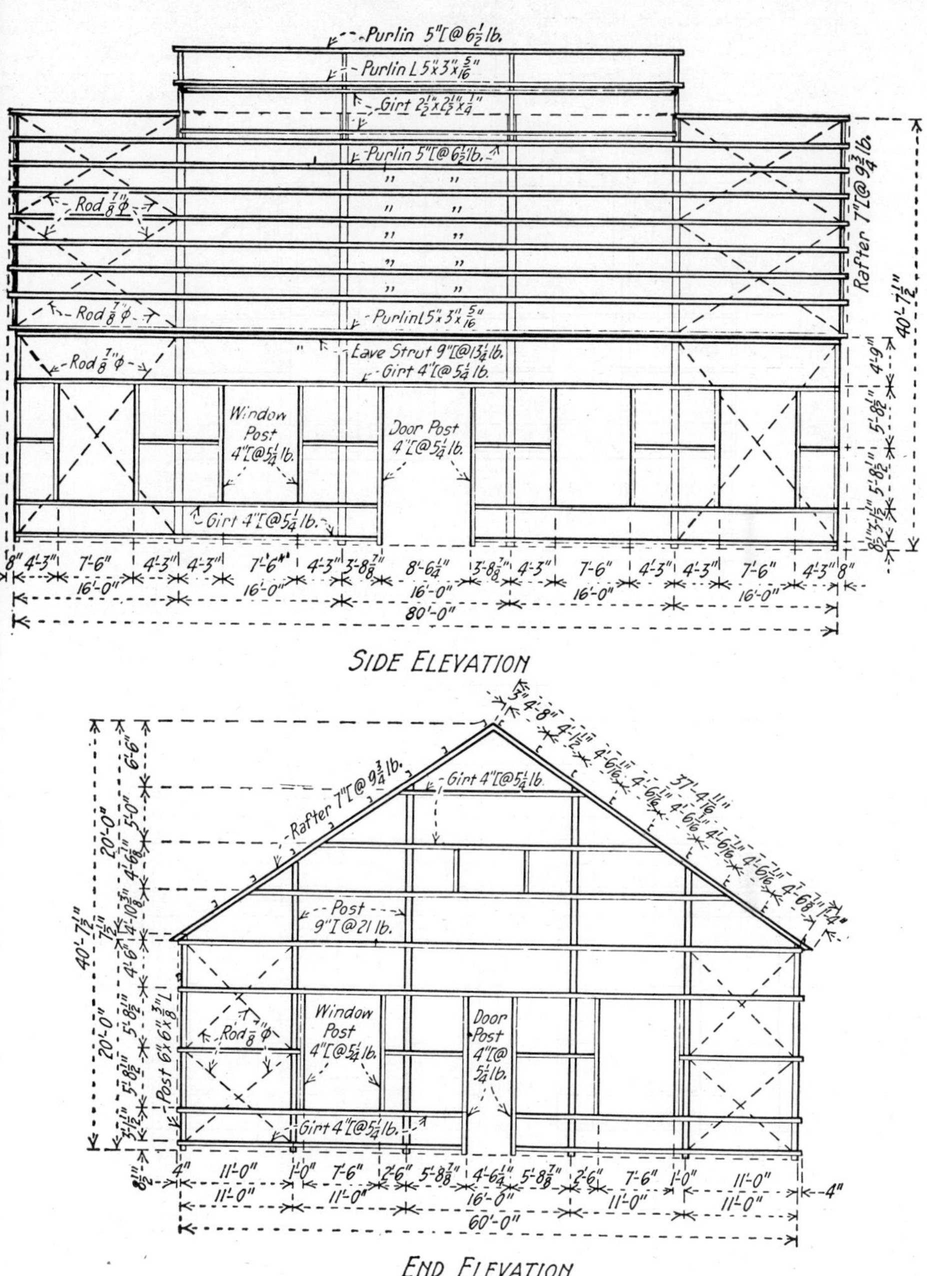

FIG. 6. PLANS OF A STEEL TRANSFORMER BUILDING.

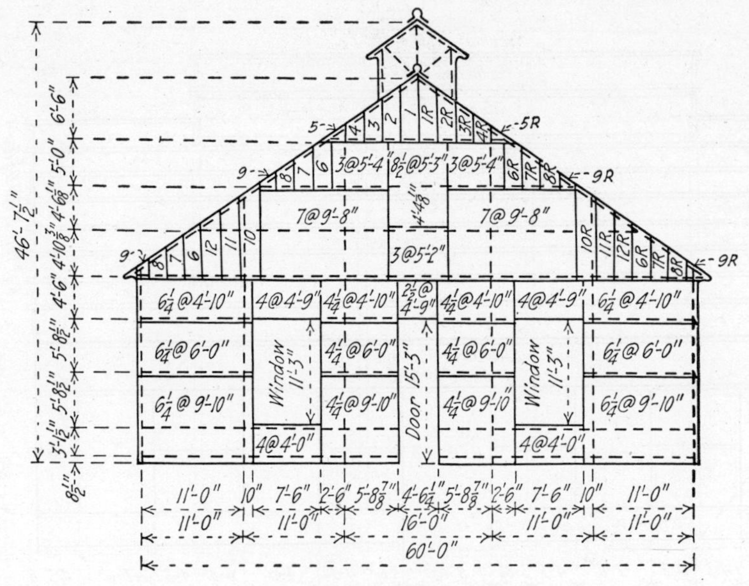

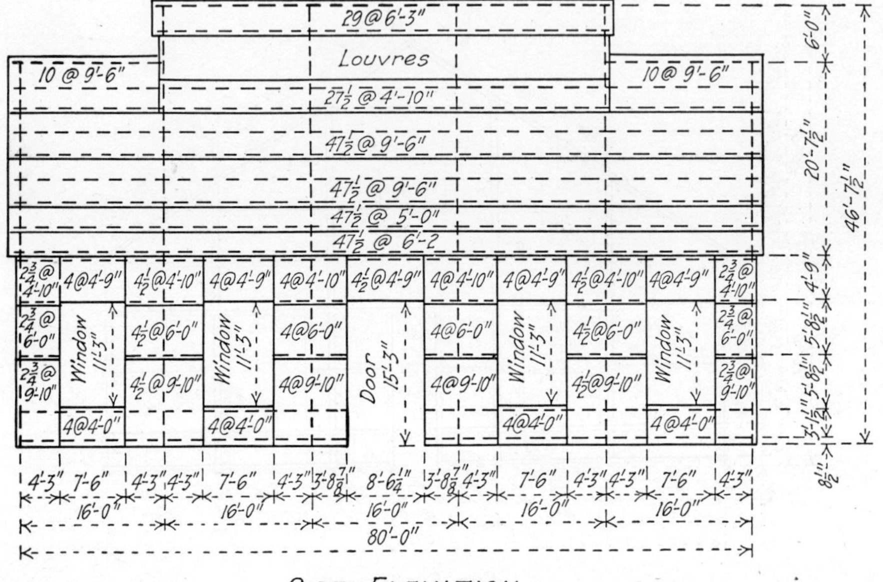

FIG. 7. CORRUGATED STEEL PLANS FOR A STEEL TRANSFORMER BUILDING.

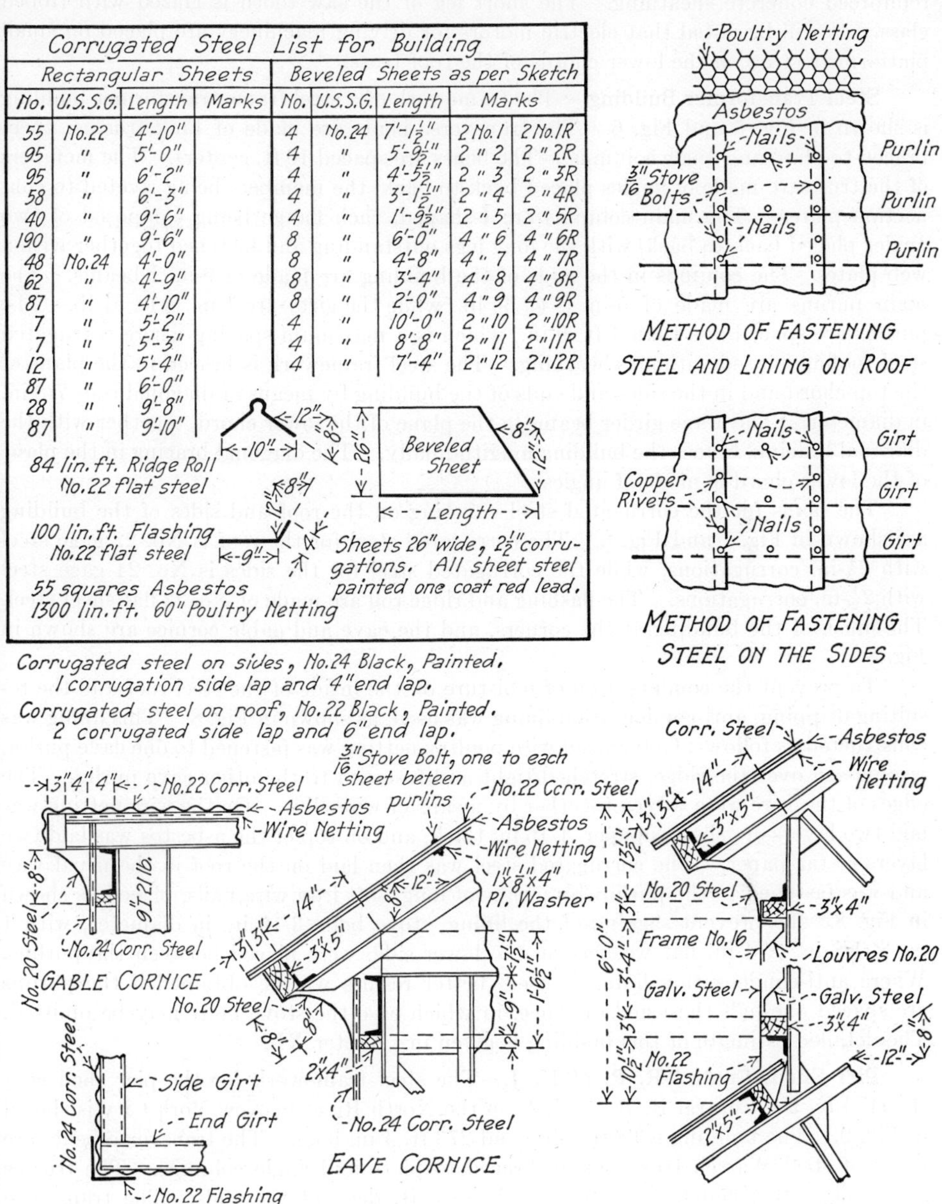

Corrugated Steel List for Building

Rectangular Sheets				Beveled Sheets as per Sketch				
No.	U.S.S.G.	Length	Marks	No.	U.S.S.G.	Length	Marks	
55	No. 22	4'-10"		4	No. 24	7'-1½"	2 No. 1	2 No. 1R
95	"	5'-0"		4	"	5'-9½"	2 " 2	2 " 2R
95	"	6'-2"		4	"	4'-5½"	2 " 3	2 " 3R
58	"	6'-3"		4	"	3'-1½"	2 " 4	2 " 4R
40	"	9'-6"		4	"	1'-9½"	2 " 5	2 " 5R
190	"	9'-6"		8	"	6'-0"	4 " 6	4 " 6R
48	No. 24	4'-0"		8	"	4'-8"	4 " 7	4 " 7R
62	"	4'-9"		8	"	3'-4"	4 " 8	4 " 8R
87	"	4'-10"		8	"	2'-0"	4 " 9	4 " 9R
7	"	5'-2"		4	"	10'-0"	2 " 10	2 " 10R
7	"	5'-3"		4	"	8'-8"	2 " 11	2 " 11R
12	"	5'-4"		4	"	7'-4"	2 " 12	2 " 12R
87	"	6'-0"						
28	"	9'-8"						
87	"	9'-10"						

84 lin. ft. Ridge Roll No. 22 flat steel
100 lin. ft. Flashing No. 22 flat steel
55 squares Asbestos
1300 lin. ft. 60" Poultry Netting
Sheets 26" wide, 2½" corrugations. All sheet steel painted one coat red lead.

FIG. 8. CORRUGATED STEEL DETAILS FOR A STEEL TRANSFORMER BUILDING.

reinforced concrete sheathing. The short leg of the saw tooth is glazed with ribbed glass. It will be noted that electric motors for driving machinery are placed on small platforms resting on the lower chords of the roof truss.

Steel Transformer Building.—The framework of a steel frame transformer building is shown in Fig. 5 and Fig. 6. The transverse bents are made of Fink trusses, knee-braced to plate and angle columns. The bents are spaced 16 ft. centers. The members of the truss are made of angles placed back to back, the members being riveted to connection plates. The main columns are I-shaped, each flange being composed of two angles placed back to back, with the long legs outstanding and fastened together with a web plate. The columns in the ends of the building are made of 9-in. I beams. The main purlins are made of 5-in. [s @ $6\frac{1}{2}$ lb., while the girts are 4-in. [s @ $5\frac{1}{4}$ lb. The purlins are spaced less than 4 ft. 9 in., which is a maximum spacing where corrugated steel roofing is used without sheathing. The steel framework is braced in the plane of the top chord and in the sides and ends of the building by means of diagonal rods 7/8 in. in diameter. The crane girder beams in the plane of the lower chord, together with the diagonal bracing, braces the building longitudinally. The diagonal bracing in the plane of the lower chord is made of angles.

The plans for the corrugated steel covering on the roof and sides of the building are shown in Fig. 7 and Fig. 8. The corrugated steel for the roof is No. 22 gage steel with $2\frac{1}{2}$-in. corrugations, while the corrugated steel for the sides is No. 24 gage steel with $2\frac{1}{2}$-in. corrugations. The flashing and ridge roll are made of No. 22 flat sheet steel. The finish of the building at the corners, and the eave and gable cornice are shown in Fig. 8.

To prevent the condensation of moisture on the inside of the steel roof and the resulting dripping, anti-condensation lining was used, as shown in Fig. 8. This lining was constructed as follows: Galvanized wire poultry netting was fastened to one eave purlin, was passed over the ridge, stretched tight and fastened to the other eave purlin. The edges of the wire were woven together by means of wire clips. On the wire netting was laid two layers of asbestos paper, 1/16 in. thick, and on top of the asbestos was laid two layers of tar paper. The corrugated steel was then laid on the roof in the usual way and was fastened to the purlins by means of long, soft iron wire nails, placed as shown in Fig. 8. To prevent sagging of the lining, stove bolts 3/16 in. in diameter, with 1 in. × 1/8 in. × 4 in. flat washers on the lower side, were placed between the purlins. Where anti-condensation lining is used, better results will be obtained if the purlins are spaced one-half the usual distance, in which case the stove bolts may be omitted. The detailed estimate of this building is given in Chapter XL.

Pier Shed, Central R. R. of N. J.—The steel framework for the pier shed constructed by the Central R. R. of N. J. on the North River in New York City is shown in Fig. 9. The building is 68 ft. wide and 273 ft. 4 in. long. The transverse bents are made of steel Warren trusses, knee-braced to plate and angle columns. The trusses are made with riveted connections and are 5 ft. deep at the ends. The transverse bents are spaced from 19 ft. 4 in. to 22 ft., as shown in Fig. 9. The transverse bents are braced in pairs in the plane of the top chords. The sides of the building are braced by means of riveted steel trusses 5 ft. deep. The purlins are made of 9-in. [s @ $13\frac{1}{4}$ lb. The purlins on the braced bays extend 3 ft. 6 in. into the adjacent panels. This method of arranging the purlins made the erection easier and resulted in a saving in the weight

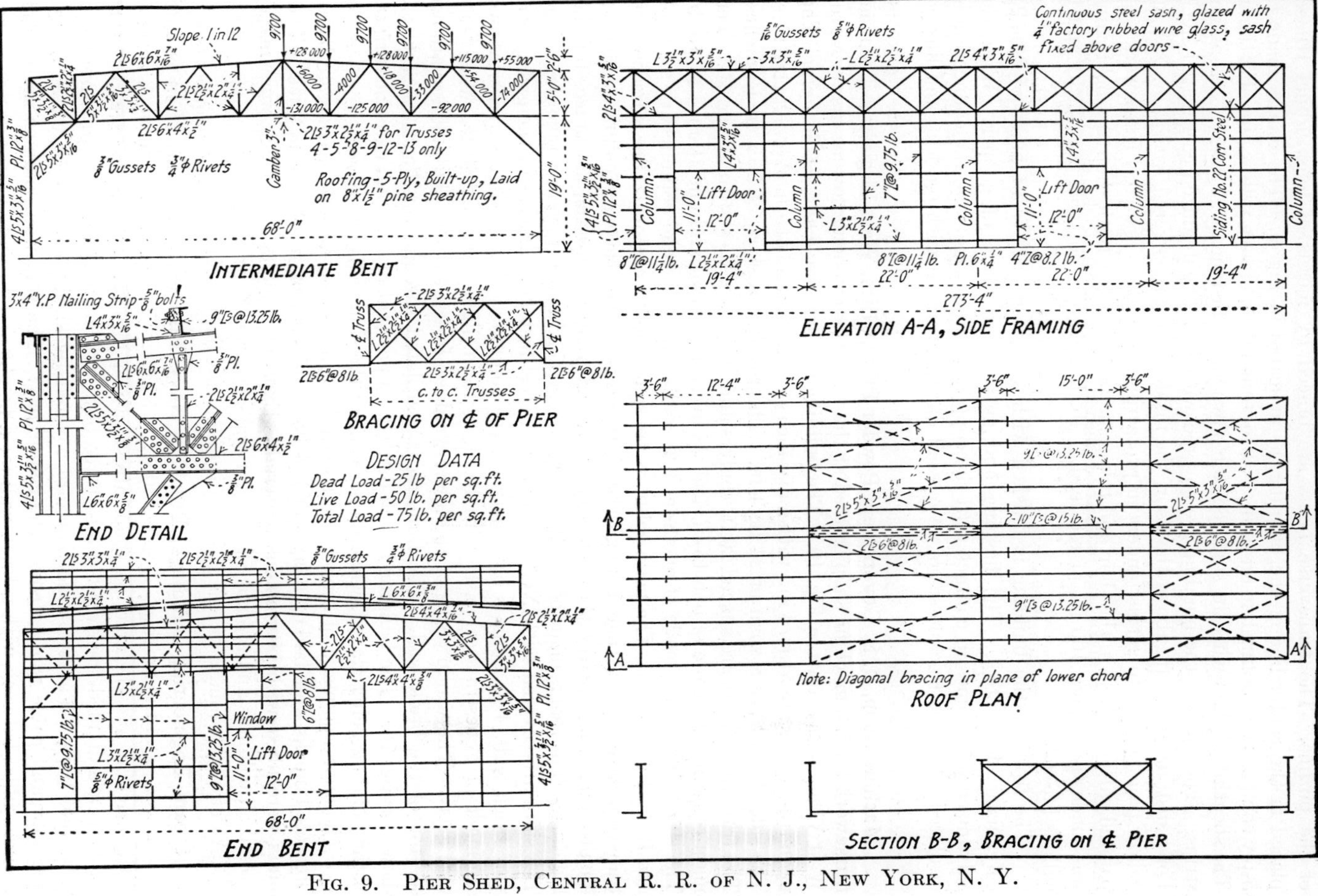

FIG. 9. PIER SHED, CENTRAL R. R. OF N. J., NEW YORK, N. Y.

of the purlins. The transverse bents are braced by means of longitudinal trusses placed in the center line of the building, as indicated in Fig. 9. The roof is made of 5-ply composition roofing laid on $1\frac{1}{2}$ in. × 8 in. tongue and groove yellow pine sheathing. The sheathing is laid with the surfaced side down and is fastened to 3 in. × 4 in. spiking strips. The sides of the building are covered with No. 22 galvanized corrugated steel. For a distance of 11 ft. above the floor, the inside walls are covered with 2 in. × 8 in. yellow pine planks, to act as fenders in protecting the wall. The steel framework was painted with one coat in the shop and two coats in the field. Both shop and field paint was made by mixing 100 lb. of red lead, 1 lb. lampblack (not coal tar black) and 6 gallons linseed oil.

The front of the building is finished with an ornamental front made of No. 24 galvanized sheet steel. The flashing and gutters are made of copper. Wherever galvanized iron comes in contact with the copper flashing or gutters, the connection is insulated with two thicknesses of 14-oz. sail duck, saturated with red lead and linseed oil.

Machine Shop, U. S. Government Powder Plant, Nitro, West Virginia.—The steel framework for the machine shop erected at the U. S. Government Powder Plant, Nitro, West Virginia, is shown in Fig. 10. The building is 100 ft. wide and 200 ft. long. The main truss spans are 51 ft. 4 in., with a distance of 33 ft. to the bottom chord of the truss. The side sheds have a span of 24 ft. 4 in. The roof has a slope of 5 in. in 12 inches. The transverse bents are spaced 20 ft. centers and are braced as shown in Fig. 10. The main columns are made of one 15-in. I @ 38 lb. (Bethlehem) and one 10-in. [@ 15 lb. The side columns are made of one 8-in. I @ 18 lb., while the end columns are made of one 12-in. I @ $31\frac{1}{2}$ lb. The main columns are spaced 40 ft. centers. The intermediate transverse bents are carried on longitudinal trusses carried on the main columns. These longitudinal trusses carry the 10-ton crane and also act as longitudinal braces for the building. The roof is made of No. 22 corrugated steel laid on 2-in. yellow pine sheathing. The sides are covered with No. 22 corrugated steel fastened directly to the girts. An 8-in. brick wall, 4 ft. high, is built between the columns. The skylights and windows are made of Fenestra steel sash, with 10 in. × 16 in. lights, and are glazed with $\frac{1}{8}$-in. wire glass. The window sills of the lower windows in the sides of the building are on the top of the brick wall. The building is ventilated through the Fenestra sash, as shown in Fig. 10. The building is well lighted, 23 per cent of the total exterior surface of the building being glazed, while 60 per cent of the side walls are glazed.

The floor was made of 3-in. creosoted timber blocks laid on a 6-in. concrete base. Creosoted blocks were laid on a layer of 1: 4 Portland cement mortar, $\frac{1}{2}$ in. thick. The joints were filled with bituminous material. Expansion joints 1 in. thick were made around all columns and around all exterior walls to provide for expansion.

A detailed estimate of this building is given in Chapter XL.

Steam Engineering Buildings, Brooklyn Navy Yard.—The erecting shop is 130 ft. × 252 ft., and the machine shop is 130 ft. × 350 ft. The general framework details of the machine and the erecting shops are shown in Fig. 11. It will be seen that the buildings are divided transversely into three bays, the center bay 70 ft. wide and two 30-ft. side bays. The two side bays are covered by shed roofs, above which rise a clerestory and gable roof to cover the center bay. The side wall columns are 12-in. I-beams, filled between with a brick wall for a height of 4 ft. and above this point are

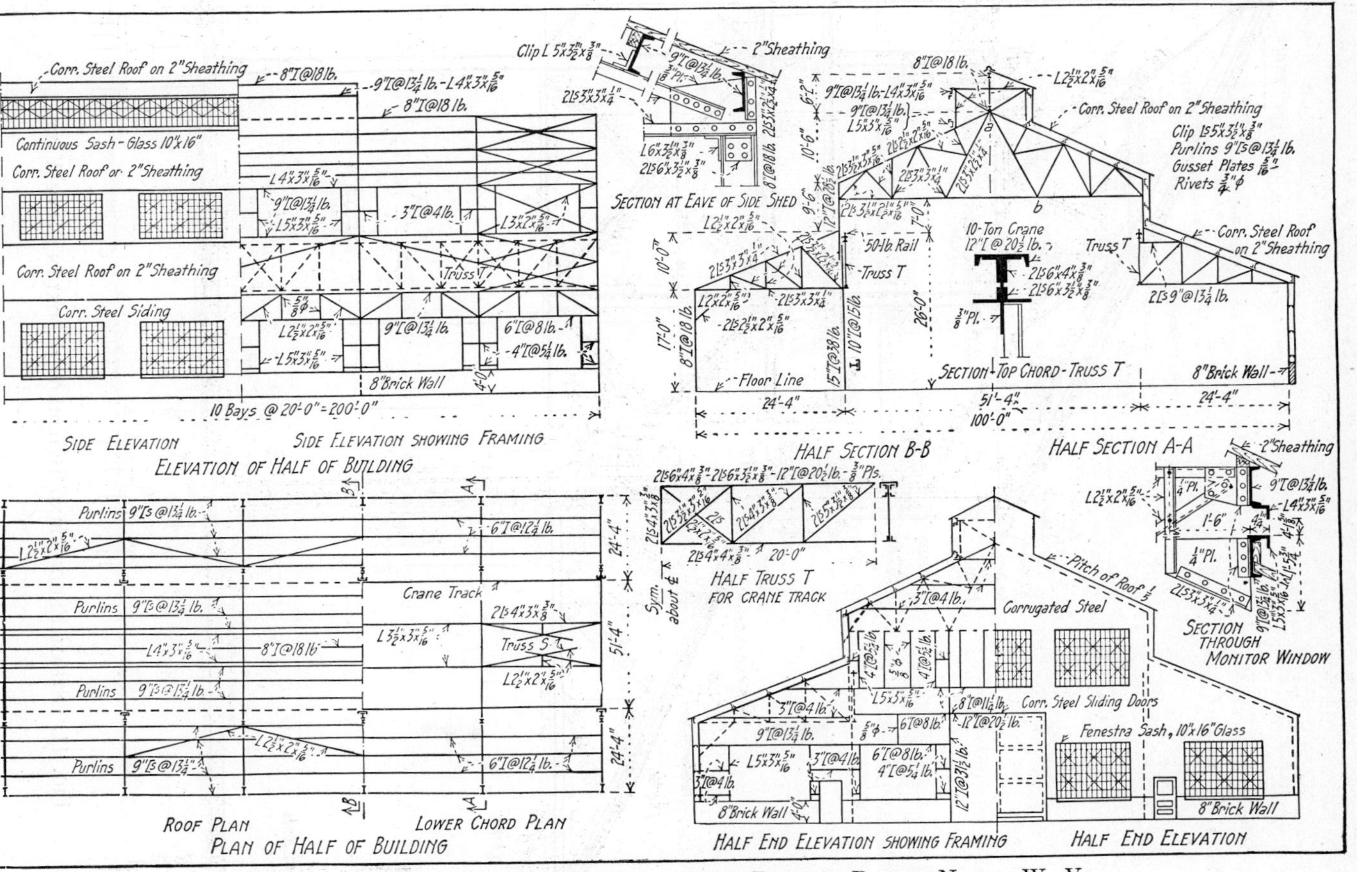

Fig. 10. Machine Shop, U. S. Government Powder Plant, Nitro, W. Va.

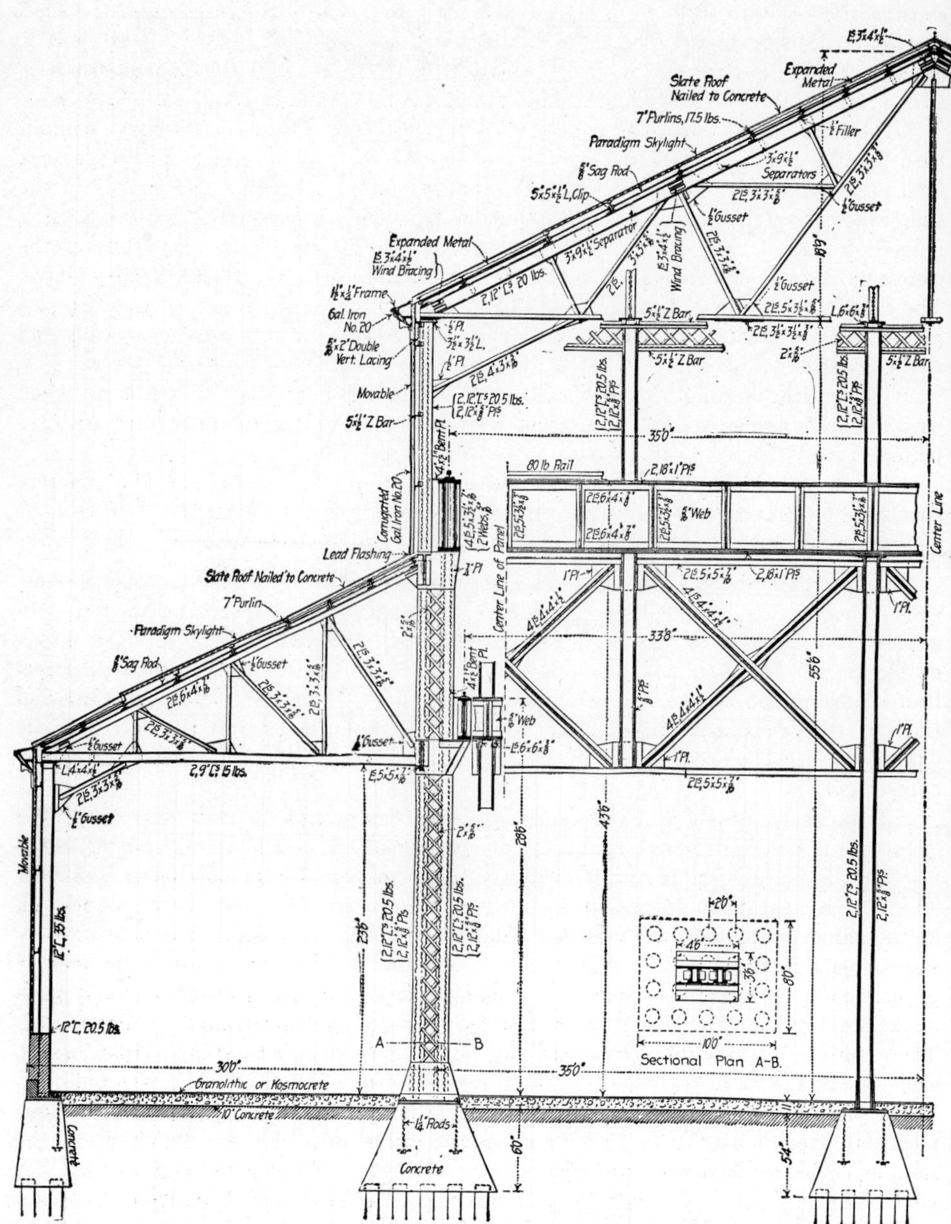

Fig. 11. Steam Engineering Building, Brooklyn Navy Yard.

covered with glazing to the cornice line. The main columns are of lattice and channel construction and are 43 ft. 6 in. high, reaching to the level of the junction of the shed roof and the clerestory. The main columns are spaced 54 ft. apart and support a double intersection truss 15 ft. deep, which in turn supports 70-ft. transverse trusses at the third points. These columns also support a box crane runway.

The foundations consist of concrete column pedestals carried on piles, the column base plates being anchor-bolted directly to the concrete. The piles were driven to a final penetration of 1 inch by a 3,000-lb. hammer falling 15 feet. The glazing in the side walls above the brick base wall is put on in panels or sections, each section being hinged so that it may be swung out to provide ventilation. The side walls of the clerestory consist of corrugated steel covering on the lower part, with glazing above. The greater part of the area of the shed roofs is skylight, and wide skylights are also placed in the clerestory roof. Fully 60 per cent of the area of the external walls and roof is glazed.

The entire building is constructed of fire-resisting materials. There is no wood used in the building except for the framework of the doors, which are covered with tin plate.

The roof is made of slate nailed directly to concrete sheathing. The concrete sheathing is composed of Portland cement and cinder, and is 3½ in. thick. The floor is made of concrete 10 in. thick, with a 1-in. granolithic wearing surface.

Locomotive Shops of the Atchison, Topeka and Santa Fe R. R., Topeka, Kas.—This building is intended for locomotive work, including boilers and tenders. In general plan it is 852 ft. long and 153 ft. 10 in. wide, the width being divided into a center span of 74 ft. 3 in. and two side spans of 39 ft. 9 in. It is of self-supporting steel frame construction, with concrete foundations and floor, 13-in. brick walls, and Ludowici tile roof. There is no sheathing under the tiles, which thus constitute the sole covering. The tiles are laid on 2 × 2-in. timber strips to which every fourth tile is fastened by copper wire.

The most striking feature of the design is that the saw tooth or weaving shed type of roof is adopted for the side spans, the glazed vertical sides of the ridges facing northward. This feature was introduced with the view of making the shop as light as possible. The arrangement could not well be used where heavy snows are frequently experienced, as the snow would pack between the ridges, but there are comparatively few heavy snow storms in the vicinity of Topeka. In addition to this arrangement, the greater proportion of the area of the side walls is composed of windows, while the exposed parts of the sides of the central span (between the ridges of the side spans) are also glazed. There are also several windows in the end walls. The roof of the central span has on each side of the ridge a skylight 12 ft. wide, extending the full length of the building. These skylights are fitted with translucent fabric instead of glass. By these various means an exceptionally good lighting effect and diffusion of light are obtained and the shop is in fact remarkably light even on a gloomy day. There is no monitor roof, but ventilation is provided for by Star ventilators 25 ft. apart along the ridge of the main roof.

The columns are built up of pairs of 15-in. channels, and independent columns of similar construction carry the double-web box girder runways for the electric traveling cranes which run the entire length of the central span. Fig. 12 shows the elevations,

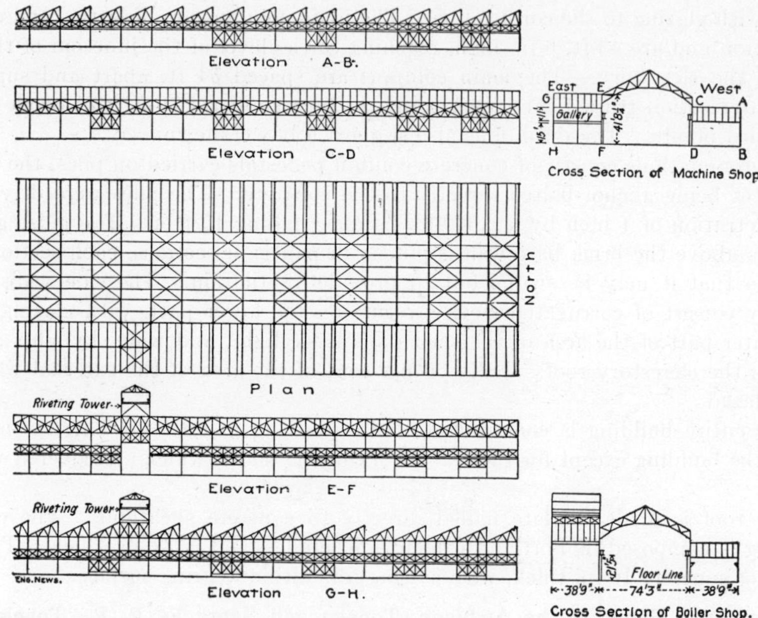

FIG. 12. PART ELEVATIONS AND PLANS OF STEEL STRUCTURAL WORK OF NEW LOCOMOTIVE SHOPS.

sections and plans of the steel structural framework, and Fig. 13 is a partial elevation on the east side. Fig. 14 shows the design of the central roof trusses and the lattice girders which form longitudinal bracing between the trusses. This longitudinal bracing is not continuous but is fitted only between alternate pairs of trusses. End trusses are built into the walls, as these walls are pierced by numerous windows and doors and are not relied upon in any way to support the roof. Portal bracing is fitted between the side or wall columns at intervals. No metal less than $\frac{3}{8}$-in. thick is used in the structural work.

The roof trusses are proportioned for a load of 15 lb. per sq. ft. for the weight of the roofing, 10 lb. per sq. ft. for snow, and 25 lb. per sq. ft. for wind pressure, or 50 lb. per sq. ft. in all. The members were calculated on a basis of 16,000 lb. per sq. in. for tension and 14,000 lb. per sq. in. for compression. Provision for expansion and contraction is made at intervals of 100 ft. The building is heated by the Sturtevant hot blast

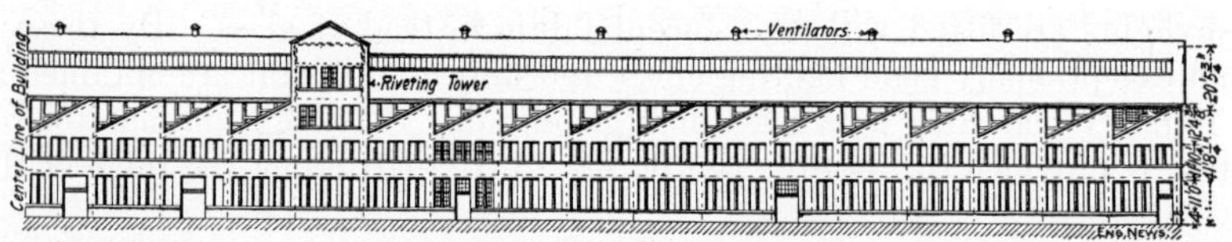

FIG. 13. HALF EAST ELEVATION OF NEW LOCOMOTIVE SHOP. (SHOWING RIVETING TOWER AND WEAVING SHED ROOF.)

system. On each side are two fan rooms, each containing a steam-driven blower fan and a heating chamber filled with coils of pipe through which passes the exhaust steam. The hot air is delivered into two longitudinal underground conduits parallel with the lines of columns, with a duct leading to the surface at each column. Each duct is fitted with a vertical sheet iron pipe 7 ft. high, with a flaring head to deliver the air horizontally. The plant is guaranteed to maintain a temperature of 70° F. throughout the shop in zero weather.

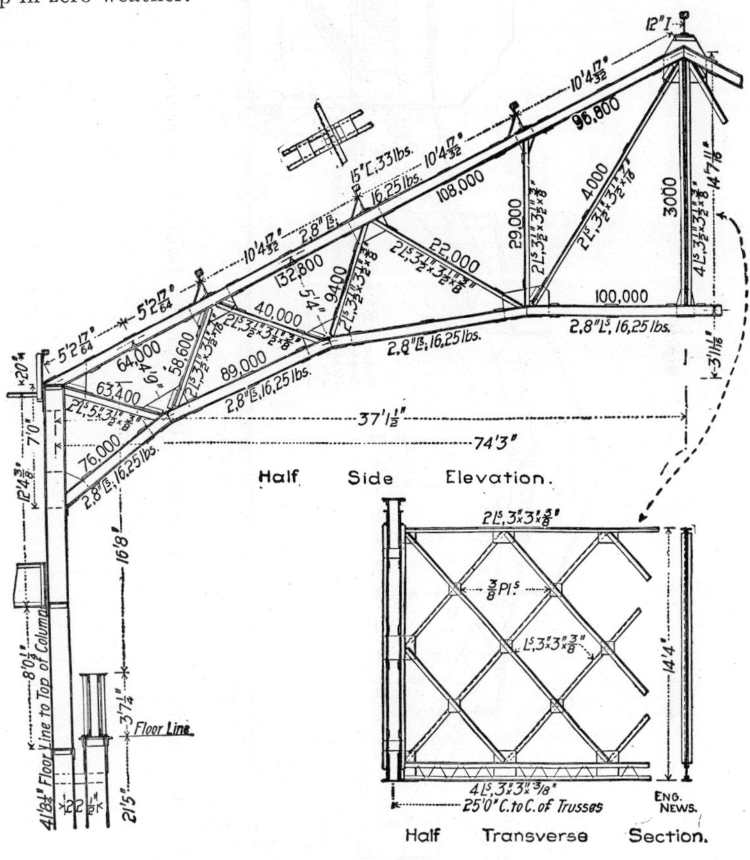

FIG. 14.

The floor foundation is formed of 6 inches of concrete resting on the natural soil well tamped. The concrete is composed of 1 part cement, 2 parts sand and 4 parts stone. On the concrete are laid yellow pine nailing strips, 3 in. × 4 in., 18 in. c. to c., to which is spiked the $1\frac{3}{4}$-in. splined hard-maple flooring. The concrete for column foundations is composed of 1 part Portland cement, 3 parts sand and 5 parts stone. These foundations are 8 to 15 ft. deep, extending to solid clay. They are built up with gas pipe sleeves to form holes for the anchor bolts, and the holes in the bed plates of the columns are slotted longitudinally so as to allow of adjustment for any slight variation.

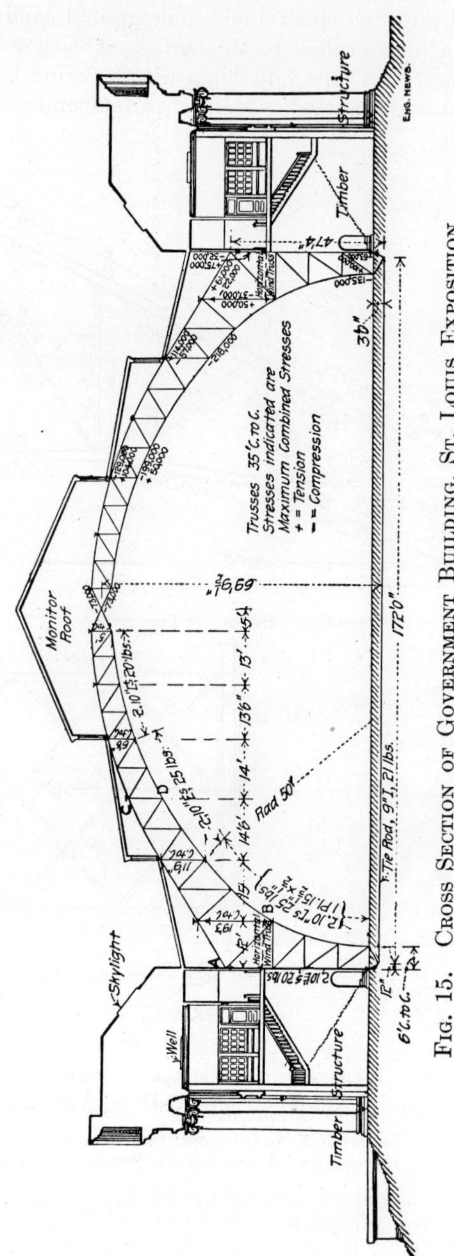

FIG. 15. CROSS SECTION OF GOVERNMENT BUILDING, ST. LOUIS EXPOSITION.

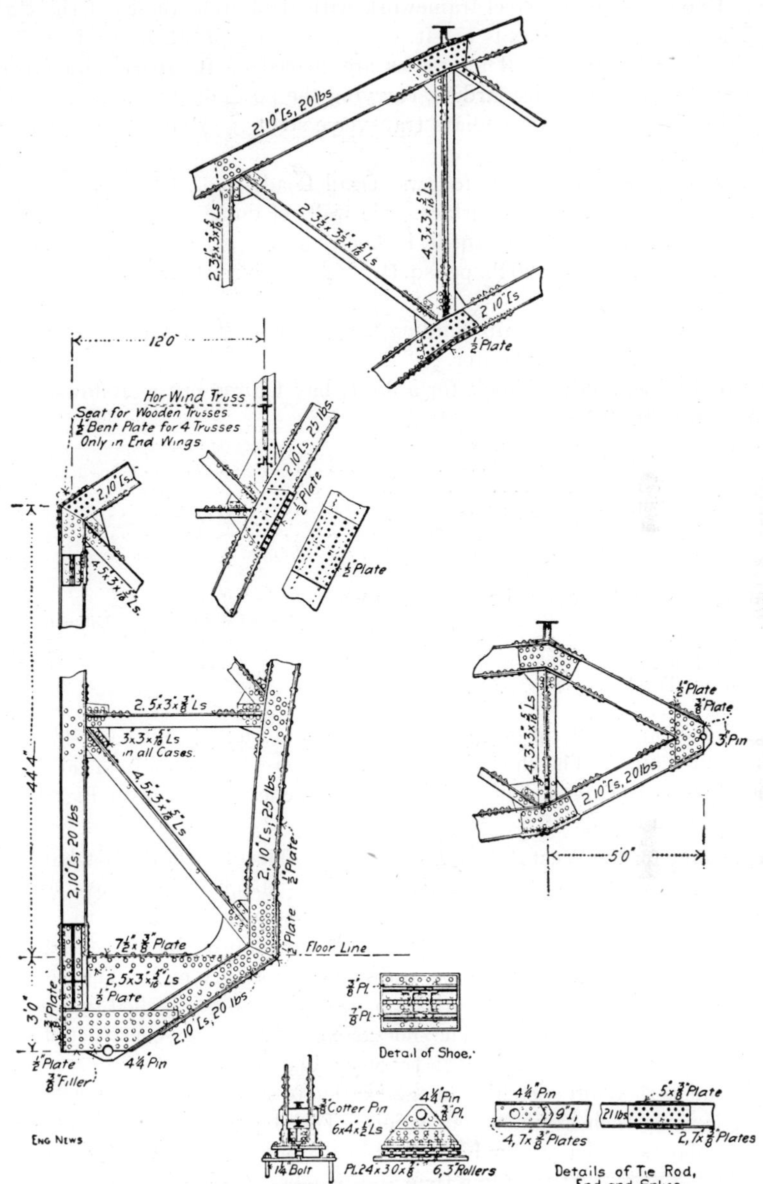

FIG. 16. DETAILS OF ARCH, GOVERNMENT BUILDING, ST. LOUIS EXPOSITION.

Government Building, St. Louis Exposition.—The Government Building at the St. Louis Exposition had a steel framework with steel arch trusses of the three-hinged type. The span of the arches is 172 ft. c. to c. of pins, and their rise from heel pins to center pins is 66 ft. $9\frac{1}{2}$ in. The trusses are spaced 35 ft. apart, and are connected laterally by six lines of lattice girders, carrying the posts of the main roof and monitor roof, and by eight other intermediate transverse struts. A horizontal wind strut truss is located as shown in Fig. 16.

The assumed loading was as follows: Dead Load: Roof, 10 lb. per sq. ft. on slope; dome, 12 lb. per sq. ft. of roof surface; side walls of dome and building, 15 lb. per sq. ft. of surface; trusses, 10 lb. per sq. ft. of floor surface.

Wind Load: Side walls, 20 lb. per sq. ft.; dome, curved, 15 lb. per sq. ft. of projection on a vertical surface.

Snow Load: On roof of main building, 20 lb. per sq. ft. horizontal; reduced to 10 lb. per sq. ft. on ventilator over center.

The revised estimate of loads for a 35-ft. bay figured out as follows, per sq. ft. of horizontal projection:

	Lb. per sq. ft.
Weight of steel	13.1
" " roof	6.6
" " tin covering	0.5
Actual roof	20.2
Calculated total	21.5

The loading on one truss for the 35-ft. bay was:

	Actual Weight in lb.	Estimated Weight in lb.
Total Dead Load	40,500	70,000
Total Steel	80,000	64,000
Grand Total	120,500	134,000

The arches are built up of channels, plates and angles, and have $4\frac{1}{2}$-in. shoe pins and 3-in. center pins. The shoe pins of each truss are connected by a tie bar consisting of a line of 9-in. I-beams. The stresses in the arches are given in Fig. 15, while the details are shown in Fig. 16.

Steel Dome for the West Baden, Ind., Hotel.*—The dome of the hotel at West Baden, Ind., is about 200 feet in outside diameter and rises about 50 feet above the bed plates. Its frame consists of 24 steel ribs, all connected at the center or crown to a circular plate drum, and tied together at the bottom by a circular plate girder tie. Each rib foots at its outside end on a built-up steel shoe, resting on a masonry pier. The rib is connected to the shoe by a steel pin, and the outside plate girder toe is attached to the gusset plate at this point, just above the shoe. The shoes of all the girders are constructed as expansion bearings, being provided with rollers in the usual manner.

The dome is therefore virtually an aggregation of two-hinged arches with the drum at the center forming their common connection. The thrust of the arches at the foot goes into the circular tie-girder, and only vertical loads (and wind loads) come upon the shoes and the bearing piers. At the same time any temperature stresses are avoided, since the expansion rollers under the shoes permit a uniform outward motion of the lower ends of all the ribs.

The outline of the dome and part of the dome framing are shown in Fig. 17. The rise is between $\frac{1}{4}$ and $\frac{1}{5}$ of the span. The outline of the top chord approximates an elliptical

* Engineering News, Sept. 4, 1902.

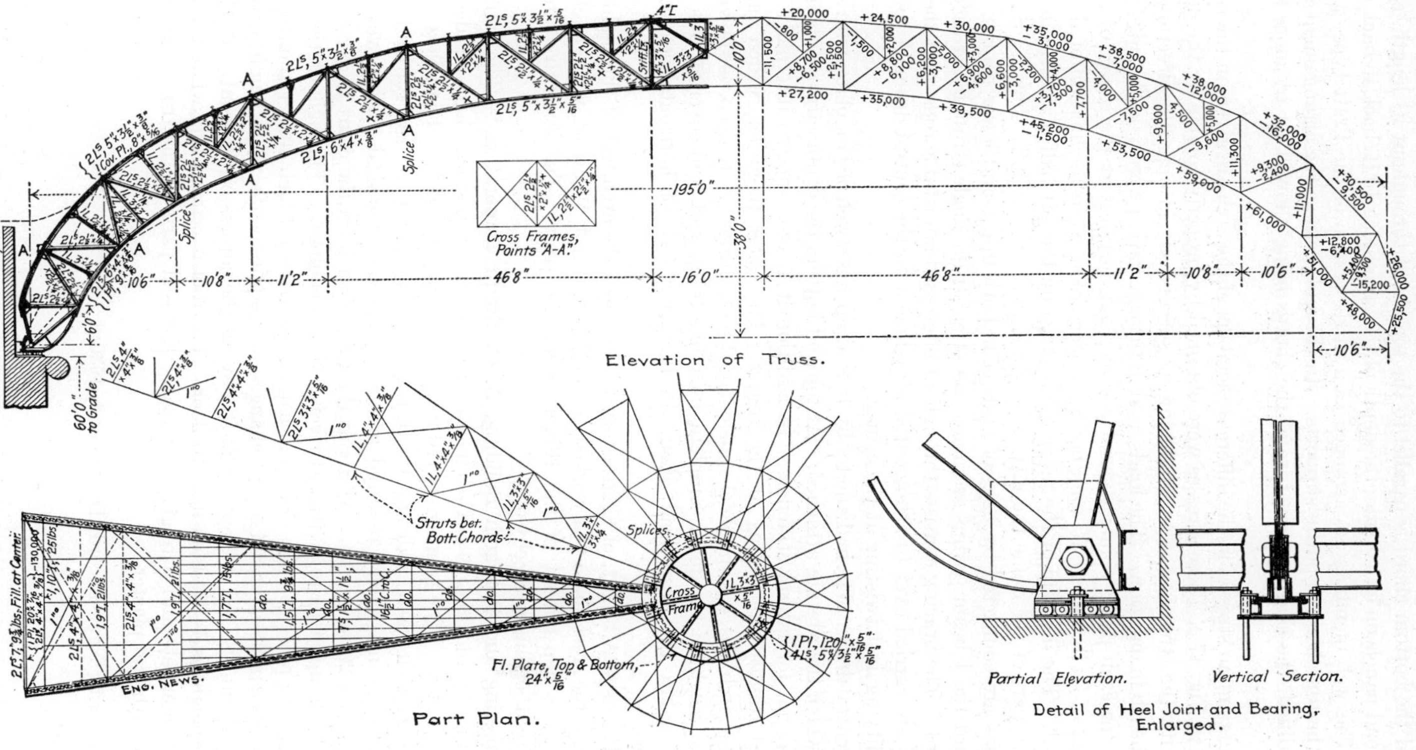

FIG. 17. STEEL DOME FOR WEST BADEN, IND., HOTEL.

curve, and the bottom chord is parallel to the top chord throughout its length, except in the three end panels on either side; the depth of the arch being 10 ft. back to back of chord angles. The web members are arranged as a single system of the Pratt type, with sub-struts to the top chord as purlin supports. In the end sections the arrangement is necessarily modified, the sharper curvature of the chords being allowed for by more frequent strutting.

The maximum stresses in the different members of the arch are given on the right half of the rib in Fig. 17. These stresses were obtained by properly combining the dead load stresses with the stresses due to wind blowing successively in opposite directions in the plane of the rib in question. The loads used in the calculation were a dead load separately estimated for each panel point, a variable snow load, heaviest at the center of the roof, a wind load of 30 lb. per sq. ft. on a normal surface reduced for inclination of the roof to the vertical. The makeup of the members is given on the left half of the rib in Fig. 17. In the plan part of the dome the method of bracing the ribs is fully shown. Successive pairs of ribs are connected by bays of bracing in both upper and lower chords. In the upper chord the I beam purlins are made use of as struts, angle struts being used in the lower chord. The bracing consists throughout of crossed adjustable rods. At the center, these rods are carried over to a tangential attachment to the central drum, so as to give more rigidity against twisting at the center.

The central drum, 16 ft. in diameter by 10 ft. deep, has a web of $\frac{3}{8}$ in. plate, with stiffener angles to which the ribs are attached. At top and bottom the drum carries a flange plate 24 in. $\times \frac{3}{16}$ in. for lateral stiffeners. In addition it is cross braced internally by four diametrical frames intersecting at the center. The outer tie-girder, which takes the thrust of the arch ribs, is a simple channel-shaped plate girder, 24 in. deep, as shown on the plan. The weight of the dome complete, including framework and covering was 475,000 lb. This makes the dead load about 15 lb. per sq. ft. of horizontal projection of roof surface.

Mr. Harrison Albright, of Charleston, W. Va., was the architect of the building and the design of the steel dome was worked out by Mr. Oliver J. Westcott, while in charge of the estimating department of the Illinois Steel Company. The structural steel was furnished by the Illinois Steel Co.

Engineering and Research Building, A. O. Smith Corporation.*—The building as shown in Fig. 18 and Fig. 19 is U-shaped in plan and is seven stories high besides a basement and an attic. The frontage is 170 ft. and the depth is 205 ft. The wings are 45 ft. wide, leaving a court 80 ft. wide and 160 ft. long. The court is to be used for testing equipment and heavy machinery required in mechanical and electrical testing work and is equipped with a 20-ton crane. At about the third floor level the court is covered by an arch roof made up of pairs of trusses riveted to the columns. Throughout the building the columns are placed in the walls and carry floor trusses which span the entire width. The partitions can be arranged to suit changes and requirements. The longitudinal spacing of the columns is 20 ft. except for 25-ft. bays at the corners of the front. In the main stories the height is 14 ft. from floor to floor. The roof is cement tile, while the court is roofed with concrete and wire-glass skylight. Exposed parts of the trusses are covered with metal lath and plaster.

* Engineering News-Record, December 4, 1930.

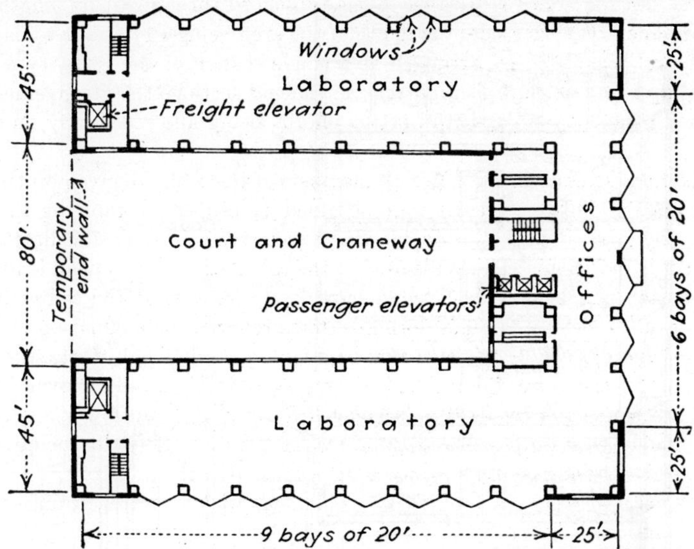

FIG. 18. GENERAL PLAN OF BUILDING.

Structural Design.—The riveted columns, Fig. 20, approximately 3 ft. square, are composed of 6 in. × 6 in. corner angles and $\frac{9}{16}$ in. cover plates, except for a panel of lacing bars in each story. There are batten plates and two exterior angles 6 in. × 4 in. on the outside face and both plates and angles on the inside face, and both plates and lacing bars on the outside face. Horizontal stiffeners angles on the outside face serve as shelf angles for the exterior architectural facing. The column is wrapped with expanded metal lath and covered with 2 inches of cement plaster. An opening or manhole is provided in the basement section of each column and the interior of the column is fitted with ladder irons to enable the repair men to reach any part of the pipe or wiring. Manholes are also provided in the attic. Framed against the side of the column are riveted trusses 20 in. deep and 3 ft. apart as shown in Fig. 20. Each chord is composed of two 5 in. × 4 in. angles with the 5 in. legs horizontal in the top chords so that the horizontal legs form seats for the 5 in. I-beams of the "battle deck" floor framing, whose upper flanges are even with the tops of the trusses. These beams tie the trusses together at the top while 6-in. channels resting on the bottom chords tie the lower chords together. The box girder thus formed has a covering of expanded metal and $1\frac{1}{2}$ inches of cement plaster. The ceiling is made of expanded metal and 1 in. of plaster and is painted the same as the columns. Manholes 23 in. × 18 in. fitted with $\frac{1}{8}$ in. steel doors give access from the columns to the girders. Pipes and wiring are carried through sleeves in the bulkhead between the columns and the girders. Pipes and wiring are extended laterally to any position in the floor.

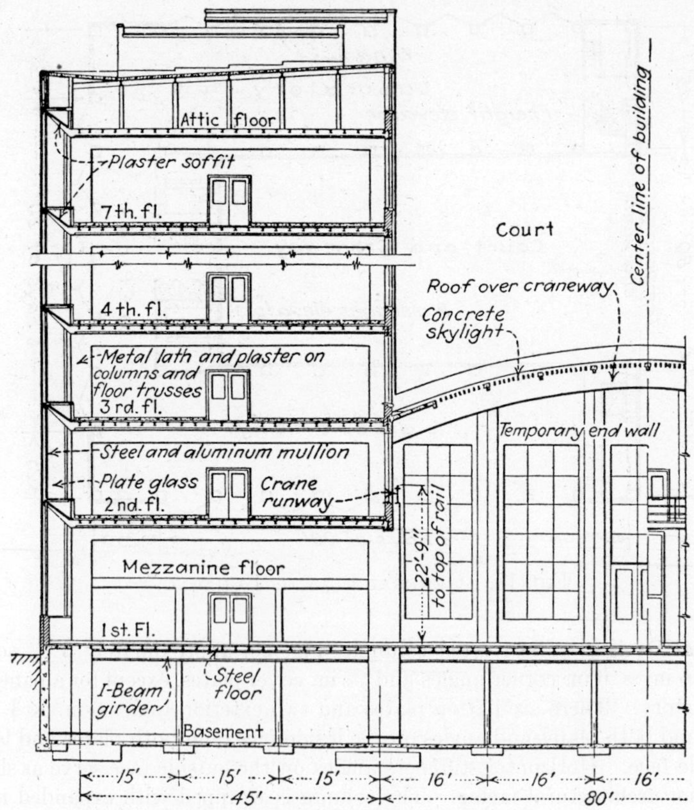

FIG. 19. TYPICAL CROSS-SECTION.

Floor and Roof Construction.—The floor consists of 5 in. I-beams spaced 2 ft. c. to c. resting on the floor trusses and carrying $\frac{3}{16}$ in. deck plates 6 ft. × 20 ft., electrically spot welded to the I-beams through 2 in. slots. The floor surface is a specially designed concrete 1 in. thick, reinforced by steel plates stamped to form 2 in. rings 1 in. deep. This reinforcement is tack-welded to the steel plates. After the concrete was set it was finished by grinding. The floor finish in the offices is $\frac{13}{16}$ in. wood blocks, $11\frac{1}{2}$ in. square attached to the steel deck plates by a mastic coat. The roof is cement tile on I-beam framing. The roof over the court has framing as shown in Fig. 21. The 9-in. I-beam purlins are spaced 8 ft. apart and are welded to the truss and carry a concrete and glass skylight.

Windows.—The greater part of the exterior surface is glazed. None of the windows can be opened as the building will be ventilated mechanically with air conditioned as required. Cool air being supplied in summer and warm air in winter. In the exterior walls each 20-ft. structural panel is a convex triangular bay the full width between columns. A typical window extends 2 ft. 7 in. above one floor to the same level of the floor above.

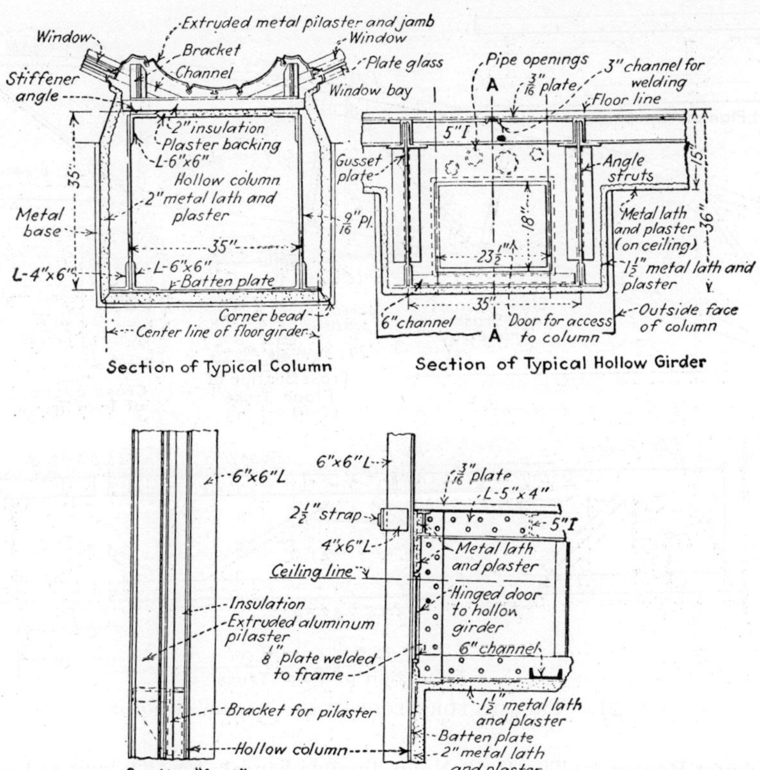

FIG. 20. HOLLOW STEEL COLUMNS AND RIVETED FLOOR TRUSSES.

This bay window slopes upward in triangular form from the ceiling of the room. Each side of the bay is formed by a fixed sash having a single sheet of $\frac{1}{4}$ in. plate glass secured in place by removable exterior stops of extruded aluminum attached to the sash. The sash and frames are aluminum and are welded to the hollow columns. In the walls fronting the court special steel sash with plate glass is used.

The research building was designed by E. W. Burgess, Construction Engineer, A. O. Smith Corporation. The architects were Holabird & Root, Chicago.

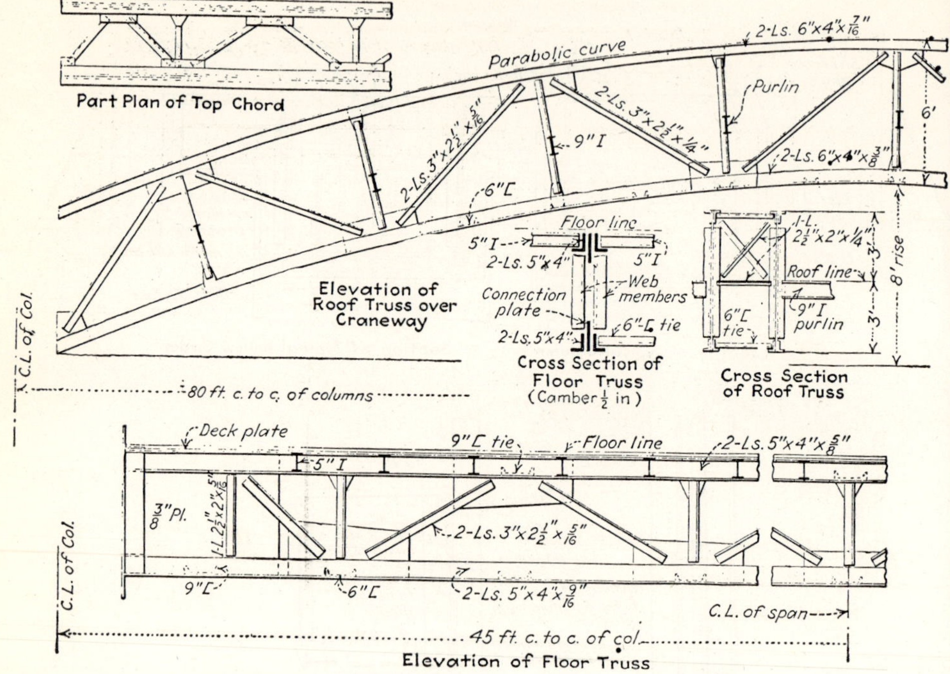

FIG. 21. TRUSSES FOR FLOORS AND CRANEWAY ROOF.

Lakehurst Hangar.*—The U. S. Navy dirigible hangar, Fig. 22, built at Lakehurst, N. J., in 1920 has the following dimensions. The outside dimensions are 954 ft. in length out to out of doors and 350 ft. in width by 200 ft. in height. The clear inside dimensions are 803 ft. by 262 ft. by 172 ft. The clear height of the roof at the crown is 172 ft. at the door and 195 ft. from the floor to the center of the center pin. The framework consists of a series of three-hinged arches supported on high triangular towers. The arch ribs are in pairs, spaced 17 ft. 4 in. center to center, the bents being 69 ft. 4 in. apart with the roof and siding supported by trusses. The outside siding follows the inclined outer chord of the arch rib down to about the junction with the outer leg of the tower at which point it extends as a roof over the space between the inner and outer legs of the towers. This space on both sides is divided into two stories for office and shop purposes. The roof is covered with a felt layer roofing and the sides with corrugated asbestos board.

Design.—The plans for the footings are shown in Fig. 23. There are separate concrete pedestals under each of the three legs of the towers. The piles were designed for a safe load of 25 tons per pile. Each arch is a three-hinged arch carried on triangular trussed towers 64 ft. high. The distance between lower pins is 264 ft. while the rise from pin to pin is 131 ft. The arches are in pairs 17 ft. 4 in. center to center and 69 ft. 4 in. apart, braced as shown in Fig. 24.

* Engineering News-Record, May 6, 1920.

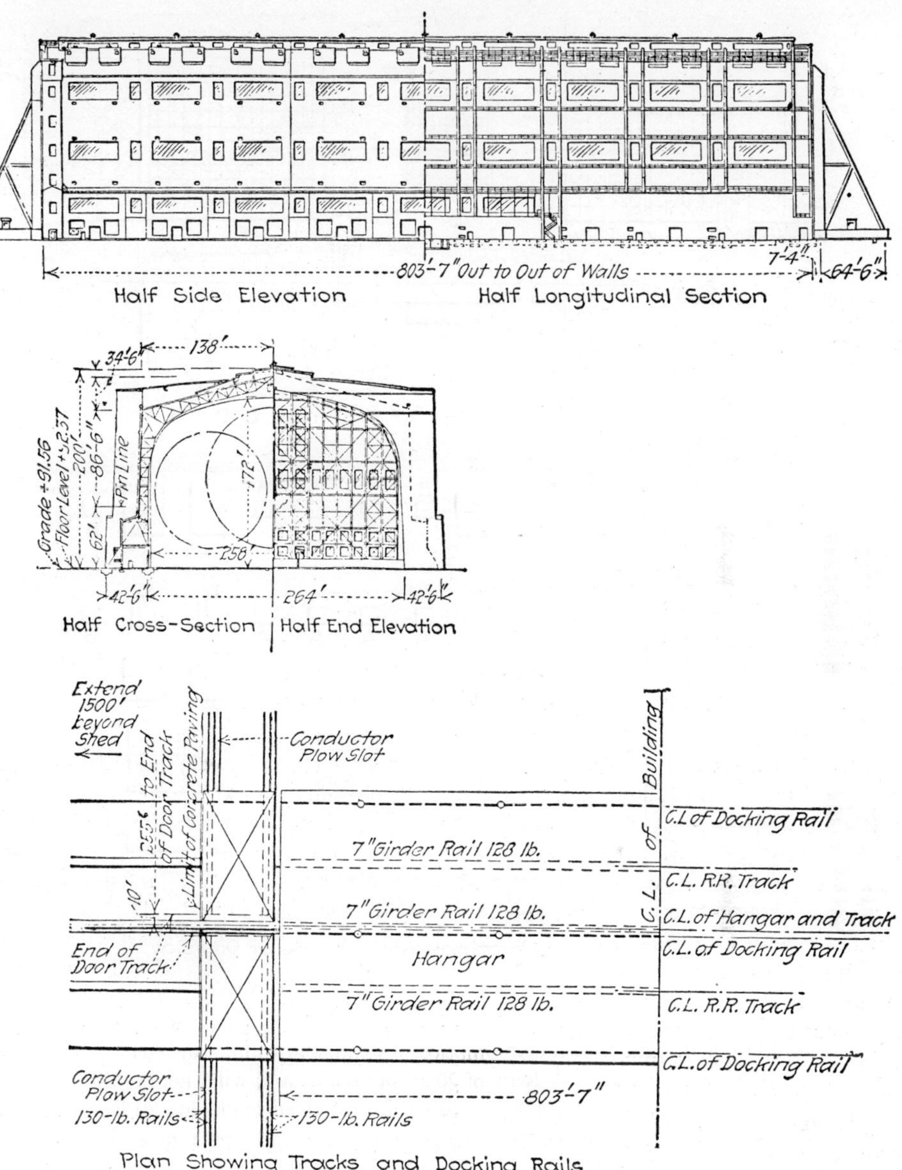

Fig. 22. General Outline and Plan of Lakehurst Steel Hangar, for U. S. Navy.

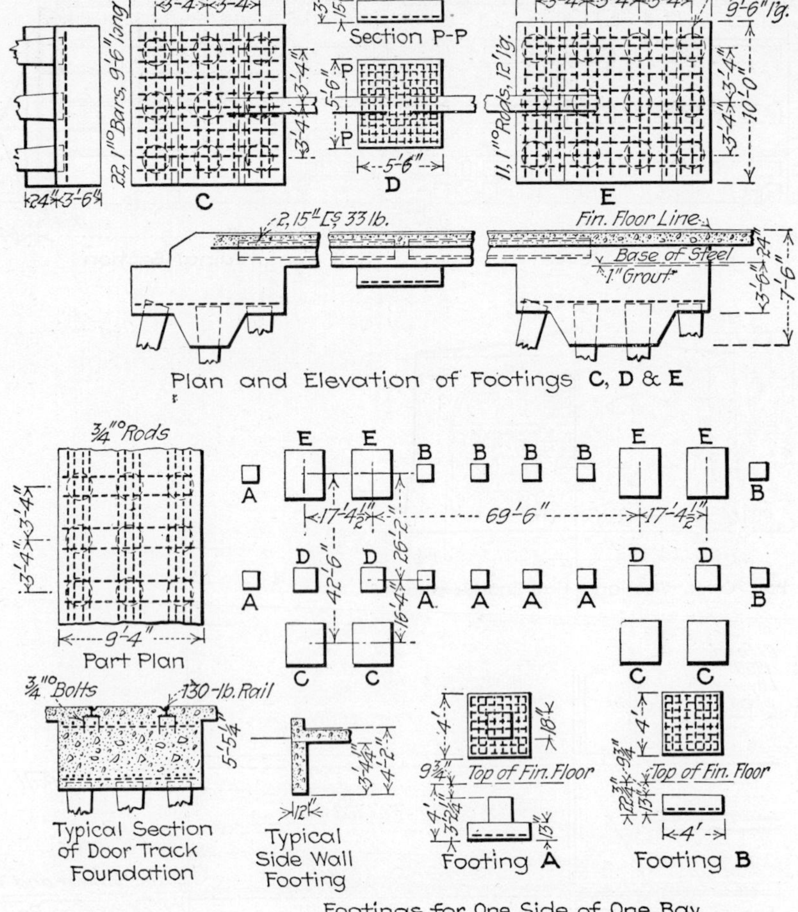

FIG. 23. PLAN OF FOOTINGS FOR COLUMNS.

The building is designed for a combination of dead, snow and wind load, with a basic dead load of 35 lb. per sq. ft., snow load of 20 lb. per sq. ft. and wind load of 30 lb. per sq. ft. The basic unit stress was 16,000 lb. per sq. in. for dead load plus 20 lb. snow load. For dead load plus 30 lb. wind load, add 10 per cent; for dead load plus 30 lb. wind load plus 20 lb. snow load, add 50 per cent, for dead load plus 10 lb. wind load plus 40 lb. snow load, add 50 per cent; for dead load plus 30 lb. wind load plus 10 lb. snow load, add 25 per cent; for dead load plus 40 lb. snow load add 25 per cent to the basic stress of 16,000 lb. per sq. in. The allowable axial compression in columns was $16,000 - 70l/r$ for l/r up to 120. The maximum l/r for main members was 100, for secondary members was 120,

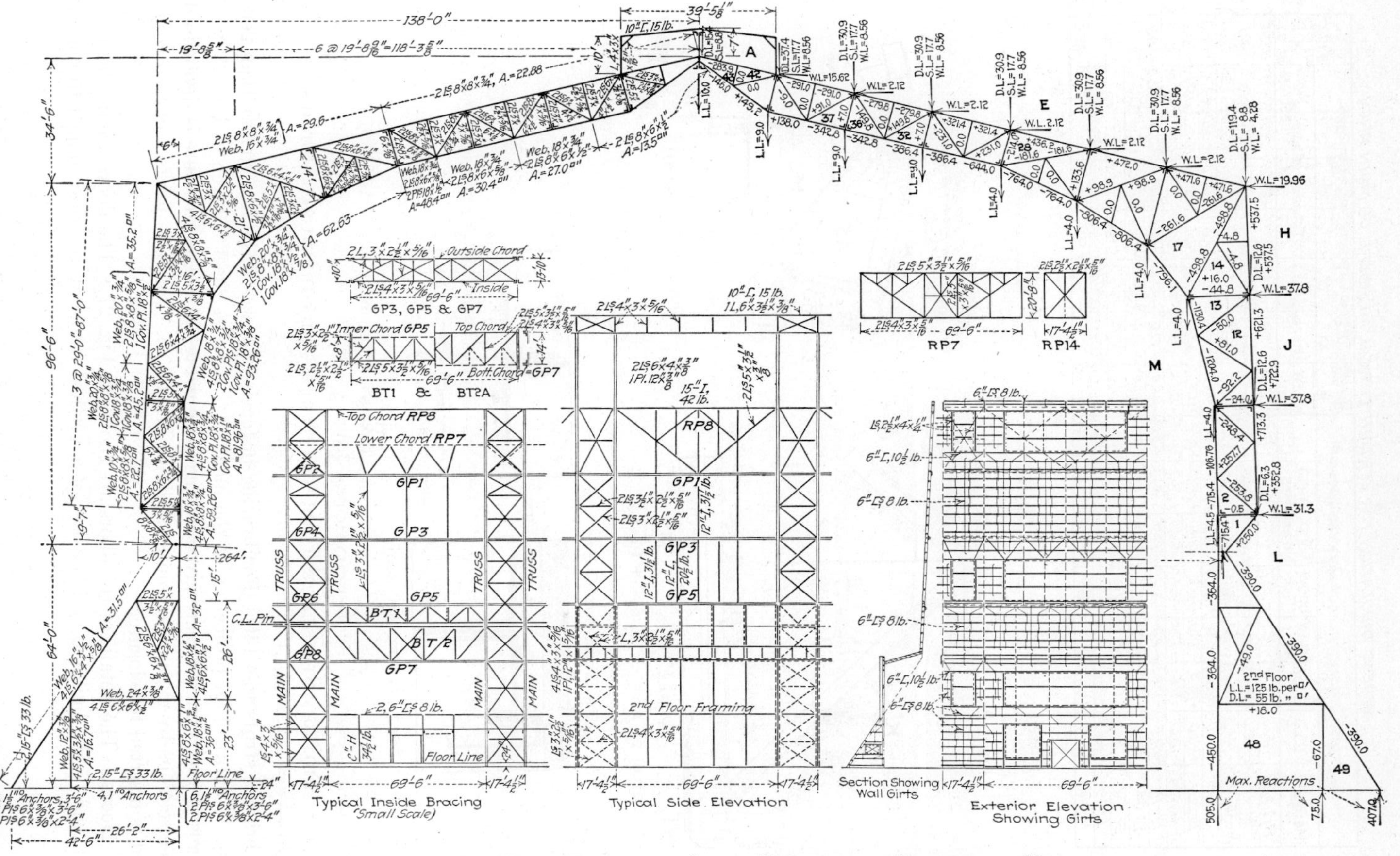

FIG. 24. DETAILS OF MAIN TRUSS AND STEEL FRAMING OF LAKEHURST HANGAR.

STRESS TABULATION FOR CERTAIN TYPICAL MEMBERS OF MAIN ARCH

− Denotes Compression + Denotes Tension								18,000#/□" e	16,000#/□" a	20,000#/□" b	24,000#/□"	24,000#/□" d	20,000#/□" c		
Member	D.L.	Snow	Snow Near	Snow Far	Wind Near	Wind Far	L.L.	D.+L+W.	D.+L.+S.	D.+L+2S.	D.+L+S+W.	D.+L+2.5+$\frac{1}{3}$W	D.+L+W+$\frac{1}{2}$S	Max. Stress	Max. Stress on Basis of 16,000#/□"
M-1. M-2	-450.0	-176.0	-108.5	- 57.7	+ 94.0	-91.0	-91.0	-632.0	-717.6	-894.2	-808.6	-924.5	-720.6	b-894.2	-715.4
M-17	-435.0	-224.0	-115.0	-103.5	+142.0	-171.0	-112.1	-718.1	-769.1	-995.1	-942.1	-1052.1	-830.1	b-995.1	-796.1
M-32, M-33	-145.0	- 71.0	+60.0	-131.0	+288.0	-213.0	-59.5	-417.5	-335.5	-462.5	-548.5	-537.5	-493.0	c-483.0	-386.4
J-12	+291.0	+188.0	+ 85.0	+108.0	-278.0	+177.0	+107.0	+515.0	+586.0	+773.0	+763.0	+833.0	+669.0	d+833.0	+555.0
E-28	+181.0	+87.4	- 54.0	+138.0	-369.0	+227.0	+68.2	+476.2	+387.2	+525.2	+614.2	+601.2	+545.2	c+545.2	+436.2
A-42, A-43	-129.0	-71.5	-77.0	+ 8.0	-154.0	+ 12.0	-33.4	-316.4	-239.4	-316.4	-393.4	-367.7	-354.9	c-354.9	-283.9
12-13	-41.5	-11.5	- 8.0	0	+ 22.0	0	- 4.0	-45.5	-57.0	-62.5	-57.0	-68.5	-51.3	b-62.5	-50.0
13-14	+35.0	+ 9.0	+ 8.0	0	-55.0	0	+ 3.0	- 17.0	+ 47.0	+56.0	+47.0	+56.0	+42.5	e-17.0 b+56.0	-16.0 +44.8
36-37	0	0	0	0	0	0	+8.7	+ 8.7	+ 8.7	+ 8.7	+ 8.7	+ 8.7	+ 8.7	c+8.7	+ 7.0
L-49	- 201.0	-110.0					-66.0			-487.0					
M-48	- 254.0			-41.0	-199.0		- 11.0				-505.0			f-505.0	-450.0

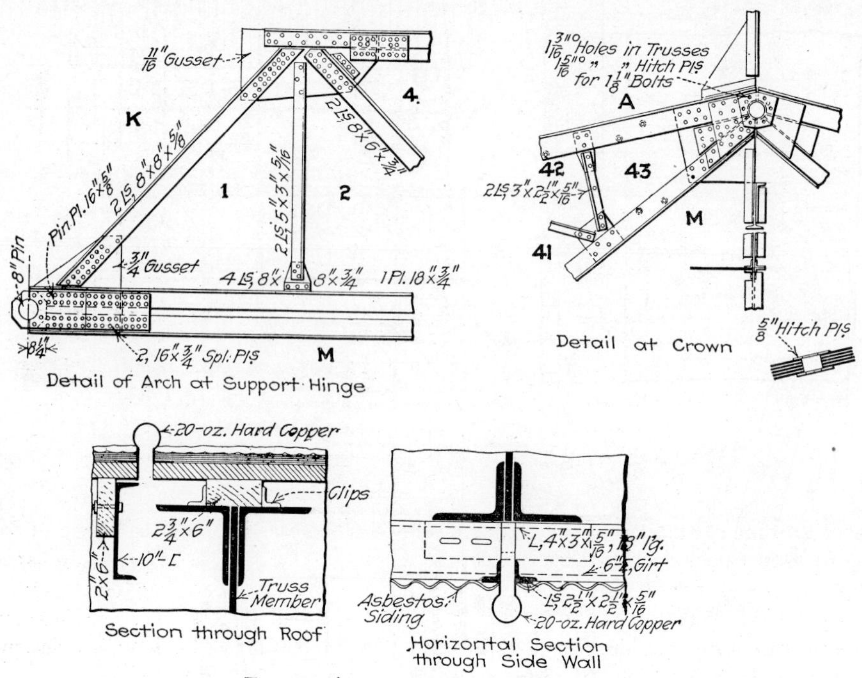

FIG. 25. STRESS SHEET FOR MAIN TRUSS AND STRUCTURAL DETAILS.

for bracing struts was 140. For bracing in tension l/r was to be not greater than 200, l being the horizontal projection of the member. A stress sheet is given in Fig. 25, while details of the framework are given in Fig. 25 and Fig. 26. The structure is divided into three sections by expansion joints as shown in Fig. 25. At these joints a curved copper joint is inserted for closure.

Doors.—The details of the doors are shown in Fig. 27. The doors are duplicates at each end of the building and consists of a vertical frame 10 ft. wide shaped to one-half

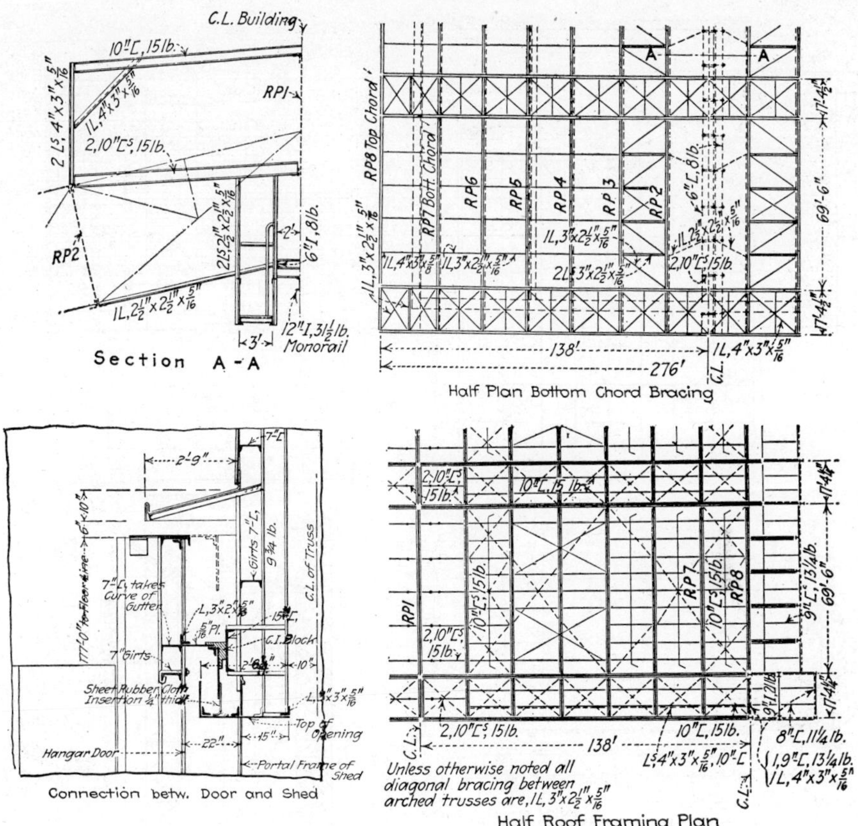

FIG. 26. STEEL FRAMEWORK.

the arch opening, with an inside sheathing of asbestos board. Each leaf is carried on four standard gage trucks each truck having eight wheels. The back braces are also carried on trucks on a standard gage track. The maximum vertical dead load per truck was estimated to be 562,000 lb. The maximum vertical live load 496,000 lb. The maximum horizontal thrust on each door for a 30 lb. load was 720,000 lb. The doors are designed to operate under a wind load of 10 lb. per sq. ft.

Windows.—Special attention was paid to the lighting of the shed because of the possible presence of an explosive mixture due to the escape of hydrogen from the dirigible. All lighting is through heavy glass covers in walls, floor and roof with electrical connections outside the structure and with gas proof glass covers. There were no exposed wires taken inside the shed.

Floor.—The floor of the hangar is asphalt block on an 8 in. concrete base. Other floors are concrete, tile or wood flooring.

The hangar was designed by the Bureau of Yards and Docks under the direction of Rear Admiral C. W. Parks, Civil Engineer Corps, U.S.N., Chief of Bureau, and Commander Kirby Smith, C.E.C., U.S.N., Project Manager.

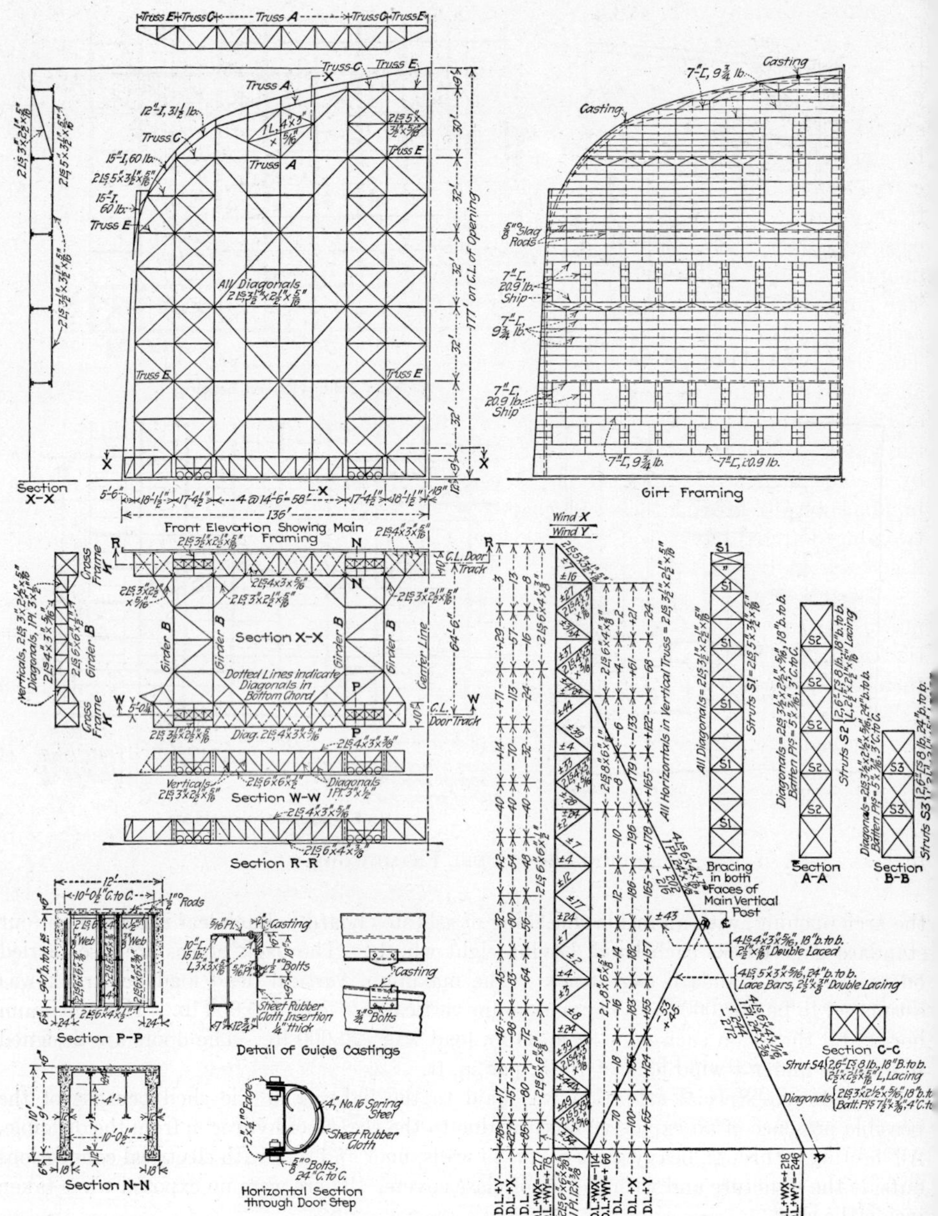

Fig. 27. Details of Framework for Steel Doors.

Akron Airship Dock.*—The airship factory and dock, Fig. 28 at Akron, Ohio, built by the Goodyear-Zeppelin Corporation, has the following main dimensions: Length 1,175 ft., width 325 ft. The vertical distance from the lower pins to the center pin is 197 ft. 6 in. The main framework consists of a series of eleven parabolic three-hinged arches, spaced 80 ft. on centers and are connected by a system of vertical and horizontal truss bracing. These trusses carry light trussed rafters spaced 10 ft. on centers which in turn carry Z-bar purlins, spaced 8 ft. on centers. At each end of the main shell, which is 800 ft. long, are two diagonal arches meeting the end arches in the door pins. The structure encloses a floor area of 360,000 sq. ft. and has a total volume of 55,000,000 cu. ft. The doors are built of similar arched and braced ribs, five arch segments being used in each door. The horizontal component of the stress of the arches is taken by the reinforced concrete arch ties placed under the building floor. There are no expansion joints in the structure. The three center arches are fixed in position while all others are carried upon rollers, allowing the building to expand freely from the center toward each end. This permits the end arches supporting the doors to move laterally about 4 in. under the maximum temperature range. The forces exerted on the shoes by expansion and contraction are transmitted by a continuous strut placed above the floor. The diagonal arches at each end of the building were treated as three-hinged arches, while the main arches were converted into two-hinged arches by riveting up the lower chord after the steel was erected. This made it necessary to design the main arches as statically indeterminate two-hinged arches.

Design Data.—The dead load was assumed as 10 lb. per sq. ft. on roofing sheets, purlins and rafters; 20 lb. on laterals and 30 lb. on the arches. The snow load in combination with the dead load only was assumed as 30 lb. per sq. ft. on all surfaces inclined less than 45 per cent; in combination with a maximum wind load, the snow load was assumed as 15 lb. per sq. ft.

Three classifications of wind loads were considered. (1) A wind load of 80 lb. per sq. ft. on roofing sheets, purlins and rafters in the upper portion of the building, and 40 lb. per sq. ft. for those in the lower, (2) a wind load of 37.5 lb. per sq. ft. combined with an internal force of 12.5 on all bracing and arches, pressures distributed in accordance with the pressure diagram derived from model experiments, Fig. 29, (3) a direct horizontal wind pressure of 15 lb. per sq. ft. on external surface only with no consideration of interior forces to be used when stresses due to this load exceed those from the wind load in (2) above.

Working Stresses.—The working stress for dead and snow load only was 18,000 lb. per sq. in. on structural steel grade, and 24,000 lb. on silicon steel. For maximum stresses due to wind load the working stress was 24,000 lb. per sq. in. on structural steel grade and 32,000 lb. on silicon steel. All material is structural grade steel except the chords of the main arches which are silicon steel. The carbon steel was required to give an ultimate strength of 55,000 to 65,000 with a yield point of 30,000 lb. per sq. in. minimum. The silicon steel was required to give an ultimate strength of 80,000 to 95,000 with a yield point of 45,000 lb. per sq. in. minimum. There are 5,500 tons of structural steel in the shell of the building.

Door Design.—Each leaf of the spherical door is approximately one-eighth of a sphere, 214 ft. wide at the base, 202 ft. high, and weighs about 600 tons. Each leaf is carried on 40 forged steel double flanged wheels 27 in. in diameter, and run on a standard gage track with 100 lb. rails curved to a radius of approximately 188 ft. The hinge pins at the top

* Engineering News-Record, July 24, 1930.

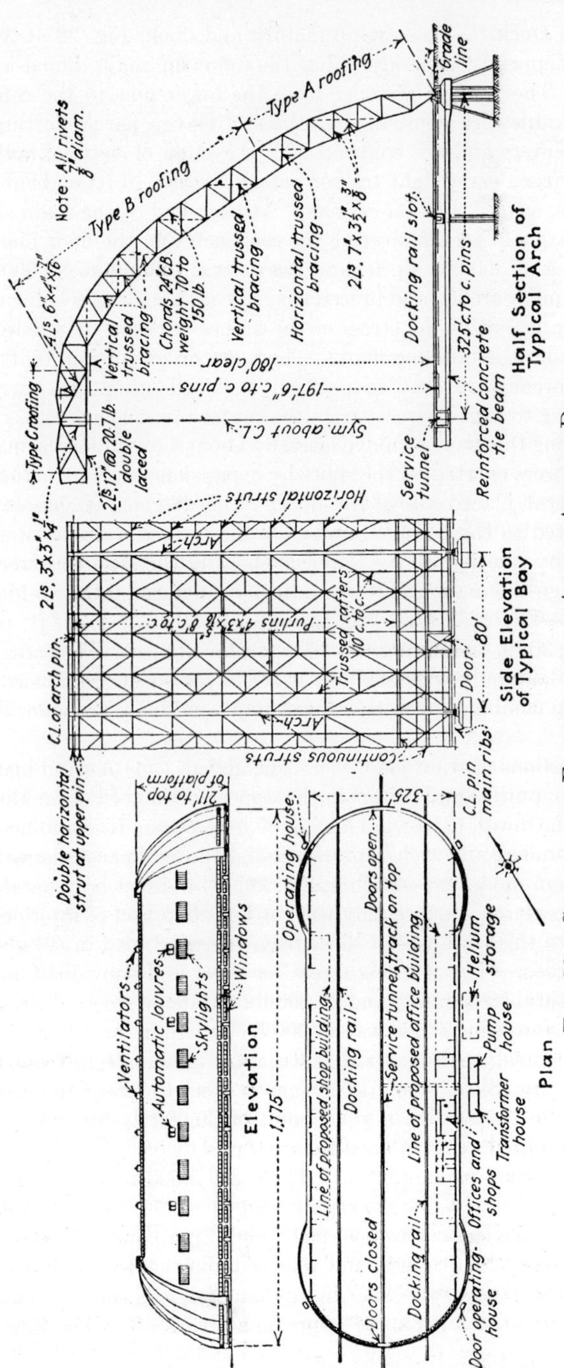

FIG. 28. STRUCTURAL FRAMEWORK OF AKRON AIRSHIP DOCK.

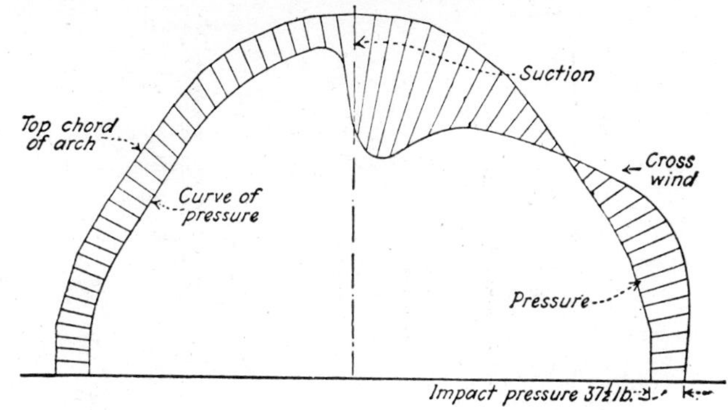

FIG. 29. WIND-PRESSURE CURVE OF AKRON AIRSHIP DOCK.

of the doors are 17 in. in diameter and 6 ft. long and are secured to the roof girders by heavy steel frames. Since a separate pin is required for each leaf of the door, there are two pins side by side 4 ft. apart. Each pin is required to resist the side pressure caused by the tendency of the door to fall inward. With doors on opposite ends open a strong wind may tend to push the doors outward. It is estimated that the pressure against the pin may reach a maximum of about 550,000 lb. inward and 450,000 lb. outward. The pins carry no vertical loads.

Roofing Design.—It was desirable that the roofing should be strong, incombustible and watertight and furnish the maximum practical insulation. The roof covering was divided into three types. Type A was to consist of metal sheets, pretreated with a protective coating and designed to carry a load of 100 lb. per sq. ft. either from the outside or the inside with a maximum deflection of 2 per cent of the span. Type B covering was to consist of metal sheets except that they were to be designed for a load of 200 lb. per sq. ft., either from outside or inside. Type C covering was similar except that flat surface waterproofing was to be applied. Tests showed that 18-gage open hearth steel satisfied the requirements for B type steel and 22-gage steel satisfied the A type loading. All steel sheets were 23½ in. wide and were corrugated with corrugations 5.25 in. wide and 1.75 in. deep. On account of the great cost of insulating the entire roof it was decided to insulate the Type C surface, Fig. 17, and 14 ft. at the top of Type B surface at the present. The insulation used consists of two layers of ½ in. wood-fiber board covered with a tar and gravel roofing for Type C and with 22-gage steel sheets for Type B roofing. Ventilators were provided along the top of the roof. Automatic relief vents were provided along the sides of the building. These relief vents open out automatically when the internal pressure is 10 lb. per sq. ft. Only a small amount of natural light is provided inasmuch as most of the manufacturing operations will require artificial light. The floor is concrete 6 in. thick on a 6 in. slag base.

The personnel in charge of the Goodyear Zeppelin airship factory and dock consisted of P. W. Litchfield, President; Dr. Karl Arnstein, Vice President and Chief Engineer; W. C. State, Consulting Engineer and Wilbur J. Watson. The structure was designed by Wilbur J. Watson and Associates.

References.—For examples of steel bins and steel grain elevators, see the author's "Design of Walls, Bins and Grain Elevators." For examples of steel head frames, steel rock houses, steel coal tipples, and other mine structures, see the author's "Design of Mine Structures."

CHAPTER XXVII.

Data for Design of Framework.

Introduction.—The framework of steel frame buildings consists of members that are designed to carry the stresses by direct tension and compression, or by bending, or by both direct and bending stresses. The members of the framework are fabricated from plates and standard sections riveted together, or from bars or structural shapes alone. The members are fastened together at the joints by means of rivets, or the trusses or the bracing may have pin connections. The trusses used in steel mill buildings are commonly made with riveted connections. The lateral bracing should preferably be made of stiff members capable of taking both tension and compression, although adjustable rods may be used in the sides and ends and in the plane of the upper chords of steel frame buildings. The standard structural sections will be described in detail.

STRUCTURAL SHAPES.—The standard rolled sections used in fabricating steel frame structures are shown in Fig. 1. Angles are made with equal legs, (a) Fig. 1, or with unequal legs, (b) Fig. 1. The maximum section for an equal legged angle is 8 in. × 8 in. by $1\frac{1}{4}$ in. thick; while the maximum section for an unequal legged angle is 8 in. × 6 in. × 1 in. thick. The maximum section for a Z-bar, (c) Fig. 1, is $6\frac{1}{8}$ in. × $3\frac{5}{8}$ in. × $\frac{7}{8}$ in. thick. The maximum standard I-beam is 24 in. deep and weighs 115 lb. per lineal foot. The Carnegie Steel Co. makes a special I-beam 27 in. deep and weighing 83 lb. per lineal foot, while the Bethlehem Steel Co. makes I-beams 30 in. deep and weighing 120 lb. per lineal foot. The maximum channel is 15 in. deep and weighs 55 lb. per lineal foot. The U. S. Steel Corporation and the Bethlehem Steel Company make girder beams 36 in. deep weighing 300 lb. and H-columns up to 18 in. deep weighing 425 lb. per ft. The maximum T-beam with equal legs is 4 in. × 4 in. × $\frac{1}{2}$ in. thick. The maximum T-beam with unequal legs is 5 in. × 3 in. × $\frac{1}{2}$ in. thick. Deck beams vary in weight from 6 in. deep, weighing 14 lb. per lineal foot to 10 in. deep, weighing 36.6 lb. per lineal foot. Bulb angles vary in weight from 4 in. × $3\frac{1}{2}$ in., weighing 11.9 lb. per lineal foot to 10 in. × $3\frac{1}{2}$ in., weighing 32 lb. per lineal foot. Z-bars and T-bars are used to a very limited extent in fabricating steel frame structures. Deck beams and bulb angles are used principally in the construction of ships.

The dimensions, weights and other data for structural shapes are given in the author's "Structural Engineers' Handbook," and also in the handbooks furnished by the steel companies.

COMPRESSION MEMBERS.—Angles may be used for struts or ties, either singly or riveted together as shown in (a) to (f), Fig. 2. Angle columns may be fabricated as shown in (g), (h) and (i), Fig. 2. The 4-angle section in (g) should be spread at the ends to admit connection plates. The 4-angle column in (i) is usually imbedded in concrete.

Channel and T-shaped chord sections made of angles and plates are shown in Fig. 3.

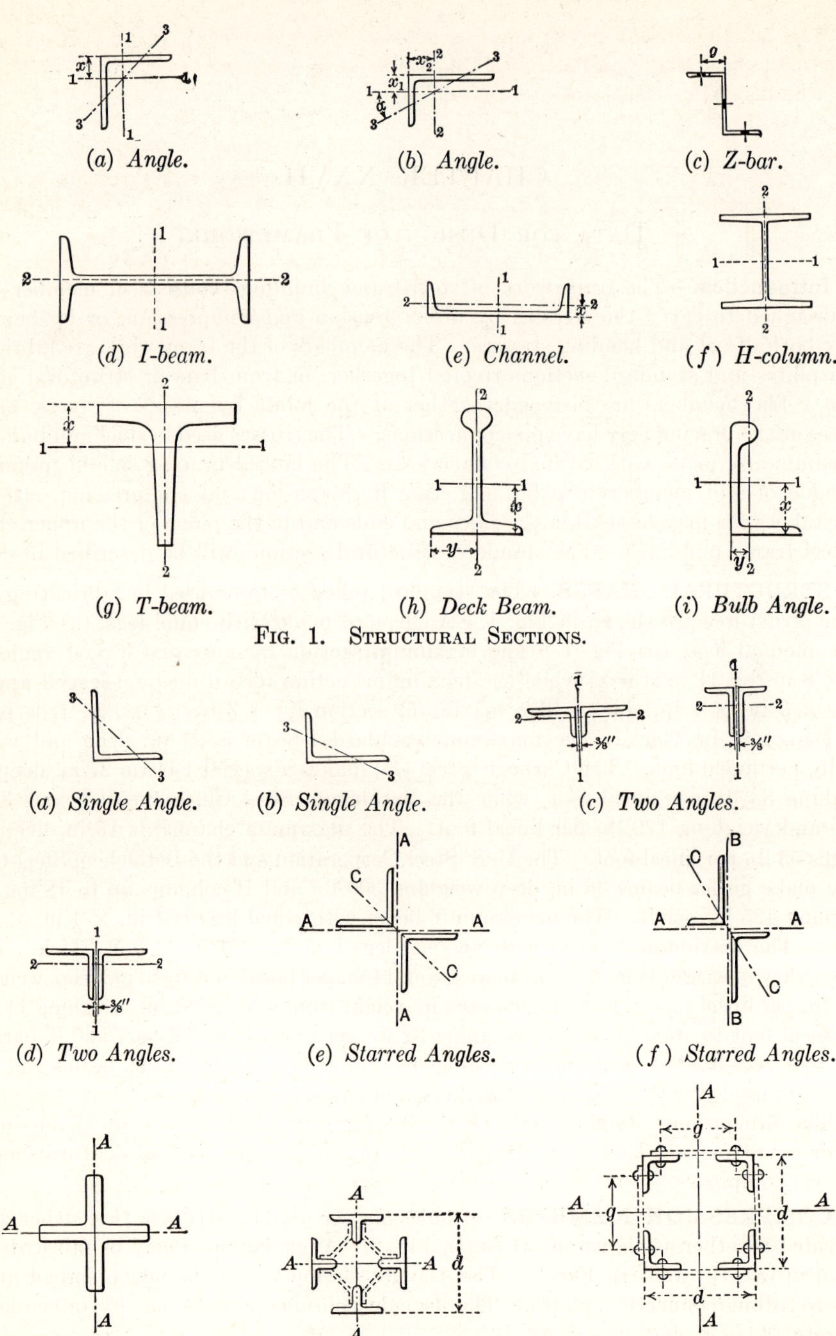

FIG. 1. STRUCTURAL SECTIONS.

FIG. 2. ANGLE STRUTS.

The built H-section in (a) Fig. 4 is made of 4 angles laced; the built H-section in (b) is made of 4 angles and a web plate, while the H-section in (c) is made of 4 angles and 3 plates. These sections are used for columns.

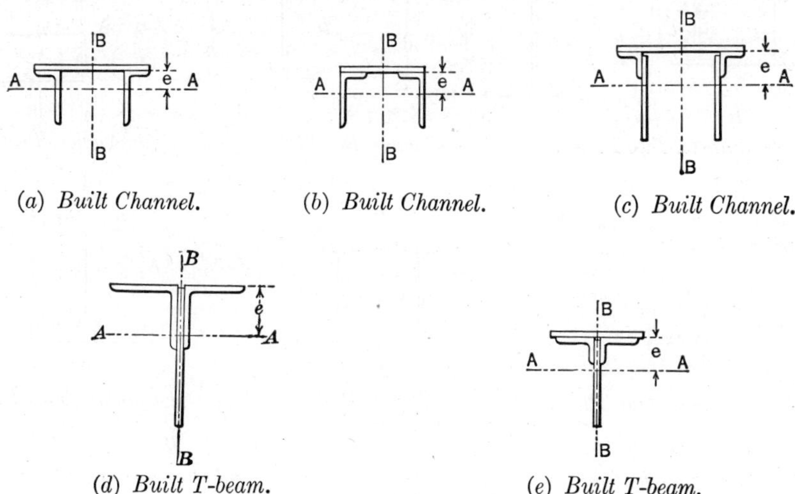

(*a*) *Built Channel.* (*b*) *Built Channel.* (*c*) *Built Channel.*

(*d*) *Built T-beam.* (*e*) *Built T-beam.*

FIG. 3. CHORD SECTIONS.

Several built column sections are shown in Fig. 5. Sections (d), (e), (f), (i), (j), (k), (l) and (m) are used for columns carrying heavy loads. The H-section in (f) is the H-section in (f) Fig. 1, with two cover plates riveted to the flanges. This section is used for office building columns in competition with the built H-column in (c), Fig. 4.

For types of columns used in steel mill buildings, see Fig. 19, Chapter XXV. For details of steel columns, see Fig. 20 to Fig. 23, Chapter XXV.

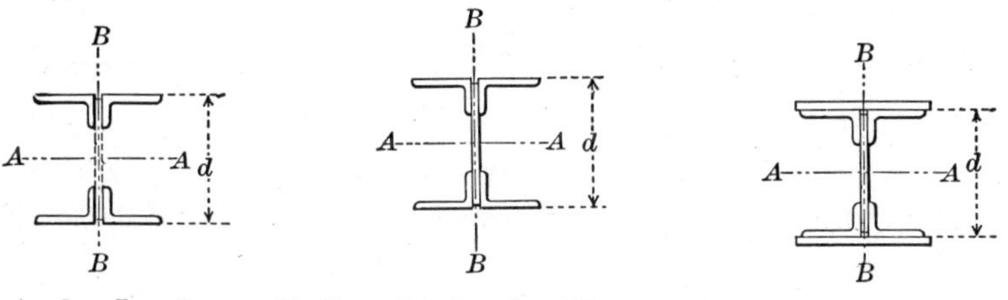

(*a*) *Four Angles, Laced.* (*b*) *Four Angles, One Plate.* (*c*) *Four Angles, Three Plates.*

FIG. 4. COMPRESSION MEMBERS MADE OF ANGLES AND PLATES.

The built chord sections shown in Fig. 6 are used in steel truss bridge construction.

Section (a) Fig. 7 is used for eave struts, while sections (b) and (c) are used for columns which carry an unsymmetrical load due to a crane girder.

The connection of an I-beam to a channel by means of connection angles is shown in (a), Fig. 8, while the connection of an I-beam to an I-beam is shown in (b), Fig. 8. Details of standard connection angles are shown in Fig. 18.

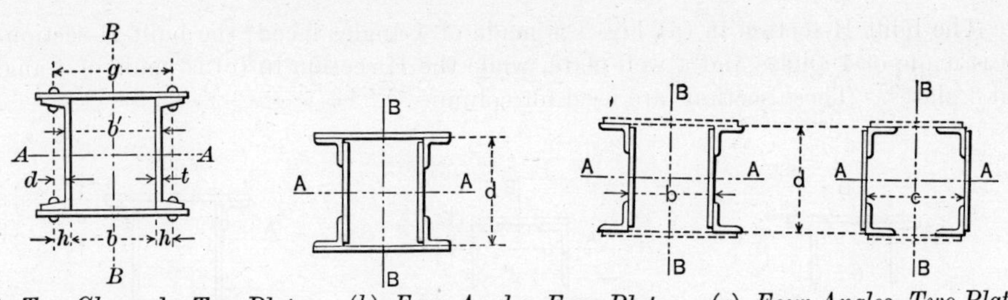

(a) *Two Channels, Two Plates.* (b) *Four Angles, Four Plates.* (c) *Four Angles, Two Plates.*

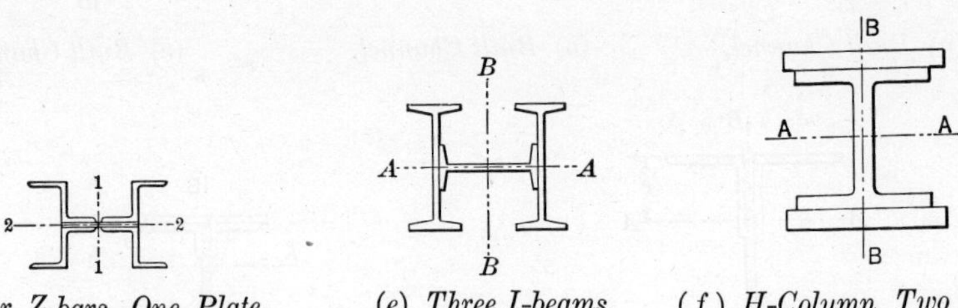

(d) *Four Z-bars, One Plate.* (e) *Three I-beams.* (f) *H-Column Two Plates.*

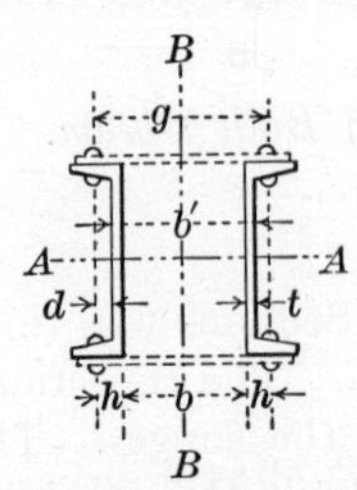

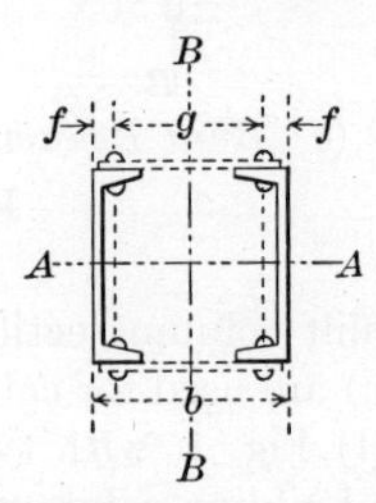

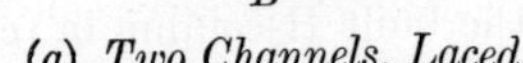

(g) *Two Channels, Laced.* (h) *Two Channels, Laced.*

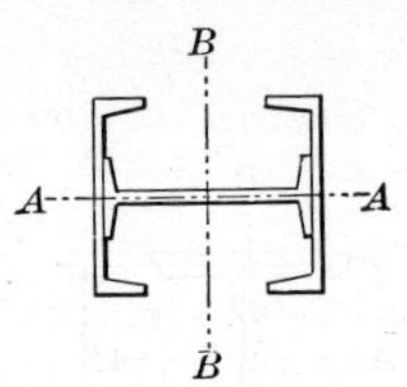

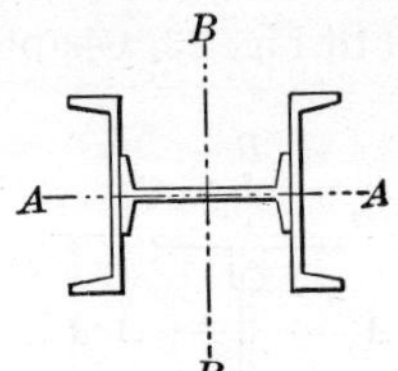

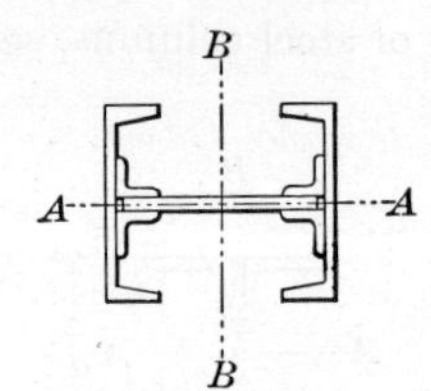

(i) *Two Channels, One I-beam.* (j) *Two Channels, One I-beam.* (k) *Two Channels, Built I-beam.*

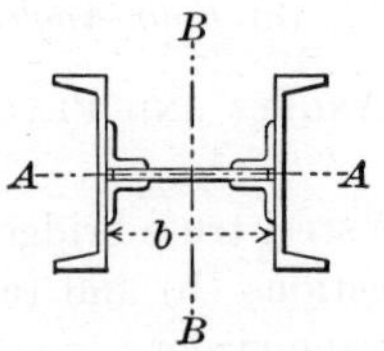

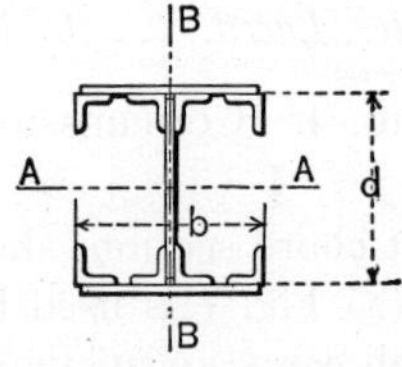

(l) *Two Channels, Built I-beam.* (m) *Two Built Channels, Built I-beam.*

FIG. 5. COMPRESSION MEMBERS.

TENSION MEMBERS.—Tension members are made (1) of eye-bars; (2) of square or round loop bars; (3) of simple shapes, and (4) of built sections.

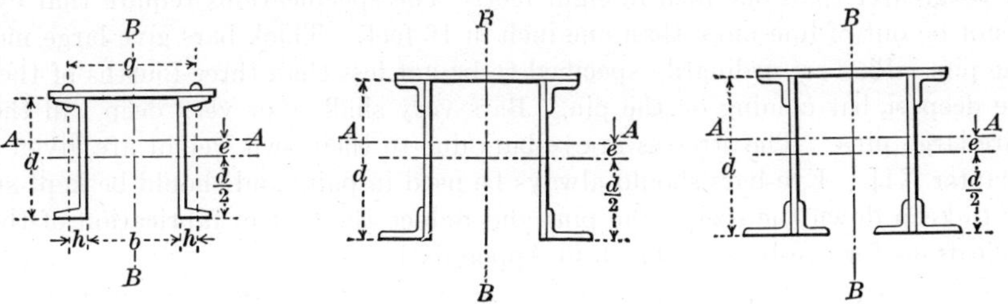

(*a*) *Two Channels, One Plate.* (*b*) *Four Angles, Three Plates.* (*c*) *Six Angles, Three Plates.*

Fig. 6. Chord Sections.

Eye-bars.—Eye-bars are used for main tension members of pin-connected trusses. The eyes may be formed (*a*) by upsetting and forging, or (*b*) by piling and welding. By the first method the bar is upset and the head is forged in a die, after which the bar is reheated and annealed and the pin hole is drilled. By the second method a " pile " of iron bars is placed on the end of the bar, the pile is heated and the head is forged in a die. The bar is then reheated and annealed and the pin hole is drilled.

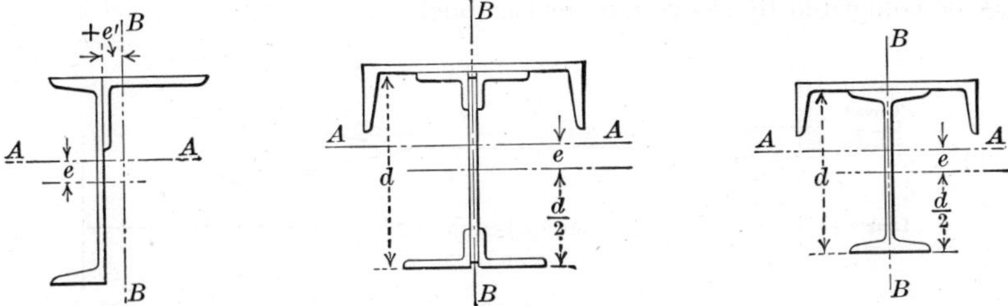

(*a*) *One Channel, One Angle.* (*b*) *One Channel, Built I-beam.* (*c*) *One Channel, One I-beam.*

Fig. 7. Eave Strut and Unsymmetrical Columns.

Steel eye-bars should always be made by upsetting and forging. The American Bridge Company's standard eye-bars are given in Fig. 9, and in the author's " Structural Engineers' Handbook." Eye-bars thinner than those specified are liable to buckle in the head. Eye-bars may be obtained in different thicknesses varying by 1/16 inch. Eye-bars are seldom made with a thickness of more than one-third or less than one-sixth of the depth of the bar. The Osborn Engineering Company specifies that bars

(*a*) *Connection Angle.* (*b*) *Connection Angles.*

Fig. 8. Connection Angles.

shall not be less than $\frac{5}{8}$ in. in thickness, and preferably not less in thickness than $\frac{1}{5}$ the depth. Eye-bars should be parallel as nearly as possible; the maximum variation should never be greater than one inch in eight feet. The specifications require that eye-bars shall not be out of line more than one inch in 16 feet. Thick bars give large moments on the pin. Pins are ordinarily specified to be not less than three-fourths of the depth of the deepest bar coming on the pin. Bars very shallow or very deep will therefore require large pins. The stresses in eye-bars due to their own weight are given in Fig. 4, Chapter XII. Eye-bars should always be used in pairs and should be kept small in order to keep down the size of the pins and reduce the cost of fabrication of the pins. Specifications for eye-bars are given in Appendix I.

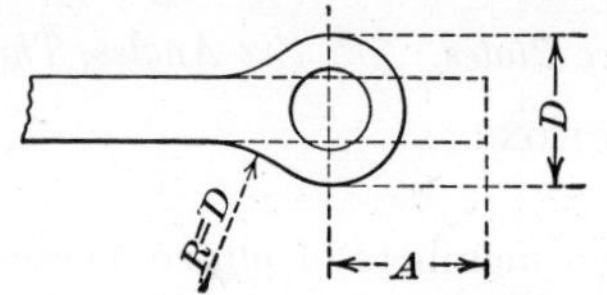

FIG. 9. ORDINARY EYE-BARS.

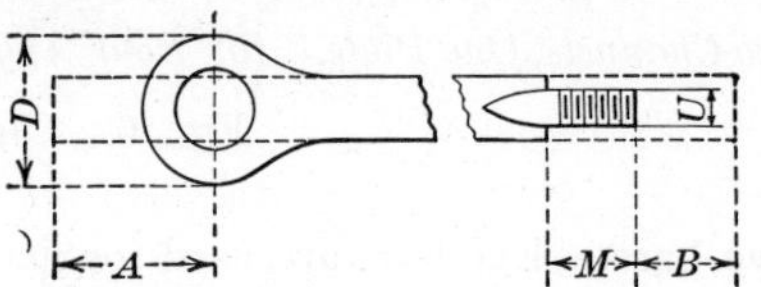

FIG. 10. ADJUSTABLE EYE-BARS.

Adjustable Eye-bars.—Where eye-bars are used for counters they are made adjustable. The American Bridge Company's standard adjustable eye-bars are given in Fig. 10, and in the author's "Structural Engineers' Handbook." The parts of the bar may be connected by sleeve nuts or turnbuckles.

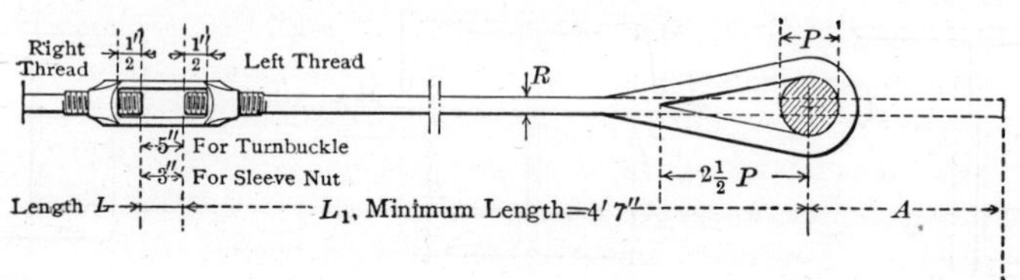

FIG. 11. LOOP-BAR.

Loop-bars.—Iron bars, both square and round, are often made with loop ends. Steel bars should never be used with loop ends for the reason that welded steel is not ordinarily considered reliable. The American Bridge Company's standard loop-bars are shown in Fig. 11, and in the author's "Structural Engineers' Handbook." Loop-bars are made with both single and double loops. Clevises are to be preferred to double loops. Loop-bars bent in the weld should not be used.

Standard Upsets.—Bars upon which screw ends are to be cut, are first upset so that the area through the base of the screw will be in excess of the main body of the bar by a required amount, varying from 16 to 40 per cent. The American Bridge Company's standard upsets for round and square bars are given in the author's "Structural Engineers' Handbook."

Clevises.—Where small round or square steel bars are used, the ends should be upset and the connection to the pin should be made by means of clevises. The American Bridge Company's standard clevises are given in Fig. 12, and in the author's "Structural Engineers' Handbook."

Turnbuckles and Sleeve Nuts.—Eye- or loop-bars are made adjustable by means of turnbuckles or sleeve nuts. Turnbuckles are more often used than sleeve nuts. The turnbuckle has the advantage that the ends of the bars are visible, while it has the disadvantage that it can be loosened with a bar. The American Bridge Company's standard turnbuckles and sleeve nuts are given in Fig. 13 and Fig. 14, and in the author's "Structural Engineers' Handbook."

Riveted Tension Members.—The problem in the design of riveted tension members is the design of the end connections. The rivets in the end connections should be sym-

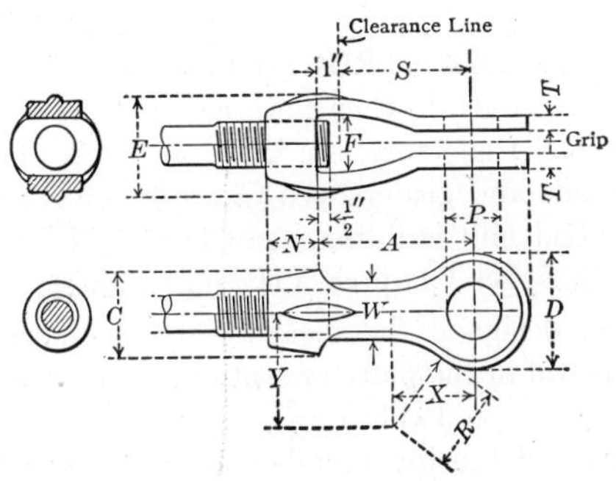

FIG. 12. CLEVIS.

metrical with the neutral axis of the member. This is sometimes difficult to attain, and results in large eccentric stresses. In riveted tension members with pin-connections it is usually specified: (1) That the net area through the pin hole must exceed the required net area of the member by 25 per cent, and (2) the area back of the pin hole on a plane through the center of the pin hole and parallel to the axis of the member must be not less than 75 per cent of the area through the pin hole. The net area of the member must be used in calculating the strength of a riveted tension member.

The net area of a tension member, A, required to carry a direct tension, T, with a safe unit stress, f, is $A = T/f$. For methods of calculating the stresses in tension members due to direct and cross-bending forces, see Chapter XII.

For the calculation of the stresses in an eccentric riveted connection, see Chapter XII.

The areas to be deducted for rivet holes in tension members are given in Table II.

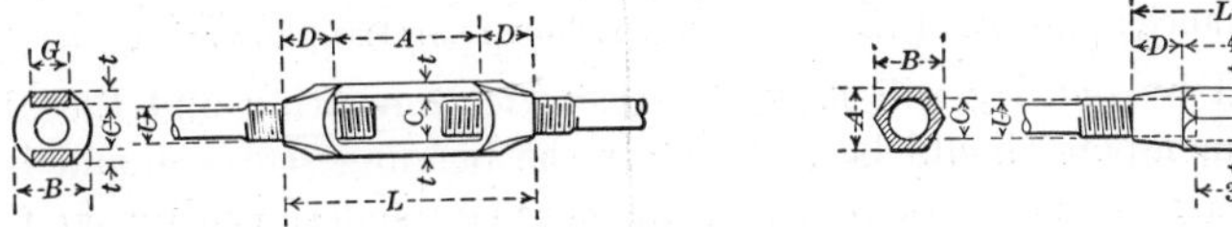

FIG. 13. TURNBUCKLE. FIG. 14. SLEEVE NUT.

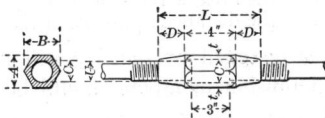

PRESSED STEEL SECTIONS.—Structural steel sections, I-beams, channels, angles, etc., are made by pressing rolled steel sheets into the desired shape. Pressed steel sections, called "steel lumber," are used as joists in floor construction, and in wall construction. Small industrial buildings or residences have been made by coating the framework of "steel lumber" with expanded metal and plaster, for the walls and with reinforced concrete floors. Details of "steel lumber" are described in "Handbook of Steel Lumber," The National Pressed Steel Co., Massilon, Ohio, and in "Berloy," The Berger Manufacturing Co., Canton, Ohio.

SPECIFICATIONS FOR STEEL FRAME BUILDINGS.—Detail specifications for the design of steel frame mill buildings are given in Appendix I. These specifications contain detailed requirements for loads, allowable unit stresses, materials and details of steel frame mill buildings. The specifications for structural steel given in Appendix I are identical with the specifications for steel for buildings adopted by the American Society for Testing Materials, except that the option of using Bessemer steel has been eliminated.

DESIGN OF STEEL FRAME STRUCTURES.—The design of steel frame structures is taken up in detail in several other chapters.

For the design of a steel roof truss, see Chapter XXXVI.

For the design of beams and girders, see Chapter XXXVII.

For the design of a steel mill building, see Chapter XXXVIII.

For the design of purlins, see Chapter XII and Chapter XXV.

RIVETS.—Rivets are designed for shearing stress on the rivet and for bearing stress of the rivet on the metal in the plate or section. The allowable stresses on rivets for shear and bearing are given in Table I.

The net area of a riveted tension member is found by deducting the number of rivet holes at any section from the gross area of the member at that section. The diameter of the rivet is to be taken as $\frac{1}{8}$ in. larger than the nominal diameter of the rivet. For example the hole for a $\frac{5}{8}$ in. rivet is to be taken as $\frac{3}{4}$ in. Areas to be deducted for rivets of different diameters and plates of different thickness are given in Table II.

Where there is more than one line of rivets in a tension member the number of rivets to be deducted should be determined by the following specification taken from Appendix I.

Net Section.—In members subject to tensile stresses full allowance shall be made for reduction of section by rivet-holes, screw-threads, etc. In calculating net area the rivet-holes shall be taken as having a diameter $\frac{1}{8}$ in. greater than the normal size of rivet.

The net section of riveted members shall be the least area which can be obtained by deducting from the gross sectional area the areas of holes cut by any plane perpendicular to the axis of the member and parts of the areas of other holes on one side of the plane, within a distance of 4 inches, and which are on other gage lines than those of the holes cut by the plane, the parts being determined by the formula:

$$A(1 - p/4),$$

in which A = the area of the hole, and

p = the distance in inches of the center of the hole from the plane.

Angles fastened by one leg will have an eccentric connection and the allowable stresses in tension members should be reduced or the bending stress should be calculated. Angles in tension that are fastened by one leg may be designed by the following specification taken from Appendix I.

Angles in Tension.—When single-angle members subject to direct tension are fastened by one leg, only seventy-five per cent of the net area shall be considered effective. Angles with lug angle connections shall not be considered as fastened by both legs.

The standard specifications for the pitch of rivets in members and the edge distance are as follows:—

Pitch of Rivets.—The minimum distance between centers of rivet holes shall be three diameters of the rivet; but the distance shall preferably be not less than 3 in. for $\frac{7}{8}$-in. rivets, $2\frac{1}{2}$ in. for $\frac{3}{4}$-in. rivets, and 2 in. for $\frac{5}{8}$-in. rivets. The maximum pitch in the line of stress for members composed of plates and shapes shall be 16 times the thickness of the thinnest outside plate or 6 in. For angles with two gage lines and rivets staggered, the maximum shall be twice the above in each line. Where two or more plates are used in contact, rivets not more than 12 in. apart in either direction shall be used to hold the plates well together.

Edge Distance.—The minimum distance from the center of any rivet hole to a sheared edge shall be $1\frac{1}{2}$ in. for $\frac{7}{8}$-in. rivets, $1\frac{1}{4}$ in. for $\frac{3}{4}$-in. rivets, and $1\frac{1}{8}$ in. for $\frac{5}{8}$-in. rivets, and to a rolled edge $1\frac{1}{4}$, $1\frac{1}{8}$ and 1 in., respectively. The maximum distance from any edge shall be eight times the thickness of the plate, but shall not exceed 6 in.

Maximum Diameter.—The diameter of the rivets in any angle carrying calculated stress shall not exceed one-quarter the width of the leg in which they are driven. In minor parts $\frac{7}{8}$-in. rivets may be used in 3-in. angles, $\frac{3}{4}$-in. rivets in $2\frac{1}{2}$-in. angles, and $\frac{5}{8}$-in. rivets in 2-in. angles.

Conventional Signs for Rivets.—The conventional signs for rivets as used on structural drawings are shown in Fig. 15.

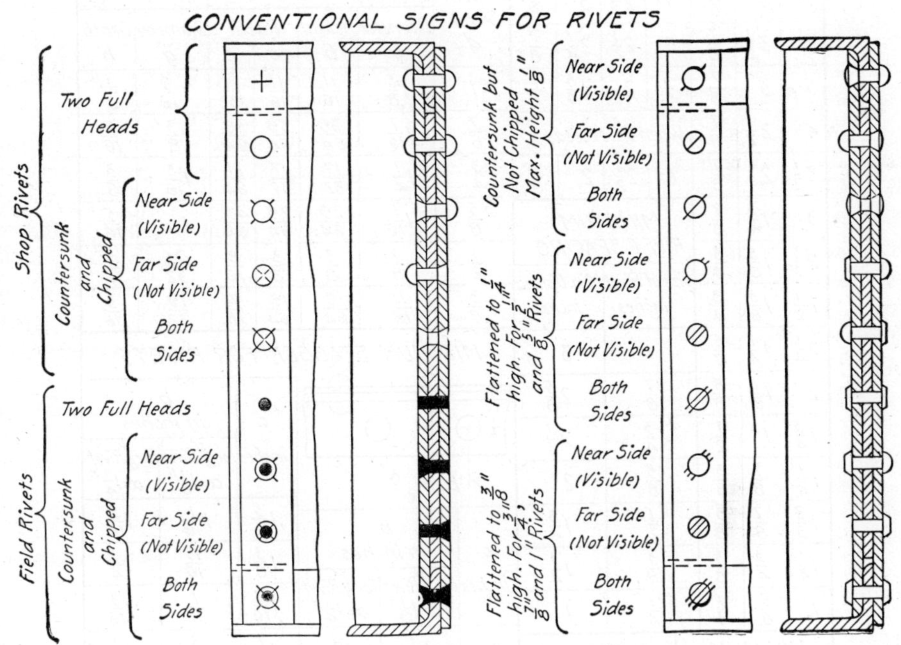

FIG. 15. CONVENTIONAL SIGNS FOR RIVETS.

Standards for Riveting.—The proportions of structural rivets, and the standards for structural riveting are shown in Fig. 16. For additional data and standards, see the author's "Structural Engineers' Handbook."

DESIGN OF LACING BARS FOR COLUMNS.—It is difficult to calculate the bending stresses in a built-up column, and since the shearing stresses depend on the bending stresses the design of lacing bars must be largely a matter of judgment until sufficient tests are made to establish empirical formulas. The following method gives results that agree with tests and with good practice.

For a column with a concentric loading, experiments show that the allowable unit stress may be represented by the straight line formula, $p = 16{,}000 - 70\, l/r$ lb. per sq. in., where p = allowable unit stress in the member; l = length of the member, c. to c.

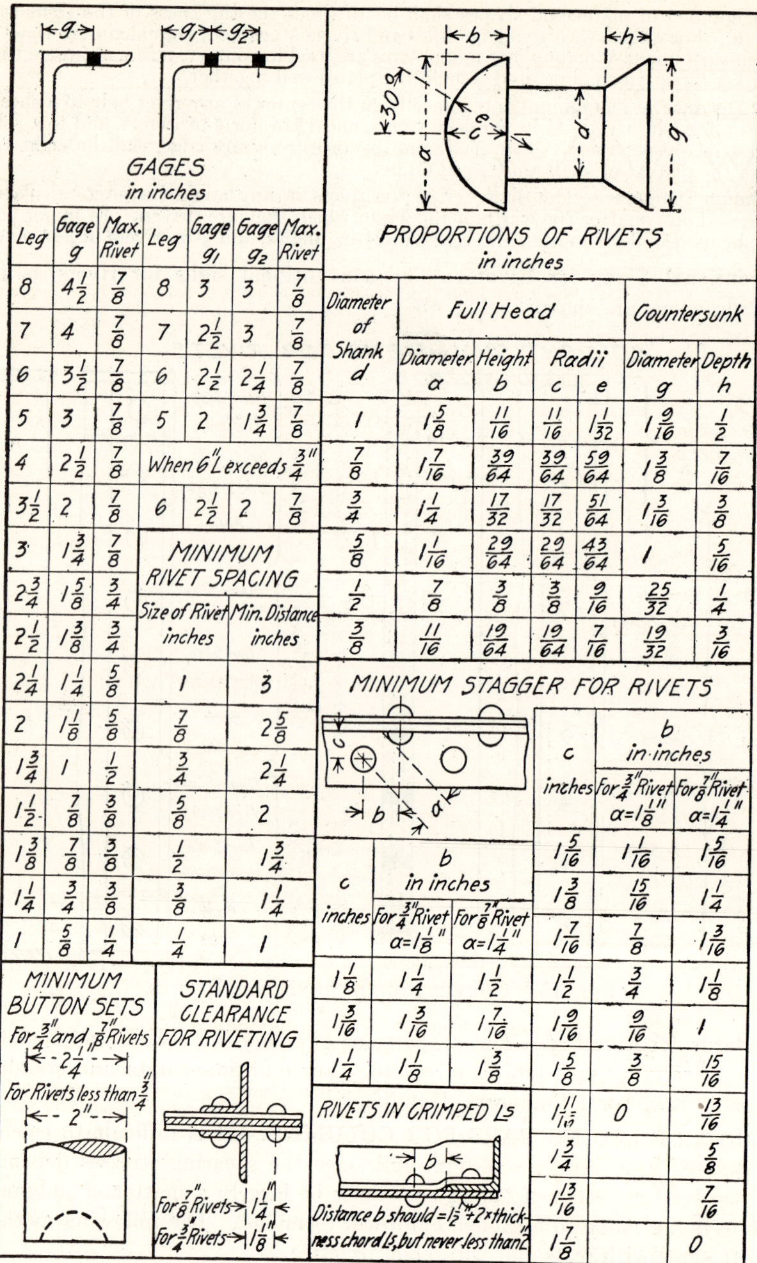

GAGES in inches

Leg	Gage g	Max. Rivet	Leg	Gage g_1	Gage g_2	Max. Rivet
8	$4\frac{1}{2}$	$\frac{7}{8}$	8	3	3	$\frac{7}{8}$
7	4	$\frac{7}{8}$	7	$2\frac{1}{2}$	3	$\frac{7}{8}$
6	$3\frac{1}{2}$	$\frac{7}{8}$	6	$2\frac{1}{2}$	$2\frac{1}{4}$	$\frac{7}{8}$
5	3	$\frac{7}{8}$	5	2	$1\frac{3}{4}$	$\frac{7}{8}$
4	$2\frac{1}{2}$	$\frac{7}{8}$	When 6″ L exceeds $\frac{3}{4}$″			
$3\frac{1}{2}$	2	$\frac{7}{8}$	6	$2\frac{1}{2}$	2	$\frac{7}{8}$
3	$1\frac{3}{4}$	$\frac{7}{8}$				
$2\frac{3}{4}$	$1\frac{5}{8}$	$\frac{3}{4}$				
$2\frac{1}{2}$	$1\frac{3}{8}$	$\frac{3}{4}$				
$2\frac{1}{4}$	$1\frac{1}{4}$	$\frac{5}{8}$				
2	$1\frac{1}{8}$	$\frac{5}{8}$				
$1\frac{3}{4}$	1	$\frac{1}{2}$				
$1\frac{1}{2}$	$\frac{7}{8}$	$\frac{3}{8}$				
$1\frac{3}{8}$	$\frac{7}{8}$	$\frac{3}{8}$				
$1\frac{1}{4}$	$\frac{3}{4}$	$\frac{3}{8}$				
1	$\frac{5}{8}$	$\frac{1}{4}$				

MINIMUM RIVET SPACING

Size of Rivet inches	Min. Distance inches
1	3
$\frac{7}{8}$	$2\frac{5}{8}$
$\frac{3}{4}$	$2\frac{1}{4}$
$\frac{5}{8}$	2
$\frac{1}{2}$	$1\frac{3}{4}$
$\frac{3}{8}$	$1\frac{1}{4}$
$\frac{1}{4}$	1

PROPORTIONS OF RIVETS in inches

Diameter of Shank d	Full Head: Diameter a	Full Head: Height b	Full Head: Radii c	Full Head: Radii e	Countersunk: Diameter g	Countersunk: Depth h
1	$1\frac{5}{8}$	$\frac{11}{16}$	$\frac{11}{16}$	$1\frac{1}{32}$	$1\frac{9}{16}$	$\frac{1}{2}$
$\frac{7}{8}$	$1\frac{7}{16}$	$\frac{39}{64}$	$\frac{39}{64}$	$\frac{59}{64}$	$1\frac{3}{8}$	$\frac{7}{16}$
$\frac{3}{4}$	$1\frac{1}{4}$	$\frac{17}{32}$	$\frac{17}{32}$	$\frac{51}{64}$	$1\frac{3}{16}$	$\frac{3}{8}$
$\frac{5}{8}$	$1\frac{1}{16}$	$\frac{29}{64}$	$\frac{29}{64}$	$\frac{43}{64}$	1	$\frac{5}{16}$
$\frac{1}{2}$	$\frac{7}{8}$	$\frac{3}{8}$	$\frac{3}{8}$	$\frac{9}{16}$	$\frac{25}{32}$	$\frac{1}{4}$
$\frac{3}{8}$	$\frac{11}{16}$	$\frac{19}{64}$	$\frac{19}{64}$	$\frac{7}{16}$	$\frac{19}{32}$	$\frac{3}{16}$

MINIMUM STAGGER FOR RIVETS

c inches	b in inches: For $\frac{3}{4}$″ Rivet $a=1\frac{1}{8}$″	b in inches: For $\frac{7}{8}$″ Rivet $a=1\frac{1}{4}$″
$1\frac{1}{8}$	$1\frac{1}{4}$	$1\frac{1}{2}$
$1\frac{3}{16}$	$1\frac{3}{16}$	$1\frac{7}{16}$
$1\frac{1}{4}$	$1\frac{1}{8}$	$1\frac{3}{8}$

c inches	b in inches: For $\frac{3}{4}$″ Rivet $a=1\frac{1}{8}$″	b in inches: For $\frac{7}{8}$″ Rivet $a=1\frac{1}{4}$″
$1\frac{5}{16}$	$1\frac{1}{16}$	$1\frac{5}{16}$
$1\frac{3}{8}$	$\frac{15}{16}$	$1\frac{1}{4}$
$1\frac{7}{16}$	$\frac{7}{8}$	$1\frac{3}{16}$
$1\frac{1}{2}$	$\frac{3}{4}$	$1\frac{1}{8}$
$1\frac{9}{16}$	$\frac{9}{16}$	1
$1\frac{5}{8}$	$\frac{3}{8}$	$\frac{15}{16}$
$1\frac{11}{16}$	0	$\frac{13}{16}$
$1\frac{3}{4}$		$\frac{5}{8}$
$1\frac{13}{16}$		$\frac{7}{16}$
$1\frac{7}{8}$		0

FIG. 16. AMERICAN BRIDGE COMPANY'S STANDARDS FOR RIVETS AND RIVETING.

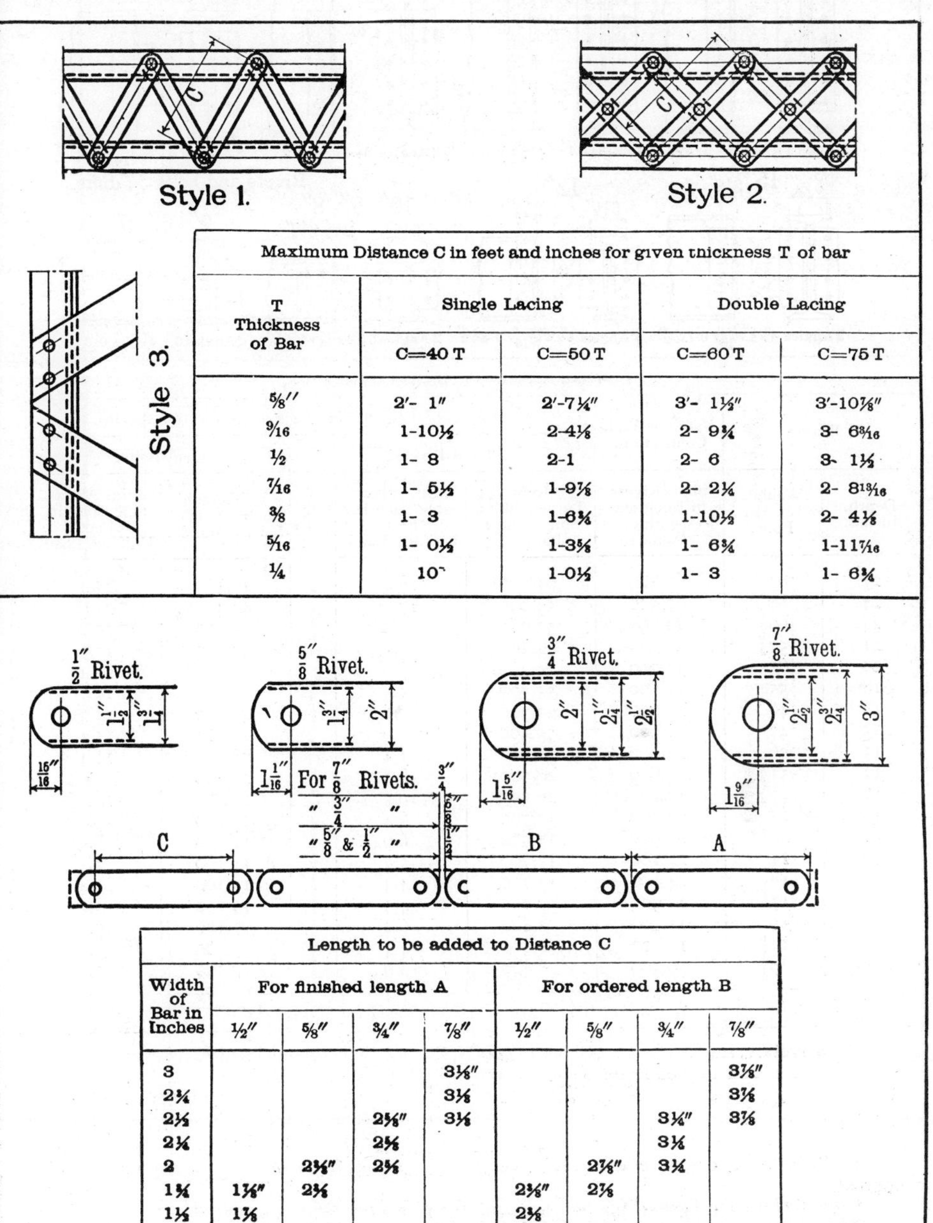

T Thickness of Bar	Single Lacing C=40 T	Single Lacing C=50 T	Double Lacing C=60 T	Double Lacing C=75 T
5/8"	2'- 1"	2'-7¼"	3'- 1½"	3'-10⅞"
9/16	1-10½	2-4⅛	2- 9¾	3- 6 3/16
1/2	1- 8	2-1	2- 6	3- 1½
7/16	1- 5½	1-9⅞	2- 2¼	2- 8 13/16
3/8	1- 3	1-6¾	1-10½	2- 4⅛
5/16	1- 0½	1-3⅝	1- 6¾	1-11 7/16
1/4	10"	1-0½	1- 3	1- 6¾

Maximum Distance C in feet and inches for given thickness T of bar

Width of Bar in Inches	For finished length A ½"	⅝"	¾"	⅞"	For ordered length B ½"	⅝"	¾"	⅞"
3				3⅛"				3⅞"
2¾				3⅛				3⅞
2½			2⅝"	3⅛			3¼"	3⅞
2¼			2⅝				3¼	
2		2⅜"	2⅝			2⅞"	3¼	
1¾	1⅞"	2⅜			2⅜"	2⅞		
1½	1⅞				2⅜			

Length to be added to Distance C

Fig. 17. Standards for Lacing Bars. American Bridge Company.

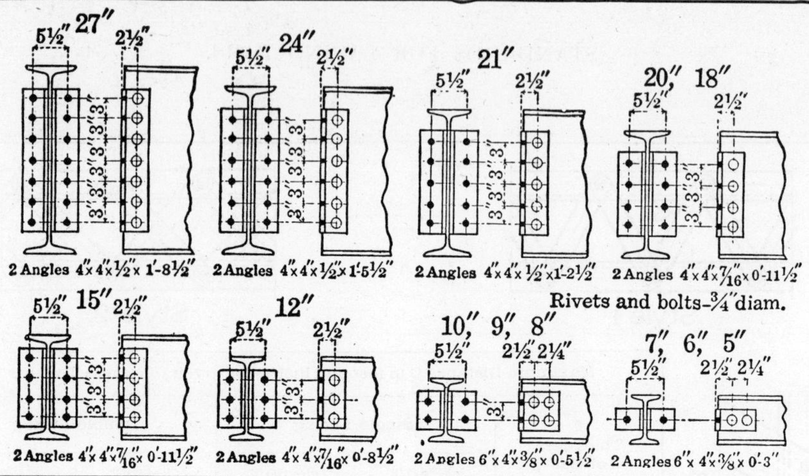

LIMITING VALUES OF BEAM CONNECTIONS.

I Beams.		Value of Web Connection.	Values of Outstanding Legs of Connection Angles.					
			Field Rivets.			Field Bolts.		
Depth, Inches.	Weight, Lb. Per Foot.	Shop Rivets in Enclosed Bearing, Pounds.	¾" Rivets or Turned Bolts, Single Shear, Pounds.	Min. Allowable Span in Feet, Uniform Load.	t, In.	¾" Rough Bolts, Single Shear, Pounds.	Min. Allowable Span in Feet, Uniform Load.	t, In.
27	83	66,800	61,900	18.4	$\frac{5}{8}$	49,500	23.1	$\frac{5}{8}$
24	80	67,500	53,000	17.5	$\frac{5}{8}$	42,400	21.9	$\frac{5}{8}$
24	69½	52,700	53,000	16.3	$\frac{5}{8}$	42,400	20.2	$\frac{5}{8}$
21	57½	40,200	44,200	15.5	$\frac{9}{16}$	35,300	17.6	$\frac{5}{8}$
20	65	45,000	35,300	17.6	$\frac{5}{8}$	28,300	22.1	$\frac{5}{8}$
18	55	41,400	35,300	13.3	$\frac{5}{8}$	28,300	16.7	$\frac{5}{8}$
18	46	29,000	35,300	15.0	$\frac{1}{2}$	28,300	15.4	$\frac{5}{8}$
15	42	36,900	35,300	8.9	$\frac{5}{8}$	28,300	11.1	$\frac{5}{8}$
15	36	26,000	35,300	11.1	$\frac{7}{16}$	28,300	11.1	$\frac{5}{8}$
12	31½	23,600	26,500	8.1	$\frac{9}{16}$	21,200	9.0	$\frac{9}{16}$
12	27½	17,200	26,500	10.3	$\frac{7}{16}$	21,200	10.3	$\frac{5}{8}$
10	25	27,900	17,700	7.4	$\frac{5}{8}$	14,100	9.2	$\frac{1}{2}$
10	22	20,900	17,700	6.9	$\frac{5}{8}$	14,100	8.6	$\frac{5}{8}$
9	21	26,100	17,700	5.7	$\frac{5}{8}$	14,100	7.1	$\frac{5}{8}$
8	18	24,300	17,700	4.3	$\frac{5}{8}$	14,100	5.4	$\frac{5}{8}$
8	17½	18,900	17,700	4.4	$\frac{5}{8}$	14,100	5.5	$\frac{5}{8}$
7	15	11,300	8,800	6.2	$\frac{5}{8}$	7,100	7.8	$\frac{5}{8}$
6	12¼	10,400	8,800	4.4	$\frac{5}{8}$	7,100	5.5	$\frac{5}{8}$
5	9¾	9,500	8,800	2.9	$\frac{5}{8}$	7,100	3.6	$\frac{5}{8}$

ALLOWABLE UNIT STRESS IN POUNDS PER SQUARE INCH.

Single Shear	Rivets................Shop 12,000 Rivets and Turned Bolts . Field 10,000 Rough Bolts..........Field 8,000	Bearing	Rivets—enclosed.........Shop 30,000 Rivets—one side. ....Shop 24,000 Rivets and Turned Bolts . . . Field 20,000 Rough Bolts....... .....Field 16,000

t = Web thickness, in bearing, to develop max. allowable reactions, when beams frame opposite.

Connections are figured for bearing and shear (no moment considered).

The above values agree with tests made on beams under ordinary conditions of use.

Where web is enclosed between connection angles (enclosed bearing), values are greater because of the increased efficiency due to friction and grip.

Special connections shall be used when any of the limiting conditions given above are exceeded—such as end reaction from loaded beam being greater than value of connection; shorter span with beam fully loaded; or a less thickness of web when maximum allowable reactions are used.

FIG. 18. NEW STANDARD CONNECTIONS FOR BEAMS AND CHANNELS. AMERICAN BRIDGE COMPANY.

of end connections, and r = radius of gyration of the column, both in inches. Now the allowable unit stress on a short block is 16,000 lb. per sq. in., and the $70l/r$ represents the increase in the fiber stress in the column. Now if we assume that this fiber stress is caused by a uniform horizontal load, W, then $\frac{W \cdot l}{8} = \frac{70I \cdot l}{r \cdot c}$, where I = moment of inertia of the cross-section of the column = $A \cdot r^2$, where A = the area of the cross-section of the column, and c = the distance from the neutral axis of column to the extreme fiber in the plane parallel to the plane of the lacing bars. Then $\frac{W \cdot l}{8} = \frac{70A \cdot r^2 \cdot l}{r \cdot c}$, and $W = 560 \frac{A \cdot r}{c}$. Now the maximum shear in the column will be $S = W/2$, and $S = 280 \frac{A \cdot r}{c}$, and the stress in a lacing bar will be $= 280 \frac{A \cdot r}{c} \times csc\ \theta$, where θ = the angle made by the bar with the axis of the column. In a laced channel column the shearing stress above will be taken by two lacing bars. This shows that the stresses in the lacing bars in the column with a concentric loading depend upon the make-up of the column, and are independent of the length of the column.

While the method for calculating the stresses in lacing bars just described gives quite satisfactory results the method described in the following specification is now the standard practice.

Lacing Bars.—The lacing of compression members shall be proportioned to resist a shearing stress of $2\frac{1}{2}$ per cent of the direct stress. The minimum width of lacing bars shall be $1\frac{3}{4}$ in. for members 6 in. in width, 2 in. for members 9 in. in width, $2\frac{1}{2}$ in. for members 12 in. in width, $2\frac{1}{2}$ in. for members 15 in. in width, or 3 in. for members 18 in. and over in width. Single lacing bars shall have a thickness not less than one-fortieth, or double lacing bars connected by a rivet at the intersection, not less than one-sixtieth of the distance between the rivets connecting them to the members. They shall be inclined at an angle not less than 60° to the axis of the member for single lacing, nor less than 45° for double lacing with riveted intersections.

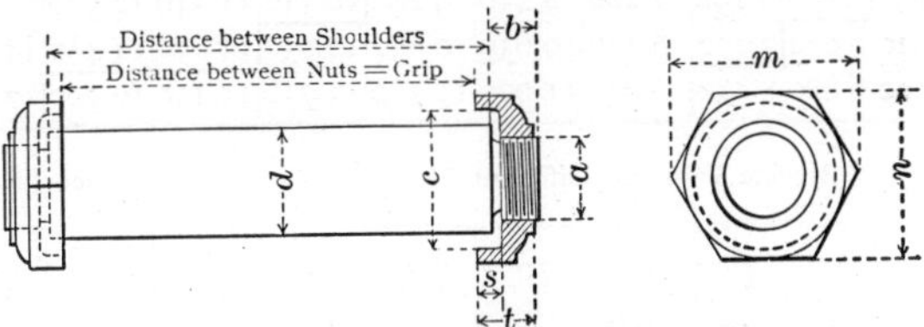

FIG. 19. BRIDGE PIN AND NUT.

Spacing of Lacing Bars.—Lacing bars shall be so spaced that the portion of the flange included between their connection shall be as strong as the member as a whole. The pitch of the lacing bars must not exceed the width of the channel plus nine inches.

Standards for lacing bars are given in Fig. 17.

CONNECTION ANGLES.—The standard connection angles for making connections of channels and I-beams to other structural members are given in Fig. 18.

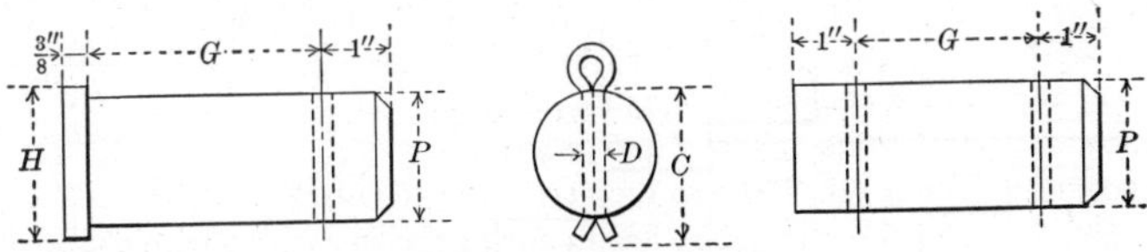

FIG. 20. COTTER PINS.

SHEARING AND BEARING VALUE OF RIVETS

Values above or to right of upper zigzag lines are greater than double shear.
Values below or to left of lower zigzag lines are less than single shear.

Rivet Diam., In.	Rivet Area, Sq. In.	Single Shear at 7 500 Pounds	Bearing Value for Different Thicknesses of Plate at 15 000 Lbs. Per Square Inch 1/4″	5/16″	3/8″	7/16″	1/2″	9/16″	5/8″	11/16″	3/4″	13/16″	7/8″	15/16″	1″
1/2	.196	1 470	1 880	2 340	2 810	3 280	3 750	....	....	....	....	....	....	....	....
5/8	.307	2 300	2 340	2 930	3 520	4 100	4 690	5 270	5 860	....	....	....	....	....	....
3/4	.442	3 310	2 810	3 520	4 220	4 920	5 630	6 330	7 030	7 730	8 440	....	....	....	....
7/8	.601	4 510	3 280	4 100	4 920	5 740	6 560	7 380	8 200	9 020	9 840	10 660	11 480	12 300	....
1	.785	5 890	3 750	4 690	5 630	6 560	7 500	8 440	9 380	10 310	11 250	12 190	13 130	14 060	15 000

Rivet Diam., In.	Rivet Area, Sq. In.	Single Shear at 10 000 Pounds	Bearing Value for Different Thicknesses of Plate at 20 000 Lbs. Per Square Inch 1/4″	5/16″	3/8″	7/16″	1/2″	9/16″	5/8″	11/16″	3/4″	13/16″	7/8″	15/16″	1″
1/2	.196	1 960	2 500	3 130	3 750	4 380	5 000	....	....	....	....	....	....	....	....
5/8	.307	3 070	3 130	3 910	4 690	5 470	6 250	7 030	7 810	....	....	....	....	....	....
3/4	.442	4 420	3 750	4 690	5 630	6 560	7 500	8 440	9 380	10 310	11 250	....	....	....	....
7/8	.601	6 010	4 380	5 470	6 560	7 660	8 750	9 840	10 940	12 030	13 130	14 220	15 310	16 410	....
1	.785	7 850	5 000	6 250	7 500	8 750	10 000	11 250	12 500	13 750	15 000	16 250	17 500	18 750	20 000

Rivet Diam., In.	Rivet Area, Sq. In.	Single Shear at 11 000 Pounds	Bearing Value for Different Thicknesses of Plate at 22 000 Lbs. Per Square Inch 1/4″	5/16″	3/8″	7/16″	1/2″	9/16″	5/8″	11/16″	3/4″	13/16″	7/8″	15/16″	1″
1/2	.196	2 160	2 750	3 440	4 130	4 810	5 500	....	....	....	....	....	....	....	....
5/8	.307	3 370	3 440	4 300	5 160	6 020	6 880	7 730	8 590	....	....	....	....	....	....
3/4	.442	4 860	4 130	5 160	6 190	7 220	8 250	9 280	10 310	11 340	12 380	....	....	....	....
7/8	.601	6 610	4 810	6 020	7 220	8 420	9 630	10 830	12 030	13 230	14 440	15 640	16 840	18 050	....
1	.785	8 640	5 500	6 880	8 250	9 630	11 000	12 380	13 750	15 130	16 500	17 880	19 250	20 630	22 000

Rivet Diam., In.	Rivet Area, Sq. In.	Single Shear at 12 000 Pounds	Bearing Value for Different Thicknesses of Plate at 24 000 Lbs. Per Square Inch 1/4″	5/16″	3/8″	7/16″	1/2″	9/16″	5/8″	11/16″	3/4″	13/16″	7/8″	15/16″	1″
1/2	.196	2 360	3 000	3 750	4 500	5 250	6 000	....	....	....	....	....	....	....	....
5/8	.307	3 680	3 750	4 690	5 630	6 560	7 500	8 440	9 380	....	....	....	....	....	....
3/4	.442	5 300	4 500	5 630	6 750	7 880	9 000	10 130	11 250	12 380	13 500	....	....	....	....
7/8	.601	7 220	5 250	6 560	7 880	9 190	10 500	11 810	13 130	14 440	15 750	17 060	18 380	....	....
1	.785	9 420	6 000	7 500	9 000	10 500	12 000	13 500	15 000	16 500	18 000	19 500	21 000	22 500	24 000

Rivet Diam. in.	Rivet Area sq. in.	Single Shear at 13 500 Pounds	Bearing Value for Different Thicknesses of Plate at 27 000 Lbs. Per Square Inche 1/4″	5/16″	3/8″	7/16″	1/2″	9/16″	5/8″	11/16″	3/4″	13/16″	7/8″	15/16″	1″
1/2	.196	2 650	3 380	4 240	5 060	5 906	6 750	....	....	....	....	....	....	....	....
5/8	.307	4 140	4 240	5 270	6 330	7 380	8 440	9 492	....	....	....	....	....	....	....
3/4	.442	5 960	5 060	6 330	7 590	8 860	10 130	11 390	12 656	11 922	....	....	....	....	....
7/8	.601	8 120	5 910	7 380	8 860	10 340	11 820	13 290	14 770	16 240	17 720	19 080	20 680	....	....
1	.785	10 600	6 750	8 440	10 130	11 810	13 500	15 190	16 880	18 560	20 250	21 940	23 620	25 320	27 000

TABLE II.

Areas to be Deducted for Rivet Holes, Maximum Rivets, and Rivet Spacing.

Areas in Square Inches, to be Deducted from Riveted Plates or Shapes to Obtain Net Areas.

Thickness of Plates.	Diameter of Hole in Inches (Diam. of Rivet + 1/8″).																
Inches.	1/4	5/16	3/8	7/16	1/2	9/16	5/8	11/16	3/4	13/16	7/8	15/16	1	1 1/16	1 1/8	1 3/16	1 1/4
1/4	.06	.08	.09	.11	.13	.14	.16	.17	.19	.20	.22	.23	.25	.27	.28	.30	.31
5/16	.08	.10	.12	.14	.16	.18	.20	.21	.23	.25	.27	.29	.31	.33	.35	.37	.39
3/8	.09	.12	.14	.16	.19	.21	.23	.26	.28	.30	.33	.35	.38	.40	.42	.45	.47
7/16	.11	.14	.16	.19	.22	.25	.27	.30	.33	.36	.38	.41	.44	.46	.49	.52	.55
1/2	.13	.16	.19	.22	.25	.28	.31	.34	.38	.41	.44	.47	.50	.53	.56	.59	.63
9/16	.14	.18	.21	.25	.28	.32	.35	.39	.42	.46	.49	.53	.56	.60	.63	.67	.70
5/8	.16	.20	.23	.27	.31	.35	.39	.43	.47	.51	.55	.59	.63	.66	.70	.74	.78
11/16	.17	.21	.26	.30	.34	.39	.43	.47	.52	.56	.60	.64	.69	.73	.77	.82	.86
3/4	.19	.23	.28	.33	.38	.42	.47	.52	.56	.61	.66	.70	.75	.80	.84	.89	.94
13/16	.20	.25	.30	.36	.41	.46	.51	.56	.61	.66	.71	.76	.81	.86	.91	.96	1.02
7/8	.22	.27	.33	.38	.44	.49	.55	.60	.66	.71	.77	.82	.88	.93	.98	1.04	1.09
15/16	.23	.29	.35	.41	.47	.53	.59	.64	.70	.76	.82	.88	.94	1.00	1.05	1.11	1.17
1	.25	.31	.38	.44	.50	.56	.63	.69	.75	.81	.88	.94	1.00	1.06	1.13	1.19	1.25
1 1/16	.27	.33	.40	.46	.53	.60	.66	.73	.80	.86	.93	1.00	1.06	1.13	1.20	1.26	1.33
1 1/8	.28	.35	.42	.49	.56	.63	.70	.77	.84	.91	.98	1.05	1.13	1.20	1.27	1.34	1.41
1 3/16	.30	.37	.45	.52	.59	.67	.74	.82	.89	.96	1.04	1.11	1.19	1.26	1.34	1.41	1.48
1 1/4	.31	.39	.47	.55	.63	.70	.78	.86	.94	1.02	1.09	1.17	1.25	1.33	1 41	1.48	1.56
1 5/16	.33	.41	.49	.57	.66	.74	.82	.90	.98	1.07	1.15	1.23	1.31	1.39	1 48	1.56	1.64
1 3/8	.34	.43	.52	.60	.69	.77	.86	.95	1.03	1.12	1.20	1.29	1.38	1.46	1.55	1.63	1.72
1 7/16	.36	.45	.54	.63	.72	.81	.90	.99	1.08	1.17	1.26	1.35	1.44	1.53	1.62	1.71	1.80
1 1/2	.38	.47	.56	.66	.75	.84	.94	1.03	1.13	1.22	1.31	1.41	1.50	1.59	1.69	1.78	1.88
1 9/16	.39	.49	.59	.68	.78	.88	.98	1.07	1.17	1.27	1.37	1.46	1.56	1.66	1.76	1.86	1.95
1 5/8	.41	.51	.61	.71	.81	.91	1.02	1.12	1.22	1.32	1.42	1.52	1.63	1.73	1.83	1.93	2.03
1 11/16	.42	.53	.63	.74	.84	.95	1.05	1.16	1.27	1.37	1.47	1.58	1.69	1.79	1.90	2.00	2.11
1 3/4	.44	.55	.66	.77	.88	.98	1.09	1.20	1.31	1.42	1.53	1.64	1.75	1.86	1.97	2.08	2.19
1 13/16	.45	.57	.68	.79	.91	1.02	1.13	1.25	1.36	1.47	1.59	1.70	1.81	1.93	2.04	2.15	2.27
1 7/8	.47	.59	.70	.82	.94	1.05	1.17	1.29	1.41	1.52	1.64	1.76	1.88	1.99	2.11	2.23	2.34
1 15/16	.48	.61	.73	.85	.97	1.09	1.21	1.33	1.45	1.57	1.70	1.82	1.94	2.06	2.18	2.30	2.42
2	.50	.63	.75	.88	1.00	1.13	1.25	1.38	1.50	1.63	1.75	1.88	2.00	2.13	2.25	2.38	2.50

Maximum Rivet in Leg of Angles or Flange of Beams and Channels.

Leg of Angle	3/4	1	1 1/4	1 3/8	1 1/2	1 3/4	2	2 1/2	3	3 1/2	4	5	6	7	8
Max. Rivet	1/4	1/4	3/8	3/8	3/8	1/2	5/8	3/4	7/8	7/8	7/8	7/8	7/8	1	1 1/8
Depth of Beam	3	4	5	6	7	8	9	10	12	15	18	20	24		
Max. Rivet	3/8	1/2	1/2	5/8	5/8	3/4	3/4	3/4	3/4	3/4	7/8	7/8	7/8		
Depth of Channel	3	4	5	6	7	8	9	10	12	15					
Max. Rivet	1/2	1/2	1/2	5/8	5/8	3/4	3/4	3/4	7/8	7/8					

Rivet Spacing in Inches.

Size of Rivet.	Minimum Pitch.		Max. Pitch in Line of Stress.				Min. Edge Dist		Max. Edge Dist.
	Allowed.	Preferred.	At Ends of Comp.Mem.	Bridges.		Bld'gs.	Sheared.	Rolled.	
1/2″	1 1/2	1 3/4	2	4	16 x thickness of thinnest outside plate.	6	1	7/8	8 x thickness of plate.
5/8″	1 7/8	2	2 1/2	4 1/2		"	1 1/8	1	
3/4″	2 1/4	2 1/2	3	5		"	1 1/4	1 1/8	
7/8″	2 5/8	3	3 1/2	6		"	1 1/2	1 1/4	

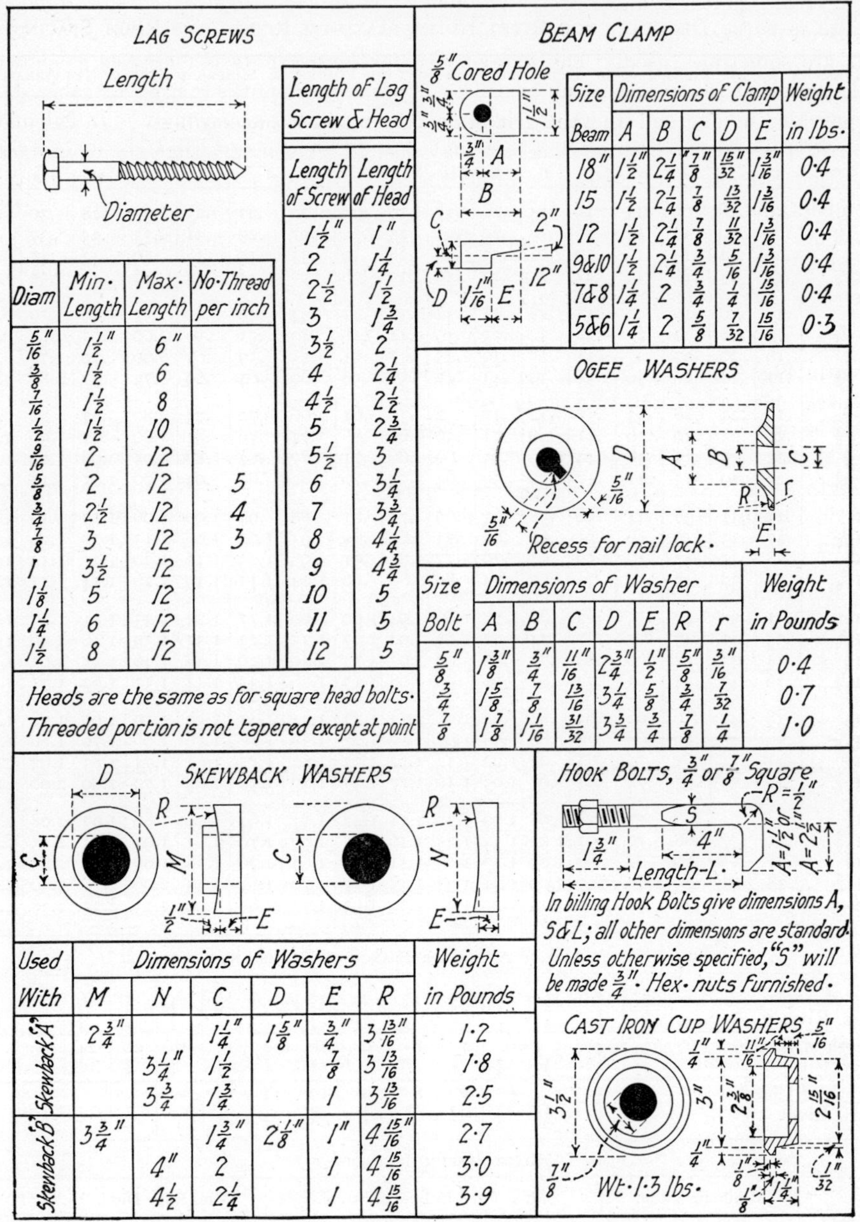

Lag Screws

Diam	Min. Length	Max. Length	No. Thread per inch
5/16"	1 1/2"	6"	
3/8	1 1/2	6	
7/16	1 1/2	8	
1/2	1 1/2	10	
9/16	2	12	
5/8	2	12	5
3/4	2 1/2	12	4
7/8	3	12	3
1	3 1/2	12	
1 1/8	5	12	
1 1/4	6	12	
1 1/2	8	12	

Length of Lag Screw & Head	
Length of Screw	Length of Head
1 1/2"	1"
2	1 1/4
2 1/2	1 1/2
3	1 3/4
3 1/2	2
4	2 1/4
4 1/2	2 1/2
5	2 3/4
5 1/2	3
6	3 1/4
7	3 3/4
8	4 1/4
9	4 3/4
10	5
11	5
12	5

Heads are the same as for square head bolts. Threaded portion is not tapered except at point.

Beam Clamp

Size Beam	Dimensions of Clamp A	B	C	D	E	Weight in lbs.
18"	1 1/2"	2 1/4	7/8"	15/32"	1 3/16"	0.4
15	1 1/2	2 1/4	7/8	13/32	1 3/16	0.4
12	1 1/2	2 1/4	7/8	11/32	1 3/16	0.4
9&10	1 1/2	2 1/4	3/4	5/16	1 3/16	0.4
7&8	1 1/4	2	3/4	1/4	15/16	0.4
5&6	1 1/4	2	5/8	7/32	15/16	0.3

Ogee Washers

Size Bolt	Dimensions of Washer A	B	C	D	E	R	r	Weight in Pounds
5/8"	1 3/8"	3/4"	11/16"	2 3/4"	1/2"	5/8"	3/16"	0.4
3/4	1 5/8	7/8	13/16	3 1/4	5/8	3/4	7/32	0.7
7/8	1 7/8	1 1/16	31/32	3 3/4	3/4	7/8	1/4	1.0

Skewback Washers

Used With	Dimensions of Washers M	N	C	D	E	R	Weight in Pounds
Skewback "A"	2 3/4"		1 1/4"	1 5/8"	3/4"	3 13/16"	1.2
		3 1/4"	1 1/2		7/8	3 13/16	1.8
		3 3/4	1 3/4		1	3 13/16	2.5
Skewback "B"	3 3/4"		1 3/4"	2 1/8"	1"	4 15/16"	2.7
		4"	2		1	4 15/16	3.0
		4 1/2	2 1/4		1	4 15/16	3.9

FIG. 21. STANDARD LAG SCREWS, HOOK BOLTS AND WASHERS. AMERICAN BRIDGE COMPANY.

PINS.—The American Bridge Company's standard bridge pins with Lomas nuts are given in Fig. 19, and in the author's "Structural Engineers' Handbook." Square nuts are sometimes used. The figured grip for Lomas nuts is increased as shown to make sure that the pin has a full bearing. Where square nuts are used a washer should be provided at one end and the grip should be increased accordingly. In calculating the grip it is usual to assume that bars may be 1/16 inch thicker than the figured thickness, that riveted members may be $\frac{1}{4}$ inch wider or narrower than the figured dimensions. Members should be packed on the pin so that the bending moments will be as small as possible. The allowable bending moments on pins for different fiber stresses are given in the author's "Structural Engineers' Handbook." The method of calculating the stresses in pins is described in detail in Chapter XII.

LATERAL PINS.—The American Bridge Company's standard cotter pins are given in Fig. 20, and in the author's "Structural Engineers' Handbook." These pins are used only for laterals and other similar members.

The Jones & Laughlin Steel Corporation rolls I-beams 6 in., 8 in., 10 in., and 12 in. deep that are about one-third the weight of standard I-beams of the same depth. For strength of J. & L. Junior beams, see University of Illinois Engineering Experiment Station Bulletin No. 241, "Tests of Light I-Beams" by Milo S. Ketchum and Jasper O. Draffin.

References.—For data on the properties of structural shapes and built sections, see the author's "Structural Engineers' Handbook."

30

CHAPTER XXVIII.

Corrugated Steel.

Introduction.—Corrugated steel is made from sheet steel of standard gages, and is either galvanized at the mill or is left black. The black corrugated steel is usually painted at the mill and is always painted after erection. Paint will not adhere well to the galvanized steel until after it has weathered unless a portion of the coating is removed by the application of an acid. The common standard for the gage of sheet steel in the United States is the United States Standard Gage, and this should be used in specifying the weight and thickness. The thickness and weights per square of 100 square feet, for black and galvanized sheet and corrugated steel are given in Table I.

Corrugated steel is made with corrugations 5, 3, $2\frac{1}{2}$, 2, $1\frac{1}{4}$ and $\frac{5}{8}$ in. wide, approximately. Corrugated steel with corrugations $2\frac{1}{2}$ in. wide and $\frac{5}{8}$ in. deep is commonly used for roofing and siding, while corrugated steel with corrugations $1\frac{1}{4}$ in. wide and $\frac{3}{8}$ in. deep is frequently used for lining buildings. Corrugated steel with $1\frac{1}{4}$-in. corrugations weighs about 4 per cent more than steel of the same gage with $2\frac{1}{2}$-in. corrugations. Corrugated sheets are commonly made from flat bessemer or open hearth steel sheets, by

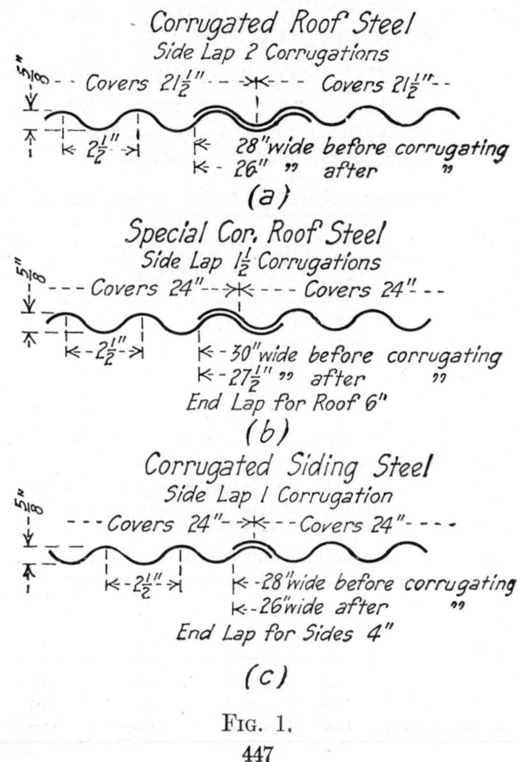

Fig. 1.

TABLE I.

Corrugated Sheets. American Sheet and Tin Plate Company Standard.

Description of Corrugated Sheets						Areas of Corrugated Sheets						
Corrugations				Width, Inches		Length of Sheet, Inches	Sq. Ft. in 1 Sheet			Sheets in 100 Sq. Ft.		
Width, Inches		Depth, Approx. Inches	Number per Sheet	Full Sheet	Covers Approx.		Corrugations			Corrugations		
Nominal	Actual						5″	3″, 2½″, 2″	1¼″, ⅝″	5″	3″, 2½″, 2″	1¼″, ⅝″
5	$4\frac{2}{3}$	$\frac{7}{8}$	6	28	24	60	11.67	10.83	10.42	8.57	9.23	9.60
3	$2\frac{8}{9}$	$\frac{5}{8}$	9	26	24	72	14.00	13.00	12.50	7.14	7.69	8.00
$2\frac{1}{2}$	$2\frac{3}{5}$	$\frac{1}{2}$	10	26	24	84	16.33	15.17	14.58	6.12	6.59	6.86
2	$2\frac{4}{11}$	$\frac{1}{2}$	11	26	24	96	18.67	17.33	16.67	5.36	5.77	6.00
$1\frac{1}{4}$	$1\frac{1}{4}$	$\frac{3}{8}$	20	25	24	108	21.00	19.50	18.75	4.76	5.13	5.33
$\frac{5}{8}$	$\frac{25}{26}$	$\frac{3}{16}$	26	25	24	120	23.33	21.67	20.83	4.29	4.62	4.80
Standard lengths 5, 6, 7, 8, 9 and 10 feet. Maximum length, 12 feet for 5″ to 1¼″ corrugation.						144	28.00	26.00	25.00	3.57	3.85	4.00

Corrugated Sheets.—Painted.
Weights in Pounds per 100 Square Feet.

Nom. Corrug. Inches	Thickness, U. S. Standard Gage and Decimals of an Inch												
	12	14	16	18	20	21	22	23	24	25	26	27	28
	.109	.078	.063	.050	.038	.034	.031	.028	.025	.022	.019	.017	.016
5	......	339	271	217	163	150	136	123	110	96	83	76	68
3	......	......	271	217	163	150	136	123	110	96	83	76	68
$2\frac{1}{2}$	474	339	271	217	163	150	136	123	110	96	83	76	68
2	......	......	271	217	163	150	136	123	110	96	83	76	68
$1\frac{1}{4}$	......	......	......	......	170	156	142	128	114	100	86	79	72
$\frac{5}{8}$	......	......	......	......	......	......	......	......	114	100	86	79	72

Corrugated Sheets.—Galvanized.
Weights in Pounds per 100 Square Feet.

Nom. Corrug. Inches	Thickness, U. S. Standard Gage and Decimals of an Inch												
	12	14	16	18	20	21	22	23	24	25	26	27	28
	.109	.078	.063	.050	.038	.034	.031	.028	.025	.022	.019	.017	.016
5	......	354	286	232	178	165	151	138	124	111	98	91	85
3	......	......	286	232	178	165	151	138	124	111	98	91	85
$2\frac{1}{2}$	488	354	286	232	178	165	151	138	124	111	98	91	85
2	......	......	286	232	178	165	151	138	124	111	98	91	85
$1\frac{1}{4}$	......	......	......	......	185	......	157	......	129	......	101	94	87
$\frac{5}{8}$	......	......	......	......	......	......	......	......	129	......	101	94	87

The weights per 100 square feet given in preceding tables do not include allowances for end or side laps. The following table gives the approximate number of square feet of sheeting necessary to cover an area of 100 square feet and is based on sheets of standard width, 96 inches long. If longer or shorter sheets are used, the number of square feet required will vary accordingly.

Square Feet of Corrugated Sheets to Cover 100 Square Feet.

Side Lap	End Lap, Inches					
	1	2	3	4	5	6
1 Corrugation..................	110	111	112	113	114	115
$1\frac{1}{2}$ "	116	117	118	119	120	121
2 "	123	124	125	126	127	128

rolling one corrugation at a time. Iron corrugated sheets can be obtained, but are very hard to get and cost extra.

The standard sheets of corrugated steel with $2\frac{1}{2}$-in. corrugations, are 28 in. wide before, and 26 in. wide after corrugating, and will cover a width of 24 in. with one corrugation side lap, and approximately $21\frac{1}{2}$ in. with two corrugations side lap, (c) and (a) Fig. 1. Special corrugated steel, (b) Fig.1, can usually be obtained that will cover a width of 24 in. with $1\frac{1}{2}$ corrugations side lap. Corrugated steel should be laid with 6 in. end lap on the roof and 4 in. end lap on the sides of buildings.

Stock lengths of corrugated steel sheets can be obtained from 5 to 10 feet, varying by one-half foot. Sheets of any length between 4 and 10 feet can usually be obtained directly from the mill without extra charge. Sheets from 48 to 5 in. long, cost 5 per cent extra. Sheets from 10 to 12 feet long are very hard to obtain and cost extra. Sheets cannot be obtained longer than 12 feet. Stock lengths of sheets should be used whenever possible as odd lengths often delay the filling of the order. Bevel sheets should preferably be ordered in multiple lengths and should be cut in the field. Sheets to fit around windows and doors should be cut in the field; no part of a sheet less than $\frac{1}{4}$ the width of a full sheet should ever be used.

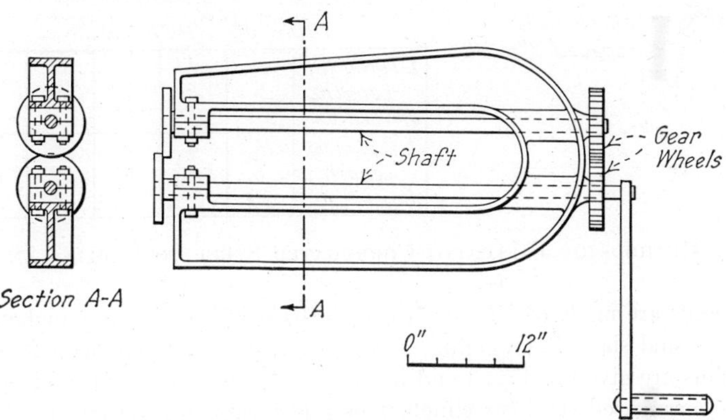

FIG. 2. ROTARY SHEAR.

For cutting and splitting corrugated sheets in the field the rotary shear shown in Fig. 2 is invaluable. It will make square or bevel cuts, or will split sheets without denting the corrugations. The shear shown in Fig. 2 is one made by the Gillette-Herzog Mfg. Co., Minneapolis, Minn., and was used by the author in the erection of a steel stamp mill in Northern Michigan, while in the employ of the above named company. The shear is not on the market, but can be made in any ordinary machine shop at a comparatively small cost.

Fastening Corrugated Steel.—Where spiking strips are used, the corrugated steel is fastened with 8d barbed roofing nails $\frac{3}{4}$ to $2\frac{1}{2}$ in. long, spaced 6 to 8 in. apart. The $2\frac{1}{2}$-in. barbed nails should be used for nailing to spiking strips and to sheathing whenever possible. Ninety-six 8d barbed roofing nails weigh one lb.

The common methods of fastening corrugated steel directly to the purlins and girts are shown in Fig. 3. Nailing pieces should preferably be used where anti-condensation roofing, Fig. 14, is used, or where the sides are lined with corrugated steel. The clinch nail is probably the most satisfactory fastening for the usual conditions. The side laps are fastened together by means of copper or galvanized iron closing rivets, spaced about 8 to 12 in. apart on the roof and about 12 in. apart on the sides. The sizes and weights of copper closing rivets are given in Fig. 5.

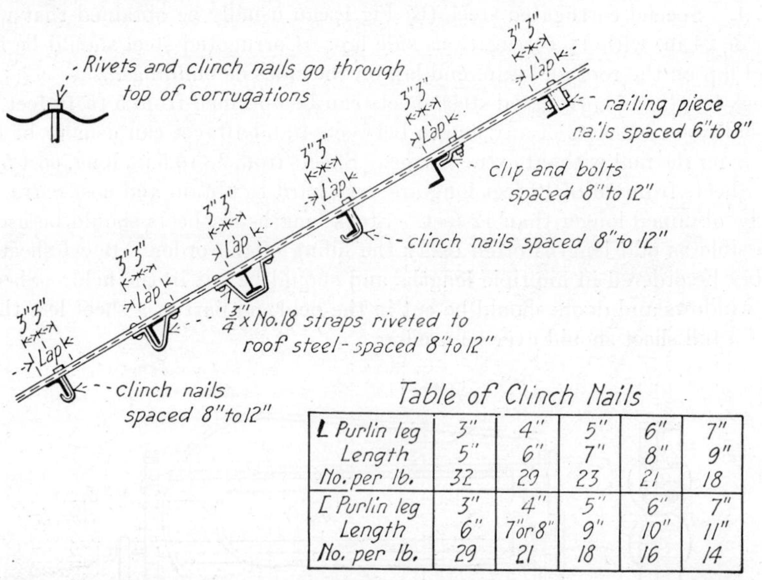

Table of Clinch Nails

L Purlin leg	3"	4"	5"	6"	7"
Length	5"	6"	7"	8"	9"
No. per lb.	32	29	23	21	18
[Purlin leg	3"	4"	5"	6"	7"
Length	6"	7" or 8"	9"	10"	11"
No. per lb.	29	21	18	16	14

Fig. 3. Methods of Fastening Corrugated Steel to Purlins and Girts.

Clinch nails are made of $\frac{1}{8}$ in. or No. 10 soft iron wire and are clinched around the purlin. The usual sizes and weights of clinch nails for different lengths of angle and channel purlins are given in Fig. 3 and in Fig. 5. Care should be used in punching the holes in the corrugated steel for clinch nails and rivets to get them in the top of the corrugations and to avoid making the hole unnecessarily large. Clinch nails are spaced from 8 to 12 in. apart. Two clinch nails are usually furnished for each lineal foot of purlin and girt.

Straps.—These are made of No. 18 U. S. gage steel, $\frac{3}{4}$ of an in. wide. These straps pass around the purlins and are riveted to the sheets at both ends by 3/16 in. diameter rivets, $\frac{3}{8}$ in. long; or, they may be fastened by bolts. Order one strap and two rivets, or bolts, for each lineal foot of girt or purlin, to which the corrugated steel is to be fastened, and add 20 per cent to the number of rivets for waste, and 10 per cent to the straps or the bolts. One thousand rivets will weigh 6 lb.; one bundle of hoop steel will weigh 50 lb. and contains 400 lineal feet.

Clips and Bolts.—These are used for fastening corrugated steel to steel purlins or girts. Clips are made of No. 16, $1\frac{1}{2}$ in. steel, about $2\frac{1}{2}$ in. long, and are slightly crimped at one end, to go over the flange of the purlin. The bolts are of the same diameter, and have the same head as the clinch rivets, except that they are supplied with threads and nut, and are about 1 in. long. These clips and bolts should not be used excepting in special cases, where the regular fastenings cannot be easily applied.

In cases where flashing, cornice work, and several thicknesses of metal are to be fastened at one point, rivets or bolts, other than standard lengths given will be needed. Closing rivets $\frac{1}{2}$ in. long and bolts $1\frac{1}{2}$ long will usually answer these cases.

If side laps of corrugated steel are to be riveted, rivets should be ordered, one for each lineal foot of side lap, plus 20 per cent for waste.

If corrugated steel is to be fastened to wooden purlins or timber sheathing, order 8d barbed nails for roofing and for siding. These nails should be spaced one foot apart, for both end and side laps; add 20 per cent for waste. Ninety-six 8d barbed nails weigh 1 lb.

Corrugated steel for roofing should be laid with two corrugations side lap if standard or $1\frac{1}{2}$ corrugations side lap if special, and 6 in. end lap. Corrugated steel for siding should have one corrugation side lap and 4 in. end lap.

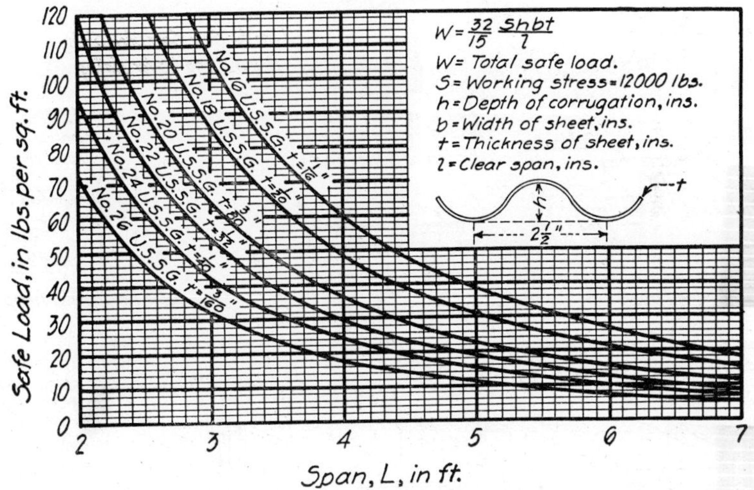

Fig. 4. Safe Uniform Load in Pounds for Corrugated Steel for Different Spans in Feet.

Copper rivets weighing about 6 pounds per 1000 rivets have commonly been used for closing rivets; but galvanized iron rivets made of very soft wire and weighing about 7 pounds per 1000 rivets are fully as good and cost less.

Standard details for corrugated steel are shown in Fig. 5.

Strength of Corrugated Steel.—The safe load per square foot for corrugated steel supported as a simple beam, for sheets with $2\frac{1}{2}$-in. corrugations and of various gages is given in Fig. 4. This diagram is based on Rankine's formula

$$W = \frac{32}{15}\,\frac{S \cdot h \cdot b \cdot t}{l}$$

where W = safe load in lb.;
S = working stress in lb.;
h = depth of the corrugations in in.;
b = width of the sheet in in.;
t = thickness of the sheet in in.;
l = clear span in in.

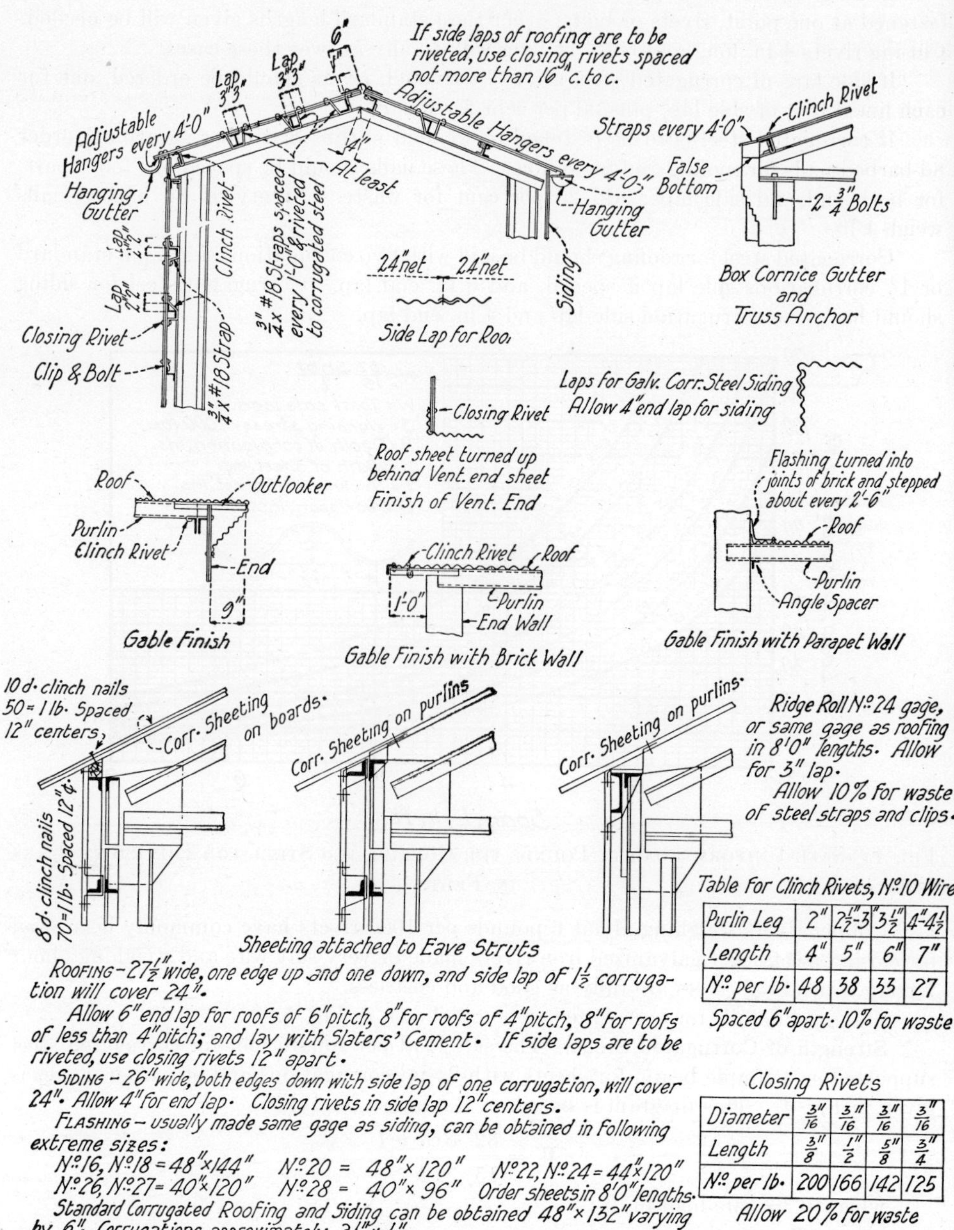
6"
1"
If side laps of roofing are to be riveted, use closing rivets spaced not more than 16" c. to c.
Lap 3"3"
Lap 3"3"
Adjustable Hangers every 4'-0"
Adjustable Hangers every 4'-0"
Hanging Gutter
Lap 2"2"
Lap 2"2"
Closing Rivet
Clip & Bolt
Clinch Rivet
3/4" x #18 Strap
3/4" x #18 Straps spaced every 1'-0" & riveted to corrugated steel
4" At least
Hanging Gutter
Siding
24"net 24"net
Side Lap for Roof
Straps every 4'-0"
Clinch Rivet
False Bottom
2-3/4" Bolts
Box Cornice Gutter and Truss Anchor
Closing Rivet
Roof sheet turned up behind Vent. end sheet
Finish of Vent. End
Laps for Galv. Corr. Steel Siding
Allow 4" end lap for siding
Roof
Outlooker
Purlin
Clinch Rivet
End
9"
Gable Finish
Clinch Rivet
Roof
1'-0"
Purlin
End Wall
Gable Finish with Brick Wall
Flashing turned into joints of brick and stepped about every 2'-6"
Roof
Purlin
Angle Spacer
Gable Finish with Parapet Wall
10 d. clinch nails 50 = 1 lb. Spaced 12" centers.
Corr. Sheeting on boards.
8 d. clinch nails 70 = 1 lb. Spaced 12" c.
Corr. Sheeting on purlins
Corr. Sheeting on purlins.
Sheeting attached to Eave Struts
Ridge Roll No. 24 gage, or same gage as roofing in 8'0" lengths. Allow for 3" lap.
Allow 10% for waste of steel straps and clips.
Table for Clinch Rivets, No. 10 Wire

Purlin Leg	2"	2½"-3"	3½"	4"-4½"
Length	4"	5"	6"	7"
No. per lb.	48	38	33	27

Spaced 6" apart. 10% for waste
Closing Rivets

Diameter	3/16"	3/16"	3/16"	3/16"
Length	3/8"	1/2"	5/8"	3/4"
No. per lb.	200	166	142	125

Allow 20% for waste
ROOFING—27½" wide, one edge up and one down, and side lap of 1½ corrugation will cover 24".
Allow 6" end lap for roofs of 6" pitch, 8" for roofs of 4" pitch, 8" for roofs of less than 4" pitch; and lay with Slaters' Cement. If side laps are to be riveted, use closing rivets 12" apart.
SIDING—26" wide, both edges down with side lap of one corrugation, will cover 24". Allow 4" for end lap. Closing rivets in side lap 12" centers.
FLASHING—usually made same gage as siding, can be obtained in following extreme sizes:
No. 16, No. 18 = 48" × 144"   No. 20 = 48" × 120"   No. 22, No. 24 = 44" × 120"
No. 26, No. 27 = 40" × 120"   No. 28 = 40" × 96"   Order sheets in 8'0" lengths.
Standard Corrugated Roofing and Siding can be obtained 48" × 132" varying by 6". Corrugations approximately 2½" × ½".

FIG. 5. STANDARD DETAILS FOR CORRUGATED STEEL.

A summary of experiments to determine the strength of corrugated steel made under the author's direction by Mr. Ralph H. Gage, is given in Technograph No. 17. These tests checked the Rankine formula very closely.

Purlins are commonly spaced for a safe load of 30 lb. per sq. ft. as given in Fig. 4; if the purlins are spaced farther apart than this, the steel will deflect a dangerous amount when walked on, and will leak snow and rain. Girts should be spaced for a safe load of

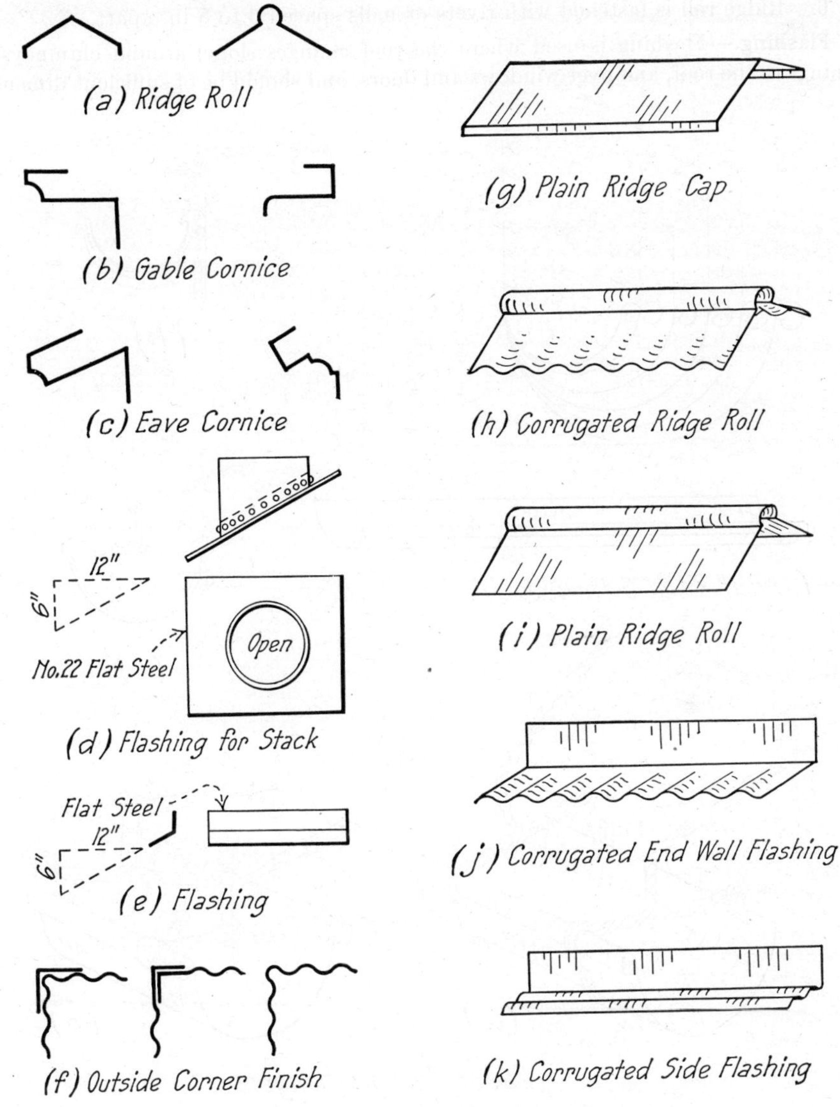

Fig. 6. Corrugated Steel Details.

about 20 lb. per sq. ft. From an inspection of Fig. 4, it is evident that corrugated steel lighter than No. 24 is of little use for mill buildings. Corrugated steel of No. 26 or 28 gage is so thin that it soon rusts out and should never be used unless for lining cheap buildings.

Corrugated Steel Details.—Ridge Roll.—The ridge roll most commonly used is made from No. 24 flat steel, and has a $2\frac{1}{2}$-in. roll and 6-in. aprons. It comes in 96-in. lengths and should be laid with 3 in. end lap. Plain and corrugated ridge roll are used, Fig. 6. Ridge roll is fastened with rivets or nails spaced 6 to 8 in. apart.

Flashing.—Flashing is used where the roof changes slope, around chimneys and openings in the roof, and over windows and doors, and should be of sufficient dimensions

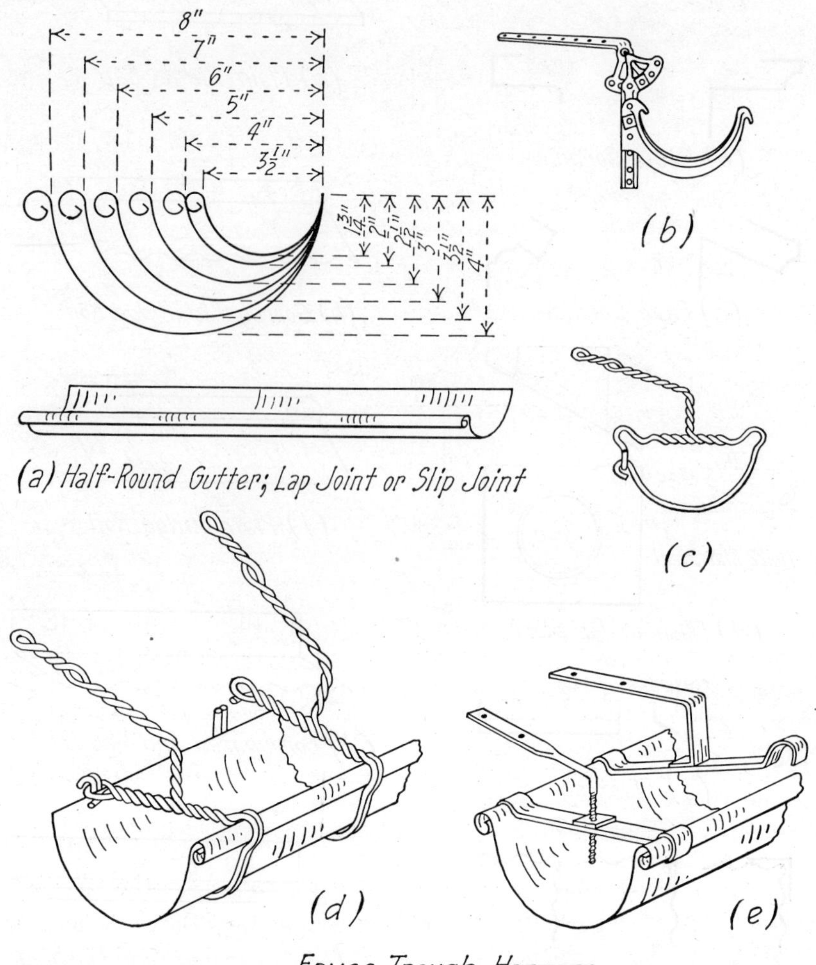

FIG. 7. SHEET STEEL GUTTERS.

and so arranged that at least 3 in. vertical height is obtained between the edge of the flashing and the end of the corrugated steel roofing. Vertical and horizontal seams of all flashing should be closely riveted. Flashing is made from flat sheets of the same gage as the corrugated steel, and can be obtained up to 96 in. in length. Flashing is made both plain and corrugated, Fig. 6.

Corner Finish.—Corner finish is made in various ways, three of which are shown in Fig. 6. Other methods are shown on the succeeding pages.

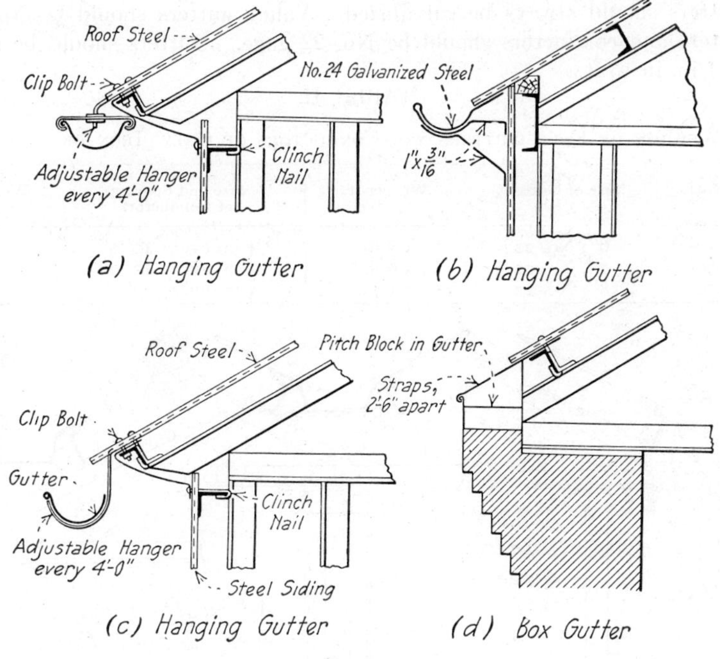

Fig. 8.

Gutters and Conductors.—Gutters for eaves are ordinarily made from No. 24, and valley gutters from No. 20 galvanized steel. Gutters may be obtained in even foot lengths up to 10 ft., and should have 4-in. end laps. Special flat sheets up to 42 in. in width can be obtained for making gutters and details.

The common sizes of half round gutters are shown in Fig. 7. Two common forms of adjustable hangers are shown in (d) and (e) in Fig. 7.

Three forms of hanging gutters and one form of box gutter used with brick walls are shown in Fig. 8.

A standard form of valley gutter is shown in (b), Fig. 12. Extreme care should be used in making valley gutters to see that the sides are carried well up, and that the laps are well soldered.

Standard eave and valley gutters designed by the American Bridge Company are given in Fig. 9.

Conductors are made plain round or square, and corrugated round or square.

Corrugated conductors are to be preferred to plain conductors for the reason that they will give when the ice freezes inside of them, and will not burst as the others often do. Common sizes of round pipe are 2 in., 3 in., 4 in., 5 in., and 6 in. diameter. Common sizes of square pipe are $1\frac{3}{4}$ in. × $2\frac{1}{4}$ in., $2\frac{3}{8}$ in. × $3\frac{1}{4}$ in., $2\frac{3}{4}$ in. × $4\frac{1}{4}$ in. and $3\frac{3}{4}$ in. × 5 in., equal to 2 in., 3 in. and 4 in. round pipe, respectively. Conductor pipes are fastened with hooks or by means of wire.

Design of Gutters and Conductors.—The specifications of the American Bridge Company for the design of gutters and conductors are as given in Table II. Eave or valley gutters should always be galvanized. Valley gutters should be No. 20 gage. Eave gutters and conductors should be No. 22 gage. Gutters should be sloped not less than 1 in. in 15 ft.

TABLE II.

WEIGHTS OF EAVE GUTTERS AND CONDUCTORS OF GALV. IRON OR STEEL.

Span of Roof.	Size of Gutter.	Wt. per ft.	Size and Spacing of Conductor.	Wt. per lin. ft. No. 22.
up to 50′	6″, No. 22	1.8 lb.	4 in. every 40′ 0″	1.5 lb.
50′ to 70′	7″, No. 22	1.9 lb.	5 in. every 40′ 0″	2.1 lb.
70′ to 100′	8″, No. 22	2.1 lb.	5 in. every 40′ 0″	2.3 lb.

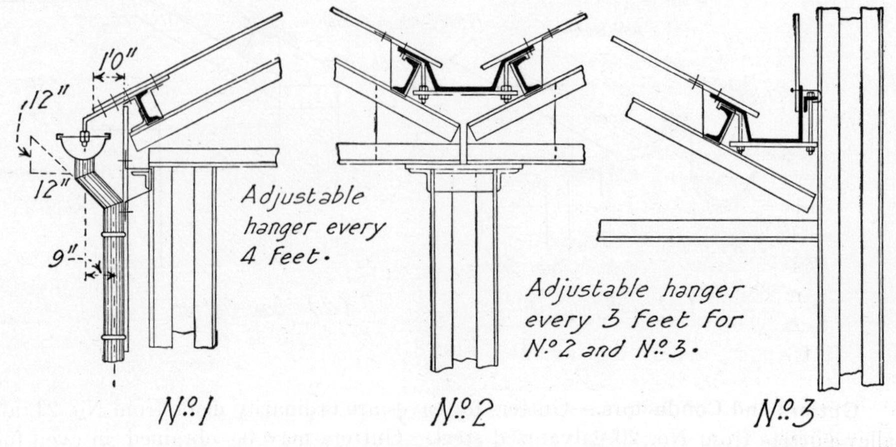

Type	Area Drained Sq. Ft.	Size of Gutter	Conductors Diam. Ins.	Conductors Spaced Ft.
	0 to 1200	6″	4	40
No. 1	1200 to 1800	7″	5	40
	1800 to 2400	8″	5	40
No. 2	0 to 2400	4″×8″	5	40
and	2400 to 3600	5″×8″	6	40
No. 3	3600 to 4800	5″×10″	6	40

Eave and Valley Gutters usually No. 20 or same gage as roofing.

Slope one inch in fifteen feet.

Order in 8 feet lengths.

Conductors usually No. 22 or same gage as siding.

FIG. 9. DETAILS OF CONDUCTORS AND DOWNSPOUTS. AMERICAN BRIDGE COMPANY.

The diagram in Fig. 10 for the design of gutters and conductors was described in Engineering News, April 17, 1902, by Mr. Emmett Steece, Assoc. M. Am. Soc. C. E., City Engineer of Burlington, Iowa, as follows:—

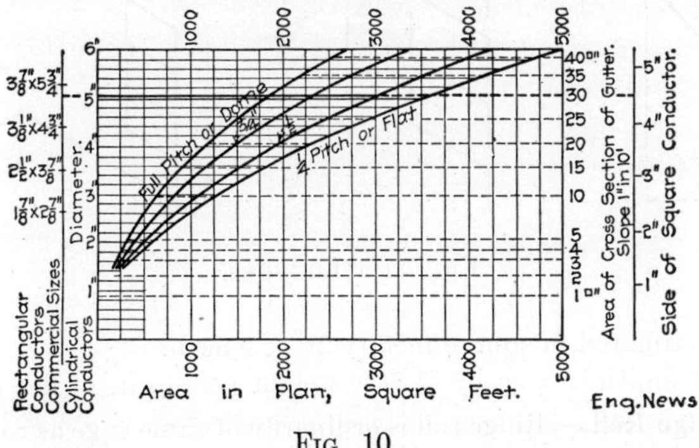

Fig. 10.

"The curves are for $\frac{1}{4}$ pitch or flat roofs, to full pitch or domes. The areas are reduced to plan as shown. The minimum sizes of circular and commercial rectangular conductors are given on the left side of the diagram and the sizes and the minimum cross-sectional areas of square gutters are given on the right hand side.

"To use the diagram: Assume an area of roof, say 30 × 100 ft., or 3000 sq. ft., $\frac{1}{2}$ pitch and one conductor for the whole area. Note the intersection of the vertical over area 3000 and the curve of $\frac{1}{2}$ pitch; following thence the horizontal line to the left it strikes a diameter of 5 in. for circular, or over $3\frac{1}{8} \times 4\frac{3}{4}$ in. for commercial size. The next larger size would be used. The minimum cross-sectional area of gutters is shown on the right to be about 30 sq. in., and the side of a square conductor about 4.5 in."

This diagram was based on a maximum rainfall of 1.98 in. per hour.

English practice is as follows: Rain-water or down-pipes should have a bore or internal area of at least one sq. in. for every 60 sq. ft. of roof surface in temperate climates, and about 30 sq. ft. in tropical climates. They should be placed not more than 20 ft. apart, and should have gutters not less in width than twice the diameter of the pipe.

The practice among American architects is to provide about one sq. in. of conductor area for each 75 sq. ft. of roof surface; no conductor less than 2 in. in diameter being used in any case.

To prevent clogging with debris the tops of all downspouts should be protected by means of wire guards. In cold climates the downspouts should be carried down inside the building, or the downspout may be kept free from ice by means of live steam, which is introduced through a cock near the bottom. Cast-iron downspouts give the best service and should preferably be used.

Louvres.—Weights of Shiffier louvres of black iron or steel are as follows:

Gage No.	Weight per Sq. Ft.
20	2.7 lb.
22	2.0 lb.

The weight is obtained from Fig. 11, as follows:

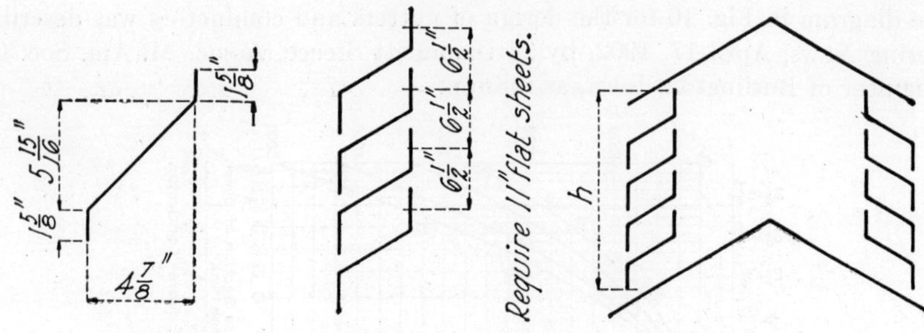

FIG. 11. LOUVRES.

Louvres are estimated in square feet $= 2h \times$ length.

To get weight multiply area by (1.7 $\times$ weight per sq. ft. of flat of material used).

Weight of Ridge Roll.—Ridge roll is ordinarily of same gage as roofing and black or galvanized to correspond with same. Ridge roll is usually made from an 18 in. flat sheet.

TABLE III.

WEIGHT OF RIDGE ROLL.

Gage No.	Weight, lb. per lineal ft.	
20	2.4	Black Iron or Steel.
22	2.0	
24	1.6	

Cornice.—There are many methods of finishing the gables and eaves of buildings. A gable finish for a steel end, and for a brick end as used by the American Bridge Company, are shown in Fig. 12. The steel end may have a cornice made by bending the corrugated steel as shown, or a molded cornice.

The flashed finish shown in (a), Fig. 12 is quite effective and gives a very neat appearance. The corrugated steel siding should preferably be carried up to the roof steel.

In (a), Fig. 13, the eave cornice is made by simply extending the roofing steel, while the gable cornice is made by bending a sheet of corrugated steel over the ends of the purlins and nailing to wooden strips as shown.

Sheets heavier than No. 22 should not be bent in the field. The corner finish is made by bending a sheet of corrugated steel.

The cornice and ridge finish shown in (b), Fig. 13, designed by Mr. H. A. Fitch, Kansas City, Mo., is very neat, efficient and economical. The galvanized rivets are much cheaper than copper rivets, and are preferred by many to the copper rivets. The detail shown was for a small dry house in which the eave strut was omitted.

In (c), Fig. 13, the eave and gable cornice are made of plain flat steel bent in the shop as shown. The eave cornice is made to mitre with the gable cornice, thus giving a neat finish at the corner. The corner finish is made by using sheets at the corners in which one-half is left plain.

In (d), Fig. 13, the eave strut and gable cornice are molded. The two cornices are so made as to mitre at the corners, the mitres being made in the field. A plain corner cap is put on as shown, after bending the corrugated steel around the corner.

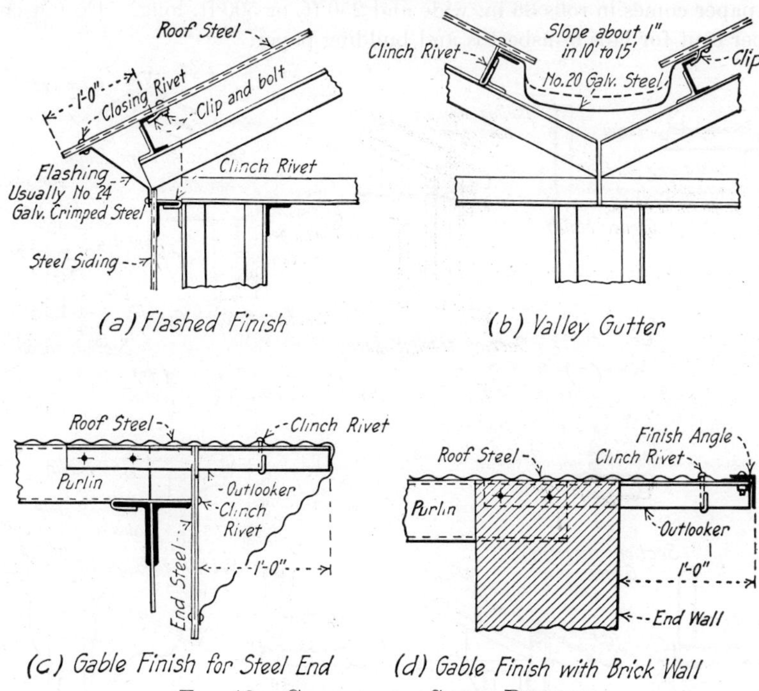

FIG. 12. CORRUGATED STEEL DETAILS.

Anti-condensation Lining.—To prevent the condensation of moisture on the inner surface of a steel roof, and the resulting dripping, the *anti-condensation lining* shown in Fig. 14 and in Fig. 15 is frequently used.

Anti-condensation lining, shown in Fig. 14, consists of asbestos felt supported on wire netting that is stretched tight and supported by the purlins. Anti-condensation lining is put on according to two systems.

Berlin System, Fig. 14.—(1) Lay galvanized wire netting, No. 19, 2-in. mesh, transversely to the purlins with edges about 1½ in. apart so that when laced together with No. 20 brass wire the netting will be stretched smooth and tight. When the purlins are spaced more than 4 ft. apart stretch No. 9 galvanized wire across the purlins about 2 ft. centers to hold up the netting.

(2) On the top of the wire netting place a layer of asbestos paper weighing 14 lb. per square of 100 sq. ft., and on this place a layer of asbestos paper weighing 6 lb. per square. All holes in the paper must be patched when laid.

(3) On top of the asbestos paper lay two thicknesses of Neponset building paper.

Note.—The asbestos and building paper should lap 3 in. and break joints 12 in. The corrugated steel is fastened with the usual connections. Use tin washers on corrugated steel bolts where there is danger of breaking or tearing the lining.

Wire netting, No. 19 gage, 2-in. mesh comes in bundles 6 ft. wide and 150 ft. long, containing 900 sq. ft. Asbestos comes in rolls 36 in. wide and is sold by the pound. No. 20 brass wire is bought by the pound, 272 lineal ft. weigh one pound. Neponset building paper comes in rolls 36 in. wide and 250 ft. or 500 ft. long. Do not cut a roll. Add 10 per cent for laps of asbestos and building paper.

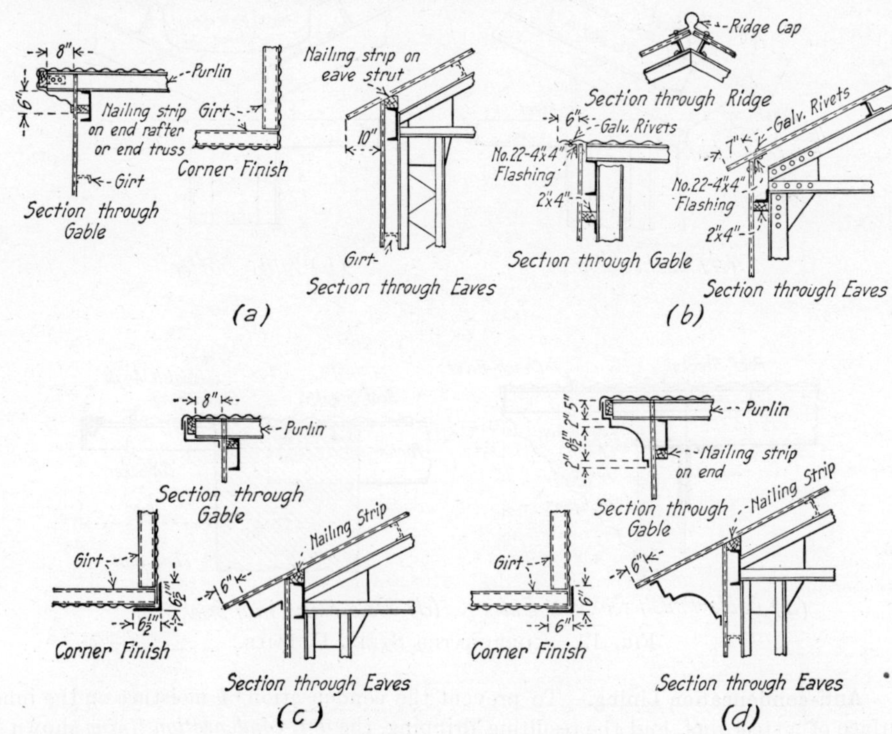

FIG. 13. CORRUGATED STEEL DETAILS.

Minneapolis System, Fig. 14 and Fig. 15.—(1) Lay wire netting, No. 19, 2-in. mesh, transversely to the purlins, with edges 1½ in. apart, so that when laced together with No. 20 brass wire the netting will be stretched smooth and tight.

(2) On the top of the netting lay asbestos paper weighing 30 lb. to the square of 100 sq. ft., allowing 3 in. for laps. For important work lay one or two thicknesses of building paper on top of the asbestos.

(3) Lay the corrugated steel and fasten to purlins in the usual manner.

Note.—If wood purlins are used the wire netting may be fastened to the nailing strips with ¾ in. staples. Where the purlins are more than 2 ft. 6 in. centers place a line of 3/16 in. bolts between purlins, about 2 ft. centers, with washers 1 in. × 4 in. × ⅛ in. to prevent netting from sagging.

Details of anti-condensation lining are shown in Fig. 14 and Fig. 15.

The author would recommend that purlins be spaced one-half the usual distance where anti-condensation lining is used; the stove bolts could then be omitted. Asbestos paper $\frac{1}{16}$ in. thick comes in rolls, and weighs about 32 lb. per square of 100 sq. ft. Galvanized poultry netting comes in rolls 60 in. wide and weighs about 10 lb. per square.

The corrugated steel used with anti-condensation roofing should never be less than No. 22, and the purlins should be spaced for not less than 30 lb. per sq. ft. A less substantial roof will not usually be satisfactory.

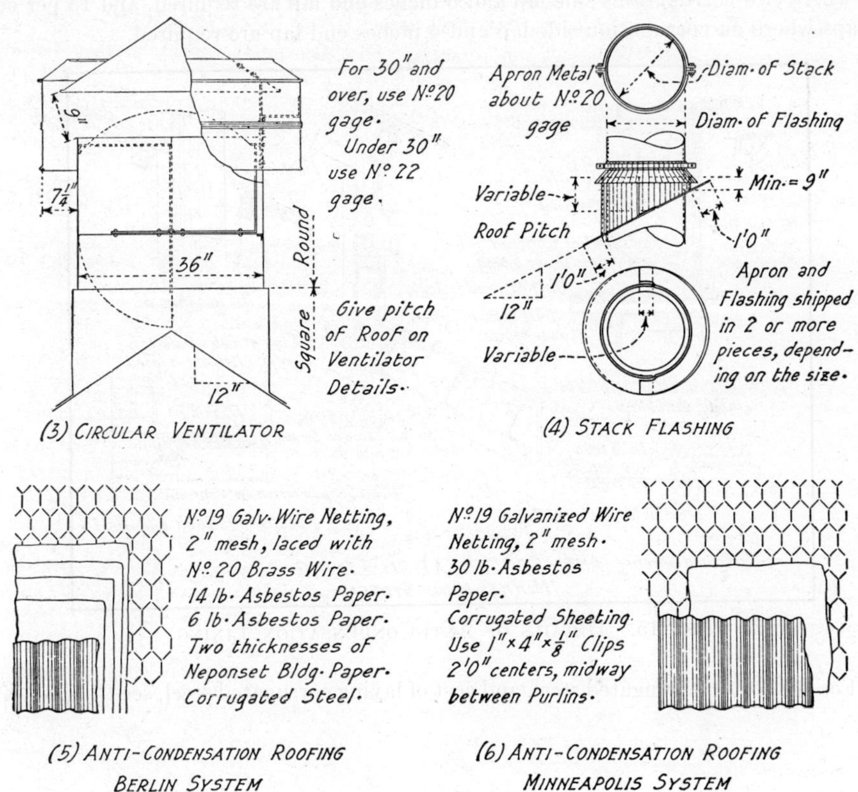

FIG. 14. DETAILS OF ROOFING, VENTILATORS AND ANTI-CONDENSATION LINING.

An engine house with anti-condensation lining on the roof and sides has been in use in the Lake Superior copper country for several years, and has been altogether satisfactory under trying conditions. The covering and lining of roof and sides are fastened by clinch nails to angle purlins and girts spaced about two feet apart.

A transformer building designed by the author and built by the Gillette-Herzog Mfg. Co., at East Helena, Montana, has anti-condensation lining on the roof as shown in Fig. 8, Chapter XXVI, and is lined on the sides with one layer of asbestos paper, and $1\frac{1}{4}$-inch No. 26 corrugated steel. The black framework, the red side lining, and white roof lining made a very pleasing interior.

Corrugated Steel Plans.—The shop plans, list of steel and details of the corrugated steel for a mill building are shown in Fig. 7 and Fig. 8, Chapter XXVI. Corrugated steel sheets should be ordered to cover two purlin or girt spaces if possible. Bevel sheets should be ordered by number, and sheets should be split and reentrant cuts should be made in the field. All sheets should be plainly marked with the number or length. Sheets No. 22 or lighter can be bent in the field, heavier metal should always be bent at the mill. In preliminary estimates of corrugated steel allow 20 per cent for laps where two corrugations side lap and 6 inches end lap are required, and 15 per cent for laps where on corrugation side lap and 4 inches end lap are required.

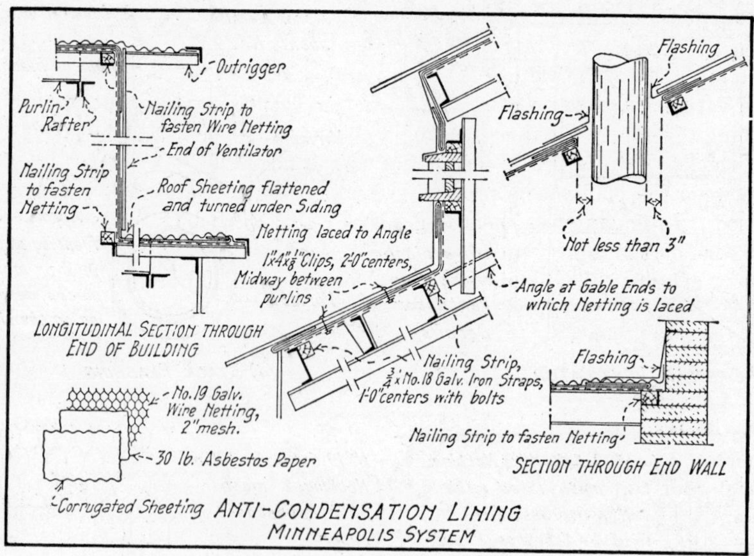

FIG. 15. DETAILS OF ANTI-CONDENSATION LINING.

For the cost of corrugated steel, and cost of laying corrugated steel, see Chapter XL.

CHAPTER XXIX.

Roof Coverings.

Introduction.—Industrial buildings are covered with corrugated steel supported directly on the purlins; by slate, clay or cement tile supported by sub-purlins; or by corrugated steel, slate, tile, shingles, tar and gravel, or other composition roof, or some one of the various patented roofings supported on sheathing. For ordinary buildings, the sheathing to support the roof covering is commonly made of a single layer of planks 1 to 3 in. thick. Two layers of planks are sometimes used, with a thin layer of lime mortar between the planks as a protection against fire. A laminated plank sheathing may be used. In making this sheathing, plank 2 to 3 in. thick, and 4 to 6 in. wide are placed on edge on the top chords of the trusses and are spiked together with 60d spikes spaced 18 in. centers. The laminated plank sheathing should be fastened to the upper chords of the trusses by means of bolts. For the thickness of wood sheathing see Table I, Chapter XXXII. Where the planks are partially continuous the allowable spans for deflection may be increased about 25 per cent. Wood sheathing with a thickness of less than $1\frac{5}{8}$ in., commercial 2 in. plank, should not be used. The allowable spans for laminated sheathing made of commercial 2 in. by 4 in. plank, and 2 in. by 6 in. plank may be obtained from Table I, Chapter XXXII. Where the planks are laid with, say, one plank in four continuous over the truss, quite satisfactory results will be obtained with a 2 in. by 4 in. laminated plank floor designed to carry a roof load of 50 lb. per sq. ft. on spans of 16 ft.

The sheathing may also be made of reinforced concrete or of reinforced gypsum. Reinforced gypsum slabs have the advantage that they may be molded on the ground and hoisted into place, that they are much lighter than concrete, and also do not sweat on the under side, as may be the case with roof sheathing that is a good conductor of heat. For the thickness of reinforced concrete slabs, see Tables II and III, Chapter XXXII.

Roofs of smelters, foundries, steel mills, mine buildings and similar structures are commonly covered with corrugated steel. Where the buildings are heated, or where a more substantial roof covering is to be desired, slate, tile, tin or a good grade of composition roofing is used. For very cheap and for temporary roofs, a composition roofing laid on plank sheathing is commonly used.

The following roof coverings will be described in the order given; corrugated steel, slate, terra cotta tile, cement tile, tin, sheet steel, tar and gravel, asphalt and gravel, shingle, and also several patented roofings.

CORRUGATED STEEL ROOFING.—Corrugated steel roofing is laid on plank sheathing or is supported directly on the purlins as described in Chapter XXVIII. For the cost of erecting corrugated steel roofing, see Chapter XL. Corrugated steel sheets covered with an asbestos preparation can now be obtained on the market.

Corrugated steel roofing should be kept well painted with a good paint. Where corrugated steel is exposed to the action of corrosive gases, as in the roof of a smelter reducing sulphur ores, ordinary red lead or iron oxide paint is practically worthless as a protective coating; better results have been obtained by using graphite or asphalt paints. Tar paint, made by mixing tar, Portland cement and kerosene in the proportions of 16 parts of tar, 4 parts of Portland cement, and 3 parts of kerosene, by volume, is an excellent protection against corrosive gases in smelters and similar structures. To prevent the condensation of vapor on the inside of the metal roof, corrugated steel roofing should be laid on sheathing or should have anti-condensation lining. The corrosion of corrugated steel is sometimes very rapid. In 1898, the author saw at the Trail Smelter, Trail, B. C., a corrugated steel roof made of No. 22 corrugated steel and painted with oxide of iron paint that had corroded so rapidly in one year that one could stick his finger through it as easily as through brown paper. The climate in that locality is moist, and the smelter was used for reducing sulphur ores. Galvanized corrugated steel is used quite extensively in many mining districts.

SLATE ROOFING.—There are many varieties of roofing slate, among which the Brownville and Monson slates of Maine, and Bangor and Peach Bottom slates of Pennsylvania are well known and are of excellent quality. Besides the characteristic slaty color, green, purple and red variegated roofing slates may be obtained. The best quality of slate has a glistening, semi-metallic appearance. Slate with a dull, earthy appearance will absorb water and is liable to be destroyed by the frost.

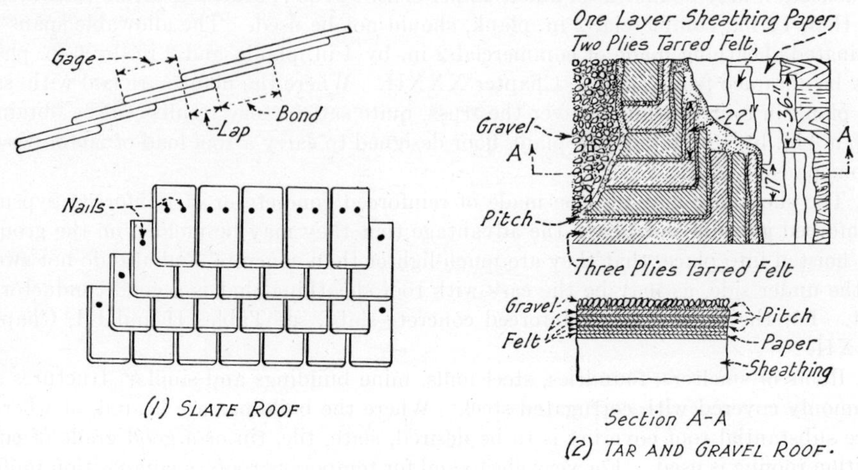

Fig. 1.

Roofing slates are usually made from $\frac{1}{8}$ to $\frac{1}{4}$ in. thick, 3/16 in. being a very common thickness. Slates vary in size from 6 in. $\times$ 12 in. to 24 in. $\times$ 44 in.; the sizes varying from 6 in. $\times$ 12 in. to 12 in. $\times$ 18 in. being the most common. Slates are laid like shingles as shown in Fig. 1. The lap most commonly used is 3 in.; where less than the minimum pitch $\frac{1}{4}$ is used, the lap should be increased. The number of slates of different sizes required for one square of 100 sq. ft. of roof for a 3 in. lap are given in Table I.

The weight of slates of various lengths and thicknesses required for one square of roofing, using a 3 in. lap, is given in Table II. The weight of slate is about 174 lb. to the cubic foot.

The weight of slate per sq. ft. of different thicknesses is given in Table III.

The minimum pitch recommended for a slate roof is $\frac{1}{4}$; but even with steeper roofs the rain and snow may be driven under the slates by the wind. This can be prevented by laying the slate in slater's cement. Cemented joints should always be used around eaves, ridges and chimneys. Slate may be laid on plank sheathing, reinforced

TABLE I.

Number of Roofing Slates Required to Lay One Square of Roof with 3-In. Lap.

Size in Inches.	No. of Slate in Square.	Size in Inches.	No. of Slate in Square.	Size in Inches.	No. of Slate in Square.
6 × 12	533	8 × 16	277	12 × 20	141
7 × 12	457	9 × 16	246	14 × 20	121
8 × 12	400	10 × 16	221	11 × 22	137
9 × 12	355	12 × 16	184	12 × 22	126
10 × 12	320	9 × 18	213	14 × 22	108
12 × 12	266	10 × 18	192	12 × 24	114
7 × 14	374	11 × 18	174	14 × 24	98
8 × 14	327	12 × 18	160	16 × 24	86
9 × 14	291	14 × 18	137	14 × 26	89
10 × 14	261	10 × 20	169	16 × 26	78
12 × 14	218	11 × 20	154	....	....

TABLE II.

The Weight of Slate Required for One Square of Roof.

Length in Inches.	Weight in pounds, per square, for the thickness.							
	$\frac{1}{8}''$	$\frac{3}{16}''$	$\frac{1}{4}''$	$\frac{3}{8}''$	$\frac{1}{2}''$	$\frac{5}{8}''$	$\frac{3}{4}''$	$1''$
12	483	724	967	1450	1936	2419	2902	3872
14	460	688	920	1370	1842	2301	2760	3683
16	445	667	890	1336	1784	2229	2670	3567
18	434	650	869	1303	1740	2174	2607	3480
20	425	637	851	1276	1704	2129	2553	3408
22	418	626	836	1254	1675	2093	2508	3350
24	412	617	825	1238	1653	2066	2478	3306
26	407	610	815	1222	1631	2039	2445	3263

TABLE III.

Weight of Slate Per Square Foot.

Thickness—in........	$\frac{1}{8}$	$\frac{3}{16}$	$\frac{1}{4}$	$\frac{3}{8}$	$\frac{1}{2}$	$\frac{5}{8}$	$\frac{3}{4}$	1
Weight—lb.........	1.81	2.71	3.62	5.43	7.25	9.06	10.87	14.5

concrete slabs, reinforced gypsum slabs, or may be laid directly on sub-purlins. The sheathing should be strong enough to prevent deflections that will break the slate. Plank sheathing should be tongued and grooved or ship-lapped, and should be dressed on the upper surface. Tar roofing felt laid between the slates and sheathing materially assists in making the roof waterproof and prevents breakage when the roof is walked on. The use of rubber-soled shoes by the workmen will materially reduce the breakage caused by walking on the roof. Roofing slates may also be supported directly on sub-purlins. The details of this method are practically the-same as for tile roofing, which see.

When roofing slates are laid on sheathing, they are fastened by two nails, one in each upper corner. When supported directly on sub-purlins, the slates are fastened by copper or composition wire. Galvanized and tinned steel nails, copper, composition and zinc slate roofing nails are used. Where the roof is to be exposed to corrosive gases, copper, composition or zinc nails should always be used.

Slate roofs, when made from first-class slate, well laid, have been known to last fifty years. When poorly put on, or when an inferior quality of slate is used, slate roofs are comparatively short-lived. Slate are easily broken by walking over the roof, and are sometimes broken by hail stones. Slate roofing is fireproof, as far as sparks are concerned, but the slate will crack and disintegrate when exposed to heat. Local conditions have much to do with the life of slate roofs, an ordinary life being from twenty-five to thirty years.

CLAY TILE ROOFING.—Baked clay or terra cotta roofing tiles are made in many forms and sizes. Plain roofing tiles are usually $10\frac{1}{2}$ in. long, $6\frac{1}{4}$ in. wide and $\frac{5}{8}$ in. thick, weigh from 2 to $2\frac{1}{2}$ lb. each, and lay one-half to the weather. There are many other forms of tile, among which book tile, Spanish tile, pan tile and Ludowici tile are well known. Tile are also made of glass, which are used in the place of skylights.

Clay tile may be laid (1) on plank sheathing, (2) on concrete or gypsum slab sheathing, or (3) may be supported directly on angle sub-purlins, as shown in Fig. 9, Chapter XXV. Tiles are laid on sheathing in the same manner as slate.

The roof shown in Fig. 9, Chapter XXV, was constructed as follows. Terra cotta tile, manufactured by the Ludowici Roofing Tile Co., Chicago, Ill., were laid directly on the angle sub-purlins, every fourth tile being secured to the angle sub-purlins by a piece of copper wire. The tiles were interlocking, requiring no cement except in exceptional cases. The tiles were 9 in. × 16 in. in size, 135 being sufficient to lay a square of 100 sq. ft. of roof. These tiles weigh from 750 to 800 lb. per square, and cost about eight dollars per square at the factory. Skylights in this roof were made by substituting glass tile for the terra cotta tile.

The roof of the two-story portion of the new laboratory building at the University of Colorado, see Fig. 2, Chapter XXX, is made of Ludowici tile, supported on sheathing made of gypsum slabs. The tile are fastened to the sheathing by means of wire which passes through lugs on the under side of the tile and through the gypsum slabs.

Tile roofs laid without sheathing do not ordinarily condense the steam on the inner side of the roof, unless the tiles are glazed, although several cases have been brought to the author's attention where the condensation has caused trouble in clay tile roofs. Anti-condensation linings should be used where there is danger of excessive sweating, or the tiles should be laid on a non-sweating sheathing. For the cost of clay tile roofs, see Chapter XL.

CEMENT ROOFING TILE.—Cement tile are made of Portland cement and clean, sharp sand and are reinforced with steel rods.

Data for "Bonanza" cement tile, manufactured by the American Cement Tile Mfg. Co., Pittsburgh, Pa., are given in Fig. 2. The exposed surface of the tile is Indian red in color, while the underside has a cement finish. The smallest desirable slope of roof is a pitch of one-fifth. Data for Federal cement tile, manufactured by the Federal

Cement Tile Co., Chicago, Ill., are given in Fig. 3, and in the upper part of Fig. 4. Cement roofing tile have been very extensively used for industrial plants. The cement tile have the following advantages: (a) are fire resisting; (b) require very simple roof construction; (c) require no sheathing; (d) are non-conductors; (e) may be erected rapidly; (f) the first cost is low for a permanent type of roof; (g) maintenance is low. Skylights are made by means of wire glass inserts as described in Fig. 2.

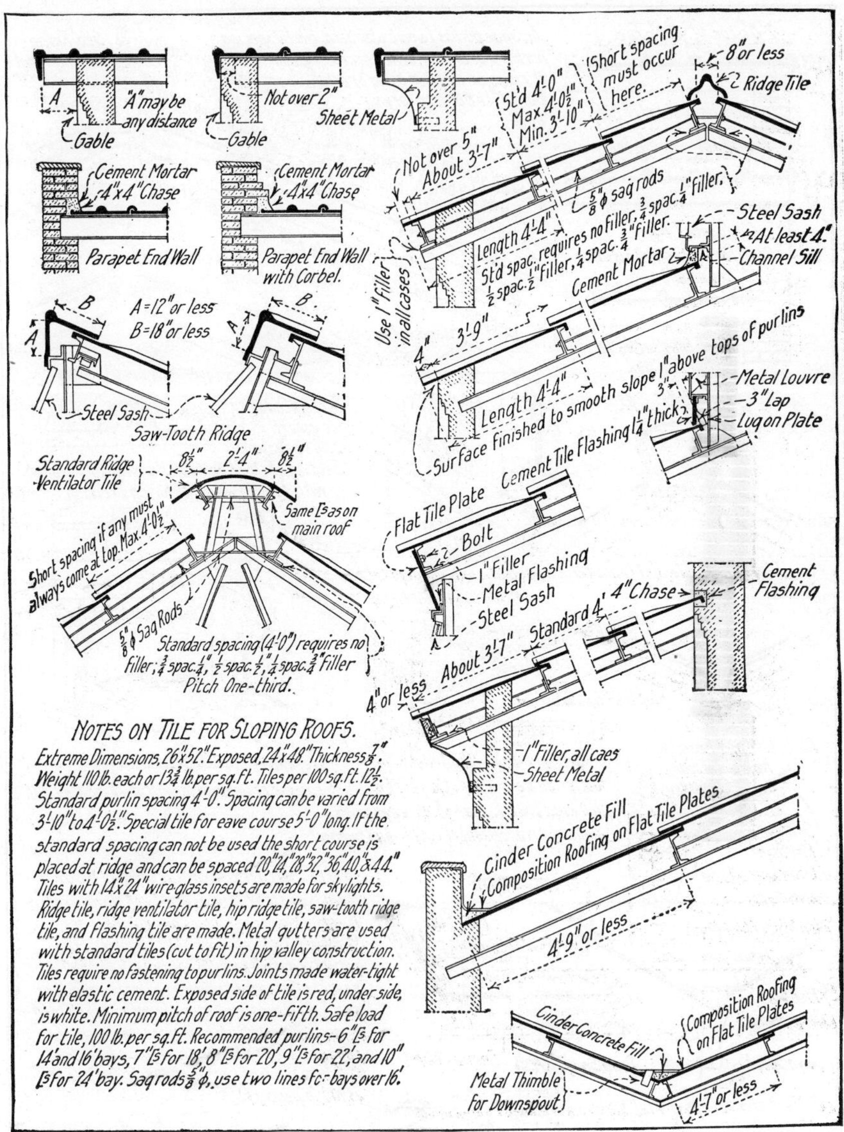

Fig. 2. Data for "Bonanza Tile."

Gypsum Roofing Tile.—Gypsum roofing tile made by the United States Gypsum Company, Chicago, are sold under the trade name of Pyrobar gypsum roof tile. The tile are 12 in. wide and 30 in. long, and weigh 13 lb. per sq. ft. Data taken from the catalog for rafters and purlins for Pyrobar gypsum roof tile are given in the lower part of Fig. 4. Gypsum roof tile have recently been used on buildings for the Navy Department at Norfolk, Va. The following advantages of gypsum roof slabs were given

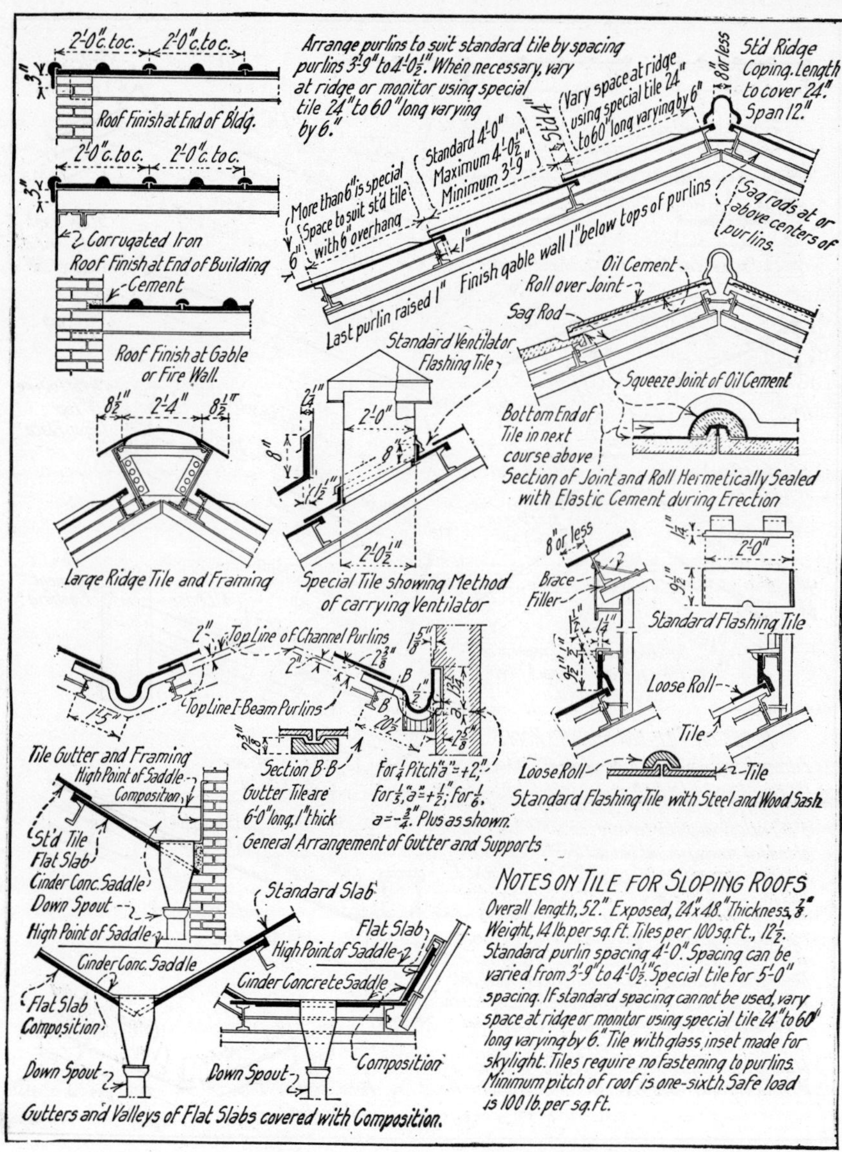

FIG. 3. DATA FOR FEDERAL CEMENT TILE.

by L. M. Cox, U. S. N., Engineering News, Jan. 25, 1917: (a) Light weight; (b) rapid construction; (c) roof slab is non-conductor and non-condensing; (d) is fire resisting; (e) shows few cracks; (f) low cost of maintenance. Gypsum roofing tile are made by several firms, and are also made at the building site. Gypsum slabs should always be covered with a roof covering.

TIN ROOFS.—Tin plates are made by coating flat iron or steel sheets with tin or with a mixture of lead and tin. The former is called " bright " tin plate and the latter " terne " plate. " Terne " plates should not be used where the roof will be subjected to the action of corrosive gases, for the reason that the lead coating is rapidly destroyed. Plates are covered with tin (1) by the dipping process, in which plates are pickled in dilute sulphuric acid, annealed, again pickled, dipped in palm oil and then in a bath of molten tin or tin and lead; or (2) by the roller process, in which the plates are dipped in the tin bath and are immediately run through rolls working in a large vessel containing oil. The latter method gives the better results.

Two sizes of tin plates are in common use; 14 × 20 in. and 20 × 28 in., the latter size being most used. Tin plates are made in several thicknesses, the IC, or No. 29 gage, weighing 8 oz. to the sq. ft. and the IX, or No. 27 gage, weighing 10 oz. to the sq. ft. being the most used. The weight of a box of 112 plates of 14 × 20 in. size will vary from 107 to 112 lb. for IC tin plate, and from 153 to 161 lb. for IX tin plate.

The value of tin roofing depends upon the amount of tin used in coating and the uniformity with which the iron has been coated. The amount of tin used in coating 112 plates 20 × 28 in. size, varies from 8 to 40 lb. The Navy Department specifies that 5 lb. of tin shall be used per 112 plates of 14 × 20 in. size. The Navy Department specification for " terne " plate requires a mixture of 20 per cent of pure tin and 80 per cent of pure lead, the coating to be thoroughly amalgamated with the black plate by the palm oil process. The amount of tin and lead coating for 112 plates of 20 × 28 in. size is 40 lb.

Tin roofing is laid (1) with a flat seam, or (2) with a standing seam. In the former method the sheets of tin are locked into each other at the edges, the seam is flattened and fastened with tin cleats or is nailed firmly and is soldered water tight. Rosin is the best flux for soldering, although some tinners recommend the use of diluted chloride of zinc. For flat roofs the tin should be locked and soldered at all joints, and should be secured by tin cleats and not by nails. For steep roofs the tin is commonly put on with standing seams, not soldered, running with the pitch of the roof, and with cross-seams double locked and soldered. One or two layers of tar paper should be placed between the sheathing and the tin.

The under side of the sheets should be painted before laying. Tin roofs should be painted every two or three years. If kept well painted a tin roof should last 25 to 30 years.

For flat seam roofing, using $\frac{1}{2}$ in. locks, a box of 14 × 20 tin will cover 192 sq. ft., and for standing seam, using $\frac{3}{8}$ in. locks and turning $1\frac{1}{4}$ and $1\frac{1}{2}$ in. edges, making 1 in. standing seams, it will lay 168 sq. ft. For flat seam roofing, using $\frac{1}{2}$ in. locks, a box of 20 × 28 tin will lay about 399 sq. ft., and for standing seam, with $\frac{3}{8}$-in. locks and turning $1\frac{1}{4}$ and $1\frac{1}{2}$ in edges, making 1 in. standing seams, it will lay about 365 sq. ft.

SHEET STEEL ROOFING.—Sheet steel roofing is sold in sheets 28 in. wide and from 4 to 12 ft. long, or in rolls 26 in. wide and about 50 ft. long. It is commonly laid with vertical standing seams and horizontal flat seams; tin cleats from 12 to 15 in. apart being nailed to the plank sheathing and locked into the seams. Sheet steel plates are also made with standing crimped seams near the edges, which are nailed to V-shaped sticks; the horizontal seams being made by lapping about 6 in.

Care should be used in laying sheet steel roofing to see that it does not come in contact with materials containing acids, and it should be kept well painted. The weight

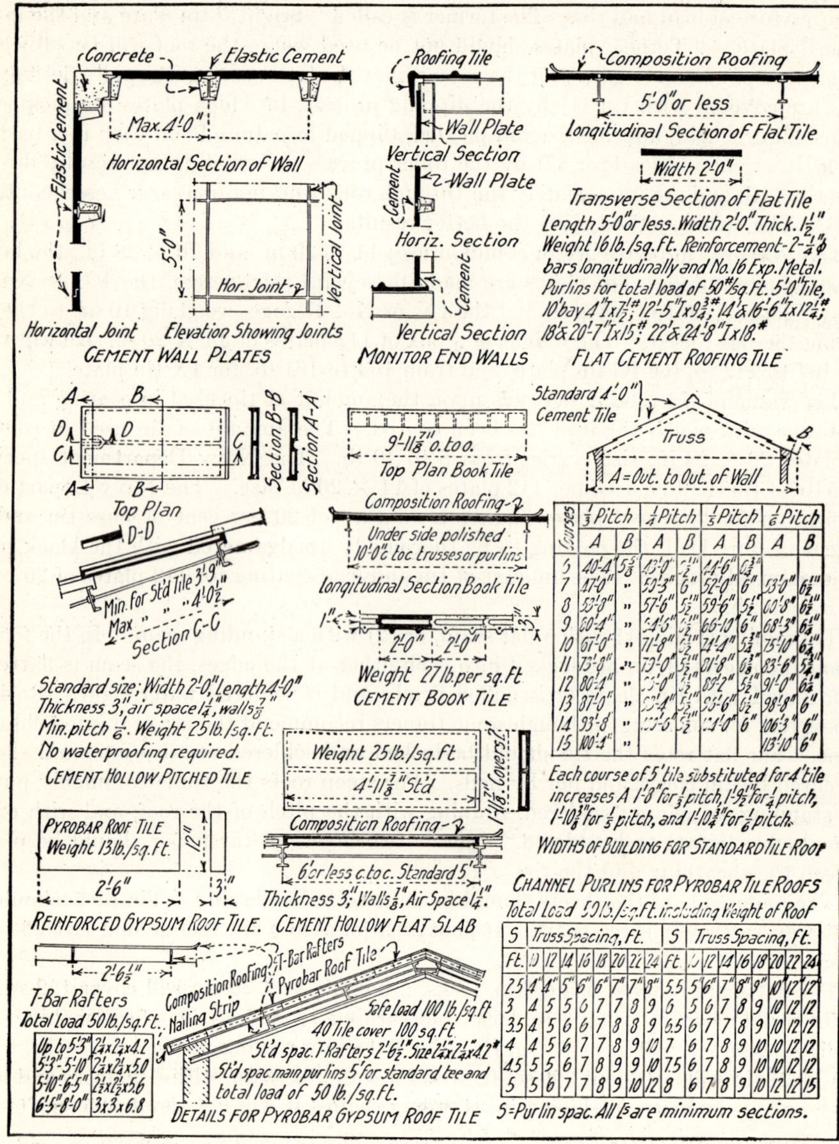

Courses	⅓ Pitch A	⅓ Pitch B	¼ Pitch A	¼ Pitch B	⅕ Pitch A	⅕ Pitch B	⅙ Pitch A	⅙ Pitch B
6	40'-4"	5⅝"	43'-0"	6½"	44'-6"	6¾"		
7	47'-0"	"	50'-3"	6"	52'-0"	6"	53'-0"	6½"
8	53'-8"	"	57'-6"	5½"	59'-6"	5½"	60'-8"	6½"
9	60'-4"	"	64'-6"	6½"	66'-10"	6"	68'-3"	6¼"
10	67'-0"	"	71'-8"	6½"	74'-4"	5¾"	75'-10"	6¼"
11	73'-8"	"	79'-0"	5½"	81'-8"	6⅜"	83'-6"	5¾"
12	80'-4"	"	[illegible]'-0"	6½"	89'-2"	5½"	91'-0"	6¼"
13	87'-0"	"	93'-4"	5½"	96'-6"	6½"	98'-8"	6"
14	93'-8"	"	100'-6"	6½"	[illegible]'-0"	6"	106'-3"	6"
15	100'-4"	"					113'-10"	6"

S Ft.	10	12	14	16	18	20	22	24	S Ft.	10	12	14	16	18	20	22	24
2.5	4"	4"	5"	6"	6"	7"	7"	8"	5.5	5"	6"	7"	8"	9"	10"	12"	12"
3	4	5	5	6	7	7	8	9	6	5	6	7	8	9	10	12	12
3.5	4	5	6	6	7	8	8	9	6.5	6	7	7	8	9	10	12	12
4	4	5	6	7	7	8	9	10	7	6	7	8	9	10	10	12	12
4.5	5	5	6	7	8	9	9	10	7.5	6	7	8	9	10	10	12	12
5	5	6	7	7	8	9	10	12	8	6	7	8	9	10	12	12	15

T-Bar Rafters	Size
Up to 5'-3"	2¼x2¼x4.2
5'-3"-5'-10"	2¼x2¼x5.0
5'-10"-6'-5"	2½x2½x5.6
6'-5"-8'-0"	3x3x6.8

FIG. 4. DATA FOR FEDERAL TILE (UPPER PART), DATA FOR PYROBAR GYPSUM TILE (LOWER PART).

of flat steel of different gages is given in Table I, Chapter XXVIII. Nos. 26 and 28 gage sheets are commonly used for sheet steel roofing. Sheet steel roofing can be laid at a somewhat less cost than tin roofing.

TAR AND GRAVEL ROOFING.—Tar and gravel roofing, Fig. 2, is made by laying several layers of roofing felt on sheathing so as to break joints; the laps are mopped and cemented together with roofing tar or pitch and the entire surface is covered with a coating of hot tar or pitch. While the tar roofing pitch is still hot, the surface of the roof is covered with a layer of clean gravel that has been screened through a $\frac{5}{8}$ in. mesh. The number of layers of felt varies with conditions, but should never be less than 4 (4-ply). Tar and gravel roofs should not be laid on roofs with a pitch greater than 3 in. in 12 in. The best results with roofs of this type are obtained with a slope of 1 in. in 12 in.

Gravel roofing under ordinary conditions will last for from 10 to 15 years. With careful attention it can be made to last longer and has been known to last 30 years.

The author's specifications for tar and gravel roofing on plank sheathing and on concrete sheathing are as follows:

Specifications for Five-Ply Tar and Gravel Roof on Timber Sheathing.—The materials used in making the roof are 1 (one) thickness of sheathing paper or unsaturated felt, 5 (five) thicknesses of saturated felt weighing not less than 15 (fifteen) lb. per square of one hundred (100) sq. ft., single thickness, and not less than one hundred and fifty (150) lb. of pitch, and not less than four hundred (400) lb. of gravel or three hundred (300) lb. of slag from $\frac{1}{4}$ to $\frac{5}{8}$ in. in size, free from dirt, per square of one hundred (100) sq. ft. of completed roof.

The material shall be applied as follows: First, lay the sheathing or unsaturated felt, lapping each sheet one in. over the preceding one. Second, lay two (2) thicknesses of tarred felt, lapping each sheet seventeen (17) in. over the preceding one, nailing as often as may be necessary to hold the sheets in place until the remaining felt is applied. Third, coat the entire surface of this two-ply layer with hot pitch, mopping on uniformly. Fourth, apply three (3) thicknesses of felt, lapping each sheet twenty-two (22) in. over the preceding one, mopping with hot pitch the full width of the 22 in. between the plies, so that in no case shall felt touch felt. Such nailing as is necessary shall be done so that all nails will be covered by not less than two plies of felt. Fifth, spread over the entire surface of the roof a uniform coating of pitch, into which, while hot, imbed the gravel or slag. The gravel or slag in all cases must be dry.

Specifications for Five-Ply Tar and Gravel Roof on Concrete Sheathing.—The materials used shall be the same as for tar and gravel roof on timber sheathing, except that the one thickness of sheathing paper or unsaturated felt may be omitted.

The materials shall be applied as follows: First, coat the concrete with hot pitch, mopped on uniformly. Second, lay two (2) thicknesses of tarred felt, lapping each sheet seventeen (17) in. over the preceding one, and mop with hot pitch the full width of the 17-in. lap, so that in no case shall felt touch felt. Third, coat the entire surface with hot pitch, mopped on uniformly. Fourth, lay three (3) thicknesses of felt, lapping each sheet twenty-two (22) in. over the preceding one, mopping with hot pitch the full width of the 22-in. lap between the plies, so that in no case shall felt touch felt. Fifth, spread the entire surface of the roof with a uniform coat of pitch into which, while hot, imbed gravel or slag.

Barrett Specification Roof.—The Barrett Company has prepared standard specifications for tar and gravel roofs. When tar and gravel roofs are put on according to the Barrett specifications, using Barrett specification tarred felt and waterproofing materials, by approved contractors, the Barrett Company will give a guaranty bond under certain conditions. The following is an abstract of the Barrett specifications for 5-ply tar and gravel roofing on plank sheathing. The slope of the roof shall not exceed 2 in. in 12 in. The roof deck shall be of seasoned lumber, smooth and free from cracks, knot-holes and loose material. The roof deck shall be properly graded to outlets.

First.—Lay one thickness of sheathing paper weighing not less than 5 lb. per square, lapping sheets 1 in.

Second.—Lay two plies of specification tarred felt, lapping each sheet 17 in. over preceding one, and nail as often as is necessary.

Third.—Coat the entire surface uniformly with specification pitch.

Fourth.—Over the entire surface lay three plies of specification tarred felt, lapping each sheet 22 in. over preceding one, and mopping with pitch the full 22 in. on each sheet, so that in no place shall felt touch felt. All nails shall be covered by not less than 2 plies of felt.

Fifth.—Cover the entire surface with a uniform coat of specification pitch, into which, while hot, imbed not less than 400 lb. of gravel or 300 lb. of slag per 100 sq. ft. The gravel or slag shall be from $\frac{1}{4}$ to $\frac{5}{8}$ in. in size, dry and free from dirt. Felt shall be laid without wrinkles or buckles. Not less than 150 lb. of pitch shall be used in constructing each 100 sq. ft. of completed roof. The pitch shall not be heated above 400° F.

The Barrett Company has also prepared specifications for 4-ply tar and gravel roofing, where the inclination of the roof does not exceed 1 in. in 12 inches.

SLAG ROOFING.—Slag is sometimes used in the place of gravel in making roofs. The method of constructing the roof and the specifications are essentially the same as for a gravel roof.

ASPHALT ROOFING.—Asphalt roofing is laid like tar and gravel roofing except that asphalt is used in the place of tar or pitch. Asphalt and gravel roofs do not ordinarily give as good service as well made tar and gravel roofs.

FLASHING OF TAR AND GRAVEL ROOFS.—The roofing should be finished against fire walls, chimneys, curbs and skylights by turning the felt up 4 in. against the wall. Over this lay 12-in. strips of felt with one-half the width on the roof. The upper edge of the strips should be inserted in a groove in the wall, or in a joint in brick work, or be fastened to wood with strips firmly nailed. The top edge of the strips may be covered with copper or galvanized flashing inserted in the wall. The strips should be pressed into the angle of the wall and should be cemented together with hot pitch. Nail the lower edge of the strips to the plank sheathing every 4 or 6 in. The flashing on pitch roofs should extend 12 in. up the slope of the roof. In flashing against a vertical wall a bevel flashing block should be inserted in the corner of the roof. Flashing blocks should be 5 in. × 5 in. with a slope of 45°. The roof felt should be finished to the top edge of the flashing block, and the flashing strips should be inserted about 2 in. into a groove in the wall at the top of the flashing block and extend to the bottom edge of the flashing block. On a concrete roof the bevel block may be made of porous concrete.

The Barrett Company furnishes a special pitch known as "Elastigum" for flashing of tar and gravel roofs. Standard details for flashing and for roof drains may be obtained from The Barrett Company.

Underwriters' Laboratories Classification of Roofs.—The Underwriters' Laboratories divide built-up roofs laid on roofs with a slope of not greater than 3 in. in 12 in., into Class A, Class B, and Class C. Class A roofs are effective against severe fire exposures, Class B roofs are effective against moderate fire exposures, Class C roofs are effective against light fire exposures.

Class A roofs include 4- and 5-ply tar and gravel roofs, 4- and 5-ply asphalt and asphalt-saturated rag-felt and gravel roofs; 4- and 5-ply asphalt and asphalt-impregnated asbestos felt roof coverings, smooth, and asbestos-shingle roof coverings, laid "American Method." Class B roofs include 3-ply asphalt and asphalt-saturated rag-felt and gravel or slag, asphalt and asphalt-impregnated asbestos felt roof coverings, smooth, and asbestos shingles, laid "French Method." Class C roofs include asphalt and asphalt-saturated rag-felt roof coverings, smooth or grit surfaced; asphalt-rag-felt prepared roof coverings, and asphalt-rag-felt shingle roof coverings.

SHINGLE ROOFS.—Shingle roofs are now very seldom used for mill buildings. Shingles have an average width of 4 in. and with 4 in. laid to the weather 900 are required to lay one square of roof. One thousand shingles require about 5 lb. of nails. One man can lay from 1500 to 2000 shingles in a day of 8 hours.

Shingles are also made of tin, sheet steel, asbestos and of various compositions.

FERROINCLAVE.—This is a patented roofing made by the Brown Hoisting Machinery Co., Cleveland, Ohio. Ferroinclave roofing is made by coating a special crimped or corrugated iron or steel on both sides with a mixture of Portland cement and sand, after which it is painted on the upper side. The sheets are made of No. 22 or No. 24 sheet steel, and full sized sheets are 20 inches wide and 10 ft. long. The steel is crimped or corrugated with corrugations about 2 inches wide and $\frac{1}{2}$ in. deep, the width of the corrugation on the outer side being less than on the inner side, thus forming a key to hold the cement mortar in place. The sheets are laid in the same manner as corrugated steel, and a coating of Portland cement mortar, composed of 1 part Portland cement and 2 parts sand, is plastered on the upper and lower surfaces to a thickness of $\frac{3}{8}$ in. above and below the corrugations, making the total thickness of the roofing $1\frac{1}{4}$ in. The weight of No. 24 sheet steel Ferroinclave is about 15 lb. per square foot when filled with cement mortar as above. A test of a sheet of Ferroinclave made as above, showed failure with a uniformly distributed load of 300 lb. per sq. ft. with supports 4 ft. 10 in. apart, the cement having set ten days. The cost of this roofing in 1913 was about $21.00 per square complete in place on the roof. The Brown Hoisting Machinery Co. has also used Ferroinclave quite extensively for floors and side walls of buildings.

PREPARED ROOFINGS.—Prepared roofings that are ready to lay on the roof may be purchased. These roofings usually come in rolls that will lay 100 sq. ft. of finished roofing. Prepared roofings are made by treating felt or burlap with some preparation that will cement the layers together and make a waterproof covering. Prepared roofings are commonly listed as one-ply, two-ply, three-ply, etc. Prepared roofings are laid shingle fashion, beginning at the foot of the slope of the roof, the sheets being lapped 2 in. to 4 in. The joints are cemented and nailed.

Prepared roofings should be laid on roofs with a slope of $\frac{1}{4}$ to $\frac{1}{3}$. Prepared roofings give the best service on pitched roofs where the tar and gravel roof is not satisfactory. A few of the well known prepared roofings will be described.

Asbestos Roofing.—The "Standard" asbestos roofing, manufactured by the H. W. Johns-Manville Co., New York, is composed of a strong canvas foundation with asbestos felt on the under side, and saturated asbestos felt on the upper side finished with a sheet of plain asbestos; the whole being cemented together with a special cement and compressed together into a flexible roofing. It does not require painting, although it is commonly painted with a special paint, one gallon of which will cover about 150 sq. ft. The roofing is laid with a lap of 2 in., beginning at the lower edge of the roof and running parallel to the eaves. The laps are cemented and are nailed with special roofing nails and caps. The roofing is laid on sheathing and is very easily and cheaply laid. It is quite flexible and may be used for flashing and for gutters. It is practically fireproof and makes a very satisfactory roof. Asbestos roofing comes in rolls and weighs about 75 lb. per square.

Asbestos roofing felts may be purchased which are used for roofing in one, two or three-ply, and are laid in the same way as for gravel roofing.

Carey's Roofing.—Carey's magnesia flexible cement roofing, manufactured by the Philip Carey Manufacturing Company, Lockland, Ohio, is made by putting a layer of asphalt cement composition on a foundation of woolen felt and imbedding a strong burlap in the upper surface of the cement. After laying, the burlap is covered with a tough elastic paint which when it dries gives a surface similar to slate. The roof is practically acid proof and burns very slowly. It comes in rolls 29 in. wide and containing sufficient material to lay one square of roof. The roofing is made in two weights, standard weighing 90 lb. per square, and extra heavy weighing about 115 lb. per square. A special flap is provided on one side to cover the nail heads. The roofing is very pliable and can be used for flashing and for gutters. It should be laid on sheathing and is very easily and cheaply applied. It may be laid over an old shingle or corrugated iron roof.

Granite Roofing.—Granite roofing, manufactured by the Eastern Granite Roofing Company, New York, is a ready-to-lay composition roofing with manufactured quartz pebbles imbedded in its upper surface. It is a very satisfactory roofing and is quite extensively used.

Ruberoid Roofing.—P. & B. ruberoid roofing, manufactured by the Standard Paint Co., New York, is quite extensively used and has given good satisfaction. The following description is taken from the maker's catalog: " No paper whatever is used in the manufacture of ruberoid roofing. It has a foundation of the best wool felt, except in the case of the ½-ply grade which is a combination of wool and hair. This is first saturated with the P. & B. water and acid proof compound, and afterwards coated with a hard solution of the same material, thereby making the roofing at once light in weight as well as strong, durable and elastic. It is thoroughly acid and alkali proof, is not affected by coal gas or smoke and can be laid on either pitched or flat roofs, proving equally effectual in both cases. Inasmuch as it contains no tar or asphalt the roofing is not affected by extremes in temperature."

Ruberoid is made ½-ply weighing 22 lb. per square; 1-ply weighing 30 lb. per square; 2-ply weighing 43 lb. per square; and 3-ply weighing 51 lb. per square. The 2-ply and the 3-ply roofing are commonly used for factories and mills. The roofing is put up in rolls 36 in. wide, containing two squares (200 sq. ft.), with an additional allowance of 16 sq. ft. for two-inch laps at the seams; sufficient tacks, tin caps and cement are included with each roll.

EXAMPLES OF ROOFS.—For examples of roofs, see Chapter XXV, Chapter XXVI, and Chapter XXX.

CHAPTER XXX.

Side Walls.

TYPES OF MILL BUILDINGS.—Steel mill buildings may be divided into three classes as follows:—(1) Steel frame mill buildings with light covering; (2) steel mill buildings with walls filled in between the columns; and (3) mill buildings with masonry walls.

Steel frame mill buildings may be covered on the roof and side walls with corrugated steel, with asbestos covered corrugated steel, or with asbestos corrugated sheets fastened to sheathing or directly to the purlins or girts. Or the side walls may be covered with expanded metal and plaster, or wire netting and plaster, or with ferroinclave and plaster fastened directly to the girts. In buildings of this type a brick, concrete or tile wall should extend to the window sills, and a considerable portion of the side walls should be glazed.

Steel frame buildings may have filled walls of brick, concrete, stone, terra cotta tile or gypsum tile. Or concrete pilasters may be built around the columns and reinforced concrete slabs may be used for the intervening side walls.

Mill buildings with steel trusses resting on self supporting walls may have side walls of brick, stone or concrete masonry, or of reinforced concrete.

Heat Transmission of Side Walls.—The transmission of heat through side walls of different materials in terms of k, the heat transmission in British Thermal Units (b.t.u.) per sq. ft. per hour, for a difference of one degree in temperature between inside and outside temperature is as follows:

Windows.—Single windows, $k = 1.03$; double windows, $k = 0.48$; double glass on single sash, $k = 0.72$.

Corrugated Steel.—Corrugated steel, on total surface, $k = 1.13$; on projected surface, $k = 1.50$.

Wood Walls.—Matched and sealed wood walls 2 in. thick, $k = 0.46$.

Plaster and Wire Lath.—Partitions made of plaster and wire lath or expanded metal, $k = 0.64$.

Brick Walls.—Brick walls 8 in. thick, $k = 0.39$; 12 in. walls, $k = 0.31$; 16 in. walls, $k = 0.26$.

Concrete Walls.—Solid concrete walls 4 in. thick, $k = 0.62$; 8 in. thick, $k = 0.50$; 12 in. thick, $k = 0.42$.

Terra Cotta Walls.—Hollow terra cotta 4 in. thick, $k = 0.42$; 6 in. thick, $k = 0.36$; 8 in. thick, $k = 0.32$.

For wind exposure add about 25 per cent to the above values. The above walls must be tight so that no air will get through the cracks.

Corrugated Steel Side Walls.—The methods of fastening corrugated steel to the sides of buildings are the same as on the roof and are described in detail in Chapter XVIII. Where warmth is desired, buildings covered with corrugated steel are often lined with No. 24 corrugated steel with $1\frac{1}{4}$-inch corrugations. Where this lining is used spiking pieces should be bolted to the girts and intermediate spiking pieces should be placed between the girts to which to nail the lining. If this is not done the corrugated steel will gape open for the reason that it is impossible to rivet the side laps of the lining. Where anti-condensation lining is used on the sides it is made the same as on the roof, except that the girts should always be placed not more than one-half the usual distance. The clinch-nail fastening is the best method for fastening the corrugated steel where the anti-condensation lining is used.

Asbestos Protected Corrugated Steel.—Corrugated steel sheets are coated on both sides with a layer of asphalt, a layer of asbestos, and a layer of waterproofing material. Asbestos protected corrugated steel has the same widths and lengths as standard corrugated steel, and is laid in the same manner. The roofing is not affected by acid fumes and is used in the construction of acid plants and similar structures. Unless the connections are specially treated the steel will corrode around the holes made by punching the sheet steel for the rivets, and the sheets will drop off the sides of the building. The steel used in commercial asbestos protected corrugated steel is much thinner than plain or corrugated steel. For mine and smelter structures asbestos protected corrugated steel does not give more satisfactory results than may be obtained at a less cost by coating No. 18 plain corrugated steel sheets with a tar paint after erection.

Asbestos Corrugated Sheathing.—Asbestos corrugated sheathing is made by mixing asbestos fiber with Portland cement and with sufficient water. The sheets are formed by hydraulic pressure. Asbestos corrugated sheets are $27\frac{1}{2}$ in. wide with corrugations $2\frac{1}{2}$ in. wide and 1 in. deep and 3/16 in. thick. Asbestos sheathing may be obtained from 4 ft. to 10 ft. in length. Asbestos sheathing is not affected by acid fumes and is a non-conductor of heat. The sheets are laid in the same manner as corrugated steel sheets, except that the clips should be non-corrosive.

Expanded Metal and Plaster.—The methods of making walls of expanded metal and plaster are shown in Fig. 1, which shows details of the construction of the soap buildings of W. H. Walker, Pittsburgh, Pa. These buildings were constructed as follows:

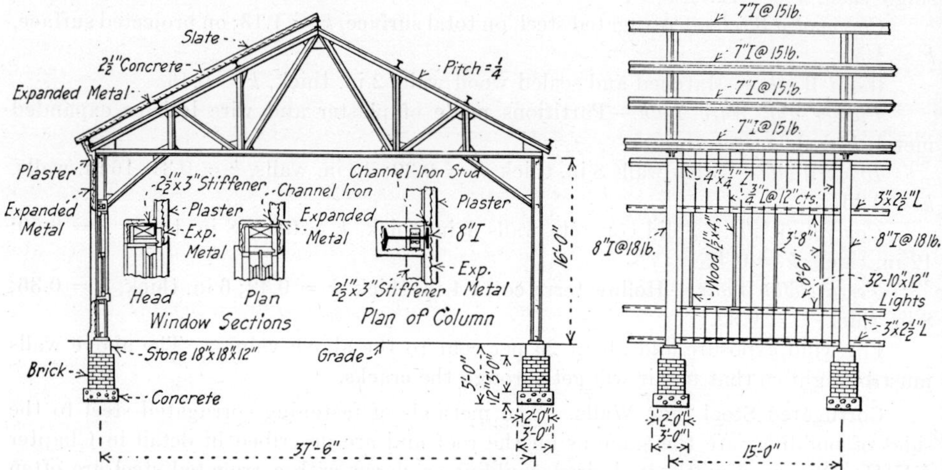

FIG. 1. CROSS-SECTION OF STEEL BUILDING COVERED WITH EXPANDED METAL AND PLASTER.

The buildings were made with a self-supporting steel frame, all connections except those for the purlins and girts being riveted. Inaccessible surfaces were painted with red lead and linseed oil before erection, and the entire framework was painted two coats of graphite paint after erection. The trusses are spaced from 14 to 18 ft. and carry 6, 7 and 8-in. channel purlins. The purlins are spaced from 6 to 7 ft. apart and carry roof slabs $2\frac{1}{2}$ to 3 in. thick made of expanded metal and concrete. The expanded metal is made from No. 16 B. W. G. steel plate with 4-in. mesh, and the concrete is composed of 1 part Portland cement, 2 parts sand and 4 parts screened furnace cinders. The roof slabs are covered with 10 × 12-in. slate nailed directly to the concrete, and are plastered smooth on the under side. The side walls were made by fastening $\frac{3}{4}$-in. channels at 12-in. centers to the steel framing, and covering this framework with expanded metal wired on. The expanded metal was then covered on the outside with a coating of cement mortar composed of 1 part Portland cement and 2 parts sand and on the inside with a gypsum plaster, making a wall about 2 inches thick. The ground floors were made by covering the surface with a 6-in. layer of cinders in which were imbedded 2 × 4-in. white pine nailing strips 16 in. apart, and on these strips was laid a floor of tongued and grooved maple boards $1\frac{1}{4}$ in. thick and $2\frac{1}{2}$ in. wide. The upper floors are made of concrete slabs reinforced with expanded metal, and supported on beams spaced 4 to 15 ft. apart. Where the spans exceed 7 ft. suspension bars 7 in. × $\frac{3}{8}$ in. were placed 3 ft. apart and were bent around the flanges of the beams. The concrete filling was composed of 1 part Portland cement, 2 parts sand and 6 parts cinders.

The Northwestern Expanded Metal Co. recommends that the first coat of the plaster used for curtain walls be composed of two parts lime paste, 1 part Portland cement and 3 parts sand, and that the wall be finished with a smooth coat composed of 1 part Portland cement and 2 parts sand.

For coating on wire lath the following has been found to give satisfactory results in Chicago and vicinity: For the first coat use a mortar composed of 1 part Portland cement and 2 parts ordinary lime mortar. The lime should be very thoroughly slaked before using as the presence of any free lime will injure the wall. After the first coat has hardened it is thoroughly soaked and a finishing coat composed of 1 part Portland cement, 2 parts sand and a small quantity of slaked lime is applied and rubbed smooth.

A method of plastering curtain walls is described by Mr. George Hill in the Transactions of the American Society of Civil Engineers, Vol. 29, as follows: " The external curtain walls were composed of hard plaster, Portland cement and sand in equal parts, the scratch coat being applied to uncoated metallic lath, making the thickness of the scratch coat about 1 in.; then a surfacing of Portland cement $\frac{1}{2}$-in. thick was applied on each side making the curtain walls a total thickness of 2 in. Good results were obtained in every case except one, where the scratch coat was alternately frozen and thawed several times, and the outer surfacing of the wall peeled off in patches."

The Northwestern Expanded Metal Co. does not recommend the use of hard or patent plasters for curtain walls.

In the standard specifications for Portland cement stucco given in Proceedings American Concrete Institute, Vol. XVI, 1920, all coats are required to be of mortar made by mixing 3 cu. ft. of coarse sand with one sack of Portland cement. If hydrated lime is used, it shall not be in excess of 20 per cent of the volume of the cement. The second coat should be applied on the day following the scratch coat. The finish coat should be applied not more than one week after the first coat. The use of hydrated lime makes the stucco more easily applied and reduces the cost of the wall.

Curtain walls are made of wire lath and plaster in the same way as expanded metal and plaster and have all the advantages of the latter.

Expanded metal is made with ribs or corrugations that make the reinforcement self-supporting, so that channel or angle framework is not necessary. Where expanded metal with ribs is used for roof slabs, the lower side of the expanded metal is first plastered, and after this coat has set the concrete is placed on top of the expanded metal, no forms being required.

The special corrugated steel known as " Ferroinclave " may be used for side walls and roof sheathing; for details see Chapter XXIX.

Expanded metal and plaster curtain walls are light, strong and efficient. They do not require the heavy foundations required by brick and stone walls and are fireproof. They can be used to advantage where it is desirable to have a large glass area in the sides of buildings. This type of construction is almost ideal for factory construction. There are quite a number of different systems but the methods of construction are essentially the same in all.

Pressed Steel Sections.—Steel I-beams, channels and angles made by pressing rolled steel sheets are used for the framework of walls, roofs and floors of industrial buildings. For details of pressed steel sections and details of construction, see "Handbook of Steel Lumber," The National Pressed Steel Co., Massilon, Ohio, and "Berloy," the Berger Manufacturing Co., Canton, Ohio.

Masonry Filled Walls.—The walls between the columns may be made of brick, of concrete, of terra cotta tile or gypsum tile. The foundation and lower courses of a wall of brick or tile should consist of hard burned brick or tile laid in Portland cement mortar, or may be made of concrete. The footing course should extend below the frost line and should have ample bearing area. For single story buildings brick or tile walls should be not less than 13 in. thick, and reinforced concrete walls should not be less than 8 in. thick. Tile walls should be stuccoed on both sides.

Masonry Walls.—Where the outside walls of factory buildings support the roof trusses the walls should not be less than 16 in. for heights of 25 ft. or less, 20 in. for heights of over 25 ft. and less than 50 ft., 24 in. for heights of over 50 ft. and less than 75 ft. The thickness of the wall under heavy trusses or under the ends of crane girders should be increased in thickness by pilasters of the depth required to give the required bearing area. Brick should be laid in Portland cement mortar with push or full bedded joints. The brick wall should be bonded together by headers every fifth course, or by some other effective bond.

The minimum thickness of curtain walls in steel skeleton buildings should be 12 in. for brick or concrete and 8 in. for reinforced concrete.

Schneider's " Specifications for Structural Steel " give the following empirical rule for calculating the thickness of walls in buildings several stories in height.

" The minimum thickness of walls will be given by the formula

$$t = L/4 + (H_1 + H_2 + \cdots + H_n)/6$$

where t = minimum thickness of wall in inches, L = unsupported length in feet, which shall be assumed as not less than 24 ft.; and H_1, H_2, H_3, etc. the heights of stories in feet beginning at the top. Cellar walls are to be 4 in. thicker than the first story walls."

For the thickness of walls for walls for office buildings, see the author's "Structural Engineers' Handbook."

Comparison of Curtain Walls for Factory Buildings.—The different types of curtain walls for factory buildings were discussed by several prominent mill engineers in Engineering Record, April 8, 1911. The most satisfactory curtain wall was decided to be a brick wall from 9 in. to 13 in. thick. Concrete walls 8 in. thick gave satisfactory results but cost about 10 per cent more than a 13 in. brick wall. Tile walls 8 in. to 12 in. thick gave satisfactory results but cost more than the brick wall. The brick walls are not only cheaper but give a better appearing building than any of the other types of curtain walls discussed.

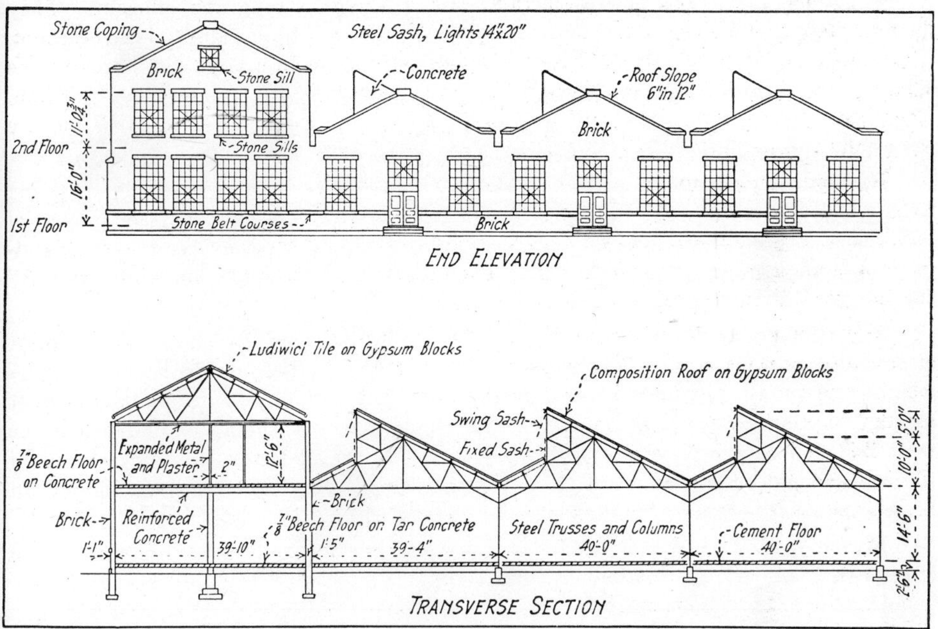

FIG. 2. ENGINEERING LABORATORY BUILDING, UNIVERSITY OF COLORADO.

Examples.—The engineering laboratory building at the University of Colorado is shown in Fig. 2. The two-story section has brick walls 13 in. thick in the front, and 17 in. thick in the first story of the rear. The outside walls of the saw tooth sections are 13 in. thick. The two-story section has Ludowici tile roofing on reinforced gypsum blocks, while the saw tooth sections have a composition roof on gypsum slabs. The windows all have steel sash with lights 14 in. by 20 in. The inner surface of all brick walls is painted white in the saw tooth sections, and are plastered in the two-story section. The partitions in the two-story section are made of expanded metal and plaster.

The shop with modified saw tooth roof shown in Fig. 2, Chapter XXVI, has brick exterior curtain walls 12 in. thick with pilasters 24 in. by 20 in. placed under the ends of the trusses. The intermediate curtain walls are 12 in. brick walls.

The machine shop for the U. S. Government powder plant at Nitro, W. Va., shown in Fig. 10, Chapter XXVI, has 8 in. brick curtain walls 4 ft. high, and the remainder of the side covering is corrugated steel.

The machine shop for the Brooklyn Navy Yard, shown in Fig. 11, Chapter XXVI, has 13 in. brick curtain walls to a height of 4 ft., while the remainder of the sides are covered with glazed sash.

The locomotive shop of the A. T. & S. F. R. R. shown in Figs. 12, 13 and 14, Chapter XXVI, has 13 in. brick curtain walls.

CHAPTER XXXI.

FOUNDATIONS.

Introduction.—The design of the foundations for mill buildings is ordinarily a simple matter for the reason that the buildings are usually located on solid ground and the loads on the columns are small. Where the soil is treacherous or when an attempt is made to fix the columns at the base the problem may, however, become quite complicated.

BEARING POWER OF SOILS.—The bearing power of a soil depends upon the character of the soil, its freedom from water, and its lateral support. The downward pressure of the surrounding soil prevents lateral displacement of the material under the foundation and adds materially to the bearing power of treacherous soils.

A soil incapable of supporting the required loads may have its supporting power increased (1) by increasing the depth of the foundation; (2) by draining the site; (3) by compacting the soil; (4) by adding a layer of sand or gravel; (5) by using timber grillage to increase the bearing area; (6) by driving piles through the soft stratum, or far enough into it to support the loads.

A method used in France for compacting foundations is to drive holes with a heavy metal plunger and then fill these holes with closely rammed sand or gravel.

When foundations are placed on solid rock, the surface of the rock should be carefully cleaned of loose and rotten rock and roughly brought to a surface as nearly perpendicular to the direction of the pressure as practicable. A layer of cement mortar placed directly on the rock surface will assist in bonding the foundations and the footing together.

When foundations are placed on sand, gravel or clay it is usually only necessary to dig a trench and start the foundation below frost. If the soil is somewhat yielding or if the load is heavy the foundation should be carried to a greater depth or the footings should be made wider than for greater depths or the bearing power should be increased by driving piles.

Pressure on Foundations.—The following allowable pressures may be used in the absence of definite data. No important structure should be built without the making of careful tests of the bearing power of the soil upon which it is to rest.

The loads on foundations should not exceed the following in tons per square foot:

Ordinary clay and dry sand mixed with clay	2
Dry sand and dry clay	3
Hard clay and firm, coarse sand	4
Firm, coarse sand and gravel	5
Shale rock	8
Hard rock	20

For all soils inferior to the above, such as loam, etc., never more than one ton per square foot

Pressure on Masonry.—The allowable stresses in masonry and pressures of beams, girders, column bases, etc. on masonry as given in Table I represent good practice.

TABLE I.

ALLOWABLE STRESSES IN MASONRY AND PRESSURES OF BEARING PLATES.

Kind of Masonry.	Safe Stresses in Masonry, Lb. per Sq. In.	Safe Pressures of Wall Plates and Columns on Masonry, Lb. per Sq. In.
Common Brick, Portland Cement Mortar........	170	250
Hard burned brick, Portland Cement Mortar.....	210	300
Rubble Masonry, Portland Cement Mortar	170	250
First Class Masonry, Sandstone...........	280	350
First Class Masonry, Crystallized Sandstone	400	600
First Class Masonry, Limestone...............	300	500
First Class Masonry, Granite................	400	600
Portland Cement Concrete, 1–2–4..............	400	600
Portland Cement Concrete, 1–3–5..............	300	400

Bearing Power of Piles.—Probably no subject has been more freely discussed and with more conflicting views and opinions than has the safe bearing power of piles. The safe load to put on a pile in any particular case is dependent upon so many conditions that any formula for the safe bearing power is necessarily simply an aid to the judgment of the engineer, and not an infallible rule to be blindly followed. All formulas for the bearing power of piles determine the safe bearing power from the weight of the hammer, the length of free fall of the hammer, and the penetration of the pile. The penetration of the pile for any blow of the hammer depends on the condition of the head of the pile, upon whether the pile is driving straight, and upon the rigidity of the pile. The penetration of a slim, limber pile with a broomed head is very misleading, and any formula will give values too large.

The Engineering News formula for the safe bearing power of piles is most used and is the most reliable. It is

$$P = \frac{2W.h}{s+1} \tag{1}$$

where P = safe load on pile in tons;
W = weight of hammer in tons;
h = distance of free fall of the hammer in feet;
s = penetration of the pile for the last blow in inches.

If the pile is driven with a steam hammer the factor unity in the denominator is changed to one-tenth. This formula is supposed to give a factor of safety of about 6, and has been shown by actual use to give values that are safe.

Where piles are to be driven through gravel or very hard ground the lower ends are often protected with cast iron or steel points. The value of these points is questionable and most engineers now prefer to drive piles without their use, simply making a very blunt point on the pile. In driving piles, care must be used where small penetrations are obtained not to smash or shiver the pile. The maximum load carried by a pile should not exceed 40,000 lb. Piles should be driven not less than 10 ft. in hard material, nor less than 15 ft. in soft material if the pile is to be loaded to full bearing.

Piles are usually driven at about 3-ft. centers over the bottom of the foundation. After the piles are driven they are sawed off below the water level, and (1) concrete is deposited around the heads of the piles, or (2) a grillage or platform is built on top of the piles to support the walls or piers. The first method is now the most common one for mill building foundations.

A common specification for piles for mill buildings is as follows:—

"All piles are to be spruce, yellow pine or oak, not less than 9 in. in diameter at the point and not more than 14 in. in diameter at the butt. Piles are to be straight and sound, and free from defects affecting their strength or durability."

Bearing piles for heavy foundations are sometimes made of reinforced concrete.

Pressure of Walls on Foundations.—In Fig. 1, let W = resultant weight of the

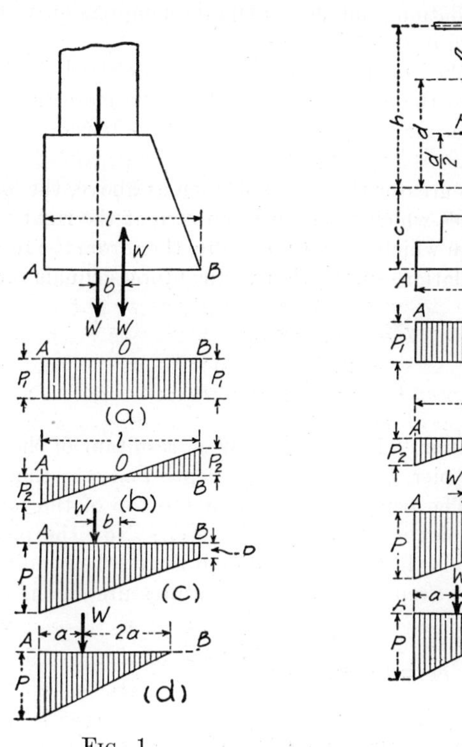

FIG. 1.

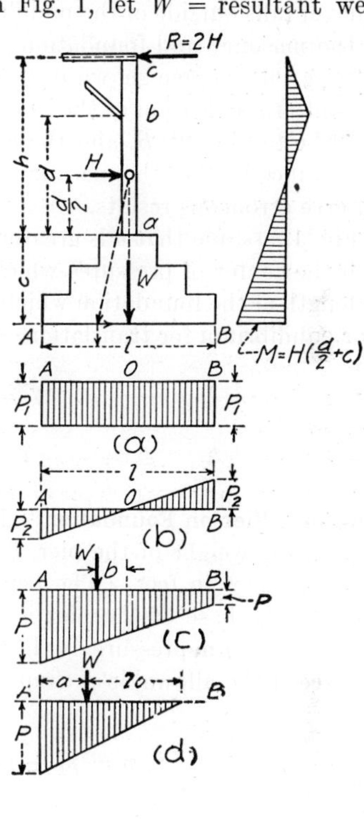

FIG. 2.

wall, the footing and the load on the wall, l = length of the footing and b = distance from center of gravity of footing to point of application of load W, and let the wall be of unit length. The pressure on the footing will be that due to direct load W, and a couple with an arm b and a moment = $+ W.b$. The pressure due to the direct W will be

$$p_1 = W/l \qquad \text{as shown in (a),}$$

and the maximum pressure due to the bending moment, $M = + W.b$, will be

$$p_2 = \frac{M \cdot c}{I} = \frac{6W \cdot b}{l^2} \tag{2}$$

The pressure at A will be

$$p = p_1 + p_2 = \frac{W}{l} + \frac{6W \cdot b}{l^2} \tag{3}$$

and at B will be

$$p = p_1 - p_2 = \frac{W}{l} - \frac{6W \cdot b}{l^2} \tag{4}$$

as shown in (c).

Now if p_1 is made equal to p_2 the pressure at B will be zero and at A will be twice the average pressure. Placing $p_1 = p_2$ in (4) and solving for b, we have $b = \frac{1}{6}l$. This leads to the theory of the middle third or kern of a section. If the point of application of the load never falls outside of the middle third there will be no tension in the masonry or between the masonry and foundation, and the maximum compression will never be more than twice the average shown in (a).

If the point of application of the load falls outside the middle third (b greater than $\frac{1}{6}\,l$) there will be tension at B, and the compression at A will be more than twice the average. But since neither the masonry nor foundation can take tension, formulas (3) and (4) will give erroneous results.

In (d) Fig. 1, assume that b is greater than $\frac{1}{6}\,l$, and then as above, the load W will pass through the center of pressures which will vary from zero at the right to P at A. If $3\,a$ is the length of the foundation which is under pressure, then from the fundamental condition for equilibrium for translation, summation vertical forces equals zero, we will have

$$W = 3p \cdot a/2$$

and

$$p = \frac{2W}{3a} \tag{5}$$

Pressure of a Pier on Foundation.—In Fig. 2, let W = resultant of the stresses in the column and the weight of the pier, l = length, c = depth and n = the breadth of the footing of the pier in feet. The bending moment at the top of the pier is $M = -\frac{1}{2}H \cdot d$, and at the base of the pier is $M_1 = -H(\frac{1}{2}d + c)$. Now the pier must be designed so the maximum pressure on the foundation due to W and the bending moment M_1 will not exceed the allowable pressure. The maximum pressure on the foundation will be

$$p = p_1 \pm p_2 = \frac{W}{l \cdot n} \pm \frac{M_1 \cdot y}{I}$$

$$= \frac{W}{l \cdot n} \pm \frac{\frac{1}{2}H(\frac{1}{2}d + c)l}{\frac{1}{12}n \cdot l^3}$$

$$= \frac{W}{l \cdot n} \pm \frac{3H(d + 2c)}{n \cdot l^2} \tag{6}$$

It will be seen from (6) that a shallow pier with a long base is most economical.

To find the relations between l and c when the maximum pressure is twice the average, place

$$\frac{W}{l \cdot n} = \frac{3H(d + 2c)}{n \cdot l^2}$$

and $$l = \frac{3H(d + 2c)}{W} \tag{7}$$

For any given conditions the value of l that will be a minimum may be found by substituting in the second member of (7).

To illustrate the method of calculating the size of a pier we will calculate the pier required to fix the leeward column in Fig. 8, Chapter X.

The sum of the stresses in column A-17 is a minimum for dead and wind load and will be, Table I, Chapter X, equal to $4{,}800 + 4{,}100 = 8{,}900$ lb.

Try a pier 3 ft. × 3 ft. on top, 6 ft. × 6 ft. on the base and 6 feet deep, weighing about 17,100 lb.

Substituting in (6) we have

$$p = \frac{26{,}000}{36} \pm \frac{3 \times 4\cdot300(14 + 12)}{6 \times 36}$$
$$= 722 \pm 1\cdot553 \text{ lb.}$$

This gives tension on the windward side which will not be allowed, and so we will reinforce the footing with steel bars and make $l = 10$ ft., and increasing weight so that

$$W = 40{,}800 \text{ lb.}$$
$$p = 680 \pm 559$$
$$= 1{,}239 \text{ or } 121 \text{ lb. per sq. ft.,}$$

which is safe for ordinary soils.

If it had been necessary to drive piles for this pier, a small amount of tension might have been allowed on the windward side if the tops of the piles had been enclosed in concrete.

Stresses in Anchor Bolts.—The stresses in the anchor bolts may be calculated as in Fig. 4, Chapter IX.

Wall Footings.—Wall footings should be calculated as cantilever beams, taking moments of the forces acting on the footing outside the line of the wall. The maximum stresses should be calculated by the usual flexure formula for plain reinforced concrete footings, and by the standard formulas for reinforced concrete beams where the footing is reinforced.

Column Footings.—In the column footing in Fig. 3 the reinforcing bars are placed at the bottom of the footing and run in both directions.

Shear.—The load on the column will produce punching shear on an area $4a\cdot d'$, where a = side of column and d' = thickness of the footing slab, both in inches. The allowable punching shear should be taken at 120 lb. per sq. in.

Bending Moment.—The maximum bending moment will occur at the face of the column. In Fig. 3, the moment about g–h will be equal to the area of the trapezoid h–g–B–D, multiplied by w, the unit pressure on the footing, multiplied by the distance x, the distance from the face of the column to the center of gravity of the area h–g–B–D, and

$$M = \tfrac{1}{2}w\cdot c(a + b)x \tag{8}$$

For two way reinforcement evenly spaced over the footing the section that may be assumed as taking the bending moment may be assumed as greater than the section g–h in Fig. 3. The tests made by Professor A. N. Talbot and described in Bull. 67, University of Illinois Engineering Experiment Station, show that for two way reinforcement uniformly spaced the resisting moment may be calculated at the face of the column base and including all bars that lie within a width of footing equal to the width of the column base plus twice the thickness of the column base, plus one-half the remaining distance on each side to the edge of the footing. This method may also be used if the bars are spaced more closely in the central part of the footing than on the outside portion. The stress in the steel may be calculated by the usual flexure formula

$$f_s = M/(A \cdot j \cdot d) \tag{9}$$

where A = area of steel calculated as above, and $j \cdot d$ = distance from center of steel to centroid of compressive stresses.

Bond Stress.—In calculating the bond stress on the steel, the total shear may be taken as $V = \frac{1}{2}w \cdot c(a + b)$, and the unit bond stress may be calculated by the usual formula

$$f_u = V/(\Sigma 0 \cdot j \cdot d) \tag{10}$$

where $\Sigma 0$ = area per lineal inch of all bars included in the section used in calculating resisting moment as above. There should be 3 or 4 inches of concrete below the steel.

Diagonal Tension.—As a measure of the diagonal tension the shearing stress should be calculated by the usual formula on a section found by taking a square with sides equal to a, the width of the column, plus twice the thickness of the slab. The unit shear will be equal to

$$f_v = V'/(h \cdot j \cdot d) \tag{11}$$

where V' = total upward pressure on the footing outside of the square and h = total distance around the outside of the square, and $j \cdot d$ = distance from center of reinforcing steel to center of compressive stresses. The allowable stress for shear where stirrups or bent-up bars are not used should not exceed 40 lb. per sq. in. Where bent-up bars and stirrups are used, a unit shear of 120 lb. per sq. in. may be used.

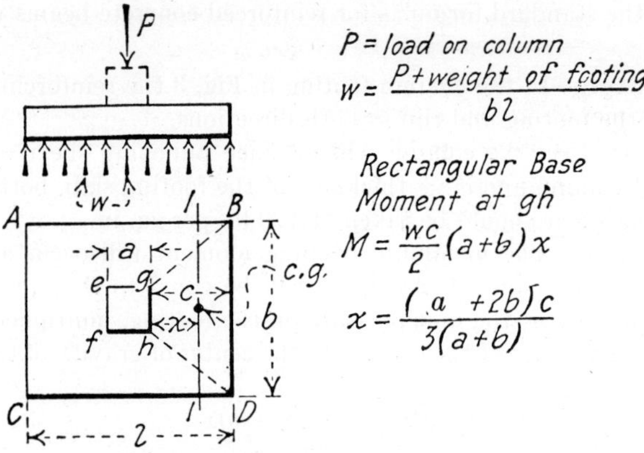

FIG. 3. REINFORCED CONCRETE FOOTING.

Retaining Walls.—For the design of retaining walls, see the author's "The Design of Walls, Bins and Grain Elevators."

Bearing Plates.—The bearing plates required for beams and columns, Fig. 4, may be determined by the following formulas.

Let R = reaction of beam or load on column.
A = area of bearing plate.
w = allowable unit pressure in masonry.
f = allowable fiber stress in plate.
p = projection of bearing plate beyond any edge of beam or column.

Area of bearing plate,

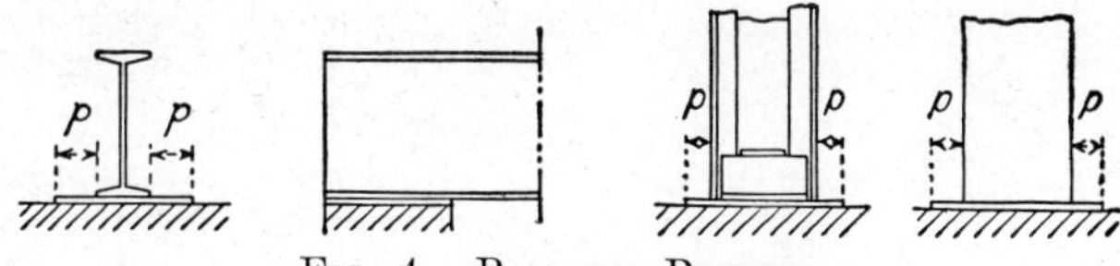

FIG. 4. BEARING PLATES.

$$A = \frac{R}{w} \tag{12}$$

Thickness of bearing plate required by a given projection,

$$t = p\sqrt{\frac{3R}{A \cdot f}} = p\sqrt{\frac{3w}{f}} \tag{13}$$

Safe projection for a given thickness of plate,

$$p = t\sqrt{\frac{A \cdot f}{3R}} = t\sqrt{\frac{f}{3w}} \tag{14}$$

The allowable pressures of bearing plates on masonry (value of w) are given in Table I. Standard bearing plates for I-beams and channels, and the length of I-beams which should bear on plates in order that the full shearing strength be developed are given in the author's "Structural Engineers' Handbook."

For a full discussion of bearing plates, see Bulletin No. 35, University of Illinois Engineering Experiment Station, entitled "A Study of Base and Bearing Plates for Columns and Beams," by Professor N. Clifford Ricker.

References.—For additional data on foundations, see the author's "The Design of Walls, Bins and Grain Elevators" and "Structural Engineers' Handbook."

CHAPTER XXXII.

Floors.

Introduction.—The best type of floor for an industrial building depends upon the requirements and local conditions. Floors will be discussed under the head of (1) ground floors, and (2) floors above ground.

GROUND FLOORS.—Types of Floors.—There are three general types of ground floors in general use in industrial plants: (1) Solid, heat conducting floors, as stone, brick or concrete; (2) semi-elastic, semi-heat conducting floors, as earth, macadam, tar macadam or asphalt macadam; (3) elastic, non-heat conducting floors of wood or with a wooden wearing surface on a bituminous base.

(1) **Solid Floors.**—Floors of this class have been used in Europe and formerly in this country to a considerable extent in shops and mills, and at present are much used in round houses, smelters, foundries, warehouses and in other buildings where the wear and tear are considerable and where men are not required to stand along side of machines. Floors of this class are cold and damp and cause the workmen considerable discomfort. The wooden shoes of the Continental workman or the wooden platforms in use in many of our shops which have floors of this class overcome the above objections to some extent. The gritty dust arising from most concrete floors is very objectionable where delicate machinery is used. The noise and danger from breakage are additional objections to floors of this class. By covering concrete floors with battleship linoleum or a similar material, most of the above objections are eliminated.

(2) **Semi-elastic Floors.**—Floors of this class have many of the objections and defects of floors of the first class. These floors are liable to be cold and damp unless properly drained, and give rise to a gritty dust that is often intolerable in a machine shop. Earth and cinder floors are very cheap and are adapted to forge shops and many other places where more expensive floors are now in use. Floors of this class should be well tamped in layers and should be carefully drained. Floors made of tar concrete or asphalt concrete give very satisfactory results when properly constructed and where they are not required to support heavy machinery. Asphalt mastic floors when properly constructed are practically acid-resisting and are especially adapted to use in chemical plants and storage battery rooms.

(3) **Elastic Non-heat Conducting Floors.**—Floors made of wood or with a wooden wearing surface on a bituminous base are the most satisfactory floors that can be used for shops, mills and factories. Wooden floors are elastic, non-heat conducting and are pleasant to work on. They are easily kept clean and do not give rise to grit or dust. This type of floor is cheap, and is easily laid, repaired and renewed.

The most satisfactory wearing surface on a wooden floor is rock maple, $\frac{7}{8}$ in. to $1\frac{1}{4}$ in. thick, and $2\frac{1}{2}$ to 4 in. wide, tongued and grooved, or with square edges, as desired. The matched floor makes a somewhat smoother floor and is on the whole the most satisfactory. The wearing floor should be laid to break joints and should be nailed to a sub-floor laid at right angles to the surface layer. The thickness of the sub-planking will depend upon the foundation and upon the use to which the floor is to be put.

For heavy service, creosoted timber blocks laid on a cement concrete or a bituminous concrete base gives very excellent results.

The different classes of floors will be briefly discussed and illustrated by examples of floors in use.

CONCRETE FLOORS.—The construction of concrete or cement floors is similar to the construction of concrete sidewalks, the principal difference being that the floor usually requires a better foundation. The foundation will depend upon the use to which the floor is to be put and the character of the material upon which the foundation is to rest. The excavation should be made to solid ground or until there is depth enough to permit a sub-foundation of gravel or cinders. Upon this sub-foundation there should be placed a layer of gravel or coarse cinders 6 to 8 in. thick, thoroughly rammed. The author's specifications for laying concrete floors are as follows:

Specifications for Concrete Floor on a Concrete Base. Materials.—The cement used shall be first-class Portland cement, and shall pass the standards of the American Society for Testing Materials. The sand for the top finish shall be clean and sharp and shall be retained on a No. 30 sieve and shall have passed the No. 20 sieve. Broken stone for the top finish shall pass a $\frac{1}{2}$ in. screen and shall be retained on the No. 20 screen. Dust shall be excluded. The sand for the base shall be clean and sharp. The aggregate for the base shall be of broken stone or gravel and shall pass a 2 in. ring.

Base.—On a thoroughly tamped and compacted subgrade the concrete for the base shall be laid and thoroughly tamped. The base shall not be less than $2\frac{1}{2}$ in. thick. Concrete for the base shall be thoroughly mixed with sufficient water so that some tamping is required to bring the moisture to the surface. If old concrete is used for the base the surface shall be roughened and thoroughly cleaned so that the new mortar will adhere. The roughened surface of old concrete shall then be thoroughly wet, so that the base will not draw water from the finish when the latter is applied. Before scrubbing the base with grout, the excess water shall be removed.

Finish.—With old concrete the surface of the base shall first be scrubbed with a thin grout of pure cement, rubbed in with a broom. On top of this, before the thin coat is set, a coat of finish, mixed in the proportions of one part Portland cement, one part stone broken to pass a $\frac{1}{2}$ in. ring, and one part sand shall be troweled on using as much pressure as possible, so that it will take a firm bond. After the finish has been applied to the desired thickness, preferably 2 in., it should be screeded and floated to a true surface. Between the time of initial and final set it shall be finished by skilled workmen with steel trowels and shall be worked to a final surface. Under no condition shall a dryer be used, nor shall water be added to make the material work easily.

Precautions in Laying Concrete Floors.—If a concrete floor is properly constructed, the wearing surface will wear away so slowly that the amount of dust which accumulates is imperceptible and will cause no inconvenience. Dusty concrete floors may be due to one or more of the following causes: (1) Dust and fine material in the aggregate; (2) the use of a soft aggregate; (3) the use of insufficient water in mixing the concrete; (4) the use of too much water in mixing the concrete; (5) the use of driers in finishing the wearing surface.

The coarse aggregate used in a concrete floor should be selected with great care. The stones should be tough and should be free from all dust and fine material. The aggregate in the top finish should all pass a $\frac{1}{2}$ in. screen and should be retained on a 30 in. mesh screen. All dust should be excluded.

A good quality of gravel passing the above screens will give results almost as satisfactory as broken stone. The important feature of any aggregate is that the particles shall be hard and durable and that the coarse sizes predominate in quantity. The concrete should be mixed so that there is no free water and should be tamped until enough moisture is brought to the surface to trowel. Where the concrete wearing surface is placed on a base which has thoroughly set, a 2-in. coat consisting of a layer $1\frac{1}{4}$ in. thick of coarse material and a $\frac{3}{4}$ in. finish coat is recommended. With a layer of concrete thinner than 2 in., there is difficulty in obtaining a proper bond between the new coat and the old base.

Dusty concrete floors can be improved by the application of one or two coats of boiled linseed oil. If the linseed oil is mixed with gasoline, the oil will penetrate the wearing surface and will be quite effective in preventing dust. Quite satisfactory results may also be obtained by treating the surface of the floor with a mixture of one part silicate of soda, or water glass, diluted with six parts of water. The solution is applied with a brush and after about 24 hours all excess is washed off, and a second application is given.

ASPHALT MASTIC FLOORS.—Asphalt mastic floors may be constructed in the same manner as asphalt mastic pavements, or may be constructed of asphalt blocks laid on a cement concrete base. The latter method is the more generally used and appears to give better results.

A floor made of asphalt blocks was laid in the storage battery building in the Philadelphia Navy Yard as follows. Asphalt blocks 8 in. long, 4 in. wide and $1\frac{1}{4}$ in. thick were laid upon a layer of 1: 4 cement mortar on a concrete sub-floor. After the blocks were laid, hot liquid asphalt was spread over the surface and was squegeed into the joints. While the liquid asphalt was hot, a thin layer of sand was spread over the surface and was swept into the joints. The blocks were made with a trap-rock aggregate. This floor is dense enough to resist deformation under the concentrated weight of the battery units giving a pressure of one-half ton per square foot; is impervious to moisture and resists acids. The cost of this floor at the Philadelphia Navy Yard in 1918 was as follows:

8 in. × 4 in. × $1\frac{1}{4}$ in. blocks at plant	$1.35 per sq. yd.
Freight and laying	.35 " " "
Concrete base and mortar pitch	1.00 " " "
Asphalt seal for joints	.20 " " "
Total cost per square yard in place	$2.90 per sq. yd.

An asphalt block floor has been in use in the boiler shop of the Brooklyn Navy Yard for four years and has given excellent results. The asphalt blocks are 2 in. thick and are laid on a dry mortar bed with sand swept into the joints and without asphalt jointing material.

An asphalt mastic floor was constructed in 1912 in the forge and structural shop of the Twin Cities Rapid Transit Company, Minneapolis, Minn. The floor consisted of a $1\frac{1}{2}$ in. layer, composed of 65 per cent gravel, rock and bank sand, and 35 per cent mastic and flux, laid on a concrete base. In 1918 this floor was reported as being in excellent condition, with the one exception that is is somewhat marked up where pieces of heavy material have been piled or where jack screws have stood. Where the floor has not been subject to excessively heavy loading, it is smooth and free from cracks.

An asphalt mastic floor has been used in a machine shop of the Jeffery Mfg. Co. of Columbus, Ohio. The asphalt mastic wearing surface is 1 in. thick. Warren asphalt mastic was melted in kettles and was mixed with an equal quantity of sharp river sand. After the mastic had been heated to a temperature of 300° F., it was spread on the concrete foundation and was rolled to the proper thickness. When the material was partially cooled, the surface was finished by rubbing in fine lake sand and Portland cement with wooden rubbing trowels.

BRICK FLOORS.—Brick floors give excellent results in forge shops, round houses and similar locations. Brick used in floors should be paving brick and should comply with standard specifications. The brick should be laid on a solid foundation of concrete or of macadam. The brick are usually laid on a layer of sand from ½ in. to 1 in. in thickness. After the brick are laid, the joints may be filled with sand, with cement grout or with a bituminous filler.

WOODEN FLOORS ON BITUMINOUS BASE.—Coal tar or asphalt concrete makes the best foundation for a shop floor. If a Portland cement concrete is used, the planking will decay very rapidly unless the top of the concrete is covered with a layer of sand, impregnated with coal tar or asphalt. Floors with a bituminous base and a wooden wearing surface are usually made with a layer of sub-planking resting directly on the bituminous base and with a finished floor spiked to the sub-planking. The sub-planking may be spiked to sleepers encased in the bituminous base, or may be laid directly upon the bituminous base. Satisfactory results may be obtained with both methods. Where sleepers are used, it is much easier to properly level up the surface of the bituminous concrete than where the sub-planking is laid directly upon the bituminous base. Where a wooden floor is placed on a cement concrete base, the best results are obtained by laying the sub-planking directly on a layer of bituminous sand mastic 1 in. thick. The author's specifications for a wood floor on a concrete base are as follows:

Specifications for Wood Floor on a Tar Concrete Base. Floor Sleepers.—Sleepers for carrying the timber floor shall be 3 in. × 3 in. placed 18 in. c. to c. After the subgrade has been thoroughly tamped and rolled to an elevation of 4½ in. below the tops of the sleepers, the sleepers shall be placed in position and supported on stakes driven in the subgrade. Before depositing the tar concrete the sleepers must be brought to a true level.

Tar Concrete Base.—The tar concrete base shall be not less than 4½ in. thick and shall be laid as follows: First, a layer three (3) in. thick of coarse, screened gravel thoroughly mixed with tar, and tamped to a hard level surface. Second, on this bed spread a top dressing 1½ in. thick of sand heated and thoroughly mixed with coal tar pitch, in the proportions of one (1) part pitch to three (3) parts tar. The gravel, sand and tar shall be heated to from 200 to 300 degrees F. and shall be thoroughly mixed and carefully tamped into place.

Plank Sub-Floor.—The floor plank shall be of sound hemlock or pine not less than 2 in. thick, planed on one side and one edge to an even thickness and width. The floor plank is to be toe-nailed with 4 in. wire nails.

Finished Flooring.—The finished flooring is to be of maple of clear stock, ⅞ in. finished thickness, thoroughly air and kiln dried and not over 4 in. wide. The flooring is to be planed to an even thickness, the edges jointed, and the underside channeled or ploughed. The finished floor is to be laid at right angles to the sub-floor, and each board neatly fitted at the ends, breaking joints at random. The floor is to be final nailed with 10 d. or 3 in. wire nails, nailed in diagonal rows 16 in. apart across the boards, with two (2) nails in each row in every board. The floor to be finished off perfectly smooth on completion.

The finished flooring is not to be taken into the building or laid until the tar concrete base and sub-plank floor are thoroughly dried.

The following specifications for a wooden floor on a tar concrete base were prepared by Lockwood, Green and Co., consulting engineers, Boston, Mass.:

SPECIFICATIONS FOR PLANK FLOOR ON TAR CONCRETE BASE. Tar Concrete Sub-Floors.—Lay tar concrete sub-floors to support planking for all wood floors resting on earth.

The surface of the ground to receive the floors shall be well rolled to a true level before laying the concrete. The floors shall be $4\frac{1}{2}$ in. thick when finished and shall be composed and laid as follows:

Base.—A base of crushed stone or coarse screened gravel, of size graded from $\frac{3}{4}$ to $1\frac{1}{2}$ in., thoroughly mixed with coal tar shall be laid and rolled to a hard, level surface to finish $3\frac{1}{2}$ in. thick.

Top Dressing.—On the bed thus laid spread the top dressing, consisting of sand *heated* and thoroughly mixed with coal tar and pitch (one part pitch and three parts tar). These shall be mixed together until the sand is completely covered, making a homogeneous mass. Spread this top dressing over the whole surface levelling off even, and of sufficient thickness to finish 1 in. thick when compacted. The floor plank shall then be bedded on this top dressing before hardening; shall be well hammered down on same and the tops of all plank brought to the proper level. Any plank below the proper level shall be taken up, before nailing, and raised with more material.

Planking on Tar Concrete.—Plank shall be of good quality thoroughly seasoned, sound kyanized spruce or hard pine, treated with an approved wood preservative. It shall be of 2 in. or 3 in. stock and planed on one side and two edges to an even thickness and width over entire length. The plank is not to exceed three different widths in the entire lot and not over 8 in. wide and may be random lengths with a minimum length of 10 ft. 0 in. It shall be as dry as possible, shall be stacked up for air drying and housed from the weather as soon as received at the site. Plank shall be laid level on the tar concrete, running across the building, following closely after the top dressing is laid, before hardening that the plank may be bedded on it, and after being brought to a proper level shall be thoroughly toe-nailed with 3 in. or 4 in. wire nails, depending on the thickness of plank used. Plank shall not be laid within 1 in. of all walls, columns and piers. Where hard pine planking is used a waterproof paper with the edges lapped at least 3 in. shall be laid under all top flooring. This paper shall weigh not less than 45 lb. per roll of 500 sq. ft.

Flooring.—Furnish and lay a maple top flooring on all floors where shown, all of No. 1 grade according to the latest rules of the Maple Flooring Manufacturers Association, viz:—All flooring shall be 1 in. stock, air-dried and kiln-dried before planing; shall be planed on one side to an even thickness, with edges jointed, making each piece the same width its entire length and the under side double channeled or plowed. All ends shall be matched. All finished flooring will admit of tight, sound knots and slight imperfections in dressing but must lay without waste; shall be 13/16 in. thick, not over 4 in. wide and in $1\frac{1}{2}$ to 16 ft. lengths but shall contain not more than 40 per cent of $1\frac{1}{2}$ to $3\frac{1}{2}$ ft. lengths. The flooring shall not be taken into the buildings or laid until the walls and planking are thoroughly dried out.

Laying.—Separate the several widths; laying each course at right angles to the planking with one width of flooring and with each piece neatly fitted at the ends. Break joints at random for every course of flooring and crowd together and hold by temporary nailing.

All top flooring, including stair landings, shall be kept 1 in. away from all walls. Cover this space with a beveled maple strip put on after the floors are finished.

Nailing.—Flooring shall be finally nailed, with 8d. ($2\frac{1}{2}$ in) wire floor nails, in diagonal rows 14 in. apart across the pieces, with two nailings in each row in every piece, except at the ends of pieces, which shall be nailed with two nails in each piece; all nails shall be set and all standing joints smoothed down to make a smooth level floor.

Where a wooden floor is laid on a cement concrete slab, the practice of Lockwood, Green and Co. is as follows: Lay a tar and sand sub-base of sufficient thickness to finish 1 in. thick when compacted. Sand shall be heated and thoroughly mixed with sufficient coal tar and pitch (one part of pitch to three parts of tar). The sand and tar shall be mixed together until the sand is completely covered, making a homogeneous mass. The concrete surface to receive this mixture shall be thoroughly cleaned and washed free from any dust or débris and allowed to dry, and as soon as the tar mixture is spread, it shall be leveled off even and rolled or troweled to a dense mass. The floor planks shall then be bedded on this top dressing while it is still hot; shall be well hammered down on same, and the tops of all plank brought to the proper level. Any plank below the proper level shall be taken up, and raised with more material. The specifications for planking and for placing the planking are the same for this type of floor as for the wood floor on a tar concrete base.

The specifications of Mr. F. W. Dean, consulting engineer, Boston, Mass., for a wood floor and tar concrete base are as follows:

"The earth is to be filled in layers 6 in. thick and rammed level. On top of this there is to be a layer 3 in. thick of hot tar concrete laid and rolled firmly and level, the upper ½ in. being of fine material laid hot and well rolled so as to prevent moisture from coming through.

"On this there is to be a layer of 4 in. unplaned, square-edged, kyanized or otherwise treated to prevent decay, spruce plank laid close and covered with a standard maple mill floor laid as specified elsewhere, at right angles to the plank.

The specifications of The Barrett Company for "Tar-rok" floors are essentially the same as the specifications of Lockwood, Green and Co. For "Tar-rok" sub-floors over earth, the tar concrete foundation is to be 5 in. thick, laid in two courses, the foundation course 4 in. thick and the damp-proof course 1 in. thick. The foundation course is made of screened gravel or crushed stone, varying in size from 2½ to ¼ in., and mixed with sufficient quantity of Barrett sub-floor tar No. 5 so that it will compact under a roller. The tar for this course is heated to not more than 200° F. and is rolled with a roller weighing not less than 300 lb. per foot of length. The damp-proof course is made of fine sand mixed with sub-floor tar No. 7, in the proportion of not less than 50 nor more than 60 gallons of tar to each cubic yard of sand. The sand and tar is not to be hotter than 225° F. when mixed together. This mixture is spread evenly 1¼ in. thick, so that it will compact to 1 in., and is leveled with a straight edge. The sub-floor is laid on this soft mixture and is bedded by hammering. The sub-plank are 3 in. thick and are toe-nailed together. The wearing plank is 1 in. in thickness and is laid at right angles to the sub-plank.

In laying "Tar-rok" sub-floors over concrete slabs, the 1 in. damp-proof course is laid directly upon the concrete slabs.

CREOSOTED WOOD BLOCK FLOORS.—Creosoted wood block floors may be laid on a cement concrete foundation or upon a tar concrete foundation. If the concrete foundation has a uniform surface and the wood blocks are uniform in height, the blocks may be laid in hot tar directly on the concrete without a cushion layer. Specifications usually permit a variation of 1/16 of an inch in the height of blocks and it is therefore necessary to use a cushion layer between the blocks and the top of the foundation. Wood blocks are laid on a sand cushion ½ in. to 1 in. thick, upon a 1:4 cement mortar cushion ½ in. thick, or upon a bituminous mastic cushion about ½ in. thick. For upper floors, wood blocks may be laid on a creosoted timber sub-floor without the use of a cushion layer. Wood blocks used in laying floors are ordinarily long leaf yellow pine, sawed 3 in. high, 3 to 4 in. wide, 5 to 10 in. long, with an average length of about 8 in. After the blocks have been sawed to size, they are impregnated by the full cell process with from 12 to 16 lb. to the cubic foot of creosote oil. The wood blocks are laid with the grain of the wood vertical. After the blocks are laid, the joints may be filled with sand, with cement grout, or with a bituminous filler. A wood block pavement or floor expands after laying, and it is therefore necessary to make adequate provision for this expansion. The following represents good practice in providing for expansion joints. "Expansion joints shall be formed by placing a 1 in. × 4 in. board on edge against the sides of the building and around columns and foundations. After the blocks are laid, and after tamping and rolling, the strips shall be removed and the voids filled with a low-melting point pitch to within ¼ in. of the wearing surface of the floor."

For additional data on creosoted wood block floors, see Chapter XL.

EXAMPLES OF FLOORS.—The floor shown in (a) Fig. 1, was constructed as follows: 2-in. plank, matched and planed on one side, were laid on 3 in. × 3 in. chestnut joists. The surface of the cinders was kept 2 in. away from the wood and this space was filled with lime mortar. After the surface of the cinders had been grouted, the 3 in. × 3 in. joists were held in place by sticks about 3 ft. apart, nailed to the joists. The lime mortar was then filled in around and slightly above the surface of the joists to allow for shrinkage. Before laying the floor, a thin layer of slaked lime was spread over the surface.

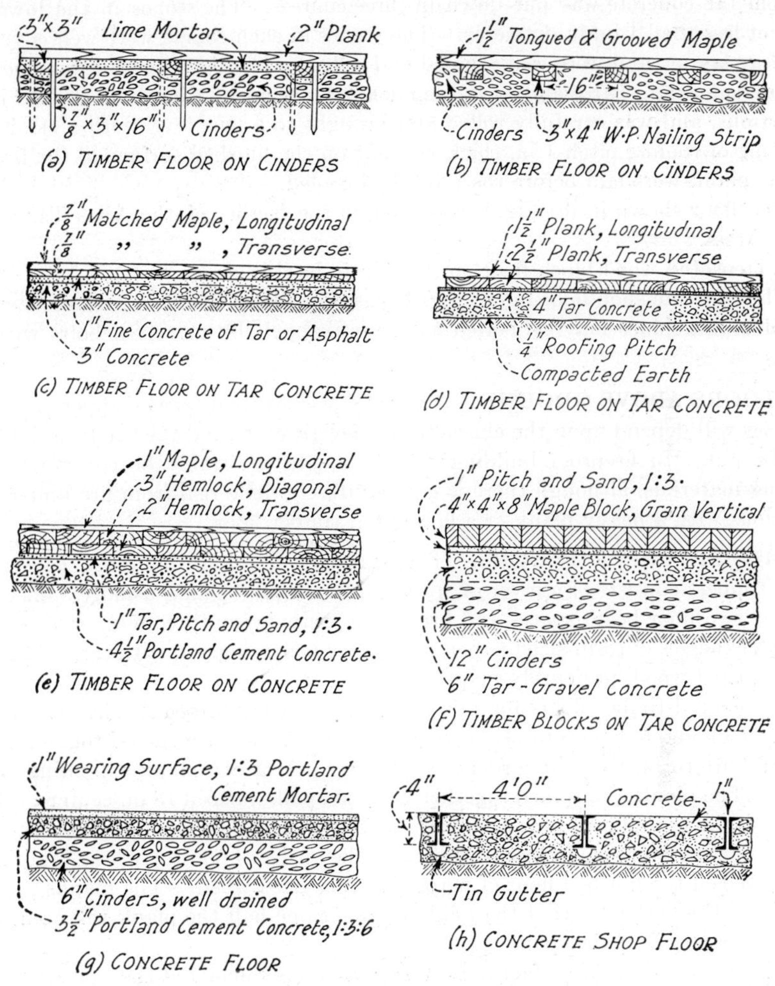

Fig. 1. Examples of Ground Shop Floors.

A cheap but serviceable floor may be made as shown in (b) Fig. 1. The soil is excavated to a depth of 12 to 15 inches, and cinders are filled in and carefully tamped. The floor planks are nailed to the sills which are embedded in the cinders. The life of the plank floor can be increased by putting a coating of slaked lime on top of the cinders.

A very good floor for mills and factories is shown in (c) Fig. 1. The pitch or asphalt will prevent the decay of the plank and will add materially to the life of the floor. Maple flooring makes the best wearing surface and should be used if the cost is not prohibitive.

The floor shown in (d) Fig. 1, was used in a shop of the Boston and Maine Railway. The earth was well compacted and brought to a proper surface and a 4-in. layer of pitch and coal tar concrete was put down in three courses. The stones in the lower course were not less than 1 in. in diameter. The stones in each course were well covered with tar before laying, and were well tamped and rolled. The third and finishing course was composed of clean, sharp sand, well dried, heated hot, mixed with pitch and tar in proper proportions, and was carefully rolled and brought to a true level with a straight edge. A coating of roofing pitch 1 in. thick was put on the finished surface of the foundation and the plank were laid before the pitch had cooled.

The floor shown in (e) Fig. 1, was used in the factory of the Atlas Tar Co., Fairhaven, Mass.

A creosoted wood block floor on a concrete base is shown in (f) Fig. 1.

The concrete shop floor in (h) Fig. 1, has 4 in. channels set in and anchored to the concrete. Machines may be bolted to these channels by means of bolts with oblong heads.

FLOORS ABOVE GROUND.—The type of floor used for the upper stories of mill buildings will depend upon the character of the structure and the use to which the floor is to be put. In fireproof buildings, floors should preferably be constructed of fire-resisting materials, although there is comparatively little risk from fire under ordinary conditions with a heavy plank or a laminated timber floor.

TIMBER UPPER FLOORS.—The standard floor for buildings constructed of heavy timbers consists of a layer of spruce or dense pine plank, usually 3 in. thick, laid to cover two floor beam spaces and break the joints every three feet. On these is laid three thicknesses of rosin-sized paper, each layer being mopped with tar. The top floor is $1\frac{1}{8}$ in. hard wood, preferably maple.

Laminated-timber floors for mill buildings are constructed as follows: Planks 2 in. or 3 in. thick and 6 in. or 8 in. wide are placed on edge and are spiked together. Planks are laid butt to butt on the girders, with every 6th or 8th plank extending across the girder. The planks are spiked together with 60d nails, spaced 18 in. centers. In laying the floor, the two planks near the wall should be omitted until the glazing is finished. The laminated floor should not be spiked to the girders. On top of the laminated sub-floor is placed the finished floor of maple or other hard wood. The planks may also be laid across the girders so that the joints in about one-half the plank will come at about the quarter points of the span.

The Yellow Pine Manufacturers Association has calculated the safe span of yellow pine when used for mill floors with fiber stresses of 1,200 to 1,800 lb. per sq. in. for live loads of 50 to 400 lb. per sq. ft. in addition to the weight of the floor, Table I. In the line marked "Deflection" is given the span which has a maximum deflection of one thirtieth of an inch per foot of span for the various live loads. The modulus of elasticity of timber was taken as 1,620,000 lb. per sq. in. The table may be used for any kind of timber by using the proper working stress. The maximum spans for fiber stresses less than 1,200 lb. per sq. in. may be found as follows: Required the maximum safe span for a timber floor $2\frac{5}{8}$ in. thick for a fiber stress of 800 lb. per sq. in. and a live load of 150 lb. per sq. ft. The span is approximately the same as for a fiber stress of 1,200 lb. per sq. in. and a live load of 225 lb. per sq. ft., = 6 ft. 11 in.; or for a fiber stress of 1,600 lb. per sq. in. and a live load of 300 lb. per sq. ft., = 6 ft. 11 in.

Table I may be used in designing laminated timber floors.

TABLE I.

Allowable Spans for Timber Floors.

Nominal Thickness. In.	Actual Thickness. In.	Fiber Stress, Lb. Per Sq. In.	Span in Feet and Inches. Live Load in Lb. Per Sq. Ft. 50	100	150	200	250	300	400
		1,200	8′ 9″	6′ 4″	5′ 3″	4′ 6″	....	....	....
2	$1\frac{5}{8}$	1,500	9′ 9″	7′ 1″	5′ 10″	5′ 1″	....	....	....
		1,800	10′ 8″	7′ 9″	6′ 5″	5′ 7″	....	....	....
		Deflection	5′ $8\frac{1}{2}$″	4′ 7″	4′ 0″	3′ 8″	....	....	....
		1,200	13′ 8″	10′ 1″	8′ 4″	7′ 3″	6′ 6″	6′ 0″	5′ 2″
3	$2\frac{5}{8}$	1,500	15′ 4″	11′ 3″	9′ 4″	8′ 2″	7′ 4″	6′ 8″	5′ 10″
		1,800	16′ 9″	12′ 4″	10′ 3″	8′ 11″	8′ 0″	7′ 4″	6′ 4″
		Deflection	9′ 0″	7′ 4″	6′ 6″	5′ 11″	5′ 6″	5′ 2″	4′ 9″
		1,200	18′ 5″	13′ 8″	11′ 5″	10′ 0″	9′ 0″	8′ 3″	7′ 2″
4	$3\frac{5}{8}$	1,500	20′ 7″	15′ 4″	12′ 9″	11′ 2″	10′ 0″	9′ 2″	8′ 0″
		1,800	22′ 7″	16′ 9″	13′ 11″	12′ 2″	11′ 0″	10′ 1″	8′ 9″
		Deflection	12′ 3″	10′ 1″	8′ 11″	8′ 2″	7′ 7″	7′ 2″	6′ 6″
		1,200	22′ 10″	17′ 8″	14′ 5″	12′ 7″	11′ 4″	10′ 5″	9′ 1″
5	$4\frac{5}{8}$	1,500	25′ 7″	19′ 3″	16′ 1″	14′ 1″	12′ 8″	11′ 8″	10′ 2″
		1,800	28′ 0″	21′ 1″	17′ 7″	15′ 5″	13′ 11″	12′ 9″	11′ 1″
		Deflection	15′ 4″	12′ 9″	11′ 3″	10′ 4″	9′ 8″	9′ 1″	8′ 4″
		1,200	27′ 0″	20′ 8″	17′ 4″	15′ 3″	13′ 9″	12′ 8″	11′ 0″
6	$5\frac{5}{8}$	1,500	30′ 1″	23′ 1″	19′ 4″	17′ 0″	15′ 4″	14′ 1″	12′ 3″
		1,800	33′ 0″	25′ 3″	21′ 2″	18′ 0″	16′ 10″	15′ 5″	13′ 6″
		Deflection	18′ 3″	15′ 4″	13′ 8″	12′ 6″	11′ 8″	11′ 0″	10′ 1″

REINFORCED CONCRETE FLOORS.—The economical bays for a reinforced concrete floor vary from about 14 ft. by 14 ft. for heavy loads to 18 ft. by 18 ft. for light loads. The most economical spacing for beams carrying reinforced concrete floors usually occurs with the cross beams placed at the third points of the girders. For 18 ft. girders the slab will have a span of 6 ft. Slabs are designed for a moment of $\frac{1}{8}\ w \cdot l^2$ with ends supported, $1/10\ w \cdot l^2$ with one end supported and one end fixed, and $1/12\ w \cdot l^2$ for interior continuous spans. The more usual thickness of floor slabs is from $3\frac{1}{2}$ in. to 5 in. A few rods should be placed at right angles to the main rods to assist in preventing contraction cracks and in distributing the load to the main rods.

Standard specifications for reinforced concrete floor slabs are as follows:—

The concrete slab shall be designed for the following allowable unit stresses; the concrete to be made of one part Portland cement, 2 parts clean, sharp sand, and 4 parts suitable gravel or broken stone that will pass a $1\frac{1}{2}$ in. ring, and that will give a compressive strength of not less than 2,000 lb. per sq. in. when tested in cylinders 8 in. in diameter and 16 in. long after having been stored for 28 days in a moist closet. Allowable compression in slabs, 650 lb. per sq. in., allowable tensile stress in steel, 16,000 lb. per sq. in., modulus of elasticity of steel to be taken as 15 times the modulus of elasticity of concrete, allowable shear as a measure of diagonal tension 40 lb. per sq. in., punching shear 120 lb. per sq. in., bond stress in slabs 80 lb. per sq. in. for plain bars.

For a concrete floor finish the thickness of the wearing surface should be from ½ to ¾ in. thick if the surface is placed at the same time as the slab, or about 2 in. thick if the wearing surface is placed after the slab has fully set.

The details of laying the wearing surface are the same as for a concrete floor on the ground, which see.

The safe loads on reinforced concrete slabs designed to comply with the above specifications are given in Table II and Table III. The spacing of reinforcing bars for reinforced concrete slabs is given in Table IV. For formulas and data for the calculation of the stresses in reinforced concrete slabs, see the author's "Design of Highway Bridges of Steel, Timber or Concrete," or "Structural Engineers' Handbook."

TABLE II.

SAFE LOADS ON REINFORCED CONCRETE SLABS. For $f_s = 16{,}000$, $f_c = 650$, $n = 15$, $M = 1/10w.l^2$

Total Thickness of Slab.	Center of Steel to Bottom of Slab.	Area of Steel Per Ft. of Width.	Weight of Slab Per Sq. Ft.	Span in Feet for Safe Live Load in Pounds per Square Foot of Slab. $M = 1/10\, w.l^2$ (For $M = 1/8\, w.l^2$ multiply span lengths by 0.894).										
In.	In.	Sq. In.	Lb.	40 Lb.	50 Lb.	75 Lb.	100 Lb.	125 Lb.	150 Lb.	200 Lb.	250 Lb.	300 Lb.	350 Lb.	400 Lb.
3	¾	0.208	38	8.4	7.9	7.0	6.3	5.8	5.4	4.8	4.3	4.0	3.7	3.6
3½	¾	0.254	44	9.6	9.3	8.3	7.5	6.9	6.5	5.8	5.3	4.9	4.5	4.3
4	1	0.277	50	10.4	9.0	8.8	8.0	7.4	7.0	6.2	5.7	5.3	4.9	4.7
4½	1	0.323	56	11.7	11.2	10.0	9.2	8.5	8.0	7.2	6.6	6.1	5.7	5.4
5	1	0.369	63	12.9	12.3	11.2	10.3	9.6	9.0	8.1	7.4	6.9	6.5	6.1
5½	1	0.416	69	14.1	13.5	12.3	11.3	10.6	10.0	9.0	8.3	7.7	7.2	6.8
6	1¼	0.439	75	14.5	13.9	12.7	11.8	11.0	10.4	9.4	8.6	8.0	7.5	7.1

TABLE III.

SAFE LOADS ON REINFORCED CONCRETE SLABS. For $f_s = 16{,}000$, $f_c = 650$, $n = 15$, $M = 1/12wl^2$

Total Thickness of Slab.	Center of Steel to Bottom of Slab.	Area of Steel Per Ft. of Width.	Weight of Slab Per Sq. Ft.	Span in Feet for Safe Live Load in Pounds per Square Foot of Slab. $M = 1/12\, w.l^2$ (For $M = 1/8\, w.l^2$ multiply span lengths by 0.817).										
In.	In.	Sq. In.	Lb.	40 Lb.	50 Lb.	75 Lb.	100 Lb.	125 Lb.	150 Lb.	200 Lb.	250 Lb.	300 Lb.	350 Lb.	400 Lb.
3	¾	0.208	38	9.2	8.6	7.6	6.9	6.4	5.9	5.2	4.8	4.4	4.1	3.9
3½	¾	0.254	44	10.8	10.2	9.1	8.2	7.6	7.1	6.3	5.8	5.3	5.0	4.7
4	1	0.277	50	11.4	10.8	9.6	8.8	8.2	7.6	6.8	6.2	5.8	5.4	5.1
4½	1	0.323	56	12.8	12.2	11.0	10.7	9.3	8.8	7.9	7.2	6.7	6.2	5.9
5	1	0.369	63	14.2	13.5	12.2	11.3	10.5	9.9	8.9	8.1	7.5	7.1	6.7
5½	1	0.416	69	15.5	14.8	13.5	12.4	11.6	10.9	9.9	9.1	8.4	7.9	7.5
6	1¼	0.439	75	15.9	15.3	13.9	12.9	12.1	11.4	10.3	9.5	8.8	8.3	7.8

BUCKLE PLATES.—Buckle plates, Fig. 2, are made from steel plates ¼ in., 5/16 in., ⅜ in., or 7/16 in. thick. The buckles are made from 2 ft. by 2 ft. 6 in. to 4 ft. by 4 ft. 6 in., with a depth of 2 in. to 3½ in. Buckle plates are made with from one to 15 buckles, all buckles in a plate having the same depth. Buckle plates are supported on a flange with a width of 2 in. to 6 in. Buckle plates are covered with Portland cement concrete, or with bituminous concrete and a wood wearing surface.

TABLE IV.

Spacing of Reinforcing Bars in Concrete Slabs

Total Thickness of Slab, In.	Center of Steel to Bottom of Slab, In.	Area of Steel Per Ft. of Width, Sq. In.	Weight of Slab Lb. per Sq. Ft.	Spacing of Bars in Inches.											
				Round Bars, In.						Square Bars, In.					
				1/4	3/8	7/16	1/2	9/16	5/8	1/4	3/8	7/16	1/2	9/16	5/8
3	$\frac{3}{4}$	0.208	38	$2\frac{3}{4}$	$6\frac{1}{4}$	$8\frac{1}{2}$	.....	.....	.....	$3\frac{1}{2}$	8	.....	.....	.....	.....
$3\frac{1}{2}$	$\frac{3}{4}$	0.254	44	$2\frac{1}{4}$	$5\frac{1}{4}$	7	.....	.....	.....	3	$6\frac{1}{2}$	9	.....	.....	.....
4	1	0.277	50	2	$4\frac{3}{4}$	$6\frac{1}{2}$	$8\frac{1}{2}$	.....	.....	$2\frac{3}{4}$	6	$8\frac{1}{4}$	.....	.....	.....
$4\frac{1}{2}$	1	0.323	56	$1\frac{3}{4}$	4	$5\frac{1}{2}$	$7\frac{1}{4}$	$9\frac{1}{4}$	.....	$2\frac{1}{4}$	$5\frac{1}{4}$	7	$9\frac{1}{4}$	.....	.....
5	1	0.369	63	$1\frac{1}{2}$	$3\frac{1}{2}$	$4\frac{3}{4}$	$6\frac{1}{4}$	8	10	2	$4\frac{1}{2}$	$6\frac{1}{4}$	8	$10\frac{1}{4}$	.....
$5\frac{1}{2}$	1	0.416	69	$1\frac{1}{2}$	$3\frac{1}{4}$	$4\frac{1}{4}$	$5\frac{1}{2}$	7	$8\frac{3}{4}$	$1\frac{3}{4}$	4	$5\frac{1}{2}$	$7\frac{1}{4}$	9	.....
6	$1\frac{1}{4}$	0.439	75	.....	3	4	$5\frac{1}{4}$	$6\frac{3}{4}$	$8\frac{1}{4}$	$1\frac{3}{4}$	$3\frac{3}{4}$	$5\frac{1}{4}$	$6\frac{3}{4}$	$8\frac{3}{4}$	$10\frac{3}{4}$
$6\frac{1}{2}$	$1\frac{1}{4}$	0.485	81	.....	$2\frac{3}{4}$	$3\frac{3}{4}$	$4\frac{3}{4}$	6	$7\frac{1}{2}$	$1\frac{1}{2}$	$3\frac{1}{2}$	$4\frac{3}{4}$	$6\frac{1}{4}$	$7\frac{3}{4}$	$9\frac{3}{4}$
7	$1\frac{1}{4}$	0.531	88	.....	$2\frac{1}{2}$	$3\frac{1}{4}$	$4\frac{1}{4}$	$5\frac{1}{2}$	7	.....	$3\frac{1}{4}$	$4\frac{1}{4}$	$5\frac{3}{4}$	7	$8\frac{3}{4}$
$7\frac{1}{2}$	$1\frac{1}{4}$	0.578	94	.....	.....	3	4	5	$6\frac{1}{4}$	.....	3	4	$5\frac{1}{4}$	$6\frac{1}{2}$	8
8	$1\frac{1}{4}$	0.624	100	.....	.....	$2\frac{3}{4}$	$3\frac{3}{4}$	$4\frac{3}{4}$	6	.....	$2\frac{3}{4}$	$3\frac{3}{4}$	$4\frac{3}{4}$	6	$7\frac{1}{2}$

Details of buckle plates are given in the author's "Structural Engineers' Handbook."

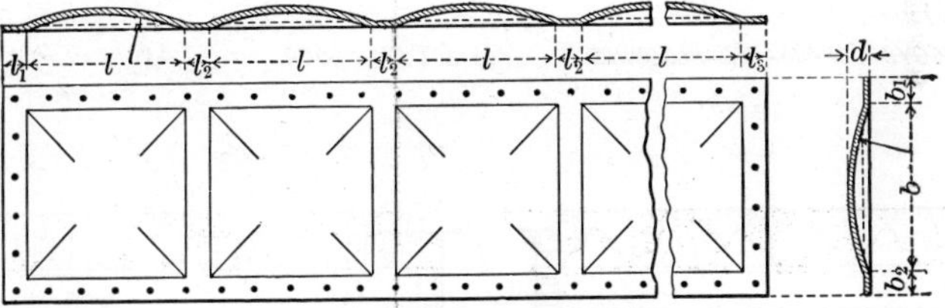

Fig. 2. Buckle Plates.

BRICK ARCH FLOOR.—The brick arch floor shown in (a) Fig. 3, was formerly much used in fireproof buildings and is still used to some extent in mills and factories. The arch is commonly made of a single layer of brick about 4 inches thick, with a span of 4 to 8 ft. and a center rise of preferably not less than $\frac{1}{8}$ the span. The space above the brick arch is filled with concrete and a wearing floor is nailed to strips imbedded in the surface of the concrete. Tie rods are commonly placed at about $\frac{1}{3}$ the height of the beam and are spaced from 4 to 6 ft. apart. The thrust of the arch per lineal foot can be found by the formula

$$T = 1.5W \cdot L^2/R$$

where T = thrust of arch in lb. per lineal ft.; W = load on arch in lb. per square ft.; L = span of the arch in ft.; R = rise of arch in in.

The weight of this floor is about 75 lb. per sq. ft.

CORRUGATED STEEL ARCH FLOOR.—The corrugated steel arch shown in (b) Fig. 3, makes a very strong floor for shops and mills. The corrugated steel acts as a center for the concrete filling above it, and in connection with the concrete makes a composite arch. The corrugated steel is ordinarily the standard $2\frac{1}{2}$-inch corrugations, and the gages are Nos. 16, 18 or 20, depending upon the load and the length of span. The rise of the arch should not be less than 1/12 the span and should have a thickness of from 2 to 4 in. of concrete over the center of the arch. Beams are spaced from 4 to 7 ft. apart for this floor, and tie rods are used as in the brick arch floor.

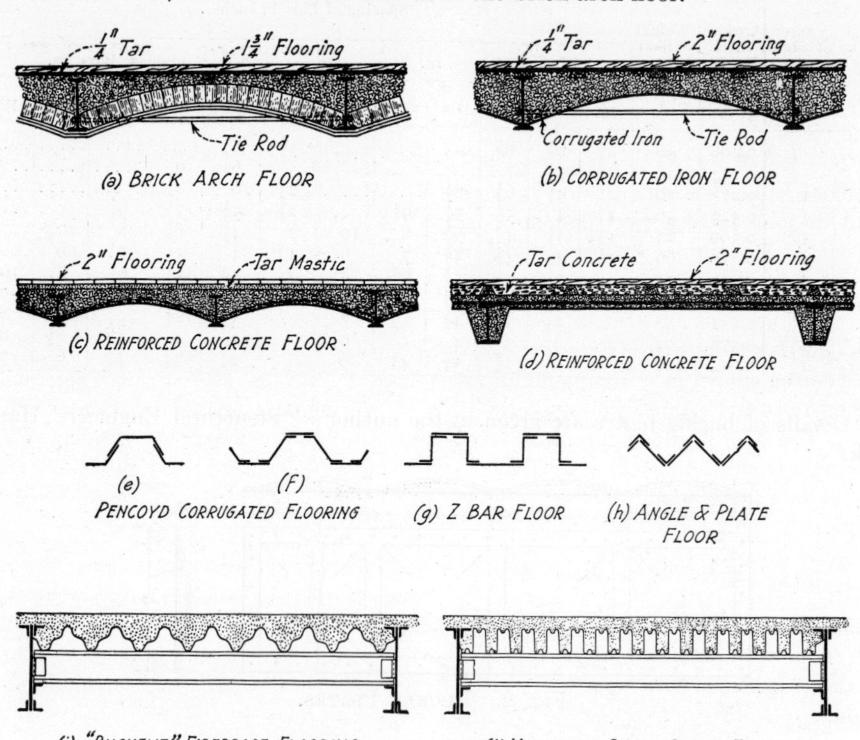

FIG. 3. EXAMPLES OF SHOP FLOORS ABOVE GROUND.

Ferroinclave.—Ferroinclave is fully described in Chapter XXIX. It has been used by the Brown Hoisting Company for floors as well as for roofing and siding. It should make a very satisfactory flooring where light loads are to be carried.

CORRUGATED FLOORING.—Corrugated flooring or trough plates shown in (e) and (f) Fig. 3, are used for fireproof floors where extra heavy loads are to be carried in mill buildings, in train sheds and for bridge floors. The troughs are filled with concrete, which is given a finishing coat of cement or is covered with a plank floor; the planks being laid directly on the plates or spiked to spiking pieces imbedded in the filling. The details, weights and safe loads for corrugated plates are given in the author's "Structural Engineers' Handbook."

Corrugated flooring or trough plates are usually very hard to get and the Z-bar and plate floor shown in (g) Fig. 3, and the angle and plate floor shown in (h) are substituted. The details, weights and safe loads for Z-bar and plate flooring are given in "Carnegie Steel." Angle and plate flooring is made of equal legged angles and plates, and the safe loads are not given in handbooks but must be calculated. The moment of inertia, I, of a section of flooring containing two angles and two plates is given by the formula

$$I = 2I' + 2A \cdot d^2 + 2I''$$

where I' = moment of inertia of one angle about an axis through the center of gravity of the angle parallel to the neutral axis of the flooring; A = area of one angle; d = distance from center of gravity of the angle to the neutral axis of the flooring; I'' = moment of inertia of the plate about the neutral axis.

The properties of the angles required in the calculations may be obtained from the handbook, and I'' is equal to one-half the sum of the moments of inertia of the plate about its long and its short diameter—since the sum of the moments of inertia about any pair of rectangular axes is a constant.

"BUCKEYE" FIREPROOF FLOORING.—The steel flooring shown in (i) Fig. 3, is manufactured by the Youngstown Iron & Steel Roofing Co., Youngstown, Ohio. This floor is made in two sizes, one for bridge floors and the other for building floors. The flooring shown in (i) is for buildings, is made in sections of four triangles each in lengths up to 10 ft., and will lay a width of 21 in. Each triangle is $5\frac{1}{4}$ in. wide and $2\frac{1}{2}$ in. deep. The flooring when complete with a concrete filling and a $1\frac{1}{2}$-in. wearing surface will weigh from 32 to 35 lb. per sq. ft. The weights of the metal troughs laid in place and the safe loads in addition to the weight of the floor are given in the manufacturer's catalog.

MULTIPLEX STEEL FLOOR.—The steel flooring shown in (j) Fig. 3, is manufactured by the Berger Mfg. Co., Canton, Ohio. This floor is made with corrugations from 2 to 4 in. deep and of Nos. 16, 18, 20 and 24 gage steel. The triangles are filled with concrete and the floor is given a cement finish, or is covered with a wooden wearing surface. Tables of safe loads for Multiplex Steel Floor are given in the manufacturer's catalog.

STEEL PLATE FLOORING.—Fireproof floors around smelters, etc., are often made of steel plates. Flat steel plates do not make a very satisfactory floor for the reasons that the plates will bulge up in the center when fastened around the edges, and because they become dangerously smooth. Flat plates should be fastened to the floor by means of bolts placed near the center of the plate.

Neverslip wrought steel floor plates are made from 24 in. × 72 in. to 36 in. × 120 in., and from 3/16 in. to 1 in. thick. These plates are designed to take the place of the cast iron checkered plates formerly used for floors, weigh about 50 per cent less and last much longer. The stock sizes, weights and safe loads for Neverslip floor plates are given in the Stock List of the Scully Steel Co., Chicago. These lists are issued about six times a year and will be sent free upon request.

The floors of the A. O. Smith engineering and research building, described in Chapter XXVI, consist of 5 in. I-beams spaced 2 ft. center to center resting on floor trusses and carrying $\frac{3}{16}$ in. deck plates 6 ft. × 20 ft., electrically spot welded to the I-beams through 2 in. slots. The floor surface is a specially designed concrete 1 in. thick, reinforced by steel plates stamped to form 2 in. rings 1 in. deep. This reinforcement is tack welded to the steel plates. After the concrete has set it is finished by grinding.

Experience with Flooring in Industrial Buildings.—In Engineering News-Record, August 18, 1932, Mr. O. C. Spurling, Engineer of Plant, Western Electric Company, summarizes the experience at the Hawthorne Plant for a period of twenty-eight years as follows:

"Concrete floors with a satisfactory wearing surface, including an integral metallic hardener, can be produced at relatively low cost. The surface requires minimum tractive effort and is easily cleaned. It is, however, generally considered to be hard and cold where employees are for the greater part of the time standing, particularly if the slabs are laid directly on fill. A concrete floor gives a very solid foundation for high speed machinery, but it is expensive to fasten the machinery in position. Tools and materials are damaged if they fall upon the floor.

"Cresoted wood-block flooring laid upon a suitable concrete foundation is very satisfactory for heavy manufacturing, although it requires more tractive effort to pull trucks over it than concrete or maple. This type of construction is more expensive than a finish concrete. A block floor is quiet but not convenient when high speed machinery is to be installed. We have found it necessary to carry holding-down bolts through the blocks into the concrete foundation.

"Maple surfaces are most satisfactory for general light manufacturing operations. They permit ready fastening of machinery and benches in position by means of lag screws. For relatively heavy trucking in the main aisles the thinner sections of maple are not satisfactory due to breaking of the tongue and groove. The square-edged maple is not satisfactory because of its tendency to curl. The $1\frac{1}{16}$ in. T. & G. maple held down by countersunk wood screws is perfectly satisfactory.

"Asphalt mastic floors require a large amount of tractive effort to pull trucks over them, and it is extremely difficult—if not impossible—to lay this flooring from time to time with uniform hardness over all areas. The quality of the workmanship has a very great effect upon the quality of the product obtained. Materials left on it over night will sink into the flooring unless the mixture is so hard that the surface will crack up in cold weather.

"Magnesite flooring depends upon the workmanship as for asphalt mastic floor, and our experience has been very erratic. A few installations have given good service, but most of them have failed from cracking and pulverizing after a short life.

"King block floor is laid herringbone fashion and does not give as smooth an aisle as heavy maple laid lengthwise of the aisle and we are somewhat concerned about the service that we shall get in our main aisles. Experience in the new multi-story buildings at Hawthorne will determine whether we will be satisfied with this flooring under heavy trucking in our main aisles."

CHAPTER XXXIII.

Windows, Skylights and Ventilators.

Introduction.—All industrial buildings should be provided with adequate window area. The windows and skylights should be so arranged and designed that the darkest work space shall be lighted with at least three times the minimum intensities required for artificial light. For satisfactory lighting conditions the light must be adequate, must be continuous and must be diffused. The windows and skylights should be so arranged as to avoid a glare due to the sun's rays; the light should be reflected light, or the direct rays of the sun should be shaded.

Daylight illumination may be provided (1) by windows in the vertical sides of the buildings or in the nearly vertical sides of saw teeth or monitors; (2) by skylights set nearly horizontal, and (3) by prismatic glass which changes the direction of the light.

The amount of glazed surface required in industrial buildings will depend upon the use to which the building is to be put, the material used in glazing, the location and angle of the windows and skylights, and the clearness of the atmosphere. In glazing windows for mills and factories in which the determination of color is a necessary part of the work, care should be used to obtain a clear white glass, for the reason that ordinary commercial glass breaks up the light passing through it so that the determination of color is difficult. For schools it is common to provide that the window area, where all lighting comes through the side walls, shall not be less than 20 to 25 per cent of the floor area.

Height of Windows.—The Wisconsin Industrial Commission requires that for factories and industrial buildings the glass area shall not be less than 20 per cent of the floor area, and that the distance of any working position from the windows shall not exceed 2.25 times the height of the top of the window, where windows are on one side only, and 4.5 times this height where the windows are on both sides.

It is usual to assume that effective reflected light coming through a vertical window is limited by planes making 60° and 26° 35′ with the vertical. If the entire floor is to be reached by effective reflected light a building with windows on one side should have a span not greater than 2 times the height of the top of the window, and a span of not greater than 4 times the height of the top of the window when windows are on two sides. This is the standard practice in Germany. The window sills should be placed at a height of 3 ft. 6 in. to 4 ft. above the floor. For a building with a span of 60 ft. the windows should have a height of not less than 15 ft. above the floor. Where the span of the building is greater than permitted by the above requirements it is necessary to provide skylights, or to use prismatic glass in the upper parts of the windows.

Design of Skylights.—The angle of reflected light coming through a horizontal skylight is usually taken as 45° with the horizontal. For effective lighting the skylights should be so spaced that all parts of the floor area at the working height shall be reached by the light coming through the skylight, as shown in Fig. 8, Chapter XXV.

Amount of Light Required.—The amount of glazed surface in an industrial building will therefore depend upon the span, the story height, the position of the glazed area and upon the quality of the glass. The present tendency in shop and factory design is to make as much of the side walls and roof as possible of glass. Many factory buildings have from 50 to 60 per cent of the exterior surface of glass.

The Steam Engineering Building of the Brooklyn Navy Yard has 60 per cent of the exterior surface made of windows and skylights.

In the shops of the Public Service Corporation shown in Fig. 2, Chapter XXVI, the skylight area is about 20 per cent of the roof area, the window area is about 45 per cent of the outside walls, while 28 per cent of the entire outside surface of the building is of glass.

In the machine shop built at Nitro, W. Va., Fig. 10, Chapter XXVI, 60 per cent of the side walls are of glass, while 23 per cent of the total exterior surface is glazed.

The Central Railway of New Jersey shops at Elizabeth, N. J., have skylights made of translucent fabric in the different buildings in per cents of the entire roof surface as follows: Blacksmith shop 30 per cent; machine shop 36 per cent; paint and repair shop 55 per cent.

About 25 per cent of the roof of the St. Louis train shed is skylight.

In the American Car and Foundry Company's shop at Detroit, about 27 per cent of the exterior surface is ribbed glass.

Specifications for Windows and Skylights.—The requirements for windows and skylights as given in the author's specifications in Appendix I are as follows:—

Windows and Skylights.—Where buildings are lighted by windows the clear window area shall not be less than 20 per cent of the floor area, nor less than 10 per cent of the area of the entire exterior surface in mill buildings, nor less than 20 per cent of the area of the entire exterior surface in machine shops, factories and other buildings in which men are required to work at machines. Skylights shall be used where the required window area cannot be provided in the sides and ends of buildings.

Where buildings are lighted by windows having the sills not more than 4 ft. above the floor, the span of the building shall not exceed 2 times the height of the top of the windows where buildings are lighted by windows in one side, or 4 times the height of the top of the windows where buildings are lighted by windows in both sides. Where the span of the building is greater than is permitted by the preceding requirement, the necessary illumination shall be provided either by prism glass in side walls or by skylights. Skylights shall have such an area and shall be so arranged that light coming through the skylight making an angle of not more than 45° with the vertical shall cover the entire horizontal area at a distance of 6 feet above the floor; or the light may be diffused by means of ribbed glass or prisms or by reflection from the ceiling to obtain equally satisfactory illumination. In saw tooth roofs the inner surface of the roof shall be light colored or shall be painted with a paint that will reflect the light and make the illumination uniform and effective. All windows or skylights admitting direct sunlight shall be provided with muslin or other satisfactory shades.

Glazing.—For glazing windows and skylights, two substances, glass and translucent fabric ("rubber glass"), are in common use.

GLASS.—The principal kinds of glass used in windows and skylights are (1) plane or sheet glass; (2) rough plate or hammered glass; (3) ribbed or corrugated glass; (4) maze glass; (5) wire glass—glass with wire netting pressed into it; (6) ribbed wire glass, and (7) prisms.

(1) **Plane Glass.**—Plane or common window glass is technically known as sheet or cylinder glass. It is made by dipping a tube in molten glass and blowing the glass into a cylinder, which is then cut and pressed out flat. Without regard to quality sheet

glass is divided according to thickness into "single strength" and "double strength" glass. Double strength glass is $\frac{1}{8}$ inch thick while single strength glass is about $\frac{1}{16}$ inch thick. In mill buildings, lights larger than 12 in. × 14 in. are usually made of double strength glass. With reference to quality sheet glass is divided into three grades AA, A, and B. The AA is the best quality, the A is good quality while the B is fair quality. For residences, offices, and similar purposes nothing poorer than A should be specified. The B grade does very well for ordinary mills, although the A grade should be used if practicable.

(2) **Plate Glass.**—Plate glass is made by casting and not by blowing, and is finished by grinding and polishing on both sides until a smooth surface is obtained. It is usually $\frac{1}{4}$ or $\frac{3}{16}$ in. thick. The price depends upon the size of the plate and the quality of the glass. The rough plate glass used in mills is not finished as carefully as for glass fronts, and it may contain many flaws that would not be allowable in the former case. The roughened surface of the glass prevents the entrance of direct sunlight and does away with the use of sun-shades. The only value of rough plate glass is in softening the light, the loss of light in passing through it being very great.

(3) **Ribbed or Corrugated Glass.**—Ribbed or corrugated glass is usually smooth on one side and has 5, 7, 11 or 21 ribs on the other side, (a) Fig. 1. It varies in thickness and shape of ribs. "Factory ribbed" glass with 21 ribs to the inch is distinctly the most effective.

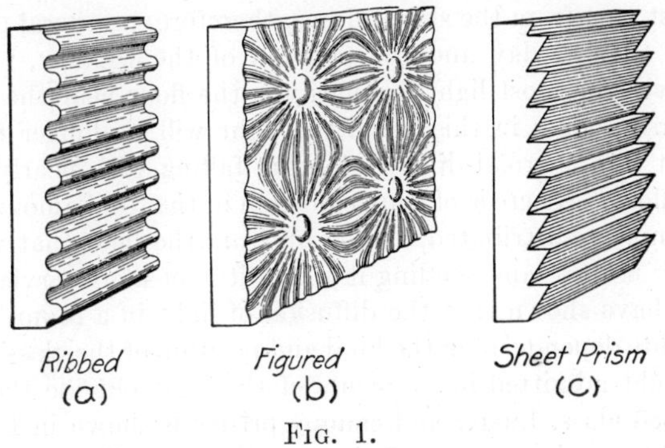

Fig. 1.

(4) **Maze Glass.**—Maze glass has one side smooth and has a raised pattern on the other side roughening practically the entire surface, (b) Fig. 1. It is quite effective.

(5) **Wire Glass.**—Wire glass is made either by the "sandwich" method in which wire netting is placed between two plates of glass which are then rolled together, or by the "solid" method where the wire netting is rolled into one plate of molten glass. The "solid" method produces a clearer and a stronger glass. Wire glass is injured but is not destroyed by the action of fire and water, and is now accepted by fire insurance companies as fire proof construction where it is set in solid metal frames as specified.

Standard specifications for wire glass for factory buildings are as follows:—

Wire glass shall have a thickness of not less than $\frac{1}{4}$ in. The wire mesh shall not be larger than $\frac{7}{8}$ in., and the thickness of the wire shall not be less than No. 24 B. & S. gage for single wire or less than No. 27 B. & S. gage for double twisted wire. The wire shall be practically midway between the two surfaces of glass. Lights shall not have a greater area than 720 sq. in., or more than 54 in. vertical and 48 in. horizontal dimension. Lights of glass shall preferably be 12 in. by 18 in. or 14 in. by 20 in. The selvage shall be removed from the glass before setting. The bearing of glass in grooves shall not be less than $\frac{5}{8}$ in. at all points, and there shall be a clearance of not less than $\frac{1}{8}$ in. between the edge of the frame and the glass.

Wire glass should be used for practically all factory and mill windows where prisms are not required. Wires of rather open mesh cause so little reduction in light as to warrant no mention of this feature. Wire or ribbed glass gives better diffusion than plane glass.

(6) Corrugated wire glass is made with corrugations $2\frac{1}{2}$ in. wide and with corrugations of two depths, deep corrugations for a corrugated asbestos roof, and shallow corrugations for a corrugated steel roof. The sheets are about $26\frac{1}{2}$ in. wide and are 42 in. and 63 in. long. Special lengths of sheet may be obtained up to 126 in. The glass is from $\frac{1}{4}$ in. to $\frac{5}{16}$ in. thick, and the weight is $4\frac{3}{4}$ lb. per sq. ft. The sheets are laid without any side lap, and with an end lap of about 2 in. The sheets are bolted to the purlins or girts and the space between the sheets is covered with a layer of asphalt roofing and a metal cover cap.

(7) **Prisms.**—Prisms are made in small sections which are set in a frame of lead or other metal, or are made in sheets as shown in (c), Fig. 1. Luxfer sheet prisms, manufactured by the American Luxfer Prism Co., Chicago, will be cut in any size desired up to 84 in. wide (parallel with the saw teeth) by 36 in. high.

Diffusion of Light.—The light entering a room through a window or skylight comes for the most part from the sky and has, therefore, a general downward direction, varying with the time of day and the position of the window. The portion of the room which receives the most light ordinarily is the floor near the windows, but if we interpose a dispersive glass in this beam the light will no longer fall to the floor but will be spread out into a broad divergent beam falling with nearly equal intensity on walls, ceiling and floor. There is of course no gain in the total amount of light admitted, the light being simply redistributed, taking up from the floor that which fell there and was comparatively useless, and sending it where it is of more service.

Experiments have shown that the diffusion of light in a room lighted by means of windows or skylights depends upon the kind and position of the glass used. The relative intensity of the light admitted in per cents of the light outside the window for plane glass, factory ribbed glass, Luxfer and canopy prisms is shown in Fig. 2.*

Fig. 2 shows a great increase in efficiency of factory ribbed glass and prisms as the sky angle increases.

The equivalent areas required to give the same intensity of light with the kinds of glass shown in Fig. 2, are given in Table I for skylights making angles of 30° and 60° with the horizontal.

TABLE I.

EQUIVALENT AREAS FOR DIFFERENT KINDS OF GLASS.

Kinds of Glass.	Angle Skylight makes with the Horizontal.	
	30°	60°
Plane	100 sq. ft.	100 sq. ft.
Factory Ribbed	25 " "	40 " "
Luxfer Prisms	17 " "	30 " "
Luxfer Canopy Prisms	13 " "	

* Report No. III. Insurance Engineering Experiment Station, Boston, Mass.

The American Luxfer Prism Co. recommends that Luxfer prisms be set at an angle of about 57 degrees with the horizontal when used in skylights.

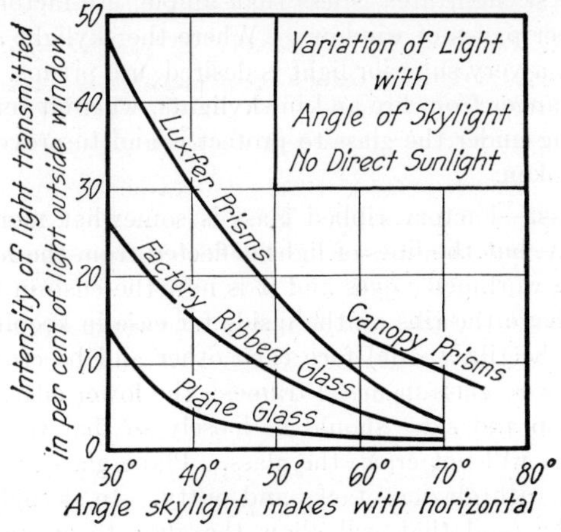

FIG. 2

The amount of indirect light passing through any skylight varies with the solid angle of exposure. A horizontal skylight on a high building where there are no disturbing influences will have an exposure represented by a solid angle of 180 degrees; while a vertical skylight will have an exposure represented by a solid angle of 90 degrees. The intensity of the light passing through the horizontal skylight will be twice the intensity of the light passing through the vertical sash. While a flat skylight will admit the largest amount of light it will also admit direct sunlight. Saw tooth skylights have the north side glazed, and the angle between the glazed surface and the horizontal is made sufficiently large to shut out the direct rays of the sun. In a latitude of 40° the glazed leg of a saw tooth roof should be set at an angle of about 70° with the horizontal to shut out all sunlight. The projection of the top of the roof will shut out some of the light, and will reduce the angle to about 60° with the horizontal. There is ordinarily no great objection to a small amount of sunlight in the early morning and in the late afternoon, and an angle of 57° to 60° with the horizontal for the glazed leg of a saw tooth roof will be found to give very satisfactory results for latitudes of 35° to 45°.

Relative Value of Different Kinds of Glass.—Ground glass is of little value except as a softening medium for bright sunlight. It becomes opaque with moisture and makes an undesirable window glass. Roughened plate glass has very little value as a diffusing medium. Of the ribbed glasses, the factory ribbed glass with 21 ribs to the inch gives the widest and most uniform distribution and is distinctly the best. There is no apparent gain in corrugating both sides. Ribbed wire glass is slightly less effective than the factory ribbed glass. When a glass of a slightly better appearance than the factory ribbed glass is wanted the maze glass is the best; the raised pattern imprinted on the back of this glass giving wide diffusion, especially in bright sunlight. The prisms are very much more effective than any of the glasses mentioned above, but their cost prevents their use under ordinary conditions.

Kind of Glass to Use.—Where the amount of skylight is large and the light is not obstructed by buildings, plane glass is very satisfactory. Where a superior light is desired, or where the skylight area is less than ample, use factory ribbed glass in skylights and in the upper panes of windows. Where the skylight area is very small, the light is obstructed, or a very superior light is desired, use prisms. Wire glass should be used where there is danger from fire and in skylights, where it removes the necessity of stretching wire netting under the glass to protect it and to prevent it from falling into the building when broken.

Placing the Glass.—Factory ribbed glass is somewhat more effective if the ribs are placed horizontally, but the lines of light deflected from the horizontal ribs may become injurious to the workmen's eyes and it is now the custom to set the ribs vertical. Ribbed glass should have the ribs on the inside for ease in keeping it clean, and where double glass is used the ribs should face each other and be crossed. Care should be used in setting thick wire glass in metal frames; the lower edge must bear directly on the frame, but the top and sides should fit loosely so that the differential expansion of the glass and frame will not crack the glass. Plane glass and small panes of other kinds of glass are set with glaziers' tacks and putty. In skylights and large windows some method must be used that will allow the glass to expand and contract freely and at the same time will be free from leakage.

Several methods of glazing skylights without putty are shown in Fig. 3. Skylight

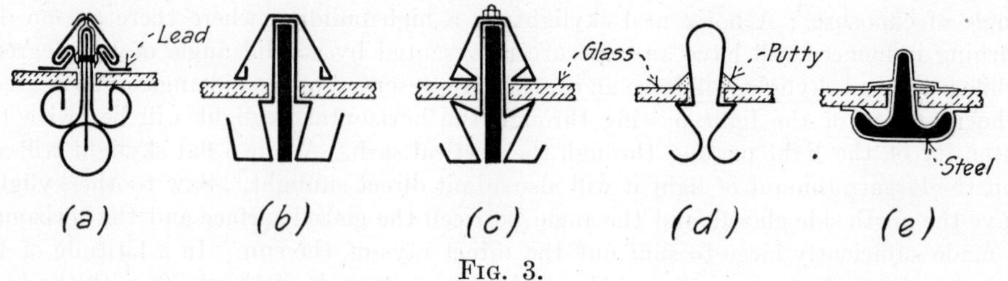

FIG. 3.

bar (a) is made of heavy galvanized iron and lead. Bars (b) and (c) are made of zinc or galvanized iron, supported by a steel bar. Bar (d) is adapted to small panes of glass and is made of galvanized iron; it is made water tight by the use of putty. The skylight bars in Fig. 3 all have condensation gutters to catch the moisture that leaks through or forms on the inner surface of the glass. For details of steel skylights see Fig. 20 and Fig. 21.

SKYLIGHTS.—Skylights may have the glazed surface (1) in the plane of the roof or (2) the glazed surface may be in surfaces not in the plane of the roof.

Skylights in Plane of Roof.—Glass tile may be used with clay tile. The Ludowici tile roof in Fig. 9, Chapter XXV, is lighted by substituting glass tile for the clay tile. In the shop building at the University of Colorado the skylights in the roof were made of glass Ludowici tile laid on sub-purlins. The results are very satisfactory. Glass inserts may be placed in cement tile. In Fig. 2, Chapter XXIX, wire glass 14 in. by 24 in. is inset in the "Bonanzo" cement tile slabs. Flat sheets of wire glass may be supported on a special frame, arranged to drain the roof water and to provide for the expansion of the glass.

Corrugated wire glass in sheets $26\frac{1}{2}$ in. wide and 42 in. to 63 in. long and $\frac{1}{4}$ in. thick may be used for skylights. Corrugated wire glass should be used on pitch roofs, and is especially satisfactory in a corrugated steel roof, or in a corrugated asbestos covered steel roof.

Translucent fabric or rubber glass is especially suitable for skylights in mining buildings or other structures subject to vibrations.

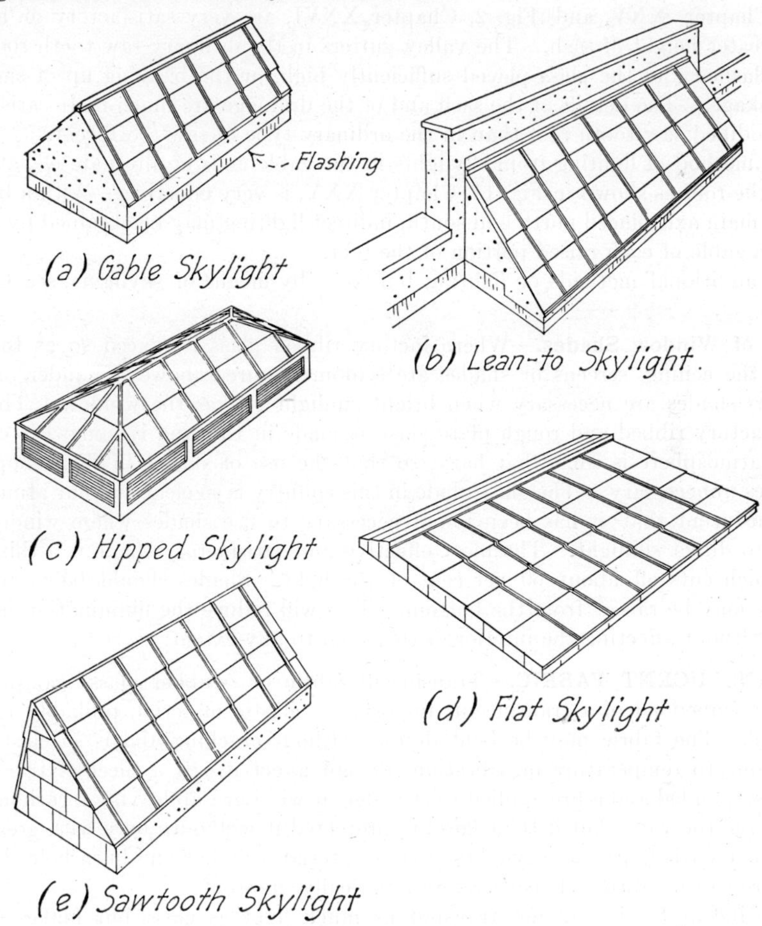

Fig. 4. Types of Skylights.

Skylights Not in Plane of Roof.—Several types of box skylights are shown in Fig. 4. For long buildings with a pitch roof the monitor skylight, Fig. 20 and Fig. 21, is very effective. The monitor skylight has the glass continuous, and usually has part of the sash hinged to give ventilation. The monitor skylight is very effective in buildings which consist of a central bay and two side sheds as in the machine shop at Nitro, W. Va., shown in Fig. 10, Chapter XXVI, and in the Steam Engineering Building at the Brooklyn Navy Yard, shown in Fig. 11, Chapter XXVI.

For buildings with roofs with a flat slope the transverse monitor, Fig. 8, Chapter XXV, is very effective. To give effective lighting the monitors should be spaced as shown in Fig. 8, Chapter XXV.

The saw tooth skylight is very effective where only north reflected light is desired. While the saw tooth skylight is somewhat more effective when the glass is placed at an angle of about 60° with the vertical, the vertical sash in the modified saw tooth roof, Fig. 5, Chapter XXV, and Fig. 2, Chapter XXVI, are very satisfactory on account of the greater height of sash. The valley gutters in the ordinary saw tooth roof must be well flashed and the glass placed sufficiently high, or the banking up of snow will cause leakage. The details of the sash and of the drainage are much more satisfactory in the modified saw tooth roof than in the ordinary type of saw tooth roof.

The method of lighting from skylights in the gable ends of alternate elevated sections of the roof as shown in Fig. 11, Chapter XXV, is very effective. With a building with the main axis placed north and south, indirect lighting may be obtained by glazing the north gable of each raised portion of the roof.

For additional methods of lighting buildings by means of skylights, see Chapter XXV

Use of Window Shades.—Where factory ribbed glass is placed so as to throw light on the ceiling, screens or shades are seldom required; however, under ordinary conditions shades are necessary when bright sunlight strikes the window. The glass used in factory ribbed and rough plate glass as made in England is somewhat opaque, and the atmosphere is somewhat hazy, so that the use of shades in their shops is in most cases unnecessary. The glass made in this country is so clear and our atmosphere is so translucent that it has been found necessary to use shades where windows are exposed to direct sunlight. The most effective and satisfactory shade is a thin white cloth, which cuts off about 60 per cent of the light. Shades should be so arranged that they may be raised from the bottom. This will reduce the illumination near the window without affecting the interior of the room to any extent.

TRANSLUCENT FABRIC.—Translucent fabric or "rubber glass" consists of a wire cloth imbedded in a translucent, impervious, elastic material, probably made of linseed oil. The fabric may be bent double without cracking and is so elastic that changes due to temperature or vibrations do not affect it. If a sheet of translucent fabric is suspended and a fire applied to the edge, it will burn up leaving a carbonaceous covering on the wire; but if the edges are protected it will burn only with great difficulty. Live coals falling on skylights of this material will char and burn holes but will not set fire to the fabric. It is therefore practically fireproof.

Translucent fabric will not transmit as much light as glass, but makes a most excellent substitute. It shuts off sufficient light so that the lighting is uniform throughout the shop and makes it possible for men to work directly under it without shading. Where one-quarter of the roof is covered with the fabric the lighting is practically perfect. The fabric should be washed with castile soap and warm water occasionally, and should be varnished every year or two with a special varnish furnished by the manufacturers. It is said to become more opaque with age. When properly cared for the fabric has been known to give good service for ten years.

The fabric is made in long rolls 34 in. and 38 in. wide. The 38 in. width is used for a spacing of 18 in. on centers, and the 34 in. width is used for a spacing of 16 in. on centers. The framework for the fabric may be made of wood or of steel. When made of wood the vertical bars are made of 2-in. stock dressed to $1\frac{7}{8}$ in. The nominal sizes for the bars for different spans are 2 in. × 4 in. for 6 ft. span, and 2 in. × 6 in. for 10 ft. span. The top of each vertical bar should be finished with a vertical symmetrical triangle $1\frac{1}{2}$ in. wide and $\frac{3}{8}$ in. high. The vertical bars should be spaced not more than 18 in. centers. The fabric is placed on this framework, is drawn tight and nailed on the outside edges of the sheet with special nails spaced from 3 in. to 6 in. The fabric is then stretched over the middle vertical bar by means of a forming block, a metal cap is then placed over the middle cap, and the cap is nailed with 8d nails, spaced 8 in. apart. When more than one sheet is used in a skylight, the laps are cemented together with rubber glass cement. Plans for skylights will be furnished on application to the Angier Mills, Quincy, Mass.

Mr. H. Kenyon Burch, consulting engineer, has used rubber glass on several large mining plants in Arizona and Mexico. Under date of Dec. 17, 1920, Mr. Burch wrote the author with reference to the use of rubber glass as follows:—"I cannot vouch for the service that rubber glass will render in colder climates, but in the southwest it is absolutely the best material I know of for skylights, as the skylights with its use can be made perfectly watertight. It is true that the material becomes slightly opaque after a few years' service, but I consider this somewhat of an advantage as it subdues the very strong sunlight which we have in Arizona and parts adjacent thereto. It is my opinion that 10 years' service is not too much to expect of rubber glass."

Double Glazing.—The condensation on the inner surface of glass can be prevented by double glazing the windows and skylights. Buildings with double glazing are also very much easier to heat than those with single glazing, the air space between the sheets of glass acting as an almost perfect non-conductor of heat. For data on heat transmission of windows, see Chapter XXX.

Details of Windows and Skylights.—The details of windows in use in different sections of the country vary a great deal on account of the varied conditions. In buildings that have to be heated and ventilated through the windows at the same time, it is necessary to provide some means of opening and closing the windows quickly and easily; while in many other cases the sash can remain fixed. The author would call especial attention to the saving in fuel by the use of double glazing; the loss of heat through a double glazed skylight has been shown by experiment to be only about one-half what it is through a single glazed skylight. To prevent condensation on the inner side of double glazed windows the outside air should be admitted to the space between the glass by means of openings about $\frac{1}{8}$ in. in diameter.

Details of windows for use in ordinary brick and stone walls can be found in books on architectural construction and will not be given here. A few of the best designs available for windows in buildings with corrugated steel, expanded metal and plaster, and similar walls, have been selected and are given on the following pages.

The different types of windows for buildings covered with corrugated steel siding as used by the American Bridge Company are shown in Figs. 7 to 12 inclusive.

The sash frames are constructed of white pine and are glazed usually with B quality American glass. The common sizes of glass used in these windows are 10 in. × 12 in., 12 in. × 12 in., 10 in. × 14 in. and 12 in. × 14 in. single strength. For lights larger than 12 in. × 14 in., double strength glass is used. Data for wooden

DIMENSIONS FOR GLAZED WOOD SASH

Size of Glass	Width W	Height H_1	Height H_2	Height H_3	Single Sash	Double Hung Sash	Height H_2	Height H_1	Width W	Size of Glass
10"×12"	2'11¼"	2'5⅝"	3'6"	4'6⅜"			6'8¼"	4'7½"	2'11¼	10"×12"
12×12	3-5¼	2-5⅝	3-6	4-6⅜			6-8¼	4-7½	3-5¼	12×12
10×14	2-11¼	2-9⅝	4-0	5-2⅜			7-8¼	5-3½	2-11¼	10×14
12×14	3-5¼	2-9⅝	4-0	5-2⅜			7-8¼	5-3½	3-5¼	12×14
10×16	2-11¼	3-1⅝	4-6	5-10⅜			8-8¼	5-11½	2-11¼	10×16
12×16	3-5¼	3-1⅝	4-6	5-10⅜			8-8¼	5-11½	3-5¼	12×16
14×16	3-11¼	3-1⅝	4-6	5-10⅜			8-8¼	5-11½	3-11¼	14×16
10×12	3-9⅝	2-5⅝	3-6	4-6⅜			6-8¼	4-7½	3-9⅝	10×12
12×12	4-5⅝	2-5⅝	3-6	4-6⅜			6-8¼	4-7½	4-5⅝	12×12
10×14	3-9⅝	2-9⅝	4-0	5-2⅜			7-8¼	5-3½	3-9⅝	10×14
12×14	4-5⅝	2-9⅝	4-0	5-2⅜			7-8¼	5-3½	4-5⅝	12×14
10×16	3-9⅝	3-1⅝	4-6	5-10⅜			8-8¼	5-11½	3-9⅝	10×16
12×16	4-5⅝	3-1⅝	4-6	5-10⅜			8-8¼	5-11½	4-5⅝	12×16
14×16	5-1⅝	3-1⅝	4-6	5-10⅜			8-8¼	5-11½	5-1⅝	14×16
10×12	3-9⅝	5-6¾	6-8¼					8-9	2-11¼	10×12
12×12	4-5⅝	5-6¾	6-8¼					8-9	3-5¼	12×12
10×14	3-9⅝	6-4¾	7-8¼					10-1	2-11¼	10×14
12×14	4-5⅝	6-4¾	7-8¼					10-1	3-5¼	12×14
10×16	3-9⅝	7-2¾	8-8¼					11-5	2-11¼	10×16
12×16	4-5⅝	7-2¾	8-8¼					11-5	3-5¼	12×16
14×16	5-1⅝	7-2¾	8-8¼					11-5	3-11¼	14×16
					SLIDING SASH					
10×12	3-11½	2-5⅝	3-6				3-6	2-5⅝	5-8¼	10×12
12×12	4-7½	2-5⅝	3-6				3-6	2-5⅝	6-8¼	12×12
10×14	3-11½	2-9⅝	4-0				4-0	2-9⅝	5-8¼	10×14
12×14	4-7½	2-9⅝	4-0				4-0	2-9⅝	6-8¼	12×14
10×16	3-11½	3-1⅝	4-6				4-6	3-1⅝	5-8¼	10×16
12×16	4-7½	3-1⅝	4-6				4-6	3-1⅝	6-8¼	12×16
14×16	5-3½	3-1⅝	4-6				4-6	3-1⅝	7-8¼	14×16

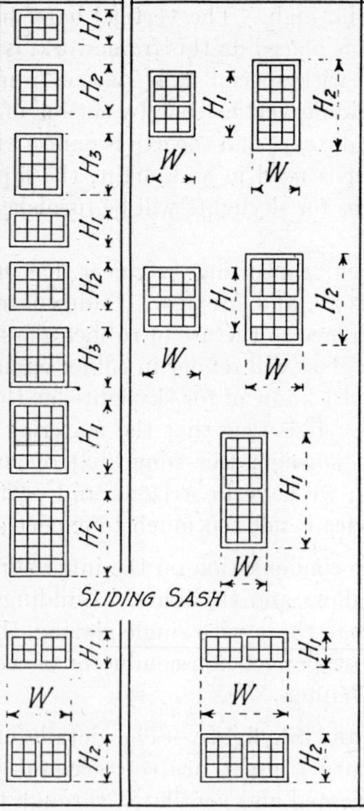

QUALITY OF GLASS

"B" American Single Strength				"B" American Double Strength		
10"×12"	12"×12"	10"×14"	12"×14"	10"×16"	12"×16"	14"×16"

All sash to be 1⅜" thick, except Sliding Sash, Pivoted Sash, and Single Sash (or one half of Double Sash) exceeding 4'6" high or 4'0" wide, which should be made 1¾" thick.

Top Rails 2¼". Stiles 2¼". Bottom Rail 3". Muntins ⅜".

Pivoted Sash, 4 lights high or over, to have one Horizontal Muntin 1½" thick; all other Sash, 6 lights high or over, to have one Horizontal Muntin 1½" thick.

Pivoted Sash, 4 lights wide or over, to have one Vertical Muntin 1½" thick; all other Sash, 6 lights wide or over, to have one Vertical Muntin 1½" thick.

For Pivoted Sash 4 and 5 lights high or wide, add 1⅛" to figures given in above tables.

FIG. 5. DIMENSIONS AND DATA FOR GLAZED WOOD SASH. AMERICAN BRIDGE COMPANY.

Distance H = Girt Spacing for Fixed, Pivoted or Sliding Windows.

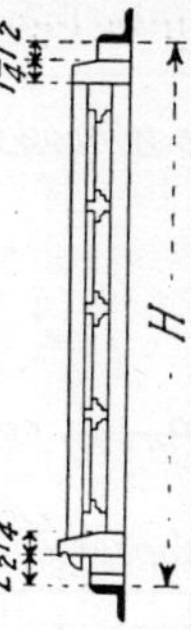

Height of Glass	No. of Lights High	Spacing H
12"	2	3'1 5/8"
12	3	4-2
12	4	5-2 3/8
12	5	6-2 3/4
12	6	7-4 1/4
12	7	8-4 5/8
14	2	3-5 5/8
14	3	4-8
14	4	5-10 3/8
14	5	7-0 3/4
14	6	8-4 1/4
14	7	9-6 5/8

Width of Glass	No. of Lights Wide	Spacing W	Spacing D	Width of Glass	No. of Lights Wide	Spacing W	Spacing D
10"	2	2'7 7/8	2'2 7/8"	12	2	2'11 7/8"	2'6 7/8"
10	3	3-6 1/4	3-1 1/4	12	3	4-0 1/4	3-7 1/4
10	4	4-4 5/8	3-11 5/8	12	4	5-0 5/8	4-7 5/8
10	5	5-3	4-10	12	5	6-1	5-8
10	6	6-2 1/2	5-9 1/2	12	6	7-2 1/2	6-9 1/2

W = Width of Single Pivoted, Fixed or Counterbalanced Window. Width of Continuous Window = No. of Windows × D, + 2 3/8" + 2 3/8" + (1/4" Clearance).

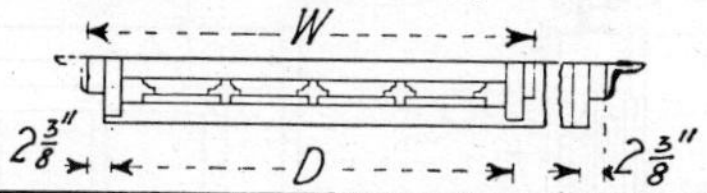

Distance H = Girt Spacing for Counterbalanced Windows.

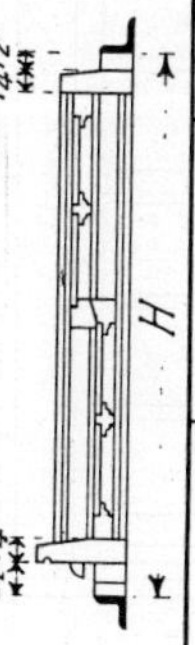

Height of Glass	No. of Lights High	Spacing H
12"	4	5'3 1/4"
12	6	7-4
12	8	9-4 3/4
12	10	11-5 1/2
12	12	13-8 1/2
14	4	5-11 1/4
14	6	8-4
14	8	10-8 3/4
14	10	13-1 1/2
14	12	15-8 1/2

Width of Glass	No. of Lights Wide	Spacing W	Spacing D	Width of Glass	No. of Lights Wide	Spacing W	Spacing D
10"	4	4'6 1/4"	4'1 1/4"	12"	4	5'2 1/4"	4'9 1/4"
10	6	6-3	5-10	12	6	7-3	6-10
10	8	7-11 3/4	7-6 3/4	12	8	9-3 3/4	8-10 3/4
10	10	9-8 1/2	9-3 1/2	12	10	11-4 1/2	10-11 1/2
10	12	11-7 1/2	11-2 1/2	12	12	13-7 1/2	13-2 1/2

W = Width of Single Sliding Window. Width of Continuous Sliding Window = D × No. Windows + 2 3/8" + 2 3/8" + (1/4" Clearance)

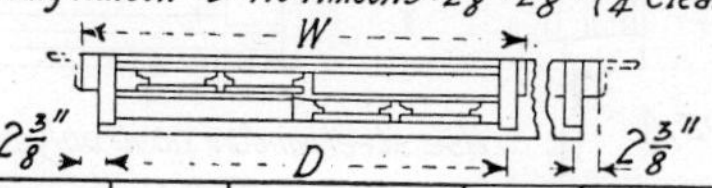

Distance H = Girt Spacing for Double Hung Weighted Windows.

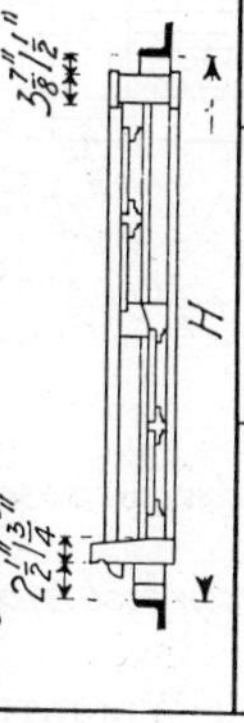

Height of Glass	No. of Lights High	Spacing H
12"	4	5'5 3/8"
12	6	7-6 1/8
12	8	9-6 7/8
12	10	11-7 5/8
12	12	13-10 5/8
14	4	6-1 3/8
14	6	8-6 1/8
14	8	10-10 7/8
14	10	13-3 5/8
14	12	15-10 5/8

Width of Glass	No. of Lights Wide	Spacing W	Width of Glass	No. of Lights Wide	Spacing W
10"	2	3'-1 3/8"	12"	2	3'5 5/8"
10	3	3-11 3/4	12	3	4-5 3/4
10	4	4-10 1/8	12	4	5-6 1/8
10	5	5-8 1/2	12	5	6-6 1/2
10	6	6-8	12	6	7-8

W = Width of Single Double Hung Weighted Window.

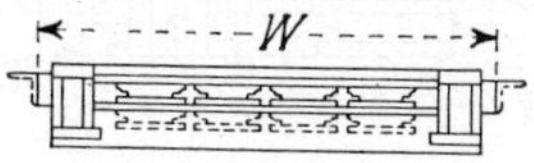

Fig. 6. Dimensions for Glazed Wood Sash. American Bridge Company.

sash are given in Fig. 5 and Fig. 6. The window shown in Fig. 11 is used where light is desired without ventilation. This detail is used principally for monitor ventilators or for windows placed out of reach. Where it is desirable to obtain ventilation as well as light the window frame with sliding sash shown in Fig. 12 is used.

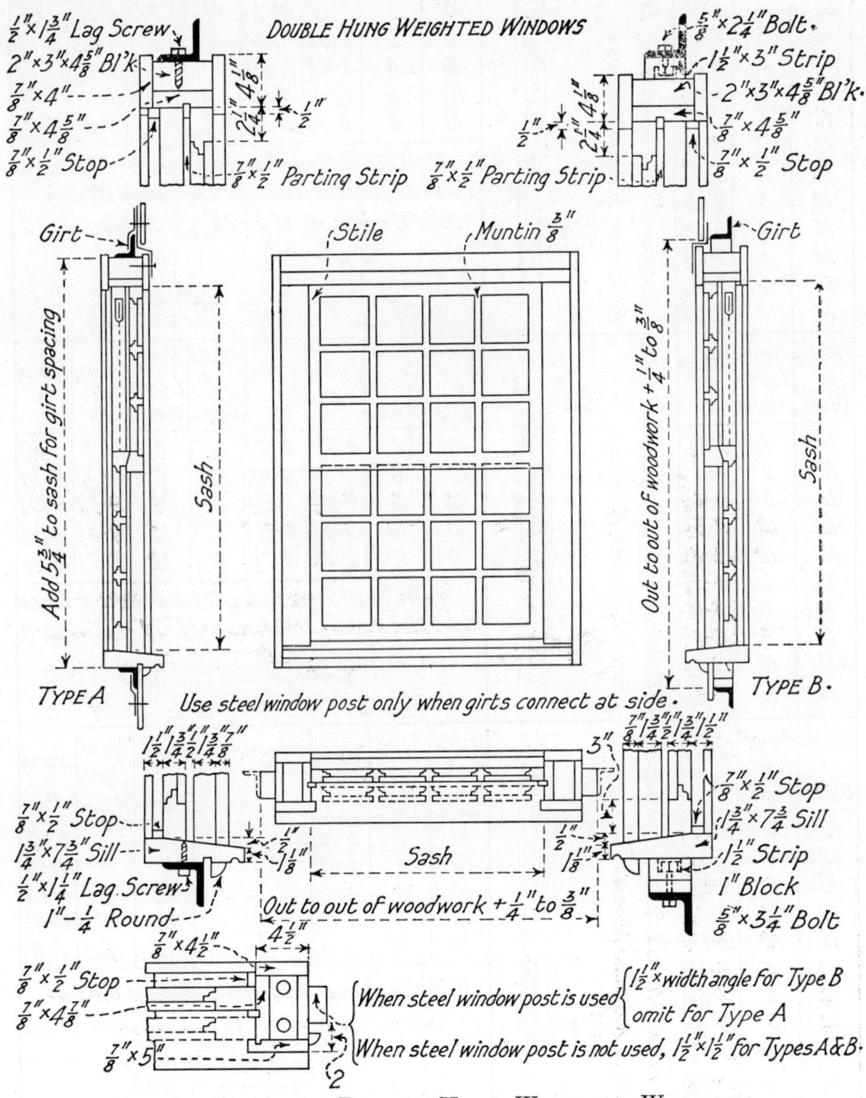

FIG. 7. DATA FOR DOUBLE HUNG WEIGHTED WINDOWS. AMERICAN BRIDGE COMPANY.

STEEL WINDOWS.—Windows with steel sash and steel frames are now used in fireproof buildings and are generally used in all industrial buildings. The windows are

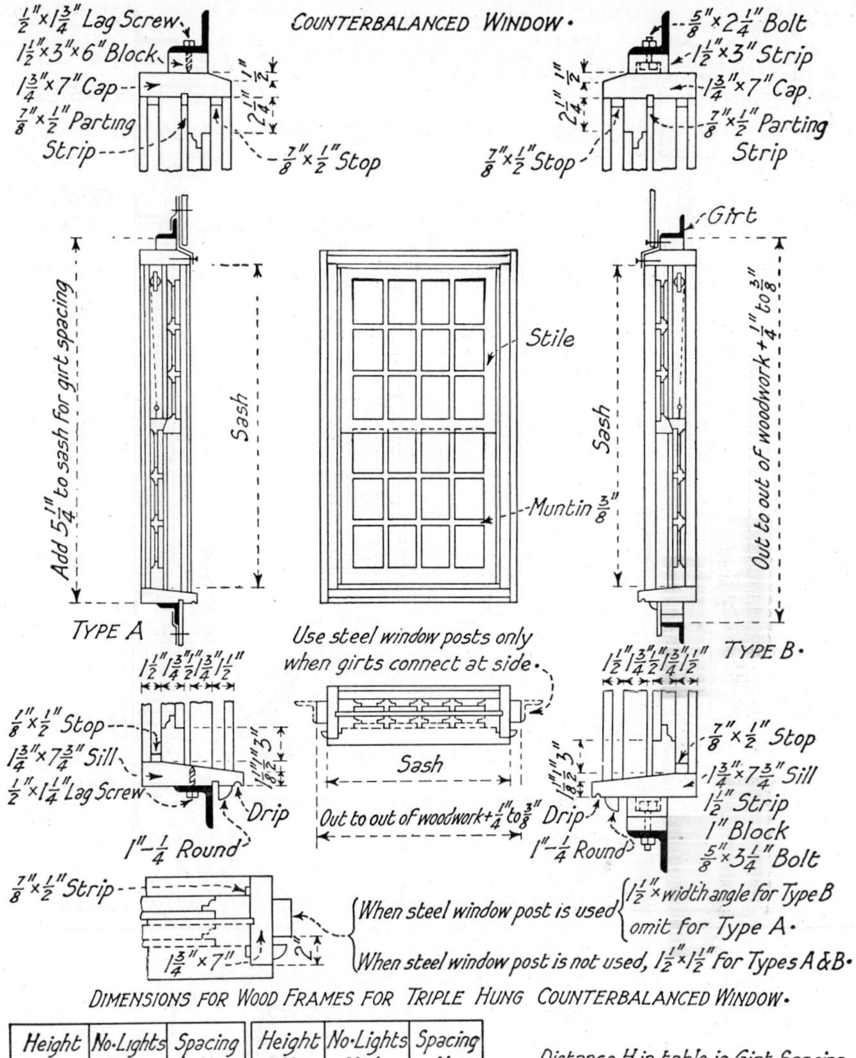

Height of Glass	No. Lights High	Spacing H	Height of Glass	No. Lights High	Spacing H
12"	6	7' 5$\frac{1}{8}$"	14"	6	8' 5$\frac{1}{8}$"
12	9	10-6$\frac{1}{4}$	14	9	12-0$\frac{1}{4}$
12	12	13-7$\frac{3}{8}$	14	12	15-7$\frac{3}{8}$
12	15	16-8$\frac{1}{2}$	14	15	19-2$\frac{1}{2}$
12	18	20-1	14	18	23-1

Distance H in table is Girt Spacing for Triple Hung Counterbalanced Windows. For width see sheet giving width of ordinary Counterbalanced Windows.

FIG. 8. DATA FOR COUNTERBALANCED WINDOWS.
AMERICAN BRIDGE COMPANY.

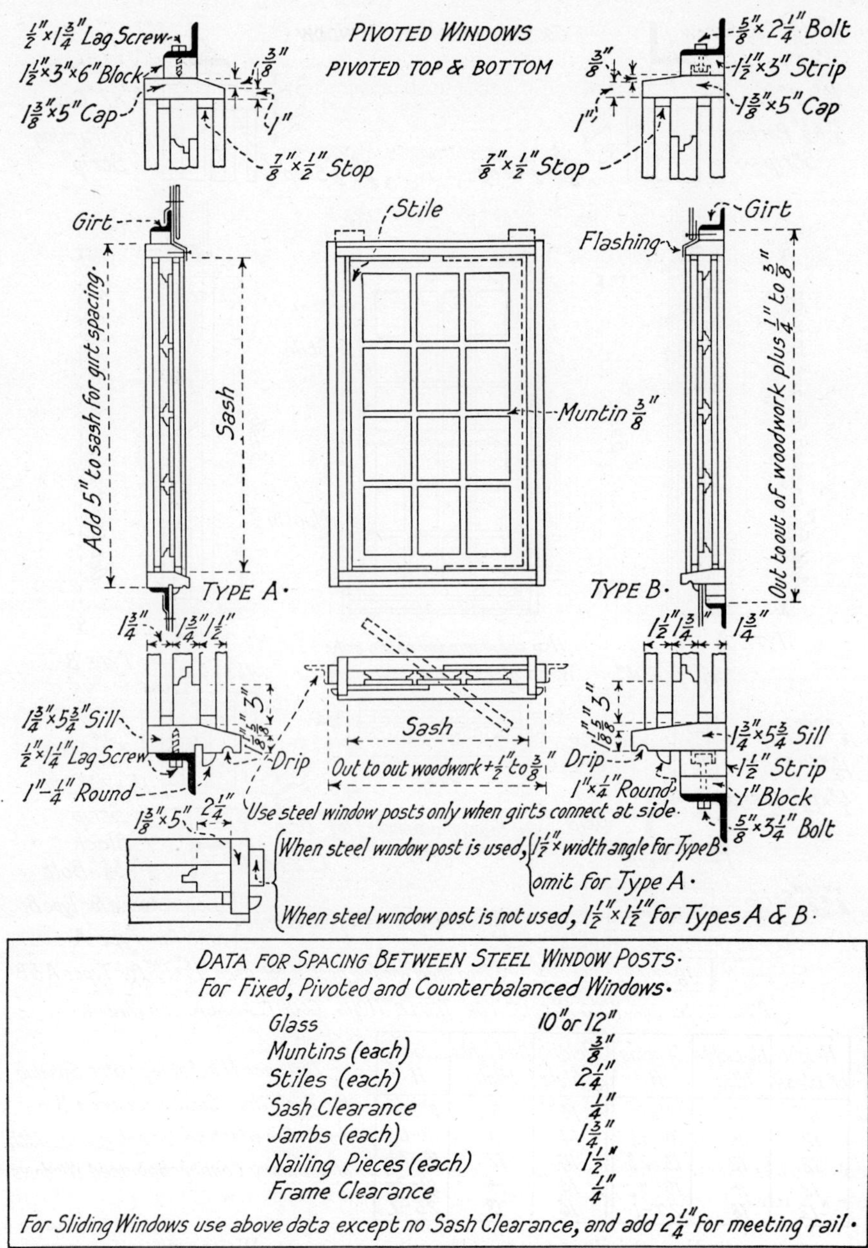

DATA FOR SPACING BETWEEN STEEL WINDOW POSTS.
For Fixed, Pivoted and Counterbalanced Windows.

Glass	10" or 12"
Muntins (each)	3/8"
Stiles (each)	2 1/4"
Sash Clearance	1/4"
Jambs (each)	1 3/4"
Nailing Pieces (each)	1 1/2"
Frame Clearance	1/4"

For Sliding Windows use above data except no Sash Clearance, and add 2 1/4" for meeting rail.

FIG. 9. DATA FOR PIVOTED WINDOWS. AMERICAN BRIDGE COMPANY.

generally glazed with wire glass $\frac{1}{4}$ in. thick. Window sash may be fixed, or may be opened by swinging, or by sliding horizontally or vertically.

In Fig. 13, (a) to (g) inclusive, are windows with fixed sash with ventilators in different positions; (h) is a window with horizontal sliding sash; (i) is a window with

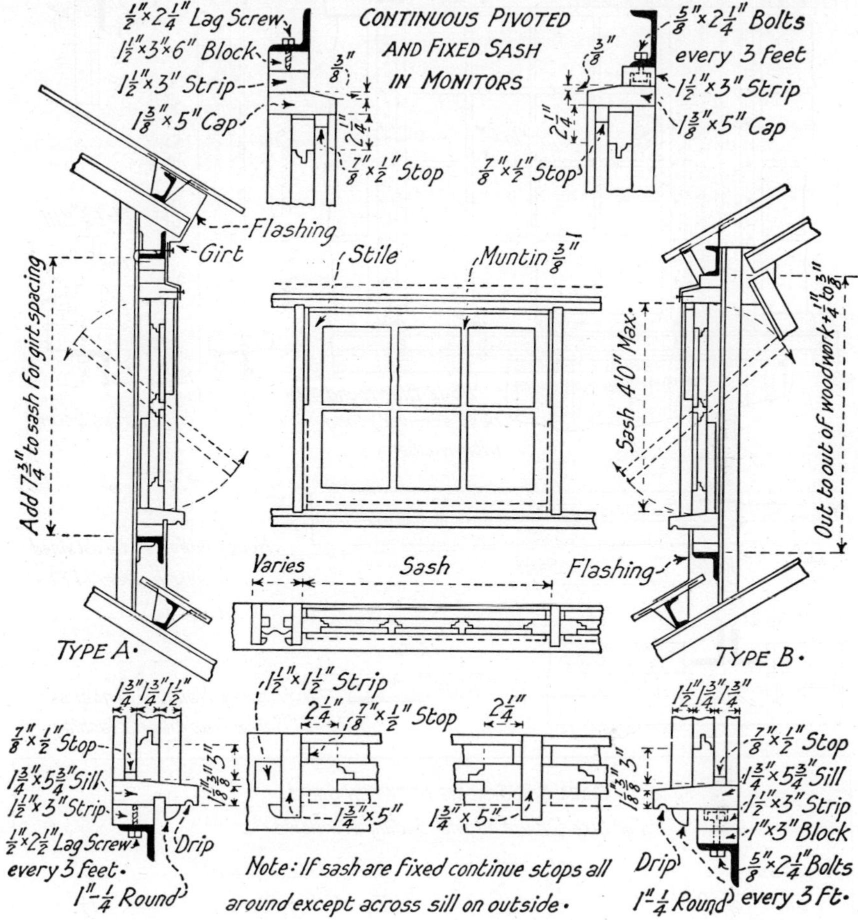

FIG. 10. DATA FOR CONTINUOUS PIVOTED AND FIXED SASH IN MONITORS. AMERICAN BRIDGE COMPANY.

a sash which swings outward; (j) is a window with counterbalanced sash; (k) is a window with a fixed sash and a swinging ventilator; (l) is a window with a swinging sash; while (m) is a window with swinging sash with weather strips to prevent the storm from beating into the building.

Steel sash are made by many different firms. While the main dimensions of the windows made by the different firms are practically standard, each firm uses different rolled-steel sections, different details and different operating devices.

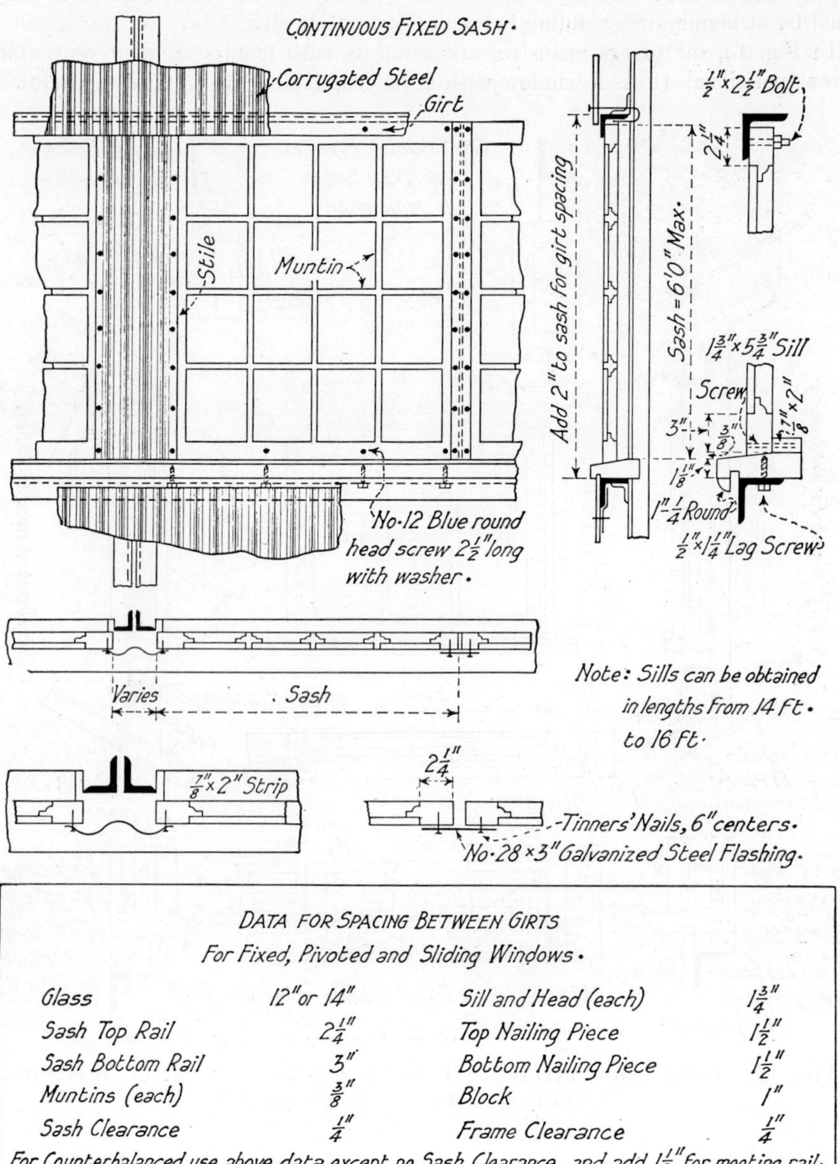

DATA FOR SPACING BETWEEN GIRTS
For Fixed, Pivoted and Sliding Windows.

Glass	12" or 14"	Sill and Head (each)	$1\frac{3}{4}$"
Sash Top Rail	$2\frac{1}{4}$"	Top Nailing Piece	$1\frac{1}{2}$"
Sash Bottom Rail	3"	Bottom Nailing Piece	$1\frac{1}{2}$"
Muntins (each)	$\frac{3}{8}$"	Block	1"
Sash Clearance	$\frac{1}{4}$"	Frame Clearance	$\frac{1}{4}$"

For Counterbalanced use above data except no Sash Clearance, and add $1\frac{1}{2}$" for meeting rail.

FIG. 11. DATA FOR CONTINUOUS FIXED SASH.
AMERICAN BRIDGE COMPANY.

Standard dimensions for steel sash are given in Fig. 14. It should be noted that more steel is used with small sizes of glass than with large sizes, and that sash with small sizes of glass are therefore stronger than sash with large sizes. The maximum sizes of sash given in Fig. 14 are for glass 14 in. by 20 in. For glass 10 in. by 16 in. the

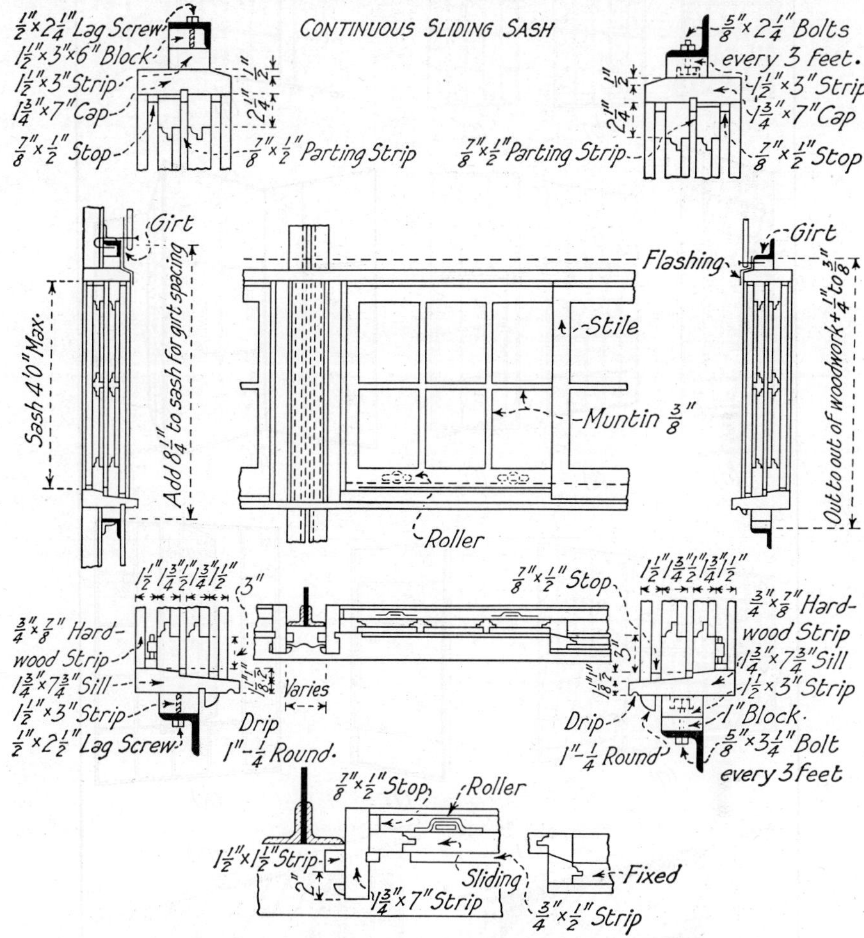

FIG. 12. DATA FOR CONTINUOUS SLIDING SASH. AMERICAN BRIDGE COMPANY.

maximum sizes may be increased 15 per cent; while for glass 18 in. by 24 in. the maximum sizes should be reduced by 15 per cent, and proportional for intermediate sizes of glass. The glass are fastened with clips and are glazed with special putty, on the inside of the sash.

Specifications for Steel Sash.—The specifications for steel sash as given in Appendix I are as follows:—

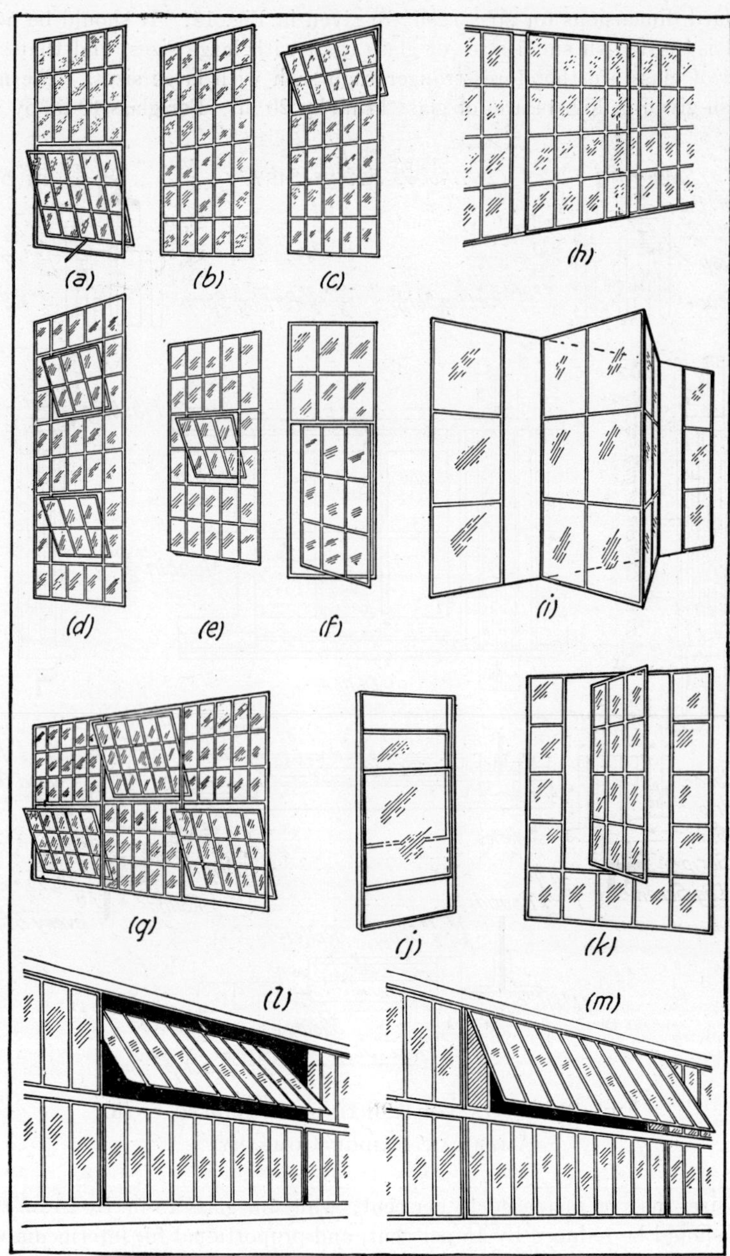

FIG. 13. TYPES OF STEEL WINDOWS.

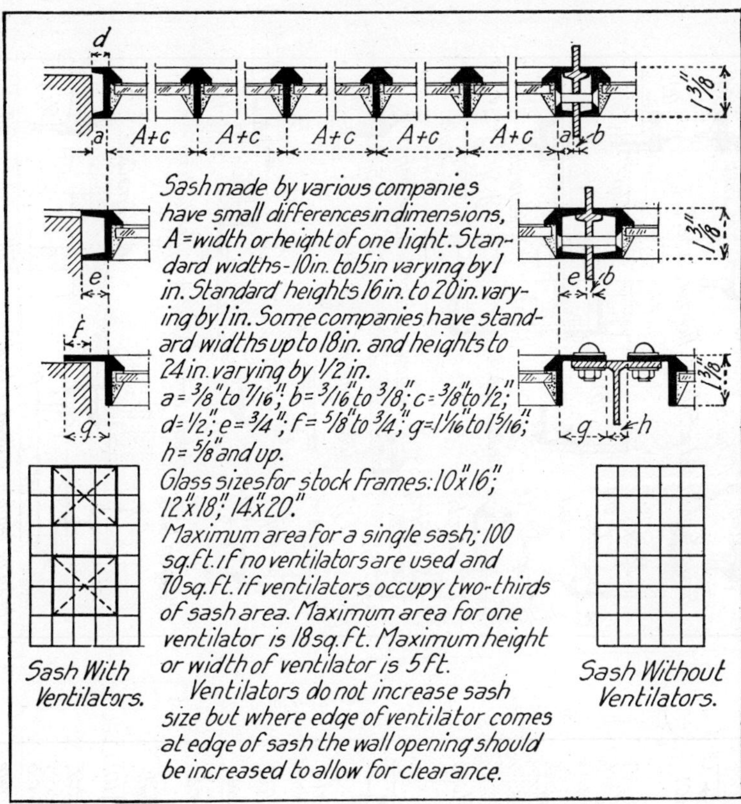

d
A+c
a
b
1 3/8"
Sash made by various companies have small differences in dimensions, A = width or height of one light. Standard widths - 10 in. to 15 in varying by 1 in. Standard heights 16 in. to 20 in. varying by 1 in. Some companies have standard widths up to 18 in. and heights to 24 in. varying by 1/2 in.
a = 3/8" to 7/16"; b = 3/16 to 3/8"; c = 3/8" to 1/2";
d = 1/2"; e = 3/4"; f = 5/8" to 3/4"; g = 1 1/16" to 1 5/16";
h = 5/8" and up.
Glass sizes for stock frames: 10"x16"; 12"x18"; 14"x20".
Maximum area for a single sash; 100 sq. ft. if no ventilators are used and 70 sq. ft. if ventilators occupy two-thirds of sash area. Maximum area for one ventilator is 18 sq. ft. Maximum height or width of ventilator is 5 ft.
Ventilators do not increase sash size but where edge of ventilator comes at edge of sash the wall opening should be increased to allow for clearance.
e
f
g
h
Sash With Ventilators.
Sash Without Ventilators.

FIG. 14. STANDARD DETAILS FOR STEEL SASH.

Steel sash shall be made with solid sections. The maximum size of steel sash shall be 100 sq. ft. where no ventilators are used, and 70 sq. ft. where ventilators occupy two-thirds of the window area, and proportional for intermediate amount of ventilators. Steel sash shall be glazed with special glazing clips and with glazing putty. All sash shall be provided with locking devices and other hardware as specified.

TABLE II.

DIMENSIONS OF FENESTRA SOLID STEEL WINDOWS.

No. of Lights High.	Height Dimensions, ft. and in. Height of Each Light in Inches.				No. of Lights Wide.	Width Dimensions, ft. and in. Width of Each Light in Inches.			
	X-16	Y-18	Z-20	P-22		X-10	Y-12	Z-14	P-16
1	1– 5¼	1– 7¼	1– 9¼	1–11¼	1	0–11¼	1–1¼	1– 3¼	1– 5¼
2	2– 9⅝	3– 1⅝*	3– 5⅝*	3– 9⅝	2	1– 9⅝	2–1⅝	2– 5⅝	2– 9⅝
3	4– 2	4– 8 *	5– 2 *	5– 8	3	2– 8	3–2 *	3– 8 *	4– 2
4	5– 6⅜	6– 2⅜*	6–10⅜*	7– 6⅜	4	3– 6⅜	4–2⅜*	4–10⅜*	5– 6⅜
5	6–10¾	7– 8¾*	8– 6¾*	9– 4¾	5	4– 4¾	5–2¾*	6– 0¾*	6–10¾
6	8– 3⅛	9– 3⅛*	10– 3⅛*	11– 3⅛	6	5– 3⅛	6–3⅛	7– 3⅛	8– 3⅛
7	9– 7½	10– 9½	11–11½	——	7	6– 1½	7–3½	8– 5½	——
8	10–11⅞	12– 3⅞	13– 7⅞	——					
9	12– 4¼	13–10¼	——	——					

Combine X Widths with X Heights, Z Widths with Z Heights, etc.

Add 2 inches to allow for Tee Bar Mullion when combining Sash.

* Indicates Warehouse Sash.

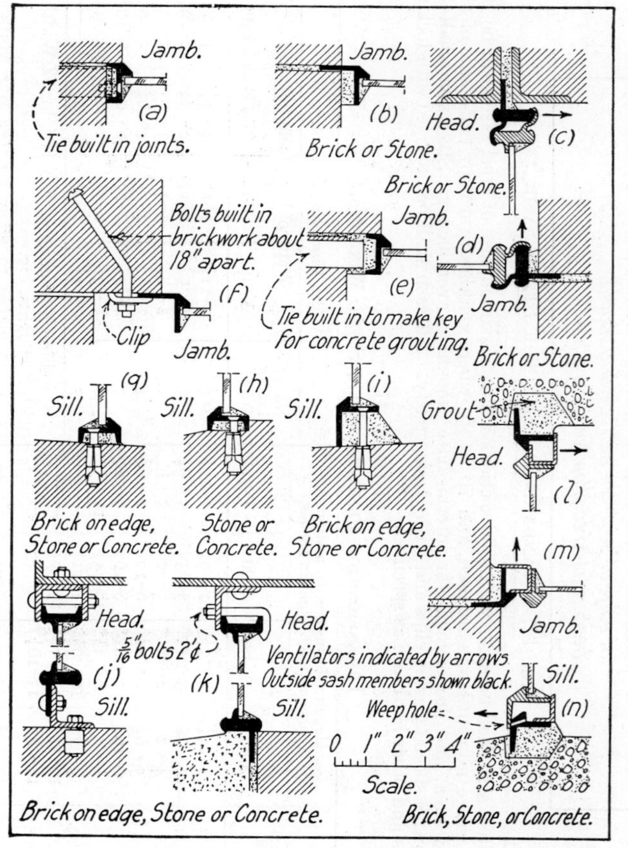

FIG. 15. DETAILS.

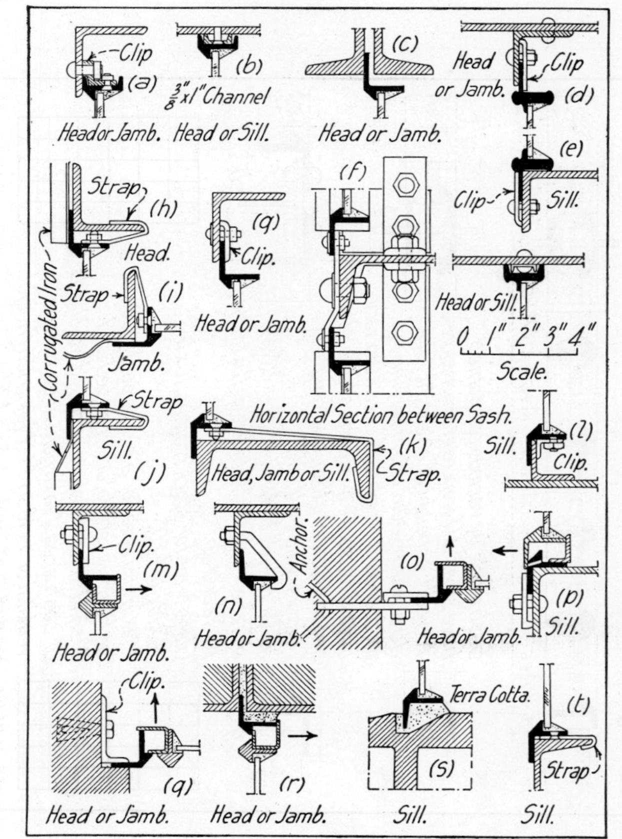

FIG. 16. DETAILS.

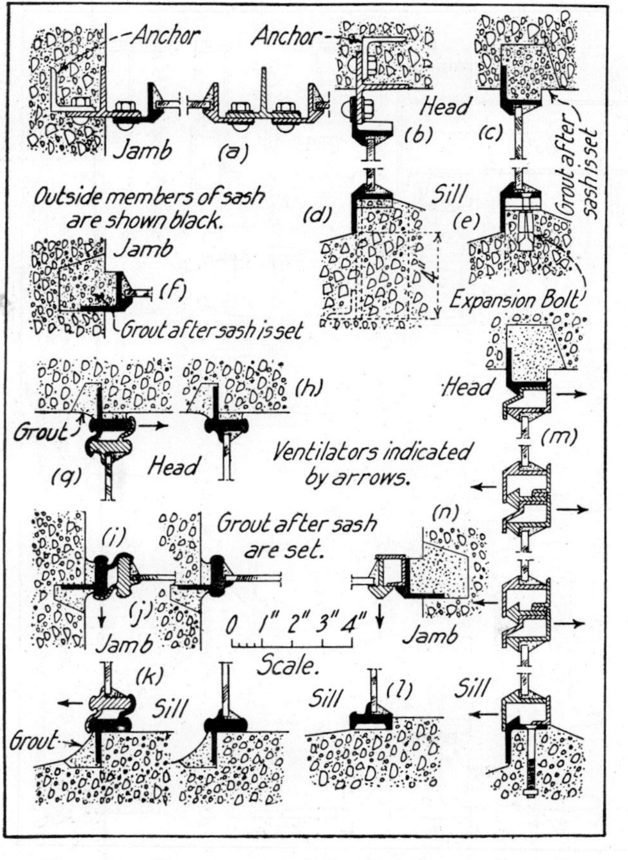

FIG. 17. DETAILS OF "UNITED STEEL SASH."

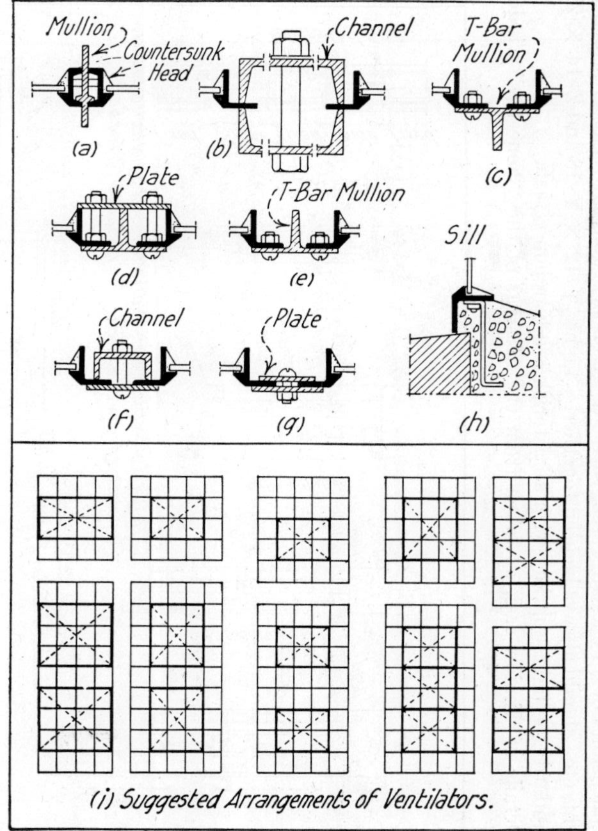

FIG. 18.

Dimensions of "Fenestra" steel sash are given in Table II. The X width and X height, etc., should always be used together. Lights Y–12 × Y–18 and Z–14 × Z–20 are standard, the lights marked with an asterisk are warehouse sash.

Details of window sash as taken from the catalogs of the "Fenestra" windows,

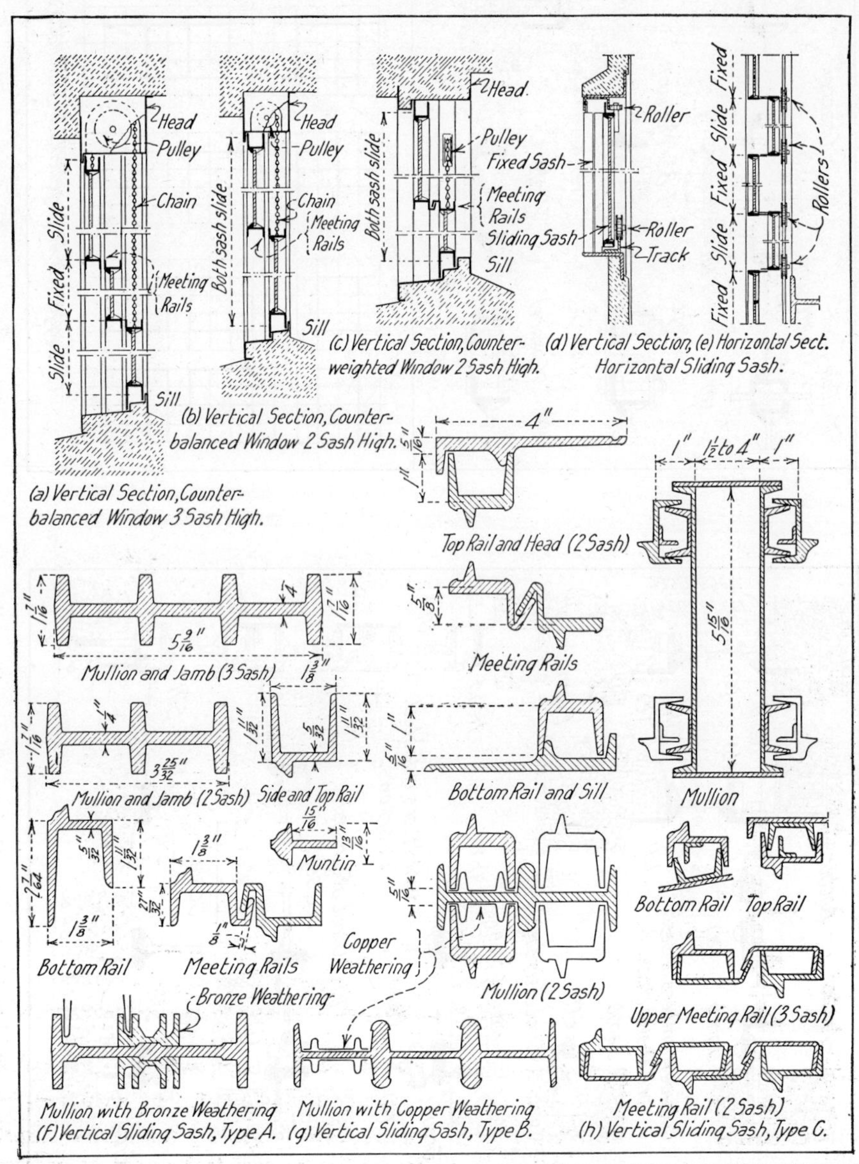

FIG. 19. DETAILS OF STEEL SASH.

((f) is "Lupton," (g) is "United Steel Sash," and (h) is "Fenestra.")

made by the Detroit Steel Products Company, Detroit, Mich.; the "Lupton" windows, made by the David Lupton Sons Company, Philadelphia, and "United Steel Sash" made by the Trussed Concrete Steel Co., Youngstown, Ohio, are shown in Fig. 15 to Fig. 18. While each company uses different rolled sections the details are essentially

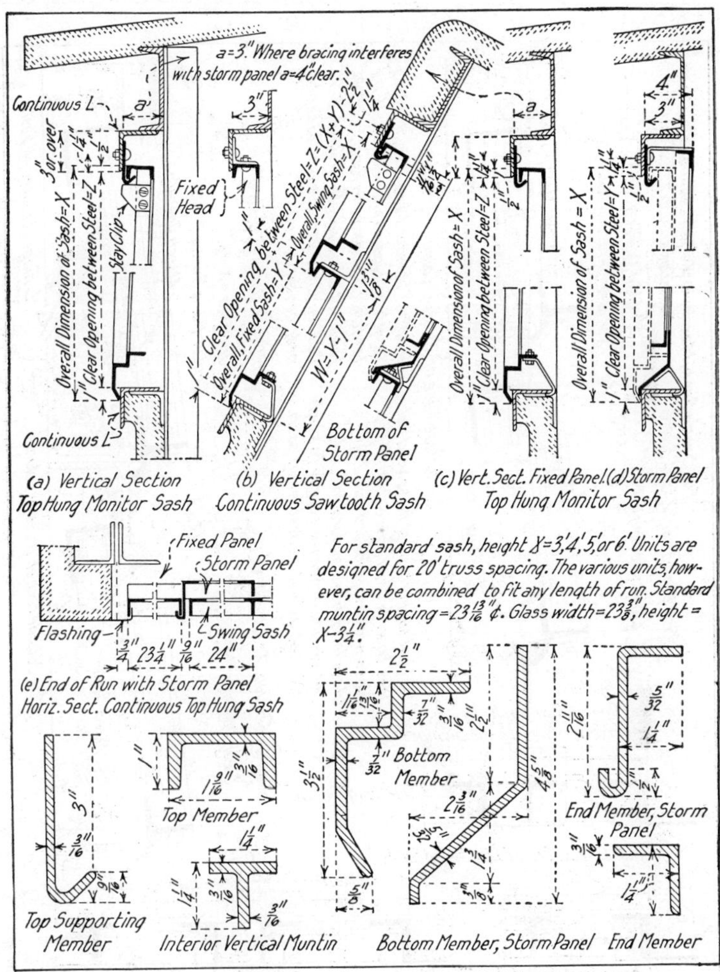

Fig. 20. Details of "United Steel Sash" Ventilators and Skylights.

the same and may be used interchangeably as far as the designing engineer is concerned. Details of counterbalanced sash are shown in (a) to (c), and details of a horizontal sliding sash are shown in (d) and (e), Fig. 19. The details of the sections used by the different firms may be determined by observing that in Fig. 19 (f) is "Lupton," (g) is "United Steel Sash," and (h) is "Fenestra." Details of construction, and details of operating devices and hardware can be obtained from the various catalogs. Details of

"United Steel Sash" monitor ventilators and skylights are shown in Fig. 20. Details of "Lupton" monitor ventilators and skylights are shown in Fig. 21. The details shown in Fig. 20 and Fig. 21 are very complete. For the addresses of other companies manufacturing steel windows, see Sweet's "Architectural Catalog" published by Sweet's Catalog Service, New York.

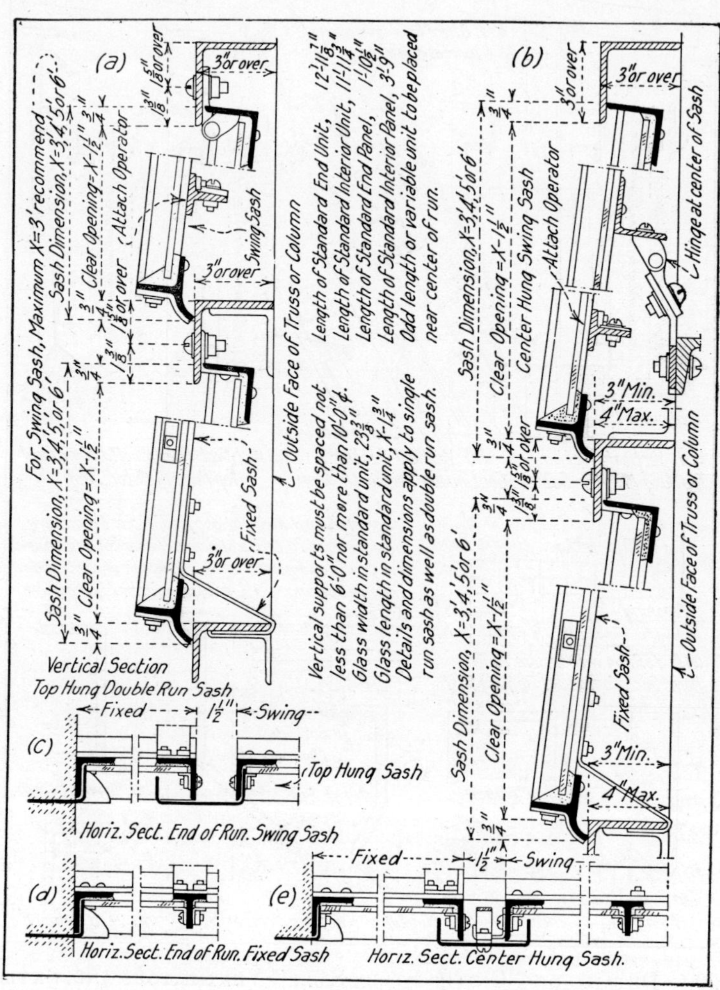

FIG. 21. DETAILS OF "LUPTON" VENTILATORS AND SKYLIGHTS

VENTILATORS.—Industrial buildings are ventilated either by forced draft or by natural ventilation. Natural ventilation is usually sufficient, although forced draft is necessary in many factories or mills such as cement mills and similar structures. The amount of air required depends upon the use to which the building is to be put. For mill and factory buildings it is usual to require 20 to 30 cu. ft. of fresh air per minute for each operative, and to require that all the air be entirely changed each hour. A common specification is to require a net ventilator opening per 100 sq. ft. of floor space of not less than one-fourth sq. ft. for clean machine shops and similar buildings; of not less than one sq. ft. for dirty machine shops; of not less than four sq. ft. for mills, and of not less than six sq. ft. for forge shops, foundries and smelters. The American Bridge Co. specifies that tubular ventilators shall have a net opening of one sq. ft. for each 200 to 400 sq. ft. of floor space.

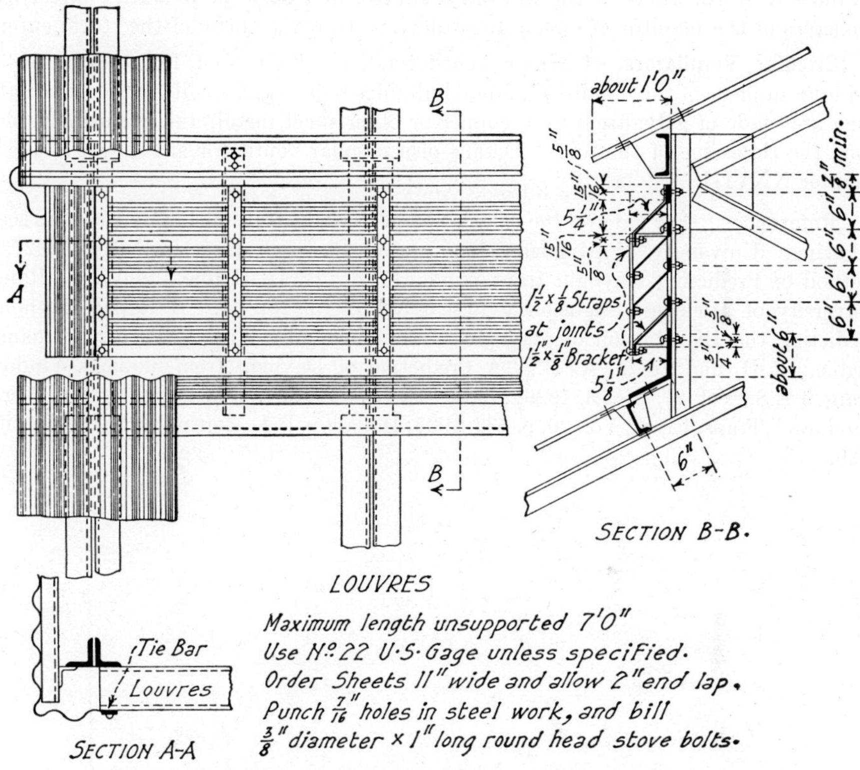

FIG. 22. DETAILS OF A STEEL MONITOR LOUVRE VENTILATOR. AMERICAN BRIDGE COMPANY.

Ventilators are more effective in high buildings than in low buildings. One sq. ft. of ventilator opening at a height of 60 ft. will be nearly twice as effective as one sq. ft. at a height of 20 ft.

Industrial buildings are ventilated (1) through monitor ventilators, (2) through tubular ventilators placed in the roof, or (3) by means of swing ventilators placed in the windows. The best ventilation is obtained with monitor or tubular ventilators in the roof and ventilators in the windows in the side of the building.

Details of a circular ventilator as designed by the American Bridge Company are shown in (3) Fig. 14, Chapter XXVIII. Details of a standard monitor steel louvre ventilator are shown in Fig. 22. The sides of the monitor ventilator in Fig. 8, Chapter

XXVI, were fitted with louvres which were to be closed in cold weather. Buildings of this type should have glazed sash so that when the ventilators are closed the light will not be cut off. Data for estimating louvre slats are given in Fig. 22.

In smelters the clerestory of the monitor is often left entirely open or is slightly protected by self-acting shutters. In the latter case the shutters are hinged at the bottom and are connected at the top with each other and with a counter-weight so that the shutter will ordinarily make an angle of about 30 degrees with the vertical. A wind or a storm will close the windward shutter and open the leeward shutter wider. The eaves of the monitor are made to project, so that very little of the storm enters.

Circular Ventilators.—Circular ventilators are often used for ventilating mill buildings in place of the monitors, and on buildings requiring a small area for ventilation. They are made of galvanized iron, copper or other sheet metal, and are usually placed along the ridge line of the roof. Details of a circular ventilator are shown in Fig. 14, Chapter XXVIII.

References.—For data on the calculation of daylight transmitted by windows see the following. University of Michigan Engineering Research Bulletin No. 6, 1927, "A Method of Predicting Daylight from Windows," by H. H. Higbie and W. C. Randall; University of Michigan Engineering Research Bulletin No. 17, "A Rapid Method for Predicting the Distribution of Daylight in Buildings," by Waclaw Turner-Syzmanaski; Higbie, H. H. and Levin, A. H., "A Prediction of Daylight from Sloping Windows," Trans. I.E.S., Vol. 21, p. 273, 1926; Higbie, H. H., "Prediction of Daylight from Vertical Windows," Trans. I.E.S., Vol. 20, p. 433, 1925; Holladay, L. L., Journal Franklin Institute, 1929.

CHAPTER XXXIV.

Doors.

WOODEN DOORS.—Wooden doors are usually constructed of matched pine sheathing nailed to a wooden frame as shown in Fig. 1. These doors are made of white pine. Doors up to four feet in width should be swung on hinges; wider doors should be made to slide on an overhead track or should be counter-balanced and raise vertically. Sliding doors should be at least 4 in. wider and 2 in. higher than the clear opening.

"Sandwich" doors are made by covering a wooden frame with flat or corrugated steel. The wooden framework of these doors is commonly made of two or more thicknesses of $\frac{7}{8}$ in. dressed and matched white pine sheathing not over 4 in. wide, laid diagonally and nailed with clinch nails. Care must be used in handling sandwich doors made as above or they will warp out of shape. Corrugated steel with $1\frac{1}{4}$ in. corrugations makes the neatest covering for sandwich doors.

For swing doors use hinges about as follows: For doors 3 ft. × 6 ft. or less use 10 in. strap or 10 in. T-hinges; for doors 3 ft. × 6 ft. to 3 ft. × 8 ft. use 16 in. strap or 16 in. T-hinges; for doors 3 ft. × 8 ft. to 4 ft. × 10 ft. use 24 in. strap hinges.

Paneled Doors.—For openings from 2 ft. × 6 ft. to 3 ft. × 9 ft. ordinary stock paneled doors are commonly used. The stock doors vary in width from 2 ft. to 3 ft. by even inches and in length by 4 in. to 6 in. up to 7 ft. for 2 ft. doors, and 9 ft. for 3 ft. doors. Stock doors are made $1\frac{3}{8}$ and $1\frac{3}{4}$ in. thick, and are made in three grades, A, B and C; the A grade being first class, B grade fair and C grade very poor. Paneled doors up to 7 ft. wide and $2\frac{1}{4}$ in. thick can be obtained from most mills by a special order.

STEEL DOORS.—Details of a steel sliding door are shown in Fig. 2. Details of a swinging steel door are shown in Fig. 3. Steel doors should be covered with corrugated steel, preferably with $1\frac{1}{4}$ in. corrugations.

Details of the track for a sliding door are shown in Fig. 4.

There are quite a number of patented devices on the market for hanging sliding doors. The Wilcox trolley door hanger and track shown in Fig. 2 and Fig. 4 are efficient and are quite generally used. Details and prices of track devices may be obtained from the Wilcox Manufacturing Co., Aurora, Ill.

Steel doors built of special steel sections are made by several firms. Details of "Lupton" tubular steel doors manufactured by David Lupton Sons Company, Philadelphia, Pa., are shown in Fig. 5. These doors are hinged to swing one way or to slide horizontally. The lower part of the door is filled with No. 12 gage steel, while the upper part is filled with wire glass set in steel sash and steel frames. "Lupton" doors have the frames welded.

Details of "Fenestra" tubular steel doors made by the Detroit Steel Products Company, Detroit, Mich., are shown in Fig. 6. The doors are hinged to swing one way or to slide horizontally. Special tubular sliding doors can be made 10 ft. wide and 25 ft. high, or with double doors for an opening 20 ft. wide and 25 ft. high. "Fenestra"

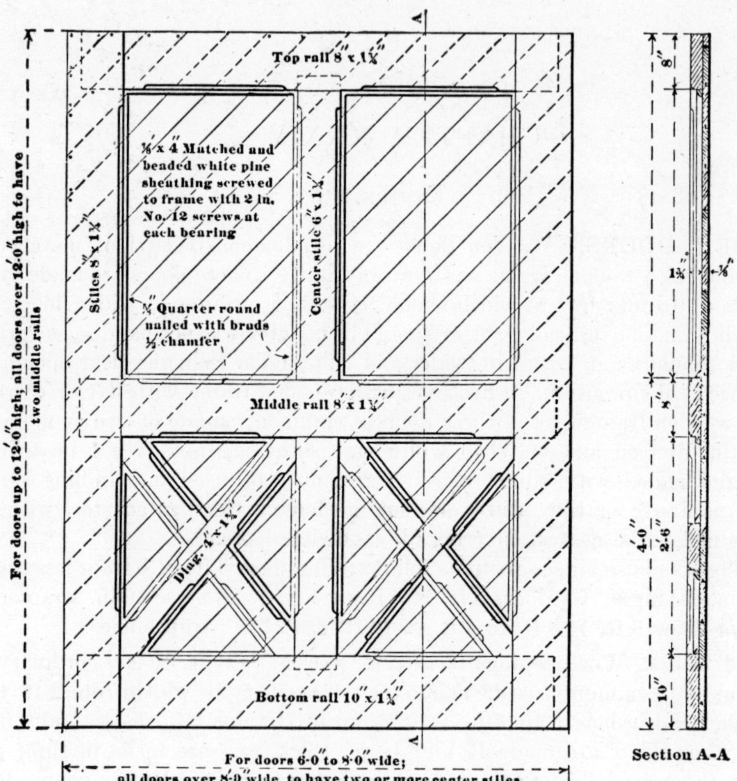

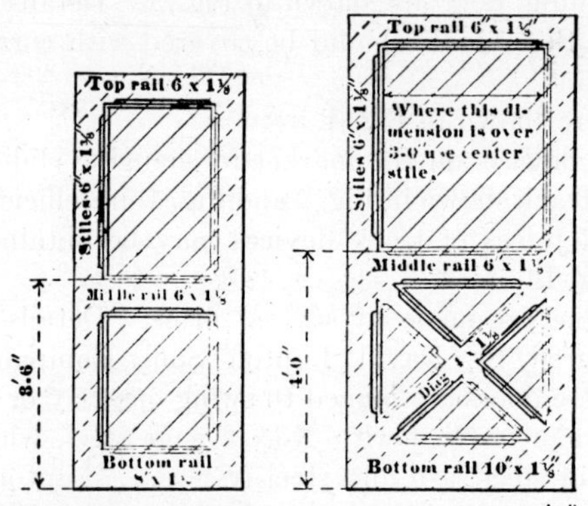

Design for door up to 3'-0" x 7'-0"

Design for doors over 3'-0" x 7'-0" and up to 6'-0" wide

3" 1⅜" ⅞" 3" Hardwood 3" ⅞"

Meeting strips for double sliding doors.

Meeting strip for double swing doors.

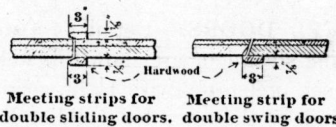

Doors may be either slide or swing. Sliding doors should be 4" wider and 2" higher than clear opening between jambs.
All doors under 6'-0" wide to have 1⅜" stiles and rails.
All doors over 6'-0" wide to have 1⅞" stiles and rails.
All stiles and rails to be halved or mortised and tenoned together.
Doors to be made of white pine
If doors are to be covered with tin or sheet metal they are to be made of two or more thicknesses of ⅞ matched white pine sheathing not over 4" wide, laid diagonally and put together with wrought nails well clinched.

FIG. 1. DETAILS OF WOODEN DOORS. AMERICAN BRIDGE COMPANY.

doors have the frames riveted. Steel doors are also made by the Trussed Steel Concrete Company.

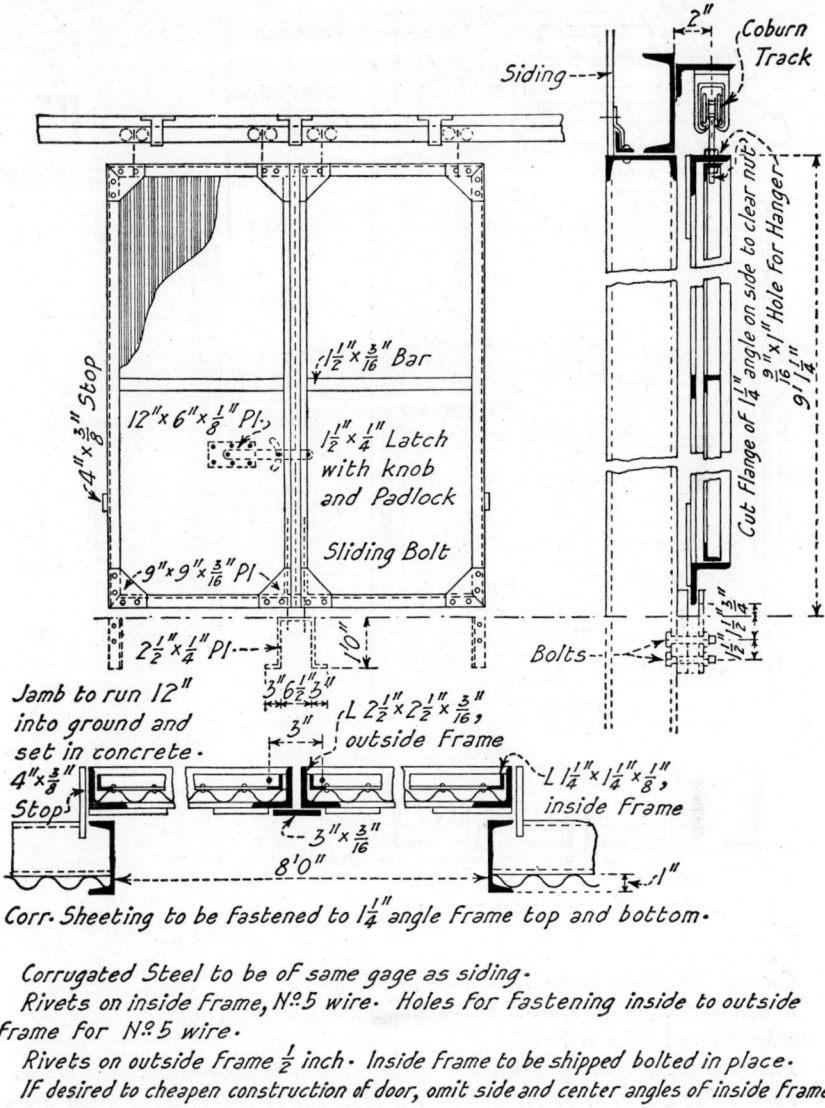

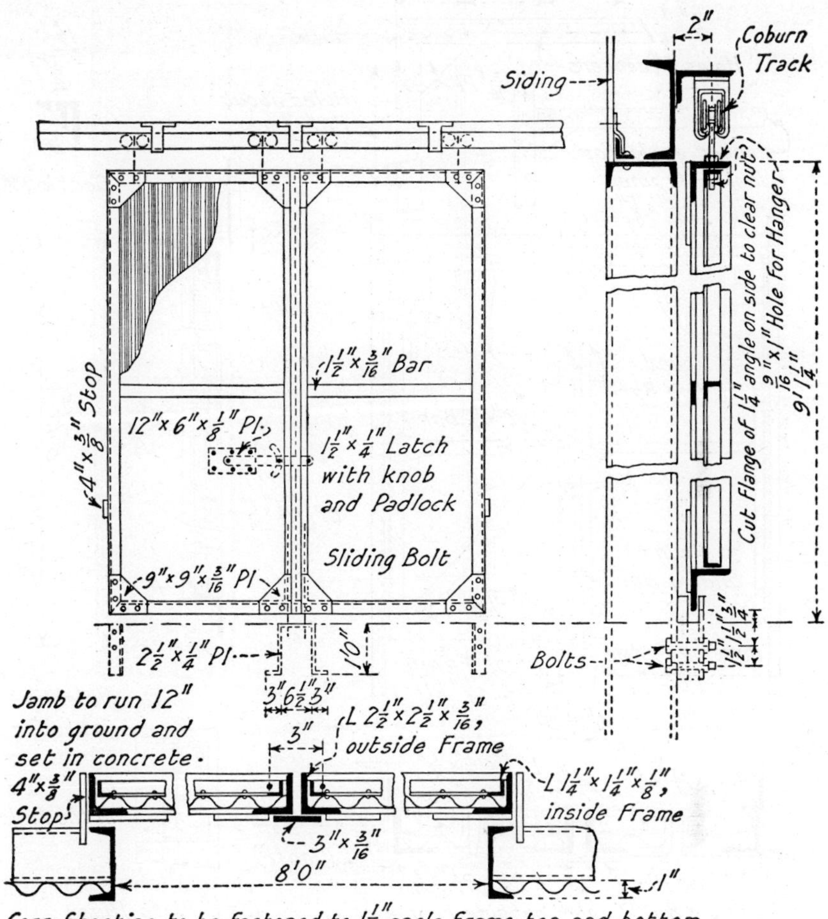

Corrugated Steel to be of same gage as siding.
Rivets on inside Frame, No. 5 wire. Holes for Fastening inside to outside frame for No. 5 wire.
Rivets on outside Frame $\frac{1}{2}$ inch. Inside Frame to be shipped bolted in place.
If desired to cheapen construction of door, omit side and center angles of inside Frame.

Fig. 2. Details of a Sliding Steel Door. American Bridge Company.

Diagrammatic sketches of several types of doors are shown in Fig. 7. These sketches represent different types of doors shown in the catalog of J. Edward Ogden, New York, N. Y. This company is prepared to furnish door hardware and mechanical

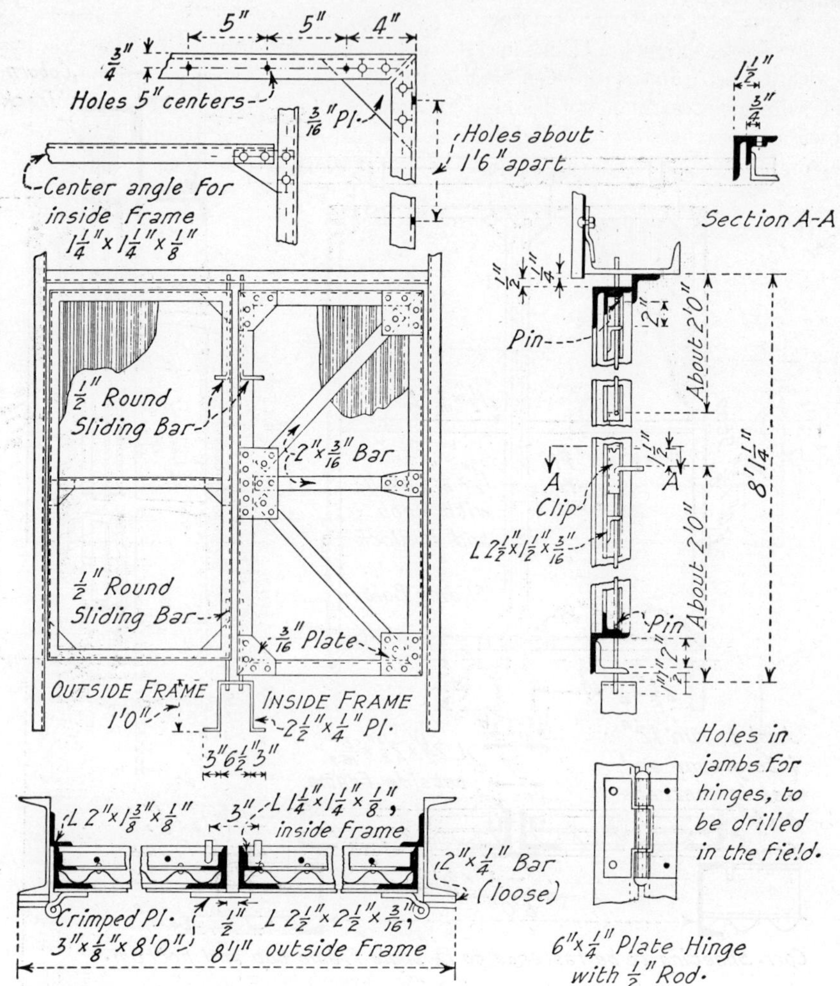

Corrugated Steel to be same gage as siding.
Rivets on inside frame, No. 5 wire. Holes for fastening inside frame to outer frame, No. 5 wire.
Rivets on outer frame 1/2" diameter. Inside frame to be shipped bolted in place.
Corrugated Steel to be riveted in field to top and bottom angles of inside frame.
If desired to cheapen construction of door, omit side and center angles of inside frame.

FIG. 3. DETAILS OF A SWINGING STEEL DOOR. AMERICAN BRIDGE COMPANY.

parts of the doors shown, or will supply the doors complete. The following data have been taken from the Ogden catalog.

Two-section Doors.—Doors may be made of wood frame and sheet-steel covering, or with a steel frame with sheet-steel covering; the upper section may be glazed with ½-in. wire glass set in metal frames. Details of doors 20 ft. wide and 22 ft. high are shown as constructed with wood frames, and also with steel frames. Counterweights are commonly made equal to one-half the total weight of the door.

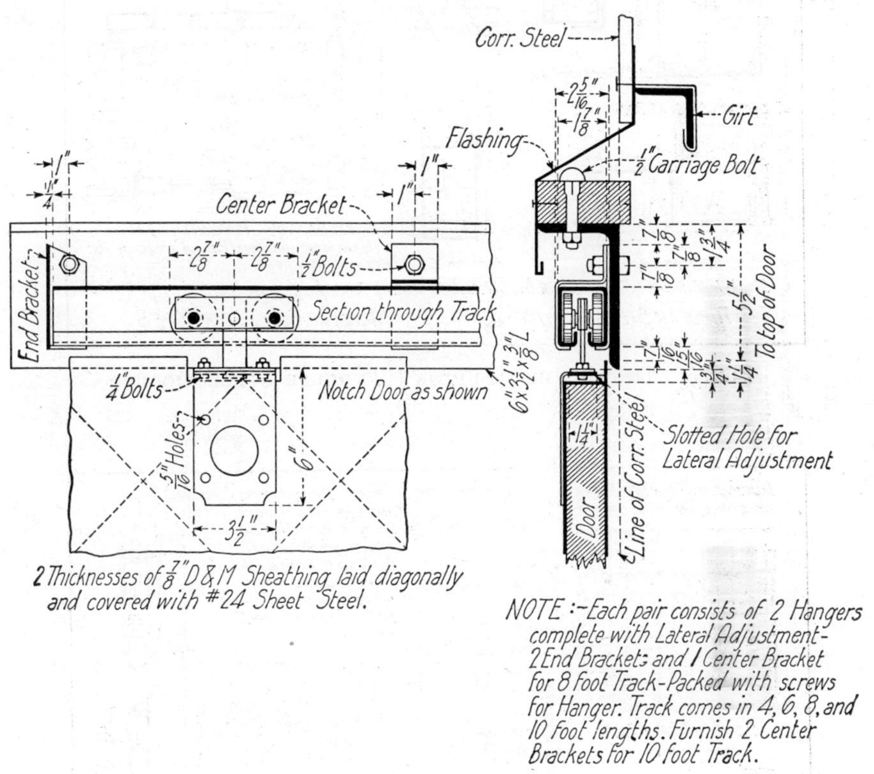

FIG. 4. DETAILS OF A TRACK FOR A SLIDING DOOR.

Single-section Doors.—Doors may be made with wood frames or with steel frames. Details of a door 27 ft. 9 in. wide and 19 ft. 6 in. high are shown.

Multi-section Door.—This door is especially adapted for locations where there is little ceiling space. Doors may be made with wood frames or with steel frames. Details of doors 18 ft. 3 in. wide and 22 ft. 2 in. high are shown.

Turn-over Door.—This door is used for small openings. There is no operating winch, the door being operated by hand.

Canopy Door.—This door protects the doorway when open. The minimum headroom above the door is 16 inches. This is a modification of the single-section door.

Single-section Vertical-sliding Door.—These doors require adequate headroom.

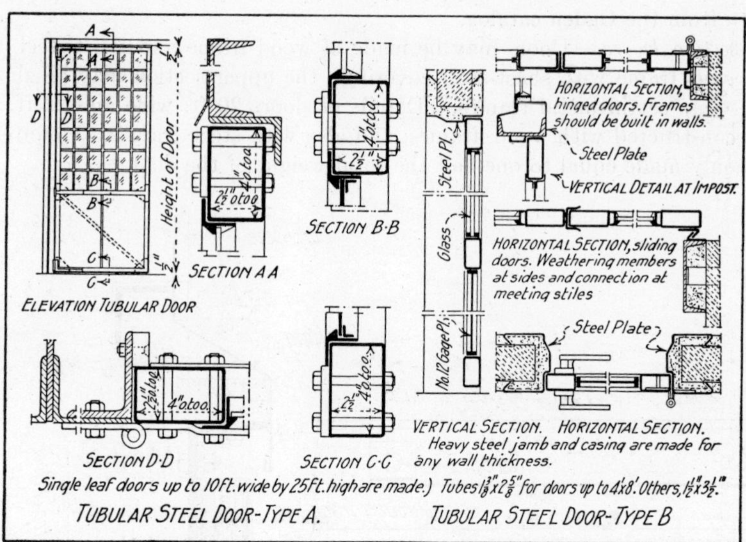

FIG. 5. DETAILS OF "LUPTON" TUBULAR STEEL DOORS.

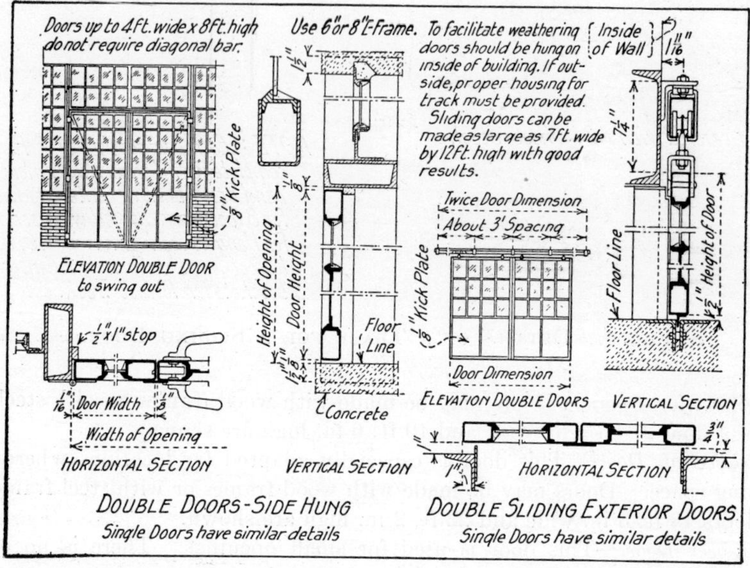

FIG. 6. DETAILS OF "FENESTRA" TUBULAR STEEL DOORS.

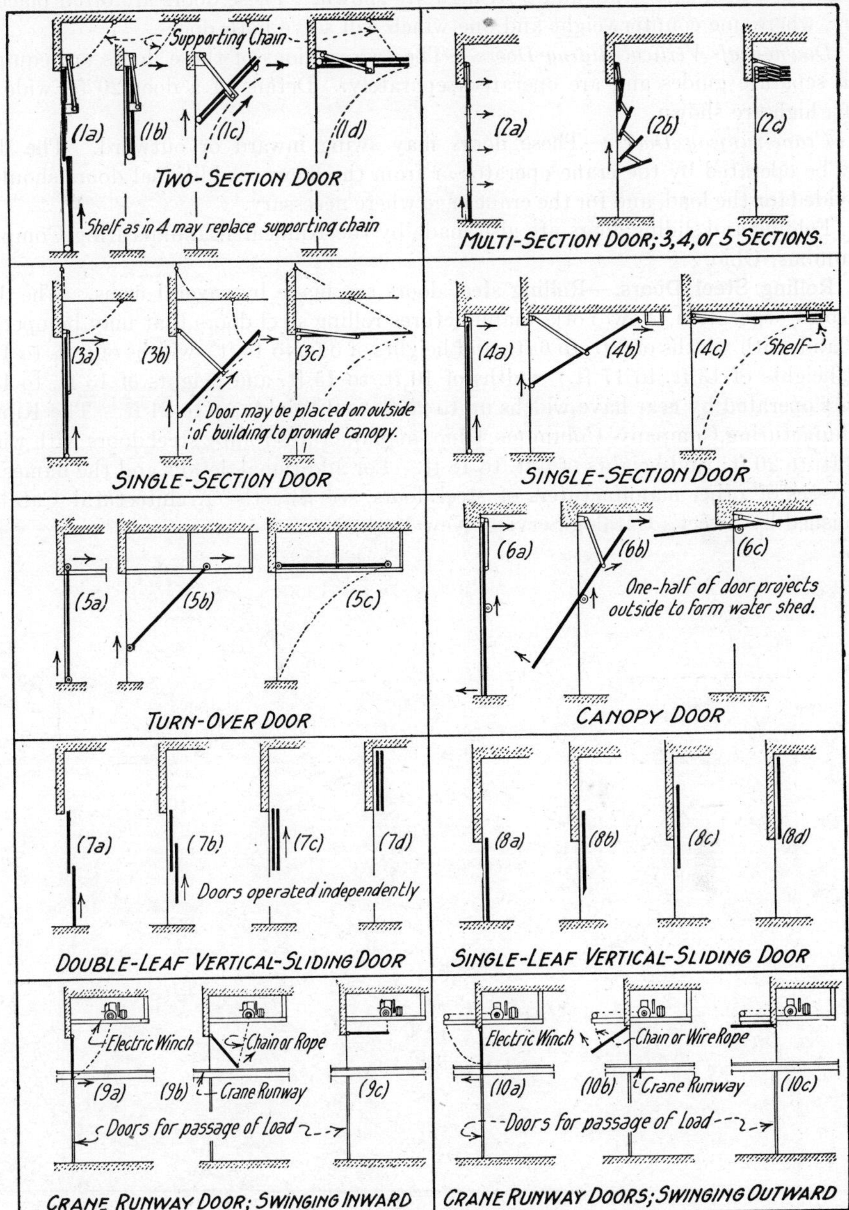

FIG. 7. DIAGRAMMATIC SKETCHES OF DOORS. COMPILED FROM CATALOG OF J. EDWARD OGDEN COMPANY.

Details of a door 8 ft. wide and 8 ft. high are shown. These doors are often placed in pairs, where one counterweight and one winch will serve both doors.

Double-leaf Vertical-sliding Doors.—The two sections of these doors are equipped with separate guides and are operated separately. Details of a door 20 ft. wide and 18 ft. high are shown.

Crane-runway Doors.—These doors may swing inward or outward. The doors may be operated by the crane operator or from the floor. Additional doors should be provided for the load, and for the crane cage where necessary.

Folding and sliding doors are also made by the Kinnear Manufacturing Company, Columbus, Ohio.

Rolling Steel Doors.—Rolling steel doors are made by several firms. The J. G. Wilson Corporation, New York, manufactures rolling steel doors that may be operated by hand, with widths of 3 ft. to 6 ft., and heights of 6 ft. to 14 ft.; widths of 6 ft. to 10 ft. and heights of 13 ft. to 17 ft.; widths of 10 ft. to 15 ft. and heights of 13 ft. to 15 ft. Doors operated by gear have widths up to 20 ft. and heights up to 21 ft. The Kinnear Manufacturing Company, Columbus, Ohio, manufactures rolling steel doors with widths of 3 ft. to 20 ft., and heights of 6 ft. to 18 ft. For additional details and the names and addresses of other manufacturers of steel doors, see Sweet's "Architectural Catalog," published by Sweet's Catalog Service, New York, N. Y.

CHAPTER XXXV.

Paints and Painting.

CORROSION OF IRON AND STEEL.—If iron or steel is left exposed to the atmosphere it unites with oxygen and water to form rust. Where the metal is further exposed to the action of corrosive gases the rate of rusting is accelerated but the action is similar to that of ordinary rusting. Neither dry air nor water free from oxygen has any corrosive effect. While not essential to corrosion acids greatly hasten its action. It seems evident that some weak electrolysis is essential for corrosive action. Where iron or steel are in contact with water electrolytic action will always take place, although the amount is very small under ordinary conditions. Where a considerable electrolytic force exists the corrosion is greatly hastened. The increase in the use of electricity has doubtless had a tendency to increase the corrosion of iron and steel and to make the problem of the preservation of iron and steel from corrosion of great importance.

In an article on "The Corrosion of Iron" in Proceedings of American Society for Testing Materials, vol. VII, 1907, pages 211 to 228, Mr. Allerson S. Cushman shows that the two factors without which the corrosion of iron is impossible are electrolysis and the presence of hydrogen in the electrolyzed or "ionic" condition. The electrolytic action can only take place in the presence of oxygen or some other oxidizing agent. Rust is a hydroxide of iron—ferric hydroxide, FeO_3H_3. The corrosion of iron or steel may be prevented or retarded by covering it with a coating that will protect it from the water or the air.

It is commonly believed, with good reason, that cast iron corrodes less rapidly than either wrought iron or steel. The graphite in the cast iron and the silicious coating that the cast iron receives in molding doubtless assist in protecting the cast iron from corrosion.

It is also commonly believed that steel corrodes more rapidly than wrought iron. The tests that have been made to determine the relative corrosion of wrought iron and steel are very conflicting, but it appears certain that the difference in the corrosion of well made steel and well made wrought iron is very slight. The acid test as a measure of natural corrosion has been used, especially by firms manufacturing and selling "ingot iron" (very low carbon open-hearth steel). Committee A-5 on the Corrosion of Iron and Steel of the American Society for Testing Materials in the Proceedings of the Society, vol. XI, 1911, page 100, states *that it considers the acid test as unreliable as a measure of natural corrosion and does not recommend its use.*

In the paper on "The Corrosion of Iron" above referred to, Mr. Cushman states: —"A very widespread impression prevails that charcoal iron or a puddled wrought iron are more resistant to corrosion than steel manufactured by the Bessemer and open-hearth processes. It is by no means certain that this is the case, but it would follow from the electrolytic theory that in order to have the highest resistance to corrosion a metal should either be as free as possible from certain impurities, such as manganese, or should be so homogeneous as not to retain localized positive and negative nodes for a long time without change. Under the first condition iron would appear to have the advantage, but under the second much would depend upon the care exercised in manufacture, whatever process was used."

In Marks' "Mechanical Engineers' Handbook," p. 555, Mr. Morgan B. Smith makes the following statement: "Under similar conditions iron and steel corrode at practically the same rate. Steel, however, corrodes more uniformly than iron."

From the preceding discussion it would appear that neither "ingot iron" nor wrought iron has any advantage in resisting corrosion over a well made structural steel.

PAINT.—The paints in use for protecting structural steel may be divided into oil paints, tar paints, asphalt paints, varnishes, lacquers, and enamel paints. The last two mentioned are too expensive for use on a large scale and will not be considered.

OIL PAINTS.—An oil paint consists of a drying oil or varnish and a pigment, thoroughly mixed together to form a workable mixture. "A good paint is one that is readily applied, has good covering powers, adheres well to the metal, and is durable." The pigment should be inert to the metal to which it is applied and also to the oil with which it is mixed. Linseed oil is commonly used as the varnish or vehicle in oil paints, and is unsurpassed in durability by any other drying oil. Pure linseed oil will, when applied to a metal surface, form a transparent coating that offers considerable protection for a time, but is soon destroyed by abrasion and the action of the elements. To make the coating thicker, harder and more dense, a pigment is added to the oil. An oil paint is analogous to concrete, the linseed oil and pigment in the paint corresponding to the cement and the aggregate in the concrete. The pigments used in making oil paints for protecting metal may be divided into four groups as follows: (1) lead; (2) zinc; (3) iron; (4) carbon.

Linseed Oil.—Linseed oil is made by crushing and pressing flaxseed. The oil contains some vegetable impurities when made, and should be allowed to stand for two or three months to purify and settle before being used. In this form the oil is known as raw linseed oil, and is ready for use. Raw linseed oil dries (oxidizes) very slowly and for that reason is not often used in a pure state for structural iron paint. The rate of drying of raw linseed oil increases with age; an old oil being very much better for paint than that which has been but recently extracted. Raw linseed oil can be made to dry more rapidly by the addition of a drier or by boiling. Linseed oil dries by oxidation and not by evaporation, and therefore any material that will make it take up oxygen more rapidly is a drier. A common method of making a drier for linseed oil is to put the linseed oil in a kettle, heat it to a temperature of 400 to 500 degrees F., and stir in about four pounds of red lead or litharge, or a mixture of the two, to each gallon of oil. This mixture is then thinned down by adding enough linseed oil to make four gallons for each gallon of raw oil first put in the kettle. The addition of four gallons of this drier to forty gallons of raw oil will reduce the time of drying from about five days to twenty-four hours. A drier made in this way costs more than the pure linseed oil, so that driers are very often made by mixing lead or manganese oxide with rosin and turpentine, benzine, or rosin oil. These driers can be made for very much less than the price of good linseed oil, and are used as adulterants; *the more of the drier that is put into the paint, the quicker it will dry and the poorer it becomes.* Japan drier is often used with raw oil, and when this or any other drier is added to raw oil in barrels, the oil is said to be "boiled through the bung hole."

Boiled linseed oil is made by heating raw oil, to which a quantity of red lead, litharge, sugar of lead, etc., has been added, to a temperature of 400 to 500 degrees F., or by passing a current of heated air through the oil. Heating linseed oil to a temperature at which merely a few bubbles rise to the surface makes it dry more rapidly than the unheated oil; however, if the boiling is continued for more than a few hours the rate of drying is decreased by the boiling. Boiled linseed oil is darker in color than raw oil, and is much used for outside paints. It should dry in from 12 to 24 hours when spread out in a thin film on glass. Raw oil makes a stronger and better film than boiled oil, but it dries so slowly that it is seldom used for outside work without the addition of a drier.

Lead.—*White Lead* (hydrated carbonate of lead—specific gravity 6.4) is used for interior and exterior wood work. White lead forms an excellent pigment on account of its high adhesion and covering power, but it is easily darkened by exposure to corrosive gases and rapidly disintegrates under these conditions, requiring frequent renewal. It does not make a good bottom coat for other paints, and if it is to be used at all for metal work it should be used over another paint.

Red Lead (minium; lead tetroxide—specific gravity 8.3) is a heavy, red powder approximating in shade to orange; is affected by acids, but when used as a paint is very stable in light and under exposure to the weather. Red lead is seldom adulterated, about the only substance used for the purpose being red oxide. Red lead is prepared by changing metallic lead into monoxide litharge, and converting this product into minium in calcining ovens. Red lead intended for paints must be free from metallic lead. One ounce of lampblack added to one pound of red lead changes the color to a deep chocolate and increases the time of drying. This compound when mixed in a thick paste will keep 30 days without hardening.

Zinc.—Zinc white (zinc oxide—specific gravity 5.3) is a white loose powder, devoid of smell or taste and has a good covering power. Zinc paint has a tendency to peel, and when exposed there is a tendency to form a zinc soap with the oil which is easily washed off, and it therefore does not make a good paint. However, when mixed with red oxide of lead in the proportions of 1 lead to 3 zinc, or 2 lead to 1 zinc, and ground with linseed oil, it makes a very durable paint for metal surfaces. This paint dries very slowly, the zinc acting to delay hardening about the same as lampblack.

Iron Oxide.—Iron oxide (specific gravity 5) is composed of anhydrous sesquioxide (hematite) and hydrated sesquioxide of iron (iron rust). The anhydrous oxide is the characteristic ingredient of this pigment and very little of the hydrated oxide should be present. Hydrated sesquioxide of iron is simply iron rust, and it probably acts as a carrier of oxygen and accelerates corrosion when it is present in considerable quantities. Mixed with the iron ore are various other ingredients, such as clay, ocher and earthy materials, which often form 50 to 75 per cent of the mass. Brown and dark red colors indicate the anhydrous oxide and are considered the best. Bright red, bright purple and maroon tints are characteristic of hydrated oxide and make less durable paints than the darker tints. Care should be used in buying iron oxide to see that it is finely ground and is free from clay and ocher.

Carbon.—The most common forms of carbon in use for paints are lampblack and graphite. Lampblack (specific gravity 2.6) is a great absorbent of linseed oil and makes an excellent pigment. Graphite (black lead or plumbago—specific gravity 2.4) is a more or less impure form of carbon, and when pure is not affected by acids. Graphite does not absorb nor act chemically on linseed oil, so that the varnish simply holds the particles of pigment together in the same manner as the cement in a concrete. There are two kinds of graphite in common use for paints—the granular and the flake graphite. The Dixon Graphite Co., of Jersey City, uses a flake graphite combined with silica, while the Detroit Graphite Manufacturing Co. uses a mineral ore with a large percentage of graphitic carbon in granulated form. On account of the small specific gravity of the pigment, carbon and graphite paints have a very large covering capacity. The thickness of the coat is, however, correspondingly reduced. Boiled linseed oil should always be used with carbon pigments.

Mixing the Paint.—The pigment should be finely ground and should preferably be ground with the oil. The materials should be bought from reliable dealers, and should be mixed as wanted. If it is not possible to grind the paint, better results will usually be obtained from hand mixed paints made of first-class materials than from the ordinary run of prepared paints that are supposed to have been ground. Many ready mixed paints are sold for less than the price of linseed oil, which makes it evident that little if any oil has been used in the paint. The paint should be thinned with oil, or if necessary a small amount of turpentine may be added; *however turpentine is an adulterant and should be used sparingly. Benzine, gasoline, etc., should never be used in paints,* as the paint dries without oxidizing and then rubs off like chalk.

Proportions.—The proper proportions of pigment and oil required to make a good paint vary with the different pigments, and the methods of preparing the paint; the heavier and the more finely ground pigments require less oil than the lighter or coarsely ground while ground paints require less oil than ordinary mixed paints. A common rule for mixing paints ground in oil is to mix with each gallon of linseed oil, dry pigment equal to three to four times the specific gravity of the pigment, the weight of the pigment being given in pounds. This rule gives the following weights of pigment per gallon of linseed oil: white lead, 19 to 26 lb.; red lead, 25 to 33 lb.; zinc, 15 to 21 lb.; iron oxide, 15 to 20 lb.; lampblack, 8 to 10 lb.; graphite, 8 to 10 lb. The weights of pigment used per gallon of oil varies about as follows: red lead, 20 to 33 lb.; iron oxide, 8 to 25 lb.; graphite, 3 to 12 lb.

Covering Capacity.—The covering capacity of a paint depends upon the uniformity and thickness of the coating; the thinner the coating the larger the surface covered per unit of paint. To obtain any given thickness of paint therefore requires practically the same amount of paint whatever its pigment may be. The claims often urged in favor of a particular paint that it has a large covering capacity may mean nothing but that an excess of oil has been used in its fabrication. An idea of the relative amounts of oil and pigment required, and the covering capacity of different paints may be obtained from Table VI, Chapter XL.

Light structural work will average about 250 square feet, and heavy structural work about 150 square feet of surface per net ton of metal; while No. 20 corrugated steel has 2,400 sq. ft. of surface per ton of metal.

It is the common practice to estimate $\frac{1}{2}$ gallon of paint for the first coat and $\frac{3}{8}$ gallon for the second coat per ton of structural steel, for average conditions.

Applying the Paint.—The paint should be thoroughly brushed out with a round brush to remove all the air. The paint should be mixed only as wanted, and should be kept well stirred. When it is necessary to apply paint in cold weather, it should be heated to a temperature of 130 to 150 degrees F.; paint should not be put on in freezing weather. Paint should not be applied when the surface is damp, or during foggy weather. The first coat should be allowed to stand for three or four days, or until thoroughly dry, before applying the second coat. If the second coat is applied before the first coat has dried, the drying of the first coat will be very much retarded.

Cleaning the Surface.—Before applying the paint all scale, rust, dirt, grease and dead paint should be removed. The metal may be cleaned by pickling in an acid bath, by scraping and brushing with wire brushes, or by means of the sand blast. In the process of pickling the metal is dipped in an acid bath, which is followed by a bath of milk of lime, and afterwards the metal is washed clean in hot water. The method is expensive and not satisfactory unless extreme care is used in removing all traces of the acid. Another objection to the process is that it leaves the metal wet and allows rusting to begin before the paint can be applied. The most common method of cleaning is by scraping with wire brushes and chisels. This method is slow and laborious. The method of cleaning by means of a sand blast has been used to a limited extent and promises much for the future. The average cost of cleaning five bridges in Columbus, Ohio, in 1902, was 3 cts. per sq. ft. of surface cleaned.* The bridges were old and some were badly rusted. The painters followed the sand blast and covered the newly cleaned surface with paint before the rust had time to form.

Mr. Lilly estimates the cost of cleaning light bridge work at the shop with the sand blast at $1.75 per ton, and the cost of heavy bridge work at $1.00 per ton. In order to remove the mill scale it has been recommended that rusting be allowed to start before the sand blast is used. One of the advantages of the sand blast is that it leaves the surface perfectly dry, so that the paint can be applied before any rust has formed.

Priming or Shop Coat.—Engineers are very much divided as to what makes the best priming coat; some specify a first coat of pure linseed oil and others a priming coat of paint. Linseed oil makes a transparent coating that allows imperfections in the workmanship and rusted spots to be easily seen; it is not permanent, however, and if the metal is exposed for a long time the oil will often be entirely removed before the second coat is applied. It is also claimed that the paint will not adhere as well to linseed oil that has weathered as to a good paint. Linseed oil gives better results if applied hot to the metal. Another advantage of using oil as a priming coat is that the erection marks can be painted over with the oil without fear of covering them up. Red lead paint toned down with lampblack is probably used more for a priming coat that any other paint; the B. & O. R. R. uses 10 oz. of lampblack to every 12 lb. of red lead. Linseed oil mixed with a small amount of lampblack makes a very satisfactory priming or shop coat.

Without going further into the controversy it would seem that there is very little choice between linseed oil and a good red lead paint for a priming coat. For data on the standard shop paints specified by different railroads, see digest of specifications in the author's "Structural Engineers' Handbook."

Finishing Coat.—From a careful study of the question of paints, it would seem that for ordinary conditions the quality of the materials and workmanship is of more importance in painting metal structures than the particular pigment used. If the priming coat has been properly applied there is no reason why any good grade of paint com-

*Sand Blast Cleaning of Structural Steel, by G. W. Lilly, Trans. Am. Soc. C. E., Feb. 1903.

posed of pure linseed oil and a very finely ground, stable and chemically non-injurious pigment will not make a very satisfactory finishing coat. Where the paint is to be subjected to the action of corrosive gases or blasts, however, there is certainly quite a difference in the results obtained with the different pigments. The graphite and asphalt paints appear to withstand the corroding action of smelter and engine gases better than red lead or iron oxide paints; while red lead is probably better under these conditions than iron oxide. Portland cement paint or coal tar paint are the only paints that will withstand the action of engine blasts.

To obtain the best results in painting metal structures, therefore, proceed as follows: (1) prepare the surface of the metal by carefully removing all dirt, grease, mill scale, rust, etc., and give it a priming coat of pure linseed oil or a good paint—red lead seems to be the most used for this purpose; (2) after the metal is in place carefully remove all dirt, grease, etc., and apply the finishing coats—preferably not less than two coats—giving ample time for each coat to dry before applying the next. The separate coats of paint should be of different colors. Painting should not be done in rainy weather, or when the metal is damp, nor in cold weather unless special precautions are taken to warm the paint. The best results will usually be obtained if the materials are purchased in bulk from a responsible dealer and the paint ground as wanted. Good results are obtained with many of the patent or ready mixed paints, but it is not possible in this place to go into a discussion of their respective merits.

ASPHALT PAINT.—Many prepared paints are sold under the name of asphalt that are mixtures of coal tar, or mineral asphalt alone, or combined with a metallic base, or oils. The exact compositions of the patent asphalt paints are hard to determine. Black bridge paint made by Edward Smith & Co., New York City, contains asphaltum, linseed oil, turpentine and Kauri gum. The paint has a varnish-like finish and makes a very satisfactory paint. The black shades of asphalt paint are the only ones that should be used.

COAL TAR PAINT.—Coal tar paint is occasionally used for painting gas tanks, smelters, and similar structures that receive rough usage. Coal tar paint mixed as described below has been used by the U. S. Navy Department for painting the hulls of ships. It should give satisfactory service where the metal is subject to corrosion. The coal tar paint is mixed as follows: The proportions of the mixture are slightly variable according to the original consistency of the tar, the use for which it is intended and the climate in which it is used. The proportions will vary between the following proportions in volume.

	Coal Tar.	Portland Cement.	Kerosene Oil.
New Orleans Mixture	8	1	1
Annapolis Mixture	16	4	3

The Portland cement should first be stirred into the kerosene, forming a creamy mixture; the mixture is then stirred into the coal tar. The paint should be freshly mixed and kept well stirred. This paint sticks well, does not run when exposed to the sun's rays and is a very satisfactory paint for rough work. The cost of the paint will vary from 10 to 20 cts. per gallon. The kerosene oil acts as a drier, while the Portland cement neutralizes the coal tar.

If it is desired to paint with oil paint a structure which has been painted with coal tar paint, the surface must be scraped and all the coal tar removed.

CEMENT AND CEMENT PAINT.—Experiments have shown that a thin coating of Portland cement is effective in preventing rust; that a concrete to be effective in preventing rust must be dense and made very wet. The steel must be clean when imbedded in the concrete. There is quite a difference of opinion as to whether the metal should be painted before being imbedded or not. It is probably best to paint the metal if it is not to be imbedded at once, or is not to be used in concrete-steel construction where the adhesion of the cement to the metal is an essential element. When the metal is to be imbedded immediately it is better not to paint it.

Portland Cement Paint.—A Portland cement paint has been used on the High St. viaduct in Columbus, Ohio, with good results. The viaduct was exposed to the fumes and blasts from locomotives, so that an ordinary paint did not last more than six months even on the least exposed portions. The method of mixing and applying the paint is described in Engineering News, April 24th and June 5th, 1902, as follows: "The surface of the metal was thoroughly cleaned with wire brushes and files—the bridge had been cleaned with a sand blast the previous year. A thick coat of Japan drier was then applied and before it had time to dry a coating was applied as follows: Apply with a trowel to the minimum thickness of $\frac{1}{16}$ in. and a maximum thickness of $\frac{1}{4}$ in. (in extreme cases $\frac{1}{2}$ in.) a mixture of 32 lb. Portland cement, 12 lb. dry finely ground lead, 4 to 6 lb. boiled linseed oil, 2 to 3 lb. Japan drier." After a period of about two years the coating was in almost perfect condition and the metal under the coating was as clean as when painted. The cost of the coating including the hand cleaning, materials and labor was 8 cts. per sq. ft.

Gunite.—The metal to be protected is covered with wire mesh or expanded metal reinforcement. The cement mortar is applied to the reinforcement by means of a cement gun. For metal exposed to engine blasts the cement mortar should be at least $1\frac{1}{2}$ in. thick. For a description of the cement gun and of its work, see Journal Western Society of Engineers, Vol. 19, 1914, pp. 272–318.

SPECIFICATIONS.—For specifications for painting steel structures, see § 190 to § 194 and § 211, Appendix I.

References.—For additional data on the subject of paints and painting, see the following:—

Wood's "Rustless Coatings," John Wiley & Sons, Inc.

Wilson's "Corrosion of Iron," McGraw-Hill Book Co., Inc.

Lang's "Corrosion of Iron and Steel," McGraw-Hill Book Co., Inc.

Cushman and Gardner's "Corrosion and Preservation of Iron and Steel," McGraw-Hill Book Co., Inc.

Gardner's "Paint Technology and Tests," McGraw-Hill Book Co., Inc.

Sabin's "Red Lead and How to Use it in Paint," John Wiley & Sons, Inc.

CHAPTER XXXVI.

DESIGN OF A STEEL ROOF TRUSS.

1. **Problem.**—Design a steel roof truss to rest on brick walls. The distance center to center of end connections is 50 ft. 0 in. The type of truss shown in (c), Fig. 4, Chapter XXV, is best suited to this span and will be used. A pitch of $\frac{1}{4}$ will be adopted, making the center height 12 ft. 6 in. Trusses will be spaced 16 ft. 0 in. center to center. The truss is to be designed to comply with the "General Specifications for Steel Frame Buildings," Appendix I.* The properties of sections will be taken from the author's "Structural Engineers' Handbook."

2. **Loads.**—The roof covering will be corrugated steel placed directly on the purlins. The purlins should be spaced for a minimum normal load of 30 lb. per sq. ft., and will be placed at the panel points, or 4 ft. 8 in. centers. From Fig. 4, Chapter XXVIII, it will be seen that No. 18 corrugated steel must be used. Condensation lining weighing about 1.0 lb. per sq. ft. of horizontal projection will be provided. A maximum snow load of 20 lb. per sq. ft. of horizontal projection will be assumed. The minimum snow load will be taken as 10 lb. per sq. ft. of horizontal projection. The wind load will be taken as the normal component of a horizontal wind pressure of 30 lb. per sq. ft. as reduced by Duchemin's formula, (6), Chapter XXIV, and $P_n = 22.4$ lb. per sq. ft. of roof area. The weight of the roof truss per square foot of horizontal projection is estimated by the formula, $w = (P/45)(1 + (L/5\sqrt{A}))$ as given in § 14, Specifications. For an assumed capacity of 40 lb. per sq. ft. of horizontal projection, $w = 3.1$ lb. per sq. ft. of horizontal projection. The approximate weight of the roof will be:—

Trusses	3.1 lb. per sq. ft.
Purlins and bracing	2.9 " " " "
Corrugated Steel	3.0 " " " "
Lining	1.0 " " " "
Total	10.0 lb. per sq. ft. hor. proj.

3. **Panel Loads.**—Each panel has $74.7 \times 0.8944 = 66.8$ sq. ft. horizontal projection, so the dead panel load will be $66.8 \times 10 = 668$ lb. (use 670 lb.). The minimum snow load on each panel is $66.8 \times 10 = 668$ lb. (use 670 lb.). The maximum snow load is $66.8 \times 20 = 1,336$ lb. (use 1,340 lb.). The wind load per panel is $74.7 \times 22.4 = 1,675$ lb.

4. **STRESS DIAGRAMS.**—The stress diagram for dead loads is shown in Fig. 1. The stresses due to snow loads are proportional to the dead load stresses and may be obtained by changing the scale of the dead load stress diagram, or by multiplying the dead load stresses by the ratio of the snow load to the dead load. The stress diagram for wind loads is shown in Fig. 1, and is drawn assuming the left end fixed and the right end free to move.

The maximum stresses are found by combining dead and maximum snow loads, dead and wind loads, and dead, minimum snow and wind loads. Each member will be

* See note on page 552.

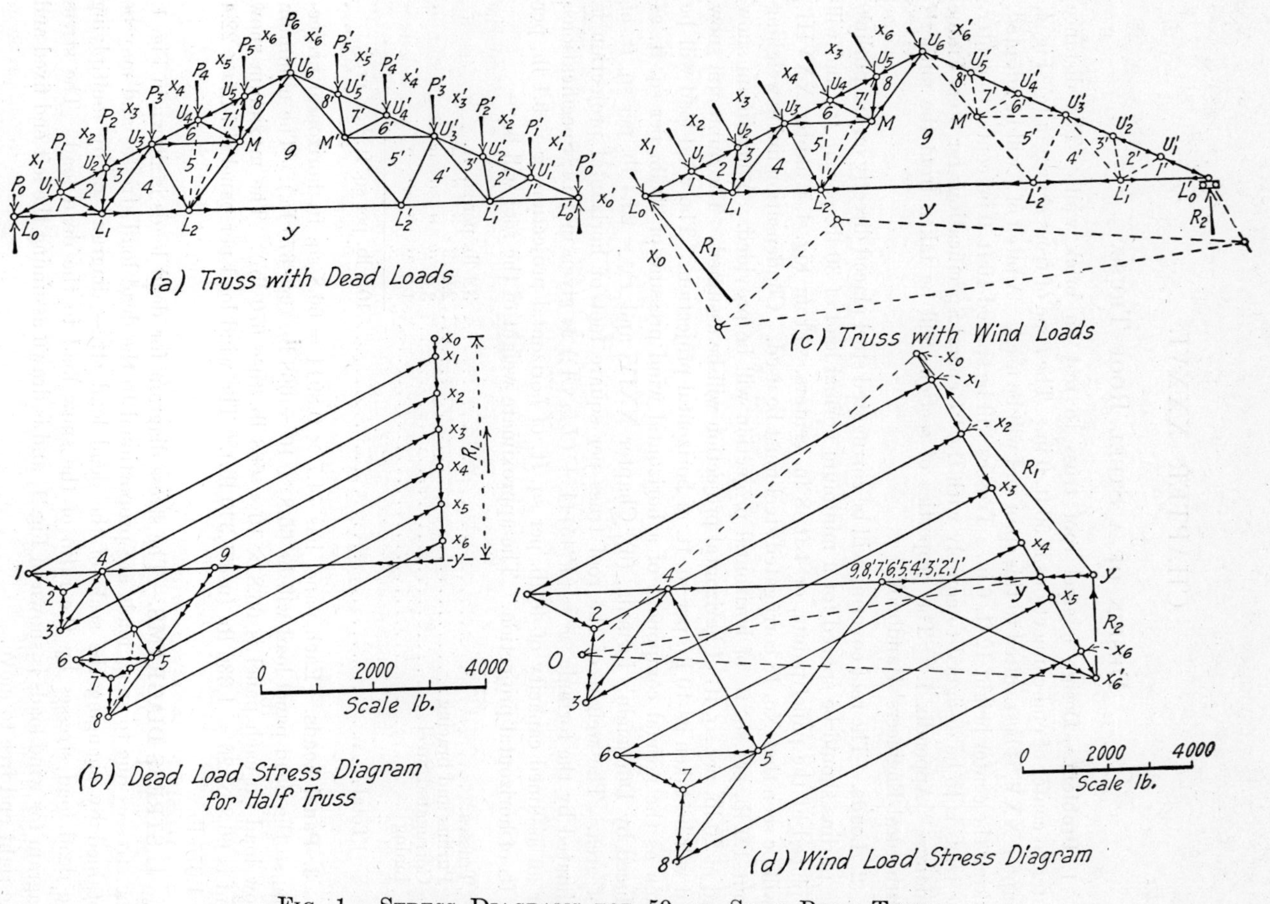

FIG. 1. STRESS DIAGRAMS FOR 50 FT. SPAN ROOF TRUSS.

designed for the combination that gives the greatest stress in that member. The stresses are given in Table I.

TABLE I.

Stresses in Roof Truss in Pounds.

Member.		Dead Load. 1	Max. Snow. 2	Min. Snow. 3	Wind Wind-ward. 4	Wind Lee-ward. 5	Combined Stress. 1 + 2	1 + 3 + 4	1 + 4	Max. Stress. Ten-sion.	Com-pres-sion.
L_0U_1	1-x	+ 8,220	+ 16,440	+ 8,220	+ 12,250	+ 5,600	+ 24,660	+ 28,690	+ 20,470		28,690
U_1U_2	2-x	+ 7,510	+ 15,020	+ 7,510	+ 11,100	+ 5,600	+ 22,530	+ 26,120	+ 18,610		26,120
U_2U_3	3-x	+ 7,615	+ 15,230	+ 7,615	+ 12,250	+ 5,600	+ 22,845	+ 27,480	+ 19,865		27,480
U_3U_4	6-x	+ 7,310	+ 14,620	+ 7,310	+ 12,250	+ 5,600	+ 21,930	+ 26,870	+ 19,560		26,870
U_4U_5	7-x	+ 6,615	+ 13,230	+ 6,615	+ 11,100	+ 5,600	+ 19,845	+ 24,330	+ 17,715		24,330
U_5U_6	8-x	+ 6,725	+ 13,450	+ 6,725	+ 12,250	+ 5,600	+ 20,175	+ 25,700	+ 18,975		25,700
L_0L_1	1-y	− 7,335	− 14,670	− 7,335	− 15,000	− 5,630	− 22,005	− 29,670	− 22,335	29,670	
L_1L_2	4-y	− 6,000	− 12,000	− 6,000	− 11,250	− 5,630	− 18,000	− 23,250	− 17,200	23,250	
L_2L_2'	9-y	− 4,010	− 8,020	− 4,010	− 5,360	− 5,360	− 12,030	− 13,650	− 9,640	13,650	
U_1L_1	1-2	+ 720	+ 1,440	+ 720	+ 2,000		+ 2,160	+ 3,440	+ 2,720		3,440
U_2L_1	2-3	+ 720	+ 1,440	+ 720	+ 2,000		+ 2,160	+ 3,440	+ 2,720		3,440
U_3L_1	3-4	− 1,335	− 2,670	− 1,335	− 3,750		− 4,005	− 6,420	− 5,085	6,420	
U_3L_2	4-5	+ 1,790	+ 3,580	+ 1,790	+ 5,030		+ 5,370	+ 8,610	+ 6,820		8,610
U_3M	5-6	− 1,335	− 2,670	− 1,335	− 3,750		− 4,005	− 6,420	− 5,085	6,420	
U_4M	6-7	+ 720	+ 1,440	+ 720	+ 2,000		+ 2,160	+ 3,440	+ 2,720		3,440
U_5M	7-8	+ 720	+ 1,440	+ 720	+ 2,000		+ 2,160	+ 3,440	+ 2,720		3,440
U_6M	8-9	− 3,345	− 6,690	− 3,345	− 9,430		− 10,035	− 16,120	− 12,775	16,120	
L_2M	5-9	− 2,010	− 4,020	− 2,010	− 5,680		− 6,030	− 9,700	− 7,690	9,700	

5. **Design of Purlins.**—The component of the dead, snow and wind loads in the plane of roof, carried by one purlin is $66.8 \times (6.9 + 10 + 0) \times 0.4463 = 505$ lb. The normal component of the dead, snow and wind loads carried by one purlin is $66.8 \times (6.9 + 10) \times 0.8944 + 74.7 \times 22.4 = 2{,}685$ lb. Sag rods will be provided at the middle of the purlins and will carry the component of the load along the roof, so the purlins need only be designed for the component normal to the roof. The maximum bending moment

$M = 2{,}685 \times 16 \times 12/8 = 64{,}500$ in.-lb. $I/C = M/S = 64{,}500/16{,}000 = 4.03$ in.^{3} A 6 in. channel at 8 lb. has a section modulus of 4.3 in.^{3}, and satisfies the requirement that the depth shall not be less than $\frac{1}{40}$ of the span, so will be used. The same size purlin is given in Table I, Chapter XXV.

6. **DESIGN OF MEMBERS.**—The specifications require, § 109, that the main members shall be composed of sections symmetrically placed, such as two angles back to back. Secondary members such as the sub-struts and the sag tie at the center of the truss are usually made of one angle. Stitch rivets will be used to insure members composed of two angles acting as a unit and the value of l/r for each angle, between stitch rivets, should not exceed l/r for the whole member. The length of a main compression member must not exceed 125 times its least radius of gyration, or 150 times its least radius of gyration for laterals and sub-struts, § 41. The length of a tension member must not exceed 200 times its least radius of gyration, § 42. The distance center to center of end connections is taken as the length of a member, § 36. $\frac{3}{8}$ in. connection

plates and $\frac{5}{8}$ in. diam. rivets will be used. Allowable stresses in rivets are given in § 36 of Specifications and in Table I, Chapter XXVII.

6. **Design of Compression Members.**—*Member* L_0U_6.—The top chord will be made of the same section throughout. Any saving in material effected by using smaller sections for the less stressed members will be overcome by the cost of the extra splices made necessary. Maximum stress = + 28,690 lb. Unsupported length will be taken as 14 ft. = 168 in. l/r must not exceed 125, so minimum r = 168/125 = 1.35 in. Two angles, $3\frac{1}{2}$ in. × 3 in. × $\frac{5}{16}$ in., $\frac{3}{8}$ in. back to back, long legs out, will be tried. r = 1.66, area = 3.86 sq. in. Allowable stress, S = 16,000 — 70 × 168/1.66 = 8,900 lb. per sq. in. Required area = 28,690/8,900 = 3.23 sq. in. Two angles $3\frac{1}{2}$ in. × 3 in. × $\frac{1}{4}$ in. or two angles $3\frac{1}{2}$ in. × $2\frac{1}{2}$ in. × $\frac{5}{16}$ in. are satisfactory as far as stress is concerned, but the larger section will be used to increase the rigidity of the top chord, particularly during erection.

Member U_3L_2.—Maximum stress = + 8,610 lb. Length = 7 ft. 0 in = 84 in. Minimum r = 84/125 = 0.67 in. Try two angles $2\frac{1}{2}$ in. × 2 in. × $\frac{1}{4}$ in., r = 0.78 in., area = 2.12 sq. in. Allowable stress = 16,000 − 70 × 84/0.78 = 8,460 lb. per sq. in. Required area = 8,610 ÷ 8,460 = 1.02 sq. in. Two angles 2 in. × 2 in. × $\frac{1}{4}$ in. (minimum section) give a value of l/r = 84/0.61 = 138, which is too large. Two angles $2\frac{1}{2}$ in. × 2 in. × $\frac{1}{4}$ in. will be used.

Sub-strut U_1L_1.—Maximum stress = + 3,440 lb. Length = 4 ft. 3 in. = 51 in. Minimum r = 51/150 = 0.34 in. Try one angle 2 in. × 2 in. × $\frac{1}{4}$ in. (minimum section). r = 0.39 in., area = 0.94 sq. in. Allowable stress, S = 16,000 − 70 × 51/0.39 = 6,840 lb. per sq. in. Required area = 3,440 ÷ 6,840 = 0.50 sq. in. Sufficient area is provided. All sub-struts will be made of one angle 2 in. × 2 in. × $\frac{1}{4}$ in.

7. **Design of Tension Members.**—*Member* L_0L_2.—Members L_0L_1 and L_1L_2 will be made of the same section. It usually will be found that any saving in material in member L_1L_2 will be offset by the extra cost of the connection at joint L_1. A field splice will be provided at joint L_2 in order to facilitate shipment of parts of the truss. Maximum stress = − 29,670 lb. Required net area = 29,670 ÷ 16,000 = 1.85 sq. in. Two angles $2\frac{1}{2}$ in. × $2\frac{1}{2}$ in. × $\frac{1}{4}$ in. furnish a net area of 2.00 sq. in. (assuming $\frac{5}{8}$ in. diam. rivets and one hole deducted). l/r = 15.6 × 12 ÷ 1.19 = 157. l/r must not exceed 200. Two angles $2\frac{1}{2}$ in. × $2\frac{1}{2}$ in. × $\frac{1}{4}$ in. will be used.

Member L_2L_2'.—Maximum stress = − 13,650 lb. Required net area = 13,650 ÷ 16,000 = 0.86 sq. in. Two angles 2 in. × 2 in. × $\frac{1}{4}$ in. will be found to give sufficient area but will not satisfy the requirement that l/r must not exceed 200. Minimum r = 18.8 × 12 ÷ 200 = 1.13 in. Two angles $2\frac{1}{2}$ in. × $2\frac{1}{2}$ in. × $\frac{1}{4}$ in., $\frac{3}{8}$ in. back to back, have a value of r = 1.19 in. Using a sag tie of sufficient strength to afford support at the middle of member L_2L_2', the minimum r around a horizontal axis must be r = 9.4 × 12 ÷ 200 = 0.57 in. Two angles $2\frac{1}{2}$ in. × $2\frac{1}{2}$ in. × $\frac{1}{4}$ in. satisfy this requirement, so will be used.

Member U_3L_1.—Maximum stress = − 6,420 lb. Required net area = 6,420 ÷ 16,000 = 0.40 sq. in. Two angles 2 in. × 2 in. × $\frac{1}{4}$ in. furnish 1.50 sq. in. l/r = 7.8 × 12/0.61 = 153. One angle 3 in. × $2\frac{1}{2}$ in. × $\frac{1}{4}$ in. or one angle $2\frac{1}{2}$ in. × $2\frac{1}{2}$ in. × $\frac{1}{4}$ in. will furnish sufficient area, but since U_3L_1 is a main member it will be made of a symmetrical section with 2 angles 2 in. × 2 in. × $\frac{1}{4}$ in.

Member U_3M will be made of the same section.

Member U_6M.—Maximum stress = − 16,120 lb. Required net area = 16,120 ÷ 16,000 = 1.01 sq. in. Two angles 2 in. × 2 in. × $\frac{1}{4}$ in. (minimum section) furnish a net area of 1.50 sq. in. $l/r = 15.6 \times 12/0.99 = 189$. Even if the section for member U_6M could be reduced, no economy would result on account of the splice at joint M. Members U_6M and ML_2 will be made of two angles 2 in. × 2 in. × $\frac{1}{4}$ in.

8. **Design of Joints.**—Sufficient rivets will be furnished at each joint to develop the full strength of all members meeting at the joint. $\frac{3}{8}$-in. gusset plates and $\frac{5}{8}$-in. rivets will be used. An allowable unit shearing stress of 12,000 lb. per sq. in. for shop rivets and 10,000 lb. per sq. in. for field rivets will be used. A bearing stress of 24,000 lb. per sq. in. for shop rivets and 20,000 lb. per sq. in. for field rivets will be used. At least two rivets will be used at the end of each member. For allowable stresses in rivets, see § 36 Specifications, and Table I, Chapter XXVII.

Member L_0U_6 will require 3.86 × 8,900 ÷ 5,630 = 6 shop rivets at L_0, since bearing on a $\frac{3}{8}$-in. plate controls the number of rivets. At joints U_1, U_2, U_3, U_4 and U_5, sufficient rivets must be provided to transfer the panel load to the gusset plate. One will be sufficient, but at least two will be provided. At joint U_6 either the right or left section of the truss will have to be field-riveted to the gusset plate, the other being shop-riveted. It is desirable to keep the gusset plate symmetrical about the center line of the truss, so the number of rivets will be determined by the field connection and will be 3.86 × 8,900 ÷ 4,690 = 8 rivets. At joint L_0, member L_0L_1 will require 2.00 × 16,000 ÷ 5,630 = 6 shop rivets. The number of rivets in the lower chord at joint L_1 will be determined by the maximum difference in stress between members L_0L_1 and L_1L_2, and will be 6,420 ÷ 5,630 = 2 shop rivets. At joint L_2, member L_1L_2 requires 2.00 × 16,000 ÷ 5,630 = 6 shop rivets. Member L_2L_2' will be field-riveted at both ends and will require 2.00 × 16,000 ÷ 4,690 = 7 field rivets. The connection plate for the bracing in the plane of the lower chord may take one-half of the rivets for these members. The sub-struts each require 0.94 × 6,840 ÷ 3,680 = 2 shop rivets. Members U_3L_1 and U_3M each require 1.50 × 16,000 ÷ 5,630 = 4 shop rivets at U_3 and 1.50 × 16,000 ÷ 5,630 = 4 shop rivets at joints L_2 and M respectively. Considerable excess cross section area is furnished in these members, in order to use a symmetrical section and, since 4 rivets require an unnecessarily large gusset plate, the number of rivets will be reduced to 3. Two rivets are ample to transfer the calculated stress in the member. Member U_3L_2 requires 2.12 × 8,460 ÷ 5,630 = 4 shop rivets. Member U_6M will be shop-riveted or field-riveted at joint U_6. The number of rivets required will be 1.50 × 16,000 ÷ 4,690 = 6 rivets. At joint M, member U_6M requires sufficient rivets to transfer the maximum difference in stress in members U_6M and ML_2, or 6,420 ÷ 3,750 = 2 shop rivets, the same as at joint L_1. At joint L_2, member ML_2 requires 1.50 × 16,000 ÷ 5,630 = 5 shop rivets.

In this design, the shoe brings the end reaction directly to the gusset plate. The resultant reaction due to dead load, wind load and minimum snow load is 15,000 lb., so the required number of rivets between the shoe angles and the gusset plate is 15,000 ÷ 5,630 = 3 shop rivets. The required area of the bed plate is determined by the vertical component of the reaction, and will be 14,300 ÷ 250 = 57 sq. in. The allowable bearing on brick masonry is taken as 250 lb. per sq. in. If the bearing value of the masonry is to develop a bending stress of 16,000 lb. per sq. in. in the plate, the thickness of the plate should be 0.54 in. A 10 in. × 12 in. × $\frac{5}{8}$ in. plate connected to the gusset plate by $2\frac{1}{2}$ in. × $2\frac{1}{2}$ in. × $\frac{3}{8}$ in. angles will be used.

TABLE II.

DETAILS OF DESIGN OF MEMBERS.

Member.		Maximum Stress.		Section.	Area, Sq. In.,		l in.	r in.	l/r		Out-standing Leg.	Unit Stresses.				Rivets $\frac{5}{8}$ in. dia.	
												Compression.		Tension.			
		Compression, lb.	Tension, lb.		Gross.	Net.			All.	Act.		Allowable, lb.	Actual, lb.	Allowable, lb.	Actual, lb.	Ends.	Int.
L_0U_1	1–x	28,690		2∠s $3\frac{1}{2} \times 3 \times \frac{5}{16}$	3.86		168	1.66	125	101	l	8,900	7,450			6	1
U_1U_2	2–x	26,120		2∠s $3\frac{1}{2} \times 3 \times \frac{5}{16}$	3.86		168	1.66	125	101	l	8,900	6,800				1
U_2U_3	3–x	27,480		2∠s $3\frac{1}{2} \times 3 \times \frac{5}{16}$	3.86		168	1.66	125	101	l	8,900	7,100				1
U_3U_4	6–x	26,870		2∠s $3\frac{1}{2} \times 3 \times \frac{5}{16}$	3.86		168	1.66	125	101	l	8,900	6,950				1
U_4U_5	7–x	24,330		2∠s $3\frac{1}{2} \times 3 \times \frac{5}{16}$	3.86		168	1.66	125	101	l	8,900	6,300				1
U_5U_6	8–x	25,700		2∠s $3\frac{1}{2} \times 3 \times \frac{5}{16}$	3.86		168	1.66	125	101	l	8,900	6,650			8*	
L_0L_1	1–y		29,670	2∠s $2\frac{1}{2} \times 2\frac{1}{2} \times \frac{1}{4}$	2.38	2.00	187	1.19	200	157				16,000	14,835	6	2
L_1L_2	4–y		23,250	2∠s $2\frac{1}{2} \times 2\frac{1}{2} \times \frac{1}{4}$	2.38	2.00	187	1.19	200	157				16,000	11,625	6	
L_2L_2'	9–y		13,650	2∠s $2\frac{1}{2} \times 2\frac{1}{2} \times \frac{1}{4}$	2.38	2.00	225	1.19	200	189				16,000	6,825	7*	
U_1L_1	1–2	3,440		1∠ $2 \times 2 \times \frac{1}{4}$	0.94		51	0.39	150	131		6,840	3,650			2	
U_2L_1	2–3	3,440		1∠ $2 \times 2 \times \frac{1}{4}$	0.94		51	0.39	150	131		6,840	3,650			2	
U_3L_1	3–4		6,420	2∠s $2 \times 2 \times \frac{1}{4}$	1.88	1.50	94	0.61	200	153				16,000	4,275	4	
U_3L_2	4–5	8,610		2∠s $2\frac{1}{2} \times 2 \times \frac{1}{4}$	2.12		84	0.78	125	108	s	8,460	4,050			4	
U_3M	5–6		6,420	2∠s $2 \times 2 \times \frac{1}{4}$	1.88	1.50	94	0.61	200	153				16,000	4,275	4	
U_4M	6–7	3,440		1∠ $2 \times 2 \times \frac{1}{4}$	0.94		51	0.39	150	131		6,840	3,650			2	
U_5M	7–8	3,440		1∠ $2 \times 2 \times \frac{1}{4}$	0.94		51	0.39	150	131		6,840	3,650			2	
U_6M	8–9		16,120	2∠s $2 \times 2 \times \frac{1}{4}$	1.88	1.50	187	0.99	200	189				16,000	10,750	6*	2
L_2M	5–9		9,700	2∠s $2 \times 2 \times \frac{1}{4}$	1.88	1.50	187	0.99	200	189				16,000	6,500	5	

* Field rivets.

Anchor bolts $\frac{3}{4}$ in. in diam. will be used. These bolts pass through slotted holes to provide for expansion. A temperature variation of 150° F. must be provided for, so the length of slot must be at least $50 \times 12 \times 150 \times 0.0000065 = 0.585$ in.

9. **Minor Details.**—Compression members composed of two angles should be riveted together at intervals such that l/r for the angle will not exceed l/r for the member. This spacing should not exceed 39 in. in the top chord and $84 \times 0.42 \div 0.78 = 45$ in. for member U_3L_2. The usual practice is to space stitch rivets about 30 in. apart. Tension members composed of two angles are generally connected by similar rivets spaced from 36 to 48 in. Ring fills, the same thickness as the gusset plates, must be placed between the angles.

Clip angles 4 in. $\times$ 3 in. $\times$ $\frac{5}{16}$ in. will be used for attaching the purlins to the top chord. One angle 2 in. $\times$ 2 in. $\times$ $\frac{1}{4}$ in. with two field rivets at each end will be used as a sag tie on the center line of the truss.

Sag rods $\frac{5}{8}$ in. in diam. will be placed at the middle points of the purlins in order to carry the component of the load along the roof. See § 58 and § 59, Specifications, and Fig. 25, Chapter XXV.

10. **Lateral Bracing.**—The trusses will be placed in units of two, braced as shown in Fig. 2. The lateral bracing will be designed to satisfy the l/r requirement, assuming the members to act in tension. Member L_0U_3 will be fastened at the middle and its length will be 10 ft. 8 in. or 128 in. l/r must not exceed 250, so minimum $r = 128/250 = 0.51$ in. One angle 3 in. $\times$ $2\frac{1}{2}$ in. $\times$ $\frac{1}{4}$ in. will satisfy this requirement. The same section will be used for all the bracing in the plane of the top chord.

Member L_0L_2 in the plane of the lower chord will be fastened at the middle, so its effective length is 11 ft. 2 in. or 134 in. Minimum $r = 134/250 = 0.54$ in. One angle 3 in. $\times$ 3 in. $\times$ $\frac{1}{4}$ in. satisfies this requirement and will be used. Member L_2L_2' has a length of 12 ft. 4 in. or 148 in. Minimum $r = 148/250 = 0.59$ in. One angle 3 in. $\times$ 3 in. $\times$ $\frac{1}{4}$ in. will be used. Member L_2L_2 will be designed as a strut; l/r must not exceed 150, so minimum $r = 16 \times 12/150 = 1.28$ in. Two angles 4 in. $\times$ 3 in. $\times$ $\frac{1}{4}$ in., *3* in. back to back, just satisfy this requirement and will be used.

11. **Drawings.**—A detail drawing of this truss is shown in Fig. 2. A detailed estimate of the weight of this truss is given in Table I, Chapter XL.

THE 1921 EDITION OF GENERAL SPECIFICATIONS FOR STEEL FRAME BUILDINGS.

The designs in Chapters XXXVI, XXXVII and XXXVIII were made to comply with the 1921 edition of General Specifications for Steel Frame Buildings. These specifications as used in the designs were the same as the revised specifications in Appendix I with the following exceptions:

36. **Compressive Stress.**—

$$S = 16{,}000 - 70\frac{l}{r}$$

The maximum value of S shall be 14,000 per sq. in.

37. **Tensile Stress.**—Shapes, main members, net section; bars, and bottom flanges of rolled beams, 16,000 lb. per sq. in.

38. **Bending.**—Rolled shapes, built sections and girders, 16,000 lb. per sq. in. Pins, 24,000 lb. per sq. in.

39. **Shearing.**—Shop driven rivets and pins, 12,000; field driven rivets and turned bolts, 10,000; plate girder webs, net section 10,000 lb. per sq. in.

40. **Bearing.**—Shop driven rivets and pins, 24,000; field driven rivets and turned bolts, 20,000 lb. per sq. in.

Rivets shall not be used in direct tension, except for lateral bracing where unavoidable, in which case the value for direct tension on the rivet shall be taken the same as for single shear.

51. **Compression Flanges.**—For $20{,}000 - 200l/b$ substitute $16{,}000 - 150l/b$.

52. **Web Stiffeners.**—For $h = t(18{,}000 - s)/100$ substitute $d = t(12{,}000 - s)/40$ where d is clear distance between stiffeners.

54. **Rolled Beams.**—For 10 times the span substitute 20 times the span, and for $20{,}000 - 200l/b$ substitute $16{,}000 - 150l/b$.

57. For 18,000 substitute 16,000 lb. per sq. in.

59. For 18,000 substitute 16,000 lb. per sq. in.

CHAPTER XXXVII.

Design of Beams and Plate Girders.

DESIGN OF BEAMS.*—A beam carrying loads acting normal to the beam is designed for shear and bending moment. If the shearing stresses were uniformly distributed the unit shearing stress would be

$$f_v = V/A \tag{1}$$

where f_v is the unit shearing stress, V is the total shear on the section, and A is the area of the section of the beam. The shearing stresses are not uniformly distributed, but vary from zero at the extreme fiber to a maximum at the neutral axis. For a rectangular beam the maximum unit shear will be $3V/2A$, for a circular beam the maximum unit shear will be $4V/3A$, while for an I-beam or for an I-shaped built-up plate girder the maximum unit shear is very closely equal to $6V/5A$. For steel I-beams and for plate girders the allowable shear in specifications is given for average shear and it will therefore be sufficiently accurate to assume the maximum unit shear as equal to the average unit shear.

The bending moment at any point in a beam is resisted by the moment of the tensile and the compressive stresses. If f = the unit stress on any fiber at the upper or lower surface of the beam due to bending moment, c = the distance of the fiber from the neutral axis of the beam, and M = the bending moment due to the external forces, then

$$M = f \cdot I/c, \quad \text{or} \quad f = M \cdot c/I \tag{2}$$

where I is the moment of inertia of the cross-section of the beam.

In designing beams it is convenient to use the ratio $S = I/c$, so that $M = f \cdot S$ or $f = M/S$. The ratio S is known as the section modulus.

Values of I, c, S, and other properties of I-beams, channels, angles and other structural shapes are given in the author's "Structural Engineers' Handbook."

The allowable stresses for shear and bending stresses in beams are given in Appendix I.

If a beam is not supported to prevent lateral deflection, the allowable bending stress must be reduced. The allowable bending stress for bending in the upper fiber in a beam that is not braced to prevent lateral deflection may be obtained from the column formula

$$f_c' = 16{,}000 - 150l/b$$

where b is the breadth of the upper flange and l is the unsupported span, both in inches. The specifications in Appendix I require that when rolled beams are used as girders, the allowable unit stress when l/b is greater than 20 shall be determined by the formula, $16{,}000 - 150l/b$.

Girders are frequently made of two I-beams fastened together, by means of bolts and separators closely spaced as shown in Fig. 2.

* See note on page 552.

DESIGN OF PLATE GIRDERS.—A plate girder consists of a vertical steel web plate to whose top and bottom edges are riveted horizontal pairs of angles to form flanges, and to whose ends are attached vertical angles which transmit the load to the supports. Where the web plate is thin as compared with its depth, stiffener angles are riveted on opposite sides of the web, usually in pairs, at intervals not greater than the depth of the girder, or six feet. Where the span is long, two or more plates are spliced together to form the web plate, and horizontal plates are riveted to the flange angles to increase the flange area.

Standard specifications limit the minimum thickness of the web plates to $\frac{3}{8}$ in. for railroad bridges and $\frac{5}{16}$ in. for highway bridges and for buildings. For heavy loads and long spans the web plates are made much thicker than the minimum thickness. Thin webs require more stiffeners and give a much shorter life to the girder.

The simplest form of a flange consists of a pair of unequal-legged angles with the long legs placed out and the short legs riveted to the web plate. When additional rivets are required in the connection of the flanges to the web plate, equal-legged angles with two rows of rivets are used. When additional area is required, one or more cover plates are usually riveted to the horizontal legs of the angles. The thickness of the flanges should be limited so that the rivets will not be longer than five times the diameter of the rivet. Flange angles should never be thinner than the web plates to which they are fastened. Where more than one flange plate is used, one plate should extend the full length of the girder, the others being continued a short distance (not less than one foot) beyond the point where the plate is required. For steam or electric railway plate girder bridges and in crane girders, the rivet heads and the variation in the thickness of the flange plates makes it necessary to notch the cross-ties unequally on bridges, or to put blocking under the rails on crane girders, so that other forms of flange are sometimes used for the upper flanges of long girders. It is quite the common practice to design the tension or bottom flange to take the stresses and then make the compression or upper flange with the same gross area.

Stresses in Plate Girders.—The maximum shears and moments are calculated as described in Chapter IV and Chapter V. Plate girders may be designed by using the moments of inertia of the cross-section of the girder, or by assuming that the flanges are concentrated at their centers of gravity, in which case one-eighth of the web is taken as effective as flange area. The shear is assumed as all taken by the web plate.

The following nomenclature will be used.

A_F = gross area of one flange, in sq. in.
A_F' = net area of one flange in sq. in.
$A_w = t \cdot h$ = area web plate in sq. in.
h = distance between centers of gravity of the flanges in in.
h' = distance between gage lines of rivets in tension and compression flanges in in.
M = resisting moment of the section in in.-lb.
V = vertical shear at the section in lb.
I = moment of inertia of gross section in in.^{4}
I' = moment of inertia of net section in in.^{4}
c = distance in in. from neutral axis to extreme fiber.
d = distance in inches from neutral axis to any rivet.
t = thickness of web plate in in.

f = allowable stresses in flanges in lb. per sq. in.
p = pitch of rivets in flanges in in.
r = allowable resistance of one rivet in lb.
$2n$ = number of rivets on one side of a web splice.
w = concentrated load in lb. per unit length of rail = P/l, where P = concentrated load in lb., and l = distance in in. over which load P is considered as uniformly distributed, usually taken for crane girders as 25 inches.

Flange Area.—The moment of inertia of the gross cross-section of a plate girder is approximately, $I = 2A_F(\frac{1}{2}h)^2 + t \cdot h^3/12$, and $c = \frac{1}{2}h$. Then from equation (2)

$$\begin{aligned} M &= f \cdot I/c \\ &= A_F \cdot f \cdot h + t \cdot f \cdot h^2/6 \\ &= A_F \cdot f \cdot h + A_w \cdot f \cdot h/6 \\ &= f(A_F + A_w/6)h \end{aligned} \tag{3}$$

This shows that approximately one-sixth of the web is available as flange area if the gross areas are considered. On account of the reduction of the flange area due to rivet holes, one-eighth of the area of the web may be taken as available as flange area, and

$$M = f(A_F' + A_w/8)h \tag{4}$$

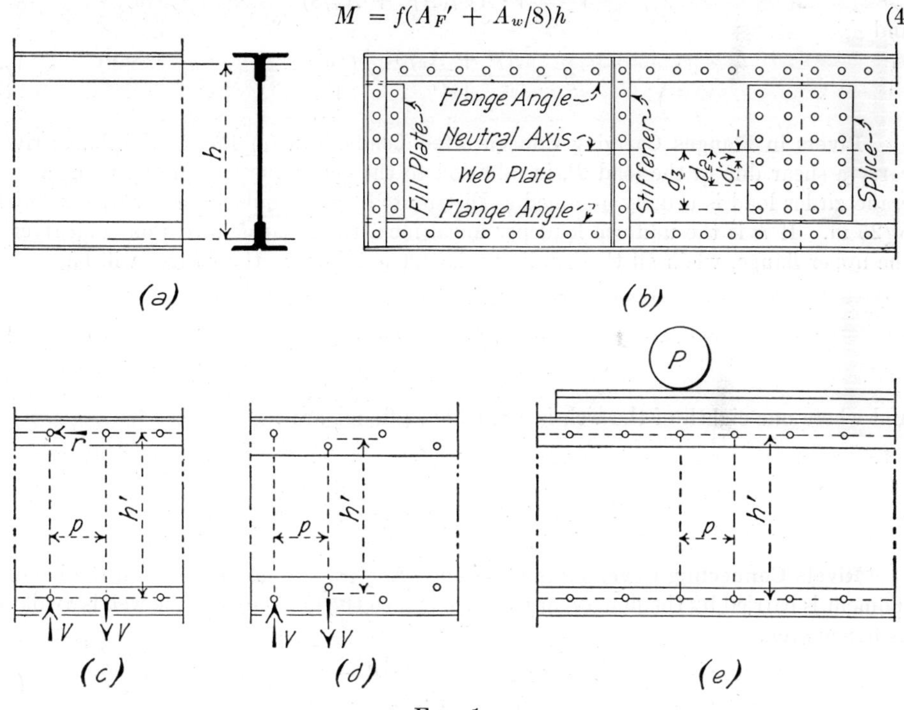

FIG. 1.

Equation (4) may be obtained from (*a*) Fig. 1, by equating the moment of the couple with forces $f(A_F' + A_w/8)$ acting with an arm h, to the resisting moment M.

If the flanges are assumed to take all the bending moment

$$M = f \cdot A_F' \cdot h \tag{5}$$

The net section of the tension flange is to be determined as described in Chapter XXVII, and as specified in § 47, Appendix I. Rivet holes are to be taken as $\frac{1}{8}$ in. larger than the nominal size of the rivet.

In designing the compression flange the unit stress should not exceed 16,000 $- 150l/b$ lb. per sq. in., where l = unsupported length of upper flange, and b = width of flange, both in inches. Tension and compression flanges should preferably have the same gross area.

Rivets in Flanges.—The loads produce shearing stresses in the web, which are transferred to the flanges by means of stresses in the rivets that fasten the flanges to the web plate. In (*c*) Fig. 1, by taking moments about the lower left hand rivet,

$$V \cdot p = r \cdot h'$$

and

$$p = r \cdot h'/V \tag{6}$$

If one-eighth of the web is available as flange area, the proportion of the shear producing flange stress will be

$$V' = V \cdot A_F'/(A_F' + A_w/8)$$

and

$$p = \frac{A_F' + A_w/8}{A_F'} \times \frac{r \cdot h'}{V} \tag{7}$$

Rivets in Flanges Carrying Concentrated Loads.—In (*e*) Fig. 1, the flange rivets carry a shear due to the load P, in addition to the shear due to bending moment. A crane girder load is usually assumed as distributed by the rail uniformly over a length of 25 in. If w is the uniform load per lineal inch, the shearing stress on each rivet in the upper flange, when all the bending moment is taken by the flanges will be

$$p = \frac{r}{\sqrt{w^2 + \left(\frac{V}{h'}\right)^2}} \tag{8}$$

and where one-eighth of the web is available as flange are

$$p = \frac{r}{\sqrt{w^2 + \left(\frac{A_F'}{A_F' + A_w/8} \cdot \frac{V}{h'}\right)^2}} \tag{9}$$

Rivets Connecting Cover Plates to Flange Angles.—Assuming that all the bending moment is carried by the flanges, or that one-eighth the gross area of the web is available as flange area,

$$p = \frac{n \cdot r \cdot d \cdot A_F}{V \cdot A_c} \tag{10}$$

where n = number of rivets on one transverse line;
r = value of one rivet in single shear or bearing;
d = distance back to back of angles;
A_c = total net area of cover plates in one flange.

Web Splice.—An ordinary web splice is shown in Fig. 1. Two lines of rivets should be used in each section of the web. The rivet most remote from the neutral axis is the most severely stressed.

(1) Assuming that all the bending moment is carried by the flanges,

$$r = V/2n, \qquad \text{and} \qquad 2n = V/r \tag{11}$$

where $2n$ is the number of rivets on one side of web splice.

(2) Assuming that one-eighth the area of web is available as flange area. The stress in the outermost rivet is given by the formula, where M' is moment carried by web and d is the distance from the neutral axis of the girder to any rivet,

$$r = \sqrt{\left(\frac{V}{2n}\right)^2 + \left(\frac{M' \cdot d_n}{2\Sigma d^2}\right)^2} \tag{12}$$

Flange Splice.—Flanges should never be spliced unless it is impossible to get material of the required length. Flange splices should always be located at points where there is an excess of flange section; no two parts of the flange should be spliced within two feet of each other. Rivets in splice plates and angles should be located as close together as possible in order that the transfer may take place in a short distance. No allowance should be made for abutting edges of spliced members of the compression flange.

Flange angles should be spliced with a splice angle of equal section riveted to both legs of the angle spliced. Where this is impossible the largest possible splice angle should be used and the difference made up by a plate riveted to the vertical leg of the opposite angle. The number of rivets required in the splice angle on each side of the joint in the angle is given by the formula

$$n = \frac{f \cdot A}{r} \tag{13}$$

where f = the allowable unit stress in the flange, A = area of spliced angle, and r = allowable stress on one rivet. Rivets which are already considered as transferring the shear may be considered as splice rivets if they are included in the splice angle.

Cover plates should be spliced with a splice plate of equal section. The number of rivets required in the splice plate on each side of the joint is determined by the above formula if the plates are in direct contact in the same way as for splice angles. Where one or more plates intervene between the splice plate and cover plate which it splices, rivets should be used on each side of the joint in excess of the number required in case of direct contact, to an extent of one-third that number for each intervening plate.

Design of Web Stiffeners.—Web stiffeners are used to prevent the buckling of the web plate, and are usually spaced somewhat less than the depth of the girder. There is no rational method for the design of stiffener angles. Tests show that the stiffener acts as a beam to prevent buckling of the web and is not appreciably stressed in the direction of its length, except where it is used at points of concentrated loading. A common specification is that "The distance between stiffeners shall not exceed that given by the following formula (and not greater than the clear depth of the web); $d = t(12{,}000 - s)/40$, where d = clear distance between stiffeners of flange angles, t = thickness of web, s = shear in lb. per sq. in. Where stiffeners are required they shall

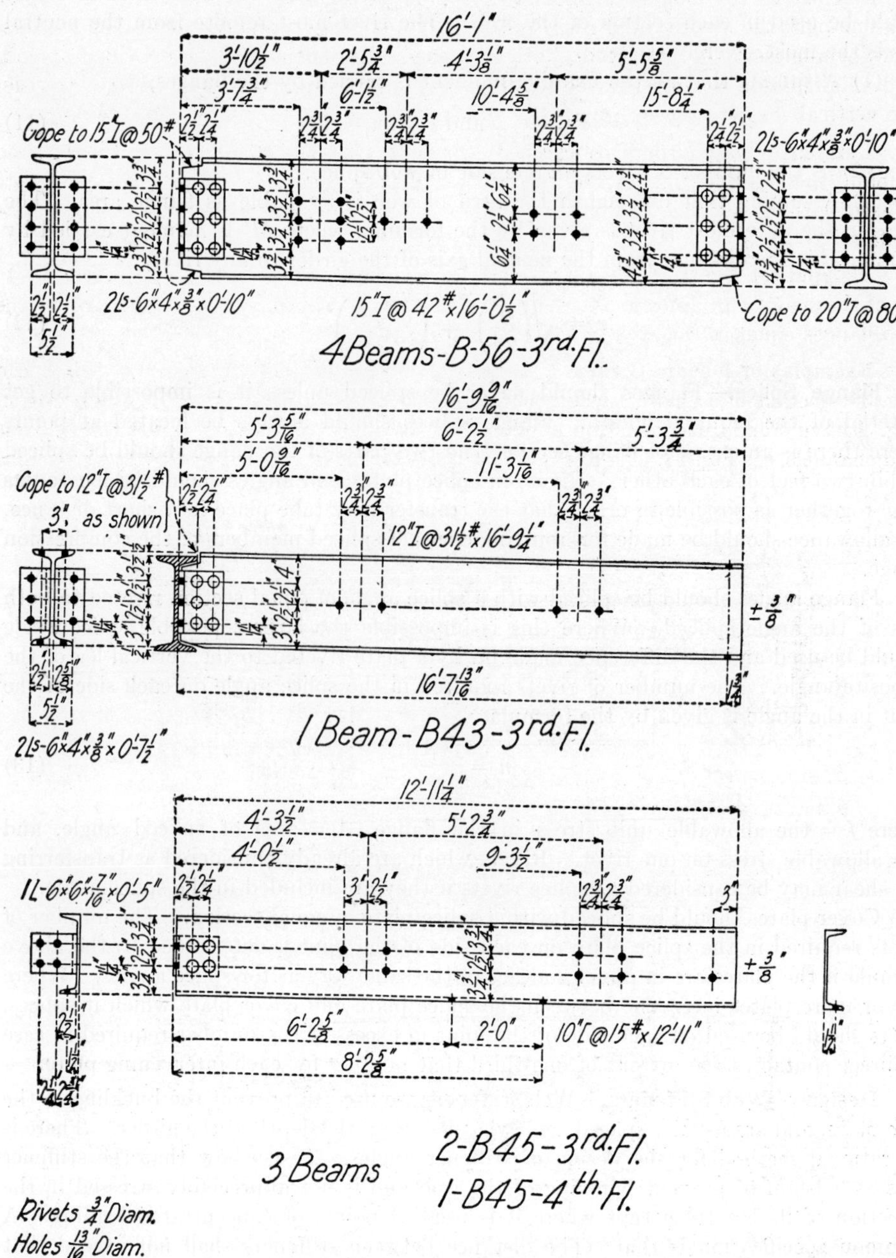

FIG. 2. STANDARD DETAILS FOR ROLLED BEAMS.

be designed as columns with an allowable unit stress of $P = 16{,}000 - 70l/r$, where l = one-half the depth of girder and r = radius of gyration of the stiffener angles at right angles to the web plate, both in inches. Stiffeners shall be provided at ends and at all points of concentrated loading, and shall contain enough rivets to transfer the vertical shear to the web plate."

Camber.—Plate girders are cambered by separating the web plates by the required amount, in the upper part of the web splice. Plate girders in which a single web plate is used without a splice cannot be cambered. Many engineers do not camber plate girders.

Economical Depth.—Plate girders are commonly made with a depth of from $\frac{1}{8}$ to $\frac{1}{12}$ of the span. An approximate empirical rule for the depth is to make the area of the two flanges equal to the area of the web plate.

Examples of I-beam Girders.—Details of I-beam girders are shown in Fig. 2 and Fig. 3. Details of a channel when used as a girder are shown in Fig. 2. The beams in Fig. 2 have standard connection angles. For standard connection angles for I-beams and channels, see Fig. 18, Chapter XXVII. The girder in Fig. 3 is made of two I-beams

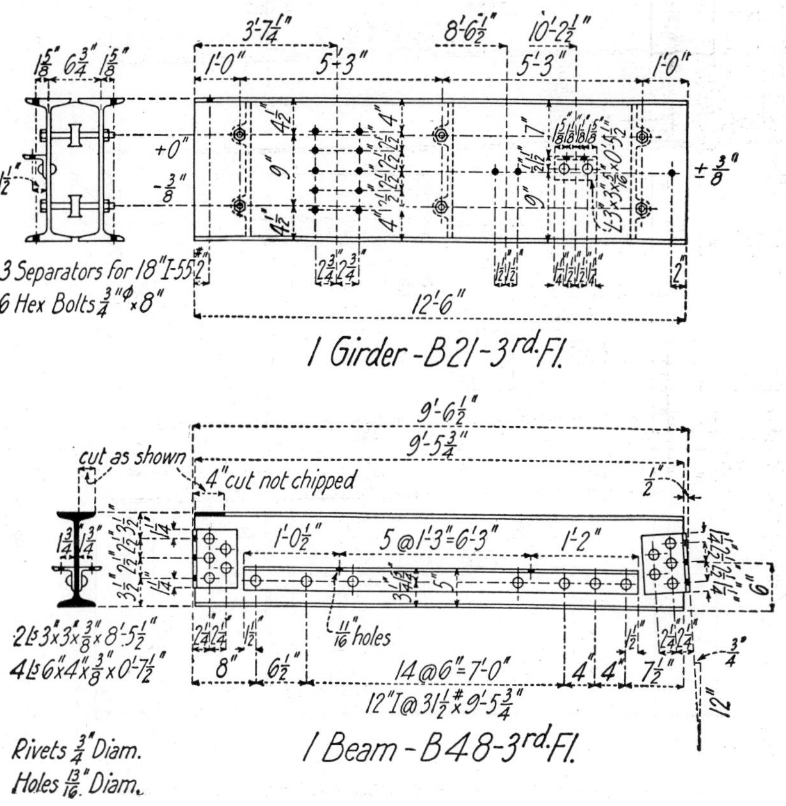

FIG. 3. STANDARD DETAILS FOR ROLLED BEAMS.

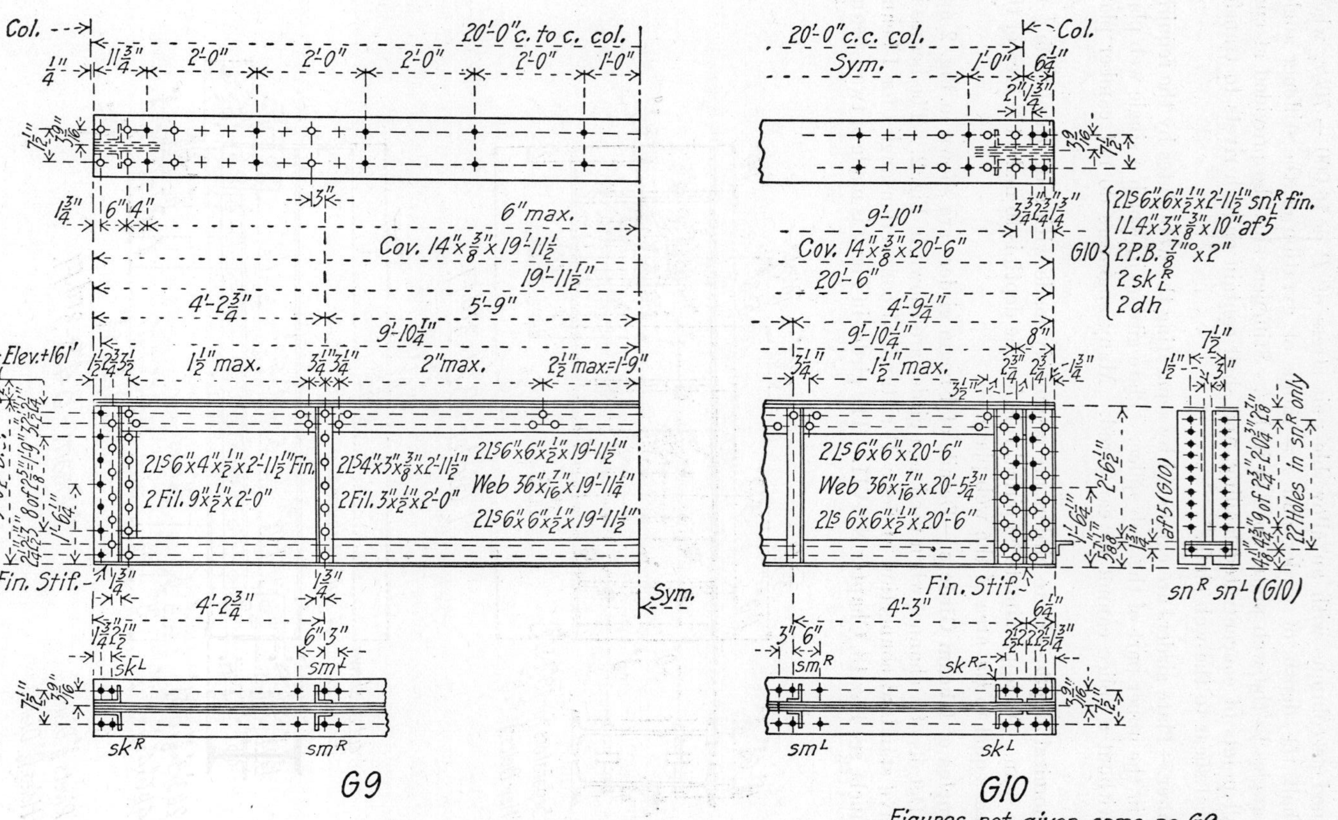

FIG. 4. DETAILS OF CRANE GIRDERS. AMERICAN BRIDGE COMPANY.

fastened together by means of bolts and cast-iron separators. For standard cast-iron separators, see the author's "Structural Engineers' Handbook."

Examples of Plate Girders.—Details of two plate girders designed to carry a moving crane are given in Fig. 4. The top flanges are made of two angles and a cover plate, while the bottom flanges are made of two angles. Girder G9 is designed to be riveted to a column, while girder G10 is designed to rest on a pedestal and also to carry a second girder which is to be riveted to the end stiffeners. The stiffeners have fillers under them, making crimping unnecessary. The intermediate stiffeners might have been crimped over the flange angles and the filler omitted. Fillers should always be used under the end stiffeners.

Design of a Plate Girder for a Crane.

1. **Problem.**—Design a plate girder to carry a 25-ton crane. Distance center to center of columns is 20 ft. 0 in. Design to comply with the specifications in Appendix I. The properties of sections will be taken from the author's "Structural Engineers' Handbook."

2. **LOADS.**—The wheel loads and spacing are shown in Fig .5. The wheel loads consist of two 46,000-lb. loads spaced 10 ft. 0 in. center to center.

3. **Weight of Girder and Fastenings.**—

Assumed weight of girder	150 lb. per lin. ft.
Weight of track (70-lb. rail) and fastenings	25 lb. per lin. ft.
Total	175 lb. per lin. ft.

4. **MOMENTS.**—Moments due to dead load, live load and impact will be computed at sections 2 ft. 6 in. apart. The bending moment due to dead loads is calculated by the formula

$$M = w \cdot l \cdot x/2 - w \cdot x^2/2$$

where M = bending moment in ft.-lb.; w = uniform load in lb. per lin. ft.; l = span in ft., x = distance in ft. of section from left end of beam. The dead load moments for the various sections are given in Table I.

In Chapter V it was shown that if the wheel spacing is less than 0.586 times the span, the maximum bending moment occurs with both wheels on the span, and the maximum moment under one wheel occurs when that wheel is as far from one end of the beam as the center of gravity of both wheels is from the other end.

The moment at any section is calculated by the formula

$$M = \frac{2P(l - x - \frac{1}{2}a)}{l} x$$

where P = one wheel load in lb.; l = span in ft.; x = distance from left end of beam to section; a = wheel spacing. The moment at any section may be obtained by substituting the proper value of x in the above equation.

It will be found that the above criterion for maximum live load bending moment will be satisfied when x = 7.5 ft. and the maximum moment is

$$M = 2 \times 46{,}000 \frac{(20 - 7.5 - 5)}{20} \times 7.5$$
$$= 258{,}750 \text{ ft.-lb.}$$

The other bending moments are shown in Table I.

TABLE I.

MOMENTS IN CRANE GIRDER.

(See Fig. 5.)

Section.	A	B	C	D	E
Dead load moment	0	3,830	6,560	8,200	8,750
Live load moment	0	143,750	230,000	258,750	230,000
Impact moment	0	35,940	57,500	64,690	57,500
Total ft.-lb.	0	183,520	294,060	331,640	296,250

The live load bending moment will be increased 25 per cent to take care of impact stresses, § 35, Specifications.

The girder will be designed for the maximum total bending moment to which it is subjected. The maximum moment at D will be found from Table I to be 331,640 ft.-lb. The maximum bending moment in the girder will be found by adding the bending moments due to dead load, live load and impact to occur at a distance of 7.55 ft. from the left end, and to be 331,640 ft.-lb. It may usually be safely assumed for crane girders that the maximum moment occurs at the point of maximum live load bending moment.

5. **SHEARS.**—The shears will be calculated at sections 2 ft. 6 in. apart. The dead load shear is calculated by the formula

$$V = \tfrac{1}{2}w\cdot l - w\cdot x$$

when w = uniform load in lb. per lin. ft.; l = span in ft.; x = distance of section from left end. The dead load shears are shown in Table II.

TABLE II.

SHEARS IN CRANE GIRDER.

(See Fig. 5.)

Section.	A	B	C	D	E
Dead load shear	1,750	1,310	875	440	0
Live load shear	69,000	57,500	46,000	34,500	23,000
Impact shear	17,250	14,375	11,500	8,625	5,750
Total lb.	88,000	73,185	58,375	43,565	28,750

The maximum live load shear at any section will occur with one load just to the right of the section and is calculated by the formula

$$V = \frac{2P(l - x - \tfrac{1}{2}a)}{l}$$

when P = one of the loads; l = span in ft.; x = distance of section from left end of beam; a = wheel spacing. The impact factor is 0.25, § 35, Specifications.

6. **DESIGN.**—The depth and thickness of the web must be chosen so that sufficient area is provided to carry the shear and the required depth for moment is obtained. The depth should not be less than $\frac{1}{12} \times 20 \times 12 = 20$ in. The distance back to back

of angles will be taken as $30\frac{1}{2}$ in. The thickness of plate will be taken as $\frac{3}{8}$ in. This is greater than $\frac{5}{16}$ in. or $\frac{1}{160}$ of $(30\frac{1}{2} - 12) = 0.12$ in. as required by § 50, Specifications.

Using a web plate 30 in. $\times \frac{3}{8}$ in. the unit shear on the gross section of the web is

$$88{,}000 \div 11.25 = 7{,}820 \text{ lb. per sq. in.}$$

From Fig. 5 it will be necessary to deduct 6 rivet holes to obtain the net section and shear on net section of web is

$$88{,}000 \div 9.00 = 9{,}800 \text{ lb. per sq. in.}$$

The allowable unit stress is 10,000 lb. per sq. in., § 39, Specifications.

It will be assumed that the distance between rivet lines is 7.5 in. less than the distance back to back of angles, and that there are 2 rows of $\frac{7}{8}$-in. rivets connecting the flange angles to the web plate. The approximate rivet spacing in the flanges near the ends will be from equation (6),

$$p = \frac{r \cdot h'}{V} = \frac{7{,}880 \times 23}{88{,}000} = 2.06 \text{ in.}$$

where p = pitch of rivets in in.; r = allowable stress on one rivet in lb., Table I, Chapter XXVII; h' = distance between gage lines of rivets in in., and V = shear in lb. Allowable stresses in rivets are given in § 36 of Specifications and in Table I, Chapter XXVII.

It is seen that a $\frac{3}{8}$-in. plate is satisfactory for rivet spacing at the ends, so will be used. The pitch of the rivets connecting the web plate to the flanges will be fully investigated later.

7. **Flanges.**—The gross area of the compression flange must not be less than the gross area of the tension flange. The allowable unit stress in the tension flange is 16,000 lb. per sq. in. on the net section, and in the compression flange is $16{,}000 - 150l/b$, where l = length between lateral supports of the top flange $= 20 \times 12 = 240$ in., and b = width of cover plate. The value of b is more easily estimated after the tension flange is determined.

Assuming the effective depth to be 3 in. less than the distance back to back of flange angles, the total net area required for the tension flanges is, equation (5),

$$A_F' = \frac{M}{f \cdot h} = \frac{331{,}640 \times 12}{16{,}000 \times 27.5} = 9.05 \text{ sq. in.}$$

where A_F' = net area in sq. in.; M = bending moment in in.-lb.; f = allowable unit stress in tension flange; h = effective depth in in. Allowing one-eighth of the web area as flange area, the required net area of the flange angles is

$$9.05 - \tfrac{1}{8} \times 11.25 = 7.65 \text{ sq. in.}$$

Deducting two holes for $\frac{7}{8}$-in. rivets, two angles 6 in. $\times$ 6 in. $\times \frac{7}{16}$ in. furnish 8.36 sq. in. and will be used. (This assumption is on the safe side. The actual net area should be calculated as required in § 47, Specifications, after the girder is partially detailed.)

The width of the cover plate, § 51, Specifications, must be at least $240 \div 30 = 8$ in. It will be desirable to use 6-in. angles in the top flange, so a 12-in. cover plate will be too narrow.

Since the top flange must be designed to take a lateral thrust due to the crane a 15 in. channel with the flanges turned down will be used as a cover plate. The allowable unit compression in the top flange, § 51, Specifications, is

$$16{,}000 - 150 \times \frac{240}{15} = 13{,}600 \text{ lb. per sq. in.}$$

The gross area required for the compression flange to take the vertical loads, from equation (5), is

$$A_F = \frac{M}{f_c \cdot h} = \frac{331{,}640 \times 12}{13{,}600 \times 27.5} = 10.64 \text{ sq. in.}$$

Allowing one-eighth of the web area as effective as flange area, the required gross area in the flange is

$$10.64 - \tfrac{1}{8} \times 11.25 = 9.24 \text{ sq. in.}$$

From § 25, Specifications, the top flange of the crane girder must be designed to take a lateral thrust of $0.2 \times 50{,}000 \div 4 = 2{,}500$ lb. on each of two wheels spaced 10 ft. apart. The maximum moment will be at section D, Fig. 5, and will be $M = 1{,}875 \times 7.5 \times 12 = 168{,}750$ in.-lb. Adding 25 per cent for impact, $M = 1.25 \times 168{,}750 = 210{,}950$ in.-lb. A top flange section made of two angles 6 in. $\times$ 6 in. $\times \frac{7}{16}$ in. and one 15 in. channel @ 33 lb. will be investigated. The section modulus of this section with reference to a vertical axis is $S = 51$ in.^{3}, and the maximum fiber stress due to lateral thrust is $f_c' = 210{,}950 \div 51 = 4{,}150$ lb. per sq. in.

From equation (5) the stress in the top flange due to transverse loads is

$$f_c = \frac{M}{A_F \cdot h} = \frac{331{,}640 \times 2}{21.42 \times 27.41} = 6{,}680 \text{ lb. per sq. in.}$$

(The effective depth, $h = 27.41$ in., is the actual distance between the centers of gravity of the top and bottom flange.) The maximum stress in the top flange will be $4{,}150 + 6{,}680 = 10{,}830$ lb. per sq. in. The section appears to be excessive. Assuming a top flange made of two angles 6 in. $\times$ 4 in. $\times \frac{7}{16}$ in. and a 12 in. channel, and making the necessary calculations, it will be found that a 12 in. channel @ 40 lb. is required, giving a weight of 68.6 lb. per lineal foot as compared with 67.2 lb. per lineal foot for the section above with a 15 in. channel @ 33 lb. The top flange section with the 15 in. channel will be adopted.

The effective depth of the section is 27.41 in., which is slightly less than the assumed depth, so no revision will be made. The average distance between gage lines is $23\frac{3}{4}$ in.

It will be assumed that the rail distributes a wheel load over 25 inches. The required pitch of rivets between the flanges and web is given by equation (9).

$$p = \frac{7{,}880}{\sqrt{\left(\frac{46{,}000}{25}\right)^2 + \left(\frac{8.36}{9.76} \times \frac{88{,}000}{23.75}\right)^2}} = 2.14 \text{ in.}$$

The other rivet spacings are calculated in a similar manner. The spacings actually used are shown in the general drawing, Fig. 5.

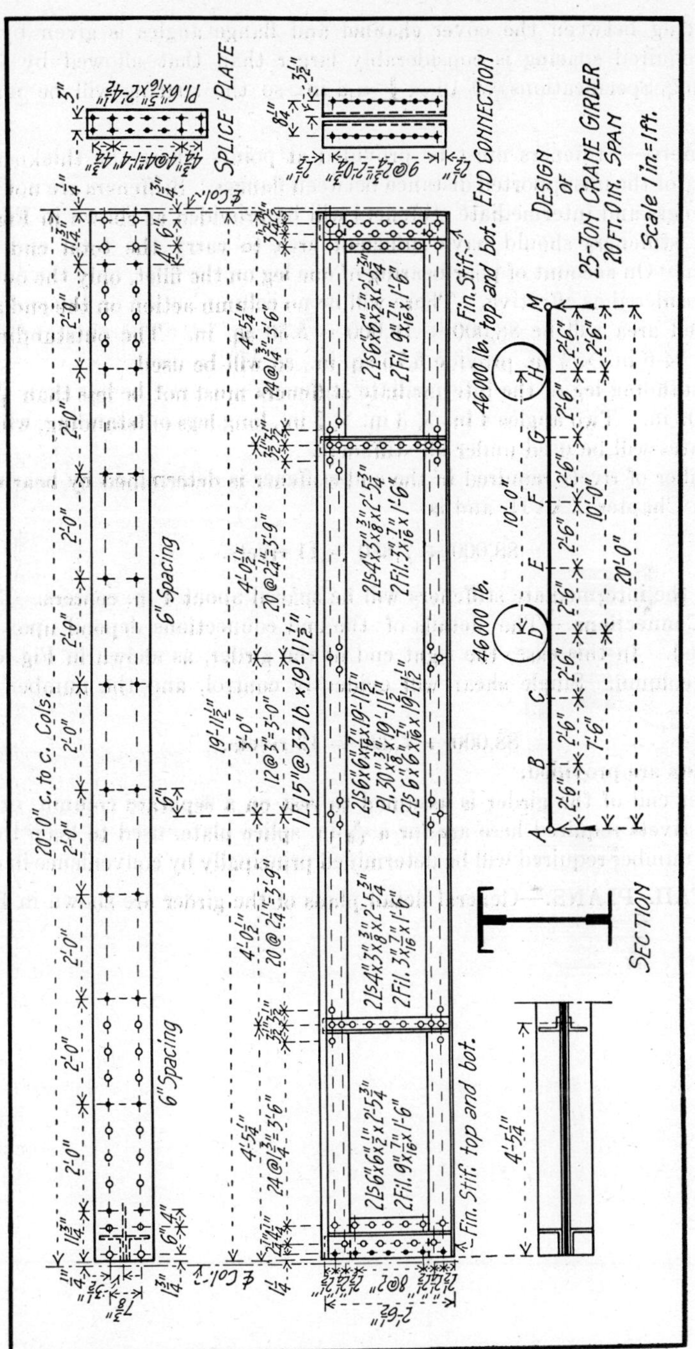
SPLICE PLATE
END CONNECTION
DESIGN
OF
25-TON CRANE GIRDER
20 FT. 0 IN. SPAN
Scale 1 in.=1 ft.
46 000 lb.
46 000 lb.
A B C D E F G H M
SECTION
Fin. Stif. top and bot.
Fin. Stif. top and bot.
6" Spacing
6" Spacing
20'-0" c. to c. Cols.
℄ Col.
℄ Col.

FIG. 5.

The spacing between the cover channel and flange angles is given by equation (10). The required spacing is considerably larger than that allowed by the specifications, § 92, Specifications, or $16 \times \frac{3}{8} = 6$ in., so the spacing will be made 6 in. throughout.

8. **Stiffeners.**—Stiffeners must be provided at points where the thickness of web is less than $\frac{1}{60}$ of the unsupported distance between flanges. Stiffeners are not required, but end stiffeners and intermediate stiffeners will be provided as shown in Fig. 5.

The end stiffeners should have sufficient area to carry the total end shear by column action. On account of poor bearing of one leg on the fillet, only the outstanding leg will be considered as effective. There will be no column action on the end stiffeners, so the required area will be $88,000 \div 16,000 = 5.50$ sq. in. The outstanding legs of 2 angles 6 in. $\times$ 6 in. $\times \frac{1}{2}$ in. provide 5.75 sq. in., so will be used.

The outstanding leg of the intermediate stiffeners must not be less than $\frac{1}{30} \times 30.5 \times 2$ in. $= 3.02$ in. Two angles 4 in. $\times$ 3 in. $\times \frac{3}{8}$ in., long legs outstanding, will be used.

Filler plates will be used under all stiffeners.

The number of rivets required in the end stiffener is determined by bearing on the web, Table I, Chapter XXVII, and is

$$88,000 \div 7,880 = 11 \text{ rivets.}$$

The rivets in the intermediate stiffeners will be spaced about 4 in. centers.

9. **End Connections.**—The details of the end connections depend upon the type of column used. In this case, the right end of the girder, as shown in Fig. 5, will be riveted to a column. Single shear will evidently control, and the number of rivets required is

$$88,000 \div 7,220 = 13 \text{ rivets.}$$

Sufficient rivets are provided.

The other end of the girder is assumed to rest on a separate column, or bracket, and the only rivets required here are for a $\frac{5}{16}$-in. splice plate, used to keep the girders in line. The number required will be determined principally by convenience in detailing.

10. **DETAIL PLANS.**—General detail plans of the girder are shown in Fig. 5.

CHAPTER XXXVIII.

Design of a Steel Mill Building.

1. **Problem.**—Design a steel mill building 60 ft. by 80 ft., with columns 24 ft. long. Building to be covered with corrugated steel. Windows to be glazed with factory-ribbed glass set in steel sash. The building is to be designed to comply with the "General Specifications for Steel Frame Buildings" in Appendix I.* The properties of sections will be taken from the author's "Structural Engineers' Handbook."

2. **General Dimensions.**—The general dimensions of the building will be: span, 60 ft. 0 in. center to center of columns, pitch $\frac{1}{4}$, distance to foot of knee brace 16 ft. 0 in., height of columns 24 ft. 0 in., total height 39 ft. 0 in., spacing of bents 16 ft. 0 in.; length 80 ft. 0 in., see Fig. 4.

3. **Loads.**—The roof covering will be corrugated steel placed directly on the purlins. Purlins are spaced for a minimum normal load of 30 lb. per sq. ft. and will be placed at panel points or 4 ft. $2\frac{5}{16}$ in. centers. From Fig. 4, Chapter XXVIII, also Table IV, Appendix I, it is seen that No. 20 corrugated steel must be used. Anti-condensation lining weighing about 1.0 lb. per sq. ft. horizontal projection will be provided. The weight of the roof truss will be estimated by the formula given in § 14, Specifications. For an assumed capacity of 40 lb. per sq. ft. horizontal projection, $w = \frac{40}{45}\left(1 + \frac{60}{5\sqrt{16}}\right) = 3.6$ lb. per sq. ft. horizontal projection. The approximate weight of the roof will be:—

Trusses	3.6 lb. per sq. ft. hor. proj.
Purlins and bracing	3.0 " " " " " "
Corrugated Steel	2.3 " " " " " "
Anti Condensation Lining	1.0 " " " " " "
Total	9.9 lb. per sq. ft. hor. proj.

Use 10 lb. per sq. ft. horizontal projection.

A maximum snow load of 20 lb. per sq. ft. horizontal projection will be assumed. The minimum snow load will be taken as 10 lb. per sq. ft. horizontal projection. The wind load will be taken as the normal component of a horizontal wind pressure of 30 lb. per sq. ft. as reduced by Duchemin's formula (6), Chapter XXIV, or 22.4 lb. per sq. ft. of roof area.

4. **Panel Loads.**—Each panel has $4.19 \times 16 = 67.0$ sq. ft. of roof area, or $67.0 \times 0.8944 = 60.0$ sq. ft. horizontal projection. The dead joint load will be $60.0 \times 10.0 = 600$ lb. The minimum snow joint load is $60.0 \times 10.0 = 600$ lb. The maximum snow joint load is $60.0 \times 20.0 = 1,200$ lb. The wind joint load is $67.0 \times 22.4 = 1,500$ lb.

5. **Stress Diagrams.**—The stress diagram for dead loads is shown in Fig. 1. The stresses due to snow loads are proportional to the dead load stresses and may be obtained by changing the scale of the dead load stress diagram or by multiplying the dead load

* See note on page 552.

TABLE I. STRESSES.

Member.		Dead Load. 1	Snow Load. Max. 2	Snow Load. Min. 3	Wind Load. Wind'd. 4	Wind Load. Leew'd. 5	Combined Stresses. I 1 + 2	Combined Stresses. II 1 + 3 + 4	Combined Stresses. III 1 + 3 + 5	Combined Stresses. IV 1 + 4	Combined Stresses. V 1 + 5	Maximum Stresses. Tension. Case.	Maximum Stresses. Tension. Stress.	Maximum Stresses. Compression. Case.	Maximum Stresses. Compression. Stress.
$A-K$	$b-y$	+ 4,800	+ 9,600	+ 4,800	+ 3,700	+ 7,100	+ 14,400	+ 13,300	+ 16,700	+ 8,500	+ 11,900		0	III	16,700
$K-L_0$	$a-c$	+ 4,800	+ 9,600	+ 4,800	+ 10,100	+ 10,050	+ 14,400	+ 19,700	− 450	+ 14,900	− 5,250	V	5,250	II	19,700
$K-L_2$	$c-y$				− 9,940	+ 26,200		− 9,940	+ 26,200	− 9,940	+ 26,200	IV	9,940	V	26,200
L_0U_1	$1-x$	+ 10,100	+ 20,200	+ 10,100	+ 21,070	− 22,600	+ 30,300	+ 41,270	− 2,400	+ 31,170	− 12,500	V	12,500	II	41,270
U_1U_2	$2-x$	+ 9,830	+ 19,660	+ 9,830	+ 21,070	− 22,600	+ 29,490	+ 40,730	− 2,940	+ 30,900	− 12,770	V	12,770	II	40,730
U_2U_3	$5-x$	+ 9,570	+ 19,140	+ 9,570	+ 21,070	− 22,600	+ 28,710	+ 40,210	− 3,460	+ 30,640	− 13,030	V	13,030	II	40,210
U_3U_4	$6-x$	+ 9,310	+ 18,620	+ 9,310	+ 21,070	− 22,600	+ 27,930	+ 39,690	− 3,980	+ 30,380	− 13,290	V	13,290	II	39,690
U_4U_5	$9-x$	+ 9,040	+ 18,080	+ 9,040	+ 13,850	− 3,500	+ 27,120	+ 31,930	+ 14,580	+ 22,890	+ 5,540		0	II	31,930
U_5U_6	$10-x$	+ 8,780	+ 17,560	+ 8,780	+ 13,850	− 3,500	+ 26,340	+ 31,410	+ 14,060	+ 22,630	+ 5,280		0	II	31,410
U_6U_7	$13-x$	+ 8,500	+ 17,000	+ 8,500	+ 13,850	− 3,500	+ 25,500	+ 30,850	+ 13,500	+ 22,350	+ 5,000		0	II	30,850
U_7U_8	$14-x$	+ 8,250	+ 16,500	+ 8,250	+ 13,850	− 3,500	+ 24,750	+ 30,350	+ 13,000	+ 22,100	+ 4,750		0	II	30,350
L_0L_1	$1-c$	− 9,050	− 18,100	− 9,050	− 9,700	+ 7,130	− 27,150	− 27,800	− 10,970	− 18,750	− 1,920	II	27,800		0
L_1L_2	$3-c$	− 8,450	− 16,900	− 8,450	− 8,050	+ 7,130	− 25,350	− 24,950	− 9,770	− 16,500	− 1,320	I	25,350		0
L_2L_3	$7-y$	− 7,250	− 14,500	− 7,250	− 7,450	+ 14,150	− 21,750	− 21,950	− 350	− 14,700	+ 6,900	II	21,950	V	6,900
L_3L_3'	$15-y$	− 4,850	− 9,700	− 4,850	+ 3,230	+ 3,230	− 14,550	− 6,470	− 6,470	− 1,620	− 1,620	I	14,550		0
U_1L_1	$1-2$	+ 530	+ 1,060	+ 530	+ 1,500	0	+ 1,590	+ 2,560	+ 1,060	+ 2,030	+ 530		0	II	2,560
U_3N	$5-6$	+ 530	+ 1,060	+ 530	+ 1,500	0	+ 1,590	+ 2,560	+ 1,060	+ 2,030	+ 530		0	II	2,560
U_5N	$9-10$	+ 530	+ 1,060	+ 530	+ 1,500	0	+ 1,590	+ 2,560	+ 1,060	+ 2,030	+ 530		0	II	2,560
U_7N	$13-14$	+ 530	+ 1,060	+ 530	+ 1,500	0	+ 1,590	+ 2,560	+ 1,060	+ 2,030	+ 530		0	II	2,560
U_2L_1	$2-3$	− 600	− 1,200	− 600	− 1,650	0	− 1,800	− 2,850	− 1,200	− 2,250	− 600	II	2,850		0
U_2N	$4-5$	− 600	− 1,200	− 600	− 1,650	0	− 1,800	− 2,850	− 1,200	− 2,250	− 600	II	2,850		0
U_6N	$10-11$	− 600	− 1,200	− 600	− 1,650	0	− 1,800	− 2,850	− 1,200	− 2,250	− 600	II	2,850		0
U_6N	$12-13$	− 600	− 1,200	− 600	− 1,650	0	− 1,800	− 2,850	− 1,200	− 2,250	− 600	II	2,850		0
U_2L_2	$3-4$	+ 1,060	+ 2,120	+ 1,060	+ 3,000	0	+ 3,180	+ 5,120	+ 2,120	+ 4,060	+ 1,060		0	II	5,120
U_6M	$11-12$	+ 1,060	+ 2,120	+ 1,060	+ 3,000	0	+ 3,180	+ 5,120	+ 2,120	+ 4,060	+ 1,060		0	II	5,120
L_2N	$4-7$	− 1,200	− 2,400	− 1,200	− 11,400	+ 21,400	− 3,600	− 13,800	+ 19,000	− 12,600	+ 20,200	II	13,800	V	20,200
U_4N	$6-7$	− 1,800	− 3,600	− 1,800	− 13,050	+ 21,400	− 5,400	− 16,650	+ 17,800	− 14,850	+ 19,600	II	16,650	V	19,600
U_4L_3	$7-8$	+ 2,120	+ 4,240	+ 2,120	+ 9,600	− 9,800	+ 6,360	+ 13,840	+ 5,560	+ 11,720	− 7,680	V	7,680	II	13,840
U_4N	$8-9$	− 1,800	− 3,600	− 1,800	− 4,950	0	− 5,400	− 8,550	− 3,600	− 6,750	− 1,800	II	8,550		0
$N-M$	$8-11$	− 1,200	− 2,400	− 1,200	− 3,300	0	− 3,600	− 5,700	− 2,400	− 4,500	− 1,200	II	5,700		0
L_3M	$8-15$	− 2,400	− 4,800	− 2,400	− 10,750	+ 10,900	− 7,200	− 15,550	+ 6,100	− 13,150	+ 8,500	II	15,550	V	8,500
$M-N$	$12-15$	− 3,600	− 7,200	− 3,600	− 14,100	+ 10,900	− 10,800	− 21,300	+ 3,700	− 17,700	+ 7,300	II	21,300	V	7,300
U_8N	$14-15$	− 4,200	− 8,400	− 4,200	− 15,750	+ 10,900	− 12,600	− 24,150	+ 2,500	− 19,950	+ 6,700	II	24,150	V	6,700

TABLE II. DESIGN OF SECTIONS.

Member.		Maximum Stress.		Section.	Area, Sq. In.,		l, in,	r, in,	l/r		Out-standing Leg.	Unit Stresses.				Rivets.	
												Compression.		Tension.		$\frac{5}{8}$ in. dia.	
		Com-pression. lb.	Ten-sion. lb.		Gross.	Net.			Allow-able.	Actual.		Allow-able. lb./sq. in.	Actual lb./sq in	Allow-able. lb./sq. in.	Actual. lb./sq. in.	Ends.	Int.
$A-K$	$b-y$	16,700	0														
$K-L_0$	$a-c$	19,700	5,250														
$K-L_2$	$c-y$	26,200	9,940	2∠s 4″ × 3″ × $\frac{5}{16}$″	4.18	3.72	148	1.27	125	117	s	7,850	6,270	16,000	2,670	7*	
L_0U_1	$1-x$	41,270	12,500	2∠s 4″ × 3″ × $\frac{3}{8}$″	4.96	4.40	201	1.94	125	104	l	8,750	8,330	16,000	2,800	8	2
U_1U_2	$2-x$	40,730	12,770	2∠s 4″ × 3″ × $\frac{3}{8}$″	4.96	4.40	201	1.94	125	104	l	8,750	8,220	16,000	2,900		2
U_2U_3	$5-x$	40,210	13,030	2∠s 4″ × 3″ × $\frac{3}{8}$″	4.96	4.40	201	1.94	125	104	l	8,750	8,110	16,000	2,960		2
U_3U_4	$6-x$	39,690	13,290	2∠s 4″ × 3″ × $\frac{3}{8}$″	4.96	4.40	201	1.94	125	104	l	8,750	8,000	16,000	3,050		4
U_4U_5	$9-x$	31,930	0	2∠s 4″ × 3″ × $\frac{3}{8}$″	4.96	4.40	201	1.94	125	104	l	8,750	6,440				2
U_5U_6	$10-x$	31,410	0	2∠s 4″ × 3″ × $\frac{3}{8}$″	4.96	4.40	201	1.94	125	104	l	8,750	6,340				2
U_6U_7	$13-x$	30,850	0	2∠s 4″ × 3″ × $\frac{3}{8}$″	4.96	4.40	201	1.94	125	104	l	8,750	6,220				2
U_7U_8	$14-x$	30,350	0	2∠s 4″ × 3″ × $\frac{3}{8}$″	4.96	4.40	201	1.94	125	104	l	8,750	6,120			10*	
L_0L_1	$1-c$	0	27,800	2∠s $3\frac{1}{2}$″ × $2\frac{1}{2}$″ × $\frac{1}{4}$″	2.88	2.50	225	1.71	200	132	l			16,000	11,100	8	2
L_1L_2	$3-c$	0	25,350	2∠s $3\frac{1}{2}$″ × $2\frac{1}{2}$″ × $\frac{1}{4}$″	2.88	2.50	225	1.71	200	132	l			16,000	10,150		2
L_2L_3	$7-y$	6,900	21,950	2∠s $3\frac{1}{2}$″ × $2\frac{1}{2}$″ × $\frac{1}{4}$″	2.88	2.50	225	1.71	150	132	l	6,800	2,400	16,000	8,800	8	
L_3L_3'	$15-y$	0	14,550	2∠s 3″ × $2\frac{1}{2}$″ × $\frac{1}{4}$″	2.62	2.24	270	1.45	200	186	l			16,000	6,500	8*	
U_1L_1	$1-2$	2,560	0	1∠ 2″ × 2″ × $\frac{1}{4}$″	0.94		25	0.39	150	64		11,500	2,720			2	
U_3N	$5-6$	2,560	0	1∠ 2″ × 2″ × $\frac{1}{4}$″	0.94		25	0.39	150	64		11,500	2,720			2	
U_5N	$9-10$	2,560	0	1∠ 2″ × 2″ × $\frac{1}{4}$″	0.94		25	0.39	150	64		11,500	2,720			2	
U_7N	$13-14$	2,560	0	1∠ 2″ × 2″ × $\frac{1}{4}$″	0.94		25	0.39	150	64		11,500	2,720			2	
U_2L_1	$2-3$	0	2,850	1∠ 2″ × 2″ × $\frac{1}{4}$″	0.94	0.56	56	0.39	200	144				16,000	5,100	3	
U_2N	$4-5$	0	2,850	1∠ 2″ × 2″ × $\frac{1}{4}$″	0.94	0.56	56	0.39	200	144				16,000	5,100	2	
U_6N	$10-11$	0	2,850	1∠ 2″ × 2″ × $\frac{1}{4}$″	0.94	0.56	56	0.39	200	144				16,000	5,100	2	
U_6N	$12-13$	0	2,850	1∠ 2″ × 2″ × $\frac{1}{4}$″	0.94	0.56	56	0.39	200	144				16,000	5,100	2	
U_2L_2	$3-4$	5,120	0	1∠ $2\frac{1}{2}$″ × 2″ × $\frac{1}{4}$″	1.06		50	0.42	150	119	s	7,660	4,830			2	
U_6M	$11-12$	5,120	0	1∠ $2\frac{1}{2}$″ × 2″ × $\frac{1}{4}$″	1.06		50	0.42	150	119	s	7,660	4,830			2	
L_2N	$4-7$	20,200	13,800	2∠s $2\frac{1}{2}$″ × $2\frac{1}{2}$″ × $\frac{1}{4}$″	2.38	2.00	113	1.19	125	95		9,350	8,500	16,000	6,900	4	2
U_4N	$6-7$	19,600	16,650	2∠s $2\frac{1}{2}$″ × $2\frac{1}{2}$″ × $\frac{1}{4}$″	2.38	2.00	113	1.19	125	95		9,350	8,240	16,000	8,330	4	
U_4L_3	$7-8$	13,840	7,680	2∠s 3″ × $2\frac{1}{2}$″ × $\frac{1}{4}$″	2.62	2.24	101	0.95	125	106	s	8,550	5,300	16,000	3,430	4	
U_4N	$8-9$	0	8,550	2∠s 2″ × 2″ × $\frac{1}{4}$″	1.88	1.50	113	0.99	200	114				16,000	5,700	4	2
$N-M$	$8-11$	0	5,700	2∠s 2″ × 2″ × $\frac{1}{4}$″	1.88	1.50	113	0.99	200	114				16,000	3,800	4	
L_3M	$8-15$	8,500	15,550	2∠s $3\frac{1}{2}$″ × $2\frac{1}{2}$″ × $\frac{1}{4}$″	2.88	2.50	225	1.71	150	132	l	6,800	2,950	16,000	6,220	4	2
$M-N$	$12-15$	7,300	21,300	2∠s $3\frac{1}{2}$″ × $2\frac{1}{2}$″ × $\frac{1}{4}$″	2.88	2.50	225	1.71	150	132	l	6,800	2,540	16,000	8,520		2
U_8N	$14-15$	6,700	24,150	2∠s $3\frac{1}{2}$″ × $2\frac{1}{2}$″ × $\frac{1}{4}$″	2.88	2.50	225	1.71	150	132	l	6,800	2,330	16,000	9,660	6	

* Field Rivets.

stresses by the proper factor. The stress diagram for wind loads is shown in Fig. 1. The structure will be designed assuming the columns as pin connected at the base. As actually built, the columns will be fixed to a certain extent by the anchor bolts provided at the base. The maximum stresses are obtained by combining dead and maximum snow load stresses; dead, minimum snow and wind load stresses; and dead and wind load stresses, as shown in Table I. Each member is designed for the combination giving the maximum stress of either kind in the member.

6. **Design of Purlins and Girts.**—The maximum component along the roof of the dead and snow loads is $60(6.4 + 20) \times 0.4463 = 710$ lb. Sag rods will be provided to carry the component along the roof, § 58 and § 59, Specifications. The load from any panel carried by a sag rod will be $\frac{1}{2} \times 710 = 355$ lb. The maximum stress in the top sag rod will be $8 \times 355 = 2{,}840$ lb. Required net area $= 2{,}840 \div 16{,}000 = 0.18$ sq. in. The area at the root of the thread in a $\frac{5}{8}$-in. rod is 0.202 sq. in., and $\frac{5}{8}$-in. sag rods will be used for all purlins.

The component of the dead, snow and wind loads normal to the roof is $60 \times (6.4 + 10) \times 0.8944 + 67 \times 22.4 = 2{,}380$ lb.; and since sag rods are provided, the purlins need be designed only for the normal component, § 57, Specifications. The maximum bending moment is

$$M = 2{,}380 \times 16 \times 12/8 = 57{,}100 \text{ in.-lb.} \quad I/c = M/S = 57{,}100 \div 16{,}000 = 3.57 \text{ in.}^3$$

A 6-in. channel @ 8 lb. has a section modulus of 4.30 and its depth satisfies the requirement that the depth must not be less than $\frac{1}{40}$ of the span, § 54, Specifications, so will be used.

The maximum spacing of the girts will be about 5 ft. 0 in. Girts must be designed for a normal component of 20 lb. per sq. ft., so No. 20 corrugated steel must be used for the sides. The weight of the siding and girts will be carried by sag rods or other supports, so only the normal component of the wind need be considered in the design of the girts. The maximum bending moment is

$$M = 5.0 \times 16.0 \times 20 \times 16 \times 12/8 = 38{,}400 \text{ in.-lb.}$$

The required section modulus is $38{,}400 \div 16{,}000 = 2.40$. A 5-in. channel @ 6.5 lb. has a section modulus of 3.00 and will be used. A 5-in. channel just satisfies § 54, Specifications. The sag rods for the girts will be made $\frac{5}{8}$ in. diameter.

7. **Design of Compression Members.**—*Top chord* L_0U_8. Maximum stress in $L_0U_1(1\text{-}x) = +41{,}270$ lb., length $= 201$ in. (after erection, the unsupported length will be about 50 in., but in order to increase the rigidity of the section, particularly during erection, the length will be taken as the length of L_0U_4). Minimum $l/r = 125$, § 41, Specifications, so minimum $r = 201/125 = 1.61$ in. Try two angles 4 in. $\times$ 3 in. $\times \frac{3}{8}$ in., $\frac{3}{8}$ in. back to back. Area $= 4.96$ sq. in., $l/r = 201/1.94 = 104$. Allowable unit stress $= 16{,}000 - 70 \times 104 = 8{,}750$ lb. per sq. in. Actual unit stress $= 41{,}270 \div 4.96 = 8{,}330$ lb. per sq. in. The section area furnished is in excess of that required, but a reduction is not advisable. This section provides ample area to carry the tension. Some of the members of the top chord are less stressed than $L_0U_1(1\text{-}x)$, but the cost of splices at the intermediate joints would offset any economy that a reduction in section would affect, so the top chord will be made of the same section throughout.

The design of the other compression members is shown in Table II.

8. **Design of Tension Members.**—*Lower chord* L_0L_3. Maximum stress = − 27,800 lb. Length = 225 in. L_0L_3 will be made of the same section throughout. There is no economy in reducing the section and using splices at L_1 and L_2. Net area required for tension = 27,800 ÷ 16,000 = 1.74 sq. in. The maximum allowable l/r for tension members in which the stress is reversed is 150, § 41, Specifications, so the minimum r = 225/150 = 1.50 in. Two angles $3\frac{1}{2}$ in. × $2\frac{1}{2}$ in. × $\frac{1}{4}$ in., $\frac{3}{8}$ in. back to back, long legs outstanding, satisfy the requirement and furnish a net area of 2.50 sq. in. with one hole deducted, and will be used. (This member also satisfies § 47, Specifications.) A smaller angle will furnish sufficient tension area but will not satisfy the l/r requirement. The allowable compressive stress in this member is 16,000 − 70 × 132 = 6,800 lb. per sq. in. The compressive stress is 6,900 ÷ 2.88 = 2,400 lb. per sq. in.

The design of the other tension members is shown in Table II.

There is no stress in the sag tie, so a minimum section will be used. The sag tie will be made of one angle 2 in. × 2 in. × $\frac{1}{4}$ in.

9. **Joints.**—The joints are designed in the same manner as in Chapter XXXVI and the rivets are given in Table II.

10. **Design of Columns.**—The leeward column carries a direct stress of 19,700 lb. and a bending moment of 6,525 × 16 × 12 = 1,253,000 in.-lb. A truss about six feet deep will extend from column to column throughout the length of the building, and will afford considerable lateral support. However, to insure a rigid column, a length of 24 ft. 0 in. will be used. Maximum l/r = 150, so minimum r_B = 24 × 12 ÷ 150 = 1.92 in. (Fig. 1). Try one plate 18 in. × $\frac{3}{8}$ in. and 4 angles 5 in. × $3\frac{1}{2}$ in. × $\frac{3}{8}$ in., $18\frac{1}{2}$ in. back to back. Area = 18.95 sq. in. I_A = 1,054.3 in.^{4}, r_A = 7.46 in.^{4}. I_B = 70.58 in.^{4}, r_B = 1.93 in.

The maximum fiber stress will be

$$S = \frac{19{,}700}{18.95} + \frac{1{,}253{,}000 \times 9.25}{1{,}054.3 - \dfrac{19{,}700 \times 288^2}{10 \times 30{,}000{,}000}}$$
$$= 1{,}040 + 11{,}050 = 12{,}090 \text{ lb. per sq. in.}$$

Allowable unit stress, § 44, Specifications, will be 1.50(16,000 − 70 × 288/7.46) = 20,000 lb. per sq. in.

Ample area is provided by the above section and no reduction is advisable, since a rigid column is desired.

The required area of the base plate must be at least 16,700 ÷ 600 = 28 sq. in., where 600 = allowable bearing pressure on concrete foundations, § 40, Specifications. For proper details, a plate 16 in. × $\frac{3}{4}$ in. × 28 in. is used, so ample area is provided.

Although pin-connected ends were assumed in this design, anchor bolts will be provided to fix the bases. Assuming that the anchor bolts fix the lower end of the column, the horizontal reaction will be 5,250 lb. acting at the point of contraflexure, which is assumed to be 8 ft. above the base. The maximum tendency to overturn the column will occur under dead load and maximum wind load. Under these conditions, the direct stress in the windward column will be 10,200 lb. Taking moments about the leeward anchor bolt, see Fig. 4, Chapter IX,

$$T \times 24.25 + 10{,}200 \times 12.13 - 5{,}250 \times 8 \times 12 = 0$$
$$T = 15{,}700 \text{ lb.}$$

where T = tension in windward anchor bolt. Using an allowable unit stress of 20,000 lb. per sq. in., the area of the anchor bolt will be 0.79 sq. in. Allowing for threads, $1\frac{1}{4}$ in. diam. anchor bolts furnish 0.89 sq. in., and will be used.

With fixed ends, the maximum pressure on the masonry will occur on the leeward edge of the base plate and will be

$$S = \frac{10{,}200}{16 \times 28} + \frac{5{,}250 \times 8 \times 12 \times 14}{16 \times 28^3/12}$$
$$= 23 + 242 = 265 \text{ lb. per sq. in.}$$

The allowable pressure is 600 lb. per sq. in.

11. **Lateral Bracing.**—The bents will be braced in units of two as shown in Fig. 4. The stresses in the lateral bracing are very small and the sections will be determined by the specifications for allowable ratio of l to r. It will be assumed that the member which will carry the stress in tension is acting. The section will be chosen to comply with the requirement that l/r must not exceed 250, § 42, Specifications. The diagonal bracing will be fastened in the middle, so the minimum radius of gyration in the plane of the upper chord will be $r = 139 \div 250 = 0.56$ in. One angle 3 in. × 3 in. × $\frac{1}{4}$ in. has a radius of gyration of 0.59 in. and will be used for the upper chord bracing.

The lower chord diagonal bracing L_0L_3 will be fastened in the middle, so minimum $r = 148 \div 250 = 0.59$ in., § 42, Specifications. One angle 3 in. × 3 in. × $\frac{1}{4}$ in. just satisfies the requirements, and will be used.

The diagonal bracing L_3L_3' will be fastened at the middle, so minimum $r = 166 \div 250 = 0.67$ in. One angle $3\frac{1}{2}$ in. × $3\frac{1}{2}$ in. × $\frac{1}{4}$ in. has a value of $r = 0.69$ in., and will be used.

The strut L_3L_3 will be designed as a compression member, so minimum $r = 16 \times 12 \div 150 = 1.28$ in. Two angles 4 in. × 3 in. × $\frac{1}{4}$ in., long legs vertical, and $\frac{3}{8}$ in. back to back, just satisfies the requirement and will be used.

An eave strut will be placed along the line of the tops of the columns. The eave strut furnishes longitudinal rigidity and also provides a means of fastening the corrugated roofing along the eave of the roof. The section will be chosen to comply with the specification that l/r must not exceed 150, so minimum $r = 16 \times 12 \div 150 = 1.28$ in. A section composed of a 10-in. channel @ 15 lb. and one angle 4 in. × 3 in. × $\frac{5}{16}$ in. as shown in the details, Fig. 4, just satisfies this requirement, so will be used. A nailing strip to which the roofing and siding may be fastened is bolted to the angle. To avoid the use of rods or other bracing in the plane of the sides and ends which would prevent free use of the ventilators in the windows, a light truss as shown in Fig. 4 will be used to secure the desired rigidity.

The stresses in the side trusses due to wind on the end of the building are calculated in Fig. 2. The bracing was designed for a horizontal wind load of 20 lb. per sq. ft. acting on the end of the building. The bracing will have to be designed so that it will take the wind load on either end of the building. The wind load applied at the top of the columns will be $P = \frac{1}{2}(60 \times 24 \times 20/2) + \frac{1}{2}(60 \times 15 \times 20/2) = 11{,}700$ lb. A value of $P = 12{,}000$ lb. will be used in the calculations. It will be assumed that each portal bent carries one-fifth of the total load or 2,400 lb. The top strut will also transmit the direct stress as shown in Fig. 2. The stresses were calculated by using the method shown in Problem 7, Chapter XXII. The shears in the interior columns will be equal to twice the shears in the end columns, and the bending moments in the interior columns will also be equal to twice the bending moments in the end columns. The windward bent, No. 5, will have maximum stresses and it will be investigated.

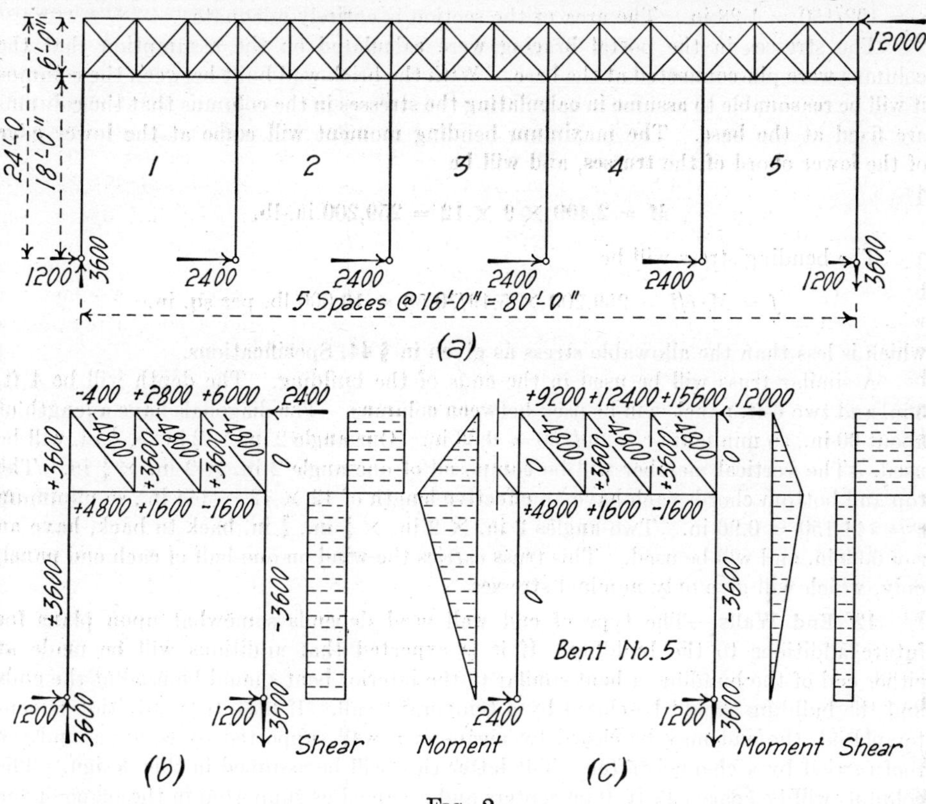

FIG. 2.

The length of the diagonal will be about 90 in. The required value of the radius of gyration will be $r = 90/250 = 0.36$ in. One angle 2 in. $\times$ 2 in. $\times \frac{1}{4}$ in. has a minimum radius of gyration, $r = 0.39$ in. and will be used if the area is sufficient. The required net area $= 4,800/16,000 = 0.30$ sq. in. The net area of a 2 in. $\times$ 2 in. $\times \frac{1}{4}$ in. angle with one $\frac{5}{8}$-in. rivet, $\frac{3}{4}$-in. hole deducted, when reduced by § 46, is 0.56 sq. in., so the angle is sufficient. The vertical members are about 58 in. center to center of connections, the required radius of gyration will be $r = 58/150 = 0.39$ in. The least radius of gyration of a 2 in. $\times$ 2 in. $\times \frac{1}{4}$ in. angle is 0.39 in. The allowable unit stress in compression will be $p = 16,000 - 70 \times 58/0.39 = 5,500$ lb. per sq. in. The required area will be $3,600/5,500 = 0.65$ sq. in. The area of a 2 in. $\times$ 2 in. $\times \frac{1}{4}$ in. angle is 0.94 sq. in., so the angle is sufficient.

The lower chord has an effective length of $16 \times 12 = 192$ in., so the minimum allowable radius of gyration will be $r = 192/150 = 1.28$ in. Two angles 3 in. $\times 2\frac{1}{2}$ in. $\times \frac{1}{4}$ in. with the long leg turned out will have a value of $r = 1.45$ in. The member has ample area to carry the stress.

The upper chord will be made of one 10-in. channel @ 15 lb. and one angle 4 in. × 3 in. × $\frac{5}{16}$ in. The radius of gyration about a vertical axis (Table 66, "Structural Engineers' Handbook") is 1.28 in. The required radius of gyration will be r = 192/150 = 1.28 in. The area of the section is entirely adequate.

The stresses in the portal bracing were calculated on the assumption that the columns were pin-connected at the base. With the brick wall built between the columns it will be reasonable to assume in calculating the stresses in the columns that the columns are fixed at the base. The maximum bending moment will come at the lower edge of the lower chord of the trusses, and will be

$$M = 2{,}400 \times 9 \times 12 = 259{,}200 \text{ in.-lb.}$$

The bending stress will be

$$f = M \cdot c/I = 259{,}200 \times 5.19/70.58 = 19{,}000 \text{ lb. per sq. in.}$$

which is less than the allowable stress as given in § 44, Specifications.

A similar truss will be used in the ends of the building. The depth will be 4 ft. 3 in. and two 6-ft. panels will be used between columns. The diagonals have a length of about 90 in., so minimum r = 90/250 = 0.36 in. One angle 2 in. × 2 in. × $\frac{1}{4}$ in. will be used. The vertical member will be composed of one angle 2 in. × 2 in. × $\frac{1}{4}$ in. The top and bottom chords each have an effective length of 12 × 12 = 144 in., so minimum r = 144/150 = 0.96 in. Two angles 2 in. × 2 in. × $\frac{1}{4}$ in., $\frac{3}{8}$ in. back to back, have an r of 0.99 in. and will be used. This truss carries the wind on one-half of each end panel, only, which will give only nominal stresses.

12. **End Walls.**—The type of end wall used depends somewhat upon plans for future additions to the building. If it is expected that additions will be made at either end of the building, a bent similar to the interior bent should be used at the ends and the building should be closed by a temporary wall. If no future addition is contemplated, the end may be closed by means of a wall supported by columns and the roof carried by a channel rafter. The latter case will be assumed in this design. The columns will be spaced 12 ft. 0 in. centers and assumed as supported in the plane of the lower chord, so their length may be taken as 24 ft. 0 in. and the uniform load = 20 lb. per sq. ft. The maximum bending moment is $\frac{1}{8}$ × 12 × 24 × 20 × 24 × 12 = 207,360 in.-lb. Using a working stress of 16,000 lb. per sq. in., the required section modulus is 12.95 in.^{3} An 8-in. I @ 18 lb. has a section modulus of 14.2 in.^{3} and will be used. The girts will give considerable lateral support, so the value of l/r is not excessively large. The truss designed for the ends of the building will take the lower chord bracing in the end bays and also afford considerable support to the columns.

An angle section will be used for the corner columns. The maximum bending moment is $\frac{1}{8}$ × 24 × 6 × 20 × 24 × 12 = 103,680 in.-lb., and the required section modulus is 6.48 in.^{3} An 8-in. × 8-in. × $\frac{1}{2}$-in. angle has a section modulus of 8.37 in.^{3}, so will be used. The lateral supports from the girts and lattice trusses in the walls will give sufficient lateral support to prevent sidewise bending.

The rafter which carries the purlins is supported by the I-beam columns and the points of support are 12 × sec 26° 34′ = 13.4 ft. apart. The component of the load normal to the roof is 35.5 lb. per sq. ft., so the load carried by one rafter is 8 × 13.4 × 35.5 = 3,800 lb. and the bending moment will be 3,800 × 13.4 × 12/8 = 76,500 in.-lb., and the required section modulus is 4.78 in.^{3} A 7-in. channel @ 9.75 lb. has a section modulus of 6 in.^{3}, so will be used.

13. **Side Walls.**—The details of the side walls are shown in Fig. 4. The brick walls will be made of paving brick laid in cement mortar, and will be laid on a concrete footing. The bottom of the footing will be below frost line or not less than 3 ft. below grade.

14. **Roofing.**—Anti-condensation lining is used and is constructed as specified in § 63, Specifications. The details of the roofing are shown in Fig. 4.

15. **Windows.**—Fenestra steel sash, or the equivalent, are used. From § 72, Specifications, the top of the windows shall be not less than 15 ft. above the floor, and the sills of the windows shall not be higher than 4 ft. above the floor. The windows shall have an area not less than 20 per cent of the floor area, nor an area less than 20 per cent. of the total exterior surface. The windows in this building are more than 50 per cent. of the floor area, and 21 per cent of the entire exterior surface.

16. **Ventilators.**—The building will be ventilated through the windows. The ventilators in the windows in the gable ends will make the use of circular ventilators on the roof unnecessary.

17. **Doors.**—Fenestra tubular steel doors, or the equivalent, will be used. For details of steel doors, see Fig. 5, and Fig. 6, Chapter XXXIV.

18. **General Drawings.**—Detail drawings of the transverse bent are shown in Fig. 3; and general plans of the building are shown in Fig. 4.

CHAPTER XXXIX.

Erection of Steel Mill Buildings.

METHODS OF ERECTION.—The method used in erecting a steel structure will depend upon the type of structure, the size of the structure, the risk to be taken, as in bridge erection, whether the structure is to be erected without interfering with traffic, as in erecting a railroad bridge to replace an existing structure, or in erecting a building over furnaces or working machinery, the available tools, and local conditions. The tendency of modern structural steel erection practice is, as far as possible, to use derrick cars for erecting railway bridges and locomotive cranes for erecting mill buildings and other structures.

Roof Trusses, Mill and Office Buildings.—Where there is sufficient room, roof trusses up to 150 ft. span may be riveted or bolted up on the ground and may then be raised into position by means of one or two gin poles. Two gin poles should be used for long trusses. Care should be used not to cripple the lower chord. With light trusses, the lower chord members should be stiffened by means of timbers or other stiff members temporarily bolted or lashed to the member. Columns and beams in office buildings may be erected with stiff-leg or guy derricks, or "A" derricks may be used for loads up to 5 tons. The bents of steel mill buildings may be erected in the same manner. Roof arches and train sheds are sometimes erected by means of falsework, which is moved as the erection proceeds. Boom-tower derricks running on tracks are found very convenient. Locomotive cranes are now used for erecting mill buildings and similar structures where tracks are available.

Elevated Towers and Tanks.—The towers for high tanks are commonly erected by means of a gin pole. A gin pole long enough to erect the entire tower may be used, or short gin poles may be lashed to the part of the tower already erected; the gin poles being moved up as the erection proceeds. Steel tanks are commonly erected from a movable platform suspended inside the tank. A movable swinging platform for the riveters is also swung outside of the tank.

For a more complete discussion of methods for the erection of steel structures, see the author's "Structural Engineers' Handbook."

Erection Plans for Steel Mill Buildings.—The method of making erection plans for steel frame mill buildings shown in Fig. 1 has been found to be very satisfactory.

Where framework is symmetrical about a center line, as trusses and end bents, the members that are reversed should be marked R (right) and L (left). The right hand side of the end bent is determined by looking outward. Mark trusses T_1, T_2, T_3, etc. Mark posts C_1, C_2, C_3, etc. Mark purlins P_1, P_2, P_3, etc. Mark struts S_1, S_2, S_3, etc. Mark girts F_1, F_2, F_3, etc. Mark bracing D_1, D_2, D_3, etc. The scheme can be modified to suit special conditions.

A foundation plan showing the piers and location of the anchor bolts should be prepared in addition to the erection plan in Fig. 1.

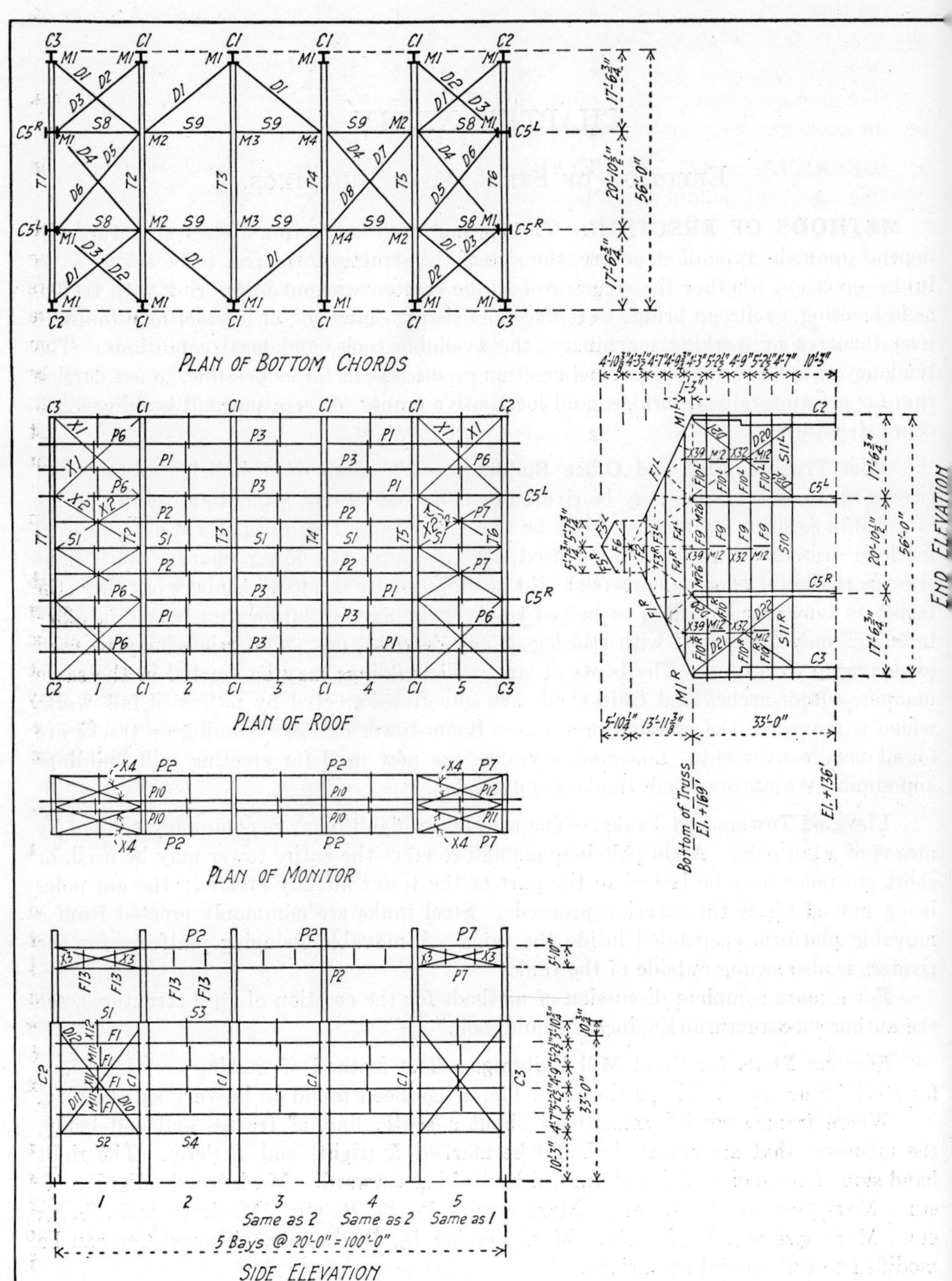

Fig. 1. Erection Plan of a Steel Mill Building.

Erection plans for corrugated steel covering on a steel mill building are shown in Fig. 7 and Fig. 8, Chapter XXVI.

Erection plans for a steel roof truss are shown in Fig. 2, Chapter XXXVI.

For erection plans for steel office buildings, steel bridges and other steel structures, see the author's "Structural Engineers' Handbook."

DERRICKS AND TRAVELERS.—The common forms of appliances used in erecting steel mill buildings will be briefly described.

Gin Pole.—A gin pole, Fig. 2, is a timber or steel mast with four guys and a block at the top through which the hoist line leads to a crab bolted near the bottom, or the hoist line may run to the hoisting engine. The foot of a gin pole is supported by timbers which are shifted with bars or on rollers. The gin pole should not be inclined more than a few degrees from the vertical, and care must be used to prevent the bottom from kicking out with heavy loads. Gin poles may be made of timber, gas pipe, or may be built structural steel masts. Gin poles are not commonly made longer than 40 to 60 ft., but a trussed gin pole 120 ft. long has been used for erecting elevated towers. The mast of a gin pole may be built up so that only two guys are necessary, resulting in "shear legs" as in Fig. 2.

Each guy is fastened at its lower end to a "deadman" (a timber, or log, or beam buried in the ground).

Guy Derricks.—A guy derrick, Fig. 2 and Fig. 3, has a vertical mast guyed with three or more guy lines, and has a boom which carries blocks and a fall line on the upper end. The boom is raised and lowered with rigging called "topping lines" or "boom lines." The load is raised by rigging called "fall lines" or "falls." The hoisting line may be run down the boom to a crab or to the hoisting engine, or the hoisting line may be run through a "rooster" placed on top of the mast and then to the hoisting engine. Guy derricks may be swung in a full circle, either by hand or by means of a bull wheel operated by a line from the hoisting engine.

"A" Derrick.—The "A" derrick or "Jinniwink" derrick is shown in Fig. 2. "A" derricks are used for light hoisting up to three to five tons. The "A" derrick is a simple form of the stiff-leg derrick.

Stiff-Leg Derrick.—The stiff-leg derrick has a mast braced by "A" frames set at right angles to each other, Fig. 2 and Fig. 3. The loads may be lifted and the boom raised and lowered by means of a crab or by a hoisting engine. The stiff-leg derrick has a free swing of about 240 degrees. The mast may be turned by hand or by means of a bull wheel operated by a line from the hoisting engine. Details of a 12-ton timber stiff-leg derrick are shown in the author's "Structural Engineers' Handbook." Stiff-leg derricks of large capacity are now commonly made of structural steel. Details of a steel stiff-leg derrick are given in Fig. 5.

Boom Travelers.—The mast of a derrick may be supported by the framework of a traveler, Fig. 2. The traveler may be made one or several stories in height. The booms may swing or may be fixed to raise and lower in one plane, and may be used single or in pairs. Boom travelers are commonly used in erecting train sheds, and structural steel buildings. Details of a steel boom traveler are given in Fig. 4 and Fig. 5.

Traveler for Erection of Armory.*—The new armory for the University of Illinois

* Engineering News, Dec. 11, 1913. The structural steel was fabricated and erected and the traveler was designed by the Morava Construction Co., Chicago, Illinois.

is 276 ft. by 420 ft. in plan, the main drill hall being covered by three-hinged arches with a span 206 ft. centers of end pins, a center height of 94 ft. 3 in., and are spaced 26 ft. 6 in. The arches have a horizontal tie of two 4 in. × $\frac{5}{8}$ in. bars, and are braced together in pairs.

Each arch was shipped in eight segments, and the four sections for each half of

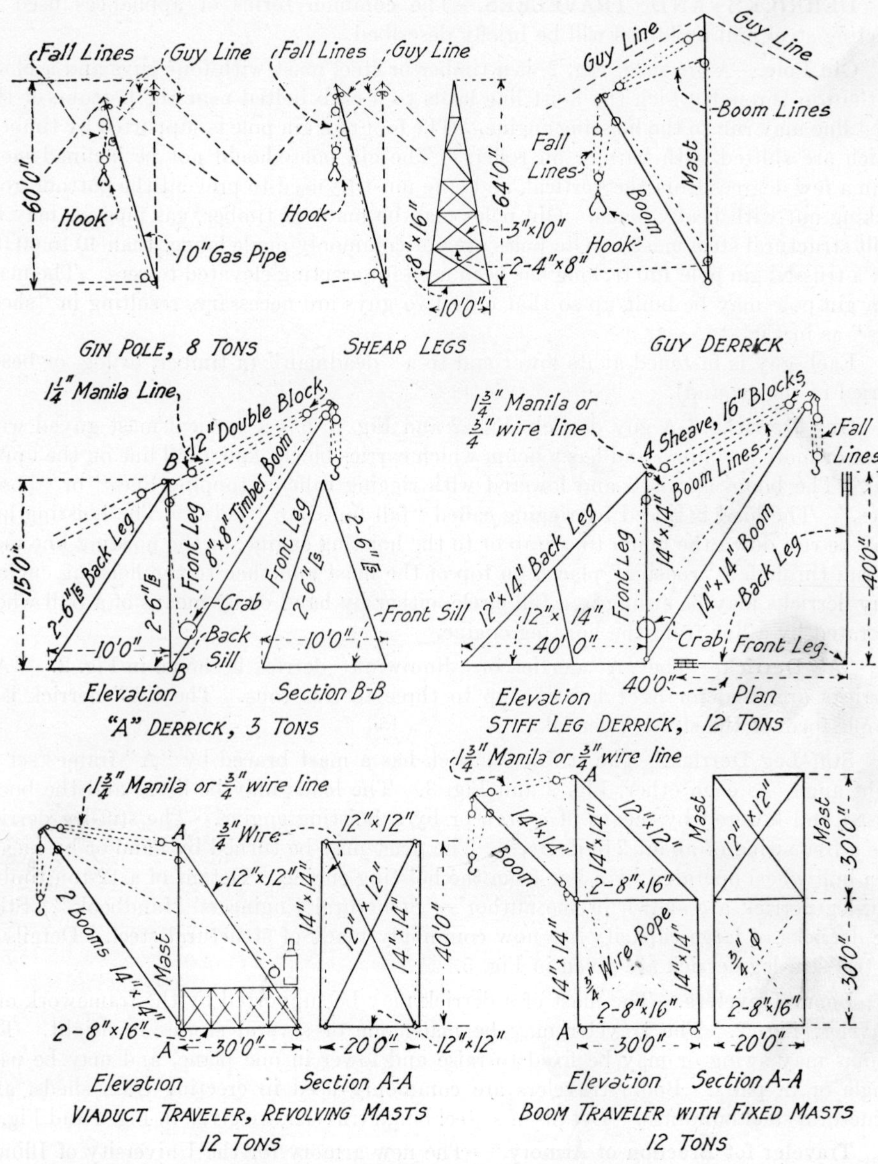

Fig. 2. Derricks and Travelers.

the arch were assembled and riveted up in horizontal position on the ground close to their final positions. One side of the arch was then lifted into a vertical plane by a two-boom traveler, and its lower end was fitted into the shoe and the shoe pin driven. The

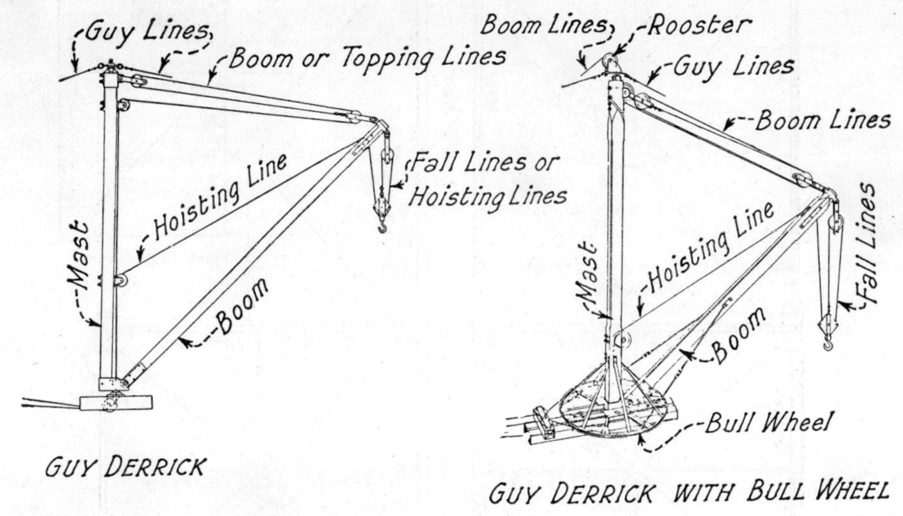

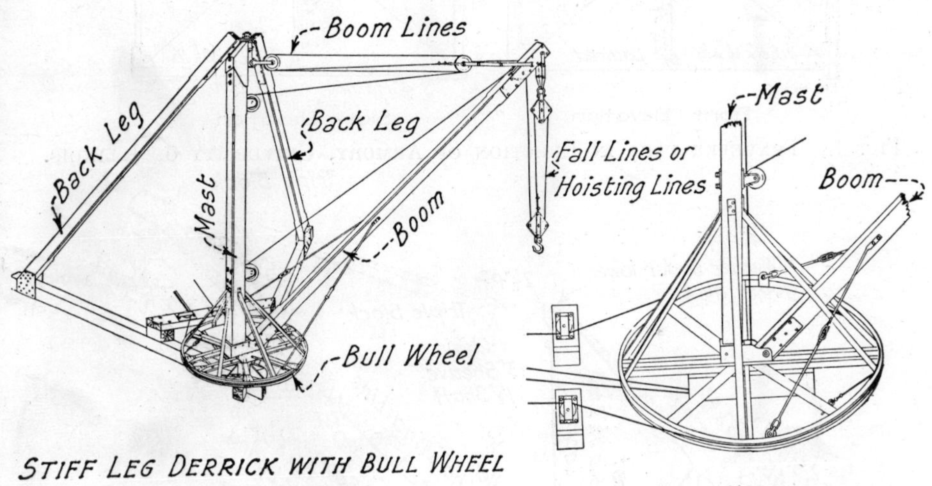

FIG. 3. DETAILS OF DERRICKS.

truss was then lowered on this pin until its head rested on the ground, the arch segment being supported by guys at the sides. The opposite segment of the arch was then raised and adjusted in the same way. The traveler was then placed at the center of the arch, and the hoisting lines of the two booms were attached near the ends of the two

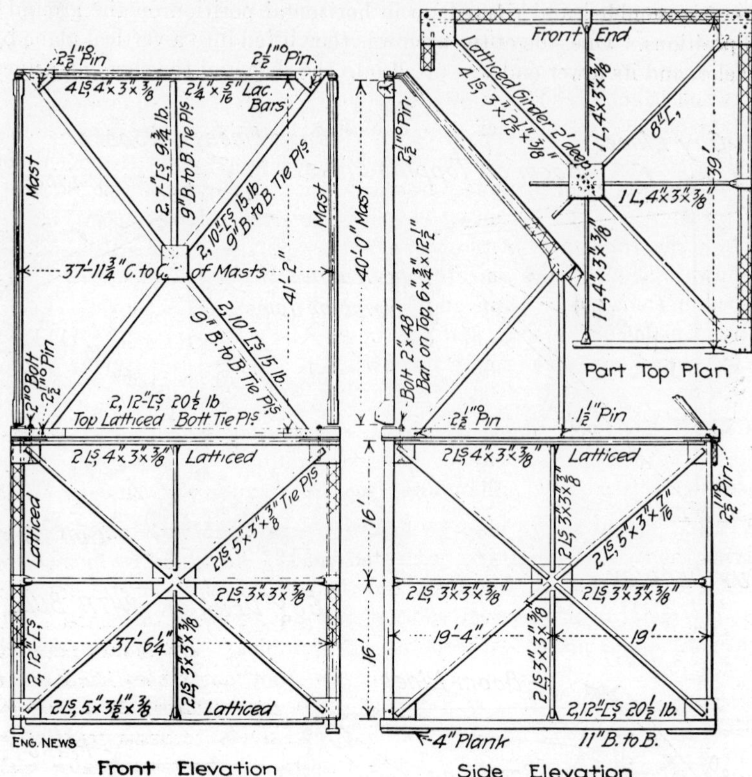

FIG. 4. TRAVELER USED IN ERECTION OF ARMORY, UNIVERSITY OF ILLINOIS.

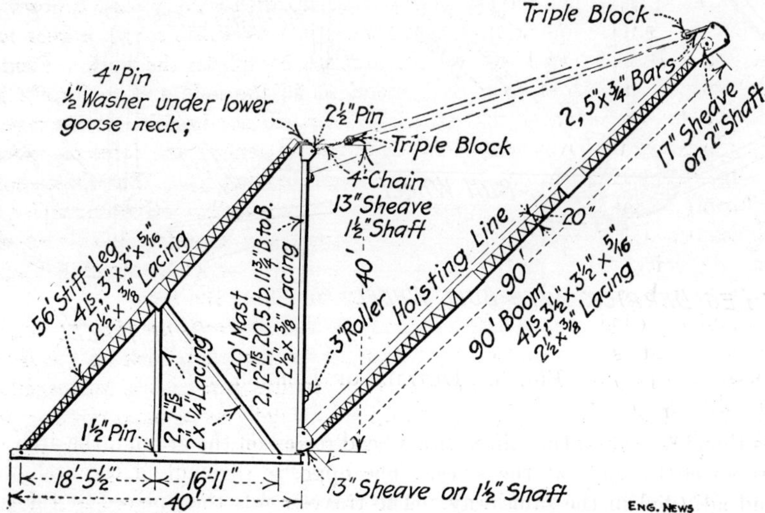

FIG. 5. STIFF-LEG DERRICK USED ON ERECTION TRAVELER FOR ERECTION OF ARMORY, UNIVERSITY OF ILLINOIS. (Two of these derricks were used on front of traveler.)

half-arches, which were then raised, the lower ends rotating on the shoe pins. The arch was then held while the center pin was driven and the purlins were placed connecting it to the adjacent arch.

The traveler, Fig. 4, consisted of a steel tower about 40 ft. square and 33 ft. high to the working deck. On this deck were two 40-ft. masts with A-frames, each carrying a 90-ft. boom, so that the top of the boom could reach about 20 ft. above the top of the arches, the maximum height from the ground to the hoisting block being 125 ft.

The traveler was supported on wood rollers on tracks of 16 × 16 in. timbers about 40 ft. apart. The upper part of the traveler was composed of two stiff-leg derricks of the type shown in Fig. 5, with one stiff-leg and one sill removed from each, the masts being stepped on the traveler frame and connected by bracing as shown. Each derrick had a lifting capacity of 15 tons, and was operated by an engine of 8 H. P., the two engines being placed on a platform on the lower sills of the traveler about 2 ft. from the ground.

ERECTION TOOLS.—Tools used in the erection of steel structures are described in detail in the author's "Structural Engineers' Handbook." For the list of the tools actually used in erecting a steel mill building, see the "Structural Engineers' Handbook."

RIVETING.—Field rivets may be driven by hand or with pneumatic riveters. Before driving the rivets the parts to be riveted must be drawn up by means of erection bolts so that the holes are fully matched and the surfaces of the metal are so close together that the metal from the rivet will not flow out between the plates. The holes are brought in line and matched by the use of drift pins; care should be used not to injure the metal with the drift pin. If the holes will not match they should be reamed. A gang for hand riveting consists of four men, (1) a rivet heater, (2) a bucker-up, (3) a rivet driver, and (4) a man to catch and enter the rivets, to assist in driving and to hold the rivet set (snap). The hot rivet is thrown by the rivet heater with rivet-pitching tongs; the rivet is caught in a bucket or keg and is put into the rivet hole with the rivet-sticking tongs. The rivet is then bucked-up with a dolly, and is upset with a rivet hammer. After the rivet is upset to fill the hole a rivet set (snap), is held over the upset rivet and a few blows with the riveting hammer completes the work. Field rivets are ordered with enough stock to furnish metal to fill the hole and to form a perfect rivet head. If the rivet is too short, either the hole will not be filled or the rivet head will be imperfect. If the rivet is too long the rivet set (snap) will force the metal out under the edge of the rivet set (snap) making a bad looking job. The rivet should be heated uniformly so that it will be upset for its entire length. Riveters prefer to use rivets with scant stock so that the rivet can be upset and a perfect head formed with little labor. To drive a rivet properly the rivet should be upset by striking it squarely on the end, as side blows will upset the rivet without filling the hole.

Where compressed air is available a pneumatic field riveter is used for driving rivets. Pneumatic field riveters are of two types: (*a*) jaw riveters that buck-up the rivet and form the head as in shop riveters; and (*b*) a pneumatic gun that is held against the rivet by the riveter, the rivet being bucked-up with a dolly as in hand riveting or with a pneumatic dolly. The pneumatic gun is more convenient and is commonly used. A rivet snap is used in the air gun. Good rivets can be driven by hand, but the work of the pneumatic riveter is more uniform and most specifications for erection of structural steel call for its use. Several railroad bridge specifications now require that hand-driven field rivets be calculated for only four-fifths of the allowable stresses on machine-driven field rivets. While more rivets can be driven with an air gun than by hand, the added expense for air makes the cost of driving nearly the same as for hand-driven rivets.

For additional data on rivets and riveting, see the author's "Structural Engineers' Handbook."

References.—For a detailed description of erection tools and methods of erection of steel structures, see the author's "Structural Engineers' Handbook." For the erection of steel and concrete bridges, see the author's "Design of Highway Bridges of Steel, Timber and Concrete."

CHAPTER XL.

Estimate of Weight and Cost of Steel Mill Buildings.

ESTIMATE OF WEIGHT.—The contract drawings for mill buildings are usually general drawings about like those in Fig. 5 and Fig. 6, Chapter XXVI, in which the main members and the outline of the building are shown, together with enough sketch details to enable the detailer to properly detail the work. In making an estimate of weight from general drawings it is necessary that the estimator be familiar with the style of the details in use at the shop, and with the per cent of the main members that it is necessary to add, to provide for details and get the total shipping weight of the structure. There are two methods of allowing for details: (1) to add the proper per cent for details to the weight of each main member in the structure, and (2) to add a per cent for details to the total weight of the main members in the structure. The first method is the safest one to follow, although the second gives good results when used by an experienced man. The best way to obtain data on the per cents of details of different members in buildings and other structures is to make detailed estimates from the shop drawings. By checking these data with the actual shipping weights, the engineer will soon have information that will be invaluable to him. Second-hand data on estimating are of comparatively little value, for the reason that the conditions under which they hold good are rarely noted, and it is better that the novice work out his own data and depend on his own resources, at least until he has developed his estimating sense. In short the only way to learn to estimate, is to estimate.

ESTIMATES OF WEIGHT OF STEEL MILL BUILDINGS.—There are three methods of estimating the weight of a steel structure. (1) Estimate from finished shop drawings; (2) estimate from detail drawings; (3) estimate from stress sheet.

(1) **Estimate from Shop Drawings.**—The method of making estimates of steel structures from the shop drawings will be illustrated by making the estimate of the steel roof truss designed in Chapter XXXVI. The details of the estimate are shown in Table I. The "main members" are those that are given on the stress sheet and are either members in which stresses occur or which are specified by the designing engineer; while the "details" are plates, angles, rivets, etc., which are necessary to develop the strength of the main members. The values given in column 10 are the weights of "details" in per cent of weights of "main members." The weights per foot given in column 7 were obtained from Ketchum's "Structural Engineers' Handbook." (May also be obtained from Carnegie or Cambria.) The weight for rivet heads should be the mean of the weight of rivet heads as made on the rivet and as driven in work. The actual shipping weight is desired, and the weights of rivet heads, only, are calculated, it being assumed that the remainder of the rivets fill the holes punched in the members. The total weights of the different parts of the roof truss and the percentage of details are shown in Table I. The total weight of details in per cent of main members is 35.5 per cent. The rivet heads are equal to about 4 per cent of the weight of the main members.

TABLE I.

ESTIMATE OF WEIGHT

STEEL ROOF TRUSS, SPAN 50 FT. 0 IN., PITCH $\frac{1}{4}$

JAN. 13, 1921 — SHEET 1 OF 2

Ref. No.	Number of Pieces	Shape	Section	Length Ft.	Length In.	Weight per ft. Lb.	Weight Main Members Lb.	Weight Details Lb.	Details per cent Main Members	Total Weight Lb.
1	4 Trusses each thus:									
	4	Ls	$3\frac{1}{2} \times 3 \times \frac{5}{16}$	28	$7\frac{1}{2}$	6.60	756			
	4	Ls	$2\frac{1}{2} \times 2\frac{1}{2} \times \frac{1}{4}$	15	2	4.10	249			
	2	Ls	$2\frac{1}{2} \times 2\frac{1}{2} \times \frac{1}{4}$	18	6	4.10	152			
	4	Ls	$2 \times 2 \times \frac{1}{4}$	14	11	3.19	190			
	4	Ls	$2\frac{1}{2} \times 2 \times \frac{1}{4}$	6	$7\frac{5}{8}$	3.62	96			
	8	Ls	$2 \times 2 \times \frac{1}{4}$	7	1	3.19	181			
	8	Ls	$2 \times 2 \times \frac{1}{4}$	3	$6\frac{5}{8}$	3.19	91			
	1	Ls	$2 \times 2 \times \frac{1}{4}$	11	5	3.19	36			
	4	Ls	$2\frac{1}{2} \times 2\frac{1}{2} \times \frac{3}{8}$	1	0	5.90		24		
	2	Pl.	$10 \times \frac{5}{8}$	1	0	21.25		43		
	2	Pl.	$12 \times \frac{3}{8}$	2	$0\frac{3}{8}$	15.30		62		
	8	Pl.	$8 \times \frac{3}{8}$	0	$4\frac{5}{8}$	10.20		31		
	2	Pl.	$13 \times \frac{3}{8}$	1	$7\frac{7}{8}$	16.58		55		
	1	Pl.	$18 \times \frac{3}{8}$	2	$0\frac{7}{8}$	22.95		48		
	4	Pl.	$12 \times \frac{3}{8}$	0	$11\frac{1}{8}$	15.30		57		
	2	Pl.	$16 \times \frac{3}{8}$	1	$3\frac{3}{4}$	20.40		54		
	1	Pl.	$6 \times \frac{3}{8}$	0	$6\frac{1}{2}$	7.65		4		
	8	Ls	$4 \times 3 \times \frac{5}{16}$	0	8	7.20		38		
	8	Pl.	$6 \times \frac{3}{8}$	0	$9\frac{5}{8}$	7.65		49		
	2	Pl.	$6 \times \frac{3}{8}$	0	$9\frac{5}{8}$	7.65		12		
	2	Pl.	$14 \times \frac{3}{8}$	1	11	17.85		68		
	30	Washers	per 100			35.00		11		
	752	$\frac{5}{8}$" Rivet Heads	per 100			8.60		65		
							1751	621	35.5	
								4 x 2372 =		9488

(2) **Estimate from Detail Drawings.**—Detail drawings show the main members partially detailed. The drawings give the number and approximate sizes of plates, the sizes of lacing bars, rivets., etc, and the approximate rivet spacing. In making an estimate from detail drawings the main members are taken from the drawings, while

part of the details are supplied by the estimater. In order that the estimate be accurate the estimater must be familiar with the shop standards of the company that will fabricate the structure.

(3) **Estimate from the Stress Sheet.**—In this method the weights of the main members are calculated directly from the stress sheet, while the weights of the details are supplied by the estimater. The weight of the details may be estimated (*a*) by adding a percentage to each member—top chord, column, etc., or (*b*) by adding a percentage to the total weight of main members. The second method is very satisfactory where a standard type of structure is used, while the first method should always be used for new types of construction.

Accuracy of Estimates.—The rolls used in rolling sections are designed to give a section of the required weight when the rolls are new, so that sections are usually slightly heavier than the figured weights due to the wear or the spreading of the rolls. It is commonly specified (see § 185, Appendix I) that the actual weight of fabricated steel work may vary not more than 2 per cent from the figured weight. This means that where fabricated structural steel is bought at a pound price, the purchaser will have to pay for the actual weight, providing it does not exceed the calculated weight by more than 2 per cent. Where fabricated structural steel work is more than $2\frac{1}{2}$ per cent lighter than the calculated weight, the purchaser may refuse to accept the material. This latter case never occurs unless sections lighter than those shown on the drawings are substituted. The estimate made from shop drawings should be used as a basis for comparison. The results obtained from the detail drawings or from stress sheets should not vary from shipping weight by more than $1\frac{1}{2}$ to 2 per cent, and should be a little heavy rather than light. Estimates from stress sheets should be made only by a skilled estimater.

Shop Waste.—The shipping weight of fabricated structural steel will be less than the weight of the rolled steel, due to the loss in rivet slugs, clippings, beveled cuts, milling, etc. This loss will vary from 3 to 5 per cent for steel mill buildings.

DETAILED ESTIMATES OF STEEL MILL BUILDINGS.—The detailed estimates of three steel mill buildings are given in Table II, Table III and Table IV. These estimates were made from the shop drawings.

Steel Frame Mill Building.—The detailed estimate of the steel frame building shown in Fig. 5 and Fig. 6, Chapter XXVI, is given in Table II. The details of the steel framework are equal to 20 per cent of the weight of the steel framework, not including the steel purlins and girts. The details are 14.6 per cent of the total weight of the steel framework and the steel covering.

Steel Frame Machine Shop.—The detailed estimate of the steel frame machine shop, shown in Fig. 10, Chapter XXVI, is given in Table III. The details of the steel framework are equal to 19.0 per cent of the weight steel of the framework, not including the purlins and girts. The details are 13.5 per cent of the total weight of the steel framework and the steel covering. The rivet heads weighed 6,400 lb., which is 3.2 per cent of the total weight of the steel framework, not including the steel purlins and girts.

Steel Pier Shed.—The detailed estimate of the steel pier shed shown in Fig. 9, Chapter XXVI, is given in Table IV. The details of the steel framework are equal to 15.9 per cent of the total weight of the steel framework, not including the steel purlins.

The rivet heads weighed 5,600 lb., which is 2.25 per cent of the total weight of the steel framework, not including the steel purlins.

Approximate Estimates.—The approximate weight of a steel frame mill building may be calculated from the sq. ft. of floor area, or the cubical contents of the building; the latter method being the more accurate. The weight of the framework of steel frame mill buildings will vary from 12 to 18 lb. per sq. ft., while the weight of the covering will vary from 3 to 4 lb. per sq. ft. of floor area. The weight of the framework of steel frame mill buildings will vary from 0.40 to 0.70 lb. per cu. ft., while the weight of the covering will vary from 0.1 to 0.2 lb. per cu. ft.

TABLE II.

ESTIMATE OF WEIGHT OF A STEEL FRAME MILL BUILDING, 60 FT. × 80 FT. × 20 FT.

(Fig. 5 and Fig. 6, Chapter XXVI).

No. Pcs.	Part of Structure.	Main Members, lb.	Details, lb.	Total Weight, lb.	Details Per cent Main Members
4	Trusses	11,284	2,736	14,020	24.6
8	Built I-posts	5,440	1,360	6,800	25.0
8	I-beam Posts	5,304	752	6,056	14.0
4	Angle-posts	1,224	444	1,668	36.3
4	End Rafters	1,460	316	1,776	22.0
2	Eave Struts	2,120		2,120	
	Angle Bracing	2,981	205	3,186	7.0
	Rod Bracing	1,760	300	2,060	17.0
	Total, not including Purlins and Girts	31,573	6,113	37,686	20.0
	Purlins	10,595		10,595	
	Girts	9,590		9,590	
	Total Framework	51,758	6,113	57,871	12.0
	Corrugated Steel	19,362	4,264	23,626	22.0
	Total	71,120	10,377	81,497	14.6

Weight of Framework per sq. ft. = 12.06 lb.
Weight of Framework per cu. ft. = 0.40 lb.
Total Weight of Steel per sq. ft. = 17.00 lb.
Total Weight of Steel per cu. ft. = 0.57 lb.
Glass = 1,040 sq. ft.

Rivet Heads.—Where the estimate is made from shop drawings the actual number of rivet heads should be determined. The weight of rivet heads in per cent of the total weight of the other material is about as follows: purlins, girts and beams, 2 per cent; trusses and bracing, 4 per cent; plate girders and columns of 4 angles and 1 pl., 5 per cent; plate girders and columns with cover plates, 6 per cent; box girders or channel columns with lacing, 7 per cent; trough floors, 8 to 10 per cent.

The rivet heads in highway bridges may be taken at 5 and 4 per cent of the total weight of steel exclusive of fence and joists for riveted and pin-connected trusses, respectively.

Bolts are usually taken off in the estimate when they occur, and entered as rivets.

TABLE III.

ESTIMATE OF WEIGHT OF STEEL MACHINE SHOP, 100 FT. × 200 FT. NITRO, W. VA.

No. Pcs.	Part of Structure.	Main Members, lb.	Details, lb.	Total Weight, lb.	Details, Per cent Main Members.
11	Main Trusses	32,495	7,074	39,569	21.8
22	Side Trusses	19,969	4,734	24,703	23.7
2	Crane Trusses	62,824	12,224	75,048	19.5
22	Main Columns	25,796	3,757	29,553	14.5
22	Side Columns	6,906	2,201	9,107	32.0
	Bracing, Main Trusses	11,135	2,120	13,255	19.0
	Bracing, Side Trusses	14,619	814	15,433	5.6
	Total Framework, not including Purlins and Girts	173,744	32,924	206,668	19.0
	Purlins	71,610	557	72,167	0.8
	Girts	21,085	1,550	22,635	7.5
	Total Framework	266,439	34,031	301,470	12.8
	Corrugated Steel Roof 230 sqs	37,490	7,498	44,988	20.0
	Sides 80 sqs	13,040	1,304	14,344	10.0
	Total	317,969	42,833	360,802	13.5

Weight of Framework per sq. ft. = 15.07 lb.
Weight of Framework per cu. ft. = 0.40 lb.
Total Weight of Steel per sq. ft. = 18.04 lb.
Total Weight of Steel per cu. ft. = 0.49 lb.
Glass = 7,860 sq. ft.
Timber, Sheathing = 45,000 ft. B.M.
Spiking Strips = 4,700 ft. B.M.
Brick = 31,500
Concrete = 80 cu. yd.
Wood Block Pavement = 2,200 sq. yd.

TABLE IV.

ESTIMATE OF WEIGHT OF STEEL PIER SHED, CENTRAL RY. OF N. J., 68 FT. × 273 FT. 4 IN.

No. Pcs.	Part of Structure.	Main Members, lb.	Details, lb.	Total Weight, lb.	Details Per cent Main Members.
13	Main Trusses	78,754	13,754	92,508	17.6
1	End Truss	4,283	889	5,172	20.8
2	Side Trusses	21,302	5,656	26,958	26.7
28	Columns	35,364	6,496	41,860	18.4
	Side Framing	33,954	898	34,852	2.7
	End Framing	23,426	3,414	26,840	14.6
	Bracing in Trusses	17,451	2,974	20,425	17.0
	Total Framework, not including Purlins	214,534	34,081	248,615	15.9
	Purlins	48,024	1,288	49,312	2.7
	Total Steel	262,558	35,369	297,927	13.5

Weight of Steel Framework per sq. ft. = 16.8 lb.
Weight of Steel Framework per cu. ft. = 0.68 lb.
Glass = 3,300 sq. ft.
Timber = 48,900 ft. B.M.

When bolts are under 6 in. in length, include bolts under the item "Bolts and Rivets." When over 6 in. in length, put the bolts under "Bars."

Miscellaneous Materials.—*Corrugated Steel.*—Always give the number of gage, whether painted or galvanized, and whether iron or steel. This remark also applies to louvres, flashing, ridge roll, gutters and conductors. State whether corrugated steel is for roofing or siding. Roofing should be estimated in squares of 100 sq. ft., adding three feet on each end of building to the distance c. to c. of end trusses to allow for cornice. Allow one foot overhang at eaves. Siding should be estimated in squares of 100 sq. ft., adding one foot at each end of building to allow for corner laps.

Louvres should be estimated in sq. ft. of superficial area, stating whether fixed or pivoted.

Flashing should be estimated in lineal feet and should be taken off over all windows where corrugated sheathing is used on the sides of building, and under all louvres and windows in ventilators.

Ridge roll should be estimated in lineal feet, adding one foot to the distance center to center of end trusses. Ridge roll is usually taken off the same gage as the corrugated steel roofing.

Gutters and conductors should be estimated in lineal feet, the conductors usually being spaced from 40 to 50 ft., depending upon the area drained.

Circular ventilators should be estimated by number, giving diameter and kind, if specified.

Stack collars should be estimated by number, giving diameter of stack.

Windows should be estimated in sq. ft. of superficial area, taking for the width the distance between girts. State whether windows are fixed, sliding, pivoted, counter-balanced or counter-weighted. State kind and thickness of glass and give list of hardware, and anything else of a special nature.

Doors should be estimated in sq. ft.; state whether sliding, lifting, rolling or swinging. Steel doors covered with corrugated steel should be estimated by including the steel frame under steel and the covering with corrugated steel siding. State style of track, hangers and latch.

Skylights should be estimated in sq. ft., giving kind of glass and frames.

Operating devices for pivoted windows or louvres should be estimated in lineal feet.

Lumber should be estimated in feet, board measure, noting kind. Note that lumber under 1 in. in thickness is classified as 1 in. Above 1 in. it varies by $\frac{1}{4}$ in. in thickness, and if surfaced will be $\frac{1}{8}$ in. less in thickness, i. e., $1\frac{3}{4}$ in. sheathing is actually $1\frac{5}{8}$ in. thick, but should be estimated as $1\frac{3}{4}$ in. Lumber comes in lengths of even feet; if a piece 10 ft. 8 in. or 11 ft. 0 in. is required, a stick 12 ft. 0 in. long should be estimated. In using lumber there is usually considerable waste, depending upon the purpose for which it is intended. In estimating tongue and groove sheathing 10 to 20 per cent should be added for tongues and grooves and from 5 to 10 per cent for waste, depending upon the widths of boards and how the sheathing is laid.

Composition roofing or slate should be estimated in squares of 100 sq. ft., allowing the proper amount for overhang at eaves and gables and for flashing up under a ventilator or on the inside of a parapet wall.

Tile roofing or slate should be estimated in squares of 100 sq. ft., adding 5 per cent for waste. Include in an estimate for tile roof, gutters, coping, ridge roll, plates over ventilator windows and plates under ventilator windows, these being estimated in lineal feet. Flat plates for the ends of ventilators should be estimated in sq. ft.

Brick should be estimated by number. For ordinary brick such as is used in mill building construction, estimate 7 brick per sq. ft. for each brick in thickness of wall, i. e., a 9-in. wall is two bricks thick and contains 14 brick for each sq. ft. of superficial area.

Always note whether walls are pilastered or corbeled and estimate the additional amount of brick required. If walls are plain, no percentage need be added for waste, but if openings such as arched windows occur add from 5 to 10 per cent.

Concrete should be estimated in cubic yards. Walls or ceiling of plaster on expanded metal should be estimated in squares of 100 sq. ft., noting thickness and kind of reinforcement. Reinforced concrete floors should be estimated in sq. ft. of floor area, noting thickness and kind of reinforcement. Paving of all kinds is estimated in square yards, but the concrete filling under the pavement itself is estimated in cubic yards. Concrete floor on cinder filling is usually estimated in square yards, specifying its proportions.

ESTIMATE OF COST.—The different types of framed steel structures vary so much with local conditions and requirements that it is only possible to give data that may be used as a guide to the experienced estimator. The cost of steel frame structures may be divided into (1) cost of material, (2) cost of fabrication, (3) cost of erection, and (4) cost of transportation. The costs of materials and labor have been abnormal for several years making cost data of relatively little value. Conditions are slowly returning to normal, but it is not possible at present to predict what the final base level will be. In the following discussion the costs are for prewar, 1914, conditions unless the actual date is given.

1. COST OF MATERIAL.—The price of structural steel is quoted in cents per pound delivered f.o.b. cars at the point at which the quotation is made. Current prices may be obtained from the Engineering-News Record, Iron Age or other technical papers.

Extras.—The base prices are for I-beams and channels 15 in. deep and under, angles with one or both legs 3 to 6 in. wide, inclusive; square or round bars, $\frac{3}{4}$ in. to 3 in., round or square, inclusive; flat bars 1 in. to 6 in. wide and $\frac{3}{8}$ in to 1 in. thick; plates $\frac{1}{4}$ in. thick and over, and 100 in. wide and under. All material other than that included above takes an extra price. For a standard card of extras, see the author's "Structural Engineers' Handbook."

COST OF FABRICATION OF STRUCTURAL STEEL.—The cost of fabrication of structural steel may be divided into (*a*) cost of drafting, (*b*) cost of mill details, and (*c*) cost of shop labor.

(*a*) **COST OF DRAFTING.**—The cost of drafting varies with the character of the structure and with the shop methods of the bridge company. There are two general methods in common use for detailing steel structures, sketch details, and complete details. The cost of drafting varies with the method of detailing and the number of pieces to be made from one detail, and costs per ton may mean but little and be very misleading. The cost per standard sheet (24 in. × 36 in.) is more nearly a constant and varies from $15 to $25 per sheet. The following approximate costs, based on a total average charge of 40 cents per hour, may be of value.

Mill and Mine Buildings.—Details of ordinary steel mill buildings cost from $2 to $4 per ton; details for headworks for mines cost from $4 to $6 per ton; details for churches and court houses having hips and valleys, cost from $6 to $8 per ton; details for circular steel bins cost from $1.50 to $3 per ton; details for rectangular steel bins cost from $2 to $4 per ton; details for conical or hopper bottom bins cost from $4 to $6 per ton.

Bridges.—Details of steel bridges will cost from $1 to $2 per ton where sketch details are used, and from $2 to $4 per ton where the members are detailed separately.

Actual Cost of Drafting.—The details of the Basin & Bay State Smelter, containing 270 tons, cost $2 per ton.

The costs of making shop details for steel structures as given in the Technograph No. 21, 1907, by Mr. Ralph H. Gage, are given in Table V.

TABLE V.
COST OF SHOP DRAWINGS.

Character of Building.	Average Cost per Ton.
Entire skeleton construction, i. e., loads all carried to the foundation by means of steel columns	$1.45
Interior portion supported on steel columns; exterior walls carry floor loads and their own weight	1.22
Interior portion carried on cast-iron columns; exterior walls support floor loads as well as their own weight	0.70
No columns and floorbeams resting on masonry walls throughout	0.85
Structure consisting mostly of roof trusses resting on columns	2.47
Structure consisting mostly of roof trusses resting on masonry walls	1.25
Mill buildings	2.56
Flat one-story shop or manufacturing buildings	0.74
Tipples, mining structures or other complicated structures	4.88
Malt or grain bins and hoppers	2.47
Remodeling and additions where measurements are necessary before details can be made	1.87

Mr. Gage makes the following comments on the cost of drafting: "The cost of drafting materials and blue prints was not included. There is always a noticeable decrease in cost of the details when the plans for the ironwork are made and designed by an engineer and separated from the general work. On the average it cost 35 per cent more to make shop drawings of the structural steel when the data were taken from the architect's plans than when the data were taken from carefully worked out engineer's plans. Inaccurate plans where the draftsman is continually finding errors which must be referred to the architect materially increase the cost of shop drawings."

(*b*) **COST OF MILL DETAILS.**—If material is ordered directly from the rolling mill the price for the necessary cutting to exact length, punching, etc., is based on a standard "card of mill extras."

CARD OF MILL EXTRAS.—If the estimate is to be based on card rates it will be necessary to have the subdivisions a, b, c, d, e, f, r, etc., as follows:

a = 0.15*cts. per lb.* This covers plain punching one size of hole in web only. Plain punching, one size of hole in one or both flanges.

b = 0.25*cts. per lb.* This covers plain punching one size of hole either in web and one flange or web and both flanges. (The holes in the web and flanges must be of same size.)

c = 0.30*cts. per lb.* This covers punching of two sizes of holes in web only. Punching of two sizes of holes either in one or both flanges. One size of hole in one flange and another size of hole in the other flange.

d = 0.35*cts. per lb.* This covers coping, ordinary beveling, riveting or bolting of connection angles and assembling into girders, when the beams forming such girders are held together by separators only.

e = 0.40*cts. per lb.* This covers punching of one size of hole in the web and another size of hole in the flanges.

f = 0.15*cts. per lb.* This covers cutting to length with less variation than $\pm \frac{3}{8}$ in.

r = 0.50*cts. per lb.* This covers beams with cover plates, shelf angles, and ordinary riveted beam work. If this work consists of bending or any unusual work, the beams should not be included in beam classification.

Fittings.—All fittings, whether loose or attached, such as angle connections, bolts, separators, tie rods, etc., whenever they are estimated in connection with beams or channels to be charged at 1.55cts. per lb. over and above the base price.

For additional data on "mill extras," see the author's "Structural Engineers' Handbook."

Mill Orders.—In mill orders the following items should be borne in mind. Where beams butt at each end against some other member, order the beams $\frac{1}{2}$ in. shorter than the figured lengths; this will allow a clearance of $\frac{1}{4}$ in. if all beams come $\frac{3}{8}$ in. too long. Where beams are to be built into the wall, order them in full lengths, making no allowance for clearance. Order small plates in multiple lengths. Irregular plates on which there will be considerable waste should be ordered cut to templet. Mills will not make reentrant cuts in plates. Allow $\frac{1}{4}$ in. for each milling for members that have to be faced. Order web plates for girders $\frac{1}{4}$ to $\frac{1}{2}$ in. narrower than the distance back to back of angles. Order as nearly as possible everything cut to required length, except where there are liable to be changes made, in which case order long lengths.

It is often possible to reduce the cost of mill details by having the mills do only part of the work, the rest being done in the field, or by sending out from the shop to be riveted on in the field connection angles and other small details that would cause the work to take a very much higher price. Standard connections should be used wherever possible, and special work should be avoided.

In estimating the cost of plain material in a finished structure the shipping weight from the structural shop is wanted. The cost of material f. o. b. the shop must therefore include the cost of waste, paint material, and the freight from the mill to the shop. The waste is variable but as an average may be taken at 4 per cent. Paint material may be taken as two dollars per ton. The cost of plain material at the shop would be

Average cost per lb. f. o. b. mill, say	2.25 cts.
Add 4 per cent for waste	.09 "
Add $2.00 per ton for paint material	.10 "
Add freight from mill to shop (Pittsburgh to St. Louis)	.24 "
Total cost per pound f. o. b. shop	2.68 "

To obtain the average cost of steel per pound multiply the pound price of each kind of material by the percentage that this kind of material is of the whole weight, the sum of the products will be the average pound price.

(*c*) **COST OF SHOP LABOR.**—The cost of shop labor may be calculated for the different parts of the structure, or may be calculated for the structure as a whole.

The cost of shop labor will depend upon the unit cost of labor, and upon the time taken to handle the parts, the number of cuts and punchings required, the assembling and bolting up and the number of driven rivets. For standard trusses and columns the number of driven rivets is an excellent measure in estimating the shop cost.

The roof trusses in Table I have 376 rivets in each truss. The present (1921) cost for driving $\frac{5}{8}$-in. shop rivets is about 7 cts. per rivet. This makes the shop cost of one truss = 376 × 0.07 = \$25.52, or about \$1.10 per 100 lb.

The framework of the steel machine shop in Table III required the driving of 30,000 rivets. The shop cost of 206,608 lb. of structural framework will be 30,000 × 0.07 = \$2,100.00, or about \$1.00 per 100 lb.

The following costs are based on an average charge of 40 cents per hour and include detailing and shop labor. The cost of fabricating beams, channels and angles which are simply punched or have connection angles loose or attached should be estimated on the basis of mill details, which see.

SHOP COSTS OF STEEL FRAME BUILDINGS.—The following costs of different parts of steel frame office and mill structures are a fair average.

Columns.—In lots of at least six, the shop cost of columns is about as follows: Columns made of two channels and two plates, or two channels laced cost about 0.80 to 0.70 cts. per lb., for columns weighing from 600 to 1,000 lb. each; columns made of 4 angles laced cost from 0.80 to 1.10 cts. per lb.; columns made of two channels and one I-beam, or three channels cost from 0.65 to 0.90 cts. per lb.; columns made of single I-beams, or single angles cost about 0.50 cts. per lb.; and Z-bar columns cost from 0.70 to 0.90 cts. per lb.

Plain cast columns cost from 1.50 to 0.75 cts. per lb., for columns weighing from 500 to 2,500 lb., and in lots of at least six.

Roof Trusses.—In lots of at least six, the shop cost of ordinary riveted roof trusses in which the ends of the members are cut off at right angles is about as follows: Trusses weighing 1,000 lb. each, 1.15 to 1.25 cts. per lb.; trusses weighing 1,500 lb. each, 0.90 to 1.00 cts. per lb.; trusses weighing 2,500 lb. each, 0.75 to 0.85 cts. per lb.; and trusses weighing 3,500 to 7,500 lb. each, 0.60 to 0.75 cts. per lb. Pin-connected trusses cost from 0.10 to 0.20 cts. per lb. more than riveted trusses.

Eave Struts.—Ordinary eave struts made of 4 angles laced, whose length does not exceed 20 to 30 ft., cost for shop work from 0.80 to 1.00 cts. per lb.

Plate Girders.—The shop work on plate girders for crane girders and floors will cost from 0.60 to 1.25 cts. per lb., depending upon the weight, details and number made at one time.

COST OF ERECTION OF STEEL FRAME OFFICE AND MILL BUILDINGS AND MINE STRUCTURES.—In estimating the cost of erection of structural steel work it is best to divide the cost into (*a*) cost of placing and bolting steel, and (*b*) cost of riveting. The cost will be based on labor at an average price of \$3.20 per day of 8 hours or 40 cts. per hour.

(*a*) **Cost of Placing and Bolting.**—The cost of placing and bolting mill buildings for ordinary conditions may be estimated at from \$6.00 to \$8.00 per ton. The cost of placing and bolting up steel office buildings may be estimated at from \$5.00 to \$9.00 per ton. The cost of placing and bolting up steel bins may be estimated at from \$10.00 to \$15.00 per ton. The cost of placing and bolting up head frames may be estimated at from \$12.00 to \$18.00 per ton.

(*b*) **Cost of Riveting.**—It will cost from 6 to 10 cts. per rivet to drive $\frac{5}{8}$- or $\frac{3}{4}$-in. rivets by hand in structural framework where a few rivets are found in one place.

A fair average is 7 cts. per rivet. The same size rivets can be driven in tank work for from 4 to 7 cts. per rivet, with 5 cts. per rivet as a fair average.

The cost of riveting by hand is distributed about as follows:

3 men, 2 driving and 1 bucking up, at \$3.50 per day of 8 hours	\$10.50
1 rivet heater at \$3.00 per day of 8 hours	3.00
Coal, tools, superintendence	1.50
Total per day	\$15.00

On structural work a fair day's work driving $\frac{3}{4}$-in. or $\frac{5}{8}$-in. rivets will be from 150 to 250, depending upon the amount of scaffolding required. This makes the total cost from 6 to 10 cts. per rivet.

On bin work when the rivets are close together and little staging is required, the gang above will drive from 200 to 400 rivets per day. This makes the total cost from about 4 to 7 cts. per rivet.

Rivets can be driven by power riveters for one-half to three-fourths the above, not counting the cost of installation and air. The added cost for power and equipment makes the cost of driving field drivets with pneumatic riveters about the same as the cost of driving field rivets by hand.

Soft iron rivets $\frac{1}{2}$ in. and under can be driven cold for about one-half what the same rivets can be driven hot, or even less.

Cost of Erection.—Small steel frame buildings will cost about \$10.00 per ton for the erection of the steel framework, if trusses are riveted and all other connections are bolted. The cost of laying corrugated steel is about \$0.75 per square when laid on plank sheathing, \$1.25 per square when laid directly on the purlins, and \$2.00 per square when laid with anti-condensation lining. The erection of corrugated steel siding costs from \$0.75 to \$1.00 per square. The cost of erecting heavy machine shops, all material riveted and including the cost of painting but not the cost of the paint, is about \$8.50 to \$9.00 per ton. Small buildings in which all connections are bolted may be erected for from \$5.00 to \$6.00 per ton. The cost of erecting the structural framework for office buildings will vary from \$6.00 to \$10.00 per ton.

Actual Costs of Erection.—The cost of erecting the East Helena transformer building, 1897, was \$12.80 per ton, including the erection of the corrugated steel and transportation of the men. The cost of erecting the Carbon Tipple was \$8.80 per ton, including corrugated steel. The cost of erection of the Basin & Bay State Smelter was \$8.20 per ton, including the hoppers and corrugated steel.

The cost of erecting the structural steel work for the Great Northern Ry. Grain Elevator, Superior, Wisconsin, was \$13.25 per ton, including the driving of all rivets. There were 10,600 tons of structural steel work, and 2,000,000 field rivets, or nearly 200 field rivets per ton of structural steel.

Erection of Structural Steel for an Armory.*—The structural framework for the new armory of the University of Illinois, consists of three-hinged arches having a span of 206 ft., and a center height of 94 ft. 3 in. The arches are spaced 26 ft. 6 in. centers and are braced in pairs. The total weight of structural steel was 985 tons, and contained 15,400 $\frac{7}{8}$-in. and 14,900 $\frac{3}{4}$-in. or a total of 30,300 field rivets. The cost of erecting the structural steel, including field riveting, was \$9.55 per ton. The average cost of driving the field rivets was 13.1 cts. each.

* Engineering and Contracting, Aug. 6, 1913.

Transportation.—Fabricated structural steel commonly takes a "fifth-class rate" when shipped in carload lots, and a "fourth-class rate" when shipped "local" (in less than carload lots). The minimum carload depends upon the railroad and varies from 20,000 to 30,000 lb. Tariff sheets giving railroad rates may be obtained from any railroad company. The shipping clerk should be provided with the clearances of all tunnels and bridges on different lines so that the car may be properly loaded.

Freight Rates.—The freight rates (1921) on finished steel products in carload shipments from the Pittsburgh District, including plates, structural shapes, merchant steel and iron bars, pipe fittings, plain and galvanized wire, nails, rivets, spikes and bolts (in kegs), black sheets (except planished), chain, etc., are as follows, in cts. per 100 lb. in carload shipments: Albany, 30; Buffalo, 17; Chicago, 27; Cincinnati, 23; Cleveland, 17; Denver, 99; Kansas City, 59; New Orleans, 38½; New York, 27; Pacific Coast (all rail), 125; Philadelphia, 24½; St. Louis, 24; St. Paul, 49½; Detroit, 33; Baltimore, 33.

COST OF PAINTING.—The amount of materials required to make a gallon of paint and the surface of steel work covered by one gallon are given in Table VI. Structural steel should be painted with one coat of linseed oil, linseed oil with lamp-black filler, or red lead paint at the shop; and two coats of first-class paint after erection. The two field coats should be of different colors; care being used to see that first coat is thoroughly dry before applying the second coat. Steel bridges and exposed steel frame buildings ordinarily require repainting every three or four years.

The steel work in the extension to the 16th St. Viaduct, Denver, Colo., was painted with red lead paint mixed in the following proportions,—100 lb. red lead, 2 lb. lamp-black and 4.125 gallons of linseed oil. This mixture made 6 gallons of mixed paint of a chocolate color, and gave 1.455 gallons of paint for each gallon of oil.

TABLE VI.

AVERAGE SURFACE COVERED PER GALLON OF PAINT.

PENCOYD HAND BOOK.

Paint.	Volume of Oil.	Pounds of Pigment.	Volume and Weight of Paint.		Square Feet.	
			Gal.	Lb.	1 Coat.	2 Coats.
Iron oxide (powdered)	1 gal.	8.00	1.2 =	16.00	600	350
Iron oxide (ground in oil)	1 gal.	24.75	2.6 =	32.75	630	375
Red lead (powdered)	1 gal.	22.40	1.4 =	30.40	630	375
White lead (ground in oil)	1 gal.	25.00	1.7 =	33.00	500	300
Graphite (ground in oil)	1 gal.	12.50	2.0 =	20.50	630	350
Black asphalt	1 gal. (turp.)	17.50	4.0 =	30.00	515	310
Linseed oil (no pigment)	1 gal.	....	....	....	875	...

Light structural work will average about 250 sq. ft., and heavy structural work about 150 sq. ft. of surface per net ton of metal, while No. 20 corrugated steel has 2,400 sq. ft. of surface.

It is the common practice to estimate ½ gallon of paint for the first coat and ⅜ gallon for the second coat per ton of structural steel, for average conditions.

For the cost of paint materials, see Engineering News-Record.

A good painter should paint 1,200 to 1,500 sq. ft. of plate surface or corrugated steel or 300 to 500 sq. ft. of structural steel work in a day of 8 hours; the amount covered depending upon the amount of staging and the paint. A thick red lead paint mixed with 30 lb. of lead to the gallon of oil will take fully twice as long to apply as a graphite paint or linseed oil. The cost of applying paint is roughly equal to the cost of a good quality of paint, the cost per ton depending on the spreading qualities of the paint. This rule makes the cost of applying a red lead paint with 30 lb. of pigment per gallon of oil from two to three times the cost of applying a good graphite paint, per ton of structural steel. For additional data on paints, see Chapter XXXV.

MISCELLANEOUS COSTS.—The following approximate costs will be of value in making preliminary estimates. The cost of construction depends so much upon local conditions that average costs should only be used as a guide to the judgment of the engineer.

MILL BUILDING FLOORS.—The following costs are for floors resting on a good compact soil and do not include unusual difficulties.

Timber Floor on Pitch-Concrete Base.—The cost varies from about $1.25 per sq. yd. for a 2-in. pine sub-floor and a $\frac{7}{8}$-in. pine finish, to about $1.75 per sq. yd. for a 2-in. pine sub-floor and a $\frac{7}{8}$-in. maple finish.

Asphalt Mastic Floor.—The asphalt mastic floor laid at the Philadelphia Navy Yard in 1918 cost $2.90 per sq. yd. For details of laying this floor and the detailed cost, see Chapter XXXII.

Concrete Floor on Gravel Sub-base.—The cost varies from $1.25 to $2.00 per sq. yd.

Creosoted Timber Block Floor.—Creosoted timber blocks 3 in. to 4 in. thick, laid on a 6-in. concrete base, will cost from $2.50 to $3.50 per sq. yd.

The Central Railway of Georgia in 1910 installed 12,140 sq. yd. of creosoted wood block floor in the machine and boiler shops at Macon, Ga. The blocks in the machine shop were 3 in. deep by 3 in. wide by 8 in. long, and were laid on a $\frac{1}{2}$-in. sand cushion on a concrete slab 5 in. thick. The joints were filled with sand and cement grout. The floor cost $2.70 per sq. yd., complete in place. The roundhouse has 5,000 sq. yd. of 4 in. creosote block floor. The blocks are $4\frac{1}{2}$ in. wide and are laid on a $\frac{1}{2}$-in. cushion on a concrete slab 5 in. thick. The floor cost $3.05 per sq. yd., complete in place. All blocks were of yellow pine treated with 18 lb. of creosote oil per cu. ft. No expansion joints were used and there has been no trouble from swelling.

The Pennsylvania Railroad laid a creosoted wood block floor during 1914 in its roundhouse at Erie, Pa. The blocks were laid on a 1-in. sand cushion on a concrete slab 6 in. thick. The floor cost $2.53 per sq. yd. in place.

ROOFING FOR MILL BUILDINGS.—The following costs include the cost of materials and the cost of laying, but do not include the cost of the sheathing.

Corrugated Steel Roofing.—The weight of corrugated steel roofing and siding may be obtained from Table I, Chapter XVIII. The price of corrugated steel may be obtained from current quotations in Engineering News-Record or Iron Age. The cost of laying corrugated steel is about $0.75 per square when laid on plank sheathing, $1.25 per square when laid directly on the purlins, and $2.00 per square when laid with anti-condensation lining. The erection of corrugated siding costs from $0.75 to $1.00 per square. Asbestos paper costs from $3\frac{1}{2}$ to 4 cts. per lb. Galvanized wire netting, No. 19, costs 25 to 30 cts. per square of 100 sq. ft. Brass wire, No. 20, costs about 20 cts. per lb. No. 9 galvanized wire costs about 3 cts. per lb. For trimmings, flashing, ridge roll, etc., add 1 ct. per lb. to the base price of corrugated steel.

Tar and Gravel Roofing.—Four- or five-ply tar and gravel roofing, for average conditions, costs from $3.75 to $4.00 per square, not including sheathing.

Cost of Five-Ply Tar and Gravel Roofing.—The cost of a roundhouse roof in the middle west, based on 1912 prices and containing 500 squares of five-ply tar and gravel roofing, was as follows:

Cost per square of 100 sq. ft. not including fixed charges or profit, not including sheathing.

Sheathing paper, 5 lb.	$0.12
Pitch, 155 lb. at 60 cents per 100 lb.	0.93
Felt, 85 lb. at $1.65 per 100 lb.	1.40
Nails and caps	0.05
Cleats for flashing	0.05
Gravel (about one-seventh yard)	.23
Labor, including hauling, board and railroad fare	1.15
Total cost per square	$3.93

Tin Roofing.—Tin roofing costs from $7.00 to $9.00 per square, not including sheathing.

Slate Roofing.—Slate roofing costs from $7.00 to $12.00 per square, not including sheathing.

Tile Roofing.—The cost of tile roofing is variable, depending upon style of roof and location and local conditions, and may vary from $13.00 to $30.00 per square, not including sheathing.

WINDOWS.—Windows with wooden frames and sash, and double strength glass, will cost from 25 to 50 cts. per sq. ft. of opening. Windows with metal frames and sash and wire glass, will cost from 45 to 55 cts. per sq. ft. of opening.

SKYLIGHTS.—Skylights with metal frames and sash and wire glass, will cost from 50 to 60 cts. per sq. ft. Skylights made of translucent fabric stretched on wooden frames, will cost from 25 to 30 cts. per sq. ft. Louvres without frames, will cost about 25 cts. per sq. ft.

CIRCULAR VENTILATORS.—Circular ventilators will cost about as follows:—12-in., $2.00; 18-in., $6.75; 24-in., $10.00; 36-in., $15.00 each, when ordered in lots of at least six.

ROLLING STEEL SHUTTERS.—Rolling steel shutters will cost $0.75 to $1.00 per sq. ft.

WATERPROOFING.—The following costs for waterproofing engineering structures are taken from the Proceedings of the American Railway Engineering Association, Vol. 12, 1911. (1) Bridge floor, 6-ply felt and pitch, $12\frac{1}{2}$ cts. per sq. ft., including protection over waterproofing. (2) Trough bridge floor, 4-ply burlap and asphalt, 10 to $16\frac{1}{2}$ cts. per sq. ft. (3) Bridge floor, 3-ply burlap and asphalt, and asphalt mastic, 16 cts. per sq. ft. (4) Concrete slab bridge floor, 5-ply felt, 1-ply burlap and pitch, $15\frac{1}{2}$ cts. per sq. ft., including a 10-year guarantee.

MISCELLANEOUS MATERIALS.—The following prices are for small lots, f.o.b. Pittsburgh (May, 1914).

Chain.—Standard chain, $\frac{3}{16}$ in., $7\frac{1}{2}$ cts. per lb.; $\frac{1}{2}$ in., 3 cts. per lb.; 1 in., 2.6 cts. per lb. For BB chain, add $1\frac{1}{2}$ cts. per lb., and for BBB chain, add 2 cts. per lb.

Nails.—Base price of nails, $2.00 per keg of 100 lb.—20d to 60d nails are base; for 10d to 16d, add 5 cts per keg; for 8d and 9d, add 10 cts. per keg; for 6d and 7d, add 20 cts. per keg; for 4d and 5d, add 30 cts. per keg; for 3d, add 45 cts. per keg, and for 2d, add 70 cts. per keg.

Gas Pipe.—Gas pipe costs about as follows:—Standard gas pipe 1 in. diam., black, $3\frac{1}{2}$ cts. per ft., galvanized, 5 cts. per ft.; 2 in. diam., black, $7\frac{1}{2}$ cts. per ft., galvanized, 11 cts. per ft.; 3 in. diam., black, $16\frac{1}{2}$ cts. per ft., galvanized, 23 cts. per ft.

Steel Railroad Rails.—Bessemer rails, $28 per gross ton (2,240 lb.); open-hearth, $30 per gross ton.

Wire Rope.—The cost of steel wire rope is about as follows:—$\frac{5}{8}$-in. rope, 10 cts. per lineal ft.; $\frac{3}{4}$-in. rope, 13 cts. per lineal ft.; 1-in. rope, 20 cts. per lineal ft.; $1\frac{1}{2}$-in. rope, 45 cts. per lineal ft.

Manila Rope.—Manila rope costs about $12\frac{1}{2}$ cts. per lb. Sisal rope costs about 9 cts. per lb.

HARDWARE AND MACHINISTS' SUPPLIES.—Prices of hardware and machinists' supplies are for the most part quoted by giving a discount from standard list prices. The "Iron Age Standard Hardware Lists" may be obtained from the Iron Age Book Department, 239 W. 39th St., New York. Discounts from these standard lists are given each week in Iron Age. The base prices of structural materials are given in the first issue of each month of Engineering News-Record, and are given in each issue of Iron Age.

ESTIMATE OF COST OF A STEEL FRAME MILL BUILDING.—An estimate will be made of the steel frame machine shop built at Nitro, West Virginia. General plans of this building are shown in Fig. 10, Chapter XXVI, and an estimate of the weight of the building is given in Table III. The prices are based on the conditions in 1918 when the building was constructed, and are slightly higher than prewar prices.

Estimate of Cost of Materials.—The base price of structural steel framework will be assumed as 2.68 cts. per lb. f.o.b. shop; shop work 1.00 cts. per lb.; and freight from shop to site 0.32 cts. per lb. This makes the total cost of structural steel 4.00 cts. per lb. f.o.b. site. Shop cost of purlins and girts will be taken as 0.30 cts. per lb., and total cost of purlins and girts will be 3.40 cts. per lb., f.o.b. site. Corrugated steel costs 3.00 cts. per lb. at mill and .30 cts. per lb. for freight from mill to site, makes a total cost of 3.30 cts. per lb., f.o.b. site.

Steel Frame Building, Cost of Materials.

Structural Steel, 206,700 lb.	@ 4.00 cts.	=	$8,268.00
Purlins and Girts, 94,800 lb.	@ 3.40 cts.	=	3,223.20
Corrugated Steel, 59,332 lb.	@ 3.30 cts.	=	1,957.96
Glass Windows, 7,860 sq. ft.	@ 50 cts.	=	3,930.00
Timber, 50,000 ft. B.M.	@ $40.00	=	2,000.00
Brick, 31,500	@ $15.00	=	472.50
Paint, 200 gallons	@ $ 2.00	=	400.00
Total Cost of Materials			$20,251.66

Steel Frame Building, Cost of Erection.

Structural Steel, 150 tons	@ $18.00 =	$2,700.00
Corrugated Steel, Roof, 230 sqs.	@ $ 2.00 =	460.00
Sides, 80 sqs.	@ $ 2.50 =	200.00
Windows, 7,860 sq. ft.	@ 15 cts. =	1,179.00
Timber, 50,000 ft. B.M.	@ $12.00 =	600.00
Brick, 31,500	@ $10.00 =	315.00
Painting		600.00
Total Cost of Erection		$6,054.00

Foundations, Cost of.

120 bbl. Portland Cement	@ $2.50 =	$300.00
40 cu. yd. Sand	@ $1.50 =	60.00
70 cu. yd. Broken Stone	@ $2.00 =	140.00
Mixing and Placing 80 cu. yd. concrete	@ $2.50 =	200.00
Total Cost of Foundations		$700.00

Wood Block Floor, Cost of.

2,200 sq. yd. wood block	@ $2.00 =	$4,400.00
500 bbl. Portland Cement	@ $2.50 =	1,250.00
180 cu. yd. Sand	@ $1.50 =	270.00
340 cu. yd. Broken Stone	@ $2.00 =	680.00
500 gal. Tar Filler	@ $ .25 =	125.00
Grading and Filling		400.00
Mixing and Placing concrete, 370 cu. yd.	@ $2.00 =	740.00
Laying wood block, 2,200 sq. yd.	@ $ .20 =	440.00
Total Cost of Floor		$8,305.00

Summary of Cost.

Steel Building, Materials	$20,251.66
Cost of Erection	6,054.00
Foundations	700.00
	$27,005.66
Profit, 15 per cent	4,050.84
Total Cost of Building and Foundations	$31,055.50
Cost = $1.51 per sq. ft.	
Cost = 4.3 cts. per cu. ft.	
Wood Block Floor, 2,200 sq. yd.	$8,305.00
Profit 10 per cent	830.00
	$9,135.00
Cost of Wood Block	$4.15 per sq. yd.
Total Cost of Building, Complete	$40,190.50
Total Cost of Building Per Sq. Ft.	$2.01
Total Cost of Building Per Cu. Ft.	0.05

REFERENCES.—For detailed estimates of steel mill buildings and additional data on the cost of steel structures, see the author's "Structural Engineers' Handbook." For detailed estimates of steel highway bridges and additional data on the cost of steel highway bridges, see the author's "The Design of Highway Bridges." For data on the cost of retaining walls, bins and grain elevators, see the author's "The Design of Walls, Bins and Grain Elevators." For data on the cost of steel head frames, coal tipples, and other mine structures, see the author's "The Design of Mine Structures."

APPENDIX I.

GENERAL SPECIFICATIONS FOR STEEL FRAME BUILDINGS.

BY

MILO S. KETCHUM,

M. Am. Soc. C. E.

FIFTH EDITION.

1932.

PART I. DESIGN.

1. **Height of Building.**—The height of the building shall be the distance from the top of the masonry to the under side of the bottom chord of the truss.

2. **Dimensions of Building.**—The width and length of the building shall be the extreme distance out to out of framing or sheathing.

3. **Length of Span.**—The length of trusses and girders in calculating stresses shall be considered as the distance from center to center of end bearings when supported, and from end to end when fastened between columns by connection angles.

4. **Pitch of Roof.**—The pitch of roof for corrugated steel shall preferably be not less than $\frac{1}{4}$ (6 in. in 12 in.), and in no case less than $\frac{1}{5}$. For a pitch less than $\frac{1}{5}$ some other covering than corrugated steel shall be used.

5. **Spacing of Trusses.**—Trusses shall be spaced so that simple shapes may be used for purlins. The spacing should be about 16 ft. for spans of, say, 50 ft. and about 20 to 22 ft. for spans of, say, 100 ft. For longer spans than 100 ft. the purlins may be trussed and the spacing may be increased.

6. **Spacing of Purlins.**—Purlins shall be spaced not to exceed 4 ft. 9 in. where corrugated steel is used, and shall preferably be placed at panel points of the trusses.

7. **Form of Trusses.**—The trusses shall preferably be of the Fink type with panels so subdivided that panel points will come under the purlins. If it is not practicable to place the purlins at panel points, the upper chords of the trusses shall be designed to take both the flexural and direct stresses. Trusses shall preferably be riveted trusses.

Trusses supported on masonry walls shall have one end supported on sliding plates for spans up to 70 ft.; for greater lengths of span, rollers or a rocker shall be used. No rollers with a diameter less than 4 in. shall be used.

8. **Bracing.**—Roof trusses supported on masonry walls or on columns, and transverse bents shall be braced in pairs. The pairs of trusses and transverse bents shall have bracing in the planes of the top and bottom chords, and, unless rigidly braced by other means, shall have transverse bracing between the trusses located approximately at the third points of the lower chord. The pairs of trusses and transverse bents shall be connected by rigid bracing in the plane of the lower chords in line with the lower chords of the transverse bracing. Steel frame buildings without effective knee braces shall have diagonal bracing extending between all pairs of trusses so arranged as to transmit the wind loads to the ends of the building, and the sides and the end bents shall be braced to transmit the wind loads.

Bracing in the plane of the lower chords shall be stiff; bracing in the planes of the top chords, sides and ends may be made adjustable.

9. **Field Connections.**—All field connections of the steel framework shall be riveted, except the connections of purlins and girts, which may be field-bolted.

10. **Proposals.**—Contractors in submitting proposals shall furnish complete stress sheets, general plans of the proposed structures giving sizes of material, and such detail drawings as will clearly show the dimensions of the parts, modes of construction and sectional areas.

11. **Detail Plans.**—The successful contractor shall furnish all working drawings required by the engineer free of cost. Working drawings shall, as far as possible, be made on standard size sheets 24 in. × 36 in. out to out, 22 in. × 34 in. inside the inner border lines.

12. **Approval of Plans.**—No work shall be commenced nor materials ordered until the working drawings are approved in writing by the engineer. The contractor shall be responsible for dimensions and details on the working plans, and the approval of the detail plans by the engineer shall not relieve the contractor of this responsibility.

PART II. LOADS.

13. The trusses shall be designed to carry the following loads:

14. **DEAD LOADS. Weight of Trusses.**—The weight of trusses per sq. ft. of horizontal projection, up to 150 ft. span, shall be calculated by the formula

$$W = \frac{P}{45}\left(1 + \frac{L}{5\sqrt{A}}\right) \tag{1}$$

where W = weight of trusses per sq. ft. of horizontal projection;
P = capacity of truss in pounds per sq. ft. of horizontal projection;
L = span of the truss in feet;
A = distance between trusses in feet.

15. **Weight of Covering. Corrugated Steel.**—The weight of corrugated steel shall be taken from Table I.

TABLE I.

WEIGHT OF FLAT, AND CORRUGATED STEEL SHEETS WITH $2\frac{1}{2}$-INCH CORRUGATIONS.

Gage No.	Thickness in inches.	Weight per Square (100 sq. ft.)			
		Flat Sheets.		Corrugated Sheets.	
		Black.	Galvanized.	Black Painted.	Galvanized.
16	.0625	250	266	271	286
18	.0500	200	216	217	232
20	.0375	150	166	163	178
22	.0313	125	141	136	151
24	.0250	100	116	110	124
26	.0188	75	91	83	98
28	.0156	63	79	68	85

When two corrugations side lap and six in. end lap are used, add 20 per cent to the above weights; when one corrugation side lap and four in. end lap are used, add 15 per cent to the above weights to obtain weight of corrugated steel laid. For paint add 2 lb. per square. The weight of covering shall be reduced to weight per sq. ft. of horizontal projection before combining with the weight of trusses.

16. **Slate.**—Slate laid with 3 in. lap shall be taken at a weight of $7\frac{1}{2}$ lb. per sq. ft. of inclined roof surface for $\frac{3}{16}$ in. slate 6 in. × 12 in., and $6\frac{1}{2}$ lb. per sq. ft. of inclined roof surface for $\frac{3}{16}$ in. slate 12 in. × 24 in., and proportional for other sizes.

17. **Tile.**—Terra-cotta tile roofing weighs about 6 lb. per sq. ft. for tile 1 in. thick; the actual weight of tile and other roof coverings not named shall be used.

18. **Sheathing and Purlins.**—Sheathing of dry pine lumber shall be assumed to weigh 3 lb. per ft. and dry oak purlins 4 lb. per ft. board measure.

19. **Miscellaneous Loads.**—The exact weight of sheathing, purlins, bracing, ventilators, cranes, etc., shall be calculated.

20. **SNOW LOADS.**—Snow loads shall be assumed as follows:—For a latitude of 40° the snow load in lb. per sq. ft. of horizontal projection shall be; for roofs with $\frac{1}{6}$ pitch (18° 15′), 25 lb.; $\frac{1}{5}$ pitch (21° 47′), 20 lb.; $\frac{1}{4}$ pitch (26° 34′), 15 lb.; $\frac{1}{3}$ pitch (33° 40′) and over, 10 lb. For a latitude of 50° the snow load in lb. per sq. ft. of horizontal projection shall be; for roofs with $\frac{1}{6}$ pitch and less, 50 lb.; $\frac{1}{5}$ pitch, 40 lb.; $\frac{1}{4}$ pitch, 30 lb.; $\frac{1}{3}$ pitch, and over 20 lb. Snow loads for other latitudes shall be taken proportional.

For Pacific coast and arid regions, use one-half of the snow loads above specified.

All roofs shall be assumed to carry a minimum snow load or ice load of 10 lb. per sq. ft. of horizontal projection, at the time of maximum wind load.

21. **WIND LOADS.**—The normal wind load on trusses shall be computed by Duchemin's formula

$$P_n = P \frac{2 \sin A}{1 + \sin^2 A} \qquad (2)$$

where P_n = normal wind pressure per sq. ft.; A = angle of roof surface with horizontal, and P = 30 lb. per sq. ft.; except for exposed locations where P = 40 lb. per sq. ft. shall be used.

Normal pressures for a horizontal wind pressure of 30 lb. per sq. ft. as calculated by Duchemin's formula are given in Table II.

TABLE II.

Normal Wind Pressure on Roofs for Horizontal Wind Pressure of 30 lb. per sq. ft. by Duchemin's Formula, (2).

Angle of Roof with Horizontal. A	Normal Pressure lb. per sq. ft. P_n	Angle of Roof with Horizontal. A	Normal Pressure lb. per sq. ft. P_n
5°	5.1	25°	21.6
10°	10.2	¼ pitch	22.4
15°	14.5	30°	24.0
⅙ pitch	17.2	40°	27.3
20°	18.3	½ pitch	28.3
⅕ pitch	20.0	55° to 90°	30.0

The sides and ends of buildings shall be computed for a normal wind load of 20 lb. per sq. ft. of exposed surface for buildings 30 ft. and less to the eaves; 30 lb. per sq. ft. of exposed surface for buildings 60 ft. to the eaves, and in proportion for intermediate heights.

22. In steel frame buildings having efficient knee-braced bents and also so braced as to transmit wind loads through the planes of the upper and lower chords and sides and ends as in § 8, the wind load may be assumed as taken equally by the two systems of bracing. In which case, the transverse bents may be designed to carry one-half the wind loads specified in § 21.

23. The wind pressure on circular tanks or chimneys shall be taken as 20 lb. per sq. ft. on the vertical projection of the surface.

24. **Mine Buildings.**—Mine, smelter and other buildings exposed to the action of corrosive gases shall have their dead loads increased 25 per cent.

25. **Live Loads.**—Concentrated loads due to cranes, shafting, etc., shall be provided for. In addition to vertical loads due to cranes, the crane girders and the structure shall be designed to withstand a lateral or a transverse loading each equal to twenty per cent. of the lifting capacity of the crane, divided equally between all the wheels of the crane, and applied in the plane of the center of gravity of the top of the flange of the crane girder.

26. **Purlins.**—Purlins shall be designed to carry the actual weight of the covering, roofing and purlins, but shall always be designed for a normal load of not less than 30 lb. per sq. ft., § 57.

27. **Girts.**—Girts shall be designed for a normal load of not less than 20 lb. per sq. ft., § 57.

28. **Roof Covering.**—Roof covering shall be designed for a normal load of not less than 30 lb. per sq. ft.

29. **Minimum Loads.**—No roof shall, however, be designed for an equivalent load of less than 30 lb. per sq. ft. of horizontal projection.

30. **Loads on Foundations.**—The loads on foundations shall not exceed the following in tons per sq. ft.:

Ordinary clay and dry sand mixed with clay	2
Dry sand and dry clay	3
Hard clay and firm coarse sand	4
Firm coarse sand and gravel	5
Shale rock	8
Hard rock	20

For all soils inferior to the above, such as loam, etc., never more than one ton per sq. ft.

31. **Stresses in Masonry.**—The allowable stresses in masonry when used in walls and foundations shall not exceed the following:

	Tons per Sq. Ft.	Lb. per Sq. In.
Common brick, Portland cement mortar	12	170
Hard burned brick, Portland cement mortar	15	210
Rubble masonry, Portland cement mortar	12	170
First class masonry, crystalline sandstone or limestone	25	350
First class masonry, granite	30	420
Portland cement concrete, 1–3–5	20	280
Portland cement concrete, 1–2–4	30	420

32. **Pressures on Masonry.**—The pressure of column bases, beams, etc., on masonry shall not exceed the following in pounds per sq. in.:

Brick work with cement mortar	250
Rubble masonry with cement mortar	250
Portland cement concrete, 1–2–4	600
First class dimension sandstone or limestone	400
First class granite	600

33. **Loads on Timber Piles.**—The maximum load carried by a pile shall not exceed 40,000 lb., or 600 lb. per sq. in. of its average cross-section. The allowable load on piles driven with a drop hammer shall be determined by the formula $P = \frac{2W \cdot h}{s + 1}$. Where P = safe load on pile in tons; W = weight of hammer in tons; h = free fall of hammer in ft.; s = average penetration for the last six blows of the hammer in in. Where a steam hammer is used, $\frac{1}{10}$ is to be used in place of unity in the denominator of the right hand member of the formula.

Piles shall have a penetration of not less than 10 ft. in hard material, such as gravel, and not less than 15 ft. in loam or soft material.

PART III. ALLOWABLE UNIT STRESSES AND PROPORTION OF PARTS.

34. **Allowable Stresses.**—In proportioning the different parts of the structure the maximum stresses due to the combinations of the dead and wind load; dead and snow load; or dead, minimum snow and wind load are to be provided for. Concentrated loads where they occur must be provided for.

35. **Impact.**—For structures carrying cranes and traveling machinery, 25 per cent shall be added to provide for the effect of vibration and impact.

36. **Compressive Stress.**—Allowable Unit Compressive Stress for Structural Steel. For direct dead, snow and wind loads

$$S = 18,000 - 60\frac{l}{r}$$

where S = allowable unit stress in lb. per sq. in.;
l = length of member in inches c. to c. of end connections;
r = least radius of gyration of the member in inches.

The maximum value of S shall be 15,000 lb. per sq. in.

37. **Tensile Stress.**—Allowable Unit Tensile Stresses for Structural Steel. For direct dead, snow and wind loads.

	Lb. per Sq. In.
Shapes, main members, net section	18,000
Bars	18,000
Bottom flanges of rolled beams	18,000
Shapes, laterals, net section	20,000
Steel bars for laterals	20,000

38. **Bending.**—Bending; on extreme fibers of rolled shapes, built sections and girders;

net section	18,000
on cast iron	3,000
on extreme fibers of pins	27,000

39. **Shearing.**—Shearing;

shop driven rivets and pins	13,500
field driven rivets and turned bolts	12,000
plate girder webs; net section	12,000
cast iron	1,500

40. **Bearing.**—Bearing; shop driven rivets and pins 27,000
field driven rivets and turned bolts 24,000
cast iron 12,000
granite masonry and Portland cement concrete 600
sandstone and limestone 400
expansion rollers; per lineal inch .... $600d$
cast iron expansion rockers; per lineal inch .... $300d$
where "d" is the diameter of the roller or rocker in inches.

Rivets may be used in direct tension, in which case the value for direct tension on the rivet shall be taken the same as for single shear.

Field bolts, when allowed, shall be spaced for stresses two-thirds those allowed for field rivets.

41. **Maximum Length of Compression Members.**—No compression member shall have a length exceeding 125 times its least radius of gyration for main members, nor 150 times its least radius of gyration for laterals and sub-members. The length of a main tension member in which the stress is reversed by wind shall not exceed 150 times its least radius of gyration.

42. **Maximum Length of Tension Members.**—The length of riveted tension members in horizontal or inclined position shall not exceed 200 times their radius of gyration except for wind bracing, which members may have a length equal to 250 times the least radius of gyration. The distance center to center of end connections of the member is to be considered the effective length.

43. **Alternate Stress.**—Members and connections subject to alternate stresses shall be designed to take each kind of stress.

44. **Combined Stress.**—Members subject to combined direct and bending stresses shall be proportioned according to the following formula:

$$S = \frac{P}{A} + \frac{M \cdot c}{I \pm \frac{P \cdot l^2}{10E}}$$

where S = stress in lb. per sq. in. in extreme fiber;
P = direct load in lb.;
A = area of member in sq. in.;
M = bending moment in in.-lb.;
c = distance from neutral axis to extreme fiber in inches;
I = moment of inertia of member;
l = length of member, or distance from point of zero moment to end of member in inches;
E = modulus of elasticity = 30,000,000 lb. per sq. in.

When combined direct and flexural stress due to wind is considered, 50 per cent may be added to the above allowable tensile and compressive stresses.

When the combined stress due to oblique loading of purlins and girts is considered, 25 per cent may be added to allowable stresses.

45. **Stress Due to Weight of Member.**—Where the stress due to the weight of the member or due to an eccentric load exceeds the allowable stress for direct loads by more than 10 per cent, the section shall be increased until the total stress does not exceed the above allowable stress for direct loads by more than 10 per cent.

46. **Angles in Tension.**—When single-angle members subject to direct tension are fastened by one leg, only seventy-five per cent of the net area shall be considered effective. Angles with lug angle connections shall not be considered as fastened by both legs.

47. **Net Section.**—In members subject to tensile stresses full allowance shall be made for reduction of section by rivet-holes, screw-threads, etc. In calculating net area the rivet-holes shall be taken as having a diameter $\frac{1}{8}$ in. greater than the normal size of rivet.

The net section of riveted members shall be the least area which can be obtained by deducting from the gross sectional area the areas of holes cut by any plane perpendicular to the axis of the member and parts of the areas of other holes on one side of the plane, within a distance of 4 inches, and which are on other gage lines than those of the holes cut by the plane, the parts being determined by the formula:

$$A(1 - p/4),$$

in which A = the area of the hole, and

p = the distance in inches of the center of the hole from the plane.

48. **Minimum Sections.**—The minimum thickness of plates shall be one-quarter ($\frac{1}{4}$) in., except for fillers. Minimum angles shall be 2 in. by 2 in. by $\frac{1}{4}$ in. The webs of channels shall have a minimum thickness of 0.18 in. The minimum thickness of connection plates of trusses shall be three-eighths ($\frac{3}{8}$) in. The minimum thickness of metal in base plates of columns shall be five-eighths ($\frac{5}{8}$) in. The minimum thickness of metal in head frames, rock houses, coal tipples, washers and breakers shall be five-sixteenths ($\frac{5}{16}$) in. except for fillers. No upset rods, except sag rods, may be less than five-eighths ($\frac{5}{8}$) in. in diameter. Sag rods may be as small as one-half ($\frac{1}{2}$) in. if the ends are properly upset.

49. **Initial Stress.**—Laterals shall be designed for the maximum stresses due to 5,000 pounds initial tension and the maximum stress due to wind.

50. **Design of Plate Girders.**—Plate girders shall be proportioned either by the moment of inertia of their net section; or by assuming that the flanges are concentrated at their centers of gravity, in which case one-eighth of the gross section of the web, if properly spliced, may be used as flange section. The thickness of web plates shall be not less than $\frac{5}{16}$ in., nor less than 1/160 of the unsupported distance between flange angles.

51. **Compression Flanges.**—Compression flanges of plate girders shall have at least the same sectional area as the tension flanges, and shall not have a stress per sq. in. on the gross area greater than $20,000 - 200\, l/b$, where l = unsupported distance, and b = width of flange, both in inches. Compression flanges of plate girders shall be stayed transversely when their length is more than thirty times their width.

52. **Web Stiffeners.**—There shall be web stiffeners, generally in pairs, over bearings, at points of concentrated loading, and at other points where the thickness of the web is less than $\frac{1}{60}$ of the unsupported distance between flange angles. The distance between stiffeners shall not exceed that given by the following formula, with a maximum limit of six feet (and not greater than the clear depth of the web): $h = t\,(18,000 - s)/100$. Where h = clear distance between stiffeners of flange angles; t = thickness of web; s = shear in lb. per sq. in.

The stiffeners at ends and at points of concentrated loads shall be proportioned by the formula of paragraph 36, the effective length being assumed as one-half the depth of girder. End stiffeners and those under concentrated loads shall be on fillers and have their outstanding legs as wide as the flange angles will allow and shall fit tightly against them. Intermediate stiffeners may be offset or on fillers, and their outstanding legs shall be not less than one-thirtieth of the depth of girder, plus 2 in.

53. **Flange Rivets.**—The flanges of plate girders shall be connected to the web with a sufficient number of rivets to transfer the total shear at any point in a distance equal to the effective depth of the girder at that point combined with any load that is applied directly on the flange. The wheel loads of crane girders shall be assumed to be distributed over 25 inches. The coefficient of friction of crane girder wheels on steel rails shall be taken as 0.20.

54. **Rolled Beams.**—Rolled beams shall be proportioned by their moment of inertia. The depth of rolled beams in floors shall not be less than one-twentieth ($\frac{1}{20}$) of the span. Where rolled beams or channels are used as roof purlins the depths shall not be less than one-fortieth ($\frac{1}{40}$) of the span. When the unsupported length of rolled beams when used as girders exceeds 10 times the width of flange, b, the unit stress in the flange shall not exceed $20,000 - 200\, l/b$ lb.

55. **Timber.**—The allowable stresses in timber purlins and other timber shall be taken from Table III.

TABLE III.

Allowable Working Unit Stresses in Timber, in Pounds per Square Inch.

Kind of Timber.	Transverse Loading, S.	End Bearing, C	Columns Under 12 Diameters	Bearing Across Fiber.	Shear.		Modulus of Elasticity, E.
					Parallel to Grain.	Longitudinal Shear in Beams	
White Oak	1,500	1,500	1,200	600	260	140	1,200,000
Long Leaf Yellow Pine	1,500	1,500	1,200	350	220	150	1,500,000
White Pine and Spruce	1,200	1,200	960	200	125	90	1,200,000
Western Hemlock	1,400	1,500	1,200	300	200	125	1,500,000
Douglas Fir	1,500	1,500	1,200	400	210	140	1,200,000

Columns may be used with a length not exceeding 40 times the least dimension. The unit stress for lengths of more than 12 times the least dimension shall be reduced by the following formula:

$$P = C - \frac{C}{60}\frac{l}{d}$$

where C = unit stress, as given above for end bearing;
P = allowable unit stress in lb. per sq. in.;
l = length of column in inches;
d = least side of column in inches.

PART IV. COVERING AND FLOORS.

56. **Corrugated Steel.**—Corrugated steel shall generally have $2\frac{1}{2}$ in. corrugations when used for roof and sides of buildings, and $1\frac{1}{4}$ in. corrugations when used for lining buildings. The minimum gage of corrugated steel shall be No. 22 for roofs, No. 24 for sides, and No. 26 for lining.

The gage of corrugated steel in U. S. standard gage and weight per sq. ft. shall be shown on the general plan.

57. **Spacing of Purlins and Girts.**—The spacing, or center to center distance of purlins carrying a corrugated steel roof without sheathing, shall not exceed the distances given in Table IV for a safe load of 30 lb. per sq. ft. Girts for corrugated steel shall be spaced for a safe load of 20 lb. per sq. ft. as given in Table IV. Corrugated steel sheets shall preferably span two purlin or girt spaces. When sag rods are provided as in § 58 and § 59, purlins and girts shall be designed to carry the normal loads with a maximum unit stress of 18,000 lb. per sq. in.

TABLE IV.

Maximum Spacing for Purlins and Girts Supporting Corrugated Steel.

Gage of Steel, No.	Spacing of Purlins and Girts.	
	Purlins, 30 lb. per sq. ft.	Girts, 20 lb. per sq. ft.
16	5 ft. 8 in.	6 ft. 9 in.
18	5 ft. 2 in.	6 ft. 2 in.
20	4 ft. 6 in.	5 ft. 4 in.
22	4 ft. 2 in.	5 ft. 0 in.
24	3 ft. 8 in.	4 ft. 6 in.

58. **Sag Rods.**—With a steel corrugated roof one sag rod, at the center, shall be used for purlin spans of 20 ft. or less, and two sag rods, spaced at the third points, for purlin spans of more than 20 ft. With clay tile, cement tile, slate, gypsum, or similar roofs, one sag rod shall be used for purlin spans of 14 ft. or less, and two sag rods spaced at the third points, for spans of more than 14 ft. Where one sag rod is used, the sag rod on each side of the roof in any panel shall be rigidly connected through the ridge purlins. Where two sag rods are used in any panel, each sag rod shall be rigidly connected with the peak of the nearest truss by means of a diagonal sag rod in the upper purlin space. Sag rods need not be used in roofs having a slope of 3 in. in 12 in., or less. With corrugated steel siding, one sag rod shall be used for all girt spacings of 20 ft. or less, and two sag rods spaced at third points for girt spacings of more than 20 ft.

59. Sag rods shall be designed to carry the component of the dead load of the purlins and roof covering and the maximum snow load parallel to the roof surface, with a unit stress of 18,000 lb. per sq. in. on net section. Sag rods for the sides shall be designed to carry the weight of the side framing and covering with the same allowable unit stresses as for sag rods for purlins. If sag rods are not upset the net section shall be taken as the section having a diameter $\frac{1}{8}$ in. less than the diameter of the root of the thread. The minimum size of sag rods shall have a diameter of $\frac{1}{2}$ in. if the ends are upset, or $\frac{5}{8}$ in. if the ends are not upset.

60. **End and Side Laps.**—Corrugated steel shall be laid with two corrugations side lap and six inches end lap when used for roofing, and one corrugation side lap and four inches end lap when used for siding.

61. **Fastening.**—Corrugated steel shall be fastened to the purlins and girts by means of galvanized iron straps $\frac{3}{4}$ in. wide by No. 18 gage, spaced 8 to 12 in. apart; by clinch nails spaced 8 to 12 in. apart; or by nailing directly to spiking strips with 8d barbed nails, spaced 8 in. apart.

Spiking strips shall preferably be used with anti-condensation lining. Bolts, nails and rivets shall always pass through the top of corrugations. Side laps shall be riveted with copper or galvanized iron rivets 8 to 12 in. apart on the roof and $1\frac{1}{2}$ to 2 ft. apart on the sides.

62. **Corrugated Steel Lining.**—Corrugated steel lining on the sides shall be laid with one corrugation side lap and four in. end lap. Girts for corrugated steel lining shall be spaced for a safe load of 20 lb. per sq. ft. as given in Table IV.

63. **Anti-Condensation Lining.**—Anti-condensation roof lining shall be used to prevent dripping in engine houses and similar buildings, and shall be constructed as follows:—(1) Lay wire netting, No. 19, 2-in. mesh, transversely to the purlins, with edges $1\frac{1}{2}$ in. apart, so that when laced together with No. 20 brass wire the netting will be stretched smooth and tight.

(2) On the top of the netting lay asbestos paper weighing 30 lb. to the square of 100 sq. ft., allowing 3 in. for laps. For important work lay one or two thicknesses of building paper on top of the asbestos.

(3) Lay the corrugated steel and fasten to purlins in the usual manner.

If wood purlins are used the wire netting may be fastened to the nailing strips with $\frac{3}{4}$ in. staples. Where the purlins are more than 2 ft. 6 in. centers place a line of $\frac{3}{16}$ in. bolts between purlins, about 2 ft. centers, with washers 1 in. × 4 in. × $\frac{1}{8}$ in. to prevent netting from sagging.

64. **Flashing.**—Valleys or corners around stacks shall have flashing extending at least 12 in. above where water will stand, and shall be riveted or soldered, if necessary, to prevent leakage. Flashing shall be provided above doors and windows. Flashing shall be made of steel not lighter than No. 20 gage.

65. **Ridge Roll.**—All ridges shall have a ridge roll, the same thickness as the corrugated steel, securely fastened to the corrugated steel.

66. **Corner Finish.**—All corners shall be covered with standard corner finish, the same thickness as the corrugated steel, securely fastened to the corrugated steel.

67. **Cornice.**—At the gable ends the corrugated steel on the roof shall be securely fastened to a finish angle or channel connected to the end of the purlins, or, where molded cornices are used, to a piece of timber fastened to the ends of the purlins. Cornice shall be made of steel not lighter than No. 20 gage.

68. **Gutters and Conductors.**—Gutters and conductors shall be furnished at least equal to the requirements of the following table:

Span of Roof.	Gutter.	Conductor.
Up to 50 ft.	6 in.	4 in. every 40 ft.
50 ft. to 70 ft.	7 in.	5 in. every 40 ft.
70 ft. to 100 ft.	8 in.	5 in. every 40 ft.

Gutters shall have a slope of at least 1 in. in 15 ft. Gutters and conductors shall be made of galvanized steel not lighter than No. 20 gage.

69. **Ventilators.**—Ventilators shall be provided and located so as to properly ventilate the building. They shall have a net opening for each 100 sq. ft. of floor space as follows: not less than one-fourth sq. ft. for clean machine shops and similar buildings; not less than one sq. ft. for dirty machine shops; not less than four sq. ft. for mills; and not less than six sq. ft. for forge shops, foundries and smelters.

70. **Shutters and Louvres.**—Openings in ventilators shall be provided with shutters, sash, or louvres, or may be left open as specified.

Shutters must be provided with a satisfactory device for opening and closing.

Louvres must be designed to prevent the blowing in of rain and snow, and must be made stiff so that no appreciable sagging will occur. They shall be made of not less than No. 20 gage galvanized steel for flat louvres, and No. 24 gage galvanized steel for corrugated louvres.

71. **Circular Ventilators.**—Circular ventilators, when used, must be designed so as to prevent down drafts. Net opening only shall be used in calculations.

72. **Windows and Skylights.**—Where buildings are lighted by windows the clear window area shall not be less than 20 per cent of the floor area, nor less than 10 per cent of the area of the entire exterior surface in mill buildings, nor less than 20 per cent of the area of the entire exterior surface in machine shops, factories and other buildings in which men are required to work at machines. Skylights shall be used where the required window area cannot be provided in the sides and ends of buildings.

Where buildings are lighted by windows having the sills not more than 4 ft. above the floor, the span of the building shall not exceed 2 times the height of the top of the windows where buildings are lighted by windows in one side, or 4 times the height of the top of the windows where buildings are lighted by windows in both sides. Where the span of the building is greater than is permitted by the preceding requirement, the necessary illumination shall be provided either by prism glass in side walls or by skylights. Skylights shall have such an area and shall be so arranged that light coming through the skylight making an angle of not more than 45° with the vertical shall cover the entire horizontal area at a distance of 6 feet above the floor; or the light may be diffused by means of ribbed glass or prisms or by reflection from the ceiling to obtain equally satisfactory illumination. In saw tooth roofs the inner surface of the roof shall be light colored or shall be painted with a paint that will reflect the light and make the illumination uniform and effective. All windows or skylights admitting direct sunlight shall be provided with muslin or other satisfactory shades.

73. **Skylights.**—Skylights shall be glazed with wire glass, or wire netting shall be stretched beneath the skylights to prevent the broken glass from falling into the building. Where there is danger of the skylight glass being broken by objects falling on it, a wire netting guard shall be provided on the outside.

Skylight glass shall be carefully set, special care being used to prevent leakage. Leakage and condensation on the inner surface of the glass shall be carried to the down-spouts, or outside the building by condensation gutters.

74. **Wood Sash.**—Window glass set in wood sash up to 12 in. × 14 in. may be single strength, over 12 in. × 14 in. the glass shall be double strength. Window glass shall be A grade except in smelters, foundries, forge shops and similar structures, where it may be B grade. The sash and frames shall be constructed of white pine. Where buildings are exposed to fire hazard the windows shall have wire glass set in metal sash and frames.

Windows with wood sash in sides of buildings shall be made with counter-balanced sash, and in ventilators shall be made with sliding or swing sash. All swinging windows shall be provided with a satisfactory operating device.

75. **Wire Glass.**—Wire glass shall have a thickness of not less than $\frac{1}{4}$ in. The wire mesh shall be not larger than $\frac{7}{8}$ in., and the thickness of the wire shall not be less than No. 24 B. & S. gage for single wire, or No. 27 B. & S. gage for twisted double wire. The wire shall be practically midway between the two surfaces of glass. Lights shall not have a greater area than 720 sq. in., or more than 54 in. vertical and 48 in. horizontal. Lights of glass shall preferably be 12 in. by 18 in. or 14 in. by 20 in. The selvage shall be removed from the glass before setting. The bearing of glass in grooves shall not be less than $\frac{5}{8}$ in. at all points, and there shall be a clearance of $\frac{1}{8}$ in. between the edge of the glass and the frame.

76. **Steel Sash.**—Steel sash shall be made with solid sections. The maximum size of steel sash shall be 100 sq. ft. where no ventilators are used, and 70 sq. ft. where ventilators occupy two-thirds of the window area and proportional for intermediate amount of ventilators. Steel sash shall be glazed with special glazing clips and with glazing putty. All sash shall be provided with locking devices, and other hardware as specified.

77. **Doors.**—Doors are to be furnished as specified and are to be provided with hinges, tracks, locks, and bolts. Single doors up to 4 ft. and double doors up to 8 ft. shall preferably be swung on hinges; large doors, double and single, shall be arranged to slide on overhead tracks, or may be counterbalanced to lift up between vertical guides.

Steel doors shall be firmly braced. Unless otherwise specified, steel doors shall be covered with No. 24 corrugated steel with $1\frac{1}{4}$ in. corrugations.

The frames of sandwich doors shall be made of two layers of $\frac{7}{8}$ in. matched white pine, placed diagonally and firmly nailed with clinch nails. The frame shall be covered on each side with a layer of No. 24 corrugated steel with $1\frac{1}{4}$ in. corrugations. Locks and all other necessary hardware shall be furnished for all windows and doors.

78. **TAR AND GRAVEL ROOF.**—Tar and gravel roofs are called three-, four-, five-ply, etc., depending upon the number of layers of roofing felt. Tar and gravel roofs may be laid upon timber sheathing or upon concrete or gypsum slabs.

79. **Specifications for Five-Ply Tar and Gravel Roof on Board Sheathing.**—The materials used in making the roof are one (1) thickness of sheathing paper or unsaturated felt, five (5) thicknesses of saturated felt weighing not less than fifteen (15) pounds per square of one hundred (100) square feet, single thickness, and not less than one hundred and fifty (150) pounds of pitch, and not less than four hundred (400) pounds of gravel or three hundred (300) pounds of slag from $\frac{1}{4}$ to $\frac{5}{8}$ in. in size, free from dirt, per square of one hundred (100) square feet of completed roof.

80. The material shall be applied as follows: First, lay the sheathing or unsaturated felt, lapping each sheet one inch over the preceding one. Second, lay two (2) thicknesses of tarred felt, lapping each sheet seventeen (17) inches over the preceding one, nailing as often as may be necessary to hold the sheets in place until the remaining felt is applied. Third, coat the entire surface of this two-ply layer with hot pitch, mopped on uniformly. Fourth, apply three (3) thicknesses of felt, lapping each sheet twenty-two (22) inches over the preceding one, mopping

with hot pitch the full width of the 22 inches between the plies, so that in no case shall felt touch felt. Such nailing as is necessary shall be done so that all nails will be covered by not less than two plies of felt. Fifth, spread over the entire surface of the roof a uniform coating of pitch, into which, while hot, imbed the gravel or slag. The gravel or slag in all cases must be dry.

81. **Specifications for Five-Ply Tar and Gravel Roof on Concrete Sheathing.**—The materials used shall be the same as for tar and gravel roof on timber sheating, except that the one thickness of sheathing paper or unsaturated felt may be omitted.

82. The materials shall be applied as follows: First, coat the concrete with hot pitch, mopped on uniformly. Second, lay two (2) thicknesses of tarred felt, lapping each sheet seventeen (17) inches over the preceding one, and mop with hot pitch the full width of the 17-inch lap, so that in no case shall felt touch felt. Third, coat the entire surface with hot pitch, mopped on uniformly. Fourth, lay three (3) thicknesses of felt, lapping each sheet twenty-two (22) inches over the preceding one, mopping with hot pitch the full width of the 22-inch lap between the plies, so that in no case shall felt touch felt. Fifth, spread the entire surface of the roof with a uniform coat of pitch, into which, while hot, imbed gravel or slag.

Tar and gravel roof shall be laid on gypsum sheathing in the same manner as on concrete sheathing.

83. **SPECIFICATIONS FOR CEMENT FLOOR ON A CONCRETE BASE. Materials.**—The cement used shall be first-class Portland cement, and shall pass the standards of the American Society for Testing Materials. The sand for the top finish shall be clean and sharp and shall be retained on a No. 30 sieve and shall have passed the No. 20 sieve. Broken stone for the top finish shall pass a ½ in. screen and shall be retained on the No. 20 screen. Dust shall be excluded. The sand for the base shall be clean and sharp. The aggregate for the base shall be of broken stone or gravel and shall pass a 2 in. ring.

84. **Base.**—On a thoroughly tamped and compacted subgrade the concrete for the base shall be laid and thoroughly tamped. The base shall not be less than 2½ in. thick. Concrete for the base shall be thoroughly mixed with sufficient water so that some tamping is required to bring the moisture to the surface. If old concrete is used for the base the surface shall be roughened and thoroughly cleaned so that the new mortar will adhere. The roughened surface of old concrete shall then be thoroughly wet so that the base will not draw water from the finish when the latter is applied. Before scrubbing the base with grout the excess water shall be removed.

85. **Finish.**—With old concrete the surface of the base shall first be scrubbed with a thin grout of pure cement, rubbed in with a broom. On top of this, before the thin coat is set, a coat of finish mixed in the proportions of one part Portland cement, one part stone broken to pass a ½ in. ring, and one part sand shall be troweled cn, using as much pressure as possible, so that it will take a firm bond. After the finish has been applied to the desired thickness, preferably 2 in., it should be screeded and floated to a true surface. Between the time of initial and final set it shall be finished by skilled workmen with steel trowels and shall be worked to final surface. Under no condition shall a dryer be used, nor shall water be added to make the material work easily.

86. **SPECIFICATIONS FOR WOOD FLOOR ON A TAR CONCRETE BASE. Floor Sleepers.**—Sleepers for carrying the timber floor shall be 3 in. × 3 in. placed 18 in. c. to c. After the subgrade has been thoroughly tamped and rolled to an elevation of 4½ in. below the tops of the sleepers, the sleepers shall be placed in position and supported on stakes driven in the subgrade. Before depositing the tar concrete the sleepers must be brought to a true level.

87. **Tar Concrete Base.**—The tar concrete base shall be not less than 4½ in. thick and shall be laid as follows: First, a layer three (3) inches thick of coarse, screened gravel thoroughly mixed with tar, and tamped to a hard level surface. Second, on this bed spread a top dressing 1½ inches thick of sand heated and thoroughly mixed with coal tar pitch, in the proportions of one (1) part pitch to three (3) parts tar. The gravel, sand and tar shall be heated to from 200 to 300 degrees F., and shall be thoroughly mixed and carefully tamped into place.

88. **Plank Sub-Floor.**—The floor plank shall be of sound hemlock or pine not less than 2 inches thick, planed on one side and one edge to an even thickness and width. The floor plank is to be toe-nailed with 4 in. wire nails.

89. **Finished Flooring.**—The finished flooring is to be of maple of clear stock, ⅞-in. finished thickness, thoroughly air and kiln dried and not over 4 inches wide. The floor is to be planed to an even thickness, the edges jointed, and the underside channeled or ploughed. The finished floor is to be laid at right angles to the sub-floor, and each board neatly fitted at the ends, breaking joints at random. The floor is to be final nailed with 10 d. or 3-in. wire nails, nailed in diagonal rows 16 inches apart across the boards, with two (2) nails in each row in every board. The floor to be finished off perfectly smooth on completion.

90. The finished flooring is not to be taken into the building or laid until the tar concrete base and sub-floor plank are thoroughly dried.

PART V. DETAILS OF CONSTRUCTION.

91. **Details.**—All connections and details shall be of sufficient strength to develop the full strength of the member.

92. **Pitch of Rivets.**—The minimum distance between centers of rivet holes shall be three diameters of the rivet; but the distance shall preferably be not less than 3 in. for $\frac{7}{8}$-in. rivets, $2\frac{1}{2}$ in. for $\frac{3}{4}$-in. rivets, and 2 in. for $\frac{5}{8}$-in. rivets. The maximum pitch in the lines of stress for members composed of plates and shapes shall be 16 times the thickness of the thinnest outside plate or 6 in. For angles with two gage lines and rivets staggered, the maximum shall be twice the above in each line. Where two or more plates are used in contact, rivets not more than 12 in. apart in either direction shall be used to hold the plates well together.

93. **Edge Distance.**—The minimum distance from the center of any rivet hole to a sheared edge shall be $1\frac{1}{2}$ in. for $\frac{7}{8}$-in. rivets, $1\frac{1}{4}$ in. for $\frac{3}{4}$-in. rivets, and $1\frac{1}{8}$ in. for $\frac{5}{8}$-in. rivets, and to a rolled edge $1\frac{1}{4}$, $1\frac{1}{8}$ and 1 in., respectively. The maximum distance from any edge shall be eight times the thickness of the plate, but shall not exceed 6 in.

94. **Maximum Diameter.**—The diameter of the rivets in any angle carrying calculated stress shall not exceed one-quarter the width of the leg in which they are driven. In minor parts $\frac{7}{8}$-in. rivets may be used in 3-in. angles, $\frac{3}{4}$-in. rivets in $2\frac{1}{2}$-in. angles, and $\frac{5}{8}$-in. rivets in 2-in. angles.

95. **Long Rivets.**—Rivets carrying calculated stress and whose grip exceeds four diameters shall be increased in number at least one per cent for each additional $\frac{1}{16}$ in. of grip.

96. **Pitch at Ends.**—The pitch of rivets at the ends of built compression members shall not exceed four diameters of the rivets, for a length equal to one and one-half times the maximum width of member.

97. **Diameter of Punch and Die.**—The diameter of the punch and die shall be as specified in § 157.

98. **Connections.**—All connections shall be of sufficient strength to develop the full strength of the member. No connections except for lacing bars shall have less than two rivets. All field connections except lacing bars shall have not less than three rivets.

99. **Flange Plates.**—The flange plates of all girders shall not extend beyond the outer line of rivets connecting them to the angles more than 6 in. nor more than eight times the thickness of the thinnest plate.

100. **Web Stiffeners.**—Web stiffeners shall be in pairs, and shall have a close fit against flange angles. The stiffeners at the ends of plate girders shall have filler plates. Intermediate stiffeners may have fillers or be crimped over the flange angles. The rivet pitch in stiffeners shall not be greater than 5 in.

101. **Web Splices.**—Web plates shall be spliced at all points by a plate on each side of the web, capable of transmitting the shearing and bending stresses through the splice rivets.

102. **Riveted Tension Members.**—Pin connected riveted tension members shall have a net section through the pin hole 25 per cent in excess of the required net section of the member. The net section back of the pin hole in line of the center of the pin shall be at least 0.75 of the net section through the pin hole.

103. **Upset Rods.**—All rods with screw ends, except sag rods, must be upset at the ends so that the diameter at the base of the threads shall be $\frac{1}{16}$ inch larger than any part of the body of the bar.

104. **Upper Chords.**—Upper chords of trusses shall have symmetrical cross-sections, and shall preferably consist of two angles back to back.

105. **Compression Members.**—All other compression members for roof trusses, except sub-struts, shall be composed of sections symmetrically placed. Sub-struts may consist of a single section.

106. **Columns.**—Side posts which take flexure shall preferably be composed of 4 angles and a plate. In calculating the least moment of inertia of columns made of 4 angles and a web plate, the web plate may be omitted. Where side posts do not take flexure and carry heavy loads they shall preferably be composed of rolled or built H-sections, or of two channels with a solid web.

107. Posts in end framing shall preferably be composed of I-beams or 4 angles laced. Corner columns shall preferably be composed of one angle.

108. **Crane Posts.**—The cross-bending stress due to eccentric loading in columns carrying cranes shall be calculated. Crane girders carrying heavy cranes shall be carried on independent columns.

109. **Batten Plates.**—The open sides of all compression members shall be stayed by batten plates at the ends and diagonal lattice-work at intermediate points. The batten plates must be placed as near the ends as practicable, and shall have a length not less than the greatest width of the member or $1\frac{1}{2}$ times its least width.

110. **Lacing Bars.**—The lacing of compression members shall be proportioned to resist a shearing stress of $2\frac{1}{2}$ per cent of the direct stress. The minimum width of lacing bars shall be $1\frac{3}{4}$ in. for members 6 in. in width, 2 in. for members 9 in. in width, $2\frac{1}{2}$ in. for members 12 in. in width, $2\frac{1}{2}$ in. for members 15 in. in width, or 3 in. for members 18 in. and over in width. Single lacing bars shall have a thickness not less than one-fortieth, or double lacing bars connected by a rivet at the intersection, not less than one-sixtieth of the distance between the rivets connecting them to the members. They shall be inclined at an angle not less than 60° to the axis of the member for single lacing, nor less than 45° for double lacing with riveted intersections. Lacing bars shall be so spaced that the portion of the flange included between their connection shall be as strong as the member as a whole. The pitch of the lacing bars must not exceed the width of the channel plus nine inches.

111. **Pin Plates.**—All pin holes shall be reinforced by additional material when necessary, so as not to exceed the allowable pressure on the pins. These reinforcing plates must contain enough rivets to transfer the proportion of pressure which comes upon them, and at least one plate on each side shall extend not less than 6 in. beyond the edge of the batten plate.

112. **Splices.**—In compression members joints with abutting faces planed shall be placed as near the panel points as possible, and must be spliced on all sides with at least two rows of rivets on each side of the joint. Joints with abutting faces not planed must be fully spliced.

113. **Splices.**—Joints in tension members shall be fully spliced.

114. **Tension Members.**—Tension members shall preferably be composed of angles or shapes capable of taking compression as well as tension. Flats riveted at the ends shall not be used.

115. Main tension members shall preferably be made of 2 angles, 2 angles and a plate, or 2 channels laced. Secondary tension members may be made of a single shape.

116. **Eye-Bars.**—Heads of eye-bars shall be so proportioned as to develop the full strength of the bar. The heads shall be forged and not welded.

117. **Pins.**—Pins must be turned true to size and straight, and must be driven to place by means of pilot nuts.

The diameter of pin shall not be less than $\frac{3}{4}$ of the depth of the widest bar attached to it.

The several members attached to a pin shall be packed so as to produce the least bending moment on the pin, and all vacant spaces must be filled with steel or cast iron fillers.

118. **Bars or Rods.**—Long laterals may be made of bars with clevis or sleeve nut adjustment. Bent loops shall not be used.

119. **Spacing Trusses.**—Trusses shall preferably be spaced so as to allow the use of single pieces of rolled sections for purlins. Trussed purlins shall be avoided if possible.

120. **Purlins and Girts.**—Purlins and girts shall preferably be composed of single sections—channels, angles or Z-bars, placed with web at right angles to the trusses and posts and legs turned down.

121. **Fastening.**—Purlins and girts shall be attached to the top chord of trusses and to columns by means of angle clips with two rivets or two bolts in each leg.

122. **Spacing.**—Purlins for corrugated steel without sheathing shall be spaced at distances apart not to exceed the span as given for a safe load of 30 lb., and girts for a safe load of 20 lb. as given in Table IV.

123. **Timber Purlins.**—Timber purlins and girts shall be attached and spaced the same as steel purlins.

124. **Base Plates.**—Base plates shall never be less than $\frac{5}{8}$ in. in thickness, and shall be of sufficient thickness and size so that the pressure on the masonry shall not exceed the allowable pressures in § 32.

125. **Cast Rockers.**—The details of cast iron rockers shall be subject to the special approval of the engineer. The vertical webs of cast iron rockers and pedestals shall be designed for an allowable unit stress of $9{,}000 - 40\, l/r$, where l = height and r = radius of gyration of vertical web, both in inches.

126. **Anchors.**—Columns shall be anchored to the foundations by means of two anchor bolts not less than 1 in. in diameter upset, placed as wide apart as practicable in the plane of the wind. The anchorage shall be calculated to resist one and one-half times the bending moment at the base of the columns.

127. **Lateral Bracing.**—Lateral bracing shall be provided in the plane of the top and bottom chords, sides and ends; knee braces in the transverse bents; and sway bracing wherever necessary, see § 8. Lateral bracing shall be designed for an initial stress of 5,000 lb. in each member, and provision must be made for putting this initial stress into the members in erecting.

128. **Temperature.**—No special provision shall be made for changes in temperature in the length and width of a building with a steel frame, except in glazed roofs where expansion joints shall be provided by bolting joints about every 30 ft. Where trusses rest on masonry walls slotted holes shall be provided in the end bearing plates, and in the purlins and roof covering to provide for a variation in temperature of 150° F. In crane runways or similar structures changes in length due to a variation in temperature of 150° F. shall be provided for either by means of slotted holes, or in calculating the stresses.

PART VI. MATERIALS.

129. **Process of Manufacture.**—Structural steel shall be made by the open-hearth process.

130. **Chemical Composition.**—The steel shall conform to the following requirements as to chemical composition:

	Structural Steel.	Rivet Steel.
Phosphorus..................	not over 0.06 per cent	not over 0.06 per cent
Sulfur......................	......	" " 0.045 "

131. **Ladle Analyses.**—An analysis of each melt of steel shall be made by the manufacturer to determine the percentages of carbon, manganese, phosphorus and sulfur. This analysis shall be made from a test ingot taken during the pouring of the melt. The chemical composition thus determined shall be reported to the purchaser or his representative, and shall conform to the requirements specified in § 130.

132. **Check Analyses.**—Analyses may be made by the purchaser from finished material representing each melt. The phosphorus and sulfur content thus determined shall not exceed that specified in § 130 by more than 25 per cent.

133. **Tension Tests.**—(*a*) The material shall conform to the following requirements as to tensile properties:

Properties Considered.	Structural Steel.	Rivet Steel.
Tensile strength, lb. per sq. in..................	55,000–65,000	46,000–56,000
Yield point, min., lb. per sq. in..................	0.5 tens. str.	0.5 tens. str.
Elongation in 8 in., min., per cent..............	$\frac{1,400,000^*}{\text{Tens. str.}}$	$\frac{1,400,000}{\text{Tens. str.}}$
Elongation in 2 in., min., per cent..............	22	....

* See § 134.

(*b*) The yield point shall be determined by the drop of the beam of the testing machine.

134. **Modifications in Elongation.**—(*a*) For structural steel over $\frac{3}{4}$ in. in thickness, a deduction of 1 from the percentage of elongation in 8 in. specified in § 133(*a*) shall be made for each increase of $\frac{1}{8}$ in. in thickness above $\frac{3}{4}$ in., to a minimum of 18 per cent.

(*b*) For structural steel under $\frac{5}{16}$ in. in thickness, a deduction of 2.5 from the percentage of elongation in 8 in. specified in § 133(*a*) shall be made for each decrease of $\frac{1}{16}$ in. in thickness below $\frac{5}{16}$ in.

135. **Bend Tests.**—(*a*) The test specimen for plates, shapes and bars, except as specified in paragraphs (*b*) and (*c*), shall bend cold through 180 deg. without cracking on the outside of the bent portion, as follows: For material $\frac{3}{4}$ in. or under in thickness, flat on itself; for material over $\frac{3}{4}$ in. to and including $1\frac{1}{4}$ in. in thickness, around a pin the diameter of which is equal to the thickness of the specimen; and for material over $1\frac{1}{4}$ in. in thickness, around a pin the diameter of which is equal to twice the thickness of the specimen.

(*b*) The test specimen for pins, rollers and other bars, when prepared as specified in § 136(*e*), shall bend cold through 180 deg. around a 1-in. pin without cracking on the outside of the bent portion.

(*c*) The test specimen for rivet steel shall bend cold through 180 deg. flat on itself without cracking on the outside of the bent portion.

(**Note.**—These Specifications for structural steel conform with Specifications for Structural Steel for Buildings adopted by American Society for Testing Materials, except that Bessemer steel is not permitted.)

136. **Test Specimens.**—(*a*) Tension and bend test specimens shall be taken from rolled steel in the condition in which it comes from the rolls, except as specified in paragraph (*b*).

(*b*) Tension and bend test specimens for pins and rollers shall be taken from the finished bars, after annealing when annealing is specified.

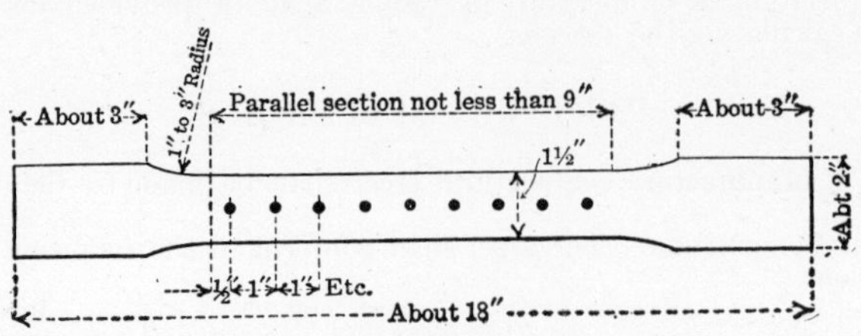

FIG. 1.

(*c*) Tension and bend test specimens for plates, shapes and bars, except as specified in paragraphs (*d*), (*e*) and (*f*), shall be of the full thickness of material as rolled; and may be machined to the form and dimensions shown in Fig. 1, or with both edges parallel.

(*d*) Tension and bend test specimens for plates over 1½ in. in thickness may be machined to a thickness or diameter of at least ¾ in. for a length of at least 9 in.

(*e*) Tension test specimens for pins, rollers and bars over 1½ in. in thickness or diameter may conform to the dimensions shown in Fig. 2. In this case, the ends shall be of a form to fit the holders of the testing machine in such a way that the load shall be axial. Bend test specimens may be 1 by ½ in. in section. The axis of the specimen shall be located at any point midway between the center and surface and shall be parallel to the axis of the bar.

(*f*) Tension and bend test specimens for rivet steel shall be of the full-size section of bars as rolled.

137. **Number of Tests.**—(*a*) One tension and one bend test shall be made from each melt; except that if material from one melt differs ⅜ in. or more in thickness, one tension and one bend test shall be made from both the thickest and the thinnest material rolled.

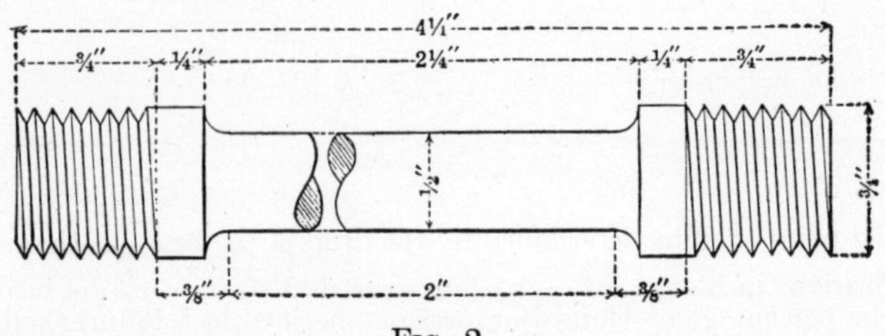

FIG. 2.

(*b*) If any test specimen shows defective machining or develops flaws, it may be discarded and another specimen substituted.

(*c*) If the percentage of elongation of any tension test specimen is less than that specified in Section 133(*a*) and any part of the fracture is more than ¾ in. from the center of the gage length of a 2-in. specimen or is outside the middle third of the gage length of an 8-in. specimen, as indicated by scribe scratches marked on the specimen before testing, a retest shall be allowed.

138. **Permissible Variations.**—The cross-section or weight of each piece of steel shall not vary more than 2.5 per cent from that specified; except in the case of sheared plates, which shall be covered by the following permissible variations. One cubic inch of rolled steel is assumed to weigh 0.2833 lb.

(*a*) *When Ordered to Weight per Square Foot:* The weight of each lot[1] in each shipment shall not vary from the weight ordered more than the amount given in Table V.

[1] The term "lot" applied to Table V means all of the plates of each group width and group weight.

TABLE V.

Permissible Variations of Plates Ordered to Weight.

Ordered Weight, Lb. per Sq. Ft.	Permissible Variations in Average Weights per Square Foot of Plates for Widths Given, Expressed in Percentages of Ordered Weights.																		Ordered Weight, Lb. per Sq. Ft.
	Under 48 in.		48 to 60 in., excl.		60 to 72 in., excl.		72 to 84 in., excl.		84 to 96 in., excl.		96 to 108 in., excl.		108 to 120 in., excl.		120 to 132 in., excl.		132 in. or over.		
Under 5....	5	3	5.5	3	6	3	7	3	...	...	...	...	...	...	...	...	...	...	Under 5
5 to 7.5 exclusive....	4.5	3	5	3	5.5	3	6	3	...	...	...	...	...	...	...	...	...	...	5 to 7.5 exclusive
7.5 to 10 exclusive....	4	3	4.5	3	5	3	5.5	3	6	3	7	3	8	3	...	...	...	...	7.5 to 10 exclusive
10 to 12.5 exclusive....	3.5	2.5	4	3	4.5	3	5	3	5.5	3	6	3	7	3	8	3	9	3	10 to 12.5 exclusive
12.5 to 15 exclusive....	3	2.5	3.5	2.5	4	3	4.5	3	5	3	5.5	3	6	3	7	3	8	3	12.5 to 15 exclusive
15 to 17.5 exclusive....	2.5	2.5	3	2.5	3.5	2.5	4	3	4.5	3	5	3	5.5	3	6	3	7	3	15 to 17.5 exclusive
17.5 to 20 exclusive....	2.5	2	2.5	2.5	3	2.5	3.5	2.5	4	3	4.5	3	5	3	5.5	3	6	3	17.5 to 20 exclusive
20 to 25 exclusive....	2	2	2.5	2	2.5	2.5	3	2.5	3.5	2.5	4	3	4.5	3	5	3	5.5	3	20 to 25 exclusive
25 to 30 exclusive....	2	2	2	2	2.5	2	2.5	2.5	3	2.5	3.5	3	4	3	4.5	3	5	3	25 to 30 exclusive
30 to 40 exclusive....	2	2	2	2	2	2	2.5	2	2.5	2.5	3	2.5	3.5	3	4	3	4.5	3	30 to 40 exclusive
40 or over ...	2	2	2	2	2	2	2	2	2.5	2	2.5	2.5	3	2.5	3.5	3	4	3	40 or over

Note.—The weight per square foot of individual plates shall not vary from the ordered weight by more than $1\frac{1}{3}$ times the amount given in this table.

(b) *When Ordered to Thickness:* The thickness of each plate shall not vary more than 0.01 in. under that ordered.

The overweight of each lot [2] in each shipment shall not exceed the amount given in Table VI.

[2] The term "lot" applied to Table VI means all of the plates of each group width and group thickness.

TABLE VI.

Permissible Overweights of Plates Ordered to Thickness.

Ordered Thickness, in.	Permissible Excess in Average Weights per Square Foot of Plates for Widths Given, Expressed in Percentages of Nominal Weights.									Ordered Thickness, in.
	Under 48 in.	48 to 60 in., excl.	60 to 72 in., excl.	72 to 84 in., excl.	84 to 96 in., excl.	96 to 108 in., excl.	108 to 120 in., excl.	120 to 132 in., excl.	132 in. or over.	
Under $\frac{1}{8}$	9	10	12	14	..	..	..	..	..	Under $\frac{1}{8}$
$\frac{1}{8}$ to $\frac{3}{16}$ excl.	8	9	10	12	..	..	..	..	..	$\frac{1}{8}$ to $\frac{3}{16}$ excl.
$\frac{3}{16}$ " $\frac{1}{4}$ "	7	8	9	10	12	..	..	..	..	$\frac{3}{16}$ " $\frac{1}{4}$ "
$\frac{1}{4}$ " $\frac{5}{16}$ "	6	7	8	9	10	12	14	16	19	$\frac{1}{4}$ " $\frac{5}{16}$ "
$\frac{5}{16}$ " $\frac{3}{8}$ "	5	6	7	8	9	10	12	14	17	$\frac{5}{16}$ " $\frac{3}{8}$ "
$\frac{3}{8}$ " $\frac{7}{16}$ "	4.5	5	6	7	8	9	10	12	15	$\frac{3}{8}$ " $\frac{7}{16}$ "
$\frac{7}{16}$ " $\frac{1}{2}$ "	4	4.5	5	6	7	8	9	10	13	$\frac{7}{16}$ " $\frac{1}{2}$ "
$\frac{1}{2}$ " $\frac{5}{8}$ "	3.5	4	4.5	5	6	7	8	9	11	$\frac{1}{2}$ " $\frac{5}{8}$ "
$\frac{5}{8}$ " $\frac{3}{4}$ "	3	3.5	4	4.5	5	6	7	8	9	$\frac{5}{8}$ " $\frac{3}{4}$ "
$\frac{3}{4}$ " 1 "	2.5	3	3.5	4	4.5	5	6	7	8	$\frac{3}{4}$ " 1 "
1 or over	2.5	2.5	3	3.5	4	4.5	5	6	7	1 or over

139. **Finish.**—The finished material shall be free from injurious defects and shall have a workmanlike finish.

140. **Marking.**—The name or brand of the manufacturer and the melt number shall be legibly stamped or rolled on all finished material, except that rivet and lattice bars and other small sections shall, when loaded for shipment, be properly separated and marked for identification. The identification marks shall be legibly stamped on the end of each pin and roller. The melt number shall be legibly marked, by stamping if practicable, on each test specimen.

141. **Inspection.**—The inspector representing the purchaser shall have free entry, at all times while work on the contract of the purchaser is being performed, to all parts of the manufacturer's works which concern the manufacture of the material ordered. The manufacturer shall afford the inspector, free of cost, all reasonable facilities to satisfy him that the material is being furnished in accordance with these specifications. All tests (except check analyses) and inspection shall be made at the place of manufacture prior to shipment, unless otherwise specified, and shall be so conducted as not to interfere unnecessarily with the operation of the works.

142. **Rejection.**—(*a*) Unless otherwise specified, any rejection based on tests made in accordance with § 132 shall be reported within five working days from the receipt of samples.

(*b*) Material which shows injurious defects subsequent to its acceptance at the manufacturer's works will be rejected, and the manufacturer shall be notified.

Rehearing.—Samples tested in accordance with § 132, which represent rejected material, shall be preserved for two weeks from the date of the test report. In case of dissatisfaction with the results of the tests, the manufacturer may make claim for a rehearing within that time.

Special Metals.

143. **Cast-Iron.**—Except where chilled iron is specified, castings shall be made of tough gray iron, with sulphur not over 0.10 per cent. They shall be true to pattern, out of wind and free from flaws and excessive shrinkage. If tests are demanded they shall be made on the "Arbitration Bar" of the American Society for Testing Materials, which is a round bar, $1\frac{1}{4}$ in. in diameter and 15 in. long. The transverse test shall be on a supported length of 12 in. with load at middle. The minimum breaking load so applied shall be 2,900 lb., with a deflection of at least $\frac{1}{10}$ in. before rupture.

144. **Wrought-Iron Bars.**—Wrought-iron shall be double-rolled, tough, fibrous and uniform in character. It shall be thoroughly welded in rolling and be free from surface defects. When tested in specimens of the form of Fig. 1, or in full-sized pieces of the same length, it shall show an ultimate strength of at least 50,000 lb. per sq. in., an elongation of at least 18 per cent in 8 in., with fracture wholly fibrous. Specimens shall bend cold, with the fiber through 135°, without sign of fracture, around a pin the diameter of which is not over twice the thickness of the piece tested. When nicked and bent the fracture shall show at least 90 per cent fibrous.

Timber.

145. **Timber.**—The timber shall be strictly first-class spruce, white pine, Douglas fir, Southern yellow pine, white oak, or other approved timber. Timber piles shall preferably be white, post or burr oak, Douglas fir, longleaf pine, tamarack, white or red cedar, chestnut, redwood or cypress.

146. **General Requirements.**—All timber shall be cut from sound live trees, and shall be sawed to standard size. It must be close grained and solid, free from defects such as injurious ring shakes and cross grain, unsound or loose knots, knots in groups, large pitch pockets, decay or other defects that will impair its strength or fitness for the purpose intended.

147. **Size of Sawed Timber.**—All timber shall be sawed true and out of wind and shall, when dry, not measure scant in thickness more than the following:

Flooring and boards up to $1\frac{1}{2}$ in. thick, may be scant $\frac{1}{16}$ in.

Planks and timbers, rough size, from $1\frac{3}{4}$ to $5\frac{3}{4}$ in. thick, may be scant $\frac{1}{8}$ in.

Dimension timber, rough size, 6 in. thick and up, may be scant $\frac{1}{4}$ in. For example, a 12 in. × 12 in. timber may be $11\frac{3}{4}$ in. × $11\frac{3}{4}$ in.

148. **Size of Dressed Timber.**—When dressed timber more than $1\frac{1}{2}$ in. in thickness is required, a reduction of $\frac{1}{8}$ in. in thickness for each surface planed will be permitted in addition to the allowance in rough timber in § 147. For example a 12 in. × 12 in. timber S.4S. may be $11\frac{1}{2}$ in. × $11\frac{1}{2}$ in.

149. **Dimension Timber.**—Dimension timber when used for beams, stringers, caps, posts and sills shall show not less than 75 per cent heart on each of four faces, measured across the sides anywhere in the length of the piece. There shall be no loose knots, or knots greater than

2 in. in diameter, or one-quarter ($\frac{1}{4}$) the width of the face of the stick in which they occur. Knots shall not be located in groups and no knot shall be nearer the edge of the stick than one-quarter ($\frac{1}{4}$) the width of the face. When used for other purposes dimension timber shall be square edged with exception of 1-in. wane on one edge or $\frac{1}{2}$-in. wane on two edges, and ring shakes shall not extend over one-eighth ($\frac{1}{8}$) the length of the piece.

150. **Flooring.**—Flooring shall preferably be yellow pine, maple or beech, as specified, and shall be furnished usually in lengths of 12 to 16 ft. and not over 4 in. face. The thickness of the flooring shall be the thickness of the finished material. Flooring shall be edge grained, kiln dried, matched, tongued and grooved, planed on the upper side, well manufactured so as to be free from planer's marks, splinters, etc. It shall show one face all heart and shall be free from knots, shakes, sap and pitch pockets.

151. **Sub-Floor Plank.**—Floor plank shall be square edged, shall show one face all heart and the other face and two edges shall show not less than seventy-five (75) per cent heart, measured across the face or sides measured anywhere in the length of the piece; and shall be free from loose knots, or sound knots more than $1\frac{1}{2}$ in. in diameter.

152. **Piles.**—Piles shall be cut from sound, live trees, shall be straight, close grained and solid, free from defects such as injurious ring shakes, large and unsound or loose knots, decay or other defects that will materially impair the strength or durability. The diameter of round piles near the butt shall not be less than 12 in. nor more than 18 in., and at the tip of piles under 30 ft. not less than 8 in., nor less than 6 in. for piles more than 30 ft. long. Piles must be cut above the ground swell and must taper evenly from butt to tip. Short bends will not be allowed. A line drawn from the butt to the tip shall lie entirely within the body of the pile. All piles shall be cut square at their ends and shall be stripped of their bark.

PART VII. WORKMANSHIP.

153. **General.**—All parts forming a structure shall be built in accordance with approved drawings. The workmanship and finish shall be equal to the best practice in modern bridge works.

154. **Straightening Material.**—Material shall be thoroughly straightened in the shop, by methods that will not injure it, before being laid off or worked in any way.

155. **Finish.**—Shearing shall be neatly and accurately done and all portions of the work exposed to view neatly finished.

156. **Rivets.**—The size of rivets, called for on the plans, shall be understood to mean the actual size of the cold rivet before heating.

157. **Rivet Holes.**—When general reaming is not required, the diameter of the punch for material not over $\frac{3}{4}$ in. thick shall be not more than $\frac{1}{16}$ in., nor that of the die more than $\frac{1}{8}$ in. larger than the diameter of the rivet. The diameter of the die shall not exceed that of the punch by more than $\frac{1}{4}$ the thickness of the metal punched.

158. **Planing and Reaming.**—In medium steel over $\frac{3}{4}$ of an in. thick, all sheared edges shall be planed and all holes shall be drilled or reamed to a diameter of $\frac{1}{8}$ of an in. larger than the punched holes, so as to remove all the sheared surface of the metal. Steel which does not satisfy the drifting test must have holes drilled.

159. **Punching.**—Punching shall be accurately done. Slight inaccuracy in the matching of holes may be corrected with reamers. Drifting to enlarge unfair holes will not be allowed. Poor matching of holes will be cause for rejection by the inspector.

160. **Assembling.**—Riveted members shall have all parts well pinned up and firmly drawn together with bolts before riveting is commenced. Contact surfaces to be painted (see § 191).

161. **Lacing Bars.**—Lacing bars shall have neatly rounded ends, unless otherwise called for.

162. **Web Stiffeners.**—Stiffeners shall fit neatly between flanges of girders. Where tight fits are called for the ends of the stiffeners shall be faced and shall be brought to a true contact bearing with the flange angles.

163. **Splice Plates and Fillers.**—Web splice plates and fillers under stiffeners shall be cut to fit within $\frac{1}{8}$ in. of flange angles.

164. **Web Plates.**—Web plates of girders, which have no cover plates, shall be flush with the backs of angles or be not more than $\frac{1}{4}$ in. scant, unless otherwise called for. When web plates are spliced, not more than $\frac{1}{4}$ in. clearance between ends of plates will be allowed.

165. **Connection Angles.**—Connection angles for girders shall be flush with each other and correct as to position and length of girder. In case milling is required after riveting, the removal of more than $\frac{1}{16}$ in. from their thickness will be cause for rejection.

166. **Riveting.**—Rivets shall be driven by pressure tools wherever possible. Pneumatic hammers shall be used in preference to hand driving.

167. Rivets shall look neat and finished, with heads of approved shape, full and of equal size. They shall be central on shank and grip the assembled pieces firmly. Recupping and calking will not be allowed. Loose, burned or otherwise defective rivets shall be cut out and replaced. In cutting out rivets great care shall be taken not to injure the adjacent metal. If necessary they shall be drilled out.

168. **Turned Bolts.**—Wherever bolts are used in place of rivets which transmit shear, the holes shall be reamed parallel and the bolts turned to a driving fit. A washer not less than $\frac{1}{4}$ in. thick shall be used under nut.

169. **Members to be Straight.**—The several pieces forming one built member shall be straight and fit closely together, and finished members shall be free from twists, bends or open joints.

170. **Finish of Joints.**—Abutting joints shall be cut or dressed true and straight and fitted close together, especially where open to view. In compression joints depending on contact bearing the surfaces shall be truly faced, so as to have even bearings after they are riveted up complete and when perfectly aligned.

171. **Field Connections.**—All holes for field rivets in splices in tension members carrying moving loads shall be accurately drilled to an iron templet or reamed while the connecting parts are temporarily put together.

172. **Eye-Bars.**—Eye-bars shall be straight and true to size, and shall be free from twists, folds in the neck or head, or any other defect. Heads shall be made by upsetting, rolling or forging. Welding will not be allowed. The form of heads will be determined by the dies in use at the works where the eye-bars are made, if satisfactory to the engineer, but the manufacturer shall guarantee the bars to break in the body with a silky fracture, when tested to rupture. The thickness of head and neck shall not vary more than $\frac{1}{16}$ in. from the thickness of the bar.

173. **Boring Eye-Bars.**—Before boring, each eye-bar shall be properly annealed and carefully straightened. Pin holes shall be in the center line of bars and in the center of heads. Bars of the same length shall be bored so accurately that, when placed together, pins $\frac{1}{32}$ in. smaller in diameter than the pin holes can be passed through the holes at both ends of the bars at the same time.

174. **Pin Holes.**—Pin holes shall be bored true to gage, smooth and straight; at right angles to the axis of the member and parallel to each other, unless otherwise called for. Wherever possible, the boring shall be done after the member is riveted up.

175. The distance center to center of pin holes shall be correct within $\frac{1}{32}$ in., and the diameter of the hole not more than 1/50 in. larger than that of the pin, for pins up to 5 in. diameter, and $\frac{1}{32}$ in. for larger pins.

176. **Pins and Rollers.**—Pins and rollers shall be accurately turned to gage and shall be straight and smooth and entirely free from flaws.

177. **Pilot Nuts and Field Rivets.**—At least one pilot and one driving nut shall be furnished for each size of pin for each structure; and field rivets 15 per cent plus 10 rivets in excess of the number of each size actually required.

178. **Screw Threads.**—Screw threads shall make tight fits in the nuts and shall be U. S. standard, except above the diameter of $1\frac{3}{8}$ in., when they shall be made with six threads per in.

179. **Annealing.**—Steel, except in minor details, which has been partially heated shall be properly annealed.

180. **Steel Castings.**—All steel castings shall be annealed.

181. **Welding.**—Fusion welding may be used for fabricating bases of columns, tie plates and lacing bars on columns, and the connections of secondary members and members carrying nominal stresses.

182. **Bed Plates.**—Expansion bed plates shall be planed true and smooth. Cast wall plates shall be planed top and bottom. The cut of the planing tool shall correspond with the direction of expansion.

183. **Shipping Details.**—Pins, nuts, bolts, rivets, and other small details shall be boxed or crated.

184. **Weight.**—The weight of every piece and box shall be marked on it in plain figures.

185. **Weight Paid For.**—The payment for pound price contracts shall be based on scale weights of the metal in the fabricated structure, including field rivets 15 per cent plus 10 rivets in excess of the number nominally required. The weight of the shop coat of paint, field paint, cement, fitting up bolts, pilot nuts, driving caps, boxes and barrels used for packing, and material used in supporting members on cars shall be excluded. If the scale weight is more than $2\frac{1}{2}$ per cent under the computed weight it may be cause for rejection. The greatest allowable variation of the total scale weight of any structure from the weights computed from the approved shop drawings shall be 2 per cent. Any weight in excess of 2 per cent above the computed weight

shall not be paid for. The weights of rolled shapes and plates shall be computed on the basis of their normal weights and dimensions, as shown on the approved drawings, deducting for all copes, cuts and open holes. With plates the percentage of overrun given in these specifications shall be added. The weight of heads of shop driven rivets shall be included in the computed weight. The weights of castings shall be computed from the dimensions shown on the approved drawings, with an addition of 10 per cent for fillets and overrun.

Additional Specifications When General Reaming and Planing are Required.

186. **Planing Edges.**—Sheared edges and ends shall be planed off at least $\frac{1}{4}$ in.

187. **Reaming.**—Punched holes shall be made with a punch $\frac{3}{16}$ in. smaller in diameter than the nominal size of the rivets and shall be reamed to a finished diameter of not more than $\frac{1}{16}$ in. larger than the rivet.

188. **Reaming after Assembling.**—Wherever practicable, reaming shall be done after the pieces forming one built member have been assembled and firmly bolted together. If necessary to take the pieces apart for shipping and handling, the respective pieces reamed together shall be so marked that they may be reassembled in the same position in the final setting up. No interchange of reamed parts will be allowed.

189. **Removing Burrs.**—The burrs on all reamed holes shall be removed by a tool countersinking about $\frac{1}{16}$ in.

Painting in Shop.

190. **Painting.**—All steel work before leaving the shop shall be thoroughly cleaned from all loose scale and rust, and be given one good coating of pure boiled linseed oil or paint as specified, well worked into all joints and open spaces.

191. In riveted work, the surfaces coming in contact shall each be painted (with paint) before being riveted together.

192. Pieces and parts which are not accessible for painting after erection shall have two coats of paint.

193. The paint shall be a good quality of red lead or graphite paint, ground with pure linseed oil, or such paint as may be specified in the contract.

194. Machine finished surfaces shall be coated with white lead and tallow before shipment or before being put out into the open air.

Inspection and Testing at Mill and the Shops.

195. The manufacturer shall furnish all facilities for inspecting and testing weight and the quality of workmanship at the mill or shop where material is fabricated. He shall furnish a suitable testing machine for testing full-sized members if required.

196. **Mill Orders.**—The engineer shall be furnished with complete copies of mill orders, and no materials shall be ordered nor any work done before he has been notified as to where the orders have been placed so that he may arrange for the inspection.

197. **Shop Plans.**—The engineer shall be furnished with approved complete shop plans, and must be notified well in advance of the start of the work in the shop in order that he may have an inspector on hand to inspect the material and workmanship.

198. **Shipping Invoices.**—Complete copies of shipping invoices shall be furnished the engineer with each shipment.

199. The engineer's inspector shall have full access, at all times, to all parts of the mill or shop where material under his inspection is being fabricated.

200. The inspector shall stamp each piece accepted with a private mark. Any piece not so marked may be rejected at any time, and at any stage of the work. If the inspector, through an oversight or otherwise, has accepted material or work which is defective or contrary to the specifications, this material, no matter in what stage of completion, may be rejected by the engineer.

201. **Full Size Tests.**—Full size tests of any finished member shall be tested at the manufacturer's expense, and shall be paid for by the purchaser at the contract price less the scrap value, if the tests are satisfactory. If the tests are not satisfactory the material will not be paid for and the members represented by the tested member may be rejected.

Erection.

202. **Tools.**—The contractor shall furnish at his own expense all necessary tools, staging and material of every description required for the erection of the work, and shall remove the same when the work is completed.

All field connections in the trusses and framework shall be riveted. Connections of purlins and girts may be bolted.

The contractor shall put in place all stone bolts and anchors for attaching the steel work to the masonry. He shall drill all the necessary holes in the masonry, and set all bolts with neat Portland cement.

203. Field rivets shall preferably be driven by pneumatic riveters of approved make. A pneumatic bucker shall be used with a pneumatic riveter. Splices and field connections shall have 50 per cent of the holes filled with bolts and drift pins (of which one-fifth shall be drift pins) before riveting. Rivets in splices of compression chords shall not be driven until the abutting surfaces have been brought into contact throughout, and submitted to full dead load stress. Field riveting shall be done to the satisfaction of the engineer.

204. The erection will also include all necessary hauling from the railroad station, the unloading of the materials and their proper care until the erection is completed.

205. Whenever new structures are to replace existing ones, the latter are to be carefully taken down and removed by the contractor to some place where the material can be hauled away.

206. The contractor shall so conduct his work as not to interfere with traffic, interfere with the work of other contractors, or close any thoroughfare.

207. The contractor shall assume all risks of accidents and damages to persons and properties prior to the acceptance of the work.

208. The contractor must remove all falsework, piling and other obstructions or unsightly material produced by his operations.

209. The contractor shall comply with all ordinances or regulations appertaining to the work.

210. The erection shall be carried forward with diligence and shall be completed promptly.

Painting After Erection.

211. **Painting.**—After the building is erected the metal work shall be thoroughly cleaned of mud, grease or other material, then thoroughly and evenly painted with two coats of paint of the kind specified by the engineer, mixed with linseed oil. All recesses which may retain water, or through which water can enter, must be filled with thick paint or some waterproof cement before final painting. The different coats of paint must be of distinctly different shades or colors, and one coat must be allowed to dry thoroughly before the second coat is applied. All painting shall be done with round brushes of the best quality obtainable on the market. The paint shall be delivered on the work in the manufacturer's original packages and be subject to inspection. If tests made by the inspector shows that the paint is adulterated, the paint will be rejected and the contractor shall pay the cost of the analyses, and shall scrape off and thoroughly clean and repaint all material that has been painted with the condemned paint. The paint shall not be thinned with anything whatsoever; in cold weather the paint may be thinned by heating under the direction of the inspector. No turpentine nor benzine shall be allowed on the work, except by the permission of the inspector, and in such quantity as he shall allow. The inspector shall be notified when any painting is to be done by the contractor, and no painting shall be done until the inspector has approved the surface to which the paint is to be applied. Paint shall not be applied out of doors in freezing, rainy, or misty weather, and all surfaces to which paint is to be applied shall be dry, clean and warm. In cool weather the paint may be thinned by heating, and this may be required by the inspector.

INDEX

Snow Load – approx. 20 lb/ft

Doctor

1005 12th

2091